Revelation

VOLUME 38A

THE ANCHOR YALE BIBLE is a project of international and interfaith scope in which Protestant, Catholic, and Jewish scholars from many countries contribute individual volumes. The project is not sponsored by any ecclesiastical organization and is not intended to reflect any particular theological doctrine.

THE ANCHOR YALE BIBLE is committed to producing commentaries in the tradition established half a century ago by the founders of the series, William Foxwell Albright and David Noel Freedman. It aims to present the best contemporary scholarship in a way that is accessible not only to scholars, but also to the educated nonspecialist. Its approach is grounded in exact translation of the ancient languages and an appreciation of the historical and cultural context in which the biblical books were written, supplemented by insights from modern methods, such as sociological and literary criticism.

John J. Collins
General Editor

THE ANCHOR YALE BIBLE

Revelation

A New Translation with Introduction and Commentary

CRAIG R. KOESTER

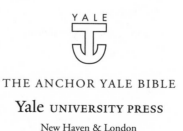

YALE

THE ANCHOR YALE BIBLE
Yale UNIVERSITY PRESS
New Haven & London

Published with assistance from the Mary Cady Tew Memorial Fund.

"Anchor Yale Bible" and the Anchor Yale logo are registered trademarks of Yale University.

Yale University Press books may be purchased in quantity for educational, business,
or promotional use. For information, please e-mail sales.press@yale.edu (U.S. office)
or sales@yaleup.co.uk (U.K. office).

Set in Garamond type by Newgen North America.
Printed in the United States of America.

Library of Congress Cataloging-in-Publication Data

Bible. Revelation. English. Koester. 2014.
Revelation : a new translation with introduction and commentary / Craig R. Koester.
pages cm.— (The Anchor Yale Bible ; volume 38A)
Includes bibliographical references and index.
ISBN 978-0-300-14488-8 (alk. paper)
1. Bible. Revelation—Commentaries.   I. Koester, Craig R., 1953–   II. Title.
BS192.2.A1 2008 .N46 vol. 38A
[BS2823]
228'.077—dc23
2013041226

A catalogue record for this book is available from the British Library.

This paper meets the requirements of ANSI/NISO Z39.48–1992 (Permanence of Paper).

10 9 8 7 6 5 4 3 2 1

I am the Alpha and the Omega,
the first and the last,
the beginning and the end.
—*Rev 22:13*

Of the Father's love begotten, ere the worlds began to be,
He is Alpha and Omega, he the source the ending he,
Of the things that are, that have been,
And that future years shall see, evermore and evermore.
—*Prudentius (ca. 400 CE)*

The end is not an event but a person.
—*G. B. Caird*

Contents

Preface

Interpreters of Revelation find themselves in a peculiar company that includes historians and fiction writers, scientists and theologians. The twelfth-century abbot Joachim of Fiore told of receiving insights into the book through mystical experience. Sir Isaac Newton, best known for his contributions to mathematics and physics, spent much of his time trying to correlate Revelation's visions with historical events. The poet and novelist D. H. Lawrence devoted one of his last works to a scathing critique of Revelation, which he considered ugly and vindictive. Few books can match Revelation's capacity to elicit curiosity and apprehension, both of which are fed by the vast amount of popular literature on the end times. Given the many interpretive possibilities, it may be helpful for me to indicate what I do in this commentary.

An important feature is the attention to the history of interpretation and influence. Interpretations of Revelation vary depending on the assumptions people make and the questions they ask. Long-standing debates about the book affect scholarship in subtle and not-so-subtle ways, and the consideration of perspectives from the past makes readers more aware of what they themselves bring to the text. When surveying interpretations, I not only ask what people have seen in Revelation, but try to identify the social, political, and theological factors that shaped their views. I do not follow the practice of grouping interpretations into four categories, often called futuristic, timeless, church historical, and preterist. These categories are more problematic than helpful. In practice, interpreters often blur the lines between categories and ask many other types of questions. I also try to show that some of the most influential views have not been those of scholars, either ancient or modern, so the sections on the history of interpretation not only mention commentaries and theological works, but consider popular literature, art, and music.

Another aspect of the commentary is attention to the world within the text of Revelation. John depicts a world inhabited by a seven-headed beast, a slaughtered and living Lamb, and fire-breathing horses with lions' heads. As narrator, he can travel to heaven above, see the door to the abyss below, and tour God's city in the age to come. Although debates about Revelation often focus on how such visions relate to the world of time and space, it is important to ask how these scenes relate to each other, creating a narrative world in which the ordinary constraints of time and space do not apply. The images are evocative and often integrate multiple aspects of meaning that work in tension with each other. In terms of structure, I read Revelation as a forward-moving spiral in which scenes of conflict lead to celebration in heaven over and over again, until "all is done" in New Jerusalem (Rev 21:6).

This literary world centers on the work of God and the Lamb. I understand the God of Revelation to be the Creator, who has made all things and whose work culminates in new creation (4:11; 21:1). Since God's dominion is based on his role as Creator, he opposes those who would destroy the earth. One aspect of God's work is the destruction of the forces of destruction, and the other is making all things new (11:18; 21:5). God's principal agent is the crucified and risen Jesus, portrayed as a Lamb. Where the agents of destruction operate through coercion and deception, characterized by the beast, the Lamb shows divine power to rule being exercised through Jesus' suffering, sacrifice, and witness to truth, which overcome sin and evil.

A major aspect of the conflict depicted in Revelation is the injustice perpetrated by earth's destroyers (6:9–11). Revelation shows that God's justice ultimately will prevail, but along the way the visions of divine judgment are repeatedly interrupted, so that the world can be called to repentance. Warning visions show the disastrous effects of allegiance to earth's destroyers (18:1–24; 19:11–21), while visions of salvation show nations, kings, and peoples receiving life in God's city (15:2–4; 21:3, 24–26). When interpreting these contrasting visions of warning and promise, I try to discern what they do as well as what they say. Their function is complex, summoning readers to a renewed trust in and commitment to God and the Lamb, while calling them to resist the forces that run counter to those commitments.

This world within the text initially addressed the social world of Christians in Asia Minor during the final decades of the first century. Although Revelation's imagery is surreal, I assume that it spoke to matters that were local and concrete for the early readers. Rather than positing a unified social setting, I envision a context with multiple dimensions, including conflict with outsiders, internal disputes over assimilation, and complacency among the more prosperous followers of Jesus. With a variety of readers in mind, I assume that the text could function in multiple ways, so that it might encourage some readers while challenging others. The writer not only addresses issues the readers could see, but seeks to provoke awareness of issues that many did not see.

I find Revelation's perspective both critical and world-engaging. The writer considers himself to be a prophetic witness who engages issues that have political, social, economic, and religious dimensions. While calling readers to separate themselves from the practices of Babylon (18:4), he also envisions his community's vocation as that of bearing witness to the reign of God (11:3). Revelation can be direct and specific when criticizing certain social and religious practices, yet I find it significant that the author does not outline a detailed program that readers are to adopt. Instead, he uses evocative imagery to create a way of seeing the world and expects readers to work out the implications in their own contexts.

This commentary relates Revelation to settings in the first century, and it is informed by studies of associations in the Roman world, along with works on inscriptions, ancient art, and Jewish and Greco-Roman texts. But while recognizing that Revelation addressed a variety of ancient readers, this commentary encourages reflection on its significance for readers of other periods. Sections on the history of interpretation and influence give examples of how this has been done, along with consideration of the effects that those interpretations have had on church and society.

Heartfelt thanks are due to many people who have made this commentary possible. I am deeply grateful to the late Raymond E. Brown for encouraging me to undertake the project after I completed a volume on Hebrews for this series. His own commentaries are models of depth and clarity, and his friendship and support were true gifts. I am indebted to the original editor of the series, the late David Noel Freedman, for his support, and to his successor, John J. Collins, who has made landmark contributions to the study of apocalyptic literature and continues to develop the series as general editor. Special thanks are due to Pheme Perkins for her careful and timely editorial work on this volume. Her questions and comments were much appreciated throughout the process. I want to thank Luther Seminary for sabbaticals during which I conducted research and the seminary's library staff for ready assistance at every phase of the work. Special credit goes to Victoria Smith for her technical work on the preparation of the manuscript, to Peter Susag for proofreading and indexing, to Imliwabang Jamir for checking references, and to Susan Laity, Sarah Miller, Heather Gold, Jessie Dolch, and the staff at Yale University Press for bringing this project to completion. Finally, my greatest debt of gratitude goes to my wife, Nancy, for her companionship and good humor throughout the years of research and writing on Revelation.

Craig R. Koester
Luther Seminary
January 6, 2013

Illustrations, Maps, and Tables

Illustrations

xvii

Maps

Tables

Abbreviations

Secondary Sources

ABD	*Anchor Bible Dictionary.* Edited by D. N. Freedman. New York: Doubleday, 1992
ACNT	Augsburg Commentaries on the New Testament
Acta Sanc.	*Acta Sanctorum.* Edited by Johannes Bolland et al. Paris: Victor Palme, 1863–
ACW	Ancient Christian Writers
AGJU	Arbeiten zur Geschichte des antiken Judentums und des Urchristentums
ANF	Ante-Nicene Fathers
ANRW	*Aufsteig und Niedergang der römischen Welt.* Edited by H. Temporini and W. Haase. Berlin: de Gruyter, 1971–
ANTF	Arbeiten zur neutestamentlichen Textforschung
ANTC	Abingdon New Testament Commentaries
AUSS	*Andrews University Seminary Studies*
AYB	Anchor Yale Bible
BDAG	W. Bauer, W. F. Arndt, F. W. Gingrich, and F. W. Danker, *A Greek-English Lexicon of the New Testament and Other Early Christian Literature.* Chicago: University of Chicago Press, 1999
BAGRW	*Barrington Atlas of the Greek and Roman World.* Edited by Richard J. A. Talbert. Princeton, NJ: Princeton University Press, 2000

BDF	F. Blass and A. Debrunner, *A Greek Grammar of the New Testament and Other Early Christian Literature*. Edited and translated by R. W. Funk. Chicago: University of Chicago Press, 1961
BETL	Biblotheca Ephemeridum Theologicarum Lovaniensium
BGU	*Aegyptische Urkunden aus den Königlichen Staatlichen Museen zu Berlin, Griechische Urkunden*. 15 vols. Berlin: Weidmann, 1895–1983
Bib	*Biblica*
BibInt	*Biblical Interpretation*
BJS	Brown Judaic Studies
BN	*Biblische Notizen*
BNTC	Black's New Testament Commentaries
BR	*Biblical Research*
BSac	*Bibliotheca Sacra*
BTB	*Biblical Theology Bulletin*
BWANT	Beiträge zur Wissenschaft vom Alten und Neuen Testament
BZNW	Beihefte zur Zeitschrift für die neutestamentliche Wissenschaft
CAM	*Civilization of the Ancient Mediterranean*. Edited by M. Grant and R. Kitzinger. New York: Scribner's, 1988
CBQ	*Catholic Biblical Quarterly*
CBQMS	Catholic Biblical Quarterly Monograph Series
CCCM	Corpus Christianorum: Continuatio mediaevalis
CCSL	*Corpus Christianorum: Series latina*
CIJ	*Corpus inscriptionum judaicarum*
CIL	*Corpus inscriptionum latinarum*
CIG	*Corpus inscriptionum graecarum*. Edited by A. Boeckh. 4 vols. Berlin, 1828–1877
CMRDM	*Corpus Monumentorum Religionis Dei Menis*. Eugene N. Lane. 4 vols. Études préliminaires aux religions orientales dans l'Empire romain. Leiden: Brill, 1971–78
ConBNT	Coniectanea biblica: New Testament Series
CSCO	Corpus Scriptorum Christianorum Orientalium
DACL	*Dictionnaire d'archéologie chrétienne et liturgie*. Edited by F. Cabrol. 15 vols. Paris, 1907–53
DJD	Discoveries in the Judaean Desert
EDNT	*Exegetical Dictionary of the New Testament*. Edited by H. Balz and G. Schneider. Grand Rapids, MI: Eerdmans, 1990–93

EDSS	*Encyclopedia of the Dead Sea Scrolls.* Edited by Lawrence H. Schiffman and James C. VanderKam. New York: Oxford University, 2000
EKKNT	Evangelisch-Katholischer Kommentar zum Neuen Testament
EpAnat	*Epigraphica Anatolica*
ESCJ	Studies in Christianity and Judaism/Études sur le christianisme et le judaïsm
EstBib	*Estudios bíblicos*
ESV	English Standard Version
ETL	*Ephemerides theologicae lovanienses*
FAT	Forschungen zum Alten Testament
FC	Fathers of the Church
FRLANT	Forschungen zur Religion und Literatur des Alten und Neuen Testaments
GCS	Griechische christliche Schriftsteller der ersten Jahrhunderte
GHG	Gesenius Hebrew Grammar
Greek Anth.	*The Greek Anthology.* Edited by W. R. Patton. 5 vols. Loeb. Cambridge, MA: Harvard University Press; London: Heinemann, 1958–63
HNT	Handbuch zum Neuen Testament
HNTC	Harper's New Testament Commentaries
HTR	*Harvard Theological Review*
HTS	Harvard Theological Studies
HvTSt	*Hervormde teologiese studies*
ICC	International Critical Commentary
Int	*Interpretation*
ISBE	*International Standard Bible Encyclopedia.* Rev. ed. Edited by G. W. Bromiley. Grand Rapids, MI: Eerdmans, 1979–88
JBL	*Journal of Biblical Literature*
JETS	*Journal of the Evangelical Theological Society*
JPTSup	Journal of Pentecostal Theology: Supplement Series
JRS	*Journal of Roman Studies*
JSJ	*Journal for the Study of Judaism in the Persian, Hellenistic, and Roman Periods*
JSJSup	Journal for the Study of Judaism: Supplement Series
JSNT	*Journal for the Study of the New Testament*

JSNTSup	Journal for the Study of the New Testament: Supplement Series
JSOT	*Journal for the Study of the Old Testament*
JSPSup	Journal for the Study of the Pseudepigrapha: Supplement Series
JTS	*Journal of Theological Studies*
KJV	King James Version
LCC	Library of Christian Classics
LCL	Loeb Classical Library
LIMC	*Lexicon Iconographicum Mythologiae Classicae*. Edited by H. C. Ackerman and J.-R. Gisler. 8 vols. Zurich: Artemis, 1981–1997
LNTS	Library of New Testament Studies
LSJ	H. G. Liddell and R. Scott, *A Greek-English Lexicon*. Revised by H. S. Jones. Oxford: Clarendon, 1968
LuthW	Luther's Works. Edited by J. Pelikan and H. Lehman. Philadelphia: Fortress, 1958–86
MAAR	Memoirs of the American Academy in Rome
MAMA	*Monumenta Asiae Minoris Antiqua*. Edited by W. M. Calder et al. Manchester: Manchester University Press, 1928–62
MeyerK	H. A. W. Meyer, Kritisch-exegetischer Kommentar über das Neue Testament
MHT	J. L. Moulton, W. F. Howard, and N. Turner, *A Grammar of New Testament Greek*. Edinburgh: Clark, 1906–63
MM	J. H. Moulton and G. Milligan, *The Vocabulary of the Greek New Testament Illustrated from the Papyri*. London: Hodder & Stoughton, 1930
NA^{27}	E. Nestle, B. Aland, et al. *Novum Testamentum Graece*. 27th ed. Stuttgart: Deutsche Bibelgesellschaft, 1993
NAB	New American Bible
NASB	New American Standard Bible
NCBC	New Century Bible Commentary
Neot	*Neotestamentica*
NET	New English Translation
NewDocs	*New Documents Illustrating Early Christianity*. Edited by G. H. R. Horsley and S. R. Llewelyn. North Ryde: Ancient History Documentary Research Centre, 1981–
NIB	*New Interpreter's Bible*

NIBC	New International Biblical Commentary
NICNT	New International Commentary on the New Testament
NIDB	*New Interpreter's Dictionary of the Bible*. Edited by J. D. Douglas and M. C. Tenney. Grand Rapids, MI: Eerdmans, 1987
NIGTC	New International Greek Testament Commentary
NIV	New International Version
NJB	New Jerusalem Bible
NJBC	*The New Jerome Biblical Commentary*. Edited by R. E. Brown et al. London: Chapman, 1995
NovT	*Novum Testamentum*
NovTSup	Novum Testamentum Supplements
NP	*Neue Pauly*. Leiden: Brill, 2002–
NPF	Nicene and Post-Nicene Fathers, 1st series
NPF	Nicene and Post-Nicene Fathers, 2nd series
NRSV	New Revised Standard Version
NTAbh	Neutestamentliche Abhandlungen
NTApoc	*New Testament Apocrypha*. Edited by Edgar Hennecke and Wilhelm Schneemelcher. Translated by R. McL. Wilson. 1st ed. Philadelphia: Westminster, 1963–64
NTApoc	*New Testament Apocrypha*. Edited by Edgar Hennecke and Wilhelm Schneemelcher. Translated by R. McL. Wilson. 2nd ed. 2 vols. Cambridge: James Clarke; Louisville, KY: Westminster John Knox, 1991–92
NTD	Das Neue Testament Deutsch
NTS	*New Testament Studies*
NW	*Neuer Wettstein: Texte zum Neuen Testament aus Griechentum und Hellenismus*. Edited by G. Strecker and U. Schnelle. 2 vols. Berlin and New York: de Gruyter, 1996–
OCD	*Oxford Classical Dictionary*. Edited by S. Hornblower and A. Spawforth. 3rd ed. Oxford: Oxford University Press, 1996
OGIS	*Orientis Graeci Inscriptiones Selectae*. Edited by W. Dittenberger. 2 vols. Leipzig: Hirzel, 1903–5
OTP	*Old Testament Pseudepigrapha*. Edited by J. H. Charlesworth. 2 vols. New York: Doubleday, 1985
PDM	*Papyri demoticae magicae*. Demotic texts in *PGM* corpus as collated in *The Greek Magical Papyri in Translation*. Edited by H. D. Betz. Chicago: University of Chicago Press, 1986

PG	Patrologia graeca. Edited by J.-P. Migne. 162 vols. Paris, 1857–86
PGM	*Papyri graecae magicae.* Edited by K. Preisendanz. Berlin, 1928
PL	Patrologia latina. Edited by J.-P. Migne. 217 vols. Paris, 1844–64
PTMS	Pittsburgh Theological Monograph Series
PzB	*Protokolle zur Bibel*
RAC	*Reallexikon für Antike und Christentum.* Edited by T. Klausner. Stuttgart: Hiersmann, 1950–
RB	*Revue biblique*
REB	Revised English Bible
RevQ	*Revue de Qumran*
RHPR	*Revue d'histoire et de philosophie religieuses*
RIC	*The Roman Imperial Coinage.* Edited by Harold Mattingly et al. 10 vols. London: Spink, 1923–94
RivBSup	Rivista biblica supplement
RLMA	*Researches in Lydia, Mysia and Aiolis.* H. Malay. Vienna: Österreichischen Akademie der Wissenschaften, 1999
Rom. Civ.	*Roman Civilization.* Edited by N. Lewis and M. Reinhold. 3rd ed. 2 vols. New York: Columbia University Press, 1990
RPC	Roman Provincial Coinage. Andrew Burnett et al. London: British Museum, 1998–
SBB	Stuttgarter biblische Beiträge
SBLDS	Society of Biblical Literature Dissertation Series
SBLRBS	Society of Biblical Literature Resources for Biblical Study
SBLSP	Society of Biblical Literature Seminar Papers
SBLSymS	Society of Biblical Literature Symposium Series
SBS	Stuttgarter Bibelstudien
SC	Sources chrétiennes
SEG	Supplementum epigraphicum graecum
Sel. Pap.	*Select Papyri.* Edited by A. S. Hunt and C. C. Edgar. 5 vols. Cambridge, MA: Harvard University; London: Heinemann, 1934.
SNTSMS	Society for New Testament Studies Monograph Series
SNTSU	Studien zum Neuen Testament und seiner Umwelt
ST	*Studia theologica*

STDJ	*Studies on the Texts of the Desert of Judah*
StPatr	Studia patristica
Str-B	H. Strack and P. Billerbeck, *Kommentar zum Neuen Testament aus Talmud und Midrasch*. 6 vols. Munich, 1922–61
SUNT	Studien zur Umwelt des Neuen Testaments
TAM	*Tituli Asiae Minoris*, vol. 5. Edited by J. Keil and P. Hermann. Vienna: Austrian Scientific Academy, 1989
TANZ	Texte und Arbeiten zum neutestamentlichen Zeitalter
TCGNT	*A Textual Commentary on the Greek New Testament*. B. M. Metzger. London and New York: United Bible Societies. 1st ed., 1971; 2nd ed., 1994
TDNT	*Theological Dictionary of the New Testament*. Edited by G. Kittel and G. Friedrich. Grand Rapids, MI: Eerdmans, 1964–76
TDOT	*Theological Dictionary of the Old Testament*. Edited by G. J. Botterweck and H. Ringgren. Grand Rapids, MI: Eerdmans, 1974–
TJ	*Trinity Journal*
TLNT	*Theological Lexicon of the New Testament*. C. Spicq. Peabody, MA: Hendrickson, 1994
TNTC	Tyndale New Testament Commentaries
TSAJ	Texte und Studien zum antiken Judentum
TynBul	*Tyndale Bulletin*
VC	*Vigiliae christianae*
VCSup	Vigiliae christianae Supplements
VTSup	Vetus Testamentum Supplements
WA.DB	*D. Martin Luthers Werke: Kritische Gesamtausgabe. Die deutsche Bibel*. Weimar: Hermann Böhlaus
WBC	Word Biblical Commentary
WMANT	Wissenschaftliche Monographien zum Alten und Neuen Testament
WTJ	*Westminster Theological Journal*
WUNT	Wissenschaftliche Untersuchungen zum Neuen Testament
ZNT	*Zeitschrift für Neues Testament*
ZNW	*Zeitschrift für die neutestamentliche Wissenschaft und die Kunde der älteren Kirche*
ZTK	*Zeitschrift für Theologie und Kirche*

Greek and Latin Authors

Achilles Tatius
    Leuc. Clit.   *Leucippe et Clitophon*

Aelian
    Nat. an.   *De natura animalium*

Aeschylus
    Ag.   *Agamemnon*
    Eum.   *Eumenides*
    Pers.   *Persae*
    Prom.   *Prometheus vinctus*
    Suppl.   *Supplices*

Aetius
    Corp. med.   *Corpus medicorum*

Alciphron
    Ep. Court.   *Epistles of the Courtesans*

Ambrose
    Ep.   *Epistolae*
    Fid.   *De fide*
    Ob. Val.   *De obitu Valentianiani consolatio*

Appian
    Bell. civ.   *Bella civilia*
    Hist. rom.   *Historia romana*

Apuleius
    Apol.   *Apologia*
    Metam.   *Metamorphoses*

Aristotle
    Hist. an.   *Historia animalium*
    Mag. mor.   *Magna moralia*
    Pol.   *Politica*
    Rhet.   *Rhetorica*

Athanasius
    C. Ar.   *Orationes contra Arianos*
    Ep.   *Epistulae*

Athenagoras
    Leg.   *Legatio pro Christianis*

Augustine
    Civ.   *De civitate Dei*

Cons.	*De consensus evangelistarum*
Doctr. chr.	*De doctrina christiana*
Ep.	*Epistolae*
Enarrat. Ps.	*Enarrationes in Psalmos*
Serm.	*Sermones*
Tract. ep. Jo.	*In epistulam Johannis*
Augustus	
Res	*Res gestae*
Aulus Gelius	
Noct. att.	*Noctes atticae*
Bede	
In Apoc.	*In Apocalypsin*
Caesar	
Bell. civ.	*Bellum civile*
Bell. gall.	*Bellum gallicum*
Callimachus	
Hymn.	*Hymni*
Iamb.	*Iambi*
Cato	
Agr.	*De agricultura*
Chariton	
Chaer.	*De Chaerea et Callirhoe*
Cicero	
Amic.	*De amicitia*
Att.	*Epistulae ad Atticum*
Caecin.	*Pro Caecina*
Cat.	*In Catalinum*
De or.	*De oratore*
Div.	*De divination*
Dom.	*De domo suo*
Fam.	*Epistulae ad familiares*
Fin.	*De finibus*
Flac.	*Pro Flacco*
Inv.	*De invention rhetorica*
Nat. d.	*De natura deorum*
Off.	*De officiis*
Phil.	*Orationes philippicae*

Pis.	*In Pisonem*
Rab. Perd.	*Pro Rabirio Perduellionis Reo*
Rosc. Amer.	*Pro Sexto Roscio Amerino*
Verr.	*In Verrem*

Clement of Alexandria

Ecl.	*Eclogae propheticae*
Exc.	*Excerpta ex Theodoto*
Paed.	*Paedagogus*
Quis div.	*Quis dives salvetur*
Strom.	*Stromata*

Columella

Rust.	*De re rustica*

Cyprian

Eleem.	*De opera et eleemosynis*
Ep.	*Epistulae*
Fort.	*Ad Fortunatum*
Hab. virg.	*De habitu virginum*
Pat.	*De bono patientiae*
Test.	*Ad Quirinum testimonia adversus Judaeos*

Demetrius

Eloc.	*De elocutione*

Didymus

Comm. Zach.	*Commentarii in Zachariam*

Dio Cassius

Rom. Hist.	*Roman History*

Dio Chrysostom

Disc.	*Discourses*

Diodorus Siculus

Libr.	*Library of History*

Diogenes Laertius

Lives	*Lives of Eminent Philosophers*

Dionysius of Halicarnassus

Ant. rom.	*Antiquitates romanae*

Dioscorides Pedanius

Mat. med.	*De material medica*

Epiphanius

Mens.	*De mensuris et ponderibus*

Pan.	*Panarion*

Euripides

Alc.	*Alcestis*
Iph. taur.	*Iphigenia taurica*
Orest.	*Orestes*
Tro.	*Troades*

Eusebius

Hist. eccl.	*Historia ecclesiastica*
Praep. ev.	*Praeparatio evangelica*

Galen

Acut.	*In Hippocrates de victu acutorum commentaria*
Progn.	*In Hippocrates prognosticum commentaria*
Simpl.	*De simplicium medicamentorum temperamentis ac facultatibus*

Gregory of Nazianzus

Or. Bas.	*Oratio in laudem Basilii*

Gregory the Great

Dial.	*Dialogues*
Moral.	*Expositio in Librum Job sive Moralium*

Hippocrates

Int.	*De affectionibis internis*
Morb.	*De morbis*
Progn.	*Prognostica*

Hippolytus

Antichr.	*De antichristo*
Comm. Dan.	*Commentarium in Danielem*
Fr. Prov.	*Fragmenta in Proverbia*
Haer.	*Refutatio omnium haeresium*

Homer

Il.	*Iliad*
Od.	*Odyssey*

Horace

Carm.	*Carmina (Odes)*
Epod.	*Epodi*
Sat.	*Satirae*

Ignatius (Ign.)

Eph.	*To the Ephesians*
Magn.	*To the Magnesians*

Phld.	*To the Philadelphians*
Pol.	*To Polycarp*
Rom.	*To the Romans*
Smyrn.	*To the Smyrnaeans*
Trall.	*To the Trallians*

Irenaeus

Epid.	*Epideixis tou apostolikou kērygmatos*
Haer.	*Adversus haereses*

Isocrates

Ep.	*Epistulae*
Or.	*Orations*

Jerome

Comm. Dan.	*Commentariorum in Danielem*
Comm. Matt.	*Commentariorum in Matthaeum*
Ep.	*Epistulae*
Hom. Mark	*Homilies on Mark*
Vigil.	*Adversus Vigilantium*
Vir. ill.	*De viris illustribus*

Josephus

Ag. Ap.	*Against Apion*
Ant.	*Antiquities*
J. W.	*Jewish War*
Life	*The Life*

Julius Frontinus

De aquis	*De aquis urbis Romae*

Julius Obsequens

Prod.	*Liber de prodigiis*

Justin Martyr

1 Apol.	*First Apology*
2 Apol.	*Second Apology*
Dial.	*Dialogus cum Tryphone*

Justinian

Dig.	*Digest*
Inst.	*Institutes*

Lactantius

Inst.	*Divinarum institutionum*

Livy

    Rom. Hist.   Roman History

Longinus

    Subl.   *De sublimitate*

Lucian

    Alex.   *Alexander the False Prophet*

    Char.   *Charon*

    Dial. mar.   *Dialogi marini*

    Dial. meretr.   *Dialogi meretricii*

    Dial. mort.   *Dialogi mortuorum*

    Electr.   *De electro*

    Fug.   *Fugitivi*

    Herc.   *Hercules*

    Ind.   *Adversus indoctum*

    Lex.   *Lexiphanes*

    Merc. cond.   *De mercede conductis*

    Nav.   *Navigium*

    Nigr.   *Nigrinus*

    Peregr.   *De morte Peregrini*

    Philops.   *Philopseudes*

    Pisc.   *Piscator*

    Salt.   *De saltatione*

    Sat.   *Saturnalia*

    Syr. d.   *De syria dea*

    Tox.   *Toxaris*

    Tyr.   *Tyrannicida*

    Ver. hist.   *Vera historia*

    Vit. auct.   *Vitarum auctio*

Lucretius

    De rer.   *De rerum natura*

Methodius

    Res.   *De resurrection*

    Symp.   *Symposium*

Origen

    Cels.   *Contra Celsum*

    Comm. Jo.   *Commentarii in evangelium Joannis*

Comm. Matt.	*Commentarium in evangelium Matthaei*
Hom. Jer.	*Homiliae in Jeremiam*
Princ.	*De principiis*

Ovid

Am.	*Amores*
Ars	*Ars amatoria*
Fast.	*Fasti*
Ib.	*Ibis*
Metam.	*Metamorphoses*
Trist.	*Tristia*

Pausanias

Descr.	*Graeciae descriptio*

Philo

Abr.	*De Abrahamo*
Cher.	*De cherubim*
Conf.	*De confusion linguarum*
Contempl.	*De vita contemplativa*
Decal.	*De decalogo*
Ebr.	*De ebrietate*
Flacc.	*In Flaccum*
Fug.	*De fuga et invention*
Her.	*Quis rerum divinarum heres sit*
Imm.	*Quod deus sit immutabilis*
Jos.	*De Josepho*
Legat.	*Legatio ad Gaium*
Migr.	*De migratione Abrahami*
Mos.	*De vita Mosis*
Plant.	*De plantatione*
Post.	*De posteritate Caini*
Praem.	*De praemiis et poenis*
Prob.	*Quod omnis probus liber sit*
QE	*Quaestiones et solutions in Exodum*
QG	*Quaestiones et solutions in Genesin*
Sacr.	*De sacrificiis Abelis et Caini*
Sobr.	*De sobrietate*
Somn.	*De somniis*

Spec. Laws	On the Special Laws
Virt.	*De virtutibus*

Philostratus
Vit. Apoll.	*Vita Apollonii*
Vit. soph.	*Vitae sophistarum*

Pindar
Isthm.	*Isthmian Odes*
Ol.	*Olympian Odes*
Pyth.	*Pythian Odes*

Plato
Apol.	*Apologia*
Crat.	*Cratylus*
Crit.	*Crito*
Gorg.	*Gorgias*
Leg.	*Leges*
Phaed.	*Phaedo*
Prot.	*Protagoras*
Resp.	*Respublica*

Plautus
Asin.	*Asinaria*
Aul.	*Aulularia*
Curc.	*Curculio*
Epid.	*Epidicus*
Pseud.	*Pseudolus*
Rud.	*Rudens*

Pliny the Elder
Nat.	*Naturalis historia*

Pliny the Younger
Ep.	*Epistulae*
Pan.	*Panegyricus*

Plutarch
Aem.	*Aemilius Paullus*
Alc.	*Alcibiades*
Ant.	*Antonius*
Art.	*Artaxerxes*
Caes.	*Caesar*

Cor.	Marcius Coriolanus
Crass.	Crassus
Demetr.	Demetrius
Luc.	Lucullus
Mor.	Moralia
Nic.	Nicias
Pel.	Pelopidas
Per.	Pericles
Rom.	Romulus
Sull.	Sulla
Them.	Themistocles
Thes.	Theseus

Polycarp (Pol.)

Phil.	To the Philippians

Ps.-Lucian

Asin.	Asinus aureus

Quintilian

Inst.	Institutio oratoria

Rufinus

Symb.	Commentarius in symbolum apostolorum

Sallust

Bell. cat.	Bellum catalinae

Seneca the Younger

Ben.	De beneficitis
Brev.	De brevitate vitae
Clem.	De clementia
Const.	De constatia
Ep.	Epistulae morales
Helv.	Ad helviam
Herc. Ot.	Hercules Otaeus
Ira	De ira
Marc.	Ad Marciam de consolatione
Nat.	Naturales quaestiones
Prov.	De providentia
Thy.	Thyestes
Tro.	Troades

Statius
  Silv.   *Silvae*
  Theb.   *Thebaid*
Suetonius
  Aug.   *Divus Augustus*
  Cal.   *Gaius Caligula*
  Claud.   *Divus Claudius*
  Dom.   *Domitianus*
  Jul.   *Divus Julius*
  Tib.   *Tiberius*
  Vesp.   *Vespasianus*
  Vit.   *Vitellius*
Tacitus
  Agr.   *Agricola*
  Ann.   *Annales*
  Hist.   *Historiae*
Tertullian
  Adv. Jud.   *Adversus Judaeos*
  An.   *De anima*
  Apol.   *Apologeticus*
  Cor.   *De corona militis*
  Cult. fem.   *De cultu feminarum*
  Fug.   *De fuga in persecutione*
  Marc.   *Adversus Marcionem*
  Or.   *De oratione*
  Paen.   *De paenitentia*
  Praescr.   *De praescriptione haereticorum*
  Pud.   *De pudicitia*
  Res.   *De resurrection carnis*
  Scorp.   *Scorpiace*
Theophilus
  Autol.   *Ad Autolycum*
Theophrastus
  Char.   *Characteres*
  Hist. plant.   *Historia plantarum*

Thucydides
  Pelop.   *Peloponnesian War*
Valerius Maximus
  Facta   *Facta et dicta memorabilia*
Varro
  Ling. lat.   *Lingua latina*
  Rust.   *De re rustica*
Vellius Paterculus
  Rom. Hist.   *Roman History*
Victorinus
  In Apoc.   *In Apocalypsin*
Virgil
  Aen.   *Aeneid*
  Ecl.   *Eclogae*
Vitruvius
  Arch.   *On Architecture*
Xenophon
  Anab.   *Anabasis*
  Cyr.   *Cyropaedia*
  Hell.   *Hellenica*
  Mem.   *Memorabilia*

Jewish and Early Christian Texts

'Abod. Zar.	*Abodah Zarah*
'Abot	*Pirqe 'Abot*
'Abot R. Nat.	*'Abot de Rabbi Nathan*
Acts Cypr.	*Acts of the Martyrdom of St. Cyprian*
Acts Paul	*Acts of Paul*
Acts Scill.	*Acts of the Scillitan Martyrs*
Apoc. Ab.	*Apocalypse of Abraham*
Apoc. El.	*Apocalypse of Elijah*
Apoc. Mos.	*Apocalypse of Moses*
Apoc. Paul	*Apocalypse of Paul*
Apoc. Pet.	*Apocalypse of Peter*
Apoc. Sed.	*Apocalypse of Sedrach*
Apoc. Zeph.	*Apocalypse of Zephaniah*

Apost. Const.	*Apostolic Constitutions*
b.	Babylonian Talmud
B. Bat.	*Baba Batra*
B. Meṣ.	*Baba Meṣiʾa*
2, 3 Bar.	*2, 3 Baruch*
4 Bar.	*4 Baruch (Paraleipomena Jeremiou)*
Barn.	*Epistle of Barnabas*
Bel	Bel and the Dragon
Ber.	*Berakot*
Cant. Rab.	*Canticles Rabbah*
CD	Damascus Document
1, 2 Clem.	*1, 2 Clement*
Deut. Rab.	*Deuteronomy Rabbah*
Did.	*Didache*
DSS	Dead Sea Scrolls
1, 2, 3 En.	*1, 2, 3 Enoch*
Ep. Arist.	*Epistle of Aristeas*
Exod. Rab.	*Exodus Rabbah*
Ezek. Trag.	Ezekiel the Tragedian
frg.	fragment
Frg. Tg.	*Fragment Targum*
Gen. Rab.	*Genesis Rabbah*
Giṭ.	*Giṭṭin*
Gos. Bart.	*Gospel of Bartholomew*
Gos. Nic.	*Gospel of Nicodemus*
Gos. Pet.	*Gospel of Peter*
Gos. Thom.	*Gospel of Thomas*
Ḥag.	*Ḥagigah*
Herm.	Shepherd of Hermas
Jos. As.	*Joseph and Asenath*
Jub.	*Jubilees*
Ket.	*Ketubbot*
L.A.B.	Pseudo-Philo, *Liber antiquitatum biblicarum*
L.A.E.	*Life of Adam and Eve*
Lam. Rab.	*Lamentations Rabbah*
Liv. Pro.	*Lives of the Prophets*

LXX	Septuagint
m.	Mishnah (tractate named)
Mand.	*Mandates*
Mart.	*Martyrdom*
Mart. Asc. Isa.	*Martyrdom and Ascension of Isaiah*
Mart. Carp.	*Martyrdom of Carpus*
Mart. Perp.	*Martyrdom of Perpetua*
Mart. Pion.	*Martyrdom of Pionius*
Mart. Pol.	*Martyrdom of Polycarp*
Meg.	*Megillah*
Mek.	*Mekilta*
Midd.	*Middot*
Midr. Ps.	*Midrash on Psalms*
Mo'ed Qaṭ.	*Mo'ed Qaṭan*
MT	Masoretic Text
Mur	Murabba'at
NT	New Testament
Num. Rab.	*Numbers Rabbah*
Odes Sol.	*Odes of Solomon*
OT	Old Testament
par.	parallel passages
Pesaḥ.	*Pesaḥim*
Pesiq. Rab.	*Pesiqta Rabbati*
Pol.	Polycarp
Pr Azar	Prayer of Azariah
Pr. Jac.	*Prayer of Jacob*
Ps.	Pseudo
Ps.-Phoc.	Pseudo-Phocylides
Pss. Sol.	*Psalms of Solomon*
1Q, 2Q, 3Q, etc.	Text from Qumran Cave 1, 2, 3, etc.
1QH^a	Qumran Hymns
Qidd.	*Qiddushim*
1QM	Qumran *War Scroll*
11QMelch	11QMelchizedek
1QpHab	Qumran Commentary ("Pesher") on Habakkuk

1QS	Qumran Rule of the Community
Sanh.	*Sanhedrin*
Shabb.	*Shabbat*
Shek.	*Shekalim*
Shem. Es.	*Shemoneh Esrei*
Sib. Or.	*Sibylline Oracles*
Sim.	*Similitudes*
Sukk.	*Sukkot*
t.	Tosefta (tractate named)
T.	*Testament*
T. 12 Patr.	*Testaments of the Twelve Patriarchs*
T. Ab.	*Testament of Abraham*
T. Adam	*Testament of Adam*
T. Ash.	*Testament of Asher*
T. Benj.	*Testament of Benjamin*
T. Dan	*Testament of Dan*
T. Gad	*Testament of Gad*
T. Iss.	*Testament of Issachar*
T. Jac.	*Testament of Jacob*
T. Job	*Testament of Job*
T. Jos.	*Testament of Joseph*
T. Jud.	*Testament of Judah*
T. Levi	*Testament of Levi*
T. Mos.	*Testament of Moses*
T. Naph.	*Testament of Naphtali*
T. Reu.	*Testament of Reuben*
T. Sim.	*Testament of Simeon*
T. Sol.	*Testament of Solomon*
T. Zeb.	*Testament of Zebulun*
Ta'an.	*Ta'anit*
Tg.	*Targum*
Tg. Neof.	*Targum Neofiti*
Tg. Onq.	*Targum Onqelos*
Tg. Ps.-J.	*Targum Pseudo-Jonathan*
Theod.	*Theodotian*
Toh.	*Tohoroth*

Vis.	*Visions*
y.	Jerusalem Talmud (tractate named)

Inscriptions and Papyri

I.Did	Inscriptions from Didyma, in Albert Rehm, *Didyma*. Vol. 2. Berlin: Mann, 1958.
I.Eph	*Die Inschriften von Ephesos*. 8 vols. Edited by H. Wankel et al. Bonn: Habelt, 1979–84.
IG	*Inscriptiones Graecae*. Editio minor. Berlin, 1924–.
IGR	*Inscriptiones Graecae ad res Romanas Pertinentes* IV. Edited by René Cagnat et al. Paris: Leroux, 1927.
IJO	*Inscriptiones Judaicae Orientis*. Edited by David Noy et al. 3 vols. TSAJ 99. 101, 102. Tübingen: Mohr Siebeck, 2004.
I.Kourion	*The Inscriptions from Kourion*. Edited by T. B. Mitford. Philadelphia: American Philosophical Society, 1971.
I.Laod	*Die Inschriften von Laodikeia am Lykos*. Edited by T. Corsten. Bonn: Habelt, 1997.
I.Leros	Inscriptions from Leros, in G. Manganaro, "Le iscrizioni delle isole Milesie." *Annuario della scuola archaologica di Atene* 46–47 (1963–64), 296–318.
I.Magn	*Die Inschriften von Magnesia am Mäander*. Edited by O. Kern. Berlin: Spemann, 1900.
I.Olympia	*Die Inschriften von Olympia*. Edited by W. Dittenberger. Berlin: Ascher, 1896.
I.Pat	Inscriptions from Patmos, in G. Manganaro, "Le iscrizioni delle isole Milesie." *Annuario della scuola archaologica di Atene* 46–47 (1963–64), 331–46.
I.Perg	*Die Inschriften von Pergamon*. 3 vols. Edited by M. Fränkel et al. Berlin: Spemann, 1890, 1895, 1969.
I.Phil	Inscriptions from Philadelphia, in G. Petzl, *Philadelpheia et Ager Philadelphenus. Tituli Lydiae* 5/3. Titula Asiae Minoris. Vienna: Östereichischen Akademie der Wissenschaften, 2007.
I.Sard	Inscriptions from Sardis, in W. H. Buckler and D. M. Robinson, *Sardis*. Vol. 7. Leiden: Brill, 1932.

I.Smyr	*Die Inschriften von Smyrna.* 2 vols. Edited by G. Petzl. Bonn: Habelt, 1982–90.
I.Strat	*Die Inschriften von Stratonikeia.* Edited by M. Ç. Sahin and A. Lozano. Bonn: Habelt, 1981–.
I.Syr	Inscriptions from Syria in *Inscriptiones Judaicae Orientis.* Vol. 3. Syria and Cyprus. Edited by David Noy and Hanswulf Bloedhorn. Tübingen: Mohr Siebeck 2004.
I.Thyat	Inscriptions from Thyatira, in *Tituli Lydiae* 5/2. Edited by P. Hermann. Titula Asiae Minoris. Vienna: Östereichischen Akademie der Wissenschaften, 1989.
I.Trall	*Die Inschriften von Tralleis and Nyssa.* Edited by F. B. Poljakov. Bonn: Habelt, 1988–.
P.Fay.	*Fayum Towns and Their Papyri.* Edited by Bernard P. Grenfell, Arthur S. Hunt, and D. G. Hogarth. London and Boston: Egypt Exploration Fund, 1900.
P.Fouad	*Les papyrus Fouad I.* Cairo: L'Institut français d'archéologie orientale, 1939.
P.Hal.	*Auszüge aus Alexandrinischen Gesetzen und Verordnungen in einem Papyrus des philologischen Seminars der Universität Halle.* Berlin: Weidmansche Buchhandlung, 1913.
P.Hib.	*The Hibeh Papyri.* Edited by Bernard P. Grenfell, Arthur S. Hunt, and E. G. Turner. London and Boston: Egypt Exploration Fund, 1906.
P.Köln	*Kölner Papyri.* Edited by Bärbel Kramer et al. Opladen: Westdeutscher Verlag; Paderborn: Schöningh, 1976–.
P.Lille	*Papyrus grecs de Lille.* Edited by Pierre Jougouet et al. 2 vols. Paris: E. Leroux, 1907–27.
P.Lond.	*Greek Papyri in the British Museum.* Edited by Frederic G. Kenyon, H. Idris Bell, and W. E. Krum. London: British Museum, 1893–.
P.Mich.	*Michigan Papyri.* Edited by C. C. Edgar, A. E. R. Boak, and J. G. Winter. Ann Arbor: University of Michigan Press, 1931–36.
P.Oslo	*Papyri Osloenses.* Edited by S. Eitrem and L. Amundsen. 3 vols. Oslo: Jacob Dybwad, 1925–36.
P.Oxy.	*The Oxyrhynchus Papyri.* Edited by Bernard P. Grenfell, Arthur S. Hunt, et al. London: Egypt Exploration Fund, 1898–.

P.Russ.   *Papyri Russischer und Georgischer Sammlungen.* Edited by
           G. Zereteli, O. Krüger, and P. Jernstedt. 5 vols. Amsterdam:
           A. M. Hakkert, 1966.
P.Ryl.   *Catalogue of the Greek Papyri in the John Rylands Library.*
           Edited by Colin H. Roberts, John de Monins Johnson, and
           Arthur S. Hunt. Manchester: Manchester University Press,
           1911–.

REVELATION: A TRANSLATION

Introduction to the Book

1 ¹A revelation from Jesus Christ, which God gave him to show his servants what things must soon take place. He made it known by sending it through his angel to his servant John, ²who bore witness to the word of God and the witness of Jesus Christ, as much as he saw. ³Blessed is the one who reads aloud and those who hear the words of the prophecy and keep the things written in it, for the time is near.

⁴John to the seven assemblies that are in Asia: Grace to you and peace from the one who is and who was and who is to come, and from the seven spirits that are before his throne, ⁵and from Jesus Christ the faithful witness, the firstborn of the dead, and the ruler of the kings of the earth. To him who loves us and released us from our sins by his blood, ⁶and made us a kingdom, priests to his God and Father, to him be glory and might for ever and ever. Amen.

⁷See, he is coming with the clouds, and every eye will see him, even those who pierced him, and all the tribes of the earth will grieve for him.

Yes. Amen!

⁸"I am the Alpha and the Omega," says the Lord God, "the one who is and who was and who is to come, the Almighty."

First Cycle: Christ and the Seven Assemblies

⁹I John, your brother and companion in the affliction and the kingdom and the endurance that we have in Jesus, was on the island called Patmos because of the word of God and the witness of Jesus. ¹⁰I was in the Spirit on the Lord's Day, and I heard behind me a loud voice that sounded like a trumpet, ¹¹saying, "Write what you see in a scroll and send it to the seven assemblies: to Ephesus, to Smyrna, to Pergamum, to Thyatira, to Sardis, to Philadelphia, and to Laodicea."

¹²So I turned toward the voice, to see who was speaking with me, and when I turned I saw seven gold lampstands. ¹³In the middle of the lampstands was someone who looked like a human being. He wore a robe that stretched down to his feet and had a gold sash wrapped around his chest. ¹⁴His head and hair were white as white wool—like snow—and his eyes were like a flame of fire. ¹⁵His feet were like shining bronze, refined as in a furnace, and his voice was like the sound of rushing water. ¹⁶He held seven stars in his right hand, and from his mouth came a sharp two-edged sword. His face was like the sun shining with all its power.

¹⁷When I saw him, I fell at his feet as if I were dead, but he put his right hand on me and said, "Do not be afraid. I am the first and the last, ¹⁸and the living one. I was dead, but see, I live forever and ever. I have the keys to Death and Hades. ¹⁹So write what you have seen, which includes things as they are now as well as things to come. ²⁰As for the mystery of the seven stars that you saw on my right hand and the seven gold lampstands: the seven stars are the seven angels of the seven assemblies and the seven lampstands are the seven assemblies.

2 ¹"To the angel of the assembly in Ephesus write: Thus says the one who holds the seven stars in his right hand, who walks among the seven gold lampstands: ²I know your works, namely your labor and your endurance, and that you are not able to bear evildoers. You tested those who say they are apostles but are not, and have found that they are liars. ³I know that you are enduring and bearing up for the sake of my name and have not gotten tired. ⁴But I have this against you, that you have let go of the love you had at first. ⁵Therefore, remember from where you have fallen. Repent and do the works you did at first. If you do not, I will come to you and move your lampstand from its place—if you do not repent. ⁶But this you have, that you hate the works of the Nicolaitans, which I also hate. ⁷Let the one who has an ear hear what the Spirit says to the assemblies. To those who conquer I will grant to eat from the tree of life that is in the paradise of God.

⁸"To the angel of the assembly in Smyrna write: Thus says the first and the last, who died and came to life: ⁹I know your affliction and poverty (even though you are rich), and the denunciation of those who say they are Jews (though they are not, but are a synagogue of Satan). ¹⁰Fear nothing you are about to suffer. You see the devil is going to throw some of you into prison so that you might be tested, and you will have affliction for ten days. Be faithful to death and I will give you the laurel wreath of life. ¹¹Let the one who has an ear hear what the Spirit says to the assemblies. Those who conquer will not be harmed by the second death.

¹²"To the angel of the assembly in Pergamum write: Thus says the one who has the sharp two-edged sword: ¹³I know where you live, where Satan's

throne is, and that you are holding on to my name and did not deny your faith in me even at the time that Antipas my faithful witness was killed among you, where Satan lives. ¹⁴But I have a few things against you, for you have some there who hold the teaching of Balaam, who taught Balak to mislead the sons of Israel so that they would eat what was sacrificed to idols and so do what is immoral. ¹⁵In the same way you also have those who hold the teaching of the Nicolaitans. ¹⁶So repent. If you do not, I will come to you soon and make war on them with the sword of my mouth. ¹⁷Let the one who has an ear hear what the Spirit says to the assemblies. To those who conquer I will give some of the hidden manna. I will also give a white stone, with a new name written on it, which no one knows except the one who receives it.

¹⁸"To the angel of the assembly in Thyatira write: Thus says the Son of God, whose eyes are like a flame of fire and whose feet are like shining bronze: ¹⁹I know your works, your love and faithfulness, your service and endurance. And I know that the works you have done most recently are even greater than those you did at first. ²⁰But I have against you that you tolerate the woman Jezebel, who calls herself a prophetess—even though she teaches and deceives my servants into doing what is immoral and eating food sacrificed to idols. ²¹I gave her time to repent, but she refuses to repent of her immorality. ²²See, I am going to put her to bed, and put those with whom she has committed adultery into terrible affliction. If they do not repent of her works, ²³I will also put her children to death with a plague. And all the assemblies will know that I am the one who examines minds and hearts, and will give to each of you what your works deserve. ²⁴But I say to the rest of you in Thyatira—those who do not hold this teaching and do not know what they call 'the deep things' of Satan—to you I say that I will not burden you with anything else. ²⁵Only hold on to what you have until I come. ²⁶To those who conquer and keep my works until the end, I will give authority over the nations. ²⁷They will rule them with an iron rod, the way one breaks clay pottery—²⁸just as I received from my Father. I will also give them the morning star. ²⁹Let the one who has an ear hear what the Spirit says to the assemblies.

3 ¹"To the angel of the assembly in Sardis write: Thus says the one who holds the seven spirits of God and the seven stars: I know your works; you have a name of being alive, even though you are dead. ²Be watchful and strengthen what you still have that is dying, for I have not found your works complete before God. ³So remember what you received and heard. Hold on to it and repent. For if you do not watch out, I will come like a thief, and you will not know at what hour I will come to you. ⁴But one could name a few in Sardis who have not defiled their clothing, and they will walk with me in white because they are worthy. ⁵Those who conquer will wear white clothing like this, and I will not blot their names out of the scroll of life, but will acknowledge their names before my Father and his angels. [6]Let the one who has an ear hear what the Spirit says to the assemblies.

[7]"To the angel of the assembly in Philadelphia write: Thus says the Holy One, the True One, the One who has the key of David, the One who opens so that no one will shut and who shuts so that no one opens: [8]I know your works. You see I have put before you an open door that no one can shut, because you have so little power and yet you have kept my word and have not denied my name. [9]See, I will make those from the synagogue of Satan—who say they are Jews but are not, but are lying—I will make them come and bow down before your feet, so that they will know I have loved you. [10]Because you kept my word of endurance, I will also keep you from the hour of testing that is coming on the whole world, to test those who live on the earth. [11]I am coming soon. Hold fast to what you have so that no one takes your laurel wreath. [12]Any who conquer I will make into a pillar in the temple of my God and they will never leave it. Moreover, I will write on them the name of God and the name of the city of my God, the New Jerusalem that comes down from heaven from my God, and my own new name. [13]Let the one who has an ear listen to what the Spirit says to the assemblies.

[14]"To the angel of the assembly in Laodicea write: Thus says the Amen, the faithful and true witness, the ruler of God's creation: [15]I know your works. You are neither cold nor hot. I wish that you were either cold or hot. [16]So, because you are tepid, and neither hot nor cold, I am about to vomit you out of my mouth. [17]For you say, 'I am rich and have become wealthy and do not need anything.' Yet you do not realize that you are miserable and pitiable and poor and blind and naked. [18]I advise you to buy from me gold that has been refined by fire so that you may be rich, and white clothing to wear so that you will not appear naked and ashamed, and salve to put on your eyes so that you may see. [19]I correct and discipline those whom I love. So be committed and repent. [20]See, I am standing at the door and knocking. If any hear my voice and open the door, I will come in to them and will dine with them and they with me. [21]As for those who conquer, I will grant that they might sit with me on my throne, just as I conquered and sat with my Father on his throne. [22]Let the one who has an ear hear what the Spirit says to the assemblies."

Second Cycle: The Seven Seals

4   [1]After these things I looked, and there was a door that had been opened in heaven. And the first voice that I heard speaking with me like a trumpet said, "Come up here and I will show you what must take place after these things." [2]At once I was in the Spirit, and there in heaven was a throne, and someone was seated on the throne. [3]The one seated there looked like jasper and carnelian,

and around the throne was a rainbow that looked like an emerald. ⁴Around the throne were twenty-four thrones and seated on the thrones were twenty-four elders, clothed in white robes with gold laurel wreaths on their heads. ⁵From the throne came flashes of lightning and rumblings and peals of thunder, and in front of the throne were seven flaming torches, which are the seven spirits of God. ⁶And in front of the throne was something like a sea of glass, like crystal. In the middle by the throne, in a circle around the throne, were four living creatures that were covered with eyes on the front and on the back. ⁷The first living creature was like a lion, the second living creature was like an ox, the third living creature had a face like a human being, and the fourth living creature was like an eagle in flight. ⁸Each of the four living creatures had six wings, and they were covered all around and inside with eyes. They never rest, day and night, saying,

> "Holy, holy, holy is the Lord God Almighty,
> who was and who is and who is to come."

⁹Whenever the living creatures give glory and honor and thanks to the one seated on the throne, who lives forever and ever, ¹⁰the twenty-four elders fall before the one seated on the throne and worship the one who lives forever and ever. They throw their laurel wreaths down before the throne and say,

> ¹¹"You are worthy, our Lord and God, to receive glory and honor and power,
> for you created all things and by your will they existed and were created."

5 ¹Then I saw in the right hand of the one seated on the throne a scroll, written on the inside and the back, sealed with seven seals. ²And I saw a powerful angel proclaiming with a loud voice, "Who is worthy to open the scroll and break its seals?" ³And no one in heaven or on earth or under the earth was able to open the scroll or to look into it. ⁴So I wept a great deal because no one was found worthy to open the scroll or to look into it. ⁵Then one of the elders said to me, "Stop weeping. You see, the Lion of the tribe of Judah, the Root of David has conquered, so that he can open the scroll and its seven seals."

⁶Then I saw in between the throne and the four living creatures and among the elders a Lamb, standing as one who had been slain. It had seven horns and seven eyes, which are the seven spirits of God that are sent into all the earth. ⁷He went and received the scroll from the right hand of the one seated on the throne. ⁸And when he received the scroll, the four living creatures and the twenty-four elders fell down before the Lamb, each with a harp and gold offering bowls filled with incense, which are the prayers of the saints. ⁹And they sang a new song, saying,

> "You are worthy to receive the scroll and to open its seals,
> for you were slain and by your blood you purchased for God
> those of every tribe and language and people and nation,

¹⁰and you made them a kingdom and priests to our God
and they will reign on the earth."

¹¹Then I looked, and around the throne and the living creatures and the elders I heard the sound of many angels. They numbered in the millions—thousands upon thousands. ¹²They said in a loud voice,

"Worthy is the Lamb who was slain
to receive power and wealth and wisdom and might
and honor and glory and blessing."

¹³And I heard every creature in heaven and on earth and under the earth and in the sea—I heard everything in them say,

"To the one seated on the throne and to the Lamb
be blessing and honor and glory and might forever and ever."

¹⁴And the four living creatures said, "Amen," and the elders fell down and worshiped.

6 ¹Then I looked, when the Lamb opened one of the seven seals, and I heard one of the four living creatures say in a voice like thunder, "Come!" ²So I looked, and there was a white horse. Its rider held a bow and a laurel wreath was given to him. And the conqueror went out in order to conquer.

³Then, when he opened the second seal, I heard the second living creature say, "Come!" ⁴And out came another horse, fiery red. Its rider was allowed to take the peace from the earth, so that people would slay one another. And a large sword was given to him.

⁵Then, when he opened the third seal, I heard the third living creature say, "Come!" So I looked, and there was a black horse. Its rider held a pair of scales in his hand. ⁶And I heard what sounded like a voice from among the four living creatures. It said, "A quart of wheat for a denarius, and three quarts of barley for a denarius, but do not damage the olive oil and the wine."

⁷Then, when he opened the fourth seal, I heard the voice of the fourth living creature say, "Come!" ⁸So I looked, and there was a pale green horse. Its rider's name was Death, and Hades was following right behind him. They were given authority over a fourth of the earth, to kill by sword and famine and disease and the wild animals of the earth.

⁹Then, when he opened the fifth seal, I saw under the altar the souls of those who had been slain because of the word of God and the witness they had given. ¹⁰They cried out with a loud voice and said, "How long, O Master, holy and true, will you wait before you pass judgment and bring justice for our blood, which was shed by those who live on the earth?" ¹¹But each of them was given a white robe, and they were told to rest for a short time, until those who were their fellow servants and their brethren—who were to be killed as they were—were finished.

¹²Then I looked, when he opened the sixth seal, and a great earthquake occurred. The sun became black as sackcloth made of hair, and the entire moon became like blood. ¹³The stars of the sky fell to the earth like a fig tree drops its fruit when shaken by a strong wind. ¹⁴The sky disappeared, like a scroll being rolled up, and every mountain and island was moved from its place. ¹⁵Then the kings of the earth and the aristocrats and the generals and the rich and the powerful and everyone, slave and free, hid themselves in caves and in the rocks of the mountains. ¹⁶They called to the mountains and the rocks, "Fall on us" and "hide us from the face of the one seated on the throne and from the wrath of the Lamb! ¹⁷For the great day of their wrath has come, and who is able to stand?"

7   ¹After this I saw four angels standing at the four corners of the earth, holding back the four winds of the earth so that no wind would blow against the earth or the sea or any tree. ²And I saw another angel coming up from the east, holding the seal of the living God, and he cried out with a loud voice to the four angels who had been given the power to damage the earth and sea. ³He said, "Do not damage the earth or the sea or the trees until we have put a seal on the foreheads of the servants of our God."

⁴Then I heard the number of the sealed, 144,000, sealed from every tribe of the sons of Israel: ⁵From the tribe of Judah 12,000 were sealed, from the tribe of Reuben 12,000, from the tribe of Gad 12,000, ⁶from the tribe of Asher 12,000, from the tribe of Naphtali 12,000, from the tribe of Manasseh 12,000, ⁷from the tribe of Simeon 12,000, from the tribe of Levi 12,000, from the tribe of Issachar 12,000, ⁸from the tribe of Zebulun 12,000, from the tribe of Joseph 12,000, from the tribe of Benjamin 12,000.

⁹After these things I looked, and there was a great crowd that no one could number, from every nation and tribe and people and language. They were standing before the throne and before the Lamb, clothed in white robes, and there were palm branches in their hands. ¹⁰They cried out with a loud voice and said,

"Salvation belongs to our God who is seated on the throne,
and to the Lamb."

¹¹And all the angels stood in a circle around the throne and around the elders and the four living creatures. They fell on their faces before the throne and worshiped God. ¹²They said,

"Amen! Blessing and glory and wisdom
and thanksgiving and honor and power and might
be to our God for ever and ever, Amen."

¹³Then one of the elders said to me, "Who are these, who are wearing white robes, and where did they come from?" ¹⁴And I said to him, "Sir, you

know." Then he said to me, "These are the people who come out of the great affliction. They have washed their robes and made them white in the blood of the Lamb. ¹⁵This is the reason they are before the throne of God. They serve him day and night in his temple, and the one seated on the throne will shelter them. ¹⁶They will not hunger anymore or thirst anymore. No sun or scorching heat will beat down on them, ¹⁷for the Lamb who is in the middle by the throne will shepherd them. He will lead them to the springs of the waters of life, and God will wipe away every tear from their eyes."

8 ¹Then, when he opened the seventh seal, there was silence in heaven for about half an hour. ²And I saw the seven angels, who stand before God, and seven trumpets were given to them. ³Then another angel came and stood at the altar holding a gold censer, and a large amount of incense was given to him to offer along with the prayers of all the saints at the gold altar that is before the throne. ⁴The smoke from the incense with the prayers of the saints went up before God from the hand of the angel. ⁵Then the angel took the censer and filled it with fire from the altar and threw it to the earth, and there were peals of thunder, rumblings, flashes of lightning, and an earthquake.

Third Cycle: The Seven Trumpets

⁶Then the seven angels who held the seven trumpets made ready to blow them. ⁷The first blew his trumpet, and there was hail and fire mixed with blood, and it was thrown down to the earth, so that a third of the earth was burned up, and a third of the trees were burned up, and all the green grass was burned up. ⁸Then the second angel blew his trumpet, and something like a great mountain burning with fire was thrown down to the sea, so that a third of the sea became blood, ⁹and a third of the living creatures in the sea died, and a third of the ships were destroyed. ¹⁰Then the third angel blew his trumpet, and a great star, burning like a torch, fell from heaven, and it fell on a third of the rivers and the springs of water. ¹¹The name of the star is Wormwood, and a third of the waters became wormwood, and many people died from the water because it became bitter. ¹²Then the fourth angel blew his trumpet, and a third of the sun was struck and a third of the moon and a third of the stars, so that a third of them were darkened, and the day lost a third of its light, and the night lost a third of its light.

¹³Then I looked and I heard an eagle flying high overhead, saying with a loud voice, "Woe, woe, woe to those who live on the earth because of the remaining blasts of the trumpet, which the three angels are about to blow."

9 ¹Then the fifth angel blew his trumpet, and I saw a star that had fallen from heaven to earth, and he was given the key to the shaft of the abyss. ²He opened the shaft of the abyss, and smoke went up from the shaft like smoke from a huge furnace, so that the sun and air were darkened by the smoke from the shaft. ³Then locusts came out of the smoke and onto the earth, and they were given power like the power of the scorpions of earth. ⁴They were told not to hurt the grass of the earth or any green plant or any tree, but only those people who do not have the seal of God on their foreheads. ⁵They were not allowed to kill them, but only to inflict pain on them for five months—and the pain they inflict is like that of a scorpion when it strikes a person. ⁶In those days people will seek death, but they will not find it. They will want to die, but death will flee from them.

⁷The locusts looked like horses ready for battle. On their heads were what seemed to be gold laurel wreaths. Their faces were like human faces, ⁸their hair was like women's hair, and their teeth were like those of lions. ⁹In the front they had what seemed to be iron breastplates, and the sound of their wings was like the sound of many chariots with horses racing into battle. ¹⁰They also have tails that sting, just like scorpions, and their power to hurt people for five months is in their tails. ¹¹Their king is the angel of the abyss, whose name in Hebrew is Abaddon, and in Greek he has the name Apollyon.

¹²The first woe has passed. See, two woes are yet to come after these things.

¹³Then the sixth angel blew his trumpet, and I heard a voice from the four horns of the gold altar that is before God. ¹⁴It said to the sixth angel who had the trumpet, "Release the four angels that are bound at the great river Euphrates." ¹⁵Then the four angels who had been made ready for that hour and day and month and year were released to kill a third of humankind. ¹⁶The number of cavalry troops was twice ten thousand times ten thousand. I heard their number. ¹⁷And this is the way I saw the horses and their riders in the vision: They had breastplates that were fiery red, dark blue, and yellow as sulfur. The horses' heads were like the heads of lions, and out of their mouths came fire and smoke and sulfur. ¹⁸By these three plagues a third of humankind was killed: by the fire and smoke and sulfur coming out of their mouths. ¹⁹For the power of the horses is in their mouths and in their tails, for their tails are like snakes with heads that inflict injuries.

²⁰The rest of humankind, who were not killed by these plagues, did not repent of the works of their hands. They did not stop worshiping demons and idols of gold and silver and bronze and stone and wood, which cannot see or hear or walk. ²¹They did not repent of their murders or their sorceries or their immorality or their thefts.

10 ¹Then I saw another powerful angel coming down from heaven. He was robed in a cloud, with the rainbow over his head. His face was like the sun, and his feet were like pillars of fire, ²and he held an open scroll in his hand. He put his right foot on the sea and his left foot on the land. ³Then he called out with a loud voice like a lion roaring, and when he called out, the seven thunders raised their voices. ⁴And when the seven thunders spoke, I was about to write, but I heard a voice from heaven say, "Seal up what the seven thunders said, and do not write it down."

⁵Then the angel, whom I saw standing on the sea and on the land, raised his right hand to heaven ⁶and he swore by the one who lives forever and ever, who created the heaven and what is in it, and the earth and what is in it, and the sea and what is in it: "There will be no more time of waiting, ⁷but in the days when the seventh angel blows the trumpet, the mysterious purpose of God will be completed, as he announced the good news to his servants the prophets."

⁸Then the voice that I heard from heaven spoke with me again and said, "Go, receive the open scroll that is in the hand of the angel who stands on the sea and on the land." ⁹So I went to the angel and told him give me the scroll. He said to me, "Receive and devour it. It will be bitter to your stomach, but sweet as honey in your mouth." ¹⁰So I took the scroll from the hand of the angel and devoured it. It was sweet as honey in my mouth, but when I ate it, it made my stomach bitter. ¹¹Then I was told, "You must prophesy again about many peoples and nations and languages and kings."

11 ¹I was given a measuring reed, which was like a staff, and was told, "Go and measure the temple of God and the altar, and those who worship there. ²But do not measure the court outside the temple. Leave that out, for it has been given to the nations, and they will trample the holy city for forty-two months.

³"I will also allow my two witnesses to prophesy for 1,260 days, wearing sackcloth." ⁴These are the two olive trees and the two lampstands that stand before the Lord of the earth. ⁵If anyone wants to hurt them, fire comes from their mouth and devours their enemies. So if anyone wants to harm them, they must be killed in this way. ⁶They have the power to close up the sky, so that no rain will fall during the days of their prophesying. They also have power over the waters, to turn them into blood, and to strike the earth with any plague, as often as they wish.

⁷When they have finished their witnessing, the beast that comes up from the abyss will make war on them and conquer them and kill them. ⁸Their dead bodies will lie on the main street of the great city, which spiritually is called Sodom and Egypt. That is also where their Lord was crucified. ⁹And for three and a half days, some from the peoples and tribes and languages and nations will look at their dead bodies, but they will not let their dead bodies be put in

a tomb. ¹⁰Those who live on the earth will rejoice over them and celebrate and give gifts to each other, because these two prophets brought such pain to those who live on the earth.

¹¹But after the three and a half days, a spirit of life from God entered them, and they stood on their feet. Great fear came over those who saw them. ¹²Then they heard a loud voice from heaven say to them, "Come up here." And they went up to heaven in a cloud, while their enemies watched them. ¹³At that hour there was a great earthquake, and a tenth of the city fell. Seven thousand people were killed by the earthquake, and the rest were afraid and gave glory to the God of heaven.

¹⁴The second woe has passed. The third woe is coming soon.

¹⁵Then the seventh angel blew his trumpet, and there were loud voices in heaven, saying,

"The kingdom of the world has become
that of our Lord and his Anointed,
and he will reign forever and ever."

¹⁶Then the twenty-four elders, who were seated on their thrones before God, fell on their faces and worshiped God. ¹⁷They said,

"We give thanks to you, Lord God Almighty, who is and who was,
for you have taken your great power and you reign.
¹⁸The nations were wrathful, but your wrath came.
It is the time for the dead to be judged,
and to reward your servants, the prophets and the saints
and those who fear your name, both the small and the great,
and to destroy those who destroy the earth."

Fourth Cycle: The Dragon, the Beasts, and the Faithful

¹⁹Then God's temple in heaven was opened, and the ark of his covenant appeared in his temple. There were flashes of lightning, rumblings, peals of thunder, an earthquake, and large hail. **12** ¹And a great sign appeared in heaven: a woman clothed with the sun, with the moon under her feet and a wreath of twelve stars on her head. ²She was pregnant and cried out in pain, for she was in the agony of giving birth. ³Then another sign appeared in heaven: a great fiery red dragon, with seven heads and ten horns, and seven diadems on its heads. ⁴Its tail swept down a third of the stars of heaven and threw them to the earth. And the dragon stood before the woman who was about to give birth, so that when she gave birth, it might devour her child. ⁵She gave birth to a son, a male, who is to rule all the nations with an iron rod. But her child was caught up to God and his throne, ⁶and the woman fled to the desert, where she had a place made ready by God. There she will be taken care of for 1,260 days.

⁷Then there was war in heaven: Michael and his angels fought the dragon, and the dragon and its angels fought back, ⁸but they were defeated and there was no longer any place for them in heaven. ⁹So the great dragon was thrown down. He is the ancient serpent, who is called devil and Satan, the deceiver of the whole world. He was thrown down to the earth and his angels were thrown down with him. ¹⁰I heard a loud voice in heaven say,

"Now the salvation and the power and the kingdom of our God,
and the authority of his Anointed have come,
for the accuser of our brethren has been thrown down,
the one who accuses them day and night before our God.
¹¹They conquered him through the blood of the Lamb
and the word of their witness.
Love for their own lives did not make them shun death.
¹²Therefore, rejoice you heavens and those who dwell in them.
But woe to the earth and sea,
because the devil has come down to you with great anger,
for he knows that his time is short."

¹³When the dragon saw that it had been thrown down to the earth, it chased the woman who had given birth to the male child. ¹⁴But the woman was given the two wings of a great eagle so that she could fly to her place in the desert, where she would be taken care of for a time and times and half a time, out of the serpent's reach. ¹⁵Then from its mouth the serpent poured a river of water after the woman, so that the river would sweep her away. ¹⁶But the earth helped the woman. The earth opened its mouth and swallowed the river that the dragon poured out of its mouth. ¹⁷So the dragon was furious at the woman, and it went off to make war on the rest of her children, who keep the commandments of God and hold firmly to the witness of Jesus.

¹⁸Then the dragon stood on the shore of the sea, **13** ¹and I saw a beast coming up from the sea. It had ten horns and seven heads. On its horns were ten diadems and on its heads were blasphemous names. ²The beast I saw was like a leopard. Its feet were like a bear's and its mouth was like a lion's mouth. The dragon gave it its power and throne and great authority. ³One of its heads appeared to have been slain and killed, but its mortal wound was healed. So the whole earth was amazed and followed the beast. ⁴They worshiped the dragon because it had given the beast its authority. And they worshiped the beast and said, "Who is like the beast and who can make war against it?"

⁵The beast was given a mouth that spoke boastful and blasphemous things, and it was given authority to act for forty-two months. ⁶It opened its mouth to speak blasphemies against God. It blasphemed his name and his dwelling place (that is, those who dwell in heaven). ⁷It was also allowed to make war on the saints and to conquer them. It was given authority over every

tribe and people and language and nation. ⁸All who live on earth will worship it, all those whose names have not been written—from the time the earth was made—in the scroll of life of the Lamb who was slain.

⁹If any have an ear, let them hear:
¹⁰If any are to go into captivity, into captivity they go.
If any are to be killed by the sword, by the sword they will be killed.

This calls for endurance and faith on the part of the saints.

¹¹Then I saw another beast coming up from the earth. It had two horns like a lamb, but it was speaking like a dragon. ¹²It exercises all the authority of the first beast in its presence. It also makes the earth and all who live in it worship the first beast, whose mortal wound was healed. ¹³It does great signs, so that it even makes fire come down from heaven to earth in the presence of the people. ¹⁴It deceives those who live on the earth by the signs that it was allowed to do in the presence of the beast. It told those who live on earth to make an image for the beast, which had been wounded by the sword and yet came to life again. ¹⁵It was allowed to give breath to the image of the beast, so that the image of the beast would even speak, and to have anyone who did not worship the image of the beast be put to death.

¹⁶It makes everyone—the small and great, the rich and poor, the free and slaves—to have a mark put on their right hand or on their forehead, ¹⁷so that no one can buy or sell anything unless the person has the mark with the beast's name or the number of its name. ¹⁸This calls for wisdom. Let the one who understands calculate the number of the beast, for it is the number of a person. Its number is 666.

14 ¹Then I looked, and there was the Lamb, standing on Mount Zion. With him were 144,000 who had his name and his Father's name written on their foreheads. ²And I heard a sound from heaven that was like the sound of rushing water and like the sound of loud thunder. The sound I heard was like that of harpists playing their harps. ³They sang what seemed to be a new song in front of the throne and the four living creatures and the elders. And no one could understand the song except the 144,000, who had been purchased from the earth. ⁴They were not defiled with women. Now these who follow the Lamb wherever he goes are maidens. They were purchased from humankind as first fruit for God and the Lamb. ⁵In their mouth no lie was found; they are blameless.

⁶Then I saw another angel flying high overhead with eternal good news to proclaim to those who live on earth, and to every nation and tribe and language and people. ⁷He said in a loud voice, "Fear God and give him glory, for the hour of his judgment has come. Worship the one who made heaven and earth and the sea and springs of water." ⁸Another angel, a second one, followed

and said, "Fallen, fallen is Babylon the great. She made all the nations drink the wine of her passionate immorality." ⁹Then another angel, a third one, followed them and said in a loud voice, "If any worship the beast and its image and receive a mark on their forehead or their hand, ¹⁰they will also drink of the wine of God's passionate anger, poured full strength into the cup of his wrath. They will suffer the pain of fire and sulfur before the holy angels and the Lamb. ¹¹The smoke of their painful suffering goes up forever and ever. There is no rest day or night for those who worship the beast and its image, or for the one who receives the mark with its name." ¹²This calls for the endurance of the saints, who keep the commandments of God and the faith of Jesus. ¹³And I heard a voice from heaven say, "Write: Blessed are the dead who die in the Lord from now on." "Yes," says the Spirit, "so they can rest from their labors, for their works follow them."

¹⁴Then I looked and there was a white cloud. On the cloud was seated someone who looked like a human being. He had a gold laurel wreath on his head and a sharp sickle in his hand. ¹⁵Another angel came out of the temple, calling in a loud voice to the one seated on the cloud: "Use your sickle to reap the harvest, for the hour to harvest has come and the harvest of the earth is ready." ¹⁶So the one seated on the cloud swung his sickle over the earth, and the earth was harvested.

¹⁷Then another angel came out of the temple in heaven, and he also had a sharp sickle. ¹⁸Still another angel, who has power over fire, came out from the altar. He spoke with a loud voice to the one who had the sharp sickle and said, "Use your sharp sickle to cut the clusters of the vineyard of the earth, because its grapes are ripe." ¹⁹So the angel swung his sickle to the earth and cut the vineyard of the earth, and he put what he reaped into the great winepress of God's passionate anger. ²⁰Then the winepress was trampled outside the city, and blood came out of the winepress as high as the horses' bridles for one thousand six hundred stadia.

15 ¹Then I saw another great and awe-inspiring sign in heaven: seven angels with seven plagues, which are the last, for with them the anger of God is completed. ²Then I saw what appeared to be a sea of glass mixed with fire. Those who conquer the beast and its image and the number of its name were standing by the sea of glass, holding harps of God. ³They sing the song of Moses, the servant of God, that is, the song of the Lamb, saying,

"Great and awe-inspiring are your works, Lord God Almighty.
Just and true are your ways, King of the nations.
⁴Who will not fear you, Lord, and glorify your name,
for you alone are holy.
All nations will come and worship before you,
for your acts of justice have been revealed."

Fifth Cycle: The Seven Bowls and the Fall of Babylon

⁵Then, after these things, I looked and the temple—that is, the tent of witness in heaven—was opened. ⁶And the seven angels, who have the seven plagues, came out of the temple. They were clothed in pure bright linen and were wearing gold sashes around their waists. ⁷Then one of the four living creatures gave the seven angels seven gold offering bowls full of the anger of God, who lives forever. ⁸The temple was filled with smoke from the glory and power of God, and no one could go into the temple until the seven plagues of the last angels were completed.

16 ¹Then I heard a loud voice from the temple say to the seven angels, "Go and pour out the seven offering bowls of the anger of God on the earth." ²So the first angel went and poured out his offering bowl on the earth, and a nasty and terrible sore appeared on the people who had the mark of the beast and worshiped its image. ³The second angel poured out his offering bowl on the sea, and it turned into blood, like the blood of a dead person, so that every living thing in the sea died. ⁴The third angel poured out his offering bowl on the rivers and the springs of water, and they turned into blood. ⁵Then I heard the angel of the waters say,

> "You are just, O Holy One, who is and who was,
> because you have given these judgments.
> ⁶Because they poured out the blood of saints and prophets,
> you have given them blood to drink. They deserve it!"

⁷And I heard the altar say,

> "Yes, Lord God Almighty, your judgments are true and just."

⁸The fourth angel poured out his offering bowl on the sun, and it was allowed to burn people with fire. ⁹The people were burned by intense heat, and they cursed the name of God, who has power over these plagues. But they did not repent and give him glory. ¹⁰The fifth angel poured out his offering bowl on the throne of the beast, and darkness covered its kingdom. People bit their tongues because of their pain, ¹¹and they cursed the God of heaven because of their pains and their sores; but they did not repent of their works.

¹²Then the sixth angel poured his offering bowl on the great river Euphrates, and its water was dried up, so that the way was made ready for the kings from the east. ¹³And I saw three unclean spirits, like frogs, come from the mouth of the dragon, the mouth of the beast, and the mouth of the false prophet. ¹⁴Now these are demonic spirits that do signs. They go out to the kings of the whole world, in order to gather them for the battle on the great day of God the Almighty. ¹⁵(See, I am coming like a thief! Blessed are those

who stay awake and clothed, so they do not go around naked and exposed to shame.) ¹⁶And they gathered them at the place that is called in Hebrew, Harmagedon.

¹⁷Then the seventh angel poured his offering bowl into the air, and there was a loud voice from the temple, from the throne, saying, "It is done!" ¹⁸There were flashes of lightning, rumblings and peals of thunder, and a great earthquake occurred, the like of which has not occurred since there have been people on the earth, so great was the earthquake. ¹⁹The great city split into three parts, and the cities of the nations fell. Babylon the great was remembered before God, so that he gave her the wine-cup of his angry wrath. ²⁰Every island fled and the mountains disappeared. ²¹Huge hailstones weighing about a hundred pounds came down from heaven on the people, so that people cursed God for the plague of hail, because the plague was so terrible.

17 ¹Then one of the seven angels who had the seven offering bowls came and said to me, "Come, I will show you the judgment of the great whore who is seated on many waters. ²The kings of the earth have committed immorality with her, and those who live on the earth have become drunk with the wine of her immorality." ³Then he brought me in the Spirit to a desert. There I saw a woman seated on a scarlet beast that was full of blasphemous names. It had seven heads and ten horns. ⁴The woman was clothed in purple and scarlet and glittered with gold and jewels and pearls. In her hand she held a gold cup full of vile things and the impurities of her immorality. ⁵On her forehead was written a name, a mystery: "Babylon the great, the mother of whores and of the vile things of earth." ⁶I saw that the woman was drunk on the blood of the saints and the blood of the witnesses to Jesus. And I was completely amazed when I saw her.

⁷Then the angel said to me, "Why are you amazed? I will tell you the mystery of the woman and the beast that carries her, the one with seven heads and ten horns. ⁸The beast that you saw was and is not, and is about to come up from the abyss and go to destruction. Those who live on the earth, whose names have not been written in the scroll of life from the time the earth was made, will be amazed when they see the beast, because it was and is not and is to come. ⁹This calls for an understanding mind. The seven heads are seven mountains on which the woman is seated. They are also seven kings. ¹⁰Five have fallen, one is, and the other has not yet come. When he comes he must remain for only a little while. ¹¹As for the beast that was and is not, it is an eighth that belongs to the seven, and it is going to destruction. ¹²The ten horns that you saw are ten kings, who have not yet received royal power, but they will receive authority as kings for an hour, along with the beast. ¹³The kings are of one mind, and they give their power and authority to the beast. ¹⁴They will make war on

the Lamb, but the Lamb will conquer them, for he is Lord of lords and King of kings, and those with him are called and chosen and faithful."

¹⁵Then he said to me, "The waters that you saw, where the whore is seated, are peoples and multitudes and nations and languages. ¹⁶As for the ten horns that you saw, they and the beast will hate the whore and will make her desolate and naked. They will eat her flesh and burn her up with fire. ¹⁷For God put into their hearts to do what is on his mind. That is why they will be of one mind and give their royal power to the beast, until the words of God have been completed. ¹⁸And the woman that you saw is the great city that has royal power over the kings of the earth."

18   ¹After these things I saw another angel coming down from heaven with great authority, and the earth was filled with light from his glory. ²He called out with a loud voice, saying, "Fallen, fallen is Babylon the great! It has become a home for demons and a lair for every unclean spirit, and a lair for every unclean bird, and a lair for every unclean and disgusting beast. ³For all the nations have fallen because of the wine of her passionate immorality, and the kings of the earth committed immorality with her, and the merchants of the earth became rich from the power of her loose and extravagant ways."

⁴Then I heard another voice from heaven say, "Come out of her, my people, so that you do not take part in her sins and do not receive any of her plagues, ⁵for her sins have stretched up to heaven, and God remembered her acts of injustice. ⁶Give her what she herself has given to others. Give her back twice as much for what she has done. In the cup that she mixed, mix her twice as much. ⁷To the extent that she glorified herself and indulged her loose and extravagant ways, give her pain and grief. For in her heart she says, 'I sit as a queen! I am not a widow. I will never see grief.' ⁸This is why her plagues will come in a single day: deadly disease and grief and hunger. She will be consumed by fire, for the Lord God who judges her is powerful.

⁹"The kings of the earth, who committed immorality and shared her loose and extravagant ways, will weep and mourn over her when they see the smoke of her burning. ¹⁰They will stand a long way off because they are afraid of the pain she suffers, and they will say, 'Oh no! Babylon, you great city, you powerful city, for in just one hour your judgment came.'

¹¹"The merchants of the earth will weep and mourn over her, for no one buys their cargo anymore—¹²cargo of gold and silver and jewels and pearls, and fine linen and purple and silk and scarlet, and all the articles of citrus wood and all kinds of articles of ivory and all kinds of articles of fine wood and bronze and iron and marble, ¹³and cinnamon and amomum and incense and fragrant ointment and frankincense, and wine and oil and fine flour and wheat, and cattle and sheep and horses and carriages, and slaves and souls of human

beings—¹⁴'The ripe fruit your soul craved has gone from you. All your glitter and glamour are lost to you, never ever to be found again.' ¹⁵The merchants who sold these things, who got so rich by her, will stand a long way off because they fear the pain she suffers. They will weep and mourn, ¹⁶and say, 'Oh, no! The great city that wore fine linen and purple and scarlet, who glittered with gold and jewels and pearls—¹⁷in just one hour such great wealth was laid waste.'

"Every sea captain and every seafarer and the sailors and all who make their living on the sea stood a long way off. ¹⁸They cried out as they saw the smoke from her burning and said, 'Who was like the great city?' ¹⁹They threw dust on their heads and were crying out, weeping and mourning, and they said 'Oh no! The great city, where all who have ships at sea became so rich by her wealth, for in just one hour she was laid waste.' ²⁰Rejoice over her, O heaven, and saints and apostles and prophets, because God has judged her as she judged you."

²¹Then a powerful angel picked up a stone that was like a large millstone and threw it into the sea. He said, "With such violent force will Babylon the great city be thrown down, and it will not be found anymore. ²²The sound of harpists and musicians and pipers and trumpeters will not be heard in you anymore. No craftsman of any kind will be found in you anymore. The sound of the hand mill will not be heard in you anymore. ²³The light of a lamp will not shine in you anymore. The sound of a bridegroom and a bride will not be heard in you anymore, because your merchants were the aristocrats of the earth, and all the nations were deceived by your sorcery. ²⁴In her was found the blood of the prophets and the saints and all who have been slain on the earth."

19 ¹After these things I heard what sounded like a huge crowd in heaven, and they said,

"Hallelujah! Salvation and glory and power belong to our God,
²for his judgments are true and just,
for he judged the great whore,
who ruined the earth with her immorality,
and he brought justice for the blood of his servants,
which was shed by her own hand."

³Then they said a second time,

"Hallelujah! Smoke goes up from her forever and ever."

⁴And the twenty-four elders and the four living creatures fell down and worshiped God, who is seated on the throne, and they said,

"Amen. Hallelujah!"

⁵Then a voice came from the throne and said,

"Praise our God, all you his servants,
and you who fear him, both small and great."

⁶And I heard something that sounded like a huge crowd, that sounded like rushing water, that sounded like powerful thunder. They said,

"Hallelujah! For the Lord our God the Almighty reigns.
⁷Let us rejoice and celebrate and give him the glory,
for the wedding day of the Lamb has come
and his wife has made herself ready.
⁸She was given fine pure white linen to wear,
for the fine linen is the just deeds of the saints."

⁹Then he said to me, "Write this: Blessed are those who have been invited to the wedding banquet of the Lamb." He said to me, "These are the true words of God." ¹⁰Then I fell at his feet to worship him. But he said, "Do not do that! I am a fellow servant with you and your brethren who hold firmly to the witness of Jesus. Worship God! For the witness of Jesus is the spirit of prophecy."

Sixth Cycle: From the Beast's Demise to New Jerusalem

¹¹Then I saw heaven opened, and there was a white horse. Its rider was called faithful and true, and he judges and makes war with justice. ¹²His eyes were like a flame of fire, and on his head were many diadems. He has a name written on him that no one knows but he himself. ¹³He wore a robe dyed with blood, and his name was called the Word of God. ¹⁴The armies of heaven were following him on white horses, and they wore fine linen that was white and pure. ¹⁵From his mouth comes a sharp sword that he will use to strike down the nations, and he is the one who will rule them with an iron rod. He is the one who will trample the winepress of the wine of the passionate wrath of God the Almighty. ¹⁶He has a name written on his robe, on his thigh: King of kings and Lord of lords.

¹⁷Then I saw an angel standing in the sun, and he called out with a loud voice and said to all the birds flying high overhead, "Come and gather for the great banquet of God. ¹⁸Come and eat the flesh of kings and the flesh of generals and the flesh of the powerful and the flesh of horses and their riders, the flesh of all, both free and slave, both small and great." ¹⁹Then I saw that the beast and the kings of the earth and their armies had gathered to make war against the rider on the horse and his army. ²⁰But the beast was captured, along with the false prophet who had done signs in its presence, the signs by which he deceived those who received the mark of the beast and worshiped its image. The two of them were thrown alive into the lake of fire that burns with sulfur. ²¹And the rest were killed by the sword that comes from the mouth of the rider on the horse; and all the birds ate their fill of their flesh.

20 ¹Then I saw an angel coming down from heaven, holding in his hand the key to the abyss and a huge chain. ²And he seized the dragon, the ancient serpent, who is the devil and Satan, and bound him for a thousand years. ³He cast him into the abyss, then locked and sealed it over him, in order that he might not deceive the nations anymore until the thousand years were over. After this he must be released for a short time.

⁴Then I saw thrones, and people sat down on them, and judgment was given in their favor. And those I saw were the souls of those who had been beheaded because of the witness of Jesus and the word of God, who had not worshiped the beast or its image and had not received the mark on their forehead or on their hand. They came to life and reigned with Christ for a thousand years. ⁵The rest of the dead did not come to life until the thousand years were over. This is the first resurrection. ⁶Blessed and holy are those who have a share in the first resurrection. Over these the second death has no power, but they will be priests of God and of Christ, and will reign with him for a thousand years.

⁷And when the thousand years are over, Satan will be released from his prison. ⁸He will go out to deceive the nations that are at the four corners of the earth, Gog and Magog, to assemble them for battle. Their number is like the sand of the sea. ⁹And they came up across the breadth of the earth and surrounded the camp of the saints, the beloved city; but fire came down from heaven and devoured them. ¹⁰And the devil who had deceived them was thrown into the lake of fire and sulfur, where the beast and the false prophet also were, and painful suffering will be inflicted on them day and night forever and ever.

¹¹Then I saw a great white throne and the one who is seated on it. Before his face the earth and heaven fled away, and no place was found for them. ¹²And I saw the dead, great and small, standing before the throne, and scrolls were opened. Another scroll was also opened, which is the scroll of life. And the dead were judged according to their works, by what was written in the scrolls. ¹³And the sea gave up the dead that were in it, and Death and Hades gave up the dead that were in them, and they were judged, each one of them, according to their works. ¹⁴Then Death and Hades were thrown into the lake of fire. This is the second death, the lake of fire. ¹⁵And if any were not found written in the scroll of life, they were thrown into the lake of fire.

21 ¹Then I saw a new heaven and a new earth, for the first heaven and the first earth passed away, and the sea was no more. ²And I saw the holy city, New Jerusalem, coming down out of heaven from God, made ready as a bride beautifully dressed for her husband. ³And I heard a loud voice from the throne, saying, "See, here is the dwelling of God with humankind. He will dwell with them and they will be his peoples, and God himself will be with them as their God. ⁴He will wipe away every tear from their eyes, and death will be no more, neither mourning nor crying nor pain anymore, for the first things have passed away." ⁵Then the one seated on the throne said, "See, I am making all things new." He also said, "Write, because these words are trustworthy and true." [6]Then he said to me, "All is done. I am the Alpha and the Omega, the beginning and the end. To the one who thirsts, I myself will give freely from the spring of the water of life. [7]Those who conquer will inherit these things. I will be their God and they will be my sons and daughters. [8]But for the cowardly and faithless and vile and murderers and immoral and sorcerers and idolaters and all the liars, their share will be in the lake that burns with fire and sulfur, which is the second death."

[9]Then one of the seven angels who had the seven offering bowls full of the seven last plagues came and spoke with me. He said, "Come, I will show you the bride, the wife of the Lamb." [10]And he transported me in the Spirit to a great high mountain, and he showed me the holy city, Jerusalem, coming down out of heaven from God. [11]It had the glory of God. Its radiance was like a jewel, like jasper that was clear as crystal. [12]It had a great high wall with twelve gates. By the gates were twelve angels, and on the gates were written the names of the twelve tribes of the sons of Israel: [13]on the east three gates and on the north three gates and on the south three gates and on the west three gates. [14]The wall of the city has twelve foundations and on them are the twelve names of the twelve apostles of the Lamb.

[15]The one who spoke with me had a gold measuring rod with which to measure the city and its gates and its wall. [16]Now the city is laid out as a square. Its length is the same as its width. He measured the city with the rod, twelve thousand stadia. The length and width and height are equal. [17]He also measured the thickness of its wall, 144 cubits as a person—or rather an angel—measures things. [18]The wall was built of jasper and the city was pure gold, like pure glass. [19]The foundations of the city wall are adorned with every kind of jewel. The first foundation is jasper, the second sapphire, the third chalcedony, the fourth emerald, [20]the fifth sardonyx, the sixth carnelian, the seventh chrysolite, the eighth beryl, the ninth topaz, the tenth chrysoprase, the eleventh jacinth, the twelfth amethyst. [21]And the twelve gates are twelve pearls, each one of the gates was of a single pearl. And the main street of the city is pure gold, as transparent as glass.

[22]Now I did not see a temple in the city, because its temple is the Lord God Almighty and the Lamb. [23]The city does not need the sun or the moon to shine on it, for the glory of God is its light and its lamp is the Lamb. [24]The nations will walk by its light, and the kings of the earth will bring their glory into it. [25]Its gates will never be shut by day, and there will be no night there. [26]They will bring the glory and the honor of the nations into it. [27]But nothing common will enter it, nor anyone who does what is vile and deceitful, but only those who are written in the Lamb's scroll of life.

22 ¹Then he showed me the river of the water of life, bright as crystal. It was flowing from the throne of God and the Lamb ²through the middle of the city's main street. On each side of the river is the tree of life, which produces twelve crops of fruit, bearing its fruit each month, and the leaves of the tree are for the healing of the nations. ³And there will be no curse anymore. The throne of God and the Lamb shall be in it, and his servants will worship him. ⁴They will see his face, and his name will be on their foreheads. ⁵Night will be no more. They will not need the light of a lamp or the light of the sun, for the Lord God will shine on them, and they will reign forever and ever.

Conclusion to the Book

⁶Then he said to me, "These words are trustworthy and true. The Lord, the God of the spirits of the prophets, sent his angel to show his servants what things must soon take place.

⁷"See, I am coming soon!

"Blessed is the one who keeps the words of the prophecy in this scroll."

⁸I, John, am the one who heard and saw these things. And when I heard and saw them, I fell down to worship at the feet of the angel who showed them to me. ⁹But he said to me, "Do not do that! I am a fellow servant with you and your brethren the prophets, and with those who keep the words of this scroll. Worship God!"

¹⁰Then he said to me, "Do not seal up the words of the prophecy contained in this scroll, because the time is near. ¹¹Let the unjust still do injustice and the filthy still be filthy. Let the just still do what is just and the holy still be holy.

¹²"See, I am coming soon, and my reward is with me to repay each according to his work.

¹³"I am the Alpha and the Omega, the first and the last, the beginning and the end.

¹⁴"Blessed are those who wash their robes so that they may have the right to the tree of life and may enter the city by the gates. ¹⁵Outside are the dogs and the sorcerers and the immoral and the murderers and the idolaters and everyone who loves and practices deception.

¹⁶"I, Jesus, sent my angel to bear witness to all of you about these things for the assemblies. I am the root and descendant of David, the bright morning star."

¹⁷The Spirit and the bride say, "Come."

Let the one who hears say, "Come."

And let the one who is thirsty come.

Let the one who wishes receive the water of life as a gift.

[18]"I myself bear witness to everyone who hears the words of the prophecy in this scroll: If anyone adds to them, God will add to that person the plagues that are written in this scroll, [19]and if anyone takes away from the words of this scroll of prophecy, God will take away that person's share in the tree of life and the holy city, which are written in this scroll." [20]The one who bears witness to these things says, "Yes, I am coming soon."

Amen. Come Lord Jesus!

[21]The grace of the Lord Jesus be with all.

INTRODUCTION

I.
History of Interpretation and Influence

Revelation has engaged the imaginations of biblical interpreters and musicians, theologians and artists. Its vision of New Jerusalem has been celebrated in songs of hope, while its portrayal of a seven-headed beast has fueled speculation about the Antichrist. Its promise of a millennial kingdom has inspired reform movements dedicated to a new age of peace on earth, and yet its depictions of fire falling from the sky has awakened fears about the imminent end of the world. An overview of ways Revelation has been interpreted provides an opportunity for us to think about the questions others have asked and the assumptions that informed their reading of the book. We will consider how their social contexts shaped their perspectives and what effect their interpretations had on church and society. Doing this helps us become aware of the questions and assumptions that contemporary interpreters bring to their work. The examples that follow are taken from works both by scholars and by leaders of popular religious movements; they include commentaries and theological treatises, architecture and hymnody. Disputed topics such as the seven seals, the Antichrist, Babylon the whore, and the millennial kingdom are noted briefly here but receive special treatment in the introductions to major sections of the commentary (§§3, 12, 18, 25, 32, 38).

A. Revelation from 100 to 500 CE

Revelation was written toward the end of the first century by an author who was sharply critical of Roman imperialism, but from the second century onward the writers who mentioned the book typically wanted to help Christians live securely under Roman rule and said little about its political dimensions. One factor shaping interpretation during this period was the need to define Christian faith in the face of issues raised by Gnostic groups, Montanists, and Arians. Another factor was the need to deal with internal disputes over the idea that history would culminate in a thousand-year reign of the saints on earth. And still another factor was the need to encourage the faithful. Writers often did so by applying the battle scenes in Revelation to the church's ongoing struggle with sin and false belief. That approach provided a way for people to read the book for moral and spiritual instruction, and it remained the most popular way to interpret the book after Christianity became the dominant religion of the Roman Empire in the fourth century.

Christians in the west generally valued Revelation and assumed that John the apostle wrote the work, along with the Fourth Gospel and one or more of the Johannine Epistles. Christians in the east held similar views until the late third century, when questions were raised about the book's authorship in the wake of controversies about its message, leading to a decline in its status in the east. Revelatory texts such as the *Shepherd of Hermas* and the *Apocalypse of Peter* circulated alongside Revelation, but as churches defined the extent of the NT canon, Revelation was the one apocalypse accepted in the west and by some, though not all, in the east.

I. THE WEST TO 350

Early reference to Revelation was made by Justin Martyr (d. ca. 165), who argued that Christians deserved fair treatment under Roman rule since they were responsible subjects of the empire (*1 Apol.* 12–17). His extant writings do not relate Revelation to imperial governance but draw from the book when explaining Christianity's relationship to Judaism. After commenting on OT passages that were fulfilled in Christ, Justin turned to Isaiah's and Ezekiel's prophecies concerning the glorification of Jerusalem, which had not been fulfilled. His response was that those prophecies would be fulfilled during the thousand years of peace envisioned by Rev 20:4–6. While noting that some Christians of his day interpreted the passage about the millennium differently, Justin thought it promised long life and prosperity on earth (*Dial.* 80–81).

Irenaeus (d. ca. 200) held similar views, which he developed when critiquing Gnostic thought. The Gnostics in question regarded the OT God as an inferior demiurge who imprisoned souls in the realm of matter from which they needed deliverance. Irenaeus countered that the OT along with the Christian Gospels, Epistles, and other writings affirmed the Creator's goodness. The OT story of creation also provided a template for history. Since the world was created in six days, according to Gen 1, Irenaeus thought that the history of the world would continue through six thousand-year periods (*Haer.* 28.3). In the final thousand years, which he identified with the vision in Rev 20, creation would be blessed with peace and abundance (*Haer.* 32–35). Since the world was created good, evil did not originate with the Creator but with the devil and human sin, which are overcome by Christ, who is the glorified Son of Man, the slain Lamb, and conquering Word of God in Revelation (*Haer.* 4.20.11; Rev 1:12–18; 5:6; 19:11–16). Although Revelation links the beast, or Antichrist, to Rome, Irenaeus was careful to note that government had rightly been established by God and should be obeyed, and he expected the Antichrist to come *after* the dissolution of the empire, before the last judgment (*Haer.* 5.24–30).

Irenaeus had become bishop of Lyons after Christians in that church were publicly harassed and killed (177 CE). A letter from the church shows how Revelation—cited as "scripture"—encouraged the faithful during persecution. On the one hand, the letter calls Jesus "the faithful witness [*martys*] and first-born from the dead" and commends those who die for the faith because they "follow the Lamb wherever he goes" (Rev 1:5; 14:4). On the other hand, the letter identifies the persecutors with the wicked of Rev 22:11, whom the faithful are to resist (Eusebius, *Hist. eccl.* 5.1.10, 58; 5.2.3).

Unfavorable views of Revelation were held by Marcion (d. ca. 160), who insisted that the OT God was one of wrath and law, who had nothing to do with the God of love revealed by Christ. He rejected the OT and used only Paul's Epistles and an edited version of Luke's gospel. He excluded Revelation, perhaps because of its violent imagery and frequent use of the OT (Tertullian, *Marc.* 4.5). But in response, Irenaeus employed a different set of theological criteria to evaluate books. His basic principles were that authoritative texts bore witness to one God, the Maker of this universe, who gave Israel the law, is attested by the prophets, and is the Father of Jesus Christ. Irenaeus apparently found those principles in Revelation, since he appealed to its vision of four creatures around God's throne when arguing that there are four authoritative gospels (Rev 4:7; *Haer.* 3.11.7–8).

Other criticisms of Revelation arose because of its use by the Montanists, who in the mid- to late second century claimed they had received the gift of prophecy. Interpreting their spiritual experiences as signs that the present age had reached its climax, they expected New Jerusalem to be centered in the Phrygian town of Pepuza (Epiphanius, *Pan.* 49.1.2–3; Tabbernee, "Appearance"). In an effort to counter Montanism, a Roman elder named Gaius sought to discredit Revelation, which seemed to support the movement's claim that prophesying had an ongoing place in the church. Gaius argued that the perspectives in Revelation could not be reconciled with those of accepted Christian texts.

He held that the book's repeated series of plagues contradicted Paul's statement that the Day of the Lord would come suddenly like a thief (1 Thess 5:2), and its visions of *angels* slaying the ungodly were incompatible with Jesus' teaching that *nation* would rise up against nation (Matt 24:7). Since Revelation's message seemed to be so problematic, Gaius attributed the book to the heretic Cerinthus (Eusebius, *Hist. eccl.* 3.28.1–2).

Hippolytus of Rome (d. 235) responded to Gaius, insisting that Revelation was congruent with other writings used by the church. Its warning about plagues at the end of the age fit the pattern of the plagues before the exodus, and those plagues would constitute the tribulations foretold by Jesus in the gospels (Gwynn, "Hippolytus"). Hippolytus also related aspects of Revelation to the current situation of the church, as would later interpreters. He thought the woman giving birth symbolized the church, laboring to bring forth Christ by its witness, while the dragon signified persecution (*Antichr.* 61). Like Irenaeus, he thought the Antichrist would appear at the close of the age, but he had no sense that the end was imminent and expected the present era to continue several centuries longer, until 500 CE (*Comm. Dan.* 9.22–24). Where Irenaeus expected the millennium to be a time of peace on earth, Hippolytus interpreted it differently, as the blessed state of the faithful immediately after death, which would be followed by resurrection on the last day. Those different views of the millennium existed side by side (C. Hill, *Regnum*, 160–69).

Revelation's importance as a source of moral instruction can be seen in the North African writers Tertullian (d. ca. 225) and Cyprian (d. 258). They regarded Babylon the whore, with her gold and opulent clothing, as a warning against ostentation (Tertullian, *Cor.* 13; Cyprian, *Hab. virg.* 12). The heavenly rewards, which Revelation promises to the martyrs, encouraged faithfulness during times of persecution (Tertullian, *Scorp.* 12; Cyprian, *Ep.* 12.1; 14.2; *Fort.* 8; 10; 11; 13). On the issue of repentance, Tertullian called for rigor, arguing that Revelation barred adulterers from New Jerusalem (*Pud.* 19; Rev 2:18–22; 21:8). Cyprian, however, wrote after the Decian persecution, when many had lapsed from the faith, and he insisted that Revelation's repeated call for repentance showed that the penitent could be restored to communion with the church (2:5; *Ep.* 19; 34).

Both writers drew on Revelation's eschatological aspects, but in different ways. Tertullian thought the Roman Empire played a positive role in history, because it now restrained the Antichrist, whose defeat at some unknown point in the future would usher in the millennial age on earth (*Fug.* 12; *Marc.* 3.25). Cyprian, however, thought the six thousand years of history were actually drawing to a close, and he saw signs that the Antichrist was already at work in the persecution by the Romans and the schisms within the church (*Fort.* pref.

1–2; *Ep.* 58.1). Like Hippolytus he also thought the millennium was the state of blessedness after death, not a coming age of earthly bliss (C. Hill, *Regnum*, 192–201).

The Christological and eschatological aspects of Revelation receive special attention in the oldest extant commentary on the book, written by Victorinus of Pettau (d. 304). In his view, the vision of the Lamb breaking the seals on God's scroll shows that Christ reveals the meaning of Scripture through his death and resurrection (*In Apoc.* 1.4; 4.1–5.3; Huber, "Aspekte"). Like many modern interpreters, Victorinus observed that the beast has traits of Roman emperors, especially Nero. He thought Revelation envisioned persecutions at the end of the age, which would culminate in the thousand-year reign of the saints on earth. But his major contribution was observing that Revelation's visions did not unfold in a linear way. Instead, they repeated the same message multiple times. The trumpet plagues gave a warning briefly, and the bowl plagues restated that warning more completely. Therefore, people were not to look for a sequential outline of future events in Revelation but were to ask about its underlying meaning (*In Apoc.* 8.2). The idea that Revelation recapitulates the same message multiple times would inform commentaries on the book until the thirteenth century, and it would influence interpreters again beginning in the mid-twentieth century.

2. THE EAST TO 350

Christians in the eastern Mediterranean interpreted Revelation in ways that fit the needs of churches seeking stability under the Roman Empire. Those who used the book included Theophilus of Antioch (d. ca. 183), who said that Christians prayed on behalf of the emperor (*Autol.* 11), and Melito of Sardis (d. ca. 190), who noted that Christianity had been founded under Augustus and was a blessing to the empire (Hall, ed., *On Pascha*, 63). Although their writings on Revelation have been lost (Eusebius, *Hist. eccl.* 4.24.1; 4.26.1–2, 7–8), the effect of Revelation's language is reflected in Melito's *On Pascha*, which defines Christianity in relation to Judaism. For him, the Passover prefigures salvation in Jesus the slain Lamb, who overcame Hades and made people into God's kingdom and priests (Rev 1:6, 18; 5:6–10). God's history of salvation therefore culminates in Jesus, who is "the Alpha and the Omega; he is the beginning and the end" (*On Pascha* 105; cf. Rev 22:13). This perspective is Christological rather than futuristic (Nicklas, "Probleme").

For writers in Alexandria, the concern was how Scripture led people to true knowledge of God. Drawing language from Revelation, Clement of Alexandria (d. ca. 215) said that God's Word was the Alpha and Omega, the beginning and end of a spiritual journey that brought people trained in faith to a place among the elders around God's throne (*Paed.* 1.6; *Strom.* 6.13; cf. Rev 1:8; 4:4; 21:6). Origen (d. 254) explored the soul's relationship to God using the Platonic distinction between the intelligible world above and the visible world below. For him, the images in Scripture pointed to higher spiritual truths. He identified the writing on the outside of the scroll in God's hand in Rev 5:1 as the simple meaning of the text, and the writing inside the scroll as Scripture's higher truth (*Comm. Jo.* 5.6; 13.28–30). Followers of Jesus are a spiritual Israel, symbolized by the 144,000 virgins (*Comm. Jo.* 1.1–9; cf. Rev 7:4–8; 14:1–5). Christ himself is God's *logos*, or reason, who overcomes the beast that symbolizes irrational elements in the soul (*Comm. Jo.* 2.42–63; cf. Rev 19:11–21), and the vision of the millennium promises spiritual transformation after death, not physical well-being on earth (C. Hill, *Regnum*, 189; Ramelli, "Origen's").

Criticism of Revelation in the east came from an anti-Montanist group known as Alogoi, who tried to discredit the book by ascribing it to Cerinthus, much as Gaius did in Rome (Epiphanius, *Pan.* 51.3.1–6; 51.32.2–33.3). A different approach was taken by Apollonius (late second century), who made use of Revelation against the Montanists—though his work has been lost (Eusebius, *Hist. eccl.* 5.18.1, 14). But the most divisive issue concerned the millennial kingdom of Rev 20:1–6. In the early second century, Papias of Hierapolis, who apparently knew Revelation, established a positive perspective on the coming age, when every vine would have a thousand branches and every grape would produce gallons of wine (Irenaeus, *Haer.* 5.33.3–4). Origen rejected the idea of a millennial age devoted to eating and drinking, since indulging in pleasure was contrary to virtue (*Princ.* 2.11.2–3), but in the third century an Egyptian bishop reasserted the notion that there would be a millennial period of bliss on earth (see §38A).

Dionysius of Alexandria (d. ca. 264) reiterated the objections to hopes for an earthly millennium and insisted that Revelation had to be understood spiritually. In his critique of millennialism, he raised questions about the apostolic authorship of Revelation. Although most people assumed that Revelation and the Fourth Gospel were both written by John the apostle, Dionysius showed that the two works could not have been written by the same person because they were so different in literary form, writing style, and theological content. Rather than ascribing Revelation to Cerinthus, as others had done, Dionysius said that the gospel was written by John the apostle and that Revelation was by another person named John, perhaps a church elder. Although Dionysius continued to accept Revelation because the church valued it, his arguments against apostolic authorship would diminish the book's credibility in the east (Eusebius, *Hist. eccl.* 7.24.1–25.27).

The effect of Dionysius's arguments was not immediately apparent, and Methodius of Olympus (d. ca. 311) continued the practice of spiritual interpretation in Asia Minor. Although he thought the millennial age would involve bodily resurrection (see §38A), he generally read Revelation symbolically. The woman clothed with the sun is the church, laboring to bring forth Christ within each person. She is threatened by the dragon, whose heads represent sins like luxury and unbelief and whose ten horns are violations of the Ten Commandments. The dragon's tail pulling stars from heaven signifies people falling into heresy. The woman seeks refuge in the wilderness, which symbolizes virtue, and she remains there for 1,260 days, a number signifying perfect knowledge of the Father, Son, and Holy Spirit (*Symp.* 8–9; McGinn, "Emergence," 264–68).

By the early fourth century Revelation was widely used as an authoritative text by churches in the west, while its status in the east was less clear. Three factors informed the question of whether a book had normative status: (1) whether the content of a work conveyed the core convictions of the Christian community; (2) whether a work was written by an apostle or preserved apostolic teaching; and (3) whether a work enjoyed long and widespread use within the church. No dimension functioned independently of the others, so arguments over authorship had more to do with judgments about a book's theological content than with historical information about the author's identity (Metzger, *Canon*, 251–54).

Different views of Revelation's status in the church are reflected in lists of canonical writings from this period. The Muratorian canon fragment could date from either the late second or the fourth century (L. McDonald, *Biblical*, 369–78). Its list of authoritative texts includes Revelation and the *Apocalypse of Peter*, both of which are assumed to be apostolic—though the fragment notes that some people do not want the *Apocalypse of Peter* read in church. In the Muratorian list another visionary text, the *Shepherd of Hermas*, is valued but not placed on the same level as other texts because it had been written too recently, after the time of the apostles (Metzger, *Biblical*, 307). Eusebius (d. 339) arranged books in three categories: texts recognized by the churches, those that are disputed but accepted by most, and those that are not genuine. He acknowledged that many put Revelation among the recognized books, although some grouped it with the rejected writings, which for him included the *Apocalypse of Peter* and *Shepherd of Hermas* (*Hist. eccl.* 3.25.2–5). Ambivalence about Revelation would continue in the eastern churches.

3. FROM 350 TO 500

Revelation's imagery expresses an anti-imperial perspective, but perspectives changed when Christianity became the dominant religion of the Roman

Empire. The last great persecution of the church occurred under Diocletian in 303–4; a decade later, Constantine's Edict of Milan (313) established religious toleration, and Christianity eventually gained wide acceptance in the imperial world. By the mid- to late fourth century, motifs from Revelation were being used in Christian art to portray Christ's victory and reign over the world. A Roman fresco shows the Lamb standing in triumph on Mount Zion (Rev 14:1), with saints extending their hands toward him, a gesture people used to honor their emperor. Churches were adorned with scenes of Christ enthroned in glory, attended by the four creatures from the heavenly throne room (4:6–8). At the front of some sanctuaries was an arch, reminiscent of the arches Roman emperors erected to celebrate their victories. For example, the triumphal arch in Santa Maria Maggiore in Rome (fifth century) is decorated with mosaics of the divine throne, the four creatures, and New Jerusalem. Similar designs were used in other churches, suggesting that the victory of the Lamb was manifested in the emergence of a Christian empire (Herrmann and van den Hoek, "Apocalyptic"; Kinney, "Apocalypse").

Interpretation of Revelation was shaped by the main theological debates of this period, which centered on the doctrine of the Trinity. In the controversy, the position of Arius was that the Son of God was a created being. His views were rejected at the Council of Nicaea (325 CE), which affirmed that the Son was coeternal with the Father. Despite that decision, the dispute persisted because Arius's views were adopted by the Goths and Vandals in Europe and by groups in North Africa. Supporters of the Nicene position, such as Ambrose of Milan (d. 397), invoked Revelation against the Arians, since it called Christ the Alpha and Omega, the beginning and the end, showing that he shared God's eternal existence (Rev 1:8; 21:6; 22:13; Ambrose, *Fid.* 2.4.34–35; 4.9.108; *Ep.* 63.49). Aurelius Prudentius Clemens (d. ca. 410) conveyed the idea in his hymn *Corde natus*:

> Of the Father's love begotten,
> ere the worlds began to be,
> he is Alpha and Omega,
> he the source, the ending he,
> of the things that are, that have been,
> and that future years shall see,
> evermore and evermore.

The Christological point was reinforced by identifying Christ with the letters Alpha and Omega in artwork (Kinney, "Apocalypse," 201–2).

Disputes over ecclesiology contributed to major development in the history of interpretation, which came with Tyconius (d. ca. 400), who applied Revelation's visions to the present situation of the church. He belonged to the

Donatists, a group that broke away from the Catholics over questions of church leadership, and he saw the present age as a time of continual struggle between the forces represented by the city of God and the city of the devil. God's city is New Jerusalem, which symbolizes the true church that now exists and will be perfected in the future. The city of the devil is Babylon, which includes pagans and false Christians. Tyconius related Revelation's conflict scenes to the ongoing struggles of the church. The horseman announcing a food shortage could signify either physical hunger or a deprivation of the word of God. The seven angels with trumpets represent the church's calling to proclaim God's message. The beast is a collective image for all who now oppose the true church under the guise of sanctity and will one day persecute it openly. The most significant move was to identify the millennium as the present time of the church, which began at Christ's first coming and would continue until his return. During the millennium, Satan is "bound" but not gone, so the battle against evil will continue until the end of the age (see §38A; Daley, *Hope*, 127–31).

Augustine (d. 430) opposed the Donatists but found that Tyconius's approach made sense of the ongoing struggle against sin and false belief within the church and each person. To some extent Augustine could assent to an apocalyptic scenario derived from a literal reading of Revelation: Elijah will return (Rev 11:6), the Jews will believe (7:4–8), the Antichrist will persecute (13:1–10), and there will be a resurrection, last judgment, and new creation (20:4–6; 21:1; *Civ.* 20.30). But by adapting Tyconius's paradigm of the city of God and city of the world, Augustine pictured a situation in which the powers of sin and grace were engaged in ongoing conflict. On one level the millennial age was the indefinite period in which the church had to contend with internal conflicts and external threats—such as the sack of Rome in 410 CE. On another level the scenario characterized the situation of individuals. People entered the millennial age when raised to new life in baptism, yet they continued to deal with sin, since Satan was now bound in the abyss of human hearts everywhere, and the power of the Antichrist could be seen wherever people denied Christ by their words or loveless actions (*Civ.* 18.53; 20.6–7). Augustine's approach made Revelation relevant to Christians of all times and places (Fredriksen, "Tyconius"; Daley, *Hope*, 131–37; McGinn, *Antichrist*, 76–77).

Jerome (d. 420) followed a somewhat different type of spiritual interpretation, which fit the growing interest in ascetic life during the fourth and fifth centuries. Like Augustine, he identified the present world with "the great city," which Revelation calls "Sodom and Egypt" because it is filled with vice (Rev 11:7–8). Rome can be pictured as a whore because it encourages opulence and pride (17:1–6). When Revelation calls people to separate themselves from Babylon, it certainly means resisting sin, but it may also involve retreating into monastic life (18:4; *Ep.* 46.6–7). When Jerome edited Victorinus's commentary on Revelation, he removed its futuristic elements, so that Satan is seen to be bound wherever people resist evil thoughts (SC 423:127; Hasitschka, "Ankunft").

Alongside spiritual interpretation, some wondered whether Revelation might show that the end of the age was approaching. Jerome thought the Arians and other heretics might fulfill prophecies concerning Gog and Magog (Rev 20:7–8), while barbarian invasions showed that the Antichrist was near (Daley, *Hope*, 101–2). A student of Augustine, Quodvultdeus (ca. 445–49), noted that some thought the Goths and Moors who ravaged North Africa might be Gog and Magog, and a Donatist chronicler concluded that the Vandal king of Carthage was the beast (Fredricksen, "Apocalypse," 167; Daley, *Hope*, 101–2). Linking Revelation to specific events and people was a way to affirm that despite the appearance of chaos, the threats had been foreseen and were ultimately subject to God's ordering of history.

Revelation was included in the canonical writings listed by western sources, such as the synod at Carthage in 397, Rufinus (d. 410; *Symb.* 37), and Augustine (*Doctr. chr.* 2.13). But its status in the east was less clear (Jerome, *Ep.* 129.3). The book was included in the fourth- and fifth-century codices Sinaiticus, Alexandrinus, and Ephraemi (INTRO VI). It was listed as a canonical work by Athanasius of Alexandria (d. 373; *Ep.* 39) and was considered apostolic by Basil the Great (d. 379), Gregory of Nyssa (d. ca. 395), and Epiphanius of Salamis (d. 403; *Pan.* 76.5). Yet Revelation was not among the books recognized by the Synod of Laodicea (360), Cyril of Jerusalem (d. 386), the Apostolic Constitutions (ca. 380), or Gregory of Nazianzus (d. 389)—though he did quote from it (*Or. Bas.* 29:17; canonical lists in Metzger, *Canon*, 310–15).

As noted above, Revelation's diminished status in the east was partly due to Dionysius's argument against apostolic authorship. The book was not used by John Chrysostom (d. 407) or Theodore of Mopsuestia (d. 428). The Syriac Peshitta, which reflects the usage of the church at Antioch during the fourth and fifth centuries, does not include Revelation, but the book did appear in the Syriac Philoxenian version, which was produced in the early sixth century and was used by some Syriac-speaking churches (Metzger, *Early*, 48, 65–66).

What gave Revelation continuing value in the east was its potential to support Nicene theology. The verse most often cited by eastern writers was Rev 1:8: "'I am the Alpha and the Omega,' says the Lord God, 'the one who is and who was and who is to come, the Almighty.'" Since similar language is used for Christ in 22:13, eastern writers argued that as the Alpha and Omega, Christ the Son is coeternal with God the Father (Basil, PG 29:599B; Gregory of Nazianzus, *Or. Bas.* 29:17; Gregory of Nyssa, PG 45:1207B; Didymus, FC 111:59–60;

Cyril of Alexandria, FC 116:349–50). When Greek commentaries on Revelation were finally composed in the sixth and seventh centuries, such Christological questions would play a major role in interpretation.

B. Revelation from 500 to 1500

By the early sixth century, the Roman Empire was divided into the Byzantine Empire in the east and Germanic kingdoms in the west. The centuries that followed were marked by invasions of Vikings and Magyars, the Islamic conquest of North Africa, and periods of plague and political instability. In the face of these challenges, medieval writers on Revelation tried to bolster cohesion within the church by synthesizing the theological and spiritual interpretations of their predecessors. Distinctly new perspectives emerged later, in the twelfth and thirteenth centuries, as writers in the west related scenes from Revelation to specific events in the church's past and future. Calls for reform of the church and society raised hopes for the coming of a spiritual age, while resistance from church leadership made some turn Revelation's vision of Babylon into a critique of the Roman papacy—a practice that continued into the sixteenth century and beyond.

I. EARLY MEDIEVAL WRITERS (500–1000)

The Council of Chalcedon of 451 shaped the theological context in which biblical interpreters of this period worked. It stated that Christ had two natures, human and divine, united in one person and substance. Although the Chalcedonian definition was widely accepted, some in the east argued that Christ's divinity and humanity were united in a single nature, and the first Greek commentary on Revelation tried to follow a mediating position. It was written in the early sixth century by Oecumenius, whose opening comments dealt with Christ's divinity and humanity in language like that of Chalcedon, even as he emphasized the unity of Christ's natures in ways that suggested openness to those who did not accept the Chalcedonian definition. Christology also shaped the rest of the commentary, which proposed that the first six seals symbolized events from Christ's birth to his resurrection and the seventh anticipated his return (Rev 6:1–8:1). Instead of construing the woman in labor as an image of the church, as most ancient interpreters had done, Oecumenius related this image to Jesus' birth (12:1–6). At the same time, he thought the visions of the beast concerned the future, as did the plague scenes, which he thought were punishments to be given to the wicked after the final judgment (Weinrich, *Greek*, xx–xxxii; de Villiers, "Coping").

Andreas of Caesarea (d. ca. 614) wrote a commentary that implicitly critiqued Oecumenius and reflected clearer Chalcedonian views. For example, he commented that the two bronzelike feet of Christ in Rev 2:18 showed that Christ's divine and human natures were both undivided and unmixed. Andreas wrote at a time when the Byzantine Empire was experiencing plague, food shortages, and attacks from Persian forces, yet he assured readers that the end was not near. His treatment of the seven seal plagues shows that the struggle with sin and hardship runs throughout the present age, and details in the visions point to the help given through the sacramental life of the church. The woman in labor stands on the moon, which signifies baptism, and the hidden manna is the Eucharist (2:17; 12:1). He also found spiritual counsel in details throughout the text. For example, the name Judah signifies confession, Reuben is spiritual vision, and Gad means patience in times of trial (7:3–8; Constantinou, "Violence"; Hernández, "Andrew").

Andreas encouraged acceptance of Revelation in the east by recalling its use by Irenaeus, Methodius, Gregory of Nazianzus, and others. He also adopted the view that the millennium was the present age of the church—thereby overcoming the common objection that Revelation falsely promised people a future thousand years of pleasure on earth. His commentary became the standard interpretation of the book in the east, informing the tenth-century commentary by Arethas of Caesarea (d. ca. 932). Nevertheless, Revelation's status in the Byzantine church remained ambiguous, even after the Council in Trullo of 691–92. The participants adopted previous church statements, including the lists of canonical writings accepted by the Council of Carthage and Athanasius, which included Revelation, while also approving statements from the Council of Laodicea and Gregory of Nazianzus, which did not include Revelation. So the book's status remained unclear. It was not included in the lectionaries of the Byzantine churches and therefore was not read during worship (Metzger, *Canon*, 216; Nikolakopoulos, "Apokalypse").

In the west, those commenting on Revelation drew mainly from two sources. First was the commentary of Victorinus, edited by Jerome. This work emphasized that Christ revealed the meaning of Scripture, since he was the Lamb who opened the book with seven seals, and it conveyed the idea that Revelation repeated the same message several times under different sets of images. Second was the commentary of Tyconius, interpreted through Augustine. As noted above, this approach related Revelation to the present life of the church; the book's visions of conflict symbolized the church's perennial struggles against sin and heresy. Like their counterparts in the east, Latin commentators addressed theological questions in light of the positions taken at Nicaea and Chalcedon, helping form the church's theological identity (Matter, "Apocalypse").

Primasius of Hadrumentum in North Africa (d. ca. 560) consolidated the patristic tradition in an influential commentary. Where Rev 1:2 says "the time is near," Primasius notes that with God, one day is like a thousand years. He takes the eschatological darkening of the sun and moon as a symbol of heresy, and when people want the rocks and hills to hide them, it means they are to take refuge in the faith of the church (6:12–17). With the Nicene tradition he invokes the expression "Alpha and Omega" against the Arians, since it shows that Father and Son are coeternal; and he notes that the numerical value of Alpha and Omega is 801, which is the same as the word *peristera*, or dove, the symbol of the Spirit, who is also coeternal (22:13; cf. Gregory of Elvira, CCSL 69:195; Didymus, PG 39:696). Primasius's contemporary Apringius of Beja (ca. 550) lived in a region ruled by Visigoths, who were Arians. To foster a sense of Catholic identity, Apringius brought the Nicene emphasis on the divinity of the Son of God into his comments, beginning with references to Jesus in Rev 1 and concluding with the vision of New Jerusalem, which reflects Christ's majesty (*Tractatus* on Rev 1:2, 4, 8; 21:2). Caesarius of Arles (ca. 540) favored ecclesial symbolism, encouraging readers to see the glory of the church in the heavenly throne room (4:1), the church's sorrows in the grief of John (5:4), and its triumphs in the rider on the white horse and other images (6:1–2; Weinrich, *Latin*, xxiv–xli).

As noted above, Tyconius and Augustine established the practice of reading Revelation as a vision of the church's struggle throughout the present age, which would end only with the resurrection and last judgment. That approach was modified by the Anglo-Saxon scholar Bede (d. 735), who thought the visions outlined the general flow of church history *within* the present age. He outlined Revelation in seven parts. The first focuses on the seven ancient churches in Asia, which include traits of the church generally. The middle parts deal with the church's many conflicts and triumphs, and the final part envisions the future defeat of the Antichrist and glory of the church as New Jerusalem. Bede could also see the general shape of history in particular series of visions. For example, the seven seals begin with the first seal and rider on the white horse, symbolizing the ancient church; then they move through various conflicts, represented by seals two through five; and they culminate in the cosmic disturbances of the sixth seal, which signifies the final persecution of the church by the Antichrist. The seventh seal brings a brief respite before the end of the age (Weinrich, *Latin*, 111, 128, 137). An alternative pattern was provided by Berengaudus (ca. 860), who related the seals to episodes in both the OT and NT, ranging from Eden and the patriarchs in the distant past up to the Roman conquest of Jerusalem in the first century, which he interprets in light of comments by the Jewish historian Josephus (PL 17:841D; Visser, *Apocalypse*, 57–58). Both Bede and Berengaudus assumed that Revelation repeated the same message multiple times, so it did not provide a consistently linear view of history, but the idea that its visions represented eras of history would become a major feature in later medieval interpretation.

A new element introduced in eighth- and ninth-century commentaries concerned the nature of John's spiritual experience. Writers prefaced their works by distinguishing several kinds of vision. First is physical vision, which involves light coming to the eye. Second is spiritual vision, which involves dreams and images that may portend the future. Such visions may come even to those without faith, such as Pharaoh and Nebuchadnezzar, who cannot understand the visions' meanings (Gen 41; Dan 2). Third is intellectual vision, which involves insight into the truth and is given only to the elect, including the biblical prophets and author of Revelation (Ambrose Autpert, d. 784 [CCL 27:10–14]; Alcuin, d. 804 [PL 100:1088–89]; Haimo, d. ca. 855 [PL 117:938–39]). Writers were also drawn to mystical themes, such as the church as the bride of the Lamb. They combined nuptial images from the Song of Songs and Revelation into a vision of salvation as the eternal wedding banquet (Matter, "Apocalypse," 46; Visser, *Apocalypse*, 52–55).

Alongside such spiritual interpretations, the futuristic aspects of Revelation attracted interest. A popular scenario appears in the "Letter on the Origin and Time of the Antichrist" by Adso of Montier en-Der (ca. 950). The letter responds to questions raised by Gerberga of Saxony at a time when Europe experienced internal conflicts between warlords as well as ongoing threats of invasion from neighboring peoples. Drawing on traditions about the Antichrist, Adso provides assurance that there is a divine plan for history. In the future the Antichrist will arise and perform miracles to win public favor. After rebuilding the temple in Jerusalem, he will demand that people worship him and unleash a persecution. The two witnesses of Rev 11 will be slain, but the Antichrist will finally be killed on the Mount of Olives. The encouraging news is that these events will not occur until the last and greatest emperor, who is yet to come, has laid down his scepter in Jerusalem. The implication is that people should remain loyal to their current rulers, who are now God's bastion against the Antichrist (McGinn, *Apocalyptic*, 81–88).

2. SPIRITUAL AND THEOLOGICAL INTERPRETATION (1000–1500)

The establishment of the Holy Roman Empire in the tenth century brought greater stability to western Europe while increasing tensions between the emperor and pope over the right to appoint church officials. Pope Gregory VII (d. 1085) asserted the church's independence from state authority and worked to curb corruption within the church. His goal was to raise clergy to a higher moral and spiritual level so they would have a preeminent role in society. When he encountered resistance, he was not surprised, since he thought the time of the Antichrist was approaching (McGinn, "Apocalypticism," 76–78).

The commentary by Rupert of Deutz (d. 1129 or 1130) supported the call for church reform. He used the messages to the churches in Rev 2–3 as occasions to denounce simony and immorality among the clergy and to condemn the secular powers that set up antipopes—an allusion to Emperor Henry V, who backed rival claimants to the papacy in 1118–19 (PL 169:877–78; van Engen, *Rupert*, 275–82). A century later the issue of reform appeared in Revelation commentaries by Dominican writers, who affirmed the virtue of poverty. Works written under Hugh of St. Cher (d. 1263) turned the admonition to the ancient church at Thyatira against current leaders who became wealthy by drawing multiple sources of income from the church. Commentators warned that the deadly flood pouring out of the dragon's mouth in Rev 12:15 represented temporal wealth, which was poisoning the church (Lerner, "Poverty").

Theological studies during the period sought to clarify and systematize Christian truth claims, and those efforts influenced biblical commentaries. The *Glossa ordinaria*, prepared at Lyons around 1120, organized Bede's and Haimo's comments on Revelation into a form useful for teaching and reference purposes. In so doing, it preserved the three categories of vision that had been used in commentaries for centuries. Richard of Saint Victor (d. 1173), however, turned the three categories into four, with the highest being pure contemplation. In his judgment, Revelation did not belong to this fourth category but only to the third, since John's visions involved images (PL 686B–87D). As theologians of the twelfth and thirteenth centuries engaged the works of Aristotle, commentators began using philosophical categories for biblical interpretation. Of special interest was the notion of causality. Nicolas de Gorran (d. 1295) wrote a preface to Revelation that identified God and Jesus as the primary and secondary efficient causes of composition, while the angel and John were the mediate and immediate efficient causes (*In Apocalypsin*, 178; Minnis, *Medieval*, 81).

Scholastic writers occasionally cited Revelation when debating theological questions but gave little attention to the eschatological dimensions of the work. Peter Lombard (d. 1164) noted that Rev 12:7–12 showed that pride led to Satan's expulsion from heaven and that Satan's activities would be limited until his final release, but he did not speculate on what that implied for the end of the age (*Sentences* Book 2 §§27, 31). He used the admonition to "hold fast to what you have so that no one takes your laurel wreath" (Rev 3:11) as an occasion to ask whether those predestined to salvation might ever be damned and demonstrated that such an idea is illogical (*Sentences* Book 1 §179). Later, Thomas Aquinas (d. 1274) mentioned Revelation's beast when defining "character" as that which distinguishes one thing from another. He said that if charity shows the character of the saints, then the beast's mark characterizes the children of perdition— though he did not indicate what the beast's mark might be (*Summa Theologiae* III.63.3). Like Peter Lombard he found Revelation more significant for the issue of predestination. Aquinas noted that Revelation spoke of being blotted out of the scroll of life (Rev 3:5) and made the case that predestination was consistent with grace and divine immutability (*Summa Theologiae* I.23.6; I.24.3).

Artistic representations of Revelation reflected contemporary moral and spiritual interpretation. The text was often copied and illustrated along with commentaries by Beatus, Berengaudus, and other writers. Details were added to bring out the implications for monastic readers. Where Rev 4:2 tells of John ascending to God's throne room, a commentator explains that the seer did so by casting aside vain cares for temporal things, which was spiritual discipline. Similarly, an illustrator showed John using a ladder to make his ascent to heaven, adopting a traditional image for the upward struggle of spiritual life (Lewis, "Exegesis," 263–65). Illustrated texts were also used devotionally by the nobility, and artists developed the motifs accordingly. For example, the whore of Babylon was pictured as an aristocratic woman holding a mirror, which was a standard image for vanity. The result was a moral lesson in which Babylon's demise showed how pride leads to a person's downfall (O'Hear, "Images").

Passages from Revelation were occasionally read in the liturgies of the western church. Selections included visions of heavenly worship (4:1–11; 7:9–17; 14:1–5; 19:5–8), New Jerusalem (21:9–22:5), and Michael's victory over the dragon (12:7–12), but not the passages about the beast and whore (*DACL* 5/ 1:335–38; Buchinger, "Johannes-Apokalypse"). The effect of liturgy on the interpretation of Revelation is shown by the altarpiece at Ghent, completed by Jan van Eyck in 1432. It is based on Rev 7:9–17, which was read on All Saints Day, and depicts a vast company of people worshiping the Lamb. Van Eyck pictures the Lamb on an altar, his blood pouring into a chalice to represent the sacrament. Before him are angelic acolytes with gold censers as in 8:3–4. Male and female martyrs hold palm branches, as in Revelation, but instead of white robes the men wear clerical garb. In the background are buildings and light suggestive of New Jerusalem, and in front of the Lamb is the fountain of life. The sense is that in the church's worship, people experience something of the life to come (Seidel, "Apocalypse," 497–500; Flanigan, "Apocalypse").

3. JOACHIM OF FIORE AND THE COMING SPIRITUAL AGE

Renewed interest in apocalyptic thought is most closely tied to Joachim of Fiore (d. 1202), who ascribed his view of history to mystical insight into Scripture. Since God is a trinity, Joachim thought time itself was a trinity: The era of the Father began at creation and extended to the first coming of Christ; the era of the Son extended from Jesus to Joachim's own time; and the era of the Spirit was coming. Where Augustine had a nonprogressive view of history, in which good and evil remained in conflict until the end, Joachim thought history was progressing toward the spiritual age in which the monastic ideal of contemplation would be realized by society as a whole. Instead of identifying the millennium with the present life of the church, as Augustine had done, Joachim related it to the future. He thought a reforming pope might lead the way to the new age but also warned that an agent of the Antichrist might occupy the papal office (McGinn, *Antichrist*, 135–42). That idea would contribute to the emerging antipapal interpretations of Revelation, which are noted below.

Joachim thought the eras of the Father and Son each had seven parts and that the same seven-part sequence was repeated during each era. He also retained the older idea that Revelation repeated its message several times, and that various images within the book traced the same historical progression. Where Bede had suggested that the seven seals reflected the flow of history in a general way, Joachim went further. He identified the seals with specific events, beginning with the early church and continuing to his own time. He thought history had progressed through the first five seals and had arrived at the sixth seal, which signaled the end of the age. Similarly, he thought the seven heads of the dragon symbolized persecutors of the church, beginning with Herod and Nero and continuing down to the sixth head, the Muslim warrior Saladin, who defeated the Crusaders in Joachim's lifetime. The seventh head was the Antichrist, who would soon appear. People could expect conflict at the turn of the ages, but Joachim predicted that two groups of "spiritual men" would soon arise, fulfilling Revelation's vision of two witnesses opposing the Antichrist (Rev 11:3–12; McGinn, *Calabrian*, 161–203; Daniel, "Joachim"; Wannemacher, "Apocalypse").

Joachim's prediction seemed to be validated by the founding of the Dominican and Franciscan orders soon after his death. An early Franciscan leader, Bonaventure (d. 1274), identified Francis as the angel who appeared during the turbulence symbolized by the sixth seal and understood the order's commitment to poverty and spiritual renewal to be signs of the coming age (Rev 6:12–17; 7:3; McGinn, *Calabrian*, 213–19). The Franciscan Gerardo of Borgo San Donnino (d. 1276) went further by claiming that Joachim was the angel with the eternal gospel, whose teachings would supplant Scripture (14:6). Where Joachim suggested that the era of the Son would last for forty-two generations, or about 1,260 years, Gerardo concluded that the end would actually arrive in the year 1260. His views scandalized many Franciscans but reflected the intensity of apocalyptic expectations among certain groups in the thirteenth century (Reeves, *Influence*, 59–70; McGinn, "Apocalypticism," 93–94).

A major development during this period was the antipapal reading of Revelation. One conflict that gave rise to this perspective involved the radical or Spiritual Franciscans, who insisted on the ideal of poverty and criticized church leaders for their wealth and corruption (Burr, "Mendicant"). The Franciscan Peter John Olivi (d. 1298) warned that the Antichrist would be a false pope who would reject the ideal of poverty. Ubertino of Casale (d. 1329) saw the prediction being fulfilled in papal opposition to the Franciscans by Boniface VIII (d. 1303) and Benedict XI (d. 1304)—whose name in Greek conveniently equaled 666. The second conflict involved the church and the empire. When Emperor Frederick II (d. 1250) seemed intent on asserting control over some papal territories, Pope Gregory IX (d. 1241) charged that he was the beast of Rev 13, and Frederick returned the accusation, calling the pope the satanic dragon of Rev 12 and the Antichrist (McGinn, *Visions*, 173–76; Lerner, "Frederick").

4. REVELATION AS A CONTINUOUS OUTLINE OF CHURCH HISTORY

Papal criticism of the apocalyptic views of the Spiritual Franciscans created the context for a new way of reading Revelation as a linear prophecy of church history. Since the third century, interpreters had assumed that Revelation repeated the same message multiple times, but in the thirteenth century some Franciscans proposed that the book was not repetitive but sequential, and that it outlined the story of the church from the time of the apostles until the end of the age.

This approach was developed by Alexander Minorita (d. 1271), who found it a useful way to ease tensions with church leaders by identifying the antagonists in Revelation with figures from the past rather than with church officials of the present. According to Alexander, Rev 1–6 traced the struggles of the early church, culminating with the appearance of a protecting angel in 7:2, who signaled the coming of Constantine, not Francis, as many had thought. Alexander said that subsequent visions progressed through the Crusades to the rise of the Franciscan and Dominican orders at the end of the millennium in 20:6. He gave the Franciscan order a key role in the consummation of history, since it helped prepare people for New Jerusalem, which would be built through good works. This approach was adopted by Peter Auriol (d. 1322), who did even more to lessen tensions with the church by identifying the antagonists in Revelation as heretics, emperors, and Muslim leaders, rather than church leaders. Unlike Alexander, he treated New Jerusalem as a heavenly rather than an earthly reality, thereby taking attention away from controversial questions about the Franciscans' role in bringing in the new age (Burr, *Olivi's*, 247–50).

Nicholas of Lyra (d. 1349) tempered the sequential approach to Revelation with an Augustinian hesitancy to see genuine historical progress toward the new age. He agreed that the angel in Rev 7:2 signified the beginning of the Constantinian era in the fourth century, but he noted that what followed were the trumpet plagues, symbolizing heretics like Arius and Eutyches in the fourth and fifth centuries. The angelic interlude in Rev 10 is the time of the emperors Justin and Justinian in the sixth century, while the angel Michael in Rev 12 is the emperor Heraclius battling the dragonlike Persians in the seventh century. Nicholas was willing to use Revelation to trace events into the twelfth century, symbolized by the plagues in Rev 16, but he refused to speculate about events after that time. His awareness of ongoing problems among the Franciscans made him unwilling to treat them as harbingers of New Jerusalem. His commentary affirmed the divine ordering of history, while dampening apocalyptic speculation by relegating the controversial visions of Babylon and the defeat of the beast in Rev 17–20 to an indefinite point in the future (Burr, *Olivi's*, 251–54; Krey, "Many").

John Wyclif (d. 1384) used this same approach in a commentary he wrote on Revelation early in his career, but his perspective changed as he grew more critical of the wealth and political influence of the church and decadence in the mendicant orders. In later works he accepted the idea that the angel in Rev 7:2 signified Constantine's reign, but he charged that the result was corruption, because special privileges were given to the clergy after that time. For Wyclif, the Antichrist was the papal office itself, and the unleashing of Satan in 20:7 occurred when the papacy attained new heights of wealth and power under Innocent III (d. 1216). After Wyclif's death, one of his followers interpreted Revelation as a depiction of papal persecution of "evangelical people" like himself, who were called to resist papal oppression (Krey, "Many," 195–99; McGinn, *Antichrist*, 181–82; Potestà, "Radical," 123).

The Bohemian reformer Jan Hus (d. 1415) followed Wyclif in distinguishing the corrupt visible church from the true invisible church, which consisted of the elect, the genuine followers of the Lamb (Rev 6:11; 14:4). Hus did not declare the papacy itself to be the Antichrist but insisted that individual popes filled that role by violating Christ's commands through vice and worldly ambition (Hus, *The Church*, chaps. 1, 2, 15). He turned Revelation's warnings about judgments on falsehood and the greed of Babylon into an indictment of simony in the church (*On Simony* 3; 9). Condemned for heresy, Hus and his associate

Jerome of Prague were both executed. Their supporters legitimated their cause by comparing them to the two witnesses in Rev 11, who were slaughtered for resisting the Antichrist (Petersen, *Preaching*, 42; McGinn, *Antichrist*, 187–87).

C. Revelation from 1500 to 1750

The sixteenth-century Reformation and Counter-Reformation redefined church and society in the west, creating new contexts for the interpretation of Revelation. Protestants followed the late medieval practice of treating Revelation as an outline of church history and adopted the antipapal interpretations that had circulated since the thirteenth century. Lutherans debated the value of Revelation as a witness to Christ, while the Reformed churches centered on the way the book showed God's providence in history. Radical and Anabaptist groups interpreted the book in light of spiritual experience, with some concluding that the end of the age was near. Roman Catholics responded to antipapal readings by relating Revelation either to the pagan Roman Empire before Constantine or to an indefinite time in the future, so that it did not pertain to the church under the papacy. Throughout the period, images from Revelation were given popular form in hymns and artwork.

I. FROM ERASMUS TO LUTHER

Desiderius Erasmus (d. 1536) reopened questions about the authorship and canonical status of Revelation that had not been debated in the west since antiquity. As a scholar in the humanist tradition, he was interested in returning to the sources of Christian theology, including the Bible and patristic writings. In 1516 he published an annotated Greek text of the NT (INTRO VI). In a note on Rev 22:12 he pointed out that Revelation had been rejected by some Greek writers and lacked apostolic weight (*gravitas*). Theologically, Erasmus's interests centered on the imitation of Christ and cultivation of an interior spiritual life, so Revelation held little appeal for him. In 1522 he added more patristic citations to the annotation, noting that some ancient writers even ascribed the book to the heretic Cerinthus. Erasmus said he accepted Revelation because the church had done so, but he did not think that all biblical books had equal value, raising doubts about the status of Revelation. It was the one book Erasmus did not include in his interpretive *Paraphrase* of the NT (Backus, *Reformation*, 3–6).

Martin Luther (d. 1546) repeated Erasmus's criticisms in his "Preface to the Revelation of St. John," published with his German translation of the NT in 1522, but he worked with a different theological perspective. For Luther, the central point of Scripture was what God had done to restore his relationship with people through the death and resurrection of Christ. Early in his career

Luther could not see that Revelation made Christ's work clear, so he declared that "Christ is neither taught nor known in it" (LuthW 35:399). The preface also made dismissive comments about "visions," in part because people had come to Luther's congregation in Wittenberg claiming direct revelations from God and announcing the imminent end of the world. Since Revelation might seem to support such claims, the preface directed people away from it. Yet Revelation was the only book that was fully illustrated in Luther's German NT. The woodcuts were created by Lucas Cranach and patterned after Albrecht Dürer's Apocalypse series, but they showed the beast and whore wearing the papal tiara. The pictures reflected Luther's conviction that papal opposition to his teaching about the work of Christ showed that the pope was against, or "anti-," Christ (see Figure 31; WA.DB 7:483–523).

Luther published a new "Preface to the Revelation of St. John" in 1530, adopting the late medieval practice of reading the book as an outline of church history. By doing so, he identified theological issues that persisted into his own time. For example, the angel with the censer signifies Athanasius and the Council of Nicaea, whose positions he approved (8:3–5). In contrast, the angels with plagues are Tatian, the Montanists, and Origen, who are charged with preaching that people are made righteous by their works instead of grace, elevating spirituality above Scripture, and corrupting the Bible with philosophy—views Luther opposed (8:6–12). The beasts and the whore are the papacy and the empire, while Gog and Magog are the Turkish armies threatening Europe (LuthW 35:402–9).

The preface concludes by developing the implications in Luther's own theological categories of law and gospel, which in Revelation take the form of warning and comfort. As a warning, the visions of beasts and plagues show that throughout its history the church will be threatened by conflict and false belief, and its flaws will be an offense to the world. As comfort, however, Revelation provides assurance that "through and beyond all plagues, beasts, and evil angels, Christ is nonetheless with his saints, and wins the final victory" (LuthW 35:411). Where the preface of 1522 did not see Christ in Revelation, the preface of 1530 concludes that Christ is central (Hofmann, *Luther*, 458–70).

Revelation's canonical status was a question for some reformers. In 1520, Andreas Bodenstein von Karlstadt (d. 1541) divided the NT books into three categories of differing value: First were the gospels and Acts; second were Paul's letters, 1 Peter, and 1 John; and third were Revelation and other writings whose authorship was disputed. Luther in turn rearranged the canonical sequence of the NT by placing Hebrews, James, and Jude at the end, along with Revelation. Printed editions of the Luther Bible numbered the first twenty-three NT books but left the last four unnumbered, which set them apart from the others, and some labeled them "apocryphal" or "noncanonical." Eventually, Johann Gerhard (d. 1637) tried to resolve the issue by arguing that even though historically, books like Revelation had been disputed, that did not mean they were "apocryphal" or theologically suspect, and so they were rightly part of the canon (Leipoldt, *Geschichte*, 2:121–33; Metzger, *Canon*, 241–45).

Passages from Revelation were woven into Lutheran doctrinal treatises. For example, the references to the righteous and holy in Rev 22:11 are linked to theological debates about justification and sanctification. The elders in 4:9–10 show that people are to do good works while ascribing worthiness to God and not to themselves. Reformers appealed to the blessed state of the dead in 14:13 when rejecting the notion of purgatory, and to the prohibition against worshiping angels in 19:10 and 22:8–9 against the invocation of the saints (Chemnitz, *Examination*, 1:472, 496, 662; 3:313, 353, 435). Commentaries on Revelation gave the Reformation a central place in God's design for history (Backus, *Reformation*, 113–29). Some even saw Luther in the book: The sermon preached at Luther's funeral identified him as the angel with the eternal gospel in Rev 14:6–7, whose twofold summons to fear and to glorify God corresponded to Luther's distinction between law and gospel. The commentary by Abraham Calov (d. 1686) gave expanded treatment to Luther's role as the angel with the gospel in Rev 14, thereby sharpening the contrast with the beast and whore, who symbolized the papacy in Rev 13 and 17 (*Biblia*, 1863–65).

Revelation played a role in Lutheran worship through the renewed emphasis on hymnody. The passages that were set to music were nonpolemical and focused on life in the presence of God. Philipp Nicolai (d. 1608) responded to a plague that took thousands of lives by composing "Wachet Auf," or "Wake, awake, for night is flying." This hymn offered hope to grieving people by blending lines from Isaiah and Jesus' parables with images of New Jerusalem. The vision of a city with gates of pearl and endless light pointed to a future life that transcended the sorrow of this age. Later, Johann Sebastian Bach (d. 1750) turned the hymn into a well-known cantata. The Pietist hymn writer Hans Adolf Brorson (d. 1764) paraphrased the vision of the countless multitude in Rev 7:9–17 in "Behold a host arrayed in white." These and other hopeful images from Revelation became regular features of Protestant hymnody.

2. REFORMED TRADITION

Revelation had a mixed reputation in the Reformed tradition. Ulrich Zwingli (d. 1531) accepted Erasmus's criticisms, especially since Revelation seemed to give credence to religious practices that Zwingli opposed. When scenes in which an angel (8:3–4) and the heavenly elders (5:8) offered prayers to God and the Lamb were used to support popular beliefs about the power of angels and the invocation of the saints, Zwingli declared that Revelation was not a biblical book (Metzger, *Canon*, 244, 273). John Calvin (d. 1564) said nothing about Revelation's authorship or canonical status, though he cited its prohibition against the worship of angels (19:10; 22:8–9), agreed that its blessing on the dead ruled out purgatory (14:13), and thought the beast symbolized the papacy (*Institutes of the Christian Religion* 1.14.10; 3.5.10; 4.7.25). Yet Revelation was the only NT book on which he did not write a commentary. Given the different viewpoints, Johannes Oecolampadius (d. 1531) and the Württemberg Confession composed by Johannes Brentz (d. 1570) ascribed primary authority to undisputed writings, like the gospels and Pauline letters. Disputed texts like Revelation, James, Jude, 2 Peter, and 2 and 3 John were canonical but of lesser value (Metzger, *Canon*, 244, 273).

Support for Revelation came from Francis Lambert (d. 1530), who published the first major Protestant commentary on it in 1528. Theologically, he identified Revelation's message with what would become a major theme in the Reformed tradition: Christ's sovereign and providential governing of his kingdom. To ensure that Revelation was taken seriously, Lambert cited patristic testimony that the book had been written by John the apostle. Sebastian Meyer (d. 1546), Theodore Bibliander (d. 1564), Heinrich Bullinger (d. 1575), and others agreed that the consensus of the church and the contents of Revelation indicated its apostolic authorship and supported its canonical status (Backus, *Reformation*, 12–36). Revelation was included among the canonical writings listed in the French (1559), Belgic (1561), and Westminster (1647) confessions, while the Thirty-Nine Articles of the Church of England (1563) affirmed the status of all NT books without listing them.

Reformed commentators construed Revelation as a prophetic outline of church history. This approach enabled them to affirm that God's sovereignty and providence would bring events to their proper end, despite the church's flaws and suffering. John Bale (d. 1563) wrote *The Image of Bothe Churches* while in exile because of religious conflict in England. Although he identified scenes in Revelation with eras of history, his understanding of the book was a variation on the Augustinian idea of perennial conflict between the city of God and the city of the world. Bale thought the struggle between the true church of the gospel and the false church of the papacy had existed for centuries, but that situation was in its final phase. People were not to be alarmed by persecution, because God had foreseen it. Satan had been set loose through the actions of the papacy after the millennium ended in 1000 CE, but the faithful could persevere knowing that God was working out his purposes. These ideas were developed by John Foxe (d. 1587), whose apocalyptic views emphasized the role of the martyrs throughout history, culminating in the Protestant martyrs of his own time (Bauckham, *Tudor*, 21–29, 68–90).

Heinrich Bullinger wrote on Revelation for Protestants who fled to Zürich to escape religious conflict in England, France, and Italy. He encouraged them by pointing to the throne vision in Rev 4–5, which affirmed the sovereign rule of God and the Lamb over history. As followers of the Lamb, they shared in his sufferings and would eventually share in his victory (Bauckham, *Tudor*, 113–15, 298–315). The Geneva Bible of 1560 popularized this approach, calling people to remain faithful despite opposition, since the papal Antichrist worked only by divine permission and his time was limited. The work identifies Catholic leaders with the demonic hordes rising from the abyss (9:1–21), which can harm the body but not the souls of the elect. When critiquing the Anabaptists, who rejected secular authority, the Geneva Bible pointed out that kings have a rightful place in God's city, implying that such offices are legitimate (21:24).

Seventeenth-century English interpretations of Revelation showed a growing sense of optimism that history was moving toward the demise of papal power. Protestant hopes were bolstered in 1588, when Britain won a seemingly miraculous victory over the armada of Catholic Spain. Interpreters assumed that Revelation prophetically outlined the future, so they tried to connect each vision to a specific past event in order to demonstrate divine providence in history. Such attempts were considered analogous to the demonstrations made in math and science. John Napier (d. 1617), who discovered how logarithms could be used for mathematical calculation, tried to discern how Revelation could be used to calculate the flow of history. He equated the trumpet with the bowl visions and postulated that each scene equaled a period of 245 years. The periods began in 71 CE and continued to the founding of the Ottoman Empire by the kings from the east at the sixth seal around 1296 (Rev 16:12). He concluded that the sixth seal period ended and the seventh began in 1541. Although that period would conclude in 1786, judgment could begin sooner, around 1688 (*Plaine*, 1–22).

Joseph Mede (d. 1638) tried to refine this approach by what he claimed was the scientific decoding of Revelation's imagery. Each image was given a definite meaning: The cosmos symbolized the state, windstorms were wars, and hail signified invasion. Recognizing that images occurred multiple times in a nonlinear sequence, he tried to synchronize parts of the book. Each scene of conflict with the beast was equated with similar scenes, so the seventh seal, trumpet, and bowl visions all signified Christ's final victory (Murrin, "Revelation," 136–41). Mede's approach appealed to Isaac Newton (d. 1727), whose interest in physics, astronomy, and calculus was matched by a fascination with

Revelation. His goal was not to predict the future, but to show how prophecies had already been fulfilled by events ranging from the rise of Constantine, signified by the exaltation of the child (Rev 12:5), to the fall of Constantinople in 1453, indicated by the devastation of the sixth trumpet (9:13–21). The precise correlations provided "a convincing argument that the world is governed by providence" (*Observations*, 251–52; Mamiani, "Newton"; Murrin, "Newton's").

Attempts to connect Revelation to progress in history were accompanied by a shift in ideas about the millennium. Early Protestants generally followed Augustine by identifying the thousand-year reign of the saints with the present era of the church, but from the seventeenth century onward, many came to see it as the era of peace and religious renewal that was yet to come (see §38A). Following the lead of British thinkers, the American Jonathan Edwards (d. 1758) identified God as the Alpha and Omega. Since God created all things in the beginning, he was now working out his designs providentially in history, and in the end all things would return to a blessed state during the millennial age. Edwards read Revelation in a linear way and thought that events had progressed to the sixth bowl vision, where the drying up of the Euphrates signified the drying up of papal resources in the post-Reformation era (Rev 16:12). For him, the vision of Babylon's fall anticipated the gradual demise of the papacy and encouraged efforts at religious renewal that would usher in the millennium (*Apocalyptic*, 15–54).

Religious conflict in Europe led the Dutch jurist and theologian Hugo Grotius (d. 1645) to develop interpretations that emphasized philology, rather than theological debate, and encouraged religious toleration. Following Luis de Alcázar—a Roman Catholic whose work is noted below—Grotius abandoned the antipapal perspective and related most of Revelation's visions to the struggles of the ancient church: Rev 1–11 depicted the early church's conflicts with Judaism, and Rev 12–19 showed the ancient struggle against Roman paganism. The millennial age began with Constantine (20:1–6). For Grotius, Revelation's antagonists belonged to the past. The beast symbolized emperors such as Claudius and Nero, and the false prophet was the first-century miracle worker Apollonius of Tyana. The result was that Revelation was not to be read as a critique of the papacy but as a message for the church under Roman imperial rule.

3. RADICAL AND ANABAPTIST MOVEMENTS

Apocalyptic perspectives in radical and Anabaptist movements emphasized the importance of spiritual experience, interpreted in light of Scripture (Barnes,

"Images," 148–51). Thomas Müntzer (d. 1525) claimed to have received revelations through dreams and visions, which gave him a sense that the last judgment was approaching and that he was to play a role in it. For him, Babylon was not only the papacy, but the entire social order, which needed to be overthrown by force (Rev 18–19). Common people were to take up arms against their rulers, for the "kingdom of the world" belonged to Christ, and the people were his agents (11:15–18). As instruments of the four horsemen, who bring the day of wrath, they were to show no pity (6:1–8; *Collected*, 69, 142, 334). Müntzer's preaching, along with that of Heinrich Pfeiffer (d. 1525), precipitated the peasants' revolt of 1524–25, which was brutally suppressed by the authorities, and both Müntzer and Pfeiffer were executed.

Hans Hut (d. 1527) was an Anabaptist who also envisioned an imminent overthrow of the social order, but he did not call the faithful to take up arms. He thought the final seven years of history began in 1521–22 with Müntzer and Pfeiffer, whom he apparently identified as the two prophetic witnesses of Rev 11:3–14. The first half of the seven-year period ended with their deaths in 1525, and the remaining three and a half years would end with the destruction of the godless by the Turkish armies invading Europe and by Christ's return at Pentecost of 1528 (Dan 9:27; Rev 11:3; 12:6). Hut identified himself with the agent of God in Ezek 9:4 and the angel in Rev 7:3, who were to put a seal on the faithful group of 144,000 in order to protect them from destruction. For him, the seal was the sign of the cross or Hebrew letter Taw, traced on the forehead. Hut was arrested and died in a prison fire in 1527, before the date set for Christ's return (Deppermann, *Melchior*, 180, 201; Petersen, *Preaching*, 71–75).

Melchior Hoffmann (d. 1543 or 1544) produced apocalyptic interpretations of Scripture along with accounts of revelatory dreams and visions. His commentary on Revelation divides history into the era of apostles and martyrs, the time of apostasy under the papacy, and the new age in which direct guidance by the Spirit would replace the letter of Scripture. For him, the harbinger of the new age was the early fifteenth-century reformer Jan Hus (noted above). Hus was the angel of the sixth seal, whose message wounded the papal beast with the sword of the Spirit (Rev 7:2; 13:1–3). Hoffmann identified his own time with the sixth trumpet, in which the two witnesses appear (9:13; 11:3–14). Visions reported by Anabaptists at Strasbourg identified Hoffmann as Elijah, who was one of the witnesses. He concluded that his role was to gather the 144,000, who would separate from the false church and evangelize the world (7:3–8; 14:1). He told his followers not to take up the sword, for the godless would be destroyed by the Turkish forces, who were Gog and Magog (20:8). Envisioning Strasbourg as the new spiritual Jerusalem, Hoffmann predicted that the age would end in 1533. Opposition forced him to flee, but he returned to face arrest, probably because Rev 11 pictured the witnesses being martyred. He died in prison a decade later (LCC 25:211–25; Packull, "Reinterpretation"; Deppermann, *Melchior*, 72–75, 255; Petersen, *Preaching*, 88–97).

Hoffmann had assumed the role of Elijah, but the role of Enoch—understood to be the second apocalyptic witness mentioned in Rev 11—was claimed by his militant follower Jan Matthijs (d. 1534), who continued the efforts to convert and seal the 144,000 before the end. Matthijs joined the growing numbers of Anabaptists in Münster, which replaced Strasbourg as the New Jerusalem. In 1534 they seized control of the city and expelled those who did not accept the new order. The city was placed under siege and Matthijs was killed—though some expected him to rise on the fourth day like the witnesses in Rev 11:7–11. The role of prophet and king was assumed by Jan van Leiden (d. 1536), who instituted polygamy and a communal use of goods. Believers were told to destroy their opponents, who belonged to godless Babylon (18:6), but the city fell in 1535 and the group's leaders were put to death (LCC 25:220–21; Deppermann, *Melchior*, 346–47).

The peaceful wing of the Anabaptist movement construed Revelation quite differently. After the disaster at Münster, Dirk Philips (d. 1568) and Menno Simons (d. 1561) fostered Anabaptist communities that emphasized purity and nonviolence. Rather than identifying New Jerusalem with a particular city, Philips interpreted it as a vision of the church's spiritual life on earth and final perfection in heaven (Rev 21:1–22:5). Its traits are unity in faith and Spirit. It expresses the peace of Christ and comes down from heaven, for Christians are not of this world but are born from above. The New Jerusalem pictures the community as the bride of the Lamb, adorned with virtue. Her dominion is spiritual and comes through faith, fed by the living water that signifies the Spirit (LCC 25:255–60).

4. ROMAN CATHOLIC TRADITION

Roman Catholic leaders took up the question of Revelation's canonical status at the Council of Trent, which was convened in 1545 to define church positions in light of issues generated by the Reformation. Given the questions that Erasmus and others had raised concerning the authorship and value of Revelation and other books, the council debated whether to distinguish undisputed writings from those that were disputed or apocryphal. But at Session IV (1546), the council stated that it followed the church fathers in receiving all OT and NT books with equal reverence, along with the unwritten traditions passed down by the church. The Latin Vulgate was the accepted text, and Revelation was listed as a canonical book. When responding to Protestant theological critiques, the decrees of the council cited Revelation to show that the good works arising from justification can be said to have genuine merit before God (Rev 14:13; 22:11–12; Session VI, chaps. 10, 16). Where Protestants used the vision of Babylon the whore polemically against the Roman church, the council found a surprising way to invoke it in support of Catholic practice: In that vision, water symbolized people (17:1, 15), so mingling wine with water in the cup during Mass signified the union of Christ and his people through the sacrament (Session XXII, chap. 7).

The lectionary approved by Pope Pius V in 1570—and used for the next four hundred years—included no readings from Revelation for Sunday Masses and only a few passages for special occasions, such as the vision of the white-robed multitude on All Saints Day (Rev 7:9–17). Yet the book contributed to Roman Catholic devotional life through artistic portrayals of Mary as the woman clothed with the sun (12:1–4). Identifying the woman of Rev 12 as Mary had grown in popularity after the feast of the Immaculate Conception received papal approval in 1476. In order to convey the idea that Mary was conceived without the taint of original sin, artists pictured her as a heavenly woman surrounded with light, standing above the moon with a wreath of stars around her head, as in Rev 12. Where Revelation pictures the woman in pain and threatened by a dragon, the artistic depictions of Mary are peaceful. This portrayal of Mary became important for Catholics in Latin America after a Native American, Juan Diego, reported seeing a vision of her in Mexico in 1531. Her image, displayed at the Basilica of Our Lady of Guadalupe, includes the radiant elements of Rev 12. Other famous versions were done by Spanish artists Francisco Pacheco (d. 1644) and Diego Velázquez (d. 1660; Drury, *Painting*, 170–75).

The most vigorous responses to Protestant uses of Revelation came from Jesuit writers. They had two strategies for showing that the visions of the beast and Babylon could not refer to the papacy. One was to insist that Revelation pertained to the distant future, and the other was that it related to the distant past. But in either case, Revelation did not deal with the church under the papacy. Francisco Ribera (d. 1591) said that the messages in Rev 1–3 pertained to Christians of John's time, while the first five seals pointed to the preaching of the apostles, Nero's persecution, the rise of false apostles, and persecution under Trajan (6:1–11). All of that was in the past. But the rest of the book relates to the end of the age, with the cosmic signs of the sixth seal anticipating Christ's second coming (6:12–17; cf. Matt 24:29) and the trumpet plagues prophesying eschatological tribulations. Most importantly, the visions of the beast and whore in Rev 12–19 point to *future* persecutions by the Antichrist.

Ribera no longer treated Revelation as a continuous history of the church but drew on the futuristic perspectives of Irenaeus and Hippolytus, who thought the Antichrist would come from the tribe of Dan and reign for a literal three and a half years at the end of the age. Where Protestants charged that Babylon was Rome under the papacy, Ribera countered that Rome would become Babylon only in the future, when it *fell away* from the papacy (*In Sacram*, 377–78). He stopped short of anticipating a future millennial kingdom on earth, however, and treated the thousand-year kingdom as the heavenly state that the faithful entered upon death (*In Sacram* 514). His views were popularized by Cornelius a Lapide (d. 1637).

The alternative to this futuristic emphasis was to say that nearly all of Revelation's prophecies were fulfilled in the past, before Constantine. This approach was developed by the Jesuit Luis de Alcázar (d. 1613), who dedicated his work to Pope Paul V and presented Revelation as a vision of the triumph of the Catholic Church. For him, the first half of the book depicts the early church's struggle against Judaism. He thought the sixth seal depicted the Jewish revolt against Rome (6:12–17), a time when the church was protected (7:1–17) and Jews suffered disasters (8:1–9:21). An angel called for the extension of the gospel to Gentiles (10:1–11), and then Jerusalem fell under siege (11:1–14). In the second half of the book, the woman symbolizing Jewish Christianity bears a child, who is the Gentile church. Threats from imperial Rome are symbolized by the beast and whore, until Babylon falls, signifying the end of paganism when the empire converted to Christianity in the fourth century (Rev 13–19). Only the final part of Revelation remains to be fulfilled, when there will be persecution by the Antichrist and the church will defeat all false religion through the Spirit, symbolized by heavenly fire (20:7–10). In New Jerusalem, Alcázar sees a vision of the church's final perfection (21:1–22:5; *Vestigatio*, 35–37). His approach was developed by Jacques-Bénigne Bossuet (d. 1704), who varied the pattern by proposing that Roman Babylon fell somewhat later, when the city was sacked in 410 (*L'Apocalypse*, 29).

Alcázar has been seen as a forerunner of modern historical interpretation of Revelation, because he related the book to Roman antiquity rather than to the history of the church. His approach is called "preterist," from the Latin *praetereo*, or "pass by," because it emphasizes that nearly all of Revelation's prophecies were fulfilled in the distant past. Yet preterists and those who read Revelation as a history of the church share a common assumption: that the book prophesies a series of specific events. The difference is that preterists think the visions were nearly all realized by events before the fifth century, while others see fulfillment continuing through the centuries of church history that follow. The kind of historical interpretation that emerged in the nineteenth and twentieth centuries was different. Instead of treating Revelation as predictive prophecy, interpreters read it as a message designed to encourage Christians in the late first century.

Their questions concerned the form of the message and the way it dealt with the immediate situation of its intended readers.

D. Revelation from 1750 to the Present

Efforts at social reform and church renewal, along with advances in technology, raised hopes for a better future during this period, even as the Napoleonic wars, the American Civil War, and then World Wars I and II called into question the prospect of genuine progress toward a new age. The older pattern of reading Revelation as an outline of history was generally abandoned, and the main options were to read it either as a prediction of the cataclysmic end of the present age or as a book that encouraged first-century Christians living under Roman rule. Awareness of contemporary religious pluralism raised questions about the book's relationship to the religious traditions of antiquity, and discoveries of the Dead Sea Scrolls encouraged renewed consideration of the apocalyptic dimensions of Judaism and early Christianity. Along the way, imagery from Revelation was given new forms of expression in worship and hymnody.

1. WORSHIP AND MUSIC

The hymns of praise in Revelation were often paraphrased by composers, who were attracted to their messages of hope. The English hymn writer Charles Wesley (d. 1788) belonged to the renewal movement known as Methodism, which in its early years experienced sharp opposition from church leaders and the public. To encourage his associates, he composed "Ye Servants of God, Your Master Proclaim," which paraphrases the cry "salvation to God" voiced by those who come through affliction into God's presence (Rev 7:10–12). His hymn "Love Divine, All Loves Excelling" culminates in praise as worshipers envision casting their crowns before God's throne (4:10). Revelation made its way into the theater through the oratorio *Messiah* by George Frideric Handel (d. 1759). The words "Hallelujah: for the Lord God Omnipotent reigneth" (19:6), which originally accompanied the fall of Babylon, became an announcement of Jesus' resurrection, and the line "Worthy is the Lamb" (5:12), which originally introduced the seal plagues, concluded the entire work with a celebration of the final resurrection. Such musical interpretations emphasized the hopeful aspects of Revelation.

Militant imagery in the book found musical expression in "The Battle Hymn of the Republic," published in 1862 during the American Civil War. The author, Julia Ward Howe (d. 1910), advocated the abolition of slavery and turned the vision of the Lord trampling "the grapes of wrath" into a song that rallied Northern support for the war effort (Rev 14:19–20; 19:11–16). At the same time, Robert Lowry (d. 1899) consoled the grieving with "Shall We Gather at the River," which gave people hope for a future life as they were reunited with loved ones by the river that flows from God's throne in New Jerusalem (22:1).

African Americans of this period gave Revelation a significant place in worship. The forms of Christianity practiced by slaves retained a West African sense of the immediacy of the spirit world, so when the author of Revelation reported seeing visions "in the Spirit," it was a recognized form of religious experience. Slave songs included images of gold crowns, the tree of life, and New Jerusalem and voiced hope for a future characterized by freedom and dignity. The lyrics blurred the lines between the future and the present, so walking the streets of New Jerusalem could signify freedom wherever it was found, whether in this world or the next. As slavery gave way to segregation after the Civil War, worshipers continued to see a hopeful element in Revelation's vision of cosmic change, because it meant that present conditions of injustice would not continue forever. The lyrics to "When the Saints Go Marching In" tell of the sun becoming dark and the moon turning to blood, while inviting singers to hope that they will be in that "number" of the redeemed when the new world is revealed (Rev 6:12; 7:4; 21:1; Genovese, *Roll*, 248–50).

2. FUTURISTIC INTERPRETATION

As we have seen, Roman Catholics from the sixteenth century on thought that Revelation prophesied events that either took place under imperial Rome before Constantine or would occur in the distant future (INTRO I.C.4). Protestants, however, assumed that the book outlined history from the time of the apostles to the coming millennial age, which they thought would occur progressively as papal power waned and evangelism and social reform brought peace on earth. Changes in outlook came when British Protestants became disillusioned with the French Revolution of 1789–99. Initially, many Protestants thought the prophecy about the wounding of the beast (Rev 13:3) was fulfilled when the revolution ended Catholic hegemony in France and led to the expulsion of the pope from Rome. But instead of bringing millennial peace closer, the conflict ushered in a reign of terror, deified human reason rather than Christ, and opened the way for Napoleon's conquests. By the 1820s, Edward Irving (d. 1836) and Henry Drummond (d. 1860) had concluded that the millennium would not arrive gradually through social progress but cataclysmically when Christ returned to establish his kingdom on earth (Sandeen, *Roots*, 3–30).

In the United States, William Miller (d. 1849) argued that passages from the books of Daniel and Revelation enabled him to calculate the time of Christ's return. Like most Protestants, he related visions in Revelation to periods of church history, the dragon being ancient pagan Rome and the beast, papal Rome. The new element was a framework derived from Dan 8:14, which said that twenty-three hundred days would pass before the sanctuary was cleansed. Miller thought that the days symbolized years and the sanctuary signified earth, which would be cleansed at Christ's return. By positing that the decree to restore Jerusalem and its sanctuary was given in 457 BCE, he concluded that fulfillment would come twenty-three hundred years later, in 1843–44.

The time Miller set passed without cataclysmic change, leading some of his followers to reconceive the system. They argued that Christ had actually returned at the expected time, but to cleanse the *heavenly* sanctuary pictured in Rev 11:19 and Heb 8:1–2. Therefore, Christ would have to cleanse the earth at some point in the future. This approach was adopted by the Seventh-Day Adventists. Later, Charles Taze Russell (d. 1916), the founder of the Jehovah's Witnesses, devised a system based on Luke 21:24 which said that Jerusalem would be trodden down by the Gentiles until their time was fulfilled. He thought the plague scenes in Rev 16 pictured the spiritual struggles of his own age, which would culminate in the battle of Armageddon in 1914. Before that time his mission was to gather the 144,000 who would reign with Christ in heaven (Rev 7:4–8; 14:1–5; Penton, *Apocalypse*, 24–46).

A more influential form of futuristic interpretation was developed by John Nelson Darby (d. 1882) and popularized by Joseph A. Seiss (d. 1904) and Cyrus Scofield (d. 1921). Abandoning the practice of relating Revelation to church history, they insisted that Rev 4–22 prophesied times yet to come. Their interpretive framework assumed that the Jewish people were to possess the land from the River of Egypt to the Euphrates and that history would not be complete until that literally occurred (Gen 15:18). They argued that God fulfilled his purposes for Israel through most of the seven-year time blocks or "weeks of years" mentioned in Dan 9:24–26, until God's Messiah was "cut off" and the city was destroyed, which they identified as the Jewish rejection of Jesus and Roman destruction of Jerusalem in the first century. At that time a Gentile church came into existence, and God stopped carrying out his purposes for the Jewish people with just one seven-year period remaining in Dan 9:27.

A defining feature of this scenario is that the current age will end when God removes the Gentile church from earth to heaven in "the rapture" and unleashes seven years of tribulation. During the tribulation the Antichrist will rise to power, and the disasters of Dan 9:27 and Rev 4:1–19:21 will occur. Darby, Seiss, and Scofield insisted that Revelation was to be interpreted as literally as possible, although in practice the literalism was selective. Although the trumpet and bowl visions are said to warn that fire will actually fall from the sky and heavenly bodies will become dark, the seven-headed beast is not a literal animal but a secular tyrant, and the whore is not a woman but a symbol for the Protestant and Catholic groups who support the tyrant (Seiss 2:46–49, 391;

3:122–24). At the end of the tribulation, the battle of Armageddon is expected to rage from Galilee to Jerusalem, and afterward the millennial age will dawn as the Jewish people accept Jesus as the Messiah and dwell in the land promised to them in Gen 15:18.

Many found this perspective appealing because it affirmed God's ultimate control over history, despite ongoing conflict on earth. Hope of being taken to heaven before the great tribulation gave people incentive to come to faith, and the approach offered a vivid sense that the end was coming without actually setting a date for Christ's return. Dwight L. Moody (d. 1899) popularized this approach during his evangelistic campaigns in the late 1800s. A century later, in the 1970s and 1980s, Hal Lindsey used it in *The Late Great Planet Earth*, which linked scenes from Revelation to conflict in the Middle East and the Cold War threat of nuclear conflagration (Boyer, *When*).

3. HISTORICAL CRITICISM

Modern historical criticism began with the assumption that Revelation was shaped by the context in which it was written. Studies by Moses Stuart (d. 1852), Friedrich Bleek (d. 1859), and others treated the book like other ancient writings, asking about the circumstances of its composition, the literary form used by its author, and its significance for the original readers. They moved away from attempts to find fulfillments of Revelation's visions in events before Constantine, as the preterist approach did, or in the centuries that followed, as was done by those who assumed that Revelation outlined church history. While acknowledging that the book looked for Christ's victory at the end of the age, they did not assume that it predicted a series of events as futuristic interpreters did. Instead, they proposed that Revelation used a rich collection of images to encourage the original readers to persevere in the face of suffering and oppression. The book's ongoing significance was to be discerned by analogy: Insofar as readers of later times found themselves in circumstances like those of the earliest readers, they could continue to benefit from its message (Stuart vi, 123–24, 160–76; Bleek, *Lectures*, 61).

Revelation's literary form was of special interest. David Pareus (d. 1622) had once suggested that Revelation was a drama with several acts, and Johann Gottfried Eichhorn (d. 1827) developed the idea, reading the book as a poetic depiction of the triumph of Christianity. But others compared Revelation's literary form to that of the *Sibylline Oracles* and *Testaments of the Twelve Patriarchs*, which claimed to present divine revelation. After the publication of the *Ascension of Isaiah* in 1819 and *1 Enoch* in 1821, Friedrich Lücke (d. 1855) wrote the first major study of apocalyptic literature and its relationship to Revelation, which appeared in 1832. By showing Revelation's similarity to other ancient texts, interpreters proposed that the author chose the literary form of an apocalypse because it was familiar to the intended readers. Modern readers needed to become familiar with the literary features of the apocalyptic genre (Stuart 97–98; on the genre, see INTRO IV.A.1).

Some historical critics challenged the idea that Revelation was a unified account of the visions John received on Patmos, proposing that it consisted of multiple sources and levels of editing. They pointed out that the messages in Rev 1–3 focus on the churches in Asia, whereas Rev 4–22 depict heaven and the future. The sequences of seal and trumpet visions are interrupted by scenes of another order (7:1–17; 10:1–11:14), while scenes of judgment (6:17; 14:8, 14–20) and victory (11:15; 12:10; 19:6–10) occur before the end has arrived. Revision theories held that Revelation was a Jewish apocalypse expanded by a Christian editor (Vischer, *Offenbarung*) or a Christian apocalypse that was revised by one or more editors (Völter, *Entstehung*; Charles 1:l–lxv). Compilation theories maintained that the author combined short vision accounts (Weizsäcker, *Apostolic*, 2:173–80) or longer Jewish and Christian documents to create Revelation (Spitta, *Offenbarung*, 235–463). None of the attempts to reconstruct the stages of composition gained wide acceptance, however (see INTRO II.B and §§18B and 22C).

More significant were studies of Revelation's use of the mythic traditions attested in many ancient cultures, especially that of the dragon threatening the woman in Rev 12. Hermann Gunkel (d. 1932) pioneered the history-of-religions approach, which assumed that myths existed in rather stable form over long periods and that texts like Revelation were particular manifestations of underlying patterns. Gunkel compared Rev 12 to Babylonian creation myths in which the dragon, which symbolized chaos, had to be overcome (*Creation*, 239–50). Others noted affinities with myths in Greek (Dieterich, *Abraxas*, 111–260) and Egyptian (Bousset 346–58) sources. Although the term "myth" had traditionally been equated with falsehood, scholars began treating myth as a form of thought that could convey abiding truths (Koch, *Drachenkampf*, 28–43).

Wilhelm Bousset (d. 1920) developed these ideas, proposing that the primeval dragon myth evolved into the legend of the Antichrist, which was included in Revelation. Although none of the earliest Jewish and Christian sources presented the legend in its entirety, Bousset argued that they presupposed it, with individual writers expressing features of the underlying tradition (*Antichrist*; *Offenbarung*, 118–19). Later studies modified this approach by showing that myths are characterized by variety rather than uniformity. Since myths change over time, it is important to compare forms of a story that circulated at the same time in the same cultural context. It is also significant that the origin of a story does not determine its meaning, since the same basic plotline can convey different and even conflicting points of view. For example, the story of conflict with a dragon can either support or critique imperial claims (§25C and D; Yarbro Collins, *Combat*; Friesen, *Imperial*, 167–79).

Historical study of Revelation was accepted in academic circles in the late nineteenth and early twentieth centuries, but interest in the book declined between World War I and II. One reason was that scholars distinguished prophetic literature, which was considered a high point in Israel's tradition, from apocalyptic writings, which were regarded as a late development that lost sight of the prophets' ideals. A second reason was that Protestants had previously coupled apocalyptic language with hope for progress toward a millennial age of peace on earth, but in the late 1800s that connection broke down. Those who looked for progress focused on the ethical aspects of Israel's prophetic writings and Jesus' teaching about the kingdom, while those who retained an interest in Revelation often read it futuristically and saw little hope for positive social change (Moorhead, "Apocalypticism").

4. FROM WORLD WAR II TO GLOBAL PERSPECTIVES

Scholarly interest in Revelation and other apocalyptic texts increased after World War II. A change was signaled in 1960 when Ernst Käsemann said that "apocalyptic was the mother of all Christian theology" (*New*, 102). For him, apocalyptic thought dealt with the problem of rightful lordship over the earth. He recalled that during the war the National Socialists had said, "Heaven is for sparrows and Christians, earth is for us"; and the world had suffered because of such ideology (*Jesus*, 134). In response, Käsemann insisted that the apocalyptic elements in the gospels and Pauline letters went beyond otherworldly piety by stressing God's rightful claim over the whole creation, exercised through the crucified and risen Christ (*New*, 180).

Elisabeth Schüssler Fiorenza identified this same issue in Revelation, which centers on the question "Who is the true Lord of this world?" (*Revelation*, 58). She maintained that Revelation's apocalyptic outlook should not be separated from the prophetic tradition, since the author called his book a prophecy, drew language from prophetic texts, and called for justice in the political, economic, and religious contexts of the Roman Empire. Her reconstruction of Revelation's social setting supported this perspective by emphasizing the role of Christian prophets in the churches of Asia Minor (*Book*, 133–56). The globalization of biblical studies is reflected in her treatment of liberation, which is informed by the work of Latin American and African interpreters, who see Revelation calling for resistance against oppression (*Revelation*, 10–12, 27–29; cf. Boesak, *Comfort*; Richard, *Apocalypse*).

Historical studies had generally assumed that Revelation originated during persecution under Domitian, but some discerned a more complex social situation. Adela Yarbro Collins noted the lack of evidence for imperial persecution in the late first century, while pointing to other issues such as local conflict with Jews, disputes over assimilating Greco-Roman religious practices, differences over wealth, and restiveness under Roman rule (*Crisis*, 84–110). Leonard Thompson went further by trying to show that Christians in Asia Minor generally fared well under Domitian and that the anti-Roman views of Revelation's author were different from those of his readers (*Book*, 95–197). Using literary and archaeological sources, Steven Friesen showed that the imperial cult enjoyed popular support in Asia Minor, so Revelation's criticisms were not directed at Domitian's excesses but at the way of life Rome fostered (*Imperial*, 150–51).

The form and function of Revelation received renewed attention as part of the broader interest in apocalyptic texts. The Dead Sea Scrolls, discovered in 1947, complicated the definition of an apocalyptic genre because some texts included apocalyptic elements, such as conflict between God and the agents of evil and the prospect of a cosmic battle at the end of the age, but their form was different from many Jewish and Christian apocalypses. Studies of the genre proposed that a literary apocalypse had a narrative framework and an intermediary, who disclosed transcendent realities (Intro IV.A.1). The function of such texts was often thought to be encouragement of those in crisis, but some observed that the effects could be more varied. Revelation could assure readers facing social conflict, while challenging those satisfied with the current order to resist the practices the author found incompatible with the faith (Intro V.A). When seen in the context of Jewish apocalypticism, the genre and its motifs have affinities with Israel's prophetic tradition, although visions of a heavenly world and cosmic conflict also have affinities with other types of ancient literature (Collins, *Apocalyptic*, 1–42).

The evocative quality of Revelation's imagery continues to generate differing responses. Some develop the contrast between scenes of God's heavenly throne hall and Roman court ceremony (Aune, *Apocalypticism*, 99–119). Feminist scholars often critique the images of the mother, the whore, and the bride, which perpetuate stereotypes concerning women's roles (Pippin, "Eros"; Keller, "Eyeing"; Levine, ed., *Feminist*, 1–16). Yet some feminist scholars find the imagery more subversive, since it uses the literary conventions to foster resistance against Roman imperialism (Schüssler Fiorenza 12–15; Rossing, *Choice*,

87–90). Similar differences surround the violent images in Revelation, with some scholars concluding that the book celebrates the prospect of violent destruction (Moyise, "Does"), while others see the violent imagery being redefined in terms of the Lamb, who redeems by suffering for others (Barr, "Lamb"; Barr, "Towards"). Some find Revelation's message to be one of merciless judgment (Royalty, *Streets*, 246), while others find in the book's repeated interruptions of judgment and visions of glory a hope for the redemption of the nations (Bauckham, *Climax*, 238–337).

We now turn to Revelation's historical and social settings and literary and rhetorical features, keeping in mind the questions raised by recent scholarship. The perspectives summarized above highlight the interplay between aspects of the book's evocative language and the complex social context envisioned by the author, creating a framework for the sustained reading of Revelation in the NOTES and COMMENTS.

II.

Historical Issues

Traditionally, Revelation is said to have been written by John the apostle about 95 CE during a period of persecution at the end of Domitian's reign. Since the Gospel and Epistles of John were also attributed to the apostle, Revelation has often been grouped with those writings. Historical studies, however, suggest a different reconstruction of the setting. The author was probably an early Christian prophet who knew several types of early Christian traditions but was not directly acquainted with John's gospel or epistles. The readers were challenged by local conflicts with those outside their communities, internal disagreements over accommodating Greco-Roman religious practice, and problems associated with complacency, but they did not face widespread persecution. The time of composition was probably 80–100, but a more precise date cannot be determined.

A. Authorship

Revelation identifies the author as "John," a "servant" of God and "brother" of the Christians to whom the book is addressed (1:1, 4, 9; 22:8). Interpreters have identified him as an apostle or a church elder, and some suggest that the name is a pseudonym. But the most plausible view is that John was the real name of the author and he was a Jewish Christian prophet active in Asia Minor. We consider these possibilities below.

I. JOHN THE APOSTLE

The writer of Revelation does not claim to be an apostle, but from the second century on many Christians assumed that he was John the son of Zebedee. It is unclear whether Papias (d. ca. 130) thought that John the apostle wrote Revelation, since his comments on the author's identity are attested only indirectly (Andreas of Caesarea, *In Apocalypsin* preface). Justin Martyr (d. ca. 165) said that John the apostle wrote Revelation (*Dial.* 81.4), and Irenaeus (d. ca. 200) added that John also wrote the Fourth Gospel and 1 and 2 John (*Haer.* 3.11.1; 3.16.5, 8; 5.30.3). Clement of Alexandria (d. ca. 215) assumed that John was the apostle (*Quis div.* 42), as did later writers (Hippolytus, *Antichr.* 35–36, 50; Origen, *Comm. Jo.* 2.41–42; Victorinus, *In Apoc.* 11.1; Muratorian canon). The tradition that it was the apostle who was banished to Patmos may have been known to Hegesippus (late second century; Nicklas, "Probleme," 42–44). Tertullian (d. ca. 225) added legendary details like the apostle surviving being boiled in oil before being banished to Patmos (*Praescr.* 36; *Marc.* 3.14.3; 3.24.4).

Some modern interpreters attribute Revelation to John the apostle for two reasons. First, one might expect the early church tradition to be accurate because it was held by Justin, who lived in Ephesus for a time, and by Irenaeus, who spent time in Smyrna. Since Revelation addresses churches in those cities, one might assume that they preserved information about its author. Some note that the *Apocryphon of John* begins with a scene in which John the son of Zebedee sees a heavenly revealer and is told that he will learn "what is [and what was] and what will come to [pass]" (1.7–8; 1.30–2.16). Given the similarities to Rev 1:13–19, the *Apocryphon* provides additional second-century evidence of the tradition that John the son of Zebedee was known to be the author of Revelation. Second, those who assume that the Fourth Gospel was written by John the apostle highlight points of similarity between Revelation and the gospel in order to show that both have the same author (Morris 27–35; Mounce 8–15; Osborne 2–6).

Both of these arguments are problematic, however. First, early Christians tended to associate writings whose content they valued with apostolic authors. Since Justin and Irenaeus valued Revelation, it would be natural for them to assume that "John" was the apostle (Yarbro Collins, *Crisis*, 29). Early Christians also mixed up references to people with the same name. Irenaeus (*Haer.* 3.12.15) confused James the son of Zebedee, who was martyred in Acts 12:2, with James the brother of the Lord (Acts 15:13–21). Similarly, Clement confused Philip the apostle with Philip the evangelist (*Strom.* 3.6.52.4; Charles 1: xlix). Second, evidence linking Revelation to the gospel and epistles is not strong (INTRO I.D.1). More importantly, John's gospel and epistles were probably not written by John the apostle (Brown, *Introduction*, 189–99; Beasley-Murray, *John*, lxvi–lxxv), so linking Revelation to those writings does not build a case for apostolic authorship.

2. "JOHN" AS A PSEUDONYM

Some in the ancient church objected to Revelation's content and tried to discredit the book by claiming that it had been written under a false name. As we have seen, in the late second to early third centuries a group in Asia Minor—the so-called Alogoi (Epiphanius, *Pan.* 51.1.3–6; 51.32.2–33.3)—and the Roman presbyter Gaius argued that Revelation had been written by the heretic Cerinthus, who used John's name to trick people into thinking that the work was apostolic (Eusebius, *Hist. eccl.* 3.28.1–5). Yet there is no evidence that the Alogoi or Gaius had historical information about the author. They attributed Revelation to Cerinthus in order to undercut its credibility because it seemingly supported the Montanist movement, which they opposed.

In the sixteenth century Desiderius Erasmus (d. 1536) and others challenged the apostolic authorship of Revelation because of its visionary content and confusing message, but they did not speculate further about the author's identity (see INTRO I.C.1). In the eighteenth century Hermann Oeder (d. 1760) and Johann Salomo Semler (d. 1791) revived the idea that Cerinthus wrote Revelation because they found the book's contents incompatible with Christ's message of love (Bousset 33–34; Kümmel, *New*, 63–64).

Modern arguments that Revelation is pseudonymous are based on its literary form. Jewish apocalypses such as Daniel, *1 Enoch*, *4 Ezra*, and *2 Baruch* are written under the names of figures from Israel's history, and Christian apocalypses such as the *Apocalypse of Peter* (second century) and *Apocalypse of Paul* (fourth century) were ascribed to apostles. Accordingly, some have proposed that Revelation is written in the name of John the apostle to give it greater authority (Weizsäcker, *Apostolic*, 174–75; Strecker, "Chiliasm," 49; Vanni, *Apocalisse*, 76, 117). Others suggest that "John" was the central figure in a Christian circle or "school" that produced the Fourth Gospel and Johannine Epistles. Attributing Revelation to such a venerable teacher would have enhanced the book's status (Frey, "Erwägungen," 425–27; Witulski, *Johannesoffenbarung*, 344–45).

But if "John" is a pseudonym, one would expect the author to call himself an "apostle" and weave in purported memories of Jesus' ministry, as is done in the *Apocalypse of Peter*. If the author used the name "John" to link Revelation to the gospel and epistles, one might expect a more direct appeal to those writings as part of the literary fiction. It is preferable to take "John" as the name of an author whose identity was known to the readers (Yarbro Collins, *Crisis*, 27–44).

3. JOHN AS AN EARLY CHRISTIAN ELDER

Dionysius of Alexandria (d. 264) wanted to distance Revelation and its vision of a millennial kingdom from the Fourth Gospel, which he believed had been written by John the apostle, so he proposed that Revelation was written by someone else named John (Eusebius, *Hist. eccl.* 7.24.7–16). Eusebius developed this approach by noting that Papias mentioned both the apostle and another John, who was a church elder. Although Papias did not say where John the elder lived, Eusebius referred to tombs in Ephesus for two different people named John. Eusebius attributed the Fourth Gospel to the apostle and Revelation to John the elder (*Hist. eccl.* 3.39.4–6). Some modern interpreters have argued that the beloved disciple of John 21:20–24 was "the elder" who wrote 2 and 3 John, suggesting that the same person wrote Revelation (Bousset 34–49).

This approach is not persuasive. The author of Revelation does not refer to himself as an elder or claim the functions of teaching and community leadership that were typical of elders (NOTE on Rev 4:4). If Papias did distinguish John the elder from the apostle, he did not claim that the elder wrote Revelation or was connected to Ephesus (Yarbro Collins, *Crisis*, 31). Finally, it is best to treat the authorship of Revelation separately from that of John's gospel and epistles (INTRO II.D.1).

4. JOHN AS AN EARLY CHRISTIAN PROPHET

The most plausible view is that John was the real name of an early Christian prophet who was active among the prophets in Asia Minor (Rev 22:9). He does not claim to be an apostle but recounts his commission to "prophesy" in a vision reminiscent of Ezekiel (Rev 10:11), and he calls this book a "prophecy" (1:3; 22:7, 10, 18–19).

The name "John," or Iōannēs, is a Greek form of the Hebrew Yoḥanan (cf. LXX *Iōanan*; 2 Kgs 25:23; 1 Chr 3:15, 24). In the Greco-Roman period, Iōannēs is attested in Jewish literary sources, papyri, and inscriptions (1 Macc 2:1–2; 13:53; 2 Macc 4:11; 11:17; Josephus, *J.W.* 2.568; 4.145; Ilan, *Lexicon*, 1:34; 3:105–8). John's name suggests that he was of Jewish background. His frequent use of biblical imagery shows familiarity with the Jewish Scriptures, while his warning against eating food sacrificed to Greco-Roman deities reflects the outlook of Jewish Christianity (Rev 2:14, 20; Acts 15:20, 29; 21:25).

Some scholars suggest that John fled from Palestine to Asia Minor during the Jewish revolt of 66–73 CE (Charles 1:xxxviii–liv; Yarbro Collins, *Crisis*, 46–50; Aune 1:l; Satake 35). Yet the evidence offered in support of this hypothesis does not allow such specificity. First, some suggest that John's peculiar Greek shows that his first language was Aramaic or Hebrew, which would be typical of Jews in Palestine but not in Asia Minor. Yet others argue that since many features of his language have analogies in non-Jewish Greek texts, he may simply be using a type of vulgar Greek that was spoken in Asia Minor (Porter, "Language").

Second, some propose that John relied primarily on a Hebrew rather than a Greek text of the Scriptures, which would suggest that he came from Palestine (Charles 1:lxvi–lxxxi, Aune 1:l). Yet there are places where his language corresponds more closely to the Greek renderings in the LXX or Theodotian than to the MT. Since manuscripts from Qumran show that Greek translations other than the LXX were available, it is difficult to know how much John worked directly with Hebrew texts and where he might rely on one of the Greek versions (INTRO IV.D.1).

Third, the apocalypses of *4 Ezra* and *2 Baruch*, which resemble Revelation, were probably composed in Palestine. Nevertheless, the apocalyptic genre was not limited to Palestine, since the Greek version of Daniel was circulating before the first century CE and *1 Enoch* was probably known outside of Palestine (Nickelsburg, *1 Enoch*, 87). The *Shepherd of Hermas* is a Christian visionary text that originated in Rome in the late first or early second century, and the second *Sibylline Oracle* shows that apocalyptic themes had a place in the Judaism of Asia Minor in the early second century CE (Collins in *OTP* 1:332).

Fourth, Revelation mentions Harmagedon, which recalls the name Megiddo, and it pictures Jerusalem under siege. Yet the siege imagery is biblical; nothing suggests personal familiarity with the topography of Palestine (NOTES and COMMENT on 11:2 and 16:16). Furthermore, if the author had fled from Judea during the Jewish revolt, one might expect him to link Rome's identity as Babylon to its destruction of the temple. Yet the Babylon vision makes no mention of the temple, focusing instead on Babylon/Rome's economic power and violence against the saints and others (17:1–18:24). John's prophetic role can best be understood within the social context of Christianity in Asia Minor. His perspectives need not be linked especially to Palestine or interpreted as those of a prophet who migrated to Asia Minor from elsewhere.

B. Unity of the Text

Revelation presents itself as an account of visions that John received on Patmos, but by the late nineteenth century some maintained that the material came from multiple sources or that the text had been revised by one or more editors. Possible marks of editorial activity include seams, such as the transition from the messages to the churches in 2:1–3:21 to the visionary journey in 4:1; repetitious elements; awkward details; and apparent differences in form or outlook among sections. Despite numerous attempts to reconstruct the stages of composition, none of the initial proposals was widely accepted (surveys in Beckwith 224–39; Aune 1:cx–cxvii). Revelation's distinctive literary style is used quite consistently throughout the work, making it improbable that an editor combined blocks of material by different authors.

As an alternative, some interpreters maintain that a single author wrote various parts of the text over a period of time and later assembled them. Recent versions of this theory hold that John was a Jewish apocalyptic writer who composed some sections before 70 CE and before his acceptance of Christianity. These units include the 144,000 from the tribes of Israel (7:1–8), John's commissioning (10:1–11), the temple (11:1–2), the dragon (12:1–17), the beasts (13:1–18), Babylon (17:1–18:24), the last judgment (20:11–15), and New Jerusalem (21:9–22:5). The references to Jesus or the Lamb in these passages are considered later additions (Aune 1:cxviii–cxxiv; Satake 59–73).

The next step, according to this reconstruction, was that during or shortly after the Jewish revolt, John created a first edition that began with his visionary ascent to heaven and culminated in New Jerusalem (4:1–22:5). The introduction to the visions in 1:7–12 might also have been included. This first edition is said to be "apocalyptic" and to give primary attention to conflict with Rome, which was of immediate concern. By this point John had adopted Christianity and added references to Jesus and the Lamb (e.g., 15:3; 17:6; 22:1, 3). For the second edition, John turned attention to the situation of the churches, adding the inaugural vision and messages (1:1–3:21) and the concluding address to the readers (22:6–20). This late material is said to be more "prophetic and parenetic" than apocalyptic (Aune 1:cxx–cxxi). The final form dates from the reign of Domitian (81–96 CE, see below) or perhaps somewhat later (cf. Tóth, "Von der Vision").

Although it is possible that Revelation was written over a period of time, the attempts to reconstruct the stages of writing and editing are not compelling. First, the criteria are problematic. It is not clear why awkward transitions should be ascribed to editing rather than to original composition, since editors may smooth out awkward passages. Moreover, Revelation was designed to be read aloud and repetitions are part of its oral style (1:3; Bauckham, *Climax*, 1–37; Barr, "Apocalypse of John"). Speakers frequently repeat key points so that listeners are able to follow (e.g., the dragon being thrown down in 12:9 and 13; the woman fleeing to her place in the wilderness in 12:6 and 14). Speakers also digress to weave in elements that may differ from the surrounding context and yet serve their overall goals. For example, by disrupting the threatening seal and trumpet visions, the vision of the redeemed (7:1–17) and call to prophetic witness (10:1–11:13) provide rhetorically powerful commentary on the purposes of God (Perry, *Rhetoric*, 209–41).

The messages to the seven churches employ a distinctive genre, but there is no reason to think that their social setting differs from that of the rest of the book. They depict a context in which some Christians faced threats of imprisonment and death under Roman rule (2:10, 13), while others felt more subtle pressures to accommodate Greco-Roman religious practices (2:14, 20), and still others seemed quite comfortable in the Roman-era economy (3:15–17). The visions of the dragon (12:1–17), beasts (13:1–18), and whore (17:1–18:24) reflect a similar range of issues, illustrating threats of violence and pressure to engage in false worship, along with the seductive power of prosperity that lulls people into complacency. It is not helpful to characterize the messages as "parenetic" and the rest of the book as "apocalyptic," since the entire book is designed to foster resistance against compromising the faith (Yarbro Collins, "Source").

Finally, it is not possible to identify some parts of Revelation as Jewish and other parts as Christian expansions. Revelation assumes strong continuity between Jewish tradition and the message of Jesus. The visions ascribed to the early phase of composition have been shaped by the stories of Jesus and his followers. For example, the two witnesses are slain and then raised after three and a half days, much like Jesus (11:3–13); the dragon is outraged by the Messiah's exaltation to heaven (12:1–17); and the portrait of the beast from the sea fuses biblical imagery with reminiscences of Nero's hostility toward the Christian community (13:1–18). Accordingly, the commentary treats the text in its final form.

C. Date

As already noted, Revelation was probably composed between 80 and 100 CE. It seems clear that it was written sometime after the death of Nero in 68, since its portrait of the beast parodies stories about Nero's purported survival of death (NOTE on 13:3). It was also written before the mid-second century since it is noted by Justin Martyr (*Dial.* 80–81; ca. 155–60) and Melito of Sardis (ca. 160–70; Eusebius, *Hist. eccl.* 4.26.2). The work was probably known to Papias (d. ca. 130; Eusebius, *Hist. eccl.*, 3.39.12; Andreas of Caesarea, *In Apocalypsin* pref.). Therefore, it had to have been composed by the late first or very early second century. A time span generally corresponding to the reign of Domitian (81–96 CE) fits the available evidence, but a more precise date cannot be determined. Rather than attempt to correlate Revelation's symbolic language with specific historical events, the present commentary interprets it in relation to common social patterns.

Proposals for a specific date of composition rely on a number of factors: comments by ancient Christian writers, Revelation's allusions to Nero, its vision of the temple, the depiction of Rome as "Babylon," the identification of the beast's heads with seven kings, and other elements. Apart from Epiphanius (d. 403), who places John's exile to Patmos in the reign of Claudius (41–54 CE; *Pan.* 51.13.33; cf. Apringius on Rev 1:9), there are several main perspectives.

I. EARLY DATES (68–70)

Two Syriac versions from perhaps the fourth century, along with the eleventh-century bishop Theophylact (PG 123.1133–34), say that John was exiled to Patmos during the reign of Nero (54–68 CE). Many nineteenth-century scholars argued that Revelation was written in the aftermath of Nero's reign and before the destruction of the Jerusalem temple in 70 CE. Some continue to hold this view (Bell, "Date"; Slater, "Dating"; Smalley, *Thunder*, 40–49; Wilson, "Problem"). One reason is that Revelation portrays a beast that personifies Roman imperial power and persecutes Christians much as Nero had done. Although Nero was said to have killed himself, some said he was still alive, like the beast that was slain and yet lived (Rev 13:3, 12, 14). A person claiming to be Nero appeared in 69 CE (Tacitus, *Hist.* 2.8). If John wrote during the late 60s, it could make sense to use images of Nero, as the memory of his persecution and the legends about his survival of death were vivid at that time. But since Nero legends remained popular for decades, a later date is also possible (NOTE on Rev 13:3).

Identifying the heads of the beast with seven kings in Rev 17:9–12 is sometimes taken as support for a date in the late 60s. The text reads:

> The seven heads are seven mountains on which the woman is seated. They are also seven kings. Five have fallen, one is, and the other has not yet come. When he comes he must remain for only a little while. As for the beast that was and is not, it is an eighth that belongs to the seven, and it is going to destruction. The ten horns that you saw are ten kings, who have not yet received royal power, but they will receive authority as kings for an hour, along with the beast.

Many assume that the passage traces a sequence of kings or emperors. John says that five have already fallen and that he is writing during the reign of the sixth. Table 1 shows ways to count the emperors. One approach would be to start with Julius Caesar and count the next five emperors. The sixth would be Nero (col. A of Table 1). The problem is that Revelation assumes knowledge of Nero's death, as noted above. Therefore, some start counting with Augustus

Table 1. The Seven Kings and the Date of Revelation

	Pre-70 date			Post-70 date		
	A	B	C	D	E	F
Julius Caesar (49–44 BCE)	1					
Augustus (31 BCE–14 CE)	2	1	1	1		
Tiberius (14 –37 CE)	3	2	2	2		
Gaius Caligula (37–41 CE)	4	3	3	3	1	
Claudius (41–54 CE)	5	4	4	4	2	
Nero (54–68 CE)	6	5	5	5	3	1
Galba (68–69 CE)		6				2
Otho (69 CE)						3
Vitellius (69 CE)						4
Vespasian (69–79 CE)			6	6	4	5
Titus (79–81 CE)				7	5	6
Domitian (81–96 CE)				8	6	7
Nerva (96–98 CE)						
Trajan (98–117 CE)						
Hadrian (117–138 CE)						

and conclude that the sixth king is Nero's successor, Galba (col. B; Bell, "Date"; Slater, "Dating"; Wilson, "Problem"). Since Galba reigned for only a short time, a variation is to count sequentially from Augustus through Nero, then to skip over the three figures who reigned briefly in 68–69 (Galba, Otho, and Vitellius), making Vespasian the sixth king, who was reigning when Revelation was written (col. C; Smalley, *Thunder*, 40–49).

Many interpreters rightly respond that the beast's heads cannot be used to determine the date of the book. The author did not count the Roman rulers from the beginning of the empire until his own time and then create a beast with a suitable number of heads. For him, the seven heads of the beast, like those of the dragon, were a given. They signify the totality of the beast's dominion (NOTES and COMMENT on 17:10–12). Moreover, the imagery is polyvalent. The heads are both kings and seven mountains or hills, which are collectively a symbol of Rome. John says that the beast that represents imperial power "is not," and yet one of its heads, or an emperor, currently "is" in power. The fluidity shows that readers cannot be expected to correlate each head with a particular emperor (Friesen, *Imperial*, 140–41).

Other arguments for a date in the 60s are based on John's vision of the holy city and its temple (Rev 11:1–2):

> I was given a measuring reed, which was like a staff, and was told, "Go and measure the temple of God and the altar, and those who worship there. But do

not measure the court outside the temple. Leave that out, for it has been given to the nations, and they will overrun the holy city for forty-two months."

Some take this vision to mean that the Jerusalem temple was still standing but was under threat, concluding that John wrote before 70 CE. But where *4 Ezra* and *2 Baruch* equate Rome with Babylon because both powers destroyed temples in Jerusalem, the Babylon vision in Rev 17:1–18:24 does not mention the temple's destruction. The most significant problem, however, is that Revelation uses images of the holy city and temple symbolically rather than literally. The temple vision portrays the church being surrounded by the nonbelieving world (Notes and Comment on 11:1–2).

2. END OF DOMITIAN'S REIGN (CA. 95)

Irenaeus (d. ca. 200) said that John, understood to be the apostle, received his visions "not long ago, almost in our own day, towards the end of Domitian's reign" (*Haer.* 5.30.3; Eusebius, *Hist. eccl.* 3.18.3; 5.8.6). Since Domitian died in 96 CE, this would date Revelation to about 95. Clement of Alexandria (d. ca. 215) knew a tradition about John the apostle leaving Patmos after the death of an unnamed "tyrant" and then appointing bishops in many churches (*Quis div.* 42; cf. Origen, *Comm. Matt.* 16.6). Eusebius assumed that the king was Domitian (*Hist. eccl.* 3.20.8–9; cf. Jerome, *Vir. ill.* 9). Irenaeus's date has continued to influence interpreters down to the present (e.g., Caird 6; Giesen 41–42; Harrington 9; Mounce 21; Reddish 16–17; Yarbro Collins, *Crisis*, 55–56).

Nevertheless, it is unlikely that Irenaeus preserves reliable historical information. His comment about the date is linked to his assumption that the author was John the apostle. If this assumption is incorrect, there is little reason to think that he was accurate about the date. Irenaeus states that Revelation had been written rather recently, even though Domitian's reign had ended nearly a century before. Clement is vague about the emperor who was in power when John was on Patmos, and his comments about the date include a legendary scenario in which John goes about appointing bishops after his release from the island. Patristic evidence for the date of Revelation is not reliable.

Evidence from the book itself generally fits a post-70 context without indicating a more specific date of composition. Memories of Nero's persecution of the church and his purported survival of death circulated during this period. People claiming to be Nero appeared in 69 (Tacitus, *Hist.* 2.8), 80 (Dio Cassius, *Rom. Hist.* 66.19.3), and 88 (Suetonius, *Nero* 57.2). References to the prospect of Nero's return were woven into various apocalyptic texts of the late first and early second centuries (*Sib. Or.* 3:63–74; 4:119–24, 138–39; 5:361–65; *Mart. Asc. Isa.* 4:2–8; Note on Rev 13:3).

The vision of the holy city and temple in Rev 11:1–2 can best be understood as a symbolic portrayal of the Christian community's struggle with its social environment. Although some think the scene originally dealt with the Roman siege of Jerusalem, they recognize that the temple imagery has been transferred to the church as a worshiping community (NOTES and COMMENT on 11:1–2). Depicting Rome as "Babylon" does not require a post-70 date. By way of analogy, some Dead Sea texts written before 70 equate Rome with Asshur, since it was an oppressive power (1QM XIX, 9; 4Q492 1 9). Yet the equating of Rome with Babylon did become common after 70, making it more likely that Revelation reflects the usage of this general period (*4 Ezra* 3:1–5:20; 10:19–48; *2 Bar.* 11:1; 67:7; 1 Pet 5:13; John Elliott, *1 Peter*, 883–84).

Interpreters who think that Revelation was composed after 70, during Domitian's reign, propose various ways to match the seven kings of Rev 17:9–12 with known emperors. The problem is that John claims to be writing under the sixth king, yet if one begins counting with Julius Caesar and includes all the emperors, then Domitian is the twelfth (see Table 1). So interpreters either start counting emperors midway through the list or find a way to include some emperors and exclude others. Few of the older proposals were widely accepted (survey and critique in Aune 1:lxii–lxii, lxx; Yarbro Collins, *Crisis*, 58–64).

One current proposal begins counting emperors with Gaius Caligula (37–41 CE) (Table 1, col. E), the first to take power after the time of Christ. He was said to have been hostile to Jewish concerns and notorious for claiming divine honors. The second and third emperors are Claudius and Nero, but since, as noted above, Galba, Otho, and Vitellius reigned only briefly, they are omitted, making Vespasian and Titus the fourth and fifth. John then writes under Domitian, the sixth emperor. Additional support is that five kings "have fallen," which suggests violent death, and the main emperors from Gaius Caligula through Vespasian were assassinated, committed suicide, or died from a violent illness (Strobel, "Abfassung"; Yarbro Collins, *Crisis*, 63–64; Prigent, *Commentary*, 69–71, 493; Müller 291–95; Murphy 44–47).

Another proposal is to begin with Nero because he set the pattern for the persecution of Christians (Table 1, col. F). If all subsequent emperors are counted, then Titus is the sixth, the one reigning at the time John initially wrote the vision. The idea is that people were afraid that when Titus's brother Domitian became the seventh king, he would be so terrible that he would have to "remain for only a little while" if the church was to survive (Rev 17:10). When John finished writing Revelation during Domitian's reign, he saw his earlier fears being realized in the blasphemous pretensions of the emperor (Court, *Myth*, 125–27, 134–37).

Alternatively, one might begin with Augustus, include all the emperors through Nero, and then skip over the three with only short reigns (Table 1, col. D). This would make Vespasian the sixth king, in whose reign this vision is set. Titus would be the seventh king, and Domitian would be the eighth, the terrible figure who brought back the practices of Nero the beast. According to this approach, Revelation was actually written in the time of Domitian, the eighth king, but John wants to give the *impression* that he received his vision earlier and that his prophecy proved to be accurate, since Titus, the seventh king, actually reigned "for only a little while" (79–81 CE; Giesen 381–83).

A major problem with these proposals was noted under the discussion of the early date: The imagery is polyvalent and does not allow readers to connect each head to a specific emperor. Especially difficult is the idea that readers could determine which emperors to include and which to omit from the list. The problem is compounded if one asks about the identity of the ten horns that signify vassal kings (17:12–14). There is no suggestion that readers are to determine which of Rome's allies might be included among the ten. It is best to treat the beast's heads and horns as a collective symbol for Roman rule (NOTES and COMMENT on 17:9–14; cf. Friesen, *Imperial*, 140–41).

It seems plausible to think that Revelation was written during Domitian's reign, but it is problematic to locate it specifically at the end of that period (ca. 95), as Irenaeus did. Positing that particular date is based on the assumption that pressure to participate in the imperial cult intensified during the 90s. Domitian purportedly demanded that everyone address him as "lord and god" in speech and writing (Suetonius, *Dom.* 13.2). Some scholars allege that he was the first emperor to enforce participation in the imperial cult (Charles 1:xciv–xcv; Mounce 16–18). Others picture him as a debauched and power-hungry tyrant, whose career ended with a reign of terror that led to the deaths of many, including Christians (Swete lxxxv–xcii; Beckwith 204).

The theory is that Revelation's visions mirror this historical setting. Accordingly, the heavenly hosts challenge Domitian's excessive claims by calling the Creator "Lord and God" (Rev 4:11). The vision of the beast from the land making people worship the statue of the sea beast corresponds to local enforcement of the imperial cult under Domitian (13:11–18). People considered Domitian to be a second Nero (Juvenal, *Satirae* 4.38; Pliny the Younger, *Pan.* 53.4; Philostratus, *Vit. Apoll.* 7.4.1); if Nero persecuted the church in the past, Revelation warns that Domitian is about to persecute the church again (Rev 13:1–10; 17:6).

Studies of Domitian, however, do not support this reconstruction. By the time Domitian assumed power, the imperial cult had been established in Asia Minor for a century, since the reign of Augustus. The cult was not imposed by the emperor but was promoted by the leading citizens of Asia, who wanted to show their gratitude for imperial favors and to forge closer ties with Rome (Price, *Rituals*; Friesen, *Imperial*, 23–121). There is no evidence that Domitian heightened the place of the cult in civic life. People may have called him "lord and god" to flatter him, just as they had done with other emperors, but those titles never appear on coins or inscriptions from Domitian's reign, even in the inscriptions in the imperial temple at Ephesus, which honored Domitian and his family (NOTES on 2:1; 4:11).

Politically, Domitian's reputation was mixed. Some said that he began as a good emperor but later became tyrannical and violent (Suetonius, *Dom.* 8.1–12.3), and it seems clear that he had some adversaries executed or banished in the early 90s (Suetonius, *Dom.* 14.4–15.1; Pliny the Younger, *Ep.* 3.11.3). What is not clear is that he had a reputation for savagery among the general public. For example, opponents later charged that he had many people executed for perceived slights against him, creating a climate of fear, but Martial and other writers continued to bring up subjects that Domitian found offensive, even during the latter part of his reign. Such writers apparently did not feel threatened (Thompson, *Book*, 107–9).

Evidence that Domitian persecuted Christians is sketchy at best. Irenaeus dated Revelation to the end of Domitian's reign but said nothing about persecution (*Haer.* 5.30.3). Some argue that the "repeated misfortunes and setbacks" in *1 Clem.* 1:1 refer to Domitian's action against the church at Rome, but the context actually says nothing about persecution (Lona, *Der erste*, 115–16). Melito said that Nero and Domitian slandered Christian teaching, leading to "the unreasonable custom of falsely accusing Christians" among the populace, yet he does not say that Domitian himself undertook a persecution (Eusebius, *Hist. eccl.* 4.26.9). Hegesippus told the legendary story that Domitian personally interrogated descendants of Jesus' brother but also said that the emperor released them and ended the persecution (Eusebius, *Hist. eccl.* 3.20.1–7; cf. Tertullian, *Apol.* 5.3–4). Eusebius said that Domitian executed Flavius Clemens and banished his wife because they were Christians (*Hist. eccl.* 3.18.4), but Dio Cassius said it was because of their attraction to Judaism, which Domitian considered atheism (*Rom. Hist.* 67.14.1–3). In either case the incident does not seem to have been part of a sustained campaign against the church. The image of widespread persecution (Eusebius, *Hist. eccl.* 3.17.1; 3.18.4) is not supported by the earlier evidence (Thompson, *Book*, 133–37; Cook, *Roman*, 117–37). Threats against Christians came from local conflicts that arose periodically during the late first century.

Finally, Domitian's policies toward the provinces were generally fair (Suetonius, *Dom.* 8.2). Some have noted an exception in 92 CE when there was ample wine production but a shortage of grain. In response, Domitian decreed that half the vineyards in the provinces were to be cut down in order to open up more land for grain, but the edict provoked such opposition in Asia Minor that he withdrew it before it could be enacted (Suetonius, *Dom.* 7.2; 14.2; Philostratus, *Vit. Apoll.* 6.42; *Vit. soph.* 1.21; Statius, *Silv.* 4.3.11–12). Some argue that the third horseman in Rev 6:6 reflects this situation by warning of a grain shortage along with ample supplies of oil and wine (Court, *Myth*, 59–60; Hemer, *Letters*, 158–59). Yet it is difficult to link Rev 6:6 directly to Domitian's edict because grain shortages occurred throughout the first century. The vision reflects a typical pattern rather than a particular event (NOTES and COMMENT on 6:6). In short, Revelation may well have been written during Domitian's reign, but there is insufficient evidence for identifying a specific date within that period.

3. LATE DATES (96–135)

Heinrich Kraft proposes that much of Revelation was written during the reign of Nerva (96–98), who is the sixth king or head of the beast (17:10) and whose name might equal 666 (13:18). In his view the messages to the churches (Rev 2–3) plus the introduction and conclusion (1:4–8; 22:21) were added around 110 CE, when Christians in the region were being denounced to the Romans (Pliny the Younger, *Ep.* 10.96–97). Since Christians were persecuted but Jews were not (Rev 2:9–11), the messages were added before the Jewish uprisings of 114–15 (Kraft 93–94, 221–22). Problems with this proposal are that it uses a form of Nerva's name (M. Neroua) that is not otherwise attested. The beast's heads cannot be readily connected with known emperors, as noted above, and there is no reason to think that the early second century was the only time that Christians were persecuted while Jews were not (NOTES and COMMENT on 2:9–10).

The reign of Trajan (98–117) has also been suggested. Of the seven kings in 17:9–12, the sixth reigns briefly, as Nerva did, so the seventh and final king would be Trajan, whose name can be abbreviated in Greek as NE. TRAI. S, which equals 666. The founding of the temple to Zeus and Trajan at Pergamum in 114 could have occasioned the critique of the imperial cult in Revelation (de Jonge, "Apocalypse," 128–29). In addition, the book must have been written long after an earthquake destroyed Laodicea in 60 CE, since residents of the city were prospering (Tacitus, *Ann.* 14.27; Rev 3:14–22; Kelhoffer, "Relevance"). Others suggest that the beast's mortal wound symbolizes the assassination of Domitian in 96 and that the beast continued to live because the imperial cult continued unabated under Domitian's successors. Certain expressions in Revelation closely resemble forms in Luke-Acts, which may date from about 90–100. Examples include not placing any other burden on those who refrain from eating what has been offered to idols (Acts 15:28–29; Rev 2:24–25), confessing the names of the faithful before both God and the angels (Luke 12:8; Rev 3:5), and the image of Jesus coming to dine with his servants (Luke 12:35–37; Rev 3:20; Witetschek, "Ein weit").

Problems with these proposals include the difficulty in relating the seven kings of 17:9–12 to specific emperors and expecting readers to know the abbreviated form of Trajan's name when doing numerical calculation. Moreover, affinities between expressions in Revelation and those in the gospels and Acts probably come from oral tradition and not reliance on the written text (Intro II.D.3 and III.B.2).

Finally, Revelation has been dated to 132–35 CE, during Hadrian's reign. This proposal argues that at this time there was heightened pressure to participate in the imperial cult. The temple to Trajan at Pergamum, dedicated in 129, is "Satan's throne" (Rev 2:13). Hadrian was also identified with Zeus Olympus at his temple in Athens, dedicated in 132. Therefore, Revelation portrays him as the beast from the sea (13:1–10). The beast from the land is the Sophist Antonius Polemon, whose oratory gave support to the imperial cult (13:11–18). The New Jerusalem vision is a polemical contrast to the popular depiction of Hadrian as the creator of a new world order (Witulski, *Johannesoffenbarung*, 346–50).

One problem with this approach is that the imperial cult is only one of the issues Revelation addresses. The book also deals with disputes over the accommodation of Greco-Roman religious practices and complacency due to wealth—issues that could have arisen at various times. Another problem with the theories of late dates is that Revelation's imagery is evocative. The images of Satan's throne and the beasts do not allow one-to-one correlations with particular figures or structures (Notes and Comment on 2:13; 13:1–18).

4. GENERAL PERIOD 80–100

Revelation was probably written during the final decades of the first century. The issues addressed by the book have more to do with persistent social patterns in Asia Minor than with specific events, such as the building of an imperial temple or changes in Roman policy. The messages to the churches in Rev 2–3 note forms of persecution that were local and sporadic, which was the case throughout this period. The portrayal of the beasts and Babylon critiques aspects of political and economic life that were part of the social fabric of this time. Although the period 80–100 CE seems most plausible, the interpretations given in the present commentary would not change significantly if the text were written somewhat earlier or later. John's critique was not focused on a particular event but on issues arising from life under imperial rule (Friesen, *Imperial*, 150–51).

D. Early Christian Traditions

As we have seen, ancient interpreters often assumed that Revelation was written by John the apostle, whose witness was also preserved in the Fourth Gospel and Johannine Epistles and was congruent with that found in the Synoptic Gospels and Pauline writings. Modern historical studies offer a more complex picture, in which early Christian traditions developed along different paths, sometimes in tension with one another. When compared with other early Christian writings, Revelation has both similarities and differences, making it difficult to place within a single well-defined stream of tradition. It seems likely that the author was acquainted with a range of Christian traditions, which he adapted in distinctive ways in his text.

I. JOHANNINE TRADITIONS

Early Christians found it plausible to think that the Fourth Gospel, Johannine Epistles, and Revelation were all written by the same author because all identify Jesus as the Word of God (John 1:14; 1 John 1:1; Rev 19:13; Irenaeus, *Haer.* 1.16.3; 3.11.1; 3.16.5, 8; 5.30.3; Origen, *Comm. Jo.* 1.1–2; 2.41–42, 149, 160). Dionysius of Alexandria challenged this consensus by arguing that Revelation's style and content were so different from the gospel and epistles that it had to have been written by someone else (Eusebius, *Hist. eccl.* 7.24.6–26). He noted that the gospel stems from Jesus' beloved disciple (John 21:20–25), but the writer of Revelation never claims to be an apostle. Thematically, the gospel and first epistle emphasize light and darkness, truth, the love commandment, believing, and other topics; but these themes do not appear in the same way in Revelation. Also, the gospel and first epistle are written in a grammatical Greek style, whereas Dionysius considered Revelation's Greek to be barbarous (INTRO V.B.2). Similar arguments appear in contemporary scholarship. There are three main ways to construe Revelation's relationship to John's gospel and epistles, the third being the most plausible.

First is the idea of common authorship. Arguments that one author wrote all the texts emphasize their common elements, such as Jesus as the Word and Lamb, the light and living water imagery, and the idea that Jesus and his followers win victory through faithful suffering. Differences in thought and style are accounted for by appealing to the various genres involved, by suggesting that they were written years apart such that the author's language and emotional state had changed, or by positing that he was assisted by different secretaries (Keener, *Gospel*, 1:126–39; Brighton 16–17).

Second, the writings may have been composed by different authors from the same Christian circle. Interpreters generally recognize that John's gospel is closely related to the Johannine Epistles and propose that those four texts were written and edited by one or more people from the same Christian community (Brown, *Epistles*, 14–35). Revelation is sometimes attributed to the same Johannine circle (Charles 1:xxix). Some think it represents an early apocalyptic phase of Johannine Christianity, which was later modified in the gospel and epistles (Strecker, "Chiliasm," 45–49, 54), whereas others see Revelation's futuristic aspect as a late phase in the Johannine tradition (Taeger, *Johannesapokalypse*, 207). Sometimes Revelation is seen as a pseudepigraphical text, which claims the authority of "John," a venerable teacher who had played a central role in the Johannine school (Frey, "Erwägungen").

Third, and most likely, is the hypothesis that different authors developed biblical and early Christian traditions independently of one another. The Fourth Gospel and three epistles are all anonymous. The gospel is linked to Jesus' beloved disciple (John 21:20–25), whereas two of the epistles are written by an elder (2 John 1; 3 John 1). By way of contrast, Revelation was written by a Christian prophet, whose name is explicitly stated and who never claims to be a disciple, elder, or apostle (Rev 1:1, 9). As noted above (INTRO II.A), there is little reason to think that "John" is either the name of the apostle or a pseudonym. Moreover, Revelation's epistolary introduction and conclusion are actually closer to the Pauline than the Johannine letter forms (Rev 1:4–6; 22:20–21; 1 Cor 1:1–3; 16:21–24; Gal 1:1–2; 6:18; 2 John 1–3, 13; 3 John 1, 15).

Elements common to Revelation and the Gospel of John can best be understood as independent developments of traditional motifs. The gospel focuses on the preexistent Word, which becomes incarnate in Jesus (John 1:1, 14), whereas Revelation envisions the Word coming at the end of the age to judge God's foes (Rev 19:13). The gospel recalls traditions that personified God's Word or wisdom residing among people (Sir 24:3; Wis 9:1–2, 9), while Revelation is closer to sources that characterized the Word as "a stern warrior carrying the sharp sword" in battle (Wis 18:15–16; Frey, "Erwägungen," 403–9). The gospel uses the word "dwell" (*skēnoun*) in association with the incarnate Word on earth (John 1:14), but Revelation uses it for the inhabitants of heaven (Rev 12:12; 13:6; cf. 7:15) and for God's presence in New Jerusalem (21:3).

The Fourth Gospel uses "I am" (*egō eimi*) in ways that recall the divine name. Whether used alone (John 8:58) or with descriptors such as bread, light, and resurrection (6:36; 8:12; 11:25), the expression identifies Jesus with his Father. When Revelation uses the expression to identify God and Jesus as the beginning and end of all things (2:17; 21:6; cf. 1:8), the language is closer to Isa 41:4, 43:10, and 48:12 than to anything in the gospel. Rather than using the gospel's imagery, Revelation links the "I am" to Jesus' role in searching people's hearts and his identity as the "root of David" and "morning star" (Rev 2:23; 22:16).

Jesus is pictured as a sacrificial Lamb in the gospel and in Revelation, but the language differs (*amnos*, John 1:29, 36; *arnion*, Rev 5:6; 7:9, 14, etc.). Both books draw the image in part from the Passover tradition. In the gospel Jesus is crucified on the day of preparation for Passover, and none of his bones is broken (John 19:14, 31, 36; Exod 12:46). Like God's "servant," he suffers for the sins of others (Isa 53:7; C. R. Koester, *Symbolism*, 219–24). In Revelation the Lamb imagery is more paradoxical. His blood cleanses (Rev 5:6–10; 7:14); he is vulnerable and yet conquers (5:5–6; 12:11); he is both warrior and bridegroom (17:14; 19:7–9; 21:9); and he is not only a sacrifice, but the temple and source of light (21:22–23).

Many writers used shepherding as an image for leadership (Ezek 37:24; Mic 5:4; *Pss. Sol.* 17:40; Heb 13:20; 1 Pet 2:25; 5:4). The gospel pictures Jesus as the shepherd who calls the sheep and lays down his life for them (John 10:1–18), whereas Revelation's shepherd imagery, which comes from Ezek 34:23 and other texts, pertains to the age to come (NOTE and COMMENT on Rev 7:17). Jesus is the "bridegroom" of the faithful in John 3:29 (Matt 19:15; Mark 2:19–20; Luke 5:34–35; *Gos. Thom.* 104), while in Revelation the imagery is applied to New Jerusalem as Jesus' bride (Rev 19:7; cf. 19:9; 21:2, 9).

John's gospel uses "living water" (*hydōr zōn*) as a symbol for the revelation and Spirit that Jesus gives. The imagery recalls the water in the wilderness and divine wisdom (Num 21:16–17; Prov 18:4; Sir 24:21–26; CD VI, 2–5; Philo, *Ebr.* 112–13). Where Zech 14:8 anticipates that "living water" will flow from Jerusalem, the gospel links it to Jesus himself (John 4:10, 13–14; 7:37–39). Revelation uses a related expression, "water of life" (*hydōr zōēs*), for a gift in the age to come (Rev 7:16–17; 21:6; 22:1–2, 17), when a river will flow from the glorified Jerusalem (Ezek 47:1; Zech 14:8; Rev 22:1–2) and people will not thirst (Isa 49:10; 55:1; Rev 7:16–17; 21:6; 22:17). Although some think that Revelation develops a distinctly Johannine motif (Taeger, *Johannesapokalypse*), it is more likely that the writers develop biblical images in different ways.

Light was a common image in early Christianity (Matt 4:16; Luke 2:32; 2 Cor 4:6; 1 Pet 2:9). Light imagery in the Fourth Gospel centers on Jesus, who reveals truth and gives life (John 1:1–5, 9; 3:19–21; 8:12; 9:5; 12:35–36; cf. 1 John 1:5–7; 2:8–10). Passages link light to creation (Gen 1:1–5), wisdom (Wis 7:26–30), leadership (Isa 42:6; 49:6), and God's presence (Pss 27:1; 36:9; Isa 60:1–2). Revelation, however, refers to the light of God and the Lamb in New Jerusalem, using imagery from Isa 60:3, 19 and Zech 14:7 (Rev 21:23–24; 22:5).

John's gospel says that Jesus cast out Satan and conquered (*nikan*) the world by his death (John 12:31; 16:33). First John says that by defeating the devil (1 John 3:8) Jesus empowers people to conquer the world through faith (2:13–14; 4:4; 5:4–5). Revelation also says that evil and the world are conquered through Jesus' death (Rev 5:5–6) and his followers' faithfulness (2:7, 11, 17; 12:11; 15:2; 21:7). Yet other Christian writers also construed Jesus' death as a victory over evil

(1 Cor 1:18–31; 2:6–8; Col 2:14–15; Heb 2:14–15) and identified faithfulness with militant resistance (1 Thess 5:8; Eph 6:10–17). When recounting the crucifixion, the gospel cites Zech 12:10: "they will look at him whom they have pierced" (John 19:37), but Revelation relates that same text to Jesus' second coming and combines it with Dan 7:13 as in Matt 24:30. The pattern is different.

Studies of vocabulary and style do not suggest that Revelation has any special connection to the Fourth Gospel or Johannine Epistles. Eight or nine words appear only in the Fourth Gospel and Revelation, but the connotations differ. For example, *arnion* (lamb) is used twenty-nine times in Revelation, regularly in the singular and almost always referring to Christ, but in the gospel it occurs only once in the plural and refers to believers (John 21:15). Sometimes the gospel and Revelation share phraseology: "prepare a place" (John 14:2–3; Rev 12:6); "do the truth" (John 3:21); "do falsehood" (Rev 22:15); and "have a share" (John 13:8; Rev 20:6). But they often express similar ideas with different words. Where the gospel has "believe" (*pisteuein*), Revelation has "faith" (*pistis*), and they use different words for a liar (*pseustēs, pseudēs*), a tomb (*mnēma, mnēmeion*), and a murderer (*anthrōpoktonos, phoneus*). The preposition *para* (with, from) and the grammatical construction *men . . . de* are common in the gospel but rare in Revelation. Prepositions that appear in John but are absent from Revelation include *hyper* (for), *pro* (before), *syn* (with), *chōris* (apart), and *anti* (in place of) (Frey, "Erwägungen," 336–58).

Finally, the Fourth Gospel is written in a grammatical Greek style, whereas Revelation's Greek often departs from common usage, making it unlikely that they were written by the same person (Mussies, *Morphology*, 351–52). By way of comparison, though the language and style of the epistles may differ from that of the gospel, the similarities are close enough to suggest that the Johannine Gospel and Epistles were composed in a community that had a distinctive style of discourse (Brown, *Epistles*, 19–28). Revelation, however, can best be treated separately from John's gospel and epistles, as a text that develops some common traditions in distinctive ways (Heinze, *Johannesapokalypse*, 355–58).

2. PAULINE TRADITIONS

Revelation has been regarded as a Jewish Christian text that has little in common with the Pauline writings (Aune 1:l, cxxvi–cxxvii). In the nineteenth century, F. C. Baur argued that John's uncompromising stance against eating food offered to Greco-Roman deities was directed against Pauline Christians, who were less rigorous (Baird, *History*, 1:266), and some continue to hold that view (e.g., Räisänen, "Nicolaitans," 1628–35). Yet there are good reasons to think that the author appropriated aspects of the Pauline tradition, which was influential in Asia Minor (Schüssler Fiorenza, *Book*, 94–95, 114–56).

Most important are Revelation's epistolary features, which resemble those of the Pauline writings. The author identifies himself and his intended recipients, extends a greeting of grace and peace, and elaborates on the identity of God and Christ using traditional material (Rev 1:4; cf. Gal 1:3–4; Rom 1:2–6). Revelation concludes with a greeting of "grace," which resembles formulas in the Pauline writings (NOTE on Rev 22:21). The way the conclusion identifies the sender in the first person, gives a warning, and expresses hope for the Lord's coming is similar to the end of 1 Corinthians (COMMENT on Rev 22:6–21).

In terms of social context, Revelation conveys "a revelation from Jesus Christ," which is a form of "prophecy" (1:1, 3). Paul also spoke of the revelations that he (Gal 1:12; 2:2; 1 Cor 12:1, 7) and members of his churches (1 Cor 14:6, 26) received. Prophetic utterances had a place in Pauline congregations (Rom 12:6; 1 Cor 12:10; 14:6, 26–33; 1 Thess 5:20). Although revelatory and prophetic speech was known in various early Christian communities (Acts 11:27; 13:1; 21:8–11), its importance in Paul's letters and Revelation shows that both writers addressed social contexts in which this type of communication was valued (Aune, *Prophecy*, 247–88).

Theologically, Revelation and the Pauline writings develop some of the same biblical and Christian traditions. Christ is compared to the Passover lamb, whose death means cleansing and deliverance (1 Cor 5:7; Rev 5:6; 7:14). Through his resurrection Christ is the "firstborn" of the dead (Rom 8:29; Rev 1:5; cf. Col 1:18; Heb 1:6). Although hope for Christ's return was common in early Christianity, Revelation and the Pauline letters are alike in picturing Christ coming to complete his triumph over the forces of evil using texts like Isa 11:1–5 and Pss 2:9 and 110:1 (1 Cor 15:25; 2 Thess 1:7–2:12; Rev 19:11, 15).

Another similarity is identifying the Christian community as God's "temple" (2 Cor 6:16; Rev 3:12; 11:1–2), which Paul links to the Spirit, though Revelation does not (1 Cor 3:16–17). In Eph 2:19–22 believers are citizens in a structure founded on the apostles, the "temple" where God dwells, and in Rev 21:1–14 such imagery is used for New Jerusalem, which has features of a sanctuary. Both Paul and Revelation develop traditional ideas concerning a heavenly or future Jerusalem (Gal 4:26; Phil 3:20; Rev 3:12; 21:10), and both expected the resurrection to liberate creation from decay (Rom 8:18–22; Rev 21:1; 22:1–5). The similarities do not indicate that the author of Revelation borrowed directly from the Pauline writings—any more than he used John's gospel or epistles—but show how these writers developed traditions in similar ways.

3. SYNOPTIC TRADITIONS

Revelation includes sayings reminiscent of those in the Synoptic Gospels, though it shows no traces of the contexts in which the gospels set the sayings.

Among these are the exhortation "Let the one who has an ear hear" (Rev 2:7, 11, 17, etc.; Matt 11:15; 13:43; Mark 4:9; Luke 8:8; cf. *Gos. Thom.* 65, 96), the warning that Jesus will come "like a thief" (Rev 3:3; 16:15; Matt 24:43–44; Luke 12:39–40), and the promise that Jesus will confess the names of the faithful before his Father and the angels (Rev 3:5; Matt 10:32; Luke 12:8).

More distant similarities include the blessing on those who hear and keep the word (Rev 1:3; Luke 11:28), Jesus arriving at the door (Rev 3:20; Mark 13:29; Matt 24:33), the hope of sitting on a throne with Christ (Rev 3:21; Matt 19:28; Luke 22:28–30), and the warning about being killed by the sword (Matt 26:52; Rev 13:10). The warning that the tribes will mourn when the Son of Man comes appears in Rev 1:7 and Matt 24:30. Since each uses language from Dan 7:13 and Zech 12:10, but in a different way, they probably drew on a common tradition (Vos, *Synoptic*, 54–111; Bauckham, *Climax*, 92–117; Penly, *Common*, 125–35).

Many have noted that Revelation's seal visions and the Synoptic warnings about the last days reflect a similar eschatological pattern, picturing threats of war, violent conflict, famine, and persecution. The sun becomes dark, the moon turns to blood, and the stars fall (Rev 6:1–8:1; Matt 24:6–9, 29–31; Mark 13:7–9, 24–25; Luke 21:9–12, 25–26). Some of these elements occur in Jewish apocalypses, but the sequence in Revelation and the Synoptic Gospels is strikingly similar. Although some have suggested that Revelation is dependent on the written gospels (Charles 1:158–60), the differences make it more likely that these texts use elements from a shared oral tradition (§12C).

As we turn to the social setting reflected in Revelation, it is helpful to keep the book's use of various early Christian traditions in mind. It suggests that the writer worked in a context in which multiple types of tradition circulated. Although his outlook was in some ways distinctive, it was informed by ideas that also found expression in other Christian sources from the period.

III.

Social Setting of Revelation

Revelation addresses congregations in Asia Minor that faced a range of issues, including conflict with outsiders, internal disputes over accommodating Greco-Roman religious practices, and the problem of complacency due to wealth. The issues have more to do with patterns of social life that persisted over a period of time than with particular events. Some of the challenges were overt, arising from confrontations with non-Christians, while others were more subtle, involving differences among Christians over the relationship of their distinctive beliefs to those of the wider society. To place the issues in context, we ask what Revelation assumes about the makeup of the Christian community and its internal dynamics, along with that community's relationship to local Jewish communities and the dominant culture of the imperial world.

A. Christian Community and Its Social Context

Revelation is written to "the seven assemblies" in cities of Roman Asia (1:4). Although John refers to "the assembly" in each location (2:1, 8, 12, etc.), certain cities had multiple Christian groups. Some suggest that John writes to all Christians in the area (Thompson, *Book*, 196), whereas others propose that he addresses only small Jewish Christian conventicles, which were separate from other groups (H. Koester, ed., *Ephesos*, 133). The situation is complex because the book presupposes a setting in which the boundaries of Christian groups are not fixed or identical in every place. The assembly at Ephesus firmly rejected some self-identified apostles and a group of Nicolaitans, while the assembly at Pergamum tolerated the Nicolaitans, and the assembly at Thyatira included the followers of a Christian prophetess, whose teachings John disputed (2:2, 6, 15, 20–23). John keeps a broad section of the church in view as he writes, recognizing that the assemblies include people with a range of perspectives, some of which are different from John's own (Trebilco, *Early*, 335–42).

I. CHRISTIAN COMMUNITY
Beliefs and Practices

Early Christian communities formed around shared faith commitments. John assumes that readers already believe that God created the world, exists throughout time, and acts justly (Rev 1:8; 4:11; 6:10; 15:3–4). They are expected to know that Jesus is God's anointed king, that he bore witness to the reign of God, that his crucifixion redeems people for God's kingdom, and that he is now alive and will return (5:9–10; 7:14; 11:8, 15; 22:20). Such beliefs were common among early Christians (NOTES on 1:4–6).

The community apparently met on "the Lord's Day," or the first day of the week, reflecting the belief that on that day Jesus rose as "the firstborn of the dead" (1:5, 9). Although Revelation's visions of heavenly worship do not directly mirror the practices of the congregations, they do suggest that prayers of thanks and intercession and hymns of praise had a place in these groups (5:8–10; 8:3–4; 15:3–4; INTRO IV.E.1). John expected his message to be read aloud in the assemblies, as was done with letters from Christian leaders (1:3; Col 4:16; 1 Thess 5:27). Given his pervasive use of biblical language and imagery as a means of communication, it seems likely that readers had become familiar with the Scriptures because they were read in their assemblies. Baptism and the Lord's Supper may be suggested by the images of cleansing and eating together, but these practices are not explicitly mentioned (NOTES on 3:20; 7:14).

Jesus' followers are to keep "the commandments of God" (12:17). Specific commands include worshiping God and rejecting idolatry, as well as refusing to engage in sorcery, murder, theft, sexual immorality, and deception (9:20–21; 19:10; 21:8, 27; 22:9, 15). Commendable patterns of discipleship express love, faithfulness, and service (2:19). Most of these ideas would have been widely shared by early Christians. Most also would have been broadly acceptable in Greco-Roman society. The exception was the prohibition of idolatry, which distinguished Jews and Christians from the majority, for whom polytheism was the norm (NOTES on 21:8).

John could assume that readers would affirm these basic patterns, while recognizing that they disagreed as to how the implications should be worked out. For example, they presumably agreed that idolatry was wrong, but they disagreed about whether eating meat offered to Greco-Roman deities actually constituted idolatry. This was a point at which the community struggled to define its identity and boundaries (2:14, 20).

Belonging to the Christian community had a public dimension, which is suggested by the term "witness" (*martys, martyria, martyrein*). In Revelation, witness involves expressing the faith, especially in contexts in which there is uncertainty or disagreement about its validity. The two figures who bear witness in Rev 11:3–13 portray the church's calling to give public testimony to the reign of God (§23 COMMENT). The risks of doing so are evident in the fate of Jesus, Antipas, and others, who were slain because of their witness (1:5; 2:13; 6:9; 12:11; 17:6; 20:4). Revelation does not equate witness with dying as a martyr but assumes that those who attest their faith may provoke conflict that can culminate in death. It seems clear that not all of Revelation's readers saw their role in this way, but John presses the issue of witness because it has to do with the way the community engages the wider society (Blount 12–14; van Henten, "Concept").

Composition of the Community

Ethnically, Christian communities in Asia Minor were probably mixed. There were Jewish Christians at Ephesus, and the conflict over the title "Jew" at Smyrna and Philadelphia suggests that some followers of Jesus in those cities were of Jewish background (2:9; 3:9). Given Revelation's apocalyptic outlook and references to prophetic leadership (22:9), some scholars propose that the book addressed Jewish Christians who had recently emigrated from Palestine, where such perspectives were common (Satake, *Gemeindeordnung*, 155–95; Witetschek, *Ephesische*, 415–16). Yet since significant numbers of Jews lived in the cities of Asia Minor, it is more likely that some of the Jesus followers came from those local Jewish communities. Neither prophesying nor apocalyptic thinking was uniquely tied to Palestine (cf. 1 Thess 1:9–10; 4:13–5:11, 19–20; 1 Cor 14:29; 15:20–25).

By the time Revelation was written, many members of the Christian community were of Gentile background. Churches connected to the Pauline mission in Asia Minor consisted mainly of non-Jews, and mixed congregations are evident in other sources linked to the region (Acts 19:26; Col 1:27; 4:15; 1 Pet 1:1; 4:2–4; John Elliott, *1 Peter*, 94–97). The issue of eating what was offered to Greco-Roman deities would have been most pressing for Gentile Christians, who had eaten such food in the past (Rev 2:14, 20). When Revelation says that Jesus redeems people of every tribe and nation, this perspective fits a context in which the Christian community included people from various backgrounds (5:9; 7:9). Ethnicity is not a defining factor for Christian identity (Tellbe, *Christ-Believers*, 57–136).

Christians probably met in house churches. The earliest house churches at Ephesus and Laodicea were established by Paul's associates (1 Cor 16:8, 19–20; Col 4:15–16). Other groups would have started in a similar way (cf. Acts 18:7; 20:8; Rom 16:5; Phlm 2). The limitations of physical space meant that household gatherings usually included no more than thirty or forty people, although larger groups might have met on occasion (Rom 16:23). A city like Ephesus would have had multiple house churches (Trebilco, *Early*, 94–99). Such groups may have included extended families, along with people who worked in the household and others who lived in the area. Using kinship terms like "brother" for those who shared the same faith fostered a sense of cohesion (NOTE on 1:9; Osiek and Balch, *Families*, 32–35; Branick, *House*).

Subgroups in these Christian communities developed their own sense of identity. One group, the Nicolaitans, were active in multiple locations. They were apparently the followers of a Christian teacher named Nicolaus, about whom nothing more is known, and they were characterized by their willingness to eat what had been offered to Greco-Roman deities (NOTE on 2:6). At Pergamum the Nicolaitans had a place within the wider Christian community, but at Ephesus their views were not accepted by the assembly, so they may have constituted a separate group there (2:6).

Other groups were local, such as the one led by Jezebel at Thyatira. Her stance on meal practices was like that of the Nicolaitans. She claimed prophetic authority for her teachings, perhaps calling them "the deep things" of God, and she had a circle of adherents (2:20–24). Some in the wider community tolerated her views without fully embracing them (2:20), while others resisted her influence (2:24–25). At Pergamum a local group held "the teachings of Balaam," which resembled those of Jezebel (2:14). It is not clear whether "Balaam" refers to a specific local leader or whether it is simply a way of equating the group's practices with the biblical Balaam, who was said to have promoted idolatry (NOTE on 2:14).

Interpreters sometimes picture Jezebel's followers, the Nicolaitans, and those linked to Balaam as a single movement within the church (Aune, *Apocalypticism*, 187; Schüssler Fiorenza, *Book*, 115; Murphy 105–11; Trebilco, *Early*, 315); but holding similar views on meal practices did not mean that these groups had shared patterns of leadership or other features that united them (Royalty, *Streets*, 28–29). All that can be said is that they agreed that eating what was sacrificed to the gods was not a problem for Christians.

Leadership

Early Christian texts refer to apostles, prophets, and teachers as types of leaders (Eph 4:11; 1 Cor 12:28). By the later first century, writings associated with Asia Minor mention elders (1 Pet 5:1–2; 1 Tim 5:17; Tit 1:5), overseers (*episkopoi*, 1 Tim 3:1; Tit 1:7), and deacons (1 Tim 3:8–13). In the early second century, Ignatius wrote as if such positions were common, and he mentions specific individuals who served in these roles (*Magn.* 2:1; 6:1; *Eph.* 1:3; 2:1). The extent to which the assemblies addressed by Revelation had such patterns of leadership is unclear, and we cannot assume that the structure described by Ignatius was the norm at the end of the first century (Schüssler Fiorenza, *Book*, 140–46). Yet it seems likely that elders played a role in at least some churches.

The elders John pictures around God's throne are the heavenly representatives of the earthly community (NOTE on 4:4). The elders in congregations did not necessarily hold specific offices but were recognized as a group whose counsel was valued. The heavenly elders sit on thrones and cast gold wreaths before God, which was presumably not true of elders in the churches (Trebilco, *Early*, 491). Yet celestial beings were not typically called "elders," and John probably uses the term because it designated respected members of the Christian community. The title enhances the heavenly elders' representative role. John addresses his message to each assembly rather than to its leaders, but early Christian epistolary conventions did not require that a writer mention local leaders when addressing congregations (Aune, *Apocalypticism*, 183–84; on the "angel" of each assembly, see the NOTE on 1:20).

Apostles are mentioned in connection with the assembly at Ephesus (2:2). An apostle is "one who is sent," and these apostles are traveling teachers who have come to the congregation from outside. The earliest apostles were those whom Jesus sent out to preach (Matt 10:2; Mark 3:14; Luke 6:13). Later, Paul claimed to be an apostle because he was sent by the risen Christ (1 Cor 9:1; Gal 1:1, 12). The title "apostle" was also used by other traveling teachers, although it is not clear that they claimed a direct commissioning by the risen Jesus (Rom 16:7; 2 Cor 11:4–5; Acts 14:4, 14; *Did*. 11:3–6). The apostles who arrived at Ephesus were tested by the congregation, and their views were rejected. The criteria that early Christians used to examine apostles often included the contents of their messages and their behavior (NOTE on Rev 2:2). One concern at Ephesus may have been whether the traveling apostles would eat what was offered to Greco-Roman deities, since that was a disputed issue on which the congregation took a firmly negative stance (2:6, 14, 20).

Prophets play a major role in the congregations addressed by Revelation. A prophet was a person who was divinely inspired to deliver messages from God, the risen Jesus, or the Spirit (Boring, *Continuing*, 38). Although God's Spirit was understood to be at work among believers generally (1 Thess 1:6; Gal 4:6; Acts 15:7–9), certain people were uniquely empowered to prophesy, so Revelation distinguishes "prophets" from the rest of the "saints" (Rev 11:18; 16:6; 18:20, 24; cf. 1 Cor 12:29). Both men and women could serve as prophets, a practice that allowed Jezebel to claim the role at Thyatira (NOTE on Rev 2:20; cf. Acts 21:9–11; 1 Cor 11:4–5).

Many prophets were resident members of their communities. Messages could be delivered in the Christian assembly, when one or more prophets might speak (1 Cor 14:29–32; Acts 13:1–2). Such prophets are mentioned alongside teachers (Acts 13:1; Rom 12:6–7; 1 Cor 12:28; Eph 4:11) and may have done teaching themselves, as Jezebel did (Rev 2:20; cf. *Did*. 11:10). On occasion, a prophet might travel to deliver a message elsewhere (Acts 11:27–29). A few adopted an ascetic lifestyle and wandered from place to place, relying on the hospitality of those they met (Aune, *Prophecy*, 190–201, 213; Boring, *Continuing*, 38–46).

The writer of Revelation presents himself as a prophet by calling his book a "prophecy" and recounting his divine commission to "prophesy" (1:3; 10:11; 22:7, 10, 18, 19). He receives his message while "in the Spirit" (1:10) and uses the first person when speaking for God (1:8; 21:5) and the risen Jesus (2:1–3:22). Scenes in which he is divinely commissioned are patterned after episodes in Ezekiel and Daniel, while his vision of the throne room includes elements from the call of Isaiah (NOTES on 1:9–20; 4:1–11; 10:1–11). His message was to be read aloud in the assembly, where prophetic messages were delivered (1:3; 1 Cor 14:29; INTRO IV.A.2). Whether John normally lived in one of the cities addressed by his book is not known. He is sometimes thought to be an itinerant prophet, who visited the seven congregations regularly, but this thinking goes beyond the evidence. He probably had visited at least some of the churches, but how often he did so is unknown, and some information about the churches could have been sent to him by others.

John belonged to a group of prophets, whom he calls his brothers (22:9). He also says that an angel told him that the message was given "to you" (plural) for the churches (22:16). The sense is that John received the visions, while others in his prophetic circle were to deliver the message to the churches. There could be multiple prophets in a single congregation (Acts 13:1; 1 Cor 14:29), but John's group may have included prophets who lived in different communities while maintaining a special connection with each other. John assumes that their viewpoints are compatible with his own, but whether he actually led a prophetic circle is unknown (Aune, *Apocalypticism*, 250–60).

Rivalry between prophets was a factor in some churches. John and Jezebel both claimed prophetic status, yet John rejected the practice of eating what was offered to Greco-Roman deities, while Jezebel did not (2:20). Revelation alludes to a prophetic confrontation in which John or someone linked to him spoke to Jezebel in the name of the risen Christ. She was told to repent but rejected the message (2:21). Although some interpreters treat rivalry between individual prophets and prophetic groups as the primary issue in Revelation (Duff, *Who*; Royalty, *Streets*, 27–34), they overstate the case. Some of John's most critical remarks are directed at assemblies in Sardis and Laodicea, where no disputes over leadership are evident (3:1–6, 14–22).

Revelation assumes that true prophets encourage faithfulness to God and Jesus, whereas false prophets deceive people into compromising those commitments. Similar criteria are employed in other Jewish and Christian texts (§8 COMMENT). To reinforce the point, John's visions depict a false prophet luring people into the cult of the ruler (13:11–18; 19:20). In Revelation, Jezebel fits the pattern of false prophecy, since she moves people to compromise their commitment to God by eating what has been offered to other gods (2:20).

John can assume that some of his readers share his viewpoint while others do not. Though he writes with prophetic authority, he must suppose that his message will be evaluated by the community to which it is sent (1 Cor 14:29; Aune, *Prophecy*, 217–29; Boring, *Continuing*, 101–7). To encourage a favorable response, John works to establish rapport with readers in the opening chapter. He also uses literary forms like those in the biblical prophets, inviting readers to see his message as an extension of the prophetic tradition and to recognize that the same God speaks through his text (§2 COMMENT; Schüssler Fiorenza, *Book*, 133–46; Mazzaferri, *Genre*, 259–330).

2. RELATIONSHIPS WITH JEWISH COMMUNITIES

The Christian communities addressed by Revelation partly defined themselves in relation to local Jewish communities. Jews had lived in Asia Minor since at least the second century BCE. By the late first century CE, Jews lived in at least six and perhaps all seven of the cities mentioned in Revelation (NOTES on 2:1, 8, 12, 18; 3:1, 7, 14). As a minority, Jews had various ways to maintain a sense of identity while fitting into the culture of Greco-Roman cities. Some showed a high degree of assimilation, while others preserved a greater sense of distinctiveness (Barclay, *Jews*, 259–81, 320–35).

Jewish groups had their own sacred writings, worshiped the God of Israel, and rejected the polytheistic worship that was common in most cities. They maintained distinctive practices such as performing circumcision, eating kosher food, and observing the Sabbath (Josephus, *Ant.* 14.241–43). Jewish communities gathered at local synagogues (Josephus, *Ant.* 14.226, 235, 259). Until the temple was destroyed in 70 CE, Jews in Asia Minor collected funds for its support and sent them to Jerusalem (Josephus, *Ant.* 16.171; Cicero, *Flac.* 26.68). Jewish tradition forbade eating food that had been offered to pagan deities (Exod 34:14–15; *Jos. As.* 8:5; 10:13; 11:9, 16; 12:5; Ps.-Phoc. 30; *Sib. Or.* 2:96), and by refusing to do so, Jews set themselves apart from the dominant practices in Greco-Roman cities (Philostratus, *Vit. Apoll.* 5.33.4).

At the same time many Jews were well integrated into society. They spoke Greek, practiced various trades, and engaged in commerce. They took part in professional associations, which included non-Jewish members, and some had Roman citizenship (Josephus, *Ant.* 14.228, 234; Trebilco, *Jewish*, 183–84). By the early second century CE, the Jews at Miletus had reserved spaces in the city's theater. At Smyrna some made contributions to the city, as did other groups (Harland, *Associations*, 200–12; Thompson, *Book*, 133–45). Though Jews did not participate in the imperial cult, they did offer prayers on behalf of the emperor. More negative Jewish perspectives on the larger culture may be reflected in the *Sibylline Oracles*, which indict Rome for its policies in Asia Minor and pronounce judgment on cities in the region (3:343–55, 471; 5:289–90). But Jewish communities in Asia Minor are not known to have given support to the revolt against Rome in Judea (Price, *Rituals*, 220–21; Barclay, *Jews*, 279–81).

The followers of Jesus shared certain features of Jewish identity. They worshiped the God of Israel, used the Jewish Scriptures, and were to keep God's commandments and reject behaviors such as idolatry, murder, sexual immorality, and sorcery, which were forbidden by Jewish law (Rev 9:20–21; 21:8; 22:15). But Revelation assumes that different groups used different words for their gatherings: Jesus' followers meet in an "assembly" (*ekklēsia*, 1:4), whereas the Jewish community constitutes a "synagogue" (*synagogē*, 2:9; 3:9). Revelation also assumes that the followers of Jesus include people from non-Jewish backgrounds (5:9; 7:9). The followers of Jesus considered the first day of the week to be "the Lord's Day," and the extent to which they observed the Sabbath is unknown (1:9). The most significant point of difference concerned the status of Jesus, which led to a conflict in which some in the Jewish community pressured Jesus' followers to deny his name (3:8–9; see below).

3. RELATIONSHIP TO GRECO-ROMAN SOCIETY

Christian communities faced the challenge of maintaining their distinctive beliefs and identity while their members lived and worked in Greco-Roman society. An ongoing task was discerning how to interact positively with others in the dominant culture and determining where they needed to resist—and not all Christians dealt with the complexity in the same way (Harland, *Dynamics*, 102–3; Harland, "Honouring").

Politically, Asia Minor had been under Roman rule since 133 BCE, when the last king of Pergamum bequeathed the region to them. Although there were periodic outbursts of violent conflict during the years that followed, conditions improved significantly under Augustus (27 BCE–14 CE). The province honored him for bringing about a new era of peace and stability, declaring that his birthday marked the beginning of each new year (*Rom. Civ.* 1:624–25). Roman proconsuls administered the region, holding court hearings in Ephesus, Pergamum, and other cities. Rome won the loyalty of many people by its benefactions, such as providing tax relief during times of disaster and constructing public buildings and water systems. Benefactors erected statutes to Roman leaders and honored them with inscriptions on city gates, streets, aqueducts, and stadiums. The Roman order provided opportunities for upward mobility, enabling some from the province to obtain positions of influence (NOTES on 2:1, 8, 12, 18; 3:1, 7, 14).

Economically, imperial rule was good for business. Residents of Asia Minor produced textiles, metal and leather goods, wine, and grain, and they traded in slaves (Broughton, *Asia*, 817–81). The Romans provided better access to markets by improving the road system. By suppressing piracy, they made sea travel safer, a boon to port cities like Ephesus and Smyrna. Groups of Roman businesspeople lived in many cities in the province, engaging in commerce locally and facilitating trade with Rome. Public rhetoric celebrated Rome's ability to provide unprecedented prosperity (Vellius Paterculus, *Rom. Hist.* 2.126.3).

In religious terms, the imperial cult was a way for the people of Asia Minor to show their gratitude for Roman rule. The cult was not imposed by Rome but established through local support. In 29 BCE provincial representatives asked Augustus for permission to dedicate sacred precincts to him. When Augustus agreed, they built him a temple at Pergamum (Dio Cassius, *Rom. Hist.* 51.20.6–9). In 23 CE they asked permission to build Tiberius a temple to show gratitude for his favorable judgments in cases pertaining to their welfare. Many cities competed for the privilege, which was finally given to Smyrna (Tacitus, *Ann.* 4.55–56). During the 80s, Ephesus erected a provincial temple to the Flavian emperors, and throughout this period other cities started local imperial cults. The art and rhetoric associated with the cults emphasized Roman military victories, which established Rome's rule over the world, along with the peace and prosperity that Rome provided for its subjects.

The imperial cult had been an accepted feature of life in Asia Minor for several generations by the time Revelation was written. As noted above (INTRO II.C), there is no evidence that people in the provinces experienced heightened pressure to participate in the cult during Domitian's reign. Throughout the period the urban elite found serving in imperial priesthoods to be a source of honor, while the festivals associated with the cult were popular public events (Price, *Rituals*, 78–132). The imperial cult was a significant issue for the writer of Revelation because it had such widespread support in Asia Minor, not because the emperor made new demands for public displays of allegiance.

Traditional polytheism flourished along with the imperial cult. Greek gods and goddesses such as Artemis, Zeus, Dionysus, and Athena were widely venerated, and there were also cults associated with Anatolian deities such as Men and Agdistis. Temples were a source of civic pride (NOTES on 2:1, 8, 12, 18; 3:1, 7, 14). Religious loyalties were generally not exclusive—in contrast to the perspective of Revelation. People could serve in the priesthoods of more than one deity, and the public took part in various religious festivals during the year. At Ephesus, religious rites jointly honored Demeter and the emperors, while at Pergamum, a festival to the emperor was held in the sacred precincts of Asclepius (Harland, *Associations*, 116–19; Friesen, *Imperial*, 74). People had the sense that divine providence undergirded Roman rule (*Rom. Civ.* 1:624, 626; Fears, "Cult," 66–80).

Support for the empire and the gods had a place in various types of associations. Some groups were explicitly religious, such as the devotees of Demeter and Dionysus. Others consisted of people involved in the same trade, such as dyers, wool workers, coppersmiths, goldsmiths, fish sellers, and physicians. Belonging to an association gave people personal connections that were helpful for business. At the same time, these groups had religious aspects. Physicians honored Asclepius (Strabo, *Geographica* 14.1.29), goldsmiths and silversmiths honored Athena (I.*Smyr* 721), and actors were devoted to Dionysus (I.*Eph* 434). The meals shared by such groups often included homage to one of the gods.

To enhance their position in society and cultivate favor among people with influence, groups posted inscriptions honoring emperors and other public figures, some of whom were priests in the cults of the emperors and traditional deities (I.Thyat 962, 972, 978). The same was true of neighborhood associations. Their primary functions involved providing social networking and support from people of influence, but the groups also showed public devotion to an emperor or god (Harland, *Associations*, 28–90, 253–55; Kraybill, *Imperial*, 110–17). Belonging to an association was voluntary to some extent. Yet those who practiced a trade or lived in a certain neighborhood probably felt pressure to participate for the sake of maintaining social and business relationships (Harland, *Dynamics*, 33). The issue for Christians was whether doing so would involve activities incompatible with their beliefs.

Christians had various attitudes toward imperial rule. Paul insisted that government was established by God and was to be respected because it restrained wrongdoing (Rom 13:1–7). Early Christians did not pray to the emperor but offered prayers on his behalf and honored his authority (1 Tim 2:1–2; 1 Pet 2:13–17). Many Christians wanted to be seen as good, law-abiding members of Roman society, and they rejected the idea that their faith threatened the public order (Acts 16:21, 37; 17:7; 18:12–17; 19:35–41; 25:11; *1 Clem.* 60:4–61:2). John's highly critical perspective differed from that of many Christians, including some of his readers. The prosperous Christians at Laodicea seemed quite comfortable under Roman rule (Rev 3:15–17), and those open to eating what had been offered to the gods showed that they did not want their beliefs to create tension with non-Christians (2:14, 20).

John's view is that there is a fundamental clash between the claims of Rome and those of God. This perspective has several aspects: Politically, Roman officials were probably responsible for putting Antipas to death and sending John to Patmos because of their witness to Jesus (NOTES and COMMENT on 1:9; 2:13). John considered such actions both unjust and an affront to God and his Messiah. They belonged to a pattern of violent conquest in which Rome subjugated the nations of the world and the followers of Jesus (13:7; 18:24). Religiously, John insisted that if what Christians believe about God and Jesus is true, then worshiping other gods must be false. For him, it was deceiving to deify human rulers and claim heavenly support for an empire that would slay Jesus and his witnesses (5:6; 13:4, 15). Economically, the prosperity provided by commerce with Rome lulled people into complacency about the arrogance and brutality of the current order. It drew people into a system driven by obsession with profit and pleasure. While draining the wealth of the provinces to enrich the few, it left others to struggle (17:1–6; 18:3, 9–20).

At the same time, John engages his Greco-Roman context in creative ways. He knows its language and imagery well enough to draw on it throughout his text, while subverting the usual meaning of these symbols. Roman rhetoric about peace and prosperity is challenged by threatening horsemen (6:3–6); the celebration of Roman conquest is turned into an indictment of Roman brutality (13:7); and popular lore about Nero surviving death is woven into the portrayal of the beast (13:3). Yet John converts the images of a laurel wreath, white stone, and white robe—all of which had positive cultural connotations— into the promises made to the faithful (2:10, 17; 3:4), and the vision of New Jerusalem fulfills and surpasses the ideals of a Hellenistic city (§42 COMMENT). John uses language from the dominant society to critique that society, while encouraging commitment to God and Jesus.

B. Issues Affecting the Readers

The issues emerging from Revelation's social setting fall into three categories: conflict with outsiders, assimilation, and complacency. Many interpreters prioritize one dimension over another. Some emphasize the threat of persecution (Mounce 16–21) or Roman oppression (Schüssler Fiorenza 127); others focus on disputes within the Christian community (Duff, *Who*; Royalty, *Streets*, 27–34); and others depict congregations that show little sign of crisis at all (Thompson, *Book*, 166, 175). But the social setting was complex, and the book's visions take the full range of issues into account when calling readers to renewed faithfulness to God, Christ, and the Christian community (Yarbro Collins, *Crisis*, 84–110; deSilva, *Seeing*, 37–63).

I. CONFLICT WITH OUTSIDERS

Readers at Smyrna and Philadelphia are threatened by conflicts with outsiders that have the potential to make them abandon their faith (2:8–11; 3:7–13). Their situations fit the pattern of first-century persecution, which was local and sporadic. The first level of hostility involved verbal harassment, when Christians were maligned because their beliefs and way of life did not conform to those of their antagonists (Acts 14:19; 17:5–9; 1 Pet 4:4, 14, 16). The second level involved denouncing Christians to the authorities as troublemakers, prompting officials to investigate the charges. The Romans did not seek out Christians for questioning, but they did respond when others accused them of posing a threat to the social order (Acts 16:16–24; 18:12–17; Pliny the Younger, *Ep.* 10.96.3–6, 9; Eusebius, *Hist. eccl.* 5.1.7). The third level involved imprisonment, interrogation, and sentencing. Officials could release the accused if they saw no cause for complaint (Acts 17:1–9; 18:12–17) or put them in prison for questioning (2 Cor 11:23; Phil 1:12–13; Acts 16:20–24; 17:1–9; Heb 10:32–34). If found to be a threat, the accused could be put to death (Pliny the Younger, *Ep.* 10.96.3).

The followers of Jesus at Philadelphia experienced the first level of conflict, as they were verbally harassed by members of a local synagogue. One source of tension was probably the status of Jesus. Although the belief that he was God's Messiah could have been an issue, more elevated Christological claims were probably involved. Note that John ascribes traits of deity to Jesus, calling him Alpha and Omega and picturing him sharing God's throne, being worshiped along with God (5:13–14; 22:3, 13). Such views could have seemed blasphemous to Jews, who felt that Christians put Jesus in the place of God. Another issue was Jewish identity. John refers to Jesus' followers as "a kingdom and priests" of God, depicting them as heirs of the promises made to Israel (Exod 19:6; Rev 1:5–6; 5:9–10; 7:4–13). From the perspective of the synagogue, however, it would have seemed illegitimate to ascribe Jewish identity to those who made extravagant claims about Jesus (2:9; 3:9).

At Philadelphia the conflict involved some Jews pressuring the followers of Jesus to deny his name or to face the prospect of being socially shut out of the Jewish community (3:8–9). There is no suggestion that the Romans were involved in this conflict. Rather, verbal harassment was designed to make Jesus' followers relinquish their faith in order to ease tensions with the local synagogue. If done publicly, such harassment also warned others not to adopt Christian beliefs, since there was a high social cost to doing so (§10 COMMENT). People who successfully denounced others also reinforced their own influence in the eyes of society (Malina and Neyrey, "Honor," 29–32).

At Smyrna the conflict took a different turn, since denunciation by the synagogue brought the followers of Jesus to the attention of Roman authorities, which is the second level of conflict noted above (2:9–11). It was not a simple matter for members of the synagogue to denounce the followers of Jesus to Roman authorities. A potential problem was that the Romans might not be able to distinguish the two groups, because synagogue members and Jesus' followers shared an aversion to Greco-Roman polytheism. Accordingly, those from the synagogue would have had to present themselves as loyal citizens of the empire, while charging that Jesus' followers had distinctive beliefs and practices that threatened the social order. For example, specific charges could have been that declaring Jesus to be sovereign showed disloyalty to the emperor (1:5; 19:16; Acts 17:7) or that those who made elevated claims about Jesus were quite different from Jews, whose peculiar beliefs were tolerable because they belonged to an ancestral tradition. Instead, Christians were to be seen as promoters of a new superstition that warranted suppression (Tacitus, *Ann.* 15.44; Pliny the Younger, *Ep.* 10.98.8–9).

Roman officials who had the legal power known as *coercitio* were allowed to have the accused beaten and imprisoned to safeguard public order. Imprisonment gave officials time to question the accused, while adding pressure for the accused to comply with the officials' directives. As proconsul in the early second century, Pliny observed that there were no standard procedures for dealing with Christians. His approach was to ask the accused whether they were Christians. If they denied it, he would have them demonstrate it by invoking the gods, offering wine and incense to the emperor's image, and reviling the name of Christ. Such procedures showed obedience to the ruler and gods of the empire (Pliny the Younger, *Ep.* 10.96.1–8; 10.97.2; Sherwin-White, *Letters*, 778–81).

Christians who proved intractable could receive various sentences. Pliny had those who refused to renounce Christianity executed because of their "stubbornness and unshakeable obstinacy" (*Ep.* 10.96.3). Before Revelation was composed, Antipas had been put to death at Pergamum because of his witness to Jesus (Rev 2:13). By way of contrast, John had apparently received a sentence of banishment to Patmos. Some have wondered whether he got a lighter sentence than Antipas because he was of a higher social status, but it more likely had to do with the way his offense was construed. Those judged guilty of spreading an insidious "superstition" were relegated to an island (NOTE on 1:9).

The messages in Rev 2–3 reflect a social setting in which persecution is a threat, but one that is limited in scope. When Antipas was put to death at Pergamum, other Christians were left alone. Those at Smyrna faced imprisonment and death, but such threats were not apparent in other cities—at Philadelphia, for instance, the threat was being shut out of the Jewish community. In the visions in Rev 4–22, conflict with the synagogue is not explicitly mentioned, although those chapters do reaffirm that Jesus' followers share the promises made to Israel and will have a place in New Jerusalem (3:12; 7:4–17; 21:7). Rather, it is conflict with Rome and its supporters that receives greatest attention. John depicts imperial power as a beast that slaughters the followers of Jesus and Rome as Babylon the whore, who is drunk with the blood of the saints (17:6; 18:24). His imagery recalls Nero's persecution of the church in Rome around 64 CE, which was known for its ruthlessness (Tacitus, *Ann.* 15.44). The bloodshed in the visions goes beyond anything that the readers would have experienced, but it shows the brutality of which the empire is capable and warns that it could happen again. For John, violence against the church is not an aberration but is what reveals the empire's opposition to God. It also heightens the questions of what it means to accommodate the religious practices that support such an empire, and how wealth makes people complacent about the empire's use of violence.

2. ASSIMILATION AND GRECO-ROMAN
RELIGIOUS PRACTICES

Assimilation has to do with the extent to which Jesus' followers could accommodate the practices of non-Christians while remaining true to their own faith. Reasons for accommodation included the desire to maintain good social and business relationships with people outside the Christian community (Yarbro Collins, *Crisis*, 88). The issue of eating food sacrificed to the gods was one point of controversy; John firmly rejected the practice, but, as we have seen, the Nicolaitans and those who followed the teachings of Balaam and Jezebel did not. A sketch of the social contexts and the range of early Christian responses shows the dynamics involved.

Religious festivals were public events that included sacrifices, banquets, and distributions of meat. Wealthy patrons bore the expense. An inscription from the late first century BCE or early first century CE tells of an official in Asia Minor inviting Roman citizens, nearby residents, and even foreigners to banquets at festivals for Dionysus and the athletic contests associated with the cult of Augustus (*NewDocs* 7:733–38; Friesen, *Imperial*, 105; cf. Plutarch, *Demetr.* 11.3; Suetonius, *Jul.* 38.2; Livy, *Rom. Hist.* 41.28.11). The Jewish refusal to share sacrifices and meals with others was considered antisocial and even offensive (Philostratus, *Vit. Apoll.* 5.33.4), and Christians who refused to participate would be seen negatively as well.

Private meals held by families or associations could include rites honoring a deity. People might be invited to dine at the table of a god (P.Oxy. 4539–40; *NewDocs* 1:5–9; Willis, *Idol*, 40–42). Banquets with religious dimensions were held in sanctuaries (P.Oxy. 110) and in private homes (P.Oxy. 523). Such meals might be held in honor of a deity (P.Fouad 76), but they could also celebrate a child's birth or coming of age (P.Oxy. 1484; 2791). On such occasions the god's image could be displayed (Aelius Aristides, *Orations* 45.27; P.Oslo 57). Members of trade and professional associations often shared meals, and at these events honors were given to various gods and deified emperors. Christians might want to participate in private meals to maintain good relationships with family, friends, and business associates, yet doing so could give the impression that they honored gods in whom they did not believe. But refusing to join in such meals was also a problem, since it risked offending people, which could make life socially and financially difficult.

Sacrificial meat that was not consumed by worshipers at a banquet or given away was sold in the city's public market along with meat from other sources (Pliny the Younger, *Ep.* 10.96.10; Sherwin-White, *Letters*, 709). A purchaser might have to ask about the origin of the meat in order to know whether it had any connection with sacrifice (1 Cor 10:25–28; Cadbury, "Macellum," 141; E. Sanders, *Jewish Law*, 279). When non-Christian family members and friends invited Christians to eat in their homes, they might serve meat that had been offered to a Greco-Roman deity. Christians had to decide whether to simply eat the food without comment, or whether doing so would give the impression that they condoned the worship of the gods (1 Cor 10:27).

Early Christian viewpoints on this issue can be grouped into three categories. First, some Christians categorically prohibited eating meat that had been sacrificed to a deity. A decree associated with the Jerusalem Council said that Christians of Gentile background did not need to be circumcised but were to abstain from things sacrificed to idols, blood, things that had been strangled, and fornication (Acts 15:20, 29; 21:25). All the prohibitions are categorical, so the decree rules out eating sacrificial meat in all situations. Other Christian sources evince a similar viewpoint: "keep strictly away from what has been sacrificed to idols, for it is the worship of dead gods" (*Did.* 6:3; cf. Justin Martyr, *Dial.* 34–35; Irenaeus, *Haer.* 1.6.3; 1.24.5; 1.28.2; Clement of Alexandria, *Paed.* 2.1; Lucian, *Peregr.* 16; Ps.-Clement, *Recognitions* 4.36; Brunt, "Rejected"; Tomson, *Paul*, 177–86).

Second, some Christians thought it acceptable to eat sacrificial meat in most if not all circumstances. Those who held this position at Corinth apparently made two arguments: One was that the gods represented by idols did not exist, which meant that a person did not actually worship other gods by eating what was sacrificed to them (1 Cor 8:1–6). The other argument was that Jewish law forbade eating what was offered to the gods (Exod 34:15), but such commands did not apply to those whom Christ had freed from the law (1 Cor 10:23). Revelation ascribes similar views to the Nicolaitans and those identified with Balaam and Jezebel (Rev 2:14–15, 20).

Third, Paul considered it acceptable to eat sacrificial meat in some contexts but not others. For him, the issue was whether the action compromised one's witness to God and Christ. On the one hand, Paul thought Christians could purchase meat in the market and eat in the homes of non-Christians without asking about its origin. If the meat was not clearly linked to idolatry in a particular social context, there was no problem eating it (1 Cor 10:23–27). On the other hand, Paul ruled out eating meals in Greco-Roman temples and in contexts in which the host made clear that meat had been offered in sacrifice (8:7–13; 10:28). He agreed that the gods represented by idols did not exist, but he also insisted that idolatry was demonic and that eating in such a religious context would condone the demonic (10:14–22).

The author of Revelation belongs to the first category since he opposes consuming any food that has been offered to a Greco-Roman deity. Like Paul and others, he associates idolatry with demonic power (Rev 2:20, 24; 9:20; 1 Cor 10:20; cf. 2 Cor 6:15–16; Ps 106:37–38; Bar 4:7; *T. Jud.* 23:1), but unlike Paul, he applies this idea categorically: If food offered to idols promotes the work of Satan, then Christians must reject it, just as they are to renounce all other aspects of Satan's work. Whether the author of Revelation knew about the apostolic decree is unclear. Both mention *eidōlothyta* (things sacrificed to idols) and *porneia* (immorality) (Acts 15:20, 29; 21:25; Rev 2:14, 20; Bauckham, *Book*, 464; Tomson, *Paul*, 180). Yet opposition to consuming sacrificial meat was sufficiently widespread among Jews and Christians that the author could have rejected the practice without knowing a specific tradition about the decree (Karrer, "Die Apokalypse").

The messages in Rev 2–3 mention the issue of meal practices, but the visions in Rev 4–22 take up the larger question of true and false worship. Scenes of heavenly worship center on the God who creates all things, acts justly, and brings salvation, and the Lamb who redeems people from every nation (4:11; 5:9–14; 7:9–14; 15:2–4; 19:1–4). Contrasting scenes show people worshiping the dragon and beast, which oppress people, slay the faithful, and ruin the earth (13:1–18). The visions of conflicting forms of worship challenge readers to ask where their loyalties lie—with God or with those who would take God's place? By making sharp contrasts in the visionary world, the writer presses readers to see the implications of worship practices in their social world. They are to live out their identity as priests of God in contexts of competing religious claims (1:5–6; 5:9–10).

3. COMPLACENCY AND WEALTH

A final problem is the attitude of complacency that arises from wealth (Yarbro Collins, *Crisis*, 132–34; Kraybill, *Imperial*, 25–31). The message to Laodicea depicts a congregation that is "tepid" in its faith commitment because its people are "rich and have become wealthy and do not need anything" (3:16–17). The issue of wealth was almost certainly more apparent to John than to many of his readers, yet it plays a major role in the visions. Babylon the whore presides over a vast commercial empire, and she speaks with the kind of self-satisfied attitude that John ascribes to the Laodiceans (18:7). The way the merchants "become wealthy" through commerce with Rome suggests that the Laodiceans also have "become wealthy" through trade (*ploutein*) (3:17; 18:3, 15, 19).

The counterpart to the wealthy Laodiceans are the Smyrneans, who are economically poor and yet faithful (2:9). The city of Smyrna was as prosperous as other places in Asia Minor, but Jesus' followers there did not benefit. The specific reasons for their poverty are unknown (NOTE on 2:9). Although early

Christian communities typically included people from various social classes (Meeks, *First*, 73), John pictures the congregation at Laodicea as mainly rich and the one at Smyrna as mainly poor. He is highly critical of the prosperous and supportive of the impoverished, yet he does not treat poverty as a virtue. He commends the faithfulness that the Smyrneans exhibit despite their poverty.

In the first century it was common for Christian circles to include people of means. Gatherings were hosted by people with homes large enough to accommodate a group (Rom 16:5; Col 4:15); for example, Gaius was able to host the whole church at Corinth (Rom 16:23). Some Christians were able to travel, because they either had their own resources or could rely on others to pay their way (1 Cor 1:11; Meeks, *First*, 55–63; Osiek and Balch, *Families*, 96–102). It was not unusual for Christians to be involved in commerce. Paul, Aquila, and Priscilla were tentmakers (Acts 18:3), and Lydia, a traveling merchant from Thyatira, dealt in the purple cloth favored by the wealthy (16:14). Many of John's readers would have considered it natural to seek a good living through trade.

John engages the question of wealth at several levels. One concerns the desire to obtain it. In Roman society the wealthy had a privileged place. The best kind of wealth was inherited, but many sought to acquire wealth through business ventures in order to advance to the upper classes. When John pictures Laodiceans boasting that they have "become wealthy" (3:17), he implies that their wealth is acquired. Greek and Latin writers pictured people scrambling to make money and imitating the lifestyle of the rich by wearing ostentatious clothing and jewelry. John invokes stereotypes of merchants, who were regarded as greedy and self-serving. Many thought that the profit motive fostered dishonesty; one might say, "Call me a scoundrel, only call me rich!" (Seneca the Younger, *Ep.* 115.10, 14). To some extent, John's perspective is similar to that of other writers, who decried Roman society's obsession with luxury. But where philosophers urged people to pursue the virtues of justice, temperance, honor, and friendship rather than wealth (Dio Chrysostom, *Or.* 3.93; 13.34), John calls readers to the kind of love, faithfulness, and service that fit the ways of God and the Lamb (Rev 2:19; §36 COMMENT).

Second, wealth makes people "blind" (Rev 3:17). The charge can be correlated with Babylon's arrogant inability to see the destructive consequences of its actions (18:7–8). Public rhetoric lauded the prosperity that Rome provided, but critics added that Rome exerted greater control over its subjects by supplying them with goods than it ever could by force of arms, since commerce lulled people into accepting political subjection (Tacitus, *Hist.* 4.64.3). However, John sees Rome as the world's ultimate consumer of goods, not its benevolent supplier. Those who engage in commerce drain the provinces of whatever they produce in order to feed the imperial city with its insatiable appetite (Rev

18:11–19; *Sib. Or.* 3:350–55). In the process, the wealth of the few is obtained at the expense of the many, including the slaves who are put on the market both body and soul (Rev 18:13; deSilva, *Seeing*, 44–48; Harland, *Associations*, 256).

Third, the aspiration for wealth draws people into the worship of the emperor and the gods. John portrays Rome's commercial empire as a whore that encourages religious promiscuity (17:1–2; 18:3). Whether at banquets or the meetings of trade associations, people involved in commerce would feel social pressure to honor the gods of their clients and business partners. John's reference to receiving the mark of the beast in order to buy and sell in the marketplace points in the same direction. It depicts people feeling pressure to condone the claims of the empire and its deified rulers for the sake of business (13:16–17).

Finally, the pursuit of wealth undermines the cohesiveness of the Christian community by prioritizing relationships based on trade over those based on a shared faith. The congregations addressed by Revelation included both poor and rich. If Christians made acquiring wealth their primary goal, then their relationships with trade associations and clients would be far more important than their bonds with believers who lacked resources. In response, Revelation not only emphasizes the destructive qualities of the quest for wealth, but presents an alternative standard of value, in which people are "purchased" by the Lamb's self-sacrifice and given a place in a community whose future extends to the glories of New Jerusalem (5:9; 14:3–4; 21–22:5).

Revelation addresses readers in a variety of social situations, and keeping this variety in mind is helpful when interpreting the visions. Readers who felt threatened might readily have agreed with John's depiction of a beastly empire and may have been encouraged by promises of divine victory. Readers who felt complacent and were accommodating, however, may have recognized that such scenes challenged their perspectives and called them to a renewed commitment to God, Christ, and the Christian community. The book's bold imagery and richly textured literary features enable it to engage the attention of a diverse audience living in diverse social contexts.

IV.

Literary Aspects

———————

Literary study of Revelation considers how the final form of the text is shaped. Its genre is complex. Visions unfold in a pattern that is both cyclical and forward moving, as threatening scenes alternate with those of hope. The plot traces the outworking of God's designs, as the forces of the Creator and the Lamb overcome the dragon, the beast, and other destroyers of the earth. Images from Jewish Scripture and Greco-Roman tradition are recast, and special literary forms such as hymns and beatitudes celebrate divine justice and redemption.

A. Genre

Interpretation of Revelation is profoundly affected by assumptions about its literary genre. The divergent perspectives that have emerged in the history of interpretation reflect different views about what kind of book Revelation is. Readers make inferences about genre by noting ways in which a book's form and contents are like those of other texts. An audience's sense of genre raises expectations about how the text will function, and assumptions are either affirmed or challenged in the reading process. The notion of genre is complex because texts often have some but not all of the same features, and literary forms change over time. Texts may also have traits from more than one kind of literature. Revelation has features of three genres: an apocalypse, a prophecy, and a circular letter. The author draws on conventions appropriate to each genre, while combining and adapting them in creative ways.

I. APOCALYPSE

The initial word in John's book is *apokalypsis*, which means "revelation" or "disclosure" (1:1). At the time Revelation was composed, the word was not a technical term for a literary genre, but it was later included in titles affixed to revelatory texts and now designates a particular type of writing (§1 COMMENT). Some Jewish texts from the third century BCE to the third century CE that are considered apocalypses are Daniel, *1* and *2 Enoch*, *2* and *3 Baruch*, the *Apocalypse of Abraham*, the *Apocalypse of Zephaniah*, and sections of *Jubilees*, the *Testament of Levi*, and the *Testament of Abraham*. Early Christian apocalypses include Revelation, the *Shepherd of Hermas*, the *Apocalypse of Peter*, the *Ascension of Isaiah*, and other texts. A useful definition of an "apocalypse" is:

> A genre of revelatory literature with a narrative framework, in which a revelation is mediated by an otherworldly being to a human recipient, disclosing a transcendent reality which is both temporal, insofar as it envisages eschatological salvation, and spatial, insofar as it involves another, supernatural world. (Collins, *Apocalyptic*, 5)

The narrative framework of Revelation begins when the writer says, "I, John, your brother . . . , was on the island called Patmos," when the exalted Christ commanded him to write a book (1:9–20). He narrates his experience using the first person "then I saw" to introduce successive visions. The book traces the progressive defeat of the agents of evil and culminates in a final judgment and new creation. The narrative framework distinguishes literary apocalypses like Revelation from other works that have similar themes. For example, the Dead Sea *War Scroll* envisions a great eschatological battle, and Paul's letters anticipate the defeat of death and liberation of creation at the end of the present age (1 Cor 15:20–28; Rom 8:18–26), but these texts are not literary apocalypses because they do not use a narrative form.

Apocalypses assume that the world is mysterious and that meaningful revelations are sent from the unseen realm above through angelic mediators (Collins, *Apocalyptic*, 8). Revelation's preface says that the book's message came from God, through the exalted Jesus, who gave it to an angel, who gave it to John, who conveyed it to the readers (Rev 1:1). The narrative follows this progression: God gives a sealed scroll to the Lamb (5:1–7), who opens it (6:1–8:1), so an angel can give the open scroll to John, who consumes it and reveals its contents through his witness (10:1–11; Mazzaferri, *Genre*, 265–79; Bauckham, *Climax*, 243–57). Along the way other heavenly beings give John insights into what he sees (5:5; 7:13–17; 17:1, 7–17; 19:9–10; 21:9–22:9; cf. Dan 10:2–8; *1 En.* 1:2; *2 En.* 1:3–9; *Apoc. Zeph.* 2:1; *4 Ezra* 4:1; *3 Bar.* 1:3–4; *Apoc. Ab.* 10:4–11:6).

Spatially, apocalypses envision a transcendent or supernatural world that lies beyond what is visible and yet shapes life in this world. Some apocalypses refer to it only briefly (Dan 7:9–10), while others recount otherworldly journeys that enable the seer to visit the celestial regions above, the hidden realms of earth, and the terrible depths of the underworld (*1 En.* 1–36; *2 En.* 1–68; *Apoc. Zeph.* 2:1–12:8; *3 Bar.* 2–16). Revelation's visionary geography extends from heaven to earth to the great abyss (Rev 4:1; 8:7; 9:1). The seer travels in the Spirit to the heavenly throne hall (4:1), to the mysterious desert where he can see Babylon the whore (17:1), and even to the new creation for a glimpse of New Jerusalem the bride (21:9).

In Revelation the realm above can be distinguished from the realm below, yet both belong to God's universe. Most vision cycles begin and end in the heavenly realm, and the decrees of God and actions of his associates affect what occurs on earth, whether through acts of worship that engage all creation or by plagues that culminate in the defeat of evil (4:1–5:13; 8:1–5; 11:15–19; 15:1–8; 19:1–8, 11). God's angels have keys to the underworld and can release and confine its demonic inhabitants (9:1–11; 20:1–3). The spatial dimension of Revelation locates true authority beyond earthly political and social structures. Readers are to show loyalty to the God who is above all powers in heaven (12:7–12), earth (17:15–18), and the underworld (1:18; 20:13–14) and who wields an authority that differs from the powers of this world.

The temporal dimension of apocalypses anticipates judgment and salvation at the end of the age. One form of judgment is the defeat of hostile nations in battle and the overcoming of demonic forces (*1 En.* 91:14–16; *4 Ezra* 12:1–39; 13:39–40; *2 Bar.* 39–40). Another form is that people are brought before God's court and held accountable for their deeds (Dan 7:10; *4 Ezra* 7:33–44; *2 Bar.* 24:2; *Apoc. Zeph.* 2–11). Both types of judgment can be combined in a single apocalypse, as in Rev 19:11–20:15. The assumption is that at present, people are vulnerable and need deliverance from hostile forces, and yet the influence of evil does not eliminate human responsibility; people are accountable for what they do.

Apocalyptic visions of salvation can include hope for resurrection (Dan 12:3; *4 Ezra* 7:32–36) along with the restoration of Israel and establishment of God's kingdom (Dan 7:27; *4 Ezra* 13:39–50). Some scenarios expect the world itself to be transformed (*1 En.* 45:4–5; 91:16–17; *2 Bar.* 29:1–8; 73:1–74:4). Revelation's vision of salvation is expansive, including resurrection, sharing in the kingdom, and having a place in the paradise of New Jerusalem (Rev 20:4–6; 21:1–22:5). The political, social, and economic forces of the present age are powerful, and in the short term readers might think that it is best to accommodate them in order to avoid conflict. But the writer takes the long view, insisting that the powers of this age will end and that hope ultimately comes from God, whose reign endures.

The temporal perspective in some apocalypses includes a survey of history. Writers may trace events from primeval times or a point in Israel's history up to the advent of the messianic kingdom (*1 En.* 83–90) or the close of the age (Dan 7–12). The impression is that the texts reveal the course of history. For this literary device to work, the events must be clear enough for readers to identify them (*1 En.* 93:1–10; 91:12–17), or the writer must explain them (Dan 8:1–26; *2 Bar.* 53–74). Such historical outlines show that the present order of things is not absolute and will give way before the greater purposes of God (Portier-Young, *Apocalypse*, 44–45).

Revelation shares the conviction that the present world order is finite, yet its cycles of visions do not outline historical periods. Historical surveys want readers to see that time is moving inexorably to its culmination, but Revelation repeats similar images in varied sequences, while adding new elements and then *interrupting* the action before judgment occurs (Rev 6:1–8:5; 8:6–11:14). Readers are assured that God's triumph will come but are not allowed to know how specific events will unfold.

Pseudonymity is a feature of all Jewish and most early Christian apocalypses. Exceptions are Revelation and the *Shepherd of Hermas*. As we have seen, pseudonymity can enhance the authority of a text by ascribing it to a notable figure, such as Enoch, Baruch, or Ezra, whose words can presumably be trusted.

By assuming the identity of someone from the past, a writer can outline a series of events as if they are still to come—even though from the real author's vantage point, the events have already occurred. Tracing the events that lead up to and go beyond the writer's own time period shows God's control over history (Collins, *Apocalyptic*, 39–40). Identifying with a figure from Israel's history also means that the writer's authority is not derived from his immediate social context. He assumes a position outside his contemporary setting, so that he can challenge its perspectives from an alternative vantage point (Portier-Young, *Apocalypse*, 42–43).

Revelation departs from the usual pattern, since it is written in the author's own name for his contemporaries (1:9–11; 22:10). Like the writers of other apocalypses, John locates himself within the tradition of Israel, but he does not use a pseudonym for two reasons. First, Revelation is a mixed genre. Although writing an apocalypse, John considers himself a prophet, and prophets typically made their messages public in their own names (Aune, *Prophecy*, 274). The book also has the qualities of a letter, whose senders regularly identified themselves by name (U. Müller, "Literarische," 608). Second, John's view of history differs from that of Jewish apocalypses. He was convinced that God had acted decisively in the death and resurrection of Jesus. He did not present himself as a writer from the past who could outline events leading up to the present and into the future. The eschatological struggle had already begun with the Messiah's exaltation and would culminate at his return. Those events define the present time (Collins, *Apocalyptic*, 271).

Apocalypses provide perspectives on the world that transcend the usual boundaries of space and time so readers can see their present situation in light of God's designs. By influencing the way people see their world, apocalypses shape the way people respond to it. Although these texts have often been regarded as sources of encouragement for people in oppressive situations, they can function in other ways (Yarbro Collins, "Introduction," 6–7). This is especially true of Revelation, where the opening chapters show that the book addressed several kinds of readers. As we have seen, some were threatened by open hostility, others dealt with questions of accommodating Greco-Roman religious practices, and still others were prosperous and complacent. Revelation's message would be heard as confrontation by some and encouragement by others, depending on their circumstances (Bauckham, *Theology*, 15).

2. PROPHECY

The writer of Revelation refers to his book as "prophecy" (1:3; 22:7, 10, 18, 19) and to his own commission to "prophesy" (10:11). The early Christian prophet has been defined as "an immediately inspired spokesperson for the risen Jesus, who received intelligible messages that he or she felt impelled to deliver to the Christian community, or as a representative of the community, to the general public" (Boring, *Continuing*, 38). Differentiating prophecy from a literary apocalypse is challenging because both included vision reports. Prophecies were often delivered orally, but they could also be written down (Herm. *Vis.* 2.4.2–3), which was the case with apocalypses. Moreover, the message of a Christian prophet could be called a prophecy (*prophēteia*) or a revelation (*apokalypsis*) with no clear difference in meaning (1 Cor 14:6, 26–30; Rev 1:1, 3).

Revelation's superscription resembles those on the prophetic writings, which told of the word of the Lord coming to the prophet and sometimes described the message. For example, "The word of the Lord that came to Micah of Moresheth . . . which he saw concerning Samaria and Jerusalem" (Mic 1:1). After this is the initial oracle: "Hear, you peoples, all of you . . . the Lord is coming out of his place" (Mic 1:2–3; cf. Isa 1:1–2; Jer 1:1–2; Hos 1:1; Joel 1:1–2; Amos 1:1–2; Zeph 1:1–2). John adapts this form: "A revelation from Jesus Christ," which came to "his servant John, who bore witness to the word of God . . . as much as he saw" (Rev 1:1–2). John varies the pattern by inserting an epistolary salutation and then giving the oracle: "See, he is coming with the clouds" and "all the tribes of the earth will grieve for him" (1:7). By using this introductory form, John locates his book within the tradition of biblical prophecy.

Another prophetic dimension is the inclusion of oracles. John says he received his message while "in the Spirit" (1:10), and in the messages to the assemblies in 2:1–3:22 the Spirit and risen Christ speak as one (2:1, 7). Christ directs John to "write" and "send" a message to the assemblies (1:11), much as biblical prophets were to "go and tell" (Isa 6:9; Jer 1:7). The address to each church begins with "thus says" (*tade legei*), a formula that prophets used for divine speech (Rev 2:1, 8, 12, etc.; Isa 3:16; Jer 2:2; Amos 2:1; Acts 21:11). The messages include oracles of salvation and judgment, like those in Israel's prophetic tradition, where the divine speaker considers the situation of listeners and calls for repentance, perseverance, and hope. The concluding summons to "hear" recalls patterns of prophetic exhortation as well as the tradition of Jesus (Aune, *Prophecy*, 275–80).

Additional oracles appear throughout the book. God identifies himself by saying "I am the Alpha and the Omega" (Rev 1:8; 21:6), and he extends promises of salvation and warnings of judgment (21:7–8). A heavenly voice says that those who die in the Lord are "blessed," and the Spirit adds that they shall rest from their labors (14:13). In the end the glorified Jesus identifies himself in the first person, telling readers "I am coming soon" and exhorting them to be faithful (22:7). As promises of salvation and warnings of judgment are given, the Spirit's voice affirms what is said (22:12–20). The way John's voice is blended with the divine voices seems to reflect the pattern of uttering prophecy in Christian worship (1 Cor 14:15–16, 29–32; Aune, *Prophecy*, 280–88).

Revelation draws heavily on the biblical prophets, encouraging readers to associate its message with that tradition. Instead of quoting texts and then interpreting them, as a teacher might do, John weaves the biblical language into his own visionary text, with the result that the older prophetic words become a vehicle for communicating a contemporary message (Boring, *Continuing*, 143–44). For example, John's description of the heavenly throne room recalls Ezek 1–2 and Isa 6. The four horsemen resemble scenes from Zech 1 and 6, and the cosmic portents in the sky appear in various prophetic texts (Isa 13:10; 34:4; Joel 2:10, 30–31). John's account of his commission to prophesy follows that of Ezekiel, who ate a scroll written on two sides (Rev 5:1; 10:1–11; Ezek 2:1–3:3).

The prophetic elements in Revelation confront readers with what John understands to be the living word of God. Where apocalypses offer a transcendent perspective on the world through visions recounted in the third person, the oracular elements in Revelation have the divine speaker address the readers directly. *They* are warned of judgment and promised salvation, and *they* are to hold firmly to the message and to persevere in hope. The prophetic framing of the book and the prophetic elements within it give immediacy and urgency to the work as a whole.

3. LETTER

Revelation is framed by a salutation and conclusion that resemble those of other ancient letters (1:4–6; 22:16–21). These epistolary features reflect early Christian adaptations of typical forms, often following Pauline patterns. Some interpreters ascribe little significance to the epistolary framework, proposing that it was simply affixed to the core apocalypse in order to facilitate its circulation among the churches (Aune 1:lxxii–lxxv). But others give more weight to the epistolary elements, noting how they shape the way Revelation is read (Boring, "Voice"; Hellholm, "Visions"; Karrer, "Text der Johannesapokalypse"; U. Müller, "Literarische"; Roloff 7–8; Schüssler Fiorenza 22–23).

Ancient letters began with a salutation that first identified the sender. The person might simply state his or her name, but senders could also add official titles, family connections, or terms of endearment (J. White, *Light*, 200). Christian letters might call the sender an "apostle" (1 Cor 1:1; 1 Pet 1:1), a "prisoner" (Phlm 1), or a "servant" (Phil 1:1) of Jesus Christ, each title affecting the way the sender was to be seen. Revelation simply gives the author's name, John (1:4), elsewhere adding that he is the "brother" and "companion" of the readers

(1:9) and like them he is God's "servant" (1:1–2). All of the expressions foster a sense of rapport with the intended recipients. But rather than saying more about himself in the epistolary introduction, John concentrates on the identity of God and Jesus, who are the authorities behind his message (1:4c–6).

Next, letters identified the recipients, in this case a group of congregations (1:4). Some early Christian salutations elaborated traits of the congregations, so the readers would know how the sender perceived them (1 Cor 1:2; 1 Thess 1:1; 1 Pet 1:1b–2; Ign. *Eph.* pref.). But John initially notes only the Roman province in which the congregations are located (Rev 1:4; cf. Gal 1:2). What the salutation shows is that Revelation is a circular letter designed to be read aloud in multiple congregations (1:3). Its public character adds rhetorical force. The text will communicate reproof and encouragement to individual congregations, yet what is said to one will be read by all. Recipients have incentive to heed the message because their reputations are at stake among churches throughout the region.

Finally there is the greeting. Greco-Roman letters began with "greetings" (*chairein*, J. White, *Light*, 101–23). Some Christian letters followed that practice (Jas 1:1; Acts 15:23; 23:26; cf. Ign. *Eph.* pref.; Barn. 1:1), but many replaced *chairein* with *charis* (grace), a word similar in form with greater theological weight, and coupled it with the Jewish greeting of "peace." The Pauline writings use the basic form "grace to you and peace" (1 Thess 1:1), usually adding "from God our Father and the Lord Jesus Christ" (Rom 1:7; 1 Cor 1:3; 2 Cor 1:2; Eph 1:2; Phil 1:2; Phlm 3). Variations are minimal (Gal 1:3; 2 Thess 1:2; cf. Col 1:2; 1 Tim 1:2; 2 Tim 1:2; Tit 1:4). Outside the Pauline tradition, other forms are used, such as "may grace and peace be multiplied to you" (1 Pet 1:2; 2 Pet 1:2; cf. Jude 2; *1 Clem.* pref.; Pol. *Phil.* pref.).

The author of Revelation adopts the Pauline form "grace to you and peace" (Rev 1:4b). His greeting also elaborates the identity of God and Jesus by employing traditional expressions such as "the one who is" and "Father" for God, and the one "who released us from our sins" for Jesus (1:4c–5). He adds distinctive elements, such as God's past existence and future coming, Jesus' role as faithful witness, and the mention of seven spirits, but then concludes with a traditional doxology (1:6). The pattern is similar to that in Gal 1:3–5, where Paul's salutation elaborates the identity of Jesus, who "gave himself for our sins," and concludes with a doxology. Revelation's expansion of the salutation includes distinctive content but fits formally within Pauline patterns.

Salutations on ancient letters were sometimes followed by thanksgiving and prayer. Early Christians often followed that practice (Rom 1:8–15; 1 Cor 1:4–9; Phil 1:3–11; 1 Thess 1:2–10) or included a blessing to God (2 Cor 1:3–11; Eph 1:3–14; 1 Pet 1:3–12). Writers could, however, move directly into the body of the letter, perhaps mentioning the circumstances that prompted them to write (2 John 4; *1 Clem.* 1:1; Ign. *Magn.* 1:1–3; Ign. *Trall.* 1:1–2). In Revelation the epistolary salutation (1:4–6) interlocks with the prophetic superscription that precedes it and the oracles that follow (1:1–3, 7–8), with the result that both forms are seen together. Then the body of the text picks up the personal tone of the salutation. The sender addresses the readers directly as "I, John, your brother" (1:9), and he explains that the occasion for his correspondence is that Christ commanded him to write. After that he begins the account of his vision (1:10–11).

Conclusions in ancient letters usually said "be well" (*errōso, errōsthe*) or "fare well" (*eutychei*), adding wishes for the recipient's good health (J. White, *Light*, 194–202). Early Christians occasionally used "be well" (Ign. *Eph.* 21:2). The Pauline letters concluded with "the grace of the Lord Jesus (Christ) be with you" (1 Cor 16:23; Rom 16:20; 1 Thess 5:28) or "with you all" (2 Cor 13:13; 2 Thess 3:18) or "with your spirit" (Gal 6:18; Phil 4:23; Phlm 25). Later forms omitted the word "peace" (Eph 6:24; Col 4:18; 1 Tim 6:21; 2 Tim 4:22; Tit 3:15). Variations appear in other texts (Heb 13:25; *1 Clem.* 65:2; *Barn.* 21:9), but not in 1 and 2 Peter, the Johannine Epistles, or Jude. Revelation's conclusion, "The grace of the Lord Jesus be with all," follows the Pauline pattern.

Other features of Revelation's conclusion resemble those in 1 Cor 16:21–23. Each includes a first-person "signature"—Paul in 1 Corinthians and Jesus in Revelation—which is followed by a curse and "our Lord, come!" or "come, Lord Jesus!" (Rev 22:16–21). Revelation also weaves in prophetic oracles from the glorified Jesus and the Spirit (22:7, 12–13, 16–20a), such that prophetic and epistolary forms appear together in the conclusion as well as the introduction. The blending of forms creates a complex fusion of voices. At points, John differentiates himself from the divine speakers, who are the authorities behind his text, and yet their words are conveyed prophetically through the words he sends to the readers (§43 COMMENT; Boring, "Voice").

The epistolary elements in Revelation have several functions. First, they frame the work as a whole in such a way that the entire text is to be read as a message to the seven churches (1:4). Second, they fit the contextual quality of the work. The book is not only "about" John's visions; it speaks "to" the situations of specific readers. The messages in Rev 2–3 deal with the issues of each church, using a literary form that combines prophetic elements with those of a "mixed letter," including approval, reproof, and admonition (see §3B). The visions in the remainder of the book are understood as relevant to the situations of seven congregations; thus, ancient and modern readers are to interpret the whole book contextually (Gradl, "Buch").

Third, the writer uses epistolary conventions from the Pauline tradition. His message may be distinctive, but introducing it with forms familiar to the readers encourages them to locate it within a wider Christian tradition (Karrer, *Johannesoffenbarung*, 73–83; Schüssler Fiorenza 39). Letters from Christian leaders were read aloud when their communities gathered, and John wants his text to receive that kind of hearing (1:3; Col 4:16; 1 Thess 5:27; Justin Martyr, *1 Apol.* 67). Through the interplay of the apocalyptic, prophetic, and epistolary genres, John brings a visionary message into the context of the readers.

B. Structure

Structure has to do with the way the parts of Revelation relate to the whole. Signals in the text encourage readers to make connections between visions, so that readers' understanding of the message is shaped by the interplay of its sections. Sometimes the writer makes clear that there are seven visions in a group, yet he also breaks literary sequences, includes unnumbered visions, and overlaps scenes. The resulting complexity has generated various proposals concerning the internal arrangement of the book (Aune 1:xc–cv; Bauckham, *Climax*, 1–37; Giesen 48–53; Müller 28–36; Schüssler Fiorenza, *Book*, 159–80).

Revelation can best be read as a series of six vision cycles, which are framed by an introduction and conclusion. The body of the text has two main parts with three cycles in each part (Yarbro Collins, *Combat*, 5–55; Murphy 47–56; Perkins, *Book*, 14–15). Detailed analysis is given in the introductions to the major sections of the commentary. The main parts are as follows:

Introduction (1:1–8)
   1. Christ and the Seven Assemblies (1:9–3:22)
   2. The Seven Seals (4:1–8:5)
   3. The Seven Trumpets (8:6–11:18)
   4. The Dragon, the Beasts, and the Faithful (11:19–15:4)
   5. The Seven Bowls and the Fall of Babylon (15:5–19:10)
   6. From the Beast's Demise to New Jerusalem (19:11–22:5)
Conclusion (22:6–21)

The introduction and conclusion create a literary frame around the book. In terms of form, both sections have epistolary elements, like those in early Christian letters, and include features of biblical or early Christian prophecy (INTRO IV.A.2). In terms of content, both sections tell readers that the message comes to John from God and Jesus through an angel, to show God's servants what must soon take place (Rev 1:1; 22:6, 16). Readers are told that this book is a prophecy (1:3; 22:7, 10, 18, 19), that those who keep it are blessed (1:3; 22:7), and that the time is near (1:3; 22:10). God and Christ are the Alpha and Omega (1:8; 22:13), and Christ is said to be coming (1:7; 22:7, 12, 20). John speaks in his own name, attesting what he heard and saw (1:1–2, 4; 22:8). He refers to his readers as those in the assemblies (1:4; 22:16) and includes responses of "yes" and "amen" (1:8; 22:20). Framing the book in this way means that its final form is designed to be read as a whole.

The body of the work consists of six cycles of visions. Four of these have numbered groups of seven scenes: seven messages, seals, trumpets, and bowls of wrath. Telling readers that there will be seven visions allows them to follow along and to know when the series is complete. The visions are "cycles" because they typically begin in the presence of God (5:1–13; 8:2, 6; 15:1, 5–8), then depict a series of threats, and conclude in the presence of God (8:1, 3–5; 11:15–18; 19:1–10). In a similar way, the seven messages to the churches begin in the presence of the risen Christ (1:9–20) and speak of the challenges facing the churches (2:1–3:22), and as the messages conclude, John comes into the presence of God (4:1–11).

There are internal arrangements within the sets of seven. The seal and trumpet visions are arranged in a pattern of 4 + 2 (interlude) +1. In each cycle, four short threatening visions are followed by two more visions, which are longer and more intense. Then the sequence is interrupted by an interlude before a final vision of heavenly worship. The bowl visions modify the sequence to 5 + 2 (interlude) + 1. There are five short visions and two longer ones, all of which are numbered. Then there is an interlude and a final unnumbered vision of heavenly worship. The interludes create a delay between the threatening visions and the final scene of celebration, and they also explain the reason for the delay. They reveal that time has been provided for people to be redeemed (7:1–17) and to bear witness (10:1–11:14; Bauckham, *Climax*, 12–13; Perry, *Rhetoric*, 209–41). The vision of Babylon's demise discloses the reason for God's judgment on the city (17:1–18:24).

Cycles of unnumbered visions follow the same pattern as the numbered series. They too move through scenes of conflict to celestial worship. The worship scenes mark the major transitions in the book. In one series the heavenly temple opens (11:19), then the faithful are threatened by the dragon and beasts, until the cycle ends with those who have conquered the beast singing praise by heaven's crystal sea (15:2–4). The other unnumbered series begins when heaven opens (19:11), so that the beasts, dragon, and death itself can be overcome, and the cycle ends with the faithful worshiping in God's presence in New Jerusalem (22:1–5).

Three devices link one major cycle to the next. First, connections can be made by juxtaposing images. The messages to the churches end with Jesus knocking on a closed door and promising the faithful a place on his throne (3:20–22), but then John sees an open door that leads to God's throne and the cycle of seven seals (4:1–2). Second, the last scene of one cycle can be interlocked with the first scene of the next cycle. The seals and visions of conflict with the beast culminate with scenes of heavenly worship (8:1, 3–5; 15:2–4), but before the worship is over, the author introduces groups of seven angels, who drive the action in the series that are about to begin (8:2, 6; 15:1, 5–8). Third, a concluding scene can foreshadow what is to come. The trumpet cycle ends by announcing the coming destruction of those who destroy the earth (11:15–18), and the next cycle introduces the dragon, who is the chief destroyer (12:1–6). Later, the celebration of Babylon's demise completes one cycle and anticipates the next by introducing the bride of the Lamb (19:7–8), who will appear as New Jerusalem in the next section (21:1–2). By connecting the cycles various ways, the writer again shows that the book is to be read as a whole.

Large forward-moving plotlines span multiple vision cycles. The three cycles in the first half of Revelation are dominated by scrolls (1:9–11:18). Initially, John is told to write what he sees in "a scroll [*biblion*] and send it to the seven assemblies" (1:11). Next, God gives a scroll (*biblion*) to the Lamb, who opens its seals. The two lines come together when an angel tells John not to write what the seven thunders say but to take the open scroll (*biblaridion, biblion*) from the angel so that John can consume it and reveal its contents (10:2, 8–11). The scroll summarizes the story of God's people bearing witness, being slain by the beast, and being raised to life by God (11:1–13). That story will be played out in the remainder of the book.

Words of the elders define the direction of the plot at the midpoint of Revelation. They reveal that the conflict between the faithful and the beast is part of a cosmic story in which the Creator and the Lamb destroy the destroyers of the earth (11:18). The writer successively introduces the destroyers as Satan, the beast and false prophet, and Babylon the whore and then traces their downfalls in reverse order:

Satan is thrown from heaven to earth (12:1–17).
    Beast and false prophet conquer (13:1–18).
        Whore rides on the beast (17:1–12).
        Whore destroyed by the beast (17:13–18).
    Beast and false prophet are conquered (19:11–21).
Satan is thrown from earth into the abyss and lake of fire (20:1–3, 7–10).

This broad movement of scenes integrates the book's last three vision cycles into the larger story of God's victory.

Interpreters of Revelation often focus on either its forward-moving aspects or its repetitive qualities. Some have construed the book as a linear outline of the church's history from the first-century congregations in Rev 2–3 to the new creation in Rev 21–22 (e.g., Nicholas of Lyra; Luther; Edwards). Dispensationalist interpreters argue that the visions from Rev 4–20 predict the events that will happen sequentially at the end of the present age (Seiss; LaHaye; Thomas). Some historical critics also assume that Revelation outlines events that the author expected to occur sequentially in the future. Where scenes disrupt the flow, they attribute the problem to faulty editing (Charles 1:xxii–xxiii, lvi–lxi; 2:144) or an uneven fusion of sources (Aune 1:xciii).

Others consider the repetitive elements integral to the book. In antiquity, Victorinus assumed that Revelation depicted events that would bring God's final victory, yet he noted that the plague scenes repeated the same message of warning several times (*In Apoc.* 8.2). Modern literary studies have shown how five of the six vision cycles move from threat to vindication, setting a pattern for the whole (Yarbro Collins, *Combat*, 5–55; Murphy 47–56). The repetition includes intensification, as plagues initially strike a fourth of the earth (6:8), then a third of it (8:7–9:19), and finally engulf the whole world (16:1–21; §18D).

The combination of elements can best be pictured as a forward-moving spiral, which repeatedly leads readers through scenes of threat and back to the presence of God, even as the broad storyline moves forward to the new creation. Vision cycles both overlap and progress, with individual sections tracing the movement from conflict to victory that shapes the book as a whole.

C. Narrative Aspects

Revelation presents readers with a narrative world inhabited by a surreal cast of characters, including monsters with seven heads, a slaughtered Lamb who lives, and grotesque beings from the nether regions. Action moves from earth to heaven and back again, as conflict spans the cosmos. Its plotline takes readers from the cities of Asia Minor through the demise of Babylon to the descent of New Jerusalem. Where historical criticism asks how the visions relate to situations in the Roman world, narrative criticism focuses on how the dimensions of the story relate to each other (Resseguie, *Revelation Unsealed*, 1–31; Barr, *Tales*). Many aspects are considered in the commentary that follows; here, we consider some select features.

I. NARRATION

John narrates in the first person and is both a participant in and an observer of the story. The style makes the action vivid and immediate. John pictures himself collapsing in fear when the risen Christ appears to him (1:12–20), then tells of entering God's heavenly throne hall and traveling to a desert to see the whore (4:1; 17:1). At a pivotal point he recalls eating a scroll and being told to prophesy (10:1–11). But John often puts himself in the background in order to focus attention on others. In the messages to the churches he is told to "write," while Christ speaks in the first person. As plagues threaten the world and the beast creates an empire, John's presence is known only by his words—"then I saw" and "then I heard."

John's perspective extends far beyond that of his readers. On his journey in the Spirit he can see God's heavenly throne hall and the door of the great abyss (4:1; 9:1). When he turns to an earthly location such as the Euphrates, he sees what an ordinary traveler would not see: angels and demonic cavalry (9:13–19). John's vantage point is fluid and sometimes indeterminate. He seems to watch from heaven as plagues fall onto the earth (8:1–9:21), but then he is on earth, writing, as an angel descends to him (10:1–11). He sees a woman clothed with the sun flee from heaven to earth, but whether he watches from heaven, earth, or some other location is not clear (12:1–17). John can look into the future, when Satan is bound and the dead rise, and he tours New Jerusalem, the city of the age to come (20:1–6; 21:9–10). John's expansive perspective engages readers who want to see what he sees.

At the same time, his perspective is not omniscient. A heavenly elder must direct John's attention to the messianic figure who can open God's scroll and explain the identity of the great multitude (5:4–5; 7:13–14). John has to be told not to write down the words of the seven thunders, and he needs angelic help to understand the significance of the beast (10:4; 17:6–7). Such limitations may make it easier for readers to identify with John as narrator, because their perspective is also limited. They share his process of discovery (D. Lee, *Narrative*, 152–61).

2. CHARACTER PORTRAYAL

Characters are portrayed by what they say and do, by what others say about them, and by the settings in which they appear. Major characters are developed in pairs: Each positive figure has a negative counterpart. Parody is integral to the pictures John creates. In parody a writer takes certain traits and distorts them in order to make a figure seem outlandish. John's assumption is that evil is a perversion of good, so his negative characters exhibit some of the traits of the positive characters, but in a distorted form. The parodies warn readers not to be deceived by evil's masquerade (Maier, *Apocalypse*, 164–70).

God is the Creator, who brought the world into being and whose purposes culminate in new creation (4:11; 10:6; 14:7; 21:1–6). As the Creator of all things, God is their rightful ruler. God is almighty (4:8), yet other powers challenge his reign. As the Creator of the world, God must defeat its destroyers (11:18). As the one who is just and true, he must overcome injustice and falsehood (6:10; 19:2). God is both judge and bringer of salvation (7:10; 20:11–12). He is and was and is to come, which is a sign of true deity (1:4). At the beginning and end of the book, God identifies himself as the Alpha and Omega (1:8; 21:6). He is before all things as their Maker and in the end makes all things new (21:5).

God's entourage reflects his character. His attendants are arranged in concentric circles that show the harmony of creation. Around the throne are four living creatures who look like a lion, an ox, a human being, and an eagle. They are heavenly representatives of the created order and honor God as Creator (4:7–8). Next are the twenty-four elders, who represent the community of faith. They recognize God's lordship by casting their laurel wreaths before his throne and leading others in worship (4:10–11). Beyond them are the angels who worship God and carry out his bidding, whether sending plagues on God's foes, holding back destruction, or disclosing the mysteries of God's designs (5:11; 7:1–3; 15:5–16:21; 17:7). In front of the throne are seven angelic spirits, who are the "eyes" God sends throughout the earth (4:5; 5:6).

Satan is God's principal opponent. God is the earth's Creator, and Satan is its chief destroyer (11:18; 12:9). He may be the angel of the abyss, whose name means "destroyer" (9:11). Satan is a red serpentine dragon, whose multiple heads and horns are terrifying. His seven diadems show his intent to rule the world (12:3). Satan tries to destroy a mother and child and relentlessly deceives the nations (12:4, 13–17; 20:7–8). Yet his activity shows weakness rather than strength, for he rages about the earth because he has been banished from heaven and his time is running out (12:7–12). As God's rival, Satan establishes a throne on earth and manifests his wrath by slaying the faithful (2:13; 12:17; 13:2). Where God works through truth, Satan operates through falsehood (12:9). Although God rejects Satan's accusations in heaven, Satan's agents condemn the faithful on earth (2:10; 12:10). Satan is incorrigible. Even after a thousand years of confinement, he persists in opposing God and is sent to the lake of fire (20:1–10).

Satan's entourage includes hideous monsters that mock the created order. Where the four beings around God's throne reflect the harmony of creation, the demonic locusts from the abyss have a ghastly pastiche of human and animal traits and raise a deafening, warlike sound. They thrive on smoke and torment people (9:1–11). Where God's angels celebrate the lordship of God and the Lamb, Satan's angels oppose it (12:7–9). While God's spirits keep watch over the world, Satan and his agents send deceptive spirits into it, luring its leaders into a disastrous revolt against the Almighty (16:13–14).

God's power is exercised through Jesus the Lamb, who was slaughtered and yet lives. From the vision of the heavenly throne room until the final chapter,

Jesus is principally identified as "the Lamb" (5:6; 22:3). He is God's Son and fulfills God's promise to send a lionlike Messiah. As the King of kings, he shares God's throne (2:18; 3:21; 5:5; 19:16), yet as the Lamb, he has exercised authority through sacrifice. The Lamb "conquered" by persevering faithfully through suffering, and his death redeems people of every tribe, nation, and language (5:9–10; 7:9–14). He is also a warrior, who will end oppression by his word of truth (19:15). The risen Jesus shares God's titles Alpha and Omega, first and last, beginning and end (22:13). He is included in true worship of God, for he is the one in whom God's purposes are accomplished (Bauckham, *Theology*, 54–65).

By way of contrast, Satan's power is exercised through the beast, which is the counterpart to the Lamb. With seven heads and ten horns, the beast resembles the satanic dragon whom it serves (13:1). Its appearance blends traits of predatory animals, and it shares Satan's throne (13:2). Like the Lamb, the beast was slaughtered and yet lives (13:3, 12, 14), but where the Lamb conquered by enduring death, the beast conquers by inflicting death on others. Where the Lamb delivers people of every tribe and nation, the beast oppresses them (13:7). People are to worship God and the Lamb for creating and redeeming them, but they are also deceived and coerced into the demonic cult of the beast (13:4, 11–18). Where the Lamb is faithful, the beast proves faithless by destroying its own ally, the whore (17:16). The beast, which "was and is not, and is about to come up from the abyss" (17:8), tries to mimic the claims of God, "who is and who was and who is to come" (1:4), but the beast ultimately goes to destruction (17:8; 19:20).

God and Satan each have their prophets. The true prophets are the two witnesses who receive authority from the Lord of all the earth. Their words are like fire from their mouths, and they can bring plagues on the earth, yet their story is like that of Jesus the Lamb, for they are slaughtered and then vindicated through resurrection. These prophets are a collective image for all faithful witnesses to God (11:3–13). Their counterpart is the false prophet, who masquerades as a lamb but speaks with the dragonlike voice of Satan. He calls fire from heaven in order to awe people into worshiping the seven-headed beast that rules the world. Where true prophets suffer death, the false prophet inflicts death on all who resist him. But in the end his deception is exposed, for he is defeated and relegated to the lake of fire (13:11–18; 16:13; 19:20).

The people of God are pictured as a bride. They are betrothed "maidens," who follow the Lamb wherever he goes (NOTE on 14:4). As they wait for the wedding day, when they will be taken to the Lamb's home, they prepare a pure bright garment of righteous deeds to wear (19:7–9). When the bride appears, she is New Jerusalem, the city where the followers or "wife" of the Lamb have a permanent place (21:9). The city has the splendor of a bride adorned for her husband, radiant with gold, jewels, and pearls (21:2, 10–11). The blending of bridal and city imagery shows that believers are now bound to Christ in faith and can anticipate a place with him in the city that is to come.

The opposite of the bride is the beast's city, portrayed as Babylon the whore. She personifies the current world order, which is driven by the desire for pleasure and profit. She is clothed in opulent purple and scarlet and draped with gold and jewels from her illicit trade (17:4). With her, life is like a bawdy banquet, where people are intoxicated with wealth and turn a blind eye to arrogance and brutality (17:2–3, 6; 18:3). Naming this city "Babylon" identifies it with the city that in Jewish tradition was remembered for the violent conquest of Jerusalem. The whore rules like a queen and consumes all that the world can provide (18:7, 11–13), but in the end she is consumed by the beast (17:16). Having destroyed others, she suffers destruction herself (18:2, 24).

These contrasting characters shape the readers' commitments by attracting them to God and his allies and alienating them from God's opponents and what they represent. The messages in Rev 2–3 depict a social context in which the activity of evil was apparent to some but not all readers. By portraying opposing forces in vivid terms, the writer seeks to deepen the readers' commitment to God and the Lamb in a society in which other forces vie for their loyalty.

3. SPATIAL AND TEMPORAL SETTINGS

Revelation envisions the universe as the creation of God, which has been invaded by hostile forces. Spatially, the writer pictures three main regions: heaven, earth, and the regions under the earth (5:3). God created and has rightful authority over all. Heaven is where God's throne is located, set within a space pictured as a temple (7:15; 11:19; 15:5). In front of the throne is an altar, where the souls of the martyrs are kept and angels offer prayers (6:9; 8:3). Below it is a sea of glass mixed with fire (4:6; 15:2).

The earth includes land, sea, and spaces underground, along with the plants and creatures that live there (5:13; 8:7, 9). Although some commentators assume that the sea is evil, it is not, because God created it (10:6; 14:7). Creatures on the land, in the sea, and underground rightly honor the Creator (5:13), yet Satan uses beasts from sea and land to further his cause (12:12; 13:1, 11). The opening chapters recognize that readers live in earthly cities in Roman Asia (1:9–3:20), but later visions depict the earth dominated by "the great city" of Babylon, whose commercial empire extends over land and sea (17:1–6; 18:11–19; cf. 11:8). Although most inhabitants of the earth engage in false worship, the Christian community is the earthly counterpart to the heavenly sanctuary. It is pictured as a temple with an altar, where true worship takes place

(11:1–2). The powers of heaven above can send plagues down onto the earth below (8:6–9:20), but the agents of evil can only show animosity toward heaven; they cannot invade it (13:6; 19:11, 19).

The underworld is an ominous region beyond the subterranean spaces where ordinary creatures live (5:13). It has several dimensions: First, Hades is where the dead are kept until the final resurrection (1:18; 20:13). Christ has the key to Hades (1:18), and in the end God compels Hades to give up the dead, before relegating Hades itself to the lake of fire (20:13–14). Second, the abyss is the demonic realm from which the satanic beast and demonic locusts come (9:1–10; 11:7; 17:8). It is different from the realm of the dead. Although the king of the abyss is an angel called "the destroyer," who is probably Satan (NOTE on 9:11), the abyss is ultimately under divine control, and God's angels use keys to open and close it (9:1; 20:1–3). Third, the lake of fire is the realm of second death, the place of torment (19:20; 20:10, 14–15; 21:8). Satan and the beast are sent to the lake of fire *after* emerging from the abyss (11:7; 17:8; 20:7, 10), and God's human opponents are sent there after being released from Hades (20:13, 15). In the end, Death and Hades itself end up on the fiery lake (20:14), as does the false prophet (19:20). This terrifying place is the opposite of the fiery sea of glass above, where the faithful celebrate in God's presence (15:2).

The story culminates with the transformation of the entire universe. The first heaven and earth pass away, and the sea no longer exists (21:1). New Jerusalem comes down, but spatial relationships no longer function as before (21:2, 10). Revelation does not end with the present heaven descending to earth. Rather, God makes "all things new" (21:5), "a new heaven and a new earth" in which evil has no place (21:1). Central to the new creation is New Jerusalem, which bears the name of a city in this world but is completely transformed. It is a space illumined by God's glory, a city with gates always open, whose only "temple" is the presence of God and the Lamb (21:9–22:5).

Time has multiple dimensions in Revelation. John's visionary experience occurs on the Lord's Day, when Christians gathered for worship (1:9). Although John is presumably alone when the visions come, he locates the experience in "worship time" and expected his message to be read aloud when readers met together (1:3). Worship time links a book interspersed with scenes of worship in heaven to the situation of worshipers on earth, including both the writer and readers (4:1–5:13; 7:9–17; 15:2–4; 19:1–10; Friesen, *Imperial*, 157–61).

Next is the flow of time within the visionary world. The main period begins when Satan is thrown down after the Messiah's birth and exaltation, and it concludes when Christ returns and Satan is bound (12:1–17; 19:11–20:3). Revelation says that this period of conflict with evil is "short" (12:12) and lasts for three and a half years, which equals forty-two months (13:5), 1,260 days (12:6), and "a time and times and half a time" (12:14). But in the visionary world this "short" period extends from Christ's first coming until his final return. Visionary time does not correspond to chronological time in the readers' world. Revelation was written decades after the death of Jesus, yet the entire period of the church's conflict with evil fits within the three and a half years of visionary time (11:2–3). The writer refers to it as three and a half years because that was a designation for the time of distress at the end of the age (Note on 11:2).

The visionary counterpart to the "short" time in which Jesus' followers are oppressed is the thousand years in which they reign with Christ (20:4–6). At present, Satan threatens the faithful with prison and death, but in the thousand years conditions are reversed, for the faithful are raised to life and Satan is imprisoned (13:8–10; 20:1–3). During the thousand years two plotlines overlap. The downward movement of evil's demise continues from previous chapters, as the devil is bound, released, and permanently banished to the lake of fire (20:1–3, 7–10). The upward movement of vindication shows the saints being raised for the thousand years and then continuing to live and reign in the new creation that follows (20:4–6; 22:3–5). For the redeemed, the thousand years is the beginning of endless life in New Jerusalem (21:1–22:5).

4. PLOT

The plot of a narrative is the sequence of events that moves the story from beginning to end. It relates *what* happens and discloses *why* it happens, so that readers can see the reasons behind the action. Plots often revolve around conflict, and Revelation is no exception. The section on "Structure" (INTRO IV.B) traced "what" occurs in the great conflict between the Creator and destroyers of the earth. Here we look more closely at the "why" questions that inform the plot (Barr, *Tales*, 10–16; Resseguie 44–47).

The first three chapters are the prelude. John says that he and his intended readers share in "the kingdom" of God. The problem is that the heirs of the kingdom now suffer "affliction" and must exhibit "endurance" (1:9). This situation implicitly raises issues of divine justice and why affliction persists despite the reign of God. The messages to the churches heighten the incongruity, because the readers who are most faithful suffer most, while those who are complacent thrive (2:1–3:22). Christ exhorts the readers to persevere, promising that reward will come in the end. Yet given the challenges of the present, readers might wonder why they should think change will come in the future.

The main plot brings the issue of divine justice into focus when John makes a visionary journey to heaven, where he sees God holding a sealed scroll. John is distraught when no one is found worthy to open the scroll. Although he wants to know God's purposes, they remain hidden. When the Lamb proves worthy to open the seals, the martyrs under the altar voice the question of divine justice that will drive the action: How long will God delay in bringing justice against a world that has shed the blood of the faithful (6:10)? No explanation is given—only a white robe and the directive to wait for a short "time" (*chronos*) until others have finished bearing witness (6:11).

Divine justice appears to come closer as the cosmos shakes and people are terrified, but then the movement toward judgment is interrupted so that during the delay people can be sealed for God (6:17–7:17). The next cycle begins with prayers rising up from the altar, but when an angel hurls fire to the earth, bringing horrific plagues, the ungodly refuse to repent (8:1–9:21). The plague visions reveal that if justice is reduced to wrath and retribution, nothing changes. So an angel halts the movement toward judgment, affirms that the time (*chronos*) of waiting will end (10:6), and gives God's scroll to John. The scroll enables John to disclose that God's purposes involve creating a time of delay, in which witness can be given to an unrepentant humanity (10:8–11:13). The point is that God has refrained from bringing final justice in order that the Christian community—represented by the two figures in 11:3–14—can bear prophetic witness to the world.

The second half of the book shows the outworking of God's purposes. Justice may seem slow, but it will come. Satan rages about the earth because he was expelled from heaven after Christ's exaltation; the intensity of the devil's activity manifests desperation, not strength (12:1–17). Satan enlists the help of a beast and his associate in his attempt to dominate the world (13:1–18), but divine pressure increases as those who shed the blood of the saints are given blood to drink (16:5–7). Yet even here the ungodly remain alive so that repentance remains a possibility.

Judgment finally falls on those who are unwavering in their ruinous attempt to dominate the world. The destroyers of the earth end up destroying each other as the beast turns against the whore (17:16). When evil destroys evil in this way, the martyrs' prayers for justice are answered (19:2). The outworking of divine justice continues as the beast and false prophet, who operate through deception, are overcome by Christ, whose weapon is the word and whose character is truth (19:11–21). Deliverance for those who have suffered comes as they are raised to life with Christ (20:4–6). The plot is fully resolved as Satan, death, and all the forces that challenge God's reign are vanquished (20:7–15). When the work of the Creator culminates in new creation, God can say "all is done," and the redeemed share in the reign of God and the Lamb in a world where affliction has no place (21:6; 22:1–5).

D. Intertextuality

Revelation communicates with readers by recasting familiar language and imagery. John assumed that his readers would be acquainted with biblical narratives and prophetic texts, as well as with stories from their Greco-Roman cultural context. As Revelation was read aloud, people would have heard expressions and themes that they knew from other settings. Some of the familiar connotations would be reaffirmed, while other aspects would be transformed in the new literary context. The role of Scripture and Greco-Roman tradition is considered throughout the commentary, but we note some main features here.

1. SCRIPTURE

Revelation employs biblical language and imagery in every chapter, but the author never quotes texts exactly. In some cases he paraphrases a biblical passage rather closely (e.g., Hos 10:8/Rev 6:16; Isa 25:8/Rev 7:17), but often the connections are less direct. Some studies note nearly three hundred possible allusions to Scripture in Revelation, yet a precise number is difficult to determine because it is not always clear what qualifies as an allusion. Moreover, a single passage in Revelation may combine elements from several biblical texts, as in the proclamation of God as holy and almighty (Rev 4:8/Isa 6:3; Amos 3:13), or may recall expressions that appear in similar forms in multiple passages of Scripture, such as the promise of God dwelling among people in a covenant relationship (NOTES on Rev 21:3–4). The clearest and most frequent allusions are to the books of Isaiah, Ezekiel, Daniel, and Psalms, but the writer also draws on all the books in the Pentateuch, along with Samuel, Kings, Job, Proverbs, Jeremiah, Hosea, Joel, Amos, Micah, Nahum, Zephaniah, and Zechariah. Some scholars note possible allusions to passages in Judges, Esther, Song of Solomon, Ecclesiastes, Habakkuk, and Malachi, though these are less apparent (Swete, cxl–cliii; Charles 1:lxviii–lxxxii; Beale, *John's*; Fekkes, *Isaiah*; Jauhiainen, *Use*; Kowalski, *Rezeption*; Mathewson, *New*; Moyise, *Old*; Sänger, ed., *Ezechielbuch*; Bandy, "Layers," 481–88).

John may have drawn from both Hebrew and Greek forms of OT books. There are points at which he clearly makes use of Greek translations of Scripture. His paraphrase of Ps 2:9 follows the LXX in saying that God's anointed will rule, or "shepherd," the nations with an iron rod. The Hebrew form of the psalm is quite different, reading "break" (NOTE on Rev 2:27). The description of a figure "coming with" the clouds in Rev 1:7 follows a Greek translation of Dan 7:13 that is traditionally associated with the second-century scholar Theodotian, although it circulated in an earlier form during the first century.

Revelation also links the coming of the figure in Dan 7:13 to the tribes grieving over the one who was pierced from Zech 12:10 and 12. Since the same texts are linked in Matt 24:30, the combination could show that John's appropriation of biblical language was shaped in part by tradition (NOTE on Rev 1:7).

At the same time, there is also evidence that John drew directly from Hebrew texts of Scripture. He notes that the name "Harmagedon" is derived from Hebrew. Since the context deals with battle on the coming day of God Almighty, the name probably recalls the reference to Megiddo in Zech 12:11, which deals with the coming Day of the Lord. That is the only place where the Hebrew Bible spells the name as "Megiddon," which is similar to John's spelling (NOTE on Rev 16:16). Yet the extent to which John relied directly on Hebrew texts of Scripture is unclear. For example, in 3:7 he says that Christ has "the key of David," an image from Isa 22:22. The allusion is not from the LXX, which refers to the "glory" of David, but the "key" is mentioned in both the Hebrew text and the Greek translation associated with Theodotian, making it difficult to know which version John used.

Some studies suggest that overall, Revelation's biblical allusions are drawn from the LXX (Karrer, "Von der Apokalypse," 99–101; Tilly, "Textsicherung"), and fragments of the *kaige* Greek translation from Qumran show that other Greek versions were also available in the first century (Tov, *Textual*, 142–43). But other scholars do note points at which allusions seem to reflect aspects of the Hebrew text and argue that both Greek and Hebrew forms should be considered when exploring John's use of Scripture (Labahn, "Septuaginta"; Labahn, "Macht"). Given John's penchant for paraphrase and the likelihood that he often worked from memory rather than from a written text, it is probably not possible to determine which form of the biblical text shaped his language at many points.

By placing older biblical language in a new literary context, Revelation creates new possibilities of meaning. A good example is saying that "the Lion of the tribe of Judah, the Root of David, has conquered" (Rev 5:5). The Lion of Judah is most closely linked to Gen 49:9–10, where the tribe of Judah is pictured as a lion and identified with kingship. That primary connection calls to mind other references to lions, which suggest power and nobility. The title "Root of David" adds another layer by recalling Isa 11:1 and 10, which speak of a righteous and victorious king from David's line. Then Revelation juxtaposes the regal imagery with the image of a slaughtered Lamb, which recalls the Passover sacrifice, as well as texts that refer to the vulnerability of sacrificial lambs and perhaps to the image of God's servant, who was like a lamb led to the slaughter (NOTE on Rev 5:6). To make sense of the imagery, readers must see that in Jesus, kingship is redefined in terms of sacrifice, and sacrifice is redefined in terms of victory.

Theologically, the interplay of older texts and a new literary context gives a sense of continuity along with change in the activity of God. John's vision of the heavenly throne room in Rev 4–5 leads to a new moment of revelation, as the Lamb takes the scroll in order to open its seals. Yet God's presence and entourage are pictured in terms reminiscent of Ezek 1 and Isa 6, so the God of the biblical prophets continues to be the focus in Revelation. Later, John is given a renewed commission to prophesy, but the angel who addresses him is much like the one who spoke with Daniel, and John is also given a scroll to eat, like the prophet Ezekiel (Rev 10:1–10; Dan 12:5–9; Ezek 2:8–3:3). The actions are new, but older patterns persist.

Biblical allusions are sometimes collected in clusters in order to convey the magnitude of divine judgment and blessing. In line after line of Rev 18, the announcement of Babylon's demise recalls oracles of judgment against Babylon, Tyre, and Nineveh, which appear in various biblical books (Isa 13; 21; 23–24; 47; Jer 50–51; Ezek 26–27; Nah 3). Those hearing the text read aloud probably would not be able to identify specific sources for the allusions, but they would have sensed that the cumulative judgment of the prophets was falling on imperial society. Since the ruling power of the readers' time exhibits traits of the cities of former times, it comes under the same prophetic condemnation. By way of contrast, the visions of the redeemed multitudes and the new creation draw language from many passages in Isaiah and Ezekiel in order to offer an expansive vision of hope for deliverance from hunger, thirst, suffering, and death. One biblical passage is recalled after another, and this cluster of allusions gives the impression that life in God's presence includes all that the prophets have said and more (NOTES on Rev 7:15–17; 21:7).

When using prophetic texts, Revelation does not move directly from promise to fulfillment but includes a transformative aspect. For example, the final chapters of Ezekiel provide a template for the end of Revelation. In Ezek 37–48 the prophet envisions the dead being given new life, God dwelling with his people, the defeat of Gog, the birds feasting on the slain, and a tour of Jerusalem with its twelve gates and the river flowing from the temple to water the trees. Revelation includes these elements while changing the order, so that the birds feast on the slain in Rev 19:17–21, Gog and Magog are defeated in 20:7–10, and the dead are raised in between (20:4–6). New Jerusalem has twelve gates and a river, but the city is a thousand times larger than the one in Ezekiel. The many trees become the single tree of life, and the city's temple is no longer a structure but the unmediated presence of God and the Lamb (21:1–22:5). The effect is to show that the prophetic word will be kept, while recognizing divine freedom in *how* it will be kept, since New Jerusalem goes beyond anything Ezekiel envisioned.

2. GRECO-ROMAN TRADITION

Stories from Greco-Roman mythology and legend contribute to Revelation's intertextual quality. At points, the primary template for a passage is biblical, with extrabiblical motifs contributing secondary allusions. For example, in Rev 15–16 seven angels pour bowls of wrath on the earth, bringing plagues of sores, blood, darkness, and hail, like those that preceded the exodus (Exod 7–12). Yet those same plagues were considered signs of divine wrath in the Greco-Roman world, and the proper response was to make amends with the gods. Readers who recognized this cultural subtext would find it remarkable that people in John's vision refuse to turn to God, since one would expect even pagans to do so (see §33 COMMENT).

In other passages the biblical and extrabiblical elements are both prominent. The beast in Rev 13 and 17 is patterned in part on the four beasts that rise from the sea in Dan 7, as well as Leviathan, the sea monster doomed to be destroyed at the end of the age (Isa 27:1). But a major subtext comes from stories about Nero, the persecutor of the church. Nero had died but was reputed to be alive and hiding among the Parthians so that he could return and take control of Rome. By blending biblical imagery with the Nero legends, John portrays the destructive potential of the empire, which at present threatens the followers of Jesus but ultimately threatens society itself (NOTE on Rev 13:3).

Finally, the vision of the woman and the dragon in Rev 12 follows a plot drawn primarily from extrabiblical stories about Python and Leto, who was the mother of Artemis and Apollo, along with similar tales. Within this mythic framework, biblical elements play a supporting role. These include equating the serpent with Satan and having the woman flee to the desert. Some interpreters find it surprising that a writer who opposed Greco-Roman religious practice could use a mythic plot for an episode in his book, but the literary context reshapes the meaning of the traditional story to serve the author's distinctive ends. The story of defeating the dragon no longer celebrates the classical tradition, which was claimed by imperial Rome, but portrays the struggle of Jesus and his followers against the destructive forces that worked through the imperial world's own political structures (see §25C)

E. Hymns and Beatitudes

Hymns and beatitudes appear throughout Revelation. These statements of praise and blessing are positive in tone, yet they function in complex ways by both encouraging and challenging readers. As these passages repeat certain themes, they shape the readers' perspectives on the actions of God and the life of faith.

I. HYMNS

Scenes of heavenly worship occur at major transition points in Revelation. In them, groups of worshipers offer hymns of praise to God and the Lamb, usually in an antiphonal style. One heavenly being or group initiates the praise, and others take it up or add "Amen." Often, the response is given in the immediate context (4:8–11; 5:9–14; 7:9–12; 11:15–18; 19:1–4, 5–8) and occasionally in the section that follows (15:3–4; 16:5–7). Praise is sometimes called "song" (*ōdē*), and the worshipers hold harps (5:9; 15:3; cf. 14:3). In other contexts the musical element is not stressed, but the praises are similar. The writer refers to praise of God and the Lamb as "worship" (*proskynein*) (4:10; 5:14; 7:11; 19:4); as an offering of glory, honor, and thanks (4:9; 7:12; 11:17); and as an action linked to prayer (5:8–9).

The lyrics in the worship scenes can be called "hymns" because they praise God and the Christ who shares God's throne by extolling their traits and actions. God and Christ may be addressed in the second person "you" (5:9; 15:3–4; 16:5–7) or in the third person (7:10–11; 19:1–8). Easy movement from the second to third person forms can occur in the same context (4:8–11; 5:9–13; 11:15–18). The conjunction "for" (*hoti*), meaning "because," is often used when identifying the reason for praise: God is worthy "for" he created all things and judges justly (4:11; 19:2); the Lamb is worthy "for" he was slaughtered and purchased people for God (5:9; cf. 11:17; 15:4; 16:5–7; 19:7). Because a heavenly voice uses similar language in order to declare the reign of God and Christ after Satan's expulsion from heaven, that section (12:10–12) is often included among the hymns, even though the context is not explicitly one of worship (Jörns, *Das hymnische*, 17–21).

Hymns of praise to God have an important place in Scripture (e.g., Pss 96; 98; 145; 1 Chr 16:8–36), and new hymns continued to be composed within Jewish communities (1QHᵃ; Philo, *Contempl.* 80). Much of Revelation's hymnic language comes from Israel's tradition. Good examples are the threefold repetition of "holy" (Rev 4:8; Isa 6:3), the Hebrew expressions "Amen" and "Hallelujah" (Rev 7:12; 19:1–6; 1 Chr 16:36; Pss 106:1; 150:1), and references to the Lord God Almighty (1 Chr 17:24 LXX; Rev 4:8; 11:17; 16:7; 19:6). Calling the redeemed "a kingdom and priests" recalls what was said of Israel (Rev 5:10; Exod 19:6). Ascribing power, glory, wisdom, and strength to God was done in Israel's worship (NOTE on Rev 5:12) and could be included in prayer (1 Chr 29:11–13; *1 En.* 9:4–5; 84:2–3).

Formally, some hymns adopt patterns of biblical poetry. For instance, the hymn celebrating victory over the beast uses parallelism. Each of the first two lines offers praise and identifies God with a title: "Great and awe-inspiring are your works, Lord God Almighty. / Just and true are your ways, King of the nations" (Rev 15:3). The last two lines envision all people worshiping God and state the reason: "Who will not fear you, Lord, and glorify your name, for you alone are holy. / All nations will come and worship before you, for your acts of justice have been revealed" (15:4). Other hymns use a three-part pattern that is typical in the psalms: a call to praise, a statement of praise, and the reason for praise (Westermann, *Psalms*, 47–52). Hymns using this pattern celebrate Babylon's demise (18:20; 19:1–4) and anticipate the marriage of the Lamb (19:5–8).

Greco-Roman worship traditions also included hymns to the gods, and the literary settings in Revelation suggest comparisons. Worshipers wear white robes and may hold palm branches, as people did at Greco-Roman festivals (4:4; 7:9; §16 COMMENT). The elders lay wreaths before God as people did when honoring a Hellenistic or Roman ruler (NOTE on 4:10). The singers in Revelation are like the choruses (*hymnodes*) that praised traditional deities such as Artemis of Ephesus, Zeus, and Dionysus or sang hymns to Augustus at his sanctuary at Pergamum (Friesen, *Imperial*, 104–13; MacMullen, *Paganism*, 15–18). There are also analogies in the way worship scenes include acclamations given by a vast company (5:11–13; 7:10; 19:1–3, 6–8), since publicly shouting praises to the ruler for salvation and lauding his majesty was a feature of imperial life. Revelation moves from hymns to acclamations without making a clear distinction between forms (Aune, *Apocalypticism*, 109–16; Vollenweider, "Hymnus," 227). For the writer, the critical question is whether the praises are being given to the Creator and the Lamb or to other figures that would take God's place.

Formally, the more poetic Greek hymns first called upon the god, then extolled the deity's traits and deeds, and concluded with a petition. Related types included the prose hymns, which orators used to praise the gods (Quintilian, *Inst.* 3.7.6–9; Vollenweider, "Hymnus," 208–21). Revelation's hymns lack the invocation of God and concluding petition, but they share themes that Greco-Roman sources ascribe to deities, such as continual existence, creative power, justice, and rule over all things (Rev 4:11; 7:12; 15:4; Aelius Aristides, *Orations* 43.7, 20, 31). The emperor was sometimes included in hymns to traditional gods (Augustus, *Res* 10; Dio Cassius, *Rom. Hist.* 51.20.1), and hymns were composed to the emperor himself. Revelation lists the glory, honor, power, wisdom, and might of God and the Lamb, who are "worthy" (4:11; 5:9, 12–13; 7:10). Orators and poets ascribed similar traits to the emperor, declaring him "worthy" of power (Martial, *Epigr.* 10.34.5; Josephus, *J.W.* 7.71; Aune 1:316–17). The literary context of Revelation reshapes these Greco-Roman conventions to show that using such forms of praise for the empire's gods and rulers is actually a perversion of the acclaim that is rightly given to God and the Lamb.

Distinctly Christian elements in Revelation's hymns include praises to the slaughtered Lamb (Rev 5:9–12), whose blood brings victory over evil (12:11). Biblical language about the Lord's "Anointed" is used for Jesus (11:15–18; cf. Ps 2:2), the Lamb is included in praise given to God (Rev 5:13; 7:10), and a hymn to God is called "the song of the Lamb" (15:3). Early Christians included psalms, hymns, and spiritual songs in their worship (1 Cor 14:26; Eph 5:19; Col 3:16). They composed new songs, some of which were sung by alternating voices (Pliny the Younger, *Ep.* 10.96.7; Yarbro Collins, "Psalms," 361–63). In form, these texts differ from poetic passages about Christ in other NT writings, which are often called hymns but are creedal in nature (John 1:1–18; Phil 2:6–11; Col 1:15–20; 1 Tim 3:16). At the same time, they reflect patterns of praising God and Christ in Christian worship.

Distinctive themes appear throughout Revelation's hymns, such as the defeat of the whore and wedding of the Lamb, which show that the writer composed the lyrics for the present literary context (Jörns, *Das hymnische*, 178–79). The placement of hymns and acclamations at pivotal points within the narrative gives perspective on the flow of the action. The hymns in Rev 4–5 identify God as the Maker of all things and Jesus as the Lamb, so readers can see that in the ensuing conflict the Creator must overcome earth's destroyers and the sacrificial Lamb must defeat the tyrannical beast. As the elders offer worship at the midpoint of the book, their lyrics announce the direction the plot will take, including the defeat of evil and redemption of God's servants (11:15–18). After Babylon's demise, worshipers announce that justice has been done and the Lamb's wedding will take place (19:1–8). Other worship scenes show the redeemed coming through affliction into God's presence, disclosing why people have incentive to remain faithful in the face of conflict (7:9–17; 15:2–4; Morton, "Glory").

The praises offered in heaven establish the focus for worship on earth. As readers join in worshiping God and the Lamb, their community below is connected to the one above. The critical dimension is that Revelation shows people making a cult of the beastlike ruler of the empire, which is a perversion of true worship. In the visionary world, the faithful consider God incomparable (15:2–4), but others find the beast incomparable (13:4). The heavenly company and all creation declare God and the Lamb worthy of power (4:8, 11; 5:9–14), but in the readers' social world, many claimed that universal consensus made the emperor uniquely worthy of power (see §13 COMMENT). The writer does not reject all Greco-Roman *forms* of praise—hymns and acclamations by white-robed multitudes have their place; the issue is the *focus* and whether the highest praise is given to God or his opponents (Aune, *Apocalypticism*, 109–16; Friesen, *Imperial*, 104–13; Schimanowski, "Connecting").

Worship expresses fundamental loyalties and commitments. As the hymns define the character of God, they shape the identities of those who worship him. The divine actions affirmed in the hymns include creation, redemption through sacrifice, and the exercise of justice and truth. By praising these acts of God and the Lamb, the hymns shape the way worshipers see their place in a world where they live with competing claims upon their loyalties, while fostering their hope in God's kingdom. As the hymns provide a means of expressing faith, they also shape the faith of readers who identify with the worshipers in the narrative (Gordley, *Teaching*, 345–46).

2. BEATITUDES

Seven times Revelation declares that a person or group is "blessed" (see Table 2). The Greek word *makarios* indicates well-being and is sometimes rendered "happy" or "fortunate." A beatitude puts hope for well-being into a formula: "Blessed is the one who . . ." The form appears in Jewish literature (Ps 1:1; 4Q525 2 II, 1–6), Greco-Roman sources (Pindar, *Pyth.* 5.46–49; Menander, frg. 114), and Christian writings (Matt 5:3–12; Luke 6:20–23). Two of Revelation's beatitudes say that those who keep the message are "blessed" without defining what that means (Rev 1:3; 22:7). The other occurrences show that being blessed means resting from one's labors and not being forgotten or ashamed. It means being invited to a wedding banquet, receiving the hope of resurrection, being elevated to the status of a priest, and sharing in Christ's kingdom. The blessed enter God's city and eat from the tree of life, which means life everlasting.

The first beatitude appears in the superscription of Revelation and defines the reason readers should take the message seriously: It offers the promise of

Table 2. Beatitudes in Revelation

1:3	Blessed is the one who reads aloud and those who hear the words of the prophecy and keep the things written in it, for the time is near.
14:13	Blessed are the dead who die in the Lord from now on . . . so they can rest from their labors, for their works follow them.
16:15	Blessed are those who stay awake and clothed, so they do not go around naked and exposed to shame.
19:9	Blessed are those who have been invited to the wedding banquet of the Lamb.
20:6	Blessed and holy are those who have a share in the first resurrection. Over these the second death has no power, but they will be priests of God and of Christ, and will reign with him for a thousand years.
22:7	Blessed is the one who keeps the words of the prophecy in this scroll.
22:14	Blessed are those who wash their robes so that they may have the right to the tree of life and may enter the city by the gates.

well-being (1:3). This beatitude sets a positive direction for the book as a whole. Through the cycles of visions that threaten and encourage, the writer wants the readers to know that he has their well-being in mind. Other beatitudes are pronounced by heavenly voices, underscoring their importance. Speakers include the exalted Jesus (16:15), the Spirit (14:13b), an angel (19:9), and unnamed voices (14:13a; 20:6). The initial beatitude is matched by two in the final chapter, which are given by the exalted Jesus to emphasize that the message is given for the good of the readers (22:7, 14; Giesen 67).

The character of Revelation's beatitudes can be seen by comparing them with broader patterns in antiquity. On one level, many writers linked being blessed to material well-being and good social relationships. The blessed were said to enjoy happiness in marriage, many children, wealth, wisdom, long life, and honor (Gen 30:13; Pss 127:4–5; 144:12–15; Prov 3:13–18; Sir 26:1; Chariton, *Chaer.* 1.3.7; 8.1.11; Plutarch, *Art.* 12.4; 15.2; Spicq, *TLNT* 2:433; F. Hauck, *TDNT* 4:363–64). On another level, being blessed involved good relationships with God. The blessed are those whom God chooses, forgives, strengthens, and gives insight (Pss 32:1–2; 33:12; Matt 16:17; Luke 10:23; Rom 4:7–8). Ideally, both levels should be congruent; that is, those who revere God should prosper (Pss 1:1–3; 128:1–4). But Revelation recognizes that experience runs counter to the hope of being blessed. The righteous may face the loss of life and freedom even if they remain true to God (Rev 2:9–11; 6:9–10), while the allies of evil prosper by trafficking with the tyrannical beast and Babylon the whore (17:2; 18:3).

One traditional response to this contradiction is to affirm that the faithful are blessed in the present. The idea is that relating rightly to God is inherently better than receiving wealth or status from the ungodly (Luke 11:28 1 Pet 3:14; 4 Macc 7:22). Accordingly, Rev 1:3 can affirm that those who read and follow the message of the book are already "blessed" because God values their obedience. A second response is that the righteous are "blessed" because God will reward them in the future. The suffering and injustice of the present will not continue forever (Matt 5:3–12; Luke 6:20–23; 14:14–15; Jas 1:12; *Pss. Sol.* 17:44; 18:6; *1 En.* 58:2; *Sib. Or.* 4.192). Accordingly, Revelation promises that in the future the faithful will find rest, life, and the joy of God's kingdom (14:13; 19:9; 20:6; 22:7, 14).

The beatitudes in Revelation may function in different ways, depending on the hearers. Well-being is promised to those who trust and follow the book's message (1:3; 22:7); who labor, remain vigilant, and wash their robes through repentance (14:13b; 16:15; 22:14); and who face death in various forms (14:13a; cf. 20:6). For readers who are complacent, the beatitudes may be heard as an admonition to be more firmly committed (Murphy 63). But for those who are struggling to remain faithful in such situations, the beatitudes provide affirmation and encouragement to persevere, knowing that God views such people favorably and will bring them to a better future (Boring 67).

V.

Rhetorical Aspects

Rhetorical study of Revelation considers the book's potential effect on readers. It looks at what the text *does* as well as what it says, asking how it might shape the perspective of an audience. The literary features discussed above contribute to Revelation's persuasive capacity; here we explore aspects that are traditionally associated with rhetoric. These include the role of logic and emotion, the character of the author, and his writing style (Aristotle, *Rhet.* 1.2.3, 7). There is no reason to think that John was trained in classical rhetoric, but his text is designed to bring readers to a renewed commitment to God, Christ, and the Christian community; and the study of rhetoric helps to show how the process of persuasion occurs (Schüssler Fiorenza 20–37; deSilva, *Seeing*, 14–27; Harland, *Associations*, 353–56).

A. Situation and Strategy

John envisions an audience of seven congregations facing different types of challenges (Intro III.B). What makes them alike is that factors in each situation work against the readers' faith and the cohesion of their communities. Readers who were overtly threatened would be aware of the challenges and needed encouragement to persevere, but those who were complacent or accommodating would not have sensed the problems. John would need to challenge them to see issues of which they were unaware, while calling for commitments that would set them at odds with the dominant social, religious, and economic patterns of the cities where they lived.

John's message ran counter to the public rhetoric of the Roman era, which celebrated the peace and prosperity that imperial rule had brought. According to the dominant discourse, Roman rule was invincible and benevolent. Under the auspices of the gods, it provided unprecedented social and economic opportunities. Its rulers were rightly venerated. The most prudent course of action would seem to be accommodation, even when it meant compromising one's beliefs concerning the reign of God and Jesus. But John argues the reverse, calling on readers to "endure" (13:10; 14:12) and to "conquer" (2:7, 11, 17; 21:7) by keeping the faith and resisting both the overt and subtle pressures to compromise.

I. REVELATION'S VISIONARY ARGUMENT

John assumes that he and his readers share certain convictions and plausibility structures. A major presupposition is that God is the one who is and was and is to come (1:4, 8; 4:8). Since God's existence spans all of time, the readers are to see their own present and future in relation to God. As the Alpha, God created all things, and as the Omega, he will bring all things to completion in the new creation (1:8; 21:5–6). God is almighty, the sovereign ruler of the world, whose throne is the center of legitimate power. Since he created all things, he has a rightful claim over the world he has made (1:8; 4:1–11). Finally, God is just. He is committed to truth and righteousness and can be expected to act on that basis (15:3).

The problem is that if God is eternal, powerful, and just, then it seems inexplicable that those who profess faith in him should suffer harassment, poverty, and death (2:9–10, 13; 3:8–10). The martyrs focus the issue by demanding to know how long God will delay in bringing justice (6:9–11). Revelation's response is twofold. First, the writer notes the scope of God's designs. In a rightly ordered universe, all living things glorify the God who made them (4:11; 5:13), and it is God's desire that all nations worship him (14:7; 15:3). Such an expansive hope is drawn from Scripture (Isa 2:2–5; 60:3; Mic 4:1–2; Pss 22:27–28; 86:9). The plague visions show that if God responds to injustice with wrath alone, his purposes will not be realized, since people will not turn to him (Rev 6:12–17; 9:20–21). Therefore, God has delayed judgment so that witness can be given and people can repent. Second, the author gives assurance that the delay will not continue indefinitely. If the perpetrators of injustice do not repent, God will defeat them in order to liberate those who suffer (17:16; 19:11–21) and hold everyone to account (20:11–15). The prophetic visions of the defeat of hostile nations and final judgment bear this out (Joel 3:1–16; Zech 14:1–5; Dan 7:9–10).

To make sense of the church's situation, readers must see it in light of Jesus, who bore faithful witness to God, was killed, and then was raised (Rev 1:5–6). Jesus was not exempted from unjust suffering; rather, he conquered through suffering to redeem people of every nation for God, and he now lives and reigns in God's presence (1:18; 5:5–10). Those who follow Jesus the Lamb are to conquer by remaining faithful and bearing witness as he did, knowing that God will bring them through death into life through resurrection (2:7, 11, 17; 7:9–17; 11:3–12; 12:11; 15:2; 20:4).

The critical side of the argument is directed at forces that work against the faith the author wants to inspire. John assumes that Satan is the one who accuses people before God, deceives the world, and promotes death (NOTES on 12:9–10). He identifies Satan's traits with aspects of the readers' experience, since some are being wrongly accused (2:9; 3:9), a few face death (2:10, 13), and others think that food linked to the worship of Greco-Roman gods is benign—an idea John considers deceptive (2:20–24).

John broadens the critique by relating local struggles to dominant patterns in the Roman Empire. He shifts from the issue of eating food offered to Greco-Roman deities (2:14, 20) to the practice of worshiping deified rulers (13:1–18). This move is plausible because the imperial cult was understood to complement the worship of traditional deities (NOTE on 13:8). A motif in the imperial cult was military conquest, which emphasized Rome's invincible rule. John agrees that conquest is central to Roman claims, but he turns the motif into a critique of a political system based on violent subjugation. To emphasize the point, he invokes the memory of Nero, an emperor who used violence against the church (NOTES and COMMENT on 13:7).

Another public claim was that imperial rule brought prosperity. John agrees, but he presses the issue by depicting a society driven by the desire for gain. The whore and her clients show how obsession with wealth makes people numb to brutality and injustice (17:1–6; 18:1–24). The force of John's critique is enhanced by his use of language from Israel's prophets and its similarity to critiques of Roman luxury made by Greek and Latin writers (§§35–36 COMMENT).

John bolsters the readers' willingness to resist the forces described above with two arguments. First, the agents of evil work intensely not because they are invincible, but because they are desperate. With the Messiah's exaltation, Satan was banished from heaven and now rages about the earth like a caged and wounded animal. Evil does not reign supreme, God and his Messiah do (12:7–12). Second, evil's destructive quality will lead to its own demise. The whore is destroyed by the beast; the society based on violence falls victim to violence; the city that consumes the world's goods finally is consumed (17:16). At present, readers might think it expedient to accommodate the forces that the writer has depicted as destructive, but they are called to resist because those who destroy the earth will inevitably be destroyed (11:18).

2. EMOTIONAL EFFECT

People are moved by what they feel as well as by what they think, so persuasion includes the emotional effect of what is said (Aristotle, *Rhet.* 2.1.8; Cicero, *De or.* 2.42 §178; Quintilian, *Inst.* 6.2.2–7). Creating pictures in the minds of an audience is a powerful means of evoking emotion (Quintilian, *Inst.* 6.2.29–31; Longinus, *Subl.* 15.1–2). Revelation uses bold images that have the potential to elicit positive feelings that encourage faithfulness to God, Christ, and the Christian community, as well as negative feelings of aversion toward God's adversaries and patterns of unfaithfulness (deSilva, *Seeing*, 175–228).

Fear is "a painful or troubled feeling caused by the impression of an imminent evil that causes destruction or pain" (Aristotle, *Rhet.* 2.5.1). Readers facing denunciation and prison have reason to fear the judgments of others in society, and the visions of a violent dragon and beast magnify the terrifying qualities of the powers that threaten them (Rev 2:9–10; 12:1–13:18). But Revelation redirects the emotion by showing that readers' adversaries have more reason to fear, since they fall under the greater judgment of God (6:17; 14:9–11; 18:10, 15).

The opposite of fear is confidence, which arises from the conviction that "the hope of what is salutary is near at hand" (Aristotle, *Rhet.* 2.5. 16). Revelation responds to fears arising from social conflict with assurances of readers' access to God and future vindication through resurrection (Rev 2:10–11; 3:8–13). The visions shake the misplaced confidence of those who feel secure in wealth or social status by warning that they are vulnerable (3:15–17; 6:12–16; 18:7–19). But when the terrified ask "who is able to stand" in the face of divine wrath (6:17), there is an encouraging vision of those who are cleansed by Christ's death "standing" in God's presence (7:9–17; cf. 15:2). The faithful may suffer at the hands of God's adversaries, but assurance of deathless life with God can evoke the confidence needed to persevere (14:12–13; 21:4–7; 22:3–5).

Feelings of indignation arise when basic standards of fairness have been violated (Aristotle, *Rhet.* 2.9.1–3). The writer portrays a dragon so cruel that it threatens a pregnant woman and tries to devour a newborn child (12:1–6). The whore amasses wealth through immorality and yet is arrogant (18:3, 7; cf. Cicero, *Inv.* 1.105). Many feel indignant when those who are undeserving prosper, while those who are worthy do not. The martyrs under the altar wrongly lost their lives because of God's word (Rev 6:9), while the beast that blasphemes heaven is able to build an empire on earth (Rev 13:1–10). Such situations evoke a sense of outrage and help move an audience to take sides against God's foes (Lausberg, *Handbook* §438).

The opposite of indignation is sympathy, which arises from "the sight of evil, deadly or painful, which befalls one who does not deserve it" (Aristotle, *Rhet.* 2.8.2). A vivid example in Revelation is the woman who endures pain to give birth to the Messiah and yet must flee to the desert because of the dragon (12:1–6). If readers feel sympathy for her, they will be more likely to identify with her, since she personifies the plight of God's people on earth. By way of contrast, readers are not to sympathize with the kings, merchants, and sailors who grieve the demise of Babylon because they have lost opportunities for immorality and profitmaking—losses that readers would presumably not find lamentable (18:9–19).

Shame "is a kind of pain or uneasiness in respect of misdeeds, past, present, or future, which seem to tend to bring dishonor" (Aristotle, *Rhet.* 2.6.1). Readers rebuked for complacency are expected to feel shame as their shortcomings are identified; the goal is that they repent (3:1–3, 15–19; cf. 16:15). Later, those doing business with Rome are likened to the clients of a whore, making such commercial involvements look shameful (17:2). The ruling power might claim supreme honors, but the climactic battle scenes show the beast and false prophet suffering ignoble defeat and the disgrace of being taken captive, making them unworthy of veneration (19:2).

The opposite of shame is honor. The writer recognizes that already readers have the dignified status of belonging to God's kingdom and serving as priests (1:5–6). After giving reproofs, he encourages readers with the promise that Christ will acknowledge them in the presence of his Father and the angels and will grant them a place on his throne, both of which convey honor (3:5, 21). Scenes of the redeemed in glory awaken the desire to share in that future (7:9–17; 15:2–4; 22:1–5).

Gratitude is evoked when help is given to someone in need. The feeling is greatest when the help is given despite great difficulty by someone who gives no thought to self-interest (Aristotle, *Rhet.* 2.7.1–2). Revelation identifies Christ as the Lamb who redeems others at the cost of his own blood, an action calling for expressions of thanks (1:5–6; 5:9–10). Gratitude is also due to God, the source of salvation, who defeats the forces of evil and brings people through suffering on earth to life in his presence (7:9–12; 11:17).

3. CHARACTER OF THE SPEAKER

People are more likely to be persuaded by someone they trust than by someone they do not trust. When readers have confidence in the character (*ēthos*) of an author, they are more receptive to the message (Aristotle, *Rhet.* 1.2–3–4; Quintilian, *Inst.* 4.1.7; deSilva, *Seeing*, 117–45; G. Carey, *Elusive*, 93–133). In its opening lines, Revelation identifies God as the ultimate source of the message, and early readers would have agreed that God is eminently trustworthy (1:1; cf. 6:10; 19:9; 21:5; 22:6). The superscription adds that the revelation is mediated through Jesus, whose credibility is of the highest order (1:1, 5; 3:14). Jesus died because of his witness to God and was vindicated through resurrection (1:5–6). Therefore, readers can assume that a message attested by Jesus is valid (22:20).

The challenge is to demonstrate John's own credibility as the prophetic mediator of the message. Since prophets were active in the churches, readers would have considered divine revelation to be a valid type of communication (Knight, "Apocalyptic," 487; deSilva, *Seeing*, 120). But congregations could test those who claimed to bring prophecies and revelations in order to see whether they were reliable. John had apparently been known in these churches for some time. He can recall past events in the communities and may have been involved in a confrontation with a rival prophet at Thyatira (2:4, 13, 19, 21). The congregations probably included some people who agreed with John and some who did not.

John fosters a sense of rapport with the readers by calling himself their "brother" and "companion" in God's kingdom, earthly affliction, and endurance (1:9). His greetings state shared beliefs about the God "who is" and the love of Jesus, whose death brings release from sin (1:4–6). He indicates that he seeks the readers' welfare, so that through his message they might be blessed (1:3). John notes that he received his visions on Patmos, where he had probably been sent by Roman authorities as punishment for his preaching (NOTE on 1:9). If readers understand that John lost his freedom "because of the word of God," they can be confident that he will now bear "witness to the word of God" with integrity (1:2, 9).

John presents himself as the recipient of the message rather than its author. In one sense, his visionary experience sets him apart from readers, who have not seen what he has. The visions place him in a unique position as communicator of a divine message. But in another sense, the pattern places him alongside the readers since he—like they—are directed to receive the word that is given. John received it in visionary form, and they receive it through his text. If the readers need help understanding God's designs, so does John, since he relates that angelic interpreters must assist him in making sense of what he sees (5:5; 7:13–17; 17:6–7). If readers receive heavenly reproof, John too is rebuked for mistakenly worshiping an angel (19:10; 22:8–9). By acknowledging his errors, John conveys the sense that his message as a whole can be trusted.

In the end, John cannot prove the authenticity of his message. But he can invite readers into his visionary world so they can see what he sees. As he directs attention to the Creator and the Lamb, he encourages readers to find that his message is congruent with the character of the God they know from Scripture and with "the witness of Jesus" that had a central place in the Christian community (1:2; 12:17; 19:10). Such congruence conveys credibility (deSilva, *Seeing*, 158–74; Thompson, *Book*, 177–79; Aune, *Apocalypticism*, 176–82).

B. Language and Style

Revelation's language can be blunt and evocative, vivid and obscure. Much of the book is narrated in simple prose, yet it is interspersed with well-crafted poetic passages. The writer both follows and violates accepted patterns of Greek grammar, resulting in an idiosyncratic style that some find intriguing and others disparage.

I. WORD PICTURES

Revelation captures the attention of readers through its word pictures. Ideas often find their most powerful expression when "you seem to see what you describe and bring it vividly before the eyes of your audience," so that attention is drawn to "the enthralling effect of the imagination" (Longinus, *Subl.* 15.1, 11). Instead of defining evil abstractly, John pictures a dragon threatening a pregnant woman. When critiquing imperial rule, he describes a seven-headed beast dominating the nations and slaughtering the saints. When offering hope for an unseen future, he provides a visual tour of New Jerusalem with its gemlike splendor. Through his use of language, he "takes you along with him . . . and turns hearing into sight" (Longinus, *Subl.* 26.2).

Satire is a feature of some word pictures. A satirist bases a picture on stock features of a subject and then exaggerates certain traits. The goal is for readers to still see the resemblance, though the subject will now seem outlandish. If people see that what appears impressive is actually ridiculous, they will be more ready to resist it. For example, imperial iconography personified Rome as a noble lady seated on seven hills, but Revelation transforms her into a drunken whore sitting on a seven-headed monster. No longer an attractive exemplar of virtue, she is arrogant and debauched—a figure that repels (17:1–18). The beast from the land is a collective image for supporters of the imperial cult. In practice, such people touted the benefits of imperial rule and erected temples and statues to the deified emperors, but Revelation satirizes them by depicting a beast that dupes and coerces the populace into worshiping a grotesque seven-headed monster (13:11–18).

Word pictures convey multiple meanings simultaneously. For example, a whore commonly signifies sexual immorality, but since she provided sexual favors for money, the image could also portray commercial dealings as immoral when they required people to compromise their principles. Since a whore was promiscuous, the image also characterized religious infidelity. All three dimensions—moral, commercial, and religious—operate in the portrait of imperial Rome in Rev 17–18. Lesser images also have multiple levels of meaning. The redeemed receive a "seal" on their foreheads, which suggests both protection and belonging (NOTE on 7:3). White robes suggest purity, holiness, and honor (NOTE on 3:5). Laurel wreaths traditionally signified victory and honor, both of which are associated with faithfulness to God and Christ (NOTE on 2:10).

Readers sometimes treat Revelation's word pictures as a code designed to hide the author's meaning from all but selected insiders. But the primary function of the imagery is to reveal, not to conceal. Word pictures offer a way of seeing the character of God, the world, and the community of faith. The writer portrays Jesus as the slaughtered Lamb in order to emphasize the sacrificial quality of his work, not to mask his identity. Similarly, the comment that the whore sits on seven hills makes clear that the image characterizes life under imperial Rome; this link to Rome would have been apparent to most ancient readers (17:9). At the same time, the images are evocative. Unlike the symbols on a map or chart, which have single well-defined meanings, the word pictures in Revelation resist simple definition. They give perspectives that stimulate reflection rather than answers that obviate the need for further thought. Their power comes from their ability to engage the imagination (Frey, "Bildersprache," 183).

2. WRITING STYLES

Ancient speakers and writers were to use a Greek style appropriate for their message. Good practice was to use an elevated style for weighty topics and a more informal one for lesser matters (Aristotle, *Rhet.* 3.7.1–2; Demetrius, *Eloc.* 120). Revelation's Greek is peculiar, and to a cultured Greek ear, the style is jarring, full of barbarisms and incongruities (Dionysius of Alexandria in Eusebius, *Hist. eccl.* 7.25.26). Copyists often corrected the grammar in order to make it adhere more closely to recognized standards.

A prime example of the problem is the greeting from the God "who is and who was and who is to come" (1:4). The preposition *apo* (from) normally takes the genitive case, but John identifies God in the nominative case. He places a definite article before the participle *ōn* (who is), as is proper, but then puts an article before the indicative verb *ēn* (was), which is *not* done. The effect is grammatically incongruous: "Grace to you and peace from he the is and he the was and he the coming one." The writer continues in a correct Greek style, extending greetings "from [*apo*] the seven spirits" and "from [*apo*] Jesus Christ" in the genitive case (1:4–5), but then he departs from correct usage by describing Jesus (genitive case) as "the faithful witness" in the nominative case (1:5).

Interpreters account for the peculiarities in several ways. First, some suggest that Greek was an imperfectly mastered second language for the writer; that is,

John wrote in Greek but thought in Hebrew or perhaps Aramaic (Charles 1: cxliii). They note constructions that are odd in Greek but appear in Semitic languages. For example, the masculine participle "saying" (*legōn*, *legontes*) functions as if it were indeclinable, like the Hebrew *lēʾmôr*. A line might begin with a participle and then shift to a finite verb (1:5–6). The writer can introduce a direct or indirect object in the nominative case and then switch to the accusative or dative (2:26; 3:12, 21). There are redundant pronouns—"to whom [*hois*] it was given to them [*autois*])" (7:2)—and *kai* (and) can introduce circumstantial clauses, like the *waw* in Hebrew (MHT 4:145–59; Aune 1:cc–cciii). Unusual word meanings and verb tenses are also attributed to the influence of Semitic languages (Charles 1:cxlii–clii; S. Thompson, *Apocalypse*, 47–50, 102–8).

Second, others think that John's primary language was Greek but his style was influenced by Greek translations of the Hebrew Scripture, which reflected Semitic forms. This view is more probable. John knew enough Hebrew to translate the word *Abaddōn* into Greek (9:11) and to formulate the name Harmagedon (NOTE on Rev 16:16), and he probably links the number 666 to a Hebrew form of Nero's name (NOTE on 13:18). But how much Hebrew John knew is not clear. Some of his allusions to Scripture are based on Greek translations (INTRO IV.D). Although features of Revelation's language appear to some degree in various Greek texts from the period, the similarities to Greek translations of Scripture give John's language a "biblical" quality (D. Schmidt, "Semitisms"; Callahan, "Language"; cf. Porter, "Language").

Third, it also seems likely that John uses peculiar grammatical forms for emphasis. He nearly always uses the genitive case after the preposition *apo* (from), so when he identifies God in the nominative case after *apo* in the greeting, he makes God seem absolute, above the normal constraints of Greek grammar. The nominative case also preserves the exact form of God's self-identification as "the one who is" (*ho ōn*) in Exod 3:14 (LXX), which might emphasize the biblical connection (Beale, "Solecisms," 426–28). Another instance is that John nearly always uses the dative case after *homoion* (like), which is correct. Only in the expression "like a human being" (*homoion huion anthrōpou*) does he use the accusative case. The effect is incongruous, yet it calls attention to the unique identity of the humanlike figure who was expected to come with the clouds according to Dan 7:13 (Rev 1:13; 14:14; cf. 1:7).

John's facility with the language is evident in the multiple styles he employs. As the narrative portion of the Apocalypse begins, John speaks in his own voice, recounting how the exalted Jesus appeared to him. But when Christ speaks in the first person, the language becomes elevated and solemn. Commands to "write" are given tersely, and the expression "thus says" (*tade legei*) has the gravity of a royal decree and prophetic word from God (see §3B).

John makes the voices of heavenly worshipers stand out by using styles that range from effusive prose acclamations of God's glory and power (4:11; 5:9–13) to poetic songs of praise that follow patterns of biblical poetry. The song in 15:3–4 is especially well-crafted, with a rhythmic quality that is enhanced as alternating lines end with the same word, *sou* (your/you). Similarly, those who lament the demise of Babylon have stylized expressions of grief. In measured lines they say "Oh no," then they briefly describe the great city and conclude with grief at its devastation in "a single hour" (18:10, 15–16, 19). The forms give powerful expression to praise and lament.

A suggestive way to construe the peculiarity of Revelation's Greek style is that it is well-suited to its nonconformist message. Greek was the language of the dominant culture in which the book was composed, and using Greek allowed the text to address a wide range of readers. Some unusual aspects of the grammar may reflect Greek translations of the OT or forms of vulgar Greek that were used in Asia Minor, but at points the writer deliberately flouts the accepted forms of grammar, which fits the idea that neither the writer nor the God to whom he bears witness is held captive by social convention (1:4; Callahan, "Language").

3. SELECTED FORMS OF EXPRESSION

Revelation uses patterns of regularity and disruption to good effect. At the beginning of a vision cycle readers may be told that there will be seven elements, such as seals, trumpets, or bowls. John counts as each successive vision occurs—first, second, third, etc.—giving the impression of inexorable movement toward the end. Readers will anticipate that after the sixth vision the seventh will follow immediately, only to find that John disrupts the sequence with interludes that delay the end (7:1–17; 10:1–11:14). The result is that readers must expect *that* the end will come, even as they suspend their expectations about *when* it will come—a literary pattern that makes an important theological point (Perry, *Rhetoric*, 209–41).

In the vision of the 144,000 John uses a similar technique when he enumerates the redeemed by repeating the same line for each of the twelve tribes: "from the tribe of _____ 12,000" (7:5–8). Readers have the impression of a large but definite number (*arithmon*, 7:4), yet John disrupts the pattern by relating that he actually saw a group so vast that it could not be numbered (*arithmēsai*, 7:9). The effect emphasizes that divine redemption exceeds expectations. Other types of speech include the following:

> *Antomasia* is the replacing of a name with a descriptive phrase or epithet. God is "the one seated on the throne" (4:9–10; 5:1, 7, 13; 6:16; 7:15;

21:5), "the one who lives forever and ever" (4:10; 10:6), and "the one who made heaven and earth" (14:7; cf. 10:6). In each of the messages to the churches, the majestic Christ is identified with phrases like the one "who holds the seven stars in his right hand, who walks among the seven gold lampstands" (2:1) and "the first and the last, who died and came to life" (2:8). The phrases used for God and the exalted Jesus preserve a respectful distance while reinforcing aspects of their characters.

Hyperbole is an exaggeration of the truth. In the visionary world, "the whole earth" follows the beast (13:3), the sins of Babylon "stretched up to heaven" (18:5), and in the city is found the blood of "all who have been slain on the earth" (18:24). Although readers might want to qualify such categorical statements, the hyperbole points to the breadth of the issues as the writer sees them. By briefly taking some aspect of a subject beyond simple description, the writer allows readers to see its character more clearly (Lausberg, *Handbook* §909).

Metaphor involves speaking of one thing in terms appropriate to another. The terms hot, cold, and lukewarm, which usually refer to physical temperature, are used for degrees of commitment (Rev 3:15–16). Similarly, being alive or dead, awake or asleep generally have to do with physical states, but in Revelation they startle readers by providing perspectives on their faith and way of life (3:1–3). References to the temple, altar, and holy city are combined in a complex metaphor, depicting the Christian community as the place where authentic worship takes place. Readers are to see that even though the "temple" or community is threatened, God preserves it (11:1–2). Metaphors are effective when readers make the shift from the ordinary sense of a word to its metaphorical application and thereby see things in a new way (*Rhetorica ad Herennium* 4.34.45).

Metonymy replaces a word with another word that has some relationship to it. When a voice comes "from the throne," the idea is that the words convey the authority of God, who is seated on the throne (16:17; 19:5; 21:3). When a voice "from the altar" declares that God's justice is done, the imagery recalls how the martyrs under the altar previously cried out for God's justice (16:7; cf. 6:9–10). Linking texts in this way emphasizes the fulfillment of the martyr's plea.

Paronomasia involves playing on different senses of a word in the same context. In the message to Ephesus, the writer commends the readers who do not "bear" evildoers but do "bear" up in faith (*bastazein*, 2:2–3) and despite their labor (*kopos*, 2:2) have not grown weary (*kopiazein*, 2:3). Such wordplays are especially helpful when they correlate an action with its result: For those who "add" (*epitithenai*) to the book of Revelation, Christ will "add" its plagues; and for those who "take away" (*aphairein*) from the book, he will "take away" their share in the tree of life (22:18–19). Those who "destroy" or "ruin" the earth morally (*diaphtheirein*) will be destroyed or annihilated through divine judgment (11:18).

Polysyndeton means connecting a series of words through a conjunction like *kai* (and). The slaughtered Lamb is worthy of "power *and* wealth *and* wisdom *and* might *and* honor *and* glory *and* praise" (5:12; cf. 4:11; 5:13; 7:12). His act of redemption and the beast's tyranny extend to those of "every tribe *and* language *and* people *and* nation" (5:9; cf. 7:9; 11:9; 13:7; 17:15). The writer lists the various social classes that are threatened by divine wrath (6:15), the varieties of idols and sins of humanity (9:20–21), and the vast number of trade goods sold in Babylon (18:11–13). By naming one item after another, the writer gives the impression that the list could go on indefinitely, emphasizing the magnitude of the subject (Demetrius, *Eloc.* 63).

Simile compares one thing to another. A writer may use similes when attempting to express something of a transcendent order in ordinary speech. The appearance of the exalted Christ defies easy description: His head and hair are "like" white wool and snow, his eyes are "like" a flame of fire, and his feet are "like" shining bronze (1:14–15). John hears voices that are "like" a trumpet (1:10), thunder (6:1), and rushing water (19:6). Similes also disclose the character of things. Words inspired by demonic spirits are as meaningless as the chirping of frogs (16:13). Noting that the beast from the land speaks "like a dragon" links it to Satan the dragon, the deceiver of the world (13:11; cf. 12:9).

Revelation's vocabulary includes 916 words, most of which are common (Aune 1:ccvii–ccxi). But the writer occasionally uses unusual words that make the writing more vivid. The woman who flees from the dragon is nearly "swept away by a river" (*potamophorētos*, 12:15). Babylon comes under judgment for her "loose and extravagant" ways (*strēnos*, 18:3; *strēnian*, 18:7, 9). The martyrs are not simply killed but are "beheaded" (*pelekizein*) for their witness (20:4). John uses the technical term "construction" (*endōmēsis*) for New Jerusalem's walls (21:18) and includes extensive lists of trade goods and gemstones, many of which do not appear in the LXX (18:12–13; 21:19–20).

Vulgar expressions catch the readers' attention. The voice that announces Satan's expulsion from heaven refers to him as the *katēgōr*, a peculiar form of the word for an accuser, which copyists often changed to the proper *katēgoros*, perhaps because the short form seemed crude (Deissmann, *Light*, 93–94). Yet a crude expression may be appropriate if it conveys disdain for the defeated Satan, who is unworthy of respect. Later, John refers to the slaves sold by the merchants as *sōmata* (bodies) rather *douloi*. The word "bodies" shows the demeaning quality of trafficking in human beings (NOTE on 18:13).

Speakers sometimes piqued the listeners' interest by coining new words based on familiar roots (Demetrius, *Eloc.* 96–98; Lausberg, *Handbook* §§547–51). John follows this practice when he coins the verb *rypareuein* (to be unclean) from the root of the previous noun, *ryparos* (22:11). The result is a balanced series of ironic warnings about wrongdoing. Other instances include *krystallizein* (to shine like crystal) for New Jerusalem (21:18), and perhaps the word for shining bronze, *chalkolibanos* (NOTE on 1:15). The unusual expressions fit the transcendent character of what John sees. By using forms of well-crafted speech, along with expressions that are novel or incorrect, Revelation draws readers into a peculiar visionary world that remains at odds with the familiar patterns of communication in the readers' world.

VI.

Text of Revelation

The Greek text of Revelation has a distinctive history. The book circulated widely in the ancient church and was cited by writers in both eastern and western parts of the Roman Empire. In the late second century, Irenaeus knew that copies of the book varied in their readings, complaining that some said the number of the beast was 616, while others read 666, which he thought was correct (*Haer.* 5.30.1). Over time, Revelation's value for Christian instruction was disputed, especially in the east, and it was not transcribed as often as other writings that became part of the NT. Some texts were copied as collections of gospels or epistles, but Revelation did not readily fit those categories. The oldest complete copies of Revelation come from fourth- and fifth-century volumes containing the entire NT (Codex Sinaiticus, ‭א‬; Codex Alexandrinus, A), but Revelation also circulated on its own, and only fragments have been preserved from manuscripts of the second and third centuries.

Latin translations of Revelation were used by western writers from the third century on, while the Greek text continued to be used in the east. The Greek commentary by Oecumenius, written in the sixth century, includes extensive quotations of Revelation. His text usually conforms to that found in fourth- and fifth-century manuscripts, although it includes some scribal errors and unusual readings. At 6:9, for example, manuscripts regularly refer to the souls who were slain for their "witness" (*martyria*), but Oecumenius says they died for their "church" (*ekklēsia*), which is theologically significant for him.

The commentary by Andreas from the early seventh century uses a different form of the text, which had been edited. Aware that manuscripts varied in quality, he reproved copyists who tried to improve Revelation's peculiar Greek style by making it more suitable to Attic tastes. At the same time, he seemed untroubled by the fact that manuscripts varied in certain details. He observed that some read "key of Hades" rather than "key of David" in Rev 3:7, and some pictured an angel clothed with "stone" (*lithon*) and others with "linen" (*linon*) in 15:6. But rather than arguing for one reading over another, he commented on both forms of the text (Hernández, "Andrew").

Medieval manuscripts include Revelation in volumes containing other NT writings, but in some cases the pages containing Revelation were copied by a different scribe and incorporated into the volume at a different time. Revelation was also placed in collections of noncanonical texts. It appears with the works of Pseudo-Dionysius, Basil the Great, Gregory of Nyssa, John Chrysostom, and other writers. Since Revelation was not regularly read in the worship services of the Greek-speaking church, the text has not been preserved in collections of lectionary readings (J. K. Elliott, "Distinctiveness").

In the sixteenth century the humanist desire to return to the sources of the Christian tradition led to a renewed interest in the Greek text of the NT. Revelation was included in the first printed edition of the Greek NT, the Complutensian Polyglot of 1514, but much more influential was the text published by Desiderius Erasmus in 1516, which was the first edition to be widely marketed. For Revelation, Erasmus had access to only one inferior manuscript from the twelfth century (minuscule 2814), which included grammatical flaws that Erasmus felt free to correct. Since the manuscript omitted words at numerous points and was missing the final page, which contained Rev 22:16–21, Erasmus filled in the gaps by retranslating from the Latin Vulgate into Greek. By doing so he created new readings that did not appear in any Greek manuscript. Erasmus later made minor corrections to his work, which became the basis for the Textus Receptus, or "received text," the standard printed Greek text for several centuries (Metzger and Ehrman, *Text*, 143–45).

Protestant translations of the NT, beginning with Martin Luther (d. 1546) and William Tyndale (d. 1536), were based on the printed Greek text rather than the Latin Vulgate. The King James Version of 1611 was based on a printed Greek text like that of Erasmus, which reflects the medieval readings in the manuscript he used. For example, when referring to the redeemed, the early manuscripts said that "they reign" or "they will reign" on earth, but Erasmus's text said "*we* shall reign" (KJV, emphasis added). Where early manuscripts said that "the nations shall walk" by the light of New Jerusalem, Erasmus's text had a longer reading, which explained that only "the nations *of them which are saved* shall walk" by its light (21:24, KJV, emphasis added; Karrer, "Text der Johannesoffenbarung," 378–81).

Subsequent studies have clarified the process of textual transmission by collecting and analyzing numerous manuscripts of the Greek NT. More than three hundred manuscripts of Revelation are known. Because of the distinctive textual histories, the manuscripts considered strongest for the gospels and Paul's letters have proved to be less reliable for Revelation (ℵ), whereas those that are less reliable for other parts of the NT have greater value for Revelation (A and Codex Ephraemi [C]). Recent studies have also explored the scribal tendencies reflected in the manuscripts. A survey of the most significant witnesses for the Greek text of Revelation follows.

Papyri

The earliest witnesses are papyrus manuscripts. All are incomplete, and many consist of small fragments. Most are from codices, but two were written on papyrus rolls ($\mathfrak{P}^{18}$ and $\mathfrak{P}^{98}$). Whether these two fragments are from the same roll is not clear (Hurtado, *Earliest*, 31–32). Another fragment includes widely separated sections of Revelation on its two sides, suggesting that it too could have been a roll ($\mathfrak{P}^{24}$). The dates and contents are listed here, followed by notes on selected manuscripts (Nicklas, "Early"):

Papyrus no.	Century	Contents
$\mathfrak{P}^{18}$	Late third–early fourth	1:4–7
$\mathfrak{P}^{24}$	Early fourth	5:5–8; 6:5–8
$\mathfrak{P}^{43}$	Sixth–seventh	2:12–13; 15:8–16:2
$\mathfrak{P}^{47}$	Late third	9:10–17:2
$\mathfrak{P}^{85}$	Fourth–fifth	9:19–10:1, 5–9
$\mathfrak{P}^{98}$	Second	1:13–20
$\mathfrak{P}^{115}$	Third–fourth	2:1–3, 13–15, 27–29; 3:10–12; 5:8–9; 6:4–6; 8:3–8; 8:11–9:5; 9:7–16; 9:18–10:4, 8; 11:5; 11:8–15; 11:18–12:6, 9–10, 12–17; 13:1–3, 6–12, 13–16; 13:17–14:3, 5–7, 10–11, 14–16; 14:18–15:1, 5–7

$\mathfrak{P}^{18}$ preserves a few verses from Rev 1 written on the back of an older biblical scroll. The text of Exodus was copied on the front in the early third century, and Revelation was copied onto the back in the later third or early fourth century. The result is that one side of the fragment has the final verses of Exodus, where God's glory fills the tabernacle, and the other side includes the initial greetings in Revelation. The implications of including the two texts in the same scroll are not clear. Its readings are generally closer to A than to other text forms.

$\mathfrak{P}^{47}$ is the most important papyrus manuscript of Revelation. It was probably copied in the late third century and preserves a large section of the book. The scribe was careless about orthography, and the text may include up to eighty readings that are not supported by other manuscripts. None of the unique readings appears to preserve the earliest text. Overall, the readings often correspond to those in ℵ.

𝔓⁹⁸, the oldest known fragment of Revelation, was probably transcribed in the late second or early third century (Hagedorn, "P.IFAO"). It appears on the back of an otherwise unknown documentary text from the late first or early second century and preserves a few verses from Rev 1. Its readings generally correspond to those in A.

𝔓¹¹⁵ is a very fragmentary and yet important witness that was copied in the late third or early fourth century. Although the copyist tended to improve Revelation's Greek style, his readings often correspond to those in the high-quality codices A and C, suggesting that it belongs to the same text type (Parker, "New"). Its most notable feature is that it states that the beast's number is 616 rather than 666, giving support to a reading attested in C and noted by Irenaeus (NOTE on 13:18).

Uncials

The earliest complete copies of Revelation are uncials from the fourth and fifth centuries (ℵ, A), while another fifth-century uncial preserves a significant amount of text (C). Most of the other early witnesses are fragmentary. The fourth-century Codex Vaticanus (B), which includes much of the NT, is incomplete and is missing Revelation.

No. (sign)	Name	Century	Contents
01 (ℵ)	Sinaiticus	Fourth	Complete
02 (A)	Alexandrinus	Fifth	Complete
04 (C)	Ephraemi	Fifth	1:1; 3:20–5:14; 7:14–17; 8:5–9:16; 10:10–11:3; 16:13–18:2; 19:5–21:21
025 (P)	Porphyrianus	Ninth	Nearly complete (missing 16:12–17:1; 19:21–20:9; 22:6–21)
046		Tenth	Complete
051		Tenth	11:15–13:1; 13:3–22:7; 22:15–21
052	Athous Pantelejmon	Tenth	7:16–8:12
0163		Fifth	16:17–20
0169	Princeton fragment	Fourth	3:19–4:3
0207		Fourth	9:2–15
0229		Seventh–eighth	18:16–17; 19:4–6
0308		Fourth	11:15–16, 17–18

Codex ℵ is the oldest complete copy of Revelation. In the early to mid-fourth century it was copied by two scribes, who made corrections to their texts. In the seventh century, three other scribes made additional corrections. Although the quality of this manuscript is high for much of the NT, it is less reliable for Revelation. It includes many scribal errors and omissions, and has 201 readings not found in other manuscripts of Revelation. Some of the unique readings arose through careless copying, whereas others may reflect theological concerns. For example, other manuscripts call Christ "the beginning of the creation [*ktiseōs*] of God," but ℵ reads "the beginning of the church [*ekklēsias*] of God" (3:14). Although the copyist might have inadvertently repeated "church" from the earlier part of the verse, the change could have been made to ensure that Christ was seen as the founder of the church but not as a creature, since that was a disputed point in the fourth century. Where Christ tells the luke-warm Laodiceans, "I am about to vomit you out of my mouth" (3:16), ℵ says Christ will "stop your mouth," avoiding the impression that Christ would engage in crude human behavior (Hernández, *Scribal*, 89–91; "Codex"; Karrer, "Text der Johannesoffenbarung," 380–83).

The fifth-century A is the most valuable manuscript of Revelation. The text was copied by a single scribe, who made an accurate transcription from a reliable exemplar. Although A is not as important for other parts of the NT, it preserves a high-quality reading of Revelation. It includes eighty-four singular readings, at least three of which may preserve the earliest form of the text: the unusual spelling *katēgōr* for "accuser" (12:10); the idea that if anyone is to "be killed" by the sword, he will be killed (13:10); and the spelling of "passed away" (*apēlthan*) in 21:4. Some scholars discern a realized eschatology in A, which refers to the reign of the saints in the present rather than the future tense as some other manuscripts do; but it is not clear that the temporal aspect can be pressed (NOTE on 5:10; cf. 20:6). Picturing priests (*hiereis*) rather than a rainbow (*iris*) around the throne (4:3) or identifying the two witnesses with the "courts" (*aulaiai*) of the sanctuary rather than "olive trees" (*elaiai*, 11:4) could reflect the copyist's cultic interests or may simply be errors. On the whole, the scribe did little editorializing. The readings generally correspond to those of C (Hernández, *Scribal*, 96–131; Karrer, "Text der Johannesoffenbarung," 383–96; Sigismund, "Schreiber").

Codex C is another manuscript that is more valuable for Revelation than for other parts of the NT. It is a palimpsest. The biblical text was copied by a single scribe in the fifth century, and a few corrections were made in the sixth century. In the twelfth century it was erased and copied over with treatises by Saint Ephraem. Its text of Revelation is incomplete and sometimes difficult to recover, but the readings are generally good and correspond to those of A. There are few signs of editorializing by the scribe (Hernández, *Scribal*, 132–54).

Minuscules

The most numerous manuscripts of Revelation are minuscules, most dating from the tenth century and later. Many preserve the text along with one of the Greek commentaries on it. Some minuscules reflect the text type represented by A, C, and the quotations in Oecumenius (2053, 2062, and 2344); others are closer to the type found in $\mathfrak{P}^{47}$ and א (1854, 2329).

Two other text types also appear. One is the text used in the commentary by Andreas, and the other is called the Koine or Byzantine text. Both represent edited versions of an earlier text form, which differed from that of A and C as well as from $\mathfrak{P}^{47}$ and א. If the textual traditions on which these edited versions are based are significantly older, perhaps dating to the fourth century, then they would be contemporary with the text types represented in the papyri and uncials. Therefore, despite the editing, manuscripts in the Andreas and Koine categories may occasionally preserve early readings. For example, in contrast to A and א, they correctly picture a rainbow (*iris*) rather than priests (*hiereis*) around the throne (4:3; Schmid, *Studien*, 2:146).

Beyond the types noted above, there are minuscules that are difficult to categorize. They show the influence of various textual traditions and are often called "mixed" texts. (For lists of minuscules, see Aune 1:cxl–cxlviii; Lembke, "Beobachtungen," 62–69.)

Patristic Quotations

Quotations of Revelation by ancient writers can be useful for textual reconstruction, though care must be taken because it is not always clear how closely an author adheres to a written form of the text. Irenaeus (d. ca. 200) quotes from Revelation, but the form of the Greek text he uses is not clear because much of his work is extant only in Latin and Armenian translation. Clement of Alexandria (d. 215) paraphrases rather than quotes Revelation, so his work is of little help for study of the text. Hippolytus (d. 235) quotes large sections of the book in his treatise on the Antichrist and smaller excerpts appear in his commentary on Daniel. Though his readings include some distinctive elements, they usually agree with those in one or more of the early uncials, over against those in the Andreas and Koine traditions. The same is true of quotations in works by Methodius (d. 311) and Eusebius (d. 339). The quotations in Origen (d. 254), however, seem most closely aligned with the text type represented by $\mathfrak{P}^{47}$ and א (Schmid, *Studien*, 2:151–72).

Summary

The Greek text of Revelation has four main types, which are summarized here in order of importance. Textual critics give priority to the manuscripts in the first two categories, but those in the third and fourth categories may on occasion preserve better readings. The text used for this commentary is the twenty-seventh edition of the Nestle-Aland *Novum Testamentum Graece* (NA[27]), which selects the best readings from witnesses in all categories. Occasional differences from the NA[27] are discussed in the Notes (Schmid, *Studien*, 2:146–47; Parker, *Introduction*, 240–41; Karrer, "Text der Johannesapokalypse," 76).

1. The most important text type is represented by the fifth-century witnesses A and C, along with the text in Oecumenius's commentary and minuscules 2053, 2062, and 2344. Additional support may come from the fragmentary $\mathfrak{P}^{115}$ and perhaps $\mathfrak{P}^{18}$, $\mathfrak{P}^{24}$, and $\mathfrak{P}^{98}$.

2. Next in importance is the type represented by $\mathfrak{P}^{47}$ and the original text of Sinaiticus ($\aleph^*$), along with the text used by Origen and some minuscules (e.g., 1854 and 2329).

3. The text type of Andreas is reflected in the uncials 025 (P), 051, and 052, as well as in corrections made to Sinaiticus ($\aleph^a$) and many minuscules (e.g., 1, 2186, and 2428).

4. Finally, the Koine group includes the uncial 046 and many minuscules (e.g., 1859, 1872, 2027, and 2256).

BIBLIOGRAPHY

The bibliography includes selected works from various periods, with preference given to recent contributions. In the NOTES and COMMENTS, commentaries are cited only by the author's last name; other works include a short title. An unnumbered footnote at the beginning of each COMMENT section lists bibliographic entries pertinent to that section.

200–500 CE

Victorinus (d. 304). *In Apocalypsin*. Pages 46–123 in *Sur l'Apocalypse et autre écrits*. Edited and translated by M. Dulaey. SC 423. Paris: Cerf, 1997. English translation in *Latin Commentaries on Revelation*. Edited and translated by William C. Weinrich. Ancient Christian Texts. Downers Grove, IL: IVP Academic, 2011.

Tyconius (d. ca. 400). *The Turin Fragments of Tyconius' Commentary on Revelation*. Edited by Francesco Lo Bue. Cambridge: Cambridge University Press, 1963. For a synopsis of sources, see Kenneth B. Steinhauser, *The Apocalypse Commentary of Tyconius: A History of Its Reception and Influence* (Frankfurt: Lang, 1987), 267–316.

Jerome (d. 420). "Prologue" and "Epilogue" to Victorinus's *Commentarii in Apocalypsin*. Pages 124–31 in *Sur l'Apocalypse et autre écrits*. Edited and translated by M. Dulaey. SC 423. Paris: Cerf, 1997.

500–1500

Oecumenius (early sixth century). *In Apocalypsin*, in *Oecumenii Commentarius in Apocalypsin*. Edited by Marc de Groote. Louvain: Peeters, 1999. English translation in *Oecumenius: Commentary on the Apocalypse*. Translated by John N. Suggit. FC 112. Washington, DC: Catholic University of America, 2006.

Primasius (d. ca. 560). *Commentarius in Apocalypsin*. Edited by A. W. Adams. CCSL 92. Turnhout: Brepols, 1985.

Caesarius of Arles (ca. 540). *Expositio in Apocalypsim Joannes*. PL 35:2417–52. English translation in *Latin Commentaries on Revelation*. Edited and translated by William C. Weinrich. Ancient Christian Texts. Downers Grove, IL: IVP Academic, 2011.

Apringius of Beja (ca. 550). *Tractatus in Apocalypsin*. Edited by Roger Gryson. CCL 107:33–97. Turnhout: Brepols, 2003. English translation in *Latin Commentaries on Revelation*. Edited and translated by William C. Weinrich. Ancient Christian Texts. Downers Grove: IVP Academic, 2011.

Cassiodorus (ca. 580). *Complexiones in Apocalypsi*. Pages 113–29 in *Commentaria Minora in Apocalypsin Johannis*. Edited by Roger Gryson. CCL 107. Turnhout: Brepols, 2003.

Unknown (ca. 550–600). *Pauca de Monogramma*. Pages in 149–57 in *Commentaria Minora in Apocalypsin Johannis*. Edited by Roger Gryson. CCL 107. Turnhout: Brepols, 2003.

Andreas of Caesarea (d. ca. 614). *In Apocalypsin*. In *Der Apokalypse-Kommentar des Andreas von Kaisareia. Studien zur Geschichte des griechischen Apokalypse-Textes*, part 1. Edited by J. Schmid. Munich: Zink, 1955. Translated by Eugenia Scarvelis Constantinou. FC 123. Washington, DC: Catholic University of America, 2011.

Unknown (ca. 650–700). *Commemoratorium de Apocalypsi Johannis Apostoli*. Pages 193–229 in *Commentaria Minora in Apocalypsin Johannis*. Edited by Roger Gryson. CCL 107. Turnhout: Brepols, 2003.

Bede (d. ca. 735). *Explanatio Apocalypsis*. PL 93:129–206. English translation in *Latin Commentaries on Revelation*. Edited and translated by William C. Weinrich. Ancient Christian Texts. Downers Grove, IL: IVP Academic, 2011.

Ambrose Autpert (d. 784). *Expositionis in Apocalypsin*. Edited by Robert Weber. 2 vols. CCCM 27–27A. Turnhout: Brepols, 1975.

Beatus of Liébana (ca. 780). *Beati in Apocalypsin libri duodecim*. Edited by H. A. Sanders. Rome: American Academy in Rome, 1985.

Alcuin (d. 804). *Commentariorum in Apocalypsin*. PL 100:1089–1156.

Haimo of Auxerre (d. ca. 855). *Expositionis in Apocalypsin B. Joannis*. PL 117: 937–1220.

Berengaudus (ca. 860). *Expositio super septem visiones libri Apocalypsis*. PL 17:765–970.

Arethas of Caesarea (d. ca. 932). *Ioannis theologi ac dilecti Apocalypsis*. PG 106: 487–786.

Anselm of Laon (d. 1117). *Enarrationes in Apocalypsin*. PL 162:1499–1586.

——— et al. *Glossa ordinaria* (ca. 1120). In *Biblia Latina cum glossa ordinaria. Facsimile Reprint of the Editio Princeps of Adolph Rusch of Strassburg 1480/81*. Turnhout: Brepols, 1992.

Bruno of Segni (d. 1123). *Expositio in Apocalypsin*. PL 165:605–736.

Rupert of Deutz (d. ca. 1129). *In Apocalypsim*. PL 169:825–1214.

Peter Lombard (d. 1164). *The Sentences*. Translated by Giulio Silano. 4 vols. Toronto: Pontifical Institute of Mediaeval Studies, 2007–10.

Dionysius bar Salibi (d. 1171). *In Apocalypsim*. Pages 3–29 in Corpus Scriptorum Christianorum Orientalum 59 (Syriac) and pages 1–22 in vol. 60 (Latin). Edited by I. Sedlacek. Leipzig: Harrassowitz, 1909–10.

Richard of St. Victor (d. 1173). *In Apocalypsim Joannis*. PL 196:683–888.

Peter of Tarantaise (d. 1174). *Apocalypsis B. Joannis Apostoli*. Pages 465–792 in *D. Alberti Magni Opera Omnia*. Vol. 38. Paris: Ludovicum Vivès, 1890.

Geoffrey of Auxerre (ca. 1188). *On the Apocalypse*. Kalamazoo, MI: Cistercian Publications, 2000.

Joachim of Fiore (d. 1202). *Enchiridion super Apocalypsim*. Edited by E. K. Burger. Toronto: Pontifical Institute of Mediaeval Studies, 1986.

———. *Expositio in Apocalypsim*. Frankfurt: Minerva, 1964.

Hugh of Saint Cher (d. 1263). *Expositio super Apocalypsim*. In *Doctoris angelici divi Thomae Aquinatis Opera Omnia*. Pages 469–661 in vol. 31 and pages 1–89 in vol. 32. Paris: Ludovicum Vivès, 1876, 1879.

———. *Libri Apocalypsis*. Pages 332v–390v in *Prima (-sexta) pars huius operis: contine[n]s textum biblie, cu[m] postilla domini Hugonis Cardinals*. Vol. 6. Basel: Johann Froben, 1504.

Alexander Minorita (d. 1271). *Expositio in apocalypsim*. *Monumenta Germaniae Historica*. Quellen 1. Weimar: Hermann Böhlaus Nachfolger, 1955.

Thomas Aquinas (d. 1274). *Summa Theologiae*. 60 vols. New York: McGraw-Hill, 1964–66.

Nicolas de Gorran (d. 1295). *In Apocalypsin Johannis Apostoli*. Pages 178–304 in *In Acta Apostolorum, et singulas apostolorum Jacobi, Petri, Johannis et Judae canonicas Epistolas, et Apocalypsin commentarii*. Antwerp, 1620.

Peter Auriol (d. 1322). *Compendium sensus literalis totius divinae scripturae*. Quaracchi: College of Saint Bonaventure, 1896.

Nicholas of Lyra (d. 1349). *Postilla super totam bibliam*. Frankfurt am Main: Minerva, 1964. Reproduction of the Strassburg 1492 edition.

Jan Hus (d. 1415). *The Church*. Translated by David S. Schaff. New York: Scribner's, 1915.

———. "On Simony." Pages 196–278 in *Advocates of Reform: From Wyclif to Erasmus*. Edited by Matthew Spinka. LCL 14. Philadelphia: Westminster, 1953.

1500–1750

Müntzer, Thomas (d. 1525). *The Collected Works of Thomas Müntzer*. Edited and translated by Peter Matheson. Edinburgh: T. & T. Clark, 1988.

Erasmus, Desiderius (d. 1536). *Adnotationes: Apocalypsis Beati Joannis Theologi*. Pages 1093–1126 in *Desiderii Erasmi Roterdami Opera Omnia*. Edited by J. Leclerc. Vol. 6. Leiden, 1703–6. Reprint. London: Gregg, 1962.

Hoffmann, Melchior (d. 1543 or 1544). *Auslegung der heimlichen Offenbarung Joannis des heyligen Apostels und Evangelisten*. Strasbourg: Beck, 1530.

Luther, Martin (d. 1546). "Preface to the Revelation of St. John." Translated by E. Theodore Bachmann. Pages 398–411 in *Word and Sacrament*. LuthW 35. Philadelphia: Fortress, 1960. German text in WA.DB 7:404–523.

Lambert, Francis (d. 1530). *Exegeseos Francisci Lamberti Auenioensis, in sanctam diui Ioannis Apocalypsim, libri VII. In academia Marpurgensi praelecti*. Marburg: Franz Rhode, 1528.

Meyer, Sebastian (d. 1546). *In Apocalypsim Iohannis Apostoli D. Sebastiani Meyer ecclesiastae Bernensis commentarius: nostro huic saeculo accommodatus, natus, & aeditus*. Tiguri: Froschouiana, 1539.

Bale, John (d. 1563). *The Image of Bothe Churches after the Moste Wonderfull and Heauenly Reuelacion of Sainct Iohn the Evangelist*. London: Richard Iugge, 1548.

Bullinger, Heinrich (d. 1575). *A Hundred Sermons vpo[n] the Apocalips of Iesu Christe*. London: Iohn Day, 1561.

Chemnitz, Martin (d. 1586). *Examination of the Council of Trent*. Translated by Fred Kramer. St. Louis, MO: Concordia, 1971–86.

Ribera, Francisco (d. 1591). *In Sacrum Beati Ioannis Apostoli, & Evangelistiae Apocalypsin Commentarij*. Antwerp: Petrum Bellerum, 1593.

Brightman, Thomas (d. 1607). *A Revelation of the Revelation that is, the Revelation of St. Iohn*. Amsterdam, 1615.

Alcázar, Luis de (d. 1613). *Vestigatio arcani sensus in Apocalypsi*. Antwerp: Ioannem Keer-bergium, 1614.

Napier, John (d. 1617). *A Plaine Discovery, of the Whole Revelation of Saint John*. Edinburgh: Robert Walde-grane, 1593.

Pareus, David (d. 1622). *A Commentary upon the Divine Revelation of the Apostle and Evangelist John*. Translated by Elias Arnold. Amsterdam: C.P., 1644. Latin original *In divinam Apocalypsim S. Apostoli et evangelistae Johannes commentarius*. Heidelberg: Jonae Rosae, 1618.

Lapide, Cornelius a (d. 1637). *Commentarius in Apocalypsin Sancti Joannis Apostoli*. Pages 1011–1368 in *Commentarii in Scripturam Sacram*. Vol. 10. Lugduni: Pelagaud et Roblot, 1875.

Mede, Joseph (d. 1638). *Clauis apocalyptica: ex innatis et insitis visionum characteribus eruta et demonstrata*. Cantabrigiae: Buck, 1627. Translated by R. Bransby Cooper. London: Rivington, 1833.

Alsted, Johann Heinrich (d. 1638). *Diatribe de Mille Annis Apocalypticis*. Frankfurt: Eifridi, 1627.

Grotius, Hugo (d. 1645). *Annotationes in Apocalypsin*. In *Annotationum in Novum Testamentum*. Vol. 3. Paris: Pepingvé & Mavcroy, 1650.

Calov, Abraham (d. 1686). *Biblia Novi Testamenti Illustrata*. Vol. 2. Frankfurt: Wustii, 1676.

Bossuet, Jacques-Bénigne (d. 1704). *L'Apocalypse avec une explication*. 1688.

Newton, Isaac (d. 1727). *Observations upon the Prophecies of Daniel and the Apocalypse of St. John*. London: Darby and Browne, 1733.

Edwards, Jonathan (d. 1758). *Apocalyptic Writings*. Vol. 5 of *The Works of Jonathan Edwards*. Edited by Stephen J. Stein. New Haven, CT: Yale University Press, 1977.

Selected Commentaries from 1750 to the Present

Aune, D. *Revelation*. 3 vols. WBC 52. Dallas: Word, 1997–98.

Barr, David L. *Tales of the End: A Narrative Commentary on the Book of Revelation*. Santa Rosa, CA: Polebridge, 1998.

Beale, G. K. *The Book of Revelation: A Commentary on the Greek Text*. Grand Rapids, MI: Eerdmans; Carlisle: Paternoster, 1999.

Beasley-Murray, G. R. *Revelation*. NCBC. Grand Rapids, MI: Eerdmans; London: Marshall, Morgan & Scott, 1974.

Beckwith, Ibson T. *The Apocalypse of John: Studies in Introduction with a Critical Exegetical Commentary*. New York: Macmillan, 1922.

Blount, Brian K. *Revelation: A Commentary*. New Testament Library. Louisville, KY: Westminster John Knox, 2009.

Boring, M. Eugene. *Revelation*. Louisville, KY: Westminster John Knox, 1989.

Bousset, Wilhelm. *Die Offenbarung Johannis*. MeyerK. Göttingen: Vandenhoeck & Ruprecht, 1906.

Boxall, Ian. *The Revelation of Saint John*. BNTC. Peabody, MA: Hendrickson; London: Continuum, 2006.

Brighton, Louis A. *Revelation*. Concordia Commentary. St. Louis, MO: Concordia, 1999.

Brütsch, Charles. *Die Offenbarung Jesu Christi*. 3 vols. Zurich: Zwingli, 1970.

Caird, G. B. *A Commentary on the Revelation of St. John the Divine*. HNTC. New York: Harper & Row, 1966.

Charles, R. H. *A Critical and Exegetical Commentary on the Revelation of St. John*. 2 vols. ICC. Edinburgh: T. & T. Clark, 1920.

Court, John M. *Revelation*. New Testament Guides. Huddersfield: Sheffield Academic Press, 1994.

Düsterdieck, Friedrich. *Critical and Exegetical Handbook to the Revelation of John*. New York: Funk & Wagnalls, 1886. German original: 1859.

Ebrard, Johannes Heinrich August. *Die Offenbarung Johannes*. Olshausen Biblisher Commentar. Königsberg: Unzer, 1853.

Elliott, Edward B. *Horae Apocalypticae*. 3rd ed. 4 vols. London: Seeley, Burnside, and Seeley, 1847.

Ewald, Heinrich. *Commentarius in Apocalypsin Johannis exegeticus et criticus*. Leipzig: Librariae Hahnianae, 1828.

Fee, Gordon D. *Revelation*. New Covenant Commentary Series. Eugene, OR: Cascade, 2011.

Ford, J. Massyngberde. *Revelation*. AYB 38. New York: Doubleday, 1975; reprint, New Haven, CT: Yale University Press.

Giblin, Charles Homer. *Revelation: The Open Book of Prophecy*. Collegeville, MN: Liturgical, 1991.

Giesen, Heinz. *Die Offenbarung des Johannes*. Regensburger Neues Testament. Regensburg: Pustet, 1997.

Harrington, Wilfrid J. *Revelation*. Sacra Pagina 16. Collegeville, MN: Liturgical, 1993.

Hengstenberg, E. W. *The Revelation of St. John*. 2 vols. Clark's Foreign Theological Library. Edinburgh: T. & T. Clark, 1851–52.

Holtz, Traugott. *Die Offenbarung des Johannes*. NTD 11. Göttingen: Vandenhoeck & Ruprecht, 2008.

Keener, Craig S. *Revelation*. NIV Application Commentary. Grand Rapids, MI: Zondervan, 2000.

Kiddle, Martin. *The Revelation of St. John*. Moffatt New Testament Commentary. London: Hodder and Stoughton, 1940.

Knight, Jonathan. *Revelation*. 2nd ed. Readings. Sheffield: Sheffield Phoenix, 2011.

Kraft, Heinrich. *Die Offenbarung des Johannes*. HNT 16a. Tübingen: Mohr Siebeck, 1974.

Krodel, Gerhard A. *Revelation*. ACNT. Minneapolis: Augsburg, 1989.

LaHaye, Tim. *Revelation Unveiled*. Grand Rapids, MI: Zondervan, 1999.

Lenski, Richard Charles Henry. *The Interpretation of St. John's Revelation*. Minneapolis: Augsburg, 1943.

Lohmeyer, Ernst. *Die Offenbarung des Johannes*. 2nd ed. HNT 16. Tübingen: Mohr Siebeck, 1953.

Lupieri, Edmundo F. *A Commentary on the Apocalypse of John*. Translated by Maria Poggi Johnson and Adam Kamesar. Grand Rapids, MI: Eerdmans, 1999.

Malina, Bruce J., and John J. Pilch. *Social-Science Commentary on the Book of Revelation*. Minneapolis: Fortress, 2000.

Michaels, J. Ramsey. *Revelation*. IVP New Testament Commentary. Downers Grove, IL: InterVarsity, 1997.

Morris, Leon. *Revelation*. Rev. ed. TNTC. Leicester: InterVarsity; Grand Rapids, MI: Eerdmans, 1987.

Mounce, Robert H. *The Book of Revelation*. Rev. ed. NICNT. Grand Rapids, MI: Eerdmans, 1998.

Müller, Ulrich B. *Die Offenbarung des Johannes*. 2nd ed. Ökumenischer Taschenbuch-Kommentar Neuen Testament 19. Gütersloh: Echter, 1984.

Murphy, Frederick J. *Fallen Is Babylon: The Revelation to John*. Harrisburg, PA: Trinity, 1998.

Osborne, Grant R. *Revelation*. Baker Exegetical Commentary on the New Testament. Grand Rapids, MI: Baker Academic, 2002.

Perkins, Pheme. *The Book of Revelation*. Collegeville Bible Commentary 11. Collegeville, MN: Liturgical, 1983.

Prigent, Pierre. *Commentary on the Apocalypse of St. John*. Translated by Wendy Pradels. Tübingen: Mohr Siebeck, 2001.

Reddish, Mitchell G. *Revelation*. Smyth & Helwys Bible Commentary. Macon, GA: Smyth & Helwys, 2001.

Resseguie, James L. *The Revelation of John: A Narrative Commentary*. Grand Rapids, MI: Baker Academic, 2009.

Richard, Pablo. *Apocalypse: A People's Commentary on the Book of Revelation*. Maryknoll, NY: Orbis, 1995.

Roloff, Jürgen. *Revelation*. Translated by John E. Alsup. Continental Commentaries. Minneapolis: Fortress, 1993.

Rowland, Christopher. *Revelation*. *NIB* 12. Nashville, TN: Abingdon, 1998.

Satake, Akira. *Die Offenbarung des Johannes*. MeyerK 16. Göttingen: Vandenhoeck & Ruprecht, 2008.

Schüssler Fiorenza, Elisabeth. *Revelation: Vision of a Just World*. Minneapolis: Fortress, 1991.

Scofield, Cyrus. *The Scofield Reference Bible*. New York: Oxford; London: Milford, 1917.

Seiss, J. A. *The Apocalypse*. 3 vols. Philadelphia: Sherman, 1881.

Smalley, Stephen S. *The Revelation to John: A Commentary on the Greek Text of the Apocalypse*. Downers Grove, IL: InterVarsity, 2005.

Stuart, Moses. *A Commentary on the Apocalypse*. Edinburgh: Maclachlan, Stewart, 1847.

Sweet, John. *Revelation*. TPI New Testament Commentaries. London: SCM; Philadelphia: Trinity, 1990.

Swete, Henry Barclay. *The Apocalypse of Saint John*. 3rd ed. London: Macmillan, 1911.

Talbert, Charles H. *The Apocalypse: A Reading of the Revelation of John*. Louisville, KY: Westminster John Knox, 1994.

Thomas, Robert L. *Revelation*. 2 vols. Chicago: Moody, 1992–95.

Thompson, Leonard L. *Revelation*. ANTC. Nashville, TN: Abingdon, 1998.

Trafton, Joseph C. *Reading Revelation: A Literary and Theological Commentary*. Macon, GA: Smyth & Helwys, 2005.

Wall, Robert W. *Revelation*. NIBC. Peabody, MA: Hendrickson, 1991.

Walvoord, John F. *The Revelation of Jesus Christ: A Commentary*. Chicago: Moody, 1966.

Witherington, Ben, III. *Revelation*. NCBC. Cambridge: Cambridge University Press, 2003.

Yarbro Collins, Adela. *The Apocalypse*. New Testament Message 22. Wilmington, DE: Glazier, 1979.

Other Books and Articles

Abir, Peter Antonysamy. *The Cosmic Conflict of the Church: An Exegetico-Theological Study of Revelation 12, 7–12*. Frankfurt am Main: Peter Lang, 1995.

Abusch, Raʿanan. "Sevenfold Hymns in *The Songs of the Sabbath Sacrifice* and the Hekhalot Literature: Formalism, Hierarchy and the Limits of Human Participation." Pages 220–47 in *The Dead Sea Scrolls as Background to Postbiblical Judaism and Early Christianity*. Edited by James R. Davila. *STDJ* 46 Leiden: Brill, 2003.

Achtemeier, Elizabeth. *The Book of Joel*. NIB 7. Nashville, TN: Abingdon, 1996.

Achtemeier, Paul J. *1 Peter*. Hermeneia. Minneapolis: Fortress, 1996.

Adams, Edward. "The 'Coming of God' Tradition and Its Influence on New Testament Parousia Texts." Pages 1–19 in *Biblical Traditions in Transmission: Essays in Honour of Michael A. Knibb*. JSJSup 111. Leiden: Brill, 2006.

———. *The Stars Will Fall from Heaven: Cosmic Catastrophe in the New Testament and Its World*. LNTS 347. London: T. & T. Clark, 2007.

Albl, Martin C. *"And Scripture Cannot Be Broken": The Form and Function of the Early Christian Testamonia Collections*. NovTSup 96. Leiden: Brill, 1999.

Allison, Dale C. "The Silence of the Angels: Reflections on the Songs of the Sabbath Sacrifice." *RevQ* 13 (1988): 189–97.

Ameling, Walter. "Der kleinasiatische Kaiserkult und die Öffentlichkeit. Überlegungen zur Umwelt der Apokalypse." Pages 15–54 in *Kaiserkult, Wirtschaft und spectacula: Zum Politischen und gesellschaftlichen Umfeld der Offenbarung*. Edited by Martin Ebner and Elisabeth Esch-Wermeling. SUNT 72. Göttingen: Vandenhoeck & Ruprecht, 2011.

Andrews, John Nevins. *Three Messages of Revelation XIV, 6–12, Particularly the Third Angel's Message*. Rochester, NY: Advent Library Office, 1855.

Arterbury, Andrew. *Entertaining Angels: Early Christian Hospitality in Its Mediterranean Setting*. New Testament Monographs 8. Sheffield: Sheffield Phoenix, 2005.

Ascough, Richard S. "Greco-Roman Religions in Sardis and Smyrna." Pages 25–39 in *Religious Rivalries and the Struggle for Success in Sardis and Smyrna*. Edited by Richard S. Ascough. ESCJ 14. Waterloo, Ont.: Wilfrid Laurier University Press, 2005.

———. "Interaction Among Religious Groups in Sardis and Smyrna." Pages 3–16 in *Religious Rivalries and the Struggle for Success in Sardis and Smyrna.* Edited by Richard S. Ascough. ESCJ 14. Waterloo, Ont.: Wilfrid Laurier University Press, 2005.

———, ed. *Religious Rivalries and the Struggle for Success in Sardis and Smyrna.* ESCJ 14. Waterloo, Ont.: Wilfrid Laurier University Press, 2005.

Aune, David E. *Apocalypticism, Prophecy, and Magic in Early Christianity.* Grand Rapids, MI: Baker Academic, 2008.

———. *Prophecy in Early Christianity and in the Ancient Mediterranean World.* Grand Rapids, MI: Eerdmans, 1983.

Aus, Roger D. "Relevance of Isaiah 66:7 to Revelation 12 and 2 Thessalonians 1." *ZNW* 67 (1976): 252–68.

Austin, M. M. *The Hellenistic World from Alexander to the Roman Conquest: A Selection of Sources in Translation.* Cambridge: Cambridge University Press, 1981.

Babcock, William S. *Tyconius: The Book of Rules.* Society of Biblical Literature Texts and Translations. 31. Atlanta: Scholars, 1989.

Bachmann, Michael. "Ausmessung vom Tempel und Stadt: Apk 11,1f und 21,5ff auf dem Hintergrund des Buches Ezechiel." Pages 61–83 in *Das Ezechielbuch in der Johannesoffenbarung.* Edited by Dieter Sänger. Neukirchen-Vluyn: Neukirchener, 2004.

———. "Die apokalyptischen Reiter: Dürers Holzschnitt und die Auslegungsgeschichte von Apk 6,1–8." *ZTK* 86 (1989): 33–58.

———. "Himmlisch: Der 'Tempel Gottes' von Apk 11.1." *NTS* 40 (1994): 474–80.

———. "Noch ein Blick auf den ersten apokalyptischen Reiter (von Apk. 6,1–2)." *NTS* 44 (1998): 257–78.

Backhaus, Knut. "Apokalyptische Bilder? Die Vernunft der Vision in der Johannes-Offenbarung." *Evangelische Theologie* 64 (2004): 421–37.

———. "Die Vision vom ganz Anderen: Geschichtlicher Ort und theologische Mitte der Johannes-Offenbarung." Pages 10–53 in *Theologie als vision: Studien zur Johannes-Offenbarung.* Edited by Knut Backhaus. SBS 191. Stuttgart: Katholisches Bibelwerk, 2001.

Backus, Irena. *Reformation Readings of the Apocalypse: Geneva, Zurich, and Wittenberg.* Oxford: Oxford University Press, 2000.

Bailey, James L. "Genre Analysis." Pages 197–221 in *Hearing the New Testament: Strategies for Interpretation.* Edited by Joel B. Green. Grand Rapids, MI: Eerdmans, 1995.

Baines, W. G. "The Number of the Beast in Revelation 13:18." *Heythrop Journal* 16 (1975): 195–96.

Baird, William. *History of New Testament Research.* 2 vols. Minneapolis: Fortress, 1992, 2003.

Balch, David L. "Two Apologetic Encomia: Dionysius on Rome and Josephus on the Jews." *JSJ* 13 (1982): 102–22.

———. "'A Woman Clothed with the Sun' and the 'Great Red Dragon' Seeking to 'Devour Her Child' (Rev 12:1, 4) in Roman Domestic Art." Pages 287–314 in *The New Testament and Early Christian Literature in Greco-Roman Context: Studies in Honor of David E. Aune.* Edited by John Fotopoulos. NovTSup 122. Leiden: Brill, 2006.

Ball, David Mark. *"I Am" in John's Gospel: Literary Function, Background and Theological Implications*. JSNTSup 124. Sheffield: Sheffield Academic, 1996.

Balsdon, J. P. V. D. *Romans and Aliens*. London: Duckworth, 1979.

Baltzer, Klaus. *Deutero-Isaiah*. Hermeneia. Minneapolis: Fortress, 2001.

Bandstra, Andrew J. "'A Kingship and Priests': Inaugurated Eschatology in the Apocalypse." *Calvin Theological Journal* 27 (1992): 10–25.

Bandy, Alan S. "The Layers of the Apocalypse: An Integrative Approach to Revelation's Macrostructure." *JSNT* 31 (2009): 469–99.

Barclay, John M. G. *Jews in the Mediterranean Diaspora from Alexander to Trajan (323 BCE–117 CE)*. Edinburgh: T. & T. Clark, 1996.

Barker, Margaret. *The Revelation of Jesus Christ: Which God Gave to Him to Show to His Servants What Must Soon Take Place (Revelation 1.1)*. Edinburgh: T. & T. Clark, 2000.

Barnes, Robin. "Images of Hope and Despair: Western Apocalypticism: ca. 1500–1800." Pages 143–84 in *Apocalypticism in Western History and Culture*. Vol. 2 of *The Encyclopedia of Apocalypticism*. Edited by Bernard McGinn. New York: Continuum, 1998.

Barnett, Paul. "Polemical Parallelism: Some Further Reflections on the Apocalypse." *JSNT* 35 (1989): 111–20.

Barr, David L. "The Apocalypse as a Symbolic Transformation of the World: A Literary Analysis." *Int* 38 (1984): 39–50.

———. "The Apocalypse of John as Oral Enactment." *Int* 40 (1986): 243–56.

———. "Doing Violence: Moral Issues in Reading John's Apocalypse." Pages 97–108 in *Reading the Book of Revelation: A Resource for Students*. Edited by David L. Barr. SBLRBS 44. Atlanta: Society of Biblical Literature, 2003.

———. "Idol Meat and Satanic Synagogues: From Imagery to History in John's Apocalypse." Pages 1–10 in *Imagery in the Book of Revelation*. Edited by Michael Labahn and Outi Lehtipun. Leuven: Peeters, 2001.

———. "The Lamb Who Looks Like a Dragon? Characterizing Jesus in John's Apocalypse." Pages 205–20 in *The Reality of Apocalypse: Rhetoric and Politics in the Book of Revelation*. Edited by David L. Barr. SBLSymS 39. Atlanta: Society of Biblical Literature, 2006.

———. "Towards an Ethical Reading of the Apocalypse: Reflections on John's Use of Power, Violence, and Misogyny." Pages 358–73 in SBLSP 36. Atlanta: Scholars, 1997.

Barth, Markus, and Helmut Blanke. *Colossians*. AYB 34B. New York: Doubleday, 1994; reprint, New Haven, CT: Yale University Press.

Bauckham, Richard. *The Book of Acts in Its Palestinian Setting*. Vol. 4 of *The Book of Acts in Its First Century Setting*. Grand Rapids, MI: Eerdmans; Carlisle: Paternoster, 1995.

———. *The Climax of Prophecy: Studies in the Book of Revelation*. Edinburgh: Clark, 1993.

———. "The List of the Tribes in Revelation 7 Again." *JSNT* 42 (1991): 99–115.

———. "The Lord's Day." Pages 221–50 in *From Sabbath to Lord's Day: A Biblical, Historical, and Theological Investigation*. Edited by D. A. Carson. Grand Rapids, MI: Zondervan, 1982.

———. "The Martyrdom of Enoch and Elijah: Jewish or Christian?" *JBL* 95 (1976): 447–58.

———. *The Theology of the Book of Revelation*. Cambridge: Cambridge University Press, 1993.

———. *Tudor Apocalypse: Sixteenth Century Apocalypticism, Millennarianism, and the English Reformation, from John Bale to John Foxe and Thomas Brightman*. Oxford: Sutton Courtenay, 1978.

Bauer, Thomas Johann. *Das tausendjährige Messiasreich der Johannesoffenbarung: Eine literarkritische Studie zu Offb 19,11–21,8*. BZNW 148. Berlin: de Gruyter, 2007.

Baynes, Leslie. *The Heavenly Book Motif in Judeo-Christian Apocalypses 200 B.C.E.– 200 C.E.* JSJSup 152. Leiden: Brill, 2012.

———. "Revelation 5:1 and 10:2a, 8–10 in the Earliest Greek Tradition: A Response to Richard Bauckham." *JBL* 129 (2010): 801–16.

Beagley, Alan James. *The "Sitz im Leben" of the Apocalypse with Particular Reference to the Role of the Church's Enemies*. BZNW 50. Berlin: de Gruyter, 1987.

Beale, Gregory K. *John's Use of the Old Testament in Revelation*. Sheffield: Sheffield Academic, 1998.

———. "Solecisms in the Apocalypse as Signals for the Presence of Old Testament Allusions: A Selective Analysis of Revelation 1–22." Pages 421–46 in *Early Christian Interpretation of the Scriptures of Israel: Investigations and Proposals*. Edited by Craig A. Evans and James A. Sanders. JSNTSup 148. Sheffield: Sheffield Academic, 1997.

———. *The Use of Daniel in Jewish Apocalyptic Literature and in the Revelation of St. John*. Lanham, MD: University Press of America, 1984.

Bean, George Ewart. *Turkey Beyond the Maeander: An Archaeological Guide*. London: Benn; Totowa, NJ: Rowan and Littlefield, 1971.

Beard, Mary, and John North, eds. *Pagan Priests: Religion and Power in the Ancient World*. Ithaca, NY: Cornell University Press, 1990.

Beard, Mary, John North, and Simon Price. *Religions of Rome*. 2 vols. Cambridge: Cambridge University Press, 1998.

Beasley-Murray, George. R. *John*. WBC 36. 2nd ed. Nashville, TN: Thomas Nelson, 1999.

Beauvery, Robert. "L'Apocalypse au risque de la numismatique: Babylone, la grande Prostituée et le sixième roi Vespasien et la décesse Rome." *RB* 90 (1983): 243–60.

Becker, Jürgen. *Untersuchungen zur Entstehungsgeschichte der Testamente der zwölf Patriarchen*. AGJU 8. Leiden: Brill, 1970.

Beirich, Gregory S. "Franciscan Poverty as a Basis for the Reform of the Church in Ubertino da Casale's Arbor vitae crucifixae Jesu." Pages 50–74 in *Reform and Renewal in the Middle Ages and Renaissance: Studies in Honor of Louis Pascoe, S.J.* Edited by Thomas Izbicki and Christopher Bellitto. Leiden: Brill, 2000.

Bell, Albert A. "Date of John's Apocalypse: The Evidence of Some Roman Historians Reconsidered." *NTS* 25 (1978): 93–102.

Benko, Stephen. *The Virgin Goddess: Studies in Pagan and Christian Roots of Mariology*. Leiden: Brill, 1993.

Berger, Klaus. *Die Amen-Worte Jesu: Eine Untersuchung zum Problem der Legitimation in apokalyptischer Rede*. BZNW 39. Berlin: de Gruyter, 1970.

————. *Die Auferstehung des Propheten und die Erhöhung des Menschensohnes: Traditionsgeschichtliche Untersuchungen zur deutung des Geschickes Jesu in frühchristlichen Texten.* SUNT 13. Göttingen: Vandenhoeck & Ruprecht, 1976.

————. "Hellenistisch-heidnische Prodigien und die Verzeichen in der jüdisch und christlichen Apocalyptik." *ANRW* II.23.2 (1980): 1428–69.

Berger, Paul R. "Kollyrium für die blinden Augen, Apk 3:18." *NovT* 27 (1985): 174–95.

Bergmann, Claudia D. *Childbirth as a Metaphor for Crisis: Evidence from the Ancient Near East, the Hebrew Bible, and 1QH XI, 1–18.* BZNW 382. Berlin: de Gruyter, 2008.

Bergmeier, Roland. "Altes und Neues zur 'Sonnenfrau am Himmel (Apk 12)': Religionsgeschichtliche und quellenkritische Beobachtungen zu Apk 12:1–17." *ZNW* 73 (1982): 97–109.

————. "Die Buchrolle und das Lamm (Apk 5 und 10)." *ZNW* 76 (1985): 25–42.

————. "Die Erzhure und das Tier: Apk 12,18–13,18 und 17f. Eine quellen- und redaktionskritische Analyse." *ANRW* II.25.5 (1988): 2899–3916.

————. "Jerusalem, du hochgebaute Stadt." *ZNW* 75 (1984): 86–106.

————. "Zeugnis und Martyrium." Pages 619–47 in *Die Johannesapokalypse: Kontexte—Konzepte—Rezeption.* Edited by Jörg Frey, James A. Kelhoffer, and Franz Tóth. WUNT 287. Tübingen: Mohr Siebeck, 2012.

Berlin, Adele. "Introduction to Hebrew Poetry." *NIB* 4 (1996): 301–15.

Bertrand, Daniel A. "L'Étang de feu et de soufre." *Revue d'histoire et de philosophie religieuses* 79 (1999): 91–99.

Betz, Hans Dieter. *The Greek Magical Papyri in Translation, Including the Demotic Spells.* Chicago: University of Chicago Press, 1986.

————. "On the Problem of the Religio-Historical Understanding of Apocalypticism." Pages 134–56 in *Apocalypticism.* Edited by Robert W. Funk. New York: Herder, 1969.

Biguzzi, Giancarlo. "The Chaos of Rev 22,6–21 and Prophecy in Asia." *Bib* 83 (2002): 193–210.

————. "Ephesus, Its Artemision, Its Temple to the Flavian Emperors, and Idolatry in Revelation." *NovT* 40 (1998): 276–90.

————. *I settenari nella struttura dell' Apocalisse. Analisi, storia della ricerca, interpretation.* RivBSup 31. Bologna: Dehoniane, 1996.

————. "Is the Babylon of Revelation Rome or Jerusalem?" *Bib* 87 (2006): 371–86.

————. "John on Patmos and the 'Persecution' in the Apocalypse." *EstBib* 56 (1998): 201–20.

Birdsall, J. N. "Irenaeus and the Number of the Beast Revelation 13,18." Pages 349–59 in *New Testament Textual Criticism and Exegesis. Festschrift J. Delobel.* Edited by A. Denaux. BETL 161. Leuven: Leuven University Press and Peeters, 2002.

Black, Matthew. *The Book of Enoch or 1 Enoch: A New English Edition.* Leiden: Brill, 1985.

————. "The 'Two Witnesses' of Rev 11:3f. in Jewish and Christian Apocalyptic Tradition. Pages 227–37 in *Donum Gentilicium: New Testament Studies in Honour of David Daube.* Edited by E. Bammel, C. K. Barrett, and W. D. Davies. Oxford: Clarendon, 1978.

Bleek, Friedrich. *Lectures on the Apocalypse*. Edinburgh: Williams and Norgate, 1875.

Blount, Brian K. *Can I Get a Witness?: Reading Revelation Through African American Culture*. Louisville, KY: Westminster John Knox, 2005.

Böcher, Otto. "Johannes der Täufer in der neutestamentlichen Uberlieferung." Pages 45–68 in *Rechtfertigung, Realismus, Universalismus in biblischer Sicht*. Darmstadt: Wissenschaftliche Buchgesellschaft, 1978.

———. *Kirche in Zeit und Endzeit: Aufsätze zur Offenbarung des Johannes*. Neukirchen-Vluyn: Neukirchener, 1983.

———. "Zur Bedeutung der Edelsteine in Offb 21." Pages 19–32 in *Kirche und Bibel: Festgabe für Bischof Eduard Schick*. Paderborn: Ferdinand Schönigh, 1979.

Bøe, Sverre. *Gog and Magog: Ezekiel 38–39 as Pre-text for Revelation 19,17–21 and 20,7–10*. WUNT II/135. Tübingen: Mohr Siebeck, 2001.

Boesak, Allan Aubrey. *Comfort and Protest: Reflections on the Apocalypse of John of Patmos*. Philadelphia: Westminster, 1987.

Boismard, Marie Emile. "Le sort des impies dans l'Apocalypse." *Lumière et vie* 45 (1996): 69–79.

Boneva, Krassimira. "La spatialisation: Élément du débrayage dans l'Apocalypse de Jean." *Sémitoque et Bible* 93 (1999): 47–53.

Borgen, Peter. "Polemic in the Book of Revelation." Pages 275–91 in *Early Christianity and Hellenistic Judaism*. Edinburgh: T. & T. Clark, 1996.

Borger, Rykle. "NA[26] und die neutestamentliche Textkritik." *Theologische Rundschau* 52 (1987): 1–58.

Boring, M. Eugene. *The Continuing Voice of Jesus: Christian Prophecy and the Gospel Tradition*. Louisville, KY: Westminster John Knox, 1991.

———. "The Voice of Jesus in the Apocalypse of John." *NovT* 34 (1992): 334–59.

Bosworth, A. B. "Arrian and the Alani." *Harvard Studies in Classical Philology* 81 (1977): 217–55.

———. "Vespasian's Reorganization of the North-East Frontier." *Antichthon* 10 (1976): 63–76.

Böttrich, Christfried. "Das 'gläserne Meer' in Apk 4,6/15,2." *BN* 80 (1995): 5–15.

Bousset, Wilhelm. *The Antichrist Legend: A Chapter in Jewish and Christian Folklore*. Atlanta: Scholars, 1999. German original: Göttingen: Vandenhoeck & Ruprecht, 1895.

Bovon, François. "John's Self-Presentation in Revelation 1:9–10." *CBQ* 62 (2000): 693–700.

———. *New Testament and Christian Apocrypha: Collected Studies II*. Edited by Glenn E. Snyder. WUNT 237. Tübingen: Mohr Siebeck, 2009.

———. "Possession or Enchantment: The Roman Institutions According to the Revelation of John." Pages 133–45 in *New Testament Traditions and Apocryphal Narratives*. Allison Park, PA: Pickwick, 1995.

Bowersock, G. W. "The Mechanics of Subversion in the Roman Provinces." Pages 291–317 in *Opposition et résistances à l'empire d'Auguste à Trajan*. Edited by Kurt A. Raaflaub et al. Geneva: Hardt Foundation, 1987.

Boyer, Paul S. *When Time Shall Be No More: Prophecy Belief in Modern American Culture*. Cambridge, MA: Belknap Press of Harvard University Press, 1992.

Bradley, Keith R. *Slavery and Society at Rome*. Cambridge: Cambridge University Press, 1994.

Brady, David. *The Contribution of British Writers Between 1560 and 1830 to the Interpretation of Revelation 13:16–18*. Tübingen: Mohr Siebeck, 1983.

Branick, Vincent. *The House Church in the Writings of Paul*. Wilmington, DE: Glazier, 1989.

Braund, David C. *Rome and the Friendly King: The Character of the Client Kingship*. London: Croom Helm; New York: St. Martin's, 1984.

Bredin, Mark R. J. *Jesus, Revolutionary of Peace: A Nonviolent Christology in the Book of Revelation*. Carlisle: Paternoster, 2003.

———. "The Synagogue of Satan Accusation in Revelation 2:9." *BTB* 28 (1999): 160–64.

Brent, Allen. *Cyprian and Roman Carthage*. Cambridge: Cambridge University Press, 2010.

———. *The Imperial Cult and the Development of Church Order: Concepts and Images of Authority in Paganism and Early Christianity Before the Age of Cyprian*. VCSup 45. Leiden: Brill, 1999.

Briggs, Robert A. *Jewish Temple Imagery in the Book of Revelation*. New York: Lang, 1999.

Brooke, George J. "Shared Intertextual Interpretations in the Dead Sea Scrolls and the New Testament." Pages 35–57 in *Biblical Perspectives: Early Use and Interpretation of the Bible in Light of the Dead Sea Scrolls*. Edited by Michael E. Stone and Esther G. Chazon. *STDJ* 28. Leiden: Brill, 1998.

Broughton, T. R. S. *Asia Minor*. Vol. 4 of *An Economic Survey of Ancient Rome*. Paterson, NJ: Pageant, 1959.

Brown, Raymond E. *The Epistles of John*. AYB 30. Garden City, NY: Doubleday, 1982; reprint, New Haven, CT: Yale University Press.

———. *The Gospel According to John*. 2 vols. AYB 29–29A. Garden City, NY: Doubleday, 1966–1970; reprint, New Haven, CT: Yale University Press.

———. *An Introduction to the Gospel of John*. Edited by Francis J. Moloney. New York: Doubleday, 2003.

Brown, Raymond E., et al., eds. *Mary in the New Testament: A Collaborative Assessment by Protestant and Roman Catholic Scholars*. Philadelphia: Fortress, 1978.

Bruce, F. F. "The Spirit in the Apocalypse." Pages 333–44 in *Christ and the Spirit in the New Testament*. Cambridge: Cambridge University Press, 1973.

Brunt, John C. "Rejected, Ignored, or Misunderstood: The Fate of Paul's Approach to the Problem of Food Offered to Idols in Early Christianity." *NTS* 31 (1985): 113–24.

Buchinger, Harald. "Die Johannes-Apokalypse im christlichen Gottesdienst: Sondierungen im Liturgie und Ikonographie." Pages 216–66 in *Ancient Christian Interpretations of "Violent Texts" in the Apocalypse*. Edited by Joseph Verheyden, Tobias Nicklas, and Andreas Merkt. SUNT 92. Göttingen: Vandenhoeck & Ruprecht, 2011.

Bucur, Bogdan G. "Hierarchy, Prophecy, and the Angelomorphic Spirit: A Contribution to the Study of the Book of Revelation's Wirkungsgeschichte." *JBL* 127 (2008): 173–94.

Burkert, Walter. *Greek Religion*. Translated by John Raffan. Cambridge, MA: Harvard University Press, 1985.

Burr, David. "Mendicant Readings of the Apocalypse." Pages 89–102 in *The Apocalypse in the Middle Ages*. Edited by Richard K. Emmerson and Bernard McGinn. Ithaca, NY: Cornell University Press, 1992.

———. *Olivi's Peaceable Kingdom: A Reading of the Apocalypse Commentary*. Philadelphia: University of Pennsylvania Press, 1993.

Burrell, Barbara. *Neokoroi: Greek Cities and Roman Emperors*. Leiden: Brill, 2004.

Busch, Peter. *Der gefallene Drache: Mythenexegese am Beispiel von Apokalypse 12*. TANZ 19. Tübingen: A. Francke, 1996.

Buttrey, Theodore V. *Greek, Roman and Islamic Coins from Sardis*. Cambridge, MA: Harvard University Press, 1981.

Byron, John. *Slavery Metaphors in Early Judaism and Pauline Christianity: A Traditio-Historical and Exegetical Examination*. Tübingen: Mohr Siebeck, 2003.

Cadbury, Henry Joel. "The Macellum of Corinth." *JBL* 53 (1934): 134–41.

Cadoux, Cecil John. *Ancient Smyrna: A History of the City from the Earliest Times to 324 A.D.* Oxford: Blackwell, 1938.

Callahan, Allen D. "Apocalypse as Critique of Political Economy: Some Notes on Revelation 18." *Horizons in Biblical Theology* 21 (1999): 46–65.

———. "The Language of the Apocalypse." *HTR* 88 (1995): 453–70.

Camille, Michael. "Visionary Perception and Images of the Apocalypse in the Later Middle Ages." Pages 276–89 in *The Apocalypse in the Middle Ages*. Edited by Richard K. Emmerson and Bernard McGinn. Ithaca, NY: Cornell University Press, 1992.

Campbell, Gordon. "Antithetical Feminine-Urban Imagery and a Tale of Two Women-Cities in the Book of Revelation." *TynBul* 55 (2004): 81–108.

———. "Findings, Seals, Trumpets, and Bowls: Variations upon the Theme of Covenant Rupture and Restoration in the Book of Revelation." *WTJ* 66 (2004): 71–96.

Campbell, R. Alastair. *The Elders: Seniority Within Earliest Christianity*. Edinburgh: T. & T. Clark, 1994.

———. "Triumph and Delay: The Interpretation of Revelation 19:11–20:10." *Evangelical Quarterly* 80 (2008): 3–12.

Carey, Greg. *Elusive Apocalypse: Reading Authority in the Revelation to John*. Macon, GA: Mercer University Press, 1999.

Carrell, Peter R. *Jesus and the Angels: Angelology and the Christology of the Apocalypse of John*. SNTSMS 95. Cambridge: Cambridge University Press, 1997.

Casson, Lionel. *The Periplus Maris Erythraei*. Princeton, NJ: Princeton University Press, 1989.

———. *Ships and Seamanship in the Ancient World*. Princeton, NJ: Princeton University Press, 1971.

Charles, J. Daryl. "An Apocalyptic Tribute to the Lamb (Rev 5:1–14)." *JETS* 34 (1991): 461–73.

———. "Imperial Pretensions and the Throne-Vision of the Lamb: Observations on the Function of Revelation 5." *Criswell Theological Review* 7 (1993): 85–97.

Charlesworth, James H., ed. *The Messiah: Developments in Earliest Judaism and Christianity. The First Princeton Symposium on Judaism and Christian Origins.* Minneapolis: Fortress, 1992.

Christe, Yves. "The Apocalypse in the Monumental Art of the Eleventh Through Thirteenth Centuries." Pages 234–58 in *The Apocalypse in the Middle Ages.* Edited by Richard K. Emmerson and Bernard McGinn. Ithaca, NY: Cornell University Press, 1992.

Clasen, Klaus-Peter. *Die Wiedertäufer im Herzogtum Württemberg und in benachbarten Herrschaften: Ausbreitung, Geisteswelt und Soziologie.* Stuttgart: Kohlhammer, 1965.

Cohen, Boaz. *Jewish and Roman Law: A Comparative Study.* Vol. 1. New York: Jewish Theological Seminary, 1966.

Cohen, Henry. *Description historique des monnaies frappées sous L'Empire Romain.* 2nd ed. Vol. 1. Paris: Rollin & Feuardent, 1880.

Collins, John J. *The Apocalyptic Imagination: An Introduction to Jewish Apocalyptic Literature.* 2nd ed. Grand Rapids, MI: Eerdmans, 1998.

———. *Daniel: A Commentary on the Book of Daniel.* Hermeneia. Minneapolis: Fortress, 1993.

———. "Introduction: Towards the Morphology of a Genre." Pages 1–20 in *Apocalypse: The Morphology of a Genre.* Semeia 14. Missoula, MT: Society of Biblical Literature, 1979.

———. *The Scepter and the Star: The Messiahs of the Dead Sea Scrolls and Other Ancient Literature.* New York: Doubleday, 1995.

Constantinou, Eugenia Scarvelis. "Violence, Free Will and the Love of God in the Apocalypse Commentary of Andrew of Caesarea." Pages 199–215 in *Ancient Christian Interpretations of "Violent Texts" in the Apocalypse.* Edited by Joseph Verheyden, Tobias Nicklas, and Andreas Merkt. SUNT 92. Göttingen: Vandenhoeck & Ruprecht, 2011.

Conzelmann, Hans. *1 Corinthians.* Minneapolis: Fortress, 1975.

Cook, John Granger. *Roman Attitudes Toward the Christians: From Claudius to Hadrian.* WUNT II/261. Tübingen: Mohr Siebeck, 2012.

Corsten, Thomas. *Die Inschriften von Laodikeia am Lykos.* Vol. 1. Bonn: Habelt, 1997.

Court, John M. *Myth and History in the Book of Revelation.* Atlanta: John Knox, 1979.

Coutsoumpos, Panayotis. "Social Implications of Idolatry in Revelation 2:14: Christ or Caesar?" *BTB* 27 (1997): 23–27.

Cross, Frank Moore. "The Hebrew Inscriptions from Sardis." *HTR* 95 (2002): 1–19.

Cuss, Dominique. *Imperial Cult and Honorary Terms in the New Testament.* Fribourg: Fribourg University Press, 1974.

Daley, Brian E. *The Hope of the Early Church: A Handbook of Patristic Eschatology.* Peabody, MA: Hendrickson, 2003.

Dalrymple, Rob. "These Are the Ones . . . (Rev 7)." *Bib* 82 (2005): 396–406.

———. "The Use of καὶ in Revelation 11,1 and the Implications for the Identification of the Temple, the Altar, and the Worshipers." *Bib* 87 (2006): 387–94.

Daniel, E. Randolph. "Joachim of Fiore: Patterns of History in the Apocalypse." Pages 72–88 in *The Apocalypse in the Middle Ages.* Edited by Richard K. Emmerson and Bernard McGinn. Ithaca, NY: Cornell University Press, 1992.

Danker, Frederick W. *Benefactor: Epigraphic Study of a Graeco-Roman and New Testament Semantic Field*. St. Louis, MO: Clayton, 1982.

Davidson, Maxwell J. *Angels at Qumran: A Comparative Study of 1 Enoch 1–36, 72–108 and Sectarian Writings from Qumran*. JSPSup 11. Sheffield: JSOT, 1992.

Davies, W. D., and Dale C. Allison. *Critical and Exegetical Commentary on the Gospel According to Saint Matthew*. 3 vols. ICC. Edinburgh: T. & T. Clark, 1988–97.

Davis, R. Dean. *The Heavenly Court Judgment of Revelation 4–5*. Lanham, MD: University Press of America, 1992.

Day, John. "The Origin of Armageddon: Revelation 16:16 as an Interpretation of Zechariah 12:11." Pages 315–26 in *Crossing the Boundaries: Essays in Biblical Interpretation in Honour of Michael D. Goulder*. Edited by Stanley E. Porter, Paul Joyce, and David Orton. Leiden: Brill, 1994.

De Boer, Martinus C. *The Defeat of Death: Apocalyptic Eschatology in 1 Corinthians and Romans 5*. JSNTSup 22. Sheffield: JSOT, 1988.

Decock, Paul B. "The Symbol of Blood in the Apocalypse of John." *Neot* 38 (2004): 157–82.

Deissmann, Adolf. *Bible Studies. Contributions Chiefly from Papyri and Inscriptions, to the History of the Language, the Literature, and the Religion of Hellenistic Judaism and Primitive Christianity*. Translated by Alexander Grieve. 2nd ed. Edinburgh: T. & T. Clark, 1909.

———. *Light from the Ancient East: The New Testament Illustrated by Recently Discovered Texts of the Graeco-Roman World*. Translated by Lionel R. M. Strachan. London: Hodder & Stoughton, 1910.

Denis, Albert-Marie. *Concordance greque des pseudépigraphes d'Ancien Testament: concordance Corpus des textes indices*. Louvain: Université catholique de Louvain, 1987.

Deppermann, Klaus. *Melchior Hoffmann: Social Unrest and Apocalyptic Visions in the Age of Reformation*. Edinburgh: T. & T. Clark, 1987.

deSilva, David A. "Final Topics: The Rhetorical Functions of Intertexture in Revelation 14:14–16:21." Pages 215–41 in *Intertexture of Apocalyptic Discourse in the New Testament*. Edited by Duane F. Watson. Atlanta: Society of Biblical Literature, 2002.

———. "The Image of the Beast and the Christians in Asia Minor: Escalation of Sectarian Tension in Revelation 13." *TJ* 12 (1991): 185–208.

———. *Seeing Things John's Way: The Rhetoric of the Book of Revelation*. Louisville, KY: Westminster John Knox, 2009.

———. "Sociorhetorical Interpretation of Revelation 14:6–13: A Call to Act Justly Toward the Just and Judging God. *Bulletin for Biblical Research* 9 (1999): 65–117.

Deutsch, Celia. "Transformation of Symbols: The New Jerusalem in Rv 21¹–22⁵. *ZNW* 78 (1987): 106–26.

Dieterich, Albrecht. *Abraxas: Studien z. Religionsgeschichte d. späteren Altertums*. Aalen: Scientia-Verlag, 1973.

DiTommaso, Lorenzo. *The Dead Sea New Jerusalem Text: Contents and Contexts*. TSAJ 110. Tübingen: Mohr Siebeck, 2005.

Dochhorn, Jan. "Beliar als Endtyrann in der Ascensio Isaiae: Ein Beitrag zur Eschatologie und Satanologie des frühen Christentums sowie zur Erforschung der Apokalypse des Johannes." Pages 293–318 in *Die Johannesapokalypse: Kontexte—*

Konzepte—Rezeption. Edited by Jörg Frey, James A. Kelhoffer, and Franz Tóth. WUNT 287. Tübingen: Mohr Siebeck, 2012.

———. "Laktanz und die Apokalypse: Eine Untersuchung zu Inst. 7.15–26." Pages 133–60 in *Ancient Christian Interpretations of "Violent Texts" in the Apocalypse*. Edited by Joseph Verheyden, Tobias Nicklas, and Andreas Merkt. SUNT 92. Göttingen: Vandenhoeck & Ruprecht, 2011.

———. *Schriftgelehrte Prophetie: Der eschatologische Teufelsfall in Apc Joh 12 und seine Bedeutung für das Verständnis der Johannesoffenbarung*. WUNT 268. Tübingen: Mohr Siebeck, 2010.

———. "Und die Erde tat ihren Mund auf: Ein Exodusmotiv in Apc 12,16." *ZNW* 88 (1997): 140–42.

Dodds, E. R. *The Greeks and the Irrational*. Berkeley: University of California Press, 1951.

Doglio, Claudio. "L'Oracolo profetico che annuncia la venuta (Ap 1,7)." *Teologia* 33 (2008): 109–34.

Doniger, Wendy. *The Implied Spider: Politics and Theology in Myth*. New York: Columbia University Press, 1998.

Dräger, Michael. *Die Städte der Provinz Asia in der Flavierzeit: Studien zur kleinasiatischen Stadt- und Regionalgeschichte*. Europäische Hochschulschriften III.576. Frankfurt: Peter Lang, 1993.

Draper, J. A. "The Heavenly Feast of Tabernacles: Revelation 7:1–17." *JSNT* 19 (1983): 133–47.

Drury, John. *Painting the Word: Christian Pictures and Their Meanings*. New Haven, CT: Yale University Press, 1999.

Du Rand, Jan A. "The New Jerusalem as Pinnacle of Salvation: Text (Rev 21:1–22:5) and Intertext." *Neot* 38 (2004): 275–302.

———. "'Now the Salvation of our God Has Come . . .' A Narrative Perspective on the Hymns in Revelation 12–15." *Neot* 27 (1993): 313–30.

———. "The Song of the Lamb Because of the Victory of the Lamb." *Neot* 29 (1995): 203–10.

Ducrey, Pierre. *Le traitement des prisonniers de guerre dans la Grèce antique*. 2nd ed. Paris: De Boccard, 1999.

Duff, Paul B. "'I Will Give Each of You as Your Works Deserve': Witchcraft Accusations and the Fiery-Eyed Son of God in Rev 2.18–23." *NTS* 43 (1997): 116–23.

———. "The 'Synagogue of Satan': Crisis Mongering and the Apocalypse of John." Pages 147–68 in *The Reality of Apocalypse: Rhetoric and Politics in the Book of Revelation*. Edited by David L. Barr. SBLSymS 39. Atlanta: Society of Biblical Literature, 2006.

———. *Who Rides the Beast? Prophetic Rivalry and the Rhetoric of Crisis in the Churches of the Apocalypse*. Oxford: Oxford University Press, 2001.

Dulk, Mattijs den. "The Promises to the Conquerors in the Book of Revelation." *Bib* 87 (2006): 516–22.

Dunbabin, Katherine M. D. *The Roman Banquet: Images of Conviviality*. Cambridge: Cambridge University Press, 2003.

———. "Wine and Water at the Roman Convivium." *Journal of Roman Archaeology* 6 (1993): 116–41.

Dunn, James D. G. *Christology in the Making: A New Testament Inquiry into the Origins of the Doctrine of the Incarnation.* 2nd ed. Grand Rapids, MI: Eerdmans, 1989.

———. *Romans.* WBC 38–38a. Dallas: Word, 1988.

———. *The Theology of Paul the Apostle.* Grand Rapids, MI: Eerdmans, 1998.

———. *Unity and Diversity in the New Testament: An Inquiry into the Character of Earliest Christianity.* 2nd ed. London: SCM; Philadelphia: Trinity, 1990.

Dyer, Charles H. "The Identity of Babylon in Revelation 17–18." *BSac* 144 (1987): 305–16 and 433–49.

Ebner, Martin, and Elisabeth Esch-Wermeling, eds. *Kaiserkult, Wirtschaft und spectacula: Zum politischen und gesellschaftlichen Umfeld der Offenbarung.* SUNT 72. Göttingen: Vandenhoeck & Ruprecht, 2011.

Ego, Beate. "Reduktion, Amplifikation, Interpretation, Neukontextualisierung: Intertextuelle Aspekte der Rezeption der Ezechielschen Thronwagenvision im antiken Judentum." Pages 31–60 in *Das Ezechielbuch in der Johannesoffenbarung.* Edited by Dieter Sänger. Neukirchen-Vluyn: Neukirchener, 2004.

Elliott, J. K. "The Distinctiveness of the Greek Manuscripts of the Book of Revelation." *JTS* 48 (1997): 116–24.

Elliott, John H. *1 Peter.* AYB 37B. New York: Doubleday, 2000; reprint, New Haven, CT: Yale University Press.

Elliott, Susan M. "Who Is Addressed in Revelation 18:6–7?" *BR* 40 (1995): 98–113.

Emmerson, Richard K., and Bernard McGinn. *The Apocalypse in the Middle Ages.* Ithaca, NY: Cornell University Press, 1992.

Engen, John H. van. *Rupert of Deutz.* Berkeley: University of California Press, 1983.

Enroth, Anne Marit. "The Hearing Formula in the Book of Revelation." *NTS* 36 (1990): 598–608.

Eriksson, Anders. *Traditions as Rhetorical Proof: Pauline Argumentation in 1 Corinthians.* ConBNT 29. Stockholm: Almqvist & Wiksell, 1998.

Esch-Wermeling, Elisabeth. "Brückschläge: Die alttestamentlichen Traditionen der Offenbarung und Anspielungen auf die Zeitgeschichte. Methodische Überlegungen und Fallbeispiele." Pages 139–64 in *Kaiserkult, Wirtschaft und spectacula: Zum Politischen und gesellschaftlichen Umfeld der Offenbarung.* Edited by Martin Ebner and Elisabeth Esch-Wermeling. SUNT 72. Göttingen: Vandenhoeck & Ruprecht, 2011.

Fàbrega, Vallentin. "Laktanz und die Apokalypse." Pages 709–54 in *Die Johannesapokalypse: Kontexte—Konzepte—Rezeption.* Edited by Jörg Frey, James A. Kelhoffer, and Franz Tóth. WUNT 287. Tübingen: Mohr Siebeck, 2012.

Farrer, Austin. *Rebirth of Images: The Making of John's Apocalypse.* London: Dacre, 1949.

Fears, J. Rufus. "The Cult of Jupiter and Roman Imperial Ideology." *ANRW* II.17.1 (1981):3–141.

Fee, Gordon. "Εἰδωλοθύτα Once Again: An Interpretation of 1 Corinthians 8–10." *Bib* 61 (1980): 172–97.

Fekkes, Jan, III. "'His Bride Has Prepared Herself': Revelation 12–21 and Isaian Nuptial Imagery. *JBL* 109 (1990): 269–87.

———. *Isaiah and Prophetic Traditions in the Book of Revelation: Visionary Antecedents and Their Development.* JSNTSup 93. Sheffield: JSOT, 1994.

Fenske, Wolfgang. "'Das Lied des Mose, des Knechtes Gottes, und das Lied des Lammes." *ZNW* 90 (1999): 250–64.

Feuillet, André. *Johannine Studies.* Staten Island, NY: Alba House, 1965.

Firth, Katharine R. *The Apocalyptic Tradition in Reformation Britain, 1530–1645.* Oxford: Oxford University Press, 1979.

Fitzmyer, Joseph A. *The Gospel According to Luke.* 2 vols. AYB 28–28a. New York: Doubleday, 1983–85; reprint, New Haven, CT: Yale University Press.

———. *Romans.* AYB 33. New York: Doubleday, 1993; reprint, New Haven, CT: Yale University Press.

Flanigan, C. Clifford. "The Apocalypse and the Medieval Liturgy." Pages 333–51 in *The Apocalypse in the Middle Ages.* Edited by Richard K. Emmerson and Bernard McGinn. Ithaca, NY: Cornell University Press, 1992.

Fontenrose, Joseph. *Python: A Study of Delphic Myth and Its Origins.* Berkeley: University of California Press, 1959.

Fox, Kenneth A. "The Nicolaitans, Nicolaus and the Early Church." *Studies in Religion/Sciences religieuses* 23 (1994): 485–96.

Frankfurter, David. "Jews or Not? Reconstructing the 'Other' in Rev 2:9 and 3:9." *HTR* 94 (2001): 403–25.

Fredriksen, Paula. "Apocalypse and Redemption in Early Christianity: From John of Patmos to Augustine of Hippo." *VC* 45 (1991): 151–83.

———. "Tyconius and Augustine on the Apocalypse." Pages 20–37 in *The Apocalypse in the Middle Ages.* Edited by Richard K. Emmerson and Bernard McGinn. Ithaca, NY: Cornell University Press, 1992.

Frenschkowski, Marco. "Die Entrükung der zwei Zeugen zum Himmel (Apk 11,11–14)." Pages 261–90 in *Der Himmel.* Edited by Martin Ebner et al. Jahrbuch für biblische Theologie 10 (2005). Neukirchen-Vluyn: Neukirchener, 2006.

———. "Utopia and Apocalypsis: The Case of the Golden City." Pages 29–42 in *Imagery in the Book of Revelation.* Edited by Michael Labahn and Outi Lehtipun. Leuven: Peeters, 2001.

Frey, Jörg. "Die Bildersprache der Johannesapokalypse." *ZTK* 98 (2001): 161–85.

———. "Erwägungen zum Verhältnis der Johannesapocalypse zu den übringen Schriften des Corpus Johanneum." Pages 326–429 in Martin Hengel, *Die johanneische Frage: Ein Lösungsversuch.* WUNT 67. Tübingen: Mohr Siebeck, 1993.

———. "The Relevance of the Roman Imperial Cult for the Book of Revelation: Exegetical and Hermeneutical Reflections on the Relation Between the Seven Letters and the Visionary Main Part of the Book." Pages 231–55 in *The New Testament and Early Christian Literature in Greco-Roman Context: Studies in Honor of David E. Aune.* Edited by John Fotopoulos. NovTSup 122. Leiden: Brill, 2006.

———. "Was erwartet die Johannesapokalypse: Zur Eschatologie des letzten Buchs der Bibel." Pages 473–551 in *Die Johannesapokalypse: Kontexte—Konzepte—Rezeption.* Edited by Jörg Frey, James A. Kelhoffer, and Franz Tóth. WUNT 287. Tübingen: Mohr Siebeck, 2012.

Friedrich, Nestor Paulo. "Adapt or Resist? A Socio-Political Reading of Revelation 2.18–29." *JSNT* 25 (2002): 185–211.

Friesen, Steven J. "The Beast from the Land: Revelation 13:11–18 and Social Setting." Pages 49–64 in *Reading the Book of Revelation: A Resource for Students*. Edited by David L. Barr. SBLRBS 44. Atlanta: Society of Biblical Literature, 2003.

———. *Imperial Cults and the Apocalypse of John: Reading Revelation in the Ruins*. Oxford: Oxford University Press, 2001.

———. "Myth and Symbolic Resistance in Revelation 13." *JBL* 123 (2004): 281–313.

———. "Revelation, Realia, and Religion: Archaeology in the Interpretation of the Apocalypse." *HTR* 88 (1995): 291–314.

———. "Sarcasm in Revelation 2–3: Churches, Christians, True Jews, and Satanic Synagogues." Pages 127–46 in *The Reality of Apocalypse: Rhetoric and Politics in the Book of Revelation*. Edited by David L. Barr. SBLSymS 39. Atlanta: Society of Biblical Literature, 2006.

———. "Satan's Throne, Imperial Cults and the Social Settings of Revelation." *JSNT* 27 (2005): 351–73.

———. *Twice Neokoros: Ephesus, Asia, and the Cult of the Flavian Imperial Family*. Religions in the Greco-Roman World 116. Leiden: Brill, 1993.

Frilingos, Christopher A. *Spectacles of Empire: Monsters, Martyrs, and the Book of Revelation*. Philadelphia: University of Pennsylvania Press, 2004.

Frye, Northrop. *Anatomy of Criticism: Four Essays*. Princeton, NJ: Princeton University Press, 1957.

Fuller Dow, Lois K. *Images of Zion: Biblical Antecedents for the New Jerusalem*. Sheffield: Sheffield Phoenix, 2010.

Furnish, Victor Paul. *II Corinthians*. AYB 32A. New York: Doubleday, 1984; reprint, New Haven, CT: Yale University Press.

Gallus, Laslo. "The Exodus Motif in Revelation 15–16: Its Background and Nature." *AUSS* 46 (2008): 21–43.

García Martínez, Florentino. *Qumran and Apocalyptic: Studies on the Aramaic Texts from Qumran*. STDJ 9. Leiden: Brill, 1992.

———. "The Temple Scroll and the New Jerusalem." Pages 431–60 in *The Dead Sea Scrolls After Fifty Years: A Comprehensive Assessment*. Vol. 2. Edited by Peter W. Flint and James C. VanderKam. Leiden: E. J. Brill, 1999.

Garnsey, Peter. *Famine and Food Supply in the Graeco-Roman World: Responses to Risk and Crisis*. Cambridge: Cambridge University Press, 1988.

Garrison, William Lloyd. *From Disunionism to the Brink of War: 1850–1860*. Vol. 4 of *The Letters of William Lloyd Garrison*. Edited by Louis Ruchames. Cambridge, MA: Belknap Press of Harvard University Press, 1975.

Gaston, Lloyd. "Judaism of the Uncircumcised in Ignatius and Related Writers." Pages 33–44 in *Anti-Judaism in Early Christianity*. Vol. 2. Edited by S. G. Wilson. Waterloo, Ont.: Wilfred Laurier University Press, 1986.

Genovese, Eugene D. *Roll, Jordan, Roll: The World the Slaves Made*. New York: Vintage, 1976.

Georgi, Dieter. "Die Visionen vom himmlischen Jerusalem in Apk 21 u 22." Pages 351–72 in *Kirche: Festschrift für Günther Bornkamm zum 75 Geburtstag*. Edited by Dieter Lührmann and Georg Strecker. Tübingen: Mohr Siebeck, 1980.

Geyser, Albert S. "The Twelve Tribes in Revelation: Judean and Judeo Christian Apocalypticism." *NTS* 28 (1982): 388–99.

Giblin, Charles Homer. "From and Before the Throne: Revelation 4:5–6a Integrating the Imagery of Revelation 4–16." *CBQ* 60 (1998): 500–13.

———. "Millennium (Rev 20.4–6) as Heaven." *NTS* 45 (1999): 553–70.

———. "Revelation 11.1–13: Its Form, Function, and Contextual Integration." *NTS* 30 (1984): 433–59.

Gieschen, Charles A. *Angelomorphic Christology: Antecedents and Early Evidence*. AGJU 42. Leiden: Brill, 1998.

Giesen, Heinz. "Das Gottesbild in der Johannesoffenbarung." Pages 162–92 in *Der Gott Israels im Zeugnis des Neuen Testaments*. Edited by Ulrich Busse. Freiburg: Herder, 2003.

———. "Lasterkataloge und Kaiserkult in der Offenbarung des Johannes." Pages 210–31 in *Studien zur Johannesoffenbarung und ihrer Auslegung: Festschrift für Otto Böcher zum 70. Geburtstag*. Edited by Friedrich Wilhelm Horn and Michael Wolter. Neukirchen-Vluyn: Neukirchener, 2005.

———. *Studien zur Johannesapokalypse*. Stuttgarter biblische Aufsatzbände 29. Stuttgart: Katholisches Bibelwerk, 2000.

Gilchrest, Eric J. *Revelation 21–22 in Light of Jewish and Greco-Roman Utopianism*. Biblical Interpretation Series 118. Leiden: Brill, 2013.

Glad, Clarence E. "Frank Speech, Flattery, and Friendship in Philodemus." Pages 21–59 in *Friendship, Flattery, and Frankness of Speech: Studies on Friendship in the New Testament World*. NovTSup 82. Leiden: Brill, 1996.

Glancy, Jennifer A. *Slavery in Early Christianity*. Minneapolis: Fortress, 2006.

Glancy, Jennifer A., and Stephen D. Moore. "How Typical a Roman Prostitute Is Revelation's 'Great Whore'?" *JBL* 130 (2011): 551–69.

Glasson, Thomas Francis. "Last Judgment in Rev 20 and Related Writings." *NTS* 28 (1982): 528–39.

Godwin, Joscelyn. *Mystery Religions in the Ancient World*. San Francisco: Harper & Row, 1981.

Gollinger, Hildegard. *Das "grosse Zeichen" von Apokalypse 12*. Würzburg: Echter; Stuttgart: Katholisches Bibelwerk, 1971.

Goodenough, Erwin R. *Jewish Symbols in the Greco-Roman Period*. 13 vols. New York: Pantheon, 1953–68.

Goranson, Stephen. "The Text of Revelation 22.14." *NTS* 43 (1997): 154–57.

Gordley, Matthew E. *Teaching Through Song in Antiquity: Didactic Hymnody Among Greeks, Romans, Jews, and Christians*. WUNT II/302. Tübingen: Mohr Siebeck, 2011.

Gordon, Robert P. "Loricate Locusts in the Targum to Nahum III 17 and Revelation IX 9." *Vetus Testamentum* 33 (1983): 338–39.

Gourgues, Michel. "The Thousand-Year Reign (Rev 20:1–6): Terrestrial or Celestial?" *CBQ* 47 (1985): 676–81.

Gradl, Hans-Georg. "Buch und Brief: Zur motivischen, literarischen und kommunikativen Interdependenz zweier medialer typen in der Johannes-Offenbarung." Pages 414–33 in *Die Johannesapokalypse: Kontexte—Konzepte—Rezeption*. Edited by Jörg Frey, James A. Kelhoffer, and Franz Tóth. WUNT 287. Tübingen: Mohr Siebeck, 2012.

———. "Kaisertum und Kaiserkult: Ein Vergleich zwischen Philos Legatio ad Gaium und der Offenbarung des Johannes." *NTS* 56 (2010): 116–38.

Grant, Frederick C. *Hellenistic Religions*. Indianapolis, IN: Bobbs-Merrill, 1953.

Grappe, Christian. "L'Immolation terrestre comme gage de la communion céleste (Apocalypse 6,9; 7,14–15; 20,6)." *RHPR* 79 (1999): 71–82.

Graz, Ursula Rapp. "Das herabsteigende Jerusalem als Bild göttlicher Präsenz." *PzB* 8 (1999): 77–84.

Grelot, Pierre. "Marie Mére de Jésus dans les Écritures." *La nouvelle revue théologique* 121 (1999): 59–71.

———. "Les Versions grecques de Daniel." *Bib* 47 (1966): 383–91.

Gummerlock, Francis X. *The Seven Seals of the Apocalypse: Medieval Texts in Translation*. Kalamazoo: Western Michigan University Press, 2009.

Gundry, Robert H. "Angelomorphic Christology in the Book of Revelation." Pages 662–78 in SBLSP 33. Atlanta: Scholars, 1994.

———. *The Church and Tribulation*. Grand Rapids, MI: Zondervan, 1973.

———. "The New Jerusalem: People as Place, Not Place for People." *NovT* 29 (1987): 254–64.

Gunkel, Hermann. *Creation and Chaos in the Primeval Era and the Eschaton: Religio-Historical Study of Genesis 1 and Revelation 12*. Translated by K. William Whitney Jr. Grand Rapids, MI: Eerdmans, 2006. German original: 1895.

Gustafson, W. Mark. "Inscripta in fronte: Penal Tattooing in Late Antiquity." *Classical Antiquity* 16 (1997): 79–105.

Guttenberger, Gudrin. "Johannes von Thyateira: Zur Perspektive des Sehers." Pages 160–88 in *Studien zur Johannesoffenbarung und ihrer Auslegung: Festschrift für Otto Böcher zum 70. Geburtstag*. Edited by Friedrich Wilhelm Horn and Michael Wolter. Neukirchen-Vluyn: Neukirchener, 2005.

Guzzo, Pier Giovanni, and Antonio d'Ambrosio. *Pompeii: Guide to the Site*. Naples: Electa, 2002.

Gwynn, John. "Hippolytus and His 'Heads Against Caius.'" *Hermathena* 14 (1888): 397–418.

Haacker, Klaus. "Neuer Himmel, neue Erde, neues Jerusalem: Zur Bedeutung von Akp 21,1–4." Pages 328–38 in *Studien zur Johannesoffenbarung und ihrer Auslegung: Festschrift für Otto Böcher zum 70. Geburtstag*. Edited by Friedrich Wilhelm Horn and Michael Wolter. Neukirchen-Vluyn: Neukirchener, 2005.

Habicht, Christian. *Die Inschriften des Asklepions*. Berlin: de Gruyter, 1969.

Hagedorn, Dieter. "P.IFAO II 31: Johannesapokalypse 1,13–20." *Zeitschrift für Payrologie und Epigraphik* 92 (1992): 243–47.

Hahn, Ferdinand. "Liturgische Elemente in den Rahmenstücken der Johannesoffenbarung." Pages 43–57 in *Kirchengemeinschaft—Anspruch und Wirklichkeit: Festschrift für Georg Kretschmar zum 60. Geburtstag*. Edited by Wolf-Dieter Hauschild, Carsten Nicolaisen, and Dorothea Wendebourg. Stuttgart: Calwer, 1986.

———. "Die Sendschreiben der Johannesapokalypse: Ein Beitrag zur Bestimmung prophetischer Redeform." Pages 357–94 in *Tradition und Glaube: Das frühe Christentum in seiner Umwelt. Festgabe für Georg Kuhn zum 65. Geburtstag*. Edited by G. Jeremias, H.-W. Kuhn, and H. Stegemann. Göttingen: Vandenhoeck & Ruprecht, 1971.

Hall, George Stuart, ed. *On Pascha and Fragments: Melito of Sardis*. Oxford: Clarendon, 1979.

Hall, Mark Seaborn. "The Hook Interlocking Structure of Revelation: The Most Important Verses in the Book and How They May Unify Its Structure." *NovT* 44 (2002): 278–96.

Hall, Robert G. "Living Creatures in the Midst of the Throne: Another Look at Revelation 4.6." *NTS* 36 (1990): 609–13.

Hanfmann, George M. *Sardis from Prehistoric to Roman Times: Results of the Archaeological Exploration of Sardis 1958–1975*. Cambridge, MA: Harvard University Press, 1983.

Hannah, Darrell D. *Michael and Christ: Michael Traditions and Angel Christology in Early Christianity*. WUNT 109. Tübingen: Mohr Siebeck, 1999.

———. "Of Cherubim and the Divine Throne: Rev 5:6 in Context." *NTS* 49 (2003): 528–42.

Haraguchi, Takaaki. "Effective Use of Duality: An Epistolographical Study of Revelation 1:4–3:22." *Asia Journal of Theology* 19 (2005): 270–83.

Hardy, Ernest George. *Christianity and the Roman Government: A Study in Imperial Administration*. London: Longmans, 1894.

Harland, Philip A. *Associations, Synagogues, and Congregations: Claiming a Place in Ancient Mediterranean Society*. Minneapolis: Fortress, 2003.

———. *Dynamics of Identity in the World of the Early Christians*. New York: T. & T. Clark, 2009.

———. "Familial Dimensions of Group Identity: 'Brothers' (Ἀδελφοί) in Associations of the Greek East." *JBL* 124 (2005): 491–513.

———. "Honouring the Emperor or Assailing the Beast: Participation in Civic Life Among Associations (Jewish, Christian and Other) in Asia Minor and the Apocalypse of John." *JSNT* 77 (2000): 99–121.

Harrill, Albert J. "The Vice of Slave Dealers in Greco-Roman Society: The Use of a Topos in 1 Timothy 1:10." *JBL* 118 (1999): 97–122.

Harris, William V. "Towards a Study of the Roman Slave Trade." Pages 117–40 in *The Seaborne Commerce of Ancient Rome: Studies in Archaeology and History*. Edited by J. H. D'Arms and E. C. Kopff. MAAR 36. Rome: American Academy in Rome, 1980.

Harrison, J. R. "Fading Crown: Divine Honour and the Early Christians." *JTS* 54 (2003): 493–529.

Harsh, Philip Whaley. *Handbook of Classical Drama*. Stanford, CA: Stanford University Press; London: Milford and Oxford University Press, 1944.

Hartman, Lars. "Form and Message: A Preliminary Discussion of 'Partial Texts' in Rev 1–3 and 22,6ff." Pages 129–49 in *Apocalypse johannique et l'apocalyptique dans le Nouveau Testament*. Edited by Jan Lambrecht and George Beasley-Murray. Gembloux: Duculot; Louvain: Leuven University Press, 1980.

Harvey, Susan Ashbrook. *Scenting Salvation: Ancient Christianity and the Olfactory Imagination*. Berkeley: University of California Press, 2006.

Hasitschka, Martin. "Ankunft des Herrn, erste Auferstehung und tausendjähriges Reich: Die Schlussabschnitte im Apokalypsekommentar von Victorinus von Pettau und die Hinzufügung des Hieronymus." Pages 118–23 in *Ancient Christian Interpretations of "Violent Texts" in the Apocalypse*. Edited by Joseph Verheyden, Tobias Nicklas, and Andreas Merkt. SUNT 92. Göttingen: Vandenhoeck & Ruprecht, 2011.

Heide, Gale Z. "What Is New About the New Heaven and the New Earth? A Theology of Creation from Revelation 21 and 2 Peter 3." *JETS* 40 (1997): 37–56.

Heil, John Paul. "The Fifth Seal (Rev 6,9–11) as the Key to the Book of Revelation." *Bib* 74 (1993): 220–43.

Heiligenthal, Roman. "Wer waren die 'Nikolaiten'? Ein Beitrag zur Theologiegeschichte des frühen Christentums" *ZNW* 82 (1991): 133–37.

Heinze, André. *Johannesapokalypse und johanneische Schriften: Forschungs- und traditionsgeschichtliche Untersuchungen.* BWANT 8. Stuttgart: Kohlhammer, 1998.

Hellholm, David. "The Problem of Apocalyptic Genre and the Apocalypse of John." Pages 13–64 in *Early Christian Apocalypticism: Genre and Social Setting.* Edited by Adela Yarbro Collins. Semeia 36 (1986).

———. "The Visions He Saw or: To Encode the Future in Writing. An Analysis of the Prologue of John's Apocalyptic Letter." Pages 109–46 in *Text and Logos: The Humanistic Interpretation of the New Testament.* Edited by Theodore W. Jennings Jr. Atlanta: Scholars, 1990.

———, ed. *Apocalypticism in the Mediterranean World and the Near East.* Edited by David Hellholm. 2nd ed. Tübingen: Mohr Siebeck, 1989.

Hemer, Colin J. *The Letters to the Seven Churches of Asia in Their Local Setting.* Grand Rapids, MI: Eerdmans; Livonia, MI: Dove, 2001.

Hengel, Martin. *Crucifixion in the Ancient World and the Folly of the Message of the Cross.* Philadelphia: Fortress, 1977.

Henten, Jan Willem van. "Balaam in Revelation 2:14." Pages 233–46 in *The Prestige of the Pagan Prophet Balaam in Judaism, Early Christianity and Islam.* Edited by George H. van Kooten and Jacques van Ruiten. Leiden: Brill, 2008.

———. "The Concept of Martyrdom in Revelation." Pages 587–618 in *Die Johannesapokalypse: Kontexte—Konzepte—Rezeption.* Edited by Jörg Frey, James A. Kelhoffer, and Franz Tóth. WUNT 287. Tübingen: Mohr Siebeck, 2012.

———. "Dragon Myth and Imperial Ideology in Revelation 12–13." Pages 181–203 in *The Reality of Apocalypse: Rhetoric and Politics in the Book of Revelation.* SBLSymS 39. Edited by David L. Barr. Atlanta: Society of Biblical Literature, 2006.

Herghelegiu, Monica-Elena. *"Siehe, er kommt mit den Wolken!" Studien zur Christologie der Johannesoffenbarung.* Europäische Hochschulschriften 23/785. Frankfurt: Peter Lang, 2004.

Herms, Ronald. *An Apocalypse for the Church and for the World: The Narrative Function of Universal Language in the Book of Revelation.* BZNW 143. Berlin: de Gruyter, 2006.

Hernández, Juan, Jr. "Andrew of Caesarea and His Reading of Revelation: Catechesis and Paranesis." Pages 755–74 in *Die Johannesapokalypse: Kontexte—Konzepte—Rezeption.* Edited by Jörg Frey, A. Kelhoffer, and Franz Tóth. WUNT 287. Tübingen: Mohr Siebeck, 2012.

———. "Codex Sinaiticus: An Early Christian Commentary on the Apocalypse?" In *From Parchment to Pixels: Studies in the Codex Sinaiticus.* Edited by David C. Parker and Scot McKendrik. London: British Library, forthcoming.

———. *Scribal Habits and Theological Influences in the Apocalypse: The Singular Readings of Sinaiticus, Alexandrinus, and Ephraemi.* WUNT II/218. Tübingen: Mohr Siebeck, 2006.

————. "A Scribal Solution to a Problematic Measurement in the Apocalypse." *NTS* 56 (2010): 273–78.

Herrmann, John, and Annewies van den Hoek. "Apocalyptic Themes in the Monumental and Minor Art of Early Christianity." Pages 81–105 in *Apocalyptic Thought in Early Christianity.* Edited by Robert J. Daly. Grand Rapids, MI: Baker Academic, 2009.

Herrmann, Peter. "Demeter Karpophoros in Sardeis." *Revue des études anciennes* 100 (1998): 495–508.

————. "Mystenvereine in Sardeis." *Chiron* 26 (1996): 315–48.

————. "Neues vom Sklavenmarket in Sardeis." *Arkeoloji Dergisi* 4 (1996): 175–87.

————. "Sardeis zur Zeit der Iulisch-Claudischen Kaiser." Pages 21–36 in *Forschungen in Lydien.* Edited by Elmar Schwertheim. Asia Minor Studien 17. Bonn: Habelt, 1995.

Herz, Peter. "Der Kaiserkult und die Wirtschaft. Ein gewinnbringendes Wechselspiel." Pages 55–80 in *Kaiserkult, Wirtschaft und spectacula: Zum Politischen und gesellschaftlichen Umfeld der Offenbarung.* Edited by Martin Ebner and Elisabeth Esch-Wermeling. SUNT 72. Göttingen: Vandenhoeck & Ruprecht, 2011.

Herzer, Jens. "Der erste apokalyptische Reiter und der König der Könige. Ein Beitrag zur Christologie der Johannesapokalypse." *NTS* 45 (1999): 230–49.

Heschel, Abraham J. *The Prophets: An Introduction.* 2 vols. New York: Harper & Row, 1962.

Hiecke, Thomas. "Der Seher Johannes als neuer Ezechiel: Die Offenbarung des Johannes vom Ezechielbuch her gelesen." Pages 1–30 in *Das Ezechielbuch in der Johannesoffenbarung.* Edited by Dieter Sänger. Neukirchen-Vluyn: Neukirchener, 2004.

Hiecke, Thomas, and Tobias Nicklas. *"Die Worte der Prophetie dieses Buches": Offenbarung 22,6–21 als Schlussstein der christlichen Bibel Alten und Neuen Testaments gelesen.* Biblisch-theologische Studien 62. Neukirchen-Vluyn: Neukirchener, 2003.

Hill, Charles E. "Antichrist from the Tribe of Dan." *JTS* 46 (1995): 99–117.

————. *Regnum Caelorum: Patterns of Millennial Thought in Early Christianity.* 2nd ed. Grand Rapids, MI: Eerdmans, 2001.

Hill, David. "Prophecy and Prophets in the Revelation of St. John." *NTS* 18 (1971–72): 401–18.

Hirschberg, Peter. *Das eschatologische Israel: Untersuchungen zum Gottesvolkverständnis der Johannesoffenbarung.* WMANT 84. Neukirchen-Vluyn: Neukirchener, 1999.

Hock, Andreas. "From Babel to the New Jerusalem (Gen 11,1–9 and Rev 21,1–22,5)." *Bib* 89 (2008): 109–18.

Hoffmann, Adolf. "The Roman Remodeling of the Asklepieion." Pages 41–61 in *Pergamon: Citadel of the Gods.* Edited by Helmut Koester. Harrisburg, PA: Trinity, 1998.

Hoffmann, Matthias Reinhard. *The Destroyer and the Lamb: The Relationship Between Angelomorphic and Lamb Christology in the Book of Revelation.* WUNT II/203. Tübingen: Mohr Siebeck, 2005.

Hofius, Otfried. "Ἀρνίον—Widder oder Lamm? Erwägungen zur Bedeutung des Wortes in der Johannesapokalypse." *ZNW* 89 (1998): 272–81.

Hofmann, Hans-Ulrich. *Luther und die Johannes-Apokalypse.* Beiträge zur Geschichte der biblischen Exegese 24. Tübingen: Mohr Siebeck, 1982.

Holladay, William L. *Jeremiah 1*. Hermeneia. Philadelphia: Fortress, 1986.

Holtz, Traugott. "Die Werke in der Johannesapokalypse." Pages 426–41 in *Neues Testament und Ethik: Für Rudolf Schnackenburg*. Edited by Helmut Merklein. Freiburg: Herder, 1989.

Homcy, Stephen L. "'To Him Who Overcomes': A Fresh Look at What 'Victory' Means for the Believer According to the Book of Revelation." *JETS* 38 (1995): 193–201.

Horn, Friedrich Wilhelm. "Johannes auf Patmos." Pages 139–59 in *Studien zur Johannesoffenbarung: Festschrift für Otto Böcher zum 70. Geburtstag*. Edited by Friedrich Wilhelm Horn and Michael Wolter. Neukirchen-Vluyn: Neukirchener, 2005.

———. "Die sieben Donner: Erwägungen zu Offb 10." *SNTSU* 17 (1992): 215–29.

———. "Zwischen der Synagoge des Satans und dem neuen Jerusalem: Die christlich-jüdische Standortbestimmung in der Apokalypse des Johannes." *Zeitschrift für Religions- und Geistesgeschichte* 46 (1994): 143–62.

Horn, Friedrich Wilhelm, and Michael Wolter, eds. *Studien zur Johannesoffenbarung und ihrer Auslegung: Festschrift für Otto Böcher zum 70. Geburtstag*. Neukirchen-Vluyn: Neukirchener, 2005.

Horst, Pieter W. van der. "The Elements Will Be Dissolved with Fire: The Idea of Cosmic Conflagration in Hellenism, Ancient Judaism, and Early Christianity." Pages 271–92 in *Hellenism—Judaism—Christianity: Essays on Their Interaction*. 2nd ed. Leuven: Peeters, 1998.

Hoz, María Paz de. *Die lydischen Kulte im Lichte der griechischen Inschriften*. Asia Minor Studien 36. Bonn: Habelt, 1999.

Huber, Konrad. "Aspekte der Apokalypse-Interpretation des Victorinus von Pettau am Beispiel der Christusvision in Off 1." Pages 94–117 in *Ancient Christian Interpretations of "Violent Texts" in the Apocalypse*. Edited by Joseph Verheyden, Tobias Nicklas, and Andreas Merkt. SUNT 92. Göttingen: Vandenhoeck & Ruprecht, 2011.

———. *Einer gleich einem Menschensohn: Die Christusvisionen in Offb 1,9–20 und Offb 14,14–20 und die Christologie der Johannesoffenbarung*. NTAbh 51. Münster: Aschendorff, 2007.

———. "Die Ernte des Menschensohngleichen. Zur Ambivalenz eines Gerichtsbildes in der Johannesoffenbarung." Pages 79–106 in *Imagery in the Book of Revelation*. Edited by Michael Labahn and Outi Lehtipun. Leuven: Peeters, 2001.

———. "Reiter auf weissem Pferd: Ein schillerndes Christusbild in der Offenbarung des Johannes." Pages 389–409 in *Im Geist und in der Wahrheit: Studien zum Johannesevangelium und zur Offenbarung des Johannes sowie andere Beiträge. Festschrift für Martin Hasitschka SJ zum 65. Geburtstag*. Edited by Konrad Huber and Boris Repschinski. NTAbh 52. Münster: Aschendorff, 2008.

Huber, Lynn R. *Like a Bride Adorned: Reading Metaphor in John's Apocalypse*. New York: T. & T. Clark, 2007.

———. "Sexually Explicit? Re-Reading Revelation's 144,000 Virgins as a Response to Roman Discourses." *Journal of Men, Masculinities and Spirituality* 2 (2008): 3–28.

Hughes, James A. "Revelation 20:4–6 and the Question of the Millennium." *WTJ* 35 (1973): 281–302.

Hughes, Julie A. *Scriptural Allusions and Exegesis in the Hodayot*. STDJ 59. Leiden: Brill, 2006.

Hughes, Kevin L. *Constructing Antichrist: Paul, Biblical Commentary, and the Development of Doctrine in the Early Middle Ages*. Washington, DC: Catholic University of America, 2005.

Hughes, Philip Edgcumbe. "First Resurrection: Another Interpretation." *WTJ* 39 (1977): 315–18.

Humphrey, Edith M. *The Ladies and the Cities: Transformation and Apocalyptic Identity in Joseph and Aseneth, 4 Ezra, the Apocalypse and The Shepherd of Hermas*. JSPSup 17. Sheffield: Sheffield Academic Press, 1995.

———. "A Tale of Two Cities and (at Least) Three Women: Transformation, Continuity, and Contrast in the Apocalypse." Pages 81–96 in *Reading the Book of Revelation: A Resource for Students*. Edited by David L. Barr. SBLRBS 44. Atlanta: Society of Biblical Literature, 2003.

Hurtado, Larry W. *The Earliest Christian Artifacts: Manuscripts and Christian Origins*. Grand Rapids, MI: Eerdmans, 2006.

———. "Revelation 4–5 in the Light of Jewish Apocalyptic Analogies." *JSNT* 25 (1985): 105–24.

Hurtgen, John E. *Anti-Language in the Apocalypse of John*. Lewiston, NY: Mellen Biblical Press, 1993.

Hylen, Susan E. "Metaphor Matters: Violence and Ethics in Revelation." *CBQ* 73 (2011): 777–96.

———. "The Power and Problem of Revelation 18: The Rhetorical Function of Gender." Pages 205–19 in *Pregnant Passion: Gender, Sex, and Violence in the Bible*. Edited by Cheryl A. Kirk-Duggan. Semeia 44. Atlanta: Society of Biblical Literature, 2003.

Ilan, Tal. *Lexicon of Jewish Names in Late Antiquity*. Vols. 1 and 3. TSAJ. Tübingen: Mohr Siebeck, 2002, 2008.

Jack, Alison M. *Texts Reading Texts, Sacred and Secular*. JSNTSup 179. Sheffield: Sheffield Academic, 1999.

Jackson, R. P. J. "Eye Medicine in the Roman Empire." *ANRW* II.37.3 (1995): 2228–51.

Janse, Sam. "'You Are my Son': The Reception History of Psalm 2 in Early Judaism and the Early Church." Leuven: Peeters, 2009.

Janzen, Ernest P. "The Jesus of the Apocalypse Wears the Emperor's Clothes." Pages 637–61 in SBLSP 33. Edited by E. H. Lovering Jr. Atlanta: Scholars, 1994.

Jart, Una. "Precious Stones in the Revelation of St. John 21:18–21." *ST* 24 (1970): 150–81.

Jauhiainen, Marko. "Ἀποκάλυψις Ἰησοῦ Χριστοῦ (Rev 1:1): The Climax of John's Prophecy?" *TynBul* 54 (2003): 99–117.

———. "The Measuring of the Sanctuary Reconsidered (Rev 11,1–2)." *Bib* 83 (2002): 507–23.

———. "The OT Background to Armageddon (Rev. 16:16) Revisited." *NovT* 47 (2005): 381–93.

———. *The Use of Zechariah in Revelation*. WUNT II/199. Tübingen: Mohr Siebeck, 2005.

Jemielity, Thomas. *Satire and the Hebrew Prophets*. Louisville, KY: Westminster John Knox, 1992.

Jobst, Werner. "Das 'öffentliche Freudenhaus' in Ephesos." *Jahreshefte des Österreichischen archäologischen Instituts* 51 (1976–77): 61–84.

Johns, Loren L. *The Lamb Christology of the Apocalypse of John: An Investigation into Its Origins and Rhetorical Force.* WUNT II/167. Tübingen: Mohr Siebeck, 2003.

Johnson, Marguerite, and Terry Ryan. *Sexuality in Greek and Roman Society and Literature: A Sourcebook.* London: Routledge, 2005.

Jones, A. H. M. *The Greek City from Alexander to Justinian.* Oxford: Clarendon, 1940.

———. *Roman Economy: Studies in Ancient Economic and Administrative History.* Edited by P. A. Brunt. Oxford: Blackwell, 1974.

Jones, C. P. "Stigma: Tattooing and Branding in Graeco-Roman Antiquity." *JRS* (1987): 139–55.

Jonge, Henk J. de. "The Apocalypse of John and the Imperial Cult." Pages 127–41 in *Kykeon: Religions in the Greco-Roman World. Studies in Honour of H. S. Versnel.* Edited by H. F. J. Horstmanshoff, H. W. Singor, F. D. van Straten, and J. H. M. Strubbe. Religions in the Graeco-Roman World 142. Leiden: Brill, 2002.

Jörns, Klaus-Peter. *Das hymnische Evangelium: Untersuchungen zu Aufbau, Funktion und Herkunft der hymnischen Stücke in der Johannesoffenbarung.* Studien zum Neuen Testament 5. Gütersloh: Gerd Mohn, 1971.

Juel, Donald. *Messiah and Temple: The Trial of Jesus in the Gospel of Mark.* SBLDS 31. Missoula, MT: Scholars, 1977.

Kahl, Werner. "Psalm 2 und das Neue Testament: Intertextuelle Aspekte anhand ausgewählter Beispiele." Pages 232–50 in *Gottessohn und Menschensohn: Exegetische Studien zu zwei Paradigmen biblisher Intertextualität.* Edited by Dieter Sänger. Biblisch-theologische Studien 67. Neukirchen-Vluyn: Neukirchener, 2004.

Kalms, Jürgen. *Der Sturz des Gottesfeindes. Traditionsgeschichtliche Studien zu Apokalypse 12.* WMANT 93. Neukirchen-Vluyn: Neukirchener, 2001.

Karrer, Martin. "The Angels of the Congregations in Revelation—Textual History and Interpretation." *Journal of Early Christian History* 1 (2011): 57–84.

———. "Die Apokalypse und das Aposteldekret." Pages 429–52 in *Beiträge zur urchristlichen Theologiegeschichte.* Edited by Wolfgang Kraus. BZNW 163. Berlin: de Gruyter, 2009.

———. "Apoll und die apokalyptischen Reiter." Pages 223–51 in *Die Johannesoffenbahrung: Ihr Text und ihre Auslegung.* Edited by Michael Labahn and Martin Karrer. Arbeiten zur Bibel und Ihrer Geschichte 38. Leipzig: Evangelische, 2012.

———. *Die Johannesoffenbarung als Brief: Studien zu ihrem literarischen historischen und theologischen Ort.* FRLANT 140. Göttingen: Vandenhoeck & Ruprecht, 1986.

———. "Der Text der Johannesapokalypse." Pages 43–78 in *Die Johannesapokalypse: Kontexte—Konzepte—Rezeption.* Edited by Jörg Frey, James A. Kelhoffer, and Franz Tóth. WUNT 287. Tübingen: Mohr Siebeck, 2012.

———. "Der Text der Johannesoffenbarung—Varianten und Theologie." *Neot* 43 (2009) 373–98.

———. "Von der Apokalypse zu Ezechiel: Der Ezechieltext der Apokalypse." Pages 84–120 in *Das Ezechielbuch in der Johannesoffenbarung.* Edited by Dieter Sänger. Neukirchen-Vluyn: Neukirchener, 2004.

Käsemann, Ernst. *Jesus Means Freedom.* Philadelphia: Fortress, 1969.

———. *New Testament Questions of Today.* Philadelphia: Fortress, 1969.

Keener, Craig S. *The Gospel of John: A Commentary*. 2 vols. Peabody, MA: Hendrickson, 2003.

Kelhoffer, James A. "The Relevance of Revelation's Date and the Imperial Cult for John's Appraisal of the Value of Christians' Suffering in Revelation 1–3." Pages 553–86 in *Die Johannesapokalypse: Kontexte—Konzepte—Rezeption*. Edited by Jörg Frey, James A. Kelhoffer, and Franz Tóth. WUNT 287. Tübingen: Mohr Siebeck, 2012.

Keller, Catherine. "Eyeing the Apocalypse." Pages 253–77 in *Postmodern Interpretations of the Bible: A Reader*. Edited by A. K. A. Adam. St. Louis, MO: Chalice, 2001.

Kerkeslager, Allen. "Apollo, Greco-Roman Prophecy, and the Rider on the White Horse in Rev 6:2." *JBL* 112 (1993): 116–21.

Kim, Jean K. "'Uncovering Her Wickedness': An Inter(con)textual Reading of Revelation 17 from a Postcolonial Feminist Perspective." *JSNT* 73 (1999): 61–81.

King, Fergus. "Travesty or Taboo? 'Drinking Blood' and Revelation 17:2–6." *Neot* 38 (2004): 303–25.

Kinney, Dale. "The Apocalypse in Early Christian Monumental Decoration." Pages 200–16 in *The Apocalypse in the Middle Ages*. Edited by Richard K. Emmerson and Bernard McGinn. Ithaca, NY: Cornell University Press, 1992.

Kirby, John T. "The Rhetorical Situations of Revelation 1–3." *NTS* 34 (1988): 197–207.

Kistemaker, Simon J. "The Temple in the Apocalypse." *JETS* 43 (2000): 433–41.

Kitzberger, Ingrid Rosa. "'Wasser und Bäume des Lebens'—Eine feministisch-intertextuelle Interpretation von Apk 21/22." Pages 206–24 in *Weltgericht und Weltvollendung: Zukunftsbilder im Neuen Testament*. Edited by Hans-Josef Klauck. Freiburg: Herder, 1994.

Klaassen, Walter. *Living at the End of the Ages: Apocalyptic Expectation in the Radical Reformation*. Lanham, MD: University Press of America, 1992.

Klauck, Hans-Josef. *Ancient Letters and the New Testament: A Guide to Context and Exegesis*. Waco, TX: Baylor University Press, 2006.

———. "Do They Never Come Back? Nero Redivivus and the Apocalypse of John." *CBQ* 63 (2001): 683–98.

———. *Der erste Johannesbrief*. EKKNT 23/1. Neukirchen-Vluyn: Neukirchener, 1991.

———. *The Religious Context of Early Christianity: A Guide to Graeco-Roman Religions*. Translated by Brian McNeil. Minneapolis: Fortress, 2003.

———. "Das Sendschreiben nach Pergamon und der Kaiserkult in der Johannesoffenbarung." *Bib* 73 (1992): 153–82.

Klein, Peter K. "The Apocalypse in Medieval Art." Pages 159–99 in *The Apocalypse in the Middle Ages*. Edited by Richard K. Emmerson and Bernard McGinn. Ithaca, NY: Cornell University Press, 1992.

Kline, Meredith G. "First Resurrection: A Reaffirmation." *WTJ* 39 (1976): 110–19.

Knibb, Michael A. *The Ethiopic Book of Enoch: A New Edition in the Light of the Aramaic Dead Sea Fragments*. 2 vols. Oxford: Clarendon, 1978.

Knight, Jonathan M. "Apocalyptic and Prophetic Literature." Pages 467–88 in *Handbook of Classical Rhetoric in the Hellenistic Period: 330 B.C–A.D. 400*. Edited by Stanley E. Porter. Leiden: Brill, 1997.

————. "The Enthroned Christ of Revelation 5:6 and the Development of Christian Theology." Pages 21–42 in *Studies in the Book of Revelation*. Edited by Steve Moyise. Edinburgh: T. & T. Clark, 2001.

Kobelski, Paul J. *Melchizedek and Melchireša'*. CBQMS 10. Washington, DC: Catholic Biblical Association of America, 1981.

Koch, Michael. *Drachenkampf und Sonnenfrau: Zur Funktion des Mythischen in der Johannesapokalypse am Beispiel von Apk 12*. WUNT II/184. Tübingen: Mohr Siebeck, 2004.

Koester, Craig R. "The Church and Its Witness in the Apocalypse of John." *Tidsskrift for Teologi og Kirke* 78 (2007): 266–82.

————. "Comedy, Humor, and the Gospel of John." Pages 123–41 in *Word, Theology, and Community in John*. Edited by John Painter, R. Alan Culpepper, and Fernando F. Segovia. St. Louis, MO: Chalice, 2002.

————. *The Dwelling of God: The Tabernacle in the Old Testament, Intertestamental Jewish Literature, and the New Testament*. CBQMS 22. Washington, DC: Catholic Biblical Association, 1989.

————. *Hebrews*. AYB 36. New York: Doubleday, 2001; reprint, New Haven, CT: Yale University Press.

————. "The Message to Laodicea and the Problem of Its Local Context: A Study in the Imagery in Rev 3.14–22." *NTS* 49 (2003): 407–424.

————. *Revelation and the End of All Things*. Grand Rapids, MI: Eerdmans, 2001.

————. "Roman Slave Trade and the Critique of Babylon in Revelation 18." *CBQ* 70 (2008): 766–86.

————. *Symbolism in the Fourth Gospel: Meaning, Mystery, Community*. 2nd ed. Minneapolis: Fortress, 2003.

————. *The Word of Life: A Theology of John's Gospel*. Grand Rapids, MI: Eerdmans, 2008.

Koester, Helmut. "The Cult of the Egyptian Deities in Asia Minor." Pages 111–35 in *Pergamon: Citadel of the Gods*. Edited by Helmut Koester. Harrisburg, PA: Trinity, 1998.

Koester, Helmut, ed. *Ephesos: Metropolis of Asia. An Interdisciplinary Approach to Its Archaeology, Religion, and Culture*. Valley Forge, PA: Trinity, 1995.

————. *Pergamon: Citadel of the Gods. Archaeological Record, Literary Description, and Religious Development*. Harrisburg, PA: Trinity, 1998.

Kolb, Robert, and Timothy J. Wengert. *The Book of Concord: The Confessions of the Evangelical Lutheran Church*. Minneapolis: Fortress, 2000.

Kooten, George H. van, and Jacques van Ruiten, eds. *The Prestige of the Pagan Prophet Balaam in Judaism, Early Christianity and Islam*. Leiden: Brill, 2008.

Kovacs, Judith, and Christopher Rowland. *Revelation: The Apocalypse of Jesus Christ*. Malden, MA: Blackwell, 2004.

Kowalski, Beate. "'Lichtfrau, Drache, Zornesschalen . . .': Zur Bedeutung eschatologischer Zeichen in der Offenbarung des Johannes." *ETL* 78 (2002): 358–84.

————. "'Prophetie und die Offenbarung des Johannes? Offb 22,6–21 als Testfall." Pages 253–93 in *Prophets and Prophecy in Jewish and Early Christian Literature*. Edited by Joseph Verheyden, Korinna Zamfir, and Tobias Nicklas. WUNT II/286. Tübingen: Mohr Siebeck, 2010.

————. *Die Rezeption des Propheten Ezechiel in der Offenbarung des Johannes*. SBB 52. Stuttgart: Katholisches Bibelwerk, 2004.

Kraabel, A. Thomas. "The Roman Diaspora: Six Questionable Assumptions." *Journal of Jewish Studies* 33 (1982): 445–64.

Kraeling, Emil J. *The Brooklyn Museum Aramaic Papyri: New Documents of the Fifth Century B.C. from the Jewish Colony at Elephantine*. New Haven, CT: Yale University Press, 1953.

Krause, M. S. "The Finite Verb with Cognate Participle in the New Testament." Pages 187–206 in *Biblical Greek Language and Linguistics: Open Questions in Current Research*. Edited by S. E. Porter and D. A. Carson. JSNTSup 80. Sheffield: Sheffield Academic, 1993.

Krauss, Franklin Brunell. *An Interpretation of the Omens, Portents, and Prodigies Recorded by Livy, Tacitus, and Suetonius*. Philadelphia: University of Pennsylvania Press, 1930.

Kraybill, J. Nelson. *Apocalypse and Allegiance: Worship, Politics, and Devotion in the Book of Revelation*. Grand Rapids, MI: Brazos, 2010.

————. *Imperial Cult and Commerce in John's Apocalypse*. JSNTSup 132. Sheffield: Sheffield Academic Press, 1996.

Krey, Philip D. W. "The Apocalypse Commentary of 1329: Problems in Church History." Pages 267–88 in *Nicholas of Lyra: The Senses of Scripture*. Edited by Philip D. W. Krey and Lesley Smith. Studies in the History of Christian Thought 90. Leiden: Brill, 2000.

————. "Many Readers but Few Followers: The Fate of Nicholas of Lyra's 'Apocalypse Commentary' in the Hands of His Late-Medieval Admirers." *Church History* 64 (1995): 185–201.

Krinzinger, Friedrich. "Spectacula und Kaiserkult." Pages 103–32 in *Kaiserkult, Wirtschaft und spectacula: Zum Politischen und gesellschaftlichen Umfeld der Offenbarung*. Edited by Martin Ebner and Elisabeth Esch-Wermeling. SUNT 72. Göttingen: Vandenhoeck & Ruprecht, 2011.

Kuhn, Heinz-Wolfgang. "Die Kreuzesstrafe während der frühen Kaiserzeit: Ihre Wirklichkeit und Wertung in der Umwelt des Urchristentums." *ANRW* II.25.1 (1982): 648–793.

Kümmel, Werner Georg. *The New Testament: The History of the Investigation of Its Problems*. Nashville, TN: Abingdon, 1972.

Labahn, Michael. "Die Macht des Gedächtnisses: Überlegungen zu Möglichkeit und Grenzen des Einflusses hebräischer Texttradition auf die Johannesapokalypse." Pages 385–416 in *Von der Septuaginta zum Neuen Testament: Textgeschichtlichen Erörterungen*. Edited by Martin Karrer, Siegfried Kreuzer, and Marcus Sigismund. ANTF 43. Berlin: de Gruyter, 2012.

————. "Die Septuaginta und die Johannesapokalypse: Möglichkeiten und Grenzen einer Verhältnisbestimmung im Spiegel von kreativer Intertextualität und Textentwicklungen." Pages 149–90 in *Die Johannesapokalypse: Kontexte—Konzepte—Rezeption*. Edited by Jörg Frey, James A. Kelhoffer, and Franz Tóth. WUNT 287. Tübingen: Mohr Siebeck, 2012.

————. "Teufelgeschichten: Satan und seine Helfer in der Johannes-apokalypse." *ZNT* 14 (2011): 33–42.

Labahn, Michael, and Martin Karrer, eds. *Die Johannesoffenbarung: Ihr Text und Ihre Auslegung*. Arbeiten zur Bibel und Ihrer Auslegung 38. Leipzig: Evangelische, 2012.

Labahn, Michael, and Outi Lehtipun, eds. *Imagery in the Book of Revelation*. Leuven: Peeters, 2001.

LaHaye, Tim, and Thomas Ice. *Charting the End Times*. Eugene, OR: Harvest House, 2001.

LaHaye, Tim, and Jerry B. Jenkins. *Are We Living in the End Times?* Wheaton, IL: Tyndale, 1999.

Lambrecht, Jan. *L'Apocalypse johannique et l'Apocalyptique dans le Nouveau Testament*. BETL 53. Gembloux: Duculot; Leuven: Leuven University Press, 1980.

———. "Jewish Slander: A Note on Revelation 2,9–10." *ETL* 75 (1999): 421–29.

———. "The Opening of the Seals (Rev 6,1–8,6). *Bib* 79 (1998): 198–220.

———. "Rev 13,9–10 and Exhortation in the Apocalypse." Pages 331–47 in *New Testament Textual Criticism and Exegesis. Festschrift for J. Delobel*. Edited by Adelbert Denaux. Leuven: Leuven University Press; Sterling, VA: Peeters, 2002.

———. "Structuration of Revelation 4,1–22,5." Pages 77–104 in *Apocalypse johannique et l'apocalyptique dans le Nouveau Testament*. Edited by Jan Lambrecht and George Beasley-Murray. Gembloux: Duculot; Louvain: Leuven University Press, 1980.

———. "'Synagogues of Satan' (Rev. 2:9 and 3:9): Anti-Judaism in the Book of Revelation." Pages 279–92 in *Anti-Judaism and the Fourth Gospel*. Edited by Reimund Bieringer, Didier Pollefeyt, and Frederique Vandecasteele-Vanneuville. Louisville, KY: Westminster John Knox, 2001.

Lampe, G. W. H. "Testimony of Jesus Is the Spirit of Prophecy (Rev 19:10)." Pages 245–58 in *The New Testament Age: Essays in Honor of Bo Reicke*. Edited by William C. Weinrich. Macon, GA: Mercer University Press, 1984.

Lampe, Peter, and Ulrich Luz. "Nachpaulinisches Christentum und pagane Gesellschaft." Pages 185–216 in *Die Anfänge des Christentums: Alte Welt und neue Hoffnung*. Edited by Jürgen Becker, Christoph Burchard, and Carsten Colpe. Stuttgart: Kohlhammer, 1987.

LaRondelle, Hans K. "The Biblical Concept of Armageddon." *JETS* 28 (1985): 21–31.

———. "The Etymology of Har-magedon (Rev 16:16)." *AUSS* 27 (1989): 69–73.

Lausberg, Heinrich. *Handbook of Literary Rhetoric: A Foundation for Literary Study*. Leiden: Brill, 1998.

Laws, Sophie. *In the Light of the Lamb: Imagery, Parody, and Theology in the Apocalypse of John*. Wilmington, DE: Michael Glazier, 1988.

Le Frois, Bernard J. *The Woman Clothed with the Sun (Ap. 12): Individual or Collective? An Exegetical Study*. Rome: Orbis Catholicus, 1954.

Lee, Dal. *The Narrative Asides in the Book of Revelation*. Lanham, MD: University Press of America, 2002.

Lee, Pilchan. *The New Jerusalem in the Book of Revelation*. WUNT II/129. Tübingen: Mohr Siebeck, 2001.

Lefebvre, Philippe. "Mystìre et disparition de Dan: de la Septante à l'Apocalypse." Pages 279–307 in *IX Congress of the International Organization for Septuagint and Cognate Studies, 1995*. Edited by Bernard A. Taylor. Atlanta: Scholars, 1997.

Leipoldt, Johannes. *Geschichte des neutestamentlichen Kanons.* 2 vols. Leipzig: Hinrichs, 1907–8.

Lembke, Markus. "Beobachtungen zu den Handschriften der Apokalypse des Johannes." Pages 19–69 in *Die Johannesoffenbarung: Ihr Text und Ihre Auslegung.* Edited by Michael Labahn and Martin Karrer. Arbeiten zur Bibel und Ihrer Auslegung 38. Leipzig: Evangelische, 2012.

Lerner, Robert E. "Frederick II, Alive, Aloft, and Allayed, in Franciscan-Joachite Eschatology." Pages 359–81 in *The Use and Abuse of Eschatology in the Middle Ages.* Edited by Werner Verbeke, Daniel Verhelst, and Andries Welkenhuysen. Leuven: Leuven University Press, 1988.

———. "The Medieval Return to the Thousand-Year Sabbath." Pages 51–71 in *The Apocalypse in the Middle Ages.* Edited by Richard K. Emmerson and Bernard McGinn. Ithaca, NY: Cornell University Press, 1992.

———. "Millennialism." Pages 326–60 in *Apocalypticism in Western History and Culture.* Vol. 2 of *The Encyclopedia of Apocalypticism.* Edited by Bernard McGinn. New York: Continuum, 1998.

———. "Poverty, Preaching, and Eschatology in the Revelation Commentaries of 'Hugh of St. Cher.'" Pages 157–89 in *The Bible in the Medieval World: Essays in Memory of Beryl Smalley.* Edited by Katherine Walsh and Diana Wood. New York: Blackwell, 1985.

Levine, Amy-Jill, ed. *A Feminist Companion to the Apocalypse of John.* London: T. & T. Clark, 2009.

Levine, Lee I. *The Ancient Synagogue: The First Thousand Years.* New Haven, CT: Yale University Press, 2005.

Lewis, Suzanne. "Exegesis and Illustration in Thirteenth-Century English Apocalypses." Pages 259–75 in *The Apocalypse in the Middle Ages.* Edited by Richard K. Emmerson and Bernard McGinn. Ithaca, NY: Cornell University Press, 1992.

Lieu, Judith. *Image and Reality: The Jews in the World of the Christians in the Second Century.* Edinburgh: T. & T. Clark, 1996.

Lincoln, Andrew T. *The Letter to the Colossians. NIB* 11. Nashville: Abingdon, 2000.

Lindsey, Hal. *The Late Great Planet Earth.* Grand Rapids, MI: Zondervan, 1970.

Loasby, Roland E. "'Har-Magedon' According to the Hebrew in the Setting of the Seven Last Plagues of Revelation 16." *AUSS* 27 (1989): 129–32.

Lohse, Eduard. "Synagogue of Satan and Church of God: Jews and Christians in the Book of Revelation." *Svensk Exegetisk Årsbok* 58 (1993): 105–23.

Lona, Horacio E. *Der erste Clemsbrief: Kommentar zu den Apostolischen Vätern.* Göttingen: Vandenhoeck & Ruprecht, 1998.

Longenecker, Bruce W. "'Linked Like a Chain': Rev 22.6–9 in Light of an Ancient Transition Technique." *NTS* 47 (2001): 105–17.

Lücke, Friedrich. *Versuch einer vollständigen Einleitung in die Offenbarung Johannis und die gesammte apokalyptische Litteratur.* Bonn: Eduard Weber, 1832.

Lülsdorff, Raimund. "Ἐκλεκτοὶ Ἄγγελοι: Anmerkungen zu einer untergegangenen Amtsbezeichnung." *Biblische Zeitschrift* 36 (1992): 104–8.

Lumsden, Douglas W. *And Then the End Will Come: Early Latin Christian Interpretations of the Opening of the Seven Seals.* New York: Garland, 2001.

Maas, Martha, and Jane McIntosh Snyder. *Stringed Instruments of Ancient Greece.* New Haven, CT: Yale University Press, 1989.

MacLeod, David J. "The Adoration of God the Redeemer: An Exposition of Revelation 5:8–14." *BSac* 164 (2007): 454–71.

———. "Heaven's Hallelujah Chorus: An Introduction to the Seven 'Last Things' (Rev 19:1–10)." *BSac* 156 (1999): 72–84.

———. "The Lion Who Is a Lamb: An Exposition of Revelation 5:1–7." *BSac* 164 (2007): 323–40.

MacMullen, Ramsay. *Enemies of the Roman Order: Treason, Unrest, and Alienation in the Empire.* Cambridge, MA: Harvard University Press, 1966.

———. *Paganism in the Roman Empire.* New Haven, CT: Yale University Press, 1981.

———. *Roman Social Relations 50 B.C. to A.D. 284.* New Haven, CT: Yale University Press, 1974.

Magie, David. *Roman Rule in Asia Minor to the End of the Third Century After Christ.* 2 vols. Princeton, NJ: Princeton University Press, 1950.

Maier, Harry O. *Apocalypse Recalled: The Book of Revelation After Christendom.* Minneapolis: Fortress, 2002.

Maitland, Samuel R. *An Enquiry into the Grounds on which the Prophetic Period of Daniel and St. John Has Been Supposed to Consist of 1260 Years.* London: Hatchard, 1826.

Malay, Hasan. *Researches in Lydia, Mysia and Aiolis.* Vienna: Österreichischen Akademie der Wissenschaften, 1999.

Malherbe, Abraham J. "Ancient Epistolary Theorists." *Ohio Journal of Religious Studies* 5 (1977): 3–77.

———. *The Letters to the Thessalonians.* AYB 32B. New York: Doubleday, 2000; reprint, New Haven, CT: Yale University Press.

———. *Moral Exhortation: A Greco-Roman Sourcebook.* Philadelphia: Westminster, 1986.

Malina, Bruce J. *On the Genre and Message of Revelation: Star Visions and Sky Journeys.* Peabody, MA: Hendrickson, 1995.

Malina, Bruce J., and Jerome H. Neyrey. "Honor and Shame in Luke-Acts: Pivotal Values of the Mediterranean World." Pages 25–65 in *The Social World of Luke-Acts: Models for Interpretation.* Peabody, MA: Hendrickson, 1991.

Mamiani, Maurizio. "Newton on Prophecy and the Apocalypse." Pages 387–408 in *The Cambridge Companion to Newton.* Edited by I. Bernard Cohen and George E. Smith. Cambridge: Cambridge University Press, 2002.

Manganaro, Giacomo. "Le iscrizioni delle isole Milesie." *Annuario della scuola archaologica di Atene* 46–47, new series 25–26 (1963–64): 293–349.

Marucci, C. "Gematrie und Isopsephie im Neuen Testament—eine wirkliche Hilfe zum Verständnis?" SNTSU 27 (2002): 179–97.

Marcus, David. *From Balaam to Jonah: Anti-Prophetic Satire in the Hebrew Bible.* BJS 301. Atlanta: Scholars, 1995.

Marshall, John W. *Parables of War: Reading John's Jewish Apocalypse.* Waterloo, Ont.: Wilfrid Laurier University Press, 2001.

Martin, Dale B. *Slavery as Salvation: The Metaphor of Slavery in Pauline Christianity.* New Haven, CT: Yale University Press, 1990.

Martyn, J. Louis. *Galatians*. AYB 33A. New York: Doubleday, 1997; reprint, New Haven, CT: Yale University Press.

Mason, Hugh J. *Greek Terms for Roman Institutions: A Lexicon and Analysis*. American Studies in Papyrology 13. Toronto: Hakkert, 1974.

Mason, Steve. "Jews, Judeans, Judaizing, Judaism: Problems of Categorization in Ancient History." *JSJ* 38 (2007): 457–512.

Matheson, Peter, ed. *The Collected Works of Thomas Müntzer*. Edinburgh: T. & T. Clark, 1988.

Mathews, Mark D. "The Function of Imputed Speech in the Apocalypse of John." *CBQ* 74 (2012): 319–38.

Mathews, Susan F. "The Power to Endure and Be Transformed: Sun and Moon Imagery in Joel and Revelation 6." Pages 35–49 in *Imagery and Imagination in Biblical Literature: Essays in Honor of Aloysius Fitzgerald, F.S.C.* Edited by Lawrence Boadt and Mark S. Smith. CBQMS 32. Washington, DC: Catholic Biblical Association of America, 2001.

Mathewson, David. "New Exodus as a Background for 'The Sea Was No More' in Revelation 21:1C." *TJ* 24 (2003): 243–58.

———. *A New Heaven and a New Earth: The Meaning and Function of the Old Testament in Revelation 21.1–22.5*. JSNTSup 238. London: Sheffield Academic, 2003.

———. "A Re-examination of the Millennium in Rev 20:1–6: Consummation and Recapitulation." *JETS* 44 (2001): 237–51.

———. "Verbal Aspect in the Apocalypse of John: An Analysis of Revelation 5." *NovT* 50 (2008): 58–77.

Matter, Ann E. "The Apocalypse in Early Medieval Exegesis." Pages 38–50 in *The Apocalypse in the Middle Ages*. Edited by Richard K. Emmerson and Bernard McGinn. Ithaca, NY: Cornell University Press, 1992.

———. "Pseudo-Alcuinian De septem sigillis: An Early Latin Apocalypse Exegesis." *Traditio* 36 (1980): 111–37.

Mattingly, Harold et al. *The Roman Imperial Coinage*. 10 vols. London: Spink, 1923–94.

Mayo, Philip L. *"Those Who Call Themselves Jews": The Church and Judaism in the Apocalypse of John*. PTMS 60. Eugene, OR: Pickwick, 2006.

Mazzaferri, Frederick David. *The Genre of the Book of Revelation from a Source-Critical Perspective*. BZNW 54. Berlin: de Gruyter, 1989.

McCann, J. Clinton, Jr. *A Theological Introduction to the Book of Psalms: The Psalms as Torah*. Nashville, TN: Abingdon, 1993.

McDermott, Gerald R. *One Holy and Happy Society: The Public Theology of Jonathan Edwards*. University Park, PA: Pennsylvania State University Press, 1992.

McDonald, Lee Martin. *The Biblical Canon: Its Origin, Transmission, and Authority*. 3rd ed. Peabody, MA: Hendrickson, 2007.

McDonald, Patricia M. "Lion as Slain Lamb: On Reading Revelation Recursively." *Horizons* 23 (1996): 29–47.

McDonough, Sean M. *YHWH at Patmos: Rev. 1:4 in Its Hellenistic and Early Jewish Setting*. WUNT II/107. Tübingen: Mohr Siebeck, 1999.

McGinn, Bernard. *Antichrist: Two Thousand Years of the Human Fascination with Evil*. New York: Columbia University Press, 2000.

———. *Apocalyptic Spirituality: Treatises and Letters of Lactantius, Adso of Montier-en-Der, Joachim of Fiore, the Franciscan Spirituals, Savonarola*. New York: Paulist, 1979.

———. "Apocalypticism and Church Reform: 1100–1500." Pages 74–109 in *Apocalypticism in Western History and Culture*. Vol. 2 of *The Encyclopedia of Apocalypticism*. Edited by Bernard McGinn. New York: Continuum, 1998.

———. *The Calabrian Abbot: Joachim of Fiore in the History of Western Thought*. New York: Macmillan, 1985.

———. "The Emergence of the Spiritual Reading of the Apocalypse in the Third Century." Pages 251–72 in *Reading Religions in the Ancient World: Essays Presented to Robert McQueen Grant on His 90th Birthday*. Edited by David E. Aune and Robin Darling Young. NovTSup 125. Leiden: Brill, 2007.

———. *Visions of the End: Apocalyptic Traditions in the Middle Ages*. New York: Columbia, 1979.

McIlraith, Donal A. "'For the Fine Linen Is the Righteous Deeds of the Saints': Works and Wife in Revelation 19:8." *CBQ* 61 (1999): 512–29.

McKelvey, R. J. "The Millennium and the Second Coming." Pages 85–100 in *Studies in the Book of Revelation*. Edited by Steve Moyise. Edinburgh: T. & T. Clark, 2001.

McKinnon, James. "The Exclusion of Musical Instruments from the Ancient Synagogue." *Proceedings of the Royal Musical Association* 106 (1979–80): 77–87.

———. *Music in Early Christian Worship*. Cambridge: Cambridge University Press, 1987.

McNicol, Allan J. *The Conversion of the Nations in Revelation*. LNTS 438. London: T. & T. Clark, 2011.

Mealy, J. Webb. *After the Thousand Years: Resurrection and Judgment in Revelation 20*. JSNTSup 70. Sheffield: JSOT, 1992.

Meeks, Wayne A. *The First Urban Christians: The Social World of the Apostle Paul*. 2nd ed. New Haven, CT: Yale University Press, 2003.

Meer, Frederick van der. *Apocalypse: Visions from the Book of Revelation in Western Art*. New York: Alpine, 1978.

Meiggs, Russell. "Sea-Borne Timber Supplies to Rome." Pages 185–95 in *The Seaborne Commerce of Ancient Rome: Studies in Archaeology and History*. Edited by J. H. D'Arms and E. C. Kopff. MAAR 36. Rome: American Academy in Rome, 1980.

———. *Trees and Timber in the Ancient Mediterranean World*. Oxford: Clarendon, 1982.

Menken, Maarten J. J. "John's Use of Scripture in Revelation 1:7." *In die Skriflig* 41 (2007): 281–93.

Metzger, Bruce M. *The Canon of the New Testament: Its Origin, Development, and Significance*. Oxford: Clarendon, 1987.

———. *The Early Versions of the New Testament: Their Origin, Transmission, and Limitations*. Oxford: Clarendon, 1977.

Metzger, Bruce M., and Bart D. Ehrman. *The Text of the New Testament: Its Transmission, Corruption, and Restoration*. 4th ed. Oxford: Oxford University Press, 2005.

Meyers, Carol L., and Eric M. Meyers. *Haggai, Zechariah 1–8*. AYB 25B. Garden City, NY: Doubleday, 1987; reprint, New Haven, CT: Yale University Press.

————. *Zechariah 9–14*. AYB 25C. Garden City, NY: Doubleday, 1993; reprint, New Haven, CT: Yale University Press.

Meynet, Roland. "Le cantique de Moïse et le cantique de l'Agneau (Ap 15 et Ex 15)." *Gregorianum* 73 (1992): 19–55.

Michael, Michael George. "666 or 616 (Rev. 13:18)." *Deltion Biblikon Meleton* 19.2 (2000): 77–83.

————. "For It Is the Number of a Man." *Deltion Biblikon Meleton* 19.1 (2000): 79–89.

Mildenberg, Leo, and Patricia Erhart Mottahedeh. *The Coinage of the Bar Kochba War.* Aarau: Sauerländer, 1984.

Millar, Fergus. *The Emperor in the Roman World.* Ithaca, NY: Cornell University Press, 1977.

Miller, Kevin E. "The Nuptial Eschatology of Revelation 19–22." *CBQ* 60 (1998): 301–18.

Minear, Paul S. "Far as the Curse Is Found: The Point of Revelation 12:15–16." *NovT* 33 (1991): 71–77.

————. "Ontology and Ecclesiology in the Apocalypse." *NTS* 12 (1965–66): 89–105.

Minnis, Alastair J. *Medieval Theory of Authorship: Scholastic Literary Attitudes in the Later Middle Ages.* 2nd ed. Philadelphia: University of Pennsylvania Press, 1988.

Mitchell, Margaret M. "New Testament Envoys in the Context of Greco-Roman Diplomatic and Epistolary Conventions: The Example of Timothy and Titus." *JBL* 111 (1992): 641–62.

Mitchell, Stephen. *Anatolia: Land, Men, and Gods in Asia Minor.* 2 vols. Oxford: Clarendon, 1993.

————. "Archaeology in Asia Minor, 1985–1989." *Archaeological Reports* 36 (1990): 83–131.

Mommsen, Theodor. *Römisches strafrecht.* Leipzig: Duncker & Humblot, 1899.

Moorhead, James H. "Apocalypticism in Mainstream Protestantism, 1800 to the Present." Pages 72–107 in *Apocalypticism in the Modern Period and the Contemporary Age.* Vol. 3 of *The Encyclopedia of Apocalypticism.* Edited by Stephen J. Stein. New York: Continuum, 1998.

Morton, Russell. "Glory to God and the Lamb: John's Use of Jewish and Hellenistic/Roman Themes in Formatting His Theology in Revelation 4–5." *JSNT* 83 (2001): 89–109.

————. "Revelation 7:9–17: The Innumerable Crowd Before the One upon the Throne and Lamb." *Ashland Theological Journal* 32 (2000): 1–11.

Moyise, Steve. "Does the Lion Lie Down with the Lamb?" Pages 181–94 in *Studies in the Book of Revelation.* Edinburgh: T. & T. Clark, 2001.

————. "The Language of the Psalms in the Book of Revelation." *Neot* 37 (1993): 246–61.

————. *Old Testament in the Book of Revelation.* JSNTSup 115. Sheffield: Sheffield Academic, 1995.

————. "Singing the Song of Moses and the Lamb: John's Dialogical Use of Scripture." *AUSS* 42 (2004): 347–60.

————. *Studies in the Book of Revelation.* Edinburgh: T. & T. Clark, 2001.

Müller, Christoph G. "Gott wird alle Tränen abwischen—Offb 21,4: Anmerkungen zum Gottesbild der Apokalypse." *Theologie und Glaube* 95 (2005): 275–97.

Müller, Ulrich B. "Literarische und formgeschichtliche Bestimmung der Apokalypse des Johannes als einem Zeugnis frühchristlicher Apokalyptik." Pages 599–619 in *Apocalypticism in the Mediterranean World and the Near East.* Edited by David Hellholm. 2nd ed. Tübingen: Mohr Siebeck, 1989.

———. *Prophetie und Predigt im Neuen Testament: Formgeschichtl. Untersuchungen z. urchristl. Prophetie.* Gütersloh: Mohn, 1975.

Müller-Fieberg, Rita. "Literarische Rezeptionen des 'neuen Jerusalem' (Offb 21f.) als Impuls für Theologie und Praxis." *ZNT* 13 (2004): 33–42.

Munck, Johannes. *Petrus und Paulus in der Offenbarung Johannis: Ein Beitrag zur Auslegung der Apokalypse.* Copenhagen: Rosenkilde og Bagger, 1950.

Murphy-O'Connor, Jerome. "Corinthian Bronze." *RB* (1983): 80–93.

Murray, James S. "The Urban Earthquake Imagery and Divine Judgement in John's Apocalypse." *NovT* 47 (2005): 142–61.

Murray, Michele. *Playing a Jewish Game: Gentile Christian Judaizing in the First and Second Centuries CE.* ESCJ 13. Waterloo, Ont.: Wilfrid Laurier University Press, 2004.

Murrin, Michael. "Newton's Apocalypse." Pages 203–20 in *Newton and Religion: Context, Nature, and Influence.* Edited by James E. Force and Richard H. Popkin. Dordrecht: Kluwer, 1999.

———. "Revelation and Two Seventeenth Century Commentators." Pages 125–46 in *The Apocalypse in English Renaissance Thought and Literature.* Edited by C. A. Patrides and Joseph Wittreich. Ithaca, NY: Cornell University Press, 1984.

Mussies, G. "Antipas." *NovT* 7 (1964): 242–44.

———. *The Morphology of Koine Greek as Used in the Apocalypse of St. John: A Study in Bilingualism.* NovTSup 27. Leiden: Brill, 1971.

Musurillo, Herbert. *The Acts of the Christian Martyrs.* Oxford: Clarendon, 1972.

———. *Acts of the Pagan Martyrs. Acta Alexandrinorum.* Oxford: Clarendon, 1954.

Nanz, Christian. "'Hinabgeworfen wurde der Ankläger unserer Brüder . . .' (Offb 12,10): Das Motiv vom Satansturz in der Johannesoffenbarung." Pages 151–71 in *Theologie als Vision: Studien zur Johannes-Offenbarung.* Edited by Knut Backhaus. SBS 191. Stuttgart: Katholisches Bibelwerk, 2001.

Neufeld, Dietmar. "Christian Communities in Sardis and Smyrna." Pages 25–39 in *Religious Rivalries and the Struggle for Success in Sardis and Smyrna.* Edited by Richard S. Ascough. ESCJ 14. Waterloo, Ont.: Wilfrid Laurier University Press, 2005.

———. "Sumptuous Clothing and Ornamentation in the Apocalypse." *HvTSt* 58 (2002): 664–89.

Newsom, Carol A. *Songs of the Sabbath Sacrifice: A Critical Edition.* Harvard Semitic Studies 27. Atlanta: Scholars, 1985.

Neyrey, Jerome H. *The Social World of Luke-Acts: Models for Interpretation.* Peabody, MA: Hendrickson, 1991.

———. "'Without Beginning of Days or End of Life' (Hebrews 7:3): Topos for a True Deity." *CBQ* 53 (1991): 439–55.

Nickelsburg, George W. E. *1 Enoch 1: A Commentary on the Book of Enoch Chapters 1–36; 81–108.* Hermeneia. Minneapolis: Fortress, 2001.

————. *Resurrection, Immortality, and Eternal Life in Intertestamental Judaism and Early Christianity*. Rev. ed. Cambridge, MA: Harvard University Press, 2006.

Nickelsburg, George W. E., and James C. VanderKam. *1 Enoch 2: A Commentary on the Book of 1 Enoch Chapters 37–82*. Hermeneia. Minneapolis: Fortress, 2012.

Nicklas, Tobias. "The Early Text of Revelation." Pages 225–37 in *The Early Text of the New Testament*. Edited by Charles E. Hill and Michael J. Kruger. Oxford: Oxford University Press, 2012.

————. "Probleme der Apokalypserezeption im 2. Jahrhundert: Eine Diskussion mit Charles E. Hill." Pages 28–45 in *Ancient Christian Interpretations of "Violent Texts" in the Apocalypse*. Edited by Joseph Verheyden, Tobias Nicklas, and Andreas Merkt. SUNT 92. Göttingen: Vandenhoeck & Ruprecht, 2011.

Nielsen, Harald. *Ancient Ophthalmological Agents*. Odense: Odense University Press, 1974.

Nielsen, Kirsten. "Shepherd, Lamb, and Blood: Imagery in the Old Testament—Use and Reuse." *ST* 46 (1992): 121–32.

Nielsen, Kjeld. *Incense in Ancient Israel*. VTSup 38. Leiden: Brill, 1986.

Nikolakopoulos, Konstantin. "Die Apokalypse des Johannes und die orthodoxe Liturgie: Anknüpfungspunkte zwischen Apokalypse und orthodoxen Kultus." Pages 775–91 in *Die Johannesapokalypse: Kontexte—Konzepte—Rezeption*. Edited by Jörg Frey, James A. Kelhoffer, and Franz Tóth. WUNT 287. Tübingen: Mohr Siebeck, 2012.

Nilsson, Martin P. *Geschichte der griechische Religion*. 2 vols. Münich: Beck, 1955–1961.

Nutton, Vivian. "The Drug Trade in Antiquity." *Journal of the Royal Society of Medicine* 78 (1985): 138–45.

————. "Healers in the Medical Market Place: Towards a Social History of Graeco-Roman Medicine." Pages 15–58 in *Medicine in Society: Historical Essays*. Edited by Andrew Wear. Cambridge: Cambridge University Press, 1992.

O'Daly, Gerard. *Augustine's City of God: A Reader's Guide*. Oxford: Clarendon, 1999.

O'Donovan, Oliver. "The Political Thought of the Book of Revelation." *TynBul* 37 (1986): 61–94.

O'Hear, Natasha. "Images of Babylon: A Visual History of the Whore in Late Medieval and Early Modern Art." Pages 311–33 in *From the Margins 2: Women of the New Testament and Their Afterlives*. Edited by Christine E. Joynes and Christopher C. Rowland. Sheffield: Sheffield Phoenix, 2009.

O'Leary, Stephen D. *Arguing the Apocalypse: A Theory of Millennial Rhetoric*. New York: Oxford University Press, 1994.

Oberweis, Michael. "Die Bedeutung der neutestamentlichen 'Rätselzahlen' 666 (Apk 13,18) und 153 (Joh 21,11)." *ZNW* 77 (1986): 226–41.

————. "Erwägungen zur apokalyptischen Ortsbezeichnung 'Harmagedon.'" *Bib* 76 (1995): 305–24.

Oesch, Josef. "Intertextuelle Untersuchungen zum Bezug von Offb 21,1–22,5 auf alttestamentliche Prätexte." *PzB* 8 (1999): 41–74.

Olson, Daniel C. "'Those Who Have Not Defiled Themselves with Women': Revelation 14:4 and the Book of Enoch." *CBQ* 59 (1997): 492–510.

Osiek, Carolyn. *Shepherd of Hermas: A Commentary*. Hermeneia. Minneapolis: Fortress, 1999.

Osiek, Carolyn, and David L. Balch. *Families in the New Testament World: Households and House Churches*. Louisville, KY: Westminster John Knox, 1997.

Oster, Richard E. "Ephesus as a Religious Center Under the Principate, I. Paganism Before Constantine." *ANRW* II.18.3 (1990): 1661–1728.

Owens, E. J. *The City in the Greek and Roman World*. London: Routledge, 1991.

Packull, Werner O. "A Reinterpretation of Melchior Hoffman's Exposition Against the Background of Spiritualist Franciscan Eschatology with Special Reference to Peter John Olivi." Pages 32–65 in *The Dutch Dissenters: A Critical Companion to Their History and Ideals*. Edited by Irvin Buckwalter Horst. Leiden: Brill, 1986.

Parke, Herbert William. *The Oracles of Apollo in Asia Minor*. London: Croom Helm, 1985.

Parker, David C. *An Introduction to the New Testament Manuscripts and Their Texts*. Cambridge: Cambridge University Press, 2008.

———. "A New Oxyrhynchus Papyrus of Revelation P[115] (P.Oxy. 4499)." *NTS* 46 (2000): 159–74.

Parker, Floyd O., Jr. "'Our Lord and God' in Rev 4,11: Evidence for the Late Date of Revelation?" *Bib* 82 (2001): 207–31.

Paschke, Boris A. "Die damnatio und consecratio der zwei Zeugen (Offb 11)." *Bib* 89 (2008): 555–75.

Pataki, András Dávid. "A Non-Combat Myth in Revelation 12." *NTS* 57 (2011): 258–72.

Pattemore, Stephen W. *The People of God in the Apocalypse: Discourse, Structure, and Exegesis*. SNTSMS 128. Cambridge: Cambridge University Press, 2004.

———. *Souls Under the Altar: Relevance Theory and the Discourse Structure of Revelation*. New York: United Bible Societies, 2003.

Patterson, Stephen J. "A Note on an Argive Votive Relief of Selene." *HTR* 78 (1985): 439–43.

Paulien, John. *Decoding Revelation's Trumpets: Literary Allusions and Interpretation of Revelation 8:7–12*. Berrien Springs, MI: Andrews University Press, 1988.

Pedley, John Griffiths. *Ancient Literary Sources on Sardis*. Cambridge, MA: Harvard University Press, 1972.

Peerbolte, L. J. Lietaert. *The Antecedents of Antichrist: A Traditio-Historical Study of the Earliest Christian Views on Eschatological Opponents*. Leiden: Brill, 1996.

Penly, Paul T. *The Common Tradition Behind Synoptic Sayings of Judgment and John's Apocalypse: An Oral Interpretive Tradition of Old Testament Prophetic Material*. LNTS 424. London: T. & T. Clark, 2010.

Penton, M. James. *Apocalypse Delayed: The Story of Jehovah's Witnesses*. 2nd ed. Toronto: University of Toronto Press, 1997.

Pernice, Erich, ed. *Gefässe und Geräte aus Bronze*. Vol. 4 of *Die Hellenistische Kunst in Pompeji*. Edited by Franz Winter. Berlin: de Gruyter, 1925.

Perry, Peter S. "Critiquing the Excess of Empire: A Synkrisis of John of Patmos and Dio of Prusa." *JSNT* 29 (2007): 473–96.

———. *The Rhetoric of Digressions: Revelation 7:1–17 and 10:1–11:13 and Ancient Communication*. WUNT II/268. Tübingen: Mohr Siebeck, 2009.

Petersen, Rodney L. *Preaching in the Last Days: The Theme of the "Two Witnesses" in the 16th and 17th Centuries*. New York: Oxford University Press, 1993.

Petzl, Georg. *Philadelpheia et Ager Philadelphenus.* Tituli Lydiae 5/3. Titula Asiae Minoris. Vienna: Östereichischen Akademie der Wissenschaften, 2007.

Peuch, Émile. "The Names of the Gates of the New Jerusalem (4Q554)." Pages 379–92 in *Emanuel: Studies in Hebrew Bible, Septuagint, and Dead Sea Scrolls in Honor of Emanuel Tov.* Edited by Shalom M. Paul, Robert A. Kraft, Lawrence H. Schiffman, and Weston W. Fields. VTSup 94. Leiden: Brill, 2003.

Pezzoli-Olgiati, Daria. *Täuschung und Klarheit: Zur Wechselwirkung zwischen Vision und Geschichte in der Johannesoffenbarung.* FRLANT 175. Göttingen: Vandenhoeck & Ruprecht, 1997.

Philonenko, Marc. "Celui qui est, qui était et qui vient (Apocalypse de Jean 1,4)." Pages 199–207 in *Le Temp et les Temps dans les literatures juives et chrétiennes au tournant de notre ère.* Edited by Christian Grappe and Jean-Claude Ingelaere. JSJSup 112. Leiden: Brill, 2006.

———. "'Dehors les chiens' (Apocalypse 22.16 et 4QMMT B 58–62)." *NTS* 43 (1997): 445–50.

———. "'Un voix sortit du trône qui disait . . .' (Apocalypse de Jean 19,5a)." *RHPR* 79 (1999): 83–89.

Pilch, John J. "Lying and Deceit in the Letters to the Seven Churches: Perspectives from Cultural Anthropology." *BTB* 22 (1992): 126–35.

Pippin, Tina. "'And I Will Strike Her Children Dead': Death and the Deconstruction of Social Location." Pages 191–98 in *Reading from This Place: Social Location and Biblical Interpretation in the United States.* Edited by Fernando F. Segovia and Mary Ann Tolbert. Minneapolis: Fortress, 1995.

———. *Death and Desire: The Rhetoric of Gender in the Apocalypse of John.* Louisville, KY: Westminster John Knox, 1992.

———. "Eros and the End: Reading for Gender in the Apocalypse of John." *Semeia* 59 (1992): 193–210.

———. "Peering into the Abyss: A Postmodern Reading of the Biblical Bottomless Pit." Pages 251–67 in *The New Literary Criticism and the New Testament.* Edited by Edgar V. McKnight and Elizabeth Struthers Malbon. Valley Forge, PA: Trinity, 1994.

Poirier, John C. "The First Rider: A Response to Michael Bachmann." *NTS* 45 (1999): 257–63.

Pollard, Leslie N. "The Function of Λοιπός in the Letter to Thyatira." *AUSS* 46 (2008): 45–63.

Porter, Stanley E. "The Language of the Apocalypse in Recent Discussion." *NTS* 35 (1989): 582–603.

———. "Why the Laodiceans Received Lukewarm Water (Revelation 3:15–18)." *TynBul* 38 (1987): 143–49.

Portier-Young, Anathea E. *Apocalypse Against Empire: Theologies of Resistance in Early Judaism.* Grand Rapids, MI: Eerdmans 2011.

Potestà, Gian Luca. "Radical Apocalyptic Movements in the Late Middle Ages." Pages 110–42 in *Apocalypticism in Western History and Culture.* Vol. 2 in *The Encyclopedia of Apocalypticism.* Edited by Bernard McGinn. New York: Continuum 1998.

Poythress, Vern S. "Genre and Hermeneutics in Rev 20:1–6." *JETS* 36 (1993): 41–54.

Price, S. R. F. *Rituals and Power: The Roman Imperial Cult in Asia Minor*. Cambridge: Cambridge University Press, 1984.

Prigent, Pierre. "L'Hérésie asiate et l'église confessante de l'Apocalypse à Ignace." *VC* 31 (1977): 1–22.

Provan, Iain. "Foul Spirits, Fornication and Finance: Revelation 18 from an Old Testament Perspective." *JSNT* 64 (1996): 81–100.

Quek, Tze Ming. "'I Will Give Authority over the Nations': Psalm 2.8–9 in Revelation 2.26–27." Pages 175–87 in *Exegetical Studies*. Vol. 2 of *Early Christian Literature and Intertextuality*. Edited by Craig A. Evans and H. Daniel Zacharias. London: T. & T. Clark, 2009.

Radt, Wolfgang. *Pergamon: Geschichte und Bauten einer antiken Metropole*. Darmstadt: Primus, 1999.

———. "Recent Research in and About Pergamon." Pages 11–40 in *Pergamon: Citadel of the Gods. Archaeological Record, Literary Description, and Religious Development*. Edited by Helmut Koester. Harrisburg, PA: Trinity, 1998.

Rainbow, Jesse. "Male μαστοί in Revelation 1.13." *JSNT* 30 (2007): 249–53.

Räisänen, Heikki. "The Nicolaitans: Apoc. 2; Acta 6." *ANRW* II.26.2 (1995): 1602–44.

Ramelli, Ilaria L. E. "Origen's Interpretation of Violence in the Apocalypse: Destruction of Evil and Purification of Sinners." Pages 46–62 in *Ancient Christian Interpretations of "Violent Texts" in the Apocalypse*. Edited by Joseph Verheyden, Tobias Nicklas, and Andreas Merkt. SUNT 92. Göttingen: Vandenhoeck & Ruprecht, 2011.

Ramsay, William M. *Letters to the Seven Churches and Their Place in the Plan of the Apocalypse*. New York: A. C. Armstrong, 1905.

Rapp, Ursula. "Das herabsteigende Jerusalem als Bild göttlicher Präsenz." *PzB* 8 (1999): 777–84.

Räpple, Eva Maria. *The Metaphor of the City in the Apocalypse of John*. New York: Peter Lang, 2004.

Rapske, Brian. *The Book of Acts and Paul in Roman Custody*. Vol. 3 of *The Book of Acts in Its First Century Setting*. Grand Rapids, MI: Eerdmans; Carlisle: Paternoster, 1994.

Reader, William W. "The Twelve Jewels of Revelation 21:19–20: Tradition History and Modern Interpretations." *JBL* 100 (1981): 433–57.

Reeves, Marjorie. *The Influence of Prophecy in the Later Middle Ages: A Study in Joachimism*. Notre Dame, IN: University of Notre Dame Press, 1993.

Rehm, Albert. *Didyma*. Vol. 2. Berlin: Mann, 1958.

Reiser, Marius. *Jesus and Judgment: The Eschatological Proclamation in Its Jewish Context*. Minneapolis: Fortress, 1997.

Reynolds, Joyce. *Aphrodisias and Rome*. London: Society for the Promotion of Roman Studies, 1982.

Ricoeur, Paul. *The Symbolism of Evil*. New York: Harper & Row, 1967.

Rissi, Mathias. *The Future of the World: An Exegetical Study of Revelation 19.11–22.15*. London: SCM, 1972.

———. *Die Hure Babylon und die Verführung der Heiligen: Eine Studie zur Apokalypse Johannes*. BWANT 136. Stuttgart: Kohlhammer, 1995.

Roloff, Jürgen. "Neuschöpfung in der Offenbarung des Johannes." *Jahrbuch für biblische Theologie* 5 (1990): 119–38.

————. "Weltgericht und Weltvollendung in der Offenbarung des Johannes." Pages 106–27 in *Weltgericht und Weltvollendung: Zukunftsbilder im Neuen Testament*. Edited by Hans-Josef Klauck. Freiburg: Herder, 1994.

Roose, Hanna. *"Das Zeugnis Jesu": Seine Bedeutung für die Christologie, Eschatologie und Prophetie in der Offenbarung des Johannes*. TANZ 32. Tübingen: Francke, 2000.

Rossing, Barbara R. *The Choice Between Two Cities: Whore, Bride, and Empire in the Apocalypse*. Harrisburg, PA: Trinity, 1999.

————. "For the Healing of the World: Reading Revelation Ecologically." Pages 165–82 in *From Every People and Nation: The Book of Revelation in Intercultural Perspective*. Edited by David Rhoads. Minneapolis: Fortress, 2005.

————. "River of Life in God's New Jerusalem: An Eschatological Vision for Earth's Future." Pages 205–24 in *Christianity and Ecology: Seeking the Well-Being of Earth and Humans*. Edited by Dieter T. Hessel and Rosemary Radford Ruether. Cambridge, MA: Harvard University Press, 2000.

Rowland, Christopher, and Ian Boxall. "Tyconius and Bede on Violent Texts in the Apocalypse." Pages 161–79 in *Ancient Christian Interpretations of "Violent Texts" in the Apocalypse*. Edited by Joseph Verheyden, Tobias Nicklas, and Andreas Merkt. SUNT 92. Göttingen: Vandenhoeck & Ruprecht, 2011.

Royalty, Robert M., Jr. "Don't Touch This Book!: Revelation 22:18–19 and the Rhetoric of Reading (in) the Apocalypse of John." *BibInt* 12 (2004): 282–99.

————. "Etched or Sketched? Inscriptions and Erasures in the Messages to Sardis and Philadelphia (Rev. 3.1–13)." *JSNT* 27 (2005): 447–63.

————. *The Streets of Heaven: The Ideology of Wealth in the Apocalypse of John*. Macon, GA: Mercer University Press, 1998.

Rudwick, M. J. S., and E. M. B. Green. "The Laodicean Lukewarmness." *Expository Times* 69 (1957–58): 176–78.

Ruiten, Jacques van. "The Intertextual Relationship Between Isaiah 65,17–20 and Revelation 21,1–5b." *EstBib* 51 (1993): 473–510.

Ruiz, Jean Pierre. *Ezekiel in the Apocalypse: The Transformation of Prophetic Language in Revelation 16,17–19,10*. European University Studies Series 23, no. 376. Frankfurt am Main: Lang, 1989.

————. "Hearing and Seeing but Not Saying: A Rhetoric of Authority in Revelation 10:4 and 2 Corinthians 12:4." Pages 91–111 in *The Reality of Apocalypse: Rhetoric and Politics in the Book of Revelation*. Edited by David L. Barr. SBLSymS 39. Atlanta: Society of Biblical Literature, 2006.

————. "Praise and Politics in Revelation 19:1–10." Pages 69–84 in *Studies in the Book of Revelation*. Edited by Steve Moyise. Edinburgh: T. & T. Clark, 2001.

————. "Taking a Stand on the Sand of the Seashore: A Postcolonial Exploration of Revelation 13." Pages 119–35 in *Reading the Book of Revelation: A Resource for Students*. Edited by David L. Barr. Atlanta: Society of Biblical Literature, 2003.

Rusconi, Roberto. "Antichrist and Antichrists." Pages 287–325 in *Apocalypticism in Western History and Culture*. Vol. 2 of *The Encyclopedia of Apocalypticism*. Edited by Bernard McGinn. New York: Continuum, 1998.

Ryan, Sean Michael. *Hearing at the Boundaries of Vision: Education Informing Cosmology in Revelation 9*. LNTS 448. London: T. & T. Clark, 2012.

Rydbeck, Lars. *Fachprosa, Vermeintliche Volkssprache und Neues Testament: Zur Beurteilung der sprachlichen Niveauunterschiede im nachklassischen Griechisch.* Uppsala: University of Uppsala Press, 1967.

Saffrey, H. D. "Relire l'Apocalypse a Patmos." *RB* 82 (1975): 385–417.

Safrai, Shemuel, and Menahem Stern. *The Jewish People in the First Century.* 2 vols. Assen: van Gorcum; Philadelphia: Fortress, 1974–76.

Sals, Ulrike. *Die Biographie der "Hure Babylon" Studien zur Intertextualität der Babylon-Texte in der Bibel.* FAT 2.6. Tübingen: Mohr Siebeck, 2004.

Sandeen, Ernest R. *The Roots of Fundamentalism: British and American Millenarianism, 1800–1930.* Chicago: University of Chicago Press, 1970.

Sanders, Edward P. *Jewish Law from Jesus to the Mishnah: Five Studies.* London: SCM; Philadelphia: Trinity, 1990.

Sanders, Jack T. "Whence the First Millennium? The Sources Behind Revelation 20." *NTS* 50 (2004): 444–56.

Sänger, Dieter. "'Amen, komm, Herr Jesus!' (Apk 22,20): Anmerkungen zur Christologie der Johannes-Apokalypse." Pages 71–92 in *Studien zur Johannesoffenbarung und ihrer Auslegung: Festschrift für Otto Böcher zum 70. Geburtstag.* Edited by Friedrich Wilhelm Horn and Michael Wolters. Neukirchen-Vluyn: Neukirchener, 2005.

Sänger, Dieter, ed. *Das Ezechielbuch in der Johannesoffenbarung.* Neukirchen-Vluyn: Neukirchener, 2004.

Satake, Akira. *Die Gemeindeordnung in der Johannesapokalypse.* WMANT 21. Neukirchen-Vluyn: Neukirchener, 1966.

Schaik, A. P. van. "Ἄλλος Ἄγγελος in Apk 14." Pages 217–28 in *Apocalypse johannique et l'apocalyptique dans le Nouveau Testament.* Edited by Jan Lambrecht and George Beasley-Murray. Gembloux: Duculot; Louvain: Leuven University Press, 1980.

Scherrer, Peter. "The City of Ephesos from the Roman Period to Late Antiquity." Pages 1–25 in *Ephesos: Metropolis of Asia.* Edited by Helmut Koester. Valley Forge, PA: Trinity, 1995.

Scherrer, Steven J. "Signs and Wonders in the Imperial Cult: A New Look at a Roman Religious Institution in the Light of Rev 13:13–15." *JBL* 103 (1984): 599–610.

Schille, Gottfried. "Der Apokalyptiker Johannes und die Edelsteine (Apk 21)." *SNTSU* 17 (1992): 231–44.

Schimanowski, Gottfried. "'Connecting Heaven and Earth': The Function of the Hymns in Revelation 4–5." Pages 67–84 in *Heavenly Realms and Earthly Realities in Late Antique Religions.* Edited by Ra'anan S. Boutstan and Annette Yoshiko Reed. Cambridge: Cambridge University Press, 2004.

———. *Die himmlische Liturgie in der Apokalypse des Johannes: Die frühjüdischen Traditionen in Offenbarung 4–5 unter Enschluss der Hekhalotliteratur.* WUNT II/154. Tübingen: Mohr Siebeck, 2002.

Schmid, Josef. *Studien zur Geschichte des griechischen Apokalypse-Textes.* 2 vols. Münich: Zink, 1955–56.

Schmidt, Daryl D. "Semitisms and Septuagintalisms in the Book of Revelation." *NTS* 37 (1991): 592–603.

Schmidt, Josef. "Νοῦς und Σοφία in Offb 17." *NovT* 46 (2004): 164–89.

———. "Die Rätselzahl 666 in Off 13:18: Ein Lösungsversuch auf der Basis Lateinischer Gematrie." *NovT* 44 (2002): 35–54.

Schmidt, Thomas E. "'And the Sea Was No More': Water as People, Not Place." Pages 233–49 in *To Tell the Mystery: Essays on New Testament Eschatology in Honor of Robert H. Gundry*. Edited by Thomas E. Schmidt and Moisés Silva. JSNTSup 100. Sheffield: JSOT 1994.

Schoedel, William R. *Ignatius of Antioch: A Commentary on the Letters of Ignatius of Antioch*. Hermeneia. Minneapolis: Fortress, 1985.

Scholtissek, Klaus. "'Mitteilhaber an der Bedrängnis, der Königsherrschaft und der Ausdauer in Jesus' (Offb 1,9): Partizipatorische Ethic in der Offenbarung des Johannes." Pages 172–207 in *Theologie als Vision: Studien zur Johannes-Offenbarung*. Edited by Knut Backhaus. SBS 191. Stuttgart: Katholisches Bibelwerk, 2001.

Schrage, Wolfgang. *Der erste Brief an die Korinther*. 4 vols. EKKNT 7. Zürich: Benzinger; Neukirchen-Vluyn: Neukirchener, 1991–2001.

Schulz, Fritz. "Roman Registers of Births and Birth-Certificates." *JRS* 32 (1942): 78–91, and *JRS* 33 (1943): 55–64.

Schürer, Emil. *History of the Jewish People in the Age of Jesus Christ*. 4 vols. Revised and edited by Geza Vermes et al. Edinburgh: T. & T. Clark, 1973–87.

Schüssler Fiorenza, Elisabeth. *The Book of Revelation: Justice and Judgment*. Philadelphia: Fortress, 1985.

———. *Priester für Gott: Studien zum Herrschafts- und Priestermotiv in der Apokalypse*. NTAbh 7. Münster: Aschendorff, 1972.

———. *Revelation: Vision of a Just World*. Minneapolis: Fortress, 1991.

Schwindt, Rainer. "Der Klageruf der Märtyrer: Exegetische und theologische Überlegungen zu Offb 6,9–11." *BN* 141–142 (2009): 117–36 and 119–30.

Scobie, Charles. H. "Local References in the Letters to the Seven Churches." *NTS* 39 (1993): 606–24.

Seidel, Linda. "Apocalypse and Apocalypticism in Western Medieval Art." Pages 467–506 in *Apocalypticism in Western History and Culture*. Vol. 2 of *The Encyclopedia of Apocalypticism*. Edited by Bernard McGinn. New York: Continuum, 1998.

Seland, Torrey. "Philo, Magic and Balaam: Neglected Aspects of Philo's Exposition of the Balaam Story." Pages 333–46 in *The New Testament and Early Christian Literature in Greco-Roman Context: Studies in Honor of David E. Aune*. Edited by John Fotopoulos. NovTSup 122. Leiden: Brill, 2006.

Selvidge, Marta. "Powerful and Powerless Women in the Apocalypse." *Neot* 26 (1992): 157–67.

Shea, William H. "Chiasm in Theme and by Form in Revelation 18." *AUSS* 20 (1982): 249–56.

———. "The Location and Significance of Armageddon in Rev 16:16." *AUSS* 18 (1980): 157–62.

Shepherd, Norman. "Resurrections of Revelation 20." *WTJ* 37 (1974): 34–43.

Sherwin-White, Adrian Nicholas. *The Letters of Pliny: A Historical and Social Commentary*. Oxford: Clarendon, 1966.

———. *The Roman Citizenship*. 2nd ed. Oxford: Clarendon, 1973.

———. *Roman Society and Roman Law in the New Testament. The Sarum Lectures 1960–61*. Oxford: Clarendon, 1963.

Shore, Fred B. *Parthian Coins & History: Ten Dragons Against Rome*. Quarryville, PA: Classical Numismatic Group, 1993.

Siew, Antoninus King Wai. *The War Between the Two Beasts and the Two Witnesses: A Chiastic Reading of Revelation 11.1–14.5.* JSNTSup 283. London: T. & T. Clark, 2005.

Sigismund, Marcus. "Schreiber und Korrektoren in der Johannes-Apokalypse des Kodex Alexandrinus." Pages 319–38 in *Von der Septuaginta zum Neuen Testament: Textgeschichtlichen Eröterungen.* Edited by Martin Karrer, Siegfried Kreuzer, and Marcus Sigismund. ANTF 43. Berlin: de Gruyter, 2012.

Siitonen, Kirsi. "Merchants and Commerce in the Book of Revelation." Pages 145–60 in *Imagery in the Book of Revelation.* Edited by Michael Labahn and Outi Lehtipun. Leuven: Peeters, 2001.

Sim, David C. "The Meaning of παλιγεννεσία in Matt 19,28." *JSNT* 50 (1993): 3–12.

Sim, Unyong. *Das himmlische Jerusalem in Apk 21,1–22,5 im Kontext biblisch-jüdischer Tradition und antiken Städtebaus.* Bochumer Altertumswissenschaftliches Colloquium 25. Trier: Wissenschaftlicher Verlag Trier, 1996.

Simpson, R. H., and J. F. Lazenby, "Notes from the Dodecanese II." *Annual of the British School at Athens* 65 (1970): 47–77.

Şimşek, Celal, and Mustafa Büyükkolanci. "The Water Springs of Laodicea and Its Distribution Systems." *Adalya* 9 (2006): 83–103.

Skaggs, Rebecca, and Thomas Doyle. "Revelation 7: Three Critical Questions." Pages 161–82 in *Imagery in the Book of Revelation.* Edited by Michael Labahn and Outi Lehtipun. Leuven: Peeters, 2001.

Slater, Thomas B. *Christ and Community: A Socio-Historical Study of the Christology of Revelation.* JSNTSup 178. Sheffield: Sheffield Academic, 1999.

———. "Dating the Apocalypse of John." *Bib* 84 (2003): 252–58.

———. "'King of Kings' and 'Lord of Lords' Revisited." *NTS* 39 (1993): 159–60.

———. "On the Social Setting of the Revelation to John." *NTS* 44 (1998): 232–56.

Smalley, Stephen S. *Thunder and Love: John's Revelation and John's Community.* Milton Keynes: Word, 1994.

Smidt, J. C. de. "A Doxology to Christ (Rev 1:5e–6)." *In die Skriflig* 40 (2006): 317–35.

Smidt, Kobus de. "The Acts of God and the Spirit in the Church(es) and in the World: A Meta-Theology of ὁ θεός and ὁ πνεῦμα in Revelations 1:4." *Acta Patristica et Byzantina* 16 (2005): 166–95.

———. "The First Μακαρισμός in Revelation 1:3." *Acta Patristica et Byzantina* 15 (2004): 91–118.

———. "A Meta-Theology of ὁ θεός in Revelations 1:1–2." *Neot* 38 (2004): 183–208.

———. "Revelation 1:5A–D: A Prolegomenon to a Theology of Ἰησοῦ Χριστοῦ in the Book of Revelation." *Acta Patristica et Byzantina* 17 (2006): 179–205.

Smith, Christopher R. "The Portrayal of the Church as the New Israel in the Names and Order of the Tribes in Revelation 7.5–8." *JSNT* 39 (1990): 111–18.

———. "The Tribes of Revelation 7 and the Literary Competence of John the Seer." *JETS* 38 (1995): 213–18.

Smith, Derwood C. "Millennial Reign of Jesus Christ: Some Observations on Rev 20:1–10." *Restoration Quarterly* 16 (1973): 219–30.

Smith, Morton. "On the History of Ἀποκαλύπτω and Ἀποκάλυψις." Pages 9–20 in *Apocalypticism in the Mediterranean World and the Near East.* Edited by David Hellholm. 2nd ed. Tübingen: Mohr Siebeck, 1989.

Smith, R. R. R. "The Imperial Reliefs from the Sebasteion at Aphrodisias." *JRS* 77 (1987): 88–138.

———. "Simulacra Gentium: The Ethne from the Sebasteion at Aphrodisias." *JRS* 78 (1988): 50–77.

Smolinski, Reiner. "Apocalypticism in Colonial North America." Pages 36–71 in *Apocalypticism in the Modern Period and the Contemporary Age*. Vol. 3 of *The Encyclopedia of Apocalypticism*. Edited by Stephen J. Stein. New York: Continuum, 1998.

Smyth, Herbert Weir. *Greek Grammar*. Cambridge, MA: Harvard University Press, 1956.

Söllner, Peter. *Jerusalem, die hochgebaute Stadt: Eschatologisches und himmlisches Jerusalem im Frühjudentum und im frühen Christentum*. TANZ 25. Tübingen: Francke, 1998.

Spatafora, Andrea. *From the "Temple of God" to God as the Temple: A Biblical Theological Study of the Temple in the Book of Revelation*. Rome: Università Gregoriana, 1997.

Spitta, Friedrich. *Die Offenbarung des Johannes*. Halle: Weisenhaus, 1889.

Stanley, Christopher D. "Who's Afraid of a Thief in the Night?" *NTS* 48 (2002): 468–86.

Staples, Peter. "Rev XVI 4–6 and Its Vindication Formula." *NovT* 14 (1972): 280–93.

Stauffer, E. "666." *ConBNT* 11 (1947): 237–44.

Stefanovic, Ranko. "The Angel at the Altar (Revelation 8:3–5): A Case Study on Intercalations in Revelation." *AUSS* 44 (2006): 79–94.

———. "The Meaning of ἐπὶ τὴν δειξίαν for the Location of the Sealed Scroll (Revelation 5:1) and Understanding the Scene of Revelation 5." *BR* 45 (2001): 42–54.

Stein, Stephen J., ed. *Apocalyptic Writings, "Notes on the Apocalypse," An Humble Attempt*. Works of Jonathan Edwards 5. New Haven, CT: Yale University Press, 1977.

Steinmann, Andrew E. "The Tripartite Structure of the Sixth Seal, the Sixth Trumpet, and the Sixth Bowl of John's Apocalypse (Rev 6:12–7:17; 9:13–11:14; 16:12–16)." *JETS* 35 (1992): 69–79.

Stenström, Hanna. "Is Salvation Only for True Men? On Gendered Imagery in the Book of Revelation." Pages 183–98 in *Imagery in the Book of Revelation*. Edited by Michael Labahn and Outi Lehtipun. Leuven: Peeters, 2001.

———. "Masculine or Feminine? Male Virgins in Joseph and Asenath and the Book of Revelation." Pages 199–222 in *Identity Formation in the New Testament*. Edited by Bengt Holmberg and Mikael Winninge. WUNT 227. Tübingen: Mohr Siebeck, 2008.

Stephens, Mark B. *Annihilation or Renewal? The Meaning and Function of New Creation in the Book of Revelation*. WUNT II/307. Tübingen: Mohr Siebeck, 2011.

Steudel, Annette. "Psalm 2 im antiken Judentum." Pages 189–97 in *Gottessohn und Menschensohn: Exegetische Studien zu zwei Paradigmen biblisher Intertextualität*. Edited by Dieter Sänger. Biblisch-theologische Studien 67. Neukirchen-Vluyn: Neukirchener, 2004.

Stevenson, Gregory. "Conceptual Background to Golden Crown Imagery in the Apocalypse of John." *JBL* 114 (1995): 257–72.

———. *Power and Place: Temple and Identity in the Book of Revelation*. BZNW 107. Berlin: de Gruyter, 2001.

Stevenson, Kenneth. "Animal Rites: The Four Living Creatures in Patristic Exegesis and Liturgy." *StPatr* 34 (2001): 470–92.

Stewart-Sykes, Alistair. *The Lamb's High Feast: Melito, Peri Pascha and the Quartodeciman Paschal Liturgy at Sardis.* VCSup 42. Leiden: Brill, 1998.

Stone, Michael Edward. *Fourth Ezra.* Hermeneia. Minneapolis: Fortress, 1990.

Strand, Kenneth A. "Some Modalities of Symbolic Usage in Revelation 18." *AUSS* 24 (1986): 37–46.

———. "Two Aspects of Babylon's Judgment Portrayed in Revelation 18." *AUSS* 20 (1982): 53–60.

Straten, F. T. van. "Did the Greeks Kneel Before Their Gods?" *Bulletin Antieke Beschaving* 49 (1974): 159–89.

Strawn, Brent A. "Why Does the Lion Disappear in Revelation 5? Leonine Imagery in Early Jewish and Christian Literatures." *Journal for the Study of the Pseudepigrapha* 17 (2007): 37–74.

Strecker, Georg. "Chiliasm and Docetism in the Johannine School." *Australian Biblical Review* 38 (1990): 44–61.

Street, Matthew J. *Here Comes the Judge: Violent Pacifism in the Book of Revelation.* LNTS 462. London: T. & T. Clark, 2012.

Streete, Gail Corrington. *The Strange Woman: Power and Sex in the Bible.* Louisville, KY: Westminster John Knox, 1997.

Strelan, Rick. "'Outside Are the Dogs and the Sorcerers . . .' (Revelation 22:15)." *BTB* 33 (2003): 148–57.

Strobel, Friedrich August. "Abfassung und Geschichtstheologie der Apocalypse nach Kap. XVII.9–12." *NTS* 10 (1963–64): 433–45.

Strubbe, J. H. M. "The Sitonia in the Cities of Asia Minor Under the Principate (I)." *EpAnat* 10 (1987): 45–82.

Stuckenbruck, Loren T. *Angel Veneration and Christology: A Study in Early Judaism and in the Christology of the Apocalypse of John.* WUNT II/70. Tübingen: Mohr Siebeck, 1995.

Sutter Rehmann, Luzia. *Geh, Frage die Gebärerin! Feministisch-befreiungstheologische Untersuchungen zum Gebärmotiv in der Apokalyptik.* Gütersloh: Gerd Mohn, 1995.

Tabbernee, William. "The Appearance of New Jerusalem in the Montanist Interpretation of the Revelation of John." Pages 651–75 in *Die Johannesapokalypse: Kontexte—Konzepte—Rezeption.* Edited by Jörg Frey, James A. Kelhoffer, and Franz Tóth. WUNT 287. Tübingen: Mohr Siebeck, 2012.

Taeger, Jens-W. *Johannesapokalypse und johanneischer Kreis: Versuch einer traditionsgeschichtlichen Ortsbestimmung am Paradigma der Lebenswasser-Thematik.* BZNW 51. Berlin: de Gruyter, 1989.

Tavo, Felise. *Woman, Mother and Bride: An Exegetical Investigation into the "Ecclesial" Notions of the Apocalypse.* Biblical Tools and Studies 3. Leuven: Peeters, 2007.

Taylor, Deborah Furlan. "The Monetary Crisis in Revelation 13:17 and the Provenance of the Book of Revelation." *CBQ* 71 (2009): 580–96.

Tellbe, Mikael. *Christ-Believers in Ephesus: A Textual Analysis of Early Christian Identity Formation in a Local Perspective.* WUNT 242. Tübingen: Mohr Siebeck, 2009.

Thimmes, Pamela. "Women Reading Women in the Apocalypse: Reading Scenario 1, The Letter to Thyatira (Rev. 2.18–29)." *Currents in Biblical Research* 2 (2003): 128–44.

Thistleton, Anthony C. *The First Epistle to the Corinthians.* NIGTC. Grand Rapids, MI: Eerdmans; Carlisle: Paternoster, 2000.

Thomas, David Andrew. *Revelation 19 in Historical and Mythological Context.* Studies in Biblical Literature 118. New York: Peter Lang, 2008.

Thomas, Robert L. "The Spiritual Gift of Prophecy in Rev 22:18." *JETS* 32 (1989): 201–16.

Thomas, Rodney Lawrence. *Magical Motifs in the Book of Revelation.* LNTS 416. London: Continuum, 2010.

Thompson, Leonard L. *The Book of Revelation: Apocalypse and Empire.* New York: Oxford University Press, 1990.

———. "Lamentation for Christ as a Hero: Revelation 1:7." *JBL* 119 (2000): 683–703.

Thompson, Steven. *The Apocalypse and Semitic Syntax.* SNTSMS 52. Cambridge: Cambridge University Press, 1985.

Thrall, Margaret E. *A Critical and Exegetical Commentary on the Second Epistle to the Corinthians.* 2 vols. ICC. Edinburgh: T. & T. Clark, 1994–2000.

Tilly, Michael. "Textsicherung und Prophetie: Beobachtungen zur Septuaginta-Rezeption in Apk 22,18f." Pages 232–47 in *Studien zur Johannesoffenbarung und ihrer Auslegung: Festschrift für Otto Böcher zum 70. Geburtstag.* Edited by Friedrich Wilhelm Horn and Michael Wolter. Neukirchen-Vluyn: Neukirchener, 2005.

Tomson, Peter J. *Paul and the Jewish Law: Halakha in the Letters of the Apostle to the Gentiles.* Compendia rerum iudaicarum ad Novum Testamentum 3.1. Assen: Van Gorcum; Minneapolis: Fortress, 1990.

Tonstad, Sigve K. *Saving God's Reputation: The Theological Function of Pistis Jesou in the Cosmic Narratives of Revelation.* LNTS 337. London: T. & T. Clark, 2006.

Tóth, Franz. "Das Gebet der Heiligen: Gebet, Räucherwerk und Räucherkult in der Johannesapokalypse vor der Hintergrund biblischer und frühjüdischer Traditionen." Pages 249–311 in *Das Gebet im Neuen Testament.* Edited by Hans Klein, Vasile Mihoc, and Karl-Wilhelm Niebuhr. WUNT 249. Tübingen: Mohr Siebeck, 2009.

———. *Das Tier, sein Bild, und der falsche Prophet: Untersuchungen zum zeitgeschichtlichen Hintergrund von Johannesoffenbarung 13 unter Einbeziehung des antiken Orakelwesens.* Biblisch-theologische Studien 126. Neukirchen-Vluyn, 2012.

———. "Von der Vision zur Redaktion: Untersuchungen zur Komposition, Redaktion und Intention der Johannesapokalypse." Pages 319–412 in *Die Johannesapokalypse: Kontexte—Konzepte—Rezeption.* Edited by Jörg Frey, James A. Kelhoffer, and Franz Tóth. WUNT 287. Tübingen: Mohr Siebeck, 2012.

Tov, Emanuel. *Textual Criticism of the Hebrew Bible.* 3rd ed. Minneapolis: Fortress, 2012.

Trebilco, Paul. *The Early Christians in Ephesus from Paul to Ignatius.* Grand Rapids, MI: Eerdmans, 2004.

———. *Jewish Communities in Asia Minor.* SNTSMS 69. Cambridge: Cambridge University Press, 1991.

Trites, Allison A. "Μάρτυς and Martyrdom in the Apocalypse: A Semantic Study." *NovT* 15 (1973): 72–80.

———. *The New Testament Concept of Witness.* SNTSMS 31. Cambridge: Cambridge University Press, 1977.

Trocmé, Étienne. "La Jezabel de Thyatire (Apoc. 2/20–24)." *RHPR* 79 (1999): 51–55.

Turner, Eric Gardner. *Greek Manuscripts of the Ancient World.* Princeton, NJ: Princeton University Press, 1971.

Ulfgard, Håkan. *Feast and Future: Revelation 7:9–17 and the Feast of Tabernacles.* ConBNT 22. Lund: Almqvist & Wiksell, 1989.

Ulland, Harald. *Die Vision als Radikalisierung der Wirklichkeit in der Apokalypse des Johannes: Das Verhältnis der sieben Sendschreiben zu Apokalypse 12–13.* TANZ 21. Tübingen: Franke, 1997.

Unnik, Willem C. van. "ΜΙΑ ΓΝΩΜΗ: Apocalypse of John 17:13–17." Pages 209–20 in *Studies in John: Presented to Professor Dr. J. N. Sevenster on the Occasion of His Seventieth Birthday.* Edited by A. S. Geyser. NovTSup 24. Leiden: Brill, 1970.

————. "De la règle μήτε προσθεῖναι μήτε ἀφελεῖν dans l'histoire du canon." *VC* 3 (1949): 1–36.

VanderKam, James, and Peter Flint. *The Meaning of the Dead Sea Scrolls: Their Significance for Understanding the Bible, Judaism, Jesus, and Christianity.* San Francisco: HarperSanFrancisco, 2002.

Vanni, Ugo. *L'Apocalisse: Ermeneutica, esegesi, teologia.* RivBSup 17. Bologna: Dehoniane, 1988.

————. "La dimension christologique de la Jérusalem nouvelle." *RHPR* 79 (1999): 119–33.

————. "Liturgical Dialogue as a Literary Form in the Book of Revelation." *NTS* 37 (1997): 348–72.

Verheyden, Joseph, Tobias Nicklas, and Andreas Merkt. *Ancient Christian Interpretations of "Violent Texts" in the Apocalypse.* SUNT 92. Göttingen: Vandenhoeck & Ruprecht, 2011.

Versnel, Hendrik Simon. *Triumphus: An Inquiry into the Origin, Development and Meaning of the Roman Triumph.* Leiden: Brill, 1970.

Villiers, Pieter G. R. de. "The Composition of Revelation 17 and Its Place in the Book as a Whole." *Acta Patristica et Byzantina* 13 (2002): 97–119.

————. "Coping with Violent Scripture in a Time of Peace and Prosperity: The Interpretation of Revelation in the Greek Commentary of Oecumenius." Pages 180–98 in *Ancient Christian Interpretations of "Violent Texts" in the Apocalypse.* Edited by Joseph Verheyden, Tobias Nicklas, and Andreas Merkt. SUNT 92. Göttingen: Vandenhoeck & Ruprecht, 2011.

————. "The Eschatological Celebration of Salvation and the Prophetic Announcement of Judgment: The Message of Revelation 8:1–6 in the Light of Its Composition." *Neot* 41 (2007): 67–96.

————. "The Lord Was Crucified in Sodom and Egypt: Symbols in the Apocalypse of John." *Neot* 22 (1988): 125–38.

————. "Prime Evil and Its Many Faces in the Book of Revelation." *Neot* 34 (2000): 57–85.

————. "The Role of Composition in the Interpretation of the Rider on the White Horse and the Seven Seals in Revelation." *HvTSt* 60 (2004): 125–53.

————. "Rome in the Historical Interpretation of Revelation." *Acta Patristica et Byzantina* 13 (2002): 120–42.

———. "The Septet of Bowls in Revelation 15:1–16:21 in the Light of Its Composition." *Acta Patristica et Byzantina* 16 (2005): 196–222.

Vischer, Eberhard. *Die Offenbarung Johannis: Eine jüdische Apokalypse in christlicher Berarbeitung.* Leipzig: Hinrichs, 1886.

Visser Derk. *Apocalypse as Utopian Expectation (800–1500): The Apocalypse Commentary of Berengaudus of Ferrières and the Relationship Between Exegesis, Liturgy, and Iconography.* Studies in the History of Christian Traditions 73. Leiden: Brill, 1996.

Vivian, Angelo. "Gog e Magog nella Tradizione Biblica, Ebraica e Cristiana." *Revista Biblica* 25 (1977): 389–421.

Vogelgesang, Jeffrey Marshall. "The Interpretation of Ezekiel in the Book of Revelation." Ph.D. diss. Harvard University, 1985.

Vögtle, Anton. "'Dann sah ich einen neuen Himmel und eine neue Erde . . .' (Apk 21,1): Zur kosmischen Dimension neutestamentlicher Eschatologie." Pages 303–33 in *Glaube und Eschatologie: Festschrift für Werner Georg Kümmel zum 80. Geburtstag.* Tübingen: Mohr Siebeck, 1985.

Vollenweider, Samuel. "Hymnus, Enkomion oder Psalm? Schattengefechte in der neutestamentliche Wissenschaft." *NTS* 56 (2010): 208–31.

Völter, Daniel. *Die Entstehung der Apokalypse: Ein Beitrag zur Geschichte des Urchristenthums.* Freiburg: Mohr Siebeck, 1882.

Vos, Louis Arthur. *The Synoptic Traditions in the Apocalypse.* Kampen: Kok, 1965.

Waddell, Robby. *The Spirit in the Book of Revelation.* JPTSup 30. Blandford Forum, UK: Deo, 2006.

Wainwright, Arthur W. *Mysterious Apocalypse: Interpreting the Book of Revelation.* Nashville, TN: Abingdon, 1993.

Walter, Nikolaus. "Nikolaos: Proselyt aus Antiochien, und die Nikolaiten in Ephesus und Pergamon: Ein Betrag auch zum Thema: Paulus und Ephesus." *ZNW* 93 (2002): 200–26.

Wannemacher, Julia Eva. "Apocalypse, Antichrists and the Third Age: Joachim of Fiore's Peaceful Revolution." Pages 267–86 in *Ancient Christian Interpretations of "Violent Texts" in the Apocalypse.* Edited by Joseph Verheyden, Tobias Nicklas, and Andreas Merkt. SUNT 92. Göttingen: Vandenhoeck & Ruprecht, 2011.

Wansink, Craig S. *Chained in Christ: The Experience and Rhetoric of Paul's Imprisonments.* JSNTSup 130. Sheffield: Sheffield Academic, 1996.

Warfield, Benjamin B. *Biblical Doctrines.* New York: Oxford University Press, 1929.

Water, Rick van de. "Reconsidering the Beast from the Sea (Rev 13.1)." *NTS* 46 (2000): 245–61.

Watson, George R. *The Roman Soldier.* Ithaca, NY: Cornell University Press, 1969.

Weima, Jeffrey A. D. *Neglected Endings: The Significance of the Pauline Letter Closings.* JSNTSup 101. Sheffield: JSOT, 1994.

Weinfeld, Moshe. "Grace After Meals in Qumran." *JBL* 111 (1992): 427–40.

Weinrich, William C. *Greek Commentaries on Revelation: Oecumenius and Andrew of Caesarea.* Ancient Christian Texts. Downers Grove, IL: IVP Academic, 2011.

———. *Latin Commentaries on Revelation: Victorinus of Petovium, Apringius of Beja, Caesarius of Arles and Bede the Venerable.* Ancient Christian Texts. Downers Grove, IL: IVP Academic, 2011.

————. *Revelation*. Ancient Christian Commentary on Scripture 12. Downers Grove, IL: InterVarsity, 2005.

Weisman, Ze'ev. *Political Satire in the Bible*. Atlanta: Scholars, 1998.

Weiss, Peter. "Ein Priester im lydischen Philadelphia—Noch einmal zu einter Münzlegende." *EpAnat* 26 (1996): 145–48.

Weizsäcker, Carl von. *The Apostolic Age*. 2 vols. Translated from the 2nd ed. by James Millar. London: Williams and Norgate; New York: Putnam, 1894–95.

Wellhausen, Julius. *Skizzen und Vorarbeiten*. Berlin: Reimer, 1899.

Wengst, Klaus. "Babylon the Great and the New Jerusalem: The Visionary View of Political Reality in the Revelation of John." Pages 189–202 in *Politics and Theopolitics in the Bible and Postbiblical Literature*. Edited by Henning Graf Reventlow, Yair Hoffman, and Benjamin Uffenheimer. JSNTSup 171. Sheffield: JSOT, 1994.

————. *Pax Romana and the Peace of Jesus Christ*. Philadelphia: Fortress, 1987.

Westermann, Claus. *The Psalms: Structure, Content & Message*. Translated by Ralph Gerke. Minneapolis: Augsburg, 1980.

Whitaker, Robyn J. "Falling Stars and Rising Smoke: Imperial Apotheosis and Idolatry in Revelation." Pages 199–218 in *Imagery in the Book of Revelation*. Edited by Michael Labahn and Outi Lehtipun. Leuven: Peeters, 2001.

White, John L. *Light from Ancient Letters*. Philadelphia: Fortress, 1983.

White, L. Michael. "Counting the Costs of Nobility: The Social Economy of Roman Pergamon." Pages 331–71 in *Pergamon: Citadel of the Gods*. Edited by Helmut Koester. Harrisburg, PA: Trinity, 1998.

————. "Urban Development and Social Change in Imperial Ephesos." Pages 27–79 in *Ephesos, Metropolis of Asia: An Interdisciplinary Approach to Its Archaeology, Religion, and Culture*. Edited by Helmut Koester. HTS 41. Valley Forge, PA: Trinity, 1995.

White, R. Fowler. "Reexamining the Evidence for Recapitulation in Rev 20:1–10." *WTJ* 51 (1989): 319–44.

Wiarda, Timothy. "Revelation 3:20: Imagery and Literary Context." *JETS* 38 (1995): 203–12.

Wick, Peter. "There Was Silence in Heaven (Revelation 8:1): An Annotation to Israel Knohl's 'Between Voice and Silence.'" *JBL* 117 (1998): 512–14.

Wilkinson, Richard H. "The Στύλος of Revelation 3:12 and Ancient Coronation Rites." *JBL* 107 (1988): 498–501.

Willis, Wendell Lee. *Idol Meat in Corinth: The Pauline Argument in 1 Corinthians 8 and 10*. SBLDS 68. Chico, CA: Scholars, 1985.

Wilson, Harry Langford. "A New Italic Divinity." *American Journal of Philology* 28 (1907): 450–55.

Wilson, J. Christian. "The Problem of the Domitianic Date of Revelation." *NTS* 39 (1993): 587–605.

Wilson, Mark W. "Revelation 19:10 and Contemporary Interpretation." Pages 191–202 in *Spirit and Renewal: Essays in Honor of J. Rodman Williams*. Edited by Mark W. Wilson. JPTSup 5. Sheffield: Sheffield Academic, 1994.

Wilson, Stephen G. "ΟΙ ΠΟΤΕ ΙΟΥΔΑΙΟΙ: Epigraphic Evidence for Jewish Defectors." Pages 354–71 in *Text and Artifact in the Religions of Mediterranean Antiquity:*

Essays in Honour of Peter Richardson. Edited by Stephen G. Wilson and Michel Desjardins. ESCJ 9. Waterloo, Ont.: Wilfrid Laurier University Press, 2000.

———. *Related Strangers: Jews and Christians, 70–170 C.E.* Minneapolis: Fortress, 1995.

Winkle, Ross E. "Another Look at the List of Tribes in Revelation 7." *AUSS* 27 (1989): 53–67.

Winston, David. *The Wisdom of Solomon.* AYB 43. Garden City, NY: Doubleday, 1979; reprint, New Haven, CT: Yale University Press.

Winter, Franz. "Aspekte der Beschreibung des himmlischen Jerusalem auf dem Hintergrund der antiken Architektur und Verfassungstheorie." *PzB* 8 (1999): 85–102.

Winter, John Garrett. *Life and Letters in the Papyri.* Ann Arbor: University of Michigan Press, 1933.

Witetschek, Stephan. *Ephesische Enthüllungen I. Frühe Christen in einer antiken Grossstadt: zugleich ein Beitrag zur Frage nach den Kontexten der Johannesapokalypse.* Biblical Tools and Studies 6. Leuven: Peeters, 2008.

———. "Der Lieblingspsalm des Sehers: Die Verwendung won Ps 2 in der Johannesapokalypse." Pages 487–502 in *The Septuagint and Messianism.* Edited by Michael A. Knibb. BETL 195. Leuven: Leuven University Press and Peeters, 2006.

———. "Ein weit geöffnetes Zeitfenster? Überlegungen zur Datierung der Johannesapokalypse." Pages 117–48 in *Die Johannesapokalypse: Kontexte—Konzepte—Rezeption.* Edited by Jörg Frey, James A. Kelhoffer, and Franz Tóth. WUNT 287. Tübingen: Mohr Siebeck, 2012.

Witherington, Ben, III. "Not So Idle Thoughts About *Eidolothuton.*" *TynBul* 44 (1993): 237–54.

Witulski, Thomas. *Die Johannesoffenbarung und Kaiser Hadrian: Studien zur Datierung der neutestamentlichen Apokalypse.* FRLANT 221. Göttingen: Vandenhoeck & Ruprecht, 2007.

———. "Zur Frage der in Apk 13 verwendeten Quellen." *BN* 144 (2010): 117–33.

Wolff, Hans Walter. *Joel and Amos.* Hermeneia. Philadelphia: Fortress, 1977.

Wong, Daniel K. K. "The First Horseman of Revelation 6." *BSac* 153 (1996): 212–26.

Worth, Ronald H., Jr. *The Seven Cities of the Apocalypse and Roman Culture.* New York: Paulist, 1999.

Wright, N. T. *The New Testament and the People of God.* Vol. 1 of *Christian Origins and the Question of God.* Minneapolis: Fortress, 1992.

———. *Resurrection of the Son of God.* Vol. 3 of *Christian Origins and the Question of God.* Minneapolis: Fortress, 2003.

Yarbro Collins, Adela. *The Combat Myth in the Book of Revelation.* Harvard Dissertations in Religion 9. Missoula, MT: Scholars, 1976.

———. *Cosmology and Eschatology in Jewish and Christian Apocalypticism.* Leiden: Brill, 1996.

———. *Crisis and Catharsis: The Power of the Apocalypse.* Philadelphia: Westminster, 1984.

———. "The Early Christian Apocalypses." Pages in 61–121 in *Apocalypse: The Morphology of a Genre.* Edited by John J. Collins. Semeia 14. Missoula, MT: Society of Biblical Literature, 1979.

————. "The History-of-Religions Approach to Apocalypticism and the 'Angel of the Waters' (Rev 16:4–7)." *CBQ* 39 (1977): 367–81.

————. "Insiders and Outsiders in the Book of Revelation and Its Social Context." Pages 187–218 in *"To See Ourselves as Others See Us": Christians, Jews, "Others" in Late Antiquity.* Edited by Jacob Neusner and Ernest S. Frerichs. Chico, CA: Scholars, 1985.

————. "Introduction: Early Christian Apocalypticism." Pages in 1–11 in *Early Christian Apocalypticism: Genre and Social Setting.* Semeia 36. Decatur, GA: Society of Biblical Literature, 1986.

————. "Numerical Symbolism in Apocalyptic Literature." *ANRW* II.21.2 (1984): 1221–87.

————. "Pergamon in Early Christian Literature." Pages 163–84 in *Pergamon: Citadel of the Gods.* Edited by Helmut Koester. Harrisburg, PA: Trinity, 1998.

————. "Persecution and Vengeance in the Book of Revelation." Pages 729–50 in *Apocalypticism in the Mediterranean World and the Near East.* Edited by David Hellholm. 2nd ed. Tübingen: Mohr Siebeck, 1989.

————. "Portraits of Rulers in the Book of Revelation." Pages 275–99 in *Neues Testament und hellenistisch-jüdisch Alltagskultur.* Edited by Roland Deines, Jens Herzer, and Karl-Wilhelm Niebuhr. WUNT 274. Tübingen: Mohr Siebeck, 2011.

————. "Psalms, Philippians 2:6–11, and the Origins of Christology." *BibInt* 11 (2002): 361–72.

————. "Revelation 18: Taunt Song or Dirge?" Pages 185–204 in *L'Apocalyptique johannique et l'Apocalyptique dans le Nouveau Testament.* Edited by Jan Lambrecht. BETL 53. Gembloux: Duculot; Leuven: Leuven University Press, 1980.

————. "Source Criticism of the Book of Revelation." *BR* 43 (1998): 50–53.

————. "Vilification and Self-Definition in the Book of Revelation." *HTR* 79 (1986): 308–20.

————. "'What the Spirit Says to the Churches': Preaching the Apocalypse." *Quarterly Review* 4 (1984): 69–84.

Young, Gary K. *Rome's Eastern Trade: International Commerce and Imperial Policy, 31 BC–AD 305.* London: Routlege, 2001.

Zabras, Konstantinos T. "Silence and Proper Intention in Late Second Temple and Early Rabbinic Prayer: The Case for mBerakhot 5,1." Pages 3–24 in *Das Gebet im Neuen Testament.* Edited by Hans Klein, Vasile Mihoc, and Karl-Wilhelm Niebuhr. WUNT 249. Tübingen: Mohr Siebeck, 2009.

Zerwick, Maximilian. *Biblical Greek.* Rome: Pontifical Biblical Institute, 1963.

Zimmermann, Ruben. "'Bräutigam' als frühjudisches Messias-Prädikat? Zur Traditionsgeschichte einer urchristlichen Metapher." *BN* 103 (2000): 85–99.

————. "Nuptial Imagery in the Revelation of John." *Bib* 84 (2003): 153–83.

————. "Die Virginitäts-metapher in Apk 14:4–5 im Horizont von Befleckung, Loskauf und Erstlingsfrucht." *NovT* 45 (2003): 45–70.

NOTES AND COMMENTS

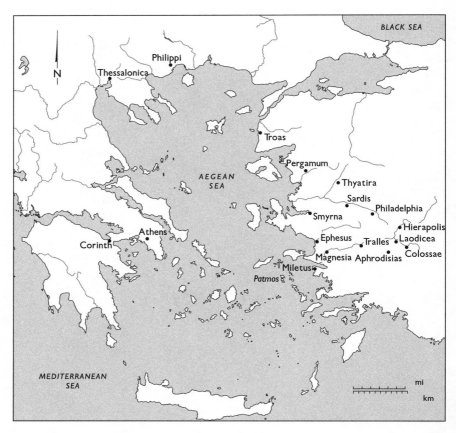

Map 1. Cities of Asia Minor and Greece (Map by Bill Nelson)

Title and Introduction to the Book

---

1. Title

NOTES

The Revelation of John. The Greek word *apokalypsis* is usually rendered in English as "apocalypse" or "revelation" (NOTE on 1:1). Placing the name "John" in the title identifies him as the book's author. Justin Martyr referred to "John, in a revelation *that* was given to him" (*Dial.* 81), using the term "revelation" for the message that was disclosed rather than a title for the work. Later, "Revelation" seems to have been used as the book title in contexts where John was assumed to be its author (Irenaeus, *Haer.* 4.14.2; 4.17.6; 4.20.11; 5.28.2; 5.35.2; Tertullian, *Marc.* 3.14.3; 4.5.2). Melito of Sardis (d. ca. 190) wrote a lost work on the devil and the Revelation of John (Eusebius, *Hist. eccl.* 4.26.2). The Latin translation of Irenaeus's works (early third century) refers to the "Revelation of John" (PG 7.687A), while the fourth-century Codex Sinaiticus (ℵ) introduces this work with the title "Revelation of John" (*Apokalypsis Iōannou*) and concludes with a subscription that uses the plural, "Revelations [*Apokalypseis*] of John." Later manuscripts sometimes used expanded titles, such as "The Revelation of John the Theologian and Evangelist" (046). On authorship, see INTRO II.A.

COMMENT

The original "title" of this book was its opening line: "A revelation from Jesus Christ" (Rev 1:1). The separate title "Revelation of John" was added later, when the book was copied and preserved alongside other writings. Titles were sometimes placed on tags attached to the outside of a scroll, so a person could identify a scroll without unrolling it. Separate titles were also inscribed inside the scroll, usually at the end of a work but sometimes at the beginning. When works were bound together in a codex, they could be given a title at the beginning, at the end, or at both places (Turner, *Greek*, 16–17; Aune 1:3–4; Kraft 17–18).

In the first century the term "apocalypse" was used for the disclosure of something hidden, but it was not a technical term for a literary genre. The prominence of the word "apocalypse" at the beginning of John's work apparently contributed to the use of this term as a title for visionary writings. The Muratorian canon fragment (either late second or fourth century CE) referred to the "apocalypses of John and Peter," indicating that the two were similar types of writings. "Apocalypse" was also used for visions of Peter (Clement of Alexandria, *Ecl.* 41.2; 48.1; 49.1; cf. Eusebius, *Hist. eccl.* 6.14.1) and in the titles affixed to works known as the *Apocalypse of Paul*, the *Testament of Abraham*, *3 Baruch*, the *Greek Apocalypse of Ezra*, and the *Apocalypse of Sedrach* (Denis, *Concordance*, 830, 866, 871, 873). Since the manuscripts that bear these titles are rather late, it is uncertain whether the texts originally called themselves "apocalypses" (M. Smith, "History," 19).

By the late second and third centuries a number of Christian texts claimed to present revelations. To distinguish these works from each other, they were given titles referring to the people who were said to have written them. To some extent, this is appropriate for Revelation, since 1:1–3 identifies John as the recipient of the visions and in 1:4 John addresses the readers in his own name. Nevertheless, the traditional title *Apokalypsis Iōannou* focuses on John as the writer, but the initial words *Apokalypsis Iēsou Christou* identify Jesus as the giver of the revelation and the authority for the message (Schüssler Fiorenza 39–40).

2. Introduction to the Book (1:1–8)

1   ¹A revelation from Jesus Christ, which God gave him to show his servants what things must soon take place. He made it known by sending it through his angel to his servant John, ²who bore witness to the word of God and the witness of Jesus Christ, as much as he saw. ³Blessed is the one who reads aloud and those who hear the words of the prophecy and keep the things written in it, for the time is near.

⁴John to the seven assemblies that are in Asia: Grace to you and peace from the one who is and who was and who is to come, and from the seven spirits that are before his throne, ⁵and from Jesus Christ the faithful witness, the firstborn of the dead, and the ruler of the kings of the earth. To him who loves us and released us from our sins by his blood, ⁶and made us a kingdom, priests to his God and Father, to him be glory and might for ever and ever. Amen.

⁷See, he is coming with the clouds, and every eye will see him, even those who pierced him, and all the tribes of the earth will grieve for him.

Yes. Amen!

⁸"I am the Alpha and the Omega," says the Lord God, "the one who is and who was and who is to come, the Almighty."

NOTES

1:1. A revelation. The noun *apokalypsis* indicates the uncovering of something hidden (Rom 16:25; Eph 3:3). The verb *apokalyptein* can be used for a person (1 Sam 20:2, 13) or God (1 Sam 3:7; 2 Sam 7:27) revealing his intentions. A divine revelation might disclose future (Dan 2:28) or heavenly (2 Cor 12:1, 7) realities, and John's book includes both. In Rev 1:1–2 God's "revelation" is synonymous with his "word." It recalls that "the Lord God does nothing without revealing [*apokalypsē*] his instruction to his servants the prophets" (Amos 3:7 LXX). There is "a God in heaven who reveals [*apokalyptōn*] mysteries" and "what things must take place" (Dan 2:27–28). Among Christians, "revelation" was used for Paul's encounter with the risen Christ and for Christ's future coming (Gal 1:12; 1 Cor 1:7; cf. 1 Pet 1:7, 13). The revelations that Christian prophets received through ecstatic experience disclosed heavenly realities and gave directions for action (2 Cor 12:1, 7; Gal 2:2; Herm. *Vis.* 3.1.2; 4.1.3). Similar aspects are reflected in John's Apocalypse.

from Jesus Christ. Here, "Christ" is a part of Jesus' name (Rev 1:1, 2, 5), although elsewhere it is a title (cf. 11:15; 12:10). The expression *Iēsou Christou* can be translated literally as a revelation "*of* Jesus Christ." The genitive case could mean that this is a revelation "about" Jesus, who is the focus of some visions (1:9–20; 5:1–14; 19:11–16). But it can better be taken as a revelation "from" Jesus, since the context identifies Jesus along with God as the source of the message (cf. 22:16). In the gospels the earthly Jesus reveals what he receives from God (Matt 11:27; Luke 10:22; John 15:15), and in the Apocalypse the risen Christ does so. John assumes that Jesus has risen from the dead and still speaks to humans (cf. 2 Cor 12:9; Acts 9:4–5, 10–16; *Odes Sol.* 31:6–13; 36:3–8), sometimes through the Spirit (Acts 13:2; John 16:13; Boring, *Continuing*, 155–84).

which God gave to him to show. God is the source of the revelation, conveying meaning by "showing" it through visionary language rather than abstract speech (Rev 4:1; 17:1; 21:9; Backhaus, "Apokalyptische").

his servants. Socially, *douloi* are slaves rather than free people (6:15; 13:16; 19:18), so one might call believers "slaves" of God. But when referring to the faithful, *douloi* can best be translated as "servants" to avoid the impression that they are the mere property of God, the slaveholder. Note that Revelation links the negative connotations of ordinary slave trade to Babylon/Rome (18:13), while using *douloi* as a positive metaphor for God's people (C. R. Koester, "Roman"). Some masters acquired slaves by purchase, but God "purchased" people through the blood of Christ (5:9; 14:3; cf. 1 Cor 6:20; 7:23). Romans acquired slaves by conquering people militarily (Josephus, *J.W.* 6.418; Strabo, *Geographica* 17.1.54; Dio Chrysostom, *Disc.* 15.25–26), but God obtained slaves through Christ, who conquered by self-sacrifice (Rev 5:5–6). God's people address him as Lord and Master and are to obey (4:8, 11; 6:10; 12:17; 14:12), but the paradox is that God's servants are truly free, since Christ freed them from subjection to other powers (1:5; cf. Rom 6:18–23; 1 Cor 9:19; Gal 5:13). The faithful remain God's servants in New Jerusalem, yet there they also reign as kings (Rev 22:3–5). In 1:1b, all Christians are God's servants (2:20; 7:3; 19:2, 5; 22:6).

what things must soon take place. Temporal expressions in Revelation include "soon" (*en tachei,* 1:1; 22:6; *tachy,* 2:16; 3:11; 11:14; 22:7, 12, 20) and "near" (*engys,* 1:3; 22:10).

Although "soon" could be used for abrupt or sudden action (Deut 28:20), it typically meant that something would happen without delay or in the near future (Acts 12:7; 1 Tim 3:14; *1 Clem.* 65:1). It could express hope for God's imminent vindication of his people and his defeat of evil (Luke 18:8; Rom 16:20). Where Dan 2:28 said that God revealed "what will happen at the end of days," Revelation speaks of what must take place "soon," bringing the message into the context of the readers (Beale). Yet Revelation couples imminence with awareness of delay (see COMMENT).

He made it known. The verb *sēmainein* was used for giving ordinary information (Acts 25:27) and for making prophetic statements about the future and vision reports (Acts 11:28; *1 En.* 106:13; 107:2). Sometimes meaning was made known through images: For example, a stone shattering a statue signified the end of earthly kingdoms and the arrival of God's kingdom (Dan 2:45 LXX; cf. Ezek. Trag., *Exagoge* 82–83; Josephus, *Ant.* 10.241). The images in Revelation are sometimes considered cryptic (Murphy 62–63), but their function is to reveal meaning rather than to conceal it. Similarly, the Fourth Gospel makes known (*sēmainein*) the character of Jesus' death by saying he would be "lifted up" in glory through crucifixion (John 12:33; 18:32).

by sending it through his angel. Superscriptions on prophetic books often tell of God's word coming to a prophet (e.g., Mic 1:1; Joel 1:1; Zeph 1:1), but a possible precedent for including an angel in the process is Mal 1:1: "The word of the Lord to Israel by the hand of his *mal'aki*." The Hebrew word is either the name Malachi or means "my messenger." In the LXX of Mal 1:1 the word is the Greek equivalent is *angelos*, which can mean either a human messenger or supernatural angel. Superscriptions in apocalyptic writings sometimes mention multiple angels. Enoch "had the vision of the Holy One . . . from the words of the watchers and holy ones I heard everything" (*1 En.* 1:2; cf. 93:2). Visionary texts often include angelic figures who show things (Ezek 40:3–4; Zech 1:7–6:15; Dan 7:16; 8:15; *1 En.* 21:5; 22:3; *2 Bar.* 55:3; *4 Ezra* 4:1; 5:31–32), and this is true of Revelation (Rev 5:5; 7:13; 17:1, 7; 19:9–10; 21:9, 15; 22:1, 6–9). The one doing the sending could be God or Christ, since both are later said to have sent the angel (22:6, 16).

to his servant John. John is the seer who narrates Revelation (on his identity, see INTRO II.A.4). He calls himself a servant (*doulos*) of God, the term he used for his readers (1:1). God's servant is dependent on God and is to be obedient to God (2 Sam 7:27; 1 Kgs 8:28; Ps 27:9; Dan 9:17). Socially, it was honorable to serve someone of high status and especially to serve God (Martin, *Slavery*, 50–68; Byron, *Slavery*, 47–55). The term "servant" was used for Moses and other prophets (1 Kgs 8:53, 56; 2 Kgs 18:12; Dan 6:20; Rev 10:7; 15:3), as well as for Abraham, Isaac, and Jacob (Ps 105:42; 2 Macc 1:2), David (1 Macc 4:30), Paul, and Christians generally (1 Cor 7:22; Gal 1:10; cf. 1 Pet 2:16). "Servant" could be used alone (Phil 1:1; Jas 1:1; Jude 1:1) or alongside "apostle," a title that warranted respect (Rom 1:1; Tit 1:1; 2 Pet 1:1). Adherents of Greco-Roman religion could be called "servants" of various deities (e.g., Euripides, *Ion* 309; Dio Cassius, *Rom. Hist.* 63.5.2). In Revelation the issue is which deity one serves (*TLNT* 1:380–84).

1:2. *who bore witness.* The verb *martyrein* and nouns *martyria* and *martys* indicate "witness," which is a statement of truth. In a formal sense, people bore witness to what they saw and heard in courtroom settings (Num 35:30; Deut 19:15; *Sel. Pap.* 254). Legal documents included the names of witnesses to attest their validity (P.Oxy. 105.13; 489.22). People also bore witness in less formal ways, typically in settings where the truth was disputed (H. Strathmann, *TDNT* 4:476–78). John follows the pattern of

Jesus' witness and exemplifies the vocation of the Christian community, which is to attest to the truth (Rev 1:5; 6:9; 11:3, 7; 12:11; 17:6; Blount).

to the word of God. "Word of God" or "word of the Lord" was a biblical expression for what God had conveyed through the prophets (Jer 1:2; Hos 1:1; Joel 1:1; Mic 1:1; Zeph 1:1; cf. Rev 10:7), including his commandments (1:9; 12:17; 14:12). When bearing witness, John uses the familiar biblical expression to show the continuity between his words (19:9; 22:6) and earlier prophetic words from God.

and the witness of Jesus Christ. The expression "the witness of Jesus Christ" (*tēn martyrian 'Iēsou Christou*) has been taken in two main ways: First, the genitive case could mean that it is the witness people make *to* Jesus through their words and actions (1:9; 6:9; 12:17; 20:4; Aune, *Apocalypticism*, 76–77; Osborne). Second, it could be the witness that comes *from* Jesus, since he and God are the source of John's message (Trites, *New*, 156–58; Tonstad, *Saving*, 179–80; Giesen). Distinguishing the two is sometimes difficult because those who receive witness from Jesus are also to bear witness to him. But in this context the emphasis is on witness "from Jesus," since the expression is parallel to the "word of God," which means that the word is "from God" (1:2; 6:9; 20:4; Slater, *Christ*, 89). On one level the earthly Jesus bore witness to the reign of God by his words, actions, and death. The legacy of Jesus' witness circulated in the Christian community alongside the word and commandments of God (12:17), and John knew of such testimony before his visionary encounter with the exalted Jesus (1:9). On another level the risen Christ continues bearing witness through prophets. John tells of receiving the word that God gave to Jesus, who in turn gave it to John (1:1). Revelation assumes that testimony purportedly given by the risen Jesus will be congruent with that received from the earthly Jesus.

as much as he saw. John received God's word and Jesus' witness by hearing and seeing (e.g., 1:10–12; 4:1, 2; 7:4, 9; 21:1, 3). Similarly, some prophetic books begin: "the word of the Lord that came to Micah . . . which he saw" (Mic 1:1; cf. Hab 1:1; Amos 1:1; Isa 1:1).

1:3. *Blessed.* There are seven references to the faithful who are "blessed" (*makarios*) (Rev 1:3; 14:13; 16:15; 19:9; 20:6; 22:7, 14). See Intro IV.E.2.

is the one who reads aloud and those who hear. There were at least three precedents for presenting a message like Revelation orally in a group setting. First, in some churches those who received prophecies and revelations delivered them orally to a group of listeners (1 Cor 14:26–31). Although John sent his revelation to the churches in written form, he expected that it would be read aloud by one person to a group. Sometimes, the person who penned a revelation read the text (Herm. *Vis.* 2.4.3), but John's message would have been sent through an envoy (Rev 1:11). Second, it was common to read Scripture aloud in Jewish and early Christian worship (Philo, *Somn.* 2.127; *m. Meg.* 4:1–6; Luke 4:16–21; Acts 13:14–15; 1 Tim 4:13). Since John calls his book a word of God, it could be read in the manner of biblical texts. Third, letters from leaders were read aloud in Christian assemblies (Col 4:16; 1 Thess 5:27; Justin Martyr, *1 Apol.* 67). Revelation has features of a letter, so it could have been read aloud in a similar way (Rev 1:4–6).

the words of the prophecy. Prophecy was understood to be a message from God sent through an inspired messenger. Readers would have been familiar with at least three types. First was biblical prophecy. Israel's prophets announced judgment, exhorted people to repent and show fidelity toward God and justice toward other people, and promised salvation. Conflict between the prophets of God and those of other gods (1 Kgs 18:19, 22), as well as between prophets within Israel (Jer 23:13–14; 28:1–17), required distinguishing true from false prophecy. Criteria included noting whether something a prophet foretold actually came to pass (Deut 18:22; Jer 28:9) and whether the prophet moved people to worship God or drew them away from God (Deut 13:1–3). John assumes that his readers considered the biblical prophetic writings genuine, and he uses language from those texts to locate his message within that tradition of accepted prophecy.

Second was prophecy in the early church. The Jewish matrix from which Christianity emerged retained an interest in prophecy. Although some texts tell of a decline in prophesying (Ps 74:9; 1 Macc 9:27), Jewish prophetic figures continued to appear (Josephus, *J.W.* 2.261–63; 6.300–309), and new revelatory texts were written (e.g., *1 En.* 1:3–9; *4 Ezra* 6:14–28). The term "prophet" fit aspects of Jesus' identity (Matt 13:57; Mark 6:4; Luke 13:33; John 9:17). Christians understood the Spirit to be active among believers (Acts 2:38; 1 Cor 12:7) and thought some people had a special gift of prophecy (Acts 15:32; 1 Cor 12:28). Prophecies dealt with eschatological salvation (1 Cor 15:51–52), instruction (Acts 13:1–2), and encouragement (1 Cor 14:3; 2 Cor 12:9), as well as upcoming events (Acts 11:27–28; 21:10–11). Again, the main criterion was whether a purportedly inspired message fostered faith in and obedience to God and Christ, or promoted false worship and unethical conduct (Matt 7:15–20; 1 John 4:1–3; 1 Cor 12:1–3; *Did.* 11–12; see Aune, *Prophecy*, 189–270; Boring, *Continuing*, 59–85, 155–84). On this basis, John distinguishes his prophetic word from those of prophets he considered to be false (Rev 2:20).

Third, prophecy was an aspect of Greco-Roman culture. People sought oracles at shrines like those dedicated to Apollo at Claros (south of Smyrna) and Didyma (near Miletus; Parke, *Oracles*). Questions were given to cultic personnel at the shrine, who sought responses. Prophets included both men and women, depending on local practice (Aune, *Prophecy*, 23–48). Individual prophets were also active in Asia Minor outside the shrines (S. Mitchell, *Anatolia*, 2:46; Malay, *Researches*, 130). The false prophets in Revelation will be pictured as promoters of Greco-Roman religion and the imperial cult (Rev 2:20; 13:11–19; 16:13; 19:20).

and keep the things written in it. To "keep" (*tērein*) what is written means maintaining fidelity to God and Christ (3:3, 8), worshiping God (22:7, 9), being obedient to God's commandments (12:17), and performing works acceptable to Christ (2:26). In Revelation, as in sayings of Jesus, those who keep God's word are "blessed" (Luke 11:28; John 13:17; cf. *1 En.* 99:10; *2 Clem.* 19:1–3; Herm. *Vis.* 5.5.5, 7; Aune).

for the time is near. Early Christian sources sometimes identify the "time" (*kairos*) with the arrival of God's kingdom, whether during the ministry of Jesus (Mark 1:14–15) or at his future coming (1 Cor 4:5; 1 Tim 6:15; 1 Pet 1:5). Some pictured the present as a time of suffering and vigilance (Rom 8:26; 13:11; 1 Cor 7:29), since evil will operate until the end comes (2 Thess 2:6; 2 Tim 3:1). In Revelation the time (*chronos*) leading up to God's ultimate defeat of evil is a time of waiting (Rev 6:11; 10:6). The concept of time is complex, however, because in the visionary world the time (*kairos*) for the final defeat of evil (11:18) has already begun with Satan's expulsion from heaven at Christ's exaltation and it continues until Christ's parousia (12:11), so the time (*kairos*) in which the faithful live is already characterized by this conflict (12:14; COMMENT on 22:6–7, 10).

1:4. *John.* The writer is an early Christian prophet (see Intro II.A.4).

to the seven assemblies that are in Asia. Revelation, like many Pauline letters, addresses congregations (1 Cor 1:2; 2 Cor 1:1; Gal 1:2; 1 Thess 1:1). In Revelation a Jewish gathering is a "synagogue" (*synagōgē*, Rev 2:9; 3:9), whereas the followers of Jesus have an "assembly" (*ekklēsia*, 2:1, 8, 12, etc.). This term was used for assemblies in Israel (Deut 31:30; *Pss. Sol.* 10:6), but in Asia Minor it commonly designated assemblies of citizens, who dealt with public affairs (Acts 19:39; I.Eph 27.22; I.Sard 8.34; Pliny the Younger, *Ep.* 110.1). Greeks rarely used the word *ekklēsia* for business or religious associations (Klauck, *Religious*, 46), but Christians regularly used the term for their gatherings. John initially identifies the addressees by province (cf. Gal 1:2; 1 Cor 16:19; 2 Cor 8:1; 1 Thess 2:14; 1 Pet 1:1) and later by city (Rev 1:11).

Grace to you and peace. Greco-Roman letters began with "greetings" (*chairein*): for example, "Apollonous to Terentianus her brother greetings" (P.Mich. 464.1–2; cf. White, *Light*, 101–23). Some Christian letters follow that pattern (Jas 1:1; cf. Ign. *Eph.* pref.; *Barn.* 1:1), but many replace *chairein* with *charis* (grace), a word similar in form but with greater theological weight (Rev 1:4; 22:21). Grace fits the redemptive work of Christ described in 1:5–6. To this was added the Jewish greeting "peace" (Hebrew *shālôm*), which connoted goodwill (Luke 10:5), concord (Dan 10:19), and well-being (2 Macc 1:1; *2 Bar.* 78:2; cf. Judg 19:20; 1 Sam 25:6; John 20:19). In Paul's letters the simple form "grace to you and peace" was sometimes used (1 Thess 1:1), but more common was "grace to you and peace from God our Father and the Lord Jesus Christ" (Rom 1:7; 1 Cor 1:3; 2 Cor 1:2; Eph 1:2; Phil 1:2; Phlm 3; cf. 1 Pet 1:2; 2 Pet 1:2; *1 Clem.* pref.).

from the one who is and who was and who is to come. This complete expression appears in Rev 1:4, 8 and 4:8 and in shortened form in 11:17 and 16:5. The language recalls Exod 3:14 LXX, where God says, "I am the one who is" (*egō eimi ho ōn*; cf. Josephus, *Ant.* 8.350; Philo, *Mos.* 1.75; *Alleg. Interp.* 3.181). Revelation expands the traditional name to include God's past existence and future coming (*Sib. Or.* 3.16; later Jewish writings said God was, is now, and will be; *Exod. Rab.* 3.6; *Tg. Ps.-J.* Deut 32:39). Instead of speaking about God's future existence ("will be"), however, Revelation tells of his coming. The language recalls that "the Lord God comes with might" to save and to judge (Isa 40:10; cf. Mic 1:3; Isa 26:21; Zech 14:5; *1 En.* 1:3). Because God exists throughout time, Jewish sources speak of his care in the past, present, and future (Jdt 9:5; 1QS III, 15; *4 Ezra* 7:136; *2 Bar.* 21:9; Philonenko, "Celui").

Greco-Roman sources sometimes used the form *to on* for God as "the existent one" or as "being" (Seneca the Younger, *Ep.* 58.7, 17; Plutarch, *Mor.* 393B–C). They also used three-part formulas for what is and was and will be to encompass all of time (Homer, *Il.* 1.70; Hesiod, *Theogonia* 1.38; McDonough, *YHWH*, 34–57). It was said that true gods were eternal (Diodorus Siculus, *Libr.* 6.1.2; Plutarch, *Pel.* 16; Cicero, *Nat. d.* 1.24 §68; Neyrey, "Without"). Therefore, one might say that Isis is "all that has been, and is, and shall be" (Plutarch, *Mor.* 354C); "Zeus was, Zeus is, Zeus shall be" (Pausanias, *Descr.* 10.12.10); or Aion, the god of time, "is and was and will be" (McDonough, *YHWH*, 51–52). In Revelation, this formula underscores God's true deity in contrast to the claims of others.

John's use of this expression does not follow typical rules of Greek grammar. The preposition *apo* (from) is regularly followed by the genitive case, but all references to God in 1:4 remain in the nominative case. Moreover, it was common to put a definite article before a participle, as in *ho ōn* (the one who is), but not before an indicative verb as John does in *ho ēn*. The Greek expression is as awkward as calling God "the was" in English. Later in this verse the seven spirits take the genitive case after *apo*, but God does not. John apparently considered God's name to be indeclinable (Aune), which heightens the impression that God is absolute. On Revelation's Greek, see INTRO V.B.2.

and from the seven spirits that are before his throne. The seven spirits are later identified with the torches before God's throne and the eyes of the Lamb (4:5; 5:6). The imagery is drawn in part from Zechariah, in which seven lamps are identified with the eyes of the Lord (Zech 4:2, 10). There are two main interpretations of the seven spirits (Waddell, *Spirit*, 7–21); the first is preferable, given the strong connection between angels and spirits in Revelation.

1. Seven angels. The seven spirits (1:4; 3:1; 4:5; 5:6) and the seven angels (8:2) are both before God's throne and seem to be the same group. Similarly, the seven stars that Christ holds are called both angels and spirits (1:20; 3:1). In 4:5, the seven spirits are flaming torches, and it was said that God "makes his angels spirits and his servants flames of fire" (Ps 104:4 [103:4 LXX]; Heb 1:7, 14). The DSS use "angels" and "spirits" as parallel expressions (4Q405 23 I, 8–10; 1QM XII, 8–9). Calling God the "Lord of the spirits" may mean he is "Lord of [angelic] hosts" (*1 En.* 37:2, 4; cf. 2 Macc 3:24; Black, *Book*, 189–92). Picturing seven angelic spirits before God's throne (Tob 12:15; *1 En.* 20:1–7; 90:21) could be analogous to seven counselors attending a king (Esth 1:14; Ezra 7:14). Including angelic spirits with God and Christ would be like referring to God, Christ, and the angels (Luke 9:26; 1 Tim 5:21). (See Oecumenius; E. Schweizer, *TDNT* 6:450; Aune; Giesen; Murphy; Roloff; Thompson; Bucur, "Hierarchy.")
2. Holy Spirit. Since Christians sometimes mentioned God, Christ, and the Holy Spirit in introductions and conclusions to letters, the seven spirits could indicate the Holy Spirit (1 Pet 1:2; 2 Cor 13:13). The lamp and eye imagery that Revelation uses for the seven spirits comes from Zech 4, which refers to God's Spirit in the singular (Zech 4:6). Therefore, the seven spirits could be the Spirit that addresses the churches (Rev 2:7, 11, 17, etc.). Moreover, some writers said that the Spirit had seven traits: wisdom, understanding, counsel, might, knowledge, reverence, and fear of the Lord (Isa 11:2–3 LXX; cf. *1 En.* 61:11), though the Hebrew of Isa 11 has only six traits (cf. 4Q161 8–10 III, 11–13). (See Victorinus; Primasius; Andreas; Beale; K. de Smidt, "Acts"; Kraft; Osborne; Smalley; Bauckham, *Climax*, 162–66.)

1:5. *and from Jesus Christ the faithful witness.* This verse uses language from Ps 89 (88 LXX) to depict Jesus as God's anointed one (89:38, 51; cf. 89:20). Where the psalm says of the moon that "the witness in heaven is faithful" (89:37), Rev 1:5 calls the exalted Christ the "faithful witness." The Greek word *martys* is not yet a technical term for one who dies for the faith; instead, witness involves attesting to the truth where the truth is disputed. John was relegated to Patmos because of his witness (1:9). For others, witness culminates in death, as in the case of Jesus, Antipas (2:13), and the two witnesses later in Revelation (11:3–10; cf. 6:9; 12:11; 17:6). Yet witness is not simply dying. Attesting to the truth can provoke the opposition that leads to death, but witness cannot simply be equated with death (6:9; 12:11; Blount; Trites, "Μάρτυς"; Roose, *Zeugnis*, 38–47; Bergmeier, "Zeugnis").

the firstborn of the dead. In Psalm 89 God says of his anointed one, "I will make him my firstborn" (89:27), and Rev 1:5 says that Christ is "the firstborn of the dead and the ruler of the kings of the earth." Calling Jesus the "firstborn" implies that he was the first of others who will rise from the dead (Rom 8:29; cf. Acts 26:23; 1 Cor 15:20–23; Heb 12:23). In Jewish tradition, the firstborn son was entitled to a double share of inheritance (Deut 21:17; Philo, *Spec. Laws* 2.133), and in a royal household, he inherited the throne (Ps 89:27; 2 Chr 21:3; *Jos. As.* 4:11). Royal connotations are evident in Colossians, where Christ is "the firstborn of the dead" and has the "first place in everything" (Col 1:18; cf. Heb 1:6). Roman practice varied; emperors occasionally had firstborn sons who rose to power, as Titus did, but some seized power for themselves or adopted sons to ensure succession (*Rom. Civ.* 2:3–7).

and the ruler of the kings of the earth. Where Ps 89:27 refers to "the highest of the kings of the earth," Revelation uses "ruler" (*archōn*) when affirming Jesus' messianic status (Herms, *Apocalypse*, 208–17; cf. *archē* in Rev 3:14). The titles "witness" and "ruler" are used for David in Isa 55:4 (Schüssler Fiorenza, *Priester*, 199–200). The term "ruler" was used for various people in authority, but the "ruler of the kings of the earth" is supreme. Roman emperors did not use "ruler" or "king" as official titles, but in popular discourse they were called "ruler" (Dio Chrysostom, *Disc.* 32.60; Aelius Aristides, *Orations* 26.107) and "king" (Josephus, *J. W.* 3.351; Appian, *Hist. rom.* 6.102). The emperors allowed vassals to use the title "king" as long as they remained obedient to Rome (Augustus, *Res* 32–33; Suetonius, *Aug.* 48; Tacitus, *Agr.* 14; Dio Cassius, *Rom. Hist.* 62.5.3; Josephus, *J. W.* 2.223; Acts 25:13; 2 Cor 11:32). The emperor ruled many of earth's kings, but Christ is "King of kings" (Rev 17:14; cf. 19:16).

To him who loves us. Early Christians spoke of the love Christ showed in the past, especially by laying down his life for others (John 13:1; 15:12–13; Gal 2:20; Eph 5:25). Revelation sees Christ's love being expressed in his death but here uses the present tense to convey the ongoing love that the risen Christ shows (cf. John 14:21).

and released us from our sins by his blood. John interprets Jesus' crucifixion as a sacrifice, where shedding blood had a salutary effect (NOTE on 5:9). The verb *lyein* (released) was used for forgiving sins, though without reference to sacrifice (Isa 40:2; Sir 28:2; Job 42:9). Christ's blood was more commonly identified with words for ransom, which were similar in form and indicate both release, as in Rev 1:5, and purchase, as in 5:9 (*lytroun*, 1 Pet 1:19; *lytōsis*, Heb 9:12; *apolytrosis*, Rom 3:24–25; Eph 1:7). Instead of "released" (*lysanti*, 𝔓[18] ℵ A C 1611 2050 2329), some manuscripts read "washed" (*lousanti*, P 1106 1841 1854 2053 2062; cf. NJB, NRSV[fn]). The concept of washing in the blood of the Lamb appears elsewhere (*plynein*, 7:14; 22:14), but "released" has better manuscript support (Aune; Smalley; *TCGNT*[2], 662).

1:6. and made us a kingdom. The language here and in the next line is from Exod 19:6 and Isa 61:6 (NOTES on Rev 5:10). To be a kingdom does not mean that the redeemed "reign" at present (Bandstra, "Kingdom"; Beale). On the one hand, belonging to the kingdom means confessing that legitimate authority belongs to the Creator and the Lamb. On the other hand, it means resisting the claims of those who would take God's place. The redeemed will "reign" only through the resurrection that enables them to participate fully in the benefits of Christ's reign (20:4; 22:5; Schüssler Fiorenza, *Book*, 76; Friesen, *Imperial*, 181–83).

priests to his God and Father. The faithful are priests because they worship the true God (see COMMENT). As blood consecrated Israel's priests, Jesus' blood sets believers apart for priestly service (Exod 29:10–21; Beale). Their role differs from that of the angels, who appear in priestly garb and whose offerings of incense and outpouring of libations bring plagues (Rev 8:3–5; 15:5–16:21). Their role also differs from that of Christ, whose blood is a sacrifice that redeems and cleanses but who is not called a priest (1:5; 5:9; 7:14). Rather than calling prayer, praise, and works of love "sacrifice" (Rom 12:1; 1 Pet 2:5; Heb 13:16), Revelation refers to these actions as "worship," which is broader (*proskynein*, Rev 4:10; 11:1; *latreuein*, 7:15; 22:3).

to him be glory and might forever and ever. Amen. Glory (*doxa*) can be the divine power, or radiance, that emanates from God (15:8; 21:11, 23), but here it is the honor that people ascribe to God (4:9, 11; 5:12–13). Giving God glory can express repentance from sin and convey both awe and joy (11:13; 14:7; 19:1, 7). "To him" in 1:6 is parallel to "to the one who loves us" in 1:5b, making clear that glory is ascribed to Christ as in heavenly worship (5:12–13; 7:12). The Hebrew word *'amēn* was sometimes translated "may it be so" (*genoito*) in the LXX, but it was also transliterated into Greek and widely used in the early church. It adds conviction to a statement (1:7; cf. 22:20) or to a doxology (5:13–14; 7:12; Rom 11:36; 16:27; Gal 1:5; Phil 4:20).

1:7. The prophetic saying of Rev 1:7 combines aspects of Dan 7:13 and Zech 12:10–12 (cf. *Did.* 16:8):

Rev 1:7	*OT*
See, he is	See, one like a human being
coming with the clouds.	coming with the clouds [Dan 7:13].
Every eye will see him,	They will look on me
even those who pierced him, and	whom they pierced and they will grieve
for him	for him [Zech 12:10]
all the tribes of the earth will grieve.	all the earth will grieve by tribes [Zech 12:12].

Like Revelation, Matt 24:30 also combines Dan 7:13 and Zech 12:10 and uses a future tense form of *oran* rather than the LXX's *epiblepsontai* as a verb for "seeing." The result suggests a wordplay: to see is to grieve (*opsetai . . . kopsetai*). Yet Matthew and Revelation link the OT passages in reverse order, with Revelation including more of Zechariah and Matthew including more of Daniel. The similarities and differences suggest that Matthew and Revelation relied on a common Christian tradition, and not that one writer drew upon the other (Albl, "*And Scripture*," 253–59; Bauckham, *Climax*, 318–22; Yarbro Collins, *Cosmology*, 159–72; Herghelegiu, *Siehe*, 86–107; Jauhiainen, *Use*, 102–7; Karrer, *Johannesoffenbarung*, 121–25; Menken, "John's").

See, he is coming with the clouds. This line recalls Dan 7:13, where one like a human being, or "Son of Man," comes on the clouds of heaven to receive dominion over all peoples forever (cf. *4 Ezra* 13:3). In Daniel this figure could be a collective image for Israel or an angelic being, but early Christians identified him as Christ (Collins, *Daniel*, 306–10; Slater, *Christ*, 67–85). The gospels relate the passage to Jesus' future coming, which will include the ingathering of God's elect (Matt 24:30; 26:64; Mark 13:26; 14:62; Luke 21:27), as in Rev 14:14–16 (NOTES and COMMENT on 22:7). Here, Revelation's language resembles Theodotian's Greek translation of Dan 7:13, which pictures the Son of Man "coming" in the present tense rather than the past (MT, LXX) and uses "with" rather than "on" the clouds (LXX). Clouds connote heavenly or divine agency (Rev 10:1; 11:12; 14:14–16).

and every eye will see him, even those who pierced him. This recalls Zech 12:10, which in the MT reads, "they will look at me, whom they have pierced." Since God is the speaker, the MT implies that God has been pierced, which could seem theologically problematic. But the LXX reads "him," making the victim someone other than God. Instead of "pierced" the LXX reads "treat spitefully," apparently reversing the Hebrew consonants *dqr* to read *dāqārû* as *rāqādû* (Albl, "*And Scripture*," 254). The *Tg.* Zech 12:10 is even more paraphrastic, rendering "look to me, whom they have pierced" as "entreat me because they were exiled." When Zech 12:10 is paraphrased in Rev 1:7 and John 19:37, "pierced" is used and it is understood to speak of "him," namely, Christ (Justin Martyr, *Dial.* 14.8; 118.1). Where the gospel relates Zech 12:10 to the crucifixion, Revelation uses it for Jesus' future coming.

and all the tribes of the earth shall grieve for him. In its original context, Zech 12:12 said that "the land" and "tribes" of Israel would grieve for a fallen victim, but Revelation says that all tribes of earth will grieve (cf. Matt 24:30). In the OT, the tribes of earth were sometimes the ungodly, who were subject to divine judgment (Ezek 20:32; Zech 14:17). Yet other passages said that God wanted all the tribes to be blessed and know him (Gen 12:3; 28:14; Ps 72:17). In Revelation the grief of the tribes has been interpreted in two ways; the first is preferable.

1. Repentance. Those who formerly condemned Christ now grieve over what was done to him, which shows a change on their part. The expression *koptesthai epi* + accusative regularly means "to grieve for" someone (NAB, NASB, NJB). Kings grieve for the fallen whore (Rev 18:9; cf. 18:11), women grieve for Jesus at his crucifixion (Luke 23:27–28), and David grieved for the slain Saul and Jonathan (2 Sam 1:12). In Zech 12:10–14, those who once "pierced" the unnamed figure receive a spirit of compassion and now grieve "for him" (cf. *T. Job* 53:4). The picture of hostile peoples changing their stance toward Christ looks for the conversion rather than the destruction of the nations (Rev 5:5, 9; 7:9; cf. 11:13; 21:24; Beale; Kraft; Bauckham, *Climax*, 319–22; Doglio, "L'Oracolo"; Jauhiainen, *Use*, 106; Thompson, "Lamentation").

2. Despair at impending judgment. Some interpreters propose that people grieve for themselves, since they will stand under judgment because of Christ (NIV, NRSV, REB). The tribes are hostile to God's witnesses and are influenced by the beast (Rev 11:9; 13:7). Those who do not repent are condemned (9:20–21; 16:9, 11; cf. Beckwith; Charles; Giesen). Grammatically, however, *koptesthai epi* + accusative (grieve for) did not have this meaning. When Revelation pictures the human one coming on the clouds, the scene has more to do with ingathering than with condemnation (NOTES on 14:14–16), and New Jerusalem offers hope for the healing of the nations (22:2). The book allows hope for the penitent.

Yes. Amen. See the NOTE on 1:6. Since a speaker could say "yes" (*nai*) when reaffirming his own words (Matt 11:26; Luke 10:21), this could be John's voice (Boring, "Voice," 387). Elsewhere, however, a second voice says "yes" to affirm what is said (14:13; 16:7; 22:20), so the voice might belong to God or other heavenly being (Karrer, *Johannesoffenbarung*, 125). Here it gives the impression of a dialog between speakers.

1:8. *"I am the Alpha and the Omega."* "I am" recalls the name of God, like the expression "the one who is" (Exod 3:14; NOTE on Rev 1:4). The Greek form *egō eimi* occurs in sayings like "I am God and there is no other" (Isa 45:22; cf. 45:18; 46:9; 47:8, 10; Deut 32:39). When used with a predicate, the "I am" identified who God was for people. This was a source of hope (Isa 43:25; 51:12). The "I am" was occasionally used for Greco-Roman deities (e.g., "I am Isis") and in magical sources (Deissmann, *Light*, 138–40; Ball, *"I Am,"* 24–45), but Revelation recalls texts that stress the singular lordship of Israel's God: "I am the first and I am the last, there is no god but me" (Isa 44:6; cf. 41:4; 48:12).

Using the letters alpha and omega as equivalent to "first" and "last" could have precedents in Jewish sources, where the first and last letters of the Hebrew alphabet (*aleph* and *tau*) indicate completeness, though the sources are late (*b. Shabb.* 55a; G. Kittel, *TDNT* 1:1–3). A link with the divine name is suggested by a Greek form of "Yahweh," which was Ιαω (*Iaō*) and includes both alpha (α) and omega (ω) (cf. the LXX of Leviticus at Qumran 4Q120 6–7, 12; 20–21, 4; manuscripts of Jer 1:6; 14:13; 39:16–17 LXX; Diodorus Siculus, *Libr.* 1.94.2). This form of the name was used in later magical sources (Aune, *Apocalypticism*, 361–64; *RAC* 17:1–11), but whether Rev 1:8 is a polemic against such magical usage is unclear.

says the Lord God, "the one who is and who was and who is to come. Lord God (*kyrios ho theos*) was the Greek equivalent of the Hebrew *yhwh 'ĕlōhîm* (Gen 2:8; Amos 5:14; *Pss. Sol.* 5:1; *Jos. As.* 7:4; 8:3; *T. Benj.* 3:1). On past, present, and future, see the NOTE on Rev 1:4.

"the Almighty." The Hebrew expression Lord "of hosts" (*ṣĕbāʾôt*) was rendered into Greek as Lord "Almighty" (*pantokratōr*, Amos 3:13; Nah 3:5). The Hebrew word "hosts" identifies God with the heavenly armies, whereas the Greek "Almighty" affirms that he is all-powerful. Inscriptions from Asia Minor often call the emperor *autokratōr*, or self-ruler (I.Eph 1523; I.Smyr 591.5; 731.2; I.Sard 8.22; I.Laod 9.1, 4; 15.1; 24.1). Revelation, however, refers to God as *pantokratōr*, ascribing to him power over all things. In Revelation God's supreme might is expressed in his acts of creation, judgment, and righteous rule (Rev 1:8; 4:8; 18:8; 19:6; 21:22; 22:5–6). Patristic writers often used Rev 1:8 to affirm the deity of Christ (Andreas; Origen, *Princ.* 2.10; Athanasius, *C. Ar.* 3.4; Gregory of Nazianzus, *Or. Bas.* 29.17; Didymus, *Comm. Zach.* 5). Here, however, God is the focus.

COMMENT

Apokalypsis, or "revelation," is the first word in this book, and it shapes the readers' expectations of what will follow. The act of revealing takes place at the boundary of human capacities, for it presupposes that God's designs are ordinarily concealed; and

---

On Rev 1:1–8, see Albl, *"And Scripture,"* 353–65; Aune, *Apocalypticism,* 191–98, 261–79, 361–64; Bandstra, "Kingship"; Boring, "Voice"; Bucur, "Hierarchy"; G. Carey, *Elusive,* 93–114; deSilva, *Seeing,* 117–37; J. C. de Smidt, "Doxology"; K. de Smidt, "First," "Meta-Theology," and "Revelation"; Hahn, "Liturgische"; Haraguchi, "Effective"; Hartman, "Form"; Hellholm, "Visions"; Herghelegiu, *Siehe,* 29–109; Jauhiainen, "Ἀποκάλυψις" and *Use,* 102–7, 142–48; Karrer, *Johannesoffenbarung,* 86–136; McDonough, *YHWH;* Menken, "John's"; Philonenko, "Celui"; Schüssler Fiorenza, *Book,* 68–81, and *Priester,* 168–262; Royalty, *Streets,* 133–49; Slater, *Christ,* 87–93; L. Thompson, "Lamentation"; Vanni, "Liturgical"; Yarbro Collins, *Cosmology,* 159–72.

because they are hidden, God must disclose them. Divine address frames the introduction. In the beginning it is God who gives the revelation to Jesus, so that it might be given to an angel, to John, and finally to the readers (Rev 1:1). At the end of this section readers are brought back to God, the source of revelation, who speaks to them in the first person: "I am the Alpha and the Omega" (1:8).

In the social world of early Christianity, God and the risen Christ were understood to speak through prophets, who might convey revelations orally (1 Cor 14:6, 26) or in writing (Herm. *Vis.* 2.4.1, 3). Since prophets were active in the churches John addressed, readers presumably would have considered revelation to be a valid type of communication (Rev 22:9; Knight, "Apocalyptic," 487; deSilva, *Seeing*, 120). The question John faced was whether they would consider his text to be a *genuine* word from God. Congregations could test purported prophecies before accepting them (NOTE on 1:3; Aune, *Prophecy*, 217–29; Boring, *Continuing*, 101–7); therefore, to encourage a favorable reception of his message, John establishes common ground with the readers by using literary forms and confessional statements that place his text within the tradition of Israel and the early church.

John uses a superscription like those on the biblical prophetic books, which often told about the word of the Lord coming to a prophet and sometimes said something about the message. For example, "The word of the Lord that came to Micah of Moresheth . . . which he saw concerning Samaria and Jerusalem" (Mic 1:1). After the superscription, the initial prophetic word would be given: "Hear you peoples . . . the Lord is coming out of his place" (Mic 1:2–3; cf. Isa 1:1; Jer 1:1–2; Hos 1:1; Joel 1:1; Aune; Murphy). John adapts this form by telling of the revelation or "word of God" that came to him (Rev 1:1–3) and including an initial prophetic word about a heavenly figure "coming" with the clouds (1:7–8). Through the use of this basic form, John locates his text within the tradition of accepted prophecy.

John also inserts a salutation like those in other early Christian letters (1:4–6). He includes the greeting "grace to you and peace," which was already in use (1:4). Furthermore, John downplays his role as the sender in order to emphasize that the greeting is from the God who is and was and is to come. In so doing, he adapts language from the biblical tradition he shared with the readers. Then he identifies Christ as witness, firstborn, and ruler; and he lists three actions, including Christ's love, deliverance from sins, and making believers into a kingdom and priests. The revelation John will present may be new, but it is said to originate with God and the risen Jesus, who are already well-known.

Revelation's introduction interconnects the prophetic (1:1–3, 7–8) and epistolary (1:4–6) forms like links of a chain. This technique also occurs in the introductions to the trumpet and bowl visions (8:1, 6; 15:1, 5–6), which overlap with the final visions in the previous sequences (8:2–5; 15:2–4), showing that the two sections are part of a whole (Schüssler Fiorenza, *Book*, 172). The interweaving of prophetic and epistolary elements occurs again at the end of Revelation, framing the book and creating a fusion of voices in which God's word addresses readers through John's written word (COMMENT on 22:9–21; Boring, "Voice"; Barr, "Apocalypse of John").

Superscription (1:1–3)

The traditional title, "The Revelation of John," was not an original part of the text but was affixed as the book was copied (§1 COMMENT). The original "title" is the opening line, a "revelation from Jesus Christ," which presents Jesus rather than John as the author (1:1). Some interpreters suggest that the internal title and introductory comments were a late edition to the text (Ford; Malina and Pilch), but this is unlikely. It was said that "authors of old used to give hints of the subject they were to treat in the prefaces or remarks which they composed as a sort of title" (Epiphanius, *Pan.* 1.1.1). John followed this practice. Some writers wrote prefaces using the first person (Luke 1:1–4), but others used the third person (Herodotus, *Historiae* 1.1), as John does. Since superscriptions were common on prophetic and apocalyptic texts (Mic 1:1; Amos 1:1; Jer 1:1–3; *1 En.* 1:1), Revelation follows the familiar pattern (Aune, *Apocalypticism*, 124; Boring, "Voice," 346).

This introduction speaks to the implied question, "Why should someone listen to what is about to be said?" Speakers understood that audiences needed to be made ready to give their attention to a message (*Rhetorica ad Herennium* 1.4.6; Quintilian, *Inst.* 4.1.5). Revelation calls for attention from the audience because its message is said to come from God and the risen Jesus, who has loved them, freed them, and made them members of God's kingdom (1:5–6). Revelation comes from the divine realm to the human addressees, warranting their most careful consideration (Schüssler Fiorenza, *Book*, 68–81; Thompson, *Book*, 177–79; deSilva, *Seeing*, 124–26).

The content concerns what "must" (*dei*) take place (Rev 1:1c). Theologically, the word "must" points to what takes place by God's will, and the visions show God's intentions culminating in his triumph over evil. The message of God's victory will be encouraging for those who suffer injustice, yet the sense of divine necessity can seem deterministic (Murphy 64). Therefore, it is important to note that the visions announce God's ultimate victory without outlining a rigid sequence by which it will be accomplished. The messages to the churches include promises and warnings about what Christ will do "if" people repent or refuse to do so, which assumes that Christ's actions will vary, depending on human response (2:5, 16, 22; 3:3, 20). The next section concerns what "must" (*dei*) take place (4:1), and the seal visions bring a relentless series of threats. But when people cry out, "Who is able to stand?" (6:17), a change occurs. The seemingly inexorable path toward judgment is interrupted so that people can be sealed (7:1–3). The trumpet visions bring another series of plagues, but when they fail to bring repentance (9:20–21), the movement toward judgment is again interrupted and John is told that he "must" (*dei*) prophesy once more, with the result that many come to glorify God (10:11; 11:13). Similarly, those who oppose God's witnesses "must" (*dei*) be struck by the word from the witnesses' mouths, but only "if" they seek to harm the witnesses (11:5). Revelation makes clear that God will prevail, but it leaves room for contingencies, such as repentance or refusal to repent, in the way things are accomplished.

The book conveys what is to take place "soon" (*en tachei*, 1:1). This approach differs from apocalyptic writings that were said to have been written for future generations (Dan 8:26; 12:4, 9; *T. Mos.* 1:17–18; *1 En.* 1:2; NOTE on Rev 22:10), and it means that the book was intended to be relevant for its original hearers. But a major question is what "soon" means, and Revelation's history of interpretation has often focused on this question (INTRO I). John does not say that "the end" must soon take place. The idea is more complex. The messages in 1:9–3:22 warn that without repentance, Christ will come "soon," not to end the present age but to discipline each congregation (2:16). Later visions continue to complicate the sense of what "soon" means, since the scenes in the middle of the book do not unfold in a linear fashion but repeatedly interrupt the movement toward the end so that people can be sealed (7:1–17) and John can prophesy (10:1–11). Readers are told of the passing of two woes (9:12; 11:14a), and they hear that a third is coming "soon" (11:14b). That third woe is apparently the seventh trumpet vision, which announces that God's kingdom has come, yet even there the end does not arrive and the conflict with evil continues for the rest of the book.

The interpretive problem is that visionary time has no straightforward connection to chronological time in the readers' world. Visions show the Christian community's conflict with evil lasting for three and a half years (12:6; 13:5); yet this period begins when Christ is exalted to heaven and Satan is thrown down to the earth (12:5, 7–9), and it ends when Christ returns and Satan is bound (19:11–20:3). So the time that Satan rages is "short" in the visionary world (12:12), but chronologically it encompasses the entire span between Christ's first and final comings. Revelation will announce that "all is done" in the new creation, but that occurs only after the saints have reigned with Christ for a thousand years, a timespan that is hardly "soon" for the intended readers (21:6; Maier, *Apocalypse*, 123–59; Bauckham, *Theology*, 157–59).

The opening line can say that Revelation conveys "what must soon take place" because its summons to perseverance and faith is immediately relevant to John's readers (Giblin; K. de Smidt, "First," 108). Yet the book's imagery, interrupted sequences, and symbolic use of time mean that readers cannot determine what "soon" means chronologically. The tension between imminence and delay is heightened, not resolved by the visions, and in this tension readers are called to live out their vocation as witnesses (COMMENT on 22:6–7).

Next the superscription elaborates the process of revelation by saying that what comes from God and Christ was given to John by an angel (*angelos*, 1:1e). This angel does not appear in the opening visions, where Christ speaks directly to the churches (1:9–3:22), but he plays a role in what follows. In the heavenly throne room God gives a scroll to Christ, who breaks the seals so that it can be opened (5:1, 8). Later, an angel brings the open scroll to John, who takes and eats it so that he can prophesy (10:2, 9). Thus the basic movement of revelatory scenes is from God to Christ to an angel to John (Mazzaferri, *Genre*, 265–79; Bauckham, *Climax*, 243–57). The introduction's focus on a single mediating angel is not sustained, since other angels show John things (Rev 17:1–18; 21:9–22:5), make announcements, offer praise, send plagues, and engage in battle (5:11; 7:1–2; 8:6; 12:7; 14:6–11; 16:1). But the single angel is mentioned again in the conclusion of the book (22:6, 16). Referring to just one mediating angel summarizes a complex chain of revelation (Carrell, *Jesus*, 119–27).

John explains that his role is to bear "witness" to what he received from Jesus (1:2). Rhetorically, people are most likely to accept the word of those they trust (Aristotle, *Rhet.* 1.2.4; Quintilian, *Inst.* 3.8.13; deSilva, *Seeing*, 117–45; G. Carey, *Elusive*, 93–133). In disputed situations speakers could sometimes gain credibility by saying little about themselves while assuming the role of reliable witnesses (Quintilian, *Inst.* 4.1.7). This is what John does when he greets readers briefly in his own name and then bears witness to God and Jesus (1:4–8). John next bears witness to his own experience, which was difficult to verify because it was not a public occurrence that was shared by others; it was a private visionary encounter with the risen Christ. To encourage acceptance of the message he received, John emphasizes that Jesus is the commissioning agent (1:9–20;

Thompson, *Book*, 177–79). To enhance the credibility of his witness, John later mentions his own mistakes, such as preparing to write the wrong words (10:4) or worshiping the wrong figure (19:10; 22:8–9). By acknowledging the times when he was mistaken and was corrected by heavenly agents, John conveys the sense that his message as a whole has integrity.

John says that he attests "the word of God and the witness of Jesus" (1:2). These expressions link John's message to traditions that were already available to the readers. The word of God included what had been conveyed through the biblical prophets, whose writings were familiar (NOTE on 1:2). For John to call his message a "word of God" suggests that it will be congruent with the words of God that have already been received through the tradition.

Similarly, "the witness of Jesus" is in one sense the witness that has come from Jesus through the tradition of the church. John summarizes aspects of Jesus' legacy in the confessional statements in 1:5–6, and he may recall traditional sayings of Jesus in the messages to the churches. These include the summons to hear, the warning that he will come like a thief, and the promise that he will confess the names of the faithful before God (2:7; 3:3, 5). Now John claims that God's word has come to him through the risen Jesus, who commissioned him to write and will add his own affidavit to the book (1:9–11; 22:18, 20). By calling the message he received the "witness of Jesus," John places it in the context of the wider tradition.

John next calls his witness "prophecy," which is understood to be a message sent from God through an inspired messenger (1:3). John says he received visions through the Spirit (1:10; 4:2; 17:3; 21:10) and that God's Spirit speaks through his text (2:7, 11, 17, 29). He even conveys words from God and the glorified Christ directly, using the first person singular (1:8; 2:1–3:22; 21:5–8). In a sense, the whole Christian community is called to make prophetic witness (11:3–10), but John also assumes that he and others have a distinctive vocation as prophets, who are inspired in ways that other people are not (22:6, 9; cf. Acts 13:1; 15:32; 1 Cor 12:10, 29; Aune, *Prophecy*, 189–231; Boring, *Continuing*, 35–47; Schüssler Fiorenza, *Book*, 135–40).

Popular treatments of Revelation sometimes equate prophecy with predicting the future (LaHaye 12–18). Revelation does look for the final defeat of evil and coming of a new creation, yet such visions cannot be reduced to predictions. Calls for repentance and warnings are made in conditional form; that is, a given threat will be carried out only if repentance does not occur (2:5, 16; 3:3). Promises of blessings express God's commitment to the faithful (2:7, 10–11, 17, 26–28; 3:5, 12, 20–21). There are exhortations to faithfulness (13:9–10), depictions of heavenly and earthly powers that are presently at work (4:1–11; 17:1–6), and scenes of eschatological judgments and salvation that recast older texts (18:1–24; 21:1–22:5; Aune, *Prophecy*, 274–88; Boring, *Continuing*, 82–83). Much of John's prophecy is designed to shape perspectives on the present, and its visions of the future affirm God's final victory and new creation without giving readers an outline of events leading up to the end (Barr, "Apocalypse as a Symbolic"). John considers his entire book to be "prophecy" (1:3; 22:7, 10, 18, 19), and its contents are as varied as those of the earlier biblical prophets.

For John, the criterion for authentic prophecy is whether the message promotes fidelity to God and Jesus (NOTE on 1:3). False prophets like Jezebel and the beast from the land are denounced for drawing people away from God through idolatrous practice

(2:20; 13:11–18; 16:13–14; 19:20). By way of contrast, true prophets include the two wit-nesses, who dress in sackcloth as a visible summons to repentance (11:3). If "the spirit of prophecy is the witness of Jesus" (19:10), then the integrity of a prophecy is reflected in promoting fidelity to Christ and his Father (Roose, *Zeugnis*, 46, 47, 188).

John expected his text to be read aloud to the community (1:3), though whether it would have been read at a single sitting or in shorter segments is not clear (Barr, "Apocalypse of John"). The one who reads aloud is "blessed," which provides assurance that conveying the message faithfully is what God desires. The opposite is falsifying the message, which leads to a loss of God's blessing (22:18–19). Next, the listeners are called "blessed" as they "keep" the message (1:3d). "Keeping" the word involves repentance and a course of life that entails faithfulness to Christ (2:26; 3:3), obedience to God's commands (12:17; 14:12), and a refusal to deny one's faith (3:8). To "keep" Revela-tion's prophecy is to "worship God" (22:9). For those who are already persevering, the promise of being "blessed" gives incentive to continue, knowing that God views them favorably despite opposition from others (Boring). And for those who are complacent, this serves as an indirect admonition to be more faithful (Murphy).

The question of time arises again when John says that those who receive the mes-sage are blessed, "for the time [*kairos*] is near" (1:3; cf. 22:10). Some assume that John thinks that the *end* of time is near (Müller) and that those who keep the message will soon receive the blessings of New Jerusalem. Evidence for this view is the way heavenly voices later announce that the time (*kairos*) has come for evil to be destroyed, the dead to be raised, and judgment to occur (11:18). Yet the time (*kairos*) of which John writes cannot be reduced to its end, since it encompasses the entire time that Satan rages on earth, from Christ's resurrection and ascension until his final coming (12:12; COMMENT on "soon" in 1:1). The time that is near is one of engaging the forces of evil, and in such a time, those who heed Revelation's call to remain faithful are "blessed" (COMMENT on 22:10).

Epistolary Introduction (1:4–6)

John now shifts to an epistolary introduction like that found in early Christian letters. A letter was to be received as one would receive the author's word in person (White, *Light*, 218–20; Mitchell, "New"; Boring, "Voice," 350). The opening lines of ancient letters regularly had three parts: identification of the sender, identification of the in-tended recipients, and greetings. These could be stated briefly or modified to shape the way the message would be received.

First is the sender's name. Personal letters typically gave only the name (White, *Light*, 108–24; 1 Thess 1:1; Ign. *Eph*. pref.; Pol. *Phil*. pref.). Others added titles such as "apostle," "one called by God," or a "servant" or "prisoner" of Christ Jesus (1 Cor 1:1; Phil 1:1; Phlm 1; 1 Pet 1:1; Jude 1:1). If a writer thought that readers might have ques-tions about the sender, a more extended self-presentation could be given (Rom 1:1–6; Gal 1:1–2a). Here, John simply gives his name, which implies that the readers knew him (cf. Rev 1:9).

Second is identification of the intended recipients. Personal letters might give the recipient's name and a description like "brother" or "esteemed"; more official corre-spondence noted the recipient's public role or office (White, *Light*, 108–18). Many Christian letters addressed congregations, which were identified by location (Gal 1:2).

The opening might also elaborate the congregation's relationship to God, Christ, and the wider Christian community (Rom 1:7; 1 Cor 1:2; 1 Thess 1:1; 1 Pet 1:1b–2; Ign. *Eph.* pref.). Revelation calls the recipients "the seven assemblies that are in Asia" (Rev 1:4), saving additional information about their locations and characteristics until later (1:11; 2:1–3:22; see Map 1).

Third is the greeting. Rather than the usual "greetings" (*chairein*), Revelation adopts a salutation like those in the Pauline letters: "Grace to you and peace" (Note on 1:4). Then John elaborates the character of God and Christ who are the source of grace and peace, adding a doxology that praises Christ for what he has done (1:4–5). Doxologies could conclude sections of a letter (Rom 11:36; 1 Tim 1:17; 1 Pet 4:11; *1 Clem.* 20:12) and were also used in greetings (Gal 1:3–5). Here, the doxology keeps John in the background so that readers focus on God and Christ, whom John invokes as the authorities behind his text (Thompson, *Book*, 177–78).

Grace and peace come from the God "who is" (Rev 1:4). This recalls the expression God used to identify himself in Exod 3:14 LXX when sending Moses to speak to Israel. John uses the same expression here and in Rev 1:8 to emphasize that this same God now addresses the readers (Aune). John also expands the name to affirm God's past existence and future coming. Jewish and early Christian sources confessed God's endless existence (Gen 21:33; Isa 40:28; Tob 14:7; Bar 4:8; *1 En.* 1:4; 9:4; Rom 16:26), and some expressed this in terms of God's past, present, and future existence (*Sib. Or.* 3:16; cf. Clement of Alexandria, *Strom.* 5.6). Revelation is unusual in referring to God's future *coming*, but this too recalls tradition. According to the prophets, God's coming was threatening, because he would judge the world (Mic 1:2–4; Isa 26:21; 66:15; Zech 14:5; *1 En.* 1:3–9), yet it was also a source of hope, for he would redeem his people (Pss 96:13; 98:9; Isa 40:10; Adams, "Coming"). In Revelation God comes in Christ to defeat evil and bring redemption (Rev 1:7; 22:7, 12, 17, 20; Roloff). Eventually, John will speak only of the God "who is and who was," dropping the reference to the future (11:17; 16:5). The implication is that when judgment and redemption take place, God has come (Bauckham, *Theology*, 29).

Affirming God's present, past, and future fits his role as Creator (Rev 4:11; cf. *4 Ezra* 8:7; Philo, *Mos.* 2.100; *Tg. Neof.* and *Tg. Ps.-J.* Exod 3:14). As the one who "was," he was present at the world's foundation (Rev 4:11; 10:6; 14:7). Living forever, he is the source of life and proper focus for the readers' faith (4:9–10; 7:2). It was common to contrast the God who truly "is" with the so-called gods that did not share authentic existence (Wis 13:1; 14:12–13; Philo, *Decal.* 8; *Sib. Or.* 3:11–16, 30–33; McDonough, *YHWH*, 153–67). Similarly, Revelation refers to idols that cannot hear, see, or walk (Rev 9:20), and it shows people giving breath to a statue in an attempt to deceive people into thinking that it too is a true living God (13:15). But Revelation makes a sharp contrast between the beast, which "was and is not and is about to ascend from the abyss and go to destruction" (17:8), and the God who exists, brings all things into being, and ushers in a new creation (21:1).

Before God's throne are seven spirits, who are probably angelic spirits (Note on 1:4). In the conflict depicted in the visions, God's throne is the center of legitimate authority, in contrast to the throne of Satan, which is given to the beast (4:1–10; 13:2; 16:10). The agents of evil may send unclean spirits (*pneumata*) into the world, fostering opposition to God through deception (16:13–14), yet God and Christ have their own active agents. The seven spirits (*pneumata*) before God's throne serve as the eyes of the Lamb. They range throughout the earth, giving God's side superior reconnaissance in the battle with evil (4:5; 5:6).

Finally, the risen Christ is introduced with three titles. The first is "faithful witness" (1:5a). In one sense, Christ was a faithful witness during his earthly ministry because he spoke the truth about God, himself, and the world in the face of opposition (John 3:12; 7:7; 18:37; 1 Tim 6:13). His death sealed his witness by showing uncompromising commitment to truth (Beale; Roloff). In another sense, the risen Christ continues to bear witness by sending God's word to people. In John's context, the conflicts with opponents make it likely that his message will be disputed (2:9–10, 14, 20; 3:8–9), but he claims that the living Jesus attests the truth of what he says (22:20; Aune; Giesen). Readers are to discern whether the Jesus who is said to speak through John's text is congruent with the Jesus who is already known through tradition.

Next, Christ is "the firstborn of the dead" (1:5b). "Firstborn" has royal connotations (NOTE on 1:5) and also anticipates that others will be raised from death (Rom 8:29; 1 Cor 15:20–23; Heb 1:6; 12:23). Just as those who follow Jesus die, they also have the promise of resurrection to endless life. This gives them incentive to remain faithful now, knowing that death itself will be defeated (Rev 20:14; 21:4).

Next, naming the risen Jesus "the ruler of the kings of the earth" affirms his messianic status and anticipates a major conflict in the book (1:5c; Ps 89:27). Jesus was put to death by earthly rulers, yet his resurrection means he is not subject to them—rather, they are subject to Jesus. The kings of earth are not inherently evil, but they are deceived by the agents of evil (Rev 16:14; 17:2, 18; 18:3, 9). The visions show two contrasting futures for these kings. One is to persist under the dominion of evil, personified by Babylon, which brings benefit now but ultimately leads to destruction (19:18–19). The other is to embrace the reign of God and the Lamb, who offer life in New Jerusalem, where the gates are open to receive earth's kings (21:24). These contrasting visions are not predictions of the kings' destruction or redemption (Herms, *Apocalypse*, 207–56); rather, they show the outcomes of differing responses to Christ (Bauckham, *Climax*, 312–16; Mathewson, *New*, 164–75).

The doxology in 1:5b–6 continues affirming what Christ has done. Glory is given to the one "who loves *us* and freed *us* from our sins by his blood and made *us* to be a kingdom, priests to his God and Father" (emphasis added). Given the use of the first-person plurals, some interpreters regard this as a baptismal confession of the community (Schüssler Fiorenza, *Book*, 71–73; Giesen), but the themes were common enough to function in other settings. Rhetorically, affirming what all can confess together is a way for John to reaffirm his relationship with the readers (Thompson, *Book*, 54–56). His reference to the love of Christ also introduces a familiar theme that will function in a complex way in the book. Christ's love was conveyed through his self-sacrifice and delivers people from sin for life in God's kingdom (1:5). For readers who experience threats, the love of Christ provides assurance that he will preserve and vindicate them (3:9). But for readers who are complacent, Christ's love will take a confrontational form, as he disciplines them (3:19; Herghelegiu, *Siehe*, 55–57). In Revelation, love is not acceptance of evil but a force that overcomes it (Blount).

The salvific effect of Christ's death is presented in four ways in Revelation. First is sin and forgiveness. Sins bring people under divine judgment, and people are "freed" by God's forgiveness, which is conveyed through the blood of Jesus (Rev 1:5). Second is bondage and liberation. Sins hold people captive, but Christ's blood purchases their freedom, as one might manumit a slave (Note on 5:9). Third is defilement and cleansing. Sins make a person unclean, and Christ's blood provides the cleansing needed to enter the presence of God. Washing one's robe in the blood of the Lamb is a way to speak of trust in Christ and the life of faith that follows (7:14). Fourth is falsehood and truth. Evil works by deceiving people about God, but the blood of Christ's self-sacrifice attests to God's true character. It empowers people to win victory over evil, since it is a triumph for truth over falsehood (12:11). Taken together, these four dimensions give a complex and dynamic perspective on the significance of Jesus' death.

Revelation considers the crucified and risen Christ to be the ruler of all of earth's kings, while referring to the Christian community as his "kingdom" in a unique sense (1:6a). The language recalls Exod 19:6, where God delivered the people of Israel from bondage and made them his priestly kingdom (Notes on 5:9–10). At present, the Christian community is *a* kingdom, but not *the* kingdom, which will encompass all creation (11:15). Jesus' followers are a kingdom in that they confess that the God who has acted through Jesus is their true sovereign. (The lordship of God and Christ is treated as a single entity in Revelation. There is only one throne, so both are honored together; 3:21; 5:6, 13; 7:10, 17; Bauckham, *Theology*, 54–65.) At present, the destroyers of the earth seek dominion over the nations (11:18; 13:7; 17:2, 15, 18). In the future, the lordship of God and Christ will bring evil to an end (19:11–21; 20:7–10). Only then will the redeemed "reign" by sharing fully in Christ's reign through resurrection (20:4–6; 22:5).

The redeemed are also "priests" of God (1:6). The language recalls that all the people of Israel had a priestly vocation, even though some had special priestly duties at the altar (Exod 19:6; Note on Rev 5:10). At present, the prayers of the Christian community are brought to God through heavenly intermediaries (5:8; 8:3–4), but in the future, Jesus' followers will have unmediated access to God, when they will see God's face through resurrection to life in New Jerusalem. They will bear God's name on their foreheads in the manner of high priests and worship in a city with traits of a sanctuary (7:7; 14:1; 22:3–4; cf. 20:6; Schüssler Fiorenza, *Priester*, 385–89). In Jewish and Greco-Roman traditions, priests offered sacrifices to God (Schürer, *History*, 292–308; Burkert, *Greek*, 95–98), but in Revelation the principal sacrifice is Jesus' self-offering. His followers serve as priests by bearing witness to what he has done (Note on 1:6).

As a priestly people, Jesus' followers are set apart from the nations by their worship of God (cf. Exod 19:5–6). Their worship differs from that of the priests devoted to other deities in Roman Asia (Comment on Rev 5:9–10). Worship is an expression of loyalty (Friesen, *Imperial*, 182). The visions show God and the Lamb being worshiped by the hosts of heaven and all creation (4:10; 5:14; 7:11), even as Satan and the beast draw people into false worship (13:4, 12, 15). As heavenly worshipers proclaim what God and the Lamb have done (4:9–11; 5:9–14; 7:9–12; 11:15–18; 15:2–4), the faithful on earth do the same. Their community is a "temple" where true worship takes place (11:1–2), and its lampstands signify the community's witness to the world (11:3–10; Beale; Boring, Sweet).

Prophetic Words (1:7–8)

Readers are now told, "See, he is coming with the clouds" (1:7a). The language is like that of prophetic and apocalyptic texts, which sometimes began by announcing God's coming (Mic 1:2–7; *1 En.* 1:3–9). Revelation's language recalls Dan 7:13, where one like a human being, or "Son of Man," comes to receive everlasting dominion over all peoples. Like other early Christians, John's readers would have taken the passage as a reference to Christ's final coming (Matt 24:30; 26:64; Mark 13:26; 14:62; Luke 21:27; *Did.* 16:8). Therefore, John reaffirms what they already believe, and by establishing common ground, he prepares them to listen favorably to what he is saying (deSilva, *Seeing*, 129–30).

Christ's coming on the clouds was traditionally envisioned as an act of sovereign power that would culminate in the ingathering of his people and judgment of the ungodly (NOTE on Rev 22:6). The paraphrase of Dan 7:13 in Rev 1:7 grounds this hope in biblical tradition, while the rest of Revelation both affirms and transforms it. The vision of Christ's coming on the clouds occurs again in Rev 14:14–16, where the redeemed are gathered in and the ungodly fall under judgment, as one might expect. But other aspects of Dan 7 are developed in surprising ways (Beale, *Use*; Moyise, *Old*, 51–63). The white hair of the figure in Dan 7:9 appears on Christ, who is already present among the churches (Rev 1:14). Where Dan 7:14 tells of the coming one being given dominion over all nations, Christ is already the ruler of earth's kings, having died to redeem those of every nation (Rev 1:5; 5:9–10). The four beasts of Dan 7:1–8 become one great beast (Rev 13:1–8), which now carries the city that rules the world (13:1–8; 17:1–18). In the end, Christ comes to defeat the beast—though no clouds are mentioned (19:11–21)—before the resurrection and judgment (Dan 7:10; Rev 20:11–15). The initial announcement of Christ's coming in 1:7 leads into a more complex vision of a Christ who is coming and yet is present already.

John says "every eye will see him, including those who pierced him" (Rev 1:7b). Taken literally, those who pierced Jesus would be those who carried out his crucifixion (cf. John 19:37). But Revelation broadens this to encompass all of Jesus' adversaries, including those of John's own time (cf. 1 Cor 2:8; Col 2:14–15; Giesen). To say that all the tribes "will grieve for him" (Rev 1:7c) is ambiguous (Osborne). Some interpreters think the tribes grieve for themselves, because they now face judgment (cf. Matt 24:30). But Revelation says they grieve "for him," that is, for Christ, which seems to show repentance (NOTE on 1:7c). The saying cannot be construed as a prediction that all who oppose Christ will one day repent. In Revelation all people are *called* to repentance and salvation, but their response is left open (15:3–4; 21:3, 24; Bauckham, *Theology*, 103; Boring 226–31).

An unnamed voice interjects—"Yes. Amen!"—giving a dialogical quality to the passage (1:7d; cf. 14:13; 16:7; 22:20). Some interpreters compare it to a liturgy in which the congregation responds to the lector (Vanni, "Liturgical," 349–55), but it is more like worshipers giving assent to a prophetic word (cf. Rev 22:10–20; 1 Cor 14:15–16, 26–31; Biguzzi, "Chaos," 206–8). The voice in the text encourages readers to do the same.

The introduction concludes when the prophetic voice becomes the voice of God, who says: "I am the Alpha and the Omega . . . the one who is and who was and who is to come, the Almighty" (Rev 1:8). Using alpha and omega, the first and last letters of the Greek alphabet, is an innovative way to identify God—and later Jesus—as the beginning and end of all things. Forms of the expression occur in the opening and final chapters of the book, creating a literary frame around the text:

God: I am the Alpha and the Omega (1:8).
Christ: I am the first and the last (1:17).
God: I am the Alpha and the Omega, the beginning and the end (21:6).
Christ: I am the Alpha and the Omega, the first and the last, the beginning and the end (22:13).

The prominence of the expression influenced the interpretation of the book in the early church, since it established a theological center from which to interpret it (INTRO I.A.3). As the Alpha, God is the Creator, the beginning of all things (4:11); as the Omega, he brings all things to completion in the new creation (21:1). His first word is spoken when the book begins (1:8), and his last word signals the fulfillment of his purposes: "All is done" (21:6; Bauckham, *Theology*, 27). Identifying God as the beginning and the end is like calling him the one "who is and who was and who is to come" (1:4); the expression emphasizes God's true deity (NOTE on 1:8). Using the same language for Jesus elsewhere shows that God and Christ must be seen together (COMMENT on 22:13).

First Cycle: Christ and the Seven Assemblies (1:9–3:22)

---

3. General Comments on the First Cycle

Revelation leads readers through six major cycles of visions, which begin in the presence of God or Christ and then depict a series of challenges or threats before returning to the presence of God or Christ again. In this first cycle, John sees a vision of the exalted Christ, who directs him to write to seven congregations about the challenges they face, while warning them of judgment and offering hope. The series ends by picturing Christ standing at a closed door, knocking (3:20–22), which prepares for the next scene, where John is taken through an open door into God's heavenly throne room (4:1–2). The messages to the congregations establish the context in which the rest of Revelation is to be understood. They identify the congregations' issues, ranging from conflict with outsiders to internal disputes over accommodation of Greco-Roman religious practices to attitudes of complacency. The visions of cosmic conflict later in the book address the situations of the readers introduced in these opening chapters.

A. HISTORY OF INTERPRETATION OF REVELATION 1–3

Interpretation of Rev 2–3 has usually focused on how the messages to first-century churches remained relevant to people of later times. Ancient and medieval interpreters looked for moral guidance. They assumed that the number seven symbolized completeness, so when the author addressed seven churches in Asia Minor, his message pertained to the church throughout the world (Muratorian canon; Victorinus; Primasius; Andreas; Bede) and throughout time (Apringius). Cyprian (d. 258) turned Christ's rebuke of the Laodiceans' complacency about wealth into an exhortation to give alms (*Eleem.* 13–14). When Christians faced persecution, he urged them to follow the example of the Smyrneans, who were to be faithful to death (Rev 2:10; *Ep.* 36; *Fort.* 10). But when people lapsed and then sought to be restored to communion with the church, he advocated forgiveness, since Revelation wants those who have sinned to repent (Rev 2:5, 20–22; *Ep.* 55.22).

Many writers saw broader implications for spiritual discipline. The ten days of affliction at Smyrna could signify the temptations people experienced throughout their lifetimes (Primasius on 2:10). Satan's throne at Pergamum could symbolize the whole world, since the devil is active everywhere (Tyconius on 2:13). Christ makes war against false belief with the sword from his mouth, which signifies Scripture (Primasius on 2:16). The lukewarm Laodiceans symbolize those who neglect the grace of baptism (Oecumenius on 3:15–16). The hidden manna is Christ himself, present in the Eucharist (Andreas on 2:17), and people dine with Christ by being nurtured by his word (Rev 3:20; Origen, *Comm. Jo.* 13.199; 32.18). With the growth of monasticism, writers warned against the complacency exhibited at Laodicea and called for spiritual striving (John Cassian, *Conferences* 4.11.2–12.3; 4.17; Caesarius, *Sermons* 235.4; Hildegard in Kovacs and Rowland, *Revelation*, 58; Geoffrey of Auxerre, *On*, 191–212).

Medieval interpreters saw Revelation as a depiction of the church's struggles throughout history. By equating each church with a particular period of time, writers could instruct readers about the kinds of leadership that they thought sustained the church, while warning against the heresies that threatened it. Peter of Tarentaise (d. 1174), a Cistercian abbot and bishop, associated Ephesus with the time of the apostles, Smyrna with the period of martyrs, Pergamum with the period of heretics, and Thyatira with the confessors and doctors of the church. He put Sardis, Philadelphia, and Laodicea nearer to his own time, when exhortations were needed for both the godly and the ungodly (*Apocalypsis*, 504–40). A more elaborate theory was developed by Joachim of Fiore (d. 1202), who thought history had progressed through five periods, from the first apostles to the dawn of the sixth period, signified by the faithful church of Philadelphia, when new orders of "spiritual men" would arise to purify the church. His interpretation gave people incentive to adopt the spiritual practices of the new age that was coming (INTRO I.B.3; Daniel, "Joachim," 80–81).

The militant reformer Fra Dolcino (d. 1307) used a similar form of interpretation in order to legitimize his call for radical social change. He located himself within the unfolding purposes of God. For him, the angels of the seven churches were a series of great church leaders who spanned the centuries. They included St. Benedict, St. Francis, St. Dominic, and others. The angel of Thyatira was Dolcino himself, who heralded a new era. Soon, the angel of Philadelphia would appear as a holy pope, who would lead the church until the Antichrist appeared. Given the resistance of established authorities to reform, however, some radicals thought the suffering symbolized by the church at Philadelphia had already arrived (Potestà, "Radical," 113–21).

Protestant reformers often followed this approach to identify the traits of true and false Christianity throughout history, which helped define their own positions. For Thomas Brightman (d. 1607) the first four churches—Ephesus, Smyrna, Pergamum, and Thyatira—signified eras from apostolic times to the early sixteenth century, and the last three churches characterized his contemporaries: the hypocrites at Sardis were Lutherans, the godly at Philadelphia were Calvinists, and the complacent at Laodicea were Anglicans (Kovacs and Rowland, *Revelation*, 54–55).

Dispensationalist interpreters of the nineteenth and twentieth centuries argued that most of Revelation pertained to the future, but they continued to use the church historical approach when reading Rev 1–3. The practice allowed them to treat these chapters as an accurate prediction of conditions throughout the present age, which gave them assurance that the book's predictions about the future were also accurate (INTRO I.D.2). Ephesus symbolized the apostolic church (30–100 CE); Smyrna was the church persecuted by Rome (100–313); Pergamum was the state church (313–590); heretical Thyatira was the papal church (590–1517); Sardis was the church of the Reformation, since a few remain pure (1517–1790); Philadelphia was the church of revival and mission (1730–1900); and Laodicea was the modern lukewarm church (LaHaye; Scofield). Problems with this approach are that Revelation gives no hint of such symbolism in chapters 2–3, and it is not viable to reduce entire periods of history to single categories, as if the early church were known only for persecution or the modern church only for complacency.

Modern historical critics shifted attention from questions about the future to the context in which Revelation was written and first read (INTRO I.D.3). William Ramsay (d. 1939) theorized that each church reflected the traits of the ancient city in which it was located. Since Christians at Ephesus were warned that Christ would move their lampstand from its place (Rev 2:5), Ramsay identified Ephesus as "the city of change," claiming that its distinctive feature was that it had been moved to a new location during the third century BCE. Since the message to Christians at Smyrna called Christ the one who died and came to life (2:8), Ramsay referred to their location as "the city of life," arguing that Smyrna once "died" when the Lydians destroyed it in the sixth century BCE, but it came to life again as a Greek city in the third century BCE (*Letters*, 210, 251). He made similar claims about the other cities.

Ramsay assumed that the promises and warnings in each message alluded to a city's topography, history, and institutions. Since Ephesian Christians were promised a share in the tree of life, Ramsay saw a contrast with the city's temple of Artemis, which originated as a tree shrine (2:7). Since Smyrnean Christians were promised a crown of life, he maintained that Smyrna itself looked like a crown (2:10; *Letters*, 246–48, 256–59). Following Ramsay's lead, other interpreters claimed that the lukewarm readers at Laodicea were like the city's water supply, which some imagined to be tepid and undrinkable (3:16; Hemer, *Letters*; Court, *Myth*, 20–28; Scobie, "Local"; Rudwick and Green, "Laodicean"; Porter, "Why"; Ford; Osborne).

A problem with this approach is that historical information about a city must be molded to fit the distinctive imagery in Revelation. Yet in almost every instance, the images used for one city would fit other locations equally well. Ephesus was called the city of change because it had been relocated, yet Smyrna too had moved to a new location. Ephesus was supposed to have been uniquely associated with a tree shrine, but Smyrna's refounding was linked to its own tree shrine (NOTE on 2:7). Smyrna was supposed to have died and risen, yet that imagery would have been even more appropriate for Sardis, Philadelphia, and Laodicea, all of which were rebuilt following earthquakes during the early imperial period (cf. Friesen, "Revelation"; Thompson, *Book*, 202–4).

The interpretations given below treat the roles of the cities differently. First, information about each city is summarized at the beginning of each message (NOTES on 2:1, 8, 12, 18; 3:1, 7, 14). This material draws on collections of inscriptions that have been published in recent years along with studies of life in Roman Asia. All the summaries use the same categories so that readers can see how the institutions and social fabric of each city resembled those in other cities. What differed was not the character of the cities, but the way the congregations responded to their social contexts. Second, critiques of proposals concerning local allusions are given in the NOTES. Third, the COMMENT sections note how the images in the messages draw on practices that were *common* in antiquity and therefore would have been widely understood.

B. LITERARY CHARACTERISTICS
OF THE SEVEN MESSAGES

The messages to the seven congregations fuse elements of prophetic and royal speech to convey majesty and authority. First, the *prophetic tradition* is reflected in the opening formula "Thus says" (*tade legei*), which resembles "Thus says the Lord." This formula occurs frequently in the LXX, especially in prophetic writings, and it was used by early Christian prophets (e.g., Isa 3:16; Jer 2:2; Amos 2:1; Acts 21:11; cf. Diodorus Siculus, *Libr.* 40.3.6; Lucian, *Sat.* 10.1). The biblical prophets warn of divine judgment, exhort listeners to repent, and give hope for deliverance, depending on the situation, and the messages in Rev 2–3 include similar emphases (Aune, *Prophecy*, 90, 330–31; U. Müller, *Prophetie*, 57–104). John puts Christ's messages in written form, which was also done by some of the prophets in Israel's tradition. The OT includes letters from Elijah and Jeremiah that begin "Thus says" and incorporate warnings, exhortations, and promises (2 Chr 21:12–15; Jer 29:4–23, 24–28, 30–32). Moreover, some biblical prophets use "Hear the word of the Lord" to capture the listeners' attention, usually at the beginning of an oracle (e.g., Isa 1:10; 7:13; Jer 2:4; 5:21; Hos 4:1; 5:1). Revelation varies this pattern by calling for attention at the conclusion of each message: "Let the one who has an ear hear" (Karrer, *Johannesoffenbarung*, 49–59; Aune 1:124–26).

Second, the messages resemble *royal decrees*, underscoring the sovereignty of Christ. In the LXX the formula "Thus says" was used by kings as well as prophets. In some situations the king speaks directly to someone, and in other contexts he sends word through a messenger. The LXX includes such sayings by the kings of Israel (1 Kgs 2:30; 2 Kgs 1:11; 9:18; 19:3; Isa 37:3), Egypt (Exod 5:10), Moab (Num 22:16), Syria (1 Kgs 20:3, 5), and Assyria (2 Kgs 18:19; Isa 36:4; Jdt 2:5). Royal decrees of the Persian kings also used the formula "Thus says" (2 Chr 36:23; Josephus, *Ant.* 11.26; Ign. *Magn.* 115; Ps.-Hippocrates, *Epistolae* 8). Similarly, a decree of a Roman emperor could declare, "Tiberius Claudius Caesar Augustus Germanicus of tribunician power says" (Josephus, *Ant.* 19.280; cf. 19.286; Appian, *Bell. civ.* 4.2.8). By way of contrast, the Christ who speaks in Revelation is "ruler of the kings of the earth" (Rev 1:5).

Ancient letter-writing patterns also shaped the seven messages. The body resembles what Greco-Roman theorists called a "mixed letter." Such a letter might begin with approval: "I know [*oida*] that you live a life of piety, that you conduct yourself as a citizen in a manner worthy of respect." Then it could turn to reproof: "But in this one thing alone do you err, that you slander your friends." Finally, it could admonish: "You must avoid that, for it is not fitting that philosophers engage in slander" (Ps.-Libanius §92; Malherbe, "Ancient," 76–77). Revelation uses a similar pattern, for Christ says, "I know [*oida*]," which is followed by approval, reproof, and admonition.

At the same time, Revelation freely departs from typical epistolary patterns. Instead of a salutation that gives the names of the sender and recipients and then extends a greeting (e.g., 1 Cor 1:1–3; 1 Thess 1:1), the messages first indicate the recipients, then give the command to write "Thus says," and only then identify the speaker. No greeting is given. The conclusion of the messages is also distinctive. Unlike Christian letters, which close with "grace" or "peace," or Greco-Roman letters, which end with "farewell" (NOTE on Rev 22:21), the messages summon people to "hear what the Spirit says to the assemblies." When John addresses his readers in his own name in 1:4–6, he generally follows the accepted epistolary styles of his day, but when the exalted Christ addresses them in 2:1–3:22, John creates new forms. This freedom accents the sense of sovereignty that the exalted Christ conveys through the words that he speaks (Aune 1:119–32; Aune, *Apocalypticism*, 212–32; Karrer, *Johannesoffenbarung*, 159–60; Murphy 103–5; Hahn, "Sendschreiben").

The seven messages share a similar structure:

Introduction: Address from the exalted Christ.
Body of the Message: Encouragement and reproof.
Conclusion: Promise to the conqueror and exhortation to listen.

Introduction

All seven messages begin with, "To the angel of the assembly in [name of the city] write, Thus says ____." Each introductory statement mentions "the angel," who is the assembly's heavenly representative (NOTE on 1:20). Addressing the angel is peculiar because each message is intended for the congregation (1:11). Moreover, since the congregation is the primary audience, the messages sometimes slip from the singular address to the angel into plural forms. For example, "The devil is going to throw some of you [plural] into prison so that you [plural] will be tested" (2:10). Nevertheless, writing to an angel rather than directly to the congregation allows readers to picture themselves maintaining a respectful distance from the overwhelming majesty of Christ while an intermediary receives the message they are to hear.

The introduction to each message includes Christ's command that John should "write." On the one hand, John, who introduced himself in 1:9–11, now fades from view. What the congregations are said to receive in Rev 2–3 is not John's assessment of their condition, but the perspective of Christ, which John communicates. On the other hand, John's obedience to the command enables him to serve as a model to be emulated. The fact that readers receive Christ's words in written form implies that John has faithfully carried out Christ's orders.

The messages in Rev 2–3 introduce Christ by recalling traits mentioned in Rev 1. His name is not given, which is unusual. Letters typically named the sender. Prophetic messages often began, "Thus says *the Lord*." Royal decrees regularly gave both the name and title of the ruler: for example, "Tiberius Claudius Caesar Augustus Germanicus Pontifex Maximus, of tribunician power, elected consul for the second time says . . ." (Josephus, *Ant.* 19.286). But Revelation never gives the name of Jesus in the messages to the churches. Readers are to know that the figure addressing them is Jesus Christ, who is named earlier (Rev 1:2, 5). Refraining from stating Jesus' name in the seven messages means that the traits listed in the opening lines function as circumlocutions that maintain a respectful distance rather than inviting undue familiarity with the majestic figure who addresses them.

The traits that introduce each message usually recall John's description of the Son of Man in 1:12–20. The references to the lampstands and stars, the first and last, the one who died and came to life, the two-edged sword, the eyes like flame and feet like bronze are all taken from the opening vision. The author varies the pattern by referring to the seven spirits and to "the Amen, the faithful and true witness, the ruler of God's creation," all of which recall the epistolary introduction (1:4–5; 3:1, 14). He also alters some images: Christ is called Son of God rather than Son of Man (1:13; 2:18), and he holds not only the keys of Death and Hades, but the key of David (1:18; 3:7). The result is interplay between constancy and development. Christ is revealed in the opening vision, but not fully revealed; there is incentive to continue reading, since more will be disclosed.

Body of the Message

The central parts of the seven messages vary in content but share several formal elements. First is the expression "I know," followed by a description of the congregation's works or situation. Such statements are to some extent conventional, since in ancient letters someone might say "I know" when extending praise or blame (1 Thess 1:4; Phlm 5; Col 1:4; Ign. *Magn.* 1:1; Ign. *Trall.* 1:1; cf. *2 Bar.* 78:4; Isocrates, *Ep.* 1.2; 2.1). Royal decrees could also indicate what the king knew before stating his will concerning a given situation. In a Persian decree, Darius begins, "I have learned that you did not obey" (Ign. *Magn.* 115). In an imperial decree, Tiberius says, "Since I have known from the beginning" (Josephus, *Ant.* 19.281; cf. Aune 1:129, 142). In Revelation the one saying "I know" is the exalted Christ, who like God searches human minds and hearts (Rev 2:23; 5:12; cf. Exod 3:7; 1 Sam 16:7; Hos 5:3; Amos 5:12). Where others see poverty, Christ discerns wealth, and where they see life, he knows there is death (Rev 2:9; 3:1, 17; Boring 89; Karrer, *Johannesoffenbarung*, 161–63).

Second, the seven messages develop an interplay between encouragement and rebuke that is suitable for each congregation. The messages to Ephesus, Pergamum, and Thyatira include both praise and blame: The readers are commended for their faithfulness and endurance and are rebuked for their lack of love or for tolerating false teaching (2:1–6, 13–16, 19–25). The situation is different in Smyrna and Philadelphia, where the readers are being denounced by opponents. Therefore, the messages include no additional reproofs but encourage readers to persevere (2:9–10; 3:8–11). Finally, the churches in Sardis and Laodicea are already receiving approval from others, so the messages to these Christians are mainly confrontational. Encouragement is not absent, however, since the faithful few at Sardis are commended, and the Laodiceans are reminded that Christ's reproofs in fact express his love for them (3:1b–4, 15–20). It was understood that using only rebuke could alienate listeners, whereas giving only approval without honest criticism could make them complacent (Dio Chrysostom, *Disc.* 77/78.38; Plutarch, *Mor.* 74D–E). The goal of each message is to evoke enduring faithfulness, and the interplay between encouragement and rebuke is designed to achieve this end.

Third, the messages often include a call to repentance accompanied by a threat or promise. The assembly at Ephesus is to repent of its lack of love, those at Pergamum and Thyatira are to repent of their acceptance of false teaching, and those at Sardis and Laodicea are to repent of their complacency (Rev 2:5, 16, 21–22; 3:3, 19). The conditional threats and promises indicate what action Christ will take if repentance does or does not occur. When the threats refer to Christ coming, they point to a provisional coming within time rather than to his final coming at the end of time. The threats are contingent: If the readers do not repent, Christ will come to remove their lampstand, make war against false teachers, or surprise them like a thief (2:5, 16; 3:3; cf. 2:23). If they do repent, Christ will not come in this way. Similarly, if the complacent open the door, Christ will come and eat with them; the implication is that if they do not repent, he will not come to share their meal (3:19–20). These provisional comings of Christ may anticipate the types of judgments and blessings that will be fully given at the end of time, but in themselves they encourage faithfulness in the present situations of the readers.

Conclusion

The conclusion of each message includes a promise to the one who conquers and an exhortation to listen. First, the promise reads, "To the one who conquers," followed by an indication of the kind of gift that will be given. What conquering means is not explained until chapter 5, where readers learn that Christ, the Lion of Judah, conquered as a Lamb whose self-sacrifice brings people into God's kingdom (5:5–10). Christ's followers are to conquer in a similar way through faithful self-sacrifice (12:11).

Promises to the one who conquers look to the final blessings that will be given at the end of the age. Some of the promises are explicitly developed later in the book. These include eating from the tree of life (2:7; 22:2, 14), not being hurt by the second death (2:11; 20:6, 14–15; 21:8), receiving power to rule and the morning star (2:26–28; 22:5, 16), being clad in white garments and having one's name in the scroll of life (3:5; 7:9–14; 20:15; 21:27), and bearing the name of the New Jerusalem (3:12; 21:2). Showing the visionary fulfillment in the later chapters of Revelation underscores the reliability of the words being spoken here.

Some of the promises, however, are not developed in subsequent visions. Readers are not shown visions of the faithful receiving the hidden manna or the stone with the new name (2:17), and there is no scene in which Christ confesses the names of the faithful before God and the angels (3:5). In some cases the promises are fulfilled in surprising ways. The faithful are told that they will rule the nations with an iron rod, yet in New Jerusalem the nations need no iron rod, for they willingly bring their glory to the city (2:26–27; 21:24, 26). The faithful are also told that they will become pillars in the temple of God (3:12), yet in the end the only temple in New Jerusalem is God and the Lamb, and it is in their presence that the redeemed worship (3:12; 21:22). The Apocalypse assures readers that the promises will be fulfilled yet leaves open the manner in which they will be fulfilled. Complete disclosure does not come within the pages of John's book, implying that the only way for readers to know the outcome of God's purposes fully is to persevere to the end.

Second, the conclusion includes the exhortation "Let the one who has an ear hear what the Spirit says to the assemblies." In the first three messages the exhortation appears before the promises to the conqueror, and in the last four it appears after the promises. This expression is reminiscent of prophetic exhortations to "hear the word of the Lord," and it also resembles sayings ascribed to the earthly Jesus (NOTE on 2:7). Both the promises to the one who conquers and the exhortation to hear are in the singular. Even though the messages address the whole Christian community, each individual is called to respond.

The introduction to each message says that the words come from the exalted Christ, but in the conclusion to each message it is the Spirit that speaks. Just as John is enabled to receive the words of Christ while in the Spirit, it will be the Spirit that conveys the message to the readers so that they too can receive it (NOTES on 1:10; 2:7, 11, etc.). Moreover, the messages begin by identifying the particular congregation being addressed, but they conclude by speaking to the assemblies. Each message takes up the specific challenges facing a given congregation, yet the words of reproof, encouragement, promise, and warning have implications for all readers (Enroth, "Hearing").

4. Christ Commissions John to Write (1:9–20)

1   [9]"I John, your brother and companion in the affliction and the kingdom and the endurance that we have in Jesus, was on the island called Patmos because of the word of God and the witness of Jesus. [10]I was in the Spirit on the Lord's Day, and I heard behind me a loud voice that sounded like a trumpet, [11]saying, "Write what you see in a scroll and send it to the seven assemblies: to Ephesus, to Smyrna, to Pergamum, to Thyatira, to Sardis, to Philadelphia, and to Laodicea."

[12]So I turned toward the voice, to see who was speaking with me, and when I turned I saw seven gold lampstands. [13]In the middle of the lampstands was someone who looked like a human being. He wore a robe that stretched down to his feet and had a gold sash wrapped around his chest. [14]His head and hair were white as white wool—like snow—and his eyes were like a flame of fire. [15]His feet were like shining bronze, refined as in a furnace, and his voice was like the sound of rushing water. [16]He held seven stars in his right hand, and from his mouth came a sharp two-edged sword. His face was like the sun shining with all its power.

[17]When I saw him, I fell at his feet as if I were dead, but he put his right hand on me and said, "Do not be afraid. I am the first and the last, [18]and the living one. I was dead, but see, I live forever and ever. I have the keys to Death and Hades. [19]So write what you have seen, which includes things as they are now as well as things to come. [20]As for the mystery of the seven stars that you saw on my right hand and the seven gold lampstands: the seven stars are the seven angels of the seven assemblies and the seven lampstands are the seven assemblies."

NOTES

1:9. *I John, your brother.* The first-person "I" plus the writer's name is a narrative feature in apocalypses (Dan 8:15; 9:2; 10:2; *1 En.* 12:3; *2 Bar.* 8:3; 13:1; *4 Ezra* 3:1). The difference here is that "John" is almost certainly the author's real name, not a pseudonym. The term "brother" affirmed social bonds among the people of Israel (Exod 2:11; Deut 18:15; 1 Macc 5:32), friends (2 Sam 1:26; Ps 35:14; Juvenal, *Satirae* 5.135), and members of a religious group (MM 8–9; Harland, "Familial"). The terms "brother" and "sister" were used for everyone in the Christian community (Rev 6:11; 12:10; 19:10; 1

Cor 8:11, 13; Phlm 16; Jas 2:15; 1 Pet 5:12; 1 John 2:9). "Brother" was also used for a subgroup of Christian prophets (Rev 22:9).

and companion in the affliction. John affirms that being a companion (*synkoinonos*) in faith involves both present affliction and a share in Christ's kingdom (next NOTE). The opposite is companionship (*synkoinein*) in the sins of Babylon, which entails sharing in the plagues that fall on it (Rev 18:4). Affliction (*thlipsis*) can mean poverty, imprisonment, and ostracism for the faith (2:9–10; cf. Matt 24:9; Acts 20:23; 2 Cor 6:4–5; Phil 1:29; 1 Pet 3:14–17).

and the kingdom and the endurance that we have in Jesus. The redeemed already constitute a "kingdom," since they acknowledge the lordship of God and Christ, and they will share in the blessings of divine rule as evil and death are overcome (NOTE on Rev 1:6). Yet given the present conflict between God and evil, "endurance" (*hymomonē*) is the shape that acknowledging God's lordship takes. "Endurance" is bearing hardship for the sake of a goal, not merely putting up with things to avoid conflict (4 Macc 7:9; 9:8; 17:23; Rom 5:3–4; Jas 1:3). Jesus both calls for and exemplifies endurance by his faithfulness to God in the face of opposition (Rev 1:5; 3:10, 14; cf. Heb 12:1–2; Ign. *Rom.* 10:3; Ign. *Pol.* 3:2). As athletes and soldiers endure for the sake of victory, Jesus' followers share in his victory over evil by showing "endurance" in faith and truth over against evil and untruth (Rev 2:7, 11, 17; 12:10–11; cf. 4 Macc 1:11; 9:30).

was on the island. The aorist tense "was" (*egenomēn*) could mean that John formerly received his visions on Patmos but was no longer there when he wrote them down (Victorinus, *In Apocalypsin* 10.3; Aune; Horn, "Johannes"). This interpretation fits the tradition that John was banished to Patmos but later released (Clement of Alexandria, *Quis div.* 42; Eusebius, *Hist. eccl.* 3.23.1, 6). Yet the verb tense could simply recall that he received his visions in the past and was still on the island when he wrote them (Jerome, *Vir. ill.* 9; Giesen). The situation is not clear.

called Patmos. Patmos is an island in the Aegean Sea about forty miles southwest of Miletus (Strabo, *Geographica* 10.5.13; Pliny the Elder, *Nat.* 4.12.69). It is seven and a half miles in length. At its northern end the island is five miles wide, while the isthmus at its center is only 400 yards wide. Formed from volcanic hills, its terrain consists of rocky slopes, meadows that could be grazed, and fields suitable for agriculture. Its main harbor is west of the central isthmus, and there are smaller bays along its sharply indented coastline.

The island was located near the juncture of two shipping routes that crossed the Aegean from east to west. Ships traveling from Asian cities like Miletus and Ephesus would sail southwest to Patmos and then west to the island of Delos and the ports near Corinth and Athens (Thycidides, *Pelop.* 3.33.1–3). On the other route, ships from the eastern Mediterranean would travel northwest from island to island: Rhodes to Cos, then to Kalymnos, Leros, and Patmos. At Patmos they turned west to the island of Delos and then toward the ports near Corinth and Athens. The mariners' handbook *Stadiasmus sive periplus Maris Magni* (§§280 and 283) used the monument to the Amazons on Patmos as a landmark when tracing these routes (Cicero, *Att.* 5.11.4; 5.12.6; Acts 18:18–19). Catering to the needs of mariners would have been one source of income for the residents of Patmos. Some, like those of neighboring islands (I.Leros 2.10–12), probably engaged in seaborne trade.

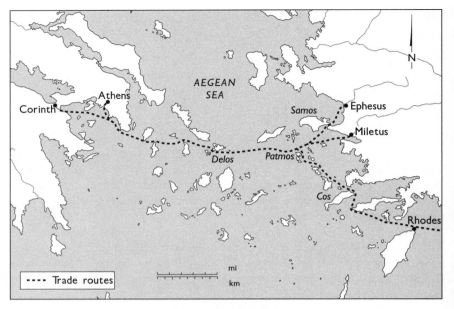

Map 2. Aegean Sea Routes near Patmos (Map by Bill Nelson)

Patmos and the nearby islands of Lepsia and Leros belonged to Miletus during the Hellenistic period. Citizens of Miletus formed garrisons on these islands to protect the shipping lanes from piracy. In the third or second century BCE a fort was built on the hill west of Patmos's harbor, providing a place of refuge in case of attack. Later, Patmos was incorporated into the Roman province of Asia. Garrison commanders were sent to the islands until the mid-first century BCE (Manganaro, "Le iscrizioni," 295, 299), but under Roman rule piracy decreased.

Socially, the dominant pattern of life on the island was the family. A Roman-era tombstone from Patmos shows a typical family scene from this period (Figure 1). Although interpreters sometimes assume that Patmos was a penal colony (next Note), the image of a family corresponds well to what is actually known about the island's population during this period. Funerary inscriptions from the first century BCE to the third century CE show that those who lived on Patmos included men, women, and children (I.Pat 36–43).

Families had a central place in village life, though alongside them were other civic and religious associations. During the Hellenistic period, the island had an athletic society, whose patron was honored for his devotion to family and community as well as his support of the local gymnasium (I.Pat 32). This patron provided the gymnasium with oil for athletes, sponsored an annual festival, and purchased a statue of Hermes. He managed the funds of the athletic society and furnished money to be lent out. Association members honored him with a gold wreath.

Religious life on Patmos centered on the goddess Artemis. An inscription from the second or third century CE suggests that the local Artemis cult had its origin in the legend of Orestes, who was sent to Scythia near the Black Sea to bring a statue of

Artemis back to Greece. Various sites claimed to have the legendary statue, and Patmos may have been one of these (I.Pat 34; Saffrey, "Relire," 399–410). A dream inspired one worshiper to set up a small marble altar to Artemis on Patmos (I.Pat 35). The island also had a monument to the Amazons. Such monuments were often built where local legends said these mythic female warriors were buried. Rites honoring them included sacrifice and dancing (*Stadiasmus sive periplus Maris Magni* 283; cf. Callimachus, *Hymn. Dian.* 237–50; Plutarch, *Thes.* 27.5–6). The Amazons were sometimes linked to the cult of Artemis (Pausanius, *Descr.* 4.31.8; 7.2.7–8; Tacitus, *Ann.* 3.61). In the second or third century CE a physician's daughter named Vera was the priestess of Artemis. She had been born on the island and later returned to celebrate the Artemis festival, paying the cost out of her family's resources (I.Pat 34).

During Hellenistic times at least part of the island was dedicated to Apollo, the brother of Artemis (I.Pat 33). Apollo had a major cult center on the mainland at Didyma, near Miletus (Parke, *Oracles*, 44–92; Aune, *Prophecy*, 24–30). Although the

Figure 1. Patmos: Grave stele showing family scene. Third century CE. © Fitzwilliam Museum, Cambridge.

apocryphal *Acts of John* ascribed to Prochorus mentions a temple of Apollo on Patmos (§§80–87), the work dates from perhaps the fifth century CE and shows no familiarity with the island's topography. Even without a temple, however, there may have been public rites honoring Apollo, since his cult was common in the region (Manganaro, "Le iscrizioni," 320). The athletic association also held an annual festival to Hermes, which included sacrifices and a torch race in which runners carried fire to an altar (I.Pat 32). Such races were also held in Didyma, Athens, and other cities on the mainland (Rehm, *Didyma*, 2:147–49; Pausanias, *Descr.* 1.30.2; Austin, *Hellenistic*, 205). The head of the gymnasium served as a priest of Hermes (I.Pat 32).

If the imperial cult had a place on Patmos, it was probably linked to the traditional gods. One inscription shows that a woman apparently served as a priestess in the imperial cult in Miletus as well as in the cult of Artemis on Patmos (I.Did 315). Although the inscription is rather late (third century CE), it reflects a practice that was common long before in mainland cities. Miletus was historically tied to Patmos, and by the mid-first century CE the worship of Roman emperors seems to have been linked to Artemis and Apollo in that city (Friesen, *Imperial*, 68–72). At some point the connection between Artemis and the emperor was apparently made on Patmos as well.

because of the word of God and the witness of Jesus. Roman authorities in Asia probably relegated John to Patmos as a punitive action. Revelation uses the expression "because of the word of God and the witness of Jesus" for those who suffer for the faith (Rev 1:9; cf. 6:9; 20:4). In 1:9 John refers to his "affliction," a term used for Christians who faced denunciation, imprisonment, and possible death (2:9–10). The specific punishment was probably "relegation to an island" (*relegatio ad insulum*). Under this sentence deportation was usually temporary and did not entail the loss of Roman citizenship or property, though in some cases it was permanent and involved a loss of property (Pliny the Younger, *Ep.* 10.56.3–4). The person could not leave the island but could associate with people there and could receive support from family and friends (Philostratus, *Vit. Apoll.* 7.16.2; Philo, *Flacc.* 166). A more severe punishment was "deportation to an island" (*deportatio ad insulum*), which was permanent and entailed the loss of property. Those sent to an island could engage in local commerce to support themselves (Justinian, *Dig.* 48.22.15).

The sentence of relegation could be given by the provincial proconsul if an island was in his jurisdiction (Justinian, *Dig.* 48.22.7.1). Patmos belonged to the province of Asia through its link to Miletus. Deportation had to be imposed by the emperor (Aune; Giesen; Yarbro Collins, *Crisis*, 102–3), but accounts of Roman action against Christians from the first through the third centuries commonly mention judgment by the provincial proconsul rather than the emperor (Pliny the Younger, *Ep.* 10.96–97; *Mart. Pol.* 3:2; 4:1; 9:2–12:1; Eusebius, *Hist. eccl.* 4.8.6–4.9.3; Musurillo, *Acts of the Christian*, 23, 87, 91). So it is likely that John was relegated by the provincial authorities rather than deported. In comparison to known places of banishment, Patmos was not as harsh as Gyaros (Plutarch, *Mor.* 602C) or as attractive as Rhodes or Samos (Dio Cassius, *Rom. Hist.* 56.27.2; see Saffrey, "Relire," 383; Balsdon, *Romans*, 114–15). Although some interpreters assume that Patmos was a penal colony (Charles; Ford; Kraft), there is no basis for this conclusion. John is the only person known to have been sent there. Relegation did not necessarily mean joining a group of prisoners. It was sometimes thought that John would have had to toil in the mines (Victorinus) or at hard labor

(Ramsay, *Letters*, 85–86; Ford); but Patmos has no mines, and relegation to an island regularly meant that a person was *not* sentenced to labor in the mines. Condemnation to the mines was a separate sentence (Justinian, *Dig.* 47.11.7; 48.13.7; 48.19.28.1, 10).

The reason John was sent to an island—instead of being killed as Antipas was (Rev 2:13)—was probably due to the way authorities construed his offense. In the late first century, Roman officials lacked standard policies concerning Christians. Individual cases were treated differently depending on the perspective of the official reviewing the case (Pliny the Younger, *Ep.* 10.96.1–4). A person deemed guilty of a particular offense might be sentenced to death by one judge but relegated to an island by another (Pliny the Younger, *Ep.* 8.14.12–15). What John referred to as "the word of God and witness of Jesus" would have been considered superstition by many Romans (Pliny the Younger, *Ep.* 10.96.8–9; Tacitus, *Ann.* 15.44; Suetonius, *Nero* 16.2). "Superstition" was the label given to religious practices that were deemed suspect. Those promoting superstition were to be relegated to an island (Justinian, *Dig.* 48.19.30), along with prophets, astrologers, and those practicing divination (Juvenal, *Satirae* 6.553–64). Although Antipas was killed because of his witness to Christ (Rev 2:13), John received the more lenient sentence of relegation. It could have been that he was of a higher social class (Aune), but it is more likely that his prophesying was judged to be pernicious superstition (Yarbro Collins, *Crisis*, 102).

Early Christian tradition elaborated reasons for John being on Patmos. Irenaeus said that John received his visions during Domitian's reign but said nothing about banishment (*Haer.* 5.30.3). Clement of Alexandria thought John remained on Patmos until an unnamed tyrant died (*Quis div.* 42). Tertullian thought John was banished after he survived being boiled in oil (*Praesc.* 36). Origen said that John was sent to Patmos by the emperor himself (*Comm. Matt.* 16.6), and others concluded that Domitian must have imposed the sentence (Eusebius, *Hist. eccl.* 3.20.8; Victorinus; Jerome, *Vir. ill.* 9). More recent interpreters suggest that John went to Patmos to seek God's word in a vision (Kraft), to spread the word by preaching (Harrington; Thompson, *Book*, 173), or to escape from difficulty on the mainland (Horn, "Johannes," 153). The most viable interpretation is that he was relegated to Patmos by the provincial authorities.

1:10. *I was in the Spirit.* The expression *en pneumati* has two dimensions. First, John has experiences "in spirit" as opposed to physically. He is taken to heaven in a vision, not bodily (Rev 4:2; 17:3; 21:10). Some interpreters call this a "trance" (Aune; Roloff). Second, John was "in the Spirit," that is, his spiritual state was brought about through God's Spirit (cf. Ezek 11:24; Mic 3:8; Zech 7:12). The language echoes Ezek 3:12, where God's Spirit moves the prophet (cf. Ezek 8:3; 37:1; 43:5). As God's Spirit brings the word of the risen Jesus to John, the Spirit speaks through him (Rev 2:7, 11; 19:10; Luke 2:27; Bauckham, *Climax*, 151; Giesen).

on the Lord's Day. This expression was used for Sunday (Ign. *Magn.* 9:1; Ign. *Did.* 14:1), the day of the week when Christians often gathered (1 Cor 16:2; Acts 20:7; Justin Martyr, *1 Apol.* 67) because it was the day that "the Lord" Jesus rose from the dead (*Gos. Pet.* 9:35; 12:50). The weekly Lord's Day was not the eschatological "Day of the Lord" (1 Thess 5:2; NOTE on Rev 6:17; Bauckham, "Lord's"). The adjective "Lord's" (*kyriakos*) was often used for what belonged to the emperor (Deissmann, *Bible*, 217–18; MM 364), but in Revelation the expression "Lord's Day" centers worship on God and Christ—who are called "Lord" (Rev 4:8; 19:16)—rather than on the ruler cult (13:1–18).

and I heard behind me a loud voice that sounded like a trumpet. John's language resembles that of Ezek 3:12, literally, "Then the Spirit lifted me up, and I heard behind me the voice of a great earthquake." The difference is that John likens the voice to a trumpet, as at God's appearance at Sinai (Exod 19:16; 20:18; Heb 12:19; cf. 2 Sam 6:15; Ps 47:5; Joel 2:1; Zech 9:14; NOTE on Rev 8:2). The sound calls John to attention before the risen Christ.

1:11. *saying, "Write what you see in a scroll."* First, writing something down makes it accessible for readers living some distance away (Herm. *Vis.* 2.1.3; 2.4.1–4). To emphasize the need for communication, the command to "write" is repeated when addressing each church (Rev 2:1, 8, 12, etc.). Second, writing makes something definite. Writing down a promise emphasizes that it will be kept (14:13; 19:9; 21:5). Third, writing preserves a message for the future (Deut 31:19, 21; Isa 30:8; Jer 30:2–3; cf. Exod 17:14; *4 Ezra* 14:22–26). John's text, however, was of immediate relevance for the readers (Rev 22:10).

"and send it to the seven assemblies: to Ephesus, to Smyrna, to Pergamum, to Thyatira, to Sardis, to Philadelphia, and to Laodicea." The scroll would have been sent through an envoy, perhaps from John's prophetic circle (22:16). Seven cities are named, though there were also churches at Colossae (Col 1:2), Hierapolis (4:13), Troas (Acts 20:6–12), and perhaps Tralles and Magnesia (Ign. *Trall.;* Ign. *Magn.*; see Map 1). Why these seven were chosen is disputed and different proposals have been made. One is that the churches symbolize the whole church. Revelation's visions are structured in groups of seven, which suggests completeness. The message to each church addresses the churches collectively (Rev 2:7, 11, 17, etc.). Therefore, by speaking to this group of churches, the book addresses the whole church (Victorinus; Muratorian canon; Andreas; Beale). This interpretation does not explain why these particular churches were selected, however.

Another proposal is that the particular churches were chosen for practical reasons. Theses churches could have been the ones that John knew best (Giesen; Smalley), that had special need of correction (Prigent; Roloff), or that would have been most receptive to the message (Oecumenius; Müller). Geographically, the sequence of cities outlines a semicircular route by which a messenger could carry the book. It begins with Ephesus, which of the seven cities was closest to Patmos; then the route moves north as far as Pergamum and finally southeast to end at Laodicea. Some interpreters suggest that each church was expected to share the message with other churches in its immediate area (Hemer, *Letters,* 14–15; Murphy; Osborne). The idea that the seven cities were postal centers (Ramsay, *Letters,* 185–96) is pure conjecture, however (Friesen, "Revelation").

The most plausible view is that seven churches are addressed because seven is a literary device used to structure major sections of the book. John almost certainly knew these particular churches, and whether he had personal ties to other congregations is unclear. Since the book is unsealed (22:10) and to be read in multiple congregations, John might have expected it to circulate more broadly. It is not necessary, however, to take the number seven itself as a symbol of the whole church.

1:12. *So I turned toward the voice, to see who was speaking with me.* The Greek is literally: "I turned to see the voice," which is peculiar, though Exod 20:18 says that at Sinai "all the people saw the voice" (cf. Deut 4:12; Dan 7:11 LXX). This expression could suggest that the divine voice was so powerful as to seem visible (Philo, *Mos.* 2.213;

Philo, *Decal.* 46–47; cf. Philo, *Migr.* 47–48; cf. Josephus, *Ant.* 1.185; 2.267–69). Some interpreters suggest that it is the voice of the Spirit (Gieschen, *Angelomorphic*, 266–29), but John more likely uses synecdoche; that is, the voice represents the speaker, who is Christ (Yarbro Collins, *Cosmology*, 178).

and when I turned I saw seven gold lampstands. The tabernacle pictured in the Pentateuch had a single gold lampstand with seven branches, each holding a lamp (Exod 25:31–40). Solomon's temple had ten lampstands (1 Kgs 7:49), but the second temple had only one (1 Macc 1:21; 4:49–50; Josephus, *J. W.* 5.217). This lampstand appears on Titus's arch, which commemorates the Roman victory in Jerusalem in 70 CE. Revelation transforms the single lampstand with seven branches into seven lampstands, which represent the seven churches (Rev 1:20). As the sanctuary's lampstand was "before the Lord" (Exod 27:20–21; Lev 24:2–4), the congregations are in the presence of Christ. A lampstand with seven lamps is also pictured in Zech 4:2, a passage Revelation uses to portray the church's vocation as a witness (Rev 11:4; cf. Matt 5:15; Phil 2:15).

1:13. *In the middle of the lampstands was someone who looked like a human being.* Here, as in 1:7, the language recalls Dan 7:13, which spoke of "one like a human being" coming to receive dominion over all peoples. The words *huios anthrōpou* can be translated "Son of Man," an expression for a messianic figure in some texts (*1 En.* 46:3; 48:2; 69:27–29; 70:1; 71:14, 17; cf. *4 Ezra* 13:3). But the expression more commonly meant "human being" (e.g., Ezek 2:1, 3, 6; Ps 144:3). In sayings of Jesus, "Son of Man" could simply mean "I" (Matt 8:20), though in several contexts the Son of Man is the heavenly figure (NOTE on Rev 1:7). Paul does not call Jesus "Son of Man," but John's gospel uses the expression for Jesus' messianic (John 12:34) and divine (1:51; 3:14) status. Revelation does not use Son of Man as a title but refers to someone who was "like" (*homoios*) a son of man or human being (Rev 1:13; 14:14). At the same time, Revelation understands Jesus to be the heavenly figure who comes on the clouds, as in Dan 7:13–14 (Rev 1:12–16; 14:14–16; Slater, *Christ*, 66–85; K. Huber, *Einer*, 123–45).

Revelation gives the "the one like a human being" of Dan 7:13 the traits of God, the ancient one with hair like wool in Dan 7:9. Some interpreters suggest that this fusion reflects a reading found in some versions of Dan 7:13 LXX. The best manuscripts picture two figures and say that the one like a human being came "to" (*heōs*) the ancient of days. But others picture only one figure, who "came like [*hōs*] a human being and was present like [*hōs*] one ancient of days" (Yarbro Collins, *Cosmology*, 179–82; Stuckenbruck, *Angel*, 213–18). While such a reading could have been a factor, the manuscript evidence is slight, and Revelation typically draws on a text of Daniel that is closer to Theodotian than to the LXX. Revelation's readiness to ascribe divine traits to Jesus is broadly based in the author's theology (NOTE on Rev 1:17).

He wore a robe that stretched down to his feet and had a gold sash wrapped around his chest. Long robes were worn by people of high social status, and shorter garments were worn by workers. Laborers wore belts around their waists so they could gird up their robes for work, whereas dignitaries wore sashes around their chests, as the figure does here (Resseguie). Some interpreters consider this priestly garb (*T. Levi* 8:2; Victorinus; Primasius; Beale; Kraft; Slater, *Christ*, 97–98). Israel's high priest wore a robe extending to his feet (Exod 28:4; Zech 3:4; Sir 45:8; Plutarch, *Mor.* 672A) and a sash of gold mixed with blue, purple, scarlet, and linen fabric around his chest (Exod 28:4–5; Josephus, *Ant.* 3.153, 159). Christ's attire does resemble that of the angels in the heavenly temple (Rev 1:13; 15:6). Yet others point out that the title "priest" is not given to Christ but to his followers (1:6; 5:10); that Christ does not lead others in worship of God but is worshiped along with God (5:11–14); and that he does not minister in the heavenly sanctuary as the angels do (8:3–5; 15:5–8). More importantly, such attire was worn by heavenly figures that did not have priestly roles (Dan 10:5; Ezek 9:2–3; *Apoc. Zeph.* 6:12; cf. Aune; Giesen; Murphy; Roloff). Here it has more to do with majesty than with priesthood.

1:14. *His head and hair were white as white wool—like snow—and his eyes were like a flame of fire.* The white hair is like that of the "ancient of days," who is God (Dan 7:9; *1 En.* 46:1; 71:10), though white hair also characterized angels (*1 En.* 106:2–6; *Apoc. Ab.* 11:2). White connotes purity (Rev 3:4; 19:14), honor (3:18; 4:4), and victory (3:5; 6:2; 7:9; 19:11). Eyes emitting flames or rays indicated divine power (19:12; Apollodorus, *Library* 2.4.9; Suetonius, *Aug.* 79.2) or angelic status (Dan 10:6; *1 En.* 106:5–6).

1:15. *His feet were like shining bronze, refined as in a furnace.* The feet are described by the rare word *chalkolibanos*, which is used only with reference to Rev 1:15 and 2:18 in ancient literature. It can best be understood as a new coinage (Demetrius, *Eloc.* 96–98; Cicero, *De or.* 3.38.154; Lausberg, *Handbook*, §§547–51). Writers sometimes coined new words from existing roots, as John does elsewhere (Rev 22:11). Here, he combines two words from Dan 10:6, the passage on which the imagery is based. In the Greek version of Theodotian, which is closest to that used in Revelation, the figure had legs like "shining bronze" (*chalkou stilbontos*). The combined word is *chalkoustilbontos*, which in Rev 1:15 is modified to *chalkolibanos*, with the *s* and *t* sounds assimilated. Less plausible is the possibility that the word means bronze and incense (Andreas) or bronze from Lebanon (Arethas), that it stems from the local brass industry at Thyatira (Hemer, *Letters*, 111–17), or that it is so rare that it conveys transcendence (Giesen). The medieval lexicon *Suda* imagined that it was a gold alloy (BDAG) (cf. bronze in *Apoc. Zeph.* 6:12).

and his voice was like the sound of rushing water. Rather than comparing the voice to the sound of a crowd (Dan 10:6), John likens it to rushing water or literally "many" waters, which may signal the approach of God (Ezek 1:24; 43:2). Similar voices are like thunder (Rev 14:2; 19:6) and the roaring sea (*Apoc. Ab.* 17:1; 1QHª II, 12, 27).

1:16. *He held seven stars in his right hand.* The right hand connoted strength (Pss 89:13; 98:1) and favor (Matt 25:33–34; Ps 110:1), implying that the stars are under his authority and protection. Some interpreters identify the seven stars with the Pleiades (Malina, *Genre*, 70), the planets (Yarbro Collins, *Cosmology*, 121–22), or Usra Major (cf. Aune), but it is not necessary to identify them with a particular constellation. Some note that many in antiquity thought that the stars shaped a person's destiny and suggest that the vision counters this idea by showing that Christ has power over the stars (Barr, *Tales*, 46–47; Boxall).

and from his mouth came a sharp two-edged sword. Greco-Roman deities sometimes appeared with traditional symbols, like Apollo holding a bow and Athena a spear (Apollonius of Rhodes, *Argonautica* 2.674–83; Royalty, *Streets*, 148). Christ's emblem is a two-edged sword, which ordinarily was used in battle (Judg 3:16; Polybius, *Histories* 6.23.6–7; cf. Ps 149:6). Here, however, the sword comes from the mouth. A sword (Pss 57:4; 59:7; cf. Ps 52:2; Ps.-Phoc. 124; Diogenes Laertius, *Lives* 5.82) or a two-edged sword (Prov 5:4; cf. Sir 21:3; cf. Isa 49:2; 4Q436 1 I, 7; Eph 6:17; Heb 4:12–13; Wis

18:15–16) was a familiar image for the power of speech. He will use the sword of his word against his adversaries (Rev 2:16; 19:15, 21).

His face was like the sun shining with all its power. The heavenly figure's face in Dan 10:6 was as bright as lightning (cf. *Jos. As.* 14:9). A face like the sun was fitting for angels (Rev 10:1; *Apoc. Zeph.* 6:11) and divinity (Matt 17:2). Light characterizes God and Christ (Rev 21:23; 22:5).

1:17. *When I saw him, I fell at his feet as if I were dead.* Jewish and Christian sources tell of people involuntarily collapsing in fear when encountering a heavenly figure (Ezek 1:28; Dan 8:17; 10:9–10; Tob 12:15–16; Luke 24:5; *1 En.* 14:14; *Apoc. Ab.* 10:2). Similar responses occur in Greco-Roman sources (Homer, *Od.* 16.179; 24.533–36; Virgil, *Aen.* 4.279–82; Apollonius of Rhodes, *Argonautica* 2.674–83; Royalty, *Streets*, 99). In some cases the person falls down as if dead (Matt 28:2–4; *4 Ezra* 10:30; *T. Ab.* 9:1; Aune). A variation is that people voluntarily prostrate themselves in worship, as John does in Rev 19:10 and 22:8.

but he put his right hand on me and said, "Do not be afraid. Traditionally, a person overwhelmed by a heavenly presence was given a word of assurance (Tob 12:17), sometimes with the touch of a hand (Dan 10:10, 12; *4 Ezra* 10:30–31; *Apoc. Ab.* 10:4). The powerful right hand that holds the seven stars is also used to give John assurance (Rev 1:16, 20).

"I am the first and the last, and the living one." Jesus introduces himself with a formula that recalls God's name, "I am" (*egō eimi*; NOTE on 1:8), and attributes: "I am the first and I am the last; besides me there is no god" (Isa 44:6); "I, the Lord, am first and with the last, I am he" (41:4; cf. 48:11b–12). These passages appear in contexts that stress God's role in the beginning as Creator, whose purposes will be accomplished in the time to come. They also contrast the singular sovereignty of Israel's God with the gods of the nations. Israel's God was "living," unlike lifeless idols (Jer 10:5, 10; 2 Cor 6:16). The living God is the source of life for others (Rev 4:9–10; 7:2; 10:6), yet he also shows wrath against his foes (15:7). These qualities are now ascribed to the risen Jesus.

1:18. *I was dead, but see, I live forever and ever.* To live forever is a characteristic of God (previous NOTE; cf. Dan 4:34; 6:26; 12:7; *1 En.* 5:1). It is also true of Jesus, who lives forever not by avoiding death, but by overcoming it through resurrection.

I have the keys to Death and Hades. Death and Hades are pictured here in spatial terms, as the realm of the dead. Later, they will be personified (Rev 6:8). Hades was the Greek god of the underworld, whose name was extended to that dark region, which was devoid of joy (I.Smyr 518.1; 523.5; 528.2; 551.12). The name could translate the Hebrew "Sheol." In the OT it is the place to which all people go when they die; it is not a place of punishment reserved for the wicked (Gen 37:35; 42:38; Pss 16:10 89:48; Sir 41:4; Ps.-Phoc. 112–13). It was pictured as a dark realm under the earth (Job 11:8; 17:13; Tob 13:2; Matt 11:23), with gates at its entrance (Job 38:17; Isa 38:10; Wis 16:13; Matt 16:18; Homer, *Il.* 5.646). In the Greco-Roman world the keys to Hades were said to belong to Pluto (Pausanius, *Descr.* 5.20.3), the hero Aecus (Apollodorus, *Library* 3.12.6; Lucian, *Dial. mort.* 20; Lucian, *Char.* 2), the goddess Hecate (Aune), and Hermes-Thoth (*Rom. Civ.* 2:535). Conversely, Jewish tradition said an angel had power over Hades (*Apoc. Ab.* 10:11; *Apoc. Zeph.* 6:15; cf. Rev 20:1). Like such angels, Christ is said to have the keys to Death and Hades; unlike them, his power over death is linked to his own resurrection (Stuckenbruck, *Angel*, 220).

Revelation has a complex view of the underworld in which Hades is where all the dead are kept until the final resurrection (Rev 20:13–14). The exceptions are the martyrs, who are said to be under the heavenly altar (6:9–11). Although some sources identified Hades with the abyss, or Abaddon (Job 26:6; Prov 15:11; 27:20), Revelation treats these as different realms: The dead are in Hades, and the abyss is a realm for demons, the beast, and Satan (9:1, 11; 11:7; 17:8; 20:1–3). Angels use keys to open the abyss so demonic agents can emerge (9:1–2), and to close the abyss so Satan is confined there (20:1–3). In some sources Hades is a fiery place of torment (Luke 16:23), but in Revelation that role is given to the lake of fire, where the wicked are sent after being released from Hades for judgment (NOTE on Rev 19:20; cf. 20:10, 14–15; 21:8). Hades itself is then thrown into the lake of fire (20:13–14). Rather than being a place of fiery judgment, Hades is subjected to fiery judgment.

1:19. *So write what you have seen, which includes things as they are now as well as things to come.* John is to write down all he sees, which refers to all of the visions (cf. 1:11). The aorist tense is used here—as elsewhere (4:1; 5:1; 6:1; etc.)—because from the readers' perspectives, the entire book recounts visions John has already seen. The *kai* is epexegetical ("which includes"), introducing John's entire visionary experience, including present and future elements (*Barn.* 1:7). Some interpreters relate this to the character of God, who is, was, and is to come (Rev 1:4, 8; Slater, *Christ*, 102–3; K. Huber, *Einer*, 191).

1:20. *As for the mystery.* A mystery (*mystērion*) was something whose meaning needed to be disclosed, like the meaning of a dream (Dan 2:18–19, 27–30). Sometimes a mystery was broad, concerning the purposes of God (Mark 4:11 par.; Rom 11:25; 1 Cor 15:51; *1 En.* 103:2), which were revealed through the prophets (Rev 10:7). But here it concerns the puzzling aspects of this vision (cf. 17:5, 7).

the seven stars are the seven angels of the seven assemblies. There are three main lines of interpretation; the first is preferable:

1. Angels as supernatural beings. Revelation regularly refers to *angeloi* as supernatural agents of God (e.g., 4:11; 8:2) or demonic beings (9:11; 12:7, 9). Angels were sometimes pictured in groups of seven, like the seven archangels (Tob 12:15; cf. 4Q403 1 I, 1–29; II, 18–37). Here, the assumption is that each congregation has an angelic representative, perhaps reflecting the idea that each nation had a corresponding angel (Deut 32:8 LXX). Michael was the angel or "prince" for Israel, and other nations had their own princes or angels (Dan 10:13, 20–21; 12:1). Individuals also had angels watching over them (Tob 2:14–16; Matt 18:10; Acts 12:15; *L.A.B.* 15:5; *1 En.* 100:5). Angels could be pictured as stars (Job 38:7 LXX) as in Rev 9:1. Positing an angel for each church has affinities with ideas in other sources (Herm. *Vis.* 5:3; *Mart. Asc. Isa.* 3:15), but this form is peculiar to Revelation (Stuckenbruck, *Angel*, 237; Carrell, *Jesus*, 20; Hannah, *Michael*, 125; Giesen; Müller; Roloff).
2. Angels as symbols of the church's spiritual condition. Just as lampstands hold lamps, the spirit of the churches may be symbolized by the stars and angels (Mounce; Lupieri; Resseguie). However, this interpretation does not fit the use of "angel" elsewhere in the book.
3. Angels as human beings. The word *angelos* can refer to human messengers (1 Macc 1:44; Luke 7:24; 9:52), including prophets (Hag 1:13; cf. Mark 1:2). Some interpret-

ers propose that these are the messengers who delivered John's text to the churches (Kraft) or else the prophets (Schüssler Fiorenza, *Book*, 145–46; Slater, *Christ*, 104) or officers (Lülsdorff, "Ἐκλεκοί") who led congregations. The consistent use elsewhere in Revelation of *angelos* for supernatural figures, however, makes this interpretation unlikely.

the seven lampstands are the seven assemblies. See the NOTE on 1:12.

COMMENT

The first cycle of visions begins with John's encounter with the exalted Jesus. Through his prose John takes readers into the visionary world. It begins when he is on the island of Patmos, where he hears a voice and then sees a radiant figure surrounded by seven gold lampstands. The figure's appearance defies easy description: hair that is white *like* wool or snow, eyes *like* a flame of fire, a voice *like* rushing water, a face *like* the sun. The comparisons show that what John describes does not fit within the confines of ordinary speech. He uses analogies from human experience to depict something from a different realm. This is not a visionary ascent into heaven—that occurs later (4:1)—but an encounter that discloses a dimension of the readers' own world. Readers find that *they* are the lampstands. They are communities in which the risen Christ is *already present*.

Biblical language shapes John's account and locates it within the tradition of recognized prophecy. The vision resembles Daniel's encounter with a figure so radiant and majestic that Daniel fell to the ground and was told not to fear (Dan 10:1–21; Theod.). Although some of the visionary elements are conventional (NOTES on Rev 1:13–17), including them suggests continuity between the one who sent a revelation to Daniel and what is given to John. Since prophetic writings sometimes recount a prophet's call into service (Isa 6:1–13; Jer 1:4–10; Ezek 1:1–3:11), some interpreters refer to Rev 1:9–20 as John's "call" vision (Kraft; Mounce). This characterization is not apt, however, because John seems to have been active in a circle of prophets before this time (Rev 22:9), and elements from the call narratives of Isaiah and Ezekiel are woven into later visions as part of his ongoing prophetic work (4:1–11; 10:1–11; Karrer, *Johannesoffenbarung*, 139–41).

Structurally, this vision has three parts arranged symmetrically. In the first and third parts, John is commissioned to write to the seven assemblies (1:9–11, 17–20). In the middle, he describes the glorified Jesus (1:12–16). The function of the vision is twofold: In one sense it introduces the entire book, since John is told to write what he sees, which encompasses everything that follows. Aspects of the opening chapter

---

On Rev 1:9–20, see Aune, *Apocalypticism*, 203–7; Bauckham, "Lord's Day"; Biguzzi, "John"; Bovon, "John's"; Carrell, *Jesus*, 129–74; Gieschen, *Angelomorphic*, 245–69; Hemer, *Letters*, 27–34; Herghelegiu, *Siehe*, 111–55; M. Hoffmann, *Destroyer*, 212–46; Horn, "Johannes"; K. Huber, *Einer*, 74–217; Janzen, "Jesus"; Karrer, *Johannesoffenbarung*, 137–220; Manganaro, "Le iscrizioni," 331–46; Pezzoli-Olgiati, *Täuschung*, 17–31; Rainbow, "Male"; Royalty, *Streets*, 39–47, 97–99, 133–49; Saffrey, "Relire"; Scholtissek, "Mitteilhaber"; Simpson and Lazenby, "Notes"; Slater, *Christ*, 93–107; Stuckenbruck, *Angel*, 205–40; Witetschek, *Ephesische*, 305–8; Yarbro Collins, *Cosmology*, 172–85.

appear again in the final chapter, framing the book as a whole. These include John's first-person attestation of what he heard, saw, and wrote in the scroll (1:9, 11; 22:6–9) and the first-person witness of Jesus, who is "the first and the last" (1:17; 22:13, 16). In another sense the inaugural vision leads directly to the messages to the seven churches in the next two chapters. The address to each church begins with traits of Christ from the opening chapter, and the command to write is repeated (2:1, 8, 12, 18; 3:1, 7, 14). The description indicates that the Christ who formerly addressed John now addresses the readers through his text.

Commission to Write (1:9–11)

The section begins in the first person: "I, John" (1:9). The previous section concluded with God speaking in the first person, "I [*egō*] am the Alpha and the Omega" (1:8). Now, however, John differentiates himself from the divine speaker and writes in his own name, "I [*egō*] John," as he will do at the end of the book (1:9; 22:8; Bovon, "John's"). John also builds rapport with his readers by drawing on what he and they have in common. He calls himself their "brother," a term that emphasizes their social bonds (1:9; Rowland; Thompson, *Book*, 178; Aune, *Apocalypticism*, 176–77; Scholtissek, "Mitteilhaber"). He notes his fear and later points out that he too has needed help in understanding what he has seen (1:17; 5:4; 7:13–14; 17:6–7). Elsewhere, John will note places where he received heavenly correction about what to write or who to worship (10:4; 19:10; 22:8–9), so when his message gives correction to the readers, John writes as one who has experienced it himself.

John is also their "companion" in three ways (1:9). First, he shares in affliction for the faith. Among the readers, affliction is clearest in the message to Smyrna, where it entails denunciation, imprisonment, and possible death (2:9–10). Although not all of John's readers were afflicted (cf. 3:17), John identifies himself with readers who suffer, which is a mark of friendship (Seneca the Younger, *Ep.* 9.10). Revelation, like other sources, also envisions a period of affliction or tribulation in the end times, before God's final victory over evil (Rev 7:14; Dan 12:1; Matt 24:21; Mark 13:19). For John, this eschatological affliction is a present reality (Boring; Murphy; Witherington). It began when Satan was banished from heaven to earth at the resurrection and exaltation of Jesus (Rev 12:5–10) and will continue until Christ's final coming to defeat the agents of evil (19:11–21; Note on 12:12; Resseguie).

Second, John and his readers share in the kingdom. Earlier, those redeemed by Jesus' blood were said to constitute a kingdom, whose members acknowledge the kingship of God and Christ in contexts where other powers vie for allegiance (1:5–6). Earth's destroyers—Satan, the beast, and Babylon—seek to establish their own kingdom, so those loyal to God and the Lamb experience affliction (16:10; 17:18). Yet the Creator and the Lamb will defeat evil and death, and the faithful will share fully in God's kingdom through resurrection (11:15; 19:6; 20:4; 22:5).

Third, the present conflict between God and evil means that the faithful must show "endurance." Endurance can occur in the face of hostility (3:9–10; 13:10; 14:12), but it is also needed when threats are more subtle, such as in the teachings that distort the Christian message and in the complacency that erodes love (2:2–3). Endurance is confrontational when it means resisting untruth, yet it also entails continued expressions of love in service to others (2:19).

John's situation on Patmos fits this complex self-presentation. He was probably banished there because of his preaching (NOTE on 1:9). Being banished sets John apart geographically from the readers in mainland cities, and hardship gives him the moral authority to call for endurance in affliction (deSilva, *Seeing*, 133). Yet exile also binds him to those who are ostracized or threatened with imprisonment, since he knows what hardship for the faith means (2:9–10; 3:8–9).

John's situation on Patmos also would have had affinities with Christians on the mainland who were not overtly threatened. Religious life on the island was much like that on the mainland. Patmos had local priesthoods and festivals devoted to Artemis, Hermes, and probably Apollo. His readers faced issues about the degree to which they could accommodate Greco-Roman religious practice. John clearly rejected eating food offered to Greco-Roman deities (2:14, 20), but like his readers, he still faced the challenge of "enduring" by maintaining a distinctive Christian identity in a social context that did not support it.

Commercial life on Patmos would have differed in scale from that in large port cities like Ephesus or Smyrna. Yet the island and the mainland were entwined in the network of trade that John associated with Babylon/Rome (18:9–19). The exhortation to the faithful to disengage from economic practices deemed incompatible with the faith (18:4) would have posed complex challenges for Christians in Asian commercial centers (Harland, *Associations*, 262–63; Bauckham, *Climax*, 376–77). John would not have been exempt from such issues, since exiles had to support themselves, and much of the island's revenue came from the empire's seaborne trade. Like the readers, he faced questions of making a living without undue entanglement in the Roman economy.

Identifying the Lord's Day as the setting of his vision reflects another point of social dislocation that John shared with the readers (1:10). Jews observed the last day of the week as the Sabbath, while Greeks and Romans in Asia Minor began the year with the birthday of Augustus and set aside special days for various deities (*Rom. Civ.* 1:623–25). Christians who worshiped on the first day of the week distinguished themselves from adherents of other traditions. The visions John received on the Lord's Day were to be read aloud in Christian gatherings, which were probably held on that day of the week (Rev 1:3). Those gathered on earth would hear about worship in heaven, inviting them to join in celebrating the lordship of the Creator and the Lamb, and in so doing to reaffirm their identity as a distinct community (4:8–11; 5:8–14; 7:9–12; 11:15–18; 15:2–4; 19:1–8; Friesen, *Imperial*, 157–58).

John says he received his revelation "in the Spirit," which links his experience to that of Israel's prophets (NOTE on 1:10). Interpreters differ over the role that genuine spiritual experience plays in the composition of John's book. Some assume that Revelation is essentially a transcription of an ecstatic experience (Lenski, *Interpretation*, 15–16). Conversely, others assume that since John wrote an apocalypse, he simply included a divine commissioning because it was part of the genre (Schüssler Fiorenza 51). It seems clear that John consciously shaped features like the groups of seven visions and the contrasts between the beast and the Lamb, Babylon, and New Jerusalem. His language also draws heavily from Scripture; for instance, the inaugural vision combines elements from Dan 7:9, 13 and 10:2–11; Ezek 3:12; Exod 19:16; and other texts. At the same time he was not bound by literary conventions. For example, he differs from other apocalyptic authors by writing in his own name rather than using a pseudonym.

Ecstatic experience was a recognized phenomenon in early Christianity, where prophets were understood to convey messages from God or Christ (2 Cor 12:2–3; Acts 10:5; 16:9; NOTES on Rev 1:3). Accordingly, interpreters cannot rule out either ecstatic experience or conscious literary shaping. If spiritual experience prompted John to write, it was an experience that he structured and interpreted through the lens of earlier prophetic texts (deSilva, *Seeing*, 121–24; Bauckham, *Climax*, 158–59).

John is told, "Write what you see in a scroll" (1:11). The command to "write" is repeated in the message to each assembly (2:1, 8, 12, etc.) and later in the book (19:9; 21:5; cf. 14:13). Culturally, various Jewish (Tob 12:20) and Greco-Roman (Pliny the Younger, *Ep.* 3.5.4; Pausanias, *Descr.* 1.21.2; Aelius Aristides, *Orations* 48.2; Dio Cassius, *Rom. Hist.* 73.23.2; Aune) authors claimed to have supernatural authorization for their writings. Early readers would have agreed in principle that an author could be divinely commissioned. The issue was whether a *particular claim* to divine authorization was true. Therefore, such claims were evaluated in Christian communities (Knight, "Apocalyptic"; Aune, *Prophecy*, 217–29; Boring, *Continuing*, 101–7). John tells of receiving the command to write in a vision, and he has no means of verifying the authenticity of that experience at the outset. Instead, he brings readers into the visionary world through his text. As they come to see what he saw, the text must become self-authenticating (Thompson, *Book*, 177–79)—or as the writer would put it, divinely authenticated.

The command to "write" includes the directive to "send" the text to the seven churches (Rev 1:11; see Map 1). This expression is like a prophetic commission to "go and tell," and it fits John's self-presentation as a messenger in Israel's prophetic tradition (Isa 6:9; Jer 1:7; Ezek 2:4; Aune). It also means that the process of revelation is complete only when the message is actually received within the churches (Murphy). The messages in Rev 2–3 are specifically addressed to these churches, but there is no evidence that they ever circulated as a separate text. According to the extant form of the text, the churches are to receive the entire book of Revelation (1:11; 22:7, 9, 10, 18, 19); therefore, interpretation of the entire Apocalypse means asking how it would have addressed the kinds of readers associated with those churches.

One Like a Human Being (1:12–16)

John takes readers into his visionary world by describing what he sees. This central section communicates through pictures and impressions rather than direct statements. John initially sees seven gold lampstands and a figure wearing a robe and gold sash. The description becomes more fantastic as he tells of the figure's eyes like flame, feet like bronze, and voice like rushing water. The awe-inspiring strangeness culminates with the description of the stars in the figure's hand, the sword extending from his mouth, and his blazing sunlike face.

The unnamed figure is "like a human being" (1:13), though his appearance is unlike that of any ordinary person. Readers might assume that the figure is Christ, since the introduction said that the book was "a revelation from Jesus Christ" (1:1). The expression "like a human being"—or literally, "like a Son of Man"—was also used in Dan 7:13, which pictured a figure coming on the clouds to receive dominion over all nations. That text was paraphrased in Rev 1:7, where the one coming on the clouds was Christ.

Yet readers could also assume that John sees an angel. The superscription said the revelation came to John through an angel (1:1), and the description of the figure John saw resembles that of the angel who spoke to Daniel (Dan 10:5–6). Other sources also pictured angels this way (*Apoc. Zeph.* 6:11–12; *Apoc. Ab.* 10:4; 11:2–3; *Jos. As.* 14:8–9; cf. *1 En.* 106:2–5). In Revelation, angels wear linen robes and gold sashes (Rev 15:6); they have faces like the sun, legs like fire, and voices that roar (10:1–3; 18:1–2; Stuckenbruck, *Angel*, 209–32; Carrell, *Jesus*, 129–74; Gieschen, *Angelomorphic*, 246–52). John will reveal that the one he sees is the risen Christ, who shares the traits of God. Yet thus far he has only hinted at this identification by referring to hair that is as white as wool, which characterizes God, the ancient one of Dan 7:9, and by comparing the voice to rushing water, which could signal the approach of God (Ezek 1:24; 43:2; M. Hoffmann, *Destroyer*, 219–46; K. Huber, *Einer*, 170–73; Herghelegiu, *Siehe*, 130–35). Clarity emerges gradually.

The section climaxes by noting that the figure holds seven stars in his right hand (Rev 1:16). This cosmic imagery conveys sovereignty. An analogy appears on a coin from Domitian's reign that depicts the emperor's deceased son as young Jupiter, sitting on the globe in a posture of world dominion. The coin's inscription calls him "divine Caesar, son of the emperor Domitian," and the imagery shows him extending his hands to seven stars in a display of divinity and power (Figure 2). John has already identified Jesus as the ruler of kings on earth (1:5), and the imagery of the seven stars fits the book's larger context, which contrasts the reign of Christ with that of imperial Rome (Janzen, "Jesus"; Barr, *Tales*, 47).

The two-edged sword coming from his mouth is fitting for royal, messianic status. Although the sword was a metaphor for speech (NOTE on 1:16), the mouth of God's servant was said to be a sword (Isa 49:2), and God's messianic king was to strike the earth with the rod or word from his mouth (Isa 11:4; *Pss. Sol.* 17:24, 35; 4Q161 8–10 III, 15–19; *1 En.* 62:2; K. Huber, *Einer*, 163–65). This imagery fits the peculiar nature of conflict in Revelation. Christ defeats evil with the force of truth, culminating in the great battle where his sword—his word—is the only weapon mentioned (Rev 19:15, 21; Resseguie). In the great battle Christ will wield the sword of truth against the nations; but here, his sword, or word, confronts Christian readers. They too are subject to his word, which in subsequent chapters includes both encouragement and rebuke.

Figure 2. Roman coin showing Domitian on one side and his son surrounded by seven stars on the other (88–96 CE). Courtesy of the Classical Numismatic Group (cngcoins.com)

Commission Repeated, Vision Explained (1:17–20)

The seer falls down at the feet of this majestic figure, as if dead. This response is to some extent typical in accounts of people meeting heavenly beings (NOTE on 1:17), but it makes a theological point. At the beginning of the book John is overwhelmed by the majesty of Christ and falls down at his feet. Yet he is given a word of encouragement: "Do not be afraid." At the end of the book, John twice falls down to worship at the feet of an angel. There, he is reproved: "Do not do that," for he is to worship God (19:10; 22:8–9). These similar and yet contrasting scenes create a pattern in which readers see that it is fitting to be awed by Christ, who shares the traits of God, and that it is also important to distinguish Christ from the angels, who are of a lesser order (M. Hoffmann, *Destroyer*, 245).

Jesus now says "I am" in a manner that recalls the divine name (1:17). Where God said "I am the Alpha and the Omega" (1:8), the exalted Christ says "I am the first and the last" (1:17). Here and at the end of the book Christ identifies himself with God, calling himself the Alpha and the Omega, the first and the last, the beginning and the end (22:13; cf. 21:6). The claim recalls texts where God says, "I am the first and I am the last; besides me there is no god" (Isa 44:6; cf. 48:12). Like the biblical prophets, Revelation opposes worship of any being other than God (Rev 19:10; 22:8–9). Yet Christ is not an alternative object of worship alongside God. He shares God's throne, such that God and Christ constitute a single focus for worship (5:13; 7:10, 17; 22:1, 3; Bauckham, *Theology*, 54–65).

Christ adds that he is "the living one," which emphasizes his oneness with the living God (1:18; cf. 7:2; 15:7). God's existence extends to past, present, and future (1:4, 8). Jesus' existence is similar (1:17–18). To say that Christ is "first" assumes that he was one with God at creation; to say that he is the "last" anticipates that he will be one with God in the new creation (22:1, 3). Like God, Jesus lives forever and ever (4:9–10; 10:6). The difference is that Jesus lives not because he avoided death, but because he overcame it through resurrection. The way the risen Jesus extends the promise of life to others is suggested here, as he speaks and restores John, who lies at his feet as if dead.

Jesus holds the keys to Death and Hades because of his resurrection. At present, the forces of evil can inflict death and send people to Hades, the realm of the underworld where people go when they die (6:8; 13:10, 15; NOTE on 1:18). Evil can destroy life, but it does not give life (11:7; 12:4; Wis 2:24; John 8:44; Heb 2:14). God, however, has the power to do both (Deut 32:39; 1 Sam 2:6; Tob 13:2). This power to bring release from death also belongs to Jesus. Revelation assumes that the faithful remain subject to death until the resurrection at the end of the age, when Death and Hades give up all whom they have held. Then, Death and Hades themselves are thrown into the lake of fire (20:13–14). For the readers, death remains real, yet it is not final. Since Jesus died and rose, he can extend to those who die the hope of release from death. Later, Jesus is also said to have the key of David, which signifies access to the presence of God (3:7). Together, the key of Death and Hades and the key of David show that release from death and access to God are two parts of the same act of redemption.

John is again commanded to "write" what he sees, including things as they are now and things to come (1:19, cf. 1:11). Some interpreters regard this expression as an outline of the book. They point out that "see" is in the aorist tense, so that it could refer to what John has seen thus far (1:9–18). Things that now "are" would be conditions in the churches (2:1–3:21), and what is to occur would be the future (4:1–22:5; Charles; Thomas). In dispensationalist interpretation this pattern is linked to the idea that the messages in Rev 2–3 concern the present era of the church, whereas the rest of the book predicts future events that will occur after the church has been raptured (Scofield). Nevertheless, the sections of the book cannot be divided into three time periods. The word "see" includes all the visions in the book (22:8). It is in the aorist tense because it looks back on a past visionary experience. Moreover, there are both present and future elements in the messages to the churches and the rest of the book. No sharp temporal distinction can be made between these sections (Aune; Smalley; cf. Beale; Osborne).

The disclosure of a "mystery" concludes this part of the vision (1:20). By revealing what is mysterious, John brings his readers into the circle of those who have special insight, helping to create community. Readers learn that the seven stars in Christ's hand signify the angels of the churches. In the visionary world groups of seven angels can have special responsibilities. The trumpet and bowl angels bring plagues on the earth and show John Babylon and New Jerusalem (8:2; 15:1, 6; 17:1; 21:9), and the seven angelic spirits are sent throughout the world and serve as Christ's eyes (Note on 1:4; cf. 4:5; 5:6). Here, seven angels have special responsibility for the churches on earth. In what follows, the message to each church will be addressed to an angel, but it is to be heard by the whole community (2:1, 7, etc.).

Finally, the lampstands represent the churches. Readers find that they are participants in the vision. The lampstand imagery suggests first that they are communities of worship within the tradition of Israel. Just as a seven-branched lampstand stood before God within the sanctuary, their congregations stand before the risen Christ (1:12). Second, it identifies them as witnesses. In a later vision lampstands will represent the whole church in its role as witness (11:3–4). Lamp imagery could be used for prophets, teachers, and other witnesses to the truth (Matt 5:14–15; John 5:35; *4 Ezra* 12:42; *2 Bar.* 77:13–16). The exalted Christ is the radiant source of light in the center of this vision, and his churches convey light in their world through their witness.

5. To the Assembly in Ephesus (2:1–7)

2 [1]"To the angel of the assembly in Ephesus write: Thus says the one who holds the seven stars in his right hand, who walks among the seven gold lampstands: [2]I know your works, namely your labor and your endurance, and that you are not able to bear evildoers. You tested those who say they are apostles but are not, and have found that they are liars. [3]I know that you are enduring and bearing up for the sake of my name and have not gotten tired. [4]But I have this against you, that you have let go of the love you had at first. [5]Therefore, remember from where you have fallen. Repent and do the works you did at first. If you do not, I will come to you and move your lampstand from its place—if you do not repent. [6]But this you have, that you hate the works of the Nicolaitans, which I also hate. [7]Let the one who has an ear hear what the Spirit says to the assemblies. To those who conquer I will grant to eat from the tree of life that is in the paradise of God."

NOTES

2:1. *To the angel of the assembly.* Each angel apparently has responsibility for a congregation (NOTE on 1:20). In ordinary public discourse the *ekklēsia* at Ephesus and other cities was the assembly of citizens, who gathered for deliberation (Acts 19:39; I.Eph 27.22). Here, it is the city's Christian community.

in Ephesus. Ephesus (near present-day Selçuk, Turkey) was the largest city in Asia Minor. The Greeks had long had a settlement in this vicinity, but in the third century BCE the city was moved to a new location and surrounded with a wall. Coming under Roman control after 133 BCE, Ephesus grew in size and importance. Probably somewhat larger than its rivals Smyrna and Pergamum, the city became the center for Roman administration in Asia, a position previously held by Pergamum. Its population was ethnically mixed, with Greeks, Romans, and Jews and people from Rhodes, Egypt, Galatia, Lydia, and Mysia (Witetschek, *Ephesische*, 58–60). Its harbor made it a hub in a network of seaborne commerce, and a well-developed road system gave it access to inland markets. It was the largest emporium in Asia (Strabo, *Geographica* 14.1.24). Enormous sums of money were kept in the temple of Artemis, making Ephesus a center for finance (Dio Chrysostom, *Disc.* 31.54–55; I.Eph 454; Broughton, *Asia*, 889–90). Groups of physicians made the city important for medicine (Broughton, *Asia*, 889–90; I.Eph 719; 1386). There were fishermen, fish merchants, linen weavers, wool dealers, bakers, potters, silversmiths, and carpenters (Harland, *Associations*, 39–40). Ephesian slave dealers sold slaves for local use and shipped many to Rome and other markets. Inscriptions from the mid-first and early second centuries CE show slave traders honoring Roman officials at Ephesus. The inscriptions use Latin rather than Greek and cultivate good relationships between Roman administrators and slave traders. Rome's role in trafficking in slaves is criticized in Rev 18 (C. R. Koester, "Roman," 776–85).

Under imperial rule the city's administrative center was redesigned, the theater was expanded, and new fountains were built. A monumental gate honored Augustus and the imperial family (I.Eph 3006). Augustus provided two new aqueducts, and a wealthy patron added a third (Figures 3, 4, 5, and 6; I.Eph 401–2; 3092; Scherrer, "City"; L. M. White, "Urban"). Inscriptions dedicate many structures jointly to the city's patron goddess Artemis and to Roman rulers: Augustus and Tiberius were named with Artemis on an aqueduct (I.Eph 3092); Artemis and Nero were honored by the new fishery tollhouse in the harbor and the stadium (I.Eph 20; 411); and Artemis and Domitian were named on sections of the theater, a new colonnade, and the stone pavement on the city's main street (I.Eph 2034; 3005; 3008).

Local religious practice was a blend of traditions. The goddess Artemis was revered as the guardian of the city's welfare. Her temple near the city was a center for pilgrimage and a place of asylum (Acts 19:23–27). Measuring about 425 feet long and 230 feet wide, it was the largest Greek temple in antiquity (Figure 7). As emperor, Augustus showed support for the cult of Artemis (I.Eph 3501). Hestia was the goddess of the public hearth, with her cult located in the city's administrative center. There were temples to Apollo and Athena and a sanctuary of Zeus and the Anatolian mother goddess. Inscriptions mention Aphrodite, Asclepius, Hecate, Herakles, and other deities. The mysteries of Demeter were celebrated with processions and sacred baskets. In addition to these traditional Greek cults, the Egyptian deities Isis and Sarapis were also venerated

Figure 3. Ephesus: Monumental gate (3 BCE). Dedicated to "the emperor Caesar Augustus, son of god and high priest," and members of his family (I.Eph 3006). Courtesy of www .HolyLandPhotos.org.

Figure 4. Ephesus: Aqueduct (4–14 CE). Dedicated to the Ephesian Artemis, emperor Caesar Augustus and Tiberius Caesar his son, and the people of Ephesus (I.Eph 3092). © Craig Koester.

Figure 5. Ephesus: Theater and harbor area. The toll house in the harbor (54–59 CE) was dedicated to Nero Claudius Caesar Augustus Germanicus, his family members, the Romans, and Ephesians (I.Eph 20). © Craig Koester.

Figure 6. Ephesus: Paved street (94–95 CE). Dedicated to the Ephesian Artemis and emperor Domitian Caesar Augustus Germanicus (I.Eph 3008). © Craig Koester.

Figure 7. Coin from Ephesus showing the emperor Claudius on one side and the temple of Artemis on the other (41–42 CE). Courtesy of the Classical Numismatic Group (cngcoins .com).

(Oster, "Ephesus"; Witetschek, *Ephesische*, 66–99). Another cult honored the Roman proconsul Publius Servilius Isauricus, a noted benefactor (Friesen, *Imperial*, 29).

The men and women who served in the priesthoods of Artemis and other deities were typically leading citizens who paid the costs of the festivals (Oster, "Ephesus," 1713–22). Associations included the worshipers of Demeter (I.Eph 4337), the devotees of Isis and Sarapis (Oster, "Ephesus," 1213), and the physicians who honored Asclepius (Strabo, *Geographica* 14.1.29). Theatrical performers identified with Dionysus (I.Eph 434). Festivals of Artemis included athletic, musical, and theatrical competitions; processions through the city; and banquets (Dionysius of Halicarnassus, *Ant. rom.* 4.25.4). The festival of Dionysus was celebrated with harps, flutes, and pipes, and for the revelry many wore ivy or dressed as Pans and Satyrs. Issues would have arisen for Christians who felt pressure to accommodate Greco-Roman religious practices in order to maintain good relationships with non-Christian family members and friends.

The imperial cult flourished at Ephesus. Traditional beliefs and Roman rule were considered to be mutually supportive. An inscription from 48 BCE honors Julius Caesar as god, and in 29 BCE he and the goddess Roma were honored with a temple at Ephesus (I.Eph 251; Dio Cassius, *Rom. Hist.* 51.20.6–9). Augustus was honored as "god" and "son of god." The main sanctuary dedicated to him was probably in the city's administrative center, connecting civic life with imperial rule (I.Eph 252; 3006; Scherrer, "City," 4–6). In 26 CE the Ephesians proposed building a provincial temple to Tiberius, but the honor went to Smyrna (Tacitus, *Ann.* 3.55). A temple to Nero might have been planned or begun at Ephesus in the sixties of the first century. Coins dating from 65/66 CE show Nero on one side and a temple—perhaps different from the Artemis temple—on the other and bear the title "temple warden" (*neokoros*). But as far as is known, no temple to Nero was actually built (Burrell, *Neokoroi*, 62–63). Only under Domitian was Ephesus finally allowed to dedicate a provincial temple to the Flavian emperors Vespasian, Titus, Domitian, and perhaps Domitian's wife (ca. 89/90 CE). Having previously called itself the temple warden of Artemis, the city extended this terminology to its imperial temple (Friesen, *Twice*, 29–59). The statue of Titus within the temple probably had a military pose, like that of Augustus at Pergamum (Figure 8; Friesen, *Imperial*, 50).

Figure 8. Statue of Titus from the imperial temple at Ephesus (89–90 CE). © Craig Koester.

In connection with the imperial cult, a bath and gymnasium complex was built near the harbor, and Olympic games were held. Some Ephesian coins featured Domitian on one side and Zeus Olympus on the other, suggesting a close relationship between imperial rule and the chief god of Olympus. Inscriptions on the imperial temple and public works called Domitian "emperor" and "high priest" but refrained from calling him "god" during his lifetime (I.Eph 232; 414; 1498; 2035; 2047; 2048; 3008; Friesen, *Imperial*, 43–55).

A Jewish community existed in Ephesus for several centuries. Under Roman rule Jews maintained their right to build a synagogue and administer their own finances (Josephus, *Ant.* 14.227–28; Philo, *Legat.* 315; Acts 18:19). Although a Jewish apocalyptic writer might warn of judgment coming on Ephesus (*Sib. Or.* 3:343, 459; 5:293–96), many Jews were well-integrated in civic life. Some were also Roman citizens (Josephus, *Ant.* 14.228, 234; Trebilco, *Early*, 37–51; Witetschek, *Ephesische*, 141–72). Later inscriptions attest to an ongoing community (*IJO* 2:147–62). Conflict between Jews and the followers of Jesus was a problem in some places (Rev 2:9; 3:9), but it is not mentioned at Ephesus.

A Christian community seems to have been established at Ephesus in the mid-50s, several decades before Revelation was written. Studies often link the earliest period to Apollos (1 Cor 1:12; Acts 18:24–26) and Prisca and Aquila (1 Cor 16:19). Others involved included Paul, Timothy, Sosthenes, and Titus (1 Cor 1:1; 16:8–12, 19; 2 Cor 7:6). In the early period Paul experienced conflict, probably with non-Christians (1 Cor 15:32; 16:9; cf. Acts 19:23–41), but whether he was imprisoned at Ephesus is unclear. An ongoing connection to the Pauline tradition is suggested by references to Ephesus in the Pastoral Epistles (1 Tim 1:3; 2 Tim 1:18; 4:12). Some scholars think there were also Johannine churches in Ephesus, though neither the gospel nor epistles of John make this explicit. Most agree that multiple forms of Christianity existed at Ephesus, but how Christian groups related to each other is not clear (Tellbe, *Christ-Believers*, 1–56). In this pluralistic context, questions of legitimate Christian teaching seem to have persisted (Acts 20:29–30; 1 Tim 1:3–7). The issues in Rev 2:1–7 have to do with accommodating Greco-Roman religious practice (Trebilco, *Early*, 99–103, 152–54, 189–96, 235–36; H. Koester, "Ephesos"; Witetschek, *Ephesische*, 350–418).

Thus says. This formula (*tade legei*) could introduce ordinary quotations (Dionysius of Halicarnassus, *Ant. rom.* 7.72; 9.9; Plutarch, *Mor.* 1052B), but its formal quality made it suitable for prophetic speech and royal decrees. Such connotations fit the exalted Christ, who shares the traits of God and rules over earth's kings (see §3B).

the one who holds the seven stars in his right hand. The stars symbolize the seven angels that represent the congregations (NOTE on 1:20; cf. 3:1).

who walks among the seven gold lampstands. Christ later speaks of coming to the readers (2:5), but here he already walks among the lampstands that symbolize the churches (1:20).

2:2. *I know your works, namely your labor and your endurance.* "I know" is a feature of the message to each church, and it often refers to the congregation's "works" (2:2, 19; 3:1, 8, 15). Commendable works (*erga*) include love for others (2:4–5) and rejecting the teachings of false apostles and Nicolaitans (2:2, 6). Both aspects involve labor (*kopos*), which continues throughout the believer's life (14:13). In some contexts endurance (*hypomonē*) means facing overt hostility (3:9–10; 13:10), but here, as at Thyatira, it means persevering in love, service, and true teaching (2:19; NOTE on 1:9; Holtz, "Werke"). Greeting a congregation by recalling its works, labor, and endurance helps to foster goodwill with readers (cf. 1 Thess 1:3; Malherbe, *Letters*, 108).

and that you are not able to bear evildoers. Elsewhere, evil deeds range from idolatry and sorcery to murder and theft (9:20–21; 21:8, 27; 22:15), but here, the "evildoers" are false apostles, whose works are more subtle and deceptive (2:2). Refusing to bear them means refusing to accept their teaching (cf. Ign. *Eph.* 6:2; 9:1).

You tested those who say they are apostles but are not, and have found that they are liars. An apostle (*apostolos*) is "one who is sent" by a person or congregation (John 13:15; 2 Cor 8:23; Phil 2:25) or by God and Christ (1 Cor 1:1; Gal 1:1). The gospels call the twelve whom Jesus sent out to preach "apostles" (Matt 10:2; Mark 3:14; Luke 6:13). In Revelation they are remembered as the foundations of the community (Rev 21:14). Some who later received the title "apostle" had followed Jesus during his ministry (Acts 1:21–26). Although that was not true of Paul, he claimed to be an apostle because he was sent out by God and the risen Jesus (1 Cor 9:1; Gal 1:1, 12). The congregations he established were evidence that his apostleship was legitimate (1 Cor 9:2).

The term "apostle" was also extended to others engaged in missionary activity, such as Barnabas (Acts 14:4, 14), Silvanus and Timothy (1 Thess 1:1; 2:7), and Andronicus and Junia (Rom 16:7). Whether each person in this wider circle of apostles would claim to have seen the risen Christ is unclear (H. D. Betz, *ABD* 1:309–11; T. Donaldson, *NIDB* 1:205–7). Because it was not evident who could claim the role of an apostle, those who came to Ephesus were to be tested.

The criteria used to distinguish true from false apostles were not fixed. The principal ones may have been whether the content of their message was compatible with the accepted beliefs of the community and whether their behavior was congruent with their message (2 Cor 11:4–5, 12–15; 12:11; cf. Matt 7:15–20; 1 John 4:1–3). Although miracles could be signs of an apostle (2 Cor 12:12; Rom 15:19; Acts 5:12), false prophets could also perform them (Rev 13:13–15; 16:13–14; 19:20; cf. Mark 13:22 par.). Improper demand for support was another sign of a false apostle (*Did.* 11:3–6; Pilch, "Lying," 130). At Ephesus, the principal test seems to have been whether a person would accommodate Greco-Roman religious practice.

2:3. *I know that you are enduring and bearing up for the sake of my name and have not gotten tired.* The congregation is commended through wordplays. Those who do not "bear" evildoers rightly do "bear" up in faith (*bastazein*, 2:2, 3); and despite their labor (*kopos*, 2:2), they have not grown weary (*kopiazein*, 2:3). The expression "for the sake of my name" could be linked to persecution (Matt 10:22; 24:9; Mark 13:13; Luke 21:17; John 15:21; Pol. *Phil.* 8:2; Herm. *Vis.* 3.2.1; Herm. *Sim.* 9.28.3), and some scholars suggest that the Ephesians were threatened (Trebilco, *Early*, 303). Nevertheless, the principal conflict is with different Christian groups, not with outsiders.

2:4. *But I have this against you, that you have let go of the love you had at first.* Love is a commitment to another's well-being, as shown by Jesus' self-sacrifice and believers' acts of service (1:5; 2:19).

2:5. *Therefore, remember from where you have fallen. Repent and do the works you did at first.* Enduring has positive connotations of strength and honor (2:3), and falling connotes weakness, defeat, and humiliation (Prov 16:18; 1 Cor 10:12; Rev 18:2). Those who have fallen have incentive to repent. Elsewhere, Revelation calls those who practice idolatry and violence to repent (2:21–22; 9:20–21; 16:9, 11). Here, the call is issued to a congregation that appears to be standing firm for Christ, but lacks love.

If you do not, I will come to you and move your lampstand from its place—if you do not repent. The lampstand is a symbol of the church (1:20). Some interpreters think moving the lampstand would mean a loss of *existence*. Since "move from one's place" can refer to creation coming undone (6:14), it could mean that the assembly at Ephesus would cease to be a church (Aune; Prigent). But it more probably means a loss of *status*. Ephesus will no longer be first among the churches or deemed legitimate (Harrington; Boxall). Although some propose that the threat of being moved recalls that Ephesus itself was once moved from its original location to a new site (Ramsay, *Letters*, 244–46; Hemer, *Letters*, 52–54; Osborne), this theory is improbable because other cities, such as Smyrna, were also rebuilt at new locations (Strabo, *Geographica* 14.1.37).

2:6. *But this you have, that you hate the works of the Nicolaitans, which I also hate.* The Nicolaitans were Christians who thought it acceptable to eat food that had been offered to Greco-Roman deities. Since Revelation links the practice to "immorality," some interpreters assume that the Nicolaitans also promoted illicit sexual behavior

(Irenaeus, *Haer.* 1.26.3; Tertullian, *Marc.* 1.29.2; Hippolytus, *Haer.* 7.36; Schüssler Fiorenza, *Book*, 116; Karrer, *Johannesoffenbarung*, 200). Nevertheless, this interpretation is unlikely, since the writer uses "immorality" (*porneia*) as a metaphor for idolatry (NOTE on 2:14).

The Nicolaitans had some followers at Pergamum and attempted unsuccessfully to promote their teachings at Ephesus (Rev 2:6, 15). At Thyatira those associated with "Jezebel" shared the Nicolaitans' views (2:20). Although some interpreters assume that Jezebel, the Nicolaitans, and the false apostles at Ephesus (2:2) were part of the same movement (Aune, *Apocalypticism*, 187; Schüssler Fiorenza, *Book*, 115; Murphy 105–11; Trebilco, *Early*, 315), it is not clear that those who held similar views on meal practices had common leadership or other features that made them a distinct group (Royalty, *Streets*, 28–29). The views of the false apostles had to be tested, whereas those of the Nicolaitans were known (2:2, 5), suggesting that such apostles were not clearly identified with the Nicolaitans.

The name "Nicolaitans" probably means that they identified with a teacher named Nicolaus. Some interpreters suggest that the name is symbolic. The name Nicolaus is based on the Greek *niką laon*, meaning "he conquers people," just as the name Balaam can be traced to Hebrew roots meaning "he devoured people" (*bālaʿ ʿam; b. Sanh.* 105a). Since Balaam and Nicolaus have similar etymologies, some infer that the teaching associated with the names is also similar (Charles; Hemer, *Letters*, 89; D. F. Watson, *ABD* 4:1106–7). This approach is unlikely, however, since the author probably would have signaled that the name "Nicolaitan" was used in a symbolic way (cf. Rev 9:11; 11:8; 16:16).

If the group was established by a figure named Nicolaus, nothing more is known about him. The name was fairly common (IG XII, 5 465.1; I.Smyr 668 II 18–19; 779.5; *MAMA* 1 #254.3; I.Delos 2598.50; P.Hib. 98.10; 107.3). Ancient interpreters linked the group to Nicolaus of Antioch, who joined the Hellenist wing of the church (Acts 6:5), though they disagreed over whether Nicolaus was responsible for the heresy (Irenaeus, *Haer.* 1.26.3; Hippolytus, *Haer.* 7.24) or whether his followers distorted his teaching (Clement of Alexandria, *Strom.* 2.20; 3.4). Some still find this approach plausible (Räisänen, "Nicolaitans," 1625–26; Fox, "Nicolaitans"; Walter, "Nikolaos"), but it is not clear that the early Christian writers had more information about the Nicolaitans than is given in Revelation (Tertullian, *Praescr.* 33; Eusebius, *Hist. eccl.* 3.29.1). It is best to acknowledge that the founder of the group is unknown.

The relationship of the Nicolaitans to other early Christian groups is unclear. Some scholars argue that the Nicolaitans followed Paul's position (Thompson, *Book*, 123; Räisänen, "Nicolaitans," 1628–31), but their views were probably closer to those of the Corinthians, who ate sacrificial food in most circumstances. Accordingly, some suggest that the Corinthians and Nicolaitans represent distortions of the Pauline tradition. They note that the approach of the Nicolaitans was like those who taught "the deep things of Satan" (Rev 2:24). This expression is probably John's parody of the Pauline expression "the deep things of God" (1 Cor 2:10; cf. Rom 11:33). If the Nicolaitans claimed to teach "the deep things of God," they could have appealed to Pauline theology when maintaining the freedom to eat sacrificial meat (Swete; Schüssler Fiorenza, *Book*, 117–20; Heiligenthal, "Wer waren"; Trebilco, *Early*, 334). This proposal is possible, but it is not certain, since Revelation does not indicate what arguments the Nicolaitans used.

Some interpreters identify the Nicolaitans as Judaizers. They connect the Nicolaitans at Pergamum, "where Satan lives" (Rev 2:13), with the "synagogue of Satan" at Smyrna and Philadelphia (2:9; 3:9). Since Revelation charges that members of those synagogues are not actually Jews, some suggest that the Nicolaitans are Gentiles who claim aspects of the Jewish tradition while advocating openness to Greco-Roman religious practices (Prigent, "L'Hérésie," 8–10; Gaston, "Judaism," 42–43). This proposal is unlikely, however, because the synagogues at Smyrna and Philadelphia almost certainly consisted of non-Christian Jews who opposed the followers of Jesus, whereas the Nicolaitans presented a more internal threat by seeking to attract Christians to their teachings (NOTE on 2:9; Schüssler Fiorenza, *Book*, 118).

Identifying the Nicolaitans as Gnostics has been common since antiquity, but it is problematic. The Corinthian Christians who ate meat sacrificed to idols claimed superior "knowledge" (*gnōsis*; 1 Cor 8:1–4), and some think that the Nicolaitans did the same. Christians in the second and third centuries identified the Nicolaitans with Gnostics of their own time but probably lacked firsthand information about the first-century Nicolaitans (Irenaeus, *Haer.* 3.11.1; Tertullian, *Praescr.* 33; Eusebius, *Hist. eccl.* 3.29.1; cf. Justin Martyr, *Dial.* 35). Gnostic texts from Nag Hammadi make no mention of eating sacrificial meat (Aune 1:149). For the interpretation of Revelation, it is enough to associate the views of the Nicolaitans with those of the people at Pergamum and Thyatira, who were willing to eat meat from offerings made to Greco-Roman deities in most if not all circumstances.

2:7. *Let the one who has an ear hear.* In the OT, the expression "Hear the word of the Lord" usually calls for attention before an oracle is given (e.g., Isa 1:10; Jer 2:4), but in Rev 2–3 the call to listen comes after the messages, emphasizing the need for response. The Greek employs assonance, as does the English translation: *ous* and *akous-* correspond to "ear" and "hear." The saying has precedent in the prophetic tradition: "Let those who hear, hear; and let those who refuse to hear, refuse" (Ezek 3:27; cf. 12:2; Jer 5:21). Most similar is the saying of Jesus: "He who has ears to hear, let him hear." This saying can call for interpretation of something obscure (Mark 4:9 par.; *Gos. Thom.* 65, 96), but more often it summons listeners to accept or act on statements whose meaning is clear (Matt 11:15; 13:43; Mark 4:23), which is the case in Revelation (Enroth, "Hearing"). Some interpreters suggest that the author drew on the gospels (Charles 1:lxxxiii–lxxxiv), but it is more likely that the saying circulated orally, since there is no trace of the Synoptic contexts in Revelation (Vos, *Synoptic*, 71–75). The ease with which this saying could circulate is evident in that it was added to some manuscripts of the Synoptic Gospels, where it now appears as a variant reading (Matt 25:29; Mark 7:16; Luke 12:21; 13:9; 21:4).

what the Spirit says to the assemblies. The Spirit was understood to inspire prophets, so God's word came through them (Num 11:25; 1 Sam 10:10; Joel 2:28; Zech 7:12). God's Spirit spoke through David and the prophets of Israel (2 Sam 23:2; Ezek 11:5; Acts 1:16; 3:7; 4:25; Heb 10:15; cf. *4 Ezra* 14:22) and the early church (Mark 13:11; Acts 20:23; 21:11; 1 Tim 4:1; Ign. *Phld.* 7:1–2). The Spirit's inspiration gave authority to the message (Philo, *Spec. Laws* 1.65; 4.49; Berger, *Amen-Worte*, 117–24).

All the messages to the churches are introduced as words of the risen Jesus, yet in the end it is the Spirit that speaks. Some interpreters maintain that the Spirit is essentially identical to the spiritual presence of the risen Jesus, noting that in Revelation the Spirit lacks the distinctive personal character that it has in later Trinitarian thought (E. Schweizer, *TDNT* 6:449–50; Bucur, "Hierarchy"). Nevertheless, the Spirit does speak with its own voice and even calls on Christ to "Come" (Rev 14:13; 22:17). The Spirit can be distinguished from Jesus yet does not work independently of Jesus. The Spirit of prophecy is the witness of Jesus (19:10; Bruce, "Spirit," 340–42; cf. Bauckham, *Climax*, 160–62; Aune 1:36; Waddell, *Spirit*, 21–38).

To those who conquer. The verb *nikan* means conquest and victory. It is a metaphor that draws from three spheres of meaning:

1. Military: Soldiers conquer on the battlefield by strength, courage, weaponry, and tactics. Roman rule was extended by victories over other peoples: Julius Caesar said, "I came, I saw, I conquered" (Plutarch, *Caes.* 50). Dates on inscriptions at Thyatira and Philadelphia reckoned time from Augustus's victory at Actium (Malay, *Researches*, no. 24; I.Phil 1434). Temples and coins at Ephesus, Pergamum, Laodicea, and other cities depicted the emperors Augustus, Titus, and Domitian in military dress receiving victory wreaths, holding trophies, or attended by Nikē, who personified victory (see Figures 8, 12, 18, 31, 32; Friesen, *Imperial*, 30, 62; R. Smith, "Imperial"). Revelation identifies this form of conquest with the beast, which slays the faithful and others (11:7; 13:7). Christian conquest will be of a different sort.

2. Athletics: The verb *nikan* was used for victory in athletic and musical competitions. Such contests were held during festivals honoring deities like Artemis at Ephesus (Dionysius of Halicarnassus, *Ant. rom.* 4.25.4) and at festivals for the emperors. At Ephesus the games inaugurated during Domitian's reign provided opportunities for athletes to "conquer" (Friesen, *Imperial*, 52). Inscriptions throughout Asia made victory in contests a form of public honor (I.Eph 1084a; 1101.5; 1106.4–5; 1117.3; I.Smyr 659.4; I.Thyat 1005; I.Sard 76.7; I.Phil 1460.9). In Revelation, conquering involves perseverance, but honor comes from God and Christ.

3. Faithfulness: Those who remained true to their convictions in the face of opposition also "conquered." Such a victory is achieved not by inflicting violence, but by enduring it. The Maccabean martyrs, who endured torture and were executed for their faithfulness to Jewish law, were compared to athletes (4 Macc 1:11; cf. 6:10; 9:30; 11:20; 17:15) and soldiers (7:4; 16:14; 17:24). In John 16:33, Christ conquers a world dominated by evil through his death and resurrection, since these actions are a triumph for divine love and life. By remaining faithful to Christ, his followers conquer the world in which hatred and untruth operate (1 John 2:13–14; 4:4; 5:4–5). Comparing perseverance in faith to the steadfastness of a soldier (1 Thess 5:8; Eph 6:10–17; 2 Tim 3–5) or an athlete (1 Cor 9:24–27; Heb 12:1–2) was common among Christians. Revelation transforms the images of conquest and victory, which brought high honor in Greco-Roman culture, into a call for Christians to resist aspects of that culture. Faithfulness to Jesus could bring dishonor in society, yet in Christ's eyes the faithful are worthy of the victory wreath (Rev 2:10; 3:11).

I will grant to eat from the tree of life. Some interpreters propose that this imagery contrasts the true tree of life with the sanctuary of Artemis at Ephesus, which could have originated as a tree shrine (Ramsay, *Letters*, 247–49; Hemer, *Letters*, 41–52; Boxall; Murphy; Osborne). But Smyrna's founding also was linked to a tree shrine (Pausanias, *Descr.* 7.5.2), and sacred trees and groves were found throughout the Greco-Roman world (Pausanias, *Descr.* 1.30.2; 2.31.8; Pliny the Elder, *Nat.* 12.3). The term *paradeisos*, which is used here, also designated sacred areas outside of Ephesus (I.Did 557.5). If the tree of life image is a contrast with Greco-Roman religious practice, it is broadly based and not uniquely tied to Ephesus. On the tree of life, see the NOTE on Rev 22:2.

that is in the paradise of God. Paradeisos is a term for a garden or park, usually filled with trees (Neh 2:8; Eccl 2:5). It was used for the garden of Eden, where the tree of life stood (Gen 2:8–9; cf. Ezek 28:13; 31:9; Isa 51:3). Because of sin, people were banished from paradise (Gen 3:24), yet tradition said that God preserved paradise after the fall (*2 Bar.* 1:3–7; *4 Ezra* 6:2). Some Jewish and Christian texts picture paradise as a distant region on earth (*1 En.* 32:3; cf. 24:3–4), while others assume a heavenly location (*Jos. As.* 16:14; *2 En.* 8:1; 2 Cor 12:4) or picture it as the place where the righteous will be rewarded at the end of time (*4 Ezra* 3:6; 7:123; 8:52; *2 Bar.* 51:11; *T. Levi* 18:10). In Luke 23:43 paradise is where the redeemed go immediately after death, but in Rev 22:1–5 paradise belongs to the new creation.

COMMENT

The message to Ephesus is the first of seven addressed to Christian communities in Asia Minor. Each message identifies the city in which the congregation is located and then deals with issues arising from life in Roman Asia. The city, or *polis*, is a major literary motif. The book begins with the seven cities in which the readers live, but the middle section treats the entire world as one "great city," which is called Babylon and has features of Rome (Rev 17–18). Through the portrayal of Babylon, the writer places the issues of conflict, worship, and wealth that readers face on local levels in the context of a larger cosmic struggle between God and the destroyers of the earth. The motif culminates in the vision of God's city, New Jerusalem, where sin, evil, and death have no place and the redeemed receive life in God's presence. The promise of that city gives readers incentive to remain faithful in the cities where they live (Rossing, *Choice*, 155–61).

Ephesus was a port city, and of the seven cities mentioned in Rev 2–3 it was the one closest to the island of Patmos (1:9). Geographically, it is appropriate for the writer to address the congregation in Ephesus first and then turn to each successive city as a messenger might do, going north to Smyrna and Pergamum, then southeast to Thyatira, Sardis, Philadelphia, and Laodicea. Interpreters have often tried to relate each message to distinctive traits of the city in which a congregation was located, but the approach taken here differs in three ways.

First, it recognizes that the seven cities had more similarities than differences. All had mixed populations that included Greeks, Romans, and Jews. Traditional forms of polytheism were popular, as was the imperial cult. Social life included gatherings of associations and public festivals with religious elements. Economically, all the cities relied

On Rev 2:1–7, see Aune, *Apocalypticism*, 175–89, 212–32; Biguzzi, "Ephesus"; deSilva, *Seeing*, 175–92, 229–38; Hemer, *Letters*, 35–56; Holtz, "Die Werke"; Homcy, "To Him"; Karrer, "Angels"; Kirby, "Rhetorical"; C. R. Koester, "Roman"; H. Koester, ed., *Ephesos*; Ramsay, *Letters*, 210–50; Tellbe, *Christ-Believers*, 100–111, 211–16; Trebilco, *Early*, 293–350; Pilch, "Lying"; Witetschek, *Ephesische*; Yarbro Collins, "Insiders" and "Vilification."

on the opportunities that the Roman Empire provided. The characteristics of the cities were much the same; it was the characteristics of the congregations that differed (NOTES on 2:1, 8, 12, 18; 3:1, 7, 14). Second, the literary context further levels the distinctions between cities. For example, Ephesus, Smyrna, and Pergamum may have been larger and more important than Thyatira and Philadelphia, but the messages make nothing of this. Each city is simply named so that attention can be focused on the particular issues facing the congregation. Third, the imagery in the messages to the churches is drawn from Scripture and contemporary cultural practices that were broadly familiar. The messages do not allude to civic history or to institutions that are unique to each city.

The Christian community at Ephesus was probably the oldest, largest, and most varied of those addressed by the Apocalypse (NOTE on 2:1). It probably included a number of house churches (Rev 2:1). The situation may have been comparable to that in Rome, where Paul writes broadly to the Christian community as a whole even though it had a number of subgroups (Rom 1:7; 16:5; cf. 1 Cor 16:8, 19; Tellbe, *Christ-Believers*, 1–56). Leadership may have taken different forms: The book of Acts pictures a church at Ephesus led by elders (20:17); the Pastoral Epistles and Ignatius refer to bishops and deacons (1 Tim 1:3; 3:1–13; Ign. *Eph.* 1:3). The author of Revelation, however, writes with prophetic authority, and some interpreters think he addresses only one subgroup, which shared his apocalyptic outlook (H. Koester, "Ephesos," 132–33) or perhaps were Jewish Christians (Witetschek, *Ephesische*, 411–14). It is more likely, however, that he envisions a wide group of Ephesian readers (Ign. *Eph.* pref.; Trebilco, *Early*, 335–42; Tellbe, *Christ-Believers*, 39). Prophets worked in Christian circles where there were other forms of authority and could deliver messages to the community directly rather than transmitting them through other leaders (Acts 11:27; 13:1; 15:32; 20:17; 21:10; Rom 12:6–8; 1 Cor 12:28; 14:29; Eph 4:11; Aune, *Prophecy*, 203–11).

One Christian group that John considers to be distinct from his intended readers is the Nicolaitans, who were open to eating what had been sacrificed to Greco-Roman deities; John and his readers rejected this practice (Rev 2:5, 15, 20). A second group of outsiders are the self-identified apostles, who came to Ephesus from elsewhere and whose views had to be tested. The author commends the Ephesian assembly for resisting these groups, but he also addresses the negative consequence of their rigor: the loss of love.

The message shares the basic literary elements of all seven messages, presenting these in symmetrical ring structure (see §3B):

Introduction (2:1)
    Commendation for resisting false teachers (2:2–3)
        Reproof for letting go of the love they had at first (2:4)
        Call to repent and to do the works they did at first (2:5)
    Commendation for resisting false teachers (2:6)
Conclusion (2:7)

The outer ring consists of an introduction that speaks of the listeners' present location in Ephesus and a conclusion that locates future hope in paradise. These elements reflect the movement of the book as a whole, which begins with the seven cities and culminates in the eschatological city, where the tree of life is found. The intermediate ring is formed by statements commending the assembly for its opposition to false teachings and words encouraging readers to continue this course. The inner ring consists of reproof and a summons to repentance. Placing these hard words in the center, surrounded by more encouraging words, allows the reproof to be heard as a correction intended for the readers' good, rather than as a dismissive judgment.

Introduction

Each message begins with the exalted Christ commanding John to "write" (2:1; see §3B). As the message unfolds, readers can assume that John shares the views of the Christ who addresses them, and yet John cannot fully identify himself with the divine speaker. The message may warn that the congregation's "lampstand" will be moved and promise that the faithful will eat from the tree of life, but John cannot enact either the warning or the promise. Both require divine action. If readers are to receive this message as a prophetic word, they must be convinced that Christ speaks through John's text.

John is told to write to "the angel of the assembly," who is the heavenly representative of the congregation (2:1). The inclusion of this angel varies a familiar pattern of contact between the divine and human worlds. John has emphasized the majesty of Christ, which is so overpowering that John fell down as though dead (1:12–18). The divine presence radiates overwhelming power. For a heavenly speaker to address a wider human audience, the encounter must be mediated. A typical pattern is that God commissions a prophet to speak to the people (Exod 20:18–19; Deut 5:25–27; Jer 1:9–10; Ezek 1:26–2:3), and sometimes an angel readies the prophet for his work (Isa 6:1–8; Rev 10:1–11). But here, the roles are reversed. Instead of the angel addressing the terrified prophet, the terrified prophet is to address the angel who represents the congregation (Boxall). There is no suggestion that the angel will take the message to the congregation. Rather, Christ's command to address the assembly through its representative angel allows people to listen to the divine voice—but at a distance (deSilva, *Seeing*, 127; Backhaus, "Vision," 10).

The exalted Christ strikes a tone of authority by saying, "Thus says" (2:1). This expression often introduced a prophetic word from the Lord, and here John uses it for a word from Christ, who shares the traits of God (1:15, 17). This expression was also used for royal decrees, and Christ speaks as the ruler of earth's kings (1:5). Christ identifies himself only by his traits, not by his name, which preserves a sense of high dignity. But despite the majestic otherness, the exalted Christ walks among the lampstands that signify the churches.

Body of the Message

The risen Jesus commends the Ephesians for their works, which establishes rapport between the speaker and listeners (2:2). In these messages praise and blame have a hortatory function (*Rhetorica ad Herennium* 3.4.7; Quintilian, *Inst.* 3.7.28). By praising the readers' labor and endurance, the speaker encourages them to continue this course. Since this affirmation is to be heard by all the congregations, it also gives others incentive to do the same.

The Ephesians receive special praise for testing those who called themselves apostles (2:2b). These apostles were apparently traveling evangelists who had come to Ephesus from elsewhere. Whether they sought support from the congregation or had other reasons for making contact is unclear, but the Ephesians questioned their authenticity. The criteria that Christians used to distinguish true from false apostles varied, but here the issue was probably whether the newcomers' teachings and manner of life were congruent with the faith of the congregation (NOTE on 2:2; cf. 2 Cor 11:4–5, 12–14). A key point may have been whether the apostles were willing to eat food offered to Greco-Roman deities. This issue led the Ephesians to oppose the Nicolaitans and John to consider Jezebel a false prophet (Rev 2:6, 20). In Revelation, truth promotes commitment to God and Christ (3:14; 6:10), whereas falsehood draws people into worship of other powers (2:20; 13:14; 16:13; 19:20; 20:10). Whatever specific test was used, the Ephesians are commended for their opposition to those whose teaching is considered deceptive.

The congregation is not exempt from criticism, however, so the speaker now shifts to reproof: "I have this against you" (2:4). Rhetorically, listeners are most likely to accept reproof when they know it arises out of concern for them. This is the case here, since the message is from Christ, who shed his blood on their behalf (1:5–6). An honest confrontation of someone's shortcomings was understood to be an act of friendship (Cicero, *Amic.* 24.89–25.96; Plutarch, *Mor.* 55DE, 59D, 66A; deSilva, *Seeing*, 186). Where the words of encouragement strengthen what is positive, the reproof seeks to change what is negative, much as a physician might administer a stinging treatment to restore the health of a patient (Plutarch, *Mor.* 55C).

The Ephesians are faulted for letting go of the love they had at first (Rev 2:4; cf. Matt 24:12). Some interpreters suggest that they have lost their love for God or Christ, and that despite their opposition to the Nicolaitans, they have become less rigorous in avoiding Greco-Roman religious practices. From this perspective the Ephesians are being called to recover their former, more rigorous stance (Trebilco, *Early*, 305; cf. Giesen; Prigent; Satake). The context, however, emphasizes the firmness of their commitment to Christ (Rev 2:3). Instead, the problem seems to be that their opposition to false teaching has led to a loss of love for other believers. Therefore, the Ephesians are called to do the works they did at first, which would have been acts of service for others (2:5, 19; Blount; Murphy; Smalley; Witherington).

The call to "repent" is given here for the first time (2:5). Later, the unbelievers will come under judgment for refusing to repent (9:20–21; 16:9, 11), but in the messages to the churches the call to repent is addressed to the followers of Jesus (2:5, 16; 3:3, 19). This need for repentance blurs the distinction between those who are outside and inside the Christian camp. All come under the scrutiny of Christ. On one level, repentance involves a renewal of commitment to God and Christ (14:6–7). On another, repentance is evident in "works" that express these commitments. If readers are committed to the Christ who loves them (1:5), it is shown by their love for others.

The call for repentance includes a warning in conditional form: "If" they do not repent, Christ will come to discipline them (2:5). A proper warning is given when both danger and hope are real. When the danger seems imminent, it may awaken fear, which motivates people to change course so that loss can be averted (Aristotle, *Rhet.* 2.5.1; Philo, *Praem.* 163). Christ is already present among the churches, yet he warns that he will "come" for disciplinary action. Some interpreters think this warning refers to Christ's final coming at the end of the age when the unrepentant will be judged (Murphy; Thomas). Yet this proposal is unlikely, since his final coming is definitive and affects all people (Rev 1:7; 22:12), whereas his coming to the Ephesians is conditional and is directed at a specific congregation (Beale; Giesen; Mounce).

The warning is that Christ will move the congregation's lampstand from its place (2:5). The sense here is that the congregation will suffer a loss of status if it fails to repent, but readers are not told how they will know whether this actually occurs. The metaphor of moving the lampstand creates a crisis of discernment, as it will in subsequent messages in which Christ warns of making war with the "sword" of his mouth, of putting Jezebel to "bed," and of spewing the complacent out of his mouth (2:16, 22; 3:16). How would readers experience the effect of such threats? As long as the congregation at Ephesus continues to gather, the readers will find it difficult to conclude that their lampstand has been moved. Yet this lack of closure also means that the imagery continues to serve as a warning about the way a loss of love threatens to bring a loss of identity.

Since the congregation has been faulted for a lack of love, it is perhaps surprising that it is now commended for hating the works of the Nicolaitans (2:6). The Nicolaitans are a Christian group open to eating food that has been offered to Greco-Roman deities. From John's perspective, the Nicolaitans foster acceptance of idolatry, which is evil (INTRO III.A.1; III.B.2), and hating evil is the opposite of loving what is good (Pss 45:7; 101:3; 119:113, 128; Rom 12:9). Traditionally, God is said to hate idolatry and wrongdoing (Deut 12:31; 16:22; Pss 5:4–5; 11:5); therefore, the faithful are to do the same (Pss 31:6; 97:10; 119:104), which according to Revelation means rejecting idolatry in all forms.

Conclusion

The message addresses the whole congregation, but it concludes with an exhortation for every individual to "hear" and heed it (2:7). The exhortation is then broadened to include all the churches, not only the one at Ephesus. The specific issues facing each congregation may vary, but the call for renewed works of love and continued resistance to false teaching applies to all. The words "Let the one who has an ear hear" may recall sayings ascribed to Jesus (NOTE on 2:7). If readers were familiar with such sayings, the appeal of the message would be enhanced, since the expression gives the sense that the Jesus known through tradition is the same one who now speaks through John's revelatory text (deSilva, *Seeing*, 238).

Although this message began as a word from Christ, it concludes by saying that "the Spirit" speaks to the assemblies (2:7). The Spirit mediates the word of the risen Jesus in two ways. First, the Spirit enables *John* to receive the words of the risen Christ through his vision. John said that he received his message while "in the Spirit" (1:9). This expression likens him to the biblical prophets, who were moved by the Spirit to convey a word from God. Second, the Spirit enables *the readers* to receive the risen Christ's words through John's text. Communication is complete when the word given to John in visionary form is received by the readers in written form. In this process the Spirit shares Christ's authority: both speak (*legei*) as one (2:1, 7).

A promise to "those who conquer" is included here, as in every message (2:7). The language anticipates scenes of holy war, where local issues facing the churches become part of a cosmic battle. The word "conquer" can have violent connotations, as in the visions of the horseman conquering by the sword and a beast slaying the faithful (6:2;

11:7; 13:7). But "conquer" is also used in a transferred sense for the Lamb and his followers, who bear witness to the truth even at the cost of their lives (5:5–6; 12:11; 15:2). The Lamb conquers in a unique way, since his death delivers people from sin and makes them into a kingdom where the reign of God is recognized (1:5–6; 5:5–9). In the present, Christ's followers share his victory and "conquer" by remaining faithful to him in the face of opposition. In the future, they will also share Christ's triumph over death by their own resurrections to life in New Jerusalem (21:7).

The call to "conquer" summons people to be faithful until death, but it does not assume that all believers will die violently. At points it seems as if all who reject idolatry will be slain (12:11; 13:7, 15), but elsewhere the writer uses the conditional "if" when referring to the possibility of death or imprisonment (13:10), and he assumes that some Christians will be alive at Christ's final coming (3:20; 16:15). The point is that people are to be faithful throughout their lives. Like the word "endurance" (2:2), the image of conquest calls for active resistance against the forces that oppose the reign of God, whether these are overt acts of hostility (2:9; 3:9), deceptive forms of false teaching (2:2, 6, 14, 20), or the seductive complacency that comes from wealth (3:17–18; cf. Bauckham, *Theology*, 88–94; Blount 13–14).

Those who conquer will eat from the tree of life in the paradise of God (2:7). This imagery recalls that at creation the tree of life stood in the "paradise" of Eden (Gen 2:9). According to the Scriptures, the first man and woman disobeyed God by eating from the tree of knowledge and were put out of the garden so they would not eat from the tree of life and live forever (3:22). Redemption required overcoming the barriers of sin and death so fullness of life could be restored. Eating from the tree of life signified salvation (*1 En.* 24:4; 25:4–6; *4 Ezra* 8:52; *T. Levi* 18:11; *Tg. Neof.* Gen 3:24–25). The final scenes in Revelation take up this hope, as the redeemed come to the tree of life in a garden within a city—New Jerusalem (COMMENT on Rev 22:1–5).

6. To the Assembly in Smyrna (2:8–11)

2   ⁸"To the angel of the assembly in Smyrna write: Thus says the first and the last, who died and came to life: ⁹I know your affliction and poverty (even though you are rich), and the denunciation of those who say they are Jews (though they are not, but are a synagogue of Satan). ¹⁰Fear nothing you are about to suffer. You see the devil is going to throw some of you into prison so that you might be tested, and you will have affliction for ten days. Be faithful to death and I will give you the laurel wreath of life. ¹¹Let the one who has an ear hear what the Spirit says to the assemblies. Those who conquer will not be harmed by the second death."

NOTES

2:8. *To the angel of the assembly.* Each angel apparently has responsibility for a congregation (NOTES on 1:20; 2:1).

in Smyrna. Smyrna (modern Izmir, Turkey) was a port city located about forty miles north of Ephesus. It was one of the largest cities in Asia, comparable to Ephesus and Pergamum. Settled in ancient times by Greeks, Smyrna was refounded at a new location in the late fourth century or early third century BCE. The Smyrneans were allies of Rome by the early second century BCE and officially came under Roman control after 133 BCE. Smyrna was one of the province's judicial centers (Pliny the Elder, *Nat.* 5.31.120). Its population included Greeks, Jews, and Roman businesspeople (Cicero, *Flac.* 71; IGR 1484). Culturally, it was known as the birthplace of Homer and one of the most beautiful cities in Asia. The first provincial athletic competitions were held at Smyrna in the first century BCE and periodically in the centuries that followed (I.Smyr 635).

Smyrna had an impressive acropolis that towered above the sea, paved streets, colonnades, a library, a theater, gymnasiums, baths, and a stadium (Strabo, *Geographica* 14.1.37; Vitruvius, *Arch.* 5.9.1; Aelius Aristides, *Orations* 17.9). One street was called the golden way (Aelius Aristides, *Orations* 17.10; 18.6). The city was supplied with water through its aqueducts, one of which was built during the reign of Domitian (I.Smyr 680). Like Ephesus, Smyrna had an excellent harbor (Philostratus, *Vit. Apoll.* 4.6–9) and access to a good road system that connected the city to inland markets (I.Smyr 823–26). There were groups of goldsmiths, silversmiths, and winemakers (I.Smyr 721; Strabo, *Geographica* 14.1.15), as well as associations for fishermen, porters, athletes, flax workers, and perhaps bankers (Harland, *Associations*, 39–40, 85). In the first century BCE a medical school was founded at Smyrna, and during the next two centuries the city was noted for its physicians (I.Smyr 536–37; Broughton, *Asia*, 851–52).

The guardian of the city's welfare was the mother goddess Meter, sometimes known as Cybele, who was worshiped throughout the region. Her temple was an important sanctuary in Smyrna (I.Smyr 655; Pliny the Elder, *Nat.* 14.4.54; Strabo, *Geographica* 14.1.37). On the acropolis was a temple to the Nemeses, who were linked to the founding of Smyrna (Aelius Aristides, *Orations* 20.20). There was a temple to Zeus, who was worshiped as Polieus, or "of the City" (Aelius Aristides, *Orations* 20.23); Akraios, or "of the Heights"; and Soter, or "Savior" (I.Smyr 680; 757). Other temples were dedicated to Tyche, Dionysus, and the Syrian goddess Atargatis (I.Smyr 697.14 728.2; 735). Areas in the city were sacred to the Ephesian Artemis and Apollo (I.Smyr 742; 750; 753), and the temple to Aphrodite Stratonikis was a place of asylum (Tacitus, *Ann.* 3.63). Dedications were made to the Greek Herakles, the Anatolian god Men, and the Egyptian deity Anubis (Tacitus, *Ann.* 768; 753.15; 765). Where Jews considered the God of Israel to be the Most High, this title was given to a Greco-Roman deity at Smyrna (Tacitus, *Ann.* 764). The cult of Asclepius would not be formally instituted until the second century CE.

Leading citizens served as priests and priestesses of various deities and underwrote the costs of festivals. Associations were dedicated to Kore and Demeter (I.Smyr 653–54) and Dionysus (I.Smyr 731–32; Harland, *Associations*, 46–47, 108, 271–72; Cadoux, *Ancient*, 202–27; Ascough, "Greco-Roman," 47–52). The association of goldsmiths and silversmiths repaired a statue of Athena (I.Smyr 721). There were also public festivals of Dionysus, which included a procession through the marketplace (Aelius Aristides, *Orations* 17.5–6), as well as athletic competitions with religious elements. For Christians in the city, social pressures to accommodate Greco-Roman practice would have been similar to those in other cities (Rev 2:6, 14–15, 20), but these are not identified in Revelation as issues at Smyrna.

Figure 9. Coin from Smyrna showing the personified Senate (left) and Livia on one side and Tiberius as a priest in the imperial temple at Smyrna (29–35 CE) on the other. Courtesy of the Classical Numismatic Group (cngcoins.com).

The imperial cult had strong popular support. Smyrna had built a temple to the goddess Roma in 195 BCE and was known as an ally of Rome (Tacitus, *Ann.* 4.56; Cicero, *Phil.* 11.2.5). After the provincial temple to Augustus was built at Pergamum, a citizen of Smyrna soon served as a high priest there (2 BCE; I.Sard 8.90). Smyrna competed with other cities for the honor of building its own imperial temple and in 26 CE received permission to erect one to Tiberius, Livia, and the Roman Senate (Tacitus, *Ann.* 4.15, 55–56; Friesen, *Twice*, 15–21). A coin from Smyrna pictures Livia and the Senate, personified as a young man, on one side and on the other the emperor Tiberius in the imperial temple at Smyrna. He is robed in the garb of a priest, rather than in military garb as Augustus was at Pergamum, and is portrayed as the ruler who carries on sacred tradition (Figure 9). The cult had a high priest and priestess, as well as hymn singers (Friesen, *Twice*, 21). Around the city, dedications were made to Julius Caesar, Augustus, and Nero (I.Smyr 617–621). Inscriptions mentioning Domitian identify him as emperor, son of god, and high priest but stop short of calling the living emperor "god" (I.Smyr 731; 826).

The Jewish community at Smyrna was well-established. A variant reading of 1 Macc 15:23 suggests that Jews lived in Smyrna by the second century BCE. In Jewish apocalyptic writing, Smyrna is among the Gentile cities that fall under divine judgment (*Sib. Or.* 3:344, 365; 5:122, 306), but that negative view was exceptional; Jews in Smyrna seem to have been well-integrated into civic life. An inscription from the early second century CE lists donations given to the city by an imperial high priest, hymn singers, and *hoi pote Ioudaioi* (I.Smyr 697.30 = *IJO* 2, no. 40). That Greek expression may refer to "former Judeans," who immigrated to Smyrna (Kraabel, "Roman," 455; Harland, *Associations*, 202), although some interpreters argue that they are "former Jews," who abandoned their faith (S. Wilson, "OI ΠΟΤΕ"). In any case, other inscriptions from the third through the fourth or fifth centuries CE attest to a Jewish community in the city (*IJO* 2:174–95).

A Christian community was probably established at Smyrna between 55 and 85 CE. There is little evidence of Christian groups in western Asia Minor before the mid-50s, yet a congregation was formed at Smyrna by the late 80s or early 90s, before Revelation was written. Some scholars connect it to Paul's work at Ephesus (Acts 19:10, 26; Cadoux, *Ancient*, 305; Murphy; Osborne; Smalley), but this is uncertain.

The apocryphal *Acts of Paul* and *Acts of John* tell of Paul and John visiting Smyrna, but these legendary accounts are unreliable for historical reconstruction (*NTApoc* 2:241, 369, 387; Neufeld, "Christian," 33–37). Nevertheless, expressions used in a letter by Polycarp, the bishop of Smyrna, show that by the early to mid-second century CE both the Pauline and Johannine traditions were known there (Pol. *Phil.* 3:2; 7:1; 11:2).

The congregation may have included Christians of Jewish background, since there was local conflict with synagogue members over who could claim to be true Jews (Rev 2:9). Nevertheless, by the time Revelation was written, Jesus' followers called their gathering an *ekklēsia*, whereas the Jewish community was a separate *synagogē*. At some point the Christians became ethnically mixed. Polycarp, for example, was not of Jewish background. By that time the congregation had adopted forms of leadership that included deacons, elders, and bishops (Ign. *Smyrn.* 8:1; 12:2; Ign. *Pol.* pref.; 6:1; Pol. *Phil.* pref.). Those roles were common in Christian assemblies but not in Jewish synagogues. In the early second century Ignatius wrote letters from Smyrna while en route to Rome as a prisoner. In a subsequent letter to the Smyrneans, Ignatius says nothing about a conflict with Judaism but warns instead against docetism, which diminished the importance of Jesus' humanity (Ign. *Smyrn.* 4).

Thus says the first and the last, who died and came to life. The phrase "thus says" has royal and prophetic connotations (NOTE on 2:1). The words "first" and "last" connote deity (NOTE on 1:17). The conviction that Jesus died and rose was integral to early Christian faith and to the hope that Christians who die will also rise (Rev 1:5; 1 Cor 15:3–4, 20; 1 Thess 4:14; Dunn, *Unity*, 56–57; Wright, *Resurrection*, 215).

2:9. *I know your affliction and poverty.* The poverty of the Christians at Smyrna contrasts with the city's general prosperity. Various reasons for the group's poverty have been suggested: The Christians could have come from the poorer classes (Smalley) or have been Jewish refugees fleeing Palestine after the revolt against Rome (Yarbro Collins, *NJBC* 1002). Given the verbal abuse and threat of imprisonment, the civic authorities might have confiscated Christian property (cf. Heb 10:34; Eusebius, *Hist. eccl.* 4.26.5; Charles; Hemer, *Letters*, 68), or Christians might have lost income by refusing to participate in trade guilds that honored Greco-Roman deities (Rev 18:4; Giesen). The cause of their poverty remains unknown. On the formula "I know," see §3B.

even though you are rich. Riches first include a present abundance of faith. Those who were economically poor could be considered rich in nonmaterial possessions such as virtue or wisdom (Philo, *Prob.* 8; Philo, *Fug.* 17; Cicero, *Fin.* 5.28 §84), grace (Eph 1:7; 2:7), or good works (1 Tim 6:18; Giesen; Roloff). Second, the faithful have the promise of blessings in the age to come, when they inherit life in New Jerusalem (Rev 21:7; Matt 6:19–21; Eph 1:18; *T. Jud.* 25:4; Aune). Present faith and future hope reinforce each other: "Has not God chosen the poor in the world to be rich in faith and to be heirs of the kingdom that he has promised to those who love him?" (Jas 2:5; cf. Luke 6:20; 12:21; 2 Cor 6:10; 8:9).

the denunciation. Here, the primary sense of *blasphēmia* is denunciation of Christians before Greco-Roman authorities. The term did not necessarily have this meaning (Duff, "'Synagogue,'" 161), but the verbal attacks in Rev 2:9 seem to lead to the threat of imprisonment in 2:10. In legal terms, those who denounce someone are *delatores*, who bring charges of wrongdoing that initiate legal proceedings (Lambrecht, "Jewish"; Yarbro Collins, "Vilification," 312–14). On a secondary level, the term suggests that those who denounce Christians in effect blaspheme the God whom the followers of Jesus worship (13:1, 5, 6; 16:9, 11, 21; 17:3). Sources from the second and third centuries include Jews among those opposing Christians at Smyrna (*Mart. Pol.* 12:2; 13:1; 17:2; 18:1; *Mart. Pion.* 3.6; 4.5, 8). But in these texts Jewish opposition may be a literary motif designed to make the martyrs' stories parallel the story of Jesus (Lieu, *Image*, 57–102), so we will not use these texts to interpret Rev 2:9.

those who say they are Jews. Factors contributing to Jewish identity included kinship and customs such as circumcision, kosher meal practices, and Sabbath observance. Jews worshiped Israel's God and were to reject polytheism (Barclay, *Jews*, 399–444; S. Mason, "Jews"). Those claiming to be Jewish probably had the usual markers of identity. John's challenge arises because he finds their actions inconsistent with loyalty to Israel's God.

though they are not. Synagogue members at Smyrna presumably considered opposition to the church to be consistent with Israel's tradition, since they thought that Jesus' followers had departed from the tradition by making elevated claims about Jesus. From John's perspective, however, their attempt to denounce Jesus' followers—especially when this could lead to imprisonment and death—was incompatible with loyalty to Israel's God. For John, those who denounce Christians thereby denounce the God to whom they bear witness, so he calls it *blasphēmia*. Moreover, the Jews who made such denunciations joined forces with civic and provincial authorities—who worshiped other gods—in their effort to have Christians arrested. For John, true Jews would not have collaborated with idolaters (Yarbro Collins, "Insiders," 203–10; Hirschberg, *Das eschatologische*, 106–27; Mayo, "*Those,*" 51–76; Tellbe, *Christ-Believers*, 105).

Other interpretations are less viable. Some assume that the inauthentic Jews are Gentile Christians. First, some argue that these Christians keep Jewish customs and affiliate with the synagogue to avoid Roman persecution. When a Gentile adopted a few Jewish practices, one might say that "he is not a Jew, he is only acting the part" (Epictetus, *Diatribai* 2.9.20). In the second century Ignatius warned against Gentile Christians who adopted Jewish ways (*Phld.* 6:1; *Magn.* 10:3). For John, seeking shelter in the synagogue would show a lack of commitment to Jesus (S. Wilson, *Related*, 163; M. Murray, *Playing*, 73–81; cf. Kraft; Rowland). Problems with this approach include the fact that individuals might affiliate with a synagogue, but they would not *constitute* a synagogue. Moreover, it is unlikely that one group of Christians would denounce another to the Roman authorities. Second, some interpreters hold that the so-called Jews are Christians like Jezebel and the Nicolaitans, who might have claimed to be part of the Jewish tradition, even though they eat what has been sacrificed to idols (Rev 2:14–15, 20; Frankfurter, "Jews"). Again, this is unlikely since the conflicts with Jezebel and the Nicolaitans were internal Christian affairs, while the so-called Jews were apparently denouncing Christians to Gentile authorities.

Other interpretations take the so-called Jews to be non-Christians. First, some assume that for John the only true Jews are those who follow Jesus. The heated polemic might be compared to that in the DSS, which deny legitimacy to Jews outside the sect (next NOTE; Borgen, "Polemic"; Lohse, "Synagogue"; Lupieri; Murphy; Roloff). Revelation does picture Jesus' followers sharing the promises made to Israel (Rev 7:4–17; 21:9–14; cf. Rom 2:28–29; Gal 3:29; 6:16; 1 Pet 2:9–10), but it is not clear that the author would deny the title "Jew" to those who did not profess faith in Jesus. Second, some interpreters suggest that the so-called Jews had assimilated into Greco-Roman society and had lost their distinctive identity (Horn, "Zwischen"; Bredin, "Synagogue"; Marshall, *Parables*, 123–34). A problem with these proposals is that most and perhaps all seven cities mentioned in Rev 2–3 had Jewish communities, yet Revelation denies a Jewish identity only to those who denounced Christians at Smyrna and Philadelphia (Rev 2:9; 3:9). The denial of their Jewish identity stems from their denunciation of Christians and cooperation with Roman authorities. Their lack of Christian faith and assimilation to Greco-Roman culture may have contributed, but these factors alone did not prompt the sharp critique.

but are a synagogue of Satan. This epithet is the opposite of expressions such as "congregation of the Lord" (Num 20:4; 1QM IV, 9; 4Q377 1 II, 3; 4Q466 3), "assembly of God" (4Q427 7 I, 14), or "synagogue of the devout" (*Pss. Sol.* 17:16). It resembles intra-Jewish polemics like those at Qumran, where one Jewish group called another an "assembly of Belial" (1QHᵃ X, 22) and an "assembly of wickedness," "futility," or "deceit" (1QM XV, 9; 1QHᵃ XIV, 5; XV, 34). The Hebrew *satan* and Greek equivalent *diabolos* (devil, Job 1:6, 7, 9 LXX) mean accuser or slanderer (Rev 2:9–10; 20:2; NOTE on 12:9).

2:10. *Fear nothing you are about to suffer.* The threat of imminent suffering regularly inspires fear (Aristotle, *Rhet.* 2.5.1). Revelation counters fear by fostering confidence that members of the community will not be abandoned but will be brought through suffering to life through resurrection.

You see the devil is going to throw some of you into prison. Some but apparently not all of the Christians are threatened. This fits the Roman practice of prosecuting only those Christians who were denounced to them (Pliny the Younger, *Ep.* 10.96.2–4; 10.97; Eusebius, *Hist. eccl.* 4.9.1–3). Persecution was generally local, rather than an empirewide campaign against the church. In the past, Antipas had been put to death at Pergamum, but the rest of the congregation was not persecuted (Rev 2:13). At the time of John's writing, Christians in Smyrna and Philadelphia were threatened, whereas those in other cities seem to have been left alone (Lampe and Luz, "Nachpaulinisches," 196–200; Hardy, *Christianity*, 166–67; S. Potter, *ABD* 5:231–35; P. Achtemeier, *1 Peter*, 34–36).

Officials who had the power known as *coercitio* could put people in prison to maintain public order even before those arrested were convicted of wrongdoing (Acts 16:23–24; A. Arbandt and W. Macheiner, *RAC* 9:322–24; Sherwin-White, *Letters*, 778–81). People were not sentenced to prison terms. Imprisonment allowed officials time to question the accused, and it pressured the accused to comply with an official's orders (Pliny the Younger, *Ep.* 10.96.3–4). People were kept in prison indefinitely until the proper sentence was imposed (e.g., fines, banishment, death; Justinian, *Dig.* 48.19.8.9, 35).

so that you might be tested. Testing might be said to come from God or Satan. God tested Abraham's faith by commanding him to sacrifice Isaac (Gen 22:1–2), and he tested Israel's faith with false prophets and other adversaries (Deut 13:3; Judg 2:22). In Rev 2:10, however, the test comes from Satan, who afflicts people (Job 1–2; Wis 2:17–20, 24; 1 Pet 5:8). In all cases the proper response to testing is to remain faithful to God (Exod 16:4; Deut 8:2). It was said that God does not abandon those who fear him "even though for a brief time he may stand aside in order to test the disposition of the soul" (*T. Jos.* 2:6; cf. 1 Cor 10:13; 1 Pet 1:6–7; Jas 1:2, 12).

you will have affliction for ten days. "Ten days" seems to be a round number to indicate a limited period (Gen 24:55; Num 11:19). Some interpreters detect an echo of Dan 1:12, 14 where Daniel and his companions are tested for ten days by eating only vegetables and water in order to avoid nonkosher food (Beale). But the context is different at Smyrna, where testing involves imprisonment.

Be faithful to death. The Roman governor Pliny said that when Christians were denounced to him, he asked them three times if they were Christians. If they admitted it, he said, "I order them to be led away for execution; for, whatever the nature of their admission, I am convinced that their stubbornness and unshakable obstinacy ought not to go unpunished" (*Ep.* 10.96.3–4). In practice, sentencing was inconsistent: Antipas was killed (Rev 2:13), whereas John was banished (1:9). In the provinces, the Roman proconsul could impose a death sentence (Justinian, *Dig.* 1.16.6, 11), which could involve beheading (Rev 20:4; Justinian *Dig.* 48.19.8.1; Sherwin-White, *Letters*, 698), crucifixion, burning, or wild animals (Tacitus, *Ann.* 15.44; *Mart. Pol.* 12:3; Ign. *Rom.* 4:1).

and I will give you the laurel wreath of life. The common wreath (*stephanos*) worn on the head was made of laurel, myrtle, ivy, or similar foliage. The most valuable wreaths were of gold (4:4; 14:14). Here, the wreath is linked to victory or conquest (2:11), and it draws on three types of associations (W. Grundmann, *TDNT* 7:615–36; G. Stevenson, "Conceptual"; Harrison, "Fading"; Aune):

1. Athletics: Wreaths were given to victors in competitions. People endured the hardships of training and contests in the hope of receiving wreaths and public acclaim (Pindar, *Ol.* 8.76; Pausanias, *Descr.* 5.15.3). During games dedicated to a deity, the victors' wreaths connoted sacred honor. Metaphorically, philosophers urged people to overcome their passions and attain a wreath of virtue (Seneca the Younger, *Ep.* 78.16). Jews and Christians spoke of engaging in a contest against sin and social conflict in order to obtain the wreath of life (Jas 1:12), glory (1QS IV, 7; 1 Pet 5:4; *2 Bar.* 15:8), or righteousness that is given to the faithful (2 Tim 4:8; 1 Cor 9:25; *T. Job* 4:10–11; 40:3) and to martyrs (4 Macc 17:15; *Mart. Pol.* 17:1; 19:2; cf. *Mart. Asc. Isa.* 9:18).
2. Military: Wreaths were worn by those who triumphed in battle (Jdt 15:13; Josephus, *Ant.* 14.299; Pliny the Elder, *Nat.* 16.3.7–8; 16.5.14; 22.4.6–8; Vellius Paterculus, *Rom. Hist.* 1.12.4; 2.81.3; Aulus Gelius, *Noct. att.* 5.6.1–27; cf. I.Smyr 609; 610). The goddess Nikē, or Victory, was associated with the wreath, and the goddess Roma was depicted giving wreaths to emperors in military dress. Revelation pictures the persecution of the church as a war in which Christians are combatants, whose weaponry is their witness to truth (11:7; 12:11; 13:7). For them, wreaths are like the honors given to soldiers. Roman soldiers were not given posthumous awards (Aune), but Christians who die are promised the "wreath" that is resurrection to life.
3. Public service: Benefactors and others who performed civic service were publicly honored with wreaths. Examples include a temple warden and judges at Smyrna (*I.Smyr* 515.7–8; 578.23–24; 579.23–24), the head of a gymnasium at Pergamum (I.Perg 459; Deissmann, *Light*, 312), a priest at Thyatira (I.Thyat 903), and patrons at Ephesus and Philadelphia (I.Eph 27.89; I.Sard 27; I.Phil 1894). Inscriptions on gravestones pictured wreaths to show that the person was publicly honored (I.Smyr

1–117; Lucian, *Funerals* 19). Recipients were commended for faithfulness, integrity, and generosity (Danker, *Benefactor*, 352–54). Similarly, Revelation promises wreaths for faithfulness to Christ.

On divine and priestly connotations of wreaths, see the Notes on Rev 4:4 and 14:14. On the diadem, see the Note on 12:3. Some scholars think that wreath imagery is uniquely suited to Smyrna, arguing that its acropolis gave the city a crownlike appearance, that its goddess was depicted with a crown, and that crown imagery was used in its oratory (Ramsay, *Letters*, 256–67; Hemer, *Letters*, 72–74; Ascough, "Interaction," 8). The opposite, however, is more plausible. The references given above show that wreath imagery was a sign of honor throughout the empire, making it suitable for readers in all the cities. Aelius Aristides used wreath or crown imagery not only for Smyrna, but even more so for Athens (*Orations* 1.184, 354, 399). It was not a trademark of Smyrna.

2:11. *Let the one who has an ear hear what the Spirit says to the assemblies.* See the Notes on 2:7.

Those who conquer. This calls for faithfulness to God (Note on 2:7).

will not be harmed by the second death. Physical death ends life in this world, whereas the second death comes through resurrection to judgment and torment in the lake of fire (Note on 20:14).

COMMENT

The second message addresses the congregation at Smyrna, where the Christian community is at odds with its social context. The contrasts are sharp. This port city was known for its culture, wealth, and beauty, but Jesus' followers are impoverished (2:9). They understood themselves to be heirs of the promises God made to Israel but were denounced by a local synagogue (1:6; 2:9). Jesus had released them from their sins by his blood, but now they faced imprisonment and perhaps the shedding of their blood (1:5; 2:10). To embolden the congregation, the message heightens the paradox: The Christians appear to be poor, but in fact they are rich. Those who denounce them claim to be Jews, but really they are not. Dying for the faith might seem to be defeat, but it is actually victory.

The social setting is similar to that at Philadelphia, where the followers of Jesus experienced conflict with a synagogue (2:9; 3:9). Sources of tension included the status of Jesus and who could rightly claim to be Jewish. What makes the setting at Smyrna distinctive is that the synagogue members are denouncing Jesus' followers to the Roman authorities, who could imprison or execute them, whereas at Philadelphia the threat was limited to people being shut out of the wider Jewish community. The way Roman authorities could put Jesus' followers to death will be underscored by the reminder of Antipas's death at Pergamum in the next message (2:13).

On Rev 2:8–11, see Ascough, ed., *Religious*; Barr, "Idol"; Beagley, *"Sitz,"* 31–35; Borgen, "Polemic"; Bredin, "Synagogue"; Cadoux, *Ancient*; Duff, "'Synagogue'"; Frankfurter, "Jews"; Friesen, "Sarcasm"; Hirschberg, *Das eschatologische*, 31–127; Horn, "Zwischen"; Lambrecht, "Jewish" and "Synagogues"; Lohse, "Synagogue"; Marshall, *Parables*, 123–34; Mayo, *"Those"*; M. Murray, *Playing*, 73–81; Ramsay, *Letters*, 251–80; Royalty, *Streets*, 159–64; Tellbe, *Christ-Believers*, 100–11; Yarbro Collins, "Insiders" and "Vilification."

The passage has a ring structure like that of the message to Ephesus:

Opening address from Christ who died and came to life (2:8)
    Warning about the synagogue of Satan (2:9a)
        Encouragement not to fear (2:10a)
    Warning that the devil will imprison them (2:10b)
Concluding promise of life and not second death (2:10c–11)

The outer ring focuses on the assurance of life despite the threat of death. The middle ring refers to the threats posed by Satan, who acts through the local synagogue and Roman authorities. At the center is the word of encouragement (2:10a). Although the messages to most congregations include reproof, this one does not. It is designed to strengthen a congregation that faces major external challenges.

Introduction

The risen Christ identifies himself in an assuring way using language from John's inaugural vision (2:8; cf. 1:17). As "the first and the last," his presence and purposes extend far beyond the congregation's present hardship; and as the one "who died and came to life," he can assure those facing death that they too have the hope of resurrection (2:8). The problem is that affirming this high Christology would also intensify the readers' alienation from the Jewish community. The Scriptures call *God* the first and the last, since he is the Creator who brought all things into existence at the beginning and the one who will bring all things to fulfillment in the end (Isa 41:4; 44:6; 48:11–12). Most Jews would have found extending such language to Jesus to be blasphemous (cf. John 8:58–59; 10:30–33; on the "angel," see the COMMENT on 2:1).

Body of the Message

Economic factors contribute to the congregation's dislocation. By the standards of a wealthy city, they are poor, yet in the eyes of Jesus their faith makes them rich (2:9). Their counterpart is the congregation at Laodicea, which is flourishing economically but poor in faith (3:17–18). Revelation does not consider poverty to be inherently virtuous and recognizes that people of all social classes are subject to divine judgment (6:15; 13:16). But the writer assumes that the desire for economic advancement can lure people into compromising their faith in order to obtain benefits from the current order. Examples might be Christians giving divine honors to the emperor or other deities in order to participate in trade associations or civic gatherings (Kraybill, *Imperial*, 16–17; Harland, *Associations*, 260–63). The message does not commend poverty but encourages those who are poor to remain true to God. To reinforce this, later visions expose the seamy side of Roman-era commerce, and they call readers to disengage from practices that are inconsistent with the faith (18:3–4, 15, 17, 19). The Smyrneans' present wealth in faith holds within it the promise of life in New Jerusalem, whose gemlike appearance is beyond that of any earthly city (21:9–22:5). The promise of a place in that city gives readers incentive to remain faithful in the city where they now live.

    Another challenge is that members of a synagogue are denouncing Jesus' followers (2:9). One reason could have been theological. If the congregation at Smyrna held a Christology like that of John—who ascribed traits of deity to Jesus (2:8)—many Jews would have considered this blasphemous (Matt 9:3; 26:65; John 10:33). Revelation, however, reverses this, assuming that if the congregation's faith is true, then those who denigrate it actually blaspheme God and Christ (Rev 2:9; cf. Yarbro Collins, "Insiders," 209; Hirschberg, *Das eschatologische*, 108–12).

Other reasons may have been social. Some interpreters suggest that the congregation provoked opposition by drawing members away from the synagogue (Mounce). Others argue that the issue was the tax that the Romans imposed on Jews after the destruction of the temple in 70 CE (Josephus, *J.W.* 7.218). The idea is that to avoid the tax, some concealed their Jewish identity until Domitian enforced the policy (Suetonius, *Dom.* 12.2). Some argue that in the face of heightened Roman pressure, the Jewish community might have felt it necessary to distinguish those who were Jewish from those who were not, resulting in expulsions of Christians from the synagogue (Schüssler Fiorenza; Tellbe, *Christ-Believers*, 105–6; cf. Hirschberg, *Das eschatologische*, 112–17; Bredin, "Synagogue"). This reconstruction of the situation remains tenuous, however, since the tax issue is not mentioned and the problem facing the congregation is not being excluded from the synagogue but being denounced to Roman officials.

Denunciation threatened to bring Jesus' followers before the municipal or provincial authorities. In the late first and early second centuries, Roman officials generally did not initiate action against Christians but responded to charges made by others. For denunciation to lead to imprisonment, officials had to be shown that Christians were a threat (Acts 16:16–24; 17:1–9; 19:37–39). This situation posed a complex challenge for Jewish opponents of the congregation. Smyrnean Jews and Christians presumably shared an aversion to Greco-Roman polytheism, while differing sharply over the status of Jesus. Yet Roman authorities would not have considered an internal theological dispute worthy of attention (Acts 18:12–17). Therefore, synagogue members would have to present themselves as loyal citizens while charging that Christians threatened the social order. One charge could have been that professing loyalty to Jesus as sovereign showed disloyalty to the emperor (Rev 1:5; 17:14; 19:16; Acts 17:7). Another could have been that those making extravagant claims about Jesus were no longer true Jews, whose beliefs were part of a recognized tradition. Instead, Christians were to be seen as promoters of a new "superstition" that warranted suppression (Tacitus, *Ann.* 15.44; Pliny the Younger, *Ep.* 10.96.8–9; Suetonius, *Nero* 16.2).

Revelation argues the reverse, insisting that those who denounce Jesus' followers cannot claim to be true Jews. If Jesus' followers belong to the God of Israel (Rev 1:4–6), then those who denounce them denigrate the God they serve (2:9). The opponents make the righteous liable to imprisonment and death, which is contrary to the will of a just God (6:10; 15:3; 19:2). For John, no one could do this and claim to be a true Jew. Moreover, the synagogue members who denounced Jesus' followers were collaborating with the Roman authorities—who served the gods of the empire. John would not consider such collaboration consistent with Jewish identity.

Instead, he calls them a synagogue of Satan (2:9). Traditionally, Satan was said to be the accuser of the righteous (12:10; cf. Job 1:6–12; 2:1–6; Zech 3:1–5), and some members of the synagogue at Smyrna accused Christians in ways that made them liable to judgment by the authorities. Satan was also the deceiver, who used falsehood to accomplish his purposes (Rev 12:9; John 8:44; 2 Cor 11:14; 2 Thess 2:9–10). Revelation's linkage of the congregation's opponents with Satan helps to define the congregation's social boundaries, giving members a sense of distinctive identity (Yarbro Collins, "Vilification," 314; Giesen). By identifying a common enemy, the message can also help to increase the group's internal cohesion (Tellbe, *Christ-Believers*, 140). Interpreters have often pointed to the dangers of John's polemical language (Borgen, "Polemic"; Lohse, "Synagogue"; Yarbro Collins, "Vilification," 320). It is crucial to note that even though most if not all of the seven cities John addresses had Jewish communities, polemical language is used in only two of them: Smyrna and Philadelphia. Nothing negative is said about synagogues elsewhere (Friesen, "Sarcasm," 141). The polemics of this local conflict cannot be extended to Jewish-Christian relations more broadly.

Polemical language is also used for Roman authorities: It is "the devil" who will put the faithful in prison (2:10). Rhetorically, identifying one's adversary with the devil helps to foster resistance (1 Pet 5:8–9; *Mart. Pol.* 3:1; 17:1; *Mart. Perpetua and Felicitas* 10.14; 20.1; Eusebius, *Hist. eccl.* 5.1.5–6, 16, 24). *Peirazein* can mean both "tempt" and "test." In other settings Satan was said to tempt people by making sin appear attractive (Matt 4:3; 1 Thess 3:5; 1 Cor 7:5), but here he tests people with affliction in order to undermine their faith (Job 1–2; Wis 2:17–20, 24; 2 Cor 12:7; 1 Pet 5:8). The devil was said to have brought death into the world (Rev 12:9; Gen 3:1–24; Wis 2:23–24; John 8:44; Heb 2:14); therefore, threatening Christians with death at Smyrna is seen as the devil's doing, as in the death of Antipas at Pergamum (Rev 2:13). Later visions of Satan's expulsion from heaven will assure readers that even though the devil may be active, he is not invincible (12:7–12). The faithful may face the prospect of prison now, but in the end the devil himself will be incarcerated and judged (20:1–3, 10).

Imprisonment is part of the "affliction" that faces the congregation (2:10). Jails commonly had stone walls, often without windows. Many had an outer room and an inner cell where prisoners could be kept in darkness (*Mart. Pion.* 11–15; cf. Isa 42:7; Diodorus Siculus, *Libr.* 31.9.2; *Mart. Marion and James* 8:3). Prisoners lived in squalor and cramped space. During the day some wore a collar and a manacle on one hand, and at night they slept on the ground with their legs in stocks (Lucian, *Tox.* 29–30; Acts 16:24; 26:29; 28:20). Prison was regarded as disgraceful, adding shame to the physical affliction (Cicero, *Caecin.* 34.100; Seneca the Younger, *Ep.* 85.41; Epictetus, *Diatribai* 2.1.35; Josephus, *J.W.* 628; Rapske, *Book*, 195–225; Wansink, *Chained*, 27–95). The threat of imprisonment could have made some Christians ready to relinquish their faith in order to avoid that fate.

Conclusion

The call to be "faithful to death" addresses readers as soldiers in battle (Rev 2:10; Appian, *Bell. civ.* 3.11.77; 4.8.48). They engage by bearing witness to the truth even at the cost of their lives (Rev 12:11; cf. *T. Job* 5:1; *Sib. Or.* 2:47). Revelation does not assume that all believers will be martyred, but it calls them all to faithfulness, which is what it means to conquer (Rev 2:11). The honor given to those who triumphed in battle was signified by a laurel wreath, an image that transforms the readers' perceptions of their situations. To suffer publicly because of one's faith would seem to be defeat, but Christ alters this judgment by identifying victory with faithfulness and promising the victory wreath that comes from God, not the public. The "wreath of life" is resurrection to life and honor in God's presence. Unlike transient honors, it is imperishable (1 Cor 9:25; *T. Job* 4:9–10; 40:3; *Mart. Pol.* 17:1).

The final promise is that the faithful will not be subject to the second death (Rev 2:11). Revelation assumes that all people are subject to death and that in the end all will be raised. The question is whether resurrection will bring life in God's presence or the "second death," which is relegation to the lake of fire (20:11–15). Ordinary death affects both the righteous and the wicked, whereas the second death afflicts only those condemned by God. At present, the followers of Jesus may be condemned for their faith by other people, but God will reverse this judgment. He will give them life at the first resurrection, and this will continue in the new creation (20:4–6; 22:3–5). For them, resurrection is God's favorable verdict, and no further condemnation or "second death" will follow (NOTES and COMMENT on 20:14).

7. To the Assembly in Pergamum (2:12–17)

2   12"To the angel of the assembly in Pergamum write: Thus says the one who has the sharp two-edged sword: 13I know where you live, where Satan's throne is, and that you are holding on to my name and did not deny your faith in me even at the time that Antipas my faithful witness was killed among you, where Satan lives. 14But I have a few things against you, for you have some there who hold the teaching of Balaam, who taught Balak to mislead the sons of Israel so that they would eat what was sacrificed to idols and so do what is immoral. 15In the same way you also have those who hold the teaching of the Nicolaitans. 16So repent. If you do not, I will come to you soon and make war on them with the sword of my mouth. 17Let the one who has an ear hear what the Spirit says to the assemblies. To those who conquer I will give some of the hidden manna. I will also give a white stone, with a new name written on it, which no one knows except the one who receives it."

NOTES

2:12. *To the angel of the assembly.* Each angel apparently has responsibility for a congregation (NOTES and COMMENT on 1:20 and 2:1).

in Pergamum. Pergamum (modern Bergama, Turkey) was a major city located about sixty-five miles north of Smyrna by road and fifteen miles from the Aegean Sea. During the Hellenistic period it was the center of an independent kingdom and a renowned cultural center (Pliny the Elder, *Nat.* 5.33.126; Strabo, *Geographica* 13.4.1–3). The heart of the city was the acropolis, which rose above the valley below. Although the city had been settled long before, the Pergamene rulers of the third and second centuries BCE transformed it by building impressive walls, temples, palaces, and a renowned library that was second only to that of Alexandria. It had a fine theater (Figure 10), markets, and several gymnasiums. Water flowed in through a sophisticated network of aqueducts and fountains (Figure 11; Radt, *Pergamon*; Radt, "Recent"). The last Pergamene king bequeathed the territory to the Romans in 133 BCE. Although Pergamum remained an important city, the hub of Roman administration for the province shifted to the port of Ephesus. Pergamum remained a judicial center.

Figure 10. Pergamum: Theater. © Craig Koester.

Figure 11. Pergamum: Aqueduct. Courtesy of Nesrin Ermis.

The city's population included residents from the nearby regions of Mysia and Lydia as well as Greeks and Roman businesspeople (Cicero, *Flac.* 70–71; IGR 315.2). The city was an important center for banking and finance. Like other cities, Pergamum relied on textile production, with people working as dyers and makers of cloth. Inscriptions also refer to makers of parchment and fine pottery, as well as fish dealers (IGR 4:352; 425; Pliny the Elder, *Nat.* 35.160; Broughton, *Asia*, 818, 823, 894). During the first century CE increasing numbers of Pergamenes obtained Roman citizenship and were upwardly mobile. The best known was C. Aulus Julius Quadratus, who was admitted to the Roman Senate in the 70s (L. M. White, "Counting").

The patron goddess of Pergamum was Athena, whose temple stood on the acropolis. She was called Nikephorus, the bringer of victories, and Polias, guardian of the city (IGR 276; 451; 460). Nearby was the great altar with its panels depicting the triumph of the Olympian gods over the giants. Among the Greek gods honored in the city were Zeus, Hermes, and Herakles (IGR 285–87; 318). Dionysus was worshiped in various forms, including Kathegemon, or the Leader, a cult associated with the city's Hellenistic rulers (IGR 468.10). A temple of Dionysus stood in the theater. Other temples were dedicated to Hera and Demeter (Radt, *Pergamon*, 186–88). Outside the city was the sanctuary of Asclepius, the god of healing, which grew in importance during the late first century and became a renowned medical center during the second century CE through the medical research of Galen and the oratory of Aelius Aristides (Habicht, *Inschriften*, 4–7). Egyptian deities such as Isis were also venerated (H. Koester, "Cult").

Men and women served in the priesthoods of deities such as Athena, Zeus, and Dionysus (I.Perg 489–518; IGR 292; 397). Typically, they were wealthy citizens who funded festivals and conducted rites. One association was devoted to Dionysus and had a hall for banquets. They called themselves "dancing cowherds," perhaps because herders were mentioned in legends about Dionysus, but their principal role was to say prayers, sing hymns, and dance in honor of the god (Harland, *Associations*, 48). A group of female singers honored Demeter (Harland, *Associations*, 45, 72, 272). The city's physicians were linked to Asclepius and its teachers to Hermes (*Rom. Civ.* 2:207). Festivals included the provincial games, held periodically in Pergamum.

The imperial cult was a source of civic pride. In 29 BCE the province of Asia obtained permission to establish sacred precincts to Augustus. Asia's first provincial temple, dedicated to Augustus and the goddess of Rome, was built in Pergamum (Tacitus, *Ann.* 4.37; Dio Cassius, *Rom. Hist.* 51.20.6–9). Coins from Pergamum depict the temple with the goddess of Rome crowning a victorious Augustus, who wears military attire (Figure 12). Such imagery informs Revelation's portrayal of the beast, whose cult is based on the impression of invincible power (Rev 13:4, 7). Games were held as part of the cult, and leaders from local gymnasiums took part (IGR 4:317; 454). Singers from cities throughout the province provided music for the imperial temple (Friesen, *Imperial*, 25–32, 105–13; Burrell, *Neokoroi*, 17–22).

Leading citizens from Thyatira, Sardis, and other cities served as priests and overseers of the games in this provincial cult (NOTES on Rev 2:18; 3:1). At Pergamum itself, the hall where the dancing cowherds met had one altar for Dionysus and another for Augustus so that honors could be given to both deities (Figure 13; Radt, *Pergamon*, 196–99). Some called themselves friends of the emperors (*philosebastoi*), and a neighborhood association honored Nero with an inscription (Harland, *Associations*, 37, 125).

Figure 12. Coin from Pergamum showing the temple of Rome and Augustus (41–42 CE). The emperor, holding a scepter, is given a laurel wreath by Nikē (Victory), who holds a cornucopia. The imagery emphasizes victory and prosperity. Courtesy of the Classical Numismatic Group (cngcoins.com).

Figure 13. Pergamum: Small altars dedicated to Augustus Caesar (left) and Dionysus Kathegemon (right) (ca. 27–25 BCE). Courtesy of the Archive of the Pergamon Excavation, German Archaeological Institute, Istanbul Department (D-DAI-IST-82/110,1). Photographer: E. Steiner.

Many groups at Pergamum ascribed divine honors to the emperor, and Christians who belonged to such groups might be expected to accommodate. For John, however, this would be an unacceptable compromise.

A Jewish community had existed at Pergamum since the second century BCE (Josephus, *Ant.* 14.247–55). At one point the funds they intended to send to Jerusalem were confiscated by a Roman official (Cicero, *Flac.* 26.68), but in general the Jewish community's relations with the city were good (Trebilco, *Jewish*, 7–8). One Jewish writer included Pergamum among the cities that would fall under divine judgment (*Sib. Or.* 5.119), but most Jews were well-integrated into civic life. Revelation does not suggest that conflict existed between the followers of Jesus and the Jewish community at Pergamum, as was the case at Smyrna and Philadelphia (Rev 2:9; 3:9).

A Christian congregation was probably established at Pergamum by the mid-80s CE, since it existed when Antipas was martyred some time before Revelation was written (Rev 2:13). Whether it was connected to Paul's work in the region is unknown (e.g., Troas in Acts 20:6). References to the apostle John at Pergamum are apocryphal (*NTApoc*[1] 2:204). Revelation assumes that readers at Pergamum will know Jewish traditions about Balaam, Balak, and manna (Rev 2:14, 17), but whether these Christians were of Jewish origin is unclear. Later sources mention a Christian from a family of Pergamum being martyred in Gaul in 177 CE (Eusebius, *Hist. eccl.* 5.1.17) and tell of several Christians being martyred at Pergamum in the late second or third century (*Mart. Carp.* 1–7; Yarbro Collins, "Pergamon," 163–66). What is most important is that Revelation depicts a Christian community in which some resisted compromise with Roman authority but others accommodated Greco-Roman religious practices.

Thus says the one who has the sharp two-edged sword. The sword from Christ's mouth is a symbol for his word (NOTE on 1:16) and could connote judicial power. In the provinces, proconsuls had "full power of the sword" (Justinian, *Dig.* 1.18.6.8) and could judge and execute those they governed (Rom 13:4; Philostratus, *Vit. soph.* 532; Justinian, *Dig.* 1.16.6; Sherwin-White, *Roman Society*, 8–11). For John, the proconsul may have had the power to condemn Antipas, but Christ has superior authority and promises to vindicate the faithful through resurrection (Rev 2:13). The sword also suggests power to wage war (Judg 4:16; 1 Sam 14:20; 1 Macc 4:15). The emperor entrusted proconsuls with authority over the military in the provinces (Mommsen, *Römisches*, 2:251). In Revelation, Christ is King of kings, who wages war with the sword of his mouth (Rev 2:16; 19:15, 21).

2:13. *I know where you live, where Satan's throne is.* Revelation locates Satan's throne at Pergamum because it is the only one of the seven cities where a Christian has been put to death (2:13). Although Ephesus, Smyrna, Sardis, and Laodicea were also judicial centers (Pliny the Elder, *Nat.* 5.105–26; Magie, *Roman*, 2:1059–63), Pergamum is the only city where a Christian has been executed (Aune; Friesen, "Satan's," 366). Calling the city where a Christian has been killed "the throne of Satan" is like giving the epithet "synagogue of Satan" to the synagogues that denounce Christians and place them in danger of imprisonment or death (Rev 2:9–10; 3:9). Other reasons for identifying Satan's throne with Pergamum are unpersuasive:

1. Great altar: The altar on Pergamum's acropolis had friezes showing Zeus and other Olympian gods battling hostile giants. During the Roman period coins and inscriptions linked the emperors to Zeus. Some interpreters propose that Revelation transforms the altar into "Satan's throne" in order to subvert imperial propaganda (Yarbro Collins, "Pergamon"; Murphy; Witherington). However, the altar had as much to do with Athena as with Zeus. Moreover, Smyrna and Sardis also had impressive acropolises adorned with temples. Pergamum's acropolis and altar would not have set it apart as "Satan's throne."

2. Temple to Augustus and Roma. Some interpreters think that Pergamum was "Satan's throne" because it was where Asia's first provincial temple to the emperor was located

(Ramsay, *Letters*, 214–15; Hemer, *Letters*, 82–87; Ford; Giesen; Müller; Osborne; Prigent; Smalley). However, there was a provincial temple to Tiberius at Smyrna and another to the Flavian emperors at Ephesus, and local imperial cults existed throughout the province (Price, *Rituals*, 249–74). Pergamum would not have been uniquely dubbed "Satan's throne" because of its imperial cult (Friesen, "Satan's," 362–64).

3. Sanctuary of Asclepius. Pergamum had a well-known sanctuary of Asclepius, the god of healing, who was sometimes called "the savior" (Aelius Aristides, *Orations* 42.4). Since Revelation ascribes salvation to God and Christ (7:10), some interpreters suggest that the writer challenges the cult of Asclepius by calling Pergamum "Satan's throne" (*NW* 2:1486; Rissi, *Hure*, 53). A pagan temple could be called a "place of Satan" (*T. Job* 3:5; 4:4); Asclepius was symbolized by a snake, an image for Satan in Rev 12:9; and Asclepius was a rival of Christ, since both were healers (Justin Martyr, *1 Apol.* 54.10). Yet there is little evidence that devotion to Asclepius ever led to persecution, as was the case with Antipas, and serpents appear in various ancient cults; there is no special link to Pergamum.

4. Pergamum as a general center for polytheism and the imperial cult (Beale; Blount; Roloff). This general sense is unlikely because many deities were worshiped in all seven cities (NOTES on 2:1, 8, 12, 18; 3:1, 7, 14). There is no reason to single out Pergamum because of its cults. What distinguishes Pergamum from other cities is that Antipas was put to death there, which is understood to be evidence of Satan's presence.

you are holding on to my name and did not deny your faith in me. Denying the faith means disowning it before other people (Rev 3:8; Matt 10:33; 26:70) or acting in ways inconsistent with one's beliefs (Tit 1:16; Jude 4). In the face of opposition, Christians might deny Christ in order to maintain their social and economic positions (Herm. *Vis.* 3.6.5). Those at Pergamum, however, have remained firm.

even at the time that Antipas. Antipas is a short form of the Greek name Antipatros, and it was used by people of both Jewish backgrounds (Matt 14:1; Josephus, *Ant.* 14.10; 17.20; Josephus, *J.W.* 1.562; 2.418) and non-Jewish backgrounds (I.Smyr 2/2:353–54; MAMA 9:57; 409; IG 2180.212; *CMRDM* 4:23; P.Russ. V, 18). In this context the name is nominative in form but genitive in function (literally, "in the days of Antipas"). Given this peculiarity, some copyists construed the name as the verb *anteipas*, "you spoke against" (א^c A; Borger, "NA^26," 45–47). The most likely reason for the form, however, is that the author considers the name indeclinable (Mussies, "Antipas"). To say that Antipas was killed "among you" could mean he came from Pergamum or another city, since Pergamum was where the proconsul heard cases for the region. Those martyred at Pergamum in the late second or third century CE were brought in from Thyatira and perhaps Gordos (Musurillo, *Acts of the Christian*, 27, 29). Later tradition pictured Antipas being interrogated by the Roman prefect and then placed in a hollow bronze bull, which was heated over a fire until he roasted to death (*Acta Sanc.* 2:3–5).

my faithful witness was killed among you, where Satan lives. A witness (*martys*) is one who makes truth claims about the Christian faith. At the time of Revelation's writing, the word did not yet have the technical sense of "martyr" (e.g., *Mart. Pol.* 19:1). Revelation pictures those who bear witness being killed as a result (Rev 11:3; 17:6), but witness is not simply dying. Attesting to the truth precedes death and provokes the opposition that can lead to death, making death the culmination of witness (Trites, "Μάρτυς";

van Henten, "Concept"; Blount, *Can*, 46–66). Jesus is called God's "faithful witness" in Rev 1:5, and use of the same expression for Antipas indicates that he follows the pattern Jesus set.

   2:14. But I have a few things against you, for you have some there who hold the teaching of Balaam, who taught Balak to mislead the sons of Israel. Balaam was a seer, perhaps from upper Syria, who was called by Balak, the king of Moab, to curse Israel (Num 22–24). The positive side of Balaam's legacy is that he pronounced blessings instead of curses. His promise that a star would rise from Jacob was understood to anticipate a messianic ruler (24:17), and the image is used this way in later Jewish sources and Revelation (4Q175 9–13; NOTES on Rev 2:28; 22:16). The negative side of Balaam's legacy is that he was implicated in Israel's sexual immorality and worship of Baal (Num 25:1–5; 31:16). Some Jewish writers considered him a false prophet (4Q339 2), a practitioner of sophistry and magic (Philo, *Migr.* 113–14; Philo, *Mos.* 1.277, 294–99), who lured Israel into apostasy (Josephus, *Ant.* 4.129–30; *L.A.B.* 18:13–14; van Kooten and van Ruiten, eds., *Prestige*; Seland, "Philo"). Revelation draws on this negative side of the Balaam tradition (van Henten, "Balaam").

   so that they would eat what was sacrificed to idols. Greco-Roman worshipers called their offerings *hierothyta* (sacred sacrifices, 1 Cor 10:28) or *theothyta* (sacrificed to gods; Pollux, *Onomasticon* 1.29.8). Revelation, however, refers to *eidōlothyta* (sacrificed to idols), a pejorative term that Jews and Christians apparently coined to parody the Greco-Roman expression (4 Macc 5:2; *Sib. Or.* 2.96; Acts 15:29; 1 Cor 8:1; *Did.* 6:3). Offerings to the gods included grain and wine, but the main issue was whether Christians could eat meat from animals offered in sacrifice (1 Cor 8:1, 13). Sheep were the most common offerings, but oxen, goats, pigs, and poultry were also used. Rites involved slaying the animal and burning a portion on the altar. The remainder of the meat was eaten in the temple, sold in the market, or distributed to the public (Burkert, *Greek*, 55–59). Some interpreters argue that Revelation's prohibition against *eidōlothyta* applies only to what was eaten in the context of pagan worship and not to meat sold in the marketplace (Fee, "Εδωλόθυτα," 181–87; Witherington, "Not"; Beale), but it is not clear that the term had such a limited sense, especially since the parallel term *hierothyta* was used for meat bought in the market (1 Cor 10:28). On this issue, see INTRO III.B.2.

   and so do what is immoral. The basic sense of *porneuein* is sexual immorality. It was also a metaphor for unfaithfulness to God and for the way some people used commerce to draw others under their influence. All three senses occur in Revelation. Here, the metaphorical sense is prominent:

1. Sexual immorality. *Porneuein* and related words (*porneia, pornē, pornos*) encompassed forms of immoral sexual behavior such as adultery (1 Cor 7:2; Heb 13:4), prostitution (1 Cor 6:15–18; Luke 15:30), and incest (1 Cor 5:1). The terms were often included in vice lists (Matt 15:19; Mark 7:21; 1 Cor 5:11; 6:9; Gal 5:19–21; Eph 5:3–5; Col 3:5; *Did.* 5:1). Although attitudes toward sexual behavior varied, the negative force of terms for immorality was recognized in Jewish (Sir 23:16–26; Ps.-Phoc. 175–98; *T. Reu.* 4:6–11; 1QS IV, 10) and Greco-Roman (*Rom. Civ.* 1:603; Dio Chrysostom, *Disc.* 32.91; 64:3; Hauck and Schulz, *TDNT* 6:579–95) moral tradition. When Revelation includes such terms in its vice lists, sexual immorality seems to be in view,

although a metaphorical dimension might also be suggested (Rev 9:21; 21:8; 22:15). Some interpreters think that the message to Pergamum envisions sexually immoral behavior at Greco-Roman festivals and banquets (Witherington; Pollard, "Function," 50), but here and in the message to Thyatira the dominant sense of the sexual imagery seems to be religious infidelity (Rev 2:20–22).

2. Idolatry. Israel's covenant relationship with God was like a marriage, so relationships with other gods were compared to prostitution and adultery (Hos 1:2; Isa 1:21; Jer 3:1–14; Ezek 16:15–22). The degree to which prostitution was actually part of Canaanite religious practice is unclear (2 Kgs 23:7; Hos 4:13; Isa 57:7), but comparing Israel's worship of other gods to sexual infidelity was a pointed indictment of polytheism (Lev 20:5; 1 Chr 5:25). Sometimes idolatry and immorality were mentioned together, with the sense that one contributed to the other (Wis 14:12; *T. Reu.* 4:6; Rom 1:23–25; Acts 15:20, 29; 21:25), but immorality can also be a metaphor for worship of deities other than God (Exod 34:15–16; Deut 31:16; Judg 2:17; 4Q169 3–4 III, 7–9). In Revelation the critique includes traditional Greco-Roman religions and the imperial cult.

3. Commercial practices. Prostitution debased sexual intimacy by reducing it to a commercial transaction. Therefore, prostitution was used metaphorically to criticize Tyre and Nineveh, which brought people under their influence by their networks of trade (Isa 23:15–18; Nah 3:1–7). Revelation's vision of Babylon portrays Rome as a prostitute, who lures people into compromising their religious principles for the sake of economic gain (Rev 14:8; 17:1–2; 18:3). This dimension is probably operative here as well, since some followers of Jesus may have accommodated Greco-Roman religious practices in order to maintain business relationships with non-Christians.

2:15. *In the same way you also have those who hold the teaching of the Nicolaitans.* The Nicolaitans were a Christian group that considered it acceptable to eat what was offered to Greco-Roman deities (Intro III.A.1; III.B.2).

2:16. *So repent. If you do not, I will come to you soon and make war on them.* Some interpreters think this passage warns against Christ's coming in judgment at the end of time (1:7; Murphy). It is best, however, to construe it as a limited disciplinary visitation before the end. Here his coming is conditional: He will come if (*ei*) people refuse to repent, which implies that if they do repent, he will not come. His coming is also limited to people at Pergamum, whereas his final coming will defeat God's opponents everywhere (1:7; 19:11–21; Aune; Beale; Giesen). On modes of Christ's coming, see the Comment on 22:7.

with the sword of my mouth. On the imagery of the sword, see the Note on 1:16.

2:17. *Let the one who has an ear hear what the Spirit says to the assemblies.* See the Note on 2:7.

To those who conquer. On this metaphor for faithfulness, see the Note on 2:7.

I will give some of the hidden manna. Manna was the food that Israel ate in the wilderness in the time of Moses. This "bread from heaven" (Exod 16:4; Neh 9:15; John 6:31–32) or "bread of angels" (Ps 78:25; Wis 16:20; 4 Ezra 1:19; *L.A.B.* 19:5) was said to come from a heavenly source (*L.A.B.* 19:10). The manna ceased appearing when Israel entered Canaan (Josh 5:12), but a jar of it was kept in the tabernacle (Exod 16:32–34). According to tradition, the manna was preserved when the temple was destroyed and would be restored in the future (*Mek.* "Vayassa" 6.82; cf. 2 Macc 2:4–8). At the end of the age "the treasury of manna will come down again from on high, and they will eat of it in those years because these are they who will have arrived at the consummation of time" (*2 Bar.* 29:8; cf. *Sib. Or.* 7:149). Some interpreters identify the manna with Jesus, who gives himself in the Eucharist (cf. John 6:31–58; 1 Cor 10:3–4; Prigent; Lupieri), but the eucharistic sense is not clear here. In Revelation the hope of eating manna will be realized through resurrection to life in New Jerusalem.

I will also give a white stone. This image signifies favorable judgment. Placing a small stone (*psēphos*) into an urn was a way in which voting was done in antiquity. A white stone was positive, and a black stone was negative (Ovid, *Metam.* 15.41–42; Aeschylus, *Eum.* 737–56; Plutarch, *Alc.* 2.22; Plutarch, *Mor.* 186F). Often, *psēphos* simply meant "vote" (LSJ 2022–23; Acts 26:10), and "white stone" was proverbial for "fortunate" (*NW* 2:1490). A white stone meant that a person "conquered" (*nikan*) or was vindicated in court (Aeschylus, *Eum.* 744; Theophrastus, *Char.* 17.8). Accordingly, in Rev 2:17 those who "conquer" by persevering in faith receive a white stone, or vindication, from God. The stone also signifies honor. Jewish inscriptions from the first centuries BCE and CE tell of white stones being cast in favor of granting public honors, including praising honorees by name and giving them laurel wreaths (Levine, *Ancient*, 89–94). This too fits Revelation, in which the white stone is a symbol of honor that is comparable to receiving a laurel wreath (2:10, 17). Where Revelation departs from common practice is by indicating that a name—apparently the name of Christ, who gives the favorable judgment—is inscribed on the stone.

An alternative interpretation is that the white stone signifies protection. Some interpreters compare it to an amulet, since it has a secret name on it, which suggests magical practice and dreams (*PDM* 12.6–20; *PGM* 12.209; 280; Betz, *Greek*, 152, 161, 164; Artemidorus, *Onirocritica* 5.26; Aune; Charles; Giesen; Murphy; Roloff). However, amulets were thought to ward off evil powers in the present, and the stone in Rev 2:17 will be given in the future, after evil has been vanquished. It is an eschatological gift, like the tree of life, wreath, and manna (2:7, 10, 17). Another proposal is that the stone is a token of admission to the messianic banquet (Beale; Mounce; Thomas). Yet this interpretation relies on tenuous combinations of references to tokens, or *tesserae*, which were not necessarily white, made of stone, or linked to dinner invitations (Hemer, *Letters*, 98; on other options, see 96–102). This approach is unlikely.

with a new name written on it, which no one knows except the one who receives it. Some interpreters propose that the stone is inscribed with the believer's own new name. This understanding recalls that Israel would receive its own "new name" when it was no longer called "forsaken" but "my delight is in her" and "married" (Isa 62:2–4; 65:15; Fekkes, *Isaiah*, 128–30; Hemer, *Letters*, 102–3). The internal movement of Revelation, however, makes it probable that the new name is Christ's name, which is written on the stone as his new name is written on the believer (Rev 3:12). The name of Christ is inscribed on the foreheads of the redeemed and on his own robe (14:1; 19:12; Aune; Beale; Giesen). To say that no one knows the name except the one who receives it does not mean that this is an esoteric name. Later, Christ's mysterious name is revealed as King of kings and Lord of lords (NOTE on 19:12). The point is that only those who receive the white stone—who are vindicated by Christ—know what his lordship means.

COMMENT

The third message is addressed to the assembly at Pergamum, which was one of the great cities of western Asia (NOTE on 2:12). The social situation has two major dimensions. One is conflict with outsiders. The writer recalls that some time in the past a Christian named Antipas was put to death at Pergamum, probably at the direction of a Roman official. At that time congregation members remained steadfast in their faith, allowing them to serve as a model for those now facing similar threats, as at Smyrna (2:9–10, 13). By the time Revelation was written, however, this conflict seems to have abated. The second and more immediate issue was the degree to which Christians could accommodate Greco-Roman religious practices, especially eating what had been sacrificed to the gods (2:14). The question arose as Christians sought to maintain good relationships with non-Christians, since public events and private gatherings of business associates and friends often had religious aspects (INTRO III.B.2).

The question of accommodation created tensions within the Christian community. Some at Pergamum advocated an open stance toward eating food that had been offered in sacrifice, as did the Nicolaitans, whom the author opposes (2:14–15). The Christians at Ephesus had resisted the Nicolaitan position (2:6), and those at Pergamum are to do the same. The author identifies the position he opposes with the teaching of "Balaam," and some interpreters take this to mean that a specific teacher or prophet promoted this view, just as "Jezebel" did at Thyatira (Friesen, *Imperial*, 174, 193). This is possible, but the reference focuses on the biblical Balaam's encounter with Balak, which makes it more likely that the name Balaam simply designates a type of teaching, not a specific teacher (cf. 2 Pet 2:15; Jude 11).

Structurally, the message follows the usual pattern of an introduction and conclusion, with words of encouragement and reproof between them. The first part introduces themes that are developed in the second part: Christ initially holds the sword and later threatens to use it (2:12, 16); those who hold firmly to Christ's name are promised a stone with a new name (2:13, 17); eating what has been sacrificed to idols is an act of infidelity, but the faithful will eat the hidden manna, which gives life (2:14–15, 17).

Introduction

The exalted Christ identifies himself as "the one who has the sharp two-edged sword" (2:12). This recalls John's inaugural vision, where the sword came from Christ's mouth, signifying his word (1:16). The imagery is appropriate because the sword could symbolize military and judicial authority, both of which appear in the message. Using a military metaphor, Christ warns that he will use the sword from his mouth to battle those who seem ready to accommodate the worship practices of other gods (2:16). As judge, his verdict will be the final one. A faithful witness like Antipas might have been

---

On Rev 2:12–17, see Coutsoumpos, "Social"; Barr, "Idol"; Friesen, "Satan's"; Hemer, *Letters*, 78–105; Klauck, "Sendschreiben"; H. Koester, ed., *Pergamon*; Pilch, "Lying"; Radt, *Pergamon*; Ramsay, *Letters*, 281–315; Schüssler Fiorenza, *Book*, 114–32; Walter, "Nikolaos"; Yarbro Collins, "Pergamon."

condemned by others in his social context, but Christ promises the faithful a white stone that signifies acquittal before God (2:17).

Body of the Message

Christ knows that the congregation lives where Satan's throne is located (2:13). Although Satan is a factor in the messages to four churches (2:9, 13, 24; 3:9), Pergamum is uniquely Satan's "throne" because it is the one city where a Christian has been put to death. Later visions will disclose the cosmic dimension of such an incident as John pictures Satan being banished from heaven to earth, where he gives his throne to the beast that persecutes Jesus' followers (13:2, 7). It is the death of Antipas that manifests the presence of Satan's throne at Pergamum. God's throne is the center of rightful power (4:2–6; 5:13; 7:9–11; 8:3; 19:4; 21:3, 5). Therefore, readers are called to be true to the God who will overthrow Satan's throne in all its forms—including those of Rome (16:10)—and will bring the faithful to life before his throne in New Jerusalem (22:1–5).

The congregation is commended for holding fast to Christ's name and not denying their faith in him in the past, when Antipas was killed. Some interpreters suggest that Antipas was killed by mob action (Schüssler Fiorenza, *Book*, 128; Boxall), but calling Antipas a "witness" suggests a trial (Yarbro Collins, "Persecution," 733). Linking his death to Satan's "throne," which is later connected to a beast with Roman traits, makes it likely that he was sentenced by an official (13:2). In practice, it was the Roman proconsul who had the authority to pass sentence on Christians in the provinces (Pliny the Younger, *Ep.* 10.96.3; *Mart. Pol.* 9:2–12:1; *Mart. Pion.* 19–20; *Acts Scill.* 16; *Acts Cypr.* 1). In the late second or third century several Christians were executed at Pergamum "while the proconsul was in residence" (*Mart. Carp.* 1), much as Antipas was killed at Pergamum "where Satan lives" (Rev 2:13).

Apart from Antipas it is unlikely that members of the Pergamum congregation were questioned by a Roman official, since they held firmly to their faith and yet were not put to death. When Pliny the Younger was proconsul, his practice was to question those who were denounced to him as Christians. If they denied their faith, reviled Christ's name, and made an offering before the statue of the emperor, he would release them, but if they refused, he would have them executed (*Ep.* 10.96.3–6). It is possible that Antipas was denounced in another city and then brought to Pergamum, where the proconsul heard legal cases for the region (*Mart. Carp.* 1; 27). Or if Antipas was from Pergamum, he might have been singled out for condemnation, as Polycarp was at Smyrna, while other Christians in the city were left alone (*Mart. Pol.* 3:2; 16:2–18:1; Klauck, "Sendschreiben," 164). The condemnation of Antipas had the potential for making other Christians abandon their faith in order to avoid a similar fate, so they are commended for identifying with the name of Christ.

They are reproved, however, because some were willing to eat what had been offered to Greco-Roman deities (2:14). The implied question is: "Having remained steadfast in the face of a severe threat, will you now compromise in the face of a much lesser threat?" (cf. Quintilian, *Inst.* 5.11.9). There were occasions when Christians might have eaten such food to maintain good relationships with non-Christians. Public festivals—whether of traditional deities or of Roman emperors—often involved sacrifices followed by banquets and distributions of food. One could downplay the religious aspect and join in the meals as a member of the broader civic community (INTRO III.B.2). Christians might have found it advantageous to belong to the professional, neighborhood, and gymnastic associations that enabled people to network with others who shared common interests. Many also would have belonged to families with non-Christian members. The question of compromise would come up when groups of family, friends, and business associates included religious rites at a gathering or met in a temple, or even when people purchased sacrificial meat in the public market to serve in their homes. As Adela Yarbro Collins puts it, "At stake here was the question of assimilation: What pagan customs could Christians adopt for the sake of economic survival, commercial gain, or simple sociability?" (*Crisis*, 88).

Social support for accommodation was given by the Nicolaitans (2:15), but the writer of Revelation calls that approach "immorality" (*porneia*, 2:14). Some interpreters think that sexual immorality was part of the problem at Pergamum (9:21; 21:8; 22:15). They note that the Balaam story included both idolatry and illicit sexual actions (Num 25:1, 6–8; 31:16; cf. Jude 4, 11; 2 Pet 2:2, 14–15). Some Christians at Corinth thought the gospel gave them sexual freedom and allowed them to eat what was offered to Greco-Roman gods (1 Cor 5:1–2; 6:12–20; 8:1–13; INTRO III.B.2), and similar views could have been held at Pergamum (Rev 2:6, 14–15, 20; Irenaeus, *Haer*. 1.26.3; Karrer, *Johannesoffenbarung*, 200; Schüssler Fiorenza, *Book*, 114–20; Murphy; Osborne). It is more likely, however, that "immorality" here is a metaphor for religious infidelity, just as committing adultery with Jezebel means adopting her open stance toward food offered to various deities (Rev 2:20–22). Later, the whore (*pornē*) is a city that practices idolatry and brutality while seducing people into commercial relationships (17:1, 5, 15, 16; 19:2). *Porneia* is the false worship that affects whole nations (14:8; 17:2, 4; 18:3; 19:2), and this seems to be the sense at Pergamum (Giesen; Kraft; Räisänen, "Nicolaitans," 1613–19; Thompson, *Book*, 122).

The critique intensifies as the message identifies religious accommodation with the teaching of Balaam, a biblical figure who was said to have led Israel into a destructive form of idolatry (2:14). The story was that Balak, king of Moab, summoned Balaam to curse the people of Israel. After a humorous incident in which Balaam's donkey began talking, Balaam ended up blessing rather than cursing Israel (Num 22:1–24:25). But immediately afterward, the Israelites engaged in sexual relations with the women of Moab, joining in worship of the Baal of Peor, and Balaam was said to be responsible (25:1–5; 31:16). Jewish tradition held that since Balaam was unable to curse Israel, he helped Balak by counseling him to have the women seduce the Israelites into idolatry so that God would judge them (Josephus, *Ant*. 4.129–30; Philo, *Mos*. 1.294–99; *L.A.B.* 18:13–14). Revelation assumes that no one would want to be associated with practices like those of Balaam (Jude 11; 2 Pet 2:15; *m. 'Abot* 5:19).

Readers are called to repent and are given a warning about what will happen "if" they refuse to do so (Rev 2:16). The dynamics of repentance were considered in the message to Ephesus (2:5). Here, we focus on the specific warning, which is that Christ will come and make war with the sword of his mouth. In the vision of Christ's final coming for battle, his weapon is the sword from his mouth (19:15), and here Christ warns that he will use the same sword against the unrepentant at Pergamum. This warning makes use of metaphor, as did the message to Ephesus, where Christ threatened to move the congregation's lampstand from its place (2:5). The metaphor creates a crisis of discernment for the readers. Since the sword comes from the mouth of the risen Christ, the implication is that Christ will wage a war of words against false teaching, but how the readers will know when this occurs is not spelled out. Would the war of words be waged by local prophets speaking on Christ's behalf? Are readers to picture victory over false teachers coming "soon," or might Christ's action "soon" instigate a more prolonged war against them? The warning is severe, and yet the way it is to be carried out remains open. As long as false teaching remains, the threat of Christ's action against it remains—and for the writer of Revelation, this gives readers ongoing incentive to repent.

Conclusion

An exhortation to hear what the Spirit says to the assemblies and a promise to the one who conquers completes the message (2:17; see the COMMENT on 2:7). The promise uses evocative imagery that fits the internal movement of the message. Earlier, readers were reproved because some thought it acceptable to eat what was offered to Greco-Roman deities, and their view was linked to the biblical figure of Balaam (2:14). The reproof is now matched by a promise that uses a different biblical image: eating the manna that is a gift of God (2:17). According to the Scriptures, Israel had nothing to eat in the wilderness and faced the prospect of death. Manna was the bread from heaven that brought life (Exod 16:3–4). For the readers, the manna no longer descended from heaven; its source was "hidden" and inaccessible, since death was real, even for the faithful. Like eating from the tree of life (Rev 2:7), receiving manna means overcoming death and entering paradise through resurrection to life in the new creation. To do so is to share in the wedding banquet of the Lamb (19:9).

Finally, Christ promises that the faithful will receive a white stone with a new name, an image signifying vindication and honor (NOTE on 2:17). The writer contrasts Christ's positive judgment of the faithful with the negative judgment by those in the readers' social contexts. If Antipas was put to death for his faith, Christ's judgment is the opposite: He calls Antipas a faithful witness, who exemplifies what it means to "conquer" (2:13; 12:11). If the prospect of having one's faith condemned can make some deny their connection with Christ's name (*onoma*), those who remain firm receive Christ's approval (2:13). The image of a stone that is inscribed with a new name (*onoma*)—apparently Christ's name—emphasizes that the verdict that ultimately matters comes from Christ, who values the faith that others condemn (2:17).

8. To the Assembly in Thyatira (2:18–29)

2   ¹⁸"To the angel of the assembly in Thyatira write: Thus says the Son of God, whose eyes are like a flame of fire and whose feet are like shining bronze. ¹⁹I know your works, your love and faithfulness, your service and endurance. And I know that the works you have done most recently are even greater than those you did at first. ²⁰But I have against you that you tolerate the woman Jezebel, who calls herself a prophetess—even though she teaches and deceives my servants into doing what is immoral and eating food sacrificed to idols. ²¹I gave her time to repent, but she refuses to repent of her immorality. ²²See, I am going to put her to bed, and put those with whom she has committed adultery into terrible affliction. If they do not repent of her works, ²³I will also put her

children to death with a plague. And all the assemblies will know that I am the one who examines minds and hearts, and will give to each of you what your works deserve. ²⁴But I say to the rest of you in Thyatira—those who do not hold this teaching and do not know what they call 'the deep things' of Satan—to you I say that I will not burden you with anything else. ²⁵Only hold on to what you have until I come. ²⁶To those who conquer and keep my works until the end, I will give authority over the nations. ²⁷They will rule them with an iron rod, the way one breaks clay pottery—²⁸just as I received from my Father. I will also give them the morning star. ²⁹Let the one who has an ear hear what the Spirit says to the assemblies."

NOTES

2:18. *To the angel of the assembly.* Each angel apparently has responsibility for a congregation (NOTES on 1:20; 2:1).

in Thyatira write. Thyatira (modern Akhisar, Turkey) was a city in a broad valley southeast of Pergamum (Pliny the Elder, *Nat.* 5.126). In the Hellenistic age it was "sacred Thyatira" (Diogenes Laertius, *Lives* 4.31). Interpreters often stress the city's insignificance, citing the older work of William Ramsay and Colin Hemer (e.g., Osborne; Guttenberger, "Johannes"). More recent publications, however, enable revision of those studies (TAM V, 2; Malay, *Researches*). Like Ephesus, Smyrna, and Pergamum, Thyatira was home to Greeks and Macedonians (Strabo, *Geographica* 13.4.4; I.Thyat 973; 989), as well as Roman businesspeople, who had their own association (I.Thyat 924; 1002). The city had several gymnasiums and eventually a theater (I.Thyat 968; 983). When it was damaged by an earthquake around 25 BCE, it was repaired with Roman help (Suetonius, *Tib.* 8), and shortly afterward nearby residents built a stoa with colonnades and dedications to Augustus as son of god (Malay, *Researches*, no. 24). During the first century CE Vespasian and Domitian ensured that local roads were well-maintained (I.Thyat 869–70). The city was supplied with water through an aqueduct (I.Thyat 991).

Thyatira had a textile industry with associations of dyers (I.Thyat 935; 945; 972), wool merchants (1019), linen workers (933), and clothing cleaners (SEG 40:1045). Other groups included coppersmiths (I.Thyat 936), potters (914), tanners (986), leather cutters (1002), and bakers (966). The city was also a regional center in the Asian slave trade network. An inscription mentions a slave trader who oversaw the public market at Thyatira and funded festivities for the imperial cult (C. R. Koester, "Roman"). Following a comment Ramsay made more than a century ago, many interpreters assume that pressure to belong to the trade associations was especially strong at Thyatira (Ramsay, *Letters*, 352; Charles; Mounce; Murphy; Osborne; Pollard, "Function"; Thimmes, "Women"). But the usual descriptions need to be qualified in three ways. First, similar trade associations existed in the other cities mentioned in Revelation, so Thyatira's social fabric was much like that of other cities (Broughton, *Asia*, 841–44; cf. 819, 824–25, 830; Harland, *Associations*, 39–40). Second, other social contexts, such as civic events and gatherings of family and friends, also had religious aspects. Third, many assume that each association at Thyatira had a patron deity, but inscriptions actually show trade associations honoring patrons who may have been priests of various gods (Hoz, *Die lydischen*, 113). Social pressures for Christians to accommodate the worship of Greco-Roman deities would have come from various sources, not only from associations.

Worship in the city centered on Apollo Tyrimnos (I.Thyat 882–83; 946; 956; 960) and Artemis Boreitene (995–96), the protectors of civic welfare. They were originally Anatolian deities, who were identified with Apollo and Artemis from the Greek pantheon. The mother goddess, Meter, whose cult was common throughout Asia Minor, was also worshiped at Thyatira (I.Thyat 955; 962; 963), as was Tyche, the goddess of fortune (894–96). Cults that may have come to Thyatira from Pergamum include Dionysus Kathegemon (the Leader), who was once linked to the ruling dynasty at Pergamum; Zeus Keraunios (Thunderbolt); Asclepius the Savior, who was associated with Hygeia, or health; and Herakles (Hoz, *Die lydischen*, 34, 53, 60–70). The cult of God Most High (*Theos Hypsistos*) was apparently devoted to a Hellenistic deity, yet the same language was used in the LXX for the God of Israel (I.Thyat 897–900; Malay, *Researches*, no. 25). The differences between religious traditions might not have been clear (S. Mitchell, *Anatolia*, 2:49–51; Trebilco, *Jewish*, 127–44). Revelation argues for a rigorous devotion to the God of Israel, but the common practice in the region was to accommodate multiple traditions.

Public honors were given to men and women from leading families, who held the priesthoods of Apollo Tyrimnos, Artemis Boreitene, and Dionysus (I.Thyat 931; 976; 995). They often held civic positions and underwrote expenses for festivals. There were cult associations for singers and speakers (*hymnodes* and *theologoi*) who were devoted to Meter (I.Thyat 955; 962). More broadly, the council and body of citizens at Thyatira set up inscriptions honoring those who performed public service and provided for the sacrifices at festivals (I.Thyat 995). Trade associations set up similar inscriptions to honor those who served in priesthoods and other public offices, thereby putting the association in a position to receive favors from people of influence (Harland, *Associations*, 143–47).

Leading citizens from Thyatira were active in the provincial cult of Augustus and Roma at Pergamum. One of these, C. Julius Xenon, became provincial high priest in the first century BCE, and after his death he was venerated as a hero by his own association (I.Thyat 1098). By 2 BCE another Thyatiran became provincial high priest and overseer of the imperial games (I.Sard 8.99). Thyatira had a municipal cult of the emperors in which a woman served as priestess (I.Thyat 972), as other women did in the cult of Augustus's wife (904–6).

A number of civic officeholders at Thyatira assumed leadership in the local and provincial cults throughout the first and second centuries CE (I.Thyat 940; 970; 978; 980). Worship of the emperors blended with that of traditional deities such that Thyatira was the city of Augustus and Tyrimnos (I.Thyat 960), and a priest or priestess could serve in the cults of Dionysus or Artemis as well as that of the emperor (976; 996). One group identified itself as friends of the emperors (I.Thyat 927; 933), and the dyers association honored benefactors and imperial cult personnel with inscriptions (Harland, *Associations*, 143–50). The most popular form of the imperial cult centered on Augustus (I.Thyat 902). Domitian was called emperor, high priest, and son of the deified Vespasian, but as a living emperor he was not officially called "god" (I.Thyat 870A). A coin from Thyatira pictures Domitian on one side and a winged victory on the other, connecting his reign to the familiar imperial theme (RPC 2:942).

Evidence for a Jewish community at Thyatira is ambiguous. A merchant named Lydia came from Thyatira. When Paul met her at Philippi, she was a "worshiper of God," that is, a Gentile who worshiped the God of Israel without formal conversion to Judaism (Acts 16:13–14). If her adherence to Judaism began in Thyatira, it would suggest that there was a Jewish community there, but if her connection to Judaism began later, it would say nothing about her home city. An inscription from the second or third century CE mentions a *sambatheion* at Thyatira. This could have been a *sabbateion*, or Sabbath house (Josephus, *Ant.* 16.164; Schürer, *History*, 3:19), but since it was located in an area linked to Chaldeans, it also could have been linked to the Sibyl Sambathe (*IJO* 2:297–302). If there was a Jewish community at Thyatira, no mention is made of conflict with the Christian congregation there.

The origins of the Christian community at Thyatira are unknown. According to Acts 16:14, the Thyatiran merchant named Lydia met Paul in Philippi, where she accepted the Christian message about 50 CE. Nothing is said about her returning to Thyatira, however. By the mid-80s there was probably a congregation in the city, since Revelation can look back to the group's former works and compare them with their present acts of service (Rev 2:19). At Thyatira, prophets were valued as leaders. John considered himself a prophet, as did the woman nicknamed Jezebel (2:20). Some in the congregation accepted Jezebel's teaching, which advocated openness to eating what was offered to Greco-Roman deities, but others did not. Later, Epiphanius claimed that Christians at Thyatira came under the influence of the new prophecy movement known as Montanism in the second or third century CE, though this did not continue (*Pan.* 51.33.1–5). A Christian from Thyatira was martyred in Pergamum during this period (*Mart. Carp.* 27; Eusebius, *Hist. eccl.* 4.15.48).

Thus says the Son of God. "Thus says" has both royal and prophetic connotations (see §3B). The title Son of God is used only here in Revelation, although some passages do refer to God as Jesus' Father (1:6; 2:28; 3:5, 21; 14:1). When related to Jewish tradition, "Son of God" shows that Jesus fulfills and goes beyond the role of messianic king. When read in light of imperial claims, it contrasts Jesus with Roman emperors:

1. Messianic kingship. In Israel's tradition "Son of God" had royal connotations. When God promised David an heir to his throne, he said: "I will establish the throne of his kingdom forever. I will be a father to him and he shall be a son to me" (2 Sam 7:13b–14; cf. Ps 89:20–37). Of the king it was said, "You are my son; today I have begotten you" (Ps 2:7). Later, this language expressed hope for a messianic ruler (4Q174 I, 10–19) who would usher in an eternal kingdom (4Q246 II, 1–9; cf. 4Q369 1 II, 1–11; *4 Ezra* 7:28–29; 13:32, 37, 52; 14:9; Collins, *Scepter*, 154–72). Early Christians understood Jesus to be the Son of God, who fulfilled the biblical promises (Matt 16:16; John 1:49; cf. Rev 1:5; 5:5).
2. Divine traits. In Jewish tradition the king was God's son by adoption. Christian sources, however, take "Son of God" in an expanded sense, to affirm that Christ shares more completely in the traits of God. Jesus was said to have been God's Son through his resurrection to deathless life (Rom 1:4; Acts 13:33), though his ministry and redemptive death were also part of his role as Son (Gal 2:20; 4:4; Rom 8:3; Mark 9:2–8). Some understood Jesus to have been God's Son in a preexistent sense, so that Jesus exercised God's power to give life and judge and he embodied God's

presence (Heb 1:1–3; John 1:14; 5:19–23; 10:30, 36; 20:28–31). In Revelation, the title "Son of God" allows readers to see Jesus as the fulfillment of messianic hopes and the one who shares the traits of God, such as Alpha and Omega (Rev 1:17; 22:13; Dunn, *Christology*, 12–64; Bauckham, *Theology*, 54–69).

3. Imperial use. Julius Caesar was deified in the first century BCE, and Augustus, his adopted son, was called "son of god." The provincial cult of Augustus, centered at Pergamum, helped to popularize this title at Thyatira (I.Thyat 902–3), Pergamum (IGR 309–11, 314), Ephesus (I.Eph 252–53), Sardis (I.Sard 8.22), Philadelphia (SEG 35:1169), and other cities. Tiberius became "son of the deified Augustus" (*Rom. Civ.* 2.631), and later, Titus (I.Laod 9.6; 15.1–2) and Domitian (I.Smyr 826) became "son of god," since their father Vespasian was deified. Revelation critiques the ruler cult and assumes that the true Son of God is Jesus. His followers will also be called "sons" of God and inherit life in New Jerusalem (Rev 21:7).

whose eyes are like a flame of fire and whose feet are like shining bronze. This imagery recalls John's initial vision of Christ (1:12–20). Fiery eyes often signified divinity (NOTE on 1:14). Some interpreters suggest that John regards his opponent Jezebel as a sorceress and a practitioner of the evil eye and therefore counters by ascribing the truly powerful eyes to Jesus (Duff, "I Will"). Yet sorcery is not mentioned, and Revelation's imagery comes from Dan 10:6. On the rare word for shining bronze, see the NOTE on Rev 1:15.

2:19. *I know your works, your love and faithfulness, your service and endurance.* The works of the congregation are specified in four ways: "Love" (*agapē*) can include love for God and acts of compassion for others. It means giving oneself for others as Christ did (1:5; 12:11; cf. 2:4). *Pistis* includes "faith" in God and Christ and "faithfulness" to God and his people. The faithful bear public witness to God in the face of conflict (1:5; 2:13; cf. 2:10; 13:10; 14:12). "Service" (*diakonia*) could include actions ranging from witnessing to the gospel to providing for the needy (Acts 6:1, 4; 11:29; 1 Cor 12:5; 2 Cor 4:1). "Endurance" (*hypomonē*) involves steadfastness in the face of open hostility (Rev 1:9; 13:10; 14:12) and the pressures of false teaching (2:2–3).

the works you have done most recently are even greater than those you did at first. The works are summarized in the previous NOTE. Rhetorically, the comment uses amplification to praise the present by making a favorable comparison with the past (Lausberg, *Handbook* §404). This builds rapport with the listeners before the words of reproof that follow.

2:20. *But I have against you that you tolerate the woman Jezebel.* Jezebel is a nickname that John gives to the woman at Thyatira in order to compare her to Queen Jezebel, the wife of King Ahab of Israel (1 Kgs 16:31). She promoted the worship of Baal and Asherah, persecuted Elijah and other prophets, and had an innocent man killed in order to seize his vineyard (1 Kgs 18:13, 19; 19:1–3; 21:1–24; 4Q382 I, 3; Josephus, *Ant.* 8.317–18). Jezebel died during a revolt fomented by Elisha, when her opponents hurled her from an upper-story window (2 Kgs 9:30–37).

who calls herself a prophetess. Women had various roles in religious leadership in antiquity. In Asia Minor, they served as priestesses for Artemis and other deities, as well as in the imperial cult (NOTE on 2:18). At some sanctuaries, they assumed prophetic functions by issuing oracles from gods like Apollo (Aune, *Prophecy*, 28; Hoz, *Die lydi-*

schen, 90). In Jewish circles in Asia Minor, some women served as leaders in synagogues (*IJO* 2:187–92). In first-century Judaism, there is little evidence of women prophesying, but the biblical tradition includes female prophets such as Miriam (Exod 15:20), Deborah (Judg 4:4), Isaiah's wife (Isa 8:3), and Huldah (2 Kgs 22:14; 2 Chr 34:22; cf. Noadiah in Neh 6:14). According to Joel 2:28, God was to inspire both men and women as prophets (cf. Acts 2:17). Early Christian sources mention female prophets such as Anna, Philip's daughters, certain women at Corinth, and Ammia of Philadelphia in Asia (Luke 2:36; Acts 21:9; 1 Cor 11:5; Eusebius, *Hist. eccl.* 5.17.3–4; Boring, *Continuing*, 120–22). There were precedents for a woman claiming a prophetic role at Thyatira. For John, the issue was whether the content of her teaching was legitimate.

even though she teaches and deceives my servants. Prophets often taught (Isa 9:15; *Did.* 11:10) or worked alongside other teachers (Acts 13:1; Rom 12:6–7; 1 Cor 12:28; Eph 4:11). Although some NT writings seem to restrict women's teaching roles (1 Cor 14:34; 1 Tim 2:12), there were female prophets (previous Note); women like Priscilla, who taught (Acts 18:26); and other women in leadership roles (Rom 16:1–7; Phil 4:3). Revelation challenges Jezebel's teaching because of its content, not because of her gender.

into doing what is immoral and eating food sacrificed to idols. Here, what is immoral (*porneuein*) is a metaphor for religious infidelity (Note on 2:14).

2:21. *I gave her time to repent, but she refuses to repent of her immorality.* God was understood to warn people and then withhold judgment so that they could repent (Wis 12:10; Rom 2:4; 2 Pet 3:9; Plutarch, *Mor.* 348–68). If delay did not bring repentance, judgment would come.

2:22. *See, I am going to put her to bed.* Use of the word "bed" (*klinē*) plays on several aspects of meaning. First, Jezebel's accommodation of Greco-Roman religious practice is compared to immorality and adultery, which were actions committed in bed (Sir 23:18). Second, the sexual imagery is used metaphorically for eating food that has been offered in sacrifice to various gods. Those dining at meals held in honor of a deity often reclined on a couch, which was also called a *klinē*, so the word could have both sexual and meal connotations (*NewDocs* 1:5). Third, the expression "put to bed" could mean contracting a severe illness (1 Macc 1:5; Jdt 8:3; cf. 2 Kgs 1:4; Ps 41:3; Matt 9:2), thereby showing symmetry in divine judgment: Jezebel teaches that it is acceptable to recline on a bed or couch at meals honoring other deities, which is like going to bed in a kind of religious adultery, so the judgment is to be put to bed with illness. Fourth, people might die in bed (Gen 49:33; 2 Chr 16:14), and ancient funerary monuments often pictured a dead person reclining on a *klinē* as a person would do at a banquet (Dunbabin, *Roman*, 103–40). Working with all four meanings, Revelation likens festive dining on a couch to sexual infidelity in bed, while intimating that it is a form of religious infidelity, which will lead to being put to bed through sickness and death (Rev 2:23; G. Carey, *Elusive*, 158).

and put those with whom she committed adultery into terrible affliction. In the sexual sense, adultery was a violation of a marriage covenant (Exod 20:14; Josephus, *Ag. Ap.* 2.215; *Rom. Civ.* 1:603). Here, adultery is a metaphor for violating a covenant relationship with God through false worship or actions inconsistent with faith (Jer 3:9; Mark 8:38; Jas 4:4; Herm. *Man.* 4.1.9). As Jezebel faces sickness, her followers are warned of "affliction," which can entail suffering an illness (Pss 22:11–17; 32:3–7) and emotional distress (2 Cor 2:4). Her co-adulterers are probably not the non-Christians with whom she associated (Boxall; Osborne), but her Christian followers, who are called "children" in the next line. Traditional versification continues the sentence to the end of Rev 2:22, but it is better to end it after "affliction," since the first two parts of the verse are parallel and concern the punishment that awaits Jezebel (2:22a) and her followers (2:22b).

2:22c–23. *If they do not repent of her works, I will also put her children to death with a plague.* The new sentence indicates what will occur *if* Jezebel's followers do not respond to affliction by repenting. Her disciples are likened to the "children" (*tekna*) of an adulteress, who were subject to judgment (Isa 57:3, 8; Wis 3:16). In contrast, followers of Jesus are the "children" who keep God's commandments (Rev 12:17). Calling believers "children" was common (1 Cor 4:14, 17; Gal 4:19; Phlm 10; cf. 1 Tim 1:2; 2 Tim 1:2; Tit 1:4; 2 John 1, 4; 3 John 4; cf. the church at Thyatira in *Mart. Carp.* 29–32). *Thanatos* can mean to strike with death, but it also means a plague or sickness (Rev 6:8; 18:8; Ezek 33:27).

And all the assemblies will know that I am the one who examines minds and hearts. This begins a paraphrase of Jer 17:10 LXX: "I am the Lord who examines hearts and tests minds to give to each according to his ways and according to the fruits of his doings." It was understood that God knows and judges what is in each person's mind and heart (1 Kgs 8:40; cf. 1 Sam 16:7; 1 Chr 28:9; Pss 7:10; 44:21; 139:1–6, 23; Jer 11:20; Sir 42:18–20; Matt 6:4; Acts 1:24; 1 Cor 4:5; Heb 4:12–13). Prophets were said to know people's thoughts and deeds (Luke 7:39; 1 Cor 14:24–25; 4Q534 I, 8), but in Revelation, the exalted Christ does so, sharing traits of God. Some spoke of Jesus knowing human hearts during his ministry (Matt 9:4; John 2:25) or disclosing their contents on the future day of judgment (Rom 2:16), but Revelation warns that the exalted Christ—with his fiery eyes (Rev 2:18)—now examines people in the time before final judgment.

and will give to each of you what your works deserve. This line continues the paraphrase of Jer 17:10, although similar statements are made elsewhere (Pss 28:4; 62:12; Prov 24:12; Sir 35:24; 2 Tim 4:14; 1 Pet 1:17; *Pss. Sol.* 2:34–35). Divine justice means that the deeds of the righteous are not forgotten but are remembered and blessed by God (Rev 14:13), and the sins of the wicked will be rightly punished (18:6). In the end, all people will be judged according to their works, yet salvation will depend on the divine favor represented by the scroll of life (20:11–15).

2:24. *But I say to the rest of you in Thyatira—those who do not hold this teaching.* Although the entire congregation is rebuked for tolerating Jezebel (2:20), only some are actually her followers. Here, Christ addresses those who tolerate her presence but do not embrace her teachings. Whether they constituted the majority of the congregation or only a minority is unclear (Pollard, "Function," 62).

and do not know what they call "the deep things" of Satan. The expression "deep things" of Satan can be taken in two ways, of which the first is preferable:

1. Parody of the expression "deep things of God." This expression appears in various sources (*T. Job* 37:6; cf. Dan 2:22; *2 Bar.* 14:8) but may be linked to the Pauline tradition, which says that the Spirit searches the "deep things of God" (1 Cor 2:10; cf. Rom 11:33). Paul also refers to Christians who argued that their deep spiritual knowledge enabled them to eat what was offered to idols without compromising

their faith, since they understood that there was only one true God and that idolatry was a sham (1 Cor 8:1–6). Revelation implies that Jezebel follows a similar logic, teaching the "deep things of God" that make people think they can eat meat from Greco-Roman religious rites while claiming a Christian identity. John identifies such teaching with Satan, since he considers idolatry to be demonic (Rev 9:20; 13:4, 11–14; cf. 1 Cor 10:20). He also thinks that blurring the distinction between God and idols is deceptive, as is the case with Satan the deceiver (Rev 12:9). The pattern is similar to that in earlier messages, where Jews might have considered themselves to be "a synagogue of God" but John calls them "a synagogue of Satan" because of their opposition to Jesus' followers (2:9; 3:9; Giesen; Osborne; Roloff; Smalley).

2. The group's own claim to understand the demonic. Jezebel could have claimed that she revealed Satan's secrets, or "deep things," in order to help others understand and resist them. Her followers could have argued that they could eat what was offered to the gods because they understood the demonic dimension of idolatry and were prepared to resist it (Bousset; Mounce; Satake). What makes this unlikely is that John is the one who uses the terms "Satan" and "the devil" to characterize his opponents (2:9–10, 13; 3:9). Some interpreters note that Gnostics claimed to know "the deep things" (Aune; Prigent), but the Gnostic sources come from the second and third centuries CE, and it is not clear that one can ascribe their theology to the Christians at Thyatira.

2:24b–25. *I will not burden you with anything else. Only hold fast to what you have until I come.* The mention of a "burden" is similar to the decree of the Jerusalem Council, which agreed not to impose on Gentile Christians any "further burden" than to "abstain from what has been sacrificed to idols and from blood and from what is strangled and from fornication" (Acts 15:28). Some interpreters suggest that Revelation recalls the decree by placing no other burden on Christians who abstained from what was sacrificed to idols and from immorality (Beale; Charles; Murphy; Prigent). It is more likely that Revelation and the decree reflect similar concerns but are not directly connected (Aune; Giesen; Harrington). "Holding fast" means continuing to show love and to resist idolatry. Doing so until Christ comes probably does not refer to his possible coming to discipline the congregation (Rev 2:5, 16; 3:3; Giesen) but to his final coming.

2:26. *To those who conquer and keep my works until the end.* Conquering is an expression for faithfulness (NOTE on 2:7). Christ's "works" include love, faithfulness, and witness to truth (1:5), and his followers "keep" them by doing the same, just as they are to "keep" God's commandments (3:8, 10; 12:17; 14:12). They are to do this "until the end" of their lives or Christ's coming at the end of the age.

I will give authority over the nations. This line paraphrases Ps 2:8, a text in which God tells his "son," the anointed king: "Ask me and I will make the nations your heritage and the ends of the earth your possession." Elsewhere, it is Jesus who has the authority, which Ps 2 likens to an iron rod (Rev 12:5; 19:15). Here, the Messiah's authority is extended to his followers. The pattern is like that attested later, where the promise "I will be his God and he will be my son" (2 Sam 7:14), which refers to the heir of David's throne, is extended to all the redeemed (Rev 21:7).

2:27. *They will rule them with an iron rod, the way one breaks clay pottery.* This continues the paraphrase of Ps 2:9, where God says: "You will rule them with an iron rod and as a clay pot you will shatter them." Instead of "rule them," the Hebrew text of the psalm reads "break them." The difference comes from the Hebrew verb *tr'm*, which in the MT seems to derive from the root *r'* (break in pieces). It is taken this way in *Pss. Sol.* 17:23 and some Greek translations of Psalms (Aquila; Symmachus). The LXX, however, assumes that it is based on the root *r'h* (to shepherd or rule). Revelation follows the LXX here.

The verb *poimainein* can mean "to shepherd" or "to rule." It indicates tending and caring when the Lamb shepherds the redeemed by springs of living water (7:17), but here the shepherd wields a rod against the flock in order to control it (Mic 5:5–6; Jer 22:22). Rulers were depicted holding a rod four or five feet long, which indicated the administration of justice and punishment (Ps 45:6–7; Isa 10:5; *ISBE* 3:409). An iron rod could inflict severe damage and death (*Num. Rab.* 12:3), but the imagery is transformed in the literary context of Revelation (see COMMENT).

Some Jewish sources treat Ps 2 as messianic because the Lord's "anointed one" is the heir to David's throne (Ps 2:2, 6). In *Pss. Sol.* 17:23–24 the image of the king smashing the arrogance of sinners like clay jars (Ps 2:9) is linked to messianic justice (Isa 11:4). At Qumran, the psalm is included alongside texts that recall God's promises to David (Ps 89:23; 2 Sam 7:11–14; Amos 9:11; 4Q174 1 I, 1–13), yet the "anointed one" of Ps 2 is taken in a collective sense, referring to all the "elect ones" in the Qumran community (4Q174 1 I, 18–19; Janse, *You*, 51–54; Steudel, "Psalm"). The messianic interpretation of Ps 2 is dominant in early Christian writings. The NT relates the psalm to Jesus when referring to the nations and kings that set themselves against him (Ps 2:1–2; Acts 4:25–26), a sense echoed in Rev 11:15–18 and 12:10–12 (Witetschek, "Lieblingspsalm"). The psalm also provides language for calling Jesus the Son whom God has begotten (Ps 2:7; Acts 13:33; Heb 1:5; 5:5; cf. Matt 3:17 par.; Janse, *You*, 77–134; Kahl, "Psalm"). This messianic sense is explicit in Rev 12:5 and 19:15, where Jesus rules the nations with an iron rod, and it is presupposed in 2:28, where the exalted Christ speaks of his authority. But in 2:26–27 the messianic language is extended to the faithful, who will share Christ's authority over the nations (Quek, "I Will").

2:28. *just as I received from my Father.* Christ was introduced as God's Son in 2:18, and here he refers to God as his Father (NOTE on 1:6).

I will also give them the morning star. The oracle of Balaam said that a star would rise from Jacob to rule the nations (Num 24:17). It also said that a scepter, or rod (Hebrew, *shebet*), would arise from Israel, and the royal rod is mentioned in Ps 2:9, which was just cited (Rev 2:27). Jewish sources took the star to be a messianic figure (*T. Levi* 18:3; *T. Jud.* 24:1; 4Q175 12). In CD VII, 18–20, the star is the interpreter of the law and his scepter is a royal figure, but in 1QM XI, 6, the star defeats Israel's foes (Collins, *Scepter*, 61–80). Revelation identifies Jesus as the messianic star (Rev 22:16). The star image also helps to contrast the claims of Jesus with those of the Roman emperors. A comet, called a "star," was said to have appeared after Julius Caesar's death, signifying his deification. The "star" was pictured on imperial coins and bequeathed to Augustus and Tiberius (Horace, *Odes* 1.12.47; Valerius Maximus, *Facta* 1 pref.; cf. the morning star in Statius, *Silvae* 4.1.1–4). In Revelation, Christ is the legitimate ruler, who grants his followers a share in his reign, signified by the star.

2:29. *Let the one who has an ear hear to what the Spirit says to the assemblies.* See the NOTES on 2:7.

COMMENT

The fourth message addresses the congregation at Thyatira, where the principal issue concerns accommodation of Greco-Roman religious practices, such as eating what has been offered to various deities (Intro III.B.2). John condemns the practice, but others do not. His opponent at Thyatira is a woman nicknamed Jezebel, whose teaching is like that of the Nicolaitans, although the text does not formally identify her with that group. Jezebel is apparently a resident member of the congregation, not an outsider like the apostles who came to Ephesus (2:2). She considers herself to be a prophetess, and some in the congregation accept her teachings (2:20, 24). John's more rigorous viewpoint is shared by some at Thyatira, yet to some extent he is an outsider who must persuade the congregation to adopt his views.

Interpreters sometimes read the message to Thyatira as a dispute over personal authority and who will set boundaries for the congregation: John or Jezebel. Some also propose that gender roles were a factor, with John using negative feminine stereotypes to undercut a female rival (G. Carey, *Elusive*, 136; Duff, *Who*, 49, 111–12; Pippin, "And I"; Royalty, *Streets*, 28; Thimmes, "Women"). The reading given below construes the issue differently, focusing on *what* the boundaries will be rather than *who* will set them. This is because the message to Pergamum deals with the same issue even though no specific resident teacher is mentioned, and the Nicolaitans are criticized for what they practice rather than who leads them (2:6, 14–15). The problem is not that Jezebel, a woman, teaches; it is the content of her message (Schüssler Fiorenza 133). Her followers are called to repent, but so are readers in congregations in which no rival leaders are mentioned (3:1–6, 14–22). John's rhetoric makes use of negative feminine imagery, like the name Jezebel and portrayal of the whore (2:20; 17:1–6), but John also invokes negative masculine imagery, including the name Balaam and depiction of the false prophet (2:14; 16:13; 19:20; 20:10; Friesen, *Imperial*, 186–87). The issue is not one of gender or personal loyalty to John, but of collective loyalty to the commandments of God and the testimony of Jesus (deSilva, *Seeing*, 69).

Like the messages to Ephesus and Smyrna, the message has a symmetrical ringlike structure:

Authority: Christ as royal Son of God (2:18)
  Encouragement: Congregation's love and faithfulness (2:19)
    Reproof: They tolerate someone teaching religious promiscuity (2:20–21)
    Warning: The teacher will be "put to bed" and her followers afflicted (2:22–23)
  Encouragement: Hold fast to what you have (2:24–25)
Authority: The conqueror will share Jesus' royal authority (2:26–28)

On Rev 2:18–28, see G. Carey, *Elusive*, 135–64; den Dulk, "Promises"; deSilva, *Seeing*, 66–69, 243–45; Duff, "I Will"; Friedrich, "Adapt"; Friesen, "Sarcasm"; Guttenberger, "Johannes"; Hemer, *Letters*, 106–28; C. R. Koester, "Roman"; Pippin, "And I"; Pollard, "Function"; Quek, "I Will"; Ramsay, *Letters*, 316–53; Siitonen, "Merchants"; Slater, *Christ*, 132–38; Thimmes, "Women"; Trocmé, "La Jezabel."

The outer ring deals with royal authority. The introduction identifies Christ as the Son of God, a royal title, and the conclusion promises authority to those who conquer by following Jesus (2:18, 26–28). The intermediate ring encourages the faithful by commending their present works and calling on them to hold fast to what they have (2:19, 24–25). The central section reproves those who follow the teachings of Jezebel and warns of the judgment they will face (2:20–23). The words of encouragement and reproof serve the same end, which is to persevere in faith.

Introduction

The message begins as John is again commanded to "write" to the angel of the congregation (2:18; COMMENT on 2:1). The message is presented as a word of the risen Jesus, and readers can assume that John shares Jesus' viewpoint. Yet he cannot simply equate himself with the divine speaker. The message may warn of the affliction threatening Jezebel and her followers, while promising blessings to the faithful, but John cannot enact either the threats or the promises. Both require divine action. If readers are to receive this message, they must hear Christ speaking through John's text (1:3).

Christ is introduced with traits from the inaugural vision. There he was called one like "a human being," or literally "Son of Man" (1:13), which now becomes "Son of God" (2:18). The two expressions had similar connotations. According to Dan 7:13, the Son of Man comes on the clouds to receive dominion over all peoples (NOTES on Rev 1:7, 13), and other passages speak of the Son of God ruling the nations (Pss 2:7–8; 89:26–27). The titles Son of God and Son of Man appear together in early Christian sources (Matt 26:63–64; Luke 22:69–70; John 5:25–27; cf. *4 Ezra* 13:3, 32). Referring to the Son of God in the message to Thyatira conveys a sense of dominion, while suggesting at least three dimensions of meaning (NOTE on 2:18).

First, "Son of God" identifies Jesus as the one who establishes the reign of God. To call Jesus the Son of God means that he is the righteous ruler promised in Scripture (Luke 1:32–35; John 1:45, 49; Heb 1:5). Therefore, Revelation also gives him royal titles like Lion of Judah (Gen 49:9–10) and Root of David (Isa 11:1; cf. Rev 1:5; 5:5). Here, the language recalls Ps 2, which identifies God's king as his "son" and promises that he will rule the nations with an iron rod. The message begins by identifying Jesus as God's Son and ends by paraphrasing the psalm in order to promise the faithful a share in Christ's reign (Ps 2:7–9; Rev 2:18, 26–27). Since the rising star was an image for God's promised ruler (Num 24:17; *T. Levi* 18:3; *T. Jud.* 24:1; 4Q175 12), the messianic Son of God also promises that the faithful will receive the "morning star," who is David's heir, Jesus himself (Rev 2:18, 28; 22:16).

Second, calling Jesus the Son of God means that he shares the traits of God. The book refers to both God and Jesus as Alpha and Omega, first and last, beginning and end—all of which connote deity (1:8, 17; cf. 21:6; 22:13). Traits like fiery eyes and feet that shine like bronze also suggest divine status (2:18), as does Jesus' ability to search minds and hearts (2:23).

Third, those who confess Jesus to be the Son of God cannot rightly give this title to anyone else, including the emperor, who was called "son of god" in inscriptions at Thyatira and other cities. Roman iconography pictured the emperor exercising power over the nations (R. Smith, "Imperial"), but Revelation makes a counterclaim, identifying Jesus as the Son of God, who has that rightful power and can extend it to his followers (2:26).

Body of the Message

Christ begins with words of praise that compare the Thyatirans favorably to other congregations. Like the Christians at Ephesus, those at Thyatira are commended for endurance (2:2–3, 19), but where those at Ephesus are faulted for lacking love and failing to do the works they did at first, those at Thyatira are commended for their love and for works that exceed those they did at first (2:4–5, 19). Like the Christians at Pergamum, those at Thyatira are praised for faithfulness (2:13, 19), but the Thyatirans alone are honored for their service (2:19). Such affirmations encourage readers at Thyatira to continue their course, while giving others incentive to do the same (*Rhetorica ad Herennium* 3.4.7; Quintilian, *Inst.* 3.7.28). Such affirmations foster rapport with listeners— which is important, since they are now given a sharp critique.

The listeners are rebuked for allowing a prophetess to teach that it is acceptable to eat what has been sacrificed to the gods (Rev 2:20). Interpreters often assume that Christians at Thyatira felt special pressure to accommodate Greco-Roman religious practices in order to participate in the trade associations there, but similar groups existed in other cities (Note on 2:18). Pressure for religious accommodation came from various directions. Public festivals like those honoring Artemis and the emperor involved sacrifices, meals, and sometimes distributions of food (I. Thyat 972; 995; 1002). Some congregants presumably had family members who were non-Christians. Members of the readers' social circles could have met in temples or purchased sacrificial meat in the public market to serve in their homes. Refusing to eat with others would have been considered antisocial (Intro III.B.2).

The assembly at Thyatira experienced a clash of prophetic perspectives over this issue. The prophetess whom John calls Jezebel apparently considered it acceptable to eat sacrificial meat in most if not all circumstances. The arguments she used are not stated, but others who held such views claimed that since the gods represented by statues did not actually exist, people could eat what had been sacrificed to them without actually worshiping. Moreover, although Jewish law forbade such practices, Christians could claim to be free from the law (1 Cor 8:1–6; 10:23). John counters by categorically prohibiting eating what had been sacrificed to the gods. He stands within a Jewish and Christian tradition that regards idols as demonic. From this perspective, eating sacrificial meat at a festival or banquet or purchasing it in the market meant receiving the benefits of evil, which was not to be done.

Questions of true and false prophecy underlie the dispute. There were cases in which people were to distinguish true from false prophets by asking whether the prophet's word came true (Deut 13:1–2; Jer 28:9), but false prophets in Revelation are not charged with making false predictions. Instead, a true prophet encourages loyalty to God and a false one draws people away from God (Deut 13:1–11; Philo, *Spec. Laws* 1.315; cf. Zech 13:2–3; 2 Pet 2:1) and works against faith in Jesus (1 John 4:1–3; 1 Cor 12:1–3; Matt 24:11; Acts 13:6–8). In some contexts a false prophet was also identified by conduct deemed incongruent with the faith (*Did.* 11:7–12; Matt 7:15–20; 24:11, 24; Aune, *Prophecy*, 217–29). In Revelation eating food offered to Greco-Roman deities is understood to compromise a person's commitment to God, which means that a person teaching this cannot be a true prophet.

Revelation seeks to foster a more rigorous sense of Christian identity by locating the conflict between true and false prophecy within a cosmic struggle (Duff, *Who*, 113–25). The great false prophet is the beast from the land, which personifies the people who reject God's lordship by promoting the ruler cult (Rev 13:1–18; 16:13). Although the Thyatiran prophetess is not explicitly linked to the ruler cult, it was common to venerate the emperor alongside traditional deities. Revelation makes the prophetess a part of that camp (Schüssler Fiorenza 133; Friedrich, "Adapt"). By way of contrast, true prophets are represented by the two witnesses in Revelation, who wear sackcloth as a call to repentance (11:3), much as John calls for repentance (2:5, 16, 21–22; 3:3, 19). The visions show that although true prophets now suffer opposition at the hands of society and its rulers, they will be vindicated (11:7–12), and false prophets and their followers will fall under the judgment of Christ (19:20; 20:10).

The message calls eating what has been offered to other deities "immoral" (2:20; cf. 2:14, 20). Although some in the congregation regarded eating food offered to idols as decent social practice, the message likens it to indecent sexual activity. The vision of Babylon the whore will show the cosmic dimensions of the issue (Duff, *Who*, 83–96). For some, eating what was offered to the gods seemed like an innocuous way to ensure good social relationships with non-Christian family members and friends, and it seemed to be necessary when fostering business relationships that produced a good living. But the vision of Babylon the whore equates the practice with the religious infidelity that is linked to the brutality and materialism that John sees in imperial society (17:1–6; 18:1–24; Siitonen, "Merchants"). Having called the accommodation of Roman-era worship practices immoral (*porneuein*), the description of the whore (*pornē*) confronts readers with the unsavory aspects of the world that some wish to embrace.

Finally, the message identifies religious accommodation with the legacy of the biblical Jezebel—much as it was previously linked to Balaam (2:14, 20). First, the biblical Jezebel was a person of status. She was the daughter of a Phoenician king and became queen by marrying king Ahab of Israel (1 Kgs 16:31). The social position of the Thyatiran woman is unclear, but by encouraging people to eat what was offered in sacrifice, she put believers in a compromising position. Those who received food from the wealthy non-Christians who paid for the banquets were expected to show gratitude to their patrons—and by implication to the gods they honored. Second, the biblical Jezebel actively promoted the worship of Canaanite deities, and her actions were called "whoredoms and sorceries," just as those of the woman at Thyatira are labeled "immoral" (2 Kgs 9:22; Josephus, *Ant.* 8.318). Third, the biblical Jezebel opposed Elijah and other prophets loyal to Israel's God (1 Kgs 18:13, 19). At Thyatira, John is the Elijah figure who confronts another "Jezebel" (Caird; Guttenberger, "Johannes," 175–75).

In the visionary message the exalted Christ says, "I gave her time to repent, but she refuses to repent of her immorality" (Rev 2:21). If this line recalls an actual encounter, it could mean that John or another prophet had previously confronted the prophetess. The word "repent" is repeated, emphasizing that the purpose of the confrontation was to move the woman to change her practice (2:5, 16; 3:3, 19). Since the prophetess has resisted change, the message makes a wordplay on the term "bed" to warn that the consequences will be fitting for her deeds (2:22). People would sometimes eat a meal in honor of a deity while reclining on a couch or bed, and Revelation depicts this as religious infidelity comparable to the sexual infidelity that is committed in bed. Therefore, the prophetess who has taught this is warned that she will be "put to bed," but in a manner that inhibits her activities (NOTE on 2:22).

Readers might see the warning to the prophetess as analogous to the story of Queen Jezebel, who came to a sordid end, but the parallels quickly break down. At Thyatira the threat depends entirely on divine action. In the older storyline, God commissioned his prophets to foment a military overthrow of the ruling house of Israel. After victory on the battlefield, the allies of the prophets hurled Jezebel out of a window, and her body was devoured by dogs (1 Kgs 19:15–17; 2 Kgs 9:1–10, 30–37). In Revelation, however, judgment belongs to Christ, not to his followers, and readers are left to discern when and how Christ will enact justice.

The question of discernment is significant because the language in Revelation is surprisingly vague. Are readers to take the warning against Jezebel in a strict literal sense, or does it have a metaphorical aspect, like those to other churches? It is not clear how one would know whether Christ had moved the Ephesians' "lampstand" from its place, made war at Pergamum with the "sword" of his mouth, or "vomit" the Laodiceans out of his mouth (Rev 2:5, 16; 3:16). So are the Thyatirans to wait for the prophetess to be physically confined to bed through an illness, or does the warning have other meanings?

The question continues as Jezebel's followers are warned that they will suffer "affliction" (2:22). What is clear is that the woman's disciples are to repent by rejecting her practice of eating what has been sacrificed to various deities. What is not clear is what "affliction" might entail. Would it be a physical ailment or an emotional, social, or economic hardship? The warning is open enough to fit many situations, thereby allowing it to serve as an ongoing call for repentance. As the warnings continue, a final step puts the most severe judgment into an indefinite future. "If they do not repent of her works, I will also put her children to death with a plague" (2:22c–23). The operative word is "if" (*ean*). Christ has recourse to more severe measures, including death, *if* people do not respond to the warnings and afflictions. But the final step belongs to him, not to his followers, and in the meantime the call for repentance remains.

A problem for readers is that the warnings seem to create sharp contradictions in Revelation's portrayal of Christ. How are they to imagine the Christ who endured suffering for the sake of others now threatening to inflict suffering on others (1:5; 2:23)? If the Son of God was once slain by the opponents of God, why would he now threaten to slay the sons and daughters of Jezebel (1:5; 2:23)? Has he adopted the tactics of his opponents? Christ may be known for commending love (1:5; 2:19), yet the warnings seem to lack all semblance of love. Do the warnings make Christ indistinguishable from the Beast (Moyise, "Does," 182)?

The tensions between Christ's severity and mercy are not resolved within the message but are played out in what follows. The opening of the seals will bring one threatening vision after another, but when people cry out in terror, the movement toward judgment is interrupted and readers are shown the scale of divine redemption (6:16–17; 7:1–17). The trumpet visions continue depicting divine wrath against the ungodly, but when the plagues fail to bring repentance, judgment is again interrupted so that the faithful can bear witness (9:20–21; 10:1–11:12). Only when many have been brought to glorify God does the final trumpet sound (11:13–15). The final visions depict Christ's judgment on kings and nations, making it remarkable that the book also holds out hope that kings and nations will have a place in New Jerusalem (19:11–21; 21:24–26). The threat of judgment is real, but warnings are given in order to move people to repent before judgment is carried out, and visions of redemption continue to call for change until the end.

The message identifies the glorified Christ as the one who examines human minds and hearts, so he is the one to whom readers are accountable (2:23). Those who eat what is offered to other deities may seek approval from non-Christians, but in the end they are subject to the authority of Christ, who judges on a different basis. Christ gives people what their works deserve, which means that his judgments are just. Other messages acknowledge that the faithful suffer (2:9–10; 3:8–10) while the complacent thrive (3:1, 14–17). Such experiences would support Jezebel's encouragement of the kind of religious accommodation that would ease tensions with society, but Revelation challenges this teaching by calling for more rigorous commitment to God and Jesus. Support comes from subsequent visions, which assume that the problem is not that divine judgment is too quick, but is too *slow*, so that the faithful suffer (6:9–11). Readers will learn that the delay in divine justice gives the ungodly the opportunity to repent (9:20–21; 16:9, 11) while calling the faithful to bear witness to the world (10:1–11:13).

The body of the message concludes by encouraging those who reject the teachings of Jezebel (2:24–25). The passage recognizes that knowledge is a form of social influence. The followers of Jezebel claim to understand things more deeply than others do, which puts them in a coveted position as insiders, while others are by implication outsiders. The message reverses this claim by commending those who do *not* know the deep things she purports to teach. Those who *lack* knowledge are in the favored position, because what she teaches pertains to Satan and not to God. In previous messages Satan has been identified with the kind of open hostility that threatens Jesus' followers with imprisonment and death (2:9–10, 13). When linked to Jezebel's teaching, Satan's work is more subtle and deceptive, but those who embrace it nonetheless join the ranks of Christ's opponents. The message fosters a sense of community by telling those who do not follow Jezebel that their circle already has what is needed: faithfulness, love, and service (2:19).

Conclusion

The message began by identifying Christ as the royal Son of God, and it concludes by promising that the faithful will share in his reign (2:26–28). On one level the passage is a collage of militant images: The faithful "conquer," they receive authority over the nations, and they rule with an iron rod as one breaks clay pottery (Ps 2:8–9). Some interpreters assume that the promise should be taken in a straightforward way, so that Jesus' followers can anticipate helping Christ destroy the wicked in the final battle (Rev 12:5; 19:15) and then join in reigning over subject nations (Charles). Yet later visions do not bear this out. A large company may come with Christ for battle, but Christ alone wins the victory with his word (17:14; 19:11–21). Alternatively, others relate this promise to the millennial kingdom, assuming that the saints will firmly rule the nations that remain on earth (Thomas). However, the faithful are resurrected to reign *with*

Christ but are not said to reign *over* the nations (20:4–6). When hostile nations appear again, it is not the saints but heavenly fire that overcomes them (20:7–10).

The promises made here can best be understood in a transformed sense. Conquering (*nikan*) is defined by Christ, who has the authority of the messianic Lion of Judah but who exercises it through his death as the Lamb (5:5–6). Through the shedding of his own blood, he builds the kingdom (1:5–6; 5:9–10). Similarly, the message to Thyatira says that Jesus' followers conquer by keeping his works, which consist of love, faithfulness, service, and endurance (2:19, 26). At present, the faithful break the power of the nations by their witness to God and Jesus. Their refusal to capitulate to the ways of the world is a victory for truth over falsehood (Beale; Caird; Harrington). The promise also points to the culmination of the book, where the faithful are resurrected to endless life and reign with Christ in New Jerusalem. The surprise is that there, the nations no longer need the iron rod, for they turn to God and the Lamb for light and healing (21:24–26; 22:2).

The final promise is that the faithful will receive the "morning star" (2:29). The significance of the image is not explained, but in the end the star proves to be Christ himself (22:16). This line recalls the oracle of Balaam, which said that a star was to rise from Jacob to rule the nations (Num 24:17). But calling the exalted Jesus "the morning star" goes further, portraying him as the harbinger of a new day (*Jos. As.* 14:1; Martial, *Epigrams* 8.21; 2 Pet 1:19). This role is most fully seen in New Jerusalem, where the redeemed reign forever in Christ's light (Rev 21:23; 22:5).

9. To the Assembly in Sardis (3:1–6)

3 [1]"To the angel of the assembly in Sardis write: Thus says the one who holds the seven spirits of God and the seven stars: I know your works; you have a name of being alive, even though you are dead. [2]Be watchful and strengthen what you still have that is dying, for I have not found your works complete before God. [3]So remember what you received and heard. Hold on to it and repent. For if you do not watch out, I will come like a thief, and you will not know at what hour I will come to you. [4]But one could name a few in Sardis who have not defiled their clothing, and they will walk with me in white because they are worthy. [5]Those who conquer will wear white clothing like this, and I will not blot their names out of the scroll of life, but will acknowledge their names before my Father and his angels. [6]Let the one who has an ear hear what the Spirit says to the assemblies."

NOTES

3:1. *To the angel of the assembly.* Each angel apparently has responsibility for a congregation (NOTES on 1:20; 2:1).

in Sardis. Sardis (modern Sartmahmut, Turkey) was located about forty miles southeast of Thyatira and fifty miles east of Smyrna at the juncture of several road systems. It had been the capital of the kingdom of Lydia in the seventh and sixth centuries

BCE. At one time gold was found in the Pactolus River near the city, and the wealth of Sardis's ancient king, Croesus, was legendary (Dio Chrysostom, *Disc.* 77/78.31–32; Ovid, *Metam.* 11.136–45). Captured by the Persians in 547 BCE, Sardis became the western terminus of the royal road that stretched eastward to the Persian capital, and it flourished through trade. Following the conquests of Alexander the Great, the city came under Hellenistic rule and was the capital of the Seleucid kingdom in the third century BCE. After 133 BCE Sardis became part of Roman Asia, where it was a judicial center (Pliny the Elder, *Nat.* 5.111). Like other cities, its population included Greeks, Macedonians, and Jews as well as Roman businesspeople (SEG 46:1521). In Roman times the river no longer yielded gold, but Sardis remained "a great city," and its council of elders met in the ancient palace of Croesus, preserving the memory of its heritage (Strabo, *Geographica* 13.4.5; Vitruvius, *Arch.* 2.8.10).

The city that existed when Revelation was composed had been rebuilt after a devastating earthquake in 17 CE. Under Tiberius, the Romans helped Sardis recover by exempting it from taxes for five years, providing financial assistance, and sending a commissioner to oversee reconstruction (Tacitus, *Ann.* 2.47). During the decades that followed, many buildings were repaired, a colonnaded street and aqueduct were built, and work was undertaken on the theater, stadium, and bath-gymnasium complex (Hanfmann, *Sardis*, 141–44). To show its gratitude, the city adopted imperial titles, calling itself "the people of the Caesarean Sardians." Tiberius was "Founder of the City," and groups of citizens honored him with monuments (I.Sard 34; 39–40; Hanfmann, *Sardis*, 144). Trade associations included textile workers, goldsmiths, and builders (Pedley, *Ancient*, 44–45; Hanfmann, *Sardis*, 10–12). Sardis was a regional center for the Roman slave trade. Those doing business in the slave market at Sardis apparently included some Italian businesspeople, and an inscription from the late first century CE shows slave traders honoring a civic benefactor, who was a priest in the imperial cult. Such connections between the slave trade and Roman rule are reflected in Rev 18 (C. R. Koester, "Roman," 783–85). The empire provided opportunities for upward social mobility. For instance, Celsus Polemaenus, a citizen of Sardis, was admitted to the Roman Senate in the 70s CE and was the first Asian to become consul in 92 (I.Sard 45).

Religious life during the Hellenistic period centered on Artemis of Sardis and Zeus Polieus, the guardians of civic welfare. Their temple, which was more than three hundred feet long, was built in the second century BCE. The Sardians also honored the Ephesian Artemis and Athena Nicephorus, "the bringer of victory" and patron of Pergamum. Hellenistic deities such Apollo and Herakles were popular, as was the festival of Dionysus. There were sanctuaries for Hera, for the Asian mother goddess Meter, and for the Anatolian moon god Men (Herrmann, "Sardeis," 30; Hoz, *Die lydischen*, nos. 21.1; 40.12; Malay, *Researches*, no. 131). Tyche, the goddess of fortune, was also venerated. When the temple of Artemis and Zeus was damaged in the earthquake of 17 CE, the structure was not fully rebuilt for decades as attention shifted to other deities. Coins from the time of Nero featured Kore the grain goddess instead of Artemis, and by 70–100 Sardis was known as the city of Demeter (Herrmann, "Demeter"). The honors given to traditional deities were combined with those of the imperial household. Coins from Sardis showed Tiberius raising a female figure representing Sardis, while on the other side his mother Livia appears as Demeter, holding sheaves of grain (Figure 14) (Dräger, *Städte*, 435).

Figure 14. Coin from Sardis: Tiberius raising up a kneeling Sardis on one side and Livia as the goddess Demeter holding a scepter and grain on the other (17–37 CE). © The Trustees of the British Museum.

Portrayals of Zeus also changed so that he appeared in Lydian form (Hanfmann, *Sardis*, 129–35). The god called Holy and Righteous (*Theos Hosios kai Dikaios*) was apparently an intermediary between the divine and human worlds (Hoz, *Die lydischen*, no. 27.15). Although Revelation uses the words "holy" and "righteous" exclusively for the God of Israel (Rev 15:3–4; 16:5), the context at Sardis shows the potential for a blending of biblical and Hellenistic religious traditions.

The priestess of Artemis (I.Sard 50–55; 91–93) and priest of Zeus Polieus (47–48) traditionally played important civic roles. They underwrote costs of festivals and conducted religious rites. Organizations included the tribe of the wine god, Dionysus; the brotherhood of the Phrygian god of vegetation, Attis; and the initiates of Apollo, the sun god and offspring of Zeus (Hoz, *Die lydischen*, 54, 67, 102; SEG 46:1528). One inscription says that those devoted to Zeus Baradates, "the lawgiver," were not to participate in the mysteries of the Thracian-Phrygian god Sabazios or the Anatolian mother goddesses Agdistis and Ma, but such exclusive religious commitments were unusual (Herrmann, "Mystenvereine"; Ascough, "Greco-Roman," 40–41).

Sardis had a cult of the goddess Roma before the end of the second century BCE. Public documents were dated by identifying the priest of Roma who held office in a given year (I.Sard 8.75; 93; 112–15). The first provincial temple to Augustus was built at Pergamum by 26 BCE, and Sardis had a municipal temple to Augustus before the end of the first century BCE (I.Sard 8.13–14). Soon, a citizen from Sardis oversaw the provincial imperial games (IGR 1611). Because of the assistance the city received after the earthquake, local officials wanted to honor Tiberius with a provincial temple, but Smyrna was given the privilege (Tacitus, *Ann.* 4.55). Nevertheless, Tiberius was honored as "god," and similar honors were given to Caligula and Claudius (Herrmann, "Sardeis," 31–36). During the Flavian period (69–96 CE) a citizen of Sardis served as provincial high priest in the imperial cult (C. R. Koester, "Roman," 784). Although some scholars suggest that Sardis dedicated its first provincial imperial temple to Vespasian in the late first century CE, this probably occurred under Hadrian, early in the second century (Burrell, *Neokoroi*, 100–3).

The large Jewish community at Sardis was prosperous and influential. Some Jews were Roman citizens. Under Roman rule they asserted their rights to have a place of worship, to adjudicate their own affairs, and to have a supply of ritually clean food.

Until the destruction of the Jerusalem temple in 70 CE, the Jews of Sardis sent money for its support (Josephus, *Ant.* 14.232, 235, 259–261; 16.171). The city's massive synagogue dates from the third century CE, but the Jewish community was well-established long before. Although the Jewish text the *Sibylline Oracles* includes Sardis in warnings of divine judgment (5:289), the Jews who lived there were an integral part of civic life (Trebilco, *Jewish*, 37–54, 183–85).

A Christian community had existed at Sardis for some time before Revelation was composed. Whether the early Jesus followers at Sardis were of Jewish origin is not known, but in the second century they coordinated their Easter observances with the Jewish festival of Passover, as did other Christians in the region. Since John's gospel places the death of Jesus on the day of preparation for Passover, some scholars suggest that Sardian Christians followed the Johannine tradition (Stewart-Sykes, *Lamb's*, 11–25). One might also wonder whether the congregation had connections to the Pauline churches in Asia, but given the paucity of data, little can be said about this (Neufeld, "Christian," 28–33). In the second century Melito, the bishop of Sardis, showed a deep interest in Scripture and was considered a prophet (Eusebius, *Hist. eccl.* 4.26.13; 5.24.5; Jerome, *Vir. ill.* 24). His treatise on the Passover is sharply critical of Judaism, but such tensions are not evident in Revelation's message to Sardis.

Thus says the one who holds the seven spirits of God and the seven stars. The seven spirits are probably angelic beings that serve as attendants of God (NOTE on 1:4), whereas the seven stars represent the angels that are associated with the seven congregations (1:20). The expression "Thus says" has royal and prophetic connotations (NOTE on 2:1).

I know your works; you have a name of being alive even though you are dead. Jesus was introduced as one who died and was raised (1:18). Similar language is used metaphorically for the Sardians. To be alive (*zēn*) is to be active or vibrant rather than dead (*nekros*) or inactive. Since sin was often identified with deadness and faith with life, the language could suggest that the Sardians appear to be faithful and yet persist in sin (Luke 15:24; Rom 6:13; 8:10; Eph 2:1–5; Col 2:13). But since no specific wrongdoing is mentioned, being alive probably means being committed to Christ and his followers, while being dead means being uncommitted (Matt 8:22; Luke 9:60). Deadness could include a failure to bear witness to one's faith (Beale; Blount), but the issue cannot be limited to that. Some interpreters contend that questions of death and afterlife were especially prominent at Sardis (Keener; Osborne) or that the word "dead" pictures Sardis as a city in decline (Smalley), but these conjectures are unlikely. Sardis was a significant urban center in Asia during the first century CE, and its religious practices were much like those in other cities (NOTE on Rev 3:1).

3:2. *Be watchful and strengthen what you still have that is dying.* Exhortations to watch (*grēgorein*) are common in apocalyptic texts that call for resisting evil and remaining faithful in anticipation of imminent divine action (Mark 13:34–37 par.; 1 Cor 16:13; 1 Thess 5:6; 1 Pet 5:8). Strengthening (*stērizein*) involved promoting a manner of life consistent with the Christian message (Rom 16:25; 1 Thess 3:13; 1 Pet 5:10). Readers are to strengthen *ta loipa*, which some interpreters take to be "the rest" of the congregation, who are weak in faith (Satake; Smalley). Since the expression is neuter plural, however, it more likely means strengthening the works of love, faithfulness, and service that were in danger of dying out (cf. Rev 2:19).

for I have not found your works complete before God. Works are complete (*peplērō-mena*) when done in full obedience to God's will. Israel was complete (Hebrew *tamim*) when following God's commandments and rejecting the practices of other nations (Deut 18:13). In the Dead Sea community, one's actions were to be completely congruent with the law as understood by the sect (1QS I, 8; III, 9–10; V, 24; VIII, 1; IX, 3). Early Christians could speak of completing their work, service (Acts 12:25; 14:26; Rom 15:19), and requirements of the law (Rom 13:8). Related expressions refer to going beyond conventional patterns or half-hearted actions to more complete expressions of love and obedience (Matt 5:48; 19:21; 1 John 2:5; 4:12, 17; cf. Jas 2:10). Revelation calls for complete fidelity to God, Christ, and the Christian community.

3:3. *So remember what you received and heard. Hold on to it and repent.* Christian communities were established when the gospel message was heard and received in faith (1 Cor 11:23; 15:1; 1 Thess 2:13; John 17:8). Christians at Sardis received a form of the tradition that the congregation can still remember. Holding on to it involves confessing Christ's name and showing love and service (Rev 2:3–4, 13, 19; 3:8). The word *pōs* could mean "what" they received, but it could also refer to "how" they received and heard the gospel message—for example, with firm conviction (1 Thess 1:5, 9).

For if you do not watch out, I will come like a thief, and you will not know at what hour I will come to you. The simile of the thief appears in traditions about Christ's return. A saying of Jesus, usually ascribed to the Sayings Source (Q) underlying the Synoptic Gospels, reads: "But understand this: If the owner of the house had known at what part of the night the thief was coming, he would have stayed awake and would not have let his house be broken into. Therefore, you also must be ready, for the Son of Man is coming at an unexpected hour" (Matt 24:43–44; Luke 12:39–40). Similarly, Paul wrote of the return of Christ, and then added "the Day of the Lord will come like a thief in the night" and exhorted Christians to be watchful (1 Thess 5:2, 4). Some forms of the saying about the thief lack an explicit reference to the coming of the Son of Man (*Gos. Thom.* 21; 103; 2 Pet 3:10), but Revelation relies on a tradition that anticipates Christ's return (Bauckham, *Climax*, 104–9). Thieves were commonly said to work at night, but daytime theft was also possible (Job 24:14; Philo, *Spec. Laws* 4.10; Dio Chrysostom, *Disc.* 69.8). Revelation does not mention night or day, leaving open the prospect that Christ could come at any time.

Some interpreters think that the congregation's lack of watchfulness recalls the history of Sardis. In 546 BCE the city's forces seemed to be in a secure position in the fortified citadel of Sardis, but the Persians surprised the defenders and won the victory (Herodotus, *Hist.* 1.84; Xenophon, *Cyr.* 7.2.2–4). The forces of Antiochus III did the same in 214 BCE (Polybius, *Histories* 7.15–18). The proposed analogy is that the congregation thinks itself secure but is warned of being surprised by Christ (Ramsay, *Letters*, 276–77; Hemer, *Letters*, 132–33; Court, *Myth*, 36; Beale; Blount; Ford; Giesen; Harrington; Keener; Osborne; Reddish; Witherington). Nevertheless, an allusion to city history is improbable. In a passage that has nothing specifically to do with Sardis, Revelation will refer again to Christ coming like a thief (Rev 16:15). Exhortations to watchfulness (Mark 13:34–37 par.; 1 Cor 16:13; 1 Thess 5:6; 1 Pet 5:8) and warnings about Christ or the Day of the Lord coming like a thief were used in many contexts (Matt 24:43–44; Luke 12:39–40; 1 Thess 5:2, 4). The saying about the thief is used for Sardis not because it fits the city's history, but because it was a typical way to warn Christians of the need for vigilance.

3:4. *But one could name a few in Sardis who have not defiled their clothing.* A literal translation would be, "you have a few names." Earlier, "name" meant reputation, but here it is "person" (cf. 11:13 Acts 1:15; *NewDocs* 2:201–2; MM 451). In ordinary usage the outer clothes (*himatia*; cf. *stolē*, Rev 6:11; 7:9, 13, 14; 22:16) were worn over the under layer or tunic. Clothes that were defiled were physically unclean and ritually unsuitable to be worn in God's presence (Exod 19:10–14; Num 8:7, 15; P.Oxy. 840.16). In Rev 3:4 clothes signify a person's condition, and defilement results from sin (Isa 59:3; Zech 3:1–5). Some interpreters suggest that the readers' "clothing" refers to the identity they received in baptism, when they "put on" Christ (Gal 3:27; Bede; Blount; Murphy). It is clear that the garment signifies Christian identity, but whether it connotes baptism is uncertain.

and they will walk with me in white because they are worthy. Worth is the value that someone has in the eyes of someone else. God and the Lamb are worthy of honor because they create and redeem, whereas sinners are worthy of punishment (Rev 4:11; 5:9–12; 16:6). Similarly, those who now resist sin and thus do not defile their garments will be worthy to walk with Christ in white garments in the future. To walk with Christ indicates his approval (Gen 5:22; 6:9).

3:5. *Those who conquer will wear white clothing like this.* White clothing has several meanings, including the following:

1. Purity. White clothes are the opposite of those that are stained, which here means tainted by sin (Rev 3:4). The multitude in 7:13–14 wears robes that have been made white in the blood of the Lamb. Those who enter New Jerusalem wash their robes, whereas those outside are unclean (21:27; 22:14–15). The heavenly armies that come with Christ wear pure white linen (19:14). Greco-Roman religious practice also associated white with purification (Aelius Aristides, *Orations* 48.31).

2. Holiness. Holiness means setting what is clean apart for service to God. Those who wear pure white are said to walk with Christ. Since Christ is holy, those who are with him must be holy (Rev 3:7). This meaning is evident in visions in which worshipers wear white as they stand before the throne of God, who is holy (4:4; 7:9). Heavenly beings were described wearing white (Dan 7:9; Matt 17:2; John 20:12; Acts 1:10; *1 En.* 14:20). Participants in Greco-Roman religious rites in Asian cities commonly wore white, since that was the color most appropriate to the gods (Plato, *Leg.* 956A; Aelius Aristides, *Orations* 48.30; Plutarch, *Mor.* 771D; P.Oxy. 471.101).

3. Honor. Honor is the positive value that people receive from others. Here, those in white are called worthy and are acclaimed as conquerors, both of which connote honor (Rev 3:4–5; 4:11; 5:12). The white robes that people receive from Christ cover their shame and give them dignity (3:18; 16:15). The martyrs who cry out for justice are given white robes to show divine approval (6:11). In apocalyptic writings, bright garments point to the glory of those who are raised (*1 En.* 62:15–16). Culturally, white garments could connote death and grief (Plutarch, *Mor.* 270F), but Revelation relates them to life and celebration (cf. Eccl 9:8).

and I will not blot out their names out of the scroll of life. The scroll of life is a register of those who have the hope of resurrection to everlasting life. It lists those who have citizenship in New Jerusalem. In the OT "the scroll of the living" (Ps 69:28) and "the scroll" God has written (Exod 32:32) identify people who are currently alive. Those passages warn of sinners being blotted out of God's scroll, meaning that they are threatened with death. Other sources expect those recorded in the scroll to have a glorious future in God's city (Isa 4:3), which came to be understood as resurrection to deathless life (Dan 12:1). Some thought people were listed in the scroll as a reward for righteous living (Herm. *Sim.* 2.9; *Apoc. Zeph.* 3:6–9), but others said they were included in the scroll through divine grace, which gave them citizenship in heaven and hope of everlasting life (Luke 10:20; Phil 3:20–4:3). This is the perspective of Revelation, in which the Creator inscribes people in the scroll from the time the world was made (Rev 13:8; 17:8). To have one's name in the scroll of life gives assurance of divine preservation (4Q504 1–2 VI, 14), and to have one's name blotted out connotes death (4Q381 31 8). When extended to the future, having one's name removed from the scroll signifies final condemnation (*Jub.* 30:22; 36:10; *1 En.* 108:3; *Shem. Es.* 12), whereas those whose names are not blotted out receive everlasting life (*Jos. As.* 15:4). In Revelation, those inscribed in the scroll find endless life in New Jerusalem (Rev 20:15; 21:27).

The scroll imagery has analogies in Greco-Roman practice where communities kept lists of their citizens. Each legitimate child of a Roman citizen was to be registered within forty days of birth so that the child could receive the benefits of citizenship, such as fair legal treatment and material help. When a person died, the name was listed among the dead (Acts 22:25–29; Seneca the Younger, *Ben.* 4.28.2; J. Winter, *Life*, 52–55, 132; Schulz, "Roman"). When authorities in some cities passed judgment on a person for a capital crime, that person's name was removed from the list of citizens and the death sentence was carried out (Dio Chrysostom, *Disc.* 31.84–85; Xenophon, *Hell.* 2.3.51). Revelation contrasts God's judgment with human judgment. The faithful may be ostracized by others in the cities where they live, but God will not blot them out of his citizenship roll: They are promised life in his city.

but [I] will acknowledge their names before my Father and his angels. Acknowledging someone means affirming a relationship with that person in a way that shows loyalty and favor. Since Christ has a position of honor before God and the angels, those he acknowledges share in the honor that belongs to him. The language resembles a traditional saying of Jesus. Often ascribed to Q, the statement circulated in various forms:

Rev 3:5c	Luke 12:8b	Matt 10:32b	2 Clem. 3:2b
and I will acknowledge his name before my Father	Son of Man will also acknowledge him before	I will also acknowledge him before my Father	I will acknowledge him before my Father in the heavens
and before his angels	the angels of God		

The verb "acknowledge" (*homologein*) occurs only here in Revelation. The author probably drew it from tradition, adding the word "name" to underscore the preceding remark about keeping the names in the scroll of life (Aune; Schüssler Fiorenza, *Book*, 104; Yarbro Collins, *Cosmology*, 186–89).

3:6. Let the one who has an ear hear what the Spirit says to the assemblies. See the NOTES and COMMENT on 2:7.

COMMENT

The fifth Christian community of Revelation is located at Sardis. What distinguishes this congregation is the absence of conflict. Historically, the citizens of Sardis asserted their loyalty to Rome through monuments to the emperors and participation in the imperial cult, yet Revelation does not suggest that Christians there had problems with Roman authority, as at Smyrna and Pergamum (2:10, 13). Sardis had a large Jewish population, but there is no mention of tension between Christians and Jews, as at Smyrna and Philadelphia (2:9; 3:9). The city had its share of social organizations, public sacrifices, and banquets, but the message does not suggest that the congregation faced questions about accommodating Greco-Roman religious practices, as at Pergamum and Thyatira (2:14, 20). And nothing is said about conflicts with false apostles, Nicolaitans, or a prophetess like Jezebel (2:2, 6, 14, 15, 20). The message rebukes the Sardian Christians for their comfort but does not charge them with anything more concrete (Murphy; Thompson, *Book*, 124–25).

With remarkable bluntness, the Sardians are told that they are alive in name only, for in reality they are dead: In Christ's judgment the readers have fallen short in their calling and must therefore examine themselves in relation to the witness they previously received from Jesus (3:3). This message draws language from the tradition of Jesus' sayings. All the messages do this when urging those with ears to hear what is being said (NOTE on 2:7), but the message to Sardis also does so when warning that Christ will come like a thief and when promising that he will acknowledge the faithful before his Father and the angels (3:3, 5). The sayings underscore the fact that the Christ who is known to the readers through tradition now speaks through John's text.

Structurally, the passage is framed by an introduction in which the speaker identifies himself and a conclusion that includes promises to the conquerors and an exhortation to listen (3:1a, 5–6). Where most previous messages began with praise and continued with rebuke, this one inverts the pattern by beginning with reproof (3:1b–3) and later giving encouragement (3:4). There is a pattern of reversal as the speaker moves from negative to positive statements about the readers' "name," from declaring them dead to promising them life, and from the problem of defiled clothing to the hope of white garments.

Introduction

John identifies the exalted Christ by recalling what was said in the first chapter: Christ holds the seven spirits and seven stars (3:1). The seven spirits are angelic beings that God sends into the world, and they serve as the eyes of the Lamb. Mentioning them reminds

---

On Rev 3:1–6, see Ascough, ed., *Religious*; Baynes, *Heavenly*, 145–49; deSilva, *Seeing*, 245–47; Hanfmann, *Sardis*; Hemer, *Letters*, 129–52; C. R. Koester, "Roman"; Ramsay, *Letters*, 259–85; Royalty, "Etched"; Slater, *Christ*, 138–42; Stanley, "Who's"; Yarbro Collins, *Cosmology*, 186–89.

readers that the Christ who calls for their vigilance is attended by the spirits that are agents of divine vigilance (NOTE on 1:4; cf. 4:5; 5:6). The seven stars are the angels that have oversight of the churches (1:16, 20). Since the initial indictment of the congregation's "name" is given in the presence of these angels, bringing disgrace to those who are complacent (3:1), Christ later promises that he will acknowledge the "name" of the faithful before his Father and the angels, giving them honor (3:5).

Body of the Message

The message contrasts the way the assembly appears to other people with the way God sees it. Christ refers to the assembly's good reputation, or "name," which means that other people regard the group favorably, giving the Sardians a sense of self-worth (3:1b; cf. Prov 22:1; Sir 41:12–13). The Christians at Sardis could have had a positive reputation within society if non-Christians considered their way of living respectable (1 Tim 3:7; Tit 2:7–8; Col 4:5–6; 1 Thess 4:11–12). But here attention focuses on their reputation among other Christians, who apparently thought that believers at Sardis exhibited a notable vitality.

The exalted Christ counters by stating that they are not alive but dead (3:1d). The statement is designed to startle readers out of their complacency. Deadness can signify spiritual and moral deficiency. The "dead" are the marginally committed (Matt 8:22; Luke 9:60), whose faith does not express itself in action (Jas 2:22, 26) and who are unconcerned about sin (Eph 2:1, 5). Similarly, the Sardians will be rebuked for works that fall short (Rev 3:2). Deadness was also linked to defilement. Those who dealt with the dead became unclean and unfit to appear before God without cleansing (Num 19:11–13). By analogy, the writer will charge that some in Sardis have spiritually defiled their clothes, thereby requiring cleansing through repentance (Col 2:13; Heb 6:1; Rev 3:3–4; 7:14; 22:14).

The reproof is followed by an exhortation to be watchful and strengthen what is dying (3:2a). Having depicted the congregation as a corpse, John now compares the readers to a seriously ill patient who needs to be tended. This imagery allows space for change. In an ordinary sense, those at the bedside of a sick person would try to strengthen the patient with medications, food, and drink (2 Kgs 20:7; Pliny the Elder, *Nat.* 23.60; cf. 20.23, 34; 22.25, 29). By analogy, the Sardians are to attend to their diminished spiritual health by repenting and holding more firmly to the message of Jesus (Rev 3:3).

The imagery shifts again as the readers are depicted as servants being brought to account before their master, who faults them for failing to carry out their responsibilities (3:2b; cf. Matt 24:45–51; 25:14–30; Luke 12:42–48). The Sardians are among God's servants, yet in Christ's judgment their works are incomplete (1:1; 3:2b). They are told *that* they have fallen short but not *how* they have done so, which means they must ask what they lack. Responses could vary. Since they had previously received God's commandments, they might conclude that they are faulted for keeping some commands but not others (12:17; 14:12). Since they are called to witness, love, and service, they might be rebuked for failing to follow through with these commitments (2:19; 11:7; 14:13; cf. Col 1:25; 4:17; 4 Macc 12:14). Or since their works have the appearance of vitality, yet mask a spiritual deadness, they might think they are being reproved for failing to act in a heartfelt way (Rev 3:1; 2 Thess 1:11; Phil 2:2).

Whatever the case, the judgment is given "before God" in order to inspire renewed commitment so the Sardians might be favorably acknowledged "before God" (Rev 3:2, 5). Although later visions will focus on the need for the world to repent (9:20–21; 14:7; 16:9, 11), the messages to the churches call for repentance within the Christian community itself. The Jesus followers at Sardis are to repent of their complacency, just as those at Ephesus must turn from their loss of love (2:4–5), those at Laodicea from their self-satisfaction (3:15–19), and those at Pergamum and Thyatira from accommodation of Greco-Roman religious practices (2:14–16, 20–22). The point of the reproofs is to motivate the readers to change.

The writer now uses a different image, picturing readers as members of a household who sit or sleep behind closed doors, unaware that an intruder is coming (3:3c). Christ identifies himself as the thief, a figure associated with stealth and violence. John's placing of Christ in this role is a startling rhetorical move, yet it suits the purpose of his message, which is to awaken the Sardian Christians to the need for vigilance. Some interpreters think the image of the thief warns of Christ's coming at the end of the age (Murphy), but it probably warns of his coming to take local action against the Sardis congregation, since his coming is contingent on their refusal to repent (cf. 2:5, 15; 3:3). If repentance occurs, Christ will not come in this way (Giesen).

Like earlier warnings, this one leaves much to the imagination, since readers are not told *what* Christ might do if he comes. In the readers' social world, the threat of being robbed cut across class lines. Both rich and poor were vulnerable (Matt 6:19–20). Some thieves slipped into a home through darkened courtyards or by climbing onto balconies (Joel 2:9). They might break a lock while someone was away or forcibly enter and intimidate homeowners while seizing property (Mark 3:27; Apuleius, *Metam.* 3.5, 28; 4.18; Stanley, "Who's").

The warning creates a crisis of discernment for the readers. It is not apparent whether they will recognize Christ's coming, as they might hear a thief breaking in, or whether his coming will be furtive, so they will recognize their loss only after it has occurred. And they learn nothing about what Christ might take from them. The problem of discernment is like that in earlier warnings, where it is unclear how one would know whether Christ had moved the "lampstand" of the Ephesians, made war with the "sword" of his mouth at Pergamum, or had spewed the Laodiceans out of his mouth (Rev 2:5, 16; 3:16). Yet the disturbing vagueness helps to rob the readers at Sardis of the complacency that they mistake for true security.

Encouragement finally comes through another abrupt change in imagery: The congregation is told that some of its members have not defiled their clothing (3:4). Rhetorically, this gives incentive for others to do the same (*Rhetorica ad Herennium* 3.4.7; Quintilian, *Inst.* 3.7.28). In a physical sense, clothing was defiled by contact with something that stained it, making the wearer unclean and unfit to be in God's presence (Isa 59:9; Lam 4:14; 1 Macc 1:37; Jer 23:11). In the message to Sardis, the image of undefiled clothing is a metaphor for those not tainted by sin. Revelation connects defilement to metaphors for illicit sexual activity (Rev 14:4), which connote religious infidelity and other practices inconsistent with the faith (2:14, 20–22). The theme of defilement culminates in the vision of Babylon the whore, whose impurities encompass the idolatry, brutality, oppression, and greed that John sees in Roman society (17:4; cf. 18:1–24).

Believers keep their clothing undefiled by resisting the religious, economic, and social practices that violate their commitments to God, Christ, and the Christian community. The author assumes that this involves struggle, yet readers have incentive to persevere because Christ values their fidelity. Those who now resist defiling their clothing through social and religious compromise are promised a future in which they will wear white and walk with Christ (3:4). Revelation does not limit salvation to those who have never sinned, however, for later visions encourage people to "wash their clothes" by repenting of sin and trusting in the redemption provided by Christ (7:14; 22:14).

Conclusion

The three promises given in the conclusion are the positive counterparts to the negative judgments made earlier. First is the promise of wearing white clothing, which connotes purity, holiness, and honor (NOTE on 3:5). This is a fitting image for resurrection because it was traditional to picture heavenly beings in radiant white attire (Dan 7:9; 2 Macc 11:8; Mark 9:3; 16:5; Acts 1:10) and to envision the dead who are raised being clothed with life and glory (*1 En.* 62:15–16; 2 Esd 2:39, 45; 1 Cor 15:53–54; 2 Cor 5:1–4; *Mart. Asc. Isa.* 4:16; 9:9, 17; Herm. *Sim.* 8.2.3; Murphy). Just as the elders around God's throne wear white, those who are raised to life will be similarly clothed (Rev 4:4; 7:9, 13). The martyrs under the altar are given white robes as a pledge of their future resurrection (6:11; cf. 20:4), and the message to Sardis extends this promise to all the faithful.

White clothing suggests several characteristics of resurrection life. One is that the redeemed will join in worship of God and the Lamb. In the readers' world worshipers sometimes wore white (NOTE on 7:9), and Revelation pictures the white-robed multitudes worshiping continuously in God's presence (7:9–17). Another aspect is victory, since the white robes are given to those who conquer (*nikan*) through faithfulness and wave palm branches in triumph (3:5; 7:9). Revelation will present the heavenly armies wearing white as they ride beside Christ as he conquers the beast (19:14). But here, the faithful are promised that they will *walk* with Christ in white, as one might accompany a leader who has already conquered (Juvenal, *Satirae* 10.45; Suetonius, *Claud.* 24.3). Finally, resurrection will be depicted as a wedding, for the people of God wear the bright linen garments of a bride as they prepare to meet Christ the bridegroom. The garments that are now being woven from their faithful way of life are transformed into bridal attire in New Jerusalem (19:8–9; 21:2, 9–11). By fusing all these aspects of meaning, the image of white garments enables readers to picture the resurrection hope in terms of worship, triumph, and a wedding celebration.

Second is the promise that the faithful will not have their names blotted out of the scroll of life (3:5b). Previously it was said that the Sardian Christians only appeared to be alive in the eyes of other people, but here they are given the hope of genuine life from God. The scroll of life is a register of those who belong to God and the Lamb now and will be raised to deathless life in the future (21:27). This passage assumes that the names of the faithful are already in the scroll and promises that they will not be blotted out. This is designed to be assuring. The readers are being called to "conquer" by remaining faithful in ways that could lead to condemnation by other people (2:9–10; 3:9). Some ancient cities blotted the names of condemned people out of their citizenship rolls before putting them to death, but readers are assured that even if the faithful lose their social status in the cities where they now live, they will have a place in God's city (3:5).

Interpreters sometimes construe this promise as a veiled threat that Christ will blot out the names of those who are disobedient (Roloff; Thomas; Royalty, "Etched"). Theologically, this question involves Revelation's complex treatment of divine grace and human accountability. On the side of grace, the writer assumes that God inscribed people's names in the Lamb's scroll of life before the time the world was made (13:8; 17:8). People's names are in the scroll because God wants them there; it is an act of divine favor. These same passages also affirm that those who worship the beast are not in the scroll and will be judged. Some understand this in terms of divine election, maintaining that those whom God has placed in the scroll never fall away, whereas those who engage in false worship were never in the scroll at all. If people who appear to be believers fall away, this is taken to mean that they were never truly in the scroll (Beale). Others find this unpersuasive, since Christ speaks of blotting out a name that was in the scroll. Such interpreters give a greater role to human agency, arguing that God places people in the scroll by grace, and their names are blotted out if they reject this gift (Caird; Harrington; Osborne).

In the end, Revelation leaves readers with a tension. There is no suggestion that God determined to exclude some people from his scroll at the dawn of time, thereby consigning them to the beast. At the last judgment, people are judged according to their works, but salvation ultimately depends on divine favor, as shown by their names being inscribed in the scroll of life (20:12–15; 21:27). Logically, the tension is awkward, but it shapes the readers' perspectives in a twofold way: On the one hand, people are accountable for what they do, so they are to resist sin and evil. On the other hand, if the world seems so dominated by evil that resistance appears futile (13:4), the scroll of life gives assurance that salvation is ultimately God's doing. The tension encourages people to resist compromise with evil without making them despair of the future.

Third is the promise that Christ will acknowledge the names of the faithful before his Father and the angels (3:5c). Earlier, the congregation's reputation, or "name," was judged negatively, since it merely gave the appearance of life. Stating this judgment in the presence of angels, spirits, and readers in other congregations meant disgrace for the Sardians (3:1), but to have one's name acknowledged before God and the angels signals vindication and honor for the faithful. Some interpreters picture a juridical context. If believers are to confess the name of Jesus in the presence of earthly judges, Jesus promises to confess their names before the heavenly judge.

The image also suggests public honor. The exalted Christ has already promised the faithful a white stone and laurel wreath, which signify honor (2:10, 17). A common Greco-Roman practice was that when someone was awarded a laurel wreath, the person's name would be announced at a civic gathering, such as an athletic contest (*Rom. Civ.* 1:624–25; Harrison, "Fading," 500–502). First-century inscriptions tell of synagogues adapting this practice by using white stones to vote honors to one of their members, then giving the person a head wreath and publicly declaring the honoree's name in their own assembly (Levine, *Ancient*, 89–93). By analogy, Revelation promises that the faithful will be named at the most important assembly, where God and the angels are present, so the honor given will be of the highest sort.

10. To the Assembly in Philadelphia (3:7–13)

3 ⁷"To the angel of the assembly in Philadelphia write: Thus says the Holy One, the True One, the One who has the key of David, the One who opens so that no one will shut and who shuts so that no one opens. ⁸I know your works. You see I have put before you an open door that no one can shut, because you have so little power and yet you have kept my word and have not denied my name. ⁹See, I will make those from the synagogue of Satan—who say they are Jews but are not, but are lying—I will make them come and bow down before your feet, so that they will know I have loved you. ¹⁰Because you kept my word of endurance, I will also keep you from the hour of testing that is coming on the whole world, to test those who live on the earth. ¹¹I am coming soon. Hold fast to what you have so that no one takes your laurel wreath. ¹²Any who conquer I will make into a pillar in the temple of my God and they will never leave it. Moreover, I will write on them the name of God and the name of the city of my God, the New Jerusalem that comes down from heaven from my God, and my own new name. ¹³Let the one who has an ear listen to what the Spirit says to the assemblies."

NOTES

3:7. To the angel of the assembly. Each angel apparently has responsibility for a congregation (Notes on 1:20; 2:1).

in Philadelphia. Philadelphia (modern Alaşehir, Turkey) was located southeast of Sardis. It was founded in the second century BCE by the king of Pergamum, Attalos II, who situated it in a broad valley with the ridge of Mount Tmolus towering behind it. Our understanding of the city in the Roman era has been enriched by recent publications. Philadelphia's population was mixed and included people from Lydia and Mysia, along with Macedonians and Roman businesspeople (I.Phil 1423; 1455). During the first century CE the city was the administrative center for nearby towns, although the judicial center for the region was in Sardis (Pliny the Elder, *Nat.* 5.111; Petzl, *Philadelpheia*, X). The soil was fertile and wine production flourished (Strabo, *Geographica* 13.4.11; Pliny the Elder, *Nat.* 14.9.74). Aqueducts were used regionally for water (I.Phil 1430; 1439). Industries included textile and leather production. The associations of wool and leather workers were official civic tribes (I.Phil 1490–92; Magie, *Roman*, 2:48–49).

The city had good relations with Rome. In imperial times Philadelphia's calendar often dated public documents to a given year after "the victory of Augustus" at Actium in 31 BCE (I.Phil 1434; 1435; 1439). When Philadelphia, like Sardis, was devastated by the earthquake of 17 CE, the emperor Tiberius granted tax exemption for five years and provided assistance for rebuilding (Strabo, *Geographica* 12.8.18; 13.4.10; Tacitus, *Ann.* 2.47). The city showed its gratitude by calling itself Neocaesarea through the reigns of Tiberius and Claudius and erecting a monument in Rome (*CIL* X, 1624).

In the later first century the city adopted the name Flavia Philadelphia to honor the Flavian emperors Vespasian, Titus, and Domitian (I.Phil 1453; 1456a; 1515). In the late first century a temple and other monumental structures were built (I.Phil 1514; S. Mitchell, "Archaeology," 97), and Philadelphia was deemed important enough to exchange official honors with a major urban center like Ephesus (I.Phil 1452–53). In the second century it had a theater.

The principal deity of Philadelphia was Anaitis, a goddess of Persian origin (I.Phil 1548; 1549; 1551). Her identity blended with that of the Anatolian mother goddess Meter as well as the Greek Artemis (I.Phil 1550; Hoz, *Die lydischen*, 74–75). About seven miles from the city was a sanctuary of the mother goddess Meter Phileis (I.Phil 1625–26). The moon god Men, who was sometimes pictured with the mother goddess, was also worshiped (I.Phil 1630–31). Deities from the Hellenistic tradition included Zeus, who was called Eumenes, or Kindly; Koryphaios, or Leader; and Soter, or Savior. His cult assumed various forms; he was identified with Helios the sun god, the Thracian-Phrygian god Sabazios, and the local Zeus of Targyenos (I.Phil 1506; 1539–44). Dionysus was honored, perhaps in a temple or theater (I.Phil 1632), and the cult of Dionysus Kathegemon, the Leader, which had been associated with the rulers of Pergamum, was popular. The cult of Apollo was also attested (I.Phil 1545–46). Some local deities were identified with language similar to that used in Jewish tradition, for example, God Most High (*Theos Hypsistos*, I.Phil 1634–35) and God Holy and Righteous (*Theos Hosios kai Dikaios*), who may have been an intermediary between the divine and human worlds (I.Phil 1637; Hoz, *Die lydischen*, 59–60). Although in Revelation John uses these terms only for the God of Israel (15:3–4; 16:5), the cultural context he addressed allowed for more blending of traits.

Leading citizens served in traditional priesthoods, like that of Artemis (I.Phil 1447), and the initiates of Dionysus Kathegemon had a religious association (1462). A household cult dating from the first century BCE included men and woman, free persons and slaves. This group formed under the auspices of Agdistis, an Anatolian mother goddess, but those same worshipers also invoked the Hellenistic deities Zeus, Hestia, and the savior gods, along with Arete, or Virtue; Hygieia, or Health; Tyche Agathe, or Good Fortune; Agathos Daimon; Mneme; Charites, or Graces; and Nikē, or Victory. Members were to follow strict standards for ritual purity and moral conduct (I.Phil 1539).

Philadelphia had its own local cult of Augustus and Rome by 27–26 BCE (I.Phil 1428). An inscription from 40 CE notes that the birthday of Augustus was celebrated with sacrifices to the deified emperors (I.Phil 1434). Both women and men served in the cult's priesthood (I.Phil 1472; 1484). When the provincial temple to the Flavian emperors was built at Ephesus during the reign of Domitian (ca. 89/90), the Philadelphians erected a monument there (I.Phil 1453; Friesen, *Twice*, 157). The civic games at Philadelphia were dedicated to both the local goddess Anaitis and the emperor (I.Phil 1480; cf. 1460; 1505), and coins from the late first century CE show the emperor Domitian on one side and the mother goddess on the other. The impression is one of harmony between the benefits provided by the city's patron deity and those of imperial rule (Figure 15; Weiss, "Ein Priester").

There was a Jewish community in Philadelphia, as in many other Asian cities (Rev 3:9). In the early second century CE, Ignatius seems to assume that Judaism at

Figure 15. Coin from Philadelphia showing Domitian on one side and a goddess on the other (81–96 CE). Courtesy of the Classical Numismatic Group (cngcoins.com).

Philadelphia was strong enough to be attractive to Gentiles, including some Christians (Ign. *Phld.* 6:1). An inscription from the third century CE refers to a synagogue of the Hebrews in the area and mentions a "godfearer," who is probably Jewish (Trebilco, *Jewish*, 162). Inscriptions from later periods also attest to a Jewish presence there (*IJO* 2:202–8).

The history of Christianity at Philadelphia before Revelation was written is unknown. Since conflict with a local synagogue involved questions of Jewish identity, some of the congregation's members may have been of Jewish origin (Rev 3:9). The complexity of Jewish-Christian relations is shown by Ignatius's letter to Philadelphia, in which the problem is not conflict with Judaism, but the fact that some Christians were moving too far toward adopting Jewish teachings (Ign. *Phld.* 6:1; 8:2; Schoedel, *Ignatius*, 195–215). The congregation apparently developed a distinctive Christian identity, however, and by the mid-second century eleven of its members were martyred (*Mart. Pol.* 19:1). The church was organized with a bishop, elders, and deacons (Ign. *Phld.* pref.), but prophetic leadership was also valued. John wrote to the congregation as a prophet, and in the early second century a woman from Philadelphia named Ammia was considered a prophetess by both Montanists and other Christians (Eusebius, *Hist. eccl.* 5.17.1–4).

Thus says the Holy One, the True One. The title "Holy One" was used for God (Rev 6:10; Hab 3:3; Isa 40:25; *1 En.* 1:3; *m. 'Abot* 3:1) and is here used for Christ (cf. Mark 1:24; John 6:69; Acts 3:14). This use of the title may stem from Isa 60:14, in which God identifies himself as the Holy One and promises that the opponents of his people will bow at their feet, a promise echoed in Rev 3:9. God was also called "true" (Rev 6:10; Exod 34:6; Isa 65:16; Ps 86:15; Jer 10:10; John 17:3; 1 Thess 1:9), and this title too is given to Christ, who shares the traits of God (Rev 3:14; 19:11). In Revelation truth is closely related to faithfulness, so what is true is reliable (19:9; 21:5; 22:6). "Thus says" has royal and prophetic connotations (NOTE on 2:1).

the One who has the key of David, the One who opens so that no one will shut and who shuts so that no one opens. The Hebrew text of Isa 22:22 refers to a servant who is given "the key of the house of David," which entails authority to "open" and "shut." The steward granted people access to the king and had administrative responsibilities. He was to be a father to the people of the realm (22:21). The LXX differs, referring not to the key, but to "the glory of David." The Greek translation associated with Theodotian, however, does mention the "key," so it is not clear whether the writer drew the image directly from the Hebrew text or from a Greek version that corresponds to it more closely than the LXX (INTRO IV.D.1). The author of Revelation may have related Isa 22:22 to Jesus because "servant" could be a messianic title (e.g., Zech 3:8) and the key was related to Davidic authority (Fekkes, *Isaiah*, 130–33). The Targum adds that the servant will have the key to the sanctuary (*Tg.* Isa 22:22). Similarly, Revelation assumes that Christ grants access to the temple (3:12). Angels sometimes use keys to open and close the underworld (9:1–2; 20:1–3), but access to the kingdom is given by Christ.

Similar imagery is used in Matt 16:19, where Jesus tells Peter, "I will give you the keys of the kingdom of heaven, and whatever you bind on earth will be bound in heaven, and whatever you loose on earth will be loosed in heaven." The difference is that the authority to bind and loose apparently has to do with teaching what is forbidden and permitted, whereas Revelation speaks of access to God's presence (Davies and Allison, *Critical*, 2:634–41). Moreover, Matthew tells of Jesus giving authority to Peter, whereas Revelation deals with authority that is unique to Jesus.

3:8. *I know your works. You see I have put before you an open door that no one can shut.* The open door means access to God. Readers already have access to God through prayer (cf. 5:8; 8:4), and in the future they have the hope of resurrection to life in God's presence (7:13–17; 22:3). Alternatively, some interpreters think the "open door" is the readers' opportunity to spread the gospel (1 Cor 16:9; 2 Cor 2:12; Col 4:3; Ramsay, *Letters*, 404; Hemer, *Letters*, 162; Charles; Caird; Harrington). The context, however, suggests that the open door has to do with the Philadelphians' need for access to God, just as the open door in Rev 4:1 brings John into God's presence (Aune; Giesen; Mounce; Murphy; Smalley).

because you have so little power and yet you have kept my word and have not denied my name. This passage assumes that those who identify with Jesus' "name" are being pressured to deny their faith. Although other sources mention both Jews and Gentiles persecuting those who identify with Jesus' name (Matt 10:22; 24:9; Mark 13:13; Luke 21:12, 17; John 15:21; Pol. *Phil.* 8:2; Herm. *Vis.* 3.2.1; Herm. *Sim.* 9.28.3), this context focuses on conflict with a synagogue. If Christians at Philadelphia had been questioned by a Roman magistrate, they might have been pressured to deny Jesus' name in order to escape punishment (Pliny the Younger, *Ep.* 10.96.3, 5; *Mart. Justin* 3.4–4.5; *Mart. Perpetua and Felicitas* 3). But since the Philadelphians refused to deny Christ's name and yet were not punished, it is unlikely that the Romans were involved (cf. COMMENT on Rev 2:13).

3:9. *See, I will make those of the synagogue of Satan, who say they are Jews but are not, but are lying.* See the NOTES on 2:9.

I will make them come and bow down before your feet. In the Greco-Roman world, throwing oneself before someone's feet could connote helpless supplication (Caesar, *Bell. gall.* 1.27, 31; Tacitus, *Ann.* 12.18; Tacitus, *Hist.* 1.66; Polybius, *Histories* 10.18) and subordination (Polybius, *Histories* 10.38; 15.1). Biblically, bowing down (*proskynein*) at someone's feet could show the utmost respect (2 Kgs 4:37; Jdt 14:7; Acts 10:25), but here the language recalls passages that speak of Israel's adversaries being brought into subjection. The dominant passage is Isa 60:14: "all who despised you shall bow down at your feet; they shall call you the City of the Lord, the Zion of the Holy One of Israel." Isaiah's promise of adversaries bowing down is picked up in Rev 3:9, and that of being called by the name of God's city, in Rev 3:12. Another passage is Isa 49:23: "With their faces to the ground they shall bow down to you, and lick the dust of your feet. Then you will know that I am the Lord; those who wait for me shall not be put to shame" (cf. 45:14; 1QM XII, 14–15; XIX, 6–7; *1 En.* 90:30). This passage repeats the motif of bowing in subjection and introduces the theme of knowing, which will be taken up in Rev 3:9 (Fekkes, *Isaiah*, 134–35). Elsewhere, Revelation shows that it is right to bow before God and the Lamb in worship (4:10; 5:14; 15:4) but idolatrous to bow to the beast and its ruler cult (13:4; 14:9). Even bowing to an angel is prohibited (19:10; 22:8–9). For synagogue members to bow at the feet of Jesus' followers is an exception to the pattern. It shows that the faithful will be vindicated, but it does not mean that they will be worshiped.

so that they will know I have loved you. The language may continue echoing Isaiah, which speaks of God's love for Israel: "Because you are precious in my sight, and honored, and I love you, I give people in return for you, nations in exchange for your life" (43:4). Divine love, however, is a broader biblical theme (e.g., Deut 7:8; Isa 41:8; 44:2; 60:10; 63:9 LXX). It is a way to speak of God's choosing and redeeming people (Fekkes, *Isaiah*, 136–37). In Revelation divine love, extended through the death of Jesus, delivers people from sin and makes them people of God (Rev 1:5). Those in the synagogue community at Philadelphia must learn that God loves the followers of Jesus, whom they oppose.

3:10. *Because you kept my word of endurance.* This expression has been taken in two ways. The first is preferable:

1. Christ's call for Christians to persevere (NIV, NRSV). "Keep" (*tērein*) can mean following divine commands (Rev 12:17; 14:12), so Christ's "word" is presumably his command to endure along with his promise of salvation (Mounce; Satake; Smalley). Such a command could have come from traditional sayings of Jesus—"the one who endures to the end will be saved" (Mark 13:13; Matt 10:22; 24:13)—or from other Christian teachings concerning endurance (2 Tim 2:12; Jas 1:12). It also could be a word of the exalted Christ, transmitted through a Christian prophet, for example: "Here is a call for the endurance and faith of the saints" (Rev 13:10; 14:12).
2. The message about Christ's own endurance. The Greek could be translated "the word of my endurance" (cf. KJV, NAB, NASB), which could refer to Christ persevering through his ministry, passion, and death. Christians would keep the word about Christ's endurance by bearing witness to it (Beale; Charles; Giesen; Prigent). Although this reading is attractive, the pronoun "my" almost certainly modifies both "word" and "endurance" (Aune). Taking this expression as Christ's command to endure fits Revelation's call for Christian perseverance.

I will also keep you from the hour of testing that is coming on the whole world. Prophetic writings pictured a time of great suffering accompanying the Day of the Lord. There would be war, famine, natural disasters, and other threats (Jer 30:7; Amos 5:18–20; Joel 2:1–32; Zeph 1:14–18). Apocalyptic writings envisioned such affliction before the future victory of God (Dan 12:1; *T. Mos.* 8:1; *2 Bar.* 26:1–27:15). Christian sources also tell of coming afflictions that will include war, natural disasters, the spread of false teachings, and threats against the faithful (Matt 24:15–31; Mark 13:7–20). The "great affliction" in Rev 7:14 recalls this tradition.

Dispensationalist interpreters argue that believers will be spared this testing by being snatched up, or "raptured," from earth to heaven before the onset of a seven-year period of tribulation that they expect to occur before Christ's return (LaHaye; Thomas). Helpful critiques of this view point out that the promise is made to a first-century congregation at Philadelphia, and if it concerns the rapture at the end of time, it would have no meaning for its intended readers. Moreover, Revelation pictures the faithful being protected from divine wrath but not from all earthly suffering (see COMMENT). An analogous idea appears in John 17:15, where the same expression (*tērein ek*) is used: "I do not ask that you take them out of the world but that you *keep them from* the evil one." The related expression *tērein apo* can also mean protection from evil for those living in the middle of evil (Prov 7:5; Jas 1:27; Gundry, *Church*, 54–61; Beale).

to test those who live upon the earth. In apocalyptic writings "those who live upon the earth" may be depicted positively as recipients of God's mercy (*1 En.* 60:5; *4 Ezra* 6:26) or negatively as sinful and subject to divine judgment (*1 En.* 65:6, 10; 67:8; *2 Bar.* 54:1; 70:2; *4 Ezra* 3:34–35; 6:18). Revelation develops the negative connotations, portraying those who live upon the earth as opponents of God (Rev 6:10; 8:13; 11:10; 13:8, 12, 14; 14:6; 17:2, 8; Bauckham, *Climax*, 239–41). The testing mentioned here is sometimes taken as God's punishment on an unbelieving world (Beale), but this is unlikely. In Revelation, testing (*peirazein*) reveals the character of both the faithful and the unfaithful (2:2, 10).

3:11. *I am coming soon.* See the NOTE on 22:7.

Hold fast to what you have so that no one takes your laurel wreath. A laurel wreath was given to those who won a victory in an athletic contest or military battle, as well as those honored for public service (NOTE on 2:10). Here, it is given to those who win victory through faithfulness to God and Christ in the face of opposition. It signifies resurrection to life in New Jerusalem.

3:12. *Any who conquer.* See the NOTE on 2:7.

I will make into a pillar in the temple of my God and they will never leave it. This metaphor is based on the image of a temple with pillars (*styloi*) in it. The LXX called the poles supporting the tabernacle its pillars (Exod 26:15–25) and said that two bronze pillars named Jachin and Boaz stood in the vestibule of Solomon's temple (1 Kgs 7:15–22). The courts of Herod's temple were adorned with porticoes supported by beautiful columns (*kiones*, Josephus, *J.W.* 5.190–91, 200, 203). Visions of a restored or glorified temple assumed that it would have pillars (Ezek 40:49; *1 En.* 90:28; 11Q19 X, 4, 11; XXXV, 10). The heavenly temple was also said to have pillars (4Q403 1 I, 41). Greco-Roman temples were built with rows of columns. Some were sculpted to look like human beings, the most famous being the six maidens that serve as pillars in a temple in Athens. Their presence suggests perpetual service to a deity (G. Stevenson, *Power*, 63–67).

Revelation uses pillar imagery to show that the faithful constitute God's temple and have a permanent place in God's presence, which was a blessing (Ps 27:4). Early Christians described the community of faith as a temple (1 Cor 3:16–17; 2 Cor 6:16; Eph 2:19–22; cf. 1 Pet 2:5; Ign. *Eph.* 9:1; Ign. *Magn.* 7:2), and this sense is developed in the temple imagery of Rev 11:1–2. The leading members of a community could be called "pillars" (Philo, *QE* 1.21; Gal 2:9; *1 Clem.* 5:2; Aeschylus, *Ag.* 897; Euripides, *Iph. taur.* 57). Revelation brings the temple and pillar metaphors together. It is unlikely that the pillar imagery recalls how Isaiah said that the bearer of the key of David—who is mentioned in Rev 3:7—would be a "peg" in his father's house (Isa 22:22–23; Beale; Kraft; Mounce; Smalley; Briggs, *Jewish*, 71–74; Fekkes, *Isaiah*, 133). The images are too different.

Moreover, I will write on them the name of God and the name of the city of my God.
Readers would have been familiar with the practice of inscribing pillars and monuments with the names of donors, gods, and cities. For example, a first-century inscription on a column at Ephesus commemorated the building of the imperial temple during Domitian's reign. It named both the city of Teos and the emperor (I.Eph 239). Columns in the temples of Artemis at Ephesus and Sardis were inscribed with the names of donors, and similar practices are attested in other cities (I.Eph 1518–19; Royalty, "Etched," 452–53; G. Stevenson, *Power*, 249). Even more common were inscriptions on steles. One from first-century Philadelphia gives the names of a god along with those of the donor and the donor's home city: "Plution son of Plutioin, from Maionia, dedicated to Zeus Koryphaios" (I.Phil 1540). Another stele refers to the god's city, as a donor honored Zeus of Targyenos (I.Phil 1542; cf. I.Sard 100). Revelation adapts the practice by including the names of God, Christ, and God's city in the inscription. Those names are inscribed on the people who are pillars of faith, identifying them with the God and city to which they belong.

There is no reason to link the image to the pillars named Jachin and Boaz in Solomon's temple (1 Kgs 7:15–22; Lupieri), since they did not bear the name of God or God's city. Some interpreters think that the imagery is especially tied to Philadelphia, which adopted the names Neocaesarea and Flavia to honor imperial rule (Ramsay, *Letters*, 409–12; Hemer, *Letters*, 176; Giesen). This is unlikely, however, because the same could be said of Sardis, which adopted the name Caesarea, or Laodicea, which was named for the wife of a Hellenistic ruler, replacing the older names Rhoas and Diospolis, or city of Zeus (Pliny the Elder, *Nat.* 5.29.105).

the New Jerusalem that comes down from heaven from my God. See the NOTES on 21:2 and 10.

and my own new name. It was said that when God vindicated his people, they would be called by "a new name," no longer "Forsaken" but "My Delight Is in Her" (Isa 62:2–4; cf. 65:15; Beale). In Revelation, however, the names are those of New Jerusalem and the "new" name of Jesus. The theme of Jesus' name is developed when he returns to defeat the agents of evil. He is inscribed with a name known only to him, but the name proves to be King of kings and Lord of lords (Rev 19:12, 19:16). If that title is his "new name," it is fitting to inscribe it on his people and on the white stone of 2:17, since both passages anticipate the vindication of the faithful.

3:13. *Let the one who has an ear listen to what the Spirit says to the assemblies.* See the NOTE on 2:7.

COMMENT

The sixth message addresses the congregation at Philadelphia, where the principal issue was conflict with a local synagogue. The followers of Jesus at Philadelphia had their own assembly (*ekklēsia*), yet they also had much in common with the wider Jewish

On Rev 3:7–13, see Beagley, "*Sitz,*" 31–36; Borgen, "Polemic"; Briggs, *Jewish*, 72–74, 107–9; Friesen, "Sarcasm"; Hemer, *Letters*, 153–77; Mayo, "*Those,*" 51–76; M. Murray, *Playing*, 73–81; Petzl, *Philadelpheia*; Ramsay, *Letters*, 391–412; Royalty, "Etched"; G. Stevenson, *Power*, 341–51; Wilkinson, "Στύλος"; Yarbro Collins, "Insiders."

community, including faith in the God of Israel and shared Scriptures. One source of tension seems to have been the status of Jesus. If members of the congregation had views like those of the writer of Revelation, they extended the traits of Israel's God to Christ, who is the Alpha and Omega, first and last, beginning and end (Rev 1:8, 17; 21:6; 22:13). Like God, Jesus is "holy" and "true" (3:7; 6:10) and can be worshiped (5:13–14; 22:3; Bauckham, *Theology*, 54–65). For many Jews, this would have seemed blasphemous (Murphy). There were also disputes over who could claim to be Jewish (3:9). Revelation assumes that the promises to Israel are realized through Christ (7:4–14), which non-Christian Jews would have contested (cf. 2:9).

The message to Philadelphia assumes that some Jews are pressuring Jesus' followers to deny the name of Christ or face being socially shut out of the Jewish community. The means used to apply this pressure are not indicated. It could have involved action by leaders of the synagogue (Matt 10:17; Mark 13:9; Luke 21:12; John 9:22; 12:42; 16:2; Acts 26:11), or it could have been in the form of informal verbal confrontations by some group "from" the synagogue (Rev 3:9; Acts 13:50; 17:13). Verbal harassment could make congregation members deny their faith in order to ease tensions with the Jewish community. If done publicly, harassment warned others not to affiliate with the followers of Jesus, since there was a high social cost to doing so (cf. Acts 13:50; 17:13; 1 Pet 4:14, 16; Neyrey, *Social*, 29–32; J. H. Elliott, *1 Peter*, 779; Mayo, *"Those,"* 67–73).

Rhetorically, the message draws on biblical language to encourage a congregation struggling in a Jewish context. Depicting Jesus as the bearer of the key of David and promising that Jesus' followers will see their opponents bow at their feet recall texts from Isaiah. The references to the temple and New Jerusalem also develop biblical themes. In the face of conflict with the synagogue, the writer encourages readers to remain faithful by emphasizing that God's promises to Israel are fulfilled in Jesus and his followers. The message is encouraging and includes no reproof. It sometimes follows a pattern of reversal: The faithful may be shut out of the local synagogue, but they will have a place in God's temple. There is also reciprocity: As they have kept Christ's word, Christ will keep them in the hour of testing. Since they have not denied his name, he will inscribe them with his own name, God's name, and the name of New Jerusalem.

Introduction

Christ identifies himself as the Holy One, the True One, the One who has the key of David, the One who opens so that no one can shut (3:7). This battery of titles is given in quick succession, giving the impression that even more could be added to the majestic portrayal of the speaker's identity (Quintilian, *Inst.* 9.3.50; Lausberg, *Handbook* §711). In previous messages the traits of Christ were taken directly from Rev 1, but here the connection is more general. In the inaugural vision, Christ appeared in majestic radiance, which suggested holiness (Rev 1:17; Exod 3:5–6; Isa 6:3–5), and Christ is now called "holy" (Rev 1:12–17). The introduction called Christ the faithful witness, and he is now called "true" (1:5; 3:14). Using this pair of titles identifies the exalted Jesus with God, who is holy and true (6:10; cf. 4:8; 15:3; 16:7; 19:2).

Christ is also the One who has the key of David, the One who opens so that no one will shut and who shuts so that no one opens (3:7). The language recalls a passage from Isaiah in which God says he will replace one servant of the king with another: "On that day I will call my servant" and "will clothe him with your robe and bind your sash on him. I will commit your authority to his hand, and he shall be a father to the inhabitants of Jerusalem and to the house of Judah. I will place on his shoulder the key of the house of David; he shall open and no one shall shut; he shall shut and no one shall open"; he will be "a throne of honor in his father's house" (Isa 22:20–22).

Revelation weaves this language into its portrait of Christ. No longer depicted as a thief, who might suddenly intrude (Rev 3:3), Christ now is the keeper of the keys, the guardian of legitimate access (3:7). The inaugural vision pictured Christ holding keys to release people from Death and Hades (1:13, 18). Now, as the bearer of the key of David, he has the authority to admit people into the presence of the king—here understood to be God. The keys of Death and Hades and the key of David show that release from death and access to God are two parts of the same act of redemption. Where Isaiah said that the bearer of the key of David would be a throne in his father's house, Revelation says that the bearer of the key is the root and descendent of David, who shares God's throne (5:5; 22:3, 6). Where Isaiah said that the bearer of the key would have authority over Judah and Jerusalem, the Christ of Revelation brings people of every realm into God's kingdom and into New Jerusalem (3:12; 5:9–10; 21:2).

Body of the Message

Christ uses his authority to place before the Philadelphians an open door that no one can shut (3:8). In relation to the Jewish community the followers of Jesus may be socially shut out, but in relation to God the door is open. In the next chapter of Revelation John himself makes a visionary journey through an open door and into the heavenly throne room, where celestial hosts give glory to the Creator and the Lamb (4:1). The promise of the open door to the splendor of God's presence contrasts with the inglorious conditions the Philadelphians face in the world. It gives them incentive to persevere, knowing that their present situation is not final.

Socially, the congregation has little power (3:8). Their opponents apparently have more social resources to use in the conflict. The Jewish community at Philadelphia could well have outnumbered the followers of Jesus and may have enjoyed greater support from the civic community. Jews were well-integrated into many Asian cities. Some had wealth and influence, and their distinctive practices were accepted because they belonged to an ancestral tradition (Trebilco, *Jewish*, 167–85; Harland, *Associations*, 200–210). Groups professing a belief in Jesus were a newer phenomenon, and their status in society was unclear, which sometimes made them suspect (Acts 17:5–7; Suetonius, *Nero* 16.2).

The opponents from the synagogue claimed to be Jews, but Revelation insists this is not true (3:9). Some interpreters have wondered whether the opponents were Gentiles who followed a few Jewish practices or were heterodox Christians (NOTE on 2:9). But the most plausible view is that they claimed to be Jews because of the usual factors of kinship, circumcision, Sabbath observance, meal practices, and rejection of polytheism (Barclay, *Jews*, 399–444; S. Mason, "Jews"). The author might challenge the opponents' claims to be Jewish because he believes that the heritage of Israel belongs to the followers of Jesus (Borgen, "Polemic"; Lohse, "Synagogue"; Lupieri, Murphy; Roloff). But more is involved. Jewish communities existed in most if not all of the cities mentioned in Rev 2–3, yet the author pointedly denies a Jewish identity only to those who oppose Jesus' followers at Philadelphia and Smyrna. From his perspective, those who identify with Jesus belong to God. Therefore, those who denounce them reject the God whom they serve—and the author considers such rejection incompatible with a professed adherence to Israel's tradition.

The author intensifies the polemic by calling the opponents "a synagogue of Satan" (Rev 3:9). Traditionally, Satan was the accuser of the righteous, and some people from the synagogue accuse those who belong to Jesus (12:10; cf. Job 1:6–12; 2:1–6; Zech 3:1–5). Satan operated through falsehood (Rev 12:9; John 8:44; 2 Cor 11:14; 2 Thess 2:9–10), and the author sees the opponents speaking falsely about Jesus' followers and wrongly claiming a Jewish identity. Pointing to the presence of evil at Philadelphia links their situation to that of other churches, where Satan works through hostility and violence (Rev 2:9, 13; 3:9) and through pressures to accommodate Greco-Roman religious practice (2:24). Later visions will show Satan working relentlessly on earth not because he is so powerful, but because he has been banished from heaven and is desperate to expand his influence on earth (12:1–17). By tracing the epic defeat of Satan in subsequent chapters, the book gives readers incentive to persevere, knowing that God and Christ will prevail in the end (20:1–14).

Socially, linking the opponents to Satan helps define the congregation's boundaries, giving the members a greater sense of distinctive identity (Yarbro Collins, "Vilification," 314). This also fosters internal cohesion, since congregation members must overcome the differences among themselves in order to meet the threat posed by a common enemy (Tellbe, *Christ-Believers*, 140). Modern interpreters have noted the dangers in John's polemical language (Borgen, "Polemic"; Lohse, "Synagogue"; Yarbro Collins, "Vilification," 320). It is therefore important to see that even though most if not all of the seven cities John addresses had Jewish communities, he uses polemical language only where there is open hostility toward the followers of Jesus. The polemics of this local conflict cannot be extended to Jewish-Christian relations more broadly (Friesen, "Sarcasm," 141).

The Philadelphians are promised a dramatic reversal of their current situation, for the opponents from the synagogue are to bow down at their feet (3:9). The language originally told of Gentile nations being subjected to Israel (Isa 49:23; 60:14). In Revelation this takes an ironic turn, so instead of receiving homage from the Gentiles, those in the synagogue will one day give homage to the followers of Jesus. This is not a simple reversal of the text, as if Jesus' followers are the Gentiles who now receive honor from Jews. Revelation works with different categories. Through their faith, the followers of Jesus belong to the people of God and are not Gentiles in the usual sense, just as their adversaries in the synagogue are no longer authentically Jewish. Ironically, they are included with the Gentile opponents of God's people (Mounce; Murphy).

The promise of vindication is vivid, yet the manner of fulfillment is left open. Readers might envision Christ taking action against local opponents at Philadelphia in the near future, much as Christ threatened to do at Pergamum and Thyatira (Rev 2:16, 22–23; Aune). But if this is so, it is not clear how readers will know that it has occurred. The messages make use of metaphor: Christ will move the Ephesians' "lampstand," make war at Pergamum with the "sword" of his mouth, put Jezebel to "bed" at Thyatira, and "vomit" the Laodiceans out of his mouth (2:5, 16, 22; 3:16). So if readers at Philadelphia expect vindication soon, they must also ask whether their opponents will physically bow at their feet or whether that is an image for vindication that will take another form.

Readers might also hear the message as a promise of vindication at the end of the age (Giesen; Müller). This interpretation would fit the futuristic perspective of the biblical passages that inform Revelation's language (Isa 60:14; cf. 60:19; Rev 3:12; 21:23). But none of the later visions shows the believers' adversaries—Jewish or Gentile—bowing down at their feet. One might therefore picture vindication happening in a transformed way, much as the notion of conquering is transformed by the death of the Lamb (5:5–6; 12:11). The promise is comparable to the message to Thyatira, which promised that the faithful would rule the nations with an iron rod (2:26–27). In the end, the faithful reign with Christ, but the nations finally need no iron rod for they willingly walk in the light of God (21:24; 22:5). By analogy, the point of the message to Philadelphia is not a simple role reversal, as if the faithful are eventually to dominate the people who tried to dominate them. Rather, the adversaries bow down in recognition of God's love for those whom they themselves had opposed.

The Philadelphians have "kept" Jesus' word by remaining faithful in the face of opposition, and Jesus promises to "keep" them from the hour of testing that is coming on the whole world (3:10). "Testing" (*peirasmos*) portends the hardships depicted later, including war, violence, and economic hardship, as well as the lure of false worship and the threats of persecution (6–19). These things "test" (*peirazein*) people by disclosing their loyalties—whether they will ally themselves with the Creator and the Lamb or with the destroyers of the earth (11:18).

In a genuine test, both faith and opposition must be open possibilities. On the negative side, the expression "those who live on the earth" usually identifies those who drink the wine of Babylon (17:2), worship the beast (13:8, 14; 17:8), oppose the faithful (6:10; 11:10), and come under God's judgment (8:13). On the positive side, the call to worship God is extended to all "those who live on earth" (14:6), which opens the possibility of repentance and redemption. Some visions depict those who oppose God falling under judgment (19:11–20; 20:7–10), while other visions hold out the hope of life for earth's peoples in New Jerusalem (21:2, 24; 22:2). "Testing" means that both faith and unbelief are possible (Bauckham, *Climax*, 238–42; Bauckham, *Theology*, 98–104).

Christ promises that the faithful at Philadelphia will be kept from this hour of testing, which means they will be preserved in faith *through* testing but not that they will be spared suffering of all sorts (3:10). Note that the Smyrneans are to face "testing" through imprisonment and possible death, and later visions assume that some will be martyred (2:9–10; 6:9–11; 17:6; 18:24). The redeemed are not exempt from affliction but are brought through and "out of" (*ek*) it to deathless life (7:14), just as those at Philadelphia will be brought "out of" (*ek*) testing to life in New Jerusalem (3:10–12). The Philadelphians are told that testing will last for an hour (3:10), but later this testing becomes three and a half years (11:3; 12:6; 13:5), and in Revelation's visionary world, this "short" time actually extends from Christ's death and exaltation to his final return (12:12). During this period of testing the faithful are pictured as a woman who is persecuted by Satan. She is preserved, but in the wilderness, and victory over Satan is won through the deaths of Christ and his followers (12:6, 11, 14; Beale; Mounce).

The words "I am coming soon" assure the beleaguered congregation of Christ's commitment to them (3:11), yet the time and mode of his coming are left open. Some interpreters assume that Christ speaks of coming to support the local congregation, much as he warned about coming to discipline opponents in specific locations (2:5, 16; 3:3; Beale; Giesen). Others think the reference is to Christ's coming for victory at the end of the age (19:11–21; Aune). Yet the Christ who speaks about coming is already present among the congregations (1:12–20; 2:1), and the book's varied references to his coming blur the lines between the prospect of his local and final comings (COMMENT on 22:7). The word "soon" calls readers to persevere in hope, even as the fluidity in the language resists attempts to calculate what "soon" means in chronological terms.

For the present, readers are to hold firmly to what they have, which is the word of Christ (3:10). The goal is that no one takes the believer's laurel wreath, which signifies life and honor in the presence of God. Wreath imagery appears in the messages to Philadelphia and Smyrna, where Jesus' followers were called to persevere in the face of conflict as one might in a battle or contest. They already have the wreath in the form of a promise, which will be fully realized through resurrection to life in New Jerusalem. Their opponents may threaten to take the wreath away by pressuring people into denying their faith, but Christ encourages the resolute faithfulness through which believers conquer in the war against evil (3:12; NOTE on 2:7).

Conclusion

The concluding promises to the faithful at Philadelphia respond to the prospect of being shut out of the local synagogue with the hope of being pillars in the temple of God (3:12). A synagogue was a local gathering place, but in Israel's tradition the temple was the one place God made his name to dwell. By the time Revelation was composed, the Jerusalem temple had been destroyed, yet the book uses temple imagery to give hope to readers. Later visions will picture the community of faith as a temple in which those redeemed by Christ serve as priests (1:5; 5:10; 11:1). Yet in the visions this earthly community or temple is besieged by adversaries, much like the congregation at Philadelphia (11:2). One might expect the author to give the readers hope for a place in heaven, where God is now attended by angels in his celestial temple (11:19; 14:15, 17; 15:5–8; 16:1, 17). This expectation is encouraged by a vision of the redeemed serving God day and night in his temple, where there is no longer any suffering or grief (7:15).

The temple imagery is transformed, however, by the vision of New Jerusalem. The city has the features of a temple, and the faithful serve as priests in a sanctuary (21:23; 22:3). But John sees no temple in the city, because God and the Lamb are its temple (21:22). No sacred building or community mediates God's presence there. The promise of the faithful becoming pillars *in* the temple is transformed through a vision in which a separate temple is no longer needed, and the redeemed have an abiding place in the presence of God and the Lamb (G. Stevenson, *Power*, 268–70; Briggs, *Jewish*, 107–8).

Readers are also promised that they will be inscribed with names. Thus far the message has drawn on part of Isa 60:14, which says that the opponents of the faithful will one day bow at their feet (Rev 3:9). That passage goes on to say that the faithful will be called "the City of the Lord, the Zion of the Holy One of Israel," which is affirmed in Rev 3:12, where the faithful are said to bear the names of God and his city. The pillar imagery also fits a related passage, where God says to those who are despised, "I will give, in my house and within my walls, a monument and a name . . . an everlasting name that shall not be cut off" (Isa 56:5). Isaiah depicts a stone monument in God's house, inscribed with the faithful person's name, but in Revelation the person is the pillar who is etched with God's everlasting name (Beale).

Like other promises, this too is transformed in later visions, which say nothing about pillars but picture the redeemed with the names of God and Jesus on their foreheads (7:3; 14:1). The names identify those who belong to God and have a place in New Jerusalem, in contrast to those who bear the name of the beast and belong to Babylon (13:16–17; 17:1–6). The readers live in cities where their adversaries may be of Jewish, Greek, or Roman background, but all are understood to be under the dominion of Babylon. For readers, the challenge is to live as citizens of New Jerusalem in a world where hostile powers are at work, knowing that Christ has a place for them.

11. To the Assembly in Laodicea (3:14–22)

3 [14]"To the angel of the assembly in Laodicea write: Thus says the Amen, the faithful and true witness, the ruler of God's creation: [15]I know your works. You are neither cold nor hot. I wish that you were either cold or hot. [16]So, because you are tepid, and neither hot nor cold, I am about to vomit you out of my mouth. [17]For you say, 'I am rich and have become wealthy and do not need anything.' Yet you do not realize that you are miserable and pitiable and poor and blind and naked. [18]I advise you to buy from me gold that has been refined by fire so that you may be rich, and white clothing to wear so that you will not appear naked and ashamed, and salve to put on your eyes so that you may see. [19]I correct and discipline those whom I love. So be committed and repent. [20]See, I am standing at the door and knocking. If any hear my voice and open the door, I will come in to them and will dine with them and they with me. [21]As for those who conquer, I will grant that they might sit with me on my throne, just as I conquered and sat with my Father on his throne. [22]Let the one who has an ear hear what the Spirit says to the assemblies."

NOTES

3:14. *To the angel of the assembly.* Each angel apparently has responsibility for a congregation (NOTE on 1:20).

in Laodicea. Laodicea (near modern Denizli, Turkey) was located in the Lycus Valley about sixty miles southeast of Philadelphia and a hundred miles west of Ephesus. It was situated where a major east-west route from Ephesus intersected other roads going north to Philadelphia and Sardis and south to the Mediterranean coast. Founded by the Seleucids in the mid-third century BCE on the site of older settlements, it came under the control of Pergamum in 188 BCE and then Rome after 133 BCE. Laodicea was home to Greeks and Roman businesspeople (I.Laod 48; 82.1). Like many of the cities in Rev 2–3, it was an administrative center where court cases were heard during the Roman period (Pliny the Elder, *Nat.* 5.29.105). Wealthy patrons, including one who became a client king of the Romans, gave large sums of money to beautify the city during the first century BCE (Strabo, *Geographica* 12.8.16). Other revenue came from trade and from the soft black wool that was produced in the region (Strabo, *Geographica* 12.8.16; Vitruvius, *Arch.* 8.3.14; Pliny the Elder, *Nat.* 8.73.190). As in other cities, professional groups included those in the textile and garment industries (I.Laod 50). On the city's role in finance, see the NOTE on Rev 3:18. Laodicea had a theater for music and drama, and in time a second theater was built. Roman entertainments were also popular, especially shows featuring gladiators from Thyatira and other cities (I.Laod 73; 75; 81A; Cicero, *Att.* 6.3.9; Bean, *Turkey*, 247–57).

Laodicea suffered earthquake damage around 20 BCE and received Roman help in rebuilding (Strabo, *Geographica* 12.8.18; Suetonius, *Tib.* 8). Another earthquake struck in 60 CE, but this time the city was rebuilt without Roman assistance, funding coming from local benefactors (Tacitus, *Ann.* 14.27; *Sib. Or.* 4.1–8). A new stadium of extraordinary size was dedicated to the emperor Titus in 79 CE (I.Laod 15). Then a patron dedicated a monumental gate to Zeus and Domitian on the east side of the city (ca. 84–85 CE; I.Laod 24). A main street flanked by colonnades ran through the city to a similar gate in the wall on the opposite side. Laodicea was well-supplied with water brought by an aqueduct and distributed through a water tower and fountains, some built during the reign of Domitian (81–96 CE; I.Laod 12–13). There is no basis for the idea that water from this aqueduct was a problem (NOTE on Rev 3:16).

Laodicea was formerly called Diospolis, or "city of Zeus." In Roman times there was a statue and altar to Zeus, who was often called the Savior, along with other dedications to Zeus and sometimes Hermes his messenger (Pliny the Elder, *Nat.* 5.105; I.Laod 24; 26; 62; 64; 82.13). A coin from the city shows Domitian on one side and Zeus on the other.

Embassies from Laodicea went to the oracle of Apollo at Claros near Ephesus. They were led by a prophet, who was a youth accompanied by his father. The father would consult the oracle, and the young prophet would report the messages (I.Laod 67–68; Bean, *Turkey*, 249–50). Other Hellenistic deities venerated at Laodicea included Hestia and Herakles (I.Laod 65–66). Thirteen miles west of the city was the temple of Men Karrou, an Anatolian god associated with the moon, the underworld, and agricultural fertility. This temple had a medical school in the tradition of the Hellenistic physician Herophilus, who was known for his studies of anatomy (Strabo, *Geographica* 12.8.20). Just as Jewish tradition referred to Israel's God as the Most High, some Laodiceans gave this title to a Hellenistic deity, as others did at Smyrna and Thyatira (I.Laod 61; Trebilco, *Jewish*, 127–44).

Special honors were given to the priest of the cult of the personified city of Laodicea. Dates on official documents were given by naming the priest of the city who was in office at the time (I.Laod 4b.9; 8.1; 53.3; 83.13–14; 85.14; 132). An association of artists was dedicated to Dionysus, who was honored by theatrical and musical performances (I.Laod 65A). In the first century Laodicea hosted the provincial games as well as those honoring the emperor Claudius (S. Mitchell, *Anatolia*, 1:219; Friesen, *Twice*, 115). An inscription from the first or second century CE honors a high priestess in the provincial cult of the emperor who oversaw the games and held other sacred offices (I.Laod 53).

The city's relations with Rome were strong. Laodicea competed for the honor of building a provincial temple to the emperor Tiberius in 23 CE, although permission was given to Smyrna (Tacitus, *Ann.* 4.55). In 79 CE a statue at Laodicea honored Titus as "son of god," since he was the son of the deified Vespasian (I.Laod 9; cf. 15). About

Figure 16. Coin from Laodicea: Domitian and Domitia on one side and their imperial temple at Laodicea on the other (81–96 CE). © The Trustees of the British Museum.

89/90 CE a provincial temple to Domitian and the other Flavian emperors was dedicated at Ephesus, but Laodicea had its own municipal cult to Domitian, which emphasized the ideology of power and victory. Coins show Domitian, his wife Domitia, and their temple. The emperor wears military attire and holds a spear and trophy to emphasize triumph. The inscription on his temple reads *Epineikios*, "for victory" (Figure 16; Price, *Rituals*, 183; Friesen, *Imperial*, 61–62; Dräger, *Städte*, 207).

There were Jewish communities at Laodicea and nearby Hierapolis. In the first century BCE Laodicea was one of the places where taxes for the Jerusalem temple were collected. In 62 BCE a Roman official confiscated these funds, which amounted to twenty Roman pounds of gold, enough to suggest that the Jewish population in the area was significant (Cicero, *Flac.* 68; S. Mitchell, *Anatolia*, 2:33). Jewish apocalyptic writers sometimes depicted Laodicea coming under divine judgment (*Sib. Or.* 3:471; 4:107; 5:290), but Jews who lived there were part of an established community. About 45 BCE magistrates at Laodicea were told that Jews were to be allowed to observe the Sabbath and other traditions (Josephus, *Ant.* 14.241–43). Inscriptions attest to the presence of a Jewish community in the second century CE and later (*IJO* 2:443–47). At the time Revelation was written, there is no indication of conflict between Jews and Christians at Laodicea, as there was at Smyrna and Philadelphia.

The local Christian community was probably founded by an associate of Paul. According to Colossians, Paul did not visit Laodicea, but his coworker Epaphras formed congregations in Laodicea and the nearby towns of Hierapolis and Colossae. These groups met in the homes of leading members, including a woman named Nympha, who hosted a house church at Laodicea (Col 1:7; 2:1; 4:12–16; Barth and Blanke, *Colossians*, 486). Although the authorship and date of Colossians are disputed, it seems likely that there was a Christian community at Laodicea by the late 50s or early 60s. Paul may have written a letter to the Laodiceans that has not survived (Col 4:16). Later, the followers of Marcion claimed that the letter to the Ephesians was the letter to Laodicea (Tertullian, *Marc.* 5.17), and others thought Marcion's followers had forged an epistle with that name (Muratorian canon). The epistle to the Laodiceans that circulated in the western church was essentially a compilation of Pauline phrases and is clearly inauthentic (*NTApoc* 2:42–46). In the mid-second century Laodicea's bishop, Sagaris, was martyred (Eusebius, *Hist. eccl.* 5.24.5).

Thus says the Amen, the faithful and true witness. "Amen" indicates affirmation, as in "Yes, Amen" (1:8; cf. 1:6; 7:12; 19:4). Here, it is a title for Christ. It recalls the Hebrew of Isa 65:16, where people are to give blessings and swear oaths "by the God of Amen," emphasizing God's faithfulness. Some ancient versions of Isa 65:15 transliterate *ʾāmēn* (Symmachus, Vulgate), while others translate it as "faithful" (Aquila) or "true" (LXX). Revelation draws together these possibilities by calling Christ "the Amen" and then adding that he is "faithful and true" (cf. 2 Cor 1:20). The terms "faithful" and "true" characterize the words of God and those who bear witness to God (Rev 21:5; 22:6).

the ruler of God's creation. Revelation uses "creation" (*ktisis*) and related words (*ktizein, ktisma*) for the present created order (4:11; 5:13; 10:6) rather than for the new creation (cf. 21:1; Beale). Calling Christ the *archē* of creation could mean that he is its "origin," though "ruler" is more likely:

1. Ruler (NIV). Revelation introduced "Jesus Christ the faithful witness" as "the ruler [*archōn*] of the kings of the earth" (1:5). Similar language is now used for Jesus, "the faithful and true witness, the ruler [*archē*] of God's creation" (3:14). The similarities suggest that *archōn* and *archē* point to Christ's rule over the world. The message to Laodicea begins with Christ's rule and concludes with his enthronement (3:14, 21). Later, all creation declares Christ's rightful power to rule (5:12), and at his final coming he is "faithful and true" and is said to rule the nations (19:11). The word *archē* was used for civic offices (I.Laod 65.3; 83.7; I.Smyr 641.7), administration of provinces, and imperial power (Dio Cassius, *Rom. Hist.* 39.9.3; 51.21.6). The word was extended from the offices to the people who held those offices, both collectively (Luke 12:11; Tit 3:1; *Mart. Pol.* 10:2) and individually, as is the case here (Hos 1:11 [2:2 LXX]; 2 Esd 19:17; P.Hal. 1.226; H. Mason, *Greek*, 110–11).

2. Origin (NRSV), source (NAB, REB), or beginning (KJV, NASB). This reading relates the word *archē* to Christ's creative activity at the beginning of time. Revelation calls God and Christ the Alpha and the Omega, the beginning (*archē*) and the end (21:6; 22:13). Because both God and Christ are called *archē*, the term conveys a sense of deity (Bauckham, *Theology*, 56). Since God is the Creator, the same can be said of Christ. Some interpreters compare Rev 3:14 to Col 1:15–17, where Christ is the firstborn of creation and the one through whom all things were made. The problem is that *archē* is not applied to Christ in Col 1:15–17 but in 1:18, where it indicates preeminence in rank. Others suggest that Revelation identifies Christ with divine wisdom, God's agent of creation "at the beginning" (Prov 8:22; John 1:1–18; Heb 1:1–4; Justin Martyr, *Dial.* 61.1; 62:4; Victorinus; Aune; Giesen; Murphy; Osborne). Revelation's high Christology does affirm Christ's existence at the beginning, but it does not develop his creative role in the message to Laodicea. The context emphasizes his power to rule (Rev 3:21).

3:15. *I know your works. You are neither cold nor hot. I wish that you were either cold or hot.* Both hot and cold are understood positively. Together, they characterize works of perseverance, faith, and love (2:2, 19; 3:8) and are synonymous with commitment (3:19). Tepidness is a contrast to both hot and cold and signifies complacency. Alternatively, some interpreters take heat as a positive term for faith and coldness as a negative term for unbelief (Victorinus; Primasius; Aune; Caird; Roloff;

Swete). From this perspective, the writer is saying that Christ wishes the Laodiceans were either cold or hot, which is a rhetorical move that is designed to startle them, since he would be saying that even cold unbelief is preferable to a tepid faith. A more straightforward reading, however, takes both hot and cold as positive images for faith (see COMMENT).

3:16. *So, because you are tepid, and neither hot nor cold, I am about to vomit you out of my mouth.* The metaphors of hot, cold, and tepid are drawn from Greco-Roman dining practices and fit the meal imagery used in this passage (see COMMENT). Many interpreters, however, argue that calling the Laodiceans "tepid" alludes to the local water supply. The idea is that since Laodicea had an aqueduct, the water that flowed into the city must have been lukewarm and undesirable. In contrast, the nearby city of Hierapolis was known for its hot springs and mineral baths, while the city of Colossae seems to have had cold water sources. Both types of water would be beneficial (Rudwick and Green, "Laodicean"; Porter, "Why"; Hemer, *Letters*, 186–91; Aune; Beale, Ford; Giesen; Harrington; Mounce; Murphy; Osborne).

This approach is untenable. Aqueducts were used in or around *all* of the cities in Revelation (NOTES on 2:1, 8, 12, 18; 3:1, 7, 14). Laodicea's water supply was like that of other cities—and water from aqueducts was considered good to drink (Athanaeus, *Deipnosophistae* 2.42c). To make their theory work, some interpreters imagine that Laodicea's water originated at the hot springs of Hierapolis northwest of Laodicea (Ford), even though the aqueduct actually comes in from the south. Others suppose that the source lying south of the city might have been a hot spring and that the water became tepid by the time it reached Laodicea (Rudwick and Green, "Laodicean"; Hemer, *Letters*, 188), but studies of the water system do not bear this out (Şimşek and Büyükkolanci, "Water"). Laodicea had access to water from two rivers and two springs, the main one located five miles south of the city. A sophisticated network of channels, pipes, reservoirs, and fountains supplied the city's needs. The system had features like those of the water systems in other cities, including provisions for keeping the pipes free-flowing. Structures were maintained and improved throughout the Hellenistic and Roman periods. The water was not "undrinkable" (Osborne) but an essential resource that enabled the city to thrive.

Laodicea's water was of good quality. A donor named Hedychrous gave his name to part of the first-century water system of the city. Since his name meant "sweet complexioned," he created a wordplay that emphasized the *pleasing* quality of the "sweet-complexioned" water being brought to the city (I.Laod 13; Corsten, *Inschriften*, 49). A fourth- or fifth-century inscription refers to a Laodicean fountain house that supplied "sweet clear water" (I.Laod 11). Revelation's imagery focuses on what was used for drinking—taken into the mouth—yet the hot water at Hierapolis was not valued for drinking but for bathing and dying fabric. Strabo said that the rivers near Laodicea were similar to those of Hierapolis in that they had a high mineral content, "although their water is drinkable" (*potimos*; *Geographica* 13.4.14). In other words, Strabo thought that Laodicea's water was *drinkable*, whereas the water from Hierapolis was not. A Jewish apocalyptic writer referred to "Laodicea . . . by the wonderful water of the Lycus" (*Sib. Or.* 3:471–72). All this attests to Revelation's imagery not being connected to the quality of local water supplies (C. R. Koester, "Message," 409–11).

3:17. For you say, 'I am rich and have become wealthy and do not need anything.' The author seeks to startle the readers by mimicking their attitude. For the rhetoric to be effective, the congregation would need to be wealthy enough for the indictment to be plausible. Some interpreters assume that it was also a special *civic* trait because after the earthquake of 60 CE Laodicea was rebuilt without Roman assistance (Tacitus, *Ann.* 14.27). Some think that Laodicea was notorious for proudly refusing Roman help (Hemer, *Letters*, 191–96; Osborne), yet ancient sources do not say that Romans offered help or that the Laodiceans refused it. Tacitus simply makes the point that the city was able to manage on its own (Magie, *Roman*, 1:564). Inscriptions honoring the wealthy benefactors who paid for the city's new gate, stadium, and other public works note that the funds came "from their own means" (I.Laod 9.9; 12.1; 13.7–8; 15.3; cf. 24.3). Yet this expression was standard language in inscriptions used by the benefactors who sponsored public works in many Asian cities during this period. Revelation does not allude to a civic trait of Laodicea but simply assumes that the congregation benefited from the Roman-era prosperity.

Yet you do not realize that you are miserable and pitiable and poor and blind and naked. The author has listed three sources of the Laodiceans' pride, but now counters with five ways in which they are lacking. Rhetorically, all five Greek adjectives end in *-os*, allowing the repetition to strike the ear. Repetition of the connective "and" (*kai*) gives the impression that the list could be expanded beyond what is actually said (Lausberg, *Handbook* §§686–87).

I advise you to buy from me gold that has been refined by fire so that you may be rich. Interpreters often argue that gold is mentioned to counter Laodicea's pride in being a banking center (Ramsay, *Letters*, 428; Osborne), but such a specific understanding is unlikely. Asia's principal banking center was Ephesus (Dio Chrysostom, *Disc.* 31.54–55; Aelius Aristides, *Orations* 23.24), with Pergamum also important for finance (IGR 352; Broughton, *Asia*, 888–97). The gold of Sardis's ancient rulers was legendary (Ovid, *Metam.* 11.136–45; Lucan, *Phar.* 3.209–10; Philostratus, *Vit. Apoll.* 6.37), and Smyrna had goldsmiths and a street named for gold (I.Smyr 721; Aelius Aristides, *Orations* 18.6). In the first century BCE Laodicea had been a banking center, where Roman tax collectors and officials kept funds (Cicero, *Fam.* 2.17.4; 3.5.4; *Att.* 5.15, 21; 6.2); but the city's importance for finance in the first century CE is unclear, since methods of tax collection changed, and communities began sending funds directly to the quaestor of the province (Magie, *Roman*, 1:165, 407). Gold was simply a common image for wealth.

and white clothing to wear. Interpreters often assume that the white clothing is a direct contrast to the local black wool that provided revenue for the city (Ramsay, *Letters*, 429; Hemer, *Letters*, 208). Again, such a specific reference is unlikely. Most cities mentioned in Rev 2–3 produced textiles. White robes were mentioned in the message to Sardis (3:4–5), yet there is no suggestion that the author was making a contrast with the garment industry in that city. The message contrasts white robes with nakedness, not with black garments.

so that you will not appear naked and ashamed. Nakedness was positive in Greco-Roman art, where athletes, gods, heroes, and emperors were pictured in the nude to show their perfection. Conversely, Revelation connects nakedness with shame (Gen 2:25; 3:7; Isa 20:4; 1QS VII, 13–14; 1QM VII, 7) and with poverty—another source of shame (Prov 14:20; 19:7; cf. Isa 58:7; Matt 25:36; Jas 2:15). Shame involves a loss of value in the eyes of other people (Aristotle, *Rhet.* 2.6.14–15). For the Laodiceans, shame would arise first from the sense that in Christ's eyes they are not wealthy and honorable, but poor and naked. Second, this message was to be read by six other congregations, so the Laodiceans would also feel ashamed by their poor reputation among other Christians. The appeal to the Laodiceans' sense of shame is designed to awaken a desire to be judged more favorably by Christ and other believers.

and salve to put on your eyes so that you may see. Many interpreters argue that eye salve counters Laodicean pride in the medical school that was located at the temple of Men Karrou some thirteen miles away (Strabo, *Geographica* 12.8.20; Ramsay, *Letters*, 429; Hemer, *Letters*, 208). Physicians at the school treated various disorders. In the early first century CE one of the doctors was the ophthalmologist Demosthenes Philalethes (*NP* 4:297–98). The idea is that the Laodiceans may have been proud of local eye treatments, but the writer of Revelation responds by warning of spiritual blindness.

A direct connection with local practice is unlikely, however. First, eye salves were produced throughout the empire. Some people who treated eyes made their own salves, while others simply purchased what was on the market. Salves were not tied to specific medical schools (Pliny the Elder, *Nat.* 34.108; Epictetus, *Diatribai* 3.21.20–21). Second, no known source says that Laodicea had a reputation for producing eye salve. The region of Phrygia produced a mineral used for eye treatment, but this mineral is not associated with Laodicea. The city was known for its nard, which was used to treat ears and liver or stomach inflammations, but this medication is never connected to eyes and it was also produced in other cities (C. R. Koester, "Message," 419). Third, other cities were at least as well-known for medicine. At Pergamum's sanctuary of Asclepius many ailments were treated, including those of the eyes (Aelius Aristides, *Orations* 39.15; A. Hoffmann, "Roman"). Smyrna had a medical school (I.Smyr 536–37; Cadoux, *Ancient*, 150–51), and Ephesus had an association of physicians (Broughton, *Asia*, 851; Nutton, "Healers," 42–43). The image of eye salve is valuable because it would have been commonly understood, not because it was uniquely tied to Laodicea.

3:19. *I correct and discipline those whom I love.* The language paraphrases Prov 3:11–12a: "My child, do not despise the Lord's discipline or be weary of his reproof, for the Lord disciplines the one whom he loves." A loving parent will correct behaviors that threaten the well-being of a child and others in the community (cf. Prov 13:24; 27:17; Eph 6:4). This idea is extended to God disciplining his people (Deut 8:5; Job 5:17; Heb 12:7–11; 4Q504 1–2 III, 6–7; cf. Seneca the Younger, *Prov.* 4.7). In Revelation the exalted Christ does the work of God by reproving and disciplining, much as he performs other actions of God, such as scrutinizing the human heart (Rev 2:23). Discipline (*paideuein*) can involve both the correction of wrongdoing and positive instruction (2 Tim 2:25; Tit 2:12; *T. Zeb.* 2:3; *1 Clem.* 56:16). The goal is to bring change. Accordingly, Christ disciplines the Laodiceans by telling them the truth about their impoverished condition and directing them to the source of authentic wealth and healing.

So be committed and repent. The term *zēleuein* (be committed) indicates intense desire or zeal. It is the opposite of being tepid (Rev 3:15–16). Although zeal can have a negative sense similar to jealousy (Gal 5:20), Revelation commends a positive commitment or zeal toward God (John 2:17). Such commitment is the outcome of repentance.

Here, repentance involves turning away from complacency, while the messages to other congregations connect repentance to rejecting false teachings that promote idolatry (Rev 2:16, 21, 22), doing works of love (2:5), and keeping the Christian message (3:3).

3:20. *See, I am standing at the door and knocking.* Knocking was a way to request admission to someone's home, and it could be accompanied by the visitor calling out (Plato, *Prot.* 310A; Luke 13:25; Acts 12:13, 16; *T. Job* 6:4). Readers are to picture Jesus asking a householder for the hospitality of a meal or a place to stay, which was a common occurrence (Gen 24:23; Job 31:32; Luke 19:5; Homer, *Od.* 7.142–45; Dio Chrysostom, *Disc.* 7.52; Arterbury, *Entertaining*, 52). It is unlikely that the imagery has a more specific origin: For example, some interpreters note that in Song 5:2 a woman's lover knocks when asking to come in (Beale; Boxall; Osborne; Prigent), but there is little else to suggest a connection. Others recall Jesus' parable about servants waiting for the master to return and knock, and when they open the door, he prepares a meal for them (Luke 12:36–37; cf. Mark 13:33–37; Roloff; Satake; Bauckham, *Climax*, 106). But since Revelation does not picture servants waiting for the master's knock, a direct connection is unlikely. Finally, the knocking and meal have been taken as a critique of magical practices in which someone prepares a meal to attract supernatural help. From this perspective, the point is that Christ initiates the relationship and is not lured into it by sorcery (Aune). There is little to suggest a critique of magic in this context, however.

If any hear my voice and open the door. Christ's voice is mediated. The readers hear Christ's voice through John's text. The message addresses the whole congregation but calls for a response from each individual.

I will come in to them and will dine with them and they with me. Interpreters have understood dining with Jesus in several ways. It can best be understood as an invitation to relationship in the present with hope for life in the future:

1. Future messianic banquet. The idea that the coming kingdom of God would be a banquet was part of Jewish tradition (Isa 25:6; *1 En.* 62:14; *2 Bar.* 29:8). Christian tradition envisioned the banquet being celebrated when Christ returned at the end of the age (Matt 8:11; Luke 13:29; 22:28–30). Similarly, Revelation anticipates that Christ's final return will be the time when the faithful will celebrate his wedding banquet (Rev 19:9). To say that he is at the door means that the end is imminent (Mark 13:29; Jas 5:9) and people must be ready (Luke 12:35–37; Mounce; Müller; Osborne; Satake; Bauckham, *Climax*, 106).

2. Present faith relationship. This approach notes that Christ is already present among the churches and now stands at the door, knocking. Revelation assumes that Christ's final coming will be unconditional and of universal significance (Rev 1:7; 19:11–20), but here, Jesus asks to be admitted, and the shared meal is contingent upon the response each person gives. The passage uses the images of the door and meal to describe the quality of the faithful relationship in the present (Origen, *Comm. Jo.* 13.199; Caesarius; Andreas; Beale; Giesen).

3. Lord's Supper. The meal imagery is sometimes related to the Christian practice of sharing bread and wine. The Lord's Supper was understood to be a way in which Christians enjoyed fellowship (*koinōnia*) with the risen Christ and other believers (1 Cor 10:16–17; 11:20; Luke 24:30–31, 35). Revelation would have been read aloud during worship (Rev 1:3), which might have included the eucharistic meal (Oecume-

nius; Blount; Boxall; Giesen; Harrington; Prigent; Reddish; Roloff). The difficulty with this approach is that Revelation does not develop eucharistic imagery here or elsewhere.

3:21. *As for the one who conquers.* This is a metaphor for persevering in faith (NOTE on 2:7).

I will grant that they might sit with me on my throne. One aspect of these words is messianic. Psalm 110:1 tells of a royal figure being seated at God's right hand, and this idea is realized through Jesus' resurrection and ascension (next NOTE). The other aspect is that Christ's authority is extended to his followers. One could say that Israel's king sits on the throne of God (1 Chr 29:23), and this prerogative is extended to those who follow Jesus. A saying of Jesus promised that the twelve disciples would sit on thrones and judge the tribes of Israel (Matt 19:28; Luke 22:30), but others expected all the faithful to reign with Christ, as is the case here (2 Tim 2:12). A similar move occurs in the message to Thyatira, where a psalm's promise that God's anointed would wield authority over the nations is fulfilled in Jesus and extended to believers (Ps 2:8–9; Rev 2:26–28). Finally, God said of the heir to David's throne, "I will be a father to him, and he will be a son to me" (2 Sam 7:14), and Revelation assumes that this promise is realized in Jesus, the Son of God (Rev 2:18), yet it is also extended to all the redeemed (21:7).

just as I conquered and sat with my Father on his throne. The picture of Christ enthroned with God in heaven is based in part on Ps 110:1: "The Lord says to my lord, 'Sit at my right hand until I make your enemies your footstool'" (cf. Matt 22:44 par.; Acts 2:34–35; 1 Cor 15:25; Heb 1:13). The psalm pictures the royal figure sitting at God's right hand, which could mean sitting on a separate throne, but Revelation tells of Christ sharing God's own throne, which underscores the unity of their reign. An analogy from the Roman period is Augustus being pictured on a coin sharing a two-person throne (*bisellium*) with his son-in-law, Marcus Agrippa, to convey shared authority (Figure 17). Augustus was also pictured sharing such a throne with the goddess Roma, and various Greco-Roman deities were depicted sharing thrones with each other (Aune). In Revelation, however, the risen Jesus shares his Father's legitimate authority over the world.

3:22. *Let the one who has an ear hear what the Spirit says to the assemblies.* See the NOTE on 2:7.

Figure 17. Roman coin showing Augustus and his designated heir, Agrippa, sharing the same throne (13 BCE). Courtesy of the Classical Numismatic Group (cngcoins.com).

COMMENT

The visionary sequence that began with Christ's appearance to John in Revelation's opening chapter now concludes with the address to the seventh assembly at Laodicea. The message focuses on the problem of complacency that arises from wealth. All of the cities in Rev 2–3 enjoyed a degree of prosperity from trade and local industry. Their wealthiest citizens were an elite group, while most of the population belonged to the lower classes. As a city, Laodicea was like Smyrna in the way it benefited from trade and the largesse of the benefactors who beautified its streets and public structures, but at Smyrna the Christian community was impoverished and threatened and at Laodicea it was affluent and at ease (2:9–10; 3:17). The tendencies at Laodicea are magnified in the vision of Babylon the whore in order to show how the pursuit of wealth leads people to accommodate a way of life that is debased and destructive (17–18).

The profile of Laodicea in the NOTE on 3:14 shows that Roman administration and the imperial cult were as important there as in other cities, yet there is no suggestion that the Laodicean Christians were threatened by Roman authorities as at Smyrna and Pergamum (2:10, 3). A Jewish community lived in Laodicea, but no mention is made of conflict between the synagogue and Christians, as at Smyrna and Philadelphia (2:9; 3:9). Civic life included popular festivals and athletic events with religious aspects, but there is no sign of tension over Christians accommodating Greco-Roman religious practices as at Pergamum and Thyatira (2:14, 20). Other congregations may have experienced conflict with Christian groups such as the Nicolaitans or followers of Jezebel (2:2, 6, 14, 20), or with false apostles, but none of this is evident at Laodicea.

The message addresses readers whose wealth made them comfortable, and the writer turns images of wealth into a critique that is designed to make them uncomfortable. Banquets were occasions for displaying wealth, when people would be served fine foods with chilled or heated wine. To challenge them, the message invokes the banquet images of hot, cold, and tepid to critique the congregation's complacency before the risen Christ and to call for the repentance that will allow him to eat with them in true friendship. The interpretation given below differs from the common practice of relating the images to unique features of Laodicea and considers them in relation to practices that were broadly familiar to Greco-Roman readers.

Like some of the previous messages, the message is presented in several concentric rings of thought:

Sovereignty: Christ is the faithful witness and ruler of God's creation.
    Dining: Christ will vomit the lukewarm out of his mouth.
        Prosperity: They think they are wealthy, but they are poor, blind, and naked.
        Prosperity: Obtain gold, eye salve, and clothing from Christ.
    Dining: Christ will eat with those who open the door to him.
Sovereignty: Christ's faithful followers will share a place on Christ's throne.

On Rev 3:14–22, see P. Berger, "Kollyrium"; Corsten, *Inschriften*; DeSilva, *Seeing*, 250–54; Hemer, *Letters*, 179–209; C. R. Koester, "Message"; Mathews, "Function"; Porter, "Why"; Ramsay, *Letters*, 413–30; Royalty, *Streets*, 164–75; Rudwick and Green, "Laodicean"; Şimşek and Büyükkolanci, "Water"; Wiarda, "Revelation."

In the outer ring Christ introduces himself as a faithful witness and the ruler of God's creation, and he concludes by recalling how he conquered and sat down on God's throne, promising that others who conquer will take their places on his throne (3:14, 21–22). The intermediate ring has to do with fellowship between Christ and the Laodiceans, drawing positive and negative images from dining practices (3:15–16, 20). The verses in the center reprove the Laodiceans for their misguided trust in wealth and their inability to see their self-satisfaction as a form of poverty, while directing them to seek the riches and insight that Christ provides (3:17–19).

Introduction

Christ introduces himself by recalling traits that were mentioned in the opening chapter of the book. When the writer gave glory to God, the praise concluded with "Amen" (1:6), and when he warned that all the tribes would grieve at Christ's coming, that too concluded with "Amen" (1:7). Now the risen Christ identifies himself as "the Amen," or the affirmation of the promises and reproofs given in the message to Laodicea. Next he gives a definition of "Amen" by calling himself "the faithful and true witness" (3:14; cf. 1:5). A witness attests to the truth in situations in which the truth is disputed. First, Christ did this through his ministry on earth, which culminated in his crucifixion. Second, the risen Christ continues to bear witness to the truth about God, the readers, and their world through John's book, which concludes with Jesus' verbal signature as the principal witness (22:20).

Next, Christ calls himself "the ruler of God's creation" (3:14), recalling how he was previously said to be "the ruler of the kings of the earth" (1:5). This expression identifies Christ with God, who will be acclaimed as earth's Creator (4:11; 10:6; 14:7). Accordingly, the next chapter will show every creature in heaven, on earth, under the earth, and in the sea ascribing rightful power to God and to Jesus the Lamb (5:8–13). In the plot of Revelation, the Creator and the Lamb stand with creation against the destroyers of the earth (11:18). The vision of Babylon/Rome will show how these destroyers amass earth's wealth in ways that ultimately lead to destruction (17:1–18:24), while the contrasting vision of New Jerusalem shows the reign of God and the Lamb leading to life and new creation (21:1–22:5). In their satisfaction with wealth, the Laodiceans are unwittingly collaborating with earth's destroyers. The one who addresses them calls for change and renewed commitment to creation's rightful sovereign.

Body of the Message

The message to Laodicea, like the one to Sardis, begins abruptly with a critique of the congregation's complacency (3:15; cf. 3:1). The reproof sets readers in the context of a banquet, where a host might offer guests something hot or cold to drink (Plato, *Resp.* 437D). A refreshing drink could consist simply of water that had been heated to a pleasant temperature or perhaps chilled with snow that had been purchased in the market or cooled in jars placed underground (Athenaeus, *Deipnosophistae* 3.123a–d).

Even more desirable was wine that had been heated or chilled. Both Greeks and Romans chilled wine by placing it in a well or mixing it with snow and ice. A common method was to cool wine by pouring it through a strainer (*colum nivarium*) filled with snow (Figure 18; Xenophon, *Mem.* 2.1.30; Athenaeus, *Deipnosophistae* 3.124cd; Seneca the Younger, *Ep.* 78.23; Martial, *Epigrams* 5.64.1–2; 14.103–4). In Roman times it was also popular to drink a heated mixture of wine and water. The public could find a hot drink stand (*thermopolium*) at Pompeii and other Roman cities, as well as in cities in Asia. But at banquets, a wealthy host might use a self-contained water heater to warm the water that was mixed with wine (Plautus, *Curc.* 292–93; Plautus, *Rud.* 1013–14; Cicero, *Rosc. Amer.* 133; Petronius, *Satyricon* 65; Lucian, *Lex.* 8). A fourth-century mosaic from Ephesus pictures a banquet with the mixing bowl (*kratēr*) in the lower center and a water heater (*miliarion*) to the right (Figure 19; Jobst, "Das 'öffentliche'"). A first-century example of such a heater has been found at Pompeii. It is a bronze cylinder that stands on three legs. A door in the side allows charcoal to be put into the base, and the water is warmed in the chamber above it (Figure 20). To cater to the wishes of guests, a good host might make both hot and cold water available so that people could choose which they wanted mixed with their wine (Martial, *Epigrams* 14.105; Dunbabin, "Wine"; C. R. Koester, "Message," 413–15).

The Laodiceans are unlike the hot or cold drink that a banqueter might desire. They are tepid, objectionable, and something to be vomited out of the mouth (Rev 3:16). The idea that someone would vomit after indulging in too much food or wine at a meal would have been familiar (Sir 31:21; Cicero, *Pis.* 10.22; Cicero, *Phil.* 2.104.41), but here, the picture is of someone spitting out the wine that does not meet his taste (Athenaeus, *Deipnosophistae* 3.124a). It was thought that lukewarm liquid was conducive to vomiting. For example, when a slave was charged with eating his master's figs, he drank lukewarm water and put his fingers down his throat to make himself vomit, so that everyone could see what was in his stomach (*Vita Aesopi* 2–3).

The message turns banquet practice into a graphic metaphor for the Laodiceans' complacency. Cold and hot beverages are valued because their temperature differs from that of the surrounding air, which makes them refreshing. In contrast, the temperature of lukewarm water is like that of its surroundings; it does not distinguish itself to the touch. By analogy, nothing distinguishes the works of the Laodicean Christians from the common practices of their society. In previous messages Christ commends perseverance, faith, and love—works that would be positively regarded as cold or hot (Rev 2:2, 19; 3:8). The call for works that are cold or hot is a summons to a way of life that differs from familiar patterns of wealth breeding complacency, expressing instead the commitment to Christ and the Christian community that sets readers apart.

The vulgar image of Christ vomiting the tepid Christians out of his mouth is designed to startle readers into an awareness of the danger of rejection (3:16; cf. Lev 18:25, 28). It is clear that the readers have not yet been rejected, and despite the severity of the threat, they are not told how they could tell whether Christ actually did reject them in the future. The metaphor creates a crisis of discernment, as has been the case in previous messages, which warned that the Ephesians' "lampstand" would be moved, that Christ would make war at Pergamum with the "sword" of his mouth, and that he would put Jezebel to "bed" (Rev 2:5, 16, 22). Discerning when and whether the threat has been carried out is problematic. Readers have no way to determine it. Instead, the warning of being vomited out is designed to bring change, preparing readers to respond favorably to the promise given later, when Christ asks that they open the door that they might eat together (3:20).

For the congregation's attitude, Revelation offers: "For you say, 'I am rich and have become wealthy and do not need anything'" (3:17). The assumption is that the

Figure 18. Strainer used for snow to chill wine. From H. L. Wilson, "A New Italic Divinity," 453.

Figure 20. Pompeii: Device for heating water to mix with wine (first century CE). From Erich Pernice, *Gefässe und Geräte aus Bronze*, pl. 7.

Figure 19. Ephesus: Mosaic of a banquet showing a water heater in the lower right (fourth century CE). Courtesy of the *Österreichisches Archäologisches Institut Archiv*e.

congregation derives security from its economic prosperity, so the writer turns this idea into insecurity by portraying the readers as arrogant. It was understood that pride goes before a fall (Prov 16:18; Aeschylus, *Pers.* 808), and those who placed their confidence in wealth were especially vulnerable (Pss 52:7; 62:10; Wis 5:8; Sir 5:1–3; Ps.-Phoc. 62; Luke 12:13–21). Putting prideful words into the mouth of one's opponent was a common way to warn of a coming demise. Jewish tradition held that judgment would come to pretentious people who said, "Ah, I am rich, I have gained wealth for myself; in all of my gain no offense has been found in me that would be sin" (Hos 12:8; cf. Zech 11:5; *1 En.* 97:8–10). From a philosopher's perspective, a person boasting "I am rich and need nothing" lacked integrity (Epictetus, *Diatribai* 3.7.29; Aune; Royalty, *Streets*, 168).

The dramatic demise of those who take refuge in wealth is played out in the vision of the fall of Babylon/Rome later in Revelation. The Laodiceans are said to be prosperous, and the attitude toward that prosperity is magnified in the portrait of Babylon, a fabulously wealthy city that appears as a whore glittering with gold, gems, and opulent clothing (Rev 17:3–4; 18:11–19). Like the message to Laodicea, the vision of Babylon includes a soliloquy: The opulent city "says in her heart, 'I sit as a queen; I am no widow, and I will never see grief'" (18:7). Yet destruction comes suddenly (17:16; 18:10). Her wealth does not save her; it merely deludes her into complacency until the end comes. The author discerns similar tendencies at Laodicea, which means that the readers there are also liable to fall (M. Mathews, "Function").

Christ knows the Laodiceans, but they do not know themselves (3:15, 17). They think they are rich, but Christ says they are impoverished. In an ordinary sense, the poor lack money, subsist on coarse food, and wear threadbare clothes. They are vulnerable (Amos 5:11; Isa 3:14–15; Sir 13:20). People flattered the rich, but the poor were considered marginal (Prov 14:4, 7; Jas 2:2–3). A rich person reduced to poverty was exposed to ridicule (Juvenal, *Satirae* 3.152). Some would "call those poor who are lapped around by silver and gold and a multitude of landed possessions and revenues" if they lacked virtue (Philo, *Prob.* 9; Epictetus, *Diatribai* 3.7.29). But the Laodiceans are poor in faith and impoverished in commitment.

The Laodiceans are also "blind" (Rev 3:17). In an ordinary sense, physical blindness often meant a life of poverty. One might more easily picture the blind begging along the street than drinking hot or cold wine at a banquet (Mark 10:46; Luke 14:13; John 9:1, 8). The Laodiceans may have physical sight, but they are "blind" to their own condition. The metaphor was common: "Who is blind but my servant," or "blind like the servant of the Lord? He sees many things but does not observe them" (Isa 42:19–20; cf. 56:10; Matt 23:16–17; John 9:40–41). Wealth was a reason people could not see the truth: "What are you doing, O wretched people? Like blind men you go tottering all around. You have left the true path and are going off upon another; you are looking for serenity and happiness in the wrong place . . . It is not in possessions" (Epictetus, *Diatribai* 3.22.26–27; cf. 3.26.3; cf. Antiphanes, *Fragments* 259; Menander, *Fragments* 77; 83; W. Schrage, *TDNT* 8 [1972] 277).

Finally, the Laodiceans are "naked" (Rev 3:17). In an ordinary sense, being naked or ill-clad was another sign of poverty (Job 31:19; Tob 1:17; Matt 25:36; Jas 2:15). The wealthy could buy clothes to give them honor, but those who were ill-clad were vulnerable to shame (Gen 2:25; 3:7; Isa 20:4–5; Rev 16:15). Later visions warn that Babylon/Rome will be devastated and stripped naked (17:16), but the Laodiceans are already considered naked by Christ. The complacent Sardians may wear defiled garments (3:4), but the Laodiceans are told that they have no garments at all. This metaphor indicates that those who fail to exhibit committed faith are naked in that they lack the works that make faith visible and clothe the faithful like a garment (19:8). Many understood that nothing was hidden from God and that all were "naked" and exposed to divine scrutiny (*1 En.* 9:5; Philo, *Cher.* 17; Heb 4:13). The inclusion of the Laodiceans' failings in a book designed to be read by others exposes them before other readers, heightening the sense of shame and need for change (deSilva, *Seeing*, 190)

A startling shift is that the Laodiceans, who have been described as destitute, are now told to purchase (*agorazein*) gold from the risen Jesus (Rev 3:18). In an ordinary sense, the Laodiceans were wealthy enough to purchase what they wished in the market. But Revelation will show that this type of purchasing binds people to the destroyers of the earth, whose commercial system is alluring but whose rule is oppressive (13:17; 18:11). Instead, the Christ who counsels them to purchase gold from him has already shed his blood to purchase (*agorazein*) people of every tribe and nation for life in God's kingdom (5:9; 14:3–4). The way Christ makes his purchase is by giving himself for the sake of others. Those who make a purchase from Christ in turn devote themselves to him.

The Laodiceans are to purchase gold "refined by fire" (3:18). Ordinary gold was a sign of wealth and status, but later visions show gold ensnaring people in the commercial web of Babylon/Rome with its ruler cult and idols made of gold (9:7; 17:4; 18:12, 16). The gold of which Christ speaks is the promise of life in the presence of God. On one level, the image of gold refined by fire anticipates New Jerusalem, whose streets are paved with pure gold. The redeemed enter the city through resurrection (21:18, 21). On another level, the imagery might suggest that those who receive the gold will be refined by fire, since nothing unclean will enter God's city (21:27). People were "refined" when sin was removed and faith was tested through conflict (Mal 3:2–3; Job 23:10; Zech 13:9; 1 Pet 1:6–9). The Laodiceans are called to the kind of commitment that will set them at odds with others in their social context and require perseverance.

Next they are to purchase white robes so they will not appear naked and ashamed (Rev 3:18). Socially, the wealthy and those who imitated them craved opulent clothing that was purple or scarlet—the colors worn by the whore (17:4; 18:16). In contrast, working people wore clothes that were less flamboyant but not white, since white was unsuitable for manual labor. Lawyers and other people of means sometimes did wear white, however, and if white was worn by the master, it could also be worn by the servants (Artemidorus, *Onirocritica* 2.3; 4.2). In a transferred sense, Revelation takes white to be a color suitable for God and Christ (Rev 1:14; 20:11; cf. Aelius Aristides, *Orations* 48.30–31; cf. Plato, *Legat.* 956A; Plutarch, *Mor.* 771D; Josephus, *Ant.* 11.327, 331). Accordingly, white is appropriate for the robes worn by the servants around God's throne (Rev 4:4; cf. Dan 7:9; Matt 17:2; John 20:12; Acts 1:10; *1 En.* 14:20).

Receiving a white robe first suggests cleansing from sin. People wash their robes and make them white in the blood of the Lamb, that is, by receiving the benefits of Christ's self-sacrifice (Rev 7:14; cf. 1:5; 5:9; NOTE on 3:5). Second, a person's actions make faith visible and are therefore depicted as the garment that clothes the believer (19:8). Compromising one's faith is likened to defiling one's garment, making cleansing necessary (3:4). Third, the white robe is the promise of deathless life in the presence of God. The martyrs receive white robes to anticipate resurrection (6:11), and those who wash their robes have a place in New Jerusalem (22:14; cf. *1 En.* 62:15–16; 2 Esd 2:39, 45; 1 Cor 15:53–54; 2 Cor 5:1–4; *Mart. Asc. Isa.* 4:16; 9:9, 17; Herm. *Sim.* 8.2.3). In the readers' social worlds, participants in a festival gathering often wore white (Aelius Aristides, *Orations* 48.30; Plutarch, *Mor.* 771D), and John's visions portray the redeemed in white robes celebrating before God's throne (Rev 7:9–14).

Finally, there is the metaphor of eye salve. Ordinary salves were produced and marketed throughout the Roman Empire. These medications were made from pulverized plants and minerals that were mixed with water, milk, wine, or other liquids (e.g., Pliny the Elder, *Nat.* 29.38.117–32; 33.27.114). They were applied externally to the eyes for sores, aches, inflammations, and other ailments. Salves were often made locally and sold in the markets of many cities (Jackson, "Eye"; H. Nielsen, *Ancient*, 9–57; Nutton, "Drug"; *NewDocs* 3:56–57). The image of eye salve is used for the words that the risen Christ speaks. By telling the Laodiceans about their poverty, nakedness, and blindness in matters of faith, the speaker seeks to open their eyes to the truth about themselves so that they heed the call for repentance and perseverance (Rev 3:19, 21). By seeing the truth in this way, readers share the promise of finally seeing God face to face (22:4).

The sharp admonitions reach a turning point when Christ says that he reproves and disciplines those he loves. The language paraphrases Prov 3:12 and recalls common ideas about divine discipline (NOTE on Rev 3:19). Earlier, John spoke in an encouraging way about the love Christ conveyed through his death (1:5). Here, Christ's love is confrontational and calls for change. Both encouragement and confrontation were understood to express devotion to a person when done for the other person's good (Seneca the Younger, *Ep.* 9.10; Cicero, *Amic.* 24.89–25.96; deSilva, *Seeing*, 186). A true friend would "use the stinging word as a medicine which restores and preserves health," not something that injures the person (Plutarch, *Mor.* 55C; cf. 59D; Aristotle, *Rhet.* 2.4.27; Glad, "Frank").

Such encouragement entails an abrupt reversal of roles. Christ called the Laodiceans miserable, pitiable, poor, blind, and naked—the kind of people who were relegated to the streets outside the banquet hall. Now Christ puts *himself* in the position of the outsider, knocking at the door of the Laodiceans, who are pictured as insiders (Rev 3:20). Instead of depicting himself as a disgusted banqueter, threatening to vomit the complacent out of his mouth, Christ wants to come in and share a meal with those who open the door.

If a visitor in the ancient world requested hospitality, it was a matter of honor to provide it. Hosts' reputations were bolstered by the care they extended to guests. Many understood that the way one treated a visitor affected one's status before God. Jews had the tradition of Abraham receiving the three strangers, who proved to be God's messengers (Gen 18:1–15; Philo, *Abr.* 107–18; *T. Ab.* 1:2, 5; Heb 13:2). Greeks were taught that visitors from Zeus might test their readiness to show hospitality, and in some cases the gods themselves might come in disguise (Homer, *Od.* 6.207–8; Ovid, *Metam.* 8.626–78; Arterbury, *Entertaining*, 15–93). In Revelation the readers find Christ meeting them as a visitor at the door. To welcome him would be an honor; to refuse him would be unthinkable.

Sharing a meal with a guest was central to hospitality. Revelation emphasizes the mutuality involved: Christ and the believer dine together (3:20). Some householders might provide food for the guest without joining in the meal (Dio Chrysostom, *Disc.* 7.57). Or the host might choose to emphasize social hierarchy by dining with a select few while other guests ate separately (Pliny the Younger, *Ep.* 2.6). The ideal situation, however, was that the host and the guest ate together, which made the table a sign of friendship (Dio Chrysostom, *Disc.* 7.65; Plutarch, *Mor.* 612D; Matt 9:10; Mark 2:16; Luke 15:2). On a primary level, Revelation uses meal imagery for the renewal of the readers' relationship with the risen Christ in the present. On a secondary level, the imagery anticipates the future, when the redeemed will wear fine linen at the marriage banquet of the Lamb, which is celebrated through resurrection (Rev 19:8–9).

Conclusion

The message began by introducing Christ as the ruler of God's creation, and it ends by recalling how he conquered and shares the throne of his Father (3:14, 21). Culturally, the movement from conquest (*nikan*) to enthronement (*thronos*) was integral to Roman imperial ideology. Images from the temple at Pergamum depicted Augustus the conqueror being crowned, and the calendar used in Philadelphia measured time from the year of Augustus's victory at Actium. The temple to the Flavian emperors at Ephesus was built under Domitian, who occupied the throne once held by his deified father Vespasian and brother Titus, who were military conquerors. The local temple to Domitian at Laodicea celebrated his reign as a military conqueror. Yet Revelation identifies such conquest and enthronement with the beast, which oppresses people of every nation and shares the throne of Satan (2:13; 13:2, 7).

In contrast, Jesus conquers through his suffering and death, which redeems people for service to God (5:5–10). His victory continues in resurrection, as he assumes his place on God's throne (3:21; 12:5). The followers of Jesus who conquer are also promised a place on his throne (3:20). They conquer by remaining faithful to him, bearing witness to the reign of God, and resisting the powers that contend for their allegiance (12:11). Like Jesus, the faithful take their place on the throne through the resurrection that completes their victory.

Later visions depict God and Christ sharing a single throne, because they rule as one and are worshiped as one (7:17; 22:1, 3). This unity of God and Christ is unique and distinguished from God's relationship to anyone else. Therefore, when the faithful are raised, they reign with Christ but are pictured on multiple thrones (20:4). They share fully in the blessings of Christ's reign, yet the differences between God and humanity remain. The faithful continue to worship God and the Lamb who uniquely share one throne, even as the faithful also reign with them by sharing in the blessings of the kingdom (22:3; Bauckham, *Theology*, 54–65).

Second Cycle:
The Seven Seals (4:1–8:5)

12. General Comments on the Second Cycle

Revelation's second cycle of visions begins in the heavenly throne room, where John sees the Creator and the Lamb, who are praised by the whole created order. The Lamb receives a scroll from God's hand and opens its seals, bringing visions of conquest, violence, food shortage, and death. The martyrs call out for justice, while everyone else cries out in fear as the created order trembles under divine wrath. But when people cry out, the movement toward judgment is interrupted so that they can be protected with a seal, and John sees a countless multitude praising God and the Lamb. The vision ends where it began, in the heavenly throne room, as silence reigns and an angel offers the prayers that introduce the next vision cycle.

This section's vision of God as Creator plays a major literary and theological role in Revelation. It depicts a God whose power is exercised in creating, whose sovereignty over the world is legitimate because he brought all things into being (4:1–11). The scene sets the Creator of the world against the destroyers, who must be defeated if life is to prevail, and it anticipates that the God who created all things in the beginning will finally make all things new (11:18; 21:5). The vision also reveals that God works through the slaughtered and living Lamb, whose self-sacrifice brings people into his kingdom (5:5–10). The evil counterpart to the Lamb is the beast, which sacrifices others in order to extend its power over the earth (13:1–10). Introducing Christ as the Lamb reveals the nature of divine power, which works for the redemption of the world.

A. HISTORY OF INTERPRETATION
The Heavenly Throne Room (Rev 4–5)

The vision of God as the Creator and Jesus as the slaughtered Lamb gave Revelation theological credibility at a time when some in the early church questioned its value. The belief that God created the world and that Jesus died to redeem it was widely held, so those aspects of Revelation were congruent with the church's faith (INTRO I.A.1–2). The vision of Jesus as the Root of David and slaughtered Lamb affirmed his role in fulfilling the promise of God's kingdom and made his death the consummation of Israel's sacrificial practices (Rev 5:5–6; Irenaeus, *Haer.* 4.20.11; Clement of Alexandria, *Strom.* 5.6; Origen, *Comm. Jo.* 6.273–74; Cyprian, *Test.* 2.11). It was common to understand the scroll in God's hand as the OT, whose true meaning was revealed by Christ the Lamb. Because the Lamb unseals the OT, he is honored by the four creatures, who signify the four gospels, along with the twenty-four elders, who are the patriarchs and apostles (Origen, *Comm. Jo.* 5.6; Victorinus).

As Christianity became the dominant religion of the Roman Empire through its acceptance by Constantine (d. 337) and his successors, artists used motifs from the heavenly throne room to celebrate the present reign of Christ over the world (INTRO I.A.3). The vision of the creatures and elders worshiping the Lamb in heaven was displayed on the façade of old Saint Peter's in Rome and in many other churches in the west, giving people the sense that through their worship on earth they entered the presence of God. During the Trinitarian controversies of the fourth and fifth centuries, theologians emphasized that Christ the Son was coeternal with God the Father. Artists reflected this emphasis by making Christ—rather than God the Father—the figure on the throne in their renditions of Rev 4. A fine example is the eleventh-century Bamberg Apocalypse (Figure 21), which shows the seated Christ holding God's scroll, attended by the four creatures and the elders, who hold seven flaming torches that symbolize the seven spirits. All attention focuses on Christ, who now reigns (INTRO I.A.3; I.B.1; Klein, "Apocalypse," 160–62; Kinney, "Apocalypse," 201–7; Christe, "Apocalypse").

During the Reformation of the sixteenth century, Martin Luther (d. 1546) shifted the focus of the passage to emphasize the centrality of proclamation in Christian worship. In his view the elders are teachers of the word, their crowns signify faith, and their harps indicate preaching (LuthW 35:401). For interpreters in the Reformed tradition, however, the vision focused on divine sovereignty, which was theologically central for them. The conviction that God governed the universe encouraged those who suffered to persevere, knowing that God's purposes would be carried out in the end (INTRO I.C.2).

Modern dispensationalists believe that the true church will be taken up, or raptured, to heaven before the seven years of tribulation at the end of this age. They equate Paul's promise that the saints will meet the Lord in the air (1 Thess 4:16–17) with John's visionary ascent into heaven (Rev 4:1). They note that the word "church" is used in Rev 2–3 but then disappears until the end of the book and argue that the church itself will disappear before the end of the age. For them, the elders in the throne room are the raptured saints, who have been removed from earth before the tribulations of the end time (Seiss; Scofield; LaHaye). Criticisms of this approach are that the words "come up here" in 4:1 address John in the singular rather than addressing all the faithful; they introduce a spiritual ascent rather than a bodily one; and John's journey was a temporary visionary experience rather than a definitive move to heaven.

The Four Creatures (4:6–8)

The creatures attending God's throne have the faces of a lion, ox, human being, and eagle. Church tradition identified them with the four gospels and often pictured each one holding a book (Figure 21). Irenaeus initiated this interpretation in the second century

Figure 21. Illustration of Rev 4 from the Bamberg Apocalypse (eleventh century). Courtesy of the Staatsbibliothek Bamberg.

during disputes over which writings were authoritative. His concern was apologetic. He argued that the four creatures showed that the church should recognize four gospels. Others followed his lead, linking each creature to the opening chapter of a gospel. Three major patterns emerged, with the third being the most common:

1. Matthew is the creature with a human face because he begins his gospel with Jesus' human genealogy; Mark is the eagle because he initially quotes the prophets, recalling the prophetic spirit; Luke is the ox, which is a sacrificial animal, because he begins his gospel in the temple; and John has the royal quality of the lion because he

begins with Jesus' glorious origin with the Father (Irenaeus, *Haer.* 3.11.8; Victorinus, *In Apoc.* 4.4; Andreas).

2. Matthew is the lion because the opening genealogy places Jesus in the royal tribe of Judah; Mark has the human face because he shows Jesus' humanity; Luke is the ox, linked to sacrifice; and John is the eagle, who discloses eternal truth (Hippolytus, CSCO 60:6; Augustine, *Cons.* 1.6.1; Augustine, *Tract. ep. Jo.* 36.5.2; Primasius; Bede).

3. Matthew has the human face because he begins his gospel with Jesus' human genealogy; Mark is the lion because he begins with a voice roaring in the desert; Luke is the ox because he begins with offering in the temple; and John is the eagle because of the book's soaring opening lines (Epiphanius, *Mens.* 64d–65a; Jerome, *Comm. Matt.* pref. 1.3; Apringius; Ambrose Autpert; K. Stevenson, "Animal").

Christians in the east sometimes took a different approach, identifying the creatures with the four elements: the lion with fire, the ox with earth, the human with air, and the bird with water (Methodius, *Res.* 2.10.4; Oecumenius), but others followed the tradition of identifying them with the gospels (Andreas).

Joachim of Fiore (d. 1202) identified the creatures with the four senses of Scripture: literal, moral, spiritual, and anagogical. The creatures also signified four events in Christ's life: his birth, passion, resurrection, and ascension. They could be identified with groups within the church as well: apostles, martyrs, doctors, and virgins; or pastors, deacons, confessors, and contemplatives (Kovacs and Rowland, *Revelation*, 66).

In the late nineteenth and early twentieth centuries, some historical critics theorized that the four creatures were astrological symbols, whose eyes represented stars. They argued that each creature was a constellation: the lion is Leo; the ox is Taurus the bull; the human face is Scorpio, which the Babylonians call the scorpion-man; and the eagle is Pegasus, which the Babylonians call the thunderbird (Bousset; Charles; cf. Malina, *On*, 97–100). Other ancient writings mention similar creatures but do not depict them as starry beings (4Q385 4 I, 9; *Apoc. Ab.* 18:1–14). A more promising line of interpretation is that the creatures are the heavenly representatives of the created order, who call every living thing to worship the Creator (Hengstenberg; Düsterdieck) (see the COMMENT).

The Seven Seals (6:1–8:5)

Irenaeus identified the first horsemen on the white horse as Christ (*Haer.* 4.21.3), and those who interpreted Revelation spiritually construed the other riders as threats against Christ's church. The sword of the second rider signifies attacks against body and soul, while the third rider warns of a famine of the Word of God (Tyconius; Primasius), and his black horse is the threat of heresy (Bede; Ambrosius; Beatus; see Lumsden, *And Then*).

The fifth seal was of special concern for interpreters who assumed that the vision gives moral guidance when it pictures martyrs crying out for justice (Rev 6:9–11). Cyprian thought the passage taught Christians not to seek revenge but to wait for God's justice (*Pat.* 21). Tertullian regarded the martyrs' plea for justice as a way to say "your kingdom come" (*Or.* 5). Augustine noted that the cry for justice seemed to fall short of Jesus' command to love one's enemies, yet he concluded that the martyrs were not vindictive but affirmed that God is just (*Enarrat. Ps.* 79.14). Cassiodorus thought the martyrs prayed that the wicked might taste divine vengeance in this life so that they might repent and ultimately be saved (*Explanations of the Psalms* 78:10). For Jerome, the vision of the martyrs calling out to God showed that it was acceptable to ask those who had died to offer petitions on behalf of the living (*Vigil.* 6).

Other interpreters thought the seal visions outlined a series of events. For Victorinus, the seals foretold what would occur at the end of the age, just as Jesus warned that war, famine, and persecution would happen before his return (Matt 24; Mark 13; Luke 21). Yet the seventh seal gives hope, since it brings silence, which signifies eternal rest (Victorinus, *In Apoc.* 6.1–4). Early medieval interpreters sometimes used the seals for catechetical instruction by identifying each one with an event in Christ's life; the seals therefore reinforced a basic understanding of Christ's incarnation, nativity, passion, death, resurrection, glory, and kingdom (Apringius, CCL 107:66; Matter, "Pseudo-Alcuinian"; Gummerlock, *Seven*, 5–7). But the most influential approach was that of Bede, who thought the seals depicted the history of the church in a general way, from the victorious preaching of the apostles under the first seal to heresies symbolized by the seals that followed, until the coming of the Antichrist at the sixth seal, and the seventh seal symbolizing rest (INTRO I.B.1).

Joachim of Fiore went further by identifying the seals with specific events in history. In his view, each seal corresponded to parallel events in the OT and NT, giving a coherent sense of God's action in history. For example, the first seal corresponds to the call of Abraham and Israel's occupation of Canaan as well as to the founding of the church through John the Baptist and the apostles. The conflicts of the second seal are the wars from Joshua to David and the early church's conflict with paganism. For Joachim, history was approaching the cosmic change depicted by the sixth seal, which would bring the present age to an end (INTRO I.C.3; Gummerlock, *Seven*, 18–20, 55–60).

Influenced by Joachim's ideas, some Franciscans thought that controversies over church reform in the thirteenth century confirmed that time had indeed advanced to the sixth seal, but papal criticism of this apocalyptic perspective led other Franciscans to relegate the seal visions more safely to the past. For Nicholas of Lyra (d. 1349), the seals showed how God's purposes were worked out over time, beginning with the success of the apostles' preaching, symbolized by the victorious rider at the first seal. Subsequent seals signified the church's endurance through persecution and war under Nero, Vespasian and Titus, Domitian, Trajan, and Diocletian, until the Christian empire of Constantine is established at the seventh seal (INTRO I.B.4; cf. Krey, "Apocalypse," 273).

Later, many Protestants found this approach theologically valuable, since it affirmed that history—despite the presence of conflict and heresy—was ultimately governed by providence (Mede, *Clauis*, 74–110). Rather than identifying the seal visions with periods leading up to Constantine, some interpreters extended the time span in order to critique later church practices. The deadly plague under the fourth seal was said to be monasticism, the papacy, or Islam; the martyrs of the fifth seal were those who suffered during the late medieval period; and the cosmic change of the sixth seal was the revival of the gospel under John Wyclif in the fourteenth century (Kovacs and Rowland, *Revelation*, 82–83). Others thought the seals related more generally to the church's suffering throughout the ages (Geneva Bible).

Modern futuristic interpretation assumes that the seals predict events that will occur during the seven-year tribulation at the end of the age. In this scenario the threats
symbolized by the horsemen unfold in a clear sequence, beginning with war, which
leads to the civil strife that produces economic hardship, and culminates in famine and
disease. After the seal plagues are over, the trumpet plagues begin (Rev 8–9), and only
then do the events predicted by the bowl plagues take place (Rev 16; Seiss; Scofield).
Objections to this approach include the fact that it overlooks the repetitive quality of
the three plague sequences and does not give due weight to the pattern of interrupted
judgments or the significance of the imagery for first-century readers.

The 144,000 (Rev 7:4–8)

Between the sixth and seventh seals, John hears that 12,000 people from each of the
twelve tribes of Israel receive God's seal on their foreheads, making a total of 144,000
(7:4–8), and then he sees a countless multitude from every tribe and nation (7:9). Later,
John sees 144,000 with the Lamb on Mount Zion (14:1–5). The group's identity has
been understood in at least three ways:

1. Jewish Christians. Oecumenius related them to the past, as the Jewish Christians
   who escaped the fall of Jerusalem in 70 CE. Most ancient interpreters, however,
   thought they signified the ethnic Jews who would accept the Christian faith at the
   end of the age (Irenaeus, *Haer.* 5.30.2; Augustine, *Ep.* 121; Augustine, *Serm.* 248.3;
   Jerome, *Hom. Mark* 82). Dispensationalists expect them to be a specific group of
   Jews who will convert to Christianity during the seven-year period of tribulation and
   serve as evangelists (Scofield; LaHaye).

2. The church. Origen referred to the 144,000 as the whole church, consisting of those
   Gentile believers who bear the name of God and Christ and are Jewish in a spiritual
   sense (*Comm. Jo.* 1.2–8). The group consists of all who belong to Israel through faith
   (Primasius; Bede; Cassiodorus; cf. Augustine, *Doctr. chr.* 3.35.51). Other interpreters regard them as one part of the church. Since they are called maidens, or virgins
   (*parthenoi*), in 14:1, some think they exemplify the virtue of virginity (Methodius,
   Symp. 1.5; 6.5). Still others suggest that the seal they receive is martyrdom, so the
   group consists of those who die for the faith, in contrast to the great multitude of
   Christians who are not martyrs (Caird; Yarbro Collins).

3. The elect of the final age. In the thirteenth century, Francis of Assisi was identified
   as the angel of Rev 7:2, whose "seal" consisted of the stigmata, or wounds, of Christ
   that Francis bore on his body. Ubertino of Casale (d. 1329) thought the 144,000
   were the Spiritual Franciscans, who were being gathered in order to follow the Lamb
   in perfect purity and contemplation (14:1–5; Beirich, "Franciscan," 66–70). For Melchior Hoffmann (d. ca. 1543 or 1544) the angel with the seal was not Francis, but
   the Bohemian reformer Jan Hus (d. 1415), who heralded the new age. Hoffmann
   and others in the Anabaptist movement thought their role was to gather the 144,000
   true believers before the imminent end of the age (INTRO I.C.3). Later, the Jehovah's
   Witnesses thought the 144,000 were a special group that would serve as priests and
   kings in heaven. Initially, they thought the 144,000 would be gathered before 1914,
   when the kingdom of God was to arrive. Yet they continued their evangelistic efforts
   after that date because they expected the great multitude of the redeemed to rule
   with Christ on earth (INTRO I.D.2).

The COMMENT section below takes the 144,000 and great multitude as two perspectives on the whole people of God. When read together with the seals, this vision offers hope in the face of threatening forces.

B. LITERARY STRUCTURE

The seven seals constitute the second major block of visions in Revelation. The cycle begins in the heavenly court, where God holds a scroll that is sealed with seven seals. The opening of the seven seals creates the overall structure of the section. The basic pattern of visions is 4 + 2 (interlude) + 1, which is also the case in the trumpet cycle that follows. The first four seal visions occur rapidly, and then the fifth and sixth are told at greater length. John stretches out the action by picturing the martyrs crying out and disasters striking the sun, moon, and stars. Terror seizes every social class until all cry out, "Who is able to stand?" (6:17). At that point the movement toward God's final catastrophic judgment is interrupted by a vision that answers this question: Those redeemed by the Lamb can "stand" before God (7:9).

A vision of the redeemed is placed between the opening of the sixth and seventh seals, as an angel intrudes to hold back the threatening forces (7:1–17). Where the Lamb has opened seals (*sphragis*) that reveal danger, the angel brings the seal (*sphragis*) that provides protection (6:1; 7:1–3). Some interpreters argue that the vision of redemption is part of the sixth seal (Biguzzi, *Settinari*, 134–46; Ulfgard, *Feast*, 32–33; Steinmann, "Tripartite"), but this interpretation is unlikely. The disruptive elements make it a section in its own right, variously called an interlude (Boxall; Mounce; Murphy; Osborne; Reddish; Schüssler Fiorenza), an intermission (Blount), an interval (Smalley), a parenthesis (Beale; Prigent), an interruption (Lambrecht, "Opening," 215–17), or a digression (Perry, *Rhetoric*, 53–79).

Rhetorically, this interlude functions like a digression in a speech. During a digression a speaker departs from the sequence of argument to call attention to something important and to make an emotional appeal (Cicero, *Inv.* 1.51.97; Cicero, *De orat.* 2.77.311). A digression can be one of the most important parts of a speech. Revelation was written for oral delivery (Rev 1:3), and the interludes in chapters 7 and 10–11 capture the hearers' attention with their unexpected shifts in focus. The interludes enhance the book's emotional appeal. The first six seal visions awaken fear, but the interlude offers a hope for salvation, inviting confidence, which is the opposite of fear (Aristotle, *Rhet.* 2.5.1, 16; Perry, *Rhetoric*, 143–44).

One function of the interlude is to *create* delay by disrupting the seemingly inexorable movement toward God's judgment. Readers know that God's scroll has seven seals, and by counting as the Lamb opens each seal, John gives the impression that God's judgments are relentlessly unfolding. Intensity is heightened when the martyrs ask "how long" God will delay bringing justice to the people of earth, and when the sun becomes black as sackcloth, it would appear that the end has come. But the end does not come. As soon as humanity asks, "Who is able to stand?," an angel interrupts to hold back the forces of destruction. Readers may have thought that they knew the end would arrive right after the sixth seal, but it does not.

Having created delay, the second literary function of the interlude is to *interpret* it. The martyrs have asked "how long" God will delay bringing justice, but they are told to rest for a short time while others complete their witness (6:9–11). The interlude does not explain "how long" the delay will be. Instead, it discloses the meaning of the delay by showing that it provides temporal space for people to be sealed or claimed for God before the final judgment. This scene places the question of justice within the context of God's wider purpose, which is the redemption of people from every tribe and nation (7:9–17).

When the seventh seal is opened, there is silence in heaven, creating the context for prayer in 8:1–5 (Prigent; Lambrecht, "Opening," 212–14). The martyrs cried out to God from the altar at the fifth seal, and the seventh seal show the prayers of the saints again rising up at the altar (de Villiers, "Role," 135–36). What complicates the pattern is that in between the onset of silence and the offering of prayers, John sees seven angels receive seven trumpets, introducing the vision series that will begin immediately after the prayers have been made (Rev 8:2, 6).

The way the seventh seal vision overlaps and interlocks with the first trumpet vision shows that the two vision cycles must be taken together. The prayers that conclude the seal visions are the reason for the trumpet visions that follow (Schüssler Fiorenza, *Book*, 172–73; Yarbro Collins, *Combat*, 16–19; Yarbro Collins, *Crisis*, 112–14; de Villiers, "Eschatological"; Stefanovic, "Angel"). The effect will be surprising, since the trumpet plagues will show that if God responds to the plea for justice with only wrath, nothing changes. People will not repent (Rev 9:20–21). That is why the next interlude will show that at present God has delayed his judgment so that the Christian community might continue bearing witness to the world (10:1–11:14).

C. THE SEALS AND THE SYNOPTIC APOCALYPSE

All three cycles of plagues in the Apocalypse reflect the idea that before the end of the age the world will suffer affliction (6:1–17; 8:2–9:21; 16:1–21). This idea is evident in Dan 12:1, which says that the close of the age will be a time of unprecedented tribulation. The tradition appears in various Jewish sources (*2 Bar.* 26:1–27:15; *T. Mos.* 8:1; *4 Ezra* 5:1–12; 13:16–19, 31; 1QM I, 11–12; XV, 1; cf. *Jub.* 23:22–25) and early Christian sources (Mark 13:7–19; Matt 24:6–28; *Did.* 16:3–5; Herm. *Vis.* 2.2.7; 4.1.1; 4.2.5; 4.3.6). The eschatological afflictions could be enumerated as in *2 Bar.* 25:1–30:5, which lists war, famine, earthquakes, demonic appearances, fire, and rape. These afflictions are followed by the end of the age and the advent of the Messiah.

The Synoptic Gospels envision troubles occurring at the end of the age, some of which are listed in a sequence similar to that found in Rev 6:1–17. The most striking similarities are shown in Table 3. Given such similarities, some interpreters suggest that John relied on the gospels in writing Revelation (Charles 1:158–60), though the variations make it more likely that he knew a tradition like that of the gospels but did not rely directly on the gospel texts (Court, *Myth*, 43–54; Boxall; Reddish; Witherington). Revelation lacks the gospels' narrative context, and many of the afflictions mentioned in the Synoptic Gospels occur in other lists of eschatological woes. Moreover, Revelation depicts the afflictions through an expanded use of OT imagery, including the visions of horses in Zech 1:8–11 and 6:1–8; the prophetic warnings about war, famine, and pestilence (Jer 14:12; 21:7; Ezek 5:17; 6:11); and the kinds of cosmic signs found in the prophets (NOTES on Rev 6:12–14).

Table 3. Troubles at the End of the Age in the Synoptic Gospels and Revelation

Matt 24:6–9, 29–31	*Mark 13:7–9, 24–25*
1. Wars	1. Wars
2. Violent conflict between nations	2. Violent conflict between nations
3. Famine	3. Earthquakes
4. Earthquakes	4. Famine
5. Persecutions	5. Persecutions
6. Heavenly signs (sun and moon darkened, stars fall, powers of heaven shaken)	6. Heavenly signs (sun and moon darkened, stars fall, powers of heaven shaken)
7. Son of Man comes on clouds	7. Son of Man comes on clouds

Luke 21:9–12, 25–26	*Rev 6:1–8:1–5*
1. Wars	1. Wars of conquest
2. Violent conflict between nations	2. Violent conflict between people
3. Earthquakes	3. Famine (grain shortage)
4. Famine	4. Violence, famine, disease, wild animals
5. Disease	5. Persecutions
6. Persecutions	6. Heavenly signs (sun darkened, moon to blood, stars fall, earth shaken)
7. Heavenly signs (signs in sun, moon, stars; roaring sea; people afraid; powers of heaven shaken)	7. Threats interrupted: Vision of redemption
8. Son of Man comes in a cloud	8. Heavenly silence and prayer

John's use of such traditions contributes to his communication with readers in at least two ways. First, the seal visions reaffirm what some readers already hold to be true. For those familiar with traditions like those in the gospels and the prophetic writings on which they draw, John's message would be plausible. The message was not a completely new or unprecedented revelation. Second, John challenges the established patterns by interrupting the sequence before it is complete. The apocalyptic passages in the gospels culminate with cosmic signs that lead directly to the coming of the Son of Man, but in Revelation the end does not arrive as anticipated. Rather than signaling the end, John's use of traditional imagery raises expectations of the end that are not realized. His vision of the redemption that must occur during the delay is a distinctive emphasis in the seal visions.

13. The Heavenly Throne Room (4:1–11)

4   ¹After these things I looked, and there was a door that had been opened in heaven. And the first voice that I heard speaking with me like a trumpet said, "Come up here and I will show you what must take place after these things." ²At once I was in the Spirit, and there in heaven was a throne, and someone was seated on the throne. ³The one seated there looked like jasper and carnelian, and around the throne was a rainbow that looked like an emerald. ⁴Around the throne were twenty-four thrones and seated on the thrones were twenty-four

elders, clothed in white robes with gold laurel wreaths on their heads. ⁵From the throne came flashes of lightning and rumblings and peals of thunder, and in front of the throne were seven flaming torches, which are the seven spirits of God. ⁶And in front of the throne was something like a sea of glass, like crystal. In the middle by the throne, in a circle around the throne, were four living creatures that were covered with eyes on the front and on the back. ⁷The first living creature was like a lion, the second living creature was like an ox, the third living creature had a face like a human being, and the fourth living creature was like an eagle in flight. ⁸Each of the four living creatures had six wings, and they were covered all around and inside with eyes. They never rest, day and night, saying,

"Holy, holy, holy is the Lord God Almighty,
who was and who is and who is to come."

⁹Whenever the living creatures give glory and honor and thanks to the one seated on the throne, who lives forever and ever, ¹⁰the twenty-four elders fall before the one seated on the throne and worship the one who lives forever and ever. They throw their laurel wreaths down before the throne and say,

¹¹"You are worthy, our Lord and God, to receive glory and honor and power,
for you created all things and by your will they existed and were created."

NOTES

4:1. *After these things I looked, and there was a door that had been opened in heaven.* Revelation's throne room scene recalls the opening chapter of Ezekiel, in which "the heavens opened" and the prophet saw God's throne and gemlike presence (Ezek 1:1). Revelation describes the moment as "a door" being opened (Gen 28:10–17; *1 En.* 14:15–25; *T. Levi* 5:1; 4Q213a 1 II, 15–18; 3 Macc 6:18). Some writings envisioned multiple doors in heaven (*3 Bar.* 2:2; 3:1; 4Q405 23 I, 7–10; 3), but Revelation mentions only one. Christ placed an open door before the Philadelphians, assuring them of access to God (Rev 3:7–8), and John now goes through an open door to reveal what the divine presence entails.

And the first voice that I heard speaking with me like a trumpet. The voice belongs to the exalted Jesus, who spoke in 1:10–11. What follows fits the pattern announced in the preface: It is a "revelation from Jesus Christ" (1:1).

"Come up here and I will show you what must take place after these things." Jewish and early Christian sources tell of people being called to embark on a visionary journey, and John fits this tradition (*1 En.* 14:8–9; *T. Levi* 2:6–5:7; 4Q213a 1 II, 18; *Mart. Asc. Isa.* 7:2–6). The language also resembles that in Dan 2:45, which depicts a series of earthly kingdoms giving way to the kingdom of God. To say things must (*dei*) take place indicates that God's purposes will be carried out, but Revelation leaves room for contingencies—such as repentance and refusals to repent—in the way God accomplishes his work (NOTES and COMMENT on 1:1).

4:2. *At once I was in the Spirit.* John's journey is a spiritual or visionary one, which occurs through God's Spirit (NOTE on Rev 1:10). John was already "in the Spirit" on Patmos (1:10), but repeating this expression here signals a change to a heavenly setting;

and later, John being shown Babylon and New Jerusalem (17:3; 21:10) will mark new phases of revelation. John portrays himself like Ezekiel, who was moved through stages of a vision by the Spirit (Ezek 8:3–4; 11:5). Some seers told of traveling through multiple levels of heaven, where there were structures of hail, snow, and fire (*1 En.* 14:8–17; *Mart. Asc. Isa.* 7:1–9:18), but John turns directly to the throne of God, which is his focus (cf. 2 Cor 12:1–10).

and there in heaven was a throne, and someone was seated on the throne. Israel's tradition told of God's throne in heaven (Pss 11:4; 103:19), where God is surrounded by a heavenly council (1 Kgs 22:19). Isaiah says that the throne is high and lofty and that six-winged seraphs declare God's holiness (Isa 6:1–3). Ezekiel describes a sapphire throne chariot drawn by creatures, each with faces of a lion, ox, eagle, and human being. God appears in fiery splendor, surrounded by a rainbow with a crystalline sea beneath him (Ezek 1:4–28). The fiery throne in Dan 7:9–10 also has wheels. God has white hair and robes. Around his throne are thrones for a heavenly court, and beyond them are countless other heavenly beings (cf. 4Q530 II, 17).

Later Jewish texts combined and varied these biblical scenes. In *1 En.* 14:18–22 the throne is wheeled and lofty and looks like ice, but fire comes from it. God wears a white robe and is attended by a vast company. In *Apoc. Ab.* 18:3–14 the throne is also wheeled and fiery. It is attended by four creatures, each with many eyes, four heads, and sixteen faces like those in Ezekiel. They have six wings like the seraphs in Isaiah. The *Songs of the Sabbath Sacrifice* from Qumran refers to a celestial throne that is wheeled, glorious, fiery, and surrounded by rainbowlike splendor. Around it heavenly beings offer praise (4Q405 20–22 8–11). Some of these elements also occur in Rev 4, although the elders play a distinctive role.

4:3. *The one seated there looked like jasper and carnelian, and around the throne was a rainbow that looked like an emerald.* Jasper referred to precious stones ranging from green to blue, purple to rose (Pliny the Elder, *Nat.* 37.115–18). Carnelian was a reddish stone, which suggests that God's presence had a fiery radiance as in Ezek 1:27. New Jerusalem, which reflects God's glory, also has traits of jasper and carnelian (Rev 21:11, 18–20). The rainbow is reminiscent of Ezek 1:28, but rather than stressing its varied colors (4Q405 20 II, 11), John compares it to a bright green emerald, emphasizing splendor. Some interpreters suggest that the rainbow recalls that after the flood God placed his bow in the sky as a sign that he would never again destroy the earth by water (Gen 9:13; Beale; Murphy). However, connections with the flood are not developed here or in Rev 10:1, where a rainbow adorns an angel.

4:4. *Around the throne were twenty-four thrones.* Revelation uses multiples of twelve in visions that depict the whole people of God. The number twenty-four suggests that the elders are heavenly representatives of God's people (see COMMENT). Some interpreters maintain that the number has more specific significance, though the referents suggested are unlikely:

1. Groups of people.
   (a) Tribes and apostles: The New Jerusalem has gates named for the twelve tribes and foundations named for the twelve apostles, so the twenty-four elders could signify both groups (21:12–14; Beale). This is possible, but it was not typical for Israelite

tribes to be identified by a single "elder" (R. A. Campbell, *Elders*, 25), and early Christians distinguished apostles from elders (Acts 15:2; 16:4). It is not clear why the two groups together would be called elders.

(b) Priestly groups: Twenty-four groups of priests and Levitical musicians served in the temple. Some interpreters suggest that the elders are the heavenly counterparts to the earthly priesthood (1 Chr 24:7–19; 25:1–31; Aune; Harrington; Keener). However, Revelation's elders do not have a distinctive priestly role. They offer prayers, but so do the four creatures and angels (Rev 5:8; 8:3); they offer praises, but so do other beings in heaven, earth, and the sea (5:11–14). Moreover, Israel's priests did not wear victory wreaths or sit on thrones, as the elders do. Instead, they ministered while standing (Deut 10:8; 2 Chr 29:11; Heb 10:11). Some priests were included among Jewish elders (Luke 22:66), but elders were also distinguished from priests (Deut 31:9; 1 Macc 7:33; Mark 8:31; 1QS VI, 8).

(c) Witness of Scripture: Some interpreters noted that there were twenty-four books in the Hebrew Bible (*4 Ezra* 14:45) and twenty-four biblical prophets (*Liv. Pro.*; *Gos. Thom.* 52), so the twenty-four elders could represent Scripture (Victorinus; Prigent). However, others thought the Hebrew Bible had only twenty-two books (Josephus, *Ag. Ap.* 1.39). The words of the elders convey biblical themes, but so do the words of other heavenly beings. There is no reason to think this number distinctively represents biblical books or prophets.

(d) Attendants of the emperor: Roman consuls usually appeared with twelve *lictores*, or attendants, whereas dictators and the emperor Domitian had twenty-four (Dio Cassius, *Rom. Hist.* 67.4.3). Therefore, the elders could contrast the attendants of God with those of the emperor (Aune). The problem is that *lictores* did not sit on thrones or wear white robes and wreaths. They walked ahead of a magistrate carrying axes protruding from bundles of rods. Domitian was sometimes accompanied by priests, but it is not clear that they were twenty-four in number (Suetonius, *Dom.* 4.4). The singers in the imperial cult wore wreaths, and there may have been twenty-four of them at Smyrna (I.Smyr 594.3); but the groups of singers varied in size, making it unlikely that this determined the number of elders in Revelation (Friesen, *Imperial*, 110).

2. Cosmic order. The Babylonians spoke of twenty-four celestial bodies, half of which were the judges of the universe (Diodorus Siculus, *Libr.* 2.31.4), and some writers referred to heavenly powers as "elders" (*2 En.* 4:1). Accordingly, some interpreters propose that the vision of the heavenly elders shows cosmic harmony (Malina, *On*, 93–97; Murphy; Yarbro Collins, *Cosmology*, 128–29). However, astral powers varied in number from twenty-four to seventy-two. Also, the functions of the elders do not correspond to those of the twenty-four heavenly powers; for example, the elders do not serve as judges in Revelation.

3. Time. There are twenty-four hours in the day and night, and twelve months in the year (John 11:9; Rev 22:2). Accordingly, some interpreters relate the number to the continual praise offered by the elders (4:8–11; Giesen; Roloff). Although this is suggestive, it cannot be pressed because the four living creatures also offer continual praise. The number twenty-four can best be related to the multiples of twelve that are used for God's people (see COMMENT).

and seated on the thrones were twenty-four elders. The elders are heavenly figures with several functions. First, they show readers the future glory of the faithful because they sit on thrones, wear white robes, and wear head wreaths—all of which were promised to believers (2:10; 3:5, 21; 4:4). Second, they exemplify true worship. They worship God with songs and harps beside a glassy sea, until all creation joins in praise (4:6–11; 5:8–14). Later, the redeemed follow their example by singing praise beside the glassy sea with harps (15:2–4) while the elders add their affirmation (7:9–12; 11:15–18; 19:1–4). Third, they interpret visions. An elder explains the identity of the Lion of Judah and multitude in white (5:5; 7:13–14). Elsewhere, they disclose the meaning of visions through hymns about the Creator and his coming conflict with the destroyers of the earth (4:10–11; 11:16–18). In such cases they function like the chorus in a Greek drama (Harsh, *Handbook*, 17–23).

The term *presbyteros*, or elder, was used for leaders among the families, tribes, and cities of Israel (Judg 11:5–11; Ruth 4:1–4; 1 Sam 16:4; 30:26; Isa 3:14; 1 Macc 13:36; Luke 7:3). Elders did not necessarily hold specific offices but were recognized as a group whose counsel was valued. Under Roman rule elders functioned at both local and national levels of Jewish life, as well as in synagogues (Luke 7:3; Acts 4:4; *CIJ* 1404.9–10). In the congregations of Jesus' followers, the elders' responsibilities included teaching, preaching, and dealing with issues such as hospitality and monetary gifts (1 Pet 5:1–2; Acts 11:30; 14:23; 20:17, 28; 1 Tim 5:17; Tit 1:5–9; 2 John 1; 3 John 1; *2 Clem.* 17:3, 5; Ign. *Magn.* 6:1; Herm. *Vis.* 2.4.3; R. A. Campbell, *Elders*). In Revelation the heavenly elders are in positions of honor, offering instruction by interpreting visions, and leading by example in worship.

The related terms *presbeus* and *presbeutēs* were used for people with seniority who served as a delegation or embassy (*presbeia*) to a ruler. Sometimes they wore wreaths and white robes. During the Hellenistic period, "Embassies [*presbeiai*] . . . came from Greece, and their envoys [*presbeis*] themselves crowned, came forward and crowned Alexander with gold crowns" (Arrian, *Anabasis* 7.23). During the imperial age, "Italian cities sent delegations [*presbeias*] of their prominent citizens, dressed in white, wearing laurel wreaths and all bringing with them . . . gold crowns" to greet the emperor (Herodian, *Historiae* 8.7.2; cf. Josephus, *J.W.* 4.620). The elders in Revelation follow the pattern in their attire and in honoring the sovereign with gold wreaths, though they differ in that they are seated around God's throne rather than approaching it as a delegation.

Interpreters debate about whether the elders are angels (Charles; Giesen) or human beings (Harrington; Prigent). But this way of framing the question is problematic, since the elders' role is distinctive. On the one hand, visions of God's throne room typically include angels who wear white (Rev 15:6; Matt 28:3), offer prayers, and interpret visions as the elders here do (Rev 5:8; 7:13–14; cf. 8:3–4; 17:7; Tob 12:12, 15). Daniel pictures a heavenly court seated on thrones around God's throne (Dan 7:9–10), but Revelation distinguishes elders from angels, who typically stand (Rev 5:8–14; 7:11; 8:2; cf. *4 Ezra* 8:21). On the other hand, the elders are like glorified human beings, who have the white robes, wreaths, and thrones promised to the faithful (Rev 2:10; 3:4–5, 11, 18; 6:11; 7:9; cf. 1QS IV, 7–8; *Mart. Asc. Isa.* 7:22; *1 En.* 108:2; *T. Job* 33:2–3; *Apoc. El.* 1:8). This does not mean that they are human in origin, however, since Revelation assumes that these rewards will be given to people at the end of the age through resurrection. A saying of

Jesus tells of the twelve disciples sitting on thrones as judges over Israel (Matt 19:28; Luke 22:30), but the elders in Revelation do not serve as judges here or elsewhere (see also the Note on Rev 20:4). The elders do not fit standard categories. Their importance can best be understood by focusing on the literary functions noted above.

clothed in white robes with gold laurel wreaths on their heads. White was widely thought to be suitable for God or the gods and for those who worshiped them. White robes connote purity, holiness, and honor. They are worn by angelic beings and the people who come into God's presence through resurrection (Note on 3:5; cf. 3:18). Laurel wreaths were traditionally given to those who won victory in battle or athletic contests, as well as to civic benefactors. The most valuable wreaths were made of gold. Wreath imagery often signified the honor God would give the faithful through resurrection (Note on 2:10). The faithful could hope for "a crown of glory with majestic raiment in eternal light" (1QS IV, 7–8). The elders in Revelation are dressed this way, showing that those in the earthly community can hope for a similar place in the heavenly circle.

4:5. *From the throne came flashes of lightning and rumblings and peals of thunder.* Storms convey the fearsome quality of divine power in Revelation (8:5; 11:19; 16:18), Jewish tradition (Pss 18:14; 77:18), and Greco-Roman sources (Homer, *Il.* 7.443). Lightning and rumbling signaled God's presence at Mount Sinai (Exod 19:16; *L.A.B.* 11:4–5) and in Ezekiel's vision (Ezek 1:4–14, 28; cf. *1 En.* 14:17; *Apoc. Ab.* 18:2).

and in front of the throne were seven flaming torches, which are the seven spirits of God. The imagery is reminiscent of Ezekiel, where a spirit moved the four creatures that attended God's throne as flaming lamps appeared (Ezek 1:12–13; 4Q385 1 12–13). In Revelation the spirits and flaming lamps are identical (cf. 4Q405 20 II, 9–10). These spirits are angelic beings, depicted as flames (Note on Rev 1:4; Ps 104:4; *2 Bar.* 21:6; *4 Ezra* 8:21). Identifying seven spirits as torches may recall that seven burning lamps stood in Israel's tabernacle and second temple, illuminating the court in front of the holy of holies where God was enthroned (Exod 27:21: Lev 24:2–4; Josephus, *J.W.* 5.217; cf. Zech 4:2). In Rev 5:6 the seven spirits become the seven eyes of the Lamb.

4:6. *In front of the throne was something like a sea of glass, like crystal.* At creation God was said to have established a dome over the earth. Above the dome were the waters of heaven, and beyond this was God's throne or dwelling place (Gen 1:6–7; Pss 104:2–3; 148:4; *1 En.* 54:7). Ezekiel said the dome, or firmament, looked like crystal beneath the throne of God (Ezek 1:22, 26; cf. *1 En.* 4:2; *2 En.* 4:2). At Mount Sinai, God had a pavement of clear blue sapphire below him (Exod 24:10). In Rev 15:2 the faithful gather around the sea of glass (Böttrich, "Das 'gläserne'").

In the middle by the throne, in a circle around the throne, were four living creatures that were covered with eyes on the front and on the back. The four living creatures are heavenly intermediaries who have two principal roles. First, they exemplify true worship (Rev 4:8–9). They sometimes initiate worship and are joined by the twenty-four elders in offering praise and prayers of petition before God (4:9–10; 5:8–10). They add "amen" to the worship offered by angels and the whole creation (5:14; 19:4), and they remain beside the throne as the redeemed join in praise (7:11; 14:3). Second, they summon divine threats against the earth. As the Lamb opens each of the first four seals on God's scroll, one of the living creatures calls out "come," and a horseman appears, threatening conquest, violence, economic hardship, and death (6:1–8). Later, one of the four creatures gives bowls of wrath to the angels, who pour them out onto the earth (19:7).

The Greek text literally says that the creatures are "in the middle of the throne and around the throne." The translation given above assumes that the second phrase describes the first phrase, so that "in the middle of the throne" is defined as being "around the throne" (cf. 7:11; 19:4). For other interpretations, see R. Hall, "Living."

4:7. *The first living creature was like a lion, the second living creature was like an ox, the third living creature had a face like a human being, and the fourth living creature was like an eagle in flight.* The four creatures resemble those attending God's throne chariot in Ezek 1:4–10, but with some changes. In Ezekiel each creature has four faces—that of a person, a lion, an ox, and an eagle—whereas in Revelation each has only one face. In Ezekiel each creature has four wings, and many eyes cover the wheels of God's throne chariot (1:18; 10:12), but in Revelation the creatures have six wings and are themselves covered with eyes, suggesting watchfulness (NOTE on Rev 4:8). In Ezekiel the four creatures are under God's throne (1:22, 26), whereas in Revelation they are beside it, allowing them to serve as exemplars of worship. Revelation also differs from the Qumran version, which follows Ezekiel (4Q385 4 8–9; Ego, "Reduktion"), and from *Apoc. Ab.* 18:3–7, where the four creatures each have sixteen faces. In Christian tradition the four creatures were often identified with the four gospels (see §12A). In the COMMENT below they are construed as representatives of creation.

4:8. *Each of the four living creatures had six wings, and they were covered all around and inside with eyes.* The six wings are reminiscent of the heavenly beings in Isa 6:2–3. Earlier, in Rev 4:6, the living creatures were said to be covered with eyes on the front and the back, and here they have eyes outside and inside. The descriptions suggest that they see in all directions and keep watch continuously, like the "sleepless ones who guard the throne of his glory" (*1 En.* 71:7; cf. 39:12–13; 61:12).

They never rest day and night, saying, "Holy, holy, holy is the Lord God Almighty. By declaring "holy" three times, the creatures identify God as supremely holy. Their praises recall those of the angelic hosts in Isa 6:3, who said, "Holy, holy, holy is the Lord of hosts" (Hebrew, *ṣābāʾôt*), which in Revelation is "Almighty" (*pantokratōr*) (NOTE on Rev 1:8). But where Isaiah says "the whole earth is full of his glory," Revelation says "who was and who is and who is to come," emphasizing God's past and present existence and future coming, which indicate true deity (NOTE on 1:4).

Some interpreters suggest that acclaiming God's holiness three times echoes Jewish or early Christian liturgical practice (Prigent), though early texts cite the "holy, holy, holy" when referring to angelic rather than human praise (*1 En.* 39:12–13; *1 Clem.* 34:6; *T. Adam* 1:4; *Mart. Perp.* 12:1; cf. *Apoc. Ab.* 16:3; 18:14; *T. Ab.* 3:3). By the second and third centuries CE the threefold "holy" was used in human prayer, and it became an element in Jewish and Christian liturgies (*4 Bar.* 9:3; *t. Ber.* 1:9; Tertullian, *Or.* 3; *Apost. Const.* 8.12.27; Schimanowski, *Die himmlische*, 131–41). Nevertheless, it is not clear that this practice was common when the Apocalypse was composed. The writer probably draws the formula from Isaiah and other sources that associate it with angelic praise (Aune).

"who was and who is and who is to come." See the NOTE on 1:4.

4:9. *Whenever the living creatures give glory and honor and thanks to the one seated on the throne, who lives forever and ever.* Calling God "the one who lives forever" underscores his true deity and sovereignty (Dan 4:34; 12:7; Sir 18:1; Rev 1:4). The verbs now shift to the future tense, which some interpreters suggest anticipates the worship offered by the heavenly company in 5:8 or 5:12–14 (Mussies, *Morphology*, 342–47;

Aune; Beale; Rowland). It is more likely, however, that John understands the heavenly praise to be a present activity that continues into the future "without ceasing" (4:8; MHT 3:86; Zerwick, *Biblical* §281).

4:10. *the twenty-four elders fall before the one seated on the throne and worship the one who lives forever and ever.* The elders prostrate themselves, which was sometimes done in the Jerusalem temple (2 Chr 20:18; 29:30; 1 Esd 9:47; 1 Macc 4:55; *m. Shek.* 6:3; *m. Midd.* 2:3) and on other occasions for Jewish prayer (Jdt 6:18; 9:1; *L.A.B.* 4:5). It could characterize angelic worship in heaven (4Q405 20–22 II, 7) and may have been an extraordinary gesture in Christian gatherings (1 Cor 14:25), because Jews and Christians often prayed while standing (Matt 6:5; Mark 11:25; Luke 18:11; *m. Ber.* 2:2) or kneeling (Dan 6:10; Acts 20:36; 21:5; Eph 3:14).

They throw their laurel wreaths down before the throne. In Greco-Roman worship, wreaths were sometimes placed at the feet of the statues of the gods (Propertius, *Elegies* 2.10.21–26). Gold wreaths were also given to generals, kings, and emperors. Civic delegations presented gold wreaths to the Roman conqueror Pompey, and the king of Parthia honored Titus with a gold wreath after his victory over the Jews (Josephus, *Ant.* 14.35; Josephus, *J.W.* 7.105). Roman emperors received gold wreaths upon accession to the throne and after victories, and such gifts were given to them by the cities of Asia (Millar, *Emperor*, 140–43, 410–11; Tacitus, *Ann.* 2.57; Livy, *Rom. Hist.* 37.46.4; 38.37.14). In some instances the members of a delegation, or *presbeia*, continued to wear wreaths while offering additional wreaths to a conqueror or ruler (Arrian, *Anabasis* 7.23.2; Herodian, *Historiae* 8.7.2), but a vassal king might remove the crown from his head and place it before the statue of the emperor to indicate subordination (Tacitus, *Ann.* 15.29). When cosmic war breaks out, Satan the dragon doggedly clings to his crowns as he is driven out of heaven, while the twenty-four elders willingly surrender theirs to God and remain in heaven (Rev 4:10; 12:7–9).

4:11. *You are worthy.* Gifts of gold wreaths given to a victor were sometimes accompanied by songs (Plutarch, *Aem.* 34.5–7). A ruler was "worthy" when the power and honor he received were commensurate with his deeds (Pliny the Younger, *Pan.* 4.4–5). One could legitimately say to the emperor, "You are worthy of power," when his position was used for the good of others (Martial, *Epigrams* 10.34.5; cf. Wis 9:12). The opposite was a tyrant, who received power and honor that he did not merit. In Revelation, God is "worthy" because he created all things (4:11) and Christ is "worthy" because of his redemptive suffering and death (5:9, 12).

our Lord and God, to receive glory and honor and power. Forms of the title "Lord God" are often used for God in Revelation, the LXX, and Jewish sources (NOTE on 1:8). The same sources occasionally include a conjunction to read "Lord *and* God" (Philo, *Somn.* 1.159–60; Philo, *Her.* 22) or "my God *and* my Lord" (Ps 35:23 [34:23 LXX]; cf. Jdt 5:21; Tob 13:4). Interpreters note that this form of the title may be Revelation's way of asserting the claims of God against those of the emperor (Charles; Müller; Roloff). This idea is often linked specifically to Domitian. Although the Senate was supposed to formally deify an emperor only after his death, Domitian is said to have departed from traditional practice by forcing others to call him "lord and god" (*dominus et deus*) during his lifetime (Suetonius, *Dom.* 13.2). However, the issue needs to be nuanced in three ways. First, using these titles for rulers was not unusual. In the first century BCE Hellenistic rulers could be called "god and lord" (BGU 1764.8; 1789.3).

This dual title was used for Augustus during his lifetime (P.Oxy. 1143), and participants in the imperial cult at Pergamum and elsewhere called Augustus "god." In the mid-first century, Gaius apparently wanted to be known as "lord" and "god" (Josephus, *J.W.* 2.184; Philo, *Legat.* 286, 356). Both titles were used separately by those honoring Nero and Vespasian (F. Parker, "'Our,'" 215–17).

Second, Suetonius said that Domitian insisted that the titles be used for him in speech and in writing (*Dom.* 13.2). Nevertheless, coins and inscriptions from Domitian's reign do not make use of these titles. Not even the inscriptions on the imperial temple at Ephesus, which was dedicated to Domitian and his family, refer to him as "god" (Note on 2:1; Thompson, *Book*, 104–7; Friesen, *Imperial*, 148).

Third, the title "lord and god" was used unofficially by those attempting to flatter the emperor (Martial, *Epigrams* 5.8.1; 7.34.8; Dio Cassius, *Rom. Hist.* 67.5.7; 67.13.4). In Asia, Domitian was called "master and god" (*despotēs kai theos*, Dio Chrysostom, *Disc.* 45.1). The titles "lord" (Martial, *Epigrams* 4.67.4; 5.2.6; Statius, *Silv.* 3.3.103, 110) and "god" were also used separately for Domitian (Martial, *Epigrams* 5.5.1; 7.8.1; Statius, *Silv.* 1.1.62). The practice of calling a living emperor "god" was repudiated after Domitian's death, but the title "lord" continued to be used (Martial, *Epigrams* 10.72.3; Pliny the Younger, *Pan.* 2.3; Aune). In short, honoring an emperor with these titles was a pattern in Greco-Roman ruler cults that began before Domitian's reign and continued through it. Revelation tacitly challenges the familiar practice by insisting that the Creator alone is worthy of these titles.

for you created all things and by your will they existed and were created. The belief that God created or made all things was a familiar reason for praise (Pss 33:6–9; 95:1–7), and it underscored his sovereignty: "You have made everything and with you is the authority for everything" (*1 En.* 9:5; cf. *Sib. Or.* 3:19–20; cf. Wis 9:1; Sir 18:1). For Revelation to say things "existed and were created" is an odd sequence, which could suggest that things existed (*ēsan*) before creation. To clarify, some manuscripts say things now "exist [*eisin*] and were created" (1854 2050), that they "came into being [*egenonto*] and were created" (2325), or that they "did *not* exist and were created" (046). Although some interpreters suggest that Revelation means that the world existed in the will of God before actually being created (1QS III, 15–16; Kraft; Mounce; Prigent), it is best to take the wording as a poetic way to speak of all things depending on God's creative action (McDonough, *YHWH*, 213–14). Reversing the usual sequence of actions occurs often in Revelation, as in referring to opening a scroll before breaking its seals (Rev 5:2). This was a known pattern of expression (Lausberg, *Handbook* §§891–92).

COMMENT

The trumpetlike voice of Christ calls John on a visionary ascent through heaven's open door, initiating Revelation's second cycle of visions (4:1; cf. 1:10). The previous cycle concluded with Christ knocking at the door, waiting for people to open to him (3:20),

---

On Rev 4:1–11, see Aune, *Apocalypticism*, 99–119; Böttrich, "Das 'gläserne'"; Brooke, "Shared," 50–52; Davis, *Heavenly*; Ego, "Reduktion"; Giblin, "From and Before"; Harrison, "Fading"; Hiecke, "Der Seher"; Hurtado, "Revelation"; F. Parker, "'Our'"; Schimanowski, *Die himmlische*; G. Stevenson, "Conceptual."

but before readers can respond, John is shown a door that already stands open (4:1). The contrast is provocative: As Christ asks readers to open their doors to him, he opens heaven's door to them through John's prose. The messages to the churches ended by promising that those who conquered by remaining faithful would share a place on Christ's throne, just as Christ had a place on God's throne (3:21). Now to encourage them to persevere, they are given a glimpse of God's throne—and at the throne they will see the Lamb, who conquered through faithful suffering (4:2; 5:5–6).

The Creator and the Lamb are the theological center of the Apocalypse. The throne vision puts them at the heart of the present created order, just as the final vision in the book gives the throne of God and the Lamb the central place in the new creation (22:1–5). The heavenly hall is arranged in concentric circles. In the middle is the throne of God, who created all things. Around the throne are four creatures that represent the created order, their appearances like those of a lion, an ox, a human being, and an eagle. Around them are twenty-four elders, who represent the community of faith and join the creatures in praising the Creator. In the next chapter the circles of worshipers will continue to expand until countless angels and all creatures in heaven, earth, and the sea praise God and the Lamb.

John's description of the throne room uses traditional biblical language. He speaks of the God who is already known through Scripture. Details from Ezekiel include the gemlike throne, the crystal sea, the rainbow, and the four faces of the creatures (Ezek 1:4–28). Isaiah saw heavenly beings with six wings, crying "holy, holy, holy" (Isa 6:2–3). Daniel mentions the other thrones around God's throne (Dan 7:9–10). Elements from these and other texts are combined and altered, so the scene shows continuity with the prophetic tradition along with dynamic newness. The heavenly worshipers give God honor, power, glory, and thanks for his acts of creation, recalling themes from Israel's worship (Pss 29:1–9; 59:16; 66:2; 86:12; 146:1, 6; 1 Chr 16:27–28). The hymns in Revelation were composed to fit their present context, but they use language that would have been familiar to many readers (Intro IV.E.1). Those who worship on earth echo the true worship in heaven; therefore, readers have incentive to continue worshiping God, despite social pressures to compromise.

The throne of the Creator will be contrasted with the throne of the destroyers, who include the dragon and the beast (Rev 4:2; 13:2). Revelation pictures a world in which the destructive forces of evil seek to dominate the world. Yet as the Creator, God has a sovereign claim over the world he has made, and he will battle the agents of evil in order to liberate the earth from their ruinous activity so that life will prevail. The throne room scene also makes a contrast with the dominant forms of worship in the social world of the readers. Greek and Roman worshipers wore white robes and head wreaths. They offered gold wreaths to the statues of the gods and the emperor, as hymn singers offered praise (G. Stevenson, "Conceptual," 261–62; Friesen, *Imperial*, 105–13; Aune, *Apocalypticism*, 99–119). The author of Revelation assumes that worship is an ongoing feature of the readers' social contexts and uses imagery that had affinities with various traditions. The question concerns the identity of the God who is worshiped.

The Heavenly Court (4:1–8a)

John is called toward heaven, the realm of God, whose purposes are mysterious (4:1). The open door signals that revelation is about to be given. The previous vision cycle began with Christ appearing to John on Patmos, whereas the new cycle takes John to heaven. Yet heaven and earth belong to the same universe. The vision of the throne room reveals the one who is sovereign over the world, the God whose reign is often hidden but is attested by all creation (5:13; Rowland). John is reserved about God's appearance (4:2). By way of contrast, Ezekiel said that the one seated on the throne had the form of a human being, who gleamed like amber from the waist up and like fire from the waist down (Ezek 1:26–27), and Daniel's throne room vision told of God's white robe and hair (Dan 7:9). But John speaks only of God's gemlike appearance, not his human form (Rev 4:3). His reserve is similar to that of Jewish writers, who likened God's presence to the sun's radiance (*1 En.* 18:20; cf. *Apoc. Ab.* 18:13), but it differs from Greek and Roman sculpture and coins, which often depicted deities. Zeus was pictured as a bearded man on a throne, often with one hand on a staff to signify his power to rule. John's reserve maintains a sense of God's transcendence so that he is not construed as a human being writ large (Friesen, *Imperial*, 169–70; G. Stevenson, *Power*, 46–48).

Twenty-four thrones encircle the throne of God (Rev 4:4). Some Jewish sources referred to a heavenly court, its members seated on thrones (Dan 7:9; cf. 1 Kgs 22:19), and to the thrones of angels (*T. Levi* 3:8; *Apoc. Zeph.* [*OTP* 1:508]; 11Q17 V, 8; Col 1:16). In the imperial world Jupiter was said to have a heavenly council (Ovid, *Metam.* 1.175–76), and at the political level the emperor dispensed justice while seated on his throne, surrounded by friends and advisors who would sometimes sit beside him (Musurillo, *Acts of the Pagan*, 18–26; Aune, *Apocalypticism*, 102–3).

Revelation alters the pattern by identifying those on the thrones as elders (*presbyteroi*). This term was not commonly used for angels or imperial officials, but it was used for leaders within Israel and in the congregations of Jesus' followers (NOTE on Rev 4:4). Socially, vulnerable readers like those at Smyrna and Philadelphia had no access to the circles of power, but the elders of Revelation show that the earthly community of faith does have representatives around the throne of God. The idea of heavenly representation might recall that at Mount Sinai God appeared to Moses and the elders above a gemlike pavement (Exod 24:9–10) as well as the prophetic hope that when God defeats the kings of earth, he "will reign on Mount Zion and in Jerusalem, and before his elders he will manifest his glory" (Isa 24:23). The glory manifested before the elders in Rev 4 anticipates the final victory of God and the manifestation of his glory in New Jerusalem (cf. Fekkes, *Isaiah*, 140–43; Hurtado, "Revelation," 113).

The number twenty-four fits the elders' representative role since Revelation uses twelve and its multiples for the people of God. The woman who represents God's people wears a wreath of twelve stars (Rev 12:1). The redeemed include twelve thousand from each of Israel's twelve tribes, though they prove to be a countless multitude from every tribe, who wear white and worship before God's throne (7:4–8; 14:1–5). New Jerusalem has twelve gates and foundations named for the twelve tribes and apostles (21:12–14). The city where the redeemed live measures twelve thousand stadia on each side (21:16–17). Revelation variously uses twelve and multiples of twelve for the whole people of God.

The portrayal of the elders gives readers a glimpse of what awaits the faithful. Christ promised that those who conquer would wear white robes (3:5), be given wreaths (2:10), and have a place on his throne (3:21). The elders, who are clothed in white, wear gold wreaths, and sit on thrones, now enjoy what the readers can hope to receive

(Boxall). Yet the elders also point to a tension in the readers' social contexts. In the imperial world people wore white robes and head wreaths as they celebrated the festivals of traditional deities and the emperors (Philo, *Legat.* 12; Plutarch, *Mor.* 771D; Beard, North, and Price, *Religions*, 254). Those greeting Augustus dressed in white (Suetonius, *Aug.* 93.2; cf. Herodian, *Historiae* 8.7.2), and the people of Sardis celebrated when Augustus's son came of age by wearing wreaths and festival garments (I.Sard 8.1–20). The elders wear traditional festival attire, but the God they honor is the Creator, not the emperor or gods of the Roman Empire.

The lightning and rumbling thunder that come from God's throne will later accompany the plagues the Creator brings against his foes (Rev 4:5; 8:5; 11:19; 16:18–21; Bauckham, *Climax*, 202–4). Although the agents of evil will send out demonic spirits in their efforts to dominate the world (16:13–14), the seven spirits before God's throne serve as the eyes of the Lamb, providing superior recognizance in the conflict (4:5; 5:6). The sea of glass below the throne recalls that the Creator established a dome over the earth to separate the waters above from those below (Gen 1:6–7). Later, Satan will stand by the earthly sea and his allies will include the beast and Babylon, who rise from the sea and seek to control it (Rev 12:18; 13:1; 17:1, 15, 18). But Revelation provides assurance that those who resist, even at the cost of their lives, will ultimately celebrate in triumph beside heaven's crystal sea (15:2–4).

The inner ring around the throne consists of four creatures, each with a different face (4:6–7). In Ezekiel's throne vision such creatures drew God's throne chariot (Ezek 1:15–21), whereas in Revelation they have a new role as representatives of creation. In Ezekiel each creature had four faces (1:10), but in Revelation each has only one. The lion was a wild animal (Ps 7:2; Jer 4:7; Amos 3:8); the *moschos* was a calf or young ox that was used for domestic work and sacrifice (Gen 12:16; Lev 1:5; 2 Sam 6:6; Luke 15:23); the eagle was known for its strength and grace (Jer 49:16; Obad 4; Ps 103:5; Prov 30:19; Isa 40:31). The four creatures show that in the proper order of things, all creation glorifies the Creator. The praises they offer surge outward, until the elders, the angels, and every creature of heaven, earth, and the sea is caught up in praising God (Rev 4:9–11; 5:8–13). Only then do the creatures say "amen" (5:14; Bauckham, *Theology*, 33; Brütsch; Prigent).

John sees the four creatures after entering heaven's open door, but when the door of the abyss is opened in a later vision, ghoulish beings appear (9:1–2) They will be agents of the Destroyer rather than the Creator. Their grotesque appearances fuse human faces with lions' teeth and scorpions' tails, and the cacophonous roar of their movement clashes with the songs around God's throne (9:3–11). The beast from the sea is a hideous blend of traits from a lion, leopard, bear, and horned monster. Its appearance shows the destructive results of deifying human authority. In the heavenly throne room, however, the Creator is in the center, and the creature with the human face is alongside the throne, rather than on it, taking its place among the other creatures. Instead of taking the Creator's place, they worship the Creator in ways that will draw all things into harmonious praise (5:8–14).

Praise of the Creator (4:8b–11)

The four creatures speak ceaselessly of God day and night (4:8). Jewish texts also told of heavenly beings repeatedly praising God (Isa 6:1–3; *T. Levi* 3:8; 4Q403 1 I, 1; 11Q17

VI, 8), though some made a place for silence (4Q405 20 II, 13; *Apoc. Ab.* 18:8). The continuous praise may subtly contribute to John's critique of imperial power, for Roman senators were said to spend "the whole day in laudations" to the emperor Gaius and to "prayers on his behalf" (Dio Cassius, *Rom. Hist.* 59.24.5). Nero was followed by a crowd of admirers: "Day and night they thundered applause" and "bestowed on the emperor's voice and person the epithets reserved for deities" (Tacitus, *Ann.* 14.15; cf. Acts 12:22; Aune, *Apocalypticism*, 112). In John's vision, acclaim is given to God and not to any rival.

The creatures say of God, "Holy, holy, holy" (Rev 4:8b). God's holiness is his "otherness," his numinous quality that sets him apart from other beings (Backhaus, "Vision," 10). On the one hand, God's holiness threatens to destroy whatever is impure. When Isaiah heard the seraphs declaring God's holiness, he cried out: "Woe is me! I am lost, for I am a man of unclean lips, and I live among a people of unclean lips" (Isa 6:5). Revelation shares this sense of holiness, warning readers about the defilement of infidelity and the abominations of the whore (Rev 3:4; 16:13; 17:4). On the other hand, God's holiness attracts, awakening a desire in readers to enter the presence of the Holy One and his holy city by cleansing themselves (4:8; 21:2; cf. 7:14; 22:14).

God is called the one "who is" (4:8; cf. 1:4), the name of God in Israel's tradition (Exod 3:14 LXX). To say that God "is" makes an implicit contrast with the so-called gods that do not have authentic existence, whether these are the traditional deities represented by mute statues or the image of the beast in the ruler cult, which is magically given breath by the beast's agent (Rev 9:20; 13:15; cf. Wis 13:1; *Sib. Or.* 3:11–16, 30–33; McDonough, *YHWH*, 153–67). God is also the Creator, the one "who was" present at the beginning and brought all things into existence (Rev 4:8, 11), and he will "come" in the future to bring his purposes to their goal. By way of contrast, the beast "was and is not, and is about to come up from the abyss and go to destruction" (17:8). The beast personifies the destructive power at work in the political and economic worlds of John's time. But where the beast's future holds destruction, the work of the Creator will culminate in new creation.

As the four living creatures give God glory and honor and thanks, the twenty-four elders join in worship (4:9–10). Giving glory, honor, and thanks to God was part of Israel's tradition (Pss 29:1; 96:6–8; 115:1; 145:10; 1 Chr 16:8; 29:11), but using wreaths to show honor reflects the Greco-Roman practice of giving gold head wreaths to military victors and civic benefactors. The elders in John's vision wear the coveted wreaths, but instead of posturing as the *recipients* of honor and thanks, they will *offer* the wreaths to God in order to return to him the glory, honor, and thanks that are due to the Creator of all (G. Stevenson, "Conceptual," 267).

The elders also prostrate themselves in worship before the throne (Rev 4:10). In John's visionary world such worship is properly directed toward God (5:14; 7:11; 11:16), not toward lesser beings, such as angels (19:10; 22:8–9). By way of contrast, the peoples of the world will prostrate themselves before the beast (13:4, 8, 12, 15; 14:9; 16:2). In John's social context prostration would show the most extreme form of devotion to the ruler. It was said that senators prostrated themselves in worship (*proskynein*) before the chair of the emperor Gaius in the temple. A vassal king did the same when coming before Nero, saying, "I have come to you, my god, to worship [*proskynein*] you as I do Mithras" (Dio Cassius, *Rom. Hist.* 59.24.2–3; 63.5.2; Aune, *Apocalypticism*, 108). For the writer of Revelation, using such gestures to honor a human ruler rather than the Creator is a mark of oppression.

The elders throw their head wreaths down before God's throne, honoring God's rightful reign (Rev 4:10b). The practice corresponds to the way people gave gold wreaths to a ruler to acknowledge his authority. In one sense this could be a purely diplomatic gesture. At Ephesus, for example, a Jewish delegation presented Marc Anthony with a gold wreath when asking for his help, and a civic delegation met Augustus there with a gold wreath (Josephus, *Ant.* 14.304; Millar, *Emperor*, 410–11). When Vespasian became emperor, the embassies (*presbeiai*) from various cities brought wreaths to him (Josephus, *J.W.* 4.620).

Yet the gesture also suggested an elevated notion of a ruler's authority, since gold wreaths were placed on the statues of Greco-Roman deities—an action Jewish writers considered idolatrous (Ep Jer 9; Dio Chrysostom, *Disc.* 12.60; Athenaeus, *Deipnosophistae* 10.437bc). Embassies (*presbeiai*) wearing wreaths came from Greece to crown Alexander the Great "with golden wreaths as if they had come on a sacred embassy to honor some god" (Arrian, *Anabasis* 7.23). Revelation presents a contrasting vision, in which the elders (*presbyterioi*), who represent the community of faith, give their wreaths to the Creator.

The elders say, "You are worthy [*axios*], our Lord and God, to receive glory and honor and power" (Rev 4:11a). The language echoes themes from Israel's worship (Pss 21:13; 59:16; 66:3). It also continues the implicit contrast between God and the beast, whose dominion is based on the illusion of its invincible might (Rev 13:4). After Vespasian suppressed the Jewish revolt, his supporters hailed him as their benefactor, savior, and "only worthy [*axios*] emperor of Rome" (Josephus, *J.W.* 7.71). The titles "lord" and "god" were also used when flattering an emperor in the hope of obtaining his favor (Note on Rev 4:11).

The words of the elders pose a contrast between the worship of God and others who claimed divine honors. The praises offered to emperors were sometimes lavish. When honoring Augustus, a group dressed in white robes with wreaths on their heads burned incense and declared that "it was through him they lived" and prospered (Suetonius, *Aug.* 93.2). So the heavenly elders take praise to another level by saying that God is the one through whom all things came into being (Rev 4:11b). Praising God for creating all things fits Israel's worship tradition (Pss 89:12; 148:5), and it also distinguishes God from all other beings (Rev 4:11). The Creator will not relinquish his creation to the Destroyer or be content when the world's inhabitants worship what their hands have made rather than the Maker of all things (9:11, 20; 10:5–6; 14:7). Having stepped down once from their thrones to acclaim God as the world's Creator, the twenty-four elders will do so again to announce the coming destruction of the world's destroyers (4:11; 11:18).

14. The Lamb Receives the Sealed Scroll (5:1–14)

5 ¹Then I saw in the right hand of the one seated on the throne a scroll, written on the inside and the back, sealed with seven seals. ²And I saw a powerful angel proclaiming with a loud voice, "Who is worthy to open the scroll and break its seals?" ³And no one in heaven or on earth or under the earth was able to open the scroll or to look into it. ⁴So I wept a great deal because no one was found worthy to open the scroll or to look into it. ⁵Then one of the elders said to me, "Stop weeping. You see the Lion of the tribe of Judah, the Root of David has conquered, so that he can open the scroll and its seven seals."

⁶Then I saw in between the throne and the four living creatures and among the elders a Lamb, standing as one who had been slain. It had seven horns and seven eyes, which are the seven spirits of God that are sent into all the earth. ⁷He went and received the scroll from the right hand of the one seated on the throne. ⁸And when he received the scroll, the four living creatures and the twenty-four elders fell down before the Lamb, each with a harp and gold offering bowls filled with incense, which are the prayers of the saints. ⁹And they sang a new song, saying,

"You are worthy to receive the scroll and to open its seals,
for you were slain and by your blood you purchased for God
those of every tribe and language and people and nation,
¹⁰and you made them a kingdom and priests to our God,
and they will reign on the earth."

¹¹Then I looked, and around the throne and the living creatures and the elders I heard the sound of many angels. They numbered in the millions—thousands upon thousands. ¹²They said in a loud voice,

"Worthy is the Lamb who was slain
to receive power and wealth and wisdom and might
and honor and glory and blessing."

¹³And I heard every creature in heaven and on earth and under the earth and in the sea—I heard everything in them say,

"To the one seated on the throne and to the Lamb
be blessing and honor and glory and might forever and ever."

¹⁴And the four living creatures said, "Amen," and the elders fell down and worshiped.

NOTES

5:1. *Then I saw in the right hand of the one seated on the throne a scroll.* The *biblion* John sees is a scroll. Although the codex form, with pages bound at the edge, was coming into use by the late first century CE, the writings in Revelation are on scrolls that can be rolled up (6:14). God's right hand connoted power to bring judgment and salvation (Exod 15:6; Ps 48:10; Isa 41:10), so his holding the scroll in his right hand suggests that its contents involve both aspects of God's work (Boxall). The expression *epi tēn dexian* could be rendered "at the right hand" or "on the right hand" (Stefanovic, "Meaning"), but John uses it to mean "in the right hand," just as he uses both *en* and *epi* for the stars "in" Christ's right hand (Rev 1:16, 20; cf. 20:1). The implied content of the scroll has been construed in different ways, with the first being the most viable:

1. Visions disclosed later in Revelation. The interpretation developed in the COMMENT follows the literary movement of the Apocalypse. Briefly, the scroll of God is received by Christ the Lamb, who opens the seals in 6:1–8:1. Then an angel gives the open scroll to John in 10:1–11, and John reveals the contents through the prophecies that follow. The scroll is summarized in 11:1–15 and disclosed more fully in 12:1–22:5. Some interpreters think the contents begin to be revealed at 6:1 as the seals are opened, so the scroll contains all of 6:1–22:5 (Satake; Smalley), but it is more likely that the contents are revealed only after all seven seals have been broken. Another variation is that the sealed scroll includes everything in the Apocalypse (Giesen). Yet this too is unlikely since the messages in Rev 1–3 were disclosed without any reference to a sealed scroll.

2. God's plan for the world. Apocalyptic writers sometimes pictured sealed books describing future events (Dan 12:4, 9) or told of sealed books in which the whole course of human actions was written (*1 En.* 81:1–4; 90:20; Harrington; Mounce). The main objection to this approach is that the sealed scroll of Rev 5 seems to be the one that is open and given to John in Rev 10, so its contents consist of what follows in Rev 11.

3. The scroll of life. Revelation says that at the last judgment the books of human deeds and the scroll of life will be opened (20:12; 21:27). Since the Lamb receives the scroll from God and later passages refer to "the Lamb's scroll of life" (13:8; 21:27), the sealed scroll in 5:1 might list the names of the redeemed (Oecumenius; Davis, *Heavenly*, 181–86; Keener). However, this scroll's seals are opened in Rev 6–7, yielding threats, whereas the scroll of life is opened only at the end (20:12; Schimanowski, *Die himmlische*, 184–91).

4. The Scriptures. In antiquity some interpreters identified the sealed scroll as the OT, whose true meaning was hidden until revealed by Christ (Luke 24:27; 2 Cor 3:15–16; Hippolytus, *Comm. Dan.* 4.33–34; Origen, *Comm. Jo.* 5.6; Victorinus; Apringius; Gregory the Great, *Dial.* 4.44). A variation is that one side of the scroll is the OT and the other is the NT (Primasius; Bede). It is true that John thinks Christ fulfilled what was spoken by Israel's prophets (Rev 10:7), but in Revelation the visions that occur when the seals are opened go beyond interpreting the older biblical texts, and the literary development of the scroll theme makes the unsealed scroll part of John's prophetic commissioning in Rev 10.

written on the inside and the back. This expression is awkward but fairly well-attested (A 2329 2344) and is preferred over the variants that smooth the language to read "on the inside and the outside" (P 046) or "on the front and the back" (א). Many scrolls were made of papyrus, where two layers of plant fiber were laid at right angles and pressed together to form writing material. Scribes normally wrote only on the front side, where the fibers ran horizontally. Also used were parchment scrolls, written on thin leather sheets that had been scraped and treated. The scroll in God's hand is of heavenly origin. There are two ways to interpret the scroll's writing. The first is the most plausible:

1. Text from the front continuing onto the back (*opistograph*). Revelation recalls Ezek 2:10, which pictures a scroll written on front and back. The sense is that the

text continues from one side onto the other. Similarly, Zech 5:1–3 pictures a flying scroll with a curse for those who steal written on one side and a curse for those who swear falsely written on the other. Hebrew, Greek, and Latin scrolls were occasionally written on both sides to economize on writing materials—although cost presumably would not be an issue for a heavenly scroll (Juvenal, *Satirae* 1.6; Lucian, *Vit. auct.* 9; Pliny the Younger, *Ep.* 3.5.17; 4Q503 + 512; 4Q415 + 414; DJD 39:211–13). Some copies of Revelation, produced in the second to fourth centuries, are scrolls written on both sides ($\mathfrak{P}^{18}$ $\mathfrak{P}^{24}$ $\mathfrak{P}^{98}$). In the vision, the point is that John *can see* that the scroll contains writing but *cannot know* the contents until the seals are broken. The contents are effectively hidden (Isa 29:11; Aune; Prigent; Smalley; Bergmeier, "Buchrolle," 230).

2. The same text on the inside and outside. Some interpreters suggest that the inside of the scroll contained the authoritative text of God's will and that the back was inscribed with a copy that could be read. In Jewish practice a legal document, such as a deed, was sealed and stored with an unsealed and readable copy (Jer 32:9–15; Mur 18; *m. B. Bat.* 10:1–2). By analogy, some think that having writing on both the inside and the outside of the scroll shows that its content has not been altered (Osborne; Roloff). A variation is that the outside is a *summary* of the message on the inside. Precedent comes from Greek and Latin texts that were inscribed on the insides of wooden tablets and then bound together with a summary of the contents on the back. By analogy, God's will was known in part before Christ, but the fullness is revealed in Christ (Beale). What makes this interpretation unlikely is that no one can "look into" the scroll until the seals are broken, meaning that its contents are inaccessible (Rev 5:3).

sealed with seven seals. Scrolls were rolled up and secured with strings to prevent them from coming unrolled. A strip of soft clay, wax, or lead was placed under the strings, then folded over the tops of the strings, and finally imprinted with a distinctive marking, often from a signet ring (Pliny the Elder, *Nat.* 37.4.8–10). The document could not be opened without cutting the strings or damaging the seal. Since individual rings had unique markings, one could tell whether there had been tampering by comparing the image on the scroll's seal with the image on the signet ring (Esth 8:8; Tob 7:14; *NP* 13:174).

5:2. *And I saw a powerful angel proclaiming with a loud voice.* Here, a powerful angel asks about the sealed scroll, and in 10:1 another powerful angel holds the open scroll. Describing the angel in similar ways links the two scenes. A powerful angel appears in 18:21, but no scroll is mentioned. Identifying some angels as powerful suggests that they have a special rank (*4 Bar.* 4:2), though Revelation does not give details of an angelic hierarchy (*1 En.* 20:1–7; *Jub.* 2:2; 1 Thess 4:16).

"Who is worthy to open the scroll and break its seals?" In practice, one must break the seals before opening a scroll, but here as elsewhere, John uses a rhetorical pattern that reverses the logical sequence (Lausberg, *Handbook*, §§891–92). In other visions God asks "who" should serve as his emissary (Isa 6:8; 1 Kgs 22:20), but here God is silent and an angel asks the question. On "worthy," see the Note on 4:11.

5:3. *And no one in heaven or on earth or under the earth was able to open the scroll or to look into it.* The realms mentioned here encompass the whole creation (Phil 2:10;

Ign. *Trall.* 9:1). Some texts referred to heaven, earth, and the water under the earth (Exod 20:4), which was known as the abyss (*T. Levi* 3:9; *Jos. As.* 12:2; *Jub.* 2:2 Greek). Although Revelation envisions the abyss as a place of demonic powers (Rev 9:1–2, 11; 11:7; 17:8; 20:1, 3), this is not the case here, since the creatures under the earth praise God (5:13).

5:4. *So I wept a great deal because no one was found worthy to open the scroll or look into it.* In visionary texts, weeping and fasting may show penitential discipline (*4 Ezra* 5:20; 6:35; *2 Bar.* 9:2), grief over conditions on earth (*3 Bar.* 1:1; *Mart. Asc. Isa.* 2:10), or sorrow over something that has been revealed (*1 En.* 90:41). Here, weeping is a spontaneous reaction to the seeming impossibility of learning the will of God.

5:5. *Then one of the elders said to me, "Stop weeping.* In some apocalypses a seer asks about what he sees, prompting a heavenly figure to explain (Dan 7:16–17; *1 En.* 25:1; 54:4; 108:5; *T. Ab.* 13:1–2; 14:1–2; *4 Ezra* 12:7–10). In Revelation, however, heavenly figures respond to John's unspoken questions. In Rev 5:5 and 7:13 a heavenly elder gives an interpretation, and later this is done by an angel (17:7; 21:9). In the readers' social contexts, the elders of a congregation might provide instruction, but here, a heavenly elder does so (NOTE on 4:4).

"You see the Lion of the tribe of Judah. The lion imagery has two main meanings:

1. Power. Jacob's blessing said, "Judah is a lion's whelp . . . he stretches out like a lion, like a lioness—who dares to rouse him up?" (Gen 49:9; cf. Deut 33:20, 22). The lion's reputation varied, from noble animal (Prov 28:1; 30:30; Pliny the Elder, *Nat.* 8.19.50) to destructive predator (Pss 7:2; 10:9; 4Q169 3–4 I, 1–8; 1 Pet 5:8; Strawn, "Why"), but its courage and forcefulness were ideal traits for a warrior (2 Sam 1:23; 17:10; 1 Macc 3:4; Homer, *Il.* 5.295; 7.225; Virgil, *Aen.* 9.792). When Israel was victorious, its army was like a lion (Num 23:24; 24:9). Revelation redefines lion imagery and victory by linking it to the Lamb (Rev 5:5–6).
2. Kingship. Lions were regal (Pliny the Elder, *Nat.* 8.19.48). The blessing of Jacob likened Judah to a lion and then said the "scepter will not depart from Judah, nor the ruler's staff from between his feet, until he comes to whom it belongs; the nations will obey him" (Gen 49:10 NET). Historically, the Davidic kings came from Judah. Lion imagery adorned the throne (1 Kgs 10:19–20), and kings were compared to lions (Prov 19:12). After the end of the Davidic monarchy, Jewish writers took Gen 49:9–10 to mean that God would send another ruler: "the messiah of righteousness . . . the branch of David" (4Q252 V, 1–4; cf. *Tg. Neof.* and *Frg. Tg.* Gen 49:10). Of this figure it was said, "God has raised you to a scepter for the rulers before you . . . all the nations will serve you . . . you will be like a lion" (1Q28b V, 28–29). In *4 Ezra* the Davidic Messiah is the lion, who comes at the end of the age to confront the eagle that signifies Rome (*4 Ezra* 11:37; 12:31–32). Although some interpreters question whether Revelation's lion imagery is messianic (Johns, *Lamb*, 164–67), the language from Gen 49:9–10 and related traditions makes clear that it is (Schimanowski, *Die himmlische*, 197–202).

the Root of David. This image recalls Isaiah: "A shoot shall come out from the stump of Jesse, and a branch shall grow out of his roots" (Isa 11:1) so that in days to come "the root of Jesse shall stand as a signal to the peoples" (11:10). Some writers used "Root" (Rev 22:16; Sir 47:22; cf. *T. Jud.* 24:4–6) and "Branch" (Jer 23:5; 33:15; Zech 3:8; 6:12;

4Q174 1 I, 1–11; 4Q252 V, 1–4) as titles for the heir to David's throne. The Christian community identified Jesus as a descendant of David in ways that emphasized his messianic role (Matt 1:1, 6; Mark 10:47; Luke 2:4; 3:31; Rom 1:3; 2 Tim 2:8).

has conquered, so that he can open the scroll and its seven seals." The word "conquer" (*nikan*) draws associations from military conquest, athletic victory, and traditions about faithfulness in suffering (NOTE on Rev 2:7). The negative side of conquering is shown by the first horseman, who threatens the earth with violence (6:2), and the beast, which slays the faithful (11:7; 13:7). Here, the sense is transformed, however, for the messianic Lion and Root conquered by suffering death as a slain Lamb. The Lamb's death is a victory because it is a refusal to capitulate to God's adversaries, it brings redemption for others, and it culminates in resurrection (see COMMENT). Similarly, John's gospel says that Jesus conquered the world through his crucifixion (John 16:33; cf. 12:32), which overcomes the world's hatred and deception (8:44; 15:18–25) with God's truth and love (14:30–31; 18:37). Paul also identified the cross with God's power to bring salvation and understood Jesus' resurrection to be the harbinger of the final resurrection, which would bring final victory over death (1 Cor 1:18; 15:54–57).

5:6. *Then I saw in between the throne and the four living creatures and among the elders.* Since the expression *en mesō* can mean "in the middle," some think that the Lamb, who shares God's throne (Rev 3:21), stands in the middle of the throne itself, reflecting a high Christology (Knight, "Enthroned"). From this perspective the four creatures could be constituent parts of the throne (Hannah, "Of Cherubim"). This is unlikely, however, because the Lamb comes to the throne where God is seated in order to receive the scroll (5:7). The expression *en mesō* is used twice, so it could reflect the Semitic *bēn* . . . *ûbēn*, which means "between." Accordingly, the Lamb would stand with the throne and creatures on one side and the elders on the other (Charles; Smalley). Or it could simply mean that the Lamb was in the middle "by" the throne and "among" the elders who surrounded it (Aune). On the elders and creatures, see the NOTES on 4:4, 6.

a Lamb, standing as one who had been slain. The Greek word translated as Lamb is *arnion*, which in form is the diminutive of *arēn*, a word for a lamb, though there is no real difference in meaning. The word could be used for lambs less than a year old (Josephus, *Ant.* 3.221, 226; cf. John 21:15). The connotations of *arnion* are like those of *amnos*, the other common word for a lamb. John sees the Lamb standing "as one who was slain." The word "as" (*hōs*) does not suggest that the Lamb merely appeared to have been slain; it refers to what has actually happened. Slaying has at least three dimensions of meaning:

1. Vulnerability. Revelation contrasts the lion, which was known for killing sheep, with the Lamb, who was killed (Rev 5:5–6). The LXX used *arnion* in metaphors connoting vulnerability: a gentle lamb led to the slaughter or dragged away by predators (Jer 11:19; 50:45 [27:45 LXX]). Other texts pictured the righteous as innocent lambs among the nations (*Pss. Sol.* 8:23) or lambs in the midst of wolves (*2 Clem.* 5:2–4). The word *amnos* was also used for vulnerable lambs, which could not live safely with predators—at least not in the current age (Mic 5:7; Sir 13:16–17; Isa 11:6; 65:25; cf. Babrius, *Fables* 89; Phaedrus, *Fabulae* 1.1)—and the word *arēn* was used similarly (*T. Gad* 1:7). The suffering servant of Isa 53:7 was like a lamb led to the slaughter.
2. Sacrifice of deliverance. Like the lambs at Passover, Jesus was slain (*sphazein*, Rev 5:6; Exod 12:6). In the Passover tradition, lambs' blood was smeared around the doors of Israelite houses. The blood did not atone for sin but protected people from death

and helped bring liberation from slavery so they could serve as God's kingdom of priests—as is accomplished by Jesus' blood (Exod 12:21–27; 19:6; Rev 5:9–10). Passover motifs appear in Revelation's plague visions (Rev 8–9; 16; Exod 7–12), the redeemed singing the song of Moses and the Lamb beside the sea (Rev 15:2–4; Exod 15), and the woman who represents God's people being carried on eagles' wings to safety in the desert (Rev 12:14; Exod 19:4). Therefore, the Lamb motif might also recall the exodus (Aune; Giesen; Osborne; Prigent; Roloff; M. Hoffmann, *Destroyer*, 117–34; cf. 1 Cor 5:7; John 1:29; 19:14, 37; 1 Pet 1:19; Justin Martyr, *Dial.* 111.3).

3. *Sacrifice of atonement.* The introduction to Revelation said that Jesus "released us *from our sins* by his blood, and made us a kingdom, priests to his God and Father" (Rev 1:5–6; emphasis added). Similar language is used in 5:9–10 without the reference to sins. But given the similarities, readers may have identified the Lamb as a sacrifice for purification and removal of guilt (Lev 14:12–13, 21; John 1:29; cf. *Sib. Or.* 3:625–26; Beckwith; Müller; Hofius, "Ἀρνίον"; Slater, *Christ*, 166). However, lambs were most commonly offered in the temple each morning and evening, and in other contexts they were not clearly linked to atonement (Exod 29:38–41; Num 28:3–4; *Sib. Or.* 3:578). So if atonement is suggested in Rev 5, it remains a subtheme (Johns, *Lamb*, 128–30).

It had seven horns. Ancient writers could picture a Passover lamb with two horns (*t. Pesaḥ.* 6:7), but the seven horns John sees set this lamb apart. The horn was a symbol of power and honor (Pss 89:17, 24; 92:10; 112:9; 1 Sam 2:1; 1QM I, 4) and the ability to save (Ps 18:2; 2 Sam 22:3). The image was used for the king and especially the Davidic ruler (1 Sam 2:10; Ps 132:17; Ezek 29:21; Sir 47:11; Luke 1:69). Jewish sources likened the horns of a messianic figure to those of a powerful bull (1Q28b V, 26–27; *1 En.* 90:37; Nickelsburg, *1 Enoch*, 406–7). The imagery in Revelation both affirms and transforms earlier connotations. The seven horns affirm Jesus' messianic identity, yet as the Lamb, he saves through his own self-sacrifice.

and seven eyes, which are the seven spirits of God that are sent into all the earth. The imagery recalls Zechariah's vision of a lampstand with seven lamps, which are the eyes of God (Zech 4:2, 10). Identifying the eyes as spirits might have been suggested by Zech 4:6, which says that God's purposes are carried out by his spirit. Revelation initially depicted the seven spirits as torches before God's throne (Rev 4:5; Note on 1:4), but now, they are the eyes of the Lamb. This idea might also have been suggested by Zechariah, where God promises to send his servant the Branch, a Davidic ruler, and adds that he will place before Joshua his priest a stone "with seven eyes" (Zech 3:8–9). Revelation assumes that the Messiah himself can be pictured as a Lamb with seven eyes (Beale; Schimanowski, *Die himmlische*, 231; cf. Jauhiainen, *Use*, 84–85). God was understood to see all things, so no one was exempt from his scrutiny (2 Chr 16:9; Prov 15:3). The same is true of the Lamb (cf. Rev 2:23).

5:7. *He went and received the scroll from the right hand of the one seated on the throne.* The Lamb receives the scroll from God, just as Jesus receives revelation from God (1:1). The verb "received" is in the perfect tense, which is unusual and may draw attention to this as a central action (Mathewson, "Verbal"). Some interpreters suggest that when the Lamb "received" the scroll, he formally received power to reign (cf. 5:12; Aune 1:336). Yet this is unlikely. Note that God is said to "receive" power even though the author assumes God reigns continuously (Rev 4:8, 11). Similarly, Jesus is already the ruler of earth's kings, so receiving the scroll makes him the agent of God's revelation, but it does not signal a change in regal status.

5:8. *And when he received the scroll, the four living creatures and the twenty-four elders fell down before the Lamb, each with a harp.* The harp, or kithara, usually had seven strings of equal length, although some had as few as six or as many as nine or ten (Note on 14:2). A stylized form is shown on a Jewish coin in Figure 22 (Mildenberg and Mottahedeh, *Coinage*, 46–48). Musicians sometimes wore robes and wreaths like the elders in Rev 4–5 (Figure 23; Maas and Snyder, *Stringed*, 53–78).

The heavenly company's posture is unusual, since musicians usually stood, and it seems incongruous to picture the creatures prostrating themselves while holding harps. Moreover, Jews and Christians typically offered prayers while standing so that they could lift up their eyes and hands (Josephus, *Ant.* 10.255; *m. Ber.* 5:1; *m. Taʻan.* 2:2; Luke 18:11, 13; 1 Tim 2:8). On occasion they might kneel down (Dan 6:11; Luke 22:41; Acts 9:40; Eph 3:14), but prostration was generally reserved for individuals making urgent prayer (Josh 7:6; Mark 14:35; *b. B. Meṣ.* 59b). Among Greeks and Romans, standing for prayer was the norm and prostration was rare (van Straten, "Did"). The group of creatures and elders engaging in prostration here show extraordinary reverence toward the Lamb.

and gold offering bowls. The *phialē*, or offering bowl, was used in Jewish and Greco-Roman worship. It was wide and shallow so its contents could easily be poured out. Some of the bowls in the Jerusalem temple were made of gold and could hold wine, flour, or incense (Josephus, *Ant.* 3.143; cf. Num 7:86; 2 Chr 4:8). Greeks used similar bowls when pouring out libations of wine. Artists sometimes depicted Apollo wearing a laurel wreath and holding a harp in one hand and a libation bowl in the other, like the heavenly beings in Revelation (Figure 23; cf. Maas and Snyder, *Stringed*, 78 pl. 19). A first-century coin from Sardis showed Nero on one side and Apollo with a harp and bowl on the other (Buttrey, *Greek*, 45 no. 247, 81–82; G. Stevenson, *Power*, 234). In Rev 5:8 the harps and bowls are used for worship, whereas in 15:7–16:21 the offering bowls bring judgment on the earth.

filled with incense, which are the prayers of the saints. Incense was offered morning and evening in the Jerusalem temple. Prayer was not mandated as part of the rite, but

Figure 22. Jewish coin from the Bar Kochba revolt showing a kithara (132 CE). Courtesy of the Classical Numismatic Group (cngcoins.com).

Figure 23. Apollo holding a kithara and libation bowl. Delphi (fifth century BCE).

the time of the incense offering was considered appropriate for prayer, with the smoke signifying the worshiper calling upon God (Jdt 9:1; Luke 1:10; Nielsen, *ABD* 3:407; Tóth, "Gebet"). Incense could also be a metaphor for prayer: "Let my prayer be counted as incense before you" (Ps 141:2). Jews used incense in the temple but apparently not in local synagogues (Harvey, *Scenting*, 16). Greek and Roman worshipers used shallow bowls when offering wine and prayer to the gods (Burkert, *Greek*, 70–73). They also burned incense on small altars and in special holders to honor the gods and deified emperors (Pausanias, *Descr.* 7.21.12; I.Smyr 753.12; Pliny the Younger, *Ep.* 10.96.5; Price, *Rituals*, 156, 209, 211, 228). Because of its popularity in the empire, the vision of Babylon/Rome names incense as a profitable commodity (NOTE and COMMENT on 18:13).

Early Christians used incense as a metaphor for acts of love (Eph 5:2; Phil 4:18) but apparently did not actually burn it during prayer; and from the second century onward, some Christians explicitly rejected its use (Justin Martyr, *1 Apol.* 13; Athenagoras, *Leg.* 13; Irenaeus, *Haer.* 4.17.5–6; Harvey, *Scenting*, 17–38). Rather than mirroring Christian practice, Revelation uses the image of incense, which was common throughout the ancient world, to emphasize that prayer can rightly be directed to Jesus. The way the heavenly beings bringing the saints' prayers before God had precedent in Jewish writings (Tob 12:12), but the more common idea was that angels interceded (*1 En.* 9:3; 40:6; 47:2; 104:1; *T. Dan* 6:2) or offered sacrifices (*T. Levi* 3:5) on behalf of the righteous.

The term "saints," or "holy ones" (*hagioi*), was used for God's people in Jewish tradition (Ps 34:10; Dan 7:21) and early Christianity (Acts 9:13; Rom 12:13; 2 Cor 1:1). Revelation uses it for the followers of Jesus (Rev 14:12; 17:6). To be holy is to be set apart for God and Christ, who are holy (3:7; 4:8). The literary context depicts the saints as those who revere God, keep his commandments, and devote themselves to righteous deeds (11:18; 14:12; 19:8). They suffer opposition from the forces of evil (13:7, 10; 16:6; 17:6; 18:24) yet have the promise of resurrection (20:6; 21:2, 10).

5:9. *And they sang a new song.* A "new song" connotes praise: "He put a new song in my mouth, a song of praise to our God" (Ps 40:3; cf. 96:1; Isa 42:10). Such new songs recalled God's saving deeds and were often accompanied by stringed instruments (Pss 33:3; 98:1, 5; 144:9; 149:1–3). Among the Greeks, new songs were said to be pleasing to listeners (Pindar, *Ol.* 9.48–49; Athenaeus, *Deipnosophistae* 1.25e; Lucian, *Zeuxis* 2; Aune). Here, the song is festive (cf. Rev 14:3).

"You are worthy to receive the scroll and to open its seals. Mystical literature spoke of those "worthy" to behold God's throne (*3 En.* 2:4; Schimanowski, *Die himmlische*, 243–46), but here the focus is on the Lamb's worthiness to reveal the purposes of God (Rev 4:11).

"for you were slain and by your blood. Slaying (*sphazein*) was usually done by the sword or other violent means (1 Sam 15:33; 2 Kgs 25:7; 1 Macc 1:24; 1 John 3:12). On one level, it recalls the brutality of Jesus' crucifixion, when his blood was shed through scourging, the nails in his hands and feet, and other wounds. On another level, the word was used for slaughtering Passover lambs (Exod 12:6; Ezra 6:20) and other sacrificial animals (Lev 14:13, 25; cf. 16:11, 15; Ezek 40:41–42). Like a sacrificial victim, Jesus was put to death by others, and as a sacrifice, his death had a salvific effect on human relationships with God.

"you purchased for God. The verb "purchase" (*agorazein*) has connotations of the marketplace (Rev 13:17; 18:11), where some people purchased others to be their slaves

(*Vita Aesopi* 15; 20). In the divine economy, however, Jesus purchases people for God, which is a redemptive action (1 Cor 6:20; 7:23; Gal 3:13; 4:5; 2 Pet 2:1; Rev 14:3–4; *TLNT* 1:26–28). Later visions identify the redeemed as those "purchased" by the Lamb, in contrast to those who capitulate to the beast in order to "purchase" goods in the marketplace (13:17; 14:3–4).

"*those of every tribe and language.* A tribe (*phylē*) could be the equivalent of a people (*laos*) or nation (*ethnos*), or it could be a subgroup, like the twelve tribes of Israel (7:4; Rom 11:1; Phil 3:5). Tribes shared kinship, language, and tradition. In Asia Minor such tribes included the Cibiani, Moxeani, Corpeni, and other groups. During the Hellenistic and Roman periods the term was also used for subgroups within a city, such as the tribe of Dionysius at Pergamum and Tymolis at Sardis (I.Sard 12; 34). Some civic tribes consisted of people in the same trade, like the tribe of shoemakers at Philadelphia (I.Phil 1491.22–23). Such civic tribes sometimes made dedications to an emperor or other figure (I.Sard 24). In terms of language (*glōssa*), Greek was widely spoken in the east, Hebrew was known in some Jewish circles (Rev 9:11), and many local languages were spoken throughout the Roman Empire (Acts 14:18; Strabo, *Geographica* 11.2.6; Pliny the Elder, *Nat.* 7.88). Maintaining one's language reinforced group identity.

"*and people and nation.* Biblical writers sometimes regarded tribes (Ezek 20:32; Zech 14:17), peoples (1 Chr 5:25; Ezra 9:1), and nations (Deut 6:14) as idolaters, who were liable to God's judgment. Similarly, Revelation shows them coming under the influence of God's adversaries (Rev 11:9; 13:7). But God's intent was that the earth's tribes (Gen 12:3; 28:14; Ps 72:17; Amos 3:2 LXX) and nations (Gen 22:18 LXX) should be blessed and that all peoples would serve God (Pss 67:3; 117:1; Mic 4:1). Similarly, Revelation calls people of every tribe and nation to worship God and shows them being redeemed by the Lamb (Rev 5:9; 7:9; 14:6).

5:10. "*and you made them a kingdom and priests to our God.* The language recalls Exod 19:6: "you shall be for me a kingdom of priests and a holy nation." The saying circulated in various forms. The MT said "a kingdom of priests" (cf. 4Q504 4 10; *Jub.* 16:18 Latin), while the LXX rendered it "a priestly kingdom" (cf. 1 Pet 2:9). But in Rev 1:6 the expression is "a kingdom, priests" (cf. Exod 19:6 in Symmachus; Theodotian; *Tg. Onq.*), and Rev 5:10 includes a conjunction, "a kingdom *and* priests" (cf. *Jub.* 16:18 Ethiopic; cf. *Tg. Neof.* Exod 19:6; Philo, *Abr.* 56; Philo, *Sobr.* 66; 2 Macc 2:17; Schüssler Fiorenza, *Priester*, 68–155). The forms used in Revelation suggest that "kingdom" and "priests" are two related yet distinguishable traits of God's people (Aune).

"*and they will reign on the earth.*" Some manuscripts read "reign" in the present tense and others in the future tense. The future tense, "they will reign" (*basileusousin*), has good manuscript support (א 1854 2050 2053) and fits the internal evidence. God's people already constitute a kingdom, but at present they may suffer at the hands of their opponents (Rev 13:8–10). Therefore, they can expect to reign only in the future (20:6; 22:5; Matt 5:5). If the future tense is original, it may have been changed to the present tense ("they reign," *basileuousin*) by a copyist inadvertently dropping an *s* through an error of the eye or ear, or perhaps intentionally to emphasize that Christians now reign in a spiritual way (Aune; Charles; Harrington; Smalley; Schüssler Fiorenza, *Book*, 75).

The present tense also has good manuscript support, including that of Alexandrinus, which is often the preferred text (A 1006 1611 2329; Andreas). The case for the present tense is weakened in that Alexandrinus may have changed the future tense of "reign" to a present tense in 20:6, suggesting that the same might have occurred in 5:10 (*TCGNT²*, 666–67). One might argue that the present tense is the more difficult and therefore preferable reading, since Christians do not now reign on earth in a visible way (Bandstra, "Kingship"; Karrer, "Text der Johannesoffenbarung," 391–96). It also departs from the style of Revelation, since "reign" (*basileuein*) appears elsewhere in the future and aorist tenses, but not in the present tense (Rev 11:15, 17; 19:6; 20:4, 6; 22:5). If the present tense is original, it could have been changed through a scribal error or perhaps intentionally to show that Christians do not now rule an earthly kingdom (Beale).

The textual uncertainty is linked to a twofold problem. On the one hand, Revelation can use the present tense in a futuristic way (Osborne; Swete; cf. Aune 1:clxxxv). On the other hand, the future tense can indicate a continuation of present circumstances: The kingdom of the world "has become [aorist tense] the kingdom of our Lord and his Anointed, and he will reign [future tense] forever and ever," since his reign will continue (Rev 11:15). Therefore, interpretation must rely more on literary context than on a strict reading of the verb tense. The most plausible sense is that the saints will share fully in Christ's reign in the future (see the COMMENT).

5:11. *Then I looked, and around the throne and the living creatures and the elders I heard the sound of many angels. They numbered in the millions—thousands upon thousands.* "Millions" in the Greek is literally "myriads of myriads." Although a myriad was ten thousand, the multiple myriads simply indicate an immense number. Around God's throne, "a thousand thousands served him, and a myriad of myriads stood attending him" (Dan 7:10 Theod.; cf. 4Q530 II, 17–18; *1 En.* 14:22; 40:1; 60:1; 71:8; *Apoc. Zeph.* 4:1; 8:1; *2 Bar.* 48:10).

5:12. *They said with a loud voice, "Worthy is the Lamb who was slain to receive power and wealth and wisdom and might and honor and glory and blessing."* Seven forms of praise are listed, each linked by the same conjunction (*kai*). Rhetorically, this creates a sense of grandeur, giving the impression that the list could go on indefinitely (Demetrius, *Eloc.* 65; Lausberg, *Handbook* §686). God was understood to possess and be the source of power (Ps 21:13; Jer 16:21), wealth (1 Chr 29:12), wisdom (Ps 104:24; Isa 31:2; Jer 10:12), and strength (Exod 15:13; Ps 147:5). Ascribing glory and honor to God was an act of worship (Pss 29:1; 96:7 [28:1; 95:7 LXX]; 1 Tim 1:17), as was blessing God (2 Chr 20:26; Neh 9:5; Tob 8:15). Power, honor, and glory could be ascribed to earthly kings (Dan 2:37), but Christians attributed these traits to Jesus (*1 Clem.* 65:2; *Mart. Pol.* 21).

5:13. *And I heard every creature in heaven and on earth and under the earth and in the sea—I heard everything in them say.* Praise expands from the angels to all creation (cf. Ps 103:20–22). The description of the created order is like that in Rev 5:3, with the addition of the sea (cf. Job 11:8–9; *Jub.* 2:16). Although some interpreters consider the sea to be the realm of evil (Osborne), it is an integral part of the created order (Rev 10:6; 14:7). The sea will be used by evil forces (13:1), but so will the land (13:11). The final disappearance of the sea does not suggest that it was especially evil (NOTE on 21:1).

"To the one seated on the throne and to the Lamb be blessing and honor and glory and might forever and ever." The word "blessing" ended the previous doxology, and it is the first word in this culminating doxology. Here, the Greek word for "might" (*kratos*) differs from those used before, but the sense is the same (Ps 59:9 [58:10 LXX]). On other elements, see the NOTE on Rev 5:12.

5:14. And the four living creatures said, "Amen," and the elders fell down and worshiped.
The "amen" is the four creatures' affirmation of what all creation has said. On "amen," see the NOTE on 1:6. On the creatures and elders, see the NOTES on 4:4 and 4:6.

COMMENT

John's vision of the heavenly court has focused on the resplendent throne of God, who is attended by four beings that represent the created order and by twenty-four elders who praise God for creating all things (4:1–11). These chapters identify the protagonists in the conflict that will dominate the second half of the book. As the Creator, God must overcome the destroyers of the earth and bring in the new creation (4:11; 11:18; 21:1). Christ is introduced as the Lamb, who has already won a victory by suffering death and must now overthrow the agents of death so that others may share the life of resurrection (5:5–6; 19:11–21; 22:1–5).

The plot is complicated because the forces of evil masquerade as good. The Lamb was slain (*esphagmenon*) and now lives, but the same is said about his adversary the beast (5:6; 13:3, 8). Moreover, the beast has an associate, which appears in the guise of a horned lamb (*arnion*), as does the agent of God (5:6; 13:11). The visions lift the veil of deception by showing that whereas the slain and living Lamb redeems people of every tribe and nation, the slain and living beast oppresses them (5:9–10; 13:7). And whereas the hosts of heaven worship God and the silent Lamb, their lamblike adversary speaks with the voice of a dragon, luring people into the worship of evil (5:11–13; 13:11).

This scene unfolds in three parts, each introduced by "Then I saw" (*kai eidon*). The first part centers on the throne, where God holds a sealed scroll in his hand, and the characters are limited in number. A single angel asks who is worthy to open the scroll. John alone weeps, until one of the elders tells him that the Lion of Judah has conquered (5:1–5). The second part expands the scope to include the slain and yet living Lamb, and all elders and creatures praise the Lamb for redeeming people of every tribe and nation (5:6–10). The third part extends the horizon outward, as countless angels in heaven join in praising the Lamb until every living thing in all creation ascribes praise and honor to God and the Lamb together (5:11–14; Murphy).

The vision gives readers a glimpse of a rightly ordered universe, in which God and the Lamb are central. There is symmetry: At the beginning, no creature in heaven, on earth, or under the earth is worthy to open God's scroll, while at the end, every creature in heaven, on earth, under the earth, and in the sea recognizes that the Lamb is worthy to do so (5:3, 12–13). The four heavenly creatures and elders begin the praise, and then after all others have joined the song, they conclude by adding "amen" and bowing down (5:9, 14). There is also internal progression: The first two hymns ascribe holiness,

On Rev 5:1–14, see Aune, *Apocalypticism*, 99–119; Bailey, "Genre"; Bandstra, "Kingship"; Barr, "Lamb"; Bergmeier, "Buchrolle"; Charles, "Apocalyptic"; Davis, *Heavenly*; Hannah, "Of Cherubim"; M. Hoffmann, *Destroyer*, 105–68; Hofius, "Ἀρνίον"; Hylen, "Metaphor"; Jauhiainen, *Use*, 84–89; Johns, *Lamb*; Jörns, *Das hymnische*, 44–76; Knight, "Enthroned"; Laws, *In the Light*, 24–35; MacLeod, "Adoration"; MacLeod, "Lion"; Mathewson, "Verbal"; P. McDonald, "Lion"; Morton, "Glory"; Moyise, "Does"; Schimanowski, *Die himmlische*; Schüssler Fiorenza, *Book*, 68–81, and *Priester*; Slater, *Christ*, 162–74; Stefanovic, "Meaning"; Strawn, "Why."

glory, and honor to God (4:8, 11); the next two give honor and glory to the Lamb (5:9, 12); and the final hymn acclaims God and the Lamb together (5:13). The hymns were probably composed for their present literary contexts, but the language would have sounded familiar to the readers, thereby encouraging them to make God and the Lamb the center of worship in their own social contexts (INTRO IV.E.1).

Some aspects of the passage are drawn from Scripture. Ezekiel described the heavenly throne room and scroll written on both sides (Ezek 1:4–28; 2:9–10). Daniel envisioned thousands of heavenly beings around God's throne (Dan 7:10). But where Daniel sees one like a human being receiving dominion, glory, and kingship, Revelation identifies the figure as the Lion of Judah, the Root of David, and the Lamb—images that evoke associations from other biblical texts (NOTES on Rev 5:5–6). In Daniel the human figure receives dominion over all peoples, nations, and languages, but in Revelation the Lamb redeems people from these groups so they become a kingdom and priests—recalling a biblical description of Israel (Dan 7:14; Exod 19:6; Rev 5:9; Aune; Beale).

The critical dimension of the passage is the way the vision of all the earth praising God and the Lamb contrasts with those in which the world worships the dragon and beast (Rev 13:4). In Revelation, the worship of the beast includes features of the imperial cult. It was common to give gold wreaths to Greek and Roman rulers, who might be called "lord" and "god," but in Revelation the wreaths and titles are given to the Creator (4:10–11). Similarly, hymns were sung to the emperors, who wanted it known that they ruled by the universal consensus of people in their realm (Aune, *Apocalypticism*, 109–16; Morton, "Glory"); however, in Rev 5, God and the Lamb are acclaimed worthy of rule by all creation.

The Sealed Scroll (5:1–5)

God holds a scroll with writing on the inside and the back (Rev 5:1). The scroll creates a sense of expectancy, since it presumably expresses the will of the God who holds it. Yet the scroll is sealed with seven seals. First, this means that the contents are hidden. John can see writing but cannot discern the message until the seals are broken (5:3). The scroll cannot be read; it is sealed in mystery (Isa 29:11; Dan 8:26; 12:4, 9; 1QH XVI, 11; 4Q300 1 II, 2–5; 4Q427 7 I, 19). Second, the seals show that the contents are valid. Seals were placed on scrolls to ensure that no one could tamper with them without being detected. Legal texts, such as wills, were sealed and to be opened only by authorized people. Similarly, Asian cities put a civic seal on official documents (I.Sard 8.19). The seals on the scroll in Rev 5:1 indicate that it is a valid statement of God's purposes.

The scroll has seven seals, underscoring the gravity of the contents. At one level this fits the literary pattern of the Apocalypse, in which the number seven is used to structure parts of the book. Accordingly, the opening of the seven seals will constitute a complete vision cycle (6:1–8:1). Some interpreters also suggest that seven seals are used because Roman wills were validated by seven witnesses, so one might expect God's scroll to attest the inheritance he will give to his people (Gaius, *Institutiones* 2.147; Justinian, *Inst.* 2.10.2–3; G. Fitzer, *TDNT* 7:950; Beale; Harrington). Yet seven seals were also used on other texts, such the letter of a Roman emperor to a petitioner (I.Smyr 597.11–13). More importantly, the scroll has the character of a royal decree. Stories were told of the archive at Persia, where among "the books was found a scroll, sealed with the seven seals of the ring" of King Darius (4Q550 5; cf. *4 Bar.* 3:10).

The disclosure of the scroll's contents will take place in several steps. Initially, God holds the scroll until the Lamb receives the scroll from him (Rev 5:1, 7). As the Lamb opens each of the seven seals, there are threatening visions and then silence (6:1–8:1). But these visions do not reveal the scroll's contents. Disclosure will occur after all the seals have been broken and another mighty angel gives the open scroll to John, who is told to eat it and prophesy (10:1–11). Only then will readers learn what the scroll contains—a message concerning the witness of the Christian community and its conflict with the beast. The message will be given in summary form in 11:1–15 and then in a more complete way in the rest of the book.

This literary progression was anticipated in Rev 1:1, which said that revelation was transmitted from God to Jesus to an angel to John. This pattern also fits the model of Ezekiel, which informs John's vision. After Ezekiel saw God's throne and the creatures with four faces, he was shown a scroll written on both front and back and then told to eat the scroll and prophesy (Ezek 2:8–3:3). Similarly, John sees God's throne and four creatures (Rev 4:1–11), then he is shown a scroll written on both sides (5:1–14), and finally he eats the scroll and is commissioned to prophesy (10:1–11; Mazzaferri, *Genre*, 270–79; Bauckham, *Climax*, 243–57; Blount; Boxall; Murphy). The contents are not revealed by the seal visions but in what follows, when the seals have been broken and John receives the open scroll.

To introduce this sequence, an angel asks, "Who is worthy to open the scroll and break its seals?" (Rev 5:2). The question is peculiar. If a sealed scroll was carried by a messenger, the person qualified to open it was the one to whom the message was addressed. If the scroll was a will, it would be opened after the testator's death by someone with a legal right to do so (Dio Cassius, *Rom. Hist.* 56.32.1). But Revelation does not compare God to the absent sender of a message or to the deceased testator of a will. The question is, who is worthy to make the will of the living God known and, by implication, to put it into effect?

God is the Creator of all things (Rev 4:11), yet in the first part of this scene nothing in the world has the qualities needed to reveal God's purposes (5:3). Theologically, this underscores the difference between the Creator and the creation, which is integral to the Apocalypse. In a negative sense, John critiques those who turn earthly materials into objects of worship and ascribe divine status to human rulers (9:20; 13:4, 12–14). In a positive sense, it means that if the Lamb is "worthy," he differs from all other beings in the created order. The heavenly company has called God "worthy" (*axios*), and the Lamb proves "worthy" to open the scroll and "worthy" to share the praises due to God himself (4:11; 5:9, 12–13).

When no one is found worthy to open the scroll, John begins to weep (5:4). Readers like those at Laodicea may be content and thus say, "I am rich and have become wealthy and do not need anything" (3:17). But John's weeping suggests that his perspective is aligned with those who suffer and ask "how long" it will be until God's just purposes are accomplished (6:10). God's designs now seem inscrutable, but when God's justice is done, the agents of injustice will weep (18:9, 11, 15, 19; Rowland).

The unfulfilled expectations heighten the suspense until an elder declares that the Lion of the tribe of Judah has conquered (5:5). The idea that worthiness in the eyes of heaven could be linked to conquest (*nikan*) had an important place in the readers' social worlds. According to Roman ideology, the gods sanctioned imperial rule, and this arrangement was celebrated with praise for imperial conquests (*Rom. Civ.* 1:624; Valerius Maximus, *Mem.* 1 pref.; Harrison, "Fading," 511–13). The imperial temple at Ephesus featured a statue of Titus in a triumphant military pose (Figure 8). Coins from Pergamum showed the goddess Nikē crowning Augustus with a victory wreath (Figure 12). The municipal temple at Laodicea showed Domitian as a conqueror (Figure 16). Reliefs in the imperial sanctuary at Aphrodisias showed the goddess Nikē attending the imperial conquests over the nations of the world (see Figures 29 and 30).

The writer of Revelation agrees that worthiness has to do with conquest, but he redefines what it means. When the elder says that the Lion of Judah has conquered, he recalls Gen 49:9–10, which compared Judah to a lion and said that the "scepter will not depart from Judah, nor the ruler's staff from between his feet, until he comes to whom it belongs; the nations will obey him" (NET). Judah was David's tribe, and the Genesis text was read as a promise concerning the righteous ruler who would inherit David's throne (NOTE on Rev 5:5). Christians identified Jesus as the one in whom the Davidic promises were realized and considered his descent from Judah to be part of his royal identity (Matt 1:3; 2:6; Luke 3:33; Heb 7:14). In Revelation the title "Lion of Judah" affirms that Jesus fulfills the biblical promise. He is the Lion and rightful ruler of earth's kings (Rev 1:5; 7:9–10).

The title "Root of David" also underscores the legitimacy of Jesus' rule (NOTE on Rev 5:5). The messianic Root, or Branch, of David was to act with justice and righteousness (Isa 11:1–4; Jer 23:5; 33:15; 4Q252 V, 3–4), and Revelation will picture Jesus bringing justice when he defeats the forces of evil at the end of the age (Rev 19:11). The Root was to strike the earth with the rod of his mouth and slay the wicked with his breath (Isa 11:4; cf. 4Q161 8–10 III, 10–22; 4Q285 5 3–4; 1Q28b V, 24–25; *Pss. Sol.* 17:24). Revelation depicts Christ doing this in his final defeat of the beast (Rev 19:15). Some writers expected the Branch to build the temple (Zech 6:12), and Christ does so by forming an earthly community that functions as the temple or place of true worship until Jesus and God become the temple of New Jerusalem (Rev 11:1; 21:22).

The lion and root imagery underscores the legitimacy of Christ's reign, but taken alone it does not adequately disclose that reign's character (Strawn, "Why"). A lionlike creature may serve the Creator (4:7), but John will also see a lion's features on monsters from the underworld and on the beast, who exercises the power of Satan and conquers by slaughtering the faithful (9:8, 17; 13:2). Therefore, what follows will reveal that the power of God's Messiah not only is greater than that of his opponents, but is different in kind (Barr, "Lamb"; Boesack, *Comfort*, 56–57; Resseguie).

The Slain Lamb (5:6–10)

John turns to see the Lion but finds "a Lamb, standing as one who had been slain" (5:6). The startling shift from Lion to slain Lamb does not negate Jesus' messianic identity. The point is that the promise of the Lion is *kept* through the slaughter of the Lamb. The love that the Lamb conveys by dying is the sovereign power that brings people into the kingdom of God (1:5–6; 5:9–10). What John *hears* about the Lion and Root recalls biblical texts that promised that God would send a righteous ruler, and what he *sees* shows how the promise is realized. The same pattern is repeated when John hears about the 144,000 being redeemed from the tribes of Israel and then turns to discover a countless multitude, redeemed from every tribe and nation (7:4, 9; Bauckham, *Theology*, 74–76).

Readers are expected to know that the slain Lamb is Jesus, though his name is not used, and that Jesus suffered death by crucifixion (Rev 1:5, 18; 2:8; 11:8). Culturally, crucifixion was understood to be a fitting penalty for someone who threatened the social order (Tacitus, *Ann.* 15.44). Some early Christian writers countered by using lamb imagery to depict Jesus as a victim of violence, yet one whose death was a sacrifice that benefited others. Crucifixion could be compared to the slaughter of a Passover lamb (1 Cor 5:7). Although the Passover sacrifice was not traditionally said to atone for sin, the Fourth Evangelist develops this idea by calling Jesus "the Lamb of God who takes away the sin of the world," telling of Jesus' death on the Day of Preparation, when the lambs were slain, and noting that his legs remained unbroken, as was fitting for a paschal lamb (John 1:29; 19:14, 37; Exod 12:46). Others identified Jesus as the suffering servant, who was like a lamb led to the slaughter and bore the iniquity of others (Isa 53:7; Acts 8:32; *1 Clem.* 16:7; *Barn.* 5:2; Justin Martyr, *Dial.* 111.3). Revelation's lamb imagery draws on a variety of such associations, but its significance is not determined by any one background (NOTE on Rev 5:6; Aune; Johns, *Lamb*, 107).

The slaughter of the Lamb is the conquest or victory that was announced in the previous verse. First, Jesus conquered by dying as a witness who remained faithful to God (1:5; 3:14). It would appear that Jesus' captors were victorious when they took his life, but in Revelation the opposite is true: Remaining loyal to God to the point of death is triumph, whereas abandoning one's faith to save one's life is defeat. Jesus' death is a victory of truth over falsehood, and his followers are to conquer in the same way— through the blood of the Lamb and the word of their own witness, even when this costs them their lives (2:7, 11, 17, 28; 3:5, 12, 21; 12:11; Blount).

Second, Jesus' death is unique in that it alone redeems people for life in God's kingdom (5:9–10). Many people suffered death by violent "slaying" (6:4, 9; 18:24), but Jesus' death has a redemptive effect. It releases people from sin (1:5–6), cleanses them so that they can come into God's presence (7:14), and purchases them for God (5:9). Each way of construing Christ's death presupposes that human beings are separated from God, whether through sin, uncleanness, or subjection to powers other than God. The crucifixion is the sacrificial act that Jesus accomplished out of love (1:5–6), giving himself over to death in order to evoke the faith that binds people to God. The power to redeem is true conquest and victory.

Third, Jesus' victory continues in resurrection. This is shown by the way John sees the Lamb "standing" by God's throne (5:6). The slain Lamb is alive, not dead, and John later sees the Lamb "standing" on Mount Zion with those redeemed from the earth (14:1, 3). Those who conquer the beast by faithfulness to God will be found "standing" beside heaven's glassy sea through resurrection (15:2; M. Hoffmann, *Destroyer*, 141).

The Lamb is peculiar in that he has seven horns, which often connoted strength or power (NOTE on 5:6). Because horns can be destructive, they seem out of place on a Lamb and better suited to the dragon and beast, whose horns symbolize the violent capacities of evil (12:3; 13:1). Yet the incongruity shows that the Lamb's death expresses the power to overcome sin and evil. Also distinctive are his seven eyes, which are the seven spirits of God (5:6). John has already described the risen Christ, whose eyes are like a flame of fire (1:14; 2:18; 19:12), and he has told of the seven flaming torches before the throne, which are the seven spirits of God (4:5). Through the fusion of the images, the torches and spirits before God's heavenly throne become the Lamb's eyes throughout the earth. The seven spirits are shared uniquely by God and the Lamb, which fits a vision in which both are honored as one (5:13; M. Hoffmann, *Destroyer*, 149–52). Revelation assumes that spirits may be either good or evil, and in the cosmic conflict the beast and its allies will send demonic spirits into the world to deceive people into a ruinous battle against God (16:13–14). But heaven has superior reconnaissance, conducted by the seven spirits, which extend the divine gaze throughout the world and serve the reign of God and the Lamb.

The reading developed above argues that the messianic hopes associated with the Lion and Root are realized and transformed by the image of the slain Lamb. The idea is not that the Lamb replaces the Lion and Root, as though the royal images no longer apply. Readers are to understand that the one John sees in Rev 5 fulfills the promises concerning the Lion and Root by confronting evil and building a kingdom. The new and surprising element is that he exercises this power as the Lamb, who is slain to redeem people of every nation for God (Bauckham, *Climax*, 213–15; Johns, *Lamb*, 150–64; Barr, *Tales*, 69–70; Laws, *In*, 24–35; cf. Hylen, "Metaphor").

Some writers argue differently and minimize the transformation. They propose that the Lion, Root, and Lamb were all traditional images for leadership. In *1 Enoch* Samuel and David are depicted as lambs that rule over the flock of Israel, and Judah Maccabee is a sheep with a horn, signifying military prowess (89:45–46; 90:9, 13). Similarly, *T. Jos.* 19:8 pictures a virgin from Judah, "and from her was born a spotless lamb." Beside him "was something like a lion, and all the wild animals rushed against him, but the lamb conquered them, and destroyed them, trampling them underfoot" (Aune; Ford; Mounce; Osborne; Malina, *On*, 101; G. Dautzenberg, *EDNT* 1:71). One problem in construing the Lamb as a traditional image for leadership is that the text of *T. Jos.* 19 is uncertain and shows signs of Christian editing (H. C. Kee in *OTP* 1:842; Becker, *Untersuchungen*, 59–68). Another problem is that *1 Enoch* recounts Israel's history by having cows, sheep, and other animals play the parts of notable figures from the past. The writer does not single out lambs as a distinctive royal image (Johns, *Lamb*, 76–107). More importantly, the lambs in *1 Enoch* and the *Testament of Joseph* are not slaughtered, whereas sacrifice defines the Lamb in Revelation (Maier, *Apocalypse*, 175; Slater, *Christ*, 164).

Other writers detect a reverse transformation, so that Revelation's literary context turns the suffering Lamb into a savage lion. They note that the Lamb is horned, like the dragon and beasts (Rev 5:6; 12:3; 13:1, 11). He opens the seals of the scroll to unleash plagues on the earth, is capable of wrath, watches the worshipers of the beast being tormented with fire, and triumphs over the beast in battle (6:1, 3, 5, 7, 9, 12, 16; 14:10; 17:14; Moyise, "Does"; Frilingos, *Spectacles*, 80–83; cf. Street, *Here*, 171–85, 236–37). However, the literary flow includes elements that move in the opposite direction. Opening the seals brings threatening visions that lead people to perceive the Lamb as wrathful, but when they ask "Who is able to stand?," the progression toward wrath is interrupted by a vision of a countless multitude, redeemed by the blood of the Lamb, "standing" before the throne and ascribing salvation to God and the Lamb (6:16–17; 7:9–13). Later, readers are to anticipate that the Lamb will conquer the kings allied with the beast, yet the messianic warrior's clothing is stained with blood *before* the battle begins, recalling the Lamb's death, and the only weapon used is the word (17:14; 19:13, 15). The Lamb who defeats kings makes a place for kings in the New Jerusalem, which is illumined by the Lamb's own light (21:23–24; Barr, "Lamb"; Johns, *Lamb*, 182–205; P. McDonald, "Lion").

Making the Lamb the dominant image for Christ in Revelation heightens the paradox that the one who was a victim is worthy of power (5:6–13) and that by losing his life he brings salvation to others (7:9–10). Instead of staining those it touches (Lam 4:14), the Lamb's blood brings the cleansing that allows access to God (Rev 7:14); and rather than being guided by a shepherd, the Lamb serves as the shepherd for his people (7:17). The Lamb suffered death, but those who belong to him are inscribed in his scroll of life (13:8; 21:27). The slaughtered Lamb does not become the meal at a banquet (Philo, *Legat.* 362), but is the host of a banquet—his own marriage feast (Rev 19:7, 9; 21:9). Rather than being offered up in a temple (Ezra 6:17), he and God become the temple of New Jerusalem (Rev 21:22–23; 22:1, 3).

Worship in heaven undergoes a change as the creatures and elders who bowed before God's throne now bow before the Lamb (4:10; 5:8). The harps that were traditionally used to praise God (Ps 150:3) sound praises to the Lamb. The bowls of incense that signified prayer to God (Ps 141:2) are placed before the Lamb (Rev 5:8). In the book of Psalms, a "new song" celebrated God's rule over the earth (Ps 96:1), and now a "new song" is sung to acclaim the Lamb's power and might. The heavenly chorus that acclaimed God "worthy" (Rev 4:11) now acclaims Christ "worthy" (5:9). Yet despite the shift in focus, the Lamb does not take God's place but is honored because he serves as God's agent, carrying out God's purposes.

The heavenly company declares that the slain Lamb purchased for God those of every tribe, language, people, and nation (5:9). The movement from conquest (*nikan*) to purchase (*agorazein*) creates a significant variation on common practice. The Babylonian and Persian empires were created through the conquest of various peoples, nations, and language groups (Dan 3:4; 5:19; 6:25; Jdt 3:8). Similarly, a vision of Rome's glory pictured Augustus enthroned in radiance, receiving gifts from the nations, as conquered peoples were paraded before him, all with their various languages (Virgil, *Aen.* 8:720–31; Dio Cassius, *Rom. Hist.* 56.34.3; Tacitus, *Ann.* 1.8). In Asia this theme was given visual form in the imperial temple at Aphrodisias, which included reliefs of imperial conquests over many peoples and nations, ranging from Egyptians, Arabs, and Judeans in the east to the Callaeci in the far west in Spain (see Figures 29, 30, 33, and 34; R. Smith, "Simulacra"; Friesen, *Imperial*, 86).

Conquest was often accompanied by the sale and purchase of war captives as slaves (Harris, "Towards," 121–22; Dio Chrysostom, *Disc.* 15.25). Those who conquered could put thousands of people onto the slave market, sometimes inviting dealers to purchase them for resale (1 Macc 8:10–11; Caesar, *Bell. gall.* 2.33; Josephus, *J. W.* 6.418). Those purchased as slaves were relegated to the lowest stratum of society. Such practices are reflected in the beast, which conquers by slaying those loyal to Jesus and exerts dominion over every tribe, people, language group, and nation (Rev 13:7). The beast carries the city of Babylon, which has traits of Rome and is a vast purchaser of human beings, who are its slaves (17:1–18; 18:13).

Where the beast conquers by inflicting death on others, the Lamb conquers by suffering death for the sake of others (5:5–6; 13:7). Where the beast dominates those of every tribe, people, language, and nation, the Lamb redeems people from all of these groups (5:9–10; 13:7). Earlier, the faithful were called slaves (*douloi*) of God, but serving the Creator of all things was considered an honor (NOTE on 1:1). The paradox is that those whom the Lamb purchases are not degraded to the status of chattels, but are elevated to membership in God's kingdom and given the honor of priestly status. The dignity of being called a priestly kingdom, which God gave to the Israelite slaves he delivered from Egypt (Exod 19:16; Isa 61:6), is now extended to people of all nations through the self-offering of the Lamb (Schüssler Fiorenza, *Book*, 74).

The redeemed constitute "a kingdom" in that they live under God's authority (5:10; cf. 1:6, 9). First, they are recipients of God's action. God is enthroned as Creator and sovereign Lord, and he exercises authority through the Lamb, whose death conveys the love that delivers people from subjection to sin (1:5–6; 14:12). Second, those who receive the benefits of the Lamb's action are to acknowledge his reign in a world where others vie for dominion (13:2–7; 16:10; 17:18). The faithful constitute *a* kingdom now by resisting the purported authority of evil, but *the* kingdom comes when evil is overthrown and the world recognizes the power of God and his Messiah (11:15; 12:10).

Those who belong to God's kingdom in the present "will reign on earth" in the future (5:10). At present, the Apocalypse pictures the reign of the beast and Babylon being supported by the kings of the earth, who oppose God and the Lamb (16:12, 14; 17:2, 14, 18; 18:3, 9; 19:16–19). Readers would have seen analogies to the vassal kings who ruled under the auspices of Rome (NOTE on 1:5). John, however, says that those redeemed by the Lamb will reign. He may recall a vision from Daniel, in which one who looks like a human being receives dominion so that all peoples, nations, and languages might serve him, and the saints receive kingly power (Dan 7:22, 27; Beale; Schimanowski, *Die himmlische*, 250). Yet Revelation does not picture a simple reversal in which Christ takes the imperial throne and the saints replace Rome's vassal kings. Readers have been told that Christ's throne and authority will be shared by those who "conquer" (Rev 2:26; 3:21). Now they find that the way Christ "conquers" is through suffering and that he exercises power over peoples, nations, and languages by redeeming them (5:5–6, 9). Like Christ, the redeemed conquer by remaining faithful, even at the cost of their lives (12:11; 15:2). The vision promises that they will reign with Christ through resurrection when they fully share the benefits of Christ's rule (20:4–6; 22:5; NOTES and COMMENT on 2:26).

One alternative interpretation relates this promise to the reign of the saints during the millennial period (20:4–6; Thomas 1:402; 2:414). But even though Revelation may depict the saints reigning "with Christ" for a thousand years, it says nothing about their location, and interpreters debate whether they are in heaven or on earth. What is clear is that in the new heaven and new earth the redeemed "will reign forever and ever" (Rev 22:5). Another alternative is that the saints *already* reign on earth (Beale; Bandstra, "Kingship"). Yet this interpretation is unlikely because the saints are now "a kingdom," not kings. As a kingdom they live under God's authority, which entails suffering because at present God's reign is contested. They will begin to reign with Christ through resurrection, and this culminates in the new creation (20:4, 6; 22:5; Giesen; Schüssler Fiorenza, *Book*, 76).

In addition to being a kingdom, the redeemed have a vocation as priests of God (1:6), which creates tensions with their social contexts (1:6). In Asia Minor there were priesthoods for Zeus, Dionysos, Asclepius, and other traditional deities, as well as those in the provincial and local imperial cults (NOTES on 2:1, 8, 12, 18; 3:1, 7, 14). People obtained priestly status through inheritance, appointment, election, or lot. The wealthy might purchase the office of priest for themselves. Priests often paid the costs of festivals and received public honor for doing so (Beard and North, eds., *Pagan*). Here, the priesthood of Jesus' followers differs. Instead of purchasing their position, they become priests when they themselves are purchased or redeemed by Christ (Harrison, "Fading," 513–18). They do not offer sacrifices but give honor to the Lamb whose death was the sacrifice that redeemed them (1:6).

Revelation's language recalls that Israel as a whole was a priestly people (Exod 19:6). What changes is that this priesthood is extended to the redeemed from every people and nation. There were biblical precedents for envisioning a priesthood that included former Gentiles (Isa 66:21), and the idea is emphasized in Revelation (Rev 5:9–10; 7:9, 15). Jewish tradition had a special class of priests who served in the temple and were influential in synagogue life (Acts 19:14; *IJO* II, 33.3; III, 84.5; Schürer, *History*, 2:237–91). In Revelation, angels perform priestly duties in the heavenly temple (Rev 8:3; 15:5–8), but on earth all of Jesus' followers have priestly status, and their community is depicted as a temple (3:12; 11:1–2). In the readers' social worlds divine honors are given to Greco-Roman deities and emperors, and in the visionary world this is mirrored in veneration of the beast (13:4, 12, 15). Accordingly, worship of God is part of the believers' current witness to society (Beale; Boring, Sweet; Friesen, *Imperial*, 181–82). In the future, priestly service will continue, as those who bear God's name on their foreheads in the manner of high priests will see his face and worship in a city that has traits of a sanctuary (22:3–4; cf. 20:6; Schüssler Fiorenza, *Priester*, 385–89).

All Creation Praises God and the Lamb (5:11–14)

The words "I saw" press the horizon outward, beyond the inner circle of creatures and elders to the incalculable number of angels who surround them (5:11). Where the creatures and elders acclaimed the Lamb worthy to open God's scroll (5:9), the angels declare him worthy of sovereign power. Where the Creator was given the threefold praise of "glory and honor and power" (4:11), the Lamb receives sevenfold praise, including "power and wealth and wisdom and might and honor and glory and praise" (5:12). The point is not to elevate the Lamb above God but to include the Lamb in the honor due to God so that both can be worshiped as one (5:13).

Many of the praises included here recall those given to God in Scripture:

> Yours, O Lord, are the greatness and the power and the glory and the victory and the majesty, for all that is in the heavens and on the earth is yours; yours is the kingdom. O Lord, you are exalted as head above all. Wealth and glory come from you, and you rule over all. In your hand are power and might; and it is in your hand to make great and to give strength to all. And now, our God, we give thanks to you and praise your glorious name (1 Chr 29:11–13).

The angelic company in John's vision follows a similar form and theme when declaring the glory of the Lamb, as prayers and incense rise in the heavenly sanctuary. An inscription from Pergamum, however, includes a contrasting scene. When the Hellenistic king Attalus arrived at the city, the temples were to be opened, incense offered up, and prayers made for his "health, salvation, victory, power" (I.Perg 246.27–31; G. Stevenson, *Power*, 285). During the Roman period, prayers were made not only *on behalf of* certain rulers, but *to* them, and hymn singers from Asian cities offered praises to the god Augustus and other emperors in imperial temples (I.Eph 19.57; 3801 II.18–19; Friesen, *Imperial*, 104–7).

Using such language to praise the crucified Jesus as the slaughtered Lamb heightens the incongruity between the claims of the visionary world and those of the readers' social worlds. Vespasian was acclaimed benefactor, savior, and "only worthy [*axios*] emperor of Rome" because of his military victories (Josephus, *J.W.* 7.71), but the victory that made the Lamb worthy was suffering slaughter by crucifixion. Praise was given to the empire's "all-wise, all-powerful, all virtuous, divinely ordained ruler" (*Rom. Civ.* 2:19), but it seemed incongruous to ascribe power and might to a slaughtered lamb or the crucified Jesus. Fabulous wealth heightened the emperor's status and influence, allowing him to be seen as his subjects' chief benefactor (Augustus, *Res* 17; Millar, *Emperor*, 189–201); but a slaughtered lamb was not a symbol of wealth, and a victim of crucifixion forfeited his property (Mark 15:24 par.; Justinian, *Dig.* 48.20.1). One might celebrate the wisdom shown by prudent imperial governance (Dio Chrysostom, *Disc.* 3.6, 10), but lambs were considered unwitting (Ps 119:176; Isa 53:6; Matt 18:12), and Jesus' career culminated in crucifixion—something deemed foolish rather than wise by those outside the Christian community (1 Cor 1:18–25; Justin Martyr, *1 Apol.* 13.4). Finally, imperial pageantry gave "glory, honor, and praise" to the ruler of a vast realm, but honoring a victim of crucifixion seemed absurd, since the cross was "the tree of shame" (Cicero, *Rab. Perd.* 13; cf. Justin Martyr, *Dial.* 32.1).

Ascribing power to the slaughtered Lamb shapes the way readers are to understand the power of God. God exercises power (*dynamis*) by creating (4:11; 11:17), whereas the dragon, the beast, and their allies exert destructive power over the world God made (13:2; 17:13). God will assert his rightful power by overthrowing the destroyers (12:10; 19:1), but power also characterizes the slaughtered Lamb, whose sacrifice conveys the love that brings people into God's kingdom (1:5–6; 5:9–10). Next, wealth (*ploutos*) was included in praise of God (1 Chr 29:12), but in Revelation it takes various forms. The readers at Smyrna are economically poor but rich in faith (Rev 2:9), while those at Laodicea are materially well-off but spiritually impoverished (3:17). Babylon uses the allure of wealth to entwine people in a social and political system that John considers antithetical to God (18:3, 15, 17, 19; Resseguie). But the wealth of the Lamb is shown in the way he "purchases" people for God at the cost of his own blood (5:9–10).

Wisdom (*sophia*) is ascribed to the slaughtered Lamb, as it is to God elsewhere (5:12; 7:12), and it fits a context in which readers face competing truth claims (2:2, 9, 20, 24; 3:9). John assumes that evil works through deception, so wisdom is needed to unmask it (12:9; 13:14; 18:23). A prophetess at Thyatira taught that those with a deep understanding of God could eat what was offered to Greco-Roman deities, and such accommodation would help the readers fit more comfortably into society. In contrast, Revelation places such accommodation among "the deep things of Satan" (2:20, 24) and identifies true wisdom with the slaughtered Lamb, who brings God's purposes to fulfillment. Finally, the hosts of heaven give honor, glory, and praise (*timē*, *doxa*, and *eulogia*) to the Lamb, as they do to the God who creates and saves (4:11; 7:12). In contrast, Revelation pictures the multitudes of earth worshiping a ruling power that generates awe by its conquests and dominion over many nations (13:1–8). The angels honor the authority that is exercised through self-offering and redemptive action.

The final expansion of the horizon occurs when every creature in heaven, the earth, the sea, and the regions below the earth praise God and the Lamb together (5:13). In Revelation, Christ is not a second object of worship alongside God but is included within the worship of the one God, since God's purposes are accomplished through him (7:10; 11:15; 22:3; Bauckham, *Theology*, 54–65; M. Hoffmann, *Destroyer*, 152–68).

The way the universe ascribes honor and power to God and the Lamb underscores the legitimacy of their reign. In the readers' social world, the emperors cultivated the impression that they ruled because people everywhere wanted them to do so (*consensus omnium*). Augustus claimed to have "attained supreme power by universal consent" (Augustus, *Res* 34), and Emperor Tiberius was called the one "in whose charge the unanimous will of gods and men has placed the governance of land and sea" (Valerius Maximus, *Mem*. 1 pref.; Tacitus, *Hist*. 1.15). As David Aune has put it, the "widespread assumption among the Romans was that imperial honors, to be both acceptable and legitimate, had to be conferred by others, not claimed by the emperor himself" (*Apocalypticism*, 115). Revelation challenges this assumption by including aspects of imperial rule in the portrait of the beast and its agents as tyrants, who impose their will on their subjects (Rev 13:7, 16), and by contrasting this with the praise that all creation gives to the Creator and the Lamb, who have a rightful claim over the world (5:13–14).

15. Six Seals Are Opened (6:1–17)

6 ¹Then I looked, when the Lamb opened one of the seven seals, and I heard one of the four living creatures say in a voice like thunder, "Come!" ²So I looked, and there was a white horse. Its rider held a bow and a laurel wreath was given to him. And the conqueror went out in order to conquer.

³Then, when he opened the second seal, I heard the second living creature say, "Come!" ⁴And out came another horse, fiery red. Its rider was allowed to take the peace from the earth, so that people would slay one another. And a large sword was given to him.

⁵Then, when he opened the third seal, I heard the third living creature say, "Come!" So I looked, and there was a black horse. Its rider held a pair of scales in his hand. ⁶And I heard what sounded like a voice from among the four living creatures. It said, "A quart of wheat for a denarius, and three quarts of barley for a denarius, but do not damage the olive oil and the wine."

⁷Then, when he opened the fourth seal, I heard the voice of the fourth living creature say, "Come!" ⁸So I looked, and there was a pale green horse. Its rider's name was Death, and Hades was following right behind him. They were given authority over a fourth of the earth, to kill by sword and famine and disease and the wild animals of the earth.

⁹Then, when he opened the fifth seal, I saw under the altar the souls of those who had been slain because of the word of God and the witness they

had given. [10]They cried out with a loud voice and said, "How long, O Master, holy and true, will you wait before you pass judgment and bring justice for our blood, which was shed by those who live on the earth?" [11]But each of them was given a white robe, and they were told to rest for a short time, until those who were their fellow servants and their brethren—who were to be killed as they were—were finished.

[12]Then I looked, when he opened the sixth seal, and a great earthquake occurred. The sun became black as sackcloth made of hair, and the entire moon became like blood. [13]The stars of the sky fell to the earth like a fig tree drops its fruit when shaken by a strong wind. [14]The sky disappeared, like a scroll being rolled up, and every mountain and island was moved from its place. [15]Then the kings of the earth and the aristocrats and the generals and the rich and the powerful and everyone, slave and free, hid themselves in caves and in the rocks of the mountains. [16]They called to the mountains and the rocks, "Fall on us" and "hide us from the face of the one seated on the throne and from the wrath of the Lamb! [17]For the great day of their wrath has come, and who is able to stand?"

NOTES

6:1. *Then I looked, when the Lamb opened one of the seven seals.* The sealed scroll conveys God's purposes (NOTES on 5:1). The word "one" can also be rendered "first" (Aune).

and I heard one of the four living creatures say in a voice like thunder, "Come!" The first living creature looks like a lion (4:7) and it roars like thunder. Thunder comes from God's throne (4:5), and thundering voices will later celebrate God's victories (14:2; 19:6). The sound is like the voices of Christ and an angel (1:15; 10:3). Thunder can portend threats against the earth, as is the case here (8:5; 11:19; 16:18). According to some manuscripts (ℵ 046 296; cf. KJV), the living creature tells John to "come and see" the horsemen, which ancient interpreters construed as an invitation to discipleship (Victorinus; Primasius; cf. John 1:46). The shorter and better reading (A C P 1 1006) is that the creature commands the horseman to "come," thereby signaling the threat of conquest.

6:2. *So I looked, and there was a white horse.* Horses and cavalry riders connoted warfare (Isa 31:1; Jer 8:6; Acts 23:23), and horse imagery appears in Revelation's battle scenes (Rev 9:7–19; 14:20; 19:11–21). The colors of the horses in Rev 6:1–8 recall those in Zechariah, who depicted riders and chariots with horses that were white and other colors (Zech 1:8; 6:3). The colors of the horses in John's vision—white, red, black, and green—did not have fixed meanings. In Revelation white characterizes God's throne (20:11), Christ's appearance (1:14; cf. 14:14; 19:11, 14), the white stone that signifies vindication (2:17), and the white robes that show purity and honor (3:4, 5, 18; 4:4; 6:11; 7:9, 13). Here, the white horse is linked to conquest and victory, which is appropriate since victorious military leaders from the Persians through Julius Caesar sometimes appeared with white horses (Herodotus, *Historiae* 7.40; 9.63; Dio Cassius, *Rom. Hist.* 43.14.3; cf. Virgil, *Aen.* 3.537; Charles). The writer Phlegon imagined that Asian armies would ride white horses when triumphing over Rome (*Rom. Civ.* 1:407).

Its rider. The rider has been identified in several ways; the third is the most plausible:

1. Christ. Some interpreters identify the rider as Christ and his conquering as the spreading of the gospel before the end, as in Matt 24:14 and Mark 13:10 (Lupieri; Rowland; Sweet; Bachmann, "Noch"; Herzer, "Der erste"; on the history of interpretation, see §12A). The rider on the white horse in Rev 19:11 is clearly Christ, so one might assume that the figure in 6:2 is also Christ. If the first horseman conquers, so does Christ (3:21; 5:5–6; 17:14). White is associated with God, Christ, and the faithful (previous NOTE). Wreaths are worn by Christ (14:14) and by those who belong to God (2:10; 3:11; 4:4, 10; 12:1). One problem with this view is that the rider holds a bow, whereas Christ wages war with the sword of his mouth (1:16; 2:16; 19:15, 21). A more important problem is that the four horsemen can best be taken as a group, and the rest of the horsemen are not Christlike. Some interpreters argue that the first rider should be separated from the others, noting that the second rider is "another" (*allos*) or different figure (6:4). Yet it is more plausible to see all four riders as interrelated threats—much like the first four trumpets in 8:7–12.

2. Evil figure. Some interpreters take the first horseman to be an evil agent or the Antichrist (Beale; Boxall; LaHaye; Thomas; Wong, "First"). He conquers violently like the beast (11:7; 13:7) and receives a wreath, much as the demonic horselike figures in 9:7 wear wreaths. If the rider resembles Christ, who appears on a white horse in 19:11–16, he shows how agents of evil mimic traits of Christ (5:6; 13:11; cf. Matt 7:15; 2 Cor 11:14). The rider's true identity is suggested by the bow, which was carried by God's adversaries, whether Gog (Ezek 39:3; Rissi, *Hure*, 23–24) or Apollo and the forces of paganism (Kerkeslager, "Apollo"; Karrer, "Apoll"). A variation is that the horseman signifies the false prophets who accompany the eschatological wars and famines according to the gospels (Michaels; cf. Matt 24:5–12 par.). These proposals rightly take the four riders as a group and perceive the first rider as a threat, but they press for too much specificity.

3. Human conquest. The most plausible view is that the horseman signifies the threat of human wars of conquest. This approach considers all four riders as a set, like the four groups of horses and riders in Zech 1:8–15 and 6:1–8, and it recognizes that all the horsemen are ominous. Like the violence, food shortages, and death represented by the other horsemen, the first rider points to a threat posed by the violent forces operative within human society (Aune; Boring; Giesen; Harrington; Kraft; Mounce; Murphy; Osborne; Roloff; Wall). The riders were pictured as a threatening group by Albrecht Dürer and in Luther's German NT of 1522 (Bachmann, "Die apokalyptischen").

held a bow. The rider with a bow raises the specter of conquest by an outside power. The Assyrians and Babylonians who conquered Israel and Judah used mounted archers (Jdt 2:15; Jer 6:23; 50:42), in contrast to the bowmen in Israel's armies, who moved on foot or in chariots (2 Kgs 9:16, 24; Isa 5:28; Amos 2:15; Zech 9:10). At the time Revelation was written some of the peoples at the borders of Rome's empire used mounted bowmen. On the northern frontier, west of the Black Sea, were the Sarmatians and Getans (Ovid, *Trist.* 5.7.13–15). In the east were the Parthians, whose mounted archers defeated the Romans in 53 BCE and again in 36 BCE and 62 CE (Plutarch, *Crass.*

24.5–25.5; Plutarch, *Ant.* 34.3–5; Tacitus, *Ann.* 15.1–19). Although the Romans began using mounted archers as auxiliary troops in the early second century CE (Bosworth, *Arrian*, 236–37), the mounted bowman was more typical of non-Roman peoples, making the rider a fitting way to depict conquest by outsiders.

Interpreters sometimes suggest that the image plays on Roman fears of a Parthian invasion, especially because later visions describe hostile forces coming from east of the Euphrates, which was Parthian territory (Rev 9:14; 16:12; Boring; Charles; Harrington; Murphy; Osborne). But the image does not have such specificity. The Parthians used mounted bowmen, but so did other peoples; and the Parthian cavalry used lances as well as bows (Plutarch, *Luc.* 28.2–4; Plutarch, *Crass.* 25.8). The bow does not limit the rider's identity to one group. Moreover, the Roman fear of Parthia is often overstated. The brother of the Parthian king formally submitted to Nero in 66 CE and served as the Roman vassal over Armenia. The king of Parthia sent Vespasian a gold crown to celebrate his victory over the revolt in Judea and later asked for Roman help, though Vespasian demurred. The Parthian king did threaten war against Rome in about 76 CE but ended up coming to terms (Bosworth, "Vespasian's"). Revelation's vision of the mounted bowman does not so much express Roman fears as it challenges presumptions of Roman strength.

and a laurel wreath was given to him. Laurel wreaths were given to victorious generals and soldiers who distinguished themselves in battle (Pliny the Elder, *Nat.* 16.10; Aulus Gellius, *Noct. att.* 5.6.1–27), as well as to victorious emperors (Dio Cassius, *Rom. Hist.* 53.16). Here, the rider—who looks more like a foreigner than a Roman—is given the wreath as he sets out to conquer, so it anticipates his coming victory. On wreath imagery, see the NOTE on Rev 2:10.

And the conqueror went out in order to conquer. The verb *nikan* indicates both conquest and victory (NOTE on 2:7). The Greek expression is awkward and might be translated "he came out conquering and to conquer" (NRSV). But instead of "conquering," the participle *nikōn* can better be taken as a substantive ("conqueror") and as the subject of the verb (Oecumenius; Krause, "Finite," 202–4). The *kai hina* ("and to") indicates purpose: to conquer (6:4; 13:17).

6:3. *Then, when he opened the second seal, I heard the second living creature say, "Come!"* The second creature has a face like an ox (4:7). On the seals, see the NOTE on 5:1.

6:4. *And out came another horse, fiery red.* Fiery red was a color for horses, cattle, and other animals (Zech 1:8; Num 19:2; Artemidorus, *Onirocritica* 2.11.39). In Zech 1:8 and 6:2 the fiery red color of the horses does not have special significance, but in Rev 6:4 it is linked to bloodshed (2 Kgs 3:22 LXX). In Rev 12:3, Satan the dragon is fiery red.

Its rider was allowed to take the peace from the earth. Peace is usually a blessing (Pss 29:11; 122:6), but when peace masks oppression, removing it can be a form of judgment. Paul warned that when people complacently say "'Peace and security,' then sudden destruction will come upon them" on the Day of the Lord (1 Thess 5:3). The Pax Romana, or Roman peace, was a celebrated source of well-being. The Senate erected an altar to the Augustan peace (Augustus, *Res* 12), and it was said that never had "the Romans and their allies thrived in such peace and plenty as that afforded them by Caesar Augustus" and his successor Tiberius (Strabo, *Geographica* 6.4.2; cf. Seneca the

Younger, *Clem.* 1.4.1–2; Plutarch, *Mor.* 824C; Epictetus, *Diatribai* 3.13.9). Nevertheless, critics charged, "They rob, butcher, plunder, and call it 'empire'; and where they make a desolation, they call it 'peace'" (Tacitus, *Agr.* 30). The vision of the second horseman challenges the idea that the prevailing peace is a source of security.

so that people would slay one another. And a large sword was given to him. Revelation uses terms for swords interchangeably (*machaira*, Rev 6:4; *hromphaia*, 6:8). Readers may have pictured the removal of peace as an outbreak of brigandage, which threatened roadways and sea lanes even under the Roman peace. Urban residents saw brigands as "an all-pervasive threat beyond the city gates" (*OCD* 261). Others may have pictured violent civil strife (Appian, *Bell. civ.* 1.intro.5; Lucan, *Pharsalia* 2.148–51; Keener). Massacres of Romans and Italians in Ephesus, Pergamum, and other places unleashed a brutal cycle of conflict in Asia in 88 BCE (Appian, *Hist. rom.* 12.4.22–23; 12.9.61–62). Jewish groups fought with Rome and each other during the revolt of 66–73 CE (Schürer, *History*, 1:484–508), and there were violent power struggles in Rome in 68 CE (Tacitus, *Hist.* 1.2). Although some interpreters suggest that the rider anticipates violence against Christians (Rev 6:9; 13:8; 18:24; Beale), slaughtering "each other" suggests a broader pattern of conflict.

6:5. *Then, when he opened the third seal, I heard the third living creature say, "Come!"* The third creature has a face like a human being (4:7). On the seals, see the NOTE on 5:1.

So I looked, and there was a black horse. Its rider held a pair of scales in his hand. In Revelation black is ominous, as in the sun turning dark (6:12; cf. 8:12; 9:2; 16:10). The rider holds the scales used in commerce. The Greek *zygon* corresponds to the Latin *libra*, a scale that consisted of a horizontal bar that was balanced on a hook or cord with a pan suspended from each end. The imagery fits the context in only a general way, since scales were used to sell goods according to weight, whereas Rev 6:6 cites grain prices according to volume. During severe food shortage, bread was rationed by weight (Lev 26:26; Ezek 4:16–17).

6:6. *And I heard what sounded like a voice from among the four living creatures.* The voice presumably belongs to God, since the living creatures are positioned around God's throne (4:6).

It said, "A quart of wheat for a denarius, and three quarts of barley for a denarius. Wheat was the preferred grain for bread, the staple food. A quart, or *choinix*, of wheat was a daily ration for one person (Herodotus, *Historiae* 7.187; Athenaeus, *Deipnosophistae* 3.98e; Diogenes Laertius, *Lives* 8.18; Charles). Barley was a lighter and less nutritious grain, which the lower classes baked into coarse bread or cooked into porridge (2 Kgs 4:42; John 6:9; Pliny the Elder, *Nat.* 18.67, 72). The denarius was a silver Roman coin that was equivalent to the Greek drachma and was a daily wage for laborers (Tob 5:14; Matt 20:1–16; Polybius, *Histories* 6.39.12–13; Tacitus, *Ann.* 1.17; *b. 'Abod. Zar.* 62a). In Asian cities a denarius would ordinarily buy about sixteen quarts of wheat, although after a hard winter the Roman legate allowed grain to be sold at twice that price (*Rom. Civ.* 2:250). Barley usually cost about half as much as wheat (Cicero, *Verr.* 2.3.81 §188). The prices in Revelation were eight to sixteen times higher than usual, rates associated with severe shortages (Josephus, *Ant.* 14.28). A worker would have to spend his entire day's pay to provide wheat bread for himself or enough barley for a small family.

"but do not damage the olive oil and the wine." Some interpreters suggest that oil and wine were luxury items (Reddish), but this is not the case. Both rich and poor, and even slaves, regularly consumed oil and wine (Deut 7:13; 1 Kgs 17:12; Lam 2:12; Joel 1:10; Cato, *Agr.* 56–58). In times of shortage, however, people would purchase bread before other foodstuffs. The command not to damage (*adikein*) the oil and wine is occasionally taken as a warning that merchants should not "charge unjustly" for oil and wine during the food crisis (Vanni, *L'Apocalisse*, 193–213), but this interpretation is unlikely since *adikein* commonly indicates damage (Rev 7:2–3; 9:4, 10, 19).

Some interpreters try to discern a progressive sequence of events in these visions, proposing that the shortage of grain, alongside adequate supplies of oil and wine, arises from the violence signified by the first two horsemen, either because troops might ruin grain fields while leaving orchards and vineyards untouched (Keener; Osborne) or because vines and olive trees would produce fruit even if grain could not be planted because of warfare (Kraft; Giesen). Others appeal to natural phenomena in which trees and vines yield fruit even when drought damages grain (Aune).

The vision more probably reflects a common economic pattern. In the imperial world a principal cause of food shortages "was the earmarking of vast quantities of grain to feed the city of Rome and the armies, while throughout the Empire large areas continued to be diverted from the cultivation of cereals to the more profitable production of wine and olive oil" (*Rom. Civ.* 2:247). Some people made handsome profits in oil and wine, but reduced grain cultivation meant that when the harvest was meager or grain shipments were disrupted, many cities faced a food crisis. Some people exacerbated the problem by hoarding grain for their own use or to sell at inflated prices. In John's vision the economic forces that create such shortages and lead to hardship are allowed to have their way. Although some interpreters think the vision refers specifically to a famine that occurred in 93 CE (Court, *Myth*, 59–60), the imagery is broader (Intro II.C.2).

6:7. *Then, when he opened the fourth seal, I heard the voice of the fourth living creature say, "Come!"* The fourth heavenly creature looks like an eagle (4:7).

6:8. *So I looked, and there was a pale green horse.* The colors of the first three horses in Rev 6:1–6 correspond to those in Zech 6:2–3. According to the MT of Zechariah, a fourth group of horses were *ʾămuṣim*, which may be a light color. The LXX called them "spotted." In Revelation the fourth horse is *chlōros*, which can be the color of plants (8:7; 9:4), but here it is the greenish-gray pallor of a person who is sick, dying, or terrified (Hippocrates, *Progn.* 2; Sappho, frg. 2.14–15; Artemidorus, *Onirocritica* 1.77; Homer, *Il.* 7.479).

Its rider's name was Death, and Hades was following right behind him. Earlier, Death and Hades were pictured as the netherworld to which people descend at death (Note on 1:18). They could be characterized as a place or condition (Ps 6:5; Prov 5:5). According to Hos 13:14 (MT), God summoned Death to bring plagues and Hades (Hebrew, *Sheol*) to wreak destruction against the unfaithful in Samaria. Here, they are personified as forces that have the power to grasp people (2 Sam 22:6; Pss 18:5; 116:3), much as Hades was described as a creature with a gaping mouth ready to consume the dying (Isa 5:14; Hab 2:5; Sophocles, *Elektra* 542; cf. Ps 18:5; *T. Ab.* 8:12). In the Greco-Roman world, Hades was god of the underworld. A first-century epitaph from Smyrna grieves for a person "whom stern Hades dragged away" (I.Smyr 552.1–2). In Revelation, Death rides like a warrior to strike a fourth of the earth.

They were given authority over a fourth of the earth. Authority over a fourth of the earth shows the magnitude of the threat as well as its limit: one-fourth, not more. In the trumpet visions the scale increases so that a third of the earth is damaged and a third of humanity is killed (Rev 8:1–12; 9:15, 18). The bowl visions tell of even more comprehensive plagues (16:1–21), yet death remains subject to the greater power of God. At the last judgment he will make Death and Hades surrender their captives before being hurled into the lake of fire (20:13–14; 21:4).

to kill by sword and famine and disease and the wild animals of the earth. The list is in part traditional (2 Chr 20:9; Jer 14:12; 21:7; Ezek 5:17; 6:11; 4Q171 II, 1; *Sib. Or.* 3:335), though it also continues the threats from previous visions. First, the sword continues the threats of violence represented by the horsemen who held the bow and sword. Second, famine extends the problem of food shortages ushered in by the third rider, when wheat and barley were costly (Lam 4:8–9; cf. 2:19–21; 2 Kgs 6:25). Third, the word *thanatos*, which often means death, here refers to infectious diseases. Ancient readers might have envisioned epidemics of typhus and smallpox, which brought fevers and delirium, sores, and often death (*OCD* 1188). Fourth, wild animals added to the causes of death. Ancient readers regarded wolves, lions, leopards, and bears as the most dangerous (Jer 5:6; Hos 13:7–8; Plutarch, *Mor.* 994A; 995B). Jackals and hyenas scavenged among the dead (Ps 63:10; Isa 13:22). Traits of the leopard, lion, and bear appear in the beast in Rev 13:2.

6:9. *Then, when he opened the fifth seal, I saw under the altar.* Revelation envisions a heavenly sanctuary with a single altar for sacrifice and prayer. This differs from Israel's tabernacle and temples, which had two altars: one for incense within the sanctuary and another for burnt offering in the courtyard (Exod 27:1–8; 30:1–10; 2 Chr 4:1, 19; Josephus, *J.W.* 5.216, 224). These sanctuaries were said to have been built according to divinely given patterns, which many thought were actual heavenly sanctuaries (Exod 25:9; 1 Chr 28:19; Wis 9:8; Heb 8:1–5). Therefore, some interpreters assume that Revelation pictures two heavenly altars (Kraft; Roloff). Yet this idea is unlikely. Revelation refers only to "the altar" in the singular, and sources similar to Revelation do not distinguish two heavenly altars (*T. Levi* 3:4–6; *b. Ḥag.* 12b; Herm. *Mand.* 10.3.2). Others identify the altar in Rev 6:9 with either the altar of burnt offering (Aune; Harrington; Murphy; Roloff; Swete) or the altar of incense (Beale; Charles; Briggs, *Jewish*, 80), but Revelation envisions only one heavenly altar with multiple functions (Boxall; Mounce).

Picturing the martyrs under the altar shows their deaths as sacrifices, since the blood of sacrificial victims was poured out at the base of an altar (Lev 4:7). Such sacrificial imagery reverses common perceptions of the martyrs' deaths. They might appear to have died pointlessly at the hands of their adversaries, but their location under the altar shows that God receives those who are slaughtered on account of their witness (Wis 3:6). Some ancient sources take sacrificial imagery further, suggesting that martyrs' deaths effect atonement (4 Macc 6:29; 17:22; Origen, *Comm. Jo.* 6.276), but this is not the case in Revelation. A martyr's blood marks a triumph for truth and faithfulness in the face of evil (Rev 12:11), whereas cleansing and redemption are accomplished by the blood of Christ (1:5; 5:9; 7:14).

An altar was a place where prayers were offered, and the martyrs do voice prayers for justice (6:10; 8:3, 5; 9:13). An altar was also a place of refuge in Jewish (1 Kgs 1:50) and Greco-Roman (G. Stevenson, *Power*, 288) tradition, and in Revelation the martyrs under the altar are in the care of God (1 Kgs 1:50). The altar stands before God's throne, so the martyrs are close to God (Rev 8:3). A saying ascribed to Rabbi Aqiba (early second century CE) is: "He who is buried in the land of Israel is as though he were buried under the altar; for the whole land of Israel is fit to be the site of the altar. And he who is buried under the altar is as though he were buried under the throne of glory" (*'Abot R. Nat.* 26; Str-B 3:803).

the souls. Revelation pictures the martyrs' souls (*psychai*) between their deaths and final resurrection. Some people thought of the soul as an immortal element trapped in a perishable body, so death released the soul from its prison for life with God or the gods (Seneca the Younger, *Ep.* 102.22). Revelation, however, refrains from calling the soul immortal and emphasizes that creatures with "souls" do die (Rev 8:9; 12:11; 16:3; 20:4). Death does not release the soul to immortality but leads to a period of waiting in the care of God. Revelation locates the souls under the altar, while other sources picture them being kept in chambers (*L.A.B.* 23:13; *4 Ezra* 4:35; 7:32; *2 Bar.* 30:1–2). The final resurrection does not involve clothing disembodied souls with new bodies (Josephus, *J.W.* 3.372–74) but bringing souls to life (*ezēsan*) in a newly embodied way (COMMENT on Rev 20:4–5; cf. Schwindt, "Klageruf," 121; Wright, *Resurrection*, 201).

of those who had been slain because of the word of God and the witness they had given. Jewish tradition told of the prophets, Maccabean martyrs, and others who died violently for their faithfulness to God (2 Macc 7:1–42; Matt 23:30, 35; Luke 13:34; Heb 11:36–38; *Liv. Pro.* 1:1; 2:1). Some interpreters think Revelation envisions both the earlier Jewish martyrs and the slain followers of Jesus under the altar (Boxall; Kraft). But the focus is on the fate of the followers of Jesus, who were "slain" like Christ himself (Rev 5:6, 9, 12; 6:9). Revelation closely links keeping the word of God to the witness of Jesus (1:9; 12:11; 20:4; Satake). By the time Revelation was written, Antipas had been killed at Pergamum (2:13). Other sources said Stephen was stoned, James was killed with the sword, Peter was crucified, and Paul was beheaded (Acts 6:60; 12:2; John 21:19; Eusebius, *Hist. eccl.* 2.25.5). The most notorious persecution occurred under Nero, when Christians in Rome were "torn by dogs and perished, or were nailed to crosses, or were doomed to the flames and burnt" (Tacitus, *Ann.* 15.44). Such traditions inform the vision of the fifth seal.

6:10. *They cried out with a loud voice and said, "How long, O Master, holy and true.* Those who suffer wrongdoing cry "how long" in the conviction that God will not let injustice continue indefinitely (Zech 1:12; Pss 6:3; 13:1; 35:17; 74:10; 79:5–10). The word "master" (*despotēs*) was used for the emperor and others in authority (Philo, *Flacc.* 4.23; Dio Chrysostom, *Disc.* 45.1), but God was also addressed in this fashion (Gen 15:2; Jer 1:6; *T. Job* 38:1; Luke 2:29). Some interpreters suggest that here Christ is the "Master" (Heil, "Fifth," 227), but the martyrs more probably cry to God, who brings judgment and vindication (Rev 19:1–2).

"will you wait before you pass judgment and bring justice for our blood, which was shed by those who live on the earth?" Revelation assumes that God is just (*dikaios*) and will not reward wrongdoing or punish righteousness (15:3; 16:5, 7). The plea for God

to bring justice (*ekdikein*) for the martyrs' deaths is the corollary to this conviction that God is just. It is common to think that the martyrs ask God to "avenge" their blood (NAB, NIV, NRSV, REB; Charles; Prigent; Yarbro Collins, "Persecution," 746–47). Some expected those who shed blood to pay with their own blood (Gen 9:5–6; Num 35:33). A tomb inscription calls God to act against those who shed "innocent blood wickedly," asking that the murderers might suffer the same fate and that God "might avenge the innocent blood" (Deissmann, *Light*, 413–24). Most interpreters, however, stress that the dominant theme of the martyrs' prayer is for God's justice rather than sheer retribution (Primasius; Oecumenius; Bede; Aune; Caird; Giesen; Osborne; see COMMENT). On those who dwell on earth, see the NOTE on Rev 3:10.

6:11. *But each of them was given a white robe, and they were told to rest for a short time.* The white robe, which connotes honor and purity, is the gift given to those who conquer (NOTE on 3:5). Rest is a sign of divine favor (14:13; cf. Heb 4:10); the followers of the beast experience torment, not rest (Rev 14:11). The idea that the faithful rest until the final resurrection is traditional (*L.A.B.* 3:10; 19:12; 28:10; 1 Thess 4:14). The rest continues for the short time (*chronon mikron*) in which Christian witness is to continue. In the visionary world this period lasts three and a half years (Rev 11:2–3; 12:6, 14; 13:5), but visionary time does not correspond to ordinary time. The short period of rest and witness is the same as the short time (*oligon kairon*) that the dragon persecutes the saints, which spans the period from Christ's resurrection and ascension until his second coming (COMMENT on 12:12).

until those who were their fellow servants and their brethren—who were to be killed as they were—were finished. "Servants" identifies people by their relationship of obedience to God, their Master (6:10), while "brethren" points to the bonds between Christians (NOTES on 1:1, 9). These expressions provide two perspectives on the same group of the faithful rather than referring to two different groups, as is sometimes suggested (Ulfgard, *Feast*, 56). What it means for them to be "finished" can be construed in two ways. The second is preferable:

1. The full number of martyrs must be reached. Many translations insert the word "number" so that the martyrs wait until "the number" of their fellow servants is "made complete" by their deaths (NAB, NIV, NRSV, REB). The idea is that God will bring judgment only after a certain number of people have been slain, so each martyrdom brings God's vindication nearer (Yarbro Collins, *Cosmology*, 209). Inserting the word "number" assumes that Rev 6:11 is based on a tradition attested in other sources. It was said that when God sat in judgment, the holy ones would rejoice because "the number of the righteous had been reached, and the prayer of the righteous had been heard, and the blood of the righteous one had been avenged" (*1 En.* 47:4). The righteous ask "how long" they must remain in their chambers and are told that their reward will come when "the number of those like yourselves is completed," referring to the full number of the righteous (*4 Ezra* 4:35–37; cf. 2:41; *2 Bar.* 23:5; Aune; Bousset; Charles; Mounce; Murphy; Reddish; Bauckham, *Climax*, 48–56; Schwindt, "Klageruf," 131–33).

But even though the extrabiblical sources cited above explicitly refer to "the number" of people being reached, Revelation does not do so. When writers use the word *plēroun* (complete, finish) to mean attaining a certain number, the context regularly makes this usage clear (Herodotus, *Historiae* 7.29; Irenaeus, *Haer.* 1.16.2). In Rev 6:11

the word "number" is not mentioned, and later visions do not suggest that a certain number of Christians must be killed before God will act. John hears "the number" of the sealed in 7:4, which is 144,000, but this number does not consist of martyrs. Instead, the 144,000 are all the redeemed, whom no one can "number" (Rev 7:9). When judgment falls on those who have shed the blood of the martyrs, there is no suggestion that it is triggered by a specific number of Christian deaths (16:4–6; 17:6; 18:20, 24; 19:2). Moreover, most of the extrabiblical sources cited above speak of the number of the righteous people rather than the number of martyrs. Some note that *1 En.* 47:4 refers to the number of the righteous being "offered," or sacrificed (*OTP* 1:35). But the focus is on the number of the righteous rather than the number of the martyrs (Black, *Book*, 209–10; Knibb, *Ethiopic*, 2:133).

2. The faithful are finished with their work. Earlier, Revelation used *plēroun* in the passive voice when telling the Christians at Sardis that their works are not complete, or finished (Rev 3:2). The point is not that the Sardian Christians need to finish a fixed number of works, but that their works are brought to completion through repentance and holding fast to the word of God in the confidence that God will clothe them in white robes. Similar expressions are used in 6:9–11. Just as the martyrs under the altar were faithful in witness up to the point of death and have received their white robes, their fellow servants on earth will finish their course in the same way. The sense is like using the passive voice of *plēroun* for a prophet who was killed when his ministry was finished (*4 Bar.* 9:31) or for the faithful being finished, or made complete, in righteousness before the day of Christ (Phil 1:11). Where Paul tells of his own readiness to "bring justice" when his readers' "obedience is complete" (*plērōthē*, 2 Cor 10:6), John tells of God's readiness to bring justice when the witnessing of the faithful is finished. He makes this point again by saying that the time (*chronos*) of waiting will continue until God's purposes are finished (*telein*, Rev 10:6–7), and this will occur when the faithful have been able to finish (*telein*) giving their testimony (11:7; cf. Blount; Lupieri).

This discussion assumes that Rev 6:11 uses the passive form *plērōthōsin*, which appears in some Greek manuscripts (A C 2344) and early versions, but the argument works equally well with manuscripts that use the active voice with an implied direct object: "they finished (their witness)" (cf. Acts 13:25). The aorist active subjunctive *plērōsōsin* appears in some sources (א 025 046; Oecumenius; Andreas). It is probably the basis of the later variant *plērōsousin* (1611 2329), which is a future active indicative, since an omega (ω) could inadvertently have been separated into the two letters *ou* (ου) in copying. Deciding between the aorist active and passive is difficult because evidence is rather evenly divided and the difference concerns only one letter: A theta (θ, *th*) makes *plērōthōsin* passive, and a sigma (σ, *s*) makes *plērōsousin* active. A copyist might have changed the passive voice to the more natural active voice (Aune), but the change could well have been a simple error, since it would be easy to confuse a theta and a sigma in either sight or hearing (*TCGNT*[1] 741). Finally, however, both the active and passive forms yield a similar sense: God's justice will take place when the faithful on earth have finished bearing witness.

6:12. *Then I looked, when he opened the sixth seal, and a great earthquake occurred.* The earthquake signals God's coming judgment. People understood that dreams of "earthquakes and landslides portend harm for all people and the destruction of themselves or of their property" (Artemidorus, *Onirocritica* 2.41). They were signs of divine displeasure (Ovid, *Metam.* 15.798). Israel's tradition told of the world shaking in the presence of God (Sir 16:18–19; Jdt 16:15; Pss 97:5; 99:1). His descent made Mount Sinai quake (Exod 19:18; *4 Ezra* 3:18; cf. *L.A.B.* 11:5). At God's judgment, the "earth quakes . . . the heavens tremble. The sun and the moon are darkened, and the stars withdraw their shining" (Joel 2:10; cf. Judg 5:4–5; Isa 24:19; Jer 51:29; Ezek 38:20; Nah 1:5–6; *2 Bar.* 32:1; 4Q418 212, 213.2–4). In Revelation, too, the earthquakes warn of God's coming judgment (Rev 6:12; 11:19; 16:18), and the final earthquake on Babylon brings it about (Bauckham, *Climax*, 199–209).

The sun became black as sackcloth made of hair, and the entire moon became like blood. Sackcloth was a coarse fabric, usually made of goat hair and dark in color: "I clothe the heavens with blackness, and make sackcloth their covering" (Isa 50:3; cf. MM 567). It was worn to show mourning and repentance (Isa 15:3; Joel 1:8; Rev 11:3). Comparing the moon's color to blood suggests violence (6:10; 14:20; 18:24). The prophets linked divine judgment to the dimming of sun and moon (Joel 2:31; Isa 13:10; Ezek 32:7–8; Amos 8:9; Fekkes, *Isaiah*, 158–66; S. Mathews, "Power"), as did the later tradition: The "earth will tremble, even to its ends it shall be shaken. And the high mountains will be made low"; "the sun will not give its light"; the moon "will be turned wholly to blood" (*T. Mos.* 10:4–5; cf. Mark 13:24–25). The ominous dimming of sun and moon were signs of divine wrath also in the Greco-Roman world (Ovid, *Metam.* 15.785; Lucan, *Pharsalia* 1.538–43; Petronius, *Satyricon* 122; cf. Livy, *Rom. Hist.* 4.9.3; Tacitus, *Ann.* 12.43; 14.12, 22; 15.47; 16.13, 16; Hierocles, *On Duties* 1.3.54; Malherbe, *Moral*, 87; H. Kleinknecht, *TDNT* 7:385–92; Berger, "Hellenistisch"; Aune 2:416–19). In Revelation the sun and moon lose their light several times, with each occurrence expressing divine judgment (Rev 6:12; 8:12; 16:10).

6:13. *The stars of the sky fell to the earth like a fig tree drops its fruit when shaken by a strong wind.* It was considered "inauspicious to see stars falling down upon the earth. For they prophesy the death of many people" (Artemidorus, *Onirocritica* 2.36). When God judges the nations "the circle of the stars will be thrown into disarray" (*T. Mos.* 10:6; *Sib. Or.* 5.512–31) and "the host of heaven shall rot away" like "fruit withering on a fig tree" (Isa 34:4). Sayings of Jesus used similar imagery (Mark 13:24–28 par.).

6:14. *The sky disappeared, like a scroll being rolled up, and every mountain and island was moved from its place.* Jewish tradition said that when God's wrath is poured out, "the skies roll up like a scroll" (Isa 34:4), and apocalyptic writers use this imagery for the end of the age (*Sib. Or.* 3.83; 8.233, 413). Although the verb *apechōristhē* could mean that the sky was "divided" (NAB), most interpreters take it to mean that it disappeared, like the writing on a scroll vanishes when the scroll is rolled up (NIV, NRSV). The passages cited in connection with the earthquake of Rev 6:12 referred to mountains being shaken at the coming of the Lord, especially in judgment (Ps 97:5; Ezek 38:20; Nah 1:5; Sir 16:19; Jdt 16:15; *T. Mos.* 10:4). The imagery showed the overwhelming power of God (cf. Ps 18:7; Isa 5:25; Aune). Islands are the more remote places of the earth (Isa 49:1 LXX; Sir 47:16; *Pss. Sol.* 11:3), and shaking them points to God's power over lands everywhere (Ezek 26:15, 18 LXX).

6:15. *Then the kings of the earth and the aristocrats and the generals.* In Roman times the term "king" was technically used for the rulers of vassal states outside the empire, but readers would have identified "the kings of the earth" as rulers of all sorts, including the emperor (NOTE on 1:5). Cosmic signs show that the kings of the earth are vulnerable (Isa 24:21). The aristocrats (*megistanes*) include various people of high rank such as provincial and civic officials, along with members of influential families (Isa 24:8; Dan 5:1; Mark 6:21). Revelation later critiques Roman social patterns by including merchants among the aristocrats as a sign that wealth had become the measure of a person's worth (Rev 18:23). Generals (*chiliarchoi*) were, strictly speaking, leaders of units of a thousand soldiers, but the term was used for various high-ranking military personnel. Inscriptions from Ephesus and Smyrna show that holding this rank might be a person's chief claim to fame (I.Eph 3032.5; I.Smyr 424.4) or one step in a successful administrative career (I.Eph 28.12–17; cf. I.Smyr 591.29).

and the rich and the powerful. Wealth and power were closely linked. Members of the Roman Senate were required to have at least one million sesterces, and members of the equestrian order had to possess at least four hundred thousand sesterces (laborers earned four sesterces, or one denarius, per day). In Asian cities the civic offices, priesthoods, and other positions were held by members of wealthy families. Cities relied on prosperous patrons to fund public works such as streets, aqueducts, temples, and stadiums, as well as to underwrite festivals and absorb the costs of civic administration. In return for these benefactions they received public honors, but in John's vision they come under God's judgment.

and everyone, slave and free. According to law "all people are either free or slaves" (Gaius, *Institutiones* 1.9). The free include those born free and manumitted slaves. As a class, slaves were not free to leave their masters, but they could serve in positions ranging from high authority and skilled trades down to menial labor (S. Bartchy, *ABD* 6:65–73).

hid themselves in caves and in the rocks of the mountains. Caves and rocky mountainous areas were places of refuge when an invasion or other threats made it unsafe to remain in one's town or camp (Judg 6:2; 1 Sam 13:6; Jer 4:29; Ezek 33:27). During the Maccabean revolt, some Jews hid in caves to escape hostile rulers (2 Macc 6:11; *T. Mos.* 9:6; Heb 11:38). Here, conditions are reversed as those with power hide in caves to escape divine wrath. Idolaters and the wealthy were told: "Enter into the rock, and hide in the dust from the terror of the Lord, and from the glory of his majesty . . . Enter the caves of the rocks and the holes of the ground, from the terror of the Lord, and from the glory of his majesty, when he rises to terrify the earth" (Isa 2:10, 19; cf. 21; Mark 13:14 par.).

6:16. *They called to the mountains and the rocks, "Fall on us."* The words recall how the unfaithful were to "say to the mountains, 'Cover us,' and to the hills, 'Fall on us'" (Hos 10:8). In the face of judgment, humanity no longer has any desire to live and would prefer being buried under rubble. According to Luke 23:30, Jesus warned that people will rather have mountains fall on them than endure the affliction of the end of the age.

"and hide us from the face of the one seated on the throne. God is not named, preserving a sense of sovereign majesty. On one level, the desire to hide from God's face stems from the difference between divine majesty and human limitation. Jewish, Christian, and Greco-Roman authors affirmed that God's power made it impossible to see him and remain alive (Exod 33:20–23; Ovid, *Metam.* 3.287–309; cf. Xenophon, *Mem.* 4.3.13–14; *Sib. Or.* 3:17; 1 Tim 6:16). Even earth and sky flee when God reveals his face (Rev 20:11). On another level, it was understood that human sin and uncleanness made people unfit to see God's face (Gen 3:8; Isa 6:5). Yet Revelation also assumes that people were created for relationship with God, so at a fundamental level they want

to see God's face and lament when it is hidden (Pss 13:1; 42:2). Therefore, when God's relationship with people is fully restored in New Jerusalem, they will see his face and live (Rev 22:4; cf. Matt 5:8; Heb 12:14; 1 Cor 13:12; 1 John 3:2).

"and from the wrath of the Lamb. On the Lamb, see the NOTE and COMMENT on Rev 5:6. Revelation uses words for wrath (*orgē*, 6:16–17; 11:18; 14:10; 16:19; 19:15) and fury (*thymos*, 14:10; 16:19; 19:15) interchangeably. God's wrath is provoked by sin and evil and is directed at those who destroy the earth (11:18), especially the beast and whore, who personify false worship, violence, and deceit. The manifestations of divine wrath aim at ending the reign of evil. First, they are designed to bring repentance. The plagues poured out on the beast and its followers pressure them to turn from evil to acknowledge the reign of God (15:1, 7; 16:1–11). Second, divine wrath ends evil by defeating it. Those who refuse to heed the call to worship God will drink the cup of God's wrath and suffer earthquakes and defeat (14:10, 19; 16:19; 19:15). The goal of wrath is not the destruction of earth but the defeat of those who would destroy the earth (11:18).

6:17. *"For the great day of their wrath has come.* Biblical references to "the day of wrath" could include experiences of defeat and destruction, as occurred at the fall of Jerusalem (Lam 1:12; 2:1, 21–22), or the future defeat of God's adversaries (Ps 110:5). The prophets said that the "great day of the Lord . . . will be a day of wrath" when God will destroy the sinful and punish the world for its evil (Zeph 1:14–15; cf. 2:2, 3; Ezek 7:19). "See, the day of the Lord comes, cruel, with wrath and fierce anger, to make the earth a desolation, and to destroy its sinners from it," as the sun, moon, and stars are darkened and rulers are laid low (Isa 13:9). Later writers also anticipate divine wrath bringing a definitive judgment (*1 En.* 91:7; *T. Mos.* 10:3; 1QS IV, 12; CD VIII, 3). Christian sources warn that sinners will flee "the wrath to come" because God will give glory to the righteous and anguish to the wicked (Matt 3:7 par.; Rom 2:5–10; Eph 5:6; Col 3:6; 1 Thess 1:10). Some manuscripts (A P 046) say that people fear "his wrath," referring to the Lamb, instead of "their wrath," referring to God and the Lamb (ℵ C 94 1611). The singular could be original, since one might speak about God and the Lamb as a unity (Bauckham, *Climax*, 139; cf. Aune). But it is more likely that the plural is original and was changed to singular since wrath is connected only with the Lamb in Rev 6:16.

"and who is able to stand?" The implied answer to the question is that no one can stand in the face of divine wrath (1 Sam 6:20; Ps 76:7; Nah 1:6; Mal 3:2). A similar apocalyptic scenario pictures humanity crying out, "Who will stand in his presence when he rises in wrath" to destroy the earth and heaven? (*Apoc. Zeph.* 12:7; Adams, *Stars*, 246). Those who do not fall down in reverence before God and the Lamb (Rev 1:17; 4:10; 5:8; 7:11) can anticipate falling in defeat under their judgment (14:8; 16:19; 18:2).

COMMENT

Scenes of cosmic harmony introduced this vision cycle as the creatures around God's throne ceaselessly gave him glory, honor, and thanks (4:8–9). Along with the white-

On Rev 6:1–17, see Adams, *Stars*, 236–51; Biguzzi, *I settenari*; de Villiers, "Role"; Fekkes, *Isaiah*, 158–66; Grappe, "L'Immolation"; Heil, "Fifth"; Herzer, "Der erste"; K. Huber, "Reiter"; Jauhiainen, *Use*, 63–68; Karrer, "Apoll"; Lambrecht, "Opening"; S. Mathews, "Power"; Pattemore, *Souls*; Poirier, "First"; Schwindt, "Klageruf"; Steinmann, "Tripartite"; Wong, "First."

robed elders, they sang a new song to the Lamb and uttered "amen" when all creation finally joined in a grand chorus of praise (5:9, 14). But as the Lamb opens the seals on the scroll that he received from God, the voices of the creatures summon horsemen to unleash threats upon the world, so instead of cosmic harmony, the readers witness threats to the world's well-being. John may have wept when the scroll in God's hand remained sealed (5:4), but with the breaking of each seal, the reasons for grief seem to multiply, for opening the seals takes peace away from the earth (6:4).

The first six seals give structure to this chapter. The seal visions are grouped 4 + 2 (interlude) + 1, like the trumpet visions that follow. The first four seals are opened in quick succession, with John narrating each one in the same way: A creature by the throne says "Come," a rider on a colored horse appears, and a threat is announced (6:1–8). The next two visions unfold at greater length, prolonging the action and heightening its intensity. The fifth seal shows the martyrs crying out under the altar in heaven, and the sixth seal shows the rest of humanity crying out on earth as the cosmos shakes around them (6:9–17).

As each seal is opened, John steadily counts the numbers—one, two, three, etc.— creating the impression that God's will is relentlessly being carried out, step by step. Since readers know that there are seven seals and can sense the threats increasing, they can expect the cosmic signs at the sixth seal to be followed immediately by the seventh, which presumably will bring the last cataclysmic judgment on the world. But this does not occur. Instead, humanity asks, "Who is able to stand" in the face of God's wrath? (6:17). When this question has been asked, an angel interrupts the seemingly inexorable movement toward judgment by restraining the forces of destruction so that readers can see a vision of the redeemed that is as expansive as the threats of the first six trumpets (7:1–17). This vision answers the question people have asked by showing that those who have been redeemed by the Lamb can stand before God (7:9). When the seventh seal is opened, it does not bring destruction but the silence that allows for prayer (8:1–5).

A disputed question is whether the seal visions in Rev 6 reveal the contents of the scroll that the Lamb received from God. Some interpreters assume that each vision does disclose a portion of the scroll's message so that the contents are presented in this chapter (Charles; Biguzzi, *I settinari*, 188–91) or perhaps continue through the next cycle to 11:19 (Yarbro Collins, *Combat*, 25–26). Others think that asking about the scroll's contents is irrelevant, since Revelation focuses only on opening the seals and not on reading the words inside (Giesen; Kraft; Roloff; Satake). The approach taken here is that the seal visions do not reveal the contents of God's scroll but *prepare* readers for the disclosure of the message. No one is able to open the scroll or look into it (5:3) until all seven seals have been broken and an angel gives the scroll to John (10:1–10). Then he reveals the contents in a summary way in 11:1–13, where the faithful are confronted by the beast, and elaborates this conflict in the second half of the book (Mazzaferri, *Genre*, 265–79; Bauckham, *Climax*, 243–57).

The threats conveyed by the seals challenge the idea that the current world or-der offers security. Rhetorically, this vision affirms what afflicted readers already know to be true. For those at Smyrna, violence and economic hardship are present realities (2:9–11), and the martyrs under the altar voice the questions about divine justice that those who suffer would ask. But for readers who flourish in the imperial world (3:17), the visions are designed to be unsettling. The four horsemen undermine impressions of abiding peace and prosperity, while the sixth seal shows that in the end what counts is God's judgment and not social status. By pressing such readers to ask the question "Who is able to stand?" (6:17), the visions also move them to a renewed desire for the hope that is depicted in the scenes that follow.

The imagery in the seal visions is drawn in part from Scripture. The horses and riders in the first four seal visions are modeled to some extent on Zech 1:8–11, in which riders on red, sorrel, and white horses patrol the earth and find it at peace—yet a peace that serves those who oppress Israel. The visions also recall Zech 6:1–8, in which four chariots drawn by red, black, white, and perhaps gray or dappled horses go out to patrol the earth. In John's vision the four riders do not merely patrol the earth, but bring threats against it, including the familiar themes of war, famine, and pestilence (Jer 14:12; 21:7; Ezek 5:17; 6:11). Similarly, the cosmic signs that occur at the sixth seal—the sun becoming black, the moon turning to blood, the stars falling, and the earth quaking—appear in Isaiah, Joel, and other prophetic texts that warn of the judgment of God as well as echo early Christian expectations about the end of the age (NOTES on Rev 6:12–14). For readers familiar with this background, the sixth seal is not so much a new revelation as a reaffirmation of established traditions concerning God's eschatological judgment.

The Four Horsemen (6:1–8)

The Lamb opens the first seal, one of the creatures beside God's throne calls out "Come," and a rider appears on a white horse, holding a bow. His character is initially ambiguous (6:1–2). On the positive side, the rider "conquers," a term previously used for Christ's victory through self-sacrifice and the readers' call to remain faithful (2:7, 11, 17; 5:5–6). The rider also receives a laurel wreath like those that were promised to the faithful and worn by the elders around God's throne (2:10; 3:11; 4:4). But on the negative side, this horseman is followed by riders who are threatening, which means that the conquest represented by the first rider comes through violence and warfare.

The image of the first horseman speaks to a social context in which Roman military triumphs were lauded in public speech and art. A coin from Pergamum depicts the goddess Nikē giving Augustus a victory wreath to celebrate his conquests (Figure 12), and a sculpture at the imperial temple at Aphrodisias shows her attending the emperor with a defeated captive at his feet (see Figures 29 and 30). An Asian inscription announced, "I, Victory, am always with Caesar" (Reynolds, *Aphrodisias*, 156). Such conquests brought territory from Spain in the west to the Euphrates in the east under Roman control, creating the social context in which the early readers of Revelation lived.

An archer on a horse creates tension by depicting the agent of conquest in non-Roman guise. Rather than a Roman legionnaire, the rider looks more like one of the mounted bowmen of the tribal peoples who lived in the outlying regions of the empire. On the northern frontier, west of the Black Sea, great "hordes of Sarmatians and Getans go and come upon their horses along the roads. Among them is not one who does not bear quiver and bow" (Ovid, *Trist.* 5.7.13–15). On the eastern frontier were the Parthians, whose mounted bowmen defeated the Romans and made the Euphrates River the eastern limit of Rome's empire (Plutarch, *Crass.* 24.5–25.5). The vision of the horseman takes readers to the frontiers of their world. Instead of commemorating the Roman conquests that produced the relatively stable social setting in which they lived, the vision raises the specter of conquests that could threaten the prevailing order. Although some interpreters suggest that the vision plays on Roman fears of invasion from the east, the opposite is more likely: The first rider challenges the perception of invincibility that was integral to imperial propaganda (NOTE on Rev 6:2). Revelation warns that the present order is not inviolable and that those who compromise their faith to accommodate it are trying to placate powers that are not supreme (2:14, 20)

The second horseman, who wields a great sword, was allowed to take peace from the earth so that people would slay each other (6:4). This rider raises the prospect of violence within the readers' own society, thus countering the idea that the world was securely at peace under Roman rule. It was said that the "Augustan peace, which has spread to the regions of the east and of the west and to the bounds of the north and of the south, preserves every corner of the world safe from the fear of brigandage" (Vellius Paterculus, *Rom. Hist.* 2.126.3). Horace wrote, "As long as Caesar is the guardian of the state, neither civil dissension nor violence shall banish peace" (*Odes* 4.15). In about 9 BCE the province of Asia altered its calendar so that each new year began on the birthday of Augustus, the "savior who put an end to war and established peace" (*Rom. Civ.* 1:624). Even after Augustus's death, the Asian league continued effusing gratitude to him, "for peace has been brought to land and sea, cities flourish, well governed, harmonious and prosperous" (*Rom. Civ.* 1:627).

The vision of the second rider warns, however, that the prevailing peace can be taken away. The vision also raises questions as to whether the tenuous peace is genuine or merely a façade that is supported by underlying violence (Rowland). Despite the appearance of universal peace, Christ the Lamb has been slain (*sphazein*, Rev 5:6, 9), Antipas has been killed at Pergamum, and the faithful at Smyrna face imprisonment and death (2:10, 13). Although some see peace, the martyrs will soon indict the peoples of the world for slaying (*sphazein*) those who are faithful to God (6:9–11). From the perspective of the victims, the specter of people slaying (*sphazein*) each other (6:4) would be an extension of the violence that some in the Christian community and Christ himself have already experienced.

Readers may have heard echoes of prophetic warnings against those who fostered corruption while creating a false sense of security by saying, "'Peace, peace,' when there is no peace" (Jer 6:14; 8:11; Ezek 13:10). The prophetic message was, "I have taken away my peace from this people" (Jer 16:5). Revelation's imagery is reminiscent of Zechariah, in which a rider on a fiery red horse reported that all the earth was at peace. For the prophet, this continuing peace was not good news, since it meant that the oppressors remained at ease while Israel struggled. For change to come, the prevailing peace would have to be disturbed (Zech 1:7–12). In a similar way, John sees a fiery red horse, whose rider can remove the current peace so that readers can see the destructive tendencies beneath it. Later, the vision of Babylon's fall shows the political order coming under judgment for the violence and injustice that had sustained it (Rev 17:16; 18:24).

The third horseman holds the scales used in commerce and signals exorbitant grain prices (6:5–6). In antiquity, wheat, barley, oil, and wine were staple foods, and city dwellers depended on networks of production and distribution to meet their needs. Later visions of Babylon/Rome introduce the seafarers who transported the empire's goods and the merchants who sold wheat to the ruling powers (18:11–13, 17). The emperor oversaw Rome's grain supply and appointed special officials to administer it (Augustus, *Res* 5). Grain commissioners were appointed in Thyatira, Philadelphia, and other cities (IGR 4:1228; 1248; 1637; 1638; Strubbe, "Sitonia"). When the system worked properly, one might boast, "When was the price of grain more reasonable, the blessings of peace greater?" (Vellius Paterculus, *Rom. Hist.* 2.126.3).

Yet grain shortages occurred when crops failed in bad weather, shipments were lost to storms and theft, or violence and disease impeded planting and harvest. When supplies dwindled, those who had grain often hoarded it, either for their own use or to obtain higher profits as prices rose. Those who depended on the public markets became afraid and protested the shortages (Cicero, *Dom.* 11–12), sometimes regarding them as signs of divine disfavor (Tacitus, *Ann.* 12.43). Food crises occurred in Rome during the reign of virtually every emperor in the first century CE (Garnsey, *Famine*, 218–25), and similar crises are attested in Asia and other provinces (Cicero, *Att.* 114.8; Reynolds, *Aphrodisias*, 151, 153; Philostratus, *Vit. Apoll.* 1.15; Dio Chrysostom, *Disc.* 46; *Rom. Civ.* 2:250; cf. Jones, *Greek City*, 350). Wealthy merchants and civic officials were expected to deal with shortages by obtaining grain from more distant sources and selling it below cost, absorbing the expense themselves in return for public honors (Reynolds, *Aphrodisias*, 153; I.Eph 1455.2–6; 3419.5; Jones, *Greek*, 217–18). Roman administrators might coax or order people to put stored grain onto the market, and they sometimes set limits on prices to keep food affordable (Cicero, *Att.* 114.8; *Rom. Civ.* 2:250).

The exorbitant grain prices in Rev 6:6 point to the failure of an economic system to provide for people. Even though oil and wine remain available, they are unaffordable for those who must spend their day's wage of a denarius to buy enough grain for themselves. The rich and powerful might be expected to intervene, but this vision cycle does not mention them until the end, when they do nothing more than seek their own safety by hiding from God and the Lamb (6:15–17). The shortages ushered in by the third horseman point to the limits of an economic system to guarantee prosperity.

The fourth horseman, who sits astride a pallid green horse, represents Death, and he is followed by Hades, who personifies the realm of the dead (6:8). In some contexts, death was a state of being and Hades a place in the netherworld, but here, both are personified as powers. Earlier in Revelation, Christ announced that he had the keys to Death and Hades, which seemed to be good news (1:18). Yet here, Christ's authority over Death and Hades allows him to unleash them, which he does by breaking the fourth seal. At the end of the book, Death and Hades will come to ruin by being thrown into the lake of fire (20:13–14), but here, they threaten to ruin a fourth of the earth through violence, famine, disease, and wild animals.

The list of ways in which death can be inflicted undercuts the readers' sense of immunity, making Death's power seem inescapable. Those who elude one form of death will inevitably be faced with another. The prophets warned: "Those far off shall die of disease, those nearby shall fall by the sword, and any who are left and are spared shall die of famine" (Ezek 6:12; cf. 2 Chr 20:9; Jer 14:12; 21:7; Ezek 5:17). During a food shortage the poor might succumb to death before the rich, but an outbreak of infectious disease would strike all social classes (Livy, *Rom. Hist.* 3.32.2–4; Garnsey, *Famine*, 32). When Revelation later tells of Babylon the whore, who was arrogant enough to think that she would never see grief, readers are reminded that even the greatest of cities can be overwhelmed by violence, disease, and famine and become a dwelling place for wild beasts (Rev 18:2, 8, 21).

Theologically, Revelation works with a tension. The threats represented by the horsemen are not directly imposed by God and yet seem subject to God. Some interpreters emphasize the role of divine restraint of evil. They understand conquest, civil strife, the attendant food shortages, and death to be products of human sin, not divine action. The Lamb does not bring war and violence into existence by opening the seals but shows that they are subordinate to the purposes of God, who limits the third horseman by protecting the oil and wine and then confining Death's sphere of operation to only a fourth of the earth (Caird). Others argue that the Lamb unleashes the threats; he does not merely curb them. The horsemen are "given" (*edothē*) a victory wreath, sword, and authority to act, which implies that their ability to work comes from God (6:2, 4, 8). Since God is just, however, one might assume that he afflicts only the wicked and not the righteous, who are sealed and protected (7:1–17; 9:4, 20–21; 16:2–11; Giesen 179–82). Still others observe that it is not clear that the righteous are exempted from the threats posed by the seals, so one might conclude that the afflictions come on all people. The difference is that they purify the faithful while punishing the ungodly (Beale, *Book*, 372–73, 384; Blount).

An alternative is to recognize that the seal visions do not explain why there is suffering. In the worldview of the Apocalypse, multiple forces are at work. Ultimate authority belongs to God, but the forces of evil, which are in rebellion against God, also operate in the world. People cannot always tell whether a threat comes from God, from Satan, or from human sin. Instead of offering explanations, the visions in Rev 6 address readers as a form of proclamation. They are designed to unsettle complacent readers—like those at Sardis and Laodicea, who may be lulled into a false sense of security by social and economic conditions that are favorable to them—reminding them that the present order will not continue forever. At the same time, the visions give the oppressed, like those at Smyrna, incentive to persevere with confidence that the veneer of peace, which enables those with influence to threaten them, will be taken away.

The Fifth Seal: Martyrs at Rest (6:9–11)

The opening of the fifth and sixth seals further challenges perceptions of peace and security: The martyrs rest in heaven (Rev 6:9–11), and the remainder of humanity is disturbed on earth (6:12–17). From an earthly point of view, the deaths of the martyrs seem to show that faith in God and the Lamb leads to suffering and loss. From that perspective, the most prudent course of action would be to abandon one's loyalty to Jesus in order to obtain a more secure place in society. The visions counter this view by insisting that the faithful who have suffered on earth find rest and reward in heaven, while the rest of humanity, who now appear to be secure on earth, will be shaken by portents of heavenly judgment. The implication is that readers cannot remain neutral; the options are to identify with the martyrs or with the rest of humanity. Revelation allows no middle ground (Bauckham, *Theology*, 93).

The fifth seal reveals the martyrs under the altar before God's heavenly throne (6:9). Their location suggests that their deaths were not meaningless tragedies but meaningful sacrifices. In the eyes of some Romans, the followers of Jesus were adherents of a new and pernicious superstition (Tacitus, *Ann.* 15.44; Pliny the Younger, *Ep.* 10.96.8). It seemed ludicrous to die out of loyalty to a crucified Messiah. A martyr was a person who would "play the fool" (*Mart. Carp.* 9). John's vision of the martyrs under the altar reveals the contrasting point of view: The martyrs under the altar have found favor with God, despite being rejected on earth. Their self-sacrifices manifest true faith, not delusion (Ign. *Rom.* 4:2).

The martyrs cry out, "How long, O Master, holy and true, will you wait before you pass judgment and bring justice for our blood, which was shed by those who live on the earth?" (Rev 6:10). When read in the context of other Christian writings, this call for judgment on the people of earth seems to fall short of the idea of loving one's enemies and praying for one's persecutors, as Jesus was said to have done (Matt 5:44; Luke 23:34; cf. Acts 7:60; Rom 12:19). Yet the way the plea is heard depends on where one stands (Boxall). In Revelation the plea for justice is uttered by the victims of injustice, and the assumption is that a just God cannot allow violence against the faithful to prevail (Luke 18:1–8; *T. Mos.* 9:6–7). If God is "true," as the martyrs confess him to be, the question becomes: Does God turn away while the wicked shed the blood of the innocent? Is mercy another name for indifference? (Schüssler Fiorenza 120).

Each martyr is given a white robe, which connotes purity, holiness, and honor (Rev 6:11). This gift shows that God honors them, despite the hostility they received from people on earth (NOTE on 3:5). The white robe also signifies the hope of resurrection. It was traditional to picture heavenly beings in radiant white attire, like that worn by the elders around God's throne (4:4; cf. Dan 7:9; 2 Macc 11:8; Mark 9:3; 16:5; Acts 1:10). Some writers also envisioned the dead being "clothed" with everlasting life and glory through resurrection (*1 En.* 62:15–16; 1 Cor 15:53–54; 2 Cor 5:1–4; *Mart. Asc. Isa.* 4:16; 9:9, 17), so giving the martyrs white robes assures them that they will share in these things (Rev 20:4–6, 11–15). Moreover, white robes were worn at festival gatherings, and John will depict resurrection life by describing a countless multitude of the redeemed, robed in white, giving thanks to God and the Lamb for salvation (7:9).

The martyrs are also told to rest, which is a sign of divine favor (6:11; 14:13). They have demanded to know "how long" God will delay in bringing justice for their deaths, and the cryptic answer is that their rest is to continue for a short time (*chronos*), which will end when other witnesses have finished their work (6:11). Revelation will carry the martyrs' question forward by returning to the heavenly altar at the seventh seal, where prayers continue to be offered (8:3–4). The martyrs asked *how long* God will delay in bringing justice, and the trumpet visions redefine the issue by disclosing *why* God delays. The trumpets bring plagues on earth without moving humanity to repent. The point is that if God responded to the martyrs' prayers by reducing his justice to wrath, then nothing would change (9:20–21). Therefore, the trumpet visions too are interrupted so that John can be commissioned to prophesy again. An angel reiterates the promise given to the martyrs by saying that the time (*chronos*) of waiting eventually will end (10:6), and God's mysterious purposes will be completed (*telein*, 10:7). Yet if one asks how long this will be, later visions simply repeat what was said to the martyrs: The time will continue until the faithful have finished (*telein*) giving their witness (11:7). Only then will the last trumpet sound.

Revelation identifies the "short time" in which the martyrs rest and others bear witness (6:11) with the "short time" in which Satan persecutes the saints on earth (12:12). In the visionary world this short time is three and a half years (11:2–3; 12:6, 14; 13:5), yet it extends from Christ's ascension, when Satan is banished from heaven, until Christ's second coming, when Satan is banished from earth (12:1–17; 19:11–21). The Apocalypse gives readers no way of knowing how long the time will last. Readers will see God's justice being worked out against the perpetrators of injustice in a way that allows for repentance. The people who have shed the blood of the martyrs will eventually be given blood to drink, which seems just (16:6); yet this is not simple retribution, since those who have killed do not suffer death but are allowed to live so that repentance is still possible (16:8, 11).

Only when resistance has proved to be unwavering does God's judgment come. One aspect of divine justice is ending the reign of injustice. This means bringing about the fall of Babylon, the city that shed the blood of the saints and others (17:6; 18:24). Babylon's penchant for bloodshed will come full circle so that the city is destroyed by its own allies. In that vision, the faithful can say that God has acted justly (17:16; 19:2). The other aspect of justice is restoring those who have suffered, which occurs when those who have been slain for their witness are brought to life through resurrection (20:4).

The Sixth Seal: The World Is Shaken (6:12–17)

At the opening of the sixth seal the earth quakes, the sun becomes dark, and the moon turns to blood as the stars fall and the sky vanishes. The fifth seal began with the martyrs' cries for justice, and God responded with the assurance of vindication (6:9–11); the sixth seal begins with God's action, and the world responds in fear of judgment (6:12–17). The martyrs were given the white robes of honor and celebration, but everyone else sees the sun turn as black as the sackcloth of grief and repentance. Those who dwell on earth have shed the blood of God's witnesses, and the moon now turns to blood over their heads. While the martyrs rest under the altar, all classes of society are unsettled as the earth shakes beneath their feet.

Previously, all parts of the created order declared God's lordship with festive praise (5:13), but now, both heaven and earth convey God's judgment with ominous signs. Biblical sources said, "The sun shall be turned to darkness, and the moon to blood, before the great and terrible day of the Lord comes" (Joel 2:31). The "day of the Lord comes, cruel, with wrath and fierce anger," when the stars "will not give their light; the sun will be dark at its rising, and the moon will not shed its light," for God "will punish the world for its evil" and "put an end to the pride of the arrogant" (Isa 13:9–11). Greek and Roman authors also referred to earthquakes and the darkening of heavenly bodies as signs of wrath (Cicero, *Nat. d.* 2.5.14). When someone had a dream in which "the sun is dim or suffused with blood, or hideous to behold, it is inauspicious and evil for all people," and the same is true of the moon (Artemidorus, *Onirocritica* 2.36).

Some interpreters take the cosmic signs as God's final response to the martyrs' plea: The victims asked for justice, and God's judgment now falls on the people of the world (Beale; Roloff; Heil, "Fifth," 230). Others note that these signs depict a cosmic collapse that is so vast that it can only be taken as the end of the world. John says that the sky disappeared and every mountain and island was moved (Rev 6:14). Jewish texts already cited associate these occurrences with the end of the age. Early Christian writers told of the sun and moon becoming dim just before Christ's final return (Mark 13:24–25 par.) and thought the whole earth would shake in the end (Heb 12:25–29). Although the sixth seal occurs rather early in Revelation, one can read the book in a cyclical way that allows the sixth seal to be taken as a vision of the end and not merely a prelude to it. If each major vision cycle traces the movement from conflict to final vindication, then the sixth seal can be seen as God's culminating judgment. It is like the visions near the end of the other series, which portray the collapse of the cosmos (Rev 16:17–21; 20:11). Thus on the day of wrath the first heaven and earth pass away before God's new creation (21:1; Adams, *Stars*, 236–51).

The approach taken here differs, noting that Revelation uses the traditional imagery in an unconventional way. At the sixth seal the darkening of sun and moon, the falling stars, and the trembling earth occur together, but in chapters to come these phenomena are spread out over multiple scenes, in varied sequences, so these cosmic signs do not show finality (8:6–12; 16:1–21). More importantly, the sixth seal gives the initial impression that the end has come, but as soon as people ask "Who is able to stand?" (6:17), the movement toward judgment is interrupted by a vision of the redeemed that lasts for an entire chapter (7:1–17). At the fifth seal the martyrs asked how long God would delay in bringing justice. The sixth seal does not end the delay but actually prolongs it by leading to a suspension of judgment. And when the end of the series does come at the seventh seal (8:1–5), it is not the end of the story, but the beginning of a new cycle that further probes the mystery of divine justice.

The function of the cosmic signs is to provoke a response from people of every social class. Seven groups are listed: "the kings of the earth and the aristocrats and the generals and the rich and the powerful and everyone, slave and free" (6:15). Revelation often uses the number seven to indicate a complete group—like the seals, trumpets, and bowls (5:1; 8:2; 15:1)—and can include seven items in a list to give a sense of magnitude (5:12; 7:12). Rhetorically, connecting the items with the repeated *kai* (and) gives the sense that the list could go on and on (Demetrius, *Eloc.* 65; Lausberg, *Handbook* §686; Bauckham, *Climax*, 29–37; Kraybill, *Imperial*, 75).

Kings, nobles, and generals enjoyed prestige in the eyes of the public, yet here they seek to hide themselves from the eyes of God (Rev 6:15) because God's judgment differs from society's judgment. Later visions show the kings of the earth as clients of Babylon/Rome, who debase themselves by their affairs with a great whore (17:2, 18; 18:3, 9) and ally themselves with the beast (16:12–14; 19:19). The nobles turn out to be merchants, who have an unsavory desire for monetary gain (18:3, 23). The rich make their profits by supplying the ruling power's insatiable appetite for gold, silver, purple and silk garments, and slaves (18:11–19).

John assumes that some of his readers are rich and content (3:17), while others are ready to accommodate the values of the dominant society, thinking they are benign. By way of contrast, the readers at Smyrna and Philadelphia suffer threats ranging from ostracism to imprisonment and death (2:9–10; 3:9). Given the options, it might seem prudent to diminish one's faith commitments in order to attain a more secure position in society, but the sixth seal shows that seeking refuge with the rich and powerful is futile, for they will ultimately come under the judgment of God.

The vision has a satirical quality as it depicts those who claimed high dignity for themselves indecorously seeking to hide in the caves and rocks of the mountains (6:15). Satire works by undermining human pretensions so those who are described appear ridiculous. When those who posture as lofty, noble, and worthy of emulation turn out to be absurd, readers will not want to identify with them (Frye, *Anatomy*, 167–69; C. R. Koester, "Comedy," 132–38). The faithful martyrs in these visions are worthy of honor;

the pretentious and self-serving are not. As they scramble for self-preservation, they cling to a world that is vanishing (Resseguie). It makes sense to fear the wrath of God, who sits on the throne, but Revelation also pictures people crying out in terror at "the wrath of the Lamb" (6:16); and if kings and generals tremble before a *Lamb*, then their power is only a façade (Maier, *Apocalypse*, 186).

The expression "wrath of the Lamb" is so incongruous that interpreters debate whether it can be taken seriously (6:16). Some note that the Lamb has seven horns (5:6), will defeat his opponents in battle, and will watch impassively as the ungodly are tormented (14:10; 17:14). These traits would fit the notion of wrath (Moyise, "Does," 182–84). The opposite view is that power is redefined by the image of the slaughtered Lamb, who is characterized by self-sacrifice. Those who ascribe wrath to the Lamb remain deluded about his true character (Caird). A third option brings the two perspectives together (Boring; Boxall; Reddish). What humanity sees in this vision is partially correct. The death of the Lamb confronted the dominion of sin and evil with the power of divine love (1:5–6). Those who oppose the Lamb will experience his coming as a threat. What they do not see is that the Lamb who threatens the current order can also redeem those of every tribe, people, nation, and language (5:9–10; 7:9–12).

The cosmic signs move people to ask, "Who is able to stand?" (6:17). The expected answer is "no one." Given what they see, it would appear that no one can stand (*histēnai*) before God. Yet as soon as this question is asked, an angel will halt the forces that threaten to destroy the cosmic order so that God's servants can be sealed (7:1–3). When John is allowed to see the redeemed, he finds a countless multitude of people who can stand (*histēnai*) before God, not by their social positions, but because they have been cleansed by the Lamb (7:9, 14; Aune; Murphy; Resseguie; Schüssler Fiorenza; Bauckham, *Climax*, 11; Heil, "Fifth," 231). Rather than closing off the future, the contrasting visions open up a way of seeing the future, in which persistent opposition to God and the Lamb brings the threat of judgment, while sacrifice of the Lamb extends the promise of redemption. John shows that those who receive it—even kings—can hope for a place in New Jerusalem (21:24).

16. Interlude: The 144,000 and Great Multitude (7:1–17)

7 ¹After this I saw four angels standing at the four corners of the earth, holding back the four winds of the earth so that no wind would blow against the earth or the sea or any tree. ²And I saw another angel coming up from the east, holding the seal of the living God, and he cried out with a loud voice to the four angels who had been given the power to damage the earth and sea. ³He said, "Do not damage the earth or the sea or the trees until we have put a seal on the foreheads of the servants of our God."

⁴Then I heard the number of the sealed, 144,000, sealed from every tribe of the sons of Israel: ⁵From the tribe of Judah 12,000 were sealed, from the tribe of Reuben 12,000, from the tribe of Gad 12,000, ⁶from the tribe of Asher 12,000, from the tribe of Naphtali 12,000, from the tribe of Manasseh 12,000, ⁷from the tribe of Simeon 12,000, from the tribe of Levi 12,000, from the tribe

of Issachar 12,000, [8]from the tribe of Zebulun 12,000, from the tribe of Joseph 12,000, from the tribe of Benjamin 12,000.

[9]After these things I looked, and there was a great crowd that no one could number, from every nation and tribe and people and language. They were standing before the throne and before the Lamb, clothed in white robes, and there were palm branches in their hands. [10]They cried out with a loud voice and said,

"Salvation belongs to our God who is seated on the throne,
and to the Lamb."

[11]And all the angels stood in a circle around the throne and around the elders and the four living creatures. They fell on their faces before the throne and worshiped God. [12]They said,

"Amen! Blessing and glory and wisdom
and thanksgiving and honor and power and might
be to our God for ever and ever, Amen."

[13]Then one of the elders said to me, "Who are these, who are wearing white robes, and where did they come from? [14]And I said to him, "Sir, you know." Then he said to me, "These are the people who come out of the great affliction. They have washed their robes and made them white in the blood of the Lamb. [15]This is the reason they are before the throne of God. They serve him day and night in his temple, and the one seated on the throne will shelter them. [16]They will not hunger any more or thirst any more. No sun or scorching heat will beat down on them, [17]for the Lamb who is in the middle by the throne will shepherd them. He will lead them to the springs of the waters of life, and God will wipe away every tear from their eyes."

NOTES

7:1. *After this I saw four angels standing at the four corners of the earth, holding back the four winds of the earth.* The "four winds" can mean all winds (Ezek 37:9; Dan 7:2), especially those from the four primary directions: north, south, east, and west (Zech 6:5–6; cf. Pliny the Elder, *Nat.* 2.46.119). Alternatively, the winds may come from the "four corners" of earth: northeast, northwest, southeast, and southwest. Some writers said that winds from the diagonal points of the compass were the most destructive, bringing heat, drought, cold, snow, locusts, and pestilence (*1 En.* 76:1–14; Charles).

Some interpreters equate the destructive powers of the four winds with those symbolized by the four horsemen in 6:1–8. They posit that John's imagery was modeled on Zech 6, in which four chariots are drawn by horses of different colors and are identified as the four winds (Zech 6:5; Beale; Caird; Osborne). Yet this is improbable. Readers would have to trace a movement from the initial destruction by the horsemen/winds (Rev 6:1–8) to the martyrs and cosmic shaking (6:9–17), then back to a previous time when the horsemen/winds are restrained so the saints can be sealed and protected (7:1–8), and then forward again to salvation (7:9–17). The text lacks the literary cues needed for such a sequence (Smalley; Jauhiainen, *Use*, 71). Another idea is that the vision recalls Dan 7:1–8, in which the four winds bring four empires that appear as beasts (Bede). Although Revelation includes traits of the four beasts in its vision of the single great beast (Rev 13:1–2), the author does not allude to that passage here.

so that no wind would blow against the earth or the sea or any tree. Winds could bring destructive storms (Ezek 13:13; 17:10; Matt 7:27), churn the sea (Ps 107:25; Mark 4:37), and strip trees of fruit (Rev 6:13). Winds are ultimately subject to God (Ps 135:7; Jer 10:13), but here they are controlled by angels (*Jub.* 2:2), just as angels have power over fire and water (Rev 14:18; 16:5). Since wind could bring divine judgment (Jer 49:36; Hos 13:15), halting them holds back judgment.

7:2. *And I saw another angel coming up from the east.* The expression for "east" here is literally "the rising [*anatolē*] of the sun." Patristic and medieval interpreters noted that the word for "east" or "rising" appeared in passages referring to the Messiah (Zech 6:12 LXX, Vulgate; Luke 1:78) and that Jesus had "risen" from the dead, so they identified this angel as Christ (Primasius; Bede; Haimo). More recently, some propose that east recalls the location of Eden and the direction from which God and the Messiah, or "Sun of righteousness," were to come (Gen 2:8; *1 En.* 32:2–3; Ezek 43:2; Mal 4:20; *Sib. Or.* 3:652; Giesen; Harrington; Kraft; Prigent; Roloff; Sweet). This seems unlikely, however, since God's foes also come from the east (Rev 16:12).

holding the seal of the living God. A seal was ordinarily made from a gemstone or metal that bore an image and was often set in a ring (Sir 32:5–6; 45:11; 49:11; *T. Sol.* 1:6–7). Images of deities, people, and animals were common on seals, although some were inscribed with names (Pliny the Elder, *Nat.* 37.4.8–10). When pressed into wax or clay, the seal left a distinctive impression that served as the owner's signature. Here, the seal (*sphragis*) apparently bears the names of God and Jesus (Rev 14:1; cf. 22:4; *Liv. Pro.* 2:16; *Apoc. El.* 1:9), just as the mark (*charagma*) conveys the beast's name (Rev 13:16–17; 14:11). God's seal is like a royal seal (*T. Mos.* 12:9; cf. Gen 41:41–42; Esth 8:8), which gave the bearer authority. God is "the living God," unlike the false gods, which are lifeless (Jer 10:5, 10; 2 Cor 6:16). The living God can bring both judgment and deliverance (Heb 10:31; Dan 6:26–27).

and he cried out with a loud voice to the four angels who had been given the power to damage the earth and sea. Some interpreters identify these angels as demonic powers like those in 9:11–14 (Haimo; Beale; Caird), but here they are God's angels, who can threaten earth and sea (cf. 8:2–12). Since they have been "given" power, they are under God's authority. The redundant Greek (literally, "to whom it was given to them") reflects a Semitic idiom (MHT 3:325; Aune 2:427).

7:3. *He said, "Do not damage the earth or the sea or the trees.* The way these potentially destructive angels are restrained is paralleled in other apocalyptic sources. The angels of punishment are held back so that Noah can build an ark before the flood (*1 En.* 66:1–2), and the angels are prevented from destroying Jerusalem until the temple vessels have been removed for safekeeping (*2 Bar.* 6:4–8:2; Murphy; Prigent; Roloff).

"until we have put a seal on the foreheads of the servants of our God." Destruction is held back until (*achri*) an angel has sealed God's servants, implying that threats will resume later (Rev 8:5–9). Although only one angel holds the seal, he speaks in the plural, "we," usage that occurs in other ancient sources (Smyth, *Greek* §§1007–8; BDF §141). Sealing has two dimensions of meaning:

1. Protection. Revelation recalls a vision of Ezekiel, who saw six men being summoned to destroy the idolatrous people of Jerusalem, but only after a sign was put on the foreheads of the faithful to ensure that they would be spared (Ezek 9:4). Other texts expect that the ungodly, who do not bear the sign, will be killed when messianic judgment is carried out (CD XIX, 10–12) and that the righteous inscribed with God's name on their foreheads will be protected from hunger, thirst, and evil powers (*Apoc. El.* 1:9–10). Some wrote of two signs: "God's sign is on the righteous for their salvation," for they will be spared famine, the sword, and death, whereas sinners will not escape, "for on their forehead is the sign of destruction" (*Pss. Sol.* 15:6–9). Similarly, God put a sign on Cain to protect him (Gen 4:15). Revelation assumes that the angelic sealing will protect the faithful from the plagues God sends on the ungodly (Rev 9:4), although the redeemed remain vulnerable to threats from God's adversaries (13:8–10).

   In the MT the protective sign mentioned in Ezek 9:4 is a Hebrew *taw* (ת). Some interpreters note that in Ezekiel's time the *taw* was written as ✕ and speculate that the faithful being sealed with an ✕ recalls the cross or the name of Christ, which in Greek begins with *chi* (χ; Krodel; Osborne; Roloff; Fitzer, *TDNT* 7:951). This is improbable, however, since the seal almost certainly bears the name of God and Christ (Rev 7:2; 14:1). Moreover, if readers of Revelation knew Hebrew, they would have thought of the first-century form of the *taw*, which was ת, not ✕.

2. Belonging. The sealed are the "servants of God" (1:1; 2:20; 10:7; 11:18; 15:3; 19:2, 5; 22:3, 6); the contrasting mark identifies those who belong to the beast (13:16–17; 14:9, 11; 16:2; 19:20; 20:4). The worshipers of God are a priestly people (1:6; 5:10), and those bearing the name of God come before his throne and see his face (14:1; 22:4). This fits the tradition in which Israel's high priest bore God's name on the turban across his forehead. The words "Holy to the Lord" were inscribed on it in the manner of a seal (Exod 28:36–38; Kraft; Hirschberg, *Das eschatologische*, 150).

Some interpreters note that the sealed are God's servants, or literally slaves (*douloi*), and argue that sealing recalls the practice of marking slaves to show ownership (Aune; Beale; Giesen; Osborne; Roloff). This is unlikely, however, because the word *sphragis* (seal) was rarely used for marking slaves. The usual word was *stigma*, which referred to the marks left by tattooing or branding (G. Fitzer, *TDNT* 7:941). More importantly, marking slaves on their foreheads or faces was done for punishment, not to show ownership. When a slave ran away or committed an offense, he or she was "punished with a mark" on the forehead that stated the transgression (Petronius, *Satyricon* 103.1–5; 105.11; cf. Plautus, *Aul.* 325–26; Valerius Maximus, *Facta* 6.8.7). Marking the forehead could be accompanied by whipping, being chained, or other punishment (P.Lille 29 II, 33–36; Herodas, *Mimes* 5.65–79; Aristophanes, *Ranae* 1508–14). It was also suitable for criminals (Cicero, *Rosc. Amer.* 57; Suetonius, *Cal.* 27.3).

In classical Greece, prisoners of war could be tattooed on the forehead and sold as slaves (Plutarch, *Per.* 26.4; Plutarch, *Nic.* 29.1), but in Roman times, slaves were not routinely marked this way. According to Roman law, freed slaves could become citizens *unless* they had been tattooed, which indicates that slaves were not regularly tattooed to show ownership but were marked as a special act of punishment (Gaius, *Institutiones* 1.13). If slaves were inscribed with the name of their master and soldiers with the name of the emperor, the names were placed on the hand or neck, not the forehead (Ambrose, *Ob. Val.* 58.5–7; Callimachus, *Iamb.* 203.55–56; Aetius, *Corp. med.* 8.12).

Marking slaves on the forehead was a demeaning act of punishment that does not fit Rev 7. The practice could, however, be reflected in the beast marking people's foreheads or hands (Rev 13:16) or the whore bearing Babylon's name on her forehead (17:5). People were sometimes tattooed to show that they were devoted to a god or goddess, but the marks were on the wrist or neck, not the forehead (Isa 44:5; P.Paris 10.8–9; Lucian, *Syr. d.* 59). The devotees of Mithras may have been marked on the forehead, but the evidence is disputed (Tertullian, *Praescr.* 40; Aune 2:458). As discussed, the main connotations of the seal in Rev 7 are protection (Rev 9:4; Ezek 9:4) and belonging (Exod 28:36–38). (See C. P. Jones, "Stigma"; Gustafson, "Inscripta.")

7:4. *Then I heard the number of those who were sealed, 144,000.* The number 144,000 is the total of the 12,000 sealed from each of the twelve tribes. Some interpreters take the number literally, as the precise count of Jewish people who will play a special role in the end times (LaHaye; Thomas), but most take it as a symbol of completeness. The same symbolism appears in the vision of New Jerusalem, which measures twelve thousand stadia on each side (Rev 21:16). The number shows that the city is a perfect cube, without suggesting that it will actually be twelve thousand stadia (fifteen hundred miles) wide and high. Biblically, the tribes were divided into thousands, hundreds, and other units for administrative purposes (Exod 18:21) and warfare (Num 31:14; 1 Macc 3:55; 1QM IV, 2). One battle included twelve thousand soldiers—one thousand from each tribe (Num 31:4–6)—but usually the numbers varied (2:4, 6, 8, etc.). The consistent numbers in Rev 7:5–8 suggest perfection. On the history of interpretation, see §12A.

In the readers' social contexts, the citizens of Ephesus were registered in civic tribes (*phylē*) and groups of a thousand (*chiliastys*; I.Eph 8.47; 941.4; I.Sard 6.2). In the visionary world, the groups of thousands from the twelve tribes are presumably citizens of New Jerusalem, since both the city and the sealed people are multiples of twelve thousand and the city's gates are named for these tribes (Rev 21:12, 16). The idea that Jesus' followers are citizens of New Jerusalem fits early Christian tradition (Phil 3:20; Heb 12:22–24).

sealed from every tribe of the sons of Israel. A list of the twelve tribes (*phylai*) that had territory in Canaan differed from the lists of the sons (*huioi*) of Jacob or Israel. The reason is that Levi was a son of Israel whose priestly descendants had no tribal territory. Moreover, Joseph's territory was divided among his two grandsons, Ephraim and Manasseh. Even with these traditional differences, Revelation's list of names is peculiar in two ways:

1. Content of the list. Instead of including either Joseph (Israel's son) or Ephraim and Manasseh (the grandsons who received tribal territory), Revelation includes Joseph and Manasseh but not Ephraim. The Bohairic translation solved the problem by retaining Joseph and replacing Manasseh with Dan, whose name was omitted, making the list conform to the usual lists of Israel's sons. The problem is that this translation departs from the best Greek manuscript evidence. Some interpreters propose that Ephraim was so sinful that the tribe was omitted (Hos 5:3; 8:11; 4Q169 3–4 II, 8; Beale; C. Smith, "Portrayal," 115), but this is unlikely because Manasseh was

also rebuked for sin (1 Chr 5:23–25; Isa 9:21) and Ephraim outranked Manasseh (Gen 48:17–20). It is more probable that Ephraim was fused with Joseph since the two were closely identified (Num 1:32; Ezek 37:16, 19; Bauckham, "List," 114).

The reason for Dan's omission is unknown. A common explanation is that Dan was known for idolatry, greed, persecution of the righteous, and alliance with Satan (Gen 49:17; Judg 18:30; *Liv. Pro.* 3:16–19; *T. Dan* 5:4–8; Beale; Blount; Mounce; Murphy; Osborne; Roloff). Nevertheless, these same passages also censure tribes such as Reuben, Levi, Simeon, and Gad (Gen 49:5–7; *Liv. Pro.* 3:16–19), and some anticipate Dan's return to the Lord (*T. Dan* 5:9), so one might expect Dan to have a place in a restored Israel (Ezek 48:1). A variation is that the Antichrist was to come from Dan. This idea is related to Jer 8:16, which said that Israel's adversaries would be heard from Dan—a prophecy concerning the Babylonian invasion from the north (Jer 4:15–16). By the late second and third centuries CE this was taken to mean that the Antichrist would come from Dan, so the tribe was eliminated from Rev 7 (Irenaeus, *Haer.* 5.30.2; Hippolytus, *Antichr.* 14.5–6). This interpretation has been favored by medieval interpreters (Andreas; Bede; Haimo; cf. Hill, "Antichrist"; Rusconi, "Antichrist," 289, 292) and some modern ones (Charles; Kraft). Nevertheless, it is unlikely, since the tradition does not appear in Jewish sources and is attested only in Christian writings that post-date Revelation. In Revelation itself, the Rome-like beast that plays the role of the Antichrist comes from the sea rather than from Dan (Aune; Bauckham, "List").

2. Sequence of names. The order of names in Rev 7 does not correspond to any other known tribal list. Jacob's sons were borne by two wives and two concubines. The birth order is given in Gen 29:31–30:24 and 35:16–21, but elsewhere the sons of the wives are listed before those of the concubines (35:22–26; *L.A.B.* 8:6; *Jub.* 33:22; Josephus, *Ant.* 2.177–83), or the sons of each concubine are listed after those of the wife she attended (Gen 46:8–27; *Jub.* 44:11–34), or the sons of wives are listed first and last, with those of the concubines in the middle (*L.A.B.* 8.11–14; *T. 12 Patr.*). The patterns vary even more widely in genealogies (1 Chr 2:1–2), blessing scenes (Gen 49; Deut 33), censuses (Num 1:5–15), distributions of land (Ezek 48:1–29), lists of cultic duties (1Q19 XXIII; 1Q20 VI), and the names on Jerusalem's gates (Ezek 48:3–34; Note on Rev 21:12). Reuben is often listed first, since he was the eldest, but Judah was a leading tribe and is occasionally named first (Num 2:3; 34:16–29; 1 Chr 12:23–37; *L.A.B.* 25:4). Revelation places Judah first because Jesus is the Lion of Judah (Rev 5:5), but given the variety in the sequence of names in ancient lists, it seems unlikely that the author expected readers to detect some special significance in the rest of the sequence (Mounce; Prigent). The list simply gives a sense of the whole.

7:5. *From the tribe of Judah 12,000 were sealed, from the tribe of Reuben 12,000, from the tribe of Gad 12,000.* Judah was blessed with the scepter (Gen 49:10) and was the tribe of King David. The Messiah was to come from Judah (4Q252 V, 1–4; *T. Jud.* 21:2), and Revelation identifies Jesus as the messianic Lion of Judah (Rev 5:5). Reuben was Jacob's eldest son, although the tribe was sometimes thought small and unstable (Gen 49:3–4; Deut 33:6; *T. Reu.* 1:6). Reuben's territory was east of the Jordan. Gad was remembered for violence and had territory east of the Jordan (Gen 49:19; Deut 33:20–21; *T. Gad* 2:1).

7:6. *from the tribe of Asher 12,000, from the tribe of Naphtali 12,000, from the tribe of Manasseh 12,000.* Asher was located along the coast in northwest Canaan, which was known for prosperity, and in the NT period the prophetess Anna was from Asher (Gen 49:20; Deut 33:24–25; Luke 1:36). Naphtali was a pleasant region by the Sea of Galilee where part of Jesus' ministry was located (Gen 49:21; Deut 33:23; Isa 9:1; Matt 4:13). Tobit was from this tribe (Tob 1:1). Manasseh, a son of Joseph and grandson of Jacob, had territory both east and west of the Jordan (Gen 48:8–22; on listing Manasseh, see the NOTE on Rev 7:4).

7:7. *from the tribe of Simeon 12,000, from the tribe of Levi 12,000, from the tribe of Issachar 12,000.* Simeon was known for violence and courage or rashness, since he and Levi avenged the rape of their sister. The tribe had territory in the south of Canaan but was eventually absorbed into Judah, which may be why Simeon is omitted from the blessings in Deut 33 (Gen 34:25–30; 49:5–7; *T. Sim.* 2). Levi was the tribe from which Moses, Aaron, and Israel's priests came (Exod 2:1–10; Deut 33:8–11; Sir 45:6). Some sources envisioned a priestly messiah emerging from Levi (1QS IX, 11; *T. Levi* 18), but this expectation is not evident in Revelation. Historically, the tribe of Levi had no territory, and members lived in various cities. Issachar was known for hard labor and had good farmland in the north (Gen 49:14–15; Deut 33:18–19; *T. Iss.* 3:1–8).

7:8. *from the tribe of Zebulun 12,000, from the tribe of Joseph 12,000, from the tribe of Benjamin 12,000.* Zebulun was considered a prosperous tribe, with land in the north of Canaan, where part of Jesus' ministry took place (Gen 49:13; Deut 33:18–19; *T. Zeb.* 1:1–7; Matt 4:13). Joseph and Benjamin were the youngest sons of Jacob. Joseph's territory in central Canaan was divided between his sons Ephraim and Manasseh (Gen 49:22–26; Deut 33:13–17; Rev 7:6), and Benjamin's territory was north of Jerusalem (Gen 49:27; Deut 33:12; Ezra 4:1). Paul was from this tribe (Rom 11:1; Phil 3:5).

7:9. *After these things I looked, and there was a great crowd that no one could number.* The vision of the crowd that no one can number (*arithmēsai*) offers another perspective on the group that was sealed in the previous section, where the group had a definite number (*arithmos*, 7:4).

from every nation and tribe and people and language. Similar lists are used for those dominated by the beast and Babylon (11:9; 13:7; 17:15), for those who are called to worship God (10:11; 14:6), and for those redeemed by God and the Lamb (5:9; 7:9). The list suggests a contrast with the claims of Rome and other empires, which were created through conquests of many peoples (NOTE on 5:9). Some interpreters suggest that John's vision points to the fulfillment of God's promise that Abraham's descendants would be countless (Gen 15:5; 22:17; 26:4; 32:12) and that he would father many nations (17:4–5; 35:11). The idea is that Israel's tribes (Rev 7:4–8) are joined by countless people of other tribes and nations (7:9), much as the gates of the New Jerusalem are named for the sons of Israel but stand open to the nations (21:12, 24–26; Bauckham, *Climax*, 224–25; Aune).

They were standing before the throne and before the Lamb, clothed in white robes. Standing is the opposite of coming under God's judgment (Rev 6:17; Ps 130:3), and it shows that the redeemed have a place in God's presence. Standing also is fitting for worship, since it shows respect for God, who is seated (Deut 18:7; Ps 24:3). Even angels were expected to stand before God (11Q17 VII, 4; Rev 7:11; 8:2). The elders in Revelation are initially seated, but they prostrate themselves before the throne (4:4, 10; 5:8,

14). The white robes signify purity, holiness, and honor. They are appropriate for people in worship as well as for heavenly beings (NOTE on 3:5).

and there were palm branches in their hands. The palm was a symbol of victory (Philo, *Imm.* 137; Caesar, *Bell. civ.* 3.105; Pliny the Elder, *Nat.* 17.244; Tertullian, *Scorp.* 12). Victorious athletes received palm branches, which they held in their right hands (Aristotle, *Mag. mor.* 1.34 1196a 36; Livy, *Rom. Hist.* 10.47.3; Virgil, *Aen.* 5.112; Plutarch, *Mor.* 723A–724F; Pausanias, *Descr.* 8.48.1–2). Victors in warfare also received palm branches (1 Macc 13:37; 2 Macc 14:4). After the Maccabean victory over the Syrians, worshipers held palm branches when offering thanks to God (2 Macc 10:7; 1 Macc 13:51). Crowds with palms greeted Jesus as a conquering hero (John 12:13). In Revelation, Jesus conquers through his death (Rev 5:5–6) and his followers conquer by faithfulness (2:7, 11, 17, etc.), so the palm is a fitting way to celebrate the victory.

7:10. *They cried out with a loud voice and said, "Salvation belongs to our God who is seated on the throne, and to the Lamb."* In Israel's tradition one might ascribe salvation to God because of his power to deliver people from threats (Pss 3:8; 38:22; Jonah 2:9). People in the Greco-Roman world gave thanks to various gods for saving them from illness, death, and similar threats; for example, "Artemidoros, the hereditary priest and son of Dionysios (made a vow) to Zeus Sabazios (together with) the people inhabiting Kidoukome on account of their salvation" (*RLMA* 55; cf. 137). Linking salvation to the throne was evident in the practice of acclaiming the emperor "savior" because of his power to save the people from danger (*Rom. Civ.* 1:624; Josephus, *J. W.* 7.67). By way of contrast, Revelation ascribes salvation to God and the Lamb.

7:11. *And all the angels stood in a circle around the throne and around the elders and the four living creatures. They fell on their faces before the throne and worshiped God.* The elders show readers the future glory of the faithful, exemplify worship, and interpret visions (NOTE on 4:4). The creatures also exemplify worship (NOTE on 4:6). Falling on the face is a way of recognizing the authority of the one being honored (NOTE on 4:10).

7:12. *They said, "Amen! Blessing and glory and wisdom and thanksgiving and honor and power and might be to our God for ever and ever, Amen."* The initial "amen" adds emphasis to the praise given by the multitude in 7:10, and the final "amen" adds emphasis to the praise given by the angels, elders, and creatures in 7:12 (Jörns, *Das hymnische*, 85–88). Rhetorically, grouping seven items of praise with the same connective (*kai*) gives a sense of magnitude, suggesting that the list of accolades could continue indefinitely (Demetrius, *Eloc.* 65; Lausberg, *Handbook* §686). Thanksgiving is given for God's creative work in 4:9 and for deliverance in 7:12. Nearly identical praises were given to the Lamb in 5:12. Theologically, Revelation assumes that God and the Lamb are worshiped as one (Bauckham, *Theology*, 54–65).

7:13–14a. *Then one of the elders said to me, "Who are these, who are wearing white robes, and where did they come from?"* Heavenly beings were regarded as knowledgeable figures who could disclose God's purposes (Judg 6:12; 13:13; Matt 1:20; Luke 1:11; 4Q400 2 1; 4Q405 23 I, 8). They could also interpret what a prophet saw in a vision (Ezek 40:3–4; Zech 1:7–6:15; Dan 7:16; 8:15; *1 En.* 21:5; 22:3; *2 Bar.* 55:3; *4 Ezra* 4:1; 5:31–32). In Revelation angels explain the significance of the great whore and New Jerusalem (Rev 17:1–18; 21:9–22:5), whereas elders comment on the Lion of Judah and great multitude (5:5; 7:14).

And I said to him, "Sir, you know." When God asked Ezekiel a question, the prophet replied, "Lord God, you know" (Ezek 37:3). John's reply is similar, but since Revelation distinguishes angels from God (Rev 19:10; 22:8–9), the word *kyrie* (sir) must indicate respect without suggesting that the angel is "lord" in the way God is.

7:14b. *Then he said to me, "These are the people who come out of the great affliction.* Revelation refers to the idea that before the final coming of God's kingdom, there would be unprecedented affliction on earth (Dan 12:1). Jewish writers described it as a time of violence, war, deprivation, and immorality (*2 Bar.* 26:1–27:15; *T. Mos.* 8:1; *4 Ezra* 13:16–19, 31; 1QM I, 11–12; XV, 1), and early Christian sources anticipated persecution of the faithful, false messiahs, and deprivation (Mark 13:7–19; Matt 24:6–28; *Did.* 16:3–5; Herm. *Vis.* 4.1.1). Some writers used the expression "great affliction" for it (Matt 24:21; Herm. *Vis.* 2.2.7; 4.2.5; 4.3.6; *2 Bar.* 25:4). There are three interpretations of this period in Revelation, the third being the most plausible:

1. Future tribulation. Many interpreters assume that in Revelation the great affliction is imminent but has not yet begun (Aune; Mounce; Murphy; Osborne; Bauckham, *Climax*, 226). Dispensationalists argue that there will be seven years of tribulation at the end of the present age (Dan 9:27), and the last half will be "the great tribulation." At that time the Jerusalem temple will be desecrated by the Antichrist (Matt 24:15–21; 2 Thess 2:4), and the conflict depicted in Rev 11–19 will occur. For those who think that Christians will be raptured, or taken up from the earth, before the tribulation begins, the crowd pictured in Rev 7:9–17 must consist of those converted to Christianity during the tribulation period (Scofield; LaHaye). A major problem with the dispensationalist view is that Revelation does not envision Christians being raptured but assumes that all Christians must be prepared to endure affliction.

2. Afflictions throughout time. This approach recognizes that early readers would have understood this group to include believers of their own time, who were redeemed by the Lamb's blood (7:14; cf. 1:5; 5:9), yet they would not have limited the group to believers of their own time because the crowd is so vast. Moreover, some readers already faced affliction (*thlipsis*) because of their faith, and they would hope to have a place within the crowd of the vision (1:9; 2:9–10). Neither the crowd nor the tribulation can be limited to the immediate context of the first readers of Revelation, and neither can be relegated to a remote future. The vision does not give a clear reference to time (Beale; Giesen; Maier, *Apocalypse*, 154; cf. Spatafora, *From*, 149–50).

3. Final affliction already occurring. This approach combines aspects of the other proposals. In Revelation, eschatological affliction begins when Satan is thrown down to earth in "great wrath" as a consequence of Christ's exaltation (12:1–17), and this wrath continues until Christ returns to defeat Satan and his agents (19:11–20:3). This period of "great wrath" is the "great affliction." In the visionary world it lasts for three and a half years, yet it encompasses the entire time between Christ's first and second comings. It is the time in which the readers live. The sense is comparable to Christ promising to protect believers at Philadelphia from "the hour of testing that is about to come over the whole world" (3:10). The promise addresses the immediate context of first-century readers, and the hour of testing is understood to be coming on the world at the time of writing. Revelation does not assume that the faithful will escape from the context of testing but provides assurance that Christ will protect them

in and through it, so they retain the hope of resurrection (NOTE and COMMENT on 3:10).

"*They have washed their robes and made them white in the blood of the Lamb.* In ordinary practice, people washed clothes to remove dirt, and fullers bleached garments white (Mark 9:3). The paradox is that even though blood normally stains, here it cleanses. The messianic Lion of Judah was to wash his garments in "the blood of grapes" (Gen 49:11; Rev 5:5), and here Revelation assumes that people are to wash their garments in the blood of the messianic Lamb. The imagery combines connotations from crucifixion and sacrifice. Jesus' blood was shed through scourging, the nailing of hands and feet, and other wounds (Matt 27:24–26; John 19:34; 20:25; cf. Josephus, *J.W.* 2.613). The blood that was shed through violent death was usually understood to bring uncleanness (Num 35:33; Ps 106:38; Isa 59:3; 1QM XIV, 2–3), but Revelation reverses this understanding so that the crucifixion is a sacrifice that brings cleansing (cf. Heb 9:14; 1 Pet 1:2; 1 John 1:7).

Thematically, those who are cleansed by the Lamb's blood bear witness to Christ's power to save (12:11), while his opponents shed innocent blood (6:10; 17:6; 18:24; 19:2). The threatening visions show the moon and water turning to blood as a sign that perpetrators of violence will one day succumb to it (6:12; 8:7–8; 11:6; 14:20; 16:3–4). In the end, Christ wears a robe stained with his own blood as he defeats the powers of evil, bringing justice to those who have suffered (19:13; Pezzoli-Olgiati, *Täuschung*, 95–97).

7:15. "*This is the reason they are before the throne of God. They serve him day and night in his temple.* The verb "to serve" (*latreuein*) was used for worship and service both inside and outside the sanctuary (Exod 3:12; Deut 6:13; Josh 24:15). It was used for priestly service (Heb 8:5), and the redeemed are a priestly people, who here serve in God's temple (Rev 1:6; 5:10). Like the four living creatures, the faithful worship day and night until New Jerusalem appears and night gives way to endless day (Rev 4:8; 21:25; 22:5). In contrast, God's opponents can anticipate judgment day and night (14:11; 20:10).

"*and the one seated on the throne will shelter them.* The verb "to shelter" (*skēnoun*) is related to the noun "tent" (*skēnē*), like the sacred tent where God met with Israel (Exod 33:7–11; Lev 26:11). The same verb can also be rendered "dwell." Here, the language recalls Ezek 37:24–28, which envisions God's restoration of Israel under a Davidic king. The promise is that God's sanctuary will be among the people of Israel and he will "shelter," or "dwell," with them. The difference is that Ezekiel says the nations will know that God sanctifies Israel, whereas in Revelation people from many nations share Israel's heritage and are therefore sheltered by God's presence in this vision. The same is true of New Jerusalem, where God's sheltering presence (*skēnē/skēnoun*) is not only among Israel, but among humankind (Rev 21:3).

7:16. "*They will not hunger any more or thirst any more.* The hope given here and in the lines that follow paraphrases Isa 49:10, so the scene points to God's faithfulness to what was promised. Hunger and thirst threatened Israel in the wilderness (Exod 16:3; 17:3) and during wartime (Deut 28:48; 2 Chr 32:11) but also arose more generally (Matt 25:35; 1 Cor 4:11). During food shortages, like those depicted by the third horseman, many were affected (NOTE and COMMENT on Rev 6:6).

"*No sun or scorching heat will beat down on them.* The paraphrase of Isa 49:10 continues here, again pointing to fulfillment of a promise to the Lamb's followers. The sun's heat beats down on the beast's allies(Rev 16:8–9). In some visions the sun's power is dimmed as a sign of God's judgment (6:12; 8:12; 9:2), but in the end the sun is replaced by the light of God and the Lamb, which shines on the redeemed (21:23; 22:5).

7:17. "*for the Lamb who is in the middle by the throne will shepherd them.* The language recalls Ezek 34:23, which tells of the Davidic king shepherding God's people. This image for leadership created a positive contrast to the negative images of rulers, or shepherds, who did not care for the people (Ezek 34:1–6; Jer 23:1–6: *Pss. Sol.* 17:40; 4Q504 1–2 IV, 5–6; John 10:11). The verb for shepherding (*poimainein*) can mean ruling with an iron rod (Rev 2:27; 12:5; 19:15), but here it means guiding the flock to water. Enhancing this positive sense are echoes of Ps 23:1–2, which identify the Lord as the shepherd who leads people beside still waters. Although some picture the Lamb in the middle "of" the throne (NIV, NRSV), the expression probably means that he is in the middle "by" the throne (5:6; cf. 4:6).

"*He will lead them to the springs of the waters of life.* The paraphrase of Isa 49:10, which began with protection from hunger, thirst, sun, and heat in Rev 7:16, continues by promising that God will lead the people by springs of water. The "waters of life" are waters that give life through resurrection and entry into New Jerusalem where the river and tree of life are found (Rev 21:6; 22:1). By way of contrast, John's gospel uses "living water" for the revelation of God that comes through Jesus and the Spirit (John 4:10–11; 7:37–39). In the gospel, "eternal life" includes resurrection, but people partake of living water during their lifetimes and experience the beginning of eternal life in faith (C. R. Koester, *Symbolism*, 175–206). Some interpreters argue that the Apocalypse also identifies the water of life with present experience (Taeger, *Johannesapokalypse*, 29–35), but this is not convincing. Revelation links the water to a resurrection that remains in the future.

"*and God will wipe away every tear from their eyes.*" Tears accompany grief at the death of a loved one (2 Sam 18:33), a loss of health (Pss 6:6; 42:3), and other situations. A bereaved family at Sardis wrote on a tomb, "there are many to whom thou hast left tears" (I.Sard 111.11). God's promise to wipe away the tears from all faces comes from Isa 25:8. God not only comforts the grieving but will remove the conditions that produce sorrow.

COMMENT

The opening of the first six seals brought an onslaught of threatening visions: The four horsemen unleashed conquest, violence, hardship, and death, and the martyrs cried out

---

On Rev 7:1–17, see Bauckham, *Climax*, 215–29, and "List"; Dalrymple, "These"; Draper, "Heavenly"; Fekkes, *Isaiah*, 166–74; Geyser, "Twelve"; Grappe, "L'Immolation"; Gustafson, "Inscripta"; C. Hill, "Antichrist"; Hirschberg, *Das eschatologische*, 129–202; C. P. Jones, "Stigma"; Jörns, *Das hymnische*, 77–89; Lefebvre, "Mystìre"; Morton, "Revelation"; K. Nielsen, "Shepherd"; Pattemore, *People*, 125–59; Perry, *Rhetoric*; Pezzoli-Olgiati, *Täuschung*, 86–101; Skaggs and Doyle, "Revelation"; Christopher Smith, "Portrayal" and "Tribes"; Spatafora, *From*, 146–60; G. Stevenson, *Power*, 251–57; Taeger, *Johannesapokalypse*, 29–35; Ulfgard, *Feast*; Wick, "There"; Winkel, "Another."

for justice, until all heaven and earth were filled with portents of wrath. The dimming of the sun, moon, and stars gave the impression that judgment was about to fall, so people of every social class cried out, "Who is able to stand?" (6:17). But as soon as this question is asked, an angel interrupts the movement toward judgment, and John hears that 144,000 from the twelve tribes of Israel are to receive a protective seal on their foreheads. When he turns he finds a vast crowd from every national background and language group giving praise to God and the Lamb (7:9–17). And when the seventh seal is opened, the final vision in the cycle brings not the cataclysmic destruction that readers might expect but a silence in which prayers are offered (8:1, 3–5).

The two scenes in Rev 7:1–17 involve the 144,000 and the great multitude. Their relationship can best be understood by contrasting what is heard with what is seen. This device was used earlier, when John *heard* that the Lion of Judah and Root of David had conquered and then *saw* that victory was won through the slaughtered and living Lamb (5:5–6). Although the Lion and Lamb images seem to be opposites, they offer two perspectives on a single person: Jesus. The promise of righteous rule, symbolized by the Lion, is kept through the death of the Lamb, whose sacrifice builds God's kingdom. Now the author uses this device to provide two perspectives on a single group: Jesus' followers. John initially *hears* the number of those who are sealed: 144,000 from the twelve tribes of Israel (7:4–8). Then he *sees* that the redeemed are actually a countless multitude from every tribe and nation (7:9–12). The point is that God's promise to preserve and restore the tribes of Israel is kept by redeeming people from every tribe and nation through the death of Jesus. This paradoxical vision takes readers into a world where a specific number refers to a crowd that is numberless, where blood makes clothing white, and where a Lamb acts as a shepherd.

The scene in 7:1–17 is variously called an interlude, an intercalation, or a digression. It is placed between the threats depicted by the first six seals and the silence and prayer of the seventh seal. From a literary perspective, the interlude has two main functions (see §12B). First, it interrupts the movement toward judgment and creates a sense of delay before the end of the vision cycle. Second, it interprets the meaning of the delay. The martyrs under the altar demanded to know how long it would take for God to exact justice against their enemies (6:9–11). But rather than answering the question directly, Revelation reframes it, disclosing that the reason God has delayed final justice is that people of every nation might be sealed for God. Rhetorically, the visions in Rev 6–7 move from warning to promise. Where the threatening visions unleashed by the first six seals are designed to awaken fear in the readers by stripping away a false sense of security, the expansive vision of the redeemed gives readers reason to claim their identity as people of God, offering a renewed sense of confidence, which is the opposite of fear (Aristotle, *Rhet.* 2.5.1, 16–17; Perry, *Rhetoric*, 143–44).

The 144,000 from the Twelve Tribes (7:1–8)

The initial part of this vision series is structured by the breaking of each seal (*sphragis*) on God's scroll. Since readers know there are seven seals, they can anticipate that after the sixth, the end will come. Yet the sense of the imagery changes when the angel interrupts the opening of the seals in order that a redemptive seal (*sphragis*) might be placed on people's foreheads (Perry, *Rhetoric*, 239). On one level, this seal apparently consists of the names of God and the Lamb, and it shows that people belong to God (cf. 14:1; 22:4). It differs from the tattoos or brands that were placed on the faces of ordinary slaves to punish them (NOTE on 7:3). God's servants are called his slaves (*douloi*), but instead of being degraded as chattel, they receive the honorable status of belonging to God's kingdom and serving as priests (5:9–10; 14:3–4). On another level, God's seal means protection from divine wrath, though not from all forms of suffering. Those who bear the seal will be spared the plagues that afflict the unrepentant (9:4; cf. 9:18–21), and yet those who bear the name of God may be persecuted and killed by God's adversaries (12:12, 17; 13:2, 7).

The seal of God is part of a literary motif, since its opposite is the mark of the beast, which is placed on the forehead or right hand of its followers and identifies those who belong to it (13:16–18). In the visionary world, all people belong to God or his opponent; there is no neutral position. Those who bear the seal of God worship him, whereas those with the beast's mark worship the beast and the evil power behind its throne (14:9, 11; 16:2; 19:20; 20:4). Where God's name is inscribed on those whom the Lamb has "purchased" (14:1–4), the beast's name is inscribed on those whose goal is to "purchase" goods in the market (13:16–17). To have one's identity defined by the beast's mark would seem to bring protection, since it allows people to escape social condemnation and find economic opportunity by accepting the claims of the ruling power. However, the Apocalypse warns that those who bear the beast's mark are subject to the judgment of God (14:9–11; 16:2). Conversely, those who bear the seal of God risk suffering under the political dominion symbolized by the beast, yet they have the promise of resurrection to eternal life (20:4).

How the sealing that takes place in the visionary world relates to the readers' world is disputed. Some interpreters assume that Revelation envisions an action that will occur at the end of the age to protect the faithful through the tribulations described in 8:2–9:21 (Thomas; Aune 2:443). However, Revelation does not provide a linear outline of future events, as if one should first expect the sky to vanish (6:14) and then people to be sealed (7:3). More importantly, the visions of the dragon, beast, and Babylon portray threats that were part of the imperial world; they were already real for John's readers. It is unlikely that the sealing is to be linked to a series of tribulations that are yet to come (Pattemore, *People*, 134).

Other interpreters propose that the sealing occurs when a person is baptized (Boring; Giesen; Prigent; Roloff; Hirschberg, *Das eschatologische*, 157–65). A link between a seal and baptism might be evident in Paul's letters, which connect sealing with the Spirit (2 Cor 1:22) and the Spirit with baptism (1 Cor 12:13); however, the seal is also mentioned in contexts that have no direct connection to baptism (Eph 1:13; 4:30; Thrall, *Critical*, 1:155–58). In the second and third centuries CE sealing came to have clearer baptismal connotations (2 Clem. 7:6; 8:6; cf. 6:9; Herm. Sim. 9.16.4; cf. 8.6.3; 9.17.4; Acts Paul 25; Irenaeus, *Epid.* 3; Clement of Alexandria, *Exc.* 83), but it is uncertain whether this usage was common in the first century (Aune; Mounce; Osborne; Fitzer, *TDNT* 7:951–52).

Sealing can best be understood as an evocative image for God's promise of salvation. It is functionally equivalent to people washing their robes in the blood of the Lamb in the next scene (7:14). Both actions mean that readers, in their present contexts, are identified as those who belong to God and the Lamb. Both actions give readers the hope of everlasting life, culminating in resurrection. The sealing is performed by an angel, which suggests divine action, whereas the washing is done by believers, as they receive the benefits of the Lamb's death; but the imagery is evocative and the distinctions cannot easily be pressed. It is difficult to limit receiving either God's seal or its opposite, the beast's mark, to single moments in the readers' experiences. Instead, the contrasting images of the seal and mark establish a framework in which people must understand their identity in terms of belonging either to God or to those who would take God's place.

John hears that the sealed number 144,000 (7:4), a number that primarily symbolizes perfection or completeness. It is the product of twelve times twelve thousand, which suggests symmetry and breadth. An identical number of people come from every tribe of Israel. A perfect consistency yields the total. By way of contrast, those who belong to the beast have a different number: 666 (13:16–18). The number is based on six, which is twelve halved, and not on 144, which is twelve squared—a more expansive number. And the 144 is multiplied by a thousand, suggesting greater magnitude. To emphasize the contrast, the writer will later juxtapose the number 666, which is placed on the right hands or foreheads of the beast's followers, with the number 144,000, which depicts those bearing the name of God and the Lamb on their foreheads (13:18; 14:1). The literary contrast between the numbers shapes the readers' sense of identity, giving the impression that belonging to the beast is a debased alternative to belonging to the Lamb.

Secondary connotations may be that listing the number from each tribe of Israel constitutes a kind of census. Biblically, some censuses determined the fighting strength of the tribes. The census ordered in Num 1:2–3 identified men twenty years of age and older who were capable of going to war. The number of warriors are listed tribe by tribe (1:21, 23, 27, etc.). The Apocalypse uses similar language and later says that the 144,000 are chaste, which was expected of men preparing for war (Rev 7:5–8; 14:4; Deut 23:9–10; 1 Sam 21:5–6). This took on eschatological dimensions for the Qumran community, which expected all twelve tribes to take part in the final battle against evil (1QM II, 2–3; III, 13–14; V, 1–2). Revelation transforms the holy war tradition by depicting a Messiah who conquers as a slaughtered Lamb. His followers share his triumph, but their weapons are witness and fidelity in the face of death. In the next scene, they hold palm branches to celebrate the victory (Bauckham, *Climax*, 217–20; Pattemore, *People*, 138–40).

Revelation's list of the tribes draws on hopes for the restoration of Israel. Historically, the Assyrian conquest of 722 BCE led to the exile of the northern ten tribes, which did not return to their lands. The Babylonian conquest of 587 BCE resulted in the exile of the southern tribes, some of whose descendants returned while others continued living elsewhere. A number of biblical passages promise the restoration of all Israel, both north and south, as one people living in the land, and this hope is taken up in later Jewish sources (Isa 11:11–16; 27:12–13; Ezek 37:15–28; Sir 36:1–13; *4 Ezra* 13:39–40; *Pss. Sol.* 11:2–9; *Sib. Or.* 2:171). Early Christians assumed that all twelve tribes would have a place in the resurrection and future judgment (Matt 19:28; Luke 22:30; Acts 26:6–7). In Revelation the hope for the restoration of the twelve tribes is affirmed, but a disputed question is the degree to which the tradition is transformed in the process (Bauckham, *Climax*, 215–16; Pattemore, *People*, 141–42).

First, some interpreters maintain that there is little transformation and that the 144,000 are ethnically Jewish. They make a clear contrast between those from the twelve tribes, who can be numbered (7:4–8), and the multitude from every nation, who cannot be counted (7:9–17). The sealed are a part of (*ek*) Israel, which fits God's promise to preserve a remnant of faithful Jews (Isa 10:20–22; Rom 9:27; cf. 11:25–26). Since the 144,000 follow the Lamb, one might consider them Jewish Christians (Rev 14:1–5; Bousset; Kraft; Rowland; Draper, "Heavenly," 136). Some interpreters object to this reading on the grounds that the ten northern tribes had lost their identity by the first century CE (Caird; Blount; Mounce), yet there is evidence that writers from the period thought that descendants of the northern tribes still existed (Tob 1:1–2; *Ep. Arist.* 46–51; Josephus, *Ant.* 11.133; *2 Bar.* 77:17–18; *T. Mos.* 4:9; Aune). A more significant problem is that this approach distinguishes Jewish from Gentile followers of Jesus in a manner that is not evident elsewhere in Revelation, where all those redeemed by Jesus are a kingdom and priests—the vocation of Israel (Rev 1:5–6; 5:9–10)—and can be considered true Jews (2:9; 3:9).

Second, some think the 144,000 are martyrs. The idea is that John lists their number and names the tribes in order to contrast them with the numberless multitude, making the martyrs a subset of the wider Christian community (Caird; Reddish; Yarbro Collins). One argument in support of this interpretation is that the martyrs under the altar are told to wait until the number of those like themselves is complete (Rev 6:9–11). Since John hears the number of the sealed in 7:4, one might conclude that the 144,000 is the complete number of martyrs. However, the message to the martyrs does not actually mention a "number," making this connection unlikely (NOTE on 6:11). Another argument is that the 144,000 follow the Lamb wherever he goes, which could include death (14:1–5). Yet following the Lamb is a general reference to discipleship, not a specific indication of violent death.

Third, the most plausible approach is that Rev 7 offers two perspectives on the identity of Jesus' followers. They are the heirs of the promises to Israel (7:4–8) and a group of people from many nations (7:9–17). The sealed are called God's servants (*douloi*), a term that includes all the faithful, irrespective of background (7:3; cf. 1:1; 2:20; 22:3, 6). Those "purchased" by the Lamb come from every tribe and nation (5:9–10) and also number 144,000 (14:1–4). God chose Israel to be his priestly kingdom, but this vocation is extended to all who are redeemed by the Lamb (Exod 19:6; Rev 1:5–6; 5:9–10). The number twelve thousand identifies those from each tribe who bear the seal on their foreheads, and the same number is used for the dimensions of New Jerusalem, where all the redeemed have God's name on their foreheads (7:4–8; 21:16; 22:4). The city's gates are named for the twelve tribes, while its foundations are named for the twelve apostles, making it a place for the whole people of God (21:12–14; Beale; Keener; Hirschberg, *Das eschatologische*, 139; Ulfgard, *Feast*, 70–79).

The Great Multitude (7:9–17)

Having heard that the sealed will be 144,000 in number (*arithmos*, 7:4), John sees the promise realized in the vision of a crowd that no one could number (*arithmēsai*) from every tribe and nation (7:9). The abrupt shift points to the broad scope of God's purposes for redemption. Readers are to take this vision as the heavenly response to the terrified people, who concluded the last chapter by asking, "Who is able to stand [*stathēnai*]" in the face of divine wrath (6:17)? The vision shows a multitude "standing" (*estōtes*) before God's throne (7:9), and the reason they can do so is that the God of wrath is also the God who provides salvation through the blood of the Lamb (7:10, 14; Aune; Murphy; Reddish; Resseguie; Schüssler Fiorenza; Pattemore, *People*, 143).

The description of the crowd includes notable details. First, they wear white robes, as do the twenty-four elders who worship at God's heavenly throne (4:4; cf. 7:11). White robes were understood to show purity, holiness, and honor (NOTE on 3:5). The robes are obtained from Christ (3:18) and are worn by those who remain true to him (3:4–5), including the martyrs (6:11). Second, they hold palm branches and celebrate the victory that came through the suffering Lamb, which was announced earlier (5:5–6). Third, their acclamation focuses on the salvation (*sōtēria*) that comes from God and the Lamb (7:10).

Such a scene would evoke different associations, depending on the reader. For some, a vision of crowds waving palm branches and ascribing salvation to God might suggest the Jewish Feast of Booths. Biblically, worshipers were to bring fruit and the branches of palms, willows, and other leafy trees to rejoice before the Lord for seven days (Lev 23:40; *Jub.* 16:31; Josephus, *Ant.* 13.372). Before the fall of Jerusalem in 70 CE worshipers in the temple waved their branches and called out "Save us, O Lord" (Ps 118:25; *m. Sukk.* 4:1–5; Ulfgard, *Feast*, 89–91). The hope was that when God's kingdom became manifest over the whole earth, the nations would join in celebrating the Feast of Booths (Zech 14:9, 16; Draper, "Heavenly"; Blount). From this perspective the vision of people from many nations giving praise to God marks the fulfillment of the eschatological promise attached to the festival.

Other readers would see a transformation of Greco-Roman practice. At festivals honoring various deities, worshipers were garbed in white and carried palm branches and other items (Apuleius, *Metam.* 11.10–11; cf. Plutarch, *Mor.* 771D; *Rom. Civ.* 2:188). Such gatherings were joyous occasions and a fitting way to depict life in the presence of God (Philo, *Legat.* 12; Heb 12:22–24). In a similar way throngs of people in white robes might greet a ruler with praises (Josephus, *Ant.* 11.327, 331). Some wore white when giving accolades to Augustus, declaring that through him they lived and prospered (Suetonius, *Aug.* 98.2), and the same was true of those who greeted the emperor in later times (Herodian, *Historiae* 8.7.2). People might hold palm branches as they sought help from a deity (Achilles Tatius, *Leuc. Clit.* 4.13.1–4) or celebrated a victory (Virgil, *Aen.* 7.655). It was common to show appreciation by declaring a benefactor or emperor to be one's savior (Josephus, *J.W.* 7.71).

A Roman coin from 135–138 CE shows how familiar these symbols were in the Roman world (Figure 24). The coin depicts Hadrian being welcomed by a woman, who personifies Judea, accompanied by boys with palm branches. The woman offers a libation on a lit altar, much as the angel offers incense on an altar in Rev 8:3–5. The woman and boys honor the ruler who imposed order on the province militarily by suppressing the Bar Kochba revolt. In John's vision the worshipers come from many nations, and they wear the festal garb that was typical throughout the Roman world. The writer of Revelation recognizes the value of the familiar symbols but shifts the focus, so that they

Figure 24. Roman coin showing Hadrian, Judea, an altar, and palm branches (134–138 CE). Courtesy of the Classical Numismatic Group (cngcoins.com).

celebrate the victory of God—not of the empire or its gods—since God brought deliverance through the sacrificial death of the Lamb (G. Stevenson, *Power*, 255–57).

This scene culminates when the four living creatures, the elders, and the angels who gave praise at the beginning of this vision cycle add their "amen" to what the redeemed have said (Rev 7:12). Then they offer their own sevenfold praise: "Blessing and glory and wisdom and thanksgiving and honor and power and might be to our God forever" (Rev 7:12). The reason for the praise is disclosed by a heavenly elder, who tells John that those dressed in white have come out of the great affliction (7:13–14). The expression "great affliction" recalls the expectation that the end of the age would be characterized by unprecedented distress, conflict, and persecution before the final coming of God's kingdom (NOTE on 7:14). In Revelation this idea is transformed, so the great affliction is a present reality, which began with Satan's expulsion from heaven after the Messiah's exaltation and will continue as Satan rages about the earth, threatening Christ's followers, until the Messiah comes back to defeat him (12:7–12; cf. the NOTE on 7:14).

The great affliction is the time in between Christ's exaltation and final return. It is the context in which the readers live. The writer assumes that threats from Satan can take various forms, ranging from overt persecution through human agents (2:9–11, 13; 3:7–13) to the more subtle pressures to accept teachings the author considers deceptive, especially those concerning the accommodation of Greco-Roman religious practices (2:20, 24). At points, Revelation gives the impression that all the faithful will die violently (13:15; 17:6), but elsewhere the writer assumes that imprisonment and death are possibilities for some but not all the faithful ("*if* any" are to be imprisoned or killed, they will be; 13:10). The point is that all are called to remain faithful in the face of the overt and more subtle forms of opposition to the reign of God and the Lamb. The assurance is that they will "come out of the great affliction" through resurrection, when they will drink the water of life in New Jerusalem (7:15–17; 22:1).

This assurance is given to those who wash their robes and make them white in the blood of the Lamb (7:14b). The language is evocative, like that of being sealed in 7:3, and it has been interpreted in various ways. Some interpreters suggest that the imagery refers specifically to baptism, which early Christians construed as cleansing and putting on a garment (Acts 22:16; Gal; 3:27). John does use the aorist tense for washing in Rev 7:14, which would fit a singular action like baptism (Kraft; Prigent; Roloff), but later he refers to washing in the present tense, which suggests ongoing action (Rev 22:14). Other interpreters propose that washing in the Lamb's blood entails martyrdom and link cleansing to purification through suffering (cf. Dan 11:35; 12:10 RSV; Bauckham, *Climax*, 226–29; Aune). Nevertheless, martyrdom is unlikely since redemption by Christ's blood benefits all Christians, not only martyrs (Rev 1:5–6; 5:9–10), and when the author has martyrs in mind, he makes it clear, as in 12:11. The most viable approach is to construe washing robes in the Lamb's blood as an evocative image for the repentance and faith through which people receive the benefits of Christ's death—something that Revelation depicts as both a singular and ongoing action (2:5–7; 3:3, 5; 22:14; Beale; Giesen; Mounce; Osborne).

The vision ends with the elder's description of the future of the redeemed, which weaves together a number of biblical texts (7:15–17). God's promise to make his dwelling, or shelter, with people (Ezek 37:27) is woven together with the hope that the redeemed will not hunger, thirst, or suffer from heat and sun, for they will be guided to springs of water (Isa 49:10). Then God will wipe away the tears from all faces (Isa 25:8; Fekkes, *Isaiah*, 170–74). This concentrated use of biblical language emphasizes that John's vision of the redeemed is congruent with expectations that are already known from Scripture. Rhetorically, this recasting of prophetic texts affirms hopes that would have been familiar to many readers. What is new is that these blessings are extended to a people that includes not only the traditional twelve tribes of Israel, but the redeemed of every nation.

The description of salvation in Rev 7:1–17 anticipates the final vision of New Jerusalem in 21:1–22:5. The principal contrast is between the present and the future, not between earthly suffering and heavenly bliss. The hope is not for escape from the world, but for creation to be made new and the redeemed to have a place within it. The literary themes in Rev 7 bind this chapter to the new creation and New Jerusalem. Those who wash their robes will enter the city (7:14; 22:14), where God will dwell (*skēnoun*) with them (7:15; 21:3). The city's gates are named for the twelve tribes (7:4; 21:12), but they are open to every nation (7:9; 21:24). The redeemed will worship before God's throne (7:9; 22:3) with God's name on their foreheads (7:3; 22:4). Thirst and hunger will end in New Jerusalem, where people receive the water of life that flows from the throne of God and the Lamb and eat from the tree of life that bears fruit year-round (7:16–17; 21:6; 22:1–2). There, God will wipe away every tear by eliminating death (7:17; 21:4).

Significantly, the promises expressed in Rev 7 are both fulfilled and transformed in the New Jerusalem vision. The sun will no longer beat down on people because in the new creation the sun is gone and people walk in the light of God and the Lamb (7:16: 21:23; 22:5). The redeemed are initially said to worship continuously, "day and night," but in New Jerusalem it is continuous day, for night has gone (7:15; 22:3–4). The place of worship is God's temple, which initially seems to be a heavenly space, but in New Jerusalem the only "temple" is God and the Lamb (7:15; 21:22). To worship in God's temple is finally to worship in his presence.

17. The Seventh Seal: Prayer in Heaven (8:1–5)

8 ¹Then, when he opened the seventh seal, there was silence in heaven for about half an hour. ²And I saw the seven angels, who stand before God, and seven trumpets were given to them. ³Then another angel came and stood at the altar holding a gold censer, and a large amount of incense was given to him to offer along with the prayers of all the saints at the gold altar that is before the throne. ⁴The smoke from the incense with the prayers of the saints went up from the hand of the angel before God. ⁵Then the angel took the censer and filled it with fire from the altar and threw it to the earth, and there were peals of thunder, rumblings, flashes of lightning, and an earthquake.

NOTES

8:1. *Then, when he opened the seventh seal, there was silence in heaven.* This silence has been explained in a number of ways. The first two are most viable:

1. Awe and reverence at the presence of God. Angelic companies were said to praise God and sometimes to fall into a reverent silence. Silence itself becomes a form of worship (4Q405 20–22 13; Allison, "Silence"; Giesen). However, even if awe is a factor, placing silence at this climactic point in the series of seven seals suggests something more.

2. Context for prayer. The silence leads directly to the offering of incense and prayers at the heavenly altar (Rev 8:2–4). According to some Jewish traditions, earthly sacrifices were to be offered in silence, so the same would fit a heavenly offering (*Ep. Arist.* 95–96; *T. Adam* 1:12; Wick, "There"; Smalley; cf. Zabras, "Silence"). A variation is that angels were to be silent so that the prayers of the faithful could be heard, as they are in the next scene (*b. Ḥag.* 12b; Charles; Bauckham, *Climax*, 70–83). Revelation does not suggest that God would have had trouble hearing prayers, but it does treat silence as a sign of reverence, just as it was common for Greek and Roman worshipers to become silent when prayers were offered (Homer, *Il.* 9.171; Thycidides, *Pelop.* 6.32.1; Pliny the Elder, *Nat.* 28.3.11). The worshipers in Rev 7 come from many nations, and they observe the practice of reverent silence that was part of their tradition. What changes is the focus. They no longer worship the gods of the empire, but the Creator and the Lamb.

3. Preparation for a theophany. Some interpreters recall that Elijah encountered earthquakes, wind, and fire, but only in the silence that followed did God communicate (1 Kgs 19:11–12). In a similar way the earthquake and threat of wind in Rev 6:12–7:3 culminate in the silence that brings both prayer and God's action (Kraft; Müller). Given previous threats of wrath, the silence could seem like the suspenseful expectation that God's judgment is about to be revealed, as it is when the trumpets are blown in the next vision cycle (8:2–9:21; cf. Hab 2:20; Zeph 1:7; Zech 2:13; Amos 8:3; Beale; Mounce; Murphy). Yet silence occurs only here in Revelation, before prayers are offered at the altar, making a general reference to theophany unlikely.

4. Anticipation of new creation. There was a Jewish tradition that the world was in silence before God spoke at creation (*4 Ezra* 6:39; *L.A.B.* 60:2; *2 Bar.* 3:7) and that at the end of the age the earth will return to silence before the resurrection, last judgment, and new creation (*4 Ezra* 7:30; Roloff; Blount). In Revelation, however, the silence is heavenly rather than earthly, and it is not clearly linked to the appearance of the new creation.

for about half an hour. Revelation sometimes uses "hour" for a particular point in time (3:3, 10; 9:15; 11:13; 14:7, 15), but here it signifies duration. The related expression "one hour" is used for a brief span of time, such as the time the ten kings reign with the beast (17:12) and the time it takes for Babylon to fall (18:10, 17, 19). A half hour is a limited amount of time (Cicero, *Rab. Perd.* 3.9; Josephus, *J. W.* 6.290).

8:2. *And I saw the seven angels, who stand before God.* Since these angels stand before God, they are often identified with the seven archangels, who "stand ready and enter before the glory of the Lord" (Tob 12:15; cf. *1 En.* 81:5; *T. Levi* 8:2). The Greek version of *1 En.* 20:1 identifies the seven archangels as Uriel, Raphael, Raguel, Michael, Sariel, Gabriel, and Remiel. But of these, Revelation names only Michael (Rev 12:7). These angels seem to have a premier place, like the seven princes in the DSS, who praise God in the inner sanctuary of heaven and have both military and priestly traits, like the angels in Revelation (4Q403 1 I, 10–29; II, 11; Abusch, "Sevenfold," 227). These angels stand ready to serve, like priests in a sanctuary or servants of a king (Judg 20:28; 1 Kgs 17:1; Luke 1:19). It was fitting for angels in heaven and the faithful on earth to "stand before" God (Rev 7:9; 11:4). The angelic representatives of the seven churches were apparently different from the trumpet angels (1:20). Since the seven trumpet angels stand before God, some interpreters identify them with the seven angelic spirits before his throne (1:4; 4:5; Aune; Giesen; Murphy; Roloff). The trumpet angels might be identical to the angels who pour out the bowls of wrath and then show John the cities of Babylon and New Jerusalem (15:1, 5; 16:1; 17:1; 21:9), though the link is not developed.

and seven trumpets were given to them. Trumpets were used in worship and warfare, and Revelation evokes associations from both contexts. Readers may have pictured the straight trumpets made of silver or bronze, which were a little longer than a person's arm. Such trumpets were sounded during religious rites among Greeks (*salpinx*; Artemidorus, *Onirocritica* 1.56), Romans (*tuba*; Varro, *Ling. lat.*, 5.117), and Jews (*ḥāṣōṣrāh*; Num 10:2; Josephus, *Ant.* 3.291). The straight trumpet could also give signals to troops in battle (Caesar, *Bell. gall.* 7.81; 2 Chr 13:12). The Qumran *War Scroll* expected such trumpets to be used in the final battle against evil, each trumpet inscribed with words like "God's mighty deeds to scatter the enemy and force all who hate justice to flee" (1QM III, 5). Less likely is that readers would have pictured the Jewish shofar, or ram's horn (2 Sam 2:2; Ps 98:6), or another type of Roman military trumpet, such as the circular *cornu* or the *buccina* and *lituus*, which were straight with bells curved in a J shape (Virgil, *Aen.* 6.167; 11.475; Tacitus, *Ann.* 1.68; Artemidorus, *Onirocritica* 1.56).

In Rev 8–9 the trumpet imagery draws on the use of military trumpets, since the angels' trumpet blasts summon plagues that attack the earth. The first trumpets do not call people to prayer, but are blown after prayer, much as trumpets mobilize an army once prayers for success in battle have been offered (1 Macc 3:54). The sound of the trumpet rouses the courage of the attackers (Josh 6:20; 1 Macc 9:12; Plutarch, *Aem.* 33.1) and strikes terror in the hearts of those being attacked (Judg 7:20–21; Polybius, *Histories* 2.29.6; Virgil, *Aen.* 9.503). The festive connotations of trumpets emerge at the blowing of the seventh trumpet, which signals a new outpouring of worship in heaven (Rev 11:15).

8:3. *Then another angel came and stood at the altar holding a gold censer, and a large amount of incense was given to him to offer along with the prayers of all the saints at the gold altar that is before the throne.* Jewish sources sometimes told of angels interceding on behalf of the righteous (*1 En.* 9:3; *T. Levi* 3:5), but in Revelation the angel brings the saints' own prayers before God (Tob 12:12; Rev 5:8). *Libanōtos* ordinarily means incense, but here it is the gold censer in which incense is burned. A censer could look like a goblet or chalice, consisting of a bowl on a stem with a base, or it could be a bowl with a long handle, a simple bowl (5:8), or even a short-handled shovel that was used for carrying coals and incense (Goodenough, *Jewish*, 4:195–97). Israel's tabernacle and temples had an altar for incense inside the sanctuary and an altar for burnt offerings in the court-yard, but Revelation envisions one heavenly altar for both purposes (NOTE on 6:9).

Incense was apparently not used in synagogues or Christian assemblies (NOTE on Rev 5:8), but it had an important place in Jewish temple tradition (Exod 30:7–8; Luke 1:10) and in Greco-Roman practice, where it was burned on small altars and in special holders to honor the gods and deified emperors (Pausanias, *Descr.* 7.21.12; I.Smyr 753.12; Pliny the Younger, *Ep.* 10.96.5; Price, *Rituals*, 156, 209, 211, 228). Since the context depicts people from many nations worshiping God and the Lamb (7:9), the writer transforms incense imagery, which was common to many nations, in order to show that God is the proper recipient for prayer, as the Lamb was in 5:8.

8:4. *The smoke from the incense with the prayers of the saints went up from the hand of the angel before God.* Incense was burned to honor God, to provide a cloud that protected priests from being harmed by the divine presence, and to establish commu-nication with God (Nielsen, *Incense*, 76–77, 86). Here, communication is the primary meaning, the smoke a visible sign of prayers coming before God: "Let my prayer be counted as incense before you" (Ps 141:1–2; cf. *4 Bar.* 9:3–4).

8:5. *Then the angel took the censer and filled it with fire from the altar and he threw it to the earth.* Priests often put coals from the altar on their censers and then placed incense on top of the coals (Lev 16:12; Num 16:46). Here, however, the incense has already been offered, and the fire is now taken from the altar to bring destruction upon the earth as in Ezek 10:1–7, in which a heavenly being gives a man burning coals to scatter over Jerusalem in destructive judgment. In dreams, seeing fire come down from heaven to earth portends danger (Artemidorus, *Onirocritica* 2.9; 2 Kgs 1:10; Ps 11:6; Luke 10:54). In the end, heavenly fire will destroy God's enemies (Rev 20:9).

and there were peals of thunder, rumblings, flashes of lightning, and an earthquake. People in the Greco-Roman world regarded earthquakes, along with sudden appear-ances of lightning and thunder, among the signs of divine disfavor and portents of coming disasters (Cicero, *Nat. d.* 2.5.14; Ovid, *Metam.* 15.798). In Revelation, thunder, rumblings, and lightning attend God's presence, and an earthquake can be the harbin-ger of divine judgment (4:8; 6:12; 11:19). Later, an earthquake will bring judgment by causing cities to fall (11:13; 16:18).

COMMENT

At the opening of the seventh seal (8:1), the echoes of celestial praise fade into silence. The quiet offers a respite from the anguished cries of the martyrs, the shaking earth, and the terrified voices of the multitudes who anticipated cataclysmic judgment (6:9–17).

On Rev 8:1–5, see Allison, "Silence"; de Villiers, "Eschatological"; Heil, "Fifth;" Paulien, *De-coding*; Lambrecht, "Opening"; Stefanovic, "Angel"; G. Stevenson, *Power*, 286–93; Vanni, *L'Apocalisse*, 215–25.

It also halts the countless voices of the redeemed, along with those of the creatures, elders, and angels who ascribe blessings to God (7:9–12). Yet rather than serving as an anticlimax, the silence adds suspense to the drama. The earth has been shaken by the mere opening of the seals on God's scroll, so one might expect something more terrible to occur when the final seal is snapped. When silence occurs instead, readers are left to wonder what will happen next.

Interpreters often assume that the seventh seal vision consists entirely of silence (8:1) and that the next cycle begins when the angels receive trumpets (8:2; Aune; Blount; Boxall; Giesen; Mounce; Müller; Osborne; Smalley). Others recognize that the seventh seal vision encompasses all of 8:1–5 (Beale; Harrington; Prigent; Reddish) or 8:1–6 (Satake; Lambrecht, "Opening"). This is the approach taken here, because the silence in 8:1 creates the context for the prayers in 8:3–5. The trumpet visions are introduced in 8:2, where the angels receive the trumpets, but they begin only in 8:6 where the angels prepare to blow them. The last seal vision and the first trumpet vision overlap and interlock like links on a chain. This technique of interlocking occurs elsewhere (e.g., 15:1, 2–4, 5–8) and shows that the joined scenes of prayer and plagues must be understood together (Schüssler Fiorenza, *Book*, 172–73; Yarbro Collins, *Combat*, 16–19; Yarbro Collins, *Crisis*, 112–14; de Villiers, "Eschatological"; Stefanovic, "Angel"). The trumpet visions will respond to the pleas of the martyrs and saints, but they will do so in an unexpected way.

Silence for Prayer (8:1–2)

The vision of the seventh seal consists of heavenly worship, which takes place before God's throne in a space called a temple (7:15). The silence fits Jewish worship traditions, in which offerings in the temple were to be made in silence (*Ep. Arist.* 95–96; *T. Adam* 1:12), but it also fits Greco-Roman practice, since silence showed reverence when a leader offered prayers (Homer, *Il.* 9.171; Thycidides, *Pelop.* 6.32.1; Pliny the Elder, *Nat.* 28.3.11). The backdrop of silence for prayer would have been as widely familiar as were the use of palm branches to celebrate victory or white robes to show purity (NOTES on 7:9). Greco-Roman practice is altered, however, in that the prayers in heaven will be offered to the God of Israel rather than to the gods of the empire.

The previous scenes envisioned countless multitudes celebrating victory by offering praises and then falling silent, so the force of this imagery in John's context can be seen by comparing it with an imperial triumph. When Vespasian and Titus prepared to celebrate their victory in Judea, a "countless multitude" stood everywhere in the city of Rome. When the conquerors took their seats before the people, the troops raised their voices in acclamation until the emperor gave the signal for silence so that "amidst profound and universal stillness" he might offer prayers (Josephus, *J. W.* 7.122–28).

In Revelation, a different kind of crowd celebrates a different kind of victory. The Lamb's triumph came through sacrifice (Rev 5:5–6), and the salvation he offers culminates in resurrection (7:12). Now, as praises fall silent, the prayers include not only those of the victors, but those of the victims, who have suffered violence from others (8:3; cf. 6:10). In the new vision cycle, God will disclose his response.

Before prayer is offered, John sees seven angels standing before God (8:2). They are given trumpets to blow, which suggests that they receive the trumpets from God or someone in God's inner circle. Earlier, the voice of the exalted Jesus sounded like a trumpet that summoned John to write down what he saw and to come up to the heavenly throne hall, but the sound of the angels' trumpets will play a more complex role (1:10; 4:1). Trumpets gave signals during battles, and the first six trumpets fit this pattern by bringing down destruction on the earth and summoning up demonic armies from the underworld (8:7–9:21). But trumpets were also used in worship, and when the last trumpet sounds, it will call the hosts of heaven to celebrate the reign of God and his Messiah (11:15–16).

Prayers Offered Up and Fire Hurled Down (8:3–5)

Along with the seven angels, another angel stands by the heavenly altar where the cries of the martyrs were heard (6:9–11; 8:3). The angel already holds a gold censer but is given a great deal of incense to offer along with the prayers (8:3). Having one's hands filled with incense was a way to signify legitimate priestly service (*T. Levi* 8:10), which is important because it was presumptuous for unauthorized people to burn incense at the altar (Lev 10:1–2; Num 16:15–35; 2 Chr 26:16–21). Since the incense is given to the angel by someone near to God's throne, this action intimates that the prayers of the saints, which are about to be offered, will receive a hearing before God.

The prayers are apparently pleas for divine help (Rev 8:4; Yarbro Collins, *Crisis*, 114; Heil, "Fifth," 224; G. Stevenson, *Power*, 291). These prayers were first mentioned when the Lamb had received the scroll from God and was about to open its seals; the rising prayers and incense conveyed hopeful expectancy that God's will would now be done (5:8). Then when John saw the heavenly altar, he heard the martyrs beneath it cry out, "How long . . . will you wait before you pass judgment and bring justice for our blood?" (6:10). The assumption is that a truly just God cannot allow the injustice against the faithful to continue forever. This issue would not seem pressing to readers comfortable in their lives, like those at Sardis and Laodicea (3:1–6, 14–21), but the urgency would be felt by readers in Smyrna and Philadelphia, who felt powerless and threatened by their adversaries (2:8–11; 3:7–13).

In the narrow sense, justice means bringing the perpetrators of injustice to account, and in due time Revelation will show this taking place (Beale; Mounce; Murphy). Yet in a wider sense, the desire for justice is a plea for God to manifest his reign on earth (Boring; Boxall; Giesen; Prigent; Reddish; Roloff). The offering of prayer at the seventh seal draws together the references to prayer that occurred earlier in the cycle (5:8; 6:9–11) and sets the direction for the trumpet cycle that culminates in the celebration of God's kingdom, which is the answer to the prayers of the saints (11:15). What will be surprising is the way the trumpet visions make a place for the suffering and witness of God's people in the process.

After the prayers and smoke of incense have risen up before God, the angel hurls fire from the altar down to the earth (8:5), and its effects are apparent in the trumpet plagues, where fire falls from heaven on earth and sea (8:6–13). The thunder, rumbling, and lightning that occur when the angel casts down the coals are like the phenomena that came from God's throne (4:5; 8:5), and the onset of an earthquake recalls how the earth quaked at the wrath of God and the Lamb when the sixth seal was opened (6:12–17; 8:5). The similarities give the impression that here again, God's power and wrath are to be revealed.

Third Cycle:
The Seven Trumpets (8:6–11:18)

18. General Comments on the Third Cycle

The third cycle of visions begins when seven angels are given trumpets and the prayers of the saints are offered at the altar before God's throne in heaven (8:2–5). As the prayers rise with the smoke of incense, an angel hurls fire from the altar onto the earth, signaling the start of a series of plagues. The angels blow their trumpets in a steady sequence, giving the impression that God's designs are being carried out step by step toward a last cataclysmic judgment. Yet after the sixth trumpet, people refuse to repent (9:20–21). Instead of a final plague, the movement toward judgment is interrupted as John is told to prophesy again; the people of God are depicted as a temple oppressed by the nations, and two figures prophesy (10:1–11:14). Only after their witness is complete is the seventh trumpet blown, calling for praise at the coming of God's kingdom (11:15–18).

This section plays a major role in shaping the way God's purposes are to be understood. The opening scene at the heavenly altar recalls an earlier vision in which the martyrs cried out from beneath the altar, asking how long God would delay in bringing justice against those who shed their blood. At that point, the martyrs were told to wait until others had finished bearing witness and then were given white robes as an assurance of salvation, but they were not told *why* any more delay was necessary (6:9–11). The trumpet series, which begins at the altar, shows what it would mean for God to reduce justice to retribution. Blood rains down from the sky and washes up in the sea around those who have shed the blood of the saints, and death engulfs a third of the world that inflicted death on the faithful. Yet nothing changes. Wrath alone does not move people to repent (9:20–21), which is why continued witness is needed. Readers are assured that God's justice will be done, but the delay allows time for the church to bear witness to the unrepentant world (10:1–11:14).

436

A. HISTORY OF INTERPRETATION
The Trumpet Plagues (Rev 8:6–9:20)

For ancient interpreters, the plague visions generated debates about God's ways of working. Marcion (d. ca. 160) objected to the idea that the true God would inflict plagues on the Egyptians before the exodus, and he rejected both the OT and Revelation. In response, Irenaeus (d. ca. 200) said that it was right for God to deliver Israel by the plagues in Egypt, and he considered those plagues to be similar to the ones through which God would redeem the saints in the future, as depicted in Revelation (*Haer.* 4.30.4). The Roman elder Gaius (early third century) argued that Revelation's visions of water turning to blood, the sky becoming dark, and locusts tormenting the wicked were inconsistent with other Christian Scriptures, which said that the Day of the Lord would come suddenly at a time when the wicked were prospering (1 Thess 5:2–3). But Hippolytus (d. 236) countered that Jesus and the prophets also foretold tribulation at the end of the age (Gwynn, "Hippolytus"). Victorinus (d. 304) agreed that God would send the trumpet plagues in the future, but he cautioned that these scenes did not foretell events in a linear way. Since the trumpet plagues of Rev 8–9 were repeated in the bowl plagues of Rev 16, readers were to assume that both scenes conveyed the same message in varying forms (*In Apoc.* 8.2).

For many interpreters, the trumpet visions symbolized the ongoing life of the church and offered moral guidance. A star falling and making water bitter shows how heretics fall from the truth and contaminate the Scriptures. The sun, moon, and stars being dimmed signifies heretics bringing spiritual darkness (Tyconius; Primasius; Bede; Rowland and Boxall, "Tyconius"). In the early sixth century, Oecumenius proposed an alternative, arguing that the trumpet visions pertained to the last judgment rather than to the present age. For example, the burning of trees in 8:7 symbolized the future punishment of sinners, whose souls are wooden. But Andreas (d. ca. 614) disagreed, arguing that the trumpets pointed to coming events. For him, the fire and blood falling from the sky warned of barbarian invasions.

The late medieval practice was to identify each trumpet with a specific heretic in the church's past. In so doing, interpreters defined their understanding of the true church throughout the ages (Intro I.B.4). For Nicholas of Lyra (d. 1349), the trumpet plagues were heretics from the fourth and fifth centuries, including Arius, Macedonius, Pelagius, and Eutyches, along with the Vandals and Goths, who shared their unorthodox positions (Krey, "Apocalypse," 273–76). In the sixteenth century, Protestants adjusted the pattern to include the papal hierarchy as one of the plagues, and they lengthened the time frame so that the fifth and sixth visions represented the Islamic conquests and Turkish invasion of Europe (Brightman, *Revelation*, 560–61). By correlating the visions with past events, they affirmed that God's purposes were being worked out in history (Intro I.C.2).

Modern futuristic interpreters construe the visions literally, as predictions that a third of the earth will be burned during the seven-year tribulation at the end of this age. Although that idea seems terrifying, it shows God's sovereign control of history (Seiss; LaHaye; Thomas). A variation is that the trumpet visions predict events that began to be fulfilled in the twentieth century. For example, the fire and hail that scorched the earth in Revelation occurred during the aerial bombings of World War II, and water poisoned with wormwood was the Soviet Union's nuclear disaster at Chernobyl in 1986. From this perspective, the end will arrive in the twenty-first century.

Contemporary literary studies of Revelation, which inform the COMMENT below, shift the focus from questions about the future to the pattern of interrupted judgment, which defines this vision cycle (§§18C and 18D). They explore the dynamics of divine judgment while recognizing that the visions cannot be directly equated with events in time and space (Boring 135; Murphy 237–38; Giesen 217).

The Temple and Holy City Besieged for Forty-Two Months (11:1–2)

John said that in his visions he was commanded to measure the temple, the altar, and those who worshiped there, even as the temple and holy city were under siege. Ancient interpreters wrote years after the destruction of the Jerusalem temple in 70 CE and sometimes concluded that John's vision pertained to a temple that would be rebuilt before the end of the age. Support came from 2 Thess 2:1–11, which said that the man of lawlessness, or the Antichrist, would one day set himself up in the temple and claim to be God (Irenaeus, *Haer.* 5.30.4). Accordingly, Hippolytus thought the Antichrist himself would rebuild the temple before occupying it (*Antichr.* 6; 63–64). This scenario was popularized during the Middle Ages by Adso of Montier-en-Der (INTRO I.B.1; K. Hughes, *Constructing*, 170) and by modern dispensationalist writers (LaHaye 183–85; cf. Boyer, *When*, 196–99).

For most ancient and medieval interpreters, however, the temple and holy city were symbols of the church. For Victorinus, measuring the temple meant assessing the church's faith. He identified the reed John uses with the church's creed; the vision therefore teaches that those who confess orthodox doctrine have a place among the worshipers, whereas the heterodox are in the outer court. Others followed a similar approach, noting that the forty-two months of siege could refer to a future period of persecution as well as to the entire period of the church's existence (Primasius; Bede).

Joachim of Fiore wove the forty-two months of conflict and the 1,260 days in which the two witnesses prophesy into a comprehensive theory of history (Rev 11:3–4). Since forty-two generations preceded the birth of Christ (Matt 1:1–17), Joachim thought there would be forty-two generations after Christ until the new spiritual age arrived. If a generation lasts for thirty years, then forty-two generations equal 1,260 years (INTRO I.B.3). Drawing out the implications, the Spiritual Franciscan Gerardo of Borgo San Donnino (d. 1276) predicted that the turn of the ages would occur in the year 1260, creating consternation in the order (McGinn, "Apocalypticism," 93–94).

Protestants of the sixteenth and seventeenth centuries accepted the idea that the temple symbolized the church (Petersen, *Preaching*, 157, 166). In the Geneva Bible the number of forty-two months of siege is said to encourage the faithful, since it meant that the time of the papal Antichrist was limited. Others took up the idea that the 1,260 days corresponded to 1,260 years during which the papacy would dominate the church. Some conjectured that the 1,260 years began with Pope Sylvester I (314–335), who made the church more worldly, or with Pope Boniface III (606–607), who was given the title Universal Bishop, affirming Rome's primacy over other churches (Petersen, *Preaching*, 164, 167). When French troops expelled the pope from Rome in 1798, some

British Protestants concluded that the 1,260-year reign of the papal Antichrist was finally ending (Sandeen, *Roots*, 6–7).

When progress toward the new age seemed slow in coming, however, some interpreters in the early nineteenth century began developing a futuristic perspective. They argued that the number 1,260 was not to be taken figuratively, as a number of years, but literally, as a number of days, which is what Revelation said. They expected the 1,260-day period to be half of the seven-year tribulation that was to occur at the end of the present age (Maitland, *Enquiry*). That perspective became a standard feature in dispensationalist interpretation (Seiss; Scofield; LaHaye; Thomas). By way of contrast, modern historical critics focused on what the temple vision suggested about the time in which Revelation was written. Some argued that if the temple was still standing, then Revelation must have been written before 70 CE, a view that some continue to hold (Bleek, *Lectures*; Ewald), though many now consider it unlikely (INTRO II.C). Others proposed that John wrote late in the first century but made use of pre-70 sources, including an oracle dating from the Roman siege of Jerusalem. While source theories continue to be discussed, there are good reasons for focusing on the final form of the text (§18B below).

The Two Witnesses (Rev 11:3–13)

This section depicts two prophets who are slain by the beast and then raised and taken to heaven. One main interpretive approach is to identify them as two individuals. Ancient writers usually identified them as Enoch (Gen 5:24; Sir 44:16; Heb 11:5; Josephus, *Ant.* 9.28) and Elijah (2 Kgs 2:11; Sir 48:9–10), both of whom were said to have been taken directly to heaven so that they remained alive. Elijah was expected to return at the end of the age (Mal 3:4–5; cf. Sir 48:9–10; John 1:21; *Sib. Or.* 2:187–89). Since Christians assumed that Elijah had returned once in John the Baptist, who announced the first coming of Christ (Matt 11:14 par.), he could return before Christ's second advent, along with Enoch (*Apoc. Pet.* 2; *Gos. Nic.* 25; *Apoc. El.* 4:7; Tertullian, *An.* 50; Hippolytus, *Antichr.* 43; Augustine, *Ep.* 193.3–5; Oecumenius; Andreas; cf. *Apoc. Paul* 20, 51; McGinn, *Apocalyptic*, 94–96). An alternative was that Elijah would be accompanied by Jeremiah, who would fulfill his calling to be a prophet to the nations at the end times (Jer 1:5; cf. Matt 16:14; Victorinus).

A few interpreters suggested that the witnesses might be Elijah, who caused a drought, and Moses, who turned water to blood (Exod 7:19; 1 Kgs 17:1; Victorinus, *In Apoc.* 11.3; Joachim of Fiore, *Enchiridion*, 148). Just as the belief that Elijah would return was common, so was it said that God would send a prophet "like" Moses (Deut 18:18), and traditions about Moses' mysterious disappearance at the end of his career might have suggested that Moses remained alive and would return (Deut 34:5–6). Accounts of the transfiguration show Moses and Elijah appearing with Jesus, which would suggest that both would return at the end of the age (Mark 9:4 par.). Dispensationalist interpreters picture Moses and Elijah returning in the time of the Antichrist (LaHaye; Thomas; Walvoord).

The two witnesses were also identified as individuals from later periods. Since Nicholas of Lyra read Revelation as a survey of history, he identified them with leaders from the sixth century: Pope Silverius of Rome and Patriarch Mennas of Constantinople, depicted as representatives of orthodox theology who resisted a heterodox emperor and empress (Krey, "Apocalypse"). More volatile were the reform movements that identified their own leaders as the persecuted witnesses in an effort to legitimate their causes. Christians in Bohemia challenged the Roman understanding of the church and its sacraments, and leaders like Jan Hus (d. 1415) and Jerome of Prague (d. 1416) were tried for heresy and burned. Some interpreters linked them to the two witnesses who were slain by the beast (Petersen, *Preaching*, 41–43). Among sixteenth-century Anabaptists, Melchior Hoffmann assumed the role of Elijah and Jan Matthijs took the part of Enoch, giving themselves key roles in God's designs (Intro I.C.3).

Modern historical critics sometimes argue that the author of Revelation modeled the two witnesses after martyrs of his own time, such as Peter and Paul (Ign. *Rom.* 4:3; *1 Clem.* 5:4–7; Eusebius, *Hist. eccl.* 2.25.8; cf. Munck, *Petrus*, 33–34) or Stephen and James (Acts 7:54–60; 12:1–2; cf. Kraft). Some note that Jesus was the promised prophet like Moses (Deut 18:18; Acts 3:22), and John the Baptist was Elijah (Matt 11:14; 14:1–12), and both were killed, like the witnesses (Böcher, "Johannes," 81–86). Still others note that the priests Ananus and Joshua were slain in Jerusalem during the revolt against Rome, and their bodies were left unburied, like those of the witnesses (Josephus, *J.W.* 4.314–17; K. Berger, *Auferstehung*, 27). The way that traits of many different figures are combined in the portrait of the witnesses, however, makes such specific references unlikely (Aune 2:603).

A second major approach is to construe the witnesses as representatives of groups. Tyconius (d. ca. 400) identified them as symbols of the pure church, which preaches during the present age by means of its two testaments, while resisting the worldly powers symbolized by the beast (Petersen, *Preaching*, 14). Others added that the two witnesses could symbolize a church of Jewish and Gentile believers or the internal witness of people's hearts and the external testimony of their deeds (Primasius; Caesarius; Bede). Joachim identified the witnesses as two monastic orders, which would arise in the near future to purify the church. For some, this idea seemed to be borne out soon after Joachim's death through the founding of the Dominican order, which focused on preaching and the correction of heresy, and the Franciscan order, which sought to renew the church through its emphasis on simplicity and poverty (Petersen, *Preaching*, 32–38).

Protestant reformers of the sixteenth and seventeenth centuries depicted the witnesses as faithful preachers of the gospel, who confronted the papal authority symbolized by the beast (LuthW 35:405). An illustration in the Wittenberg Bible of 1534 showed two Protestant witnesses breathing fire in the face of a beast that wears the papal tiara (van der Meer, *Apocalypse*, 307). The Geneva Bible likened the witnesses to Joshua and Zerubbabel, who were types of the true preachers who rebuild the temple or church—like the Protestant reformers themselves (Petersen, *Preaching*, 120, 160). The approach taken below construes the witnesses as representatives of the church, but the primary factors are literary: These figures encompass traits from important figures in the history of Israel and the early church (§23 Comment).

B. SOURCE CRITICISM OF REVELATION 11

In the nineteenth and twentieth centuries, source critics proposed that the visions of the temple and two witnesses were compilations of earlier materials. They generally favored a post-70 date for the Apocalypse and argued that the vision of the temple in 11:1–2 might have come from an earlier Jewish source. They noted the abrupt transition between the measuring of the temple in 11:1–2 and the two witnesses in 11:3–13 and pointed out that Revelation does not otherwise show any interest in the Jerusalem temple. In 1899 Julius Wellhausen proposed that 11:1–2 originated as a Zealot oracle that promised the inviolability of the temple during the siege of Jerusalem in 70 CE. He drew evidence from Josephus, who said that during the final stages of the Jewish revolt against Rome, the Zealots retreated into the sanctuary and holy of holies. There, prophecies were made that urged the militants to stand firm in the temple because God would deliver them (Josephus *J.W.* 6.121–22, 283–87). The fall of the temple appeared to disprove the oracle, but Wellhausen suggested that John reinterpreted the oracle about the preservation of the temple to mean the preservation of the Christian community during the conflicts of the end times (Wellhausen, *Skizzen*, 221–23; cf. Bousset 325–26; Charles 1:270–73; Aune 2:585–603; Yarbro Collins, *Crisis*, 65–67).

Other interpreters find it implausible to think that John relied on an oracle from the Jewish war. Given his freedom in composition, the imagery would not need to derive from such a source. It is also unlikely that he would have found it necessary to validate an older oracle by reinterpreting it. These interpreters suggest that John draws imagery from the siege of Jerusalem in a general way to symbolize threats against the Christian community, which is depicted as a temple (Caird; Giesen; Roloff; Schüssler Fiorenza; Hirschberg, *Das eschatologische*, 216–17). The approach taken below does not assume that John relied on a specific source, such as an oracle. Instead, attention will be given to the way the vision recasts material from Daniel and Ezekiel in light of early Christian traditions that portray the church as a temple. Allusions to the Jewish war are secondary. John's primary interest concerns the readers' social contexts in imperial Asia Minor.

The vision of the witnesses has also been ascribed to an earlier source. In 1895 Wilhelm Bousset argued that the material in 11:3–13 adapted a tradition about prophetic figures in conflict with an adversary at the end of time (*Antichrist*, 203–11). David Aune has more recently tried to uncover a similar pattern in *Apoc. El.* 4:7–19, a Christian text from the late-second or third century that may include older materials. He also draws on Lactantius, *Inst.* 7.17.1–3, which was written in the third or fourth century (Aune 2:588–93; cf. Frenschkowski, "Entrückung," 278–83). The form and style of the vision are unusual in Revelation, and the only distinctively Christian component is the reference to Jesus' crucifixion in 11:7 (cf. Satake 261–64).

One reason to question the use of an identifiable source for the story of the witnesses is that the materials from the *Apocalypse of Elijah* and Lactantius are considerably later than Revelation. The way they interweave Jewish and Christian elements also makes recovering a source that predates Revelation problematic. More importantly, the portrayal of the witnesses combines motifs from various passages of Scripture with elements from the readers' Greco-Roman contexts to create a multilayered image, which is comparable to those of the woman and dragon, the beast, and Babylon in later chapters. Given the lack of clear evidence for a source older than Revelation and the use of literary techniques found elsewhere, we will not posit an older source when interpreting this passage.

C. LITERARY STRUCTURE

The trumpet visions constitute the third major block of visions in John's Apocalypse. They interlock with the seal visions that precede them and the visions of the dragon and beast that follow. The seal visions concluded with a reverent silence in heaven, allowing the prayers of the saints to be offered at the altar (Rev 8:1, 3–5). But in between the silence and the offering of prayer, seven angels are given trumpets, which they blow after the prayers are made (8:2, 6). The way the seal and trumpet visions overlap shows that they must be taken together so that the silence and prayers that conclude the seal visions are the reason for the plagues that follow (Schüssler Fiorenza, *Book*, 172–73; Yarbro Collins, *Combat*, 16–19; Yarbro Collins, *Crisis*, 112–14; de Villiers, "Eschatological"; Stefanovic, "Angel"). A variation on the pattern occurs at the end of the trumpet cycle, where the final scene does not formally overlap with the new vision series but introduces its main themes. At the seventh trumpet, the heavenly voices announce the kingdom of God, and the elders declare that the time has come to judge the dead, to reward God's servants, and to destroy the destroyers of the earth (11:15–18). In the scenes that follow, these words come to pass. John will identify the destroyers of the earth as the dragon, the beast from the sea, and the beast from the land and introduce the process that will lead to their demise (11:19–15:4).

The seven trumpets create the overall structure of this section. As in the seal visions, the basic pattern is 4 + 2 (interlude) + 1. The first four trumpets are narrated in rapid succession, with brief descriptions of the threats they bring (8:6–12). Then the fifth and sixth visions constitute a pair of scenes that stretch out the action and climax with humanity's response to the threats (9:1–21). At this point the series is interrupted by a lengthy interlude depicting the vocation of God's people (10:1–11:14). Only then is the seventh trumpet sounded, bringing the series to its culmination with worship in heaven (11:15–18).

A pattern of three "woes" is overlaid on the basic series of seven, adding a unique structural element. After the first four trumpets have sounded, an eagle declares, "Woe, woe, woe to those who live on the earth because of the remaining blasts of the trumpet, which the three angels are about to blow" (8:13). Since four trumpets have already been blown, readers are to identify the three woes to come with the last three trumpets in the series. When the fifth trumpet plague is over, readers are told that the first woe has passed (9:12). Then, when the sixth plague is over, they expect to hear that the second woe has passed, but this announcement is delayed until John has been told to prophesy again and God's witnesses have completed their work (11:14). This means that the sixth trumpet plague, which brings no repentance, is bracketed with the visions depicting God's witnesses, so together they constitute the second woe (9:13–11:13). Linking these scenes shows that God's way of confronting those who dwell on earth is not limited to the wrath of the sixth trumpet but includes the prophetic witness of the church (Bauckham, *Climax*, 11–12; Perry, *Rhetoric*, 80).

The third woe corresponds to the seventh trumpet, which announces the arrival of God's kingdom (11:14–18). The kingdom will bring the rewarding of God's servants (20:4–6; 21:1–22:5), the judging of the dead (20:11–15), and the destruction of the destroyers of the earth (11:19–20:10), all of which occur in the second half of the book. Identifying the final woe with the celebration envisioned by the seventh trumpet points to two different perspectives on God's action. For the agents of evil, God's justice will bring the "woe" of defeat, but for those who now suffer under those powers, God's action will bring deliverance and rejoicing.

A lengthy interlude between the sixth and seventh trumpet visions is a notable feature of the series (10:1–11:14). One of its functions is to *create* delay in the seemingly inexorable movement toward final judgment. Readers know that there are seven trumpets, and the way John counts as each trumpet is blown gives the impression of a relentless outworking of God's designs. When the sixth trumpet unleashes death on a third of the world and humanity refuses to repent, readers expect the seventh trumpet to bring a final catastrophic plague. But this does not occur. Instead, an angel tells John not to write down what the seven thunders have said but to prophesy again, and John recounts a vision of the temple, or worshiping community, and its two prophets, who represent the community's witness (10:1–11:14). Only after the witnesses have finished their testimony does the seventh trumpet sound, announcing God's kingdom.

A second function of the section is to *interpret* the delay in judgment. In the seal visions the martyrs under the heavenly altar asked how long God would delay in bringing justice for their deaths; the trumpet visions take up the issue as prayers are offered at the heavenly altar (6:10; 8:3–4). The first six trumpets show wrath being unleashed on the earth, with no sign that such plagues will move people to repent (9:20–21). So the final trumpet is delayed until further witness can be given to an unrepentant world (10:1–11:14). The visions between the sixth and seventh trumpets show that if God's justice seems slow in coming, the delay allows time for witness. A similar interruption occurred between the sixth and seventh seals, where the forces of destruction were restrained in order that there might be opportunity for people from every nation to be redeemed for life with God (7:1–17). Where the interlude in the seal visions depicts the identity of the redeemed, the interlude in the trumpet visions shows their vocation as prophetic witnesses (Perry, *Rhetoric*, 207–41; Bauckham, *Theology*, 80–88).

D. RELATIONSHIP OF THE SEAL, TRUMPET, AND BOWL VISIONS

The trumpet visions are patterned closely after the seal visions and also resemble the bowl visions later in the book. All of these series are structured in groups of seven and include plagues that threaten the world. Some content is repeated. Images of war occur in all three series, and death is unleashed in two of them, at seal four and trumpet six. At the same time, each series includes elements not found in the others, such as economic hardship at the third seal, the wormwood at trumpet three, the demonic beings at trumpets five and six, the sores at bowl one, and the froglike spirits at bowl five. The sequences also differ, as shown in Table 4.

Interpreters have construed the relationships among these three series in different ways. Some assume that Revelation unfolds in a linear way. Futuristic interpreters usually think that the end of the age will begin with the outbreak of conquest depicted at the first seal, then the breakdown in civil order at the second seal, then food shortages at the third seal, and so on. Once these things have occurred, the trumpet plagues will begin, and then the bowl plagues complete the process (LaHaye; Walvoord).

Table 4. Comparison of the Seal, Trumpet, and Bowl Visions

	Seals (Rev 6)	Trumpets (Rev 8–9)	Bowls (Rev 16)
1	Conquest	Hail, fire, and blood; burning of earth, trees, grass.	Sores on worshipers of the beast.
2	Violence	Burning mountain; sea turns to blood; sea creatures die; ships are destroyed.	Sea turns to blood.
3	Economic hardship	Falling star makes rivers and springs wormwood; people die.	Rivers and springs turn to blood.
4	Death	Sun, moon, and stars darkened.	Fierce heat.
5	Martyrs	Demonic locusts afflict the ungodly.	Darkness on the kingdom of the beast.
6	Darkening of sun, moon, and stars *Interlude concerning the redeemed*	Demonic hordes from the Euphrates slay people. *Interlude concerning witness*	Demonic froglike spirits gather kings for battle.
7	Heavenly silence and prayer	Heavenly voices announce God's kingdom.	Earthquake and hail. *Interlude concerning Babylon* Heavenly voices celebrate God's justice (19:1–10).

Other interpreters think the plague sequences repeat a similar message in different ways. They emphasize that Revelation does not unfold in a linear way. For example, on multiple occasions the heavenly bodies become dark (6:12–14; 8:12; 16:1–11) and the sea turns to blood (8:8; 16:3), and there are incongruities between vision cycles. The sun is dark, the stars have fallen, and the sky has vanished by the end of the sixth seal (6:12–17), yet all the heavenly bodies are still in place in the trumpet series, where they become partially dark again (8:12). There are also incongruities within particular series. For example, all the grass is burned at the first trumpet, but it is apparently thriving at the fifth trumpet, where it receives special protection (8:7; 9:4).

The recurring patterns and non sequiturs are sometimes understood in literary terms, as a means of showing an intensification of divine wrath. The afflictions are initially limited to a fourth of the world, then expand to a third of the world, and finally are all-encompassing (Boring 135). Another interpretation sees one series telescoping into the next. For example, the seal plagues culminate with threats against earth and sky (6:12–17), and the trumpet plagues develop the theme (8:6–12). Therefore, one could argue that the sixth seal summarizes what unfolds in the trumpet series (Murphy 236). Another proposal is that the vision cycles are not fully repetitive or sequential but offer different theological perspectives on the same situation. Where the seals begin with threats brought about by human sin (conquest, violence, economic hardship), the trumpets show God actively punishing the wicked (Mounce 176–77; cf. Beale).

The approach taken here relates the three plague sequences to the theme of interrupted judgment. The first six seal visions culminate with cosmic signs of wrath that move people to ask a question: "Who is able to stand?" (6:17). At that point, the movement toward judgment is interrupted so readers can see the redeemed standing in the presence of God (7:1–17). The first six trumpet visions also display divine wrath but elicit a different response: People refuse to repent (9:20–21). Then the movement toward judgment is interrupted so witness can be given (10:1–11:14). The bowl visions continue to show divine wrath falling on God's adversaries, only to have their resistance intensify so that they curse God as the beast does (16:9, 11, 21). Only when repeated opportunities for repentance have been refused does God bring judgment by turning evil against itself so Babylon falls. These visionary cycles cannot be correlated with a specific series of events in the realm of time and space. The interplay between visions of wrath and the interruption of wrath shows readers different aspects of God's justice.

E. PLAGUES IN REVELATION, THE EXODUS TRADITION, AND THE GRECO-ROMAN WORLD

Apocalyptic writings often envisioned a time of severe distress at the end of the present age (see §12C), but only rarely do they suggest that the coming afflictions will be analogous to the plagues of the exodus (*Apoc. Ab.* 29:14–17). Nevertheless, interpreters frequently discern a connection in Revelation. The similarities and differences are summarized in Table 5. The main biblical account of the plagues in Egypt appears in Exod 7–12, which lists ten plagues. These are closely followed by later Jewish sources such as *Jub.* 48:5–8 and *L.A.B.* 10:1. Other versions occur in Ps 78:43–53 (seven plagues) and Ps 105:27–36 (eight plagues). In Wis 11–19 there are seven contrasts between Israel and Egypt. These incorporate elements from six plagues, along with Egypt's defeat at the Red Sea. The narrative of Artapanus combines the plague of locusts with lice and the hail with earthquakes (*OTP* 2:901–3; cf. Aune 2:499–506).

The influence of the exodus tradition is strongest on Revelation's bowl visions, where each plague includes an element from the plagues in Egypt. Most of these correspond to biblical accounts. Where special elements exist, such as Revelation's emphasis on fire (Rev 16:8–9; cf. Wis 16:15–29) and earthquake (Rev 17–20; cf. Artapanus), there are analogies to later forms of the exodus tradition. The bowls are also prefaced by a victory scene in which the redeemed sing the song of Moses and the Lamb beside heaven's fiery red sea, much as Israel sang beside the Red Sea (Exod 15; Rev 15:2–4). Where the biblical narrative of the exodus is followed by the building of the tabernacle, or tent of meeting (Exod 25–40), the bowl sequence is linked to the heavenly tent of meeting (Rev 15:5–8).

Many interpreters also see the exodus tradition as the basic pattern for the trumpet series, but the approach taken here differs. Connections with the biblical plagues will be noted, but weight will also be given to Greco-Roman materials. One reason for this shift is the literary context. The bowl visions begin with allusions to Moses and the exodus (15:2–4), but the trumpet visions do not. Another reason is that the content of the trumpet visions differs significantly from the exodus tradition. The focus of the first trumpet vision is fire rather than hail, as in Exodus, and it includes the new element of blood from the sky. At the second trumpet an object like a flaming mountain falls

Table 5. The Plagues in Revelation and the Exodus Tradition

Exod 7–12 (Jub. and L.A.B).	Ps 78	Ps 105	Artapanus	Wisdom	Rev 8–9 (trumpets)	Rev 16 (bowls)
River changes to blood	x	x	(River floods)	x	(Rivers become bitter) (Sea changes to blood)	x (Sea changes to blood)
Frogs	x	x	x			(Froglike spirits)
Gnats	x	x				
Flies		x	x	x		
Cattle disease	(x)					
Sores			x	x		x
Hail, fire, thunder	x	x	x		x	x
Locusts	x	x	x	x	x	
Darkness		x		x	x	x
Death	x	x		x	x	

from heaven and turns a third of the seawater to blood. At the third trumpet another star falls and turns the rivers and springs to wormwood. By way of contrast, the exodus narrative says nothing about stars falling; it tells of the Nile rather than the sea turning to blood; and it says nothing about wormwood. Revelation includes the destruction of ships, which also has no place in the exodus tradition. At the fourth trumpet the heavenly bodies are partially darkened, but in Exodus the darkness over the Egyptians is complete.

Differences are even greater at the fifth trumpet, which describes a plague of locusts that are quite different from those that affected Egypt. Before the exodus the locusts devoured plants, but in Revelation they leave the plants alone and hurt only people. At the sixth trumpet the agents of death come from the Euphrates, not from Egypt. In these trumpet plagues the agents of destruction have a surreal, demonic quality that is not paralleled in the exodus tradition.

Interpreters who stress the similarities between the exodus plagues and trumpet visions often discern important theological implications (Murphy 238; Mounce 177; Court, *Myth*, 80). In a positive sense, the plagues in Egypt were a prelude to Israel's deliverance from slavery, so if the trumpet plagues are similar, they too signal the coming of salvation (Boring 135; Giesen 181). In a negative sense, God sent plagues on those who oppressed Israel, and the trumpet plagues show him sending plagues on the ungodly people of earth. For some, this means that the trumpet plagues were intended to harden people in their unbelief, just as the plagues in Egypt hardened the heart of Pharaoh in order to reveal God's power over him (Beale 465–67; cf. Aune 2:496). But others argue that the plagues on the Egyptians were intended to move them to repentance, so the plagues in Revelation should also be interpreted as incentives to repent, even if repentance does not occur (Rev 9:20–21; 16:9, 11; Blount; Osborne; Prigent; Schüssler

Fiorenza). The approach taken below is that the trumpet visions do focus on the question of repentance, given the internal literary movement of the series. By explicitly noting that the first six trumpet plagues did not move people to repent (9:20–21), John indicates that repentance would have been the proper response (Caird 124; Bauckham, *Theology*, 82, 86).

The NOTES and COMMENT also show how Rev 8–9 describes plagues that could be recognized as evidence of divine wrath throughout the Greco-Roman world. This aspect heightens the incongruity of humanity's refusal to repent, since John could assume that even pagans would know that these disasters conveyed wrath and called for people to make amends with the powers of heaven. This approach also suggests why such displays of wrath might *not* move people to repent. These plagues do not distinguish the God of the Christian community from the gods of the empire. Given only the plagues of wrath, there is no reason people should move away from the traditional polytheism that John condemns (9:20–21) in order to worship the God he considers to be Lord of all creation (14:7). For that to occur, a different kind of testimony is needed. This is why the path toward final judgment is interrupted in the wake of humanity's refusal to repent—so that John and others can bear witness.

19. Four Trumpets Affect Land, Sea, and Sky (8:6–13)

8 ⁶Then the seven angels who held the seven trumpets made ready to blow them. ⁷The first blew his trumpet, and there was hail and fire mixed with blood, and it was thrown down to the earth, so that a third of the earth was burned up, and a third of the trees were burned up, and all the green grass was burned up. ⁸Then the second angel blew his trumpet, and something like a great mountain burning with fire was thrown down to the sea, so that a third of the sea became blood, ⁹and a third of the living creatures in the sea died, and a third of the ships were destroyed. ¹⁰Then the third angel blew his trumpet, and a great star, burning like a torch, fell from heaven, and it fell on a third of the rivers and the springs of water. ¹¹The name of the star is Wormwood, and a third of the waters became wormwood, and many people died from the water because it became bitter. ¹²Then the fourth angel blew his trumpet, and a third of the sun was struck and a third of the moon and a third of the stars, so that a third of them were darkened, and the day lost a third of its light, and the night lost a third of its light.

¹³Then I looked and I heard an eagle flying high overhead, saying with a loud voice, "Woe, woe, woe to those who live on the earth because of the remaining blasts of the trumpet, which the three angels are about to blow."

NOTES

8:6. *Then the seven angels who held the seven trumpets made ready to blow them.* Greco-Roman sources say that when "fear-inspiring trumpets and horns" are heard in the sky, they forewarn people that destructive forces are about to be unleashed on earth (Ovid, *Metam.* 15.784–88; Petronius, *Satyricon* 122; Lucan, *Pharsalia* 1.578). According to

Israel's prophets, a trumpet would announce the coming day of the Lord's wrath, and later Jewish writings link the trumpet sound to the devastation at the end of the age (Joel 2:1; Zeph 1:16; *4 Ezra* 6:23; *Apoc. Ab.* 31:1–2). Although some early Christians expected a trumpet to signal the return of Christ, the ingathering of the faithful, and the resurrection of the dead (Matt 24:31; 1 Cor 15:52; 1 Thess 4:16), Revelation does not use trumpet imagery in this way but depicts a series of trumpets that bring devastating plagues on earth, sea, and sky.

8:7. *The first blew his trumpet, and there was hail and fire.* Hailstorms mixed with fire displayed God's power and wrath against the Egyptians before the exodus (Exod 9:13–26; Pss 78:48; 105:32) and later against Gog and other adversaries (Ezek 38:22; cf. Josh 10:11; Isa 30:30; Wis 16:22; Sir 39:29; Paulien, *Decoding*, 366–67). In the Greco-Roman world lightning and hail awakened awe toward the gods (Cicero, *Nat. d.* 2.5.14). Dreams of fire from heaven portended danger, while hail indicated confusion and despair (Artemidorus, *Onirocritica* 2.8–9).

mixed with blood, and it was thrown to the earth. The plagues before the exodus did not include blood falling from the sky, though Wis 16:16 mentions "strange rains." Red droplets could be construed as a natural occurrence, since red dust from the desert can mix with rain (Roloff). But blood raining from heaven—either alone or with other phenomena—was often considered to be a portent of war in Greco-Roman sources (Statius, *Theb.* 7.408; Lucan, *Pharsalia* 1.578; Petronius, *Satyricon* 122; Cicero, *Nat. d.* 2.5.14) and Jewish writings: "For fire will rain on men from the floors of heaven, fire and blood, water, lightning bolt, darkness, heavenly night, and destruction in war" (*Sib. Or.* 5:377–79; cf. 2:20; 12:56–57; 14:89–90; Joel 2:30). The portents of war are borne out by the unleashing of demonic armies in Rev 9.

so that a third of the earth was burned up. Many interpreters have suggested that the mention of "a third" in this passage recalls prophetic texts (Primasius; Ambrose Autpert; Aune; Beale; Lupieri; Prigent); however, a direct connection is unlikely. Zechariah warns that two-thirds of the land will perish and one-third will be saved and refined by fire (13:8–9), yet this pattern differs from that in Rev 8, where a third is destroyed or damaged by fire rather than saved. Ezekiel cuts off his hair and burns a third, strikes a third with the sword, and scatters a third to the wind to show that a third of the people will die by famine and pestilence, a third will die by the sword, and a third will be scattered (Ezek 5:2, 12). Yet Ezekiel expects that all the people will suffer one of the three forms of devastation, whereas in Rev 8 two-thirds of the earth, sea, freshwater sources, and heavenly bodies are spared. In *Sib. Or.* 3:543–44 fire falls from heaven and only one-third of the earth is spared (Beale), but in Rev 8 a third of the world is struck and the remaining two-thirds is spared.

and a third of the trees were burned up, and all the green grass was burned up. Fire conveyed divine wrath in the OT (Isa 29:6; Amos 1:4, 7, 10) and Greco-Roman sources (Tacitus, *Ann.* 4.64; Julius Obsequens, *Prod.* 8; 19; 25; 39; 65), although the scale of fires in Revelation goes far beyond the usual portents. Here, the focus is on the devastation of plant life. Ordinarily, trees were valued for wood for fuel and timber for ships, buildings, and furniture (Lev 26:4; Deut 8:7–8; Ps 104:14–16; Broughton, *Asia*, 607–20; Magie, *Roman*, 1:42–47; Meiggs, "Sea-Borne"). Pastures of green grass were also a blessing for livestock (Ps 23:2; Isa 30:23). Trees and grass were important to the Asian economy (Cicero, *Leg. man.* 6.14), and their loss would be devastating.

8:8. *Then the second angel blew his trumpet, and something like a great mountain burning with fire was thrown down to the sea.* The fiery object can best be understood as a star. It is not a burning mountain but is "like" one (cf. *1 En.* 18:13; 21:3; Charles). Some interpreters think the vision portends the fiery demise of Babylon in Rev 17–18 because Jer 51:25 calls Babylon a destroying mountain that will become a burned-out mountain under God's judgment (Caird; Boxall). However, Rev 8:8 is not mainly about the destruction of a mountain or city but concerns the sea. Others compare the plague to a volcanic eruption like that of Vesuvius in 79 CE (Pliny the Younger, *Ep.* 6.16, 20; Blount; Osborne; Witherington). Yet this approach does not fit the context. This is not an earthly mountain that spews fire but a fiery mountainlike object that comes from heaven and is "thrown down to the sea" (cf. *Sib. Or.* 5:158–59), just as the fire, hail, and blood from heaven were "thrown down to the earth" at the first trumpet.

so that a third of the sea became blood. On one level the vision conveys an ominous sense of divine power. Moses turned the Nile River and other water sources in Egypt into blood, showing that the God of the Hebrews was behind the demand that Pharaoh let the people go (Exod 7:16–21). In Revelation the plague also demonstrates divine power. The specter of the sea becoming bloody, like the blood raining from heaven in Rev 8:7, was also a portent of catastrophic war. It was among the signs that were to move people to seek out the divine will (Lucan, *Pharsalia* 1.547–48; Tacitus, *Ann.* 14.32).

8:9. *and a third of the living creatures in the sea died.* Sea creatures can include all forms of marine life, ranging from dolphins, sharks, and sea turtles to shellfish and sponges (Gen 1:20–21; Lev 11:10; Pliny the Elder, *Nat.* book 9). Many people included fish in their diets, and the tollhouse at Ephesus helped regulate the fishermen and fish sellers who were active in coastal cities (I.Eph 20; cf. I.Smyr 719.5; *NewDocs* 5:95–114). The death of sea creatures imperils human welfare.

and a third of the ships were destroyed. Early readers might have pictured small fishing vessels that worked along the coasts, the more imposing ships used by the Roman navy, and the large cargo ships that contributed wealth to the empire (Rev 18:17–19). Commercial ships were typically 60–75 feet long and carried 100–150 tons of freight, although large ships could hold two or three times that amount. A seafaring ship could transport two hundred to six hundred passengers (Casson, *Ships*, 169–90). Destruction at sea meant that "your riches, your wares, your merchandise, your mariners and your pilots . . . and all your warriors within you, with all the company that is with you, sink into the heart of the seas" (Ezek 27:27). Many regarded the destruction of ships at sea as an act of God. Those leasing ships promised to return them undamaged unless "some act of God occur by storm," and those returning safely from a voyage offered thanks to heaven (P.Köln 147.5–6; *NewDocs* 6:82–86; cf. Jonah 1:6, 16).

8:10. *Then the third angel blew his trumpet, and a great star, burning like a torch, fell from heaven.* Readers would have pictured this falling star as a meteor, which were sometimes called "torches" (Pliny the Elder, *Nat.* 2.25.96). Comets were also described as torches, and such phenomena could be "tokens of impending doom" by death and war (Manilius, *Astronomica* 1.874–76; Julius Obsequens, *Prod.* 45; 54; 56). In dreams it was "inauspicious to see stars falling down upon the earth. For they prophesy the death of many men: large stars, the death of important men" (Artemidorus, *Onirocritica* 2.36).

and it fell on a third of the rivers and the springs of water. Rivers and springs are part of God's creation, providing water for all living things (Pss 24:2; 104:24). The readers of Revelation lived in cities near rivers like the Meander, Hermos, and Kaikos or the "the wonderful water" of the Lycus River that flowed by Laodicea (*Sib. Or.* 3:471). Rome was built beside the Tiber. Spring water was channeled through aqueducts in and around all of the seven cities addressed by Revelation, as it was for Rome and cities throughout the empire (Notes on Rev 2:1, 8, 12, 18; 3:1, 7, 14). The poisoning of springs would imperil human life.

8:11. *and the name of the star is Wormwood, and a third of the waters became wormwood, and many people died from the water because it became bitter.* Ancient descriptions of the heavens do not mention a star named Wormwood, which suggests that readers would have understood it to be a new and ominous phenomenon in the sky (Lucan, *Pharsalia* 1.526; Petronius, *Satyricon* 122). The star is named for what it does: contaminate water with wormwood (*apsinthion, apsinthos*). This small gray-leafed plant was so bitter that even a small amount could make food and water unpalatable (Prov 5:4; Herm. *Man.* 5.1.5). Ordinarily, consuming wormwood was not fatal, and it was used medicinally (Hippocrates, *Morb.* 3.11; Hippocrates, *Int.* 52; Theophrastus, *Hist. plant.* 7.9.5; Dioscorides Pedanius, *Mat. med.* 3.23.1–6). The lethal quality of wormwood in Revelation reflects the biblical comparison of wormwood to poison (Jer 9:15; 23:15).

8:12. *Then the fourth angel blew his trumpet, and a third of the sun was struck and a third of the moon and a third of the stars.* The ninth plague that preceded the exodus surrounded the Egyptians by darkness for three days, while the people of Israel had light where they lived (Exod 10:21–23). Revelation is similar in that it includes darkness, but it differs because the writer does not suggest that it fell on some people but not others. Instead, the whole earth is partially darkened. In prophetic texts the darkening of heavenly bodies signals divine wrath: "For the stars of the heavens and their constellations will not give their light; the sun will be dark at its rising, and the moon will not shed its light," and God "will punish the world for its evil" (Isa 13:10–11; cf. Ezek 32:7–8; Amos 8:9; cf. Mark 13:24–25). Greco-Roman writers included the dimming of sun and moon among portents of coming disasters (Ovid, *Metam.* 15.785; Lucan, *Pharsalia* 1.538–43; Petronius, *Satyricon* 122; Artemidorus, *Onirocritica* 2.36).

so that a third of them were darkened, and the day lost a third of its light, and the night lost a third of its light. The text seems to picture the sun and moon losing a third of their surface light, as they do during partial eclipses, and a third of the stars being darkened, so the intensity of the light during the day and night is reduced by a third (Aune; Giesen). Alternatively, some interpreters take the last line to mean that no light shines at all for a third of the daytime and a third of the nighttime (NAB, NIV; Mounce; Murphy; Osborne). This approach is less plausible.

8:13. *Then I looked and I heard an eagle flying high overhead, saying with a loud voice.* In the Greco-Roman world the eagle was regarded as a revealer of the divine will (*Greek Anth.* 9.223). Ancient sources say that along with heavenly trumpets, earthquakes, and showers of blood, warnings of disaster were given by birds (Statius, *Theb.* 7.404; cf. Ovid, *Metam.* 15.791; Lucan, *Pharsalia* 1.558). The eagle was associated with Zeus and was thought to be one of heaven's surest messengers (Homer, *Il.* 8.242; Homer, *Od.* 2.146; *Greek Anth.* 9.223). The eagle in Revelation is a messenger from the Creator, in whose throne hall a creature that looked like an eagle was in attendance (Rev 4:7).

Romans sometimes tried to discern the divine will by the movement or position of an eagle and especially whether it flew or called from the right or left of the viewer (Suetonius, *Aug.* 94.7; 96.1; Suetonius, *Vit.* 9; Suetonius, *Dom.* 6.2; Tacitus, *Ann.* 2.17; Tacitus, *Hist.* 1.62; Xenophon, *Anab.* 6.1.23). John says only that the bird was directly above him, or "high overhead" (NAB), using the term *mesouranēma*, which was the point at which the sun reached the highest point between its rising and setting (Strabo, *Geographica* 2.5.1; Plutarch, *Mor.* 284E; *Sib. Or.* 5:208). The best manuscripts say that an eagle (*aetou*) uttered the woes ($\mathfrak{P}^{115}$ ℵ A 046), but some say that an angel (*angelou*) did so (P 1 680 2059; KJV). The variant might be a mistake, as the Greek words for eagle and angel are similar, though it could be an intentional change, since one might expect a heavenly announcement to come from an angel as in Rev 14:6 (*TCGNT*² 669). The Greek literally says that John saw one eagle, but here "one" (*eis*) seems equivalent to the indefinite article "an" (BDF §247 [2]). The term *aetou* could refer to a vulture, which lived on carrion (cf. Matt 24:28; Luke 17:37), but the word refers to an eagle in Rev 4:7 and 12:14, and that is the case in 8:13.

"Woe, woe, woe to those who live on the earth because of the remaining blasts of the trumpet, which the three angels are about to blow." The Greek *ouai* (woe) is used for the Hebrew *'oy*, or *hoy*. Pronouncing a woe against others usually warns that divine judgment will strike (Isa 5:8; 10:1; Jer 13:27; Ezek 24:9; *1 En.* 94:6–8; Matt 11:21; 23:13). Revelation depicts "those who live on the earth" as God's opponents, who are threatened by divine judgment (NOTE on 3:10).

COMMENT

The third cycle of visions began in the heavenly throne room, where seven angels were given seven trumpets (8:2). The seventh seal had just been opened to a reverent silence, in which the prayers of the saints would be offered (8:1, 3–5). By overlapping the final seal vision and the first trumpet vision, John shows that the prayers and the plagues must be understood together. The heavenly altar was where the martyrs had cried out, "How long, O Master, holy and true, will you wait before you pass judgment and bring justice for our blood, which was shed by those who live on the earth?" (6:10). Now the saints' petitions rise up with the smoke of incense from the altar, the angel takes fire from the altar and hurls it down to earth, signaling the onset of devastating judgments. Connecting the plagues to the prayers in this way takes up the question of how God should respond to the pleas of his people. One might put it as a counterquestion: "Suppose God takes the prayers for justice and turns them into wrath. What will that accomplish?"

As the angels blow their trumpets, fire falls from heaven in a dazzling display of wrath. Yet in the wake of devastation, the ungodly refuse to give up their idolatry and murder (9:20–21). What the first six trumpet visions reveal is that wrath alone does not move people to repent. Then, to depict the nature of God's response, Revelation again uses the pattern of interrupted judgment. Instead of the final trumpet sounding immediately, an angel interrupts the movement toward judgment in order that further

---

On Rev 8:6–13, see K. Berger, "Hellenistisch"; Paulien, *Decoding*; G. Stevenson, *Power*, 286–93; Vanni, *L'Apocalisse*, 215–25.

witness might be given to the unrepentant world (Caird 124; Bauckham, *Theology*, 82, 86). The saints under the altar demanded to know how long God would delay in bringing justice, but the trumpet visions reveal *why* God's justice seems slow in coming: God's will is that the world should worship its Creator—something so vividly depicted in Rev 4 and 5—but wrath alone cannot achieve it. Other means are necessary, and these will include the suffering and witness of God's people (Perry, *Rhetoric*, 209–10; Bauckham, *Climax*, 10–13).

Interpreters have often noted that aspects of the trumpet visions resemble the plagues that led to Israel's exodus from Egypt (see §18E). By developing the analogy, one might construe both the Egyptian and trumpet plagues as signs calling God's adversaries to repentance (Prigent; Osborne), as punishments designed to harden the hearts of God's foes as part of his judgment against them (Aune; Beale; Paulien, *Decoding*, 336), or as harbingers of coming liberation (Boring; Giesen). The approach taken here is that the trumpet visions draw on the exodus tradition, but the imagery is also broader. The visions depict divine wrath in ways that would have been comprehensible throughout John's cultural context. From a Greco-Roman perspective the plagues could be understood as warnings of the disasters that will occur if people persist in a course of action that God or the gods view unfavorably (Berger, "Hellenistisch"; Krauss, *Interpretation*; Beard, North, and Price, *Religions*, 2:172–75; Aune 2:416–19). Including such threats in the trumpet visions shows people receiving warnings of heavenly judgment in ways that they should have been able to recognize. This makes their refusal to repent more remarkable and, at a deeper level, more plausible (COMMENT on 9:20–21).

The First Four Trumpets Bring Disaster on Earth (8:6–12)

The first trumpet brings a vision of hail, fire, and blood being hurled down onto the earth. In Israel's tradition and the Greco-Roman world, hail and fire were familiar means of heavenly judgment (NOTE on 8:7). The reason for the plague is suggested by the inclusion of blood along with hail and fire. The martyrs cried out for justice against those who shed their blood (6:10), as the adversaries of God once shed the blood of Christ (1:5; 5:9). The blood falling from the sky now warns of God's judgment against the world that perpetrated the violence. Blood raining from heaven was widely understood to portend war (NOTE on 8:7), and in the next chapter war will come when the demonic armies are unleashed.

The main element in this plague is fire, which consumes a third of the earth and trees and all the green grass (8:7). The angels in the previous chapter were prevented from harming the earth, sea, and trees (7:1–3), but now those who blow the trumpets threaten to destroy them. In the previous vision cycle, Death held sway over a fourth of the earth (6:8), but now the damage level is raised to one-third. At the same time, the threat remains controlled. A third of the earth suffers fire damage, but by implication, the remaining two-thirds is kept safe. The element of restraint is important, because life must continue for there to be an opportunity for repentance.

Rather than beginning with a direct assault on human life, the plagues successively damage the parts of the created order that support life (8:7). The first plague strikes the trees that for John's readers included the olive tree, which yielded oil, and the fig and other fruit trees. Oak, fir, cedar, and ash trees were used for building, and pine trees provided pitch for waterproofing ships. Furniture was made from some of these woods, as well as from citrus and other expensive woods, which were profitable trade items that support the empire of Babylon/Rome according to 18:12. Grass provided food for the sheep and cattle that provided milk and meat, as well as for the horses used for transportation (NOTES on 18:13). Damage to trees and grass threatens all who depend on them.

The second trumpet extends the threat by bringing fire, like a burning mountain, down to the sea so that a third of its waters are turned to blood (8:8). For some readers this would have been reminiscent of the exodus plague that turned the Nile into blood and all of its fish died (Exod 7:14–24). But in this vision Revelation focuses on the sea, rather than a river. In the Greco-Roman context the waves of blood in the sea would have been an ominous portent of war, calling people to seek out the divine will (NOTE on Rev 8:8). In Revelation itself, the ocean of blood gives a vivid sense that God has heard the cry of the martyrs and is now bringing judgment on those who shed the blood of his witnesses (6:10). The idea is made explicit in 16:3–7.

What is striking is that the second trumpet vision does not say anything about the deaths of the ungodly. Instead, the blood in the sea leads to the deaths of a third of the sea creatures, which is peculiar, given Revelation's theology of creation (8:9). John assumes that God created the sea (10:6; 14:7), and when the countless hosts in the heavenly throne room praise God for making all things, the song is taken up by every creature in heaven, on earth, under the earth, and in the sea (5:13). The incongruity is that the martyrs asked God to judge their adversaries, but here the plagues are felt by the sea creatures that praised the Creator. Later, the problem intensifies when the entire sea turns to blood so that all of its creatures perish (16:3). If one asks why the sea creatures should suffer, the text offers no answer.

Instead, the devastation leads to a different point: Why should the ungodly survive? Allowing the creation that praises its Creator to suffer while the ungodly survive seems as inexplicable as allowing the people who serve God to suffer while the perpetrators of injustice live on. What the visions will disclose, however, is that as long as the ungodly survive, both the need and the call for repentance remain (9:20–21; 16:9, 11). In visions to come, God's witnesses may have power to turn water into blood, yet they do so wearing sackcloth as a visible exhortation that the world repent of sin in order to worship the God who made it (11:3, 6, 13, 15–18).

The aspect of human life most directly affected by the second trumpet plague is shipping. For the writer of Revelation, the ruling power sheds the blood of the innocent yet maintains world dominion by luring people into its glittering network of trade, which thrived because of its ships that plied the seas of its empire (17:1–6; 18:17–19, 24). John personifies the ruling power as a woman who sits on many waters, arrogantly thinking she is immune from judgment (17:1; 18:7–8). But the second trumpet plague warns that the seas are subject to God, who can transform them from a vehicle for commerce into a means of judgment.

At the third trumpet a star called Wormwood falls from heaven, contaminating the world's rivers and springs of water (8:10). A falling star was often taken to be a harbinger of death (Artemidorus, *Onirocritica* 2.36), though the falling star in this plague actually makes death occur (Berger, "Hellenistisch," 1450). In the story of the exodus, the Nile and canals and pools of Egypt were turned into blood so that people could not drink the water (Exod 7:14–24). The trumpet plagues vary the pattern, since it is the sea that turns to blood (Rev 8:8), while a falling star pollutes a third of the sources of freshwater with the bitterness of wormwood (8:10–11). As in the other trumpet plagues, a Greco-Roman audience would have regarded the turning of freshwater into poison as a sign of divine wrath (Lucan, *Pharsalia* 1.648).

Calling the star Wormwood discloses the character of divine judgment. The trumpet visions depict plagues falling on "those who live on the earth" (8:13), who slay the martyrs and engage in idolatry (6:10; 9:20–21). Traditionally, the fruits of idolatry and injustice were deemed to be as bitter as wormwood (Deut 29:18; Amos 5:7), so God would mete out a bitter judgment, "feeding this people with wormwood and giving them poisonous water to drink" (Jer 9:15; 23:15). Revelation assumes that there is symmetry in divine judgment: "one is punished by the very things by which one sins" (Wis 11:16; cf. 2 Macc 5:10; 13:8; *T. Gad* 5:10; *L.A.B.* 43:5; 44:10; *m. Soṭah* 1:7–9; *t. Soṭah* 3–4; Winston, *Wisdom*, 232–33). What people perpetrate against others becomes their own undoing (Rev 16:6; 18:4–8). The earth dwellers who are liable for the deaths of the saints come to taste death themselves by drinking water made bitter by wormwood (6:10; 8:11). The plague is severe; yet since two-thirds of the rivers and springs are protected, many earth dwellers will live on. The question is how they will respond to these manifestations of divine judgment.

The fourth trumpet shifts attention from the world below to the heavens above by depicting a partial dimming of the sun, moon, and stars (8:12). What is peculiar is that only a third of the light is lost, whereas at the sixth seal the sun became completely dark, the moon turned red as blood, and the stars fell from the sky (6:12–13). Instead of the threat being increased from one series to the next, the darkness seems less ominous here than it did before or than it will later, when the beast's kingdom is engulfed in darkness (16:10; on the issue, see §18D). Nevertheless, the threat seems clear. Darkness was one of the plagues meted out on the Egyptians, and in prophetic and Greco-Roman writings it portended divine wrath (Note on Rev 8:12). People throughout John's social context would have understood this as a warning.

An Eagle Announces Three Woes (8:13)

An eagle's cry from high overhead marks a transition in this plague sequence. Greeks and Romans often regarded the eagle as a messenger from the gods, so when this eagle issues a heightened warning, the sense is that "those who dwell upon the earth" have every reason to take it seriously (Note on Rev 8:13). As in the previous visions, the warning signs are given in forms that people throughout the ancient world could be expected to understand. The eagle warns that the remaining blasts of the trumpets will bring three "woes," one for each trumpet. The warning raises expectations of the continued outworking of divine wrath.

From a literary perspective, these woes structure the next several chapters (§18C). The first woe corresponds to the fifth trumpet plague, which brings demonic locusts out of the abyss (9:1–12). The second woe includes the visions of surreal armies sweeping across the Euphrates, as well as the visions of prophetic witness, all of which happen after the blowing of the sixth trumpet (9:13–11:14). Finally, the third woe apparently comes through the blowing of the seventh trumpet, which announces the arrival of God's kingdom (Note on 11:14). The festive vision of heavenly worship does not seem to be "woe" at all—and for the redeemed it is not. But the worshipers also declare that the time has come to judge the dead, to reward the saints and prophets, and to destroy the destroyers of the earth (11:15–18). They anticipate that the reign of God must be seen from two perspectives. At present, the forces of evil rage about the earth, bringing woe to many (12:12), but through God's action those powers will be defeated, and God's victory will bring woe to the destroyers of the earth (18:10, 16, 19).

20. Fifth Trumpet: Demonic Locusts (9:1–12)

9 ¹Then the fifth angel blew his trumpet, and I saw a star that had fallen from heaven to earth, and he was given the key to the shaft of the abyss. ²He opened the shaft of the abyss, and smoke went up from the shaft like smoke from a huge furnace, so that the sun and air were darkened by the smoke from the shaft. ³Then locusts came out of the smoke and onto the earth, and they were given power like the power of the scorpions of earth. ⁴They were told not to hurt the grass of the earth or any green plant or any tree, but only those people who do not have the seal of God on their foreheads. ⁵They were not allowed to kill them, but only to inflict pain on them for five months—and the pain they inflict is like that of a scorpion when it strikes a person. ⁶In those days people will seek death, but they will not find it. They will want to die, but death will flee from them.

⁷The locusts looked like horses ready for battle. On their heads were what seemed to be gold laurel wreaths. Their faces were like human faces, ⁸their hair was like women's hair, and their teeth were like those of lions. ⁹In the front they had what seemed to be iron breastplates, and the sound of their wings was like the sound of many chariots with horses racing into battle. ¹⁰They also have tails that sting, just like scorpions, and their power to hurt people for five months is in their tails. ¹¹Their king is the angel of the abyss, whose name in Hebrew is Abaddon, and in Greek he has the name Apollyon.

¹²The first woe has passed. See, two woes are yet to come after these things.

NOTES

9:1. *Then the fifth angel blew his trumpet, and I saw a star that had fallen from heaven to earth.* The star that fell in 8:10 was a heavenly body, but the star in 9:1 is an angel. John identified seven stars with seven angels in 1:20, and Jewish tradition also referred to angels as stars (Judg 5:20; Job 38:7). The disputed question is whether this star is a demonic being, whose fall is really an expulsion from heaven, or whether it is an angel of God, whose fall is simply a descent from heaven. The second interpretation is preferable.

1. Satan or a demonic being. The star is said to have "fallen from heaven to earth," which could connote falling out of favor with God, like the devil and his angels being cast down from heaven to earth (Rev 12:7–9). A similar idea is evident in

Isa 14:12, in which the king of Babylon comes under God's judgment like the morning star that has "fallen from heaven," and in Luke 10:18, in which Jesus' disciples see Satan fall from heaven like lightning. Comparison of heavenly beings or other figures to falling stars usually casts them in a negative light (*1 En.* 86:3; 88:1–3; 90:24–26; *T. Sol.* 20:14–16; *Apoc. El.* 4:11); therefore, many interpreters have identified the fallen star of Rev 9:1 as Satan or a demonic angel, perhaps the angel of the abyss who is called the Destroyer in 9:11 (Primasius; Haimo; Beale; Caird; Prigent; Swete). Although it seems strange for an evil angel to be given the key to the abyss by God or one of God's associates, later visions imply that the beast from the abyss is given divine permission to exercise authority on earth (13:7).

2. Angel of God. Another interpretation holds that the star's fall simply refers to the angel's descent from heaven. When stars fall in 6:13 and 8:10, it does not signify God's judgment against the stars, but against the earth. When an angel descends with the key to the abyss in 20:1, it is clear that the angel is from God. To be sure, the angel in 9:1 opens the abyss to release demonic plagues, and the angel in 20:1 closes the abyss to confine Satan, but in both passages God is behind the action. It seems unlikely that the angel with the key in 9:1 is the same as the demonic angel known as the Destroyer in 9:11 since the first angel opens the abyss from outside, whereas the second angel is king of the locusts that are inside the abyss (Oecumenius; Andreas; Giesen; Murphy; Osborne; Thomas). Some interpreters associate the angel in 9:1 with the angel that was said to have charge of Tartarus, or Hades, in the Greek version of *1 En.* 20:2, but Hades and the abyss are two different parts of the underworld in Revelation (next NOTE). The angel is simply one of many.

and he was given the key. This is the third key or set of keys mentioned in Revelation. The first were the keys of Death and Hades, which belong to Jesus, who has power to release others from death (1:18). The second is the key of David, which Jesus uses to open the way to God's presence (3:7). The third key is entrusted to one of God's angels, empowering him to open the shaft to the abyss, releasing the demonic forces that dwell there. In the end, this key will be used in the opposite way—to confine Satan to the abyss before his final defeat (20:1–3).

to the shaft of the abyss. An *abyssos* is a place without a limit to its depth, a "bottomless pit" (NRSV). Revelation depicts the abyss as a region beneath the earth that is inhabited by demonic beings and ruled by a sinister angel called Abaddon, or Destruction, and Apollyon, or Destroyer (9:11). The terrifying beings that emerge from the abyss include the locustlike creatures that torment people (9:3–10) and the beast that persecutes the saints (11:7; 17:8). Eventually, Satan himself is confined to the abyss for a thousand years before being released and thrown into the lake of fire (20:1–3).

In Revelation the abyss is the demonic realm. First, it must be differentiated from the area "under the earth," which is home to creatures from the natural world. These creatures praise the lordship of the Creator along with others in heaven, on earth, and in the sea (5:13). Second, the abyss is different from Hades, where the dead are kept until the last judgment (NOTES on 1:18; 20:13). Although some writers referred to the abyss as the realm of the dead, Revelation does not do so (Rom 10:7; *Jos. As.* 15:12; Diogenes Laertius, *Lives* 4.27). Third, both the abyss and Hades are different from the lake of fire, which is the place of eternal punishment. The beast may come up from the abyss (Rev 11:7; 17:8), and Satan may be confined there (20:1–3), but in the end both are thrown into the lake of fire (19:20; 20:10), as are Death and Hades themselves (20:14–15). Some writers use the word "abyss" for the realm of fiery torment (Matt 13:42, 50) or combine the abyss, Hades, and the lake of fire into a composite portrait of hell, but each region remains distinct in Revelation (Charles; Giesen).

Revelation's depiction of the abyss has affinities with those in some Jewish writings. According to *1 En.* 20:7, Enoch was taken to a place where he was shown "terrible things—a great fire burning and flaming there. And the place had a narrow cleft (extending) to the abyss, full of great pillars of fire, borne downward" (Nickelsburg, *1 Enoch*, 297). The fiery cleft resembles the shaft in Rev 9:1–2. The difference is that Enoch sees an abyss in which fallen angels are imprisoned forever, whereas Revelation pictures an abyss from which demonic beings can be released. In this respect Revelation resembles *Jubilees*, which says that nine-tenths of the demons are confined to the abyss until the day of judgment and the other one-tenth are allowed to roam the earth, testing people along with the devil (*Jub.* Greek frg. 10:1–9; cf. Luke 8:31). In Rev 9 the demonic beings are released to afflict the ungodly.

In the Greco-Roman world some traditions identified local caves and crevasses as openings to the underworld. Such caves emitted noxious vapors that suffocated any living thing that entered or any bird that flew overhead, and at the caves' mouths people built sacred precincts to the god of the underworld (Strabo, *Geographica* 5.4.5; 14.1.11). One of these was located at Hierapolis, near Laodicea (Strabo, *Geographica*, 13.4.14). Tales were also told about a hero, such as Aeneas, venturing into such a cave and returning to relate what he saw below (Virgil, *Aen.* 6.235–64). But John writes as a visionary, who sees heaven, earth, and the underworld from a cosmic vantage point (cf. *1 En.* 19:3; 21:1–10). Rather than entering the abyss, he sees demonic creatures emerge.

9:2. *He opened the shaft of the abyss, and smoke went up from the shaft like the smoke from a huge furnace.* The term *abyssos* often referred to the depths of the sea and the deeps from which waters flowed (Gen 7:11; Ps 78:15), but in Revelation and parts of *1 Enoch* the abyss is filled with fire and smoke. John compares the smoke to that of a furnace, which readers might have pictured as a furnace used for smelting ore (Strabo, *Geographica* 9.1.23; 13.1.56) or perhaps as a kiln for firing pots (Sir 27:5). Roman-era furnaces were made of masonry. Some were tapered cylinders six to eight feet high. Charcoal was burned in a chamber at the bottom, and smoke billowed out the top (*OCD* 965–66; *NP* 8:782; cf. Diodorus Siculus, *Libr.* 5.13.1; Ezek 22:20–22). Ancient writers likened large quantities of smoke to that produced by furnaces (Gen 19:28; Exod 19:18; Sir 22:24). When the smoke rose from a shaft below the earth, it portended disaster (Philostratus, *Vit. Apoll.* 8.7.27).

so that the sun and air were darkened by the smoke from the shaft. An abyss could be filled with darkness (Gen 1:2; *Jub.* 2:2; Diogenes Laertius, *Lives* 4.27), but here it conveys darkness by emitting smoke to enshroud the sun (Rev 6:12; 8:12; cf. Joel 2:20–31). In heaven, the smoke of incense accompanies prayer (Rev 8:4) and the smoke of divine glory fills the celestial temple (15:8), but the smoke from the abyss comes from the realm of the Destroyer (9:11). It is sinister, like the smoke from the mouths of the demonic cavalry, which destroys life (9:17–18); the smoke rising from Babylon's destruction (18:9, 18; 19:3); and the smoke of endless torment (14:11).

9:3. *Then locusts came out of the smoke and onto the earth, and they were given power like the power of the scorpions of earth.* Natural locusts periodically migrate in swarms, consuming all the vegetation in their path. When locusts swarm, the "sun and the moon are darkened, and the stars withdraw their shining" (Joel 2:10; cf. Exod 10:15; Pliny the Elder, *Nat.* 11.35.104). Natural locusts could be compared to scorpions because both had wings and brought plagues (Nicander, *Theriaca* 801–2; Pausanias, *Descr.* 9.21.6), but the locusts from the abyss resemble scorpions because of their stinging tails—something natural locusts do not have.

9:4. *They were told not to hurt the grass of the earth or any green plant or any tree.* This command, which comes from God or the heavenly court, prevents these demonic beings from the ordinary action of locusts, which is to devour vegetation. Before the exodus a plague of natural locusts "ate all the plants in the land," so "nothing green was left, no tree, no plant in the field" (Exod 10:15). Grain fields, orchards, and grazing lands were devastated (Joel 1:4–7; Amos 4:9). With rare exceptions (Wis 16:9), it was understood that locusts did not injure people. In Revelation the natural pattern is reversed, so instead of harming plants and leaving people alone, the locusts torment people and do not damage plant life.

In this vision cycle all the grass was burned up in 8:7, but here it seems unharmed. Interpreters who assume that Revelation provides a sequential outline of coming events must posit a time lapse between plagues, so the grass can recover between 8:7 and 9:4 (Thomas), but it is better to take the incongruity as a form of communication (Boring; Giesen; Murphy). The visions disclose the nature of divine wrath while undermining attempts to outline a clear sequence of coming events.

but only those people who do not have the seal of God on their foreheads. The seal consists of the name of God and the Lamb (Rev 14:1). It identifies those who belong to God and protects them from divine wrath (NOTE on 7:3). The imagery recalls Ezek 9:3–6, in which a man is sent to "put a mark on the foreheads" of those who deplore the sins of Jerusalem. Afterward, others are told to cut down all the people but to "touch no one who has the mark." Revelation's vision is similar in that those who bear God's seal are protected from a plague meted out on sinners. Some interpreters also detect an echo of the plagues that preceded the exodus, which afflicted the Egyptians but not the Hebrews (Exod 8:22; 9:4, 26; 10:23; 11:7; Beale; Giesen; Mounce). In Revelation the seal does protect people from demonic locusts, but it does not exempt them from all forms of affliction, since later visions indicate that the faithful suffer at the hands of evil powers (Rev 13:7; 17:6).

9:5. *They were not allowed to kill them, but only to inflict pain on them for five months.* Scorpions were regarded as "a horrible plague, poisonous like snakes, except that they inflict a worse torture by dispatching the victim with a lingering death" (Pliny the Elder, *Nat.* 11.29.86). Ordinarily, a scorpion's sting was fatal only in some cases, but many people assumed that scorpions could kill (Diodorus Siculus, *Libr.* 3.30.2; Aelian, *Nat. an.* 5.14; 6.20; 10.23). John's vision implies that there is a divinely set limit to the lethal power of the scorpion-like locusts.

The meaning of torment for "five months" is disputed. Some interpreters suggest that this was the lifespan of a locust (Beale; Charles; Harrington), but it is more likely that "five" is simply a round number indicating a period of time. Five can mean "a few" (e.g., five words, 1 Cor 14:19; five sparrows, Luke 12:6; A Weiser, *EDNT* 3:70). From this perspective the time of torment is limited; the locusts may afflict people for five months but not more (Aune). Yet for those who suffer, five months is a very long time (Giesen).

and the pain they inflict is like that of a scorpion when it strikes a person. Pain (*basanismos*) could be intense, like the feeling of being burned (Rev 14:10–11; 18:9–10). In antiquity is was said that one type of scorpion brings "a swift and burning fever in men's mouths," while another "inflicts shivering fits, and after them a horrid eruption appears" (Nicander, *Theriaca* 770–79). When someone "is bitten by a scorpion, the place immediately begins to burn and become hard, red, and swollen with pain." The person sweats and shivers and senses "a pain like that of being stabbed with a sharp needle" (Ps.-Dioscorides, *De iis* 6; cf. Seneca the Younger, *Herc. Ot.* 1218–24; *NW* 2:1522).

9:6. *In those days people will seek death, but they will not find it. They will want to die, but death will flee from them.* This saying contrasts desire and lack of fulfillment in parallel lines. The first line uses language of seeking and finding to depict death as something whose location is hidden. The second line intensifies the imagery with death actively fleeing from the afflicted person: "It is from the wretched that death first flees" (Seneca the Younger, *Tro.* 954). It was common to say that some forms of torment make death preferable to life: "Why is light given to one in misery, and life to the bitter in soul, who long for death, but it does not come, and dig for it more than for hidden treasures, who rejoice exceedingly and are glad when they find the grave?" (Job 3:20–22; cf. Jer 8:3; cf. *Sib. Or.* 2:307–8). The idea is that death "is a release from suffering, a boundary beyond which our ills cannot pass" (Seneca the Younger, *Marc.* 19.5; cf. Plato, *Apol.* 41D). Therefore, the prospect of lingering in pain could be turned into a curse: "May neither your body nor your sick mind be free from querulous pain" and "may you have cause enough for death, but no means of dying" (Ovid, *Ib.* 115–24; cf. Dio Cassius, *Rom. Hist.* 69.17.2–3; Diodorus Siculus, *Libr.* 3.13).

9:7. *The locusts looked like horses ready for battle.* Comparison of the locusts to horses emphasizes their military aspect (Isa 31:1; Hag 2:22; Polybius, *Histories* 5.53.9–10). In Joel 2:4–5, which informs John's imagery, the locusts "have the appearance of horses, and like war-horses they charge"; they are like "a powerful army drawn up for battle." The comparison also suggests that the force is vast in size and ready to devour everything in its path (Judg 6:5; 7:12; Jer 46:23; 51:27; Jdt 2:20).

On their heads were what seemed to be gold laurel wreaths. Gold wreaths were symbols of public honor, athletic triumph, and military victory (NOTE on Rev 2:10). Here, the military aspect is dominant, as in the case of the first horseman (6:2).

Their faces were like human faces. Ancient mythical figures often had both human and nonhuman traits (Giesen; Roloff). The Babylonians depicted a creature with a human head and scorpion's body, and in the Greco-Roman period the constellations Scorpio the scorpion and Sagittarius the archer were fused into images that had human, animal, and scorpion-like traits (Ford; Malina, *On*, 144–47). Some interpreters suggest that the human faces show that these demonic locusts are rational beings (Mounce; Prigent; Swete) or that they manifest human sin (Caird; Harrington). It is more helpful, however, to consider how this combination of human and nonhuman fits Revelation's sense of symmetry in divine justice. The visions shows that those who embrace the gods of the mythic tradition are tormented by creatures like those from that tradition.

9:8. *their hair was like women's hair.* The faces of the locusts are compared to those of *anthrōpoi*, which in one sense means "human beings," though it also suggests "men." If readers picture the faces as masculine, the mention of women's hair heightens the strangeness of their appearance. They are a bizarre combination of human and nonhuman, masculine and feminine. Women in the Greco-Roman world, including Jewish women, kept their hair long, whereas men's hair was usually shorter (1 Cor 11:14–15; John 12:3; Plutarch, *Mor.* 267B). There were exceptions; some philosophers, priests, stage performers, and farmers had long hair, as did some barbarians and others (Dio Chrysostom, *Disc.* 35.10–12; Artemidorus, *Onirocritica* 1.18; Judg 16:13; 2 Sam 14:25–26; Herodotus, *Historiae* 1.82). But John's description presupposes that women's hair and a masculine face did not go together (Lucian, *Fug.* 27; Ps.-Phoc. 211–12). Some apocalyptic texts picture demonic beings with loose or disheveled women's hair, which gave them a threatening appearance (*Apoc. Zeph.* 4:4; 6:8; *T. Sol.* 13:1; Aune; Giesen).

and their teeth were like those of lions. A lion's teeth were as sharp as spears and capable of tearing apart prey (Ps 57:4; Sir 21:2). The imagery recalls Joel 1:6, which compares locusts to an invading army and says "its teeth are lions' teeth, and it has the fangs of a lioness." In Revelation, however, the locusts inflict pain through their tails rather than with their teeth.

9:9. *In the front they had what seemed to be iron breastplates.* The Greek term translated as "front" is *thorax*, which can be used for the chest of a locust and breastplate worn by a soldier. A soldier's breastplate had a metallic sheen that could be compared to that of a locust (*Tg. Nah* 3:17; Gordon, "Loricate"). Roman breastplates were often made of iron scales or plates fastened onto leather, creating a layered or segmented armor that resembled the thorax of a locust. Like soldiers, horses could also be outfitted with armor. In some cavalry units, troops were "blazing in helmets and breastplates" of shiny iron and had "horses clad in plates of bronze and iron" (Plutarch, *Crass.* 24.1; cf. Polybius, *Histories* 30.25.9; Propertius, *Elegies* 3.12.10–14; Ps.-Caesar, *Spanish War* 26). Since the demonic locusts look like horses ready for battle, the mention of breastplates sustains the imagery.

and the sound of their wings was like the sound of many chariots with horses racing into battle. The sound is not that of individual locusts, which made a strumming or grating noise with their wings (Aelian, *Nat. an.* 6.19; Pliny the Elder, *Nat.* 11.35.106). Instead, John compares the sound of the whole horde of locusts to the rumbling of chariot wheels and horses' hooves. Similar imagery is used in Joel's description of a locust plague: "As with the rumbling of chariots they leap on the tops of mountains" and "the earth quakes before them" (Joel 2:5, 10). The imagery had military connotations (Jer 8:16; 2 Kgs 7:6; Caesar, *Bell. gall.* 4.33).

9:10. *They also have tails that sting, just like scorpions, and their power to hurt people for five months is in their tails.* Scorpions have eight legs and a tail that curves up and forward with a stinging tip that injects venom into its victims. It was said that the "tail is always engaged in striking," and "it strikes both a sideways stroke and one with the tail bent up" (Pliny the Elder, *Nat.* 11.30.87; see the NOTE on Rev 9:5).

9:11. *Their king is the angel of the abyss.* There are two main interpretations of this angel's identity. The first is most viable:

1. Satan. The DSS refer to Belial—another name for Satan—as "the angel of the pit, the spirit of destruction [*'ăbaddôn*]," who exercises a wicked form of dominion (4Q286 7 II, 7). Belial is "the angel of enmity" who was made for the pit, so darkness is his dominion (1QM XIII, 11–12; cf. 11Q11 II, 1–5). He seems to be the evil angel known as Melchiresha', or king of wickedness, whose work is described as darkness (4Q544 2 1–4; Kobelski, *Melchizedek*, 75–83). In Jewish and Christian writings the devil is the prince of demons (Matt 9:34; 12:24; Mark 3:22; Luke 11:15; *T. Sol.* 2:9) and angel of Sheol (*Mart. Asc. Isa.* 10:9; 11:19). Although Satan is not called an angel in Revelation, he does wear royal diadems, and the beast from the abyss is under his dominion, which suggests Satan's kingship over the abyss itself (Rev 11:7; 13:1–2; 17:8). The COMMENT below explores the literary motif (cf. Andreas; Haimo; Aune; Blount; Prigent).

2. Agent of Satan. Since Satan is not called an angel but has angels under him (12:7), some interpreters propose that the angel of the abyss is one of his subordinates. Just as Satan brings the kings of the earth under demonic influence (16:14; 17:2, 18:3), he might exercise his influence through the angel who is king of the abyss (9:11; Giesen; Mounce; Osborne). Some sources said that earthly locusts have no king (Prov 30:27), but the LXX of Amos 7:1 envisions a horde of locusts being led by "king Gog"—and Gog is the name of one of Satan's allies in Rev 20:8 (Bøe, *Gog*, 61–71, 276). Nevertheless, the strong precedents identifying Satan as the leader of demons, together with literary developments in Revelation (see the COMMENT), make it more probable that the king of the abyss is Satan himself.

whose name in Hebrew is Abaddon. The Hebrew word *'ăbaddôn* means destruction. Revelation's usage is unusual since the name Abaddon was ordinarily used for a place rather than a demonic being. The term was used for Sheol, or the realm of the dead (Prov 15:11; Ps 88:11; Job 26:6; 1QH³ XI, 19), a region of fire and darkness (4Q491 8–10 I, 15), an accursed abyss suitable for Belial (1QH³ XI, 32; 11Q11 IV, 10). Death and Abaddon were occasionally personified (cf. Job 28:22; Rev 6:8), but Revelation transfers the name from a region of the underworld to its demonic overlord. On John's use of Hebrew, see INTRO IV.D.1 and V.B.2.

and in Greek he has the name Apollyon. The Greek name Apollyon, or Destroyer, is based on the verb *apollynai* (to destroy) and is related to *apōleia*, the Greek translation of *'ăbaddôn* in the LXX. Some interpreters suggest that the designation recalls Apollo, whose name was said to connote destructive power (Aeschylus, *Ag.* 1080–82; cf. A. Oepke, *TDNT* 1:397). Since some Roman emperors styled themselves as bearers of Apollo's power, linking Apollyon to Apollo allows the passage to be read as a critique of Roman authority (Aune; Ford; Mounce; Osborne; Sweet). Given the absence of any other allusions to imperial claims in this context, however, it is best to take Apollyon simply as a translation of Abaddon (Charles; Giesen; Prigent).

9:12. *The first woe has passed. See, two woes are yet to come after these things.* The three woes were announced in 8:13, and the locust plague of 9:1–11 constitutes the first. The words "after these things" usually begin sentences (7:9; 15:5; 18:1; 19:1; 20:3); therefore, some manuscripts conclude 9:12 with "come" and join "after these things" to the next sentence (1006 1854 2329), occasionally omitting the initial *kai* (and) to improve the sentence flow ($\mathfrak{P}^{47}$ ℵ 2344). Nevertheless, the expression "after these things" can conclude sentences (1:19; 4:1), and there is good manuscript support for including the words at the end of 9:12 (A P 1 172 2015). Accordingly, the next vision begins with "then the sixth angel blew his trumpet" (9:13), which fits the previous pattern (8:7, 8, 10; 9:1). See *TCGNT*[2] 669–70.

COMMENT

The first four trumpets culminated with the eagle's warning, "Woe, woe, woe to those who live on the earth because of the remaining blasts of the trumpet, which the three angels are about to blow" (8:13). Readers in the Greco-Roman world would have recognized that the disasters brought by the previous trumpets communicated divine wrath. Trumpets in heaven, blazing light in the sky, drops of blood coming down like rain, stars falling from their places, waves of blood in the sea, the sun and moon growing dim, and birds uttering strange cries—such phenomena were among the warnings that war was imminent (Lucan, *Pharsalia* 1.524–60; Petronius, *Satyricon* 126–43; Ovid, *Metam.* 15.779–800). The demonic locusts that now appear at the fifth trumpet seem like horses ready for battle, with armor-plated bodies and wings that sound like rumbling chariots (Rev 9:7–9). The sixth trumpet unleashes a cavalry force that rides ghastly horses whose heads are like those of lions and whose tails are like snakes (9:16–19).

The victims in this war are the ungodly, who worship demons and idols (9:4, 20). For many readers it would seem fitting for them to suffer, since the trumpet cycle began with an angel offering prayers at the heavenly altar where the martyrs had cried out for God to bring justice against the people of earth who had shed their blood (6:10; 8:3–5). When the angel takes fire from the altar and hurls it down onto the earth, readers see what it would mean to turn the saints' prayers into wrath. There is symmetry in the way that wrath is unleashed. Blood rains down from the sky and surges up in the sea against a world that shed the blood of the saints (8:7–8).

This symmetry continues in the fifth and sixth trumpet visions. The prayers of the saints rose to God with the smoke of incense, and the fifth plague begins when the abyss is opened, bringing smoke and suffering to the rest of humanity (8:3–5; 9:1–2). Revelation depicts a world where people either wittingly or unwittingly worship demons (9:20–21), and the fifth and sixth trumpet plagues show demonic powers being turned loose on their own devotees. For John's readers the main forms of false worship were associated with Greco-Roman traditions, so the demonic forces attacking the idolaters resemble mythic creatures from those traditions.

Yet the next section will show that despite the terrible displays of wrath, people do not repent (9:20–21). The martyrs may have asked God to bring justice against those who shed their blood, but these visions show that if justice is reduced to wrath, then nothing changes. If change is to come, God must use other means—and visions to come will show that God's designs entail the prophetic witness of God's people (10:1–11:14).

On Rev 9:1–12, see Gordon, "Loricate"; Pippin, "Peering"; Ryan, *Hearing*.

Opening the Abyss (9:1–6)

The fifth angel blows his trumpet, and John sees a star that has fallen from heaven (9:1). The star is an angel, who is given a key that can open the shaft of the demonic abyss that lies beneath the earth (NOTE on 9:1). The abyss is the demonic realm. The shaft leading down to its dark and smoky depths is the counterpart to the door in heaven, which leads to the brightness of God's presence (Rev 4:1; 9:2). The hosts of heaven declare that God is the Creator, but the hordes in the abyss serve the angel known as the Destroyer (9:1, 11). During the trumpet plagues the differences between the Creator and the Destroyer may seem unclear, since the disasters depicted in 8:6–12 are instigated by heavenly powers. But the interruption of judgment after the sixth plague will clarify the nature of the conflict: God's design is not to destroy the earth, but to destroy *the destroyers* of the earth (11:18).

When the abyss is opened at the fifth trumpet, smoke and swarms of locusts emerge (9:3). In antiquity, even ordinary locust plagues could be taken as signs of divine wrath. Before the exodus a plague of locusts struck those who had enslaved Israel in Egypt (Exod 10:10–14; Pss 78:46; 105:34; Wis 16:9), and later, such plagues were signs that Israel should repent and turn to God (2 Chr 7:13–14; Amos 4:9; Joel 1–2; cf. *Sib. Or.* 5:454). Some people in the Greco-Roman tradition also responded to locust plagues by trying to make amends with the gods (Pliny the Elder, *Nat.* 11.35.104; Livy, *Rom. Hist.* 42.2.5). John intensifies the threat by picturing demonic locusts with scorpion-like tails that are agents of divine punishment (Rev 9:3; cf. Sir 39:30).

Many traits of these demonic beings invert natural patterns. Ordinary locusts could be stunned by clouds of smoke (Diodorus Siculus, *Libr.* 3.29.3; Strabo, *Geographica* 16.4.12), but the demonic locusts thrive on the smoke wafting up from the abyss (Rev 9:3). Natural locusts brought destruction by devouring with their teeth (Joel 1:4–7), but the demonic ones inflict pain with their tails (Rev 9:5, 10). An ordinary swarm of locusts attacked plant life and left people alone, but here the demonic locusts are prevented from harming grass, plants, and trees and attack only human beings (9:4).

The scorpion-like locusts torment those who do not bear the seal of God on their foreheads (9:4). The seal identifies the people who are servants of God and consists of the names of God and the Lamb (7:3; 14:1). John heard that the sealed numbered 144,000 from the twelve tribes of Israel, but he saw them as a countless multitude from every nation who are cleansed by the Lamb and follow him (7:4–17; 14:1–5). By way of contrast, those who do not bear the seal serve other powers, including demons and idols (9:20). In later visions they serve the beast and bear its mark on their foreheads or hands (13:16–18; 14:9, 11; 16:2; 19:20).

Like other ancient writers, John assumes that those who worship idols actually serve demons (NOTE on Rev 9:20). His vision also reflects the principle that "one is punished by the very things by which one sins" (Wis 11:16). Accordingly, the fifth trumpet vision shows the unsealed, who worship demonic powers, being tormented by those powers. At the same time, God does not allow demonic powers free reign. They can inflict pain on people but are not permitted to kill them, and they can operate only for a specified time: five months (9:5). Such divine restraint allows the ungodly to live on, and as long as they do, the possibility remains of their responding in a different way to God.

Yet the plague does not evoke a positive response. Instead, it again inverts a typical pattern. People ordinarily seek to escape from death and hold on to life, but the plague makes them do the opposite: They "will seek death, but they will not find it. They will want to die, but death will flee from them" (9:6). Instead of moving people to seek the God who lives and gives life (4:9–11; 11:11; 22:1), it elicits a desire for death, and death is a power that God must overcome (20:14; 21:4).

Armies of the Destroyer (9:7–12)

John says that the swarm of demonic locusts resembles a vast company of horses ready for battle. The comparison was conventional (Note on 9:7), but the impression is terrifying. In an ordinary battle, civilians and foot soldiers were intimidated when facing troops with horses (Jer 4:1:13; Hab 1:8; Plutarch, *Sull.* 16.2). The appearance of these warriors from the abyss gives even greater cause for alarm. They wear gold laurel wreaths on their heads as a sign of their coming victory. Usually, such wreaths were awarded only after a battle had been won (Aulus Gellius, *Noct. att.* 5.6.1–7, 19), but these locusts wear the gold wreaths already, making their triumph seem inevitable.

The description of the locusts contrasts the agents of the Creator with those of the Destroyer. The Creator was attended by four heavenly creatures, each with its own distinct appearance: one like a lion, another like an ox, another with a human face, and one like an eagle. Each represented a part of the created order (4:7). In contrast, the Destroyer is served by hordes that combine the traits of humans, animals, and insects into a hideous collage: lions' teeth protrude from human faces, while their chests are plated with iron and they have tails like scorpions (9:7–10). The sense of created order is gone, replaced by a repulsive confusion of elements. The sounds made by each group are also different. The harmonious praises offered to the Creator were echoed by every creature in heaven, on earth, under the earth, and in the sea (4:6–11; 5:13), but the demonic locusts pound and roar like chariots going into battle (9:9). Whereas the elders in the heavenly throne room cast their gold wreaths before God in praise, the demonic locusts continue wearing theirs as they set out to attack their victims (9:7).

John's readers would have assumed that idolaters were devotees of Greco-Roman traditions, and in this vision such worshipers are threatened by the kind of hybrid monsters that those traditions included. The creatures from the abyss resemble the legendary manticore, which was said to have a human face with three rows of sharp teeth, a lion's body, and a scorpion's tail, which it used to inflict a fatal sting (Aristotle, *Hist. an.* 2.1 501a; Aelian, *Nat. an.* 4.21; Pliny the Elder, *Nat.* 8.30.75–76). The manticore would kill human beings, but the demonic beings John sees are divinely kept from doing so; their role is to inflict pain (Rev 9:10).

The king of these locusts is the angel of the abyss. If God is the Creator (4:11; 10:6; 14:7), his opposite is called Destruction and Destroyer, names that probably refer to Satan (Note on 9:11). As king of the demonic abyss, Satan wears diadems in his attempt to extend his royal authority over the earth (9:11; 12:3). Later he will be assisted by the beast from the abyss, which derives its own royal power from Satan (11:7; 13:1–2; 17:8), along with the false prophet (13:11–18) and Babylon, who rules like a queen (17:18:18:7). The second half of the Apocalypse will show what it means for God to defeat these adversaries and "destroy the destroyers of the earth" (11:18).

The fifth trumpet vision ends with the solemn announcement that the first woe has passed and two more are yet to come (9:12). Readers know that there are three woes, which correspond to the last three trumpets in this series. By enumerating the woes in addition to the trumpets, John heightens the impression that everything is unfolding according to plan. The next trumpet will continue the pattern by taking the horror of divine wrath a step further, only to interrupt the pattern by delaying the announcement of the completion of the second woe until John has been commissioned to bear witness again.

21. Sixth Trumpet: Demonic Cavalry (9:13–21)

9 ¹³Then the sixth angel blew his trumpet, and I heard a voice from the four horns of the gold altar that is before God. ¹⁴He said to the sixth angel who had the trumpet, "Release the four angels that are bound at the great river Euphrates." ¹⁵Then the four angels who had been made ready for that hour and day and month and year were released to kill a third of humankind. ¹⁶The number of cavalry troops was twice ten thousand times ten thousand. I heard their number. ¹⁷And this is the way I saw the horses and their riders in the vision: They had breastplates that were fiery red, dark blue, and yellow as sulfur. The horses' heads were like the heads of lions, and out of their mouths came fire and smoke and sulfur. ¹⁸By these three plagues a third of humankind was killed: by the fire and smoke and sulfur coming out of their mouths. ¹⁹For the power of the horses is in their mouths and in their tails, for their tails are like snakes with heads that inflict injuries.

²⁰The rest of humankind, who were not killed by these plagues, did not repent of the works of their hands. They did not stop worshiping demons and idols of gold and silver and bronze and stone and wood, which cannot see or hear or walk. ²¹They did not repent of their murders or their sorceries or their immorality or their thefts.

NOTES

9:13. *Then the sixth angel blew his trumpet, and I heard a voice from the four horns of the gold altar that is before God.* Altars in Jewish tradition had four horns, one protruding from each of its upper corners, and such altars were also known among Greeks (Exod 27:2; 30:2; Josephus, *J.W.* 5.225; Friesen, *Imperial*, 154). In the OT the gold altar that stood in Israel's tabernacle and temple was used for incense, and a second altar in the outer courtyard was used for sacrifice, but Revelation pictures a single heavenly altar for both prayer and sacrifice (NOTE on 6:9). John hears a voice from the altar, and some interpreters think the altar itself speaks (cf. 16:7; Lupieri; Resseguie). Some manuscripts do read that John heard the altar "saying" (*legontos*; 1006 1841 1854 2329), but it is more likely that the voice belongs to an angel who serves at the altar (8:3; 14:13). Since the voice is singular, it probably does not belong to the martyrs or saints (Harrington;

Mounce; Murphy), but it does remind readers that the altar is where the martyrs' pleas for justice rose before God (6:10; 8:3–4; Beale; Giesen).

Some manuscripts state that the heavenly altar has four horns (025 046 1006; cf. ESV, NAB, NRSV), but many others omit the number four ($\mathfrak{P}^{47}$ $\aleph^1$ A 027; cf. NET, NIV). If original, the number could have been accidentally omitted, perhaps through an error of the eye, since the Greek words for "four" and "horns" both end in -ōn (*TCGNT*², 670). It may be more likely, however, that the repeated mention of four angels in 9:14–15 prompted a scribe to add that the altar also had four horns (Charles; Aune; Osborne).

9:14. *He said to the sixth angel who had the trumpet, "Release the four angels that are bound at the great river Euphrates."* The angels set loose here do not appear elsewhere in Revelation. The four angels in 7:1 stood at the four corners of the earth and held back destructive winds, while here the four angels are at the Euphrates and are themselves held back from destroying. The angels are bound, as Satan later will be (20:2; cf. Mark 3:27), suggesting that they are demonic beings like those released from the abyss in the previous vision (Giesen; Osborne). Some evil angels were said to be confined in a dark netherworld until the judgment (Jude 6; 2 Pet 2:4), but those in Revelation are bound on earth and released to wreak destruction.

Both the sixth trumpet and sixth bowl visions are set at the Euphrates River, but they have quite different meanings (9:13–19; 16:12–16). Where the trumpet sends demonic forces to attack the ungodly, the bowl parts the Euphrates so that Satan and his agents can gather kings for an attack against God. At the sixth trumpet, the armies destroy one-third of humanity, but the sixth bowl anticipates a battle in which Satan's forces will meet their own destruction (19:11–21). The sixth trumpet vision shows that wrath alone does not bring repentance (9:20–21), while the sixth bowl warns that the destroyers of the earth will be overthrown.

9:15. *Then the four angels who had been made ready for that hour and day and month and year.* Emphasizing the exact time of the angels' release indicates that God's purposes are being carried out and events are not out of control (*1 En.* 92:2).

were released to kill a third of humankind. Previously, opening the fourth seal brought death to a fourth of humankind (6:8). In this cycle, plagues have affected a third of the created world (8:7–12), and that is now true of death. John shows little interest in whether the death toll increases from one-fourth to one-third of humanity, or whether one should think of one-fourth being killed and then another third being added to their number. The mention of a third shows that the devastation is extensive, since it affects a third of humanity, yet also limited, since it does not go beyond one-third.

9:16. *The number of cavalry troops was twice ten thousand times ten thousand. I heard their number.* John describes a cavalry force that is incalculably large. The best reading for their number is *dismyriades myriadōn* (A 2344 2351), an unusual expression that was modified for clarity in some manuscripts. The first word probably means "twice ten thousand," for a total of twenty thousand. Less likely is the possibility that the plural form of the first word means "twenty thousands," or multiple groups of twenty thousand (BDAG 252). Rather, the initial word seems to mean twenty thousand, which in turn is multiplied by ten thousand to yield a sense that the group is incomprehensibly large. The immensity is also clear if one assumes that the prefix *dis-* on *dismyriades* reflects the Hebrew dual form, which does not mean "twice" but "times." This would mean that John speaks of "ten thousand times ten thousand" (*dismyriades*) multiplied again by "ten thousands" (*myriadōn*; Mussies, *Morphology*, 222–25). Although the total is two hundred million, the point is not that John knew an exact number. Rather, the number is so vast that it pushes beyond the limits of human calculation, just as referring to "ten thousand times ten thousand" heavenly beings means their numbers are countless (5:11; Dan 7:10; *1 En.* 40:1; cf. *Jos. As.* 16:17; Beale; Giesen).

9:17. *And this is the way I saw the horses and their riders in the vision.* John regularly says "I saw" (e.g., 6:1; 7:1; 8:2), and here he reminds readers that what he sees occurs in a vision (cf. Dan 7:2; 8:1). Ancient and medieval interpreters distinguished physical from spiritual sight and rightly recognized that John's seeing was of a spiritual sort (Camille, "Visionary," 276).

They had breastplates that were fiery red, dark blue, and yellow as sulfur. The breastplates are worn by the riders, who are the focus of Rev 9:17b. Soldiers in antiquity wore breastplates made of layered metal plates (NOTE on 9:9), and the sheen of ordinary armor "presented a flaming and fearful sight" that conveyed invincibility (Plutarch, *Sull.* 16.2–3). The breastplates of the demonic riders give a similar impression of power. Armor protected the wearer from harm, but comparing it to fire anticipates that those wearing it can also inflict harm. The surreal armor is fiery (Sir 48:6; cf. *1 En.* 14:11), which heightens its threatening appearance and suggests that it is red, like the horseman who brings bloodshed upon the earth and the dragon that persecutes the saints (Rev 6:4; 12:3), and like sulfur. The bluish tone suggests the color of a flame or smoke. Comparing something to sulfur probably means that it is greenish yellow and capable of emitting a foul smell (Pliny the Elder, *Nat.* 35.50.174; 37.21.81; Strabo, *Geographica* 1.3.18; Diodorus Siculus, *Libr.* 2.12.2).

The horses' heads were like the heads of lions, and out of their mouths came fire and smoke and sulfur. The horses in John's vision resemble mythical beings from Greco-Roman tradition such as the "raging Chimera." It was "in front a lion, in back a serpent, and in the middle a goat, breathing out the force of blazing fire" (Homer, *Il.* 6.181–82). In artistic representations the lion-shaped head and the tail with the head of a snake are often the main parts of the body, while a goat's head sits on the back where the rider would be (*LIMC* 3/2.197–217). Descriptions sometimes mentioned only the lion's head and snakelike tail—the main elements in Revelation (Ovid, *Trist.* 4.7.13; Seneca the Younger, *Ep.* 113.9). The mythic creature was known for spitting fire from its mouth (Hesiod, *Theogonia* 319–24; Apollodorus, *Library* 2.31; Euripides, *Ion* 203–4; Lucretius, *De rer.* 5.905–7; Horace, *Carm.* 2.17.13; Aune; Keener).

Other mythical fire-breathing creatures included the bull conquered by Jason (Pindar, *Pyth.* 4.225) and the horses defeated by Herakles (Euripides, *Alc.* 493), but these traditions have few affinities with Rev 9 (Aune). Some interpreters note that Leviathan could breathe fire (Job 41:12–21; Beale; Mounce; Murphy; Smalley), but Leviathan was a sea monster and John is describing demonic cavalry. The point is that these hybrid beings are hideous (Dio Chrysostom, *Disc.* 32.28), in contrast to those representing the created order in Rev 4–5.

9:18. *By these three plagues a third of humankind was killed: by the fire and smoke and sulfur coming out of their mouths.* Fire kills by burning, and smoke and sulfur suffocate people. Sulfur is known for its foul odor, which was associated with fire and lightning

(Homer, *Il.* 14.415; Homer, *Od.* 12.417). Sulfurous fumes, like those wafting up from cracks in the earth, killed people by impairing their breathing (Diodorus Siculus, *Libr.* 2.12.2; Pliny the Elder, *Nat.* 31.28.49). In the stories of Sodom and Gomorrah, fire and sulfur from heaven destroyed the cities (Gen 19:24; Deut 29:23; Luke 17:29). God's judgment was pictured as a storm of fire and sulfur (Ps 11:6; Isa 30:33; Ezek 38:22), and in Revelation the wicked are tormented in a lake of fire that burns with sulfur (Rev 14:10; 19:20; 20:10; 21:8).

9:19. *For the power of the horses is in their mouths and in their tails, for their tails are like snakes with heads that inflict injuries.* The power in the horses' mouths comes from the fire that burns and the smoke and sulfur that asphyxiate (9:18). Like the tails of the locusts in the previous vision, which inflicted torment like a scorpion's sting, the tails of the demonic cavalry threaten to harm like snakes. It was said that when one type of snake bites, "a swelling of dark unhealthy hue rises, and a sore pain freezes the heart." With the bite of other snakes "all the skin upon the flesh, dry, loathsome, and bloated with putrid sores, breaks out from below," while fiery pangs overcome the victim (Nicander, *Theriaca* 298–304, 334–39, 359–65, 403–4).

9:20. *The rest of humankind, who were not killed by these plagues, did not repent.* Some interpreters argue that the plagues were not intended to bring repentance but to punish the ungodly and reveal the depth of their unbelief. They note that in the plague visions the ungodly persistently refuse to repent (9:20–21; 16:9, 11). They also compare the plagues to those of the exodus narrative, in which they argue the plagues were not designed to make Pharaoh repent but to demonstrate God's power by hardening Pharaoh's heart (Aune; Beale). More plausible is that Revelation's plagues are designed to bring repentance. The trumpet visions put increasing pressure on the ungodly as parts of the created order suffer damage, the ungodly are tormented but not killed, and finally some but not all suffer death. As the pressure increases, response is still possible. Moreover, when the churches are called to repent of eating what is offered to idols (2:16, 21–22), of complacency (3:3, 19), and of a lack of love (2:5), the call seems genuine, as also seems to be the case in later visions (Osborne; Smalley). On the complex relationship of the trumpet plagues and the exodus narrative, see §18E.

of the works of their hands. This expression could encompass all forms of sinful conduct (Ps 28:4), but here and elsewhere it refers to idols: "Their land is filled with idols; they bow down to the work of their hands" (Isa 2:8; cf. 17:8; Jer 1:16; Mic 5:13). This usage runs counter to views in the Greco-Roman world, in which making religious statues was an art form (Dio Chrysostom, *Disc.* 12.44–45; Pausanias, *Descr.* 1.25.7; 2.17.4). Israel's tradition held that the work of human hands could be a good thing (Ps 90:17; Isa 65:22) but insisted that it was misused when it involved fashioning images of the gods (Exod 20:1–6).

They did not stop worshiping demons. Jewish and Christian writers linked idols to evil powers. Paul acknowledged that in itself, an idol was nothing, but he added that "what pagans sacrifice, they sacrifice to demons and not God" and that a pagan altar is a "table of demons" (1 Cor 10:19–21). In Jewish tradition, those who worshiped false gods "sacrificed to demons, not to God" (Deut 32:17; cf. Ps 106:37; *1 En.* 19:1; 99:7–9; *Jub.* 1:11; 22:17; 2Q23 1 7–8; *T. Job* 3:3–4). Where the MT of Ps 96:5 says that the gods of the peoples are "idols," the LXX says those gods are "demons," and evil spirits were said to have lured people into making idols (*Jub.* 11:4–6). Revelation will develop this theme by insisting that those who worship the beast and its image worship Satan, the power behind the throne (Rev 13:4).

and idols of gold and silver and bronze and stone and wood. Idols were venerated in Greco-Roman temples, which included a sacred area with a central building where a statue of a god or goddess was displayed (Vitruvius, *Arch.* 4.5.1; 4.9.1). Asian coins show a statue of Artemis in her temple at Ephesus, a statue of Tiberius in the temple at Smyrna, statues of Augustus and the goddess Nikē in the temple at Pergamum, and images of Domitian and his wife in a temple at Laodicea (Figures 7, 9, 12, and 16; Friesen, *Imperial*, 30, 38, 62; G. Stevenson, *Power*, 46). In addition to the central statue, sanctuaries often included other images of the gods, given by patrons. Religious images were also set up in public areas and private homes, and small ones were worn as amulets (Philostratus, *Vit. Apoll.* 5.20.10; Burkert, *Greek*, 88–92).

Golden statues were known from the Scriptures—Nebuchadnezzar was said to have made one (Dan 3:1)—and were also placed in Greco-Roman sanctuaries. The faces and hands of the gold statues were often made of ivory, making them more lifelike (Pausanias, *Descr.* 1.24.5; 2.17.4; 5.11.1–4; Pliny the Elder, *Nat.* 34.19.54). Silver was not used for the central statues in temples, but it was used for smaller images and votive offerings, like those of Artemis at Ephesus (Acts 19:24; cf. Pausanias, *Descr.* 1.5.1). Bronze statues of deities were erected at many places, including one of Apollo at Pergamum (Pausanias, *Descr.* 8.42.7; cf. 3.17.6). Stone images, usually of marble, were widely used for deities in sanctuaries and other settings (Pausanias, *Descr.* 2.13.5; 2.22.7). Wooden images of the gods were often viewed with high regard because many of them were quite old. Temples in the Ephesus area and other places had wooden statues, and some were carried in processions (Pausanias, *Descr.* 3.20.7; Strabo, *Geographica* 13.1.41; 14.1.20; 15.3.15).

which cannot see or hear or walk. Critiques of idolatry frequently stress the inanimate character of idols: "Their idols are silver and gold, the work of human hands. They have mouths, but do not speak; eyes, but do not see. They have ears, but do not hear; noses, but do not smell. They have hands, but do not feel; feet, but do not walk; they make no sound in their throats" (Ps 115:4–7; cf. 135:15–17; Isa 44:9–20; Dan 5:23; Wis 15:15; Bel 4–7; Ep Jer 4–73).

Many people who followed Greco-Roman religious practices recognized that the statue was not actually the god, but in popular practice some treated the statue as though it were a god (Livy, *Rom. Hist.* 38.43.4–5; Diodorus Siculus, *Libr.* 17.41.7–8; Ps.-Lucian, *Asin.* 41). A religious procession might include mythic figures that were mechanically animated, so they could sit and stand (Athenaeus, *Deipnosophistae* 198f), and some people thought statues could talk (Plutarch, *Cor.* 37.3) or hear words whispered into their ears (Pausanias, *Descr.* 7.22.3; G. Stevenson, *Power*, 45). Revelation will critique such popular piety in its vision of the statue of the beast, which is part of the ruler cult. The beast's associate can make the statue speak, but John portrays such a talking statue as the product of sorcery (*pharmakeia*, cf. 9:21), which was officially disparaged in the Roman world (NOTES and COMMENT on 13:15).

9:21. *They did not repent of their murders or their sorceries or their immorality or their thefts.* There are three lists of wrongful behaviors in Revelation, and all include murder, immorality, sorcery, and idolatry (9:20–21; 21:8; 22:15). On such lists in ancient literature, see the COMMENT on 21:8. Murder and theft were universally condemned and punished (Exod 20:13, 15; 21:12–14; 22:1; Justinian, *Dig.* 47.2; 48.8.3.5). Immoral people engaged in illicit sexual relations. In practice, some forms of immorality were tolerated though disparaged, whereas others, such as adultery, were punished (Josephus, *Ag. Ap.* 2.215; *Rom. Civ.* 1:603). Earlier in Revelation, *porneia* primarily referred to religious infidelity, especially eating what had been sacrificed to idols (Rev 2:14–21), but the vice lists point to illicit sexual relations (21:8; 22:15).

Sorcery in the literal sense involves a potion (*pharmakon*), often blended from herbs, roots, and parts of animals (Horace, *Epod.* 5). Since potions were typically used with incantations, they connote the various practices performed by a sorcerer (*pharmakos*, Rev 21:8; 22:15; cf. *pharmakeia* in 18:23). For example, a spell in the Egyptian magical papyri calls for a mixture of cumin and the hair from a black donkey, a dappled she-goat, and a black bull. The petitioner is to call on the demons of the abyss, earth, and heaven, uttering a series of mysterious words (Betz, *Greek*, 63–64). Magical practices were familiar throughout the ancient world (Aune, *Apocalypticism*, 368–84; R. Thomas, *Magical*, 22–44). Among the cities mentioned in Revelation, Ephesus was noted for magic (Acts 19:11–19). The "Ephesian letters" were nonsense syllables used in magical rites (Plutarch, *Mor.* 706E).

At an official level, Greeks and Romans considered sorcery to be socially deviant and potentially dangerous (Apuleius, *Metam.* 3.16; Apuleius, *Apol.* 47; *Rom. Civ.* 2:511; MacMullen, *Enemies*, 121–27). An inscription from Philadelphia (late second to early first century BCE) said that upon entering the building, people should swear by all the gods that they "perform no malevolent magic [*pharmakon ponēron*] or malevolent charms against others" and that they refrain from love potions, immorality, and actions that kill children (I.Phil 1539.18–19). Similarly, Jews and Christians included sorcery in lists of wrongful behavior (Exod 22:18; Deut 18:10; Mal 3:5; Wis 12:4–6; Ps.-Phoc. 149; Gal 5:20; Rev 21:8; 22:15; *Did.* 2:2). The way Revelation lists sorcery between murder and immorality is suggestive, because some potions could kill people (*T. Ab.* 19:16; P.Oxy. 472.6), and others bewitched people into love relations, sometimes of an immoral sort (Josephus, *Ant.* 15.93; *T. Reu.* 4:9).

Revelation links sorcery and immorality in its visions of the beast and Babylon the whore (R. Thomas, *Magical*, 45–81). John expands immorality to include illicit religious behavior as well as sexual behavior. Accordingly, the ruler cult includes a statue that is magically animated to lure people into false worship (NOTES and COMMENT on Rev 13:15). Later, Babylon the whore, who personifies the imperial city, lures people into debased commercial and social relationships with the ruling power through the power of her sorcery (18:23).

COMMENT

The first four trumpets occurred in rapid succession, hemming people in with disasters on earth, sea, rivers, springs, and sky. In Greco-Roman tradition, many of these plagues would have been construed as portents of war (NOTES on 8:6–12). With the fifth trumpet, a vision of war begins as an angel unleashes demonic locusts, which are like cavalry

---

On Rev 9:13–21, see Giesen, "Lasterkataloge"; Ryan, *Hearing*; Steinmann, "Tripartite"; Rodney Thomas, *Magical*, 22–44.

troops that torment the ungodly. The theme of war continues with the sixth trumpet, where the scene shifts to the Euphrates River and demonic troops are unleashed to slaughter a third of humankind. Through these plagues it would appear that justice has been carried out. The people of earth, who had shed the blood of the saints, have now been subjected to death on a catastrophic scale. Yet people still do not repent but continue worshiping demons and idols and persist in their desire to commit murder and other crimes (9:20–21).

The trumpet visions are a literary sequence that focuses on the question of divine justice. Revelation assumes that God is just, so the saints can rightly expect him to take action against the perpetrators of injustice. But these visions also show that if God's justice is reduced to retribution, then nothing changes. Humanity continues its idolatry and murder. This insight sets the stage for what is to come, for instead of moving from humanity's resistance to a final devastating judgment, God's angel halts the seemingly relentless series of plagues so that prophetic witness can be given (10:1–11:14). God responds to the prayers of the saints by showing that even if his judgment seems slow, his purpose is to allow his witnesses to continue testifying to an unrepentant world.

Demonic Hordes at the Euphrates (9:13–19)

A voice from the heavenly altar commands the release of four angels who are bound at the Euphrates River (9:14). Since these angelic agents of destruction "are bound," they are apparently demonic beings, like the devil who is bound in 20:2. The vision assumes that God can restrain the destructive forces of evil and also unleash them. John describes what occurs from a visionary perspective in which the ordinary constraints of time and space are suspended. He has taken readers from the heavenly altar above to the door of the abyss below, and now he turns to the Euphrates River.

Locating the forces of destruction at the Euphrates fits the way Revelation uses place names to characterize something rather than to give geographical information. Elsewhere, for example, the city that dominates the world is Babylon, even though it includes features of Rome, Tyre, and Nineveh (17:5), and the kings of the earth gather at Harmagedon, because the name Megiddo was linked to the defeat of God's opponents (16:16). Similarly, referring to the Euphrates is suggestive, because for John's readers it connoted a realm of foreign powers. In Scripture the Euphrates, or "great river," was the idealized boundary of the promised land (Gen 15:18; Deut 1:7; Josh 1:4). Beyond it is foreign territory. The Assyrians and Babylonians, who conquered Israel and Judah, came from the Euphrates region (2 Kgs 23:29; 24:7). Babylon was located beside the Euphrates, and Babylonian horsemen, clad in armor, defeated the Egyptians there (Jer 46:2, 6, 10). After the exile Jewish communities continued to exist along the Euphrates (*m. Ta'an.* 1:3), but the region beyond it was known for its alien peoples (1QM II, 11).

In the first century CE the Euphrates marked the eastern border of the Roman Empire and beyond it was Parthia (Strabo, *Geographica* 16.1.28). Interpreters often assume that Rome feared a Parthian invasion, but this idea is overstated since the Romans were in a rather strong position over against Parthia in the late first century (Note on Rev 16:12). Nevertheless, the river's role as a boundary figured into apocalyptic writings. According to one scenario, the angels unleash the Parthians and Medes, who live along the Euphrates, and these armies sweep westward on a course of destruction (*1 En.* 56:5–6; Charles). Revelation is similar in that it pictures angels turning cavalry loose along the Euphrates, but the rest of the vision differs. In *1 Enoch* the forces are human armies, who attack the chosen people in Palestine, but fail. In contrast, Rev 9:17–19 depicts demonic beings, who attack the ungodly rather than the chosen (9:20–21), and they are successful in their attempt.

Another tradition held that the emperor Nero had not actually committed suicide in Rome, as many thought, but had fled to the Parthians and planned to return. Some expected that "having crossed the Euphrates with his many myriads," Nero would return to bring war to the eastern part of the empire (*Sib. Or.* 4:139; cf. 4:119–24; 5:361–65; Bauckham, *Climax*, 407). Revelation's sixth trumpet vision is similar to this tradition in that it pictures threatening armies from the Euphrates, but it differs because the attackers are demonic beings, not people. Later, kings from the east cross the Euphrates (Rev 16:12), but that is not the case at the sixth trumpet, where the bizarre horses and riders do not resemble any human army.

The four angels have been "made ready," presumably by God, who designated "that hour and day and month and year" for them to carry out their work (9:15). Rhetorically, listing one aspect of the timing after another magnifies the sense that the plague is unleashed according to God's design (Lausberg, *Handbook* §686). The wording leaves the impression that God has foreordained events, which was a theme in apocalyptic writing: God "weighed the age in the balance, and measured the times by measure, and numbered the times by number; and he will not move or arouse them until that measure is fulfilled" (*4 Ezra* 4:36–37; cf. 7:74; 13:58; *2 Bar.* 48:2–3). According to the DSS, the forces of wickedness are allowed to operate now, but they will be annihilated on "the day determined by [God] since ancient times" (1QM I, 10; cf. XIII, 14; 1QS III, 13–18; IV, 18–19, 25). Such times could be divinely revealed to human seers (*4 Ezra* 3:14; 12:9; 14:5; *2 Bar.* 56:2; Stone, *Fourth*, 98).

Revelation invokes this traditional view and assumes that God is more powerful than the forces of evil. Yet Revelation does not evince a determinism in which every event is foreordained as if part of a script. Having affirmed God's authority to carry out his purposes, step by step, the writer will interrupt the seemingly inexorable movement toward destruction in the next chapter so that witness can be given (Rev 10:1–11:14). As noted earlier, the book speaks of what "must" (*dei*) take place, yet it leaves room for contingencies, such as repentance or a refusal to repent, in the way God's victory is accomplished (COMMENT on 1:1c).

From his focus on the four angels who have been bound at the Euphrates, John expands the horizon to include the cavalry troops who will be the agents of destruction. John hears their number, which is "twice ten thousand times ten thousand" (9:16). The scale is so vast that the number given points to forces that are beyond numbering. In the visionary world they are the demonic counterpart to the angelic hosts of heaven, who number "thousands upon thousands" (5:11), and the great company of the redeemed, who were said to number 144,000 but are actually countless (7:4, 9). Where the innumerable hosts of heaven praise the Creator and the Lamb, the countless hordes at the Euphrates devastate the earth. Such immense companies of angels and demonic cavalry convey the magnitude of divine power to bring both redemption and judgment.

The description of the destructive horses and riders will fit the pattern of symmetry in justice that informs many of the trumpet visions. It was said that "one is punished by the very things by which one sins" (Wis 11:16; cf. 2 Macc 5:10; 13:8; *T. Gad* 5:10;

L.A.B. 43:5; 44:10; *m. Soṭah* 1:7–9; *t. Soṭah* 3–4; Winston, *Wisdom*, 232–33). Accordingly, the world's idolaters, who are said to worship demons (Rev 9:20), are turned over to demonic beings, who slaughter them.

The cavalry John sees are not human but have heads like lions and tails like snakes, and they snort out lethal fire, smoke, and sulfur. In Greco-Roman circles these monsters would have recalled stories about the fire-breathing Chimera, which had a lion's head and a snake for a tail. The Chimera was said to have been slain long ago, but it was a vivid example of the creatures that lurked in the underworld (Virgil, *Aen.* 6.288). Readers in the Greco-Roman world would have recognized such creatures as both evil and surreal (Cicero, *Nat. d.* 1.38.108; 2.2.5; Virgil, *Aen.* 6.292–4; Lucian, *Philops.* 2–3), and the connection with Rev 9 was noted in antiquity (Methodius, *Symp.* 9.12).

Similarly hideous combinations of traits occur in other evil figures in Revelation, such as the demonic locusts with human faces, lions' teeth, and scorpions' tails (Rev 9:1–12) and the beast from the sea, which has seven heads, ten horns, and features of a lion, bear, and leopard (13:1–2). These distorted images are the counterpart to the harmonious visions of God's throne hall, where four living beings represent each part of the created order and lead all creation in praising God and the Lamb (4:6–11; 5:13). The chaotic combinations of traits on the agents of evil fit their role in bringing destruction rather than harmony to the world.

The trumpet plagues culminate in the sixth trumpet vision where the fire, smoke, and sulfur of the demonic cavalry bring death to the world that killed God's witnesses. The pattern of justice seems to be an eye for an eye, a life for a life (Exod 21:23–25; Lev 24:18–21; Deut 19:21; Philo, *Spec. Laws* 3.182). The world that inflicts death on the faithful now suffers death, and the idolaters who serve demonic powers are now killed by those powers. The question is what this devastation has accomplished.

Wrath Alone Does Not Bring Repentance (9:20–21)

John takes up this question by focusing on "the rest of humankind, who were not killed by these plagues." What he reveals is that despite the catastrophic plagues, they "did not repent of the works of their hands" (9:20a). In the context of Revelation, repentance means worshiping the God who created all things rather than the gods represented by idols, which human hands created (4:11; 14:7). Yet the plagues do not evoke this response; instead, people keep worshiping their idols and familiar religious practices continue. In the cities of Asia Minor, as in the rest of the Greco-Roman world, statues of deities were displayed in temples (Notes on 2:1, 8, 12, 18; 3:1, 7, 14). Civic festivals included processions to temples where statues were displayed, and the devout washed and anointed the images and then adorned them in robes and garlands. People placed statues in the marketplace and alongside roads in order to show gratitude for divine help. Such images expressed the piety of the patrons who paid for them and fostered belief in the gods and goddesses they represented (Dio Chrysostom, *Disc.* 12.44, 60–61; Burkert, *Greek*, 88–92).

John's comments emphasize how incongruous it is for humanity to persist in idolatry in the face of the trumpet plagues. The disasters that struck the world manifested divine power, but people continue turning to powerless images that cannot see or hear or walk (Rev 9:20b). They cannot be compared with the living God (4:9–10). Similar critiques were common among Jews and Christians, who argued that the gods represented by lifeless statues have no power to save anyone (Isa 44:17–18; Hab 2:18–19; Dan 5:23; Acts 17:29; Ep Jer 49; *1 En.* 99:7; 4Q242 1–3, 7–8). Then John presses the incongruity by insisting that those who venerate images actually worship demons. Again, the critique is traditional (NOTE on 9:20). What is striking is that people in John's vision persist in worshiping demons even though they have suffered attacks by demonic beings, pictured as locusts and cavalry (9:1–19). This raises the issue of why they might respond in such a way.

Rather than providing a direct answer, John expands his critique by linking idolatry with murder, sorcery, immorality, and theft (9:21). Among Jews and early Christians this link was a familiar one, reflecting the Decalogue, which banned religious images and then forbade murder, adultery, theft, and other actions (Exod 20:1–17; Deut 5:6–21). Later writers treated idolatry as the source from which other wrongful conduct flowed (Wis 14:12; Rom 1:18–32; *Sib. Or.* 3:8–45; T. Naph. 3:3–5; Fitzmyer, *Romans*, 272).

The seeming incongruity between God's actions and the human response provides perspective on the problem of divine justice. Readers have been allowed to see what it would mean for God to equate justice with retribution. When God deals with a world that kills the faithful by sending a plague of death in return (6:10; 9:18), nothing changes. If the powers of heaven operate by inflicting death, the people of earth simply do the same (9:21). Similarly, the plague visions showed God's angels harnessing demonic forces to do his bidding, and the people of earth respond by doing the same through sorcery (*pharmakeia*, 9:21). Using potions and incantations, sorcerers might summon the demons of the abyss and leaders of the underworld who punished mortals, or they might seek the help of the goddess of darkness, who brings death and destruction (*PGM* 4.1350–75; 4.2851–70).

The first six trumpet plagues work with a profound irony. The plagues manifest divine wrath in ways that would have been broadly familiar in the Greco-Roman world. Yet this complicates the issue: Given only the plagues, people have no reason to distinguish the wrath of the Jewish and Christian God from the wrath of the Greco-Roman gods. Therefore, since wrath alone does not move people to repent, the pattern of wrath will be interrupted, so that prophetic witness can be given before the seventh trumpet is blown (10:1–11:13). John will emphasize the importance of witness by creating a literary connection between the end of the sixth trumpet vision and the beginning of the seventh. The sixth trumpet shows a third of humanity being killed and "the rest" (*hoi loipoi*) refusing to repent (9:20–21). Yet after God's witnesses have finished giving their testimony, the threat of judgment is moderated, and "the rest" (*hoi loipoi*) of the people come to glorify God (11:13). When change has occurred, then the seventh trumpet can sound, announcing the coming kingdom of God (Caird 124; Bauckham, *Theology*, 80–88).

22. Interlude: The Open Scroll (10:1–11:2)

10 ¹Then I saw another powerful angel coming down from heaven. He was robed in a cloud, with the rainbow over his head. His face was like the sun, and his feet were like pillars of fire, ²and he held an open scroll in his hand. He put his right foot on the sea and his left foot on the land. ³Then he called out with a loud voice like a lion roaring, and when he called out, the seven thunders raised their voices. ⁴And when the seven thunders spoke, I was about to write, but I heard a voice from heaven say, "Seal up what the seven thunders said, and do not write it down."

⁵Then the angel, whom I saw standing on the sea and on the land, raised his right hand to heaven ⁶and he swore by the one who lives forever and ever, who created the heaven and what is in it, and the earth and what is in it, and the sea and what is in it: "There will be no more time of waiting, ⁷but in the days when the seventh angel blows the trumpet, the mysterious purpose of God will be completed, as he announced the good news to his servants the prophets.

⁸Then the voice that I heard from heaven spoke with me again and said, "Go, receive the open scroll that is in the hand of the angel who stands on the sea and on the land." ⁹So I went to the angel and told him give me the scroll. He said to me, "Receive and devour it. It will be bitter to your stomach, but sweet as honey in your mouth." ¹⁰So I took the scroll from the hand of the angel and devoured it. It was sweet as honey in my mouth, but when I ate it, it made my stomach bitter. ¹¹Then I was told, "You must prophesy again about many peoples and nations and languages and kings."

11 ¹I was given a measuring reed, which was like a staff, and was told, "Go and measure the temple of God and the altar, and those who worship there. ²But do not measure the court outside the temple. Leave that out, for it has been given to the nations, and they will trample the holy city for forty-two months."

NOTES

10:1. *Then I saw another powerful angel coming down from heaven. He was robed in a cloud, with the rainbow over his head.* Clouds were said to accompany the coming of God (Exod 13:21; 34:5; 40:34; 1 Kgs 8:10) and the Son of Man or human figure who receives dominion over the world (Dan 7:13). A cloud suggests divine presence (Mark 9:7). Ancient readers would have pictured the rainbow above the head as a halo, a sign of glory. When Augustus assumed imperial power, people "saw above his head the orb of the sun with a circle about it, colored like the rainbow, seeming thereby to place a crown upon the head of one destined soon to greatness" (Vellius Paterculus, *Rom. Hist.* 2.59.6; cf. Seneca the Younger, *Nat.* 1.2.1; *NW* 2:1533). Angels were pictured wearing turbans like rainbows (*Apoc. Ab.* 11:3), and in Greek art gods were depicted with halos (*DACL* 12:1272–75). Some interpreters suggest that here the rainbow recalls God's promise not to destroy the earth again by flood, as in Gen 9:13 (Giesen; Mounce), but this theme is not developed.

His face was like the sun, and his feet were like pillars of fire. A sunlike face characterizes the glorified Jesus (Rev 1:16; cf. Matt 17:2) and could depict angelic messengers

(*Apoc. Zeph.* 6:11). Comparing the angel's feet to pillars of fire may recall that Christ's feet gleamed like bronze in Rev 1:15. Although *podes* means feet (10:2), comparing them to pillars includes the legs. Some interpreters suggest that the imagery recalls how God accompanied Israel in a pillar of fire at the time of the exodus, offering protection and guidance (Exod 13:21; 14:19, 24; Beale; Caird; Mounce; Osborne); however, John does not develop the exodus connection, and the pillars of fire seem simply to describe a shape (*1 En.* 21:7).

Some interpreters maintain that the angel is Christ because he resembles the exalted Christ of Rev 1:15–16. There are several reasons for this understanding: Christ is the Lion of Judah, and this angel roars like a lion (5:5; 10:3). Christ took the scroll from God, and this angel holds a scroll (5:7; 10:2). Christ's power was acclaimed by creatures of land and sea, and the angel stands on land and sea (5:11–13; 10:2). The LXX of Isa 9:5 calls the heir to David's throne an "angel" of great counsel (Victorinus; Primasius; Geneva Bible; Beale; Gundry, "Angelomorphic"; Gieschen, *Angelomorphic*, 256–60). This interpretation is unlikely, however, because Revelation distinguishes Christ, who can be worshiped (Rev 5:8), from the angels, who must not be worshiped (19:9–10; 22:8–9). They belong to different categories. When John speaks of "another" angel or a "powerful" angel, these angels are not Christ (5:2; 18:1, 21). The angel in Rev 10:1 has an exalted appearance because he mediates divine revelation (Carrell, *Jesus*, 131–38; Stuckenbruck, *Angel*, 229–32; Boring; Boxall).

10:2. *and he held an open scroll in his hand.* John calls the scroll a *biblaridion*, which in form is a diminutive of *biblos*. Many translate it as "small scroll," but it is better to render it "scroll" because John uses words for scrolls interchangeably. The scroll in the angel's hand can be called a *biblaridion* (10:2, 9, 10) and a *biblion* (10:8), with no distinction in meaning. Although manuscripts vary and some consistently use either the short ($\mathfrak{P}^{47}$) or the long (2351) form of the word, others use both forms in Rev 10 (A C; cf. ℵ Herm. *Vis.* 2.4.1–3), showing that the terms are synonyms. It is simply a stylistic variation, like calling the scroll of life both a *biblion* and a *biblos* (Rev 20:12, 15). Interpreters relate the sealed scroll of Rev 5 to the open scroll of Rev 10 in different ways, the first being most plausible:

1. Same scroll: sealed and open. The same scroll is pictured in Rev 5 and 10, using the synonyms *biblion* and *biblaridion*. The sealed scroll is given to Christ, who opens the seals so that an angel can give the open scroll to John. This fits the pattern in Ezekiel, in which a scroll written on both sides was given to the prophet to eat (Ezek 2:9–10; 3:1–3). In the same way, Revelation first pictures a scroll written on both sides (Rev 5:1) and then tells of a scroll being given to John to eat so that he can prophesy (10:1–11). The contents of the scroll are disclosed in summary form in Rev 11 but are elaborated in the visions that follow, so the scroll's contents encompass the rest of Revelation (Mazzaferri, *Genre*, 265–79; Bauckham, *Climax*, 243–57; Boring; Boxall; Osborne; Satake).

2. Two scrolls: large and small. Many interpreters distinguish the sealed scroll, or *biblion*, that God held in Rev 5:1, from the open scroll, or *biblaridion*, that the angel holds in 10:2. They assume that John uses different words to distinguish the scrolls. He could have identified them by saying that the angel held "the" scroll in his hand, but he does not do so. Interpreters variously propose that the scroll in Rev 5 encom-

passes the visions in Rev 6–9 (Charles), Rev 6–22 (Mounce), the whole Apocalypse (Giesen), or the OT (Prigent), while agreeing that the small scroll includes only the visions in Rev 11. Others suggest that the large scroll extends from 4:1 to 19:10 but is interrupted by the small scroll that is set within it (10:1–15:4; Schüssler Fiorenza, *Book*, 175; Humphrey, *Ladies*, 97–100). One problem with this view is that the word *biblion* does describe both scrolls (5:1; 10:8). Also, it is unlikely that the contents of the first scroll were disclosed while the Lamb was opening the seals. It is more likely that the contents will be disclosed now that the scroll is open.

3. Two parallel scrolls. In each scene a heavenly figure holds a scroll, which is given to someone else. As the seals on the first scroll are opened, a series of visions occur, which might reveal the contents of that scroll. Since the seal visions lead directly into the trumpet visions, the contents of the first scroll would encompass Rev 6–11. The second scroll is opened in Rev 10. Since its prophecies concern nations and kings, its contents would be the visions in Rev 12–22. Although the second scroll is opened before the visions from the first scroll have been completed, vision series in Revelation often overlap (Yarbro Collins, *Combat*, 19–32; Murphy; cf. Baynes, "Revelation"; Baynes, *Heavenly*, 149–62). Problems with this approach are like those noted above.

He put his right foot on the sea and his left foot on the land. To have things under one's feet shows one having dominion over them (Pss 8:6; 110:1; Rom 16:20). People recognize the power of others by falling at their feet (Rev 1:17; 19:10). God made the heavens from which the angel descends and the land and sea on which the angel stands. Earth is the footstool under God's feet (Isa 66:1; Matt 5:35), and the angel is subordinate to God (Rev 10:6).

10:3. *Then he called out with a loud voice like a lion roaring.* When God roars like a lion, he can awaken fear (Amos 3:8), but his roar can also signal redemption (Hos 11:10). In *4 Ezra* 12:31–32 the lionlike voice of the Messiah brings judgment for oppressors but deliverance for others. In Rev 10:3 the angel's voice is more promising than threatening because it interrupts the movement toward increasingly destructive judgments.

and when he called out, the seven thunders raised their voices. The seven thunders have been interpreted in two main ways. The first is most plausible:

1. Heavenly powers. A group of seven heavenly powers fits the pattern in Revelation, which has groups of seven angels (1:20; 8:2; 15:1) and seven angelic spirits (1:4). Like the four creatures beside God's throne, they speak with a voice of thunder (6:1). The thunders are plural, whereas the voice from God's throne is singular, and they respond to the lionlike roar of the angel, much as groups in heaven might speak with thundering voices (14:2; 19:6). Since the passage refers to "the" seven thunders, some interpreters assume that these heavenly powers were well-known (Bousset). Although this is possible, the tradition is not attested in other sources. In *3 Bar.* 11:3–4 there is triple thunder as the angel Michael descends, but those thunders do not convey a message. It is sufficient to consider them as one among the many groups of heavenly powers in Revelation (Oecumenius; Andreas; Beale).

2. God's voice. Some interpreters construe the thunders as God's voice (Aune; Blount; Harrington; Reddish; Smalley). Psalm 29 refers seven times to God's voice, which is like thunder. Other biblical passages identify God's voice with thunder at Mount

Sinai and in battle or judgment against the world (Exod 19:16, 19; 1 Sam 2:10; 7:10; 2 Sam 22:14; Job 37:2–5; Ps 18:13). Revelation also links thunder to God's throne (Rev 4:5). Nevertheless, this approach is not compelling. Psalm 29 refers to God's voice seven times, but it does not enumerate them, and it mentions thunder only once. Some texts compare God's voice to thunder, but in Rev 10:3 the thunders speak with their own voices, and it will be the single voice from God's throne that tells John not to write down what the thunders said.

Thunder could connote either blessing or curse (*1 En.* 59:3; Cicero, *Div.* 2.42, 84; W. Speyer, *RAC* 10.1128–31). After prayer, thunder could signal a favorable response (Homer, *Od.* 20.101–4; Pindar, *Pyth.* 4.23; cf. John 12:28–29), but at other times it was ominous (4Q318 2 II, 9). The seven thunders have been interpreted in a positive sense as harbingers of the messianic age (Horn, "Die sieben"), but more likely, they are menacing (Rev 8:5; 11:19; 16:18; Wis 19:13; Caird; Mounce; Bauckham, *Climax*, 259).

10:4. *And when the seven thunders spoke, I was about to write, but I heard a voice from heaven say.* The voice could belong to God, Christ, or an angelic being. Elsewhere, an unnamed voice from the throne belongs to God (Rev 16:17; 21:3) or perhaps Christ, who shares the throne (cf. 3:21). When a voice simply comes "from heaven," the identity is less clear. The voice commanding the witnesses to "come up here" in 11:12 echoes what Christ said in 4:1, although in that context the unnamed speaker could be God or other heavenly being. A voice announces the kingdom of God and Christ (12:10), says that those who die in the Lord are blessed (14:13), commands angels to pour out God's wrath (16:1), warns people to leave Babylon since God judges the city (18:4–8), and calls everyone to praise God (19:5). One might assume that in these passages an angel speaks because the voice refers to God in the third person, but the voice from the throne also speaks of God in the third person (21:3–5). Some sources make clear that an anonymous heavenly voice comes from God (John 12:28; *L.A.B.* 53:3–5; *T. Ab.* 10:12–14), but others leave the speaker's identity unspecified (Dan 4:31; *4 Ezra* 6:13; *2 Bar.* 13:1; 22:1; Aune). This preserves a sense of mystery while conveying heavenly authority.

"Seal up what the seven thunders said, and do not write it down." Ordinarily, something must be written down before it can be sealed, just as Daniel was told to write down his visions and then seal them until the end of the age (Dan 8:26; 12:4, 9; cf. Rev 22:10). John, however, is not to write down the words of the thunders at all. The command to seal up what they said interrupts the movement toward increasingly devastating judgments, showing that they represent threats that are not to be carried out (Caird; Harrington; Mounce; Bauckham, *Climax*, 259).

An alternative interpretation is that John heard divine things that were inexpressible (cf. 2 Cor 12:4; Origen, *Comm. Jo.* 13.28, 33; Origen, *Cels.* 6.6) or were like the truths that Jesus' disciples could not bear (John 16:12; Ambrose Autpert; Haimo). Therefore, when John did not write down what the thunders said, some suggest that he recognized the limits of his understanding (Boring). A variation is that the thunders conveyed things about the end time that John may have understood but God did not want revealed to others (Schüssler Fiorenza 75; Horn, "Die sieben"; Aune; Osborne; Roloff; Ruiz, "Hearing"; G. Carey, *Elusive*, 123–24). However, John thought what the thunders said could be communicated, since he was about to write it down, so there is no reason to think that the words of the thunders are more esoteric than those of other heavenly beings, which John did write down (Giesen).

10:5. *Then the angel, whom I saw standing on the sea and on the land, raised his right hand to heaven.* Raising the right hand to heaven invokes God as the guarantor of an oath. The gesture was customary, as in Deut 32:40 LXX: "I lift up my hand to heaven and I swear by my right hand." Similarly, the oath in Gen 14:22 begins, "I have lifted my hand to the Lord, God Most High, who made heaven and earth." Sometimes people lifted both hands when swearing an oath (Philo, *Spec. Laws* 4.34). John's vision recalls the action of the angel in Dan 12:9, but where Daniel's angel raised both hands, the one here raises only the right hand.

10:6. *and he swore by the one who lives forever and ever.* Oaths gave assurance that a person was telling the truth or would keep a promise (*Sel. Pap.* 249; 310; Philo, *Decal.* 86; Philo, *Somn.* 1.12). By swearing an oath, people held themselves accountable to a deity or other authority, who would punish them if the oath was not kept (Pausanias, *Descr.* 2.2.1). According to Jewish sources, one was to call on God in oaths, although people also were to avoid using God's name wrongfully, which meant that some swore by heaven or by sacred objects instead (Deut 6:13; Josh 9:19; Matt 5:34; 23:16; 26:63). In the Greco-Roman world people swore by one or more gods and sometimes by the king or emperor (I.Smyr 573.60–61; Apuleius, *Metam.* 2.5; P.Oxy. 263.4).

The angel must swear by God since there is no higher authority. That is why in some contexts God had to swear by himself. Some writers thought it unsuitable for God to make an oath since his integrity neither needed nor could have any outside guarantee, but others deemed it proper for God to swear in order to assure people of his intentions, as the angel does here (Philo, *Legat.* 3.207; Philo, *Sacr.* 91–94; Philo, *Abr.* 273; Heb 6:17). Biblical oaths often begin with "as the Lord lives," recognizing that only the living God can guarantee an oath (Judg 8:19; 1 Kgs 1:29; Jer 4:2; Amos 8:14). God's oaths follow the same pattern, beginning with "as I live" (Num 14:21; Deut 32:40; Jer 46:18). The angel in Revelation now swears by the God "who lives forever and ever," and since God lives forever, his guarantee of the oath has abiding validity (Dan 12:7; Rev 4:9–10; 15:7).

who created the heaven and what is in it, and the earth and what is in it, and the sea and what is in it. Swearing by heaven and earth was common (Apollonius of Rhodes, *Argonautica* 3.699; Philo, *Spec. Laws* 2.4–5; Matt 5:34). In Revelation, however, the angel calls on the Creator rather than the creation, swearing by the one who made heaven, earth, and sea (Exod 20:11; Neh 9:6; Ps 146:6; Acts 4:24). Rabbi Eleazar (ca. 100 CE) said: "Lord of all the world, if you had sworn to them by heaven and earth, I would say that even as heaven and earth pass away, so shall your oath pass away. But now you have sworn to them by your great name, and just as your great name endures forever and ever, so shall your oath endure forever and ever" (*b. Ber.* 32a).

"There will be no more time of waiting. A literal translation is "there will be no more time." This expression has been taken in several ways, the fourth being the most plausible:

1. Time itself will end. Since antiquity, many interpreters have argued that the angel's comment anticipates the close of the age, when time ceases and people are freed from temporal limitations through the gift of eternal life (Primasius; Andreas; Bede;

Richard of St. Victor; Osborne; Lupieri; cf. KJV). When heaven and earth flee, temporal space is undone (Friesen, *Imperial*, 155). While Revelation does culminate with an end to temporal existence and the saints reign forever and ever (22:5), the internal thematic connections make it preferable to relate the angel's words to the issue of perceived delay in God's action (6:10).

2. No more delay before the end. Modern translations usually read that there will be no more delay in fulfilling God's purposes, which gives the impression that the end will come immediately (NAB, NASB, NIV, NRSV; Blount; Reddish). However, the end does not come. The announcement of the kingdom is delayed until 11:15–18, and what is announced there is the final defeat of evil, judging of the dead, and rewarding of the saints—all of which occur only at the end of the book. Accordingly, some interpreters suggest that the angel might be saying that the persecution pictured in 11:1–13 is to begin without delay (Caird; Boring; Bauckham, *Climax*, 263). But the remainder of the angel's comment in 10:7 makes clear that the delay will end only after the seventh trumpet (Beale; Morris; Swete).

3. No more time for repentance. The word *chronos* was used for the time given to Jezebel for repentance ("I gave her time to repent," Rev 2:21). On a wider scale, the disasters in 8:6–9:19 called humanity to repent, though people refused to do so (9:20–21). One might argue that now the time allotted for repentance is over (Boxall). However, the witnesses do wear sackcloth as an ongoing summons to repentance (11:3), and later visions continue calling for repentance (16:9, 11; cf. 14:7).

4. Assurance that the time of waiting will end. The Greek word for time is *chronos*, which recalls the vision of the martyrs, who asked how long God would delay in bringing justice. They were told to wait for "a short time" (*chronon mikron*) until others who would be killed had finished giving their witness (6:11). In that context the martyrs were assured that the apparent delay would end but were not told how long it would be. The same is true here. The angel reaffirms that the present situation will not continue forever, using the future tense to say that this time of waiting *will* (*estai*) end when the seventh trumpet heralds the kingdom of God and Christ, the defeat of evil, and the rewarding of the saints (11:15–18). No further information is given about how long that will be.

10:7. *"but in the days when the seventh angel blows the trumpet.* The Greek is awkward and can literally be translated, "but in the days of the voice [*phonē*] of the seventh angel, when he is about to sound his trumpet." Since the seventh angel does not speak, however, the word *phonē* must refer to the "sound" that the angel's trumpet makes. Fulfillment does not come when the angel is "about to" blow the trumpet but occurs after the trumpet sounds.

"the mysterious purpose of God will be completed. The Greek word *mystērion* can be used for visionary images that need interpretation (Rev 1:20; 17:5, 7), but here it suggests secret purposes. Just as a king forms secret plans to defeat an enemy (Jdt 2:2), God has hidden purposes to overcome the wicked and vindicate the righteous (*1 En.* 38:3; 103:2–4; Wis 2:22). God's secret purposes were understood to include the rise and fall of earthly kingdoms and the establishment of his kingdom at the end of time (Dan 2:27–47). Similarly, Revelation assumes that God's secret purpose will culminate in the coming of the kingdom, the rewarding of the righteous, and the final

defeat of the powers of evil (Rev 11:15–18; cf. Mark 4:11; Rom 16:25–26; 1 Cor 2:7–9; Eph 1:9–10). This purpose will be complete (*telein*) when the prophets have finished their work, God's wrath has been poured out, and the reign of the beast has ended (Rev 11:7; 15:1, 8; 17:17). In its full sense, completion occurs after the vision of the millennial kingdom (20:3, 5, 7), when Satan is destroyed, the New Jerusalem appears, and God and Christ announce that they are the end, or completion (*telos*), of all things (21:6; 22:13).

"as he announced the good news. The verb introducing God's purposes is *euangelizein*, or "announce good news" (14:6). The word could convey the good news that enemies had been defeated in battle and that God had prevailed (2 Sam 18:19, 31; Ps 68:11–12). Similar language was used for God's deliverance of his people: "Get you up to a high mountain, Zion herald of good news," and say, "Here is your God! See, the Lord God comes with might, and his arm rules for him . . . and his recompense before him" (Isa 40:9–10; cf. 52:7; Ps 40:9; Nah 1:15). Among Christians this was a vivid way to announce God's kingdom (Mark 1:14–15) and the message about Jesus the Messiah (Acts 8:12; Rom 15:20; Gal 1:16).

Since the "good news" in Revelation involves God's victory over forces in the Roman imperial system, it is helpful to contrast imperial usage. In Asia Minor the calendar began with the birthday of Augustus. The decision to do this, made in Smyrna about 9 BCE, affirmed that "the providence that ordains our whole life" brought forth Augustus, the "savior who put an end to war and brought order to all things," the god whose birth "was the beginning of good news [*euangelia*] to the world." To honor him, the province of Asia would calculate "time to have begun with his birth" (OGIS 458; Friesen, *Imperial*, 34). Sardis held a festival to celebrate the "good news" that Augustus's son had come of age (I.Sard 8.14), and an inscription from Laodicea calls such occasions "festivals of good news" (*euangelia*; I.Laod 82.12). By way of contrast, Revelation centers time on the reign of God and his Messiah, identifying "good news" with the establishment of their kingdom, which differs from the Roman Empire (Rev 11:15).

"to his servants the prophets." The prophets are the recipients of the good news. Although John uses the accusative case, this form can identify those who receive the news (Luke 3:18; Acts 8:25, 40; 13:32; 14:21; 16:10). On one level, God's "servants the prophets" are the biblical prophets (2 Kgs 9:7; Dan 9:6; Zech 1:6; 1QS I, 3; 1QpHab II, 9–10). On a secondary level, the prophets include Christian prophets such as John and others, who stand within the prophetic tradition while continuing to receive and convey God's message (Rev 1:1; 22:9). Some interpreters think that 10:7 refers only to Christian prophets (Charles; Giesen), but it more probably includes OT and early Christian prophets (Mounce; Roloff).

The language recalls Amos 3:7, which says, "Surely the Lord God does nothing without revealing his mysterious purpose to his servants the prophets." Yet instead of saying that God has "revealed" his mystery to the prophets, John says that he "announced" it to them. This wording leaves open the possibility that the prophets did not have the full meaning of the message. This idea is reflected in a Dead Sea text, which says that God told Habakkuk "to write down what was going to happen to the last generation, but he did not let him know the consummation of the era," for "the final age will be extended and go beyond all that the prophets say, because the mysteries of God are wonderful" (1QpHab VII, 1–8). According to this text, the fuller meaning of Habakkuk's message is later disclosed to a member of the group, known as the Teacher of Righteousness. In

Revelation, John is more of a prophet than a teacher (Schüssler Fiorenza 136), but his role is similar to that of the Teacher, since John too discloses the fuller meaning of what was conveyed through the biblical prophets (Bauckham, *Climax*, 262–63).

10:8. *Then the voice that I heard from heaven spoke with me again and said, "Go, receive the open scroll that is in the hand of the angel who stands on the sea and on the land."* The scene recalls Ezek 2:8–3:3, where the prophet is told to take a scroll that is handed to him, evidently by God. In John's vision the scroll is held by the angel, whose posture with feet on sea and land connotes dominion (Note on Rev 10:2). The unnamed voice speaking to John may or may not belong to God, but it bears divine authority (Note on 10:4). The contents of the scroll are sometimes identified with Rev 12–22 (Yarbro Collins 64–66) or 10:1–15:4 (Schüssler Fiorenza, *Book*, 174; Humphrey, *Ladies*, 97–100), but more probably the scroll's message is summarized in 11:1–14 and then elaborated in the remainder of the book (Charles; Giesen; Mounce; Prigent; Smalley).

10:9. *So I went to the angel and told him to give me the scroll. He said to me, "Receive and devour it. It will be bitter to your stomach, but sweet as honey in your mouth."* Asking for the scroll shows John's readiness to obey. The command to take and eat the scroll could come from either the heavenly voice or the angel. Eating the scroll associates John with Israel's prophets, as God told Ezekiel: "'Mortal, eat this scroll that I give you and fill your stomach with it.' Then I ate it; and in my mouth it was as sweet as honey" (Ezek 3:3). Also, when God called Jeremiah, he said, "I have put my words in your mouth," and Jeremiah later said, "your words were found, and I ate them, and your words became to me a joy" (Jer 1:9; 15:16). Eating the scroll indicates empowerment to communicate God's word (*4 Ezra* 14:38–41).

10:10. *So I took the scroll from the hand of the angel and devoured it. It was sweet as honey in my mouth, but when I ate it, it made my stomach bitter.* In John's cultural context dreaming about eating a book could signify future benefits for people who made their livings by words or death to those who did not (Artemidorus, *Onirocritica* 2.45). Ezekiel found the scroll to be sweet, but John experiences both sweetness and bitterness. The significance has been taken in three ways; the third is most plausible:

1. The message holds sweet salvation for the righteous and bitter judgment for the unrepentant. Traditionally, God's word and wisdom were sweet because they brought benefits to those who received them (Pss 19:10; 119:103; cf. Prov 16:24; 24:13–14). John might experience the scroll as sweet because God's word and purposes lead to the vindication of the righteous and to God's own glory (Rev 11:15–18). Bitterness occurs because the message warns of judgment of the unrepentant, for whom the Day of the Lord is bitter (Zeph 1:14). Ezekiel ate a scroll filled with words of mourning and woe, and John must do the same (Ezek 2:10; Stuart; Beale). A problem with this view is that the faithful do suffer in subsequent visions.

2. The vocation of a prophet includes the sweetness of a call from God and the bitterness of rejection by other people. Jeremiah experienced joy when he consumed God's word because it showed that he belonged to God (Jer 15:16), and when Ezekiel found that eating the scroll was sweet, he implied that being called by God was positive (Ezek 3:3). The bitterness arises from rejection by other people (Jer 15:15–16). After God warned Ezekiel that his words would be rejected, the prophet left "in bitterness" (Ezek 3:7, 14). For John, too, bearing God's message will entail affliction (Giesen;

Roloff). This interpretation is helpful, but limited, since John's own commissioning is followed by a vision of the prophetic vocation of the community, which also includes rejection and suffering.

3. The Christian community will learn that the scroll is sweet because of its message of salvation, but it is bitter because God's purposes will be accomplished in part through the suffering and witness of his people. This interpretation is the most plausible because the next vision pictures faithful worshipers being besieged and two witnesses suffering martyrdom (11:1–10). God's kingdom will come, and his people will receive their rewards (11:15–18), but the way of redemption entails the suffering of the faithful (Caird; Harrington; Mounce; Osborne; Smalley).

10:11. *Then I was told, "You must prophesy again about.* Prophesying is inspired speech that is designed to shape the commitments of the hearers. The risen Christ previously commissioned John to write down what he saw and to send it to the seven churches (1:9–11), and Rev 1–9 stems from that initial commission. In 10:11 John is called to prophesy again, and the remainder of the book comes from this renewed calling. The expression "I was told" in Greek is literally the plural "they said." The plural could indicate that both the heavenly voice and the angel speak (Giesen; Rowland), but it is probably an impersonal plural, which functions like the passive "I was told." Some interpreters regard this as a Semitism, but it appears in Hellenistic Greek (Rydbeck, *Fachprosa*, 27–45).

The expression *prophēteuein epi* can mean "prophesy about" someone when the prophecy is positive (Ezek 13:16; 36:6 LXX). Although it could indicate that John was to prophesy "to" the nations (cf. Rev 14:6; 22:16; cf. Ezek 36:1; 37:2, 9; Mazzaferri, *Genre*, 291), the visions do not show John addressing the nations directly. He prophesies *about* the nations but *to* his readers (Rev 22:16). A few interpreters maintain that John is to prophesy "against" the nations (Jer 25:29–30 [32:29–30 LXX]; Ezek 4:7; 11:4; 25:2; Aune; Beale), but this is unlikely because John's visions include both negative and positive messages about the nations (e.g., Rev 11:2, 9; 15:4; 21:24).

many peoples and nations and languages and kings." On the first three groups, see the NOTE on 5:9. On kings in John's social context, see the NOTE on 1:5.

11:1. *I was given a measuring reed, which was like a staff.* Reeds were used as measuring tools. Ezekiel described a similar scene in which an angelic figure had a reed that was six long cubits in length (Ezek 40:5), and in the DSS the reed was seven cubits long (4Q554 1 III, 18–19; 5Q15 1 I, 2–4). Both types were about ten feet long. In Roman times, measuring reeds ranged from seven and a half to nine and a half feet in length (Heron, *Geometria* 4.11; 21.13). John compares the reed to a staff, perhaps like those used by shepherds and travelers, which were often a little shorter than a person's height. In Rev 21:15 an angel uses a measuring reed that seems to be of extraordinary size, but nothing unusual is said about the reed given to John.

and was told. The word "told," or literally "saying," has no subject. Some manuscripts assume that the angel of Rev 10 continues speaking in 11:1 (א² 046 1854), but since previous commands came from a heavenly voice (10:8; cf. 10:11) and the voice in 11:3 refers to "my" two witnesses, the speaker could be God or Christ.

"Go and measure. Measuring will define the place where true worship takes place and show that it is protected. This modifies a pattern in earlier prophetic texts, in

which measuring had more to do with restoration (Ezek 40–48; Zech 2:1–2; Isa 28:17; Jer 31:38–39) or judgment (2 Sam 8:2; 2 Kgs 21:13; Lam 2:8; Amos 7:7–9) than with protection. Some interpreters suggest that the description of angels measuring in *1 En.* 61:1–5 might indicate that the action is for protection (e.g., Boxall; Prigent), but the passage from Enoch has more to do with identifying the inheritance of the righteous than with protection (Black, *Book*, 231–32; Jauhiainen, "Measuring," 513–19).

The idea of protection fits a common social pattern in antiquity, when temples and altars were places of asylum. During wartime, invaders were not to violate temples. In the OT people sought protection at the altar (Exod 21:13–14; 1 Kgs 1:50) and took refuge in the temple (Josephus, *Life* 17–21; Josephus, *Ant.* 14.339, 447). Greco-Roman temples were also considered to be islands of safety from prosecution or conquest (Strabo, *Geographica* 14.1.23; Dio Chrysostom, *Disc.* 31.54; *NewDocs* 4:168; G. Stevenson, *Power*, 103–13, 161–64, 293). John's being told to measure the temple and altar means he is to mark out a sphere of asylum for those who worship there.

"the temple of God. The term "temple" (*naos*) was used for the Jerusalem temple and Greco-Roman temples. Calling it "the temple of God" identifies it with Israel's tradition (Matt 26:61; Luke 1:9). At Jerusalem the *naos* was the central temple building, which included an entrance hall, a forecourt, and an inner chamber, or holy of holies. This design was used for Solomon's temple, the temple in Ezek 40–48, and the Herodian temple. In the first century CE a table, lampstand, and incense altar stood in the forecourt; the holy of holies was empty. The altar for burnt offerings stood outside the temple (Josephus, *J.W.* 5.216–25). On the history of interpretation, see §18A. In current scholarship there are two principal interpretations of the temple. The first is preferable:

1. Image of the Christian community. Readers have been told that each faithful person will be "a pillar in the temple of my God" (Rev 3:12). A temple with human pillars is a community, whose members are considered priests (1:6; 5:10). Israel's temples had golden lampstands among their furnishings, and the lampstands in Revelation signify congregations and the people who bear prophetic witness (1:20; 11:3–4). Calling the worshiping community a temple was common among early Christians (1 Cor 3:16; 2 Cor 6:16; Eph 2:20; 1 Pet 2:5; Ign. *Eph.* 9:1; Ign. *Magn.* 7:2; cf. Aune; Charles; Giesen; Mounce; Murphy; Prigent; Hirschberg, *Das eschatologische*, 217; Spatafora, *From*, 164–68).

2. Heavenly temple. Some interpreters identify the temple as heaven, where the saints are fully protected (Rev 7:9–17; 12:11). They regard the outer court as the earth, which is dominated by the ungodly. Elsewhere, the temple (7:15; 11:19; 14:15–17; 15:5–8; 16:1, 17) and the altar (6:9; 8:3–5; 9:13; 14:18; 16:7) are in heaven, where worship takes place (e.g., 4:10; 5:14; 7:11). Some Jewish sources equate the sanctuary's inner chamber with heaven and its outer courts with earth (Wis 9:8; Josephus, *Ant.* 3.123, 181). Earthly sanctuaries were said to have been patterned after a heavenly model, which was the true temple (Exod 25:9; Wis 9:8; Giblin, "Revelation," 438; Bachmann, "Himmlisch"; Yarbro Collins, *Crisis*, 68). A problem with this approach is that John usually makes explicit when he is referring to the temple "in heaven," which he does not do here; and when angels come out of the heavenly temple, they do not enter an earthly courtyard but remain in heaven (Rev 11:19; 14:17; 15:5–6).

In Revelation, the followers of Jesus constitute the temple on earth. Their community is the terrestrial counterpart to the temple in heaven.

"*and the altar.* Altars stood alongside temples throughout the ancient world (Vitruvius, *Arch.* 4.5.1). The most common term for a Greco-Roman altar was *bōmos* (Strabo, *Geographica* 14.1.3; I.Smyr 753.17; I.Sard 98.3), but John uses *thysiastērion*, the term for altars in Israel's tabernacle and temples. As already noted, these sanctuaries had an incense altar inside the central structure and another for burnt offering in the open court outside. Revelation combines the functions of the two altars in the single altar before God's throne within the temple building (NOTE on Rev 6:9). The vision does not elaborate the function of the altar but includes it as a way of showing that God is preserving a community where true worship (*proskynein*) can take place.

"*and those who worship there.* John refers to God's temple and altar and those who worship there, or literally "in it." He could mean "in the temple" or "in the altar [area]" (*4 Bar.* 2:10) or "at the altar" (1 Cor 9:13). Whatever is meant, people are in the place of worship. Some translations read that John is to "count" the worshipers (NAB, NIV), but John would not use a measuring reed for counting. The worshipers are in the area that is to be measured by the reed.

11:2. "*But do not measure the court outside the temple. Leave that out, for it has been given to the nations.* John envisions a sanctuary with two parts: the enclosed temple building (*naos*) and the open court (*aulē*) around it. The basic pattern is like that of the tabernacle, which had an enclosed central structure and a surrounding open court (Exod 26:1–37; 27:9–19). The Herodian temple was more complex, with a court for priests, a court for the men of Israel, and another court where Jewish women could go. These were separated from the plaza that surrounded the temple by a low wall that warned Gentiles not to enter (Josephus, *J. W.* 5.190–94). Gentiles could enter the outer plaza or court of the Gentiles, but that space did not belong to Gentiles. It was part of the temple complex and was one of God's "courts" (Pss 84:10; 100:4; Schürer, *History*, 2:285–86; V. Hamp, *TDOT* 5:135–37). Revelation, however, simply distinguishes the enclosed temple from the open court. There are three main interpretations of the imagery. The first is preferable:

1. Outer court as the vulnerable aspect of the church. The enclosed temple (*naos*) that is measured signifies the worshiping community, which God preserves on earth. The open court (*aulē*) signifies the church, as it is vulnerable to affliction in an unbelieving world. The same community is both preserved and vulnerable. The message is repeated in the story of the two witnesses, who are preserved so they can prophesy, yet exposed to martyrdom and the scorn of the nations (Rev 11:8–10; Caird; Mounce; Murphy; Osborne; Prigent; Resseguie; Satake; Smalley; Bauckham, *Climax*, 270–72; Minear, "Ontology," 98; G. Stevenson, *Power*, 257–65).

2. Outer court as the unbelieving world. Some interpreters read the command to "leave out" (*ekballein*) the outer court as a rejection of those outside the community of faith, whether non-Christian Jews (Feuillet, *Johannine*, 237; Beagley, "*Sitz,*" 63) or unbelievers generally (Charles; Ford; Giesen; Reddish). Yet it seems redundant to think of unbelievers in the outer court being given over to unbelieving nations.

3. Outer court as the part of the church that accommodates false worship. Some of John's readers were rebuked for tolerating the teachings of those who thought it

acceptable to eat food sacrificed to Greco-Roman deities (Boxall; Kiddle; Spatafora, *From*, 170–73). They would be like the idolaters in the outer court in Ezek 8:16 (Jauhiainen, "Measuring"). The difficulty is that the outer court is connected to the city that is called "holy," and it seems to be downtrodden rather than apostate in Rev 11:2b.

"and they will trample the holy city. Ordinarily, the holy city was Jerusalem, where the sanctuary was located (Isa 48:2; 1 Macc 2:7; Matt 4:5). For the city to be trampled, or overrun, indicates conquest and political domination, but not necessarily destruction (1 Macc 3:45; 2 *Bar.* 67:2; *Pss. Sol.* 2:2, 19; 7:2; 17:22). The imagery is drawn primarily from Dan 8:10 and 13, which refer to the sanctuary being trampled for about three and a half years. Secondary echoes are from Zech 12:3 LXX, which refers to the coming day when God "will make Jerusalem a stone trampled on by all the nations." In a similar way Luke says that Jerusalem will be surrounded by armies and "will be trampled by the nations until the times of the nations are fulfilled" (Luke 21:24). He describes the period of Gentile domination of Jerusalem after the Roman conquest of 70 CE (Fitzmyer, *Gospel*, 2:1343–47).

Jewish apocalyptic writers grappled with the problem of Jerusalem's fall to the Romans (4 *Ezra* 10; 2 *Bar.* 1–13), but Revelation transfers the language to the social situation of early Christians in Asia Minor and elsewhere. Although the book was probably written after the fall of Jerusalem, it does not depict the destruction of the temple or deal with the future of the earthly city (COMMENT on Rev 21:10). The idea that Revelation draws on a source from the time of the revolt is unlikely (see §18B). The book describes a peculiar situation in which the temple continues to stand even as the city is trampled. There are two main approaches to the significance of the city in this context. The first is preferable:

1. The city as Christian community. The details in the vision—altar, temple, outer court, holy city—are one extended image for the church. The courts of the temple and the altar were constituent parts of the holy city, and both are included in Revelation's description of the Christian community, which has a vulnerable place in the unbelieving world (Beale; Bauckham, *Climax*, 272).
2. The city as unbelieving world. Since the city is trampled by the nations, some interpreters argue that it represents the unbelievers themselves. In scenes that follow, "the great city" has traits of Jerusalem, where Jesus was crucified, and it can be called Sodom, Egypt, and the place where all the inhabitants of the earth live (11:8–10; Jerome, *Ep.* 46.6–7; Giesen; Giblin, "Revelation," 439–40; Hirschberg, *Das eschatologische*, 216–23). Nevertheless, equating the city in Rev 11:2 with the unbelieving world does not fit the way John calls it "holy," and picturing an unbelieving city being overrun by unbelieving nations does not fit a context that depicts threats against the community of faith.

"for forty-two months." Periods of three and a half years appear in several forms in Revelation (11:2, 3; 12:6, 14; 13:5). The specific time indicates that the nations' power to dominate is real and yet is limited by God. They can trample it for forty-two months, but not longer. Precedents come from Daniel, which tells of God's people being oppressed for "a time and [two] times and half a time," which equals three and a half years (Dan 7:25; 12:7). Daniel reinterpreted Jeremiah's prophecy that Jerusalem was to be

oppressed for seventy years after the Babylonian conquest (Jer 25:11; 29:10; Dan 9:2). Daniel extended the prophecy to mean that seventy *weeks* of years would elapse before iniquity was ended. Since a week of years is seven years, the period is 7×70 years, for a total of 490 years. The period concludes when Jerusalem and its sanctuary are dominated by a hostile power, and burnt offering is halted for half a week, which equals three and a half years (Dan 9:24, 27). Other passages vary the length of time. In one passage it lasts for 2,300 mornings and evenings (i.e., 1,150 days), which is less than three and a half years (8:14). In another it is 1,290 days, which could equal three and a half years if one counts forty-two months of thirty days each, plus one intercalated month (12:11). Yet another extends it to 1,335 days, a more protracted period of oppression (12:12; cf. Collins, *Daniel*, 322). Historically, it is approximately the period of the temple's desecration under Antiochus IV Epiphanes (167–164 BCE).

The fluidity in Daniel's calculations is reflected in Revelation, which uses different expressions for the period of three and a half years. The writer can say that "a time and times and half a time" (Rev 12:14) equals 1,260 days (11:3; 12:6), which differs from Daniel's reference to 1,290 days but is equivalent to forty-two months of thirty days each (11:2; 13:5). John also plays on the number by shifting from three and a half *years* of oppression to three and a half *days* during which God's witnesses lie dead before the inhabitants of the world (13:9, 11). Forms of the number three and a half identify a time of oppression and preservation, but the fluid ways in which this period is depicted work against a strict chronological interpretation (Yarbro Collins, *Cosmology*, 67–68; Maier, *Apocalypse*, 157).

COMMENT

The mounting specter of God's final catastrophic judgment upon the world seems to continue into Rev 10, only to be interrupted by a voice from heaven. When the disasters brought by the first six trumpets do not move people to repent (Rev 9:20–21), an angel descends with a voice like thunder, and when seven thunders roar, one might expect this to bring the last, devastating series of punishments on the earth. But a voice tells John not to write down what the seven thunders said (10:4). Instead, he is given a scroll and told to prophesy again, and the visions in the next section reveal the scroll's contents by showing the people of God being afflicted, protected, and bearing prophetic witness (11:1–14). After the death and vindication of two witnesses, an earthquake brings judgment on some, but many others give glory to God; and at the blowing of the seventh trumpet, heavenly voices announce the kingdom of God and his anointed (11:15–18).

The visions in 10:1–11:14 constitute an interlude between the sixth and seventh trumpets, like that between the sixth and seventh seals (7:1–17). As already noted, these interludes create delay in the seemingly inexorable movement toward final judgment

---

On Rev 10:1–11:2, see Bachmann, "Ausmessung"; Bauckham, *Climax*, 243–66; Baynes, "Revelation" and *Heavenly*, 149–62; G. Carey, *Elusive*, 123–25; Carrell, *Jesus*, 131–38; Dalrymple, "Use"; de Villiers, "Lord"; Gieschen, *Angelomorphic*, 256–60; M. Hall, "Hook"; Hirschberg, *Das eschatologische*, 216–23; Horn, "Die sieben"; Kistemaker, "Temple"; Marshall, *Parables*, 163–65; Mazzaferri, *Genre*, 265–96; Perry, *Rhetoric*; Ruiz, "Hearing"; Siew, *War*, 88–107; Stuckenbruck, *Angel*, 229–32.

and interpret the meaning of the delay (§18C). The interlude in Rev 10–11 redefines the question raised by the martyrs—*how long* will God delay in bringing justice—by showing *why* God's final judgment seems to be delayed. Since wrath alone does not bring repentance, God uses other means, which include the witness of the believing community in a world dominated by unbelieving nations (Bauckham, *Theology*, 80–88; Perry, *Rhetoric*, 102). John narrates from a perspective within the visionary world and therefore is not constrained by ordinary limits of time and space. When he sees an angel descend from heaven, it might appear that John is on earth, yet in previous visions he could see prayers offered in heaven, fire fall on earth, and demonic beings rise from the abyss below the earth without any clear change in his location (Rev 8–9). John writes from a cosmic vantage point, rather than a physical space, and he takes part in the action. Although poised to write down what he sees, he remains part of the visionary world, so that he can approach the angel to receive the scroll and then be given a measuring reed.

John's account of receiving the open scroll is his second commissioning in Revelation. The book began when the exalted Jesus told John to send a prophetic message to the seven churches (1:9–20), and now an angel commissions him to prophesy again (*palin*), signaling a continuation of his work (10:11). Both episodes include elements from Dan 10, setting John within the prophetic tradition of Israel (Mazzaferri, *Genre*, 259–96). Yet neither chapter constitutes an initial prophetic call (cf. Isa 6:1–13; Jer 1:4–10; Ezek 1:1–3:11). John seems to have been active in prophetic circles before he was relegated to Patmos (Rev 1:9; 22:9), so the commissioning visions in Rev 1 and 10 do not mark the beginning of his prophesying but give direction to the work he has already begun.

The Angel with the Open Scroll (10:1–7)

John sees an angel coming down from heaven, and his appearance signals a change from the unrelenting disasters that have occurred (10:1). Six angels have blown the first six trumpets, but this angel is uniquely "powerful," and his traits are fitting for a special emissary of God. He is robed in a cloud and a rainbow adorns his head, reminding readers that Christ is expected to come from heaven on the clouds (1:7; 14:14–16) and that a rainbow encircles God's throne (4:3). The angel's sunlike face and fiery feet are reminiscent of the face and feet of the exalted Christ (1:16). In the appearance of this angel, readers can sense the presence of God and Christ, who sent him (Boring).

The angel plays a key role in mediating God's revelation. The opening lines of the book said that the message came from God to Jesus through an angel to John (1:1). The first half of the book follows this pattern. God holds a sealed scroll, and "a powerful angel" asks who is worthy to open it (5:1–2). The Lamb takes the scroll from God and opens its seals so it can be read (5:7–8:1). Now John sees "another powerful angel" with an open scroll (10:2). The angel gives the scroll to John, who eats it so that he can prophesy and reveal its contents (10:8–11). This completes the narrative depiction of the chain of mediation that was outlined in 1:1 (Mazzaferri, *Genre*, 265–79; Bauckham, *Climax*, 243–57; Boring; Boxall; Osborne; Satake).

Readers familiar with the biblical background will find that Revelation both follows and alters traditional patterns. John has just seen a vision at "the great river" Euphrates, and now an angel with a sunlike face and fiery feet appears (Rev 9:14; 10:1). This pattern was set by Daniel, who saw a vision at "the great river" Tigris, where he was met by a messenger with a face like lightning and feet like burnished bronze (Dan 10:2–6). After the angelic messenger told Daniel about the coming conflict of the nations and heavenly powers, someone asked him:

> "How long shall it be until the end of these wonders?" The man clothed in linen . . . *raised his right hand* and his left hand *toward heaven. And I heard him swear by the one who lives forever* that *it would be for a time*, two times, and half a time, and that when the shattering of power of the holy people *comes to an end*, all these things would be accomplished. I heard but could not understand; so I said, "My lord, what shall be the outcome of these things?" He said, "Go your way, Daniel, for the words are to remain secret and *sealed* until the time of the end." (Dan 12:6–9; italics added)

This portion of Dan 12 deals with the question "How long?" which was the question asked by the martyrs in Rev 6:10 and implicitly included in the prayers at the beginning of the trumpet cycle (8:3–5). This question of God's timing and purposes now informs the vision of John's commissioning, which incorporates the elements from Dan 12 noted in italics.

The angel John sees resembles the one in Daniel. A new element is that the angel places his right foot on the sea and left foot on the land as a sign of dominion over the created order (10:2). The angel calls out with a loud voice, which prompts the seven thunders to respond (10:3). Occasionally, voices in heaven give thunderous praises to God (14:2; 19:6), but thunder more often accompanies plagues, which suggests that the thunders' message is ominous (8:5; 11:19; 16:19). Moreover, John has counted as six successive trumpets have sounded, each one bringing a disaster worse than those before. So when six plagues are complete and humanity has refused to repent, readers would expect "seven" thunders to signal the most cataclysmic judgment thus far. Yet this is precisely where the interruption occurs, so judgment is not carried out.

Instead, John is told, "Seal up what the seven thunders said, and do not write it down" (10:4). In Daniel, sealing meant that a message was to remain hidden until the end of time. But in Revelation, sealing up the message of the thunders means that it is not to be written down at all. John reshapes the older motif. By commanding John to "seal" the words of the thunders, the voice creates a contrast with the scroll the Lamb received from God, whose seals were broken so that the scroll's contents could be read and enacted (Bauckham, *Climax*, 260; Smalley). The angel holds the open scroll of God, and it is to be this unsealed scroll rather than the sealed words of thunder that establishes what is to come.

As the thunders fade, the angel raises his hand to swear that God's intentions will be fulfilled (10:5), an action much like that of the angel in Dan 12. An oath is sworn to show that a person is telling the truth in a context in which the truth is disputed or to guarantee that a promise will be kept. In John's vision the underlying issue concerns "the mysterious purpose of God" (10:7). If God is both powerful and just, as the author assumes (1:8; 6:10), then God's purposes should bring in his righteous rule (NOTE on 10:7). But questions have arisen because these purposes seem to be contradicted by the continued presence of evil and injustice, so the martyrs demand to know how long God will delay bringing justice (6:10). A similar question was raised in Dan 12:6–7—the passage that informs John's vision—and it too concerns how long oppression will last (Beale; Giesen; Mounce; Thomas).

In Daniel the angel swears by the living God (Dan 12:7), which the angel in Revelation also does. But John's vision adds that God "created heaven and what is in it, the earth and what is in it, and the sea and what is in it" (Rev 10:6). In the throne room vision, the living God was identified as the Creator, and every creature in heaven, earth, and sea praised his rightful reign (4:11; 5:13). But in the trumpet visions, the difference between creation and destruction was blurred when God's angels unleashed the forces of the Destroyer, bringing suffering to the world (9:1–21). Now, the angelic emissary of the Creator reasserts the character of God's reign by reminding readers that God is the Creator rather than the destroyer of all things.

The angel places one foot on the sea and the other foot on the land, affirming the dominion of the God who sent him (10:5; cf. 14:7). This gesture anticipates the direction that the visions will take when Satan the dragon is thrown down and threatens both sea and land (12:12). Satan will assert dominion by conjuring up a beast from the sea to afflict the saints and oppress the world (13:1–10). Then a beast from the land will promote the ruler cult through coercion and deception (13:11–18). They will work in league with Babylon, which controls and profits from commerce on sea and land (17:1, 18; 18:11–19).

This cosmic conflict reflects the political aspects of the world in which Revelation was written. A basic issue is, "Who is the true Lord of this world?" (Schüssler Fiorenza 58). The beasts and Babylon reflect Roman claims to rule over land and sea (*Pss. Sol.* 2:29). A first-century relief from Aphrodisias in Asia Minor shows the emperor in a posture like that of the angel in Rev 10 (Figure 25). Encircling his head is a billow of cloth, similar to the rainbow around the angel's head in Revelation. At the emperor's right foot is a figure personifying the land, and the fruitful nature of imperial dominion is shown by the cornucopia in the emperor's right hand. At his left foot is a figure personifying the sea, and he shows his providential care over the oceans by grasping the steering oar that the figure extends to him. The sculpture portrays land and sea at the emperor's feet in order to show the world flourishing under imperial rule (R. Smith, "Imperial," 104–6; Friesen, *Imperial*, 94; Friesen, "Myth," 296–97). The angel in John's vision assumes a similar posture, reasserting the prerogatives of God over those who would take God's place.

The angel's posture is consistent with his message, though his words are confusing. The sense of 10:6c–7 can be paraphrased as follows:

The time of waiting will end when the seventh angel blows his trumpet.
That is when the mysterious purpose of God will be complete.
This promise reaffirms what God announced to his servants the prophets.

The angel raises the issue of time (*chronos*, 10:6), which recalls the question asked by the martyrs: How long will God wait before bringing justice against those who shed their blood? (6:10). The initial reply to the martyrs was cryptic, since they were given white robes and told to wait for a short time (*chronos*) until the others who would be killed had finished giving witness (6:11). The angel in Rev 10 confirms that the time of waiting will not continue forever, and he uses the future tense to say that it will end when

Figure 25. The Roman emperor standing on sea and on land. Relief from the imperial temple at Aphrodisias (first century CE). New York University Excavations at Aphrodisias.

the seventh trumpet sounds. At that point in the future, there "will" (*estai*) be no more time of waiting (10:6c).

The angel's oath in 10:6–7 states that the present time of waiting will end with the establishment of God's kingdom at the seventh trumpet; and the seventh trumpet vision will affirm that the kingdom will bring the defeat of the powers that now destroy the earth, along with God's rewarding of the saints and prophets (11:15–18). The crucial question is what happens before the consummation, during the time of waiting. The martyrs under the altar were told that others needed to finish bearing witness before the end would come (6:11), and the angel gives John a scroll that will disclose more about what such witness entails. John receives and consumes the scroll in 10:8–10, then reveals its contents in summary form in 11:3–14. The message concerns two prophets, who symbolize the faithful bearing witness during the interlude before the end. Nothing is said about how long the interlude will last. Readers learn only that the time of waiting continues because the need for witness continues, and that the time will culminate in God's kingdom, where justice will be done.

The angel affirms that this message about the kingdom was the good news that was announced to the prophets, who include Daniel (10:7c). The principal prophetic text informing this vision is Dan 12, as noted above. In that context, an angelic figure told of the coming victory over evil and resurrection of the dead but said these words were to be kept hidden (Dan 12:1–4). He also disclosed that the temple would be defiled and the holy people threatened for "a time, two times, and half a time"—or three and a half years (Dan 12:7; cf. 9:27; 11:31). When these things are finished, the end will arrive. Accordingly, when John receives the scroll, he elaborates Daniel's vision by picturing the worshiping community as a temple threatened by the nations for three and a half years (Rev 11:2). What John adds is that this is the period during which the faithful are called to bear witness (11:3). Later visions will show that the prophetic period of three and a half years is not to be understood in terms of ordinary chronology; in the Apocalypse this period extends from Christ's ascension until his final return to defeat evil at the end of the age (12:6, 12).

John Receives the Scroll (10:8–10)

The angel's oath shifts attention to John's own prophetic calling. The same heavenly voice that prevented John from writing down the message of thunder now directs him to take the open scroll from the angel and eat it (10:8–9), which makes John's commissioning similar to those of Jeremiah (Jer 1:9; 15:6) and especially Ezekiel (Ezek 2:8–3:3), who also consumed God's word. Ezekiel saw God's heavenly throne and four creatures with faces like a lion, an ox, an eagle, and a human being (Ezek 1:4–28). Then God commissioned him to prophesy:

> I looked, and a hand was stretched out to me, and a written *scroll* was in it. He spread it before me; it had *writing on the front and on the back*, and written on it were words of lamentation and mourning and woe . . . He said to me, "Mortal, *eat this scroll* that I give you and fill your stomach with it." Then I ate it; and *in my mouth it was sweet as honey*. He said to me, "Mortal, go to the house of Israel . . . not to many *peoples* of obscure speech and difficult *language*, whose words you cannot understand. Surely, if I sent you to them, they would listen to you." (Ezek 2:9–3:6; italics added)

John includes aspects of Ezekiel's call narrative in his own commissioning story (italics above) but spreads them out over different parts of his book. John told of seeing God's throne, the four creatures, and the scroll written on both sides at the beginning of the seal visions (Rev 4:1–5:1), but only now does he take the scroll and eat it (10:8–9). The action has implications for John's self-understanding.

John identifies himself as the recipient of this message rather than its author. He wants readers to accept his message as a word from God, not one that is merely his own opinion. Early Christians assumed that God could disclose his purposes through prophets (Knight, "Apocalyptic," 487; deSilva, *Seeing*, 120). For them, the question was whether a particular message was a *genuine* word from God, and it was apparently common to test purported prophecies (Aune, *Prophecy*, 217–29; Boring, *Continuing*, 101–7). The congregations John addressed faced questions of whether to accept the teachings of some people who claimed special apostolic or prophetic authority (Rev 2:2, 6, 14, 20), and in this conflicted situation, John encourages a favorable reception of his message by describing the way he received it. In doing this, he locates his experience of receiving the word of God within the tradition of accepted prophecy, like that associated with Ezekiel and Jeremiah (Mazzaferri, *Genre*, 259–96).

By eating the scroll, John takes the message into himself (10:9b–10a), so it becomes part of the prophet's own life and can be conveyed in the prophet's own words (Schüssler Fiorenza, *Book*, 136; Ruiz, "Hearing," 104; G. Carey, *Elusive*, 123). In scenes to come, John initially speaks in the first person when recounting how he was commissioned to prophesy and directed to measure the temple (10:11–11:2), then seamlessly he uses the first person for a divine speaker, who tells about the witnesses (11:3). Other parts of the Apocalypse exhibit similar fluidity as John both differentiates himself from God and Christ and yet speaks directly from God and Christ (e.g., 1:4, 8; 22:8, 16; Boring, "Voice"; Biguzzi, "Chaos"). The tension is never resolved, since John wants readers to receive his message as God's word and yet one that comes through John's words. The authenticity of the message cannot be determined at the outset. If readers can accept it, it will be because they enter John's visionary world and find their perspectives being shaped by its message (L. Thompson, *Book*, 177–79).

John says that the scroll was sweet in his mouth (Rev 10:9c, 10b), which was also true for Ezekiel (Ezek 2:8–3:3), but the message makes his stomach bitter. This change from Ezekiel anticipates the dual character of the message John will bring in the following chapters. His message is sweet in that it concerns the arrival of God's kingdom, but it is bitter in that the accomplishment of God's designs includes the witness and suffering of his people (NOTE on Rev 10:10). The trumpets may have brought plagues on the unbelieving world, making the water bitter so that many died (8:10–11), but people did not repent. Therefore, the faithful experience the bitter taste of suffering as they bear witness.

Ezekiel was commissioned to prophesy to Israel and *not* to the many other peoples, who spoke different languages, even though those other peoples would listen (Ezek 3:4–6). By way of contrast, John is to make the world's many "peoples and nations and languages and kings" the focus of his prophesying (Rev 10:11). This command fits a major theme in Revelation. Previously, John has said that the Lamb redeems people of every tribe, language, people, and nation for life in God's kingdom (5:9–10) (7:9). Yet the visions to come will show these groups allying themselves with the beast (11:9, 18; 13:6; 14:6; 17:15) and Babylon (14:8; 17:15; 18:3, 23), so they are liable to being struck down by Christ himself (19:15). But despite their animosity, it is God's will that all nations worship him (14:6; 15:3–4). Therefore, the gates of New Jerusalem remain open to the nations (21:24, 26), where the leaves of the tree of life offer them healing (22:2).

The same dynamics fit the portrayal of the kings, who are included in John's prophesying (10:11). Many kings oppose God and the Lamb (16:12–14) and consort with Babylon the whore (17:2, 18; 18:3, 9). The most powerful kings are the heads of the beast (17:9) and its ten horns, who join the beast in destroying Babylon (17:12, 16). With boundless hubris these kings attempt to do battle with Christ, only to be destroyed by his word (17:14; 19:18–19). Yet God is the rightful King of the nations (15:3) and Jesus is the true ruler of the earth's kings (1:6; 17:14; 19:16); the kings who recognize this will bring their glory into New Jerusalem (21:24). For nations, peoples, languages, and kings, John's prophetic message warns of the destructive consequences of opposing God, but it extends the promise of life to them by showing what it would mean to join in celebrating the reign of God and his Messiah (11:15; Bauckham, *Climax*, 238–337).

Measuring the Temple (11:1–2)

After John is commanded to prophesy (10:8–11), he is given a reed to measure the temple, altar, and worshipers (11:1). John continues to be a participant in his own vision (Schüssler Fiorenza 74–76; Murphy). The directive to measure the temple can best be understood as an extension of what precedes it, rather than the beginning of a new section. John has been giving an account of his prophetic commissioning, which has drawn on Dan 10–12 and tells of an angelic figure raising his hands to swear by the living God that the time until the end will last for three and a half years. During the three and a half years, the city and holy people will be trampled and the temple will be defiled (Dan 8:11–14; 9:27; 11:31; 12:7). These themes continue to be developed in Rev 11. Having told about an angel raising his hand to swear by the living God that the time will end at the seventh trumpet (Rev 10:1–7), John now turns to the temple, the holy city, and the three-and-a-half-year period during which they are trampled (11:1–2).

John apparently thought that Daniel envisioned only a part of the temple being trampled for three and a half years. John has been drawing on Dan 12:6–7, which dealt with how long oppression would last. That passage is related to an earlier one that asked the same question and told of a foe that "took the regular burnt offering away" and "threw down the place of his sanctuary" (Dan 8:11). This "giving over of the sanctuary and the host to be trampled" was to last for about three and a half years (8:13). John adapts this language by noting that the sanctuary had two parts: the enclosed temple building (*naos*) and the open court (*aulē*) beside it. John equates Daniel's reference to "the place of his sanctuary" with the open court outside the temple. Since burnt offerings were made in the open court, not inside the temple building, John assumes that the open court is the part of the sanctuary that is given to the nations, which trample the city, while the temple and altar within it are preserved. Daniel says that the place is to be "thrown down," but John says the open court is to be left out—or literally "thrown out" (*ekbale*)—of the measuring process, so it is vulnerable to oppression for the three and a half years depicted in Daniel (Bauckham, *Climax*, 267–73; Beale 568–70).

John's account of his commissioning has also drawn on Ezek 2–3, in which the prophet was given a scroll to eat and told to prophesy (Rev 10:8–11). Now John is handed a reed and told to measure the temple (11:1), much as Ezekiel envisioned the sanctuary being measured by a figure holding a reed (Ezek 40:3–8; 41:8; 42:16–20). Although the act of measuring occurs in various sources, the use of a reed (Greek, *kalamos*; Hebrew, *qāneh*) to measure a temple is tied especially to Ezekiel and texts derived from it, including Revelation's New Jerusalem vision (Rev 21:15–16; cf. 4Q554 1 III, 18–19; 5Q15 1 I, 2–4). Where Daniel pictured the temple being trampled, Ezekiel envisioned its restoration. Yet where Ezekiel saw an angel use a reed to measure the court around the temple (Ezek 40:3–8; 41:8; 42:16–20), John is told *not* to measure the outer court, since it is given over to the nations. The result is that Rev 11:1–2 combines aspects of Daniel and Ezekiel in a new way in order to portray a temple that is both threatened and preserved.

John's vision transforms the temple, the altar, and those who worship there into an image for the Christian community (NOTE on 11:1). Revelation has already said that faithful people are to be pillars in the temple (*naos*) of God (3:12), and this idea is now given expanded visual form. Thus far, the scenes of true worship (*proskynein*) have been centered in heaven (4:8–11; 5:8–14; 7:9–12), where an altar stands before God's throne (6:9; 8:3, 5; 9:13; 14:18; 16:7), which is in the celestial temple (14:15; 15:5). The congregations of Jesus' followers are the earthly counterpart. Their community is God's temple on earth, where true worship takes place and the redeemed serve as priests (1:6; 5:10).

The use of temple imagery for the Christian community fostered a sense of distinctive identity in the face of competing religious claims. John's readers lived in Greco-Roman cities that had temples to Artemis, Athena, and other traditional deities, as well as the deified emperors. Cities depicted their temples on coins as a mark of civic identity (Figures 7, 9, 12, 16), and the festivals associated with the temples forged social bonds among the residents (NOTES on 2:1, 8, 12, 18; 3:1, 7, 14; G. Stevenson, *Power*, 37–114). Christians did not have temples in the ordinary sense, and some felt pressure to eat what had been offered to various deities. The messages to the churches directly warned against such religious accommodation (2:14, 20), while the vision of measuring the temple gives readers a positive incentive to maintain their identity as God's true temple on earth.

Revelation regards worship as a major point of contention. At the end of the first six trumpet plagues, the mass of humanity continued to worship (*proskynein*) idols, which were displayed in temples and other places (9:20–21). In visions to come, the conflict intensifies, as the people of earth are lured and coerced into worshiping (*proskynein*) in the cult of the beast (13:4, 8, 12, 15). Yet despite this widespread alienation from God, the Apocalypse shows that true worship (*proskynein*) still occurs in the Christian community (11:1). Through their worship, Christians bear witness to the reign of God among them.

The temple imagery also gives the followers of Jesus a place in Israel's tradition, which held that there was to be only one temple because there was only one God (Philo, *Spec. Laws* 1.67; Josephus, *Ant.* 4.200–1; Josephus, *Ag. Ap.* 2.193). John pictures the Christian community as a single temple in which God is worshiped. Believers may live in various places, but together they constitute one sanctuary. Historically, the Jerusalem temple was destroyed in 70 CE. Some people looked for the restoration of the building, but John does not. Like the temple in this vision, New Jerusalem will be measured with a reed, but John sees no temple in the city (Rev 21:15–17, 22). The worship that now takes place in the temple of the community anticipates what will take place in New Jerusalem, where the only true temple is the unmediated presence of God and the Lamb.

The nations trample the holy city for forty-two months, a time period derived from Daniel (NOTE on 11:2). The way John uses different expressions for this period creates a literary pattern that suggests different perspectives on it. On the one hand, the references to forty-two months identify this as a time of oppression, when the holy city is trampled and the beast makes war on the saints (11:2; 13:5). On the other hand, references to 1,260 days depict it as a time of divine preservation, when the witnesses prophesy to the world and the woman representing God's people is protected in the wilderness (11:3; 12:6). The juxtaposition of these perspectives in 11:2–3 identifies a time in which the nations threaten yet God's witnesses are active. For John's readers, both aspects characterize the time in which they live (Resseguie 50–52).

At present the faithful, or holy city, are trampled (*patein*) by the nations, but in the end the hostile nations are trampled (*patein*) outside the city in the winepress of God's wrath (14:20; 19:15). Readers are now called to identify with the afflicted community that is pictured as "the holy city," yet the final visions of the book hold out the promise of life in New Jerusalem, which is "the holy city" in final form (21:2, 10). The measurements John is to make are partial (11:1–2), but the measurements of New Jerusalem show completeness (21:15–17). The faithful enter that future holy city through resurrection, and the nations there no longer threaten but offer glory to God (21:24, 26).

23. Interlude Continued: The Two Witnesses (11:3–14)

11 ³"I will also allow my two witnesses to prophesy for 1,260 days, wearing sackcloth." ⁴These are the two olive trees and the two lampstands that stand before the Lord of the earth. ⁵If anyone wants to hurt them, fire comes from their mouth and devours their enemies. So if anyone wants to hurt them, they must be killed in this way. ⁶They have the power to close up the sky, so that no rain will fall during the days of their prophesying. They also have power over the waters, to turn them into blood, and to strike the earth with any plague, as often as they wish.

⁷When they have finished their witnessing, the beast that comes up from the abyss will make war on them and conquer them and kill them. ⁸Their dead bodies will lie on the main street of the great city, which spiritually is called Sodom and Egypt. That is also where their Lord was crucified. ⁹And for three and a half days, some from the peoples and tribes and languages and nations will look at their dead bodies, but they will not let their dead bodies be put in a tomb. ¹⁰Those who live on the earth will rejoice over them and celebrate and give gifts to each other, because these two prophets brought such pain to those who live on the earth.

¹¹But after the three and a half days, a spirit of life from God entered them, and they stood on their feet. Great fear came over those who saw them. ¹²Then they heard a loud voice from heaven say to them, "Come up here." And they went up to heaven in a cloud, while their enemies watched them. ¹³At that hour there was a great earthquake, and a tenth of the city fell. Seven thousand people were killed by the earthquake, and the rest were afraid and gave glory to the God of heaven.

¹⁴The second woe has passed. The third woe is coming soon.

NOTES

11:3. *"I will also allow my two witnesses to prophesy.* The witnesses have been understood in several ways. The first is most viable:

1. Representatives of the whole church. The witnesses combine the traits of a number of figures in Israel's history. They are called olive trees, like Zerubbabel the governor and Joshua and the priest, who led the postexilic renewal of Jerusalem (Zech 4:3, 14). They stop the rain from falling for three or three and a half years, as Elijah did (1 Kgs 17:1; 18:1; Luke 4:25; Jas 5:17). Like Moses, they turn water into blood and bring plagues on the earth (Exod 7:19). The fire from their mouths recalls the preaching of Jeremiah (Jer 5:14), while their deaths, resurrection after three and a half days, and exaltation to heaven reflect the story of Jesus (Mark 8:31). John's combining of the characteristics of various figures from Israel's history enhances the witnesses' exemplary quality. It was said of the whole people of Israel, "You are my [God's] witnesses" so that it may be known that "no god was formed [before me], nor shall there be any after me . . . you are my witnesses" (Isa 43:10–12; cf. 44:8). The witnesses are also called lampstands, an image that Revelation used for the readers' congregations (Rev 1:20), which reinforces the interpretation of the witnesses representing the Christian community (Aune; Beale; Blount; Giesen; Mounce; Resseguie; Smalley; Bauckham, *Climax*, 273; Perry, *Rhetoric*, 87–88; Tavo, *Woman*, 220–22).
2. Representatives of a part of the church. The opening chapter identified all seven churches as lampstands, but here, only two lampstands are mentioned. Some interpreters take this to indicate a reduction from the whole church to a part of the church. The two witnesses could be the congregations that are persecuted and yet faithful at Smyrna and Philadelphia (Witherington). However, the use of two figures is probably not a reduction from seven; rather, it comes from the principle that the agreement of two witnesses indicates valid testimony (Deut 17:6; 19:15; Matt 18:16; 2 Cor 13:1; 1 Tim 5:19). Alternatively, the two figures could represent only the martyrs (Caird; Reddish). Yet witness was not limited to those who died violently; it was a task for the whole church. Finally, some interpreters suggest that the two figures signify those Christians who have the special gift of prophecy (Rev 10:11; cf. 1 Cor 12:10, 28; Boxall; Murphy). But again, prophecy is linked to witness, which is broader.
3. Two individuals. Ancient and medieval interpreters usually identified the witnesses as Enoch and Elijah because it was said that both Enoch (Gen 5:24; Sir 44:16; Heb 11:5) and Elijah (2 Kgs 2:11; Sir 48:9–10) were taken directly to heaven and remained alive so that they could return in the future (see the history of interpretation in §18A). The idea of their return at the close of the age could predate Revelation (*1 En.* 90:31), but most of the evidence is from later periods (*Apoc. Pet.* 2; *Apoc. El.* 4:7; *Gos. Nic.* 25). It is not clear that John expected readers to know this tradition (Black, "'Two'"; Bauckham, "Martyrdom").

Other interpreters identify the witnesses as Moses and Elijah because the witnesses turn water into blood and cause drought, as these two prophets did. Tradition said that Elijah would return before the day of wrath at the end of the age (2 Kgs 2:11; Mal 3:4–5; Sir 48:9–10; *Sib. Or.* 2:187–89). Moses was generally thought to have died (Deut 34:5), but God was to send another prophet like him, and traditions about Moses' mysterious disappearance at the end of his career might have suggested that he remained alive (Deut 18:18; Josephus, *Ant.* 3.96; 4.326; Philo, Sacr. 8). According to the gospels, Moses appeared with Elijah at Christ's transfiguration (Mark 9:4 par.), and a rabbinic tradition said that Moses and Elijah would return together (*Deut. Rab.* 3.17; Charles; LaHaye; Thomas; Walvoord; Osborne). A problem with this approach is that Rev 11 ascribes the traits of both prophets to both witnesses, so there is no reason to think that one is Elijah and the other is Moses. Also, it is unlikely that the beast would "make war" on two individuals (Rev 11:7), since war is carried out on a larger scale (9:7, 9; 12:7; 16:14; 19:19; 20:8) against the saints collectively (12:17; 13:7; Giblin, "Revelation," 441–43).

"for 1,260 days. The period of 1,260 days is the same as forty-two months, using a round number of thirty days per month. It equals three and a half years, a period of oppression in Daniel (NOTE on Rev 11:2). In the history of interpretation this number has been taken both literally and figuratively (see §18A). In Revelation's visionary world the three and a half years signify the time from Christ's ascension and Satan's expulsion from heaven to Christ's return to defeat evil at the end of the age.

wearing sackcloth." Sackcloth was a coarse fabric often made of dark goat hair. Wearing it showed grief over a disaster that had occurred or was impending, such as the conquest of a city (Isa 3:24; 32:11; Jer 6:26). It could express repentance and grief over sin and might be accompanied by prayers of confession and pleas that God would turn from judgment (Jonah 3:5–8; Matt 11:21; *Jos. As.* 10:14–15). Prophets often wore coarse garments (Zech 13:4; Mark 1:6) but donned sackcloth to show grief over the sins of the people and coming disasters (Isa 20:2; *Mart. Isa.* 2:10). In the Greco-Roman world one might see a penitent, who "sits outside in sackcloth, girt with filthy rags, and frequently he rolls naked in mire and publicly confesses some sins" (Plutarch, *Mor.* 168d; cf. Menander, frg. 544).

11:4. *These are the two olive trees and the two lampstands that stand before the Lord of the earth.* Most translators assume that the heavenly voice stops speaking after mentioning "my" two witnesses in the previous line and include quotation marks after 11:3 (as here), since the interpretation that begins at 11:4 comes from John himself.

The imagery recalls Zech 4:2–3, which pictures a single lampstand with seven lamps and two olive trees beside it. The olive trees are "the sons of oil, who stand by the Lord of the whole earth" (4:14) and represent Zerubbabel and Joshua, the governor and priest who led the postexilic Jerusalem community. Many interpreters take "sons of oil" in Zech 4:14 to mean that they are "anointed ones," that is, royal and priestly leaders of the people (ESV, NET, NIV, NRSV). If this is so, then Revelation's olive tree imagery could emphasize that the Christian community has both a royal and priestly character (Rev 1:5; 5:10; Boring; Giesen; Harrington; Murphy). Anointing is not clear in Zechariah, however, in which the sons of oil supply oil for the lamp, suggesting that they provide for the temple (Meyers and Meyers, *Haggai*, 276). Olive tree imagery can also suggest a firm trust in God (Ps 52:8). In the Greco-Roman world olive trees in sanctuaries and by altars were considered witnesses to divine power (Pausanias, *Descr.* 1.27.2; 1.42.7; 5.15.3). The olive trees in Revelation attest the power of the God of Israel.

11:5. *If anyone wants to hurt them, fire comes from their mouth and devours their enemies.* Fire from the prophets' mouths is a vivid metaphor for the word of God. God said to Jeremiah, "I am now making my words in your mouth a fire, and this people wood, and the fire shall devour them" (Jer 5:14). Similarly, Elijah's word was like a burning torch (Sir 48:1), and the Messiah could be pictured breathing fire to signify his power to confront people with the law (*4 Ezra* 13:10, 37–38). The same sense of confrontational speaking characterizes the two witnesses. Elsewhere, the speech of Jesus is depicted as a two-edged sword from his mouth (1:16; 2:16; 19:15, 21), whereas the mouths of the dragon, beast, and false prophet emit spirits like frogs, which symbolize the deceptive words that lure people into war against God (16:13). Revelation sees a war of words, using metaphors to depict the speech of Christ, his witnesses, and their adversaries.

So if anyone wants to hurt them, they must be killed in this way. John assumes a kind of symmetry in judgment: Those who want to hurt the witnesses suffer hurt themselves (cf. Rev 16:6; Osborne). The witnesses' power is defensive, allowing them to prophesy, and it is limited in scope since they are killed when their work is complete (11:7). More importantly, the fire from their mouths signifies speech. To say that their adversaries "must be killed *in this way*" (11:5) means that they are overcome by the prophets' speech, just as Jesus will slay the beast and its allies with his word, symbolized by the sword from his mouth (2:16; 19:15, 21).

11:6. *They have the power to close up the sky, so that no rain will fall throughout the days of their prophesying.* Their prophesying is like that of Elijah, who brought a drought on the land of Israel for three years (1 Kgs 17:1; 18:1). According to later tradition, no rain fell for three and a half years, which is the length of time the two witnesses in Revelation prophesy (Luke 4:25; Jas 5:17). The drought is a sign of divine judgment against the world's idolatry and sin (Rev 9:20–21). The proper response to a drought is to turn to God (Deut 11:16–17; 1 Kgs 8:35; 2 Chr 7:13; Jer 3:3; 14:2–7; Amos 4:7–8; 1Q22 II, 10). Similarly, those facing drought in a Greco-Roman context were to make amends with the gods (Pausanias, *Descr.* 1.24.3; 1.44.9; 2.29.7; Tacitus, *Hist.* 4.26; Julius Obsequens, *Prod.* 6).

They also have power over the waters, to turn them into blood. The action recalls the way Moses changed the water in Egypt, demonstrating divine authority in the face of Pharaoh's obstinacy (Exod 4:1, 9; 7:14–19). Greco-Roman readers believed that if a river or spring turned to blood, it was a sign of divine anger and coming disaster (Cicero, *Div.* 1.43.98; Livy, *Rom. Hist.* 22.1.10; Julius Obsequens, *Prod.* 25). The implication was that repentance was needed.

and to strike the earth with any plague, as often as they wish. Plagues recall how Moses struck the Egyptians with various plagues—of frogs, gnats, flies, cattle disease, boils, hail, locusts, darkness, and the deaths of the firstborn (Exod 7–11; 1 Sam 4:8). Plagues in Revelation also convey divine wrath (Rev 15:1). The proper response is to repent, although the ungodly refuse to do so (9:18–21; 16:9; Giesen). On the exodus plagues and Revelation, see §18E.

11:7. *When they have finished their witnessing, the beast that comes up from the abyss.* The beast is introduced here without explanation. Some interpreters propose that John drew on an established tradition concerning a final mythic adversary (Bousset, *Antichrist*), but Jewish and early Christian writings envision several types of eschatological opponents, such as false prophets and messiahs, a tyrant, and the evil Belial (Peerbolte, *Antecedents*). A more likely reason for this introduction is a literary one: John introduces the beast briefly so that he can elaborate in the visions that follow.

will make war on them and conquer them and kill them. According to tradition, Israel's prophets were persecuted and slain (2 Chr 36:15–16; Neh 9:26; Matt 5:11–12; 23:37; Luke 11:50–51; 13:34; Acts 7:52; 1 Thess 2:15; *Liv. Pro.* 1:1; 2:1; Aune, *Prophecy*, 157–59). Such prophets were sometimes called witnesses, as they are in Revelation: "I shall send to them witnesses so that I might witness to them, but they will not hear. And they will even kill the witnesses" (*Jub.* 1:12). The fate of the two witnesses in Revelation fits this pattern. The beast conquers (*nikan*) them through violence (Rev 13:7), whereas the Lamb and his followers "conquer" by remaining faithful to the point of death (Notes on 2:7; 5:5–6). From the perspective of the world, the deaths of the witnesses are the beast's victory, since the beast seems to prevail over its opponents (11:7). But from the perspective of heaven, the witnesses' deaths are their way of winning victory over the beast, for their refusal to capitulate is a triumph for truth and fidelity (12:11).

11:8. *Their dead bodies will lie on the main street.* After people were executed or died in hostile circumstances, the usual practice was for their opponents to carry the bodies out of the city (Tob 1:17–18; Philo, *Mos.* 1.39; Acts 14:19). During a war, corpses were removed from cities because decaying bodies spread disease (Appian, *Hist. rom.* 12.11.76). In some cases, however, the victors in war allowed unburied bodies to decay inside the city or along roads, which publicly humiliated the victims (Josephus, *J.W.* 4.317, 380–82). This also emphasized the victor's power to rule and warned against further challenges. The "main street" (*plateia*) probably refers to the central thoroughfare in ancient cities. Sometimes a large street linked different parts of a city. When a city was well-planned, a main street ran through the center and often was connected to the agora, or forum (Note on Rev 21:21). The degradation and death of the two witnesses "on the main street of the great city" on earth also contrasts with the glory that John ascribes to the main "street of the city" in New Jerusalem, where God honors the faithful and gives them life (Rev 21:21; 22:1–5).

of the great city. Revelation consistently identifies "the great city" as Babylon, which was filled with the blood of witnesses and prophets (17:18; 18:10, 16, 18, 21; cf. 17:6; 18:20, 24). Since Babylon has traits of imperial Rome in Revelation, on one level the great city symbolizes Roman authority. It was within Rome's empire that Jesus was crucified and Christians were persecuted (Schüssler Fiorenza; Smalley; Marshall, *Parables*, 171). The "great city" in Rev 11:8 and the "great city" of Babylon (17:18) have a representative significance (Caird; Mounce); that is, the traits of the great city encompass those of Sodom, Egypt, and Jerusalem, along with Babylon/Rome. Its residents include the inhabitants of the whole world—all the peoples, tribes, languages, and nations who oppose God's reign (11:8–10; Minear, "Ontology"; Giblin; Osborne). The great city has sometimes been identified with Jerusalem (Jer 22:8; *Sib. Or.* 5:154, 226), since Jesus was crucified there (Rev 11:8c; Aune; Charles; Ford; Lupieri; Thomas), but given the connections to Babylon/Rome in later visions (Rev 17–18) and to many nations here (11:9), the great city represents the larger empire of which Jerusalem is a part.

which spiritually is called Sodom and Egypt. The nature of the place where the witnesses are killed is discerned "spiritually," that is, by means of the Spirit (Bauckham, *Climax*, 168–69). Sodom was remembered for its violent and degrading ways. When visitors arrived at the city, the inhabitants sought to rape rather than care for them, and as a result the city was destroyed by fire from heaven (Gen 19:1–25). The prophets used the analogy of Sodom when indicting sins such as violence and injustice (Isa 1:9–10), immorality and deception (Jer 23:14), arrogance, neglect of the poor, and religious infidelity (Ezek 16:46–50). The city's wealth was seen as a factor in its pride and brutality (Philo, *Abr.* 227–28; Josephus, *Ant.* 1.170–206), and it was infamous for immorality (*T. Levi* 14:6; *T. Naph.* 4:1; *T. Benj.* 9:1). These same traits appear in Revelation's vision of Babylon/Rome (Rev 17–18). Those who followed the ways of Sodom were warned that they too would fall under divine judgment (Amos 4:11; Zeph 2:9; Matt 10:15; 11:24; Jude 7; 2 Pet 2:6; *Jub.* 13:17; *L.A.B.* 8:2), and Babylon the great meets a fiery end (Rev 17:16; 18:2, 9, 20).

Egypt's reputation had positive aspects, but in Revelation the connotations are negative. It was the place where Israel was enslaved (Exod 1:8–14; 2:23; Ezek 20:7; Mic 6:4) and where the newborn in Israel were to be killed (Exod 1:16). Egypt was the house of slavery (20:2) and the iron furnace (Deut 4:20; Jer 11:4) from which God delivered Israel. It was known for idolatry and aspirations to conquer, and the prophets warned Egypt of God's judgment (Isa 19:1–15; Ezek 29:1–21; cf. *Sib. Or.* 3:314–18, 596–97; 5:52–93, 179–99; 2 Esd 15:11–12). Such oppression is said to characterize Babylon/Rome (Rev 17:18; 18:20, 24).

That is also where their Lord was crucified. Historically, Jerusalem was the site of Jesus' crucifixion (Acts 10:39; cf. Tacitus, *Ann.* 15.44), and his death was linked to the tradition about prophets being killed in Jerusalem (Matt 23:37; Luke 13:33–34; Acts 7:52; 1 Thess 2:15; cf. *Liv. Pro.* 1:1; 23:1). For the two prophetic witnesses to be killed in a place with traits of Jerusalem fits this pattern. Only here does Revelation specifically mention the manner of Jesus' death. Crucifixion was physically cruel and painful and also degrading, as victims died publicly upon the "tree of shame" (Cicero, *Rab. Perd.* 4.13; cf. Mark 15:29–32 par.; Heb 12:2; Hengel, *Crucifixion*). Similarly, the witnesses are subjected to public disgrace in John's vision.

11:9. *And for three and a half days, some from the peoples and tribes and languages and nations will look at their dead bodies.* Variations of this list appear a number of times in Revelation (NOTE on Rev 5:9). In 10:11 John was told to prophesy concerning most of these groups, though his commission also involved kings. On the one hand, these groups can be swayed by those opposed to God, such as the beast and Babylon (13:7; 17:15). On the other hand, people from all these groups are called to worship God (14:6), and the Lamb can redeem them (5:9; 7:9). Here, these groups are hostile to the witnesses, but later, many will glorify God, which is God's intent (11:13; cf. 15:3–4; 21:24). On the three and a half days, see the NOTE on 11:11.

but they will not let their dead bodies be put in a tomb. John's language is reminiscent of Psalm 79, which lamented that when the nations defiled the temple and destroyed Jerusalem, they gave "the bodies of your servants to the birds of the air" and "there was no one to bury them" (Ps 79:2, 3; cf. 1 Macc 7:16–18; 4Q176 1–2 I, 1–4). The book of Jeremiah said that those who trusted false prophets should be killed and thrown into the streets of Jerusalem with no one to bury them (Jer 14:16), but in Revelation the true prophets meet this fate. It was said that no grave should be dug for those who rejoice in the suffering of the righteous (*1 En.* 98:13–14), but in Revelation the opposite occurs, for the wicked rejoice and the righteous have no grave. Only at the end is the injustice overcome when the witnesses are vindicated by resurrection.

11:10. *Those who live on the earth will rejoice over them.* Society's gloating over the deaths of God's witnesses is noted here and in later accounts of the Christian martyrs. At Lyons in the second century it was said that the bodies were thrown out and treated with contempt for six days as guards kept anyone from burying them: "Some raged and gnashed their teeth at the remains, seeking some further vengeance from them, others laughed and jeered, glorifying their idols and ascribing to them the punishment of the

Christians." Others mocked, "Where is their god and what good to them was their worship, which they preferred beyond their lives?" (Eusebius, *Hist. eccl.* 5.1.57–61).

and celebrate and give gifts to each other, because these two prophets brought such pain to those who live on the earth. This gift exchange is reminiscent of the Roman Saturnalia festival, which was celebrated for seven days beginning on December 17. Both slaves and free people joined in drinking wine, feasting, and playing games. Wealthier people gave gifts of furniture, clothing, money boxes of wood or ivory, dice, combs, writing tablets, books, baskets, jugs, and cups. Poorer people made presents of wax candles and clay figurines (Martial, *Epigrams* 14; Lucian, *Sat.* 14; Suetonius, *Aug.* 75; Macrobius, *Saturnalia* 1.11.49). During Domitian's reign, one writer referred to "the glad festival of our merry Caesar and the banquet's drunken revel" and hoped that as long as Rome stood, the festival would continue (Statius, *Silv.* 1.6.7–8, 101–2). In Revelation, however, the celebration is interrupted at its midpoint, after three and a half days, when the witnesses are raised and an earthquake shakes the city where the festival is taking place (Rev 11:11–13). Here, the great city rejoices when the beast slaughters the prophets, but later, the prophets will rejoice when the beast destroys the great city itself (18:20).

Some interpreters see an ironic comparison to the Jewish festival of Purim. That festival celebrated a Jewish victory over non-Jewish opponents (Esth 9:19), whereas the vision of the witnesses shows Gentiles celebrating the deaths of witnesses from Israel's tradition (Bauckham, *Climax*, 281–82; Keener). The stronger connections, however, are to the Saturnalia, since early readers presumably would picture the non-Jewish world celebrating in a non-Jewish way (Paschke, "Die *damnatio*," 569).

11:11. *But after the three and a half days*. This detail fits the theme of the "time, [two] times, and half a time" of oppression (Dan 7:25; Rev 12:14). Usually, the three and a half "times" are taken as three and a half years (forty-two months, or 1,260 days; see 11:2–3), but here they become three and a half days. This suggests that the three and a half days the witnesses lie dead is analogous to the three and a half years that the beast oppresses the saints (13:5). Both are periods of apparent victory for hostile forces (Yarbro Collins, *Cosmology*, 69).

The time period also links the story of the two witnesses to Jesus, "the faithful witness" (1:5). The two witnesses are killed in the world where Jesus was crucified, and they are raised after three and a half days, as Jesus was raised "after three days" (Matt 27:63; Mark 8:31; 9:31; 10:43) or "on the third day" (Matt 16:21; 1 Cor 15:4). Just as Elijah's original three years of drought is extended to three and a half in tradition, the three days before Jesus' resurrection is extended to three and a half (1 Kgs 18:1; Luke 4:25; Jas 5:17).

a spirit of life from God entered into them, and they stood on their feet. John uses a biblical idiom that recalls the way God formed human beings and breathed the breath, or spirit, of life into them at creation (Gen 2:7; Wis 15:11). The same was true of resurrection. Ezekiel was to prophesy to a valley filled with dry bones; "and the spirit came into them, and they lived, and stood on their feet," indicating a complete return to life (Ezek 37:10; cf. 2 Kgs 13:21). In Ezekiel the vision of the spirit enlivening the bones was a collective image for Israel's restoration, and this idea fits the story of the witnesses, who represent the entire community of faith. Although many translations say that the "breath" of life entered them (ESV, NET, NIV, NRSV), "spirit" is used here because the vision also recalls Zech 4:6, where God's spirit is mentioned (see COMMENT). The way the spirit of life enters the bodies means that this is a resurrection, not a release of the soul to heaven.

Great fear came over those who saw them. The witnesses do not ascend immediately to heaven but are visibly raised to life on earth as Jesus was (1 Cor 15:3–8; Matt 28:17; Luke 24:15; John 20:11–28; Acts 1:3; *Barn.* 15:9). The difference is that according to Christian tradition Jesus was seen only by his followers, who might have been afraid because they thought he was a ghost (Luke 24:36–43); but in Revelation the witnesses are seen by their enemies, who have reason to fear because by opposing the witnesses they oppose God and face divine judgment (Rev 18:10, 15; Berger, *Auferstehung*, 24; Smalley).

11:12. *Then they heard a loud voice from heaven say to them, "Come up here."* An unnamed voice could belong to God or another heavenly being (Note on 10:4), but here it could be the voice of Christ, who told John to "come up here" in 4:1. The resurrection hope is pictured as the faithful being restored to life and then caught up in the clouds to meet the returning Jesus (1 Thess 4:16–17). Since the witnesses in Revelation signify the Christian community, John's description of the scene resembles the Pauline tradition in some respects. Yet it seems unlikely that there is a direct connection, since Rev 11:11–12 tells of the witnesses' resurrection and ascension without mentioning the return of Christ, which is central in the Pauline passage.

And they went up to heaven in a cloud, while their enemies watched them. The cloud fits the pattern of divine agency, just as a cloud cloaks God's angel and carries the returning Son of Man (1:7; 10:1; 14:14). Early Christian tradition assumed that Jesus' resurrection was followed by his ascension to God in heaven. Often, the ascension was presupposed rather than described. For example, Jesus' resurrection was linked to Ps 110:1: "The Lord says to my lord, 'Sit at my right hand until I make your enemies your footstool.'" The assumption was that the risen Jesus also sat at God's right hand (Mark 12:36 par.; Acts 2:34–35; 1 Cor 15:25; Heb 1:3, 13; cf. Rom 1:3–4; 8:34; Eph 1:20–21; Heb 8:1). Some writers speak generally of the risen Jesus going through the heavenly regions (Eph 4:8–10; 1 Pet 3:22; Heb 4:14; *Barn.* 15:9). Revelation's vision of the woman and dragon pictures the messianic child being taken to God's heavenly throne without giving the details of the process (Rev 12:5). Luke describes Jesus' ascension on the clouds as a visible event distinct from the resurrection (Acts 1:9–10; cf. Luke 24:50–53). Revelation 11 presupposes a similar tradition.

The story of the witnesses follows that of Jesus but differs from those of other ancient figures. First, it was said that Enoch and Elijah were taken to heaven without dying (Gen 5:25; 2 Kgs 2:11). Later tradition said the same of Ezra and Baruch (*4 Ezra* 14:9; *2 Bar.* 76:5; Stone, *Fourth*, 172). It was also said that Moses was engulfed in a cloud at the end of his life, which could suggest that he was taken to God (Josephus, *Ant.* 4.326). By way of contrast, the witnesses in Rev 11 die and are raised before being taken to heaven. Second, some Jewish and Christian writers assumed that martyrs' souls went directly to heavenly glory (4 Macc 17:5; 18:23; Josephus, *J.W.* 2.154–55; *1 Clem.* 5:4, 7). This pattern lacks a place for the resurrection appearances of the witnesses, and it distinguishes mortal bodies from immortal souls in a way that Rev 11 does not: The witnesses died, were visibly raised to life, and then were taken to heaven in bodily form. Third, there were accounts of the dead being visibly raised to life but not taken to heaven (1 Kgs 17:17–24; cf. 2 Kgs 4:32–35; Matt 27:52–53; Luke 7:11–15; John 11:43–44). Such cases, however, are temporary resuscitations rather than resurrections to deathless life, as in the case of the witnesses. The story of the witnesses presupposes that Jesus' resurrection is the basis for the hope that his followers will be raised as he was.

11:13. *At that hour there was a great earthquake, and a tenth of the city fell.* Several earthquakes in Revelation portend judgment (Rev 6:12; 8:5), and the last makes the cities of the nations fall (16:18). The earthquake in 11:13 is a partial judgment since only a tenth of the city falls. Usually, "a tenth" identifies the limited number who survive judgment (Isa 6:13; Amos 5:3; *Jub.* 10:9), but here it refers to the limited number who suffer it; nine-tenths survive.

Seven thousand people were killed by the earthquake. Some interpreters have tried to identify the city in John's vision by using the seven thousand killed to calculate its size: If seven thousand people constitute a tenth of the city, then the total population would be seventy thousand, which would be closer to the size of ancient Jerusalem than ancient Rome (Aune; Beale; Charles; Beagley, "*Sitz,*" 68). But the way the vision shifts from the holy city (11:2) to the great city where the nations and inhabitants of the earth live (11:8–10) shows that it is unwise to press such calculations.

and the rest were afraid and gave glory to the God of heaven. Referring to "the God of heaven" (Neh 1:4; Ps 136:26; Dan 2:18; *T. Mos.* 2:4) is fitting because the witnesses are called up to heaven where God is enthroned. Some interpreters argue that the people show fear and not conversion. Reasons for this are that later visions show the nations repeatedly opposing God (Rev 11:18; 16:9, 11, 21) and show that fear can arise from the prospect of being harmed (18:10, 15; Giesen; Rowland). But others more plausibly point out that fear can include reverence for God and can indicate conversion (11:18; 19:5; Dan 4:34 LXX; Acts 13:48). Construing the response in this way conveys the hope that the nations will worship and glorify God (Rev 14:6–7; 15:3–4; 21:26; Aune; Caird; Prigent; Roloff; Schüssler Fiorenza; Bauckham, *Climax,* 278; Berger, *Auferstehung,* 35; Pattemore, *People,* 161–64; Tavo, *Woman,* 214).

11:14. *The second woe has passed.* After the first four trumpets sounded, an eagle announced that three woes would strike the people of earth (Rev 8:13). The first was completed by the fifth trumpet (9:12). The second woe presumably begins at the sixth trumpet, and some interpreters think it includes only the plague in 9:13–21 (Beale; Murphy). John, however, refrains from saying that this woe is completed until the two witnesses have been killed, raised, and exalted to heaven (11:14), which suggests that John's prophetic commission and the visions of the faithful being afflicted in Rev 10–11 must be part of the woe (Giblin; Prigent). The woe includes both the plagues and the preaching of the witnesses against the ungodly.

The third woe is coming soon. Readers may expect the third woe to come at the seventh trumpet, but instead of calamity, the heavenly chorus announces the kingdom of God. Since John does not tell readers when the third woe is completed, various interpretations have been offered. Some identify it with the woe proclaimed when Satan is thrown down to earth (12:12; Bousset; Sweet; Resseguie 164), or the plagues in Rev 16 (Mounce), or the woes over the fall of Babylon (18:10, 16, 19; Aune 2:524; Maier, *Apocalypse,* 101). But given the pattern of connecting the three woes to the last three trumpets, it seems best to identify the final woe with the seventh trumpet, since the coming of God's kingdom does bring woe to those who destroy the earth (Rev 11:15–18). The seventh trumpet outlines events in the second half of Revelation, including the defeat of earth's destroyers, the giving of judgment, and the rewarding of the faithful (Beale; Murphy; Prigent).

COMMENT

The story of the two witnesses is part of the interlude between the sixth and seventh trumpets. The first six trumpets unleashed plagues on earth, sea, and sky, and fiendish hordes brought pain and death to many. But despite the terrors, "the rest" (*hoi loipoi*) refused to repent (9:20–21), so the movement toward final judgment was interrupted. John was given a scroll to eat and commissioned to prophesy again about many peoples, nations, languages, and kings (10:8–11), and Rev 11 reveals the contents of the scroll (Charles; Giesen; Mounce; Prigent; Smalley). Thus far, attention has focused on the worshiping community, which was pictured as the temple besieged by the nations (11:1–2). Now, the community is represented by the two witnesses, who prophesy, are slain, and are treated with contempt by peoples, tribes, languages, and nations (11:9). Yet when God's power to give life is revealed by raising the witnesses and judgment falls in more moderate form, the writer makes a literary connection by repeating an earlier expression and noting that "the rest" (*hoi loipoi*) do what they have not done before: They give glory to God, which is what God desires (11:13).

The vision of the two witnesses (*martyres*) shows that the witness of the Christian community has an integral place in God's designs for the world. Their story is part of Revelation's response to the question raised by those under the altar, who were slain for their witness (*martyria*; 6:9). They demanded to know how long God would delay before bringing justice against the people of earth, who had shed their blood, but they were told to rest for a while until others had finished their work (6:10–11). Then, as prayers continue to rise from the altar, the trumpet visions redefine the issue (8:3–5). Instead of revealing *how long* the delay will last, the visions show *why* it continues. The trumpet plagues reveal that if divine justice is reduced to retribution, then nothing changes. People persist in false worship and violence (9:20–21). That is why a delay has been created—so that witnesses can continue calling the world to repentance (10:1–11).

Personifying the community of faith as two prophetic witnesses shows readers their vocation during this time before the end. This story is something like a parable. The narrative uses figurative language, yet it is not an allegory in which each detail has a distinct symbolic meaning. Each part contributes to the whole (Bauckham, *Climax*, 273–74; Barr, *Tales*, 91–92). To gain a sense of the passage, it can be helpful to consider its narrative features.

Characterization of the two witnesses is done by combining the traits of several biblical characters into a single picture. The witnesses are called olive trees, recalling the description of Zerubbabel the governor and Joshua the priest, who led the postexilic

---

On Rev 11:3–14, see Bauckham, *Climax*, 266–83; Bauckham, *Theology*, 83–88, and "Martyrdom"; K. Berger, *Auferstehung*, 9–149; Black, "'Two'"; de Villiers, "Lord"; Frenschkowski, "Entrückung"; Giblin, "Revelation"; Hirschberg, *Das eschatologische*, 216–23; Jauhiainen, *Use*, 89–93; Minear, "Ontology"; Paschke, "Die *dammnatio*"; Pattemore, *People*, 161–64; Peerbolte, *Antecedents*, 121–28; Perry, *Rhetoric*, 79–105, 224–41; Petersen, *Preaching*, 257–65; Siew, *War*, 103–22; G. Stevenson, *Power*, 257–65; Tavo, *Woman*, 197–223.

renewal of Jerusalem (Zech 4:3, 14). Like the prophet Jeremiah, the words of the witnesses are a fire that devours their foes (Jer 5:14). They can stop the rain from falling for three or three and a half years, as Elijah did (1 Kgs 17:1; Luke 4:25; Jas 5:17), and like Moses they can turn water into blood and bring plagues on the earth (Exod 7:19). Yet in the end they die, are resurrected after three and a half days, and exalted to heaven in a way that follows the story of Jesus (Mark 8:31). The traits of the two prophets form a collage, giving a composite picture of God's people in their vocation as witnesses. The author uses a similar form of composite characterization for the beast and Babylon in later chapters. The technique encourages readers to see the conflict between the people of God and the forces of evil—which occurs at many times and places—as part of one great story (Minear, "Ontology").

The setting of the story is cosmic rather than local. The witnesses' work affects the heavens, the earth, and the water, while the beast that opposes them rises from the demonic realm of the underworld (Rev 11:6–7; cf. 9:1, 11). The witnesses' bodies lie in the street of "the great city," an expression used for the oppressive city known as Babylon, which has the traits of Rome and dominates the whole earth (16:19; 17:18; 18:10, 16, 18, 19, 21). This same great city is called Sodom, which was remembered for its sinfulness, and is also like Egypt, where Israel was enslaved (NOTES on 11:8). Finally, the great city is where Jesus was crucified (11:8). This detail, however, does not reduce the scale of the great city to the site of Jerusalem, where the crucifixion took place; rather, it assumes that the site of the crucifixion is within the realm of Babylon/Rome. Like Jesus, the witnesses are slain within an empire that sheds the blood of the prophets, saints, and witnesses (17:6; 18:24). The great city's population encompasses "those who live on earth" (11:10), who come from the world's many peoples, tribes, languages, and nations (11:9). The setting is the Roman imperial world, which in turn represents the world alienated from God.

The plot has three parts. In scene one, the witnesses prophesy with remarkable power and are protected from their foes (11:3–6). In scene two, readers find that despite the prophets' power, the beast slays them, and their bodies lie unburied in the street of the great city while their foes rejoice (11:7–10). Then in scene three, the witnesses are raised and taken to heaven, judgment falls on earth, and many come to glorify God (11:11–13). The narrative does not outline a series of coming events, as if to say that God will protect the church for a time, allow it to be slaughtered, and then bring the world to repentance after the Christian community has been resurrected. Instead, the three scenes must be taken parabolically as a whole and the message brought to bear on the issue that lies before the audience.

This issue concerns the nations. Since John is prophesying "about many peoples and nations and languages and kings," the readers are to ask what the story says about these groups (10:11). In the first scene God's witnesses wear sackcloth as a visible call for repentance, which is what God desires (11:3). Initially, they replicate the ferocity of the previous trumpet plagues, which brought fire from heaven, turned water into blood, and inflicted pain (*basanizein*) on the people of earth. The same occurs through the witnesses' words and actions (8:7–12; 9:5; 11:4–6, 10). Then the second scene shows that despite the witnesses' power and plagues, nothing changes. The world remains hostile, as it did after the first six trumpet plagues (9:20–21; 11:9–10). Change comes in the third scene, where the witnesses participate in the story of Jesus, sharing in a death and resurrection like his. What moves the world to glorify God is not the plagues; rather, it is God's measured judgment and the manifestation of his power to overcome death with life (11:11–12; Bauckham, *Climax*, 280–82; Tavo, *Woman*, 216).

This vision introduces themes that unfold in the second part of the book. The beast appears briefly to persecute the faithful in 11:7 but becomes a major figure in the chapters to come (13:1–18; 17:1–18; 19:11–21). The witnesses are slain in "the great city," which anticipates the vision of Babylon, the city that slaughters the witnesses to Jesus (17:5–6). The three-and-a-half-year period of affliction in 11:2–3 is developed in scenes of the woman fleeing from the dragon and the world being oppressed by the beast (12:6; 13:4–7). The resurrection of the witnesses in 11:11–12 foreshadows the resurrection of all the faithful (20:4–6, 11–15; 21:1–4). In short, the message John receives in his commissioning vision (10:1–11:2) is revealed in summary form in the vision of the witnesses (11:3–13) and developed at greater length in the remainder of Revelation (Charles; Giesen; Mounce; Prigent; Smalley).

The Two Witnesses Prophesy (11:3–6)

Revelation does not give names to the two witnesses. In the history of interpretation, many have tried to identify them, with suggestions including Enoch, Elijah, Moses, and Jeremiah (see §18A). Many now recognize that the figures represent the church as a whole, which is the approach taken here (NOTE on 11:3). Rather than asking whether readers can identify the figures, we might ask how the text encourages readers to identify *with* them, since they embody the public testimony and perseverance to which the Christian community is called (Yarbro Collins, *Crisis*, 151; Perry, *Rhetoric*, 226; deSilva, *Seeing*, 223–25).

Calling the figures "witnesses" (*martyres*) helps engage the readers. John assumes that readers will identify with Jesus, who is God's "faithful witness" (Rev 1:5; 3:14; cf. 22:20). They in turn are to hold firmly to "the witness of Jesus," which includes what they have received from Jesus through both the tradition of the church and the words of his prophets (NOTE on 1:5). In the case of Jesus, bearing witness led to death, which was also true for Antipas, another "faithful witness" (2:13). John identifies himself as someone sharing affliction because of his witness (1:9), and when the slain witnesses under the altar cry out for justice, the assumption is that readers will want to identify with them (6:9–10; cf. 12:11; 17:6; 20:4). To be clear, Revelation does not equate witness with violent death (Trites, "Μάρτυς"; van Henten, "Concept"). Rather, by holding firmly to the testimony that comes *from* Jesus, people become witnesses *to* Jesus and the God who sent him, whether or not they die violently for the faith (1:2, 9; 6:9; 12:11, 17; 20:4).

Revelation envisions witness as a public calling. The two witnesses "stand before the Lord of the earth" and address their message to all "those who live on the earth" (11:4, 10). They attest the reign of the Creator in a context where other powers vie for dominion (10:6; 11:7). The witnesses also prophesy (11:3). In some contexts prophecy is a form of inspired speech that is done by some but not all members of the community. Among Jesus' followers, prophets can be a subgroup (11:18; 16:6; 18:20, 24) who are moved by the Spirit in a unique way and can convey revelation (1:1–2; 22:6, 9). If prophesying has this sense here, then the witnesses represent only a special group of prophets (Boxall; Murphy). But the way prophecy is now identified with witness suggests that in this context prophesying describes the vocation of the whole church (Blount 206).

In Revelation, witnessing and prophesying serve the same end, which is to direct people to God. Discerning which prophetic messages were valid was a matter of dispute in the congregations addressed by Revelation. A woman at Thyatira claimed special knowledge and called herself a prophet while adopting a latitudinarian approach to polytheism (2:20), and later visions show a prophet doing signs and wonders in the service of the beast (13:11–18; 16:13; 19:20; 20:10). Revelation draws on biblical and early Christian traditions that insisted that true prophecy moves people to worship God, while false prophecy draws people away from God (cf. Deut 13:1–11; Zech 13:2–3; Philo, *Spec. Laws* 1.315; 2 Pet 2:1), works against faith in Jesus (1 John 4:1–3; 1 Cor 12:1–3; Matt 24:11; Acts 13:6–8), and is characterized by conduct that is incongruent with the faith (*Did.* 11:7–12; Matt 7:15–20; 24:11, 24; Aune, *Prophecy*, 217–29). Revelation also identifies the "spirit of prophecy" with "the witness" that the community has received from Jesus and makes to Jesus. The point of such witness is that people "worship God" (Rev 19:10). As members of the Christian community bear witness, they share a prophetic vocation (D. Hill, "Prophecy," 413; Roose, *Zeugnis*, 156–60).

This understanding of the witnesses' role is congruent with their attire. They wear sackcloth as a visible call for the world to repent (11:3; cf. 14:6). The symbolism reshapes a familiar pattern. When Jerusalem and its sanctuary were threatened, people put on sackcloth to show grief (1 Macc 2:12–14; *Pss. Sol.* 2:20; cf. 2 Kgs 6:30) or to pray for Israel's deliverance (Dan 9:1–6; Bar 4:20; Joel 1:6–8, 13–14). One might expect this to be the case in Revelation, since the previous scene pictured the Christian community as a besieged temple and holy city (Rev 11:1–2). But those who wear sackcloth are not shown grieving over the city's plight. Instead, they wear sackcloth while witnessing to the nations.

Some interpreters think sackcloth is primarily a portent of God's judgment on the world (Beale; Satake) and argue that Revelation condemns the nations without extending any real hope for repentance and redemption (G. Carey, *Elusive*, 160–63). But others note that a warning of judgment can function as a call for repentance. In the previous vision cycle, the sun became black as sackcloth as a sign of divine wrath (6:12), but when people asked who could stand, the movement toward judgment was interrupted by a vision of redemption (6:17; 7:1–17). In the present cycle, humanity has refused to repent (9:20–21), but the movement toward judgment is again interrupted so that witness can be given by figures wearing sackcloth. Repentance remains the goal, and at the end of the episode the inhabitants of earth come to glorify God (11:12–13; Giesen; Smalley; Bauckham, *Climax*, 278; Perry, *Rhetoric*, 90; Tavo, *Woman*, 204; de-Silva, *Seeing*, 69–78).

The witnesses are called "the two olive trees and the two lampstands" (11:4). The imagery is from Zech 4:1–14, which has a single lampstand with seven lamps and two olive trees beside it. In Zechariah, the olive trees symbolize the priest and governor who led the community in Jerusalem after the exile. In that context a single lampstand signified God's presence, and its seven lamps symbolized his eyes (Zech 4:10). Revelation has drawn from this passage when picturing the seven torches before God's throne and the seven eyes of the Lamb (Rev 4:5; 5:6). What changes in Rev 11 is that Zechariah's single lampstand becomes two lampstands, which are equated with the two olive trees, and the trees are no longer individuals but representatives of the whole community (Tavo, *Woman*, 205–7).

The lampstand in Zechariah had to do with worship, and it fits the temple imagery in Rev 11:2. But in Revelation the function of the lampstand is not so much to illumine the sanctuary as it is to bear witness to God's reign over the world. The imagery also encourages readers to see their own vocation in this vision. The opening chapter of Revelation pictured Christ among seven gold lampstands, which represented the churches (1:12–13, 20). In the messages that followed, a major question was the Christian community's relationship to the unbelieving world. Situations ranged from congregations experiencing open hostility (2:9; 3:9), to those willing to accommodate Greco-Roman religious practice (2:14, 20), to those that were complacent (3:1, 16–17). Accordingly, the witnesses in Rev 11 neither retreat from nor assimilate to a context that challenges them. Instead, they challenge others with the claims of God.

John adds layer after layer to the portrait of the witnesses in order to magnify their power (*exousia*) in the first part of the vision before abruptly shifting to their seemingly senseless deaths in the second part. Rhetorically, this is called "amplification" (Quintilian, *Inst.* 8.4.3–14; Lausberg, *Handbook* §§402–3). The vision shows the witnesses' power over their foes, and then their power to affect the sky, the waters, and the earth. As is common in amplification, the final point is the most expansive, for the witnesses can strike the earth with "any plague" and do so "as often as they wish" (Rev 11:6). So by the end of the scene, the witnesses have power over each part of the created order, which makes their ensuing deaths seem incomprehensible.

The Beast Slays the Witnesses and People Celebrate (11:7–10)

The deaths of the witnesses occur in scene two, when they have finished their witness and the beast makes war against them and kills them (11:7). The beast's role will be developed later in Revelation (NOTES and COMMENT on 13:1). But here the brief mention of the beast slaying the witnesses raises again the question of injustice, which was voiced by the martyrs (6:9–10). The witnesses die even though they are faithful to God. For the wicked to slay the righteous runs counter to principles of justice, and it seems inexplicable that God would allow it (Hab 1:2–4; Job 4:7–8).

The question continues as the witnesses' dead bodies lie on the street of the great city, which has features of Babylon, Rome, Sodom, and Egypt (11:8). John adds that the great city was where "their Lord was crucified" (11:8). The memory of Jesus' crucifixion underscores the problem of injustice. God exercises power through Jesus, whom the witnesses call their Lord (*kyrios*; 11:8). Yet Jesus was crucified (*stauroun*), the brutal form of execution the Roman state used for slaves, violent criminals, and those guilty of treason (Hengel, *Crucifixion*, 33–63; Kuhn, "Kreuzesstrafe"). Jesus' death showed Rome's wrongful judgment on the agent of God. But readers also believed that through this act of human injustice God's redemptive action took place, for through Jesus' blood people are brought into God's kingdom (1:5; 5:9; 7:14). As Jesus' followers bear faithful witness, they will suffer unjustly as Jesus did, and yet out of their suffering and witness, God's redemptive purposes will be accomplished.

For three and a half days the witnesses' opponents look at their corpses without allowing the bodies to be put into a tomb (11:9). People expected the dead to be decently buried, even if they were criminals or foes killed on the battlefield. Providing for burial displayed the victor's magnanimity since it allowed the defeated to retain some dignity (Josephus, *Ag. Ap.* 2.211; Pausanias, *Descr.* 1.32.5). But refusing to allow enemy corpses to be buried showed "passionate and determined hatred" (Polybius, *Histories* 1.82.9–10; cf. Tob 1:17–18). It magnified the victor's power by degrading the conquered (*Pss. Sol.* 4:19; Suetonius, *Aug.* 13.1–2; Suetonius, *Vesp.* 2.3; Tacitus, *Ann.* 6.29). Nevertheless, the result could be the opposite, since those who refused burial actually disgraced themselves by such callousness, thereby diminishing their own status (Pausanias, *Descr.* 9.32.9; Josephus, *J. W.* 4.317, 381). This is the case in Rev 11, which is designed to elicit sympathy for the witnesses and indignation toward their oppressors.

In ordinary practice, Roman authorities allowed criminals who were executed to be buried before a festival began (Philo, *Flacc.* 83; John 19:31), but in this macabre vision the custom is reversed, and the public display of the corpses is the *occasion* for celebration. The beast that slew the witnesses has traits of a Roman emperor (Rev 13:1–4), and the festival celebrating the beast's victory has traits of the Roman Saturnalia, for people rejoice, celebrate, and "give gifts to each other" (11:10). During Saturnalia the usual forms of work and social status were put aside, and people of all classes feasted, played games, and exchanged presents. It was said, "let us enjoy ourselves, clap hands, and live on freedom's terms" (Lucian, *Sat.* 9). Saturnalia offered a merry respite from ordinary life, and the festivities in John's vision occur when the world receives a respite from the witnesses. Just as the trumpet plagues made people more entrenched in the traditional worship of idols (Rev 9:20–21), the plagues of the witnesses make people all the more ready to celebrate their deaths with a typical Roman festival.

Resurrection, Lesser Judgment, and Glory to God (11:11–14)

The climax of the story comes in the third scene, in which a spirit of life from God infuses the slain witnesses (11:11). A suggestive intertextual aspect in this part of the vision, which relates to the agency of God's spirit, comes from Zech 4, which included the lampstand and olive tree imagery. In that vision Zechariah said that God's purposes would be accomplished "'Not by might, nor by power, but by my spirit [LXX *pneuma*],' says the Lord of hosts" (Zech 4:6). Revelation puts this idea into narrative form. The two witnesses, symbolized by the olive trees, have the power to bring plagues against the earth, but their actions do not achieve God's purposes, since the world remains hostile and the witnesses are slain. Therefore, God uses different means by sending his spirit (*pneuma*) into his witnesses, thereby demonstrating his power to give life (Rev 11:11). This work of the spirit of life in the witnesses will accomplish God's designs by bringing many people to worship him.

The spirit of life enters the witnesses after they have been dead for three and a half days, suggesting that their resurrection is patterned after that of Jesus, who was raised after three days; and like him they stand on their feet and are seen by others. Since Jesus is the firstborn of the dead, those who share in a death like his will share in a resurrection like his (1:5; cf. Rom 6:5; Phil 3:10; 1 Thess 4:14; Bauckham, *Climax*, 280; Wright, *Resurrection*, 471–72). Where this vision differs from tradition is that the risen Jesus was usually said to have been seen by his followers (Matt 28:9–10, 16–20; Luke 24:13–49; John 20:11–21:23; Acts 1:3; 1 Cor 15:5–8), whereas the witnesses are seen by their enemies (Rev 11:11). In Revelation it is a public vindication. Although the witnesses were condemned by the world and slain by the beast, God overturns this judgment by restoring them. Vindication continues when a voice from heaven tells the witnesses to "come up here," and they go up to heaven in a cloud much as Jesus' resurrection was followed by his exaltation to God's throne in heaven (NOTE on 11:12; cf. 12:5). The world left their bodies on the street in dishonor, but God elevates them to honor.

Revelation's emphasis on people seeing (*theōrein*) the witnesses' resurrection is integral to the vision's theological import. God's ability to raise the dead reveals his character. If people are to give glory to the God of heaven, they need to know who God is. Here, God is the one who brings his witnesses through death to life. The visions show that what brings the nations to glorify God is not prophetic acts of power, but the way God gives life to his afflicted witnesses. Again, this follows the pattern set by Jesus. Previously, the sight of the slaughtered and living Lamb prompted angels and the whole created order to give glory to God (5:6, 11–14), and in this scene the people of earth give glory to God after they see his witnesses participating in that same story of death and life (Bauckham, *Climax*, 280–81).

The witnesses' clash with the beast in the great city gives a critical perspective on the church's conflict with Roman authority. The witnesses' bodies had been on public display in the city, where they were subjected to contempt by many nations and peoples (11:7–10). By way of contrast, when an emperor died, a facsimile of his body was put on public display in Rome for some days so that he could be honored by various classes and peoples. When the funeral pyre was burned, it was said that the emperor ascended to heaven. Artwork depicted Julius Caesar ascending visibly while others looked on (Suetonius, *Jul.* 81.3; Beard, North, and Price, *Religions*, 1:187). At the funeral of Augustus, a witness swore that he saw the emperor ascending to heaven (Suetonius, *Aug.* 100.4). Later, an eagle was released at funerals to symbolize the emperor's ascent to the gods; this imagery is included in the first-century CE Arch of Titus. The image of the visibly ascending emperor was patterned after the story of Rome's legendary founder, Romulus, and others (Herodian, *Historiae* 4.2.1–11; Dio Cassius, *Rom. Hist.* 1.5.12; 56.46.2; 75.4.2–5.5; Justin Martyr, *1 Apol.* 21.3; Beard, North, and Price, *Religions*, 2:52; Paschke, "Die *damnatio*"). In Revelation the pattern is reversed; the witnesses who were slaughtered under imperial rule and whose bodies were displayed in the street are the ones who receive a place of honor in heaven.

The story also shows a lessening of God's judgment on the world. The first six trumpet visions portrayed disasters afflicting a third of the earth, culminating in the specter of death for a third of humanity (Rev 9:18). But after the resurrection of the witnesses, an earthquake occurs and affects only one-tenth of the great city, which means that nine-tenths of the people are spared. In the literary context, judgment has been dramatically moderated. Comparisons to biblical patterns underscore the point. For example, Isaiah warned that God's judgment would be so vast that only a tenth of the people would survive it and that even that tenth would be burned again (Isa 6:13). Amos warned that when God's judgment came, nine-tenths would meet destruction (Amos 5:3). But in the story of the witnesses, the opposite is true, for nine-tenths are saved and only one-tenth is destroyed.

This pattern continues in the comment that in the earthquake "seven thousand people were killed" (Rev 11:13). On its own, the number seems large, but in contrast to the prospect of death for a third of humanity, the judgment is far less (9:13). This number again inverts a typical pattern. The two witnesses had traits of Elijah, who was told that among the faithless people of Israel, God would preserve a remnant of seven thousand who were true worshipers of God (1 Kgs 19:18). In Revelation, however, the numbers are reversed: Seven thousand are killed while the rest of those who live on earth glorify God. Since seven thousand die in John's vision, it is clear that judgment is present, but it falls only on some, and most of the people are spared. John shows the restraint in divine judgment (Giblin, "Revelation," 446; Bauckham, *Climax*, 282–83).

The climax of the story is the rest of the people giving glory to the God of heaven (Rev 11:13). After the earth experienced the horrors of the first six trumpets, people stubbornly persisted in idolatry and refused to repent (9:20–21), but here, nine-tenths of the people give glory to God, as the heavenly chorus did before (4:11; 5:13; 7:12). The witness, death, and vindication of the community of faith help to accomplish what judgment alone does not do. Through these acts the people of many tribes and nations are brought to fear God and to give him glory. The conversion of the nations, rather than their destruction, is God's will for the world. This theme continues in the second half of the book, where an angel calls all people to "fear God and give him glory" (14:6–7); the redeemed sing, "Who will not fear you, Lord, and glorify your name, for you alone are holy" and "all nations will come and worship before you" (15:4); and the nations give glory to God in New Jerusalem (21:24–26).

24. The Seventh Trumpet: The Kingdom (11:15–18)

11 ¹⁵Then the seventh angel blew his trumpet, and there were loud voices in heaven, saying,

> "The kingdom of the world has become
> that of our Lord and his Anointed
> and he will reign forever and ever."

¹⁶Then the twenty-four elders, who were seated on their thrones before God, fell on their faces and worshiped God. ¹⁷They said,

> "We give thanks to you, Lord God Almighty, who is and who was,
> for you have taken your great power and you reign.
> ¹⁸The nations were wrathful, but your wrath came.
> It is the time for the dead to be judged,
> and to reward your servants, the prophets and the saints
> and those who fear your name, both the small and the great,
> and to destroy those who destroy the earth."

NOTES

11:15. *Then the seventh angel blew his trumpet.* Six angels have blown trumpets in a threatening manner, but the seventh sounds a festive tone. A horn could acclaim a new king over Israel, and here the trumpet announces God's kingship over the world (2 Sam 15:10; 1 Kgs 1:39; Pss 47:5–6; 98:6). Trumpets also summoned people to worship, and this occurs as the elders give thanks to God (Num 10:2–3, 10; 2 Chr 7:6; 29:28). Some sources expected a trumpet to signal the Lord's judgment, and Revelation's seventh trumpet portends doom for the destroyers of the earth (Joel 2:1; Zeph 1:16; *4 Ezra* 6:23; *Apoc. Zeph.* 12:1–8; Rev 11:18). Others expected a final trumpet to herald the resurrection of the dead and ingathering of the faithful (Matt 24:31; 1 Cor 15:52; 1 Thess 4:16). In a variation on the theme, Revelation's seventh trumpet announces the judgment and reward that are to occur at the final resurrection, although this is not described until the end of the book, where no trumpet is mentioned (Rev 20:1–15).

and there were loud voices in heaven, saying. The voices are variously identified as the four living creatures (4:8; Ford; Prigent; Roloff), the angels (Kraft), or the redeemed (7:9–10; 19:1, 6; Beale; Giesen; Jörns, *Das hymnische*, 91–92). More important than the voices' identity, however, is the way they interpret events and encourage worship (cf. 12:10; 19:1).

"The kingdom of the world. On one level the contrast between the kingdom of the world and the kingdom of God reflects an apocalyptic worldview. The visions in Dan 7:1–14 contrast a series of four oppressive and yet transient earthly kingdoms with God's everlasting kingdom. Other sources characterize the present world as a single realm or kingdom that is dominated by Belial, the Angel of Darkness, who has dominion over the sons of deceit and can influence the faithful to some extent. His dominion is to last until the end of the age when he will be defeated (1QS I, 18; II, 19; III, 20–21; 1QM I, 1–5; XVIII, 1–3; 11Q13 II, 12–13). Belial, or Beliar, is "the angel of iniquity who rules this world" by luring people into sin (*Mart. Asc. Isa.* 2:4; cf. 1:3; 10:29). Early Christians spoke of the present kingdom of Satan, who exercises power through demon possession (Matt 12:26). As "the ruler of this world," Satan operates through deception, hatred, and death (John 12:31; cf. 8:44; 15:18; 1 John 5:19). He foments unbelief and sin (2 Cor 4:4; Eph 2:2; 6:12; Ign. *Eph.* 17:1; 19:1; Ign. *Magn.* 1:2; Ign. *Trall.* 4:2; Ign. *Rom.* 7:1). One could speak of "the present evil age" (Gal 1:4).

On another level the expression "kingdom of the world" fits Revelation's imperial context. For early readers, the world was under the dominion of Rome (Rev 17:9, 18). The Romans were reluctant to call themselves a kingdom and preferred to use the title "king" for the rulers of the vassal states rather than for the emperor (NOTE on 1:5). But admirers called the emperor the "lord of the world" (Martial, *Epigrams* 7.5.5; 8.2.6; 8.32.6), and the Romans were said to rule the world (Dio Cassius, *Rom. Hist.* 53.17.1–5; Tacitus, *Ann.* 1.1; 12.37; Tacitus, *Hist.* 2.78; cf. John 19:15; 1 Pet 2:13). Putting the dimensions together, one can see how Revelation seeks to show the cosmic forces of evil exercising power through the political, social, and economic structures of the world.

"has become that of our Lord. In Jewish and early Christian sources the hope for God's kingdom relates to the contradiction between the claim that God is Lord of the earth and the experience of oppressive powers. On the one hand, the kingdom means defeat for the wicked and the subjection of powers opposed to God. On the other hand, it means salvation for the righteous. Some envisioned the kingdom as national liberation from foreign powers and the establishment of a blessed life for Israel (*Pss. Sol.* 17:3, 21–32; 18:5). Others expanded the hope to include the defeat of the devil and the manifestation of God's reign throughout all creation (*T. Mos.* 10:1; D. C. Duling, *ABD* 4:49–56).

Revelation reflects the more expansive view since it envisions the defeat of hostile nations and Satan, along with God reigning in a new creation (Rev 19–22). In the

COMMENT below the statement that the world "has become" (*egeneto*) the kingdom of God and Christ is read in light of the previous scene of the world glorifying God in 11:13 and also as an anticipation of what is to come. Alternatively, some interpreters argue that the world does not "become" God's kingdom and that 11:15 simply affirms that God always "was" its ruler (Rowland). This approach is unlikely, however, because change does come to the world when God exercises royal power in Christ, who made (*epoiēsen*/*epoiēsas*) people a kingdom through his death (1:5; 5:10) and will alter conditions on earth by overthrowing the powers of evil so that the reign of God and Christ alone is acknowledged (19:1–5).

"*and his Anointed.* The passage recalls Psalm 2 (Boxall; Murphy): "Why do the nations conspire . . . against the Lord and his anointed," for the Lord "will speak to them in his wrath, and terrify them in his fury," telling his anointed, "You are my son; today I have begotten you. Ask of me and I will make the nations your heritage . . . You shall rule [Hebrew, "break"] them with a rod of iron" (Ps 2:1–2, 5, 7–9 LXX). This psalm supplies the expression "our Lord and his Anointed" in Rev 11:15, and it may also inform Revelation's reference to God's wrath meeting the hostility of the nations in 11:18 (cf. Acts 4:26; Murphy; Witetschek, "Lieblingspsalm"). Elsewhere, the psalm's reference to divine sonship may contribute to the use of the expression Son of God for Jesus (Rev 2:18). The promise of ruling with an iron rod is taken up in Revelation's visions of Christ's ascension and return to defeat the nations (12:5; 19:15) and is part of the inheritance he gives to the faithful (NOTE on 2:26–28; Janse, *You*, 95–96, 131–34; Kahl, "Psalm"; Quek, "I Will").

The seventh trumpet vision uses the word "anointed" (*christos*) as a title rather than a part of Jesus' name (1:1, 2, 5). The title once identified the reigning king of Israel and later was used for the Messiah, who would inherit David's throne (1 Sam 12:5; *Pss. Sol.* 17:21–32; 18:5–9; *1 En.* 48:10; 52:4; Charlesworth, ed., *Messiah*). Early Christians considered Jesus to be the Davidic Messiah, while holding various views on whether Jesus had already established the kingdom or whether it would come dramatically in the future. The present dimension is suggested by sayings about the kingdom being near (Mark 1:14–15; Luke 10:9), the idea that it is secretly growing (Mark 4:26–29; Luke 13:19–21) and that those with insight are not far from it (Mark 12:34). The future dimension is conveyed by sayings about the kingdom coming with cosmic signs, the arrival of the Son of Man on the clouds, and the resurrection and final judgment (Matt 8:11–12; 13:41–43; 25:31–34; Luke 13:28–29; 19:11; 21:25–33; 22:30; 1 Cor 15:50–57; 2 Tim 4:1; D. C. Duling, *ABD* 4:56–69).

Revelation reflects a similar tension. On the one hand, Jesus is the Davidic Messiah (Rev 5:5; 22:16), the ruler of earth's kings, who has already established a kingdom by redeeming people of many nations (1:5–6; 5:10). Where people honor God, the kingdom now exists in a provisional way. On the other hand, the kingdom is fully established when the powers who oppose God are finally defeated (19:11–21). Both present and future dimensions play a role in the book.

"*and he will reign forever and ever.*" The verb "reign" (*baslieusei*) is singular, and the following verses use the singular for God's power, wrath, and name (11:17–18). Biblical hymns declare God's reign to be everlasting, unlike the kingdoms of earthly rulers (Exod 15:18; Ps 145:13; 146:10; Dan 4:34; 6:26; *1 En.* 84:2–3). From this perspective, the mention of God's Anointed in the previous line is a secondary element that reflects Christ's dependence on God (Jörns, *Das hymnische*, 94; Aune). Alternatively, other interpreters plausibly see a higher Christology in which God and Christ reign as one (Rev 3:21; 5:13; 22:3; Boxall; Giesen; Prigent; Osborne). The promise of an heir to David's throne said that God would "establish the throne of his kingdom forever" (2 Sam 7:13; cf. Isa 9:7). Daniel envisions the human one, or Son of Man, receiving "an everlasting dominion that shall not pass away" (Dan 7:14). Early Christians said the Davidic promises of the everlasting kingdom were realized through Jesus' resurrection to deathless life (Luke 1:33; John 12:34; Heb 1:8). Revelation depicts Christ sharing God's throne eternally (Rev 22:3).

11:16. *Then the twenty-four elders, who were seated on their thrones before God, fell on their faces and worshiped God.* The elders are seated on thrones in positions of honor yet prostrate themselves before God, the world's true sovereign (4:10; 5:8, 14; 19:4). In a context in which sovereignty is disputed, as it is in Revelation, bowing down is an act that shows allegiance (Friesen, *Imperial*, 197). On the elders, see the NOTE on 4:4.

11:17. *They said, "We give thanks to you, Lord God Almighty.* Hymnic passages in Revelation sometimes praise God directly, as is done here (cf. Rev 4:11; 15:2–4), and sometimes use the third person (4:8; 7:10, 12; 19:1–8). Both forms are vivid. By giving thanks to God, the elders exemplify the worship to which the readers are called (4:9; 7:12; *Did.* 10:2). Addressing prayer to the "Lord God Almighty" underscores God's power to reign (NOTE on Rev 1:8).

who is and who was. Previously, God was called the one "who is and who was and who is to come" (NOTE on 1:8). Here, the idea that God is "to come" is omitted— though it is added in some manuscripts (051 1006 1841)—which suggests that the vision takes readers to that point in the future when God no longer is *to* come but *has* come (cf. 16:5; Charles).

for you have taken your great power and you reign. Prayers usually give reasons for thanking God, often mentioning deliverance and guidance (2 Macc 1:11; 1QH^a XI, 19; XII, 5; XV, 6–7). Earlier, the redeemed thanked God for salvation (Rev 7:12), and here, the elders give thanks for God's power and reign. Saying that God has "taken" his power does not mean that he obtained power from others but that he has used his power to establish the kingdom. The Roman emperor was said to have received his power from the Senate and the people (*Rom. Civ.* 2:11–12; Suetonius, *Cal.* 14.1; Dio Cassius, *Rom. Hist.* 53.17.11), but Revelation assumes that no one could confer power on God. Saying "you reign" (*ebasileusas*) in the aorist tense may show that God's reign has begun (BDF §318; NAB, NIV, NRSV), but it does not suggest that God lacked power before. The verb sums up the situation: God reigns (Pss 93:1; 96:10; 97:1; 99:1; Rev 19:6). What is new is the way the God who reigns in heaven uses his power to save on earth (Isa 52:7; Zech 14:9).

11:18. *"The nations were wrathful, but your wrath came.* The wrath of the nations shows their opposition to God's actions: "the Lord reigns, the peoples are wrathful" (Ps 99:1 [98:1 LXX]; cf. Exod 15:14 LXX). The language may be reminiscent of Ps 2:5, which asks, "Why do the nations rage?" and warns of God's wrath against them (NOTE on Rev 11:15). The way the nations' wrath provokes God's wrath shows symmetry in judgment (18:6; Murphy; Osborne). Divine wrath is not an indiscriminate outburst but a response against the wicked (Isa 13:9, 11; 1QH^a II, 27–28; *Pss. Sol.* 15:4–5; Luke 3:7; Rom 1:18; Rev 9:4).

"It is the time for the dead to be judged. Revelation anticipates that the dead will be resurrected for judgment at the end of the age (20:11–15). Some Jewish sources expected the righteous to be resurrected for a glorious future and the unrighteous resurrected for punishment (Dan 12:1–3; *4 Ezra* 7:26–32; *2 Bar.* 30:1–5; cf. Reiser, *Jesus*, 154–63, 307). A variation was that the unrighteous would be left in the realm of the dead, while the righteous were raised to a blessed life (2 Macc 7:14; *Pss. Sol.* 3:11–12; *1 En.* 91:10; 92:3; Nickelsburg, *Resurrection*, 94–95). Some sources did not specify whether judgment would occur immediately after death or at the end of the age (Wis 3–5). In the Greco-Roman context, some insisted that death was the end and that there would be no post-mortem judgments (Lucretius, *De rer.* 3.861–69; Diogenes Laertius, *Lives* 9.124–25). But others thought the souls of the wicked would be punished by being sent to Tartarus, while the souls of the righteous would go to the Islands of the Blessed (Plato, *Phaed.* 63b; 69d–e; 113d–114c; Plato, *Gorg.* 522d–526d; Plato, *Leg.* 10.904d–905d; Plato, *Resp.* 2.363c–e; Wright, *Resurrection*, 49–50).

In early Christian writings the idea that both the righteous and unrighteous would be raised for judgment at the end of the age was common (Matt 25:31–46; John 5:28–29; Acts 24:15). Some interpreters hold that Rev 11:18 refers to the judgment of only the unrighteous, since the faithful are mentioned in the next line (cf. 20:5–6; Giesen; Osborne). In either case, the statement of judgment is broad and assumes that all people are accountable to God (NOTES and COMMENT on 20:1–15).

"and to reward your servants, the prophets. Reward can mean receiving either benefits or punishments (22:12), but the rewards God gives to his servants are blessings (11:18c; 14:13; Isa 40:10; 62:11; Matt 5:12; Heb 10:35). Although reward can be construed as a crude inducement to remain faithful in the hope of obtaining some benefit, this is not the case here. In commercial life employers obtained the services of laborers by offering to pay a stated wage, or reward (*misthos*); but according to Rev 5:9–10 relationships with God were established through Christ, who "purchases," or redeems, people through his death (*TLNT* 2:502–15). In this context God's servants probably include all the faithful (Rev 1:1; 7:3; 19:5). Some interpreters assume that the prophets, who are mentioned next, also include all the faithful since the two witnesses in 11:3–10 represented the prophetic vocation of the whole church (Beale; Giesen; Prigent). But here it is more likely that the prophets are a special group (cf. 22:6, 9; Mounce; Osborne; Thomas).

"and the saints and those who fear your name, both small and great. The saints, or holy ones, belong to the God who is holy and constitute the whole Christian community (5:8). They fear God's name. This is a suitable way to describe worshipers of all backgrounds (14:7; Ps 118:4; Acts 10:2; 13:16; *1 Clem.* 21:7), all of whom are to glorify God (cf. Rev 11:13; Caird; Harrington; Bauckham, *Climax*, 278). The "small" are those of lower social status, such as slaves and poor people, and the "great" are of higher status, such as civic or military officials and wealthy people (6:15). Revelation recognizes that social status does not determine belief or unbelief: Both small and great may wear the mark of the beast and oppose the Lamb (13:6; 19:18) but are also called to praise God and will be judged by God (19:5; 20:12).

"and to destroy those who destroy the earth." The verb *diaphtheirein* can mean to destroy physically and to ruin morally. When used of the opponents of God, both ideas are operative. There are four principal agents of destruction in Revelation:

1. Satan. The king of the demonic abyss is the Destroyer, who is probably Satan (NOTE on 9:11). He seeks to destroy the Messiah and his followers (12:1–6, 17), bringing death to faithful witnesses like Antipas (2:9–10, 13). Satan also ruins people through deceptive teachings that foster idolatry, which the writer calls "immorality" (2:20, 24). Satan's ruin is the abyss and lake of fire (20:1–3, 7–10).
2. The beast. The beast receives political power from Satan and comes up from the demonic abyss and the sea (11:7; 13:1; 17:8). It destroys by slaughtering God's witnesses (11:7; 13:2, 7, 10) and burning Babylon (17:16). The beast ruins or corrupts the world by usurping the names of God for itself and making itself the object of worship (13:4–8). As an agent of destruction, it ultimately goes to destruction (17:8).
3. The false prophet. This figure is pictured as the beast from the land and destroys those who refuse to worship the beast from the sea (13:15). It ruins people by deceiving and coercing them into participation in the ruler cult and imprinting them with the mark of the great beast (13:12–18; 16:13). It too is destroyed (19:20; 20:10).
4. Babylon. Biblically, Babylon was known as the city that destroyed the earth by conquests (Jer 51:24–25 [28:24–25 LXX]). John's portrayal of Babylon links this imagery to Rome, which could also be destructive. Tacitus wrote of the Romans: "They rob, butcher, plunder, and call it 'empire'; and where they make a desolation, they call it 'peace'" (*Agr.* 30). The city is filled with blood (Rev 17:6; 18:24). In a moral sense, Babylon is a corrupting whore, who entwines the nations through the allure of profit and luxury (17:1–6; 18:3, 9–19). Portraying the city as morally ruinous challenges the idea that Rome achieved dominion through virtue and good fortune (Strabo, *Geographica* 6.4.2; Plutarch, *Mor.* 317C). The way it ruins others finally leads to its own ruin (Rev 17:16; 18:1–24).

COMMENT

Scenes of heavenly worship often occur at the end of major vision cycles; in this way, readers are repeatedly led through episodes of earthly conflict to ones of celestial praise (Rev 7:9–8:1; 11:15–18; 15:2–4; 19:1–8). This scene is structured antiphonally in two parts. First, loud voices in heaven announce that God's kingdom has come (11:15). Second, the twenty-four elders respond by giving thanks to God for his reign and outlining how God's justice will be carried out by judging the dead, rewarding the saints, and destroying the destroyers of the earth (11:16–18). Similar antiphonal patterns occur elsewhere (4:8–11; 5:8–14; 7:9–12; 14:13; 19:1–8).

The style encourages readers to identify with the type of worship depicted in the text. Whereas the description of the world's idolatry after the sixth trumpet was designed to alienate readers from false worship, the praise of God after the seventh trumpet gives them a kind of worship to emulate (9:20–21; 11:15–18). It is unlikely that the words of the heavenly company replicate actual hymns from the congregations in Roman Asia, because the lyrics seem fitted to the present literary context (INTRO IV.E.1). But the scene focuses worship on God and his anointed one and directs readers to do the same.

On Rev 11:15–18, see Jörns, *Das hymnische*, 90–108; G. Stevenson, *Power*, 293–95; L. Thompson, *Book*, 53–73.

The heavenly company invokes themes from Israel's worship to celebrate God's kingdom and victory over the nations. First, the announcement that God reigns (*basileuein*), which is made by the heavenly voices and echoed by the elders (11:15, 17), is reminiscent of the enthronement psalms that declare that "the Lord reigns" (*basileuein*) and celebrate his dominion over the earth and its peoples (Pss 93:1; 96:10; 98:1; 99:1). Such psalms could also anticipate that God is coming "to judge the world with righteousness, and the peoples with equity" (98:9) much as the elders announce God's coming acts of judgment and reward (Rev 11:18). Second, the elders say, "We give thanks to you, Lord God Almighty," and then add the reason, "for [*hoti*] you have taken your great power" (11:17). This pattern is reminiscent of the thanksgiving psalms, in which praise is given to God "for" a particular reason (Pss 106:1; 107:1; 118:1; 136:1–2; 1 Chr 16:34). Traditional themes of God's kingship and human thanks are joined in Rev 11:15–18.

Biblical poetry comes from a Jewish and Christian subculture, and Revelation uses its language to celebrate victory over the forces associated with the dominant imperial culture. Poetic forms announce victory over the kingdom of the world, the beast, and Babylon (15:3–4; 19:1–8). The scenes have a militant edge, since they challenge competing claims in the readers' social world. Traditional Greco-Roman worship included hymn singing. For example, groups regularly sang hymns to Artemis at Ephesus, and inscriptions expressed gratitude: "I give thanks to you, Lady Artemis" (I.Eph 957.9–10; 960.2–3; 961.1; G. Stevenson, *Power*, 294). At the provincial temple at Pergamum, groups from around the province sang hymns to the deified emperor (Friesen, *Imperial*, 104–13). The elders in the Apocalypse point to a form of divine rule that is both higher than the state and different in kind.

This heavenly worship scene both concludes the trumpet visions and introduces the second half of Revelation (Jörns, *Das hymnische*, 90). Looking back, one can see that readers have been told that seven angels will blow their trumpets and that the end will come with the seventh (Rev 8:2, 6; 10:7). Announcing God's kingdom at the seventh trumpet signals the fulfillment of his purposes (11:15). This scene concludes the first half of Revelation, since three of the six major vision cycles—the assemblies, the seals, and the trumpets—are now complete. Looking ahead, one will find that the second half of the book consists of three more cycles, which tell of God's coming victory over the forces of evil. These cycles begin with Rev 12 and culminate in New Jerusalem in Rev 22. So the elders, like the chorus in a Greek drama (Harsh, *Handbook*, 17–23), help readers anticipate what is about to unfold. They do not offer a linear outline of the plot but summarize key themes: the outworking of divine wrath, the judgment of the dead and rewarding of the saints, and the destruction of earth's destroyers (11:18).

The elders' words also disclose what it means for this scene to be the third woe that readers were told to expect (Note on 11:14). The arrival of God's kingdom is a cause for celebration among those who have been oppressed by hostile powers, since God's reign brings deliverance. But God's exercise of power will mean woe for the destroyers of the earth, since their dominion will end and they will be dealt with according to divine justice. The message of God's kingdom includes both deliverance and judgment, so it can be heard as either promise or threat, depending on one's position in the current order of things.

The Kingdom of the Lord and His Anointed (11:15)

At the seventh trumpet, heavenly voices announce that change has come for "the king-dom of the world" (11:15). The visions have depicted the world as God's creation. The elders praised God for bringing all things into being, and every creature in heaven, earth, and sea joined in praising the Creator and the Lamb (4:11; 5:11–14). But Rev-elation also assumes that the world is threatened by destructive forces. Therefore, an angel reiterated that God was the Creator and placed his feet on land and sea in order to reassert the claims of God over creation (10:2, 6, 8). The angel also directed John to focus his prophesying on the peoples, nations, languages, and kings who belong to the world (10:11). The assumption is that the world's hostility to its Creator takes political form (NOTE on 11:15). The vision of the witnesses showed the ruling power, personified as a beast, slaying the faithful, and the many people who inhabited the world joined in celebrating their deaths.

Yet the heavenly voices now say that the kingdom of the world has become "that of our Lord and his Anointed" (11:15). When this line is read as a summary of what has happened, it emphasizes the conversion of the nations, which was just described (11:13). The term "kingdom" is linked to acknowledging divine rule. Jesus makes people "a kingdom" by redeeming them, so that they recognize the rightful reign of God in a world where other powers vie for dominion (1:6; 5:9–10). From this perspective, the kingdom arrives when the people of earth give glory to the God of heaven (NOTE on 11:13; Blount; Caird; Bauckham, *Climax*, 242, 336).

An alternative perspective emerges when the announcement of the kingdom is read in light of what is to come. In the second half of Revelation, Satan is thrown down to earth, where he persecutes the people of God (12:7–17). Then evil assumes social and political form when Satan gives authority to the beast, seeking to make the world the beast's kingdom (13:4; 16:10). The beast works with Babylon the whore, who lures people into relationships through economic enticements and is the kingdom that dominates the kings of earth (17:18). Under the beast's regime, the faithful suffer and are killed (17:6; 18:24), while others are intoxicated by the glamour of the ruling power and seem indifferent to its brutality (17:1–2; 18:3). From this angle the coming of God's kingdom means the elimination of the destructive forces that operate within the world (Schüssler Fiorenza 79).

Also in the second half of the book, the agents of evil are successively overthrown. The broad literary movement shows the beast destroying Babylon, so the victims can rejoice when justice is finally accomplished (17:16; 18:20; 19:1–2). Then the Messiah exercises his royal power as King of kings when he defeats the beast and false prophet through his word (19:11–21), and then Satan himself is banished from earth to the abyss (20:1–3). When read in this way, the announcement that the world "has become" the kingdom of God and Christ is given not because this has happened, but because it is certain to happen. The heavenly company declares the end of the story before it has occurred (Aune; Beale; Giesen; Mounce; Osborne; Thomas).

The Elders Give Thanks (11:16–18)

The twenty-four elders respond to the announcement of the kingdom by bowing in worship before God (11:16; cf. 4:4, 10–11; cf. 5:8–14). From a literary perspective, the elders show that true worship is directed toward God (11:16; 19:4). Socially, the term "elders" (*presbyteroi*) was also used for leaders in Jewish and early Christian congregations, so readers could see in them the heavenly representatives of the earthly communities to which they belong (NOTE on 4:4). By way of contrast, the visions show the people of the world prostrating themselves (*proskynein*) before the beast (13:4, 8, 12, 15; 14:9; 16:2), which in the readers' social worlds means giving divine honors to the ruler (Dio Cassius, *Rom. Hist.* 59.24.2–3; 63.5.2; Aune, *Apocalypticism*, 108). In such a context, the elders give readers encouragement to resist.

The elders begin, "We give thanks to you, Lord God Almighty" (Rev 11:17). The titles "Lord," "God," and "Almighty" appeared at the beginning of Revelation, where God spoke in the first person (NOTE on 1:8). There, the creatures and elders used these titles in ways that suggested a contrast with imperial practice. If the one enthroned as Lord and God is the Creator, who is Almighty (*pantokratōr*), the implication is that such honors cannot be given to the one enthroned as emperor (*autokratōr*; NOTE on 4:11; cf. 15:3; 16:7, 14; 19:6, 15; 21:22).

These same passages call God "the one who is and who was and who is to come" (1:8; 4:8). This drew on the biblical tradition in which God is "the one who is," expanding the usual designation to include his past existence and future coming (NOTE on 1:4). Revelation will parody this formula when portraying the beast, which "was and is not and is about to come up from the abyss and go to destruction" (17:8). When the formula is used for God, it shows that true deity includes continuous existence and creative power, whereas the formula used for the beast includes nonexistence and vulnerability to destruction—traits that belie the beast's pretensions to divinity. Although conflict with the beast will continue through the second half of Revelation, the elders in 11:17 anticipate the end of the story by calling God the one "who is and who was," leaving out the reference to his future coming. God reigns and the time of justice has arrived (cf. 16:5).

When the elders first appeared, they declared God worthy to receive (*lambanein*) glory, honor, and power because he had created all things (4:10–11). When they now give thanks that God has taken (*lambanein*) his power and reigns, the assumption is that God has used his power to defeat the evil at work in the world he created (11:17). The elders' words may look back to the previous scene, in which God exercised power by bringing judgment against the inhabitants of the great city and giving life to the witnesses (11:13). But their announcement that God reigns will be repeated in chapters to come when God's justice brings about the fall of Babylon and the vindication of those who suffer (19:6).

The elders say "the nations were wrathful, but your wrath came," which again looks backward and forward (11:18). In previous scenes the hostile nations overran the holy city, which symbolized the people of God (11:2), and refused to let the bodies of God's witnesses be buried (11:2, 9). Given the terrifying visions of wrath at the first six trumpet visions, readers might have expected divine wrath to strike God's opponents in a final and climactic way at the end of the series (8:6–9:21), but this did not occur. During the interlude before the last trumpet, an earthquake caused the deaths of seven thousand, but most of the hostile world survived to glorify God (11:13). The sense was that God acted against his adversaries in a manner that left room for repentance.

In scenes to come, the theme of wrath (*orgē, thymos*) is more fully developed and reflects the principle of symmetry in divine judgment (18:6; cf. Wis 11:17; 2 Macc 5:10; 13:8; *T. Gad* 5:10; *L.A.B.* 43:5; 44:10; *m. Soṭah* 1:7–9; *t. Soṭah* 3–4). Those who inflict wrath on others come to suffer wrath themselves. When Satan is defeated in heaven, he comes to earth in great wrath (Rev 12:12, 17). There, he enlists the beast and false prophet, who gather the kings of the earth for battle against God (16:13–14). They are joined by Babylon the whore, who intoxicates the nations with "the wine of her passionate immorality"—or literally, her wrath (*thymos*)—which involves the debased pursuit of luxury, false worship, and brutality (14:8; 18:3). The ruling power that made the nations drunk with the wine of her immoral passion, or wrath, will drink the cup of God's wrath (14:8, 10; 16:19).

The theme of wrath also includes surprising elements. The seven bowl plagues are said to bring God's wrath to completion (15:1, 5–8), and they affect all of earth and sea (16:1–21), rather than only a portion of it, as before (8:6–9:21). Yet despite the magnitude, these plagues do not turn wrath into simple retribution; those who have shed blood are given blood to drink, but their own blood is *not* shed (16:4–7). Instead, they remain alive so that there is still room for repentance. Elsewhere, there are warnings of wrath against the nations allied with the beast, for they will be trampled in the winepress of God's anger (14:10, 19–20; 19:15). Yet in the end the nations still have a place in the city of God (21:24–26; 22:2). Rhetorically, the warnings of wrath are designed to alienate readers from the ways of the nations, while the visions of redemption call for renewed commitment to God and his anointed one.

The heavenly elders continue by declaring that the time has come for the dead to be judged (11:18). Although their words have a sense of immediacy, the cycles of visions delay the judgment scene until later (20:11–15). Readers are assured that the judgment will come but are not told how soon. Like many people in antiquity, the writer assumes that individuals are accountable to God for their actions and that death is no escape, since there will be a postmortem judgment (NOTE on 11:18). Revelation's final judgment scene involves both accountability, as signified by the scrolls of deeds, and divine grace, as symbolized by the scroll of life (20:11–15).

The positive side of judgment is that God will give a reward (*misthos*) to his servants (11:18). Revelation assumes that it would be unjust for God to abandon those who have been faithful—and especially those who have suffered—and allow the perpetrators of injustice to triumph (14:13; 17:6; 18:24). Although society may condemn the faithful, they are to persevere, knowing that God will overturn the verdict. Vindication has been symbolized by the wreath of life and white stone (2:10, 17), as well as by the white robes given to the martyrs (6:11). Resurrection to share in Christ's reign is God's favorable judgment on behalf of the faithful (20:4), and this extends to deathless life in New Jerusalem (21:1–22:5).

Finally, God will "destroy those who destroy the earth" (11:18). This line continues the symmetry in justice, which was noted above, and it is the lens through which the second half of the book should be read. God is the Creator of all things, and his reign is to be acknowledged by the whole created order (4:11; 5:8–11; 10:6; 14:7). His adversaries are the destroyers, who include Satan, the beast, the false prophet, and Babylon the whore. Revelation portrays these four powers as both corrupting and destructive for the people of the world (NOTE on 11:18). The broad literary movement traces the way in which the powers that bring destruction finally suffer it themselves. Babylon is destroyed by the beast (17:16), the beast and false prophet are defeated by Christ (19:11–21), and Satan is confined to the abyss and finally sent to the lake of fire (20:1–10). The Creator's work issues into new creation, where death is banished and only life remains (NOTES on 21:1–4).

Fourth Cycle:
The Dragon, the Beasts,
and the Faithful (11:19–15:4)

25. General Comments on the Fourth Cycle

The previous cycle of visions concluded with the announcement that "the kingdom of the world has become that of our Lord and his Anointed" (Rev 11:15). Yet the heavenly chorus warned that the story was not over, for the time had come "to destroy those who destroy the earth" (11:18). Revelation has two main parts. The first is now over, and the second is about to begin; the conflict between the Creator and the destroyers of the earth will be the dominant theme. The battle begins when Satan is cast down from heaven to earth in Rev 12, and it culminates when he is cast down from earth to the abyss and lake of fire in Rev 20. In between, evil takes several forms. The author successively introduces Satan, the beast and false prophet, and finally the whore. Then he describes the defeat of each one in reverse order:

Satan is thrown from heaven to earth (12:1–17).
    Beast and false prophet conquer (13:1–18).
        Whore rides on the beast (17:1–12).
        Whore destroyed by the beast (17:13–18).
    Beast and false prophet are conquered (19:11–21).
Satan is thrown from earth into the abyss and lake of fire (20:1–3, 7–10).

The followers of Jesus play an important part in this confrontation with evil. Intimations of their role were given in the interlude near the end of the trumpet visions. In Rev 10, John was given a scroll and commanded to prophesy. The scroll's message was then summarized in Rev 11, in which two unnamed prophets represented the community of faith bearing witness to the world. The witnesses were attacked by the beast, who slaughtered them and left their bodies in the street of "the great city" until God breathed new life into them (11:3–13). This conflict is portrayed at greater length in the second part of the book, where the beast threatens the followers of Jesus (13:1–18), who live in the world dominated by "the great city" of Babylon/Rome (17:1–18:24). These visions disclose the forces of evil at work in the social, political, and economic structures of the imperial world. Readers are to resist these powers and remain true to God and the Lamb, who will destroy the destroyers of the earth and give life to the faithful (11:18). The scope of the story is cosmic, and in the end the vision of God's triumph offers hope to the churches, the nations, and the creation itself (21:1–22:5).

A. LITERARY STRUCTURE

The visions in 11:19–15:4 are the first major section in the second half of Revelation. The section is a microcosm of the larger story because it traces the basic movement from conflict to victory. Initially, a woman gives birth to the Messiah, whose enthronement in heaven is followed by Satan's banishment to earth (12:1–17). Satan is the seven-headed dragon, who conjures up a beast from the sea to rule the world (13:1–10). That beast is assisted by a beast from the land, which makes people worship the sea beast (13:11–18). Contrasting visions follow, portraying the redeemed as followers of the Lamb, not the beast. Angels call the world to worship God and warn that those who refuse will be condemned. The earth is harvested, a battle is fought, and in the end the redeemed stand in victory, singing praises to God.

This section begins when the heavenly temple opens and the ark of the covenant appears. There is lightning, thunder, an earthquake, and hail (11:19), and two "signs" appear: a woman and a dragon (12:1–3). Some interpreters discern a sharp break between 11:19 and 12:1 (Roloff; Ulland, *Vision*, 169–70) or regard 11:19 as a bridge between the vision series (Beale; Koch, *Drachenkampf*, 100–101). But the action in the heavenly temple introduces the new series, as it does in other cycles (4:1; 8:3–5; 15:5–8; cf. 19:11). The repetition of the word *ōphthē* (appeared) links the manifestation of the ark in 11:19 to the heavenly signs of 12:1–2. Similar patterns occur in other sources, in which thunder and an earthquake precede the appearance of dragons (Add Esth 11:5–6) and a voice from the temple introduces the image of a woman giving birth (Isa 66:6–7; Aune; Barr; Talbert; Gollinger, *Das "grosse,"* 124–25).

The section concludes with the vision of the conquerors in heaven (Rev 15:2–4), much as other series conclude with heavenly praise or worship (8:1; 11:15–18; 19:1–10). The final vision in this series interlocks with the first vision of the next series. Like links on a chain, the present cycle concludes with a song in 15:2–4, and the next series of plagues is announced in 15:1 and begins in 15:5. This interlocking technique shows that the two cycles are part of a greater whole (Yarbro Collins, *Combat*, 16–19; Schüssler Fiorenza 92). Given the overlap, some interpreters maintain that the present section encompasses all of 11:19–16:21 (Aune) or 11:15–16:1 (Lambrecht, "Structuration," 86) or that it should be limited to 12:1–14:20 (Giesen; Mounce; Thompson). But the interlocking technique joined the last of the seven seal visions (8:1, 3–5) to the first of the trumpet visions (8:2, 6), and that same pattern is used here.

Some sections in Revelation consist of seven numbered visions: the seven messages to the churches and the seven seals, trumpets, and bowls. Accordingly, some scholars conclude that there must be seven unnumbered visions in 11:19–15:4. They identify seven parts by noting the repeated use of "I saw" (*eidon*) and "it appeared" (*ōphthē*; Farrer, *Rebirth*, 45–47; Yarbro Collins, *Combat*, 13–14; Beale 621–24; Murphy 276). Yet it is unlikely that readers are to count unnumbered visions. Moreover, there are actually nine expressions for "seeing" in this section: The verb *ōphthē* occurs twice in the first vision (12:1, 3), and *eidon* occurs twice in the last vision (15:1, 2). It is sufficient to treat 12:1–15:4 as a unit that moves from conflict to triumph without assuming a sevenfold pattern (Bauckham, *Climax*, 15–18; Osborne 453).

Structurally, the visions in this section move toward the concluding song of victory in 15:2–4, while internal connections are created through repeated themes. The vision of Satan's expulsion from heaven (11:19–12:17) provides a backdrop for the vision of the beasts from sea and land (12:18–13:18). Although the sea beast seems to be invincible in violent conquest (*nikan*), it is the agent of Satan, who was defeated in heaven and conquered (*nikan*) by the blood of the Lamb and the witness of his followers (12:11; 13:4, 7).

In the next chapter John contrasts the followers of the Lamb (14:1–5) with the worshipers of the beast (14:6–11) and juxtaposes the ingathering of the redeemed (14:14–16) with judgment on the ungodly (14:17–20). Those who belong to the Lamb are compared to the first fruits of God's harvest (14:4), and the worshipers of the beast are warned that they will receive the wine of God's wrath (14:10). The redeemed share the harvest of salvation (14:16), while the rest of the earth is thrown into the winepress of divine wrath (14:19).

The technique of juxtaposition links the visions of the dragon and beasts in Rev 12–13 to those of judgment and salvation in Rev 14. Those who worship the beast are marked on the forehead or right hand, which allows them to purchase (*agorazein*) in the marketplace (13:16–17). But in the next verse the faithful bear the name of the Lamb and his Father on their foreheads (14:1), and they have been purchased (*agorazein*) by the Lamb for life with God (14:3–4). The number of the beast is 666, which consists of multiples of twelve halved (13:18). In the next verse the Lamb's followers number 144,000, which is twelve squared times a thousand. This juxtaposition suggests that belonging to the beast is a debased alternative to belonging to the Lamb.

The contrasts within this section shape the way readers are to see the world. From an earthly perspective, the beast seems invincible, and those who refuse to worship the beast suffer. The best response might appear to be that people accommodate the beast's wishes in order to avoid judgment. But from a heavenly perspective, the opposite is true. The beast is not invincible, since its power comes from the dragon, which has already lost the war in heaven. Those who resist the beast may fall under the beast's judgment in the present, but in the end, those who ally themselves with the beast will fall under God's judgment, whereas the Lamb's followers obtain life.

B. HISTORY OF INTERPRETATION: REVELATION 12

Revelation 12 depicts a cosmic struggle of good and evil. The protagonist is a woman clothed with the sun, who has the moon under her feet and a wreath of twelve stars on her head; she labors to bear the child who is to rule the nations. The antagonist is a seven-headed dragon that prepares to devour her child, but the plot is foiled, for the child is taken to heaven and the woman flees to the wilderness. Interpretation has often focused on the identity of the woman and her significance for readers.

First, she has been understood to symbolize the people of God. For Victorinus (d. 304), the woman encompassed both ancient Israel and the followers of Jesus. She groans as the patriarchs, prophets, and apostles groaned for the coming of the Messiah. Her twelve stars relate to Israel's early history, since they symbolize the sons of Jacob. The dragon's threat against the child corresponds to the time of Jesus, when the devil tempted him in the wilderness. Finally, the dragon's horns are ten kings who will reign at the end of the age. For modern versions of this view, see the NOTE on 12:1.

Second, the woman has been identified with the church. Ancient and medieval interpreters understood the woman's twelve stars as symbols of the apostles (Hippolytus, *Antichr.* 61; Tyconius; Bede) and her robe as the Word of God (Methodius, *Symp.* 8:5). The moon under her feet showed that the true church was firmly established (Methodius, *Symp.* 6; cf. Primasius; Gregory the Great, *Moral.* 34.14.25) and that it tramples down evil and heresy (Caesarius). As the church, she does not give birth to Jesus himself but labors until Christ is formed in the hearts of believers (Gal 4:19; Hippolytus, *Antichr.* 61; Tyconius; Methodius, *Symp.* 8.7; Andreas; Bede; Geneva Bible).

From this perspective the dragon signifies the sin and evil that threaten the church, which must find refuge in the wilderness that symbolizes virtue (Methodius, *Symp.* 8.11–13; Andreas). The two wings that carry the woman are the OT and NT, which sustain the church's faith (Primasius). The dragon's tail sweeping down stars from heaven shows Christians falling into heresy (Caesarius). Interpretations of Rev 12 as a vision of the church's spiritual struggle continued to appear in medieval texts and in Protestant works from the sixteenth century (Geneva Bible; Backus, *Reformation*, 107–8, 126–27).

The dragon's heads were also identified with political leaders who opposed the church. Victorinus thought the heads were Roman kings from whom the Antichrist would come. For Bede (d. ca. 735), the heads were the rulers of every age who fell under the sway of evil. Joachim of Fiore (d. 1202) identified the heads with specific rulers from the first century until the end of the age: Herod and Nero (first century); the Arian emperor Constantius (fourth century); Muhammad (seventh century); Mesemoth, who was apparently a medieval North African; and Saladin, the Muslim leader who opposed the Crusaders in Joachim's time (twelfth century). What remained was the seventh head, or Antichrist, who was soon to appear (Figure 26; McGinn, *Apocalyptic*, 135–41).

Some Protestant interpreters related the dragon's heads to threats ranging from the serpent's temptation of Eve to ancient Israel's fall into idolatry, and to the wars of the OT and the Roman conquest of Judea. But for many, who considered their own groups to be the true church, the dragon's power was seen at work in the papacy that opposed them, along with the Turkish armies that threatened Europe during the sixteenth century (Bauckham, *Tudor*, 258–68; cf. Backus, *Reformation*, 46–49, 64, 130–31; Kovacs and Rowland, *Revelation*, 143).

Third, the woman has been identified as Mary, since she gives birth to the Messiah. Oecumenius (sixth century) said that Revelation pictures Mary in glory because she is a citizen of heaven. The devil's attempt to devour the child occurred when Herod the Great ordered all the children in Bethlehem to be slain, and the woman's escape to the wilderness was the holy family's escape to Egypt, as reported in Matt 2:1–18. Epiphanius (d. 403) wondered whether being kept safe in the wilderness meant that Mary never died but was taken directly to everlasting life—an issue that would figure into later discussions of Mariology (*Pan.* 78.11.3–4). For some interpreters, the basic mean-

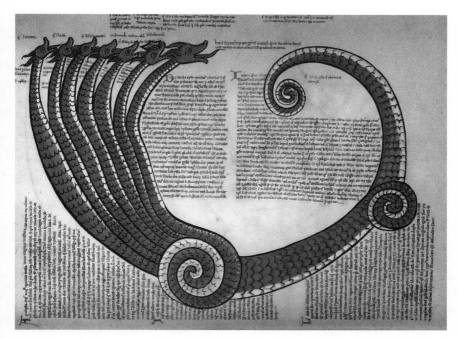

Figure 26. Joachim of Fiore's seven-headed dragon (twelfth century). Courtesy of the Centro internazionale di studi gioachimiti.

ing of Rev 12 concerns Mary bearing Jesus, but they added that Mary is also the mother and representative of the church as a whole (Quodvultdeus, CCSL 60.349; Ambrose Autpert; Haimo; Berengaudus; Richard of St. Victor). New impetus was given for the Marian interpretation through the artwork associated with the Immaculate Conception (INTRO I.C.4).

Fourth, the woman has been identified as Israel. Dispensationalist interpreters make a sharp distinction between Israel and the church. The woman is understood to personify the Jewish people, from whom the Messiah comes. Her other children, who hold the witness of Jesus, are Jewish Christians (Rev 12:17). Although the woman is interpreted symbolically, her flight into the wilderness is taken literally, as Jewish Christians escaping to a desert, perhaps in southern Jordan, at the end of the age (Scofield; LaHaye; Thomas).

C. MODERN HISTORICAL CRITICISM AND REVELATION 12

Source critics often regard Rev 12 as a combination of several elements: the story of the woman and dragon (12:1–6, 13–17), that of Satan's expulsion from heaven (12:7–10), and the explanatory comments by the heavenly voice (12:11–12). The repeated references to the woman's escape into the desert in 12:6 and 13–14 are taken as seams joining the sources. The main components are then related to different mythic patterns—one depicting conflict between a hero and dragon, or serpent, and another telling of the expulsion of rebellious beings from heaven (Charles 1:305–14; Yarbro Collins, *Combat*, 101–16; Aune 2:664–66; Roloff 142–45; Murphy 277–96).

Other scholars plausibly argue that each section of Rev 12 creatively combines elements from various ancient traditions, so one cannot assume that John was using two distinct sources. The repeated references to the woman's escape into the desert can be considered stylistic devices that help the listeners follow the movement of the story, especially since the text was meant to be read aloud (1:3; Busch, *Der gefallene*, 165; Kalms, *Sturz*, 28–29; Witulski, "Zur Frage"). Composition of Rev 12 can better be characterized as the creative use of multiple traditions than as a fusion of two relatively fixed sources with redactional elements.

Since the nineteenth century, interpreters have debated the relationship of Rev 12 to the tales of conflict between good and evil that were common in ancient cultures. The protagonist was usually a god or semi-divine hero who represented life and order, while the antagonist, sometimes pictured as a dragon or monster, signified chaos and death. The plotlines traced the struggle between these powers, culminating in the victory of life and order. Scholars working in the history of religions connected Rev 12 to Babylonian, Egyptian, and Greek myths (Gunkel, *Creation*, 239–50; Bousset 346–58). Others argued that the author of the Apocalypse—who opposed false belief of all sorts—would not have included images drawn from pagan mythology. They insisted that the chapter developed biblical motifs (Beckwith 615; Ford 188; Mounce 230; Prigent 369; Thomas 2:118). Recent studies have noted, however, that Rev 12 has affinities with both Jewish and Greco-Roman traditions and does not follow any one tradition exactly. It is also important to note that the origins of mythic images do not determine their meanings. Authors could shape the mythic images to make different, even contradictory, points in different contexts (Doniger, *Implied*, 81, 97–107; Friesen, "Myth," 286).

Older history-of-religions studies looked for the one basic myth that might inform Rev 12, but more recent writers point out that myths are characterized by variety rather than uniformity. Mythic patterns share certain typical elements while exhibiting variations in detail. Sometimes, ancient plotlines were combined. For example, tales about Leto being pursued by the serpent Python could be combined with those about the goddess Isis facing the monster Typhon (Herodotus, *Historiae* 2.156). It is most helpful to note that these stories have a *pattern* that is similar to that of Rev 12, even though the specifics vary at many points (Charles 1:310–16; Kalms, *Sturz*, 113–22; van Henten, "Dragon," 501; Koch, *Drachenkampf*, 303–5; Aune 2:672; Balch, "Woman"; Perkins 54–55).

The flexible way Revelation uses traditional imagery can be shown by comparing the woman in Rev 12 with figures and images in other sources. The woman is clothed with the sun, has the moon under her feet, and wears a wreath of stars around her head. Interpreters relating Rev 12 to Greco-Roman sources often refer to the woman as the Queen of Heaven, who is surrounded by cosmic symbols in the manner of a goddess. Artemis and her Roman counterpart Diana were depicted with the moon and stars beside them or on the ornaments they wore. A moon goddess could be shown with stars encircling her head. The twelve stars might suggest the constellations of the zodiac (Yarbro Collins, *Combat*, 71–76; Yarbro Collins, *Cosmology*, 108; Patterson, "Note"; Benko, *Virgin*, 87–115; Godwin, *Mystery*, plates 3, 54, 125). Unlike the woman in Rev 12, however, Artemis had little connection with the sun, and artists usually pictured the figures representing the signs of the zodiac, such as a scorpion, archer, or ram, rather than twelve single stars (Godwin, *Mystery*, plates 2, 8, 54, 75, 125).

Alternatively, the woman resembles the goddess Isis. It was said that Isis "showed the paths of the stars," "ordered the course of the sun and the moon," and was "the rays of the sun" (Grant, *Hellenistic*, 132–33). She could be pictured with a brilliant white robe and had the moon on her forehead and cloak. Her garments were trimmed with stars, and sometimes the earth was at her feet (Apuleius, *Metam.* 11.2–4; *LIMC* 5.2:513; Bergmeier, "Altes"). Yet Isis was not typically shown standing on the moon or with stars around her head like the woman in Rev 12.

Interpreters who construe the woman in terms of Jewish sources note that God was said to be robed with light and to have the earth under his feet and stars surrounding him (Ps 104:2; *Sib. Or.* 1:137–40). The cosmic imagery could also be used for God's people. Joseph dreamed of the sun, moon, and eleven stars bowing down to him (Gen 37:7–11), while postbiblical sources told of Isaac being wrapped in light with the glory of the sun and moon above his head, of Levi being like the sun, and of Judah as the moon with rays under his feet (*T. Ab.* 7:1–7; *T. Naph.* 5:2–4). A figure clothed in radiance could be God's emissary (*Jos. As.* 5:5), and the stars could represent the twelve tribes (Beale; Osborne; Prigent; Gollinger, *Das "grosse,"* 73–83). The woman's birth pains are like those of Jerusalem or Zion (Isa 26:17–18; 66:7–8; Jer 4:31).

Although John's portrayal of the woman has affinities with some OT and later Jewish texts, other interpreters rightly note that the differences are striking (Yarbro Collins, *Combat*, 67–69; Kalms, *Sturz*, 46–49; Busch, *Der gefallene*, 58–60). Celestial imagery was not typically used for female figures in Jewish sources. Zion was pictured as a woman in labor, and the sons of Jacob were associated with the sun, moon, and stars, but Jewish texts do not combine the two types of imagery in the way John does. The image of the woman has similarities to Greco-Roman deities and Jewish traditions but does not fully correspond to either one.

The fluidity of the imagery can be further illustrated by one of the hymns from Qumran (Gollinger, *Das "grosse,"* 138–50). Like the writer of Revelation, the author of the scroll compares the distress of his community to that of a woman giving birth—though the wider context also likens it to that of a ship tossed about on the sea and a city under siege:

> I was in distress like a woman giving birth to her firstborn, when pangs and painful labour have come upon her womb opening, causing spasms in the crucible of the pregnant woman. For children come to the womb opening of death, and she who is pregnant with a manchild is convulsed by her labour pains. For in the breakers of death she delivers a male, and in the cords of Sheol there bursts forth from the crucible of the pregnant woman a wonderful counselor with his power, and the manchild is delivered from the breakers by the one who is pregnant with him. (1QHᵃ XI, 7–11 [III, 11–12]; DJD 40:155)

Of special interest is that the woman gives birth to a "wonderful counselor," the expression used for the coming heir to David's throne in Isa 9:6. It is clear that the woman in Revelation gives birth to the Messiah (Rev 12:5), though whether the woman in 1QHᵃ does so is disputed. Some scholars assume that the "wonderful counselor" in the hymn is the Messiah, while others challenge this idea (Bergmann, *Childbirth*, 170–71, 186–89). Given the way biblical allusions are woven into the text, it seems likely that 1QH[a] is linking the community's distress and hope for deliverance to the promises God made concerning Jerusalem and the line of David (Julie Hughes, *Scriptural*, 203; Collins, *Scepter*, 66–67). Nevertheless, the Dead Sea text does not make the birth of the messianic child its focus.

Also of interest is that 1QH[a] includes serpent imagery, though it functions differently than it does in Revelation. In the passage above, the suffering of the righteous woman leads to a good outcome, for she gives birth to a child. Afterword the text tells of a woman who is pregnant with works of wickedness—comparing this to a serpent in the womb. Readers are warned that the works of wickedness will lead to destruction, for the gates of Sheol will open up and devour her works, as if devouring a serpent. The Dead Sea text is like Rev 12 in that it depicts a struggle that has cosmic dimensions, but it does not use the serpent as an image for Satan. Rather, it contrasts two different types of pregnancies in order to show that the suffering of the righteous can lead to redemption while the affliction of the wicked portends destruction.

Comparison of various ancient texts with the vision of the woman and dragon in Rev 12 shows that the imagery would have engaged the interest of a wide spectrum of readers. At the same time, the author of Revelation is not constrained by the use of these images in other sources. The characters and plotline in John's vision take on a distinctive form that is designed to shape his readers' perspectives on the situation of Jesus' followers in the world.

D. TRADITIONS OF ESCHATOLOGICAL ADVERSARIES AND REVELATION 13

Revelation's portrayal of the beast from the sea and beast from the land, or false prophet, draws on traditions about the adversaries of God who were to appear at the end of the age. At the time Revelation was composed, there was no unified belief about an eschatological opponent. Rather, traditions anticipated that various types of adversaries would pose a threat in the end time. Some Jewish and early Christian sources envisioned a final assault of the Gentile nations against God and his people, while others thought that an eschatological tyrant would appear. A few warned about false prophets, and still others spoke in mythic terms about conflict with Belial, or Satan. Revelation combines traditions in a distinctive way. Later, in the second and third centuries CE, elements from Revelation were combined with those from other early Christian writings in order to produce a composite picture of the Antichrist (discussed below).

Jewish Sources on Eschatological Adversaries

The biblical prophetic writings sometimes envision Gentile nations making a final assault against Israel, leading to the nations' defeat and a new era of peace for Jerusalem (Zech 12:1–9; 14:1–15; Joel 3:1–21). The battle could be pictured as a time when sun and moon are darkened and the foes are trampled like grapes in a winepress (Joel 3:11–15; cf. Isa 63:1–6). A similar image is used in Rev 14:19–20 and 19:16. In later apocalyptic writings, the nations sometimes turn against each other (*1 En.* 56:5–8), and Revelation varies this pattern by showing the beast destroying its ally the whore (Rev 17:16).

Another scenario is that a redeemer destroys the nations with the breath from his lips (*4 Ezra* 13:1–13); in Revelation, Christ wins victory with the sword from his mouth (Rev 19:15–21). Yet another variation is that God sends fiery swords, hail, and brimstone from heaven to destroy them (*Sib. Or.* 3:663–97), a pattern reflected at the end of Revelation, where fire from heaven destroys the nations before the final judgment (Rev 20:7–9).

One biblical form of the tradition identifies Gog from the land of Magog as the leader of the hostile nations. Although Gog is confident of victory, he is defeated by the power of heaven, and his armies become food for the birds (Ezek 38–39). In later apocalyptic writings, the nations assembled by Gog could be identified with the armies of Belial, or Satan, who are defeated at the end of the age (1QM XI, 8, 16; NOTE on Rev 20:8). The beast in Revelation has features of Gog, since it gathers the nations for the final assault, and its armies become food for the birds (6:12–16; 19:17–21). But Gog can also be distinguished from the beast, since Gog appears in the very last battle, which occurs after the beast's defeat (NOTES and COMMENT on 20:7–10).

The book of Daniel envisions kings and nations battling for power at the end of the age. Struggles in the kingdoms of Media and Persia lead to the rise of Greece and battles among the factions of the Greek empire. Eventually, Egypt, Libya, Ethiopia, and other nations become embroiled before the nations are defeated and a new age begins with the resurrection of the dead (Dan 8:15–26; 11:2–45; 12:1–3). Daniel depicts successive empires as four beasts: a lion, a bear, a leopard, and a ten-horned monster. From these empires arises the tyrant, pictured as a horn, who speaks haughtily against God and tries to alter the holy law. This oppressive ruler makes war against the holy ones, and for three and a half years they are under his power (7:19–27). Supremely arrogant, he presses upward to heaven and casts down the stars. He ends the practice of lawful burnt offering and sets up a desolating sacrilege. The tyrant reigns through deceit and destruction (8:9–11, 23–25; 9:27). Finally, however, God intervenes, breaks the oppressor's power, and establishes an everlasting kingdom (7:27; 8:25).

Historically, the pattern for Daniel's tyrant was Antiochus IV Epiphanes, who suppressed observance of Jewish customs and turned the Jerusalem temple into a sanctuary of Zeus in 167 BCE. By depicting the tyrant in visionary form, Daniel shaped the way later writers thought of the end of the age. In Revelation the beast from the sea assumes the role of the tyrant, and it has the traits of all the empires that Daniel pictures as beasts (Rev 13:2). Supremely arrogant, the beast blasphemes God, shows contempt for the sanctuary, and persecutes the faithful for three and a half years (13:5–7). Its associate manipulates people through deception (13:14). Revelation goes beyond Daniel in making the tyrannical beast the leader of the great assault by the nations (16:12–16; 19:19), but like Daniel's tyrant, the beast is defeated by the power of God and burned with fire (19:20; Dan 7:11; 8:25).

Expectations of an eschatological tyrant also appear in other apocalyptic writings. Some focus on conditions in Israel, warning that the people will have debauched leaders who will spread impiety. Then a terrible foreign ruler will ruthlessly persecute faithful Jews until some are forced to choose martyrdom. But God will intervene with signs in heaven and on earth; the nations will be defeated and the devil brought to an end, so that God's kingdom is manifest throughout the creation (*T. Mos.* 7–9). Other writers picture a series of empires oppressing the earth, with the last of these exhibiting the traits of the Roman Empire. The final king will be cruel and arrogant, fomenting ungodliness throughout his realm. Then God's Messiah will defeat the hostile nations (*4 Ezra* 12–13) and perhaps judge the tyrant himself (*2 Bar.* 36–40).

Some scenarios include the eschatological demise of the sea monster Leviathan and the land monster Behemoth, who symbolized chaos (*1 En.* 60:24; *4 Ezra* 6:49–52; *2 Bar.* 29:4). None of these sources equates the monsters with the tyrant. In a creative adaptation of the tradition, Revelation ascribes traits of Leviathan to the eschatological tyrant and likens the tyrant's associate to Behemoth (Rev 13:1, 11). Where the tradition expected the monsters to become food for the righteous, Revelation pictures them being cast into the lake of fire (19:20).

Satan, or Belial, sometimes assumes a central role in scenarios of eschatological conflict. Some of the DSS identify the present age as the dominion of Belial, the evil angel who leads other evil angels and reigns over the human sons of darkness. Belial is wicked but is ultimately subject to God, and one text warns that God will send Belial to punish apostates (CD VIII, 2). The scrolls see Belial's reign culminating in the final battle against the nations, when the angel Michael helps the sons of light defeat Belial and the sons of darkness (1QM XVII, 5–8). In other scrolls God's agent is called Melchizedek, or "king of righteousness" (11QMelch II, 12–13), and the satanic figure is Melchiresha', or "king of wickedness" (4Q544). Similar expectations appear in the *Testaments of the Twelve Patriarchs*, in which Beliar is the evil figure who draws people into sin. These texts anticipate that the forces of God will make war against Beliar (*T. Dan* 5:10–11) and that Beliar will be taken captive (*T. Zeb.* 9:8), bound (*T. Levi* 18:2), cast into the fire forever (*T. Jud.* 25:3), and destroyed (*T. Benj.* 3:8).

Some Jewish texts combine traditions about the defeat of Satan with those of the coming tyrant. Writers envision this present age culminating in a breakdown of the social and natural order and the world falling under oppressive rule (*Sib. Or.* 3:75–92, 611–15). They warn that deceivers will appear and that Beliar will do signs, even imitating God by raising the dead. Beliar will resemble Nero, for he will come from the Sebastenoi, or line of Augustus, recalling a tradition that expected Nero to return with destructive power. God, however, will destroy Beliar and his allies (2:154–73; 3:63–74; cf. 4:119–24, 137–39; 5:28–34).

Revelation varies the traditions about Satan's final defeat. Like others, the writer portrays a beast that is a Nero-like tyrant which receives its authority from Satan (NOTES on Rev 13:2–3). What is distinctive is that the defeat of Satan and the beast occurs in stages: Satan suffers an initial defeat in heaven at the hands of the angel Michael (12:7–12), but he continues seeking dominion over the world through the beast (13:2–4). When the beast is defeated, Satan is bound for a thousand years (20:1–3) but then is released to lead the final assault of the nations along with Gog and Magog before being vanquished and hurled into the lake of fire (20:7–10).

Early Christian Writings

Jesus' discourse in the Synoptic Gospels about the last days warns that several types of opponents will threaten the faithful at the end of the age. Some will come in Jesus' name, claiming to be the Messiah, so the faithful must not be deceived (Mark 13:6; Matt 24:5). When wars and persecutions occur, false messiahs and false prophets will try to lead people astray, performing miracles to demonstrate their power (Mark 13:22;

Matt 24:23–26) like the false prophet in Revelation (Rev 13:11–18; 16:13–14; 19:20). Yet these pseudo-prophets and messiahs are not said to be the agents of violent persecution, and no eschatological tyrant is mentioned. The synoptic discourse reaffirms Daniel's warning about the desecration of the temple by picturing a "desolating sacrilege" (Dan 9:27; Mark 13:14). Then the gospels picture the sun, moon, and stars becoming dark and the Son of Man coming on the clouds to gather the elect together (13:24–27 par.; Rev 14:14–16).

The motif of the eschatological tyrant appears in 2 Thessalonians, which warns that rebellion against God will occur at the end of the age, before Christ's return. The mystery of lawlessness is already at work and will climax in "the man of lawlessness" (2 Thess 2:3), or "son of destruction," who will lead many away from the truth. The lawless one will receive power from Satan and exhibit it in signs and wonders (2:9–11). At present, the son of destruction is restrained by an unnamed power (2:6–7), but after he has been allowed to deceive people for a time, Christ will destroy him (2:8).

Second Thessalonians develops themes from Daniel, for the lawless one will show contempt for every type of worship and exalt himself above the gods of the nations. He will also take his seat in the temple and declare himself to be God (2:4). Where Daniel pictured a "desolating sacrilege" being set up in the temple, 2 Thessalonians expects the satanic miracle-worker himself to become the object of worship (Malherbe, *Letters*, 420–21). By way of comparison, Revelation treats these motifs separately. The writer portrays the community of faith as a temple that is threatened by the nations (Rev 11:1–2). Then he pictures people making the tyrannical beast the focus of worship (13:4), while a wonder-working false prophet promotes the ruler cult. But Revelation does not actually picture the tyrant being worshiped in the temple.

The Johannine Epistles refer to an adversary known as Antichrist (*antichristos*), whose coming signals "the last hour" (1 John 2:18). There is no clear evidence that the notion of an anti-Messiah was part of Jewish thought at this time. The term *antichristos* appears for the first time in the Johannine Epistles, though it was apparently coined in Christian circles before the epistles were composed (2:18, 22; 4:3; 2 John 7). The next known occurrence is in the letter of Polycarp (*Phil.* 7:1), who wrote in the early second century CE and used Johannine language. The term *antichristos* begins with the Greek prefix "anti-," which can mean "against," indicating that the figure is "against Christ." The prefix can also indicate a substitution or replacement for Christ (Brown, *Epistles*, 333). The Synoptic Gospels warn about the false messiahs (*pseudo-christoi*) who will come in Jesus' name and say "I am he" (Matt 24:24; Mark 13:6), but in the Johannine Epistles the Antichrist does not claim to be the Messiah or make himself the object of worship. Rather, the Antichrist replaces true belief with a faith that from the writer's perspective is actually false.

The principal trait of the Antichrist is to deny claims about Jesus, especially that the Messiah came in the flesh (1 John 4:2–3; 2 John 7). For the writer of the epistles, this denial of the value of Jesus' humanity makes the Antichrist the deceiver. Nothing is said about an antichrist who works miracles or persecutes the faithful like Daniel's eschatological tyrant or the beast in Revelation. Moreover, these epistles extend the notion of the Antichrist from that of a single eschatological adversary to a plurality of antichrists: Every person who denies the value of Jesus' humanity is an antichrist (1 John 2:22–23; 2 John 7). Such antichrists include some people who have left the author's own community (1 John 2:18–19). If the Spirit of God moves people to faith in Jesus as the Christ, the spirit of the Antichrist is the spirit of error at work in the false prophets who negate the humanity of Jesus (4:1–3, 6). The issues addressed in the Johannine Epistles are different from those in Revelation, in which deception and false prophecy have to do with accommodating Greco-Roman religious practices and the imperial cult (Rev 2:20; 13:11–18; 19:20).

The Johannine Epistles assume that the last hour has already come and that the eschatological battle is now under way (Klauck, *Der erste*, 150–51). A major assault was made by Jesus, who came to destroy the works of the devil (1 John 3:8), and yet the world remains under the power of the evil one (5:19). The Christian community plays a role in the conflict, for as Christians confess the truth about Jesus, the human being who is God's Messiah, they share Christ's victory (2:13–14; 4:4; 5:4–5). Revelation also identifies faithfulness to God and Christ in the face of opposition as victory or conquest (Rev 12:11; 15:2; 21:7; NOTE on 2:7).

Christian writings from the late first to mid-second centuries reflect the diversity of traditions noted above. The *Didache* warns that in the last days false prophets will appear and the deceiver will come as the Son of God, doing miracles, and the world will be handed over to him. But unlike Jesus, this deceiver will commit lawless deeds of an unprecedented kind (*Did.* 16:3–4). The *Epistle of Barnabas* recalls Daniel's vision of the coming tyrant, who seems to be an agent of Satan (*Barn.* 4:1–14). The *Martyrdom and Ascension of Isaiah* warns that the church will be persecuted in the end times by Satan, or Beliar, who will come in the form of a king like Nero while usurping the place of Christ by claiming to be God's Beloved. Beliar will do miracles and the world will worship him, but in the end Christ and his angels will defeat him (*Mart. Asc. Isa.* 4:1–14; Dochhorn, "Beliar"). Revelation fits within this range of expectations concerning eschatological adversaries, while offering a distinctive form of the tradition.

E. HISTORY OF INTERPRETATION: THE ANTICHRIST AND REVELATION 13

Christians from the second century onward combined biblical passages about eschatological opponents to create a composite portrait of the Antichrist. Such efforts were part of an attempt to gain a coherent understanding of how evil functioned in the present and future, and how it would be overcome. Some thought of the Antichrist as an individual tyrant (cf. Dan 7:20–21; 2 Thess 2:3–4), while others spoke of the Antichrist in collective terms, as a group influenced by evil (cf. 1 John 2:18). Some expected the Antichrist to be of Jewish origin, while others thought he would have Roman traits like Nero (cf. Rev 13:2–3), and still others assumed he would come from the Christian community itself (cf. 1 John 2:18–19).

A dominant form of the tradition was established by Irenaeus (d. ca. 200), who responded to Gnostic teachings that linked evil to the Creator of this world. For Irenaeus, the Creator was not the originator of evil but its opponent. He identified the Antichrist as the final enemy, who would sum up all evil, just as Christ summed up all goodness. Since the Word became flesh in Christ, evil would be incarnate in the Antichrist (cf. 1 John 2:18). Receiving power from the devil, the Antichrist would be an evil king, the tyrannical beast (Rev 13:1–3), and the man of lawlessness, who would take God's place in the temple (2 Thess 2:4). He would be the desolating sacrilege (Matt 24:15) and would persecute the saints for three and a half years (Dan 7:24–25; Rev 13:5–7). Irenaeus pointed out that the numerical values of the letters in the word *Lateinos* added up to 666. Yet he did not identify the Antichrist's kingdom with the present Latin or Roman Empire and thought that the Antichrist would come from Dan, the tribe not listed with the redeemed in Rev 7:4–8 (Irenaeus, *Haer.* 5.25–30). He did not take up the anti-Roman aspects (INTRO I.A).

Hippolytus (d. 236) developed the tradition in his treatise *On Antichrist*. If Christ was a lion because of his royalty and glory (Rev 5:5), the Antichrist will be a lion because of his tyranny and violence. If Christ raised up a new "temple" in the form of his resurrected body (John 2:19), the Antichrist will build an idolatrous temple of stone in Jerusalem (2 Thess 2:4) and slay the two witnesses who refuse to glorify him (Rev 11:3–13). Hippolytus differs from Irenaeus in that he identifies the beast from the sea with the Roman Empire (13:1–10) and makes the beast from the land the kingdom of the Antichrist (13:11). A similar scenario appears in Lactantius (d. ca. 325), though he combines the traits of the first tyrannical beast with those of the miracle-working second beast in his warning about the final enemy (*Inst.* 7.17; Dochhorn, "Laktanz").

The author of Revelation depicted imperial Rome as the adversary of Christ and his followers, but Tertullian (d. ca. 225) identified the Roman Empire as the stabilizing force that *restrained* the Antichrist, whose persecution would come after the empire split into multiple kingdoms (*Res.* 24–25; cf. 2 Thess 2:1–10). For Tertullian, the Antichrist's influence was not limited to political threats but appeared in heresies threatening the church (*Marc.* 3.8; 5.16; *Praescr.* 4; 33). Cyprian (d. 258) thought the persecutions under Decius and Valerian were a sign that the Antichrist was approaching, and he associated imperial demands to sacrifice to the gods with pressure to worship the image of the beast (*Ep.* 58.1–4; 8). Yet he stopped short of identifying current emperors as the Antichrist and regarded schism in the church as another sign of the Antichrist's coming, since the disintegration of the community reflected the disintegration of the world at the end of the age (Brent, *Cyprian*, 109–16).

Victorinus (d. 304) identified the Antichrist as the beast from the sea, whose seven heads represent Rome and seven of its emperors. He made the observation—reaffirmed by modern interpreters—that the beast has the traits of Nero, since one of its heads was slain and brought back to life in order to persecute Christians (*In Apoc.* 13.1–3). The second beast, or false prophet, would put a statue of the Nero-like tyrant in the Jerusalem temple. Jerome (d. 420) expected the future Antichrist to be the man in whom Satan would dwell and that the Antichrist's "temple" would be the church (*Comm. Dan.* 7.8; *Ep.* 121.11). Since Christ ascended to heaven from the Mount of Olives, Jerome expected the Antichrist to die there—a detail that recurs later in the tradition (K. Hughes, *Constructing*, 74–79).

An alternative was to interpret the Antichrist in a collective sense, as the body of people in the church who deny Christ by their words and actions. Tyconius (d. ca. 400) thought the church throughout its history consisted of true and false believers and that the Antichrist was at work wherever sin operated under the pretense of piety. Tyconius affirmed that the Antichrist would be overcome at the end of the age, but his emphasis was on resisting sin within the church of his own time (K. Hughes, *Constructing*, 84–94). Augustine (d. 430) sometimes affirmed the traditional idea that the Antichrist would persecute the church at the end of the age (*Civ.* 20.13, 30), but he also followed Tyconius in construing the Antichrist in a collective sense. He warned that those who professed to believe in Christ could deny him by loveless deeds, so even those within the church had to ask whether they might be an antichrist (*Tract. ep. Jo.* 3.4, 8). Similar ideas were found in Gregory the Great and others in the Latin tradition (McGinn, *Antichrist*, 77, 82, 278–80; K. Hughes, *Constructing*, 94–114).

Eastern Christianity included both individual and collective interpretations of the Antichrist. Origen (d. 254) wrote of good and evil as opposing tendencies within humanity, with their ultimate forms occurring in the goodness of Jesus and the evil of the Antichrist (*Cels.* 6.45). He interpreted Christ's great battle against the beast as a conflict within each person. Revelation depicts the heavenly warrior as God's logos—the divine Word, or Reason—who comes to battle the irrational forces of sin, and victory is won whenever the divine logos gives people the light of truth and destroys all that is sinful in the soul (*Comm. Jo.* 2.42–63; Ramelli, "Origen's").

Other eastern writers took the opposite approach, assuming that the Antichrist would be a particular person. One thought the Antichrist would have a tuft of gray hair on his forehead, eyebrows reaching to his ears, and a leprous spot on his hands (*Apoc. El.* 3). Another said he would have a fiery head with one bloodshot eye and another blue-black eye (Syriac *Testament of the Lord* 11). The most common approach, however, was to follow the scenario attested by western writers, where the Antichrist is the ruler who persecutes the church at the end of the age as either Revelation's beast from the sea (Andreas) or its beast from the land (Oecumenius).

The Antichrist tradition took new forms through the legend of the last world emperor. Building on the idea that the Roman Empire now restrained the Antichrist, some expected the age to continue until the last and greatest emperor laid down his crown in Jerusalem. Only then would the Antichrist be unleashed, setting his throne on the Mount of Olives before meeting his ultimate demise there (Ps.-Methodius in McGinn, *Visions*, 75–76). In the tenth century, Adso of Montier-en-Der popularized the story, which encouraged loyalty to one's rulers (INTRO I.B.1).

Ancient interpreters generally refrained from identifying the Antichrist with known figures, but by the eleventh century that practice was changing. One factor was that interpreters began relating the visions in Revelation to historical events from the time of Christ to the end of the age. For example, Joachim of Fiore (d. 1202) identified the seven heads of the satanic dragon with seven persecutors of the church, from Herod in the time of Christ up to Saladin, who defeated the Crusaders in the twelfth century. The seventh head would be the Antichrist, whom Joachim thought had already been born. The Antichrist would not be of Jewish background but would be a false Christian from the west, who would imitate Christ's roles of prophet, priest, and king. Joachim compared the Antichrist's priestly aspect to being a false pope, an idea that later contributed to antipapal interpretations of Revelation (McGinn, *Antichrist*, 140–42).

A second factor was the struggle between popes and emperors. In the eleventh century, Pope Gregory VII castigated a rival pope, who had been set up by the emperor. Each side used "antichrist" as an epithet against the other (McGinn, *Antichrist*, 121). In the thirteenth century, clashes over control of territory in Europe and failed promises to conduct a crusade to the Holy Land prompted Pope Gregory IX to identify Emperor Frederick II as the beast from the sea (Rev 13:1–2). In response, Frederick charged that the pope was the satanic dragon and the Antichrist. After Frederick's death, some speculated that he was hiding and would return to oppose the church—like the beast that came to life in Rev 13:3 (McGinn, *Visions*, 173–75; Lerner, "Frederick").

A third factor was conflict over the reform of the church. A flashpoint was the clash between the wealth of the established church and the ideal of poverty, espoused by Francis of Assisi and others. One of the Franciscans, Peter Olivi (d. 1298), thought that the mystical Antichrist was already at work among worldly Christians and clergy and that the great Antichrist was yet to come. The power of the Antichrist would have a dual aspect, including an Islamic leader and a Christian pope who would attack the ideal of poverty (Burr, *Olivi's*, 141–45). When popes Boniface VIII and Benedict XI attacked the Spiritual Franciscans, Ubertino of Casale (d. 1330) identified the popes with the mystical Antichrist (McGinn, *Visions*, 214). For the Bohemian reformer Jan Hus (d. 1415), the Antichrist was still to come and would be an individual pope. A more radical approach was that of John Wyclif (d. 1384), who thought the entire institution of the papacy was the Antichrist (McGinn, *Antichrist*, 181–85).

Martin Luther (d. 1546) followed this trend when his call for reform brought resistance from church authorities and condemnation by papal decree in 1520. In response, he too identified the papacy with the kingdom of the Antichrist. For him, the two beasts in Rev 13 showed the unity of the empire and the papacy, which Christ would destroy (LuthW 35:406–9; 36:72). Since Turkish armies threatened Europe, they belonged to the sphere of the Antichrist (WA.DB 52:549). The writings of the Lutheran movement continued identifying the papacy with the Antichrist, while also noting that all false teachers were the Antichrist in some sense (Kolb and Wengert, *Book*, 309, 337; cf. 174, 187).

John Calvin (d. 1564) held that the kingdom of the Antichrist was manifested in the papacy throughout the ages (*Institutes* 4.2.12) and in the threat posed by Muslim Turks (Firth, *Apocalyptic*, 32–37). The antipapal view was repeated in the Reformed theological tradition (*Westminster Confession* 25.6). In England, William Tyndale (d. 1536) used antichrist language for the papacy while giving it a broader meaning, referring to the Antichrist as a spiritual force at work throughout the ages (Firth, *Apocalyptic*, 25). Linking the Antichrist to the papacy was a standard feature of Protestant interpretation from the sixteenth to the nineteenth centuries (Intro I.C.2).

The radical wing of the Reformation included Thomas Müntzer (d. 1525), who thought the entire social and religious hierarchy was the kingdom of the Antichrist and that the pope was the Antichrist's herald. Müntzer advocated using force to overthrow the established social order. A nonviolent form of resistance was advocated by Melchior Hoffmann (d. 1543), who thought Luther and other reformers were allies of the papal Antichrist in their opposition to Anabaptists like himself (Intro I.C.3; McGinn, *Antichrist*, 213–15).

Roman Catholics responded to the antipapal charges in a number of ways. Some returned the accusation, identifying Luther as the Antichrist; others linked the Antichrist to the Islamic threat, since the Turkish armies had pressed into Europe. Some drew on the tradition of spiritual exegesis, identifying the Antichrist as a principle that was operative in all times and places (Bauckham, *Tudor*, 92–94). The Jesuit Robert Bellarmine (d. 1621) argued that the Antichrist was still in the future, which meant that he could not be the present pope. Another Jesuit, Luis de Alcázar (d. 1613), argued that

Rev 1–19 described events before Constantine, which meant that Revelation did not portray the popes of later generations (INTRO I.C.4; McGinn, *Antichrist*, 226–28).

Futuristic interpreters from the early nineteenth century onward identified the beast from the sea (13:1–10) with the individual who would dominate the world at the end of the age. The beast from the land would be the promoter of false religion, which would center in the papacy and yet include Protestant churches that had departed from the true Christian message (13:11–18). Some referred to the Antichrist as a political figure (Seiss), and others as an apostate religious leader (Scofield). As papal political power declined during the eighteenth and nineteenth centuries, speculation about the Antichrist shifted to figures such as Napoleon and Adolf Hitler. After World War II, some interpreters speculated that the Antichrist might arise from the European Common Market, since Revelation portrayed the beast as engaging in economic coercion and building a coalition of ten kings (Boyer, *When*, 254–90).

Historical interpretation shifted attention to the way Revelation portrayed Rome and its emperors at the time that the book was composed. Nineteenth-century interpreters such as Friedrich Bleek, Moses Stuart, and Friedrich Düsterdieck noted allusions to Roman imperialism and possible connections to stories about Nero and Domitian. The history-of-religions approach explored possible antecedents for a unified myth about the Antichrist that might have predated the writing of Revelation (Bousset, *Antichrist*). But subsequent work has shown that various traditions about eschatological adversaries were in circulation in the first century CE and that Revelation drew on these ideas in creative ways (Peerbolte, *Antecedents*).

The Number 666

One of the most disputed points in Revelation's portrayal of the beast concerns the number 666. The beast's associate has all people put a mark "on their right hand or on their forehead, so that no one can buy or sell anything unless the person has the mark with the beast's name or the number of its name. This calls for wisdom. Let the one who understands calculate the number of the beast, for it is the number of a person. Its number is 666" (Rev 13:16–18).

Ancient interpreters of Revelation assumed that 666 was related to familiar words through the technique of gematria—adding up the numerical values of the letters of the beast's name—and they favored names that described the beast rather than proper names. Irenaeus noted that *euanthas*, or "blooming," yielded 666, but he could not see that it suited the context. He therefore adjusted the spellings of words to make them fit the number. As already noted, spelling *Latinos* with an extra *e* as *Lateinos* linked the beast to the Latin kingdom of Rome, and adding an *e* to Titan produced *Teitan*, a mythic opponent of the gods (*Haer.* 5.30.3). Later writers changed *arnoumai* (I deny) to *arnoume* and formulated the odd word *antemos*, which might connote opposition or dishonor. Still others rearranged the Roman numerals for 666—DCLXVI—into the Latin expression DIC LVX, or *Dic Lux*, referring to Satan, who "calls himself light" (2 Cor 11:14). In the sixteenth century, Protestants argued that the number meant *Lateinos*, signifying the Roman Catholic Church, which they regarded as the agent of the Antichrist, or suggested that the number corresponded to the word "Roman" in Hebrew letters or "Italian Church" (*Ekklēsia Italika*) in Greek letters (Brady, *Contribution*, 250–85).

Proper names were later identified with the beast's number. Most interpreters preferred the names of their own contemporaries, usually for polemical purposes. During thirteenth-century conflicts over imperial and papal authority, the followers of Emperor Frederick II linked Pope Innocent IV to the Antichrist by noting that *Innocencius papa* totaled 666. In the fourteenth century, the radical Franciscans, who criticized papal worldliness, found that the pope's name, *Benediktos*, fit the number (Kovacs and Rowland, *Revelation*, 158–59). Protestants in the sixteenth century regarded the papacy as the Antichrist, but Catholics found ways to make Martin Luther's name add up to 666 by adjusting its spelling. Others related the Antichrist to the threat posed by Muslim conquests, writing Muhammad's name in Greek as *Maometis* to equal 666. In the seventeenth century, critics of William Laud, the archbishop of Canterbury, wrote his name as Will Laud in Roman numerals that fit the number (VVILL LaVD). Later, Napoleon's quest to expand his empire made him an antichrist figure. Leo Tolstoy's *War and Peace* (9.19) shows how the words *l'empereur Napoléon* and the number of months in the beast's reign—*quarante-deux*, or forty-two—each could total 666.

A different approach was to take the number as a distorted abbreviation for the name of Christ. In Greek the number 666 was written χξϛ and the variant 616 as χιϛ. Both begin with chi (χ) and end with the numerical digamma, or stigma (ϛ), which many mistook for a final sigma (ς). The result was that they thought the first and last letters in the number were identical to the first and last letters in *Christos* (Χριστός) and that the middle letter signaled the Antichrist's perversion of Christ's name (CCL 107:149–51). Another alternative was to link 666 to the period of the Antichrist's reign. A scurrilous ninth-century life of Muhammad erroneously said that he had died in the year 666 (Emmerson and McGinn, *Apocalypse*, 229), and in the thirteenth century, Innocent III thought that 666 might indicate the duration of the Islamic empire. Later, Protestant writers thought the number foretold the rise of papal power in the seventh century and wondered whether 1666 might mark the end of the Antichrist's reign (Brady, *Contribution*, 180–201).

Modern futuristic interpretation of Revelation originated in the seventeenth century among Roman Catholics who insisted that the Antichrist was not the pope but a figure yet to come. They argued that the meaning of the number could not be known at present because the Antichrist had not yet appeared. Some Protestants also adopted this approach (Thomas). Some propose that the multiples of six point to human arrogance, because humankind was created on the sixth day (Walvoord; LaHaye). Others equate the number with a specific secular ruler. For example, Hitler's name works if the letters of the Latin alphabet are numbered consecutively beginning with 100 (H = 107, i = 108, t = 119, l = 111, e== 104, r = 117). Many assume that the number will be stamped on people or merchandise through some means like social security cards or international product codes (LaHaye; Lindsey, *Late*, 113; see Boyer, *When*, 275–76, 285–87).

Modern historical interpretation assumes that the name would have been known to first-century readers. Gaius Caligula (37–41 CE) was remembered for his attempt to have a statue of himself put in the Jerusalem temple, and his name in Greek adds up to 616, though not to 666. The name of Claudius (41–54 CE) has been made to work by adjusting the spelling and using Roman numerals (J. Schmidt, "Rätselzahl"), and Vespasian (69–79 CE), who helped to crush the Jewish revolt against Rome, had titles that yield the required total if abbreviated and transliterated into Hebrew (Baines, "Number"), but both of these solutions seem forced. Domitian (81–96 CE) was said to have been a Nero figure (Juvenal, *Satiriae* 4.37–38; Pliny the Younger, *Pan.* 53), but he fits the number only when one uses a complex series of abbreviations for his name and titles (Stauffer, "666"). His successor, Nerva (96–98 CE), has a name that can be made to fit the number (Kraft 222), but Nerva does not seem to have been particularly beast-like. Beginning in 1831, scholars proposed spelling the name of Nero (54–68 CE) using the Hebrew alphabet (NOTE on 13:18). This theory is the most viable one.

26. The Woman, the Child, and the Dragon (11:19–12:17)

11 [19]Then God's temple in heaven was opened, and the ark of his covenant appeared in his temple. There were flashes of lightning, rumblings, peals of thunder, an earthquake, and large hail. **12** [1]And a great sign appeared in heaven: a woman clothed with the sun, with the moon under her feet and a wreath of twelve stars on her head. [2]She was pregnant and cried out in pain, for she was in the agony of giving birth. [3]Then another sign appeared in heaven: a great fiery red dragon, with seven heads and ten horns, and seven diadems on its heads. [4]Its tail swept down a third of the stars of heaven and threw them to the earth. And the dragon stood before the woman who was about to give birth, so that when she gave birth, it might devour her child. [5]She gave birth to a son, a male, who is to rule all the nations with an iron rod. But her child was caught up to God and his throne, [6]and the woman fled to the desert, where she had a place made ready by God. There she will be taken care of for 1,260 days.

[7]Then there was war in heaven: Michael and his angels fought the dragon, and the dragon and its angels fought back, [8]but they were defeated and there was no longer any place for them in heaven. [9]So the great dragon was thrown down. He is the ancient serpent, who is called devil and Satan, the deceiver of the whole world. He was thrown down to the earth and his angels were thrown down with him. [10]I heard a loud voice in heaven say,

"Now the salvation and the power and the kingdom of our God,
and the authority of his Anointed have come,
for the accuser of our brethren has been thrown down,
the one who accuses them day and night before our God.
[11]They conquered him through the blood of the Lamb
and the word of their witness.
Love for their own lives did not make them shun death.
[12]Therefore, rejoice you heavens and those who dwell in them.
But woe to the earth and sea,
because the devil has come down to you with great anger,
for he knows that his time is short.[11]

¹³When the dragon saw that it had been thrown down to the earth, it chased the woman who had given birth to the male child. ¹⁴But the woman was given the two wings of a great eagle so that she could fly to her place in the desert, where she would be taken care of for a time and times and half a time, out of the serpent's reach. ¹⁵Then from its mouth the serpent poured a river of water after the woman, so that the river would sweep her away. ¹⁶But the earth helped the woman. The earth opened its mouth and swallowed the river that the dragon poured out of its mouth. ¹⁷So the dragon was furious at the woman, and it went off to make war on the rest of her children, who keep the commandments of God and hold firmly to the witness of Jesus.

NOTES

11:19. *Then God's temple in heaven was opened.* The door of an earthly temple being opened by an unseen power could portend either divine favor (Cicero, *Div.* 1.34.74; Virgil, *Aen.* 3.90–96) or misfortune (Dio Cassius, *Rom. Hist.* 64.8.1–2; Josephus, *J.W.* 6.293–96; Tacitus, *Hist.* 5.13). Here and in Rev 15:5 the opening of the heavenly temple is encouraging for those whom God will redeem and ominous for the powers of evil, who will be defeated.

and the ark of his covenant appeared in his temple. The ark was the chest in which the tablets of the law or covenant were kept. The earthly ark stood in the holy of holies and was said to have been made according to a heavenly pattern, which might have suggested that there was an ark in heaven (Exod 25:9–16; Josephus, *Ant.* 3.181; Philo, *QE* 2.68). Some sources assumed the ark was plundered by the Babylonians when the first temple was destroyed (*4 Ezra* 10:22), but others thought it had been hidden and would be restored in the future (2 Macc 2:4–8; *Liv. Pro.* 2:11–19). A coin from the Bar Kochba period (ca. 134–135 CE) shows the façade of the Jerusalem temple with what is probably the ark inside it (Figure 27). The image conveyed hope for the temple's restoration (Mildenberg and Mottahedeh, *Coinage*, 33–42). Rather than focusing on the earthly ark that disappeared during the Babylonian conquest, the vision of the heavenly ark announces judgment on the oppressive powers that Babylon represents (Rev 17–18; Briggs, *Jewish*, 85–103; Spatafora, *From*, 173–85; G. Stevenson, *Power*, 233–36, 263–65, 293–95).

There were flashes of lightning, rumblings, peals of thunder, an earthquake, and large hail. These phenomena show God's presence and power (4:5), inflict judgment (8:7; 11:13; 16:18–21), and here portend divine wrath (cf. 6:12; 8:5).

12:1. *And a great sign appeared in heaven.* A sign (*sēmeion*) is communication in symbolic form. John's whole revelation communicates by signs (*sēmainein*), using images to represent larger realities (1:1). Here, the woman symbolizes the people of God and the dragon signifies Satan. Later, a sign will point to the future outworking of God's wrath (15:1), but here it looks back to the birth of the Messiah. Some interpreters liken the signs in Rev 12 to the darkening of heavenly bodies that people on earth would witness before a time of affliction (Luke 21:25; Acts 2:19; Appian, *Bell. civ.* 4.1.4; Giesen). But the signs John sees are a woman and dragon rather than unusual

Figure 27. Jewish coin from the Bar Kochba revolt depicting the temple with the ark of the covenant inside (ca. 134–135 CE). Courtesy of the Classical Numismatic Group (cngcoins .com).

celestial phenomena, and they appear to him privately in a vision rather than publicly to people on earth. Others identify the signs with constellations, linking the woman to Virgo and the dragon to Scorpio, or Draco (Malina, *On*, 153–73; Aune; Roloff). Such astrological connotations are possible, but John develops the imagery in distinctive ways, since the woman ends up on earth.

a woman. John depicts the woman using elements from both Jewish and Greco-Roman traditions (see §25C). Apart from the eccentric figures who claimed to be the woman (Wainwright, *Mysterious*, 93–97), there are four main ways of understanding her identity. The ancient and medieval material is summarized in §25B; more recent work is considered here. The first proposal is the most plausible:

1. The people of God both before and after Jesus' birth. In this interpretation, the woman represents a community rather than an individual. Some of her traits are those of ancient Israel. The initial scene pictures the woman suffering the pain of labor, which was an image for Israel's distress (Rev 12:1–6; Isa 26:17; Jer 4:31). Her child is the messianic ruler, who comes from Israel (Rev 12:5; Ps 2:9). Later, the woman's experience is like that of Israel's exodus from Egypt, for she escapes danger and is carried on an eagle's wings into the desert, where she is nourished, much as Israel was fed with manna (Rev 12:13–17; Exod 16:4; 19:4). Yet the woman's children include those who keep the commandments of God and the witness of Jesus, which means that her identity is broad enough to encompass the Christian community (Rev 12:17). This approach fits Revelation, which uses traits of the twelve tribes and those of Jesus' followers for the community as a whole (7:1–17; 21:12–14; Beale; Giesen; Mounce; Osborne; Smalley; Busch, *Der gefallene*, 60; Kalms, *Sturz*, 100–107; Tavo, *Woman*, 289–94).

   Personifying a people or city as a female figure was common. In Revelation, Babylon is depicted as a whore and New Jerusalem as a bride (17:1–6; 19:7–8; 21:9). Biblically, Israel or Zion was depicted as a wife, mother, or daughter (Isa 52:2; 66:7–8; Jer 4:31; 6:23–24; Lam 1:6; Mic 4:10; Zeph 3:14). In ancient art, Rome could appear as a woman at ease on seven hills (see Figure 32), and conquered nations were depicted as female captives (see Figures 33 and 34). The image of the woman clothed with the sun—like those of the whore and the bride in Rev 17 and 21—conveys the situation of a group by personification as a single figure (Rossing, *Choice*, 17–59).

2. The Christian church. The woman has a crown of twelve stars, which could signify the twelve apostles (12:1; cf. 21:14), and her children keep the testimony of Jesus (12:17), so she could represent the church. The problem with this approach is how the church can be pictured giving birth to the Messiah. Ancient interpreters took the child's birth as a symbol of Christ being born in the hearts of believers through faith (Gal 4:19; see §25B). A more recent proposal notes that the child is to rule the nations with an iron rod (12:5), an image used for Jesus and his followers, who share in his reign (Rev 2:27–28; 19:15; Resseguie 144). Other interpreters suggest that the agony of giving birth simply describes the affliction of the Christian community (John 16:19–23; Roloff; cf. Gollinger, *Das "grosse,"* 166). These suggestions are unlikely because the many layers of biblical images noted above relate the woman's identity to the broader story of Israel, not only the church.

3. Mary. If the messianic child is Jesus, one might assume that the woman is Mary (Rev 12:5). The Marian interpretation emerged during the patristic period and was later popularized by linking this vision to the Feast of the Immaculate Conception (see INTRO I.C.4). Those who relate the vision to Mary suggest that the dragon is Herod the Great, who sought to kill the infant Jesus, and that the woman's escape into the wilderness is the holy family's journey into Egypt (Matt 2:13–18). A variation is that the woman Mary represents the whole church (Le Frois, *Woman*; Grelot, "Marie"). A more cautious assessment is that on a primary level the woman personifies the people of God collectively and that on a secondary level there may be allusions to Mary, since she gave birth to the Messiah (Brown et al., *Mary*, 235–39; Boxall). From a literary perspective, the reminiscences of Jesus' mother as an individual may contribute to the portrait of God's people as a whole. The pattern is similar to including the traits of Moses, Elijah, and other individual figures in the portrait of Revelation's two witnesses, who also signify God's people (Rev 11:3–6), and weaving traits of Nero into the portrait of the beast, which signifies the imperial system.

4. The Jewish community. Some interpreters suggest that the woman is Israel, understood to be the Jewish community. The sun, moon, and stars may recall the dream of Joseph (Gen 37:9–11). Israel was likened to a woman in labor (Isa 26:17–18; Jer 4:31). Jesus the Messiah came from the Jewish people. Those who follow a historical approach suggest that the way the woman is protected recalls how the Jewish community escaped destruction when the Romans conquered Jerusalem in 70 CE and later had a protected status within the empire. At the same time, the Christians, who were offspring of Judaism, suffered persecution, like the woman's other children, who are threatened by the Roman dragon (Court, *Myth*, 106–21). Alternatively, dispensationalists relate the first part of the vision to the Messiah being born from the Jewish people and the last part to threats against Jewish Christians at the end of the age. For them, the Jewish community is to be sharply distinguished from the Gentile church (Walvoord; LaHaye; Thomas). Such a sharp distinction between Christians of Jewish and non-Jewish background does not fit the perspective of Revelation, however.

clothed with the sun, with the moon under her feet and a wreath of twelve stars on her head. The imagery conveys a sense of majesty. In Jewish tradition, God was robed with light, had the earth under his feet, and was surrounded by stars (Ps 104:2; *Sib.*

Or. 1:137–40). Joseph dreamed that the sun, moon, and stars bowed down to him (Gen 37:7–11), and some said that celestial lights gave glory to Isaac, Levi, and Judah (*T. Ab.* 7:1–7; *T. Naph.* 5:2–4). In Greco-Roman tradition, images of the moon and stars highlighted the grandeur of Artemis and Isis (Apuleius, *Metam.* 11.2–4; see §25C). Writers personified virtue as a woman in radiant attire (Xenophon, *Mem.* 2.1.22; Dio Chrysostom, *Disc.* 1.70–71; Rossing, *Choice*, 17–59). The imagery would have been broadly appealing and need not be confined to any one background.

Some interpreters try to determine more specific meanings. They identify the twelve stars around the woman's head with the sons of Israel, who were symbolized by stars, or with Joseph's dream (Gen 37:7–11; Beale), or they link the stars to the twelve apostles (Bede) or the signs of the zodiac (Yarbro Collins, *Combat*, 71–76). While Revelation uses twelve and multiples of twelve when picturing the people of God and New Jerusalem (Rev 7:4–8; 21:12, 14, 16), it is not necessary to assume that the stars have such specific meanings. Putting something "under" someone's feet often suggested that the person had dominion over it (3:9; 10:2; 22:8; Matt 22:44; Ps 8:7), so one might assume that the woman had power over the moon (cf. Plutarch, *Mor.* 282A). Yet the idea of dominion is not developed here, since the woman must flee from heaven to earth.

12:2. *She was pregnant and cried out in pain.* Childbearing meant receiving honor from family and community (1 Sam 2:5). Mothers of several children received privileges under Roman law (*Rom. Civ.* 1:605–7). At the same time, giving birth was both painful and dangerous. The risk of the mother, child, or both dying was high (Gen 35:16–20; 1 Sam 4:20; *Greek Anth.* 7.165–67; Sutter Rehmann, *Geh*, 225–33). During ordinary births a woman would sit on a birthing stool, attended by a midwife and other women, but in John's vision she seems to be alone. Some women called out for divine help during labor (Terence, *Andria* 473; Soranus, *Gynecology* 2.2–6 [68–70]), but this woman utters only cries of agony.

for she was in the agony of giving birth. Giving birth is a vivid metaphor for a community in distress (1QHᵃ XI, 7–12; John 16:21–22). When prophets spoke of judgment falling on Israel, they said, "Like a woman with child, who writhes and cries out in her pangs when she is near her time, so were we" (Isa 26:17); "For I heard a cry as of a woman in labor, anguish as of one bringing forth a first child, the cry of daughter Zion gasping for breath" (Jer 4:31; cf. 6:24; Mic 4:9–10). Similar imagery was used for tribulations at the end of the age (Mark 13:8; 1 Thess 5:3).

12:3. *Then another sign appeared in heaven: a great fiery red dragon.* A dragon was usually pictured as a serpent (Rev 12:9; Exod 7:10; Deut 32:33 LXX; Wis 16:10). Some were red (Homer, *Il.* 2.308; 12.202). In Revelation the dragon has the qualities of a mythic monster. The LXX calls sea monsters (Hebrew, *taninim*) and Leviathan "dragons" (Ps 74:13–14 [73:13–14 LXX]). Such dragons represented the chaotic forces that needed divine control (Job 7:12; 26:13; 41:1; Ezek 32:2 LXX). Dragons were arrogant and combative creatures, whose coming could signify war (*Pss. Sol.* 2:25; Add Esth 11:6; *Sib. Or.* 5:29). This is the case here, since war breaks out in Rev 12:7. Dragons devoured the vulnerable (Jer 51:34 [28:34 LXX]). Jewish writers said that the Babylonians worshiped a dragon—which was idolatry (Bel 1:23–26)—while insisting that God could defeat dragons (Ps 74:13; Isa 27:1; Ezek 32:2). In Revelation, God and his allies will conquer the dragon in three stages: the heavenly battle in Rev 12:7–12, the thousand-year incarceration in 20:1–3, and the final defeat in 20:7–10.

In Greco-Roman writings, the dragonlike serpent that guarded the legendary golden fleece had sleepless eyes and made a horrible hiss. It "raised its horrific head" to grasp victims "in its horrific jaws" (Apollonius of Rhodes, *Argonautica* 4.153–55). A serpentine dragon named Python tried to kill Leto, the mother of the gods Apollo and Artemis (Hyginus, *Fabulae* 140). In Revelation the dragon's fiery red color also resembles that of the monster Typhon, which could be called a dragon (Plutarch, *Mor.* 359E; 362F). Typhon was the adversary of the goddess Isis and her son Horus, as well as the opponent of Zeus. Half human, half serpent, Typhon breathed fire (Strabo, *Geographica* 16.2.7; Apollodorus, *Library* 1.6.3; Fontenrose, *Python*, 13–22, 70–76). Revelation's fiery red dragon seeks to inflict death, like the rider on the fiery red horse (Rev 6:4) and the scarlet beast that is the dragon's agent (13:1–4; 17:3).

with seven heads and ten horns. Mythic beasts often had multiple heads, emphasizing their threatening quality. Some dragons had seven heads (Aune); Leviathan had an unspecified number (Ps 74:14). Typhon was sometimes pictured with a hundred dragons' heads, and the Hydra had nine or perhaps one hundred snakelike heads (Apollodorus, *Library* 1.6.3; 2.5.2; Diodorus Siculus, *Libr.* 4.11.5). A vision of seven fiery red dragon heads could signify death (*T. Ab.* 17:14; 19:7; cf. *Odes Sol.* 22:5; *Pistis Sophia* 2.66). In Revelation the number seven is a literary device that designates a complete set. Here, the seven heads suggest the magnitude of the threat. Both the dragon and the beast have seven heads and ten horns (Rev 12:3; 13:1; 17:3). The imagery is based in part on Dan 7:2–8, in which four beasts appear that have a total of seven heads and the fourth beast has ten horns.

and seven diadems on its heads. The dragon's diadems are the counterpart to the woman's wreath of stars. A diadem was a band worn around the head, sometimes by priests, but more often by kings (Esth 1:17; 1 Macc 1:9). Roman emperors generally refused to wear diadems in order to avoid the impression that they were instituting monarchy, preferring the wreath, which symbolized the triumph of the empire. But Rome did confer diadems on vassal kings (Dionysius of Halicarnassus, *Ant. rom.* 3.61.3; Suetonius, *Jul.* 79.2; Suetonius, *Cal.* 22.1; Tacitus, *Ann.* 15.2; G. Stevenson, "Conceptual," 259–60). The seven diadems suggest that the dragon claims broad powers. The assertion of power will intensify when its agent the beast appears with ten diadems (Rev 13:1). Diadems signify authority, but not necessarily legitimacy: A tyrant's diadems connote oppression (Dio Chrysostom, *Disc.* 1.79; 4.25; Aune). Claiming a diadem for oneself could be a sign of rebellion against a reigning sovereign (Josephus, *Ag. Ap.* 1.98–100). Here, the dragon illegitimately claims power, but it will be overcome by Christ, who wears many diadems since he is the true King of kings (Rev 19:12).

12:4. Its tail swept down a third of the stars of heaven and threw them to the earth. The image of a monster accosting heaven was familiar. Silius Italicus described a serpent so huge that it was like "the snakes that armed the Giants when they stormed heaven." The serpent "raised his glittering head to heaven, and first scattered his slather into the clouds and marred the face of heaven with his open jaws" (*Punica* 6.180–81, 185–87). Similarly, the serpentine Typhon "rose up against the gods, hissing terror from his formidable jaws, while fierce radiance flashed from his eyes" (Aeschylus, *Prom.* 354–57; cf. Pindar, *Pyth.* 1.15). This kind of mythic language was used for Antiochus Epiphanes, whose domination of Jerusalem in the second century BCE was pictured as casting down stars (Dan 8:10).

Some interpreters take the stars to be Christians, whom Satan makes to fall through false teaching (Irenaeus, *Haer.* 2.31.3; Bede) or persecution (*Mart. Pion.* 12; Beale). However, stars do not represent saints elsewhere in Revelation. Others suggest that the stars are angels who have come under Satan's power (*1 En.* 21:3–6; 86:1–3; Victorinus; Aune; Osborne; Thomas). Stars do represent angels in Rev 1:20, but there is no evidence of that here.

And the dragon stood before the woman who was about to give birth, so that when she gave birth, it might devour her child. The dragon is a serpent, so it "stood" by holding the front of its body erect (Aelian, *Nat. an.* 2.21). Dragons and monstrous serpents were said to be voracious. One "filled his vast maw and poison-breeding belly" with lions, cattle, and birds, which constituted "a hideous meal"; and when a man drew near, "the serpent seized him and swallowed him down" before devouring his companion in "a dreadful form of death" (Silius Italicus, *Punica* 6.151–203). A conquering tyrant was like a dragon that filled its belly with victims (Jer 51:34). Some interpreters link the dragon's action in Rev 12 to a specific moment in Jesus' career, such as Herod's massacre of children at Bethlehem (Matt 2:16; Haimo), the various plots during Jesus' ministry (Mark 3:6; Osborne), or the crucifixion (Caird). But the dragon's threat simply reflects a pattern of opposition.

12:5. *She gave birth to a son, a male.* Repeating that the woman bore "a son, a male" reflects a Hebrew idiom (*bēn zākār*, Jer 20:15). Some interpreters also suggest that using both "son" and "male" for the child echoes key biblical passages. Both Rev 12:1–5 and Isa 7:14 LXX tell of a sign (*sēmeion*) in which a woman is pregnant (*en gastri echein*) and gives birth to a son (*tiktein huion*). In Isaiah the child is Immanuel, or "God with us," a title with messianic associations (Matt 1:23). In Revelation the child is the messianic ruler of the nations, whose iron rod is mentioned in Ps 2:9, a passage that was understood as messianic (NOTE on Rev 2:27). Although the Greek noun for "son" (*huios*) is masculine, Revelation describes it with the adjective "male" (*arsen*), which is neuter in form. The peculiar grammar could recall Isa 66:7, which uses birth imagery for God's redemption of Zion: "Before she was in labor she gave birth; before her pain came upon her she delivered a male [*arsen*]." The details of the Immanuel passage are not developed in John's vision (Fekkes, *Isaiah*, 179–85), but possible echoes of Isa 7:14 and 66:7 enhance the messianic quality of the scene (Aus, "Relevance"; Beale; Peerbolte, *Antecedents*, 130–31; Tavo, *Woman*, 271).

It is best to take this scene as a portrayal of Jesus' birth; other interpretations are not compelling. First, some interpreters propose that the labor pains and satanic threats recall Jesus' passion, when Satan acted against him (John 12:31–32; 13:3, 27; 14:30; Luke 22:3, 53). Then the rapid movement from the Messiah's birth to his exaltation, without mention of his ministry, could suggest that what is depicted as birth is actually his resurrection, since Jesus is the firstborn from the dead (Rev 1:5) and other writers use birth imagery for resurrection (John 16:21–22; Acts 13:33; Feuillet, *Johannine*, 257–67; Prigent; Talbert). However, the context of Rev 12 does not prepare readers to see birth as a metaphor for resurrection. Second, others see the child as a symbol for the Christians whom the church births into faith, since Jesus promises that his followers will be like him in ruling the nations with an iron rod (2:26–27; Resseguie 144). This view is unlikely because that rule over the nations primarily belongs to Christ and only secondarily to others, who participate through their relationship with him (Kalms,

Sturz, 58). Third, the child has been taken as a symbol of the messianic age, which comes through pain (Gollinger, *Das "grosse,"* 166; Roloff), but since none of the other figures in the vision represents time periods, it is unlikely that the child does.

who is to rule all the nations with an iron rod. This line recalls what was said of God's anointed king in Ps 2:9. The wording fits the LXX, which says that God's king is to rule, or "shepherd" (*poimanein*), the nations. The MT differs and says that he will use the rod to "break" (*rā'a'*) the nations. The psalm was understood as a reference to the Messiah in some Jewish sources and the NT (NOTE on Rev 2:27). In the psalm, God is the one who is said to have "begotten" the son who rules the nations (Ps 2:7), whereas Revelation focuses on the woman, who personifies the community of people from whom this figure is born.

But her child was caught up to God and his throne. The comments about the child are so brief that some interpreters think the passage simply follows a mythic plot, like the escape of Leto, Apollo, and Artemis from Python the dragon. The passage moves directly from the child's birth to ascension without any reference to crucifixion (Charles; Aune; Murphy; Yarbro Collins, *Combat*, 105). Others observe that the pattern does have precedents in early Christian tradition. Writers who ascribed great significance to the crucifixion could summarize Jesus' career by focusing on his Davidic descent and resurrection (Rom 1:3–4), his entering and departing from the world (John 13:3; 16:28), or his birth and ascension (Justin Martyr, *1 Apol.* 54.8). Similarly, the comments about the child in Rev 12:5 encapsulate the story of Jesus by focusing on its beginning and end, while the voices in 12:11 remind readers about the integral role of the crucifixion (Beale; Giesen; Busch, *Der gefallene*, 31–32; Kalms, *Sturz*, 62–65).

12:6. *and the woman fled to the desert, where she had a place made ready by God. There she will be taken care of.* See the NOTE on 12:14. In this context, the Greek word that tells of the care given to the woman is in the impersonal third person plural (*trephōsin*, literally, "they could take care of her"), which is equivalent to the passive voice.

for 1,260 days. This is one way of designating a period of three and a half years (cf. 11:3). Other expressions are "forty-two months" (11:2; 13:5) and "a time and times and half a time" (12:14). The duration reflects passages from Daniel that spoke of affliction lasting for three and a half years (NOTE on 11:2). Some interpreters have equated the 1,260 days with the same number of years to determine when the end of the present age will come (see §18A). Dispensationalist interpreters take it to be half of the seven-year tribulation that they expect to occur after the church has been removed from earth. From a literary perspective, however, the three-and-a-half-year period symbolizes the time from Christ's exaltation until his second coming.

12:7. *Then there was war in heaven.* Battle erupts after Christ's enthronement. The victory over evil that is coming seems to manifest the power of God and the authority that the risen Christ exercises through his exaltation (12:5, 10; Giesen). For many readers the sound of armies clashing in heaven was a supernatural sign that conflict would break out on earth (2 Macc 5:1–4; Lucan, *Pharsalia* 1.578; Josephus, *J.W.* 6.298–99; Tacitus, *Hist.* 5.13; Abir, *Cosmic*, 92–93). In John's vision, Satan's defeat in heaven actually generates conflict on earth.

Michael and his angels fought the dragon. Michael was one of the best-known angels in Judaism and early Christianity. Called a prince (Dan 10:13) or archangel (Jude 9), he belonged to a special group of four or seven archangels, of whom he was sometimes regarded as the chief (*1 En.* 20:1–7; 24:6; 40:9–10; 1QM IX, 15; 4Q285 10 3; *Mart. Asc. Isa.* 3:16). He had two primary roles, eschatological and primordial:

1. Eschatological role. There was a tradition that each nation was overseen by an angel (cf. Deut 32:8–9). Michael protected Israel (Dan 12:1; *1 En.* 20:5) and helped it in battle (*1 En.* 90:14; 2 Macc 11:6–8; Black, *Book*, 275). He was to fight the angelic prince of the Persians and deliver Israel at the end of the present age (Dan 10:13–21; 12:1). According to the Qumran *War Scroll*, Michael was expected to help the covenant community when God's agents defeated the satanic angel Belial and ended the reign of evil. That text linked Michael to everlasting light and expected him to hold sway above the gods (1QM XVII, 5–9). Michael may be the Prince of Light and the heavenly Melchizedek, the angelic ruler of the righteous (Collins, *Daniel*, 375; Hannah, *Michael*, 70–75; Dochhorn, *Schriftgelehrte*, 260–72). Revelation follows this militant pattern by naming Michael as the one who defeats Satan. What is different is that the victory occurs in heaven and does not end the devil's reign altogether. Instead, it results in even greater threats for the faithful living on earth. Moreover, Revelation depicts Satan's defeat coming in three stages: In Rev 12:7–12, Satan is banished from heaven to earth after his defeat by Michael. In 20:1–3, he is bound by an unnamed angel and banished from earth to the abyss. Then in 20:7–10, Satan is thrown into the lake of fire.

2. Primordial role. Other scenarios said that at the beginning of time Michael ordered the devil to bow down to Adam. When the devil refused, God expelled him from heaven (*L.A.E.* 12–16). Some texts told of Michael binding the sinful angels until they were punished at the last judgment (*1 En.* 10:11–13; 54:6). Revelation varies the pattern by making Michael's action against Satan a consequence of Christ's exaltation to God's throne. The writer also places the binding of Satan at the end of the age rather than at the beginning (Rev 20:1–3).

3. Other roles. Michael could serve as an advocate for the faithful. He contended with Satan for the body of Moses, evidently to ensure that it was properly buried (Jude 9; *L.A.E.* 48), and he may also have struggled against Satan on behalf of others (4Q544). He could intercede for people (*1 En.* 9:4–11; *T. Ab.* 14:5–6, 12), bless them (*Apoc. Ab.* 10:17), and lead the righteous to paradise (*4 Bar.* 9:5). He disclosed the mystery of the tree of life and the secrets of righteousness (*1 En.* 24:6–25:7; 71:3; cf. 4Q529 1) and mediated the law (Herm. *Sim.* 8.3.3; Osiek, *Shepherd*, 204). Revelation focuses primarily on Michael's combative side. Only at a secondary level does Rev 12 suggest advocacy, since Michael's victory results in the removal of the accuser from the heavenly court (Hannah, *Michael*, 25–75).

Grammatically, the nominative subject with the articular infinitive *tou polemēsai* is awkward. A finite verb might be implied: "Michael and his angels [went] to make war" (cf. Dan 10:20 Theod.). Alternatively, the form might correspond to a Hebrew idiom in which the infinitive has imperative force: Michael and his angels "[had] to make war" (Charles; MHT 3:141).

and the dragon and its angels fought back. Some writers thought of Satan as the leader of the angelic beings who rebelled against God by breeding with people in primeval times (Gen 6:1–4; *1 En.* 6–10) or who refused to bow before Adam (*L.A.E.* 12–16).

Satan, or Mastemah, was the ruler of evil spirits (*Jub.* 10:7–14; Mark 3:22). Some pictured the devil's angels engaging in heavenly conflict from the dawn of time onward (*Mart. Asc. Isa.* 7:9–12). Revelation simply assumes that the devil has angelic allies (*1 En.* 54:6; *T. Dan* 6:1; Matt 25:41).

12:8. *but they were defeated and there was no longer any place for them in heaven.* Satan once had a place (*topos*) in heaven to accuse people before God (Rev 12:8, 10; cf. Job 1:6–12; 2:1–6; Zech 3:1). But Satan and his angels have now lost their place. By way of contrast, the woman who eludes the dragon is given a place (*topos*) of refuge prepared by God (Rev 12:6, 14).

12:9. *So the great dragon was thrown down. He is the ancient serpent.* A dragon was usually pictured as a serpent (NOTE on 12:3). The threatening quality of snakes was evident in the serpentine tails of the demonic horses (9:19), and a snake could signify tyranny (Plutarch, *Mor.* 551F). Here, the "ancient serpent" identifies Satan with the snake that tempted Eve in Gen 3:1. The serpent is not identified with Satan in Genesis, but that link had been made before Revelation was composed (*1 En.* 69:6; Wis 2:24; *Apoc. Mos.* 16 [*OTP* 2:277]; *Apoc. Ab.* 23:1–11; cf. *3 Bar.* 9:7). Paul speaks of Satan being crushed under the feet of the faithful, much as the serpent was to be crushed by Eve's offspring (Rom 16:20; Gen 3:15; Bauckham, *Climax*, 193; Dochhorn, *Schriftgelehrte*, 301–5).

who is called the devil and Satan. Satan appears in Jewish and Christian sources, whereas Greco-Roman tradition did not include a principal supernatural being who personified evil. The Hebrew word *śāṭān* means adversary or accuser. It could be used for human opponents (Ps 71:13) as well as the demonic being of later tradition (*Jub.* 23:29; Matt 4:10; 2 Cor 2:11; *T. Job* 3:6; *T. Dan* 3:6). In the LXX the term was translated *diabolos*, or devil, which means slanderer (1 Chr 21:1; Job 1:6; Zech 3:1; cf. Wis 2:24; Matt 4:1; *T. Naph.* 8:4). In Jewish and Christian tradition both names were given to the principal angelic opponent of God. This figure was also known as Belial (1QS I, 18; 1QM I, 1) or Beliar, the worthless one (2 Cor 6:15; *T. Sim.* 5:3; *Mart. Asc. Isa.* 4:4); Mastemah, the hostile one (*Jub.* 10:7); Beelzebul, the prince of demons (Matt 12:24; Mark 3:22); and "the evil one" (Matt 13:19; John 17:15).

Satan was the evil figure who dominated the present age. His claim to dominion is reflected in the royal diadems the dragon wears in Rev 12:3. Similar views appear in the DSS, in which Belial is the angel of darkness at work in the world (1QS I, 18; III, 20–21). He was called the ruler of this world (John 12:31; 16:11; cf. 1 John 5:18) and the ruler of the power of the air (Eph 2:2). Satan exercised dominion through human agents, whom he incited to acts of sin (1QS III, 20–21; *T. Benj.* 3:3–4) and betrayal (Luke 22:3; John 13:2), as well as through demon possession (Mark 3:22). In Revelation, Satan is said to have a throne, which means death for the faithful (Rev 2:13). He exerts power through the political system of the beast, which brings the people of the world under the sway of evil (13:2, 7). Satan's other roles included that of deceiver (next NOTE) and accuser (NOTE on 12:10).

the deceiver of the whole world. The devil lured people into transgression, often through deception (1 Chr 21:6; Matt 4:1–11; 1 Cor 7:5; *T. Job* 3:3, 6). He was the prince of deceit (*T. Sim.* 3:5; *T. Jud.* 19:4), the liar and father of lies (John 8:44), who disguised himself in order to gain trust (2 Cor 11:14; *T. Job* 6:4; *Mart. Asc. Isa.* 4:4–7). Satan, or

Belial, was associated with the spirit of falsehood (1QS I, 18; III, 18–21; *T. Dan* 3:6; *T. Jud.* 25:3). In Revelation the devil persistently deceives the nations (Rev 20:7–8). Deception is integral to his character.

He was thrown down to the earth and his angels were thrown down with him. Satan is said to have angelic allies in heaven above and in the abyss below (9:12). Readers would have thought of them as the demons that brought illness and misfortune (Busch, *Der gefallene*, 145–59; BDAG 210). Satan's expulsion from heaven has been interpreted in at least three ways. First, and most plausible, Satan's defeat is seen as the result of Jesus' death, resurrection, and exaltation. The literary context places Michael's victory after Christ's exaltation. The placement shows that Satan's defeat manifests the authority of the risen Christ, who now shares a place on God's throne (Rev 12:5, 10; cf. Giesen; Bauckham, *Climax*, 186). Moreover, a heavenly voice says that triumph over the devil comes through the blood of the Lamb and the testimony of those whom he redeems (12:11). Christ's death means that Satan no longer has the right to enter the heavenly court in order to denounce people (5:9–10; 12:10–11). So as a consequence of Christ's exaltation to the throne, the angel Michael evicts Satan from the room.

Some interpreters modify this understanding by taking Michael's battle to be a dramatic portrayal of the victory Christ won on the cross. Michael's victory over the dragon in scene two (12:7–12) is said to repeat the child's escape from the dragon in scene one (12:1–6). The idea is that the conflict in scene one focuses on the real battle, which is won on earth, while the vision of Michael's victory is a symbol of that victory's heavenly significance. An analogous reference might be found in John 12:31–32, which says that the demonic ruler of this world is cast out when Jesus is lifted up on the cross (Rev 16:2–3; Caird; Harrington; Hannah, *Michael*, 129–30). This association is unlikely, however, because the victory won through the blood of the Lamb includes Christ's enthronement in heaven, where he continues to exercise authority (Rev 12:5, 10). A variation is that Satan is said to have fallen when Jesus sent out seventy disciples to perform exorcisms (Luke 10:18–19), but John's vision is different, linking the defeat of Satan to Jesus' death and resurrection rather than to events in Jesus' ministry (Kalms, *Sturz*, 207–73).

The second approach to interpreting Satan's fall assumes that the heavenly battle is a flashback to primeval history. The story of Satan's primeval fall draws from various biblical passages and Jewish traditions. In Isa 14:12–15 a figure called the Day Star is cast down to Sheol for arrogantly trying to exalt his throne above the stars to become like God (cf. Ezek 28:16–17). The Isaiah passage uses mythic language to speak of the defeat of a tyrant. Originally, the villain was an Assyrian king, but later tradition identified him as a supernatural being. The Latin word for a day star is *lucifer*, which became a name for Satan. As the tradition developed, it was said that one of the archangels, determined to be like God, rebelled at the time of creation (*2 En.* 29:4–5). Some said Satan had refused to bow down to Adam, and when he vowed to set his own throne above the stars, God cast him down (*L.A.E.* 12–16; *2 En.* 31:3; *Gos. Bart.* 4.51–55).

This tradition appears in later Christian writings (Cassiodorus; Oecumenius; Andreas) and the Qur'an (15.28–44; 38.71–83). In the seventeenth century it was given classic form by John Milton, who told how the "infernal Serpent" aspired to become like God, and, gathering a host of rebel angels, "raised impious war in heaven," only to be defeated and "hurled headlong flaming from the ethereal sky" (*Paradise Lost*

1.34–49; cf. Nanz, "Hinabgeworfen," 151–52). The tradition was popular because it explained the origin of evil in the world that God created to be good, and it accounted for the fact that the garden of Eden included a malicious serpent that lured human beings into sin. The literary flow makes this idea unlikely here, however, since the heavenly battle against the serpent is set after the exaltation of Christ. A variation is that some interpreters identify the vision of Satan's fall with the story of angels incurring divine wrath in primeval times when they left heaven to breed with human beings (Gen 6:1–4; *1 En.* 6–10; Jude 6; Osborne). But this proposal also seems unlikely, since the tradition based on Gen 6 tells of the angels sinning by leaving heaven rather than being expelled by a battle (Aune).

The third interpretation looks to Satan's future expulsion at the end of this age. Dispensationalist interpreters argue that Revelation anticipates that Satan will be expelled from heaven during the seven years of tribulation at the end of the present age. According to this view, the fall of Satan that occurs in Rev 12 leads to the rise of the beast in Rev 13, and the assumption is that the beast's reign will occur during the final three and a half years of the great tribulation that is yet to come (12:6, 14; 13:5). They note that Dan 10–12 anticipates that Michael will play a major role at the end time and this prophecy is fulfilled in Rev 12 (LaHaye; Thomas; Walvoord). The modern dispensationalist framework posits a gap of thousands of years in between the exaltation of the Messiah, which took place in the past (12:5), and the woman's escape to the desert for the three and a half years, which remains in the future (12:6). But there are no literary signals to suggest that readers must discern a lengthy gap between 12:5 and 6.

12:10. *I heard a loud voice in heaven say, "Now the salvation and the power and the kingdom of our God, and the authority of his Anointed have come.* The voice praising "our God" for acting on behalf of "our brethren" could come from the twenty-four elders (4:11; Mounce), the angels (4:8–11; 19:10; 22:9; Beasley-Murray), the martyrs (6:9–11; Aune), or more probably the whole company of the redeemed (7:9–10; 19:1; Jörns, *Das hymnische*, 110; Giesen). On salvation, power, and the kingdom, see the NOTES on 7:10 and 11:15. The authority God gives to his anointed one is twofold. First, Christ has the power to bring people into the kingdom through his death on their behalf (1:5–6; 5:9–10). Second, he is the King of kings, whose reign will culminate in the defeat of evil forces that now ruin the earth (11:18; 17:14; 19:16). The authority of the anointed one, who is enthroned in 12:5, will be evident in Satan's expulsion from heaven and will lead to Satan's removal from earth (20:1–3, 7–14).

"for the accuser of our brethren was thrown down, the one who accuses them day and night before our God. Satan, who accused people of sin, was a member of God's heavenly court. He could point out sins that had already been committed (Zech 3:1, 4) or test a person like Job in order to make him sin so an accusation could be made (Job 1:6–12; 2:1–6). According to tradition, Satan, or Mastemah, accused Abraham of loving Isaac more than God, prompting God to test Abraham (*Jub.* 17:15–16). Other writers thought that two angels wrote down people's sins and gave them to an angel who had a serpent's body and would accuse people after death (*Apoc. Zeph.* 3:8–9; 6:8, 17).

Satan's accusations, however, could be rejected by God, who could cleanse and forgive people (Zech 3:1–5; *1 En.* 40:7). In Revelation God does not simply disregard the accusations Satan brings but actually bars Satan from the heavenly court. The unusual word for accuser (*katēgōr*), which is attested in only one manuscript (A), may be original. But it seems more likely that this unusual form was changed to the more common *katēgoros* in other manuscripts (*TCGNT*² 673).

12:11. *"They conquered him through the blood of the Lamb and the word of their witness.* The word *nikan* (conquer) was used for military and athletic triumphs (Rev 6:2). Those who died for their faith were said to conquer, or win victory, because they refused to capitulate to their adversaries (4 Macc 1:11; 6:10; 9:30; 11:20; 17:15). Christ conquered in this way, as a slaughtered Lamb (Rev 5:5–6), whereas the beast conquers by inflicting death on others (11:7; 13:7). Here, Revelation gives special attention to those who lose their lives for the faith, but elsewhere, conquering characterizes all who persevere in faith (2:7, 11, 17; 21:7; cf. 1 John 2:13–14; 4:4; 5:4–5; *T. Job* 27:3–9; Beale; Osborne). In Revelation, the martyrs are emblematic of the faithful. The writer does not assume that every faithful Christian will die violently, but the martyrs show readers the kind of steadfast faith to which the whole community is called (Bauckham, *Theology*, 93).

"Love for their lives did not make them shun death. Facing death rather than capitulating to evil was highly regarded. The Maccabean martyrs exhibited this virtue (Josephus, *Ant.* 13.198), and Polybius wrote how "utterly craven" one would be to "reject the greatest of goods and choose the greatest of evils from mere love of life" (*Histories* 15.10.5; cf. Plutarch, *Nic.* 26.4). Sayings of Jesus present the paradox that those who love their lives lose them, and those who hate or lose their lives in this world keep that life for eternal life (John 12:25; Mark 8:35 par.; Luke 17:33 par.). In these sayings losing one's life has more to do with self-renunciation than martyrdom, but Rev 12 focuses on faithfulness in the face of physical death (cf. 13:10).

12:12. *"Therefore, rejoice you heavens and those who dwell in them.* The language echoes biblical texts that call for rejoicing when God has defeated his foes and brings redemption and just rule for his people (Deut 32:43; Isa 49:13). The inhabitants of the earth rejoiced when the beast slew God's witnesses (Rev 11:20), but now the inhabitants of heaven can rejoice at the defeat of Satan through the action of God's faithful witnesses (12:12). This anticipates the future joy that will come at the demise of Babylon (18:20).

"But woe to the earth and sea, because the devil has come down to you with great anger. Previous woes warned of God's wrath, which is provoked by evil and directed at those who destroy the earth (8:13; 11:18). Here, woe comes because of the devil's fury, which is provoked by the frustration of his plans and is directed against those who live on the earth. The devil will use beasts from the sea and land to promote false worship and the whore to draw those on the earth and in the sea into a web of violence, greed, and idolatry (13:1–18; 17:2; 18:17, 19, 24). If the proper response to God's wrath is repentance and faith, the right response to the devil's fury is resistance (6:17; 13:10). For the faithful, the devil's fury means the woe of persecution, and for the ungodly, it means being seduced into alliances with evil that will bring woe when the powers of evil destroy themselves (17:16; 18:10, 16, 19).

"for he knows that his time is short." In the visionary world this short time is three and a half years, a period that has more theological than chronological significance (Note on 11:2).

12:13. *When the dragon saw that it had been thrown down to the earth, it chased the woman who had given birth to the male child.* The dragon's designs were foiled once when it was unable to devour the child (12:1–6) and again when it was thrown out of heaven (12:7–12). Its persecution of the woman reflects frustrated outrage rather than invincibility.

12:14. *But the woman was given the two wings of the great eagle.* The language recalls that of Exod 19:4, when God brought Israel safely to himself "on eagles' wings" (cf. 4Q504 6 6–7). God sustained Israel in the desert like an eagle hovering over its young (Deut 32:10–12). The image connoted strength: "those who wait for the Lord shall renew their strength, they shall mount up with wings like eagles" (Isa 40:31; cf. Ps. 103:5). It also suggested eschatological salvation (*T. Mos.* 10:8; *1 En.* 96:2; cf. Plutarch, *Them.* 26.3). The eagle imagery depicts deliverance as a divine gift (Boring).

so that she could fly to her place in the desert, where she would be taken care of. Stories were told of Hagar, Moses, David, the prophets, the Maccabees, and others fleeing into the desert to escape their adversaries (Gen 16:1–13; 21:8–19; Exod 2:15–3:1; 1 Sam 23:25; 1 Macc 2:28–29; 2 Macc 5:27; *Ps. Sol.* 17:17; *Mart. Asc. Isa.* 2:7–11; 4:13). Like the woman, some were nourished there: Israel with manna and Elijah with bread and meat (Exod 16; 1 Kgs 17:1–7; 19:4–8). The Dead Sea sect moved physically into the desert (1QS VIII, 13–14), but in Revelation the desert symbolizes the readers' social situations. In the cities where they live, the faithful face a wilderness consisting of various social challenges, and yet God preserves the Christian community.

for a time and times and half a time, out of the serpent's reach. The period, which amounts to three and a half times, is a formula used in Dan 7:25 and 12:7. In Revelation the two witnesses lie dead for three and a half days (Rev 11:11), but elsewhere, the period equals three and a half years, which is 1,260 days, or forty-two months. This period can signify protection (11:3; 12:6) and affliction (11:2; 13:5); both characterize the situation of the faithful during the time between Jesus' exaltation and return (Note on 11:2).

12:15. *Then from its mouth the serpent poured a river of water after the woman, so that the river would sweep her away.* The imagery reverses ordinary patterns. Dragons were said to lurk in water and to be so voracious that they could drink a river dry (Ps 74:13; Ezek 29:3; *Greek Anth.* 9:128, 129; *NW* 2:1556). But here, the dragon goes to the desert and spews water out of its mouth. The dragon's goal is indicated by the rare word *potamophorētos*, which was something carried away by a stream (MM 530). The image of a torrent could signify warfare (Isa 8:7–8; Dan 11:10, 40), enemies (Ps 18:3–4; 2 Sam 22:4–5), and a false teacher, "who poured over Israel waters of lies and made them stray into a wilderness without path" (CD I, 14–15; Beale). This imagery encompasses various threats from which people seek protection: At "a time of distress the rush of mighty waters shall not reach them. You are a hiding place for me; you preserve me from trouble" (Ps 32:6–7; cf. 69:12; Isa 43:2; Artemidorus, *Onirocritica* 2.27). The counterpart to the dragon's destructive river is the life-giving water that flows from the throne of God and the Lamb (Rev 22:1–2; cf. 7:17; 21:6).

12:16. *But the earth helped the woman. The earth opened its mouth and swallowed the river that the dragon poured out of its mouth.* The earth takes an active role in deliverance, much as the earth was personified in Greco-Roman stories and art (Friesen, *Imperial*, 186). Some interpreters suggest biblical precedents for the picture of the earth swallowing the river, but the differences are more striking than the similarities. The earth swallowed Abel's blood as a result of his death (Gen 4:11; Minear, "Far"), but here it swallows water to prevent the woman's death. During the exodus the earth swallowed Israel's adversaries in the water of the sea (Exod 15:12), but here the earth swallows the water itself while letting the adversary go. Later, the earth swallowed Korah for opposing God's will (Num 16:32–34), yet in Revelation the opponent is not swallowed up but allowed to continue threatening people.

Revelation shows creation serving the will of the Creator by helping the woman, who represents God's people. The Wisdom of Solomon noted that at the time of the exodus, the elements of nature threatened the Egyptians through the plagues and yet spared the Israelites. Earth and water helped the people of Israel as they fled through the sea. The "universe defends the righteous," for "creation, serving you who made it," aids "those who trust in you"; one sees creation "complying with your commands, so that your children might be kept unharmed" (Wis 16:17, 24; 19:6). Revelation varies this theme by picturing the earth—a part of the creation—helping the woman.

12:17. *So the dragon was furious at the woman, and it went off to make war on the rest of her children.* Anger and the desire for revenge are aimed at whoever frustrates one's desires (Aristotle, *Rhet.* 2.1.2–23). Since the woman eluded the dragon, it seeks revenge against her children. It is incapable of attacking those most directly responsible for foiling its plans, namely, God, Michael, and the earth (Rev 12:5, 7, 16). Therefore, attacking the woman's children underscores the meanness of the action. Earlier, the woman's offspring was the messianic child, but now her offspring include the Christian community. Showing that the dragon becomes wrathful or furious (*ōrgisthē*) out of defeat (12:17) anticipates the fact that the nations that become wrathful (*ōrgisthēsan*) will ultimately be defeated, as already announced (11:18).

who keep the commandments of God and hold firmly to the witness of Jesus. The commandments presumably include those in the OT, especially those that promote the worship of God and warn against idolatry, blasphemy, sorcery, theft, murder, and the other sins mentioned in Revelation (2:15, 20; 9:20–21; 13:6, 12; 14:7). The "witness of Jesus" could refer to the witness that Jesus bore to God, which is preserved by the Christian community (Abir, *Cosmic*, 206–9). Yet as members of the community hold onto the witness that comes from Jesus, they also bear witness to Jesus, and it is their public testimony that elicits opposition (NOTES on 1:2, 9; 19:10).

COMMENT

Scenes of God's conflict with Satan frame the last half of Revelation. The drama begins in chapter 12, where Satan the dragon threatens a woman giving birth to the messianic child. The devil's plot is foiled and he is then defeated in heaven and hurled down to the earth, where he turns his anger against Jesus' followers. The struggle reaches its denouement in chapter 20, in which an angel binds Satan and imprisons him in the abyss for

---

On Rev 11:19–12:17, see Abir, *Cosmic*; Balch, "Woman"; Bauckham, *Climax*, 185–98; Benko, *Virgin*, 83–136; Busch, *Der gefallene*; Dochhorn, "Und die Erde" and *Schriftgelehrte*; Gollinger, *Das "grosse"*; Humphrey, "Tale," 85–88; Jörns, *Das hymnische*, 109–20; Kalms, *Sturz*; Kowalski, "Lichtfrau"; Labahn, "Teufelsgeschichten"; Pataki, "Non-Combat"; Peerbolte, *Antecedents*, 129–41; Sutter Rehmann, *Geh*, 214–50; Tavo, *Woman*, 225–94; Ulland, *Vision*; van Henten, "Dragon"; Vanni, *L'Apocalisse*, 227–51; Yarbro Collins, *Combat*.

a thousand years. Upon his release, the evil one mounts a last futile attack against the faithful before being cast into the lake of fire. In the chapters in between the devil is rarely mentioned, but he works behind the scenes to influence the world through the beast and false prophet (13:2; 16:13). Readers learn that earthly conflicts over worship, political domination, and commerce are part of a cosmic struggle in which they are being called to resist the encroachments of evil while remaining true to the Creator and the Lamb. The conflict is ongoing, but the heavenly chorus has announced its outcome: The time has come for God to destroy those who destroy the earth (11:18).

The opening of the heavenly temple (11:19) introduces an episode that has three scenes arranged in a symmetrical pattern (A-B-A). The main plot, which concerns the woman and her children, appears in scenes one and three. In scene one the woman gives birth to the child who is to rule the nations. The dragon wants to devour the newborn, but the child is taken to God's throne while the woman flees to the desert (12:1–6). In scene three the dragon again tries to destroy the woman who has fled to the desert; when it fails, it persecutes the woman's other children, who belong to the community of faith (12:13–17). Where the child in the first scene was snatched away from the dragon's jaws, the children in the third scene find the dragon following close behind. These scenes raise a pointed question: Why does evil so persistently threaten the faithful?

The middle scene provides the theological key to the episode. In it, the Messiah's enthronement leads to a war in heaven, with the result that Satan is defeated and banished to earth (12:7–9). Then a heavenly voice announces the victory of God, the Lamb, and the faithful and warns that the devil is furious because he has only a short time left in which to work (12:10–12). The point is that the evil one does not rage so fiercely on earth because he is so powerful, but because he is losing and desperate. Satan lashes out like a caged and wounded animal, seeking to do as much damage as he can before his final defeat. This scene is designed to shape the readers' responses to their social situations. If evil seems invincible, the natural response is to accommodate it. But if readers can see that evil is actually losing, they will have incentive to resist it, knowing that God will triumph in the end.

The author's theological point concerns the victory of God and the Lamb, but he conveys the message through images that were broadly familiar in the ancient world. Some of this background was summarized above (see §25C). Here, we bring together the main proposals, beginning with the story of the woman and the dragon in scenes one and three.

Greco-Roman sources tell of a woman named Leto, who was pregnant by Zeus. Her antagonist was Python the dragon, who tried to kill her in order to prevent her from giving birth. She was rescued by the north wind, which carried her away to the island of Delos in the Aegean Sea. There she gave birth to Apollo and Artemis, who received arrows as gifts. Four days later, Apollo pursued the dragon, soon slaying the monster to avenge his mother (Hyginus, *Fabulae* 140; Lucan, *Pharsalia* 5.79–81; Lucian, *Dial. mar.* 9). The plot is broadly similar to John's vision of a woman giving birth to a hero and escaping from a dragon, and in some artistic renderings the mother and children could all be pictured fleeing from the dragon (Figure 28; Yarbro Collins, *Combat*, 63–67; Saffrey, "Relire"; Boring 151). But there are also differences, since the woman in Revelation gives birth before she flees rather than afterward, and she finds

Figure 28. Leto with Artemis and Apollo escaping from Python (Greek, fourth to third century BCE). Marble. 2003.23.6. Anonymous gift. Courtesy of the Michael C. Carlos Museum of Emory University (http://www.carlos.emory.edu). Photo by Bruce M. White, 2011.

refuge in the desert rather than on an island. Moreover, the dragon is not quickly slain by the son but is thrown down from heaven to earth where it persecutes the woman and her other children (Aune 2:671–72). Only later does Christ return to end the dragon's tyrannical reign (Rev 19:11–20:3).

Other mythic stories focused on the goddess Isis and her opponent, the monster Typhon, or Seth, who killed and dismembered her consort Osiris. The murder was later avenged either by Isis's son Horus or by Isis and her son together when they defeated Typhon in battle (Diodorus Siculus, *Libr.* 1.21.1–22.7; 1.88.4–6; Plutarch, *Mor.* 355D–358E; cf. Apollodorus, *Library* 1.6.3; Nonnus, *Dionysiaca* 1.163–205; Strabo, *Geographica* 16.2.7; van Henten, "Dragon"; Balch, "Woman," 292–302). Some interpreters have suggested that the story of Isis provided the dominant pattern for Rev 12 (Bousset), yet many stories shared common features with Rev 12 and yet varied in details (Aune 2:672–74; Busch, *Der gefallene*, 75–81). What is important is that tales of Isis and Typhon reflect a pattern of conflict similar to that in the tales of Leto and Python. The ease with which ancient sources equated Isis with Leto shows how one form of the story could shape another (Herodotus, *Historiae* 2.156). Revelation follows a basic pattern in which a woman and her child are threatened by a dragonlike monster, but the author does not fully adhere to any one form of the story.

Into this plotline of danger and deliverance Revelation weaves biblical elements. On one level there are echoes of the story of Eve, who faced "the ancient serpent" who lures people into wrongdoing (Gen 3:1–5; Rev 12:4, 9). Eve was warned that she would have great pain in childbearing, and yet her offspring would strike the serpent's head (Gen 3:15–16). Similarly, the woman in Rev 12 experiences pain while giving birth to the messianic child whose exaltation will lead to a victory over the serpent (12:5). On a second level the woman is like the people of Israel, who escaped destruction at the time of the exodus and were carried on eagles' wings into the desert, where God nourished them (12:6, 14; cf. Exod 19:4; Deut 8:3). On a third level the woman is like Zion, which the prophets depicted as a woman giving birth (Isa 66:7–9). Zion was threatened by Babylon, a dragon filling its belly with victims (Jer 51:34). On a fourth level the woman's story is that of Jesus' followers, for her children are those who keep the commandments of God and witness of Jesus (Rev 12:17). The multiple layers of imagery allow John's readers to recognize the experiences of conflict and threat within their own social settings as part of the broader story of God's people.

The middle scene, which tells of the dragon's defeat and expulsion from heaven, draws on different patterns (12:7–12). Some focused on the remote past. In Greco-Roman tradition, the many-headed monster Typhon was not only an opponent of Isis, but was also the adversary of Zeus. When the fiery Typhon sought dominion over the world, a terrible battle occurred, shaking heaven and earth. But Zeus defeated him, hurling the dragon down to the depths (Hesiod, *Theogonia* 820–68; Aeschylus, *Prom.* 351–76).

Jewish traditions told of a conflict in primeval times as well. One text said that heavenly beings incurred God's wrath by coming to earth to breed with human beings (Gen 6:1–4). Later, these heavenly beings were identified as evil angels, who were bound by the archangel Michael until the end of the age when they would be punished (*1 En.* 10:11–13). Another tradition was based on Isa 14:12–15, in which a tyrant called the Day Star tried to exalt his throne above the stars but was thrown down to Sheol:

> How you are fallen from heaven, O Day Star, son of Dawn!
> How you are cut down to the ground, you who laid the nations low!
> You said in your heart . . . "I will raise my throne above the stars of God;
> "I will sit in the mount of the assembly . . . I will ascend to the tops of the
> clouds, I will make myself like the Most High."
> But you are brought down to Sheol, to the depths of the Pit.

Originally, this figure was an Assyrian king, but later sources identified him with Satan, who was understood to be an evil angel who rebelled against God at the dawn of time and was therefore hurled down to the earth (*2 En.* 29:4–5; 31:3; *L.A.E.* 12–16; Note on Rev 12:9).

Other traditions expected Satan to be defeated at the end of time. Some writers referred to the evil one as Belial, the angel of darkness who fomented wickedness on earth. At the end of this age, however, God's agent Michael was expected to defeat Belial and his allies (1QM XIII, 11–12; XVII, 5–8). Others thought Belial would come in the guise of a figure like the emperor Nero, who would also work signs and wonders before being destroyed (*Sib. Or.* 3:63–74; *Mart. Asc. Isa.* 4:1–14). For some, the final defeat of Belial would mean that he would be bound and cast into the fire forever (*T. Levi* 3:3; 18:12; *T. Dan* 5:10; *T. Sim.* 6:6).

The Scriptures use dragon imagery as part of God's conflict with the forces of chaos at both the beginning and end of the age. Recalling primeval times, it was said: "God my King is from of old, working salvation in the earth. You divided the sea by your might; you broke the heads of the dragons in the waters. You crushed the heads of Leviathan" the sea monster (Ps 74:12–14a; cf. Job 26:12–13; Ps 89:9–10). Such images could be blended with those of the exodus: "Was it not you who cut Rahab in pieces, who pierced the dragon? Was it not you who dried up the sea, the waters of the great deep; who made the depths of the sea a way for the redeemed to cross over?" (Isa 51:9–10; cf. Rev 12:7–9, 13–16). A similar blend of dragon and exodus motifs occurs in Rev 12:13–17. Finally, God's eschatological victory can be portrayed using this imagery: "On that day the Lord with his cruel and great and strong sword will punish Leviathan the fleeing serpent, Leviathan the twisting serpent, and he will kill the dragon that is in the sea" (Isa 27:1; Murphy 281–82). In Revelation the future defeat of the dragon becomes the defeat of Satan himself (cf. *T. Mos.* 10:1).

Revelation's vision of Satan's heavenly defeat uses familiar images to create a new perspective on its readers' situations. The antagonist is "the ancient serpent" (Rev 12:9), but its defeat is not a flashback to primeval times. It is the result of Jesus' birth and exaltation. As in Greco-Roman stories, a woman gives birth to the hero who is destined to defeat the dragon, but in Revelation the defeat occurs in stages: The initial defeat of Satan comes after Jesus' exaltation, and it increases tension on earth, for the devil is wounded and angry (12:7–12). Next is the binding of Satan after Christ's return (20:1–3). The final victory comes a thousand years later, when the devil is released and sent to the lake of fire (20:7–10). Michael plays a role in this victory over evil, as in Jewish tradition (Dan 12:1; 1QM XVII, 5–8). But rather than simply ending the threat from evil, Michael restricts the devil's sphere of operation, so between Christ's first and second comings the faithful experience a heightened sense of threat on earth (Rev 12:17). Through this adaptation of familiar imagery, readers are to see that present threats are not signs of evil's strength but of its desperation.

Presenting a vision of conflict that develops patterns from Jewish and Greco-Roman sources would have engaged the imagination of early readers (Friesen, *Imperial*, 172; Busch, *Der gefallene*, 159; Koch, *Drachenkampf*, 316). The language is vivid and memorable, drawing people into the story. The point could have been made directly by saying, "God's people will be threatened, they must resist, God will prevail." But dynamic scenes of conflict allow readers to *see* the assaults of evil and the resistance of the faithful in their mind's eye so that they can imagine themselves taking part in the drama (Humphrey, *Ladies*, 115). Readers would have been sympathetic toward a woman giving birth and repelled by a dragon so terrible that it seeks to devour a newborn child. This attraction and repulsion, which occurs even before readers learn the identities of the woman and dragon, is rhetorically powerful since it fosters a sense of loyalty to those whom the woman represents and a readiness to resist what the dragon symbolizes (Schüssler Fiorenza 31; Yarbro Collins, *Crisis*, 144; Koch, *Drachenkampf*, 224; deSilva, *Seeing*, 198–203).

From a literary perspective, this story unfolds on a cosmic scale in which the ordinary limitations of time and space do not apply. The warring parties traverse a battlefield that stretches from the heights of heaven to the deserts of earth. The scenes are surreal, for the woman is initially in heaven with the moon under her feet, but she gives birth to the Messiah, which one would assume took place on earth. Her adversary the dragon also appears in heaven, its tail brushing down myriads of stars, yet the woman's child is taken up to God's throne in heaven to escape the dragon's wrath, while the woman flees to a desert that is apparently on earth. The lines between the world above and the world below seem clearer when angelic warriors send the dragon tumbling from heaven to earth, but the vision's fantastic quality continues as the woman is given wings to fly and the personified earth drinks the water gushing from the dragon's mouth (Kalms, *Sturz*, 32).

The writer takes readers into this strange visionary world in order to shape how they perceive their social worlds. Rather than pointing out specific instances of Satan's activity in the cities of Asia Minor, as the author did in the messages to the churches (2:9–10, 13, 24; 3:9), the vision characterizes the conflict between good and evil in ways that the readers themselves must relate to the realm of time and space (Yarbro Collins, *Combat*, 126; Doniger, *Implied*, 9; Friesen, "Myth," 295; Koch, *Drachenkampf*, 299, 308; Ricoeur, *Symbolism*, 348).

One way in which early readers might have done this is by reading the story of the woman and the dragon as a polemic against the imperial cult—a major issue in the next chapter of Revelation (13:1–18). In Greco-Roman tradition the hero born to the woman was Apollo, whose defeat of the evil dragon ushered in peace and prosperity. Caesar Augustus was hailed as a new Apollo, whose reign marked the beginning of a golden age (Virgil, *Ecl.* 4.6–10). Later, Nero styled himself as Apollo; his image on coins bore the radiant beams from his head that were Apollo's trademark, and his admirers acclaimed him as the god (Dio Cassius, *Rom. Hist.* 62.20.5).

Those who read Rev 12 with this background in mind will see John reversing the story of Apollo's birth and victory so that the hero is not the emperor's proto-type, Apollo, and the dragon is not the chaos that Rome subdues but the threats that Rome creates for Christ and his followers. There were precedents for using dragon imagery for leaders who threatened Israel, like Pharaoh (Ezek 29:3–6; 32:2–8), Nebu-chadnezzar (Jer 51:39), and the Roman general Pompey (*Pss. Sol.* 2:29). Nero was compared to a serpent (Plutarch, *Mor.* 367F; *Sib. Or.* 5:28–29), and both Nero and Domitian were described as Typhonlike tyrants (van Henten, "Dragon," 507–10). From this perspective the mythic stories that some writers used when celebrating impe-rial rule were transformed in a way that encourages readers to resist that rule (Caird 148; Yarbro Collins, *Combat*, 188–90; Van Henten, "Dragon"; Kalms, *Sturz*, 122–26; Schüssler Fiorenza 80; Boring 151; Maier, *Apocalypse*, 180; Abir, *Cosmic*, 251; Barnett, "Polemical," 118).

Other interpreters point out that the vision in Rev 12 could be applied to mul-tiple life settings (Koch, *Drachenkampf*, 270; Friesen, *Imperial*, 172; Labahn, "Teufel-geschichten"). At points, the messages in Rev 2–3 link the agency of Satan to imperial authority, since Roman officials were presumably involved in the execution of Antipas (2:13) and could imprison Christians at Smyrna (2:10). The messages also associated Satan with the synagogue members who denounced Christians at Smyrna and Phila-delphia (2:9; 3:9), as well as Christians like Jezebel, who taught that it was acceptable to eat what had been offered to Greco-Roman deities. Such offerings could have come from many different cults, including the cult of Leto's children, Apollo and Artemis, the cult of Isis, and the imperial cult—all of which were practiced in Asia Minor. The imagery in Rev 12 is flexible enough to encompass various kinds of threats that early readers faced.

The Dragon Threatens the Woman and Her Son (11:19–12:6)

The opening of the celestial temple introduces this new series of visions (11:19). The counterpart to this temple is the community of faith, which serves as God's "temple" on earth because it is where true worship takes place (11:1). The earthly community is vulnerable, so John has depicted it as a temple whose outer court is trampled by the nations (11:2). But the heavenly temple remains inviolate, and from it God will take action against the forces that threaten his people (G. Stevenson, *Power*, 264).

A distinctive element is the manifestation of the heavenly ark (11:19). According to tradition, the earthly ark once housed the tablets of the covenant that God had made with Israel (Exod 25:21; 1 Kgs 8:9). This ark was known for its destructive power (Lev 16:2; 2 Sam 6:6–7), and Israel's armies carried it into battle (Judg 6:4; 1 Sam 4:3). Accordingly, the sight of the heavenly ark introduces visions in which God will do battle against the forces of evil. These will culminate in the destruction of those who destroy the earth (Rev 11:18).

John sees a woman clothed with the sun, with the moon under her feet and a wreath of twelve stars about her head (12:1). The woman is not named; interpreters from ancient to modern times have proposed different ways of identifying her, but she can best be understood as the personification of the people of God, including ancient Israel and the followers of Jesus. Since the arguments were considered above (see §25B; NOTE on 12:1), here we can shift the focus: Instead of asking how readers are to identify the woman, we will ask how the text invites them to identify *with* her so that they see the action from her perspective.

The woman's majestic appearance shows that she belongs to God, who created all things (4:11). The sun, moon, and stars belong to the created order and give glory to the woman as similar images do for other agents of God. The exalted Jesus and angels have faces that shine like the sun (1:16; 10:1; cf. 18:1), and this woman is robed with the sun. God has power over the stars (6:13; 8:12), the exalted Jesus holds seven stars (1:16), and the woman wears a wreath of stars (12:1). Like New Jerusalem the bride, the woman clothed with the sun shares the glory of God but is not herself divine (21:10–11). In Revelation, God's radiance is beyond that of sun and moon (21:23; 22:5).

The woman wears radiant attire, and the faithful have been promised white robes that signify purity, holiness, and honor (3:4–5, 18; 6:11), as well as the wreaths that symbolize true honor (2:10; 3:11). The elders around the heavenly throne give a glimpse of the fulfillment of these promises, for they wear white robes and golden wreaths (4:4). The redeemed before God's throne are adorned in white (7:9), and the faithful who are the bride of the Lamb are clothed in pure bright linen (19:7–8). Readers who identify with the redeemed and the bride will also identify with the woman robed in sunlight and wreathed with stars.

Readers are to continue identifying with the woman as her situation goes from majesty to the agony of childbirth (12:2). Elsewhere, agony (*basanizein/basanismos*) is what the wicked undergo as punishment (9:5; 11:10; 14:10–11; 18:7, 10, 15; 20:10), and labor pain could be an image for divine judgment (Isa 26:17; Jer 4:31). But the woman in Rev 12 endures agony while giving birth to the messianic child. Her suffering is for a good purpose, so the readers' response is to be one of sympathy (Aristotle, *Rhet.* 2.8.2). Just as the woman suffers while bearing God's Messiah, those who identify with her may suffer while bearing witness to the Messiah—a point made explicit in scenes to come (Rev 12:11; Humphrey, *Ladies*, 115).

John next sees a huge dragon, which is the woman's adversary (12:3). The dragon was a powerful image for the forces that opposed God and threatened human beings. As noted above, dragons were associated with the chaotic power of Leviathan and serpentine monsters such as Python and Typhon (NOTE on 12:3). The common response to dragons was horror (Silius Italicus, *Punica* 6.170; Apollonius of Rhodes, *Argonautica* 4.136–37). Just as the radiance of the woman would have attracted readers, the hideousness of the dragon would have repelled them.

The woman has a crown of stars, which is a symbol of honor (12:1), but the dragon pulls down a third of the stars in the sky. The gesture shows hostile arrogance, which in classical terms is called hubris (Aristotle, *Rhet.* 2.2.5). The gesture is reminiscent of Dan 8:10, in which a tyrant exalted himself "as high as the host of heaven"; and in his effort to take the place of God, he "threw down to earth some of the host and some of the stars." Similarly, Greco-Roman tradition told how the serpentlike monster Typhon arrogantly attacked the heavens (Apollodorus, *Library* 1.6.3; Nonnus, *Dionysiaca* 1.163–205). In scenes to come, however, the dragon that casts down the stars will itself be cast down from heaven (Rev 12:9).

The dragon stands before the woman in order to devour her child (12:4). Although fear that a child might be hurt or killed by demonic powers at birth was common (*NP* 2:667), Revelation heightens the sense of horror by depicting a monster that not only wants to kill a newborn, but wants to devour it. Rhetorically, such premeditated cruelty intensifies the readers' animosity toward the dragon and strengthens their readiness to oppose what the dragon represents (Cicero, *Inv.* 1.100–105; Lausberg, *Handbook* §438).

The woman gives birth to the child, who is to rule all the nations with an iron rod (Rev 12:5). This juxtaposition discloses the heart of the conflict. The dragon wears seven diadems, which show its appetite for regal power. Since the child is the dragon's rival, the monster wants to devour him. The description of the child recalls Ps 2, which said that God's king would wield the iron rod; and even though his foes plotted against him, the king would have the nations as his heritage (NOTE on 2:27). Revelation will later use the language of the psalm in the scene of Christ's return as the King of kings, who will defeat evil and rule the nations with an iron rod (19:15–16).

Readers will find that Jesus' dominion over the nations is not a simple matter. On the one hand, Revelation assumes that the nations are now swayed by the forces of evil so that they oppose the reign of God and Christ (11:2; 18:3) and will be liable to judgment (19:17–21). On the other hand, Jesus offers redemption to people of every nation (5:9–10; 7:9–10), and New Jerusalem's gates stand open to receive the nations—which will need no iron rod when they walk willingly in the light of God and find healing at the tree of life (21:24–26; 22:2). Revelation assumes that Christ is the legitimate ruler of the nations, but whether this means judgment or redemption for them depends on whether they reject or receive his reign.

At this point in the vision, the child is caught up to God and his throne (12:5). First, the action means deliverance for the messianic child, who escapes from the dragon. The point is made so briefly that deliverance seems miraculous and complete, but the literary context shows that there is more to the story. Readers already know that Jesus was slaughtered before being exalted to reign with God (1:5–6). In scenes to come, they will be reminded that the Messiah escaped death not by avoiding it, but by dying and being raised to life again—and the same will be true for the Messiah's followers (12:11; cf. 1:18; 5:6).

Second, the Messiah's exaltation is his enthronement (12:5). Previous visions have described the majesty of God's throne hall (4:1–11) and have pictured Jesus sharing the throne with God (3:21; cf. 5:6, 13; 7:9, 17). In Revelation, the throne of God and the Lamb is singular because the activity of Jesus is integral to the way God rules the world (22:1–3; Bauckham, *Theology*, 54–65). The dragon is correct in seeing the child as a rival, for when the child is enthroned in heaven, the dragon will no longer be able to operate there. The child's exaltation to the throne will occasion the dragon's expulsion from heaven, marking a step toward its final defeat (12:7–12).

The child may be safe in heaven, but the woman must seek refuge in a desert (12:6), which recalls Israel's sojourn in the desert, where the people were fed with manna (Exod 16:4; Deut 8:3; Ps 78:23–25). The woman's situation has analogies to that of Revelation's readers. The Messiah may have been exalted to heavenly glory, but his followers have not. They remain in a world where evil is active. The vision presents a paradox: The woman initially appeared in celestial majesty, but she seemed to find no help in heaven. Rather, help is given to her on earth, in a desert. Her wreath of stars may have signified glory and triumph, but at this point her victory is that of a refugee escaping destruction. For the woman and those she represents, God's action is not seen in an absence of threat but in the hope for sustenance in the face of threat (Sutter Rehmann, *Geh*, 224–25).

The woman remains in the desert for 1,260 days, which is three and a half years (Rev 12:6). This distinctive length of time comes from the book of Daniel, in which God's people are oppressed for three and a half years or "a time, [two] times, and half a time" (Dan 7:25; 12:7; Note on Rev 11:2). Revelation will use this formula (12:14) as well as the equivalents of 1,260 days and forty-two months. When the author speaks of this period as forty-two months, he emphasizes the reality of the threat: It is the period in which the community is like the temple besieged by the nations (11:2) and the world is dominated by the beast (13:5). But when the author speaks of 1,260 days, he emphasizes the way God preserves the community despite the threat, so that God's witnesses can testify (11:3) and the woman who represents his people can be nourished (12:6).

In the visionary world, the three and a half years encompass the entire time between the Messiah's exaltation and final return. The author says that the messianic child "was caught up to God and his throne, and the woman fled into the desert" for 1,260 days (12:5–6). In the visionary world, the woman's 1,260 days in the desert begin when the child is taken to God's throne. The Messiah's enthronement also leads directly to Satan's expulsion from heaven (12:7–12). That is when the devil comes down to earth in great wrath, knowing that "his time is short" (12:12). During this short time, Satan pursues the woman—who needs protection for three and a half years (12:14). Satan rages on earth until Christ returns (19:11–21). Only then is he removed from earth and bound in the abyss (20:1–3). In the visionary world the time that Satan rages is "short," lasting three and a half years, yet it extends from the Messiah's exaltation until his final return.

Time in the visionary world is not equivalent to time in the readers' world. By the time Revelation was composed, many more than three and a half years had elapsed since the end of Jesus' ministry. The writer does not use the traditional period of three and a half years in a simple chronological sense. Rather, it is his way of characterizing his own time as the end of the age, when Satan rages against the community of faith. Dispensationalist interpreters argue differently. They assume that the period of three and a half years is half of the seven-year tribulation that is yet to come (Walvoord 191; Thomas 2:127). To make this idea work, they posit a gap of at least two millennia between the exaltation of Jesus in Rev 12:5 (which occurred in the past) and the woman's escape to the desert for three and a half years in 12:6 (which is still in the future). Yet in the text there is no suggestion of such a gap. Time does not function in the same way in the visionary world as it does in the ordinary world. Rather, the three-and-a-half-year period depicts the time from Jesus' exaltation to his return, which is the time in which the readers live, the period in which Satan threatens and God sustains (Giesen 284; Maier, *Apocalypse*, 157; Abir, *Cosmic*, 149; Wall 158).

Michael and the Dragon (12:7–12)

The next scene is the literary and theological center of the episode. War breaks out in heaven as a divine response to the dragon's attempt to overpower God's Messiah (12:7). Heaven was where the dragon displayed its aspiration for royal dominion by wearing seven diadems and where it swept down a third of the stars in an intimidating show of force (12:3–4). When the child who is the world's legitimate ruler is taken to God's throne, angelic warriors do battle on his behalf. Since God is the Creator, his kingdom comes by his doing away with the forces that bring destruction so that life can flourish (11:15, 18; Abir, *Cosmic*, 87).

Readers familiar with tales of Leto and Apollo might have expected the hero born of woman to now slay the dragon, but Revelation alters the pattern, and this battle is won by the angel Michael (12:7). The writer uses the last chapter of Daniel to disclose the meaning of the time between Christ's exaltation (12:5) and his final return to defeat the agents of evil (19:11–20:3). The key verses read:

> At that time Michael, the great prince, the protector of your people, shall arise. There shall be a time of anguish, such as has never occurred since nations first came into existence. But at that time your people shall be delivered, everyone who is found written in the book. Many of those who sleep in the dust of the earth shall awake, some to everlasting life, and some to everlasting shame and everlasting contempt. . . . How long shall it be until the end of these wonders? . . . it would be for a time, two times, and half a time. (Dan 12:1–2; 6–7)

Revelation identifies the three and a half years of distress that are mentioned in Dan 12:7 with the time between the Messiah's exaltation and return. It is the time in which the woman seeks protection from the dragon (Rev 12:6, 14) and the Christian community, or temple, is threatened (NOTES and COMMENT on 11:1–2). Daniel 12:1 first mentions Michael's activity and then the time of great distress. Revelation follows the pattern by placing Michael's activity at the beginning of the period of trouble that follows the Messiah's exaltation. Daniel also assumes that the time of distress will end with the resurrection of the dead, and Revelation again follows the pattern but adds that the time of distress will culminate in the Messiah's return (Rev 19:11–16; 20:4–15).

Michael was traditionally understood to be the foe of Satan (NOTE on 12:7), and Revelation identifies him as the warrior angel who drives Satan out of heaven (12:8). Revelation does not assume that defeat in heaven sends the devil to earth for the first time. Up to this point, Satan has been able to denounce people before God's heavenly throne (12:10), and he is also the "the ancient serpent" that tempted people in Eden at the dawn of time and has been deceiving the world ever since (12:9; Gen 3:1). So the outcome of the heavenly battle is to *restrict* the devil's range of operation.

The dragon is "the deceiver of the whole world," promoting evil under the guise of goodness (Rev 12:9). One of its allies is Jezebel, who deceives people by insisting that it is acceptable to eat what has been offered to idols (2:20). From the author's perspective, that notion is false and "of Satan" (NOTE on 2:24). Later, the beast from the land, or the false prophet, deceives people into supporting the ruler cult (13:14; 19:20). And Babylon will deceive people into accepting a brutal and materialistic regime by promises of wealth that actually debase people and society (18:23). Throughout Revelation, God and Christ are called "true," and the truth of their reign will finally prevail (3:7, 14; 6:10; 15:3; 19:11). By disclosing the true character of God and evil, the writer of Revelation seeks to bolster the readers' readiness to resist the claims of a world that he understands to have fallen prey to deceit (21:5; 22:6).

In the second half of this scene, a voice from heaven reveals the meaning of Satan's defeat (12:10). Echoing the songs of celebration in previous scenes (5:12–13; 7:10, 12; 11:15–18), the voice speaks like the chorus in a Greek play, helping audience members interpret what they see (Harsh, *Handbook*, 17–23). Virtually everything that is said seems to be negated in the scenes that follow. The voice declares that God's power (*dynamis*) has come, but the dragon, the beast, and Babylon defy God's claims by their own displays of power (13:2; 18:3). God's kingdom (*basileia*) has arrived, but Satan's agents have established their own kingdom on earth (16:10; 17:18). God has given authority (*exousia*) to Jesus, the ruler of the nations, but the dragon gives authority to the beast, which dominates the nations (13:2, 12).

The one remaining term, salvation (*sōtēria*), can be ascribed only to God and not to his adversaries (12:10; cf. 7:10; 19:1). But even here the meaning is not obvious, since Satan's expulsion from heaven will mean woe for the earth (12:11). In the visionary world, Satan can no longer influence human destiny by accusing people before God. In legal terms, the devil not only loses the case, but is barred from further appearances in court. The faithful are not entirely exempt from divine judgment, as is clear from Rev 2–3, where Christ rebukes the readers for their shortcomings; but Christ's reproofs are given by one who seeks their well-being, not their destruction, and whose blood brings redemption from sin (3:19; 12:11).

Satan's accusations against the faithful may have no place in the visionary world, but in the readers' social worlds, charges continued to be leveled against Jesus' followers. At Smyrna, some were denounced before the authorities, who had the power to imprison and kill them (2:9–10). Imperial practice called for formal accusations to be made before an authority such as the governor (Acts 16:19–20; 18:12–17; 24:1–2; 25:6–7; Sherwin-White, *Roman Society*, 17, 48). From John's perspective, such denunciations were incited by Satan, who could not make charges before God but opposed the faithful through human agents on earth. The threat of negative judgment by human authorities had the potential to make people relinquish their faith, but John's vision shows that accusations heard on earth are not admitted as evidence in heaven's higher court.

The faithful are said to have conquered Satan in two ways. First, their victory comes through the blood of the Lamb (Rev 12:11), which releases people from sin so they become priests of God (1:5; 5:9–10; 7:14–15). When the message about the Lamb's self-sacrifice evokes faith, it moves people to resist the claims of the other powers that vie for dominion over them—and this is a defeat for the evil one. Second, the faithful conquer Satan through their witness (12:11). People bear witness (*martyrial martyrein*) by speaking what they believe to be true in contexts where the truth is disputed. The devil uses deception to persuade the world that he reigns supreme, so the faithful are to counter by testifying that the Creator has the right to rule the universe and that legitimate power is exercised through the Lamb (5:9–10), not the beast (13:1–10). Where the faithful give such witness, truth is victorious over falsehood.

The Lamb's witnesses conquer by losing their lives for the faith (12:11). Their deaths can be understood in contrasting ways. On the one hand, Satan's agent, the beast, makes war against God's witnesses and conquers them by putting them to death (11:7; 13:7). On the other hand, the faithful who lose their lives conquer the agent of evil. As Richard Bauckham has put it, "The point is not that the beast and the Christians each win some victories; rather, the same event—the martyrdom of Christians—is described both as the beast's victory over them and as their victory over the beast" (*Theology*, 90). For early readers, Satan's designs were carried out through the Roman state, which appeared to win when it took the lives of Christians with impunity. But from a heavenly perspective, the opposite is true. When Jesus' followers bear witness to God and the Lamb and reject the claims of Satan and his allies, they win a victory for truth over the forces that would suppress it. The victory will culminate in resurrection (15:2), but even as the faithful die, they share in the victory of the slaughtered Lamb (5:5–6), for the force of the lie does not prevail over the truth of God.

The question of perception continues at the end of this scene (12:12). Here, the same event—the defeat of Satan—means joy in heaven, for Satan has been banished; and yet it brings woe to earth, for the evil one now rages there. Spatially, the sphere of Satan's operation is restricted, and temporally, he has only a short time left. Revelation likens Satan to a rogue animal that the angels have driven off the expansive plains of heaven into the fenced-in area of earth. The monster rampages within its newly limited circumstances, seeking to do as much damage as possible during the time that remains until God's angel chains it up so that it can do no further harm (12:11; 20:2). Those who recognize that Satan rages on earth because he has already lost heaven and is now desperate have reason to resist him, confident that God will prevail.

The Dragon Pursues the Woman and Her Children (12:13–17)

The woman who bore the messianic ruler of the nations fled to the desert at the end of scene one (12:6), and the dragon that threatened her was thrown down in scene two (12:9). The final scene tells of the heightened conflict that results, for the dragon pursues the woman in the desert (12:13). The setting recalls Israel's escape from Pharaoh, which could be compared to God defeating a dragon (Isa 51:9–10; cf. Ps 74:13–14; Ezek 29:3). The people were carried as if on eagles' wings to the desert, where God cared for them (Exod 19:4). In Revelation, the woman is given the two wings of a great eagle, which enable her to find refuge in the desert (Rev 12:14). Where Israel's wilderness sojourn lasted for forty years, the woman's time there lasts for three and a half years—the time of distress that Daniel envisioned at the end of the age (Dan 7:25; 12:7).

Like other early Christian writers, John finds the image of the wilderness helpful because it was where the people of Israel lived between their deliverance from Egypt and entry into the promised land (1 Cor 10:1–13; Heb 2:10–4:11). The lambs' blood in Egypt protected the people from the destroyer and led to their release from bondage (Exod 12:1–13), and now the blood of Jesus the Lamb delivers people from sin (Rev 1:5; 5:9–10) and brings victory over the dragon (12:11). Yet the Lamb's sacrifice does not take people directly to the promised New Jerusalem but into a situation that requires perseverance—a wilderness.

The wilderness imagery gives readers a way to accept dislocation from imperial society. Those who feel marginalized or threatened because of their faith might relinquish their commitments in order to find greater acceptance. But if they compare themselves to Israel in the desert, then they know that their present dislocation is temporary and will end when the forces that threaten are finally defeated. The call for social dislocation will be repeated later, when an angel warns of the demise of Babylon/Rome and urges people to "come out of her" (18:4). Leaving Babylon means disengaging from social, economic, and religious practices that are deemed incompatible with the faith. Rather than giving detailed directions for how readers are to do this, Revelation uses images like fleeing to the wilderness or leaving a city in order to urge the need for readers to accept social dislocation for the sake of the faith.

The exodus imagery continues as the dragon spews a river from its mouth to sweep the woman away (12:15). Interpreters often compare the river to the threat that the sea posed to Israel when the people fled from Egypt (Beale; Resseguie; Smalley). But it can better be read as a parody of Israel's sojourn in the desert since the woman, like Israel, has already been borne into the desert on eagle's wings (Exod 19:4). In the OT it was God who made rivers come out of the rock in the desert to give life to the people (Exod 17:6; Ps 78:16). But here, it is the dragon that sends a river into the desert, and the goal is not to give life but to sweep the woman away. Ordinarily, a river in the desert was a welcome gift (Ps 105:41; Isa 43:19), but here, the dragon turns it into a destructive force.

The imagery is evocative, allowing readers to relate it to various threats in their lives. At one level, the imagery is violent. Since the river flows from the mouth of the dragon, readers at Smyrna may have likened it to the denunciations that came from the mouths of their accusers and threatened them with imprisonment and death. Such threats were said to be the work of Satan (2:9–11). At another level, the imagery could be linked to a less obvious threat, namely, the teachings that encouraged people to accommodate Greco-Roman worship practices (Beale). Such teachings were linked to Satan at Thyatira (2:20; 24), and later the mouth of the satanic dragon will emit spirits to deceive kings into opposing God (16:13–14). The river image is not part of an allegory in which each detail has a well-defined meaning; rather, the scene is suggestive enough that readers could relate the imagery to various kinds of threats around them.

The earth saves the woman by swallowing up the river (12:16). The earth was subject to woe because of the devil's expulsion from heaven (12:12), but it is not a passive victim of the devil, for it comes to the aid of the woman. The dragon opens its mouth (*stoma*) to bring destruction, but the earth opens its mouth (*stoma*) to bring deliverance (12:15–16). When the dragon tried to consume the woman's child, it failed (12:4–5), but when the earth seeks to consume the water the dragon sends after the woman, it succeeds (12:16). Yet the story takes an ominous turn. At the time of the exodus, the adversaries of Israel were swallowed up by the water; in Revelation, the water itself is swallowed up by the earth—and the adversary is allowed to go free.

The dragon is enraged at the woman, who is protected, and makes war with the rest of her offspring, who are persecuted (12:17). How readers are to understand this renewed threat is disputed, since both the woman and her children represent the people of God. Some interpreters suggest that the woman represents the church as a whole, which is preserved despite persecution; and the woman's children, who are persecuted, are the individuals within the church who are subjected to affliction and death (Giesen). A variation is that the woman shows the community being protected spiritually even as the children show the community being threatened physically (Beale; Murphy). The vision's message is paradoxical. Protection and persecution are aspects of the same situation, and if readers include themselves among those who keep the commandments of God and the testimony of Jesus, they have to live with the tension.

The woman remains in the desert at the end of the vision, giving it an unfinished quality (Yarbro Collins, *Combat*, 29). Some scholars argue that the woman is abandoned (Pippin, *Death*, 76; Selvidge, "Powerful"), but this interpretation does not fit the context because the wilderness is where the woman is protected. Moreover, the feminine imagery must be carried forward into the contrast between Babylon the whore and Jerusalem the bride. Babylon wears the opulent clothing associated with earthly wealth; the mother in Rev 12 is clothed with the sun and has stars about her head as signs of heavenly majesty. Babylon is the mother of earth's abominations and drinks the blood of the faithful (17:5); the woman in Rev 12 is the mother of the Messiah and the faithful. The whore rides a seven-headed monster; the mother is persecuted by one. The whore will be destroyed in the desert; the mother is protected there. The whore suffers torment when divine judgment falls upon her; the mother suffers torment while giving birth.

The final feminine image in the book is New Jerusalem, the bride of the Lamb. Although the woman in Rev 12 is the mother of the Messiah and the New Jerusalem in Rev 21 is the bride of the Lamb, these images frame the second half of the book and encompass Israel and the church (Humphrey, *Ladies*, 103–11; Koch, *Drachenkampf*, 217–24; Dochhorn, *Schriftgelehrte*, 140–59). The woman clothed with the sun is a precursor to the New Jerusalem; there is both continuity and transformation in the imagery. The mother appears in heaven and then flees to the earth that is part of this creation, while the bride descends majestically from heaven when the new earth appears. The mother experiences pain, but in New Jerusalem there is no more pain. The woman is threatened by streams in the desert, but the New Jerusalem offers people streams of the water of life. The woman is clothed with sun and stands above the moon, but the bride needs neither sun nor moon for she is illumined by God (Kalms, *Sturz*, 19). The images foster loyalty toward those represented by the mother and alienate them from what Babylon signifies.

27. The Beast from the Sea (12:18–13:10)

12 ¹⁸Then the dragon stood on the shore of the sea, **13** ¹and I saw a beast coming up from the sea. It had ten horns and seven heads. On its horns were ten diadems and on its heads were blasphemous names. ²The beast I saw was like a leopard. Its feet were like a bear's and its mouth was like a lion's mouth. The dragon gave it its power and throne and great authority. ³One of its heads appeared to have been slain and killed, but its mortal wound was healed. So the whole earth was amazed and followed the beast. ⁴They worshiped the dragon because it had given the beast its authority. And they worshiped the beast and said, "Who is like the beast and who can make war against it?"

⁵The beast was given a mouth that spoke boastful and blasphemous things, and it was given authority to act for forty-two months. ⁶It opened its mouth to speak blasphemies against God. It blasphemed his name and his dwelling place (that is, those who dwell in heaven). ⁷It was also allowed to make war on the saints and to conquer them. It was given authority over every tribe and people and language and nation. ⁸All who live on earth will worship it, all those whose names have not been written—from the time the world was made—in the scroll of life of the Lamb who was slain.

⁹If any have an ear, let them hear:
¹⁰If any are to go into captivity, into captivity they go.
If any are to be killed by the sword, by the sword they will be killed.

This calls for endurance and faith on the part of the saints.

NOTES

12:18. Then the dragon stood on the shore of the sea. The dragon's movement from the desert to the sea introduces a new section. Some manuscripts read *estathēn* (I stood), picturing John standing by the sea (P 046 051; KJV), but the best read *estathē* (he stood), referring to the dragon ($\mathfrak{P}^{47}$ ℵ A C).

13:1. and I saw a beast coming up from the sea. The beast is Satan's agent and opponent of the church. The term "beast" (*thērion*) could be used in a neutral way (Gen 1:24; Ps 104:11), but it often referred to wild and dangerous animals (Lev 26:6; Wis 12:9; Mark 1:13). Beasts kill (Rev 6:8; cf. Deut 32:24; *Pss. Sol.* 13:3) and are unclean (Rev 18:2). Sometimes, beasts were monsters, like the many-headed hydra (Pausanius, *Descr.* 2.37.4). By extension, the term was used for people who had vile and dangerous qualities (Tit 1:12; Philo, *Abr.* 33). Revelation uses traits of wild and mythic beasts for the political order and its human leaders.

Revelation's beast rises from the sea, like the four beasts in Dan 7:2–8, which resembled a winged lion that stood and thought like a man, a ravenous bear, a winged leopard, and a ten-horned monster. Those beasts represented kings and empires (7:17). Greco-Roman writers compared tyrants to beasts (Plutarch, *Mor.* 147B). Of Nero, Philostratus wrote, "as for this beast, generally called a tyrant, I have no idea how many heads it has," but "its nature is wilder than the beasts of mountains or forests" because "this beast is incited by those who stroke it" so that flattery makes it even more savage (*Vit. Apoll.* 4.38.3; cf. *Sib. Or.* 8:157).

Jewish writers called the Romans the Kittim, the invading force from the sea (Dan 11:30; 1QpHab III, 9–11). The apocalypse of *4 Ezra* pictures Roman rule as an eagle from the sea (11:1). Some interpreters connect the beast rising from the sea in Rev 13:1 with the way Roman troops arrived at eastern ports (Mounce) or the proconsul landed at Ephesus (Caird). But the imagery need not signify such specific actions.

Revelation sometimes says that the beast rises up from the abyss within the underworld (11:7; 17:8), which was the demonic realm (9:1–11). Although the sea was an abyss and could connote chaos (Ps 33:7), Revelation affirms that God created the sea (Rev 5:13; 10:6; 14:7). It is a part of the creation that God's opponents will use as they attempt to carry out their designs.

It had ten horns and seven heads. The beast's heads and horns replicate those of the dragon (12:3). Its seven heads give it a fearsome appearance like that of monsters such as Typhon, who had a hundred heads, and the Hydra, which had nine or perhaps a hundred (Apollodorus, *Library* 1.6.3; 2.5.2; Diodorus Siculus, *Libr.* 4.11.5). Revelation's beast recalls Dan 7:2–8, in which the four beasts together have a total of seven heads and ten horns. Multiple horns connote strength, like the Lamb's seven horns (Rev 5:6), but they also suggest destructive power, like the ten horns of the ravaging beast in Dan 7:7 (cf. Deut 33:17; Ps 22:21).

On its horns were ten diadems. The beast has traits of Rome and its emperors. Later, the ten horns will be identified as vassal kings (Rev 17:12). The emperors generally did not wear the diadems that signified kingship, preferring the wreaths that signified the victory of the empire, but diadems were worn by the vassals (NOTE on 12:3).

and on its heads were blasphemous names. The beast's heads signify kings (17:9). From a Jewish and early Christian perspective, it was blasphemous for a ruler to claim divine titles for himself (Lev 24:16; 2 Kgs 19:6–7; John 10:33). Although some manuscripts refer to a single name ($\mathfrak{P}^{47}$ ℵ C 025; NIV), others refer to multiple names, as in Rev 17:3 (A 046 051; NRSV). Early readers probably would have identified the beast's blasphemous names with the practice of calling emperors "god" (*Rom. Civ.* 1:624), "son of god" (I.Eph 252–53; I.Smyr 826), "lord and god" (Suetonius, *Dom.* 13.2; Martial, *Epigrams* 5.8.1), "master" (Philo, *Flacc.* 4.23; Dio Chrysostom, *Disc.* 45.1), and "savior" (Philo, *Flacc.* 74; Josephus, *J.W.* 7.64)—titles used for God and Christ (Rev 2:18; 4:11; 6:10; 7:10). Nero's admirers "kept up a thunder of applause, and applied to the emperor's person the voice and epithets of deities" (Tacitus, *Ann.* 14.15).

13:2. *The beast I saw was like a leopard. Its feet were like a bear's and its mouth was like a lion's mouth.* The leopard was swift and cunning; the bear and the lion were ferocious (Hos 13:7–8; Aelian, *Nat. an.* 1.31; Artemidorus, *Onirocritica* 2.12; 4.56). Lion imagery is noble when used for the messianic Lion of Judah (Rev 5:5) and the creature beside God's throne (4:7). But here, it is fused with the traits of other predators, creating a hideous pastiche, like the demonic beings depicted earlier (9:8, 17). For ancient readers such "a multifarious and dreadful beast" was an image of tyranny, which embodied many vices (Dio Chrysostom, *Disc.* 32.28). The beast has seven heads but only a single mouth, suggesting fearsome qualities rather than giving a physical description. The beast's traits combine those of the four beasts in Dan 7, which signified four successive empires: the Babylonians, the Medes, the Persians, and the Greeks. Some later writers identified Daniel's fourth beast with the Roman Empire (*4 Ezra* 12:11; *Mek.* "Baḥodesh" 9.30–41; *Gen. Rab.* 44.17), but Revelation combines all of them in a single beast.

And the dragon gave it its power and throne and great authority. Satan's throne signifies power. His throne at Pergamum was evident in the way a Christian was put to death there (Rev 2:13). Here, Satan gives the beast its throne, leading to the persecution of Christians (13:7). The way the beast shares the throne of Satan is a demonic imitation of the way the Lamb shares the throne and authority of God (2:21; 7:17; cf. 2 Thess 2:9). By analogy, Roman emperors were said to receive authority from the gods (Pliny the Younger, *Ep.* 10.102). To Jupiter it was said, "Father and protector of the human race . . . may you have Caesar as vice regent of your kingdom" (Horace, *Odes* 1.12.49–52). In Revelation, however, the authority of the beast comes from Satan (Friesen, *Imperial*, 30, 202).

13:3. *One of its heads appeared to have been slain and killed, but its mortal wound was healed.* The word "slain" (*esphagmenē*) is used for the beast (13:3, 8) and the Lamb (5:6), depicting the beast as the demonic counterfeit of Christ. Saying that the Lamb and beast appeared (*hōs*) to have been slain (5:6; 13:3) does not suggest that death was mere appearance. Readers are to assume that each actually died, so the beast's restoration is comparable to Christ's resurrection (2:8; 13:14). Where the dragon was beaten in a heavenly battle and yet lives to persecute the faithful on earth (12:7–17), the beast too received a mortal wound and yet lives to persecute the saints (13:3, 7). Both dragon and beast show the resilience of evil.

Here *one head* is said to have been slain (13:2), but later Revelation says that *the beast itself* suffered a mortal wound (13:14). Since the beast's heads are later identified with Rome's hills and kings (17:9), there are analogies in Roman ideology: The emperor was the head of the empire, so what happens to the head affects the whole (Seneca the Younger, *Clem.* 1.5.1). Some interpreters compare the wounding of the beast's head to the assassination of Julius Caesar and the beast's return to life to the survival of the empire (Barr, *Tales*, 107). Later, Caligula had a near fatal illness yet recovered (Suetonius, *Cal.* 14). Alternatively, Nero's death in 68 CE was followed by months of political and social instability, yet the empire recovered under Vespasian (Harrington).

Most interpreters see in the beast's resurrection an allusion to tales about Nero's survival of death and possible return (Aune; Boring; Giesen; Keener; Müller; Murphy; Bauckham, *Climax*, 407–52; Friesen, *Imperial*, 136–37; Klauck, "Do They"; Yarbro Collins, "Portraits"). Although Nero had his admirers (Tacitus, *Ann.* 14.15), others regarded him as a tyrannical beast who arranged for his mother's murder (*Sib. Or.* 8:157; Philostratus, *Vit. Apoll.* 4.38). Revelation pictures the beast carrying Babylon on its back, much as imperial power carried Rome (Rev 17:3). During Nero's reign, Rome suffered a devastating fire, and rumors spread that Nero was responsible (Tacitus, *Ann.* 15.44). To deflect criticism, he blamed the Christians and had many of them killed (Tacitus, *Ann.* 15.44). Similarly, the beast in Revelation makes war on the saints (Rev 13:7). Like Nero's Rome, the beast's city flows with their blood (17:6). In a final Nero-like move, the beast turns against its own city and burns it with fire (17:16).

Where the beast was mortally wounded by the sword, Nero reportedly died by putting a dagger to his own throat (Rev 13:14; Suetonius, *Nero* 49:3–4). Because few saw the body, rumors circulated that he had not died but remained alive, perhaps hiding in the east among the Parthians. Over the next twenty years, as many as three individuals claimed to be Nero (Tacitus, *Hist.* 2.8–9; Dio Cassius, *Rom. Hist.* 66.19.3; Suetonius, *Nero* 57; Dio Chrysostom, *Disc.* 21.10). By weaving stories about Nero's purported death and return into his vision, John makes the beast the mirror opposite of the Lamb, who died and rose. Critics of this theory point out that the legend did not say that Nero died and returned to life but that he never really died (Beale; Resseguie 124–26; Siew, *War*, 257; Ulland, *Vision*, 244–53). Revelation transforms traditions about Nero's survival of death into a story of death and resurrection in order to make the beast the demonic counterpart to the Lamb.

Forms of the Nero legends appear in other apocalyptic writings. One was that at the end of the age Satan, or Beliar, would appear in the guise of Nero to deceive people and persecute the faithful, claiming to be god and being worshiped by all (*Sib. Or.* 3.63–74; *Mart. Asc. Isa.* 4:2–8). The pattern is similar to that in Rev 13, where Satan gives authority to the deceptive beast, which persecutes and is worshiped (Rev 13:2–8). Later, the beast's name is conveyed by the number 666, which seems to mean Nero Caesar (NOTE on 13:18). A second form of the story anticipated that Nero would return from the east, crossing the Euphrates with his armies to seize control of the empire (*Sib. Or.* 4:119–24, 138–39; 5:361–65). The prospect of Nero's return has shaped the beast's return from death in Rev 13, and it is developed later in the book, where the beast's allies come from the Euphrates and destroy Babylon, the city that resembles Rome (Rev 16:12; 17:16; Bauckham, *Climax*, 407–52; Klauck, "Do They").

Nothing suggests that John expected Nero himself to return. Some interpreters think he saw Nero return in the tyranny of Domitian, who was likened to Nero (Juvenal, *Satirae* 4.38; Pliny the Younger, *Pan.* 53.4; Philostratus, *Vit. Apoll.* 7.4.1; Giesen; Klauck, "Do They," 697). But it is more probable that Nero's tyranny characterizes Roman rule as a whole. For those who regarded Roman rule as benign, this vision warns them not to be fooled. In Nero, the Roman beast reveals its true nature.

So the whole earth was amazed and followed the beast. The earth is understood to have fallen prey to deception, since the faithful are to marvel at God's works, not those of his beastly opponent (15:1, 3; 17:6–8). The Greek is awkward and literally says "they were amazed after the beast," which implies that they followed, becoming the beast's allies (BDF §196).

13:4. *They worshiped the dragon because it had given the beast its authority.* The way Revelation equates worshiping the ruler with worshiping Satan draws on Jewish and early Christian perspectives on idolatry. Jewish tradition held that those who worshiped false gods "sacrificed to demons, not to God" (Deut 32:17; cf. *1 En.* 19:1; 99:7–9; *Jub.* 22:17; 2Q23 1 7–8; *T. Job* 3:3–4). Where the MT of Ps 96:5 says that the gods of the peoples are "idols," the LXX says those gods are "demons." Evil spirits were said to have lured people into making idols (*Jub.* 11:4–6; cf. *Mart. Asc. Isa.* 2:4, 7). Similarly, Paul said that "what pagans sacrifice, they sacrifice to demons and not to God," and that a pagan altar is a "table of demons" (1 Cor 10:19–21).

And they worshiped the beast and said, "Who is like the beast. People were normally repulsed by hideous monsters (Virgil, *Aen.* 6.288), but this one they adore. The tone is satirical. Worship given to the beast mimics that given to God in Israel's tradition, which says, "O Lord, who is like you?" (Ps 35:10; cf. 113:5; Isa 46:5; 1QH^a XV, 28; 1QM X, 8). The faithful recognize that God is incomparable (Jer 10:6; Ps 88:8). In John's vision, however, the beast's unrivaled power is praised. It resembles the way the province of Asia declared that Augustus had surpassed all the benefactors born before him and that none who came later would surpass him. He was incomparable (*Rom. Civ.* 1:624).

"and who can make war against it?" Awe is evoked by the beast's military strength, recalling public admiration for Rome's military victories. Reliefs in the imperial temple at Aphrodisias depict Augustus and Nikē, the goddess of victory, holding a trophy over a captive; Claudius overpowering Britannia; Nero in triumph over Armenia; and other figures displaying Rome's invincible military strength (see Figures 29, 30, 33, 34; R. Smith, "Imperial"). The people who are awed by the beast assume that no one can succeed in war against it, so the only realistic course of action is to accept its dominion. When seen through the lens of John's vision, however, venerating rulers in this way is an affront to God.

13:5. *The beast was given a mouth that spoke boastful and blasphemous things.* The language recalls Dan 7:8, in which one horn of a beast had "a mouth speaking arrogantly" (cf. 7:11, 20). This figure is a tyrant, who shall "exalt himself and consider himself greater than any god, and shall speak horrendous things against the God of gods" (11:36). Daniel was commenting on Antiochus Epiphanes, whose attempt to suppress Jewish religious practice was the height of arrogance toward God (2 Macc 9:10, 12, 28). Revelation applies such traits to the beast. Previously, the dragon gave the beast its power, but here, the passive voice implies that its speaking ability "was given" by God (Rev 6:8; 9:3; 13:7), implying further that God allows the beast to display the hubris that will lead to the beast's demise (Dan 7:11; Sophocles, *Antigone* 1.127–33).

and it was given power to act for forty-two months. This period of three and a half years of oppression is mentioned in Dan 7:25 and 12:7. Daniel is reinterpreting Jeremiah's prophecy that Jerusalem would be oppressed for seventy years after the Babylonian conquest (Jer 25:11; 29:10; Dan 9:2). To make the prophecy applicable to threats against Jerusalem centuries later, Daniel extends the time of the prophecy. Instead of seventy years, the writer says that seventy *weeks* of years will elapse before iniquity is ended. Since a week of years equals seven years, seventy such weeks equal 490 years. The period concludes when a hostile ruler ruins the sanctuary in Jerusalem and stops sacrifices and offerings for half a week, which is three and a half years. In place of the regular sacrifice, the abomination that desolates is set up until the desolator is destroyed at the end of the period (9:26–27).

Historically, Daniel depicts the desecration of the temple under the Seleucid ruler Antiochus IV Epiphanes, who set up a statue of Zeus in the Jerusalem temple and banned the regular offering for three years (167–164 BCE; 1 Macc 1:10, 41–63; 4:54; 2 Macc 6:1–11). In Daniel, the number of days in this period varies. The time could be 2,300 mornings and evenings (i.e., 1,150 days), which is less than three and a half years (Dan 8:14). Or it could be 1,290 days, which seems to be forty-two months of thirty days each, plus one intercalated month (12:11). Or it could be 1,335 days, which is even longer (12:12; cf. Collins, *Daniel*, 322). Revelation recasts the material from Daniel to depict the community of faith as the temple and holy city that are threatened for three and a half years (Rev 11:2).

Christian tradition identified the period of three and a half years with the reign of the Antichrist. At the end of the age Beliar, or Satan, will come in human form. Like Nero, he will murder his mother and persecute the church, and he will be worshiped as god (*Mart. Asc. Isa.* 4:1–11). The length of his terrible reign will be three years, seven months, and twenty-seven days, which recalls the 1,335 days of Dan 12:12 (*Mart. Asc. Isa.* 4:12). Christian writers from the second and third centuries onward expected the eschatological adversary to reign for three and a half years (Justin Martyr, *Dial.* 32.3–4; Irenaeus, *Haer.* 5.25.3; Hippolytus, *Antichr.* 61.9; Victorinus, *In Apoc.* 11.2). Futuristic interpreters in the middle ages (Adso; see McGinn, *Apocalyptic*, 94) and modern times (LaHaye; Thomas) take this to be the literal length of the Antichrist's rule. On the Antichrist tradition, see §25E.

Thus far, the writer has described the beast by fusing the traits of the four beasts in Dan 7:2–8. Now he says that the beast was given a mouth that spoke boastful and blasphemous things (Rev 13:5). This is reminiscent of the fourth beast in Daniel, which had a horn with a mouth that spoke such things (Dan 7:8). The fourth beast has ten horns and is especially destructive. Daniel reads: "He shall speak words against the Most High, shall wear out the holy ones of the Most High, and shall attempt to change the sacred seasons and the law; and they shall be given into his power for a time, two times, and half a time" (7:25). Revelation follows this pattern by picturing a beast that blasphemes God (Rev 13:5a), assumes power for three and a half years (13:5b), and wears out the holy ones, or saints, by persecuting them (13:7). But Revelation also recasts the material to fit the Roman imperial context. In Daniel the tyrant attempts to change the law by suppressing Jewish worship practices, whereas in Revelation the beast itself is the object of worship (13:4, 8).

13:6. *It opened its mouth to speak blasphemies against God. It blasphemed his name.* Blaspheming could mean declaring God to be false, impotent, or evil (2 Kgs 19:4; Philo, *Fug.* 84; Rev 16:11, 21). To blaspheme God's dwelling showed contempt for his sanctuary (4Q372 1 13). Revelation draws on Daniel's depiction of a tyrannical ruler (Dan 7:20, 25; cf. 4Q388a 3). Daniel's model was Antiochus Epiphanes, whose suppression of Jewish religious practice showed that he considered himself equal to God, which was blasphemy (2 Macc 9:10, 12, 28). In Revelation blasphemy against God's name probably means that the beast claims divine titles for itself (Dan 11:36; Ezek 28:2; *Mart. Asc. Isa.* 4:6; *Sib. Or.* 5:34; NOTE on Rev 13:1), which the writer of Revelation would have seen as a violation of the command not to misuse the name of God (Exod 20:11).

and his dwelling place (that is, those who dwell in heaven). Some manuscripts refer to blasphemy against only God's dwelling ($\mathfrak{P}^{47}$), presumably God's heavenly dwelling (*skēnē*, 15:5). Other manuscripts refer to God's dwelling *and* those who dwell in heaven ($\aleph^2$ 046). Most, however, lack the conjunction. They say the beast blasphemes "God's dwelling, those who dwell in heaven." The appositive explains that when the beast denigrates God's dwelling, the attack is aimed at the heavenly company within it. Those who dwell (*skēnoun*) in heaven include angelic beings and the redeemed, whom God's tabernacling presence protects (7:15). The beast rails against them because these heavenly dwellers rejoiced at Satan's fall (12:12).

13:7. *It was also allowed to make war on the saints and to conquer them.* The language recalls Dan 7:21, in which a beast's horn, symbolizing Antiochus Epiphanes, makes war on God's holy ones. Revelation contrasts two forms of conquering: One is through violence, as in the first horseman and the tyrannical beast (Rev 6:2; 11:7); the other is through the example of the Lamb and his followers, who remain faithful in the face of suffering, even when it means dying (5:5–6; 12:11; 15:2). This is the form of conquest to which the churches are called (2:7, 11, 17, 26; 3:5, 12, 21). Seen from an earthly perspective, the deaths of the faithful are victories for the beast, since they lose their lives. But seen from a heavenly perspective, their refusals to capitulate are victories over the beast. Their resistance is also a victory of truth over falsehood, and its outcome will be resurrection (Bauckham, *Theology*, 90–91).

It was given authority over every tribe and people and language and nation. On these groups, see the NOTE on 5:9.

13:8. *All those who live on earth will worship it.* Earlier, false worship meant the usual forms of idolatry (9:20), but now, attention centers on the ruler cult (Biguzzi, "Ephesus"). Centers of the imperial cult in Asia included the provincial temples at Pergamum, Smyrna, and Ephesus, as well as the municipal cults of emperors in other cities. It was especially strong in cities (Price, *Rituals*, xxv, 78–100; Ebner and Esch-Wermeling, *Kaiserkult*). Temples to emperors were scattered across the provinces from Caesarea Philippi near Roman Syria (Josephus, *Ant.* 15.363–64) to Tarraco in Spain (Tacitus, *Ann.* 1.78). Along with temples, one could find statues, altars, and sacred areas for the emperors within the sanctuaries of traditional Greco-Roman deities as well as in public areas such as theaters and gymnasiums. Of Augustus it was said, "Because people address him in this way [as Sebastos] in accordance with their estimation of his honor, they revere him with temples and sacrifices over islands and continents, organized in cities and provinces, matching the greatness of his virtue and repaying his benefactions towards them" (Nicolaus of Damascus; adapted from Price, *Rituals*, 1).

Worship of the emperors was included in the festivals of traditional deities such as Artemis at Ephesus. Festivals also were dedicated especially to the emperor and featured competitions in athletics and music. Some celebrations honored the emperor's birthday or commemorated an event in his family. People dressed in white and wore laurel wreaths on their heads as they processed through the city. An imperial temple might be adorned with garlands while animals were sacrificed at the altar. Sometimes the sacrifices were made in the city's central square, and banquets were held after them. Incense was burned in theaters, and imperial statues were displayed (Price, *Rituals*, 101–14). The cities of Asia sent groups of hymn singers to the provincial temple of Augustus at Pergamum, where they sang songs in the emperor's honor (Friesen, *Imperial*, 104–13; Ameling, "Der kleinasiatische").

Some Jews and Christians were willing to pray to God on behalf of the emperor but would not offer prayer to him as though to a god (Philo, *Gaius* 356–57; 1 Tim 2:1–2). Revelation, however, assumes that at the popular level worshipers treated the emperors as gods. They might pray that the gods preserve the ruler, but they also offered prayers to the emperors themselves (Aelius Aristides, *Or.* 26.32; Price, *Rituals*, 232–33). For example, mysteries and sacrifices "were made to Demeter . . . and to the gods Sebastoi by the initiates in Ephesus every year" (I.Eph 213.3–6; Friesen, *Twice*, 148–52; Price, *Rituals*, 75, 105, 207–20). In Revelation, worshiping a deified human being—whether living or dead—is an act of opposition to God.

all those whose names have not been written—from the time the world was made—in the scroll of life of the Lamb who was slain. The scroll of life, also called the Book of Life, identifies those people who have the hope of resurrection to everlasting life in the New Jerusalem. In the OT "the scroll of the living" or "the scroll" God has written identifies those who are alive. Being blotted out of the scroll is equated with death

(Ps 69:28; Exod 32:32). Other sources link being recorded in God's scroll with resurrection to a future life (Dan 12:1) and removal from the scroll with final condemnation (*1 En.* 108:3). This is similar to Revelation, in which those written in the scroll do die but are resurrected and favorably judged at the end of the age (Rev 20:11–15). The scroll was a registry of citizens in God's city (Isa 4:3), and for NT writers this meant a place in the heavenly or New Jerusalem (Phil 3:20–4:3; Heb 12:22–24; Rev 21:27).

Some writers assumed that people's names were placed in the scroll as a reward for righteous living (Herm. *Man.* 8.6; Herm. *Sim.* 2.9; *Apoc. Zeph.* 3:6–9). In Revelation, however, people's names are placed there through divine grace. Since God has inscribed people in the scroll from the time the world was made, their place is a divine gift (Rev 13:8; 17:8; cf. *Jos. As.* 15:4). Divine grace stands in tension with human accountability. At the last judgment, people are accountable for their actions, as inscribed in the scrolls of deeds, but saved by grace, by having their names in the scroll of life (Rev 3:5; 20:12–15; 21:27). Revelation does not assume that those in the scroll are sinless and assumes that all people—inside and outside the church—need to repent (2:5, 16, 21, 22; 3:3, 19; 9:20, 21; 16:9, 11). Some ancient writers assume that people will be blotted out of God's scroll through sin, but Revelation affirms only that God will not blot out those who are faithful (NOTE on 3:5).

The Greek word order is confusing. Some interpreters take it to mean that the Lamb was "slain from the time the world was made," reading it as a way of speaking about Christ's preexistence and the idea that his death was foreordained (KJV, NIV; cf. 1 Pet 1:19–20; Bede; Harrington; Osborne; Prigent; Reddish; Rowland). This interpretation seems forced, however, since pressing the Greek word order does not suggest that the Lamb's death was simply foreordained but that he was actually slain from the time the world was made, which is incongruous. Therefore, many take the word order to mean that the names in the Lamb's scroll are "written from the time the world was made," an idea that is clear in Rev 17:8 (NAB, NRSV; Aune; Giesen; Thomas; Matt 25:34; Eph 1:4).

13:9. *If any have an ear, let them hear.* This expression concluded the messages to each of the churches and now calls attention to what follows (NOTE on Rev 2:7).

13:10. *If any are to go into captivity, into captivity they go.* Captivity (*aichmalōsia*) typically means being taken captive in war. In the wake of battle, both soldiers (Num 21:1; Caesar, *Bell. civ.* 5.42) and civilians (Isa 20:4; Amos 1:6; Lam 1:5; 2 Macc 8:36) could become prisoners. War captives could be taken away from their homelands to live and work in other places at the will of the victors (2 Kgs 24:14; 1 Macc 10:33; Luke 21:24; Suetonius, *Nero* 31). Prisoners were often sold as slaves (2 Macc 8:10; Cicero, *Att.* 5.20.5; Dio Chrysostom, *Disc.* 15.25). The Romans sometimes marched their captives in the processions with which they celebrated their victories. Such displays magnified the victories and humiliated their opponents (Caesar, *Bell. civ.* 2.35; Augustus, *Res* 4; Josephus, *J.W.* 7.153–54; Tacitus, *Ann.* 2.41). To be taken captive in war was considered a disgrace, especially among the Romans (Livy, *Rom. Hist.* 22.59.1; Tacitus, *Hist.* 4.80). Legally, the status of a war captive was like that of a dead person (Justinian, *Dig.* 49.15.18). Many manuscripts omit the second reference to "into captivity" ($\mathfrak{P}^{47}$ ℵ C 051), but the repetition fits the verse's epigrammic style and is probably original (A).

If any are to be killed by the sword, by the sword they will be killed. In warfare, one might either be killed in battle or be taken captive (2 Chr 28:5–8; 1 Macc 5:12–13,

22–23; 8:10; Caesar, *Bell. civ.* 3.33), although some were taken prisoner first and put to death later (2 Kgs 25:5–7; Thucydides, *Pelop.* 3.50, 68; Caesar, *Bell. civ.* 3.59; Suetonius, *Aug.* 15; Tacitus, *Agr.* 37; Tacitus, *Hist.* 1.37). Captivity and death by the sword are part of the beast's war against the saints. The language is reminiscent of Jer 15:2 LXX: "Those to go to pestilence, to pestilence; and those to the sword, to the sword; and those to famine, to famine; and those to captivity, to captivity" (cf. 43:11 [50:11 LXX]). Where Jeremiah warned that these forms of affliction come upon sinners, Revelation warns that the faithful may also suffer in these ways. Imprisonment and death are not divine punishments but acts of an evil power, as in the persecution at Smyrna (Rev 2:9–10).

Most manuscripts use active verb forms, stating, "If anyone kills with the sword, by the sword he must be killed" (C 051*; cf. ℵ, KJV, NRSV). This echoes warnings that those who take the sword will die by the sword (Matt 26:52) and could either warn that persecutors of the church will be punished or caution readers against violent resistance. Nevertheless, the passive voice "if anyone is to be killed" best fits a context that exhorts readers to bear suffering faithfully (A; cf. NIV, NAB; *TCGNT²*, 674–75).

This calls for endurance and faith on the part of the saints. Endurance means bearing hardship for a noble goal, not merely putting up with things to avoid conflict (*TLNT* 3:414–20). Readers are to endure by remaining faithful to God, the Lamb, and the Christian community (Pezzoli-Olgiati, *Täuschung*, 137–40). Faith first involves trust in God for ultimate redemption; second, it means showing fidelity to God during life on earth (Rev 14:12; Lambrecht, "Rev 13,9–10").

COMMENT

The heavenly battle has led to Satan the dragon being cast down to earth, where he has unleashed a violent campaign against the faithful (12:1–17). Satan now enlists an agent, a seven-headed beast from the sea, which blasphemes God, persecutes the Christian community, and asserts dominion over the peoples of the world (13:1–10). This horrific tyrant will be joined by a beast from the land, or false prophet, who will beguile the world into worshiping the seven-headed monster (13:11–18). The evil alliance will be complete with the addition of Babylon the whore, who rides on the beast and represents the city reveling in brutality and greed (17:1–6). After successively portraying these agents of oppression, John will trace their demise in reverse order, as the whore is destroyed by the beast (17:16), the beast and false prophet are defeated by Christ (19:20), and Satan is finally imprisoned and thrown into the lake of fire (20:1–10; see §25A).

John's description of the beast weaves multiple layers of biblical imagery together with elements from the Roman world. This same approach to character portrayal is found in the visions of the two witnesses (11:3–13), the woman and the dragon (12:1–17),

---

On Rev 12:18–13:10, see Ameling, "Der kleinasiatische"; Bauckham, *Climax*, 384–452; Baynes, *Heavenly*, 162–64; Beale, *Use*, 229–48; Biguzzi, "Ephesus"; G. Carey, *Elusive*, 145–54; Cuss, *Imperial*; deSilva, "Image," and *Seeing*, 198–203; Friesen, *Imperial* and "Myth"; Herz, "Kaiserkult"; Klauck, "Do They"; Lambrecht, "Rev 13,9–10"; Peerbolte, *Antecedents*, 142–53; Pezzoli-Olgiati, *Täuschung*, 123–41; Ruiz, "Taking"; Siew, *War*, 168–74; L. Thompson, *Book*, 95–167; Tóth, *Tier*, 15–43; Ulland, *Vision*, 233–336; Yarbro Collins, *Combat*, 161–206, and "Portraits."

and Babylon the whore (17:1–18). The main biblical traits of Revelation's beast are those of Leviathan the sea monster and the four beasts in Dan 7, in which a lion, bear, leopard, and ten-horned monster representing empires rise from the sea. Daniel's final beast speaks against God, afflicts the saints, and imposes its policies for three and a half years, like the beast in Revelation (cf. Rev 13:1–2, 5–8). The Roman layer draws elements from imperial practice: giving emperors divine titles and worshiping them (13:1, 4, 8), fostering an impression of invincibility (13:4), and asserting dominion over the world's nations and peoples (13:7). Specific elements are taken from stories about Nero, who supposedly had died but was thought to be alive (13:3) and who was remembered for persecuting the church (13:7).

John develops the portrait in chapter 17, where he notes that the beast has a scarlet color, like the reddish hue of Satan the dragon (12:3) and the opulent scarlet worn by the whore who sits on the beast's back (17:4). This later vision emphasizes the Roman features, for the beast carries the city that rules the world (17:18). Its "heads" are rulers and seven hills, like the seven hills of Rome (17:9), and its horns are vassal kings, like those who served under Roman auspices (17:12–13). The Nero-like traits continue when the beast, like Nero, burns its own city with fire (17:16). There is symmetry in the story of the beast. At first, people worship the monster because it seems invincible (13:4), but later, the beast turns its destructive capacities against its own allies (17:16). Initially, the beast makes war on the saints and is able to slay and take captive any who oppose it (13:7, 10). But when it makes war on the Lamb, it is taken captive, and its allies are slain by the sword from Christ's mouth (17:14; 19:19–21).

Readers are to see the beast as the demonic counterpart to the Lamb. The Lamb's power is not merely greater than that of the beast, it is different in kind. The Lamb shares the throne of God the Creator (3:21; 4:11; 5:6–13; 7:17), whereas the beast receives its throne from Satan the destroyer (11:18; 13:2). The Lamb conquered by suffering death on behalf of others (5:5–6; 12:11), but the beast conquers by inflicting death on others (13:7). The Lamb was slain (*esphagmenon*) and yet is alive (5:6; 13:8), building God's kingdom by redeeming those of every tribe, people, nation, and language (5:9–10). The beast too was slain (*esphagmenēn*) and yet is alive (13:3); but it establishes a tyrannical empire by dominating those of every tribe, people, nation, and language (13:7). Those purchased by the blood of the Lamb are sealed on their foreheads with the names of God and the Lamb as a sign of their identity (5:9; 7:3; 14:1–4). In contrast, those whose identity centers on the desire to purchase goods in the marketplace are marked on their foreheads or right hands with the name of the beast (13:16–18; 14:9).

The Lamb and the beast present readers with contrasting forms of power. The writer's goal is to heighten the readers' sense of loyalty to the Lamb and his followers, while alienating them from the social and political practices symbolized by the beast. The contrasts between God and evil are clearer in the visionary world than they were in the readers' social worlds. Some readers may have sensed evil at work in the threats of imprisonment and death against believers (2:8–11), but for others the issues were not so clear-cut. Some were prosperous and complacent (3:1, 15–17), while others seemed ready to accommodate practices linked to the gods of the empire (2:14, 20). The contrast between the Lamb and the beast gives readers a way of seeing the forces at work in the world. By shaping the way readers see their world, the visions shape the way they respond to it.

Interpreters have sometimes assumed that John's portrait of the beast mirrored a heightened threat of persecution by the emperor Domitian, who is said to have taken violent action against suspected opponents during the final years of his reign. Roman writers charged that Domitian made excessive claims about his own divinity, arrogantly demanding that people call him "lord and god" (Suetonius, *Dom.* 13.2). In Christian tradition, Domitian was remembered as a persecutor, second only to Nero in his attacks against the church (Eusebius, *Hist. eccl.* 3.17; cf. Charles 1:xcv; Kiddle xxxvi–lxiii; Morris 36–37).

Yet there is surprisingly little evidence that people in the Roman provinces experienced a rising threat of violence under Domitian. Asian coins and inscriptions refer to him as "emperor" and "high priest," but not as "lord and god" (NOTE on Rev 4:11). Because his father Vespasian was formally deified, Domitian, like others before him, was called "son of god." Such standard titles were used for him in inscriptions from Ephesus (I.Eph 2034; 3005; 3008), Smyrna (I.Smyr 731; 826), Thyatira (I.Thyat 870A), Laodicea (I.Laod 24), and other cities. Coins from Ephesus displayed Zeus on one side and Domitian on the other, implying that the emperor ruled under the auspices of the gods, but the inscriptions dedicating the temple to Domitian and his family stop short of calling the living emperor "god" (Friesen, *Imperial*, 43–55). Domitian acted harshly against those he suspected of disloyalty, but little evidence has been found that Christians were singled out for persecution. The messages to the churches reflect a situation in which persecution was locally initiated and sporadic, not a sustained state-sponsored campaign against the church (Yarbro Collins, *Crisis*, 69–73; L. Thompson, *Book*, 95–167; Friesen, *Imperial*, 143–51).

John's negative perceptions of Roman authority might have been shared by some of his readers, like those at Smyrna, who faced imprisonment at the hands of Roman officials (Rev 2:9–11). But John's views were probably not shared by readers who prospered under imperial rule (3:17; L. Thompson, *Book*, 132; Gradl, "Kaisertum"). Many Christians affirmed the legitimacy of the Roman state. Paul insisted that government was established by God and was to be respected as a means for restraining wrongdoing (Rom 13:1–7; Dunn, *Romans*, 2:757–74). Early Christians offered prayers on the emperor's behalf and honored his authority (1 Tim 2:1–2; 1 Pet 2:13–17; P. Achtemeier, *1 Peter*, 179–82; J. H. Elliott, *1 Peter*, 484–502).

Revelation had to alter the way in which at least some readers perceived imperial authority. The vision of the beast—like that of the whore (17:1–6)—uses parody to unmask the hubris of imperial claims. Parody and satire were used by biblical prophets (Marcus, *From*; Jemielity, *Satire*; Weisman, *Political*), Roman writers such as Juvenal and others (cf. Quintilian, *Inst.* 10.1.93–94), and early Christians (C. R. Koester, "Comedy"). Three factors are needed for parody to work (*NP* 10:546). First, the writer must deal with a text or topic whose main features are known to the readers. Second, the writer must alter and exaggerate certain features of the subject, while leaving enough intact that readers still recognize the basic elements of the topic. Third, the effect must be comic or satirical. Making something serious into the object of ridicule was a means of critiquing "those persons and institutions which seemed untouchable" (G. Carey, *Elusive*, 150–51; cf. deSilva, *Seeing*, 201; Ruiz, "Taking," 130).

The basis for the parody in Rev 13 is the idea that Rome's power to rule rests on its ability to conquer. This idea was featured in the art and rhetoric that supported the imperial cult (Friesen, *Imperial*, 204). John accepts the Roman emphasis on the centrality of conquest in its claim to dominion. But where supporters of the empire saw conquest as the basis for Roman legitimacy and invincibility, John makes it a hallmark of Roman tyranny. He parodies the ruling power by picturing it as a savage beast. Emperors claimed to have authority from the gods, but Revelation shows their authority coming from Satan. For John, deifying human rulers is not a sign of piety but of blasphemy. The people in the vision stand in awe of the monster, but John's parody shows that such a response is absurd and that faithfulness to God entails resistance to imperial claims (deSilva, "Image," 202).

Later readers of Revelation would construe the significance of the beast in different ways. Some saw John's parody as a prediction and blended Rev 13 with other NT texts in order to form a composite picture of the Antichrist, who was to appear at the end of the age (see §25E). Others explored connections to older Jewish and early Christian traditions about an eschatological adversary (see §25D). Underlying John's vision is the assumption that evil takes tangible political and social forms. It is not merely an abstraction. Yet Satan is "the ancient serpent," who was active long before the Roman Empire appeared (12:9) and who will remain active even after the beast and its city are overthrown (17:16; 19:16–21; 20:7–10). The beast encompasses the traits of empires from various times and places (Dan 7:2–8; Rev 13:2). The vision speaks to the imperial context in which Revelation was composed, but it does so with images that go beyond that context, depicting the powers at work in the world in ways that continue to engage readers of subsequent generations (Bauckham, *Theology*, 154–55; Friesen, *Imperial*, 177).

The Appearance of the Beast and Its Worshipers (12:18–13:4)

This vision begins when the dragon takes its stand beside the sea (12:18). Revelation affirms that the sea is God's creation. In a rightly ordered world, sea creatures praise their Maker in concert with those who worship God by heaven's crystal sea (4:6; 5:13; 10:6; 14:7; 15:2). But the dragon comes to the sea as an intruder. Defeated in heaven, it now brings woe to sea and earth (12:12). Beasts will rise from the sea and earth to do the dragon's bidding (13:1, 11). The sea and its ordinary creatures will suffer in God's battle against evil (16:3), and the sea will hold some of the dead until the end of the age (20:13). But in the new creation the sea will disappear, giving way to the water of life that flows from the throne of God and the Lamb (21:1; 22:1).

The monster from the sea has seven heads and ten horns, like its satanic master (12:3; 13:1). This is a kind of demonic incarnation. Just as the Lamb embodies the power and authority of God, the beast incarnates the power and authority of Satan. Although the dragon is banished from heaven, the beast extends the dragon's dominion on earth. Where the dragon wore seven royal diadems, the beast increases the number to ten, and they are displayed on the horns that show the beast's intimidating strength (12:3; 13:1). The mounting conflict is apparent in the "blasphemous names" on the beast's heads. Revelation assumes that it is right for the faithful to bear the names of God and the Lamb on their foreheads as a sign of belonging (7:3; 14:1); but when names suitable for God are claimed by the heads, or rulers, of the empire, it is a blasphemous attempt to take God's place (NOTE on 13:1).

The beast coming up from the sea resembles Leviathan, the many-headed monster of the sea (Ps 74:13–14; Job 41:1). Its associate, the false prophet, will resemble

Behemoth, the mythic beast from the land (Job 40:15–24; Rev 13:11). Leviathan was terrifying and seemingly invincible. One could not hope to make war against Leviathan any more than against the beast; the monster had "no equal" (Job 41:8, 33; Rev 13:4). Although Leviathan was one of God's creatures (Ps 104:26), it signified chaos and destruction. Therefore, God would destroy Leviathan and Behemoth at the end of the age—like the beast from the sea (Rev 19:20; Isa 27:1; *1 En.* 60:7–9, 24; *4 Ezra* 6:49–52; *2 Bar.* 29:1–4).

Revelation's beast from the sea also has traits of the most ferocious animals on land: the body of a leopard, the paws of a bear, and the mouth of a lion (Rev 13:2). The passage recalls Dan 7:2–8, in which four beasts rise from the sea: the first like a lion, the second like a bear, and the third like a leopard. The fourth has ten horns, one of which speaks arrogantly against God (7:8, 11, 20, 25), makes war on the saints (7:21), and holds power for three and a half years (7:25). In the end, this fourth great beast is burned with fire (7:11). All these traits appear in Revelation's beast (Rev 13:1–8; 19:20). Yet Revelation does not simply repeat Dan 7; the writer recasts it. In Daniel the beasts symbolize a series of empires, from the Babylonians, Medes, and Persians to the Hellenistic kingdoms of Alexander the Great and his successors. Daniel's arrogant horn was Antiochus Epiphanes, whose suppression of Jewish practice in the second century BCE fueled the Maccabean revolt (Collins, *Daniel*, 295). But in Revelation those four beasts become a single beast, so that readers see the tyrannical qualities of many empires as part of the same reality.

Revelation's portrayal of the beast also includes traits of the Roman Empire, which encircled the Mediterranean basin such that the Romans called it "our sea" (*mare nostrum*; Caesar, *Bell. gall.* 5.1.2). Augustus rose to power in part through his victories on the sea and then suppressed piracy, making the sea safer for Roman commerce (*Rom. Civ.* 1:627; Augustus, *Res* 13, 25). John transforms this scenario by picturing the sea giving rise to a blasphemous tyrant (Friesen, "Myth," 309–10). Then he blends the traits of Rome with those of Babylon, the debauched city that is seated on many waters (Rev 17:1). Babylon/Rome turns the sea into a highway for the swarms of merchants who bring vast quantities of merchandise to the city, hoping to make hefty profits by supplying its insatiable appetite for goods (18:17–19). Many touted Rome as the power that delivered the sea from hostile agents, but from Revelation's perspective, the sea was being degraded into a means for advancing the empire's relentless quest for world domination.

According to Revelation, it was Satan the dragon who gave the beast "its power and throne and great authority" (13:2). The dragon's action imitates the activity of God. Revelation recognizes that God's power (*dynamis*) over the world is legitimate because he created all things (4:11). God shares his power and throne with the slain and living Lamb who redeems (5:6, 12; 7:17; 22:3). But the dragon is earth's destroyer (11:18) and wields power through a beast, not a Lamb. Where Satan's throne is present, one can expect death rather than life to result (2:13).

The scene parodies the conventional idea that the emperors occupied their thrones by the will of heaven. Asian inscriptions declared that divine providence brought Caesar Augustus to power for the good of all humanity (*Rom. Civ.* 1:624, 627). Augustus was said to rule the world on behalf of Jupiter and the gods of Olympus (Manilius, *Astronomica* 1.916; Ovid, *Metam.* 15.858–70). Similarly, it was said that the gods gave

Nero power over the human race (Seneca the Younger, *Clem.* 1.1; 1.5.6–7). Later, Domitian was identified as the one who ruled the world on behalf of Jupiter, or Zeus (Statius, *Silv.* 4.3.128–29; Fears, "Cult," 66–80). Coins from Ephesus displayed Domitian's portrait on the front and on the back showed Zeus sitting on his throne with a ruler's staff in one hand and the temple of Artemis in the other. The impression is that Zeus and Artemis granted legitimacy to Domitian's rule (Friesen, *Twice*, 119; van Henten, "Dragon," 200). For the author of Revelation, however, the power behind the throne is the destructive power of the devil, who works through the imperial system.

Thus far the beast has characterized imperial rule as a whole. Now attention focuses on one particular head of the beast, or ruler, who had apparently been slain and restored to life (Rev 13:3). In antiquity, Victorinus identified this head with Nero (*In Apoc.* 13.3), and modern interpreters have made a similar connection. Nero was one of the heads of the empire who died violently. He reportedly "was slain" when he committed suicide by putting a dagger to his own throat (Rev 13:3; Suetonius, *Nero* 49.3–4). Yet stories arose that Nero was not dead but alive and that he would one day return to take power. Revelation transforms the story of Nero's purported survival of death into a vision of the beast's death and resurrection (NOTE on Rev 13:3).

Revelation invokes the Nero legend to show that Nero's legacy defines Roman rule as a whole. Various emperors claimed the names of God (13:2), purportedly ruled on behalf of God (13:3), were worshiped in the ruler cult (13:4), and exerted authority over the peoples of the world (13:7). But the tale of surviving death was linked particularly to Nero, who was remembered as the great persecutor (13:7; Tacitus, *Ann.* 15.44). By giving prominence to the beast's Nero-like traits, John presses readers to see that the violence perpetrated by Nero is an essential part of the empire's character. Some readers may have considered Roman rule to be benign, but John challenges this idea. He wants them to see that in Nero the empire shows its true face.

John's adaptation of the Nero legend sharpens the contrast between the kingdom of God and the claims of the state. Where God's Messiah is Jesus, the slain and living Lamb (Rev 5:6), the dragon's Nero-like vicegerent is the slain and living beast (13:3). Where the death and resurrection of the Lamb convey the redemptive power of sacrifice, the purported death and healing of the beast disclose the resilient power of evil. The question for readers is which form of power and authority will claim their loyalty.

Revelation recognizes that social pressure can play a major role in making people accept the claims of the empire. The writer says that "the whole earth was amazed and followed the beast" (13:3). If the vast majority of people think the current regime is impressive, others will find it hard to disagree. So promoters of the empire cultivated the idea that its rulers held office through universal public support. Augustus claimed that he "attained supreme power by universal consent" (Augustus, *Res* 34). His successor Tiberius was said to govern land and sea by "the unanimous will of gods and men" (Valerius Maximus, *Facta* 1.pref.). When the emperor traveled, all ranks of society were expected to turn out to greet him, showing popular support for his rule (Aune, *Apocalypticism*, 114–15).

Revelation challenges this, however, by showing the universe giving support to the rightful claims of God and the Lamb. The whole host of heaven and the creatures of earth and sea declared them worthy of legitimate power (Rev 4:11; 5:6, 11–14). In the readers' social worlds, "universal consent" affirmed the reign of the emperor and his gods, but in John's visionary world, the vast company of heaven and earth point to the supremacy of God and the Lamb, who alone are deemed worthy of the readers' trust.

A central issue concerns worship (*proskynein*, 13:4). In the heavenly throne hall the elders worship the God who creates all things and exercises authority through the slain and living Lamb (4:11; 5:13–14). Meanwhile, the world worships the dragon that gives its authority to the slain and living beast (13:4). In the readers' world, worshipers showed gratitude to the gods of the empire for Augustus and his successors. At Sardis, news that Augustus's son had come of age occasioned a festival in which local leaders were to "offer sacrifices to the gods and render prayers through the sacred heralds for his preservation" (*Rom. Civ.* 1:635). Vows were made for the emperor and the eternity of the empire, along with sacrifices to the gods (*Rom. Civ.* 2:521; Beard, North, and Price, *Religions*, 2:71; Price, *Rituals*, 214–15). Honoring the ruler meant venerating the gods who supported him. For the author of Revelation and other Jews and Christians, such polytheistic worship was opposed to the worship of the true God and was therefore demonic (NOTE on Rev 13:4). When the emperor called forth devotion to the gods of the empire, he effectively moved people to worship Satan, the power behind the throne (13:2).

People also make the beast itself the object of worship (13:4). The ruler cult was noted in the book of Daniel, where King Nebuchadnezzar demanded that people bow down before his statue (Dan 3:1–7) and others insisted that everyone pray to King Darius (6:6–7). The heroes in Daniel refused to worship the ruler—and the author of Revelation wants readers to show similar resistance toward the Roman imperial cult. By the end of the first century CE, the cult of the Roman emperors had been part of life in Asia for more than a century. In 29 BCE permission was given for a provincial temple to be built for Augustus and the goddess Roma at Pergamum. In the first century CE a provincial temple for Tiberius and the Roman Senate was built at Smyrna, and another for the Flavian emperors was constructed at Ephesus. Local forms of the ruler cult were popular in the other cities where John's readers lived (NOTES on Rev 2:1, 8, 12, 18; 3:1, 7, 14).

John's satirical portrait of the beast and general public is designed to shape the way readers see a society that deifies human authority. In Asia Minor, the most common form of the imperial cult centered on Augustus. The cults of Tiberius and the Flavian emperors also had some following, but Revelation parodies the cult by making a beast with the traits of Nero the center of devotion (NOTE on 13:3). Although Nero had at most a minor role in the imperial cult (NOTE on 13:12), Revelation shows people in awe of a Nero-like beast that not only conquers the nations, but makes war against Jesus' followers (13:7). Where one might object that the imperial cult did not center on Nero, John's vision insists that it does, because in Nero's legacy the character of imperial authority is disclosed. In common practice, the emperors were worshiped alongside traditional gods such as Zeus and Artemis, but Revelation parodies this as well, showing the Nero-like beast being worshiped alongside Satan the dragon (13:4).

The crowd utters two questions that disclose why the cult was so popular (13:4). First they ask, "Who is like the beast?," expecting the response, "No one is like the beast; the beast is incomparable." One pillar on which the legitimacy of imperial rule depended was the claim that emperors brought incomparable peace and prosperity. It was said of Augustus that "Emperor Caesar, son of god, god Sebastos has by his benefactions to humankind outdone even the Olympian gods" (I.Olympia 53; Price, *Rituals*, 55). Later, Nero's admirers called him "Our Apollo, our Augustus," declaring, "no one surpasses you" (Dio Cassius, *Rom. Hist.* 62.20.5). Similar praises were lavished on Domitian: "Lo, a god is he, at Jupiter's command he rules for him the happy world; none worthier than he has held this sway" (Statius, *Silvae* 4.3.128–30).

Second, the crowd asks of the beast, "Who can make war against it?" (Rev 13:4). The expected response is, "No one can fight against the beast; the beast is invincible." This takes up another pillar of imperial rule, which was that Rome was unconquerable in war. Years of military victories were thought to have demonstrated the supremacy of Rome and its rulers. Coins depicting the imperial temple at Pergamum showed Augustus in military garb being given a victory crown (Figure 12). The temple to the Flavian emperors at Ephesus featured a statue of Titus in a triumphant military pose (Figure 8). Other coins showing the temple at Laodicea portrayed Domitian in military dress holding a trophy. The inscription on the temple was *Epineikios*, "for victory" (Figure 18). The reliefs in the imperial temple at Aphrodisias fit this pattern. They show various emperors standing in triumph, holding trophies of battle in their hands with figures of defeated nations at their feet (Figures 29 and 30; Friesen, *Imperial*, 30, 50, 62).

The crowd in John's vision accepts the claims of the empire, but Revelation presses readers to make a different response. The writer has the crowd show awe toward a

Figure 29. Augustus and Nikē (Victory). Relief from the imperial temple at Aphrodisias (first century CE). New York University Excavations at Aphrodisias.

Figure 30. Unidentified Roman emperor and Nikē (Victory). Relief from the imperial temple at Aphrodisias (first century CE). New York University Excavations at Aphrodisias.

beast, whose image connoted tyranny. Their first question uses language that recalls what was said about the God who delivered Israel: "Who is like you, O Lord, among the gods? Who is like you, majestic in holiness, awesome in splendor, doing wonders?" (Exod 15:11). Readers familiar with such texts could be expected to say that it is God and not the beast who is incomparable. Previous visions declared God and the Lamb to be uniquely worthy to rule (4:11; 5:9–14). The literary context has also shown that it is false to think that the beast is unconquerable. God's angels defeated the dragon in heaven, and a voice announced that Satan was conquered by the blood of the Lamb and the witness of the saints (12:7–12). Who can make war against the beast? If the allies of God and the Lamb can throw down the dragon, they can presumably fight against its ally the beast.

The Actions of the Beast and Its Worshipers (13:5–8)

The people of the world are impressed with the beast, but the writer portrays the ruling power in a manner that is designed to replace awe and gratitude with enmity and indignation (deSilva, *Seeing*, 198–99). The beast is given "a mouth that spoke boastful and blasphemous things" (13:5). Its posture couples arrogance with blasphemy, which denigrates God. Since reverence for God or the gods was a value that was widely held in antiquity, the beast's flagrant disregard for this value would have evoked a negative judgment from readers.

Before commenting further on the blasphemy, John says the beast was given authority to act for forty-two months (13:5). This detail identifies the reign of the beast with that of the worst of the tyrants in Daniel (NOTE on 13:5). During this period of three and a half years the believing community, described as a temple, is threatened by the nations (11:2); the woman who represents God's people must flee from the dragon into the desert (12:6, 14); and the saints are persecuted (13:5–7). The previous chapter showed that this period begins with the Messiah's birth and exaltation, which lead to Satan's banishment from heaven to earth, and it will end with the Messiah's return to defeat Satan and the beast at the end of the age (19:11–20:3). Time does not unfold at the same pace in the visionary world and the readers' world. The forty-two months of the beast encompass the period between Christ's first and second comings. It is the time in which the readers live.

The reference to time challenges the idea that the beast is invincible. God has limited the time during which the beast and dragon can operate, which counters the idea that the empire will endure forever. One Asian inscription from the first century was inscribed "on behalf of the eternal continuation of Tiberius Claudius Caesar Sebastos Germanicus and of his whole house" (I.Eph 3801.2–4). Another said, "On behalf of the health of our Lord Emperor Titus Caesar and the permanence of the rule of the Romans" (I.Eph 412). Such sentiments emphasized that people were not to imagine an end to the Roman order (Friesen, *Imperial*, 130). In John's vision, however, the beast's time for operation is limited, as is Satan's (Rev 12:12), whereas God works from the time the world was made and forever (11:15; 13:8).

The beast blasphemes God's name and those who dwell in heaven (13:6). Such defiant speech displays arrogance, yet it also manifests the beast's impotence. Its master the dragon was forcibly expelled from heaven, and those who dwelled in heaven rejoiced at its downfall (12:12). Now the beast can only hurl angry words at heaven and its inhabitants from below, as the followers of the beast will do when they curse God for the plagues they receive (16:9, 11, 21). Railing at heaven is what one might expect of a tyrant (2 Kgs 19:4; Dan 7:25; Giesen). Readers could be expected to deplore anyone who took such a stance (deSilva, *Seeing*, 202).

The picture of an impious ruler runs counter to the official pictures of Roman emperors, who were publicly devoted to the traditional gods. Augustus was a member of all the major priestly colleges in Rome and eventually held the office of *pontifex maximus*, or high priest (Augustus, *Res* 10). Scholars have pointed out that "portraits of the emperor, both on coins and on statues, frequently showed him veiled in a toga, in the stance of sacrifice," and "virtually no one else is depicted on a Roman public monument conducting sacrifice" (Beard, North, and Price, *Religions*, 1:186). Coins from Smyrna show Tiberius offering sacrifice (Figure 9; Friesen, *Imperial*, 38). At the public gathering that celebrated Rome's victory in Judea, the emperor Vespasian cloaked his head in the manner of a priest and offered prayers (Josephus, *J. W.* 7.128). Domitian was devoted to the Capitoline gods and presided at events wearing a crown with the images of Jupiter, Juno, and Minerva (Suetonius, *Dom.* 4.4).

An emperor would not openly deride the inhabitants of heaven, but in portraying the beast, Revelation is not directly mirroring imperial behavior. Instead, John interprets conventional practices as an assault against God, for he does not consider the gods revered by the emperors to be true deities. Honoring false gods is an affront to the true God (Rev 9:20). Moreover, John links blasphemy to the claims made about the "heads" of state, who were given titles such as "god," "son of god," "lord," and "master." In Revelation these titles are appropriate only for God and Christ (NOTE on Rev 13:1; cf. 17:3). From John's perspective, deifying human authorities shows contempt for God and the whole company of heaven.

The beast's hostility toward God is extended through acts of violence against God's people (13:7a). Such violent campaigns have already been seen in the beast's slaughter of the two witnesses and the dragon's pursuit of the woman, and they intensify as the beast from the land slays the faithful and Babylon becomes drunk on the blood of the saints (11:7; 12:17; 13:15; 17:6; 18:24). Persecution likens the beast to the tyrant of Dan 7:21. It also evokes memories of Nero, whose features have been woven into John's portrait of the beast. After a fire devastated Rome in 64 CE, rumors spread that Nero was responsible. To deflect criticism, Nero fixed the blame on the Christian community and persecuted them:

> Accordingly, an arrest was first made of all who pleaded guilty; then, upon their information, an immense multitude was convicted, not so much of the crime of firing the city, as of hatred against mankind. Mockery of every sort was added to their deaths. Covered with the skins of beasts, they were torn by dogs and perished, or were nailed to crosses, or were doomed to the flames and burnt, to serve as a nightly illumination, when daylight expired . . . it was not, as it seemed, for the public good, but to glut one man's cruelty, that they were being destroyed. (Tacitus, *Ann.* 15.44)

Readers in the Asian churches would not have experienced a threat of this magnitude. Nero's actions had occurred in the past and were confined to Rome, and in the decades that followed these actions, persecution of Christians was sporadic. Christians at Smyrna and Philadelphia experienced local opposition (Rev 2:9–10; 3:9); Antipas had been killed at Pergamum (2:13), but other Christians there had apparently been left alone; and Christians at Sardis and Laodicea were prosperous and were not persecuted at all (3:1, 17). Some interpreters assume that the vision predicts a new outburst of persecution in John's immediate future (Mounce) or at the end of the age (LaHaye). But the passage might better be taken as a disclosure of the ruling power's character. The empire may seem benign, but it has shown its true character by persecuting the church. The beast conquers by violence (13:7). Where persecution occurs, the beast is present; where Christians are put to death, Satan reigns (2:13). The Lamb and his followers conquer in a different way: by faithful witness to the reign of God (5:5–6; 12:11; 15:2).

The beast's dominion extends over those of every tribe, people, language, and nation (13:7b–8a). It challenges the Lamb, who sacrifices himself to free people of "every tribe and language and people and nation" for God's kingdom (5:9–10; 7:9). Revelation recalls biblical descriptions of various empires, such as Babylon (Dan 3:4; 5:19; Jdt 3:8) and Persia (Dan 6:25), which wielded authority over many peoples, nations, and language groups. The description also fits Roman dominion. Virgil told of the triumph of Augustus, who marched conquered peoples— Africans, Leleges, Carians, Gelonians, and many others—in a procession where they were "as diverse in fashion of dress and arms as in tongues" (*Aen.* 8.720–28). In Augustus's funeral procession representations of the conquered nations were carried in display (Dio Cassius, *Rom. Hist.* 56.34.3; Tacitus, *Ann.* 1.8). In Asia Minor, the imperial temple at Aphrodisias featured sculptures of the emperors standing in triumph over beaten figures representing nations ranging from the Egyptians, Arabs, and Judeans in the east to the Callaeci of western Spain (see Figures 29, 30, 33, 34; R. Smith, "Imperial," 96; Friesen, "Myth"). The conflicting claims of the beast and the Lamb present readers with a question: Whom do you confess to be Lord of the world? The beast, which conquers every tribe and nation by military conquest, or the Lamb, who redeems people of every tribe and nation by suffering on their behalf?

Readers have learned that people worship the beast because of its seemingly invincible power (Rev 13:4). But Revelation also says that their names have not been written in the Lamb's scroll of life, which identifies those who have the hope of resurrection to life in New Jerusalem (13:8; 20:15; 21:27). Since people are inscribed in the scroll "from the time the world was made," they do not obtain this status as a reward for their faithfulness (13:8; 17:8). Their names are placed in the scroll because God wants them there; it is an act of divine grace (Notes on 3:5; 13:8; Giesen).

Theologically, an issue is whether most of earth's people—who here worship the beast—were excluded from the scroll at the dawn of time and therefore permanently consigned to judgment. Here it is important that Revelation has a dynamic rather than a static view of redemption. The author can say that people worship the beast because their names are not in the scroll (13:8), yet he also calls people of every nation, tribe, and language to worship God (14:6–7). The assumption is that repentance is possible and it is what God wants. John assumes that the Lamb died to redeem people of every nation and language, who are countless in number (5:9–10; 7:9–17). Periodically, the movement toward judgment has been interrupted to provide opportunity for those of every nation to repent and glorify God (9:20–10:11; 11:13). Revelation warns of the judgment that awaits those who worship the beast (14:9–11), while picturing the gates of New Jerusalem standing open to receive the nations (21:24–26). The idea of being inscribed in the Lamb's scroll of life gives readers incentive to remain faithful without closing off hope for the redemption of the nations (Boring 226–31).

An Exhortation with Double Meaning (13:9–10)

This part of the vision concludes with a couplet that has two parallel lines warning about the threats of captivity and death by the sword (13:10). Repeating the key words in each line makes the warning memorable, yet the saying is cryptic and yields a double meaning. On one level, the warning pertains to the faithful, who may lose their freedom and lives if they refuse to worship the beast. From this perspective the paradox could not be sharper. Those who do not worship the beast have a place in the Lamb's scroll of life. Yet the faithful also face the prospect of losing their lives through conflict with the beast. Being written in the scroll does not exempt people from death but extends the promise of overcoming death through resurrection (20:11–15). Sometimes, Revelation speaks as if every faithful person will be killed in the war against the beast (13:15). But each line in 13:10 begins with the word "if" (*ei*), which leaves open the possibility that some will be imprisoned or killed and that others will not. As Richard Bauckham notes, "Not every faithful witness will actually be put to death, but all faithful witness requires the endurance and the faithfulness (13:10) that will accept martyrdom if it comes" (*Theology*, 94).

On another level, the warning includes a twist, reflecting the idea of symmetry in justice. The beast and its agents now threaten the faithful with imprisonment (13:10; cf. 2:10), but when Christ returns for battle, the beast and false prophet will become war captives (19:20). Moreover, the followers of Jesus now face death by the sword of the beast, but in the end the followers of the beast will face destruction by the sword from the mouth of Christ (19:21). When read in light of Revelation's ending, the saints have reason to persevere, since capitulating to the beast brings no escape from danger. When the apocalyptic war reaches its climax, those who deprive others of freedom and life will undergo these same things.

28. The Beast from the Land (13:11–18)

13 ¹¹Then I saw another beast coming up from the earth. It had two horns like a lamb, but it was speaking like a dragon. ¹²It exercises all the authority of the first beast in its presence. It also makes the earth and all who live in it worship the first beast, whose mortal wound was healed. ¹³It does great signs, so that it even makes fire come down from heaven to earth in the presence of the people. ¹⁴It deceives those who live on the earth by the signs that it was allowed to do in the presence of the beast. It told those who live on earth to make an image for the beast, which had been wounded by the sword and yet came to life again. ¹⁵It was allowed to give breath to the image of the beast, so that the image of the beast would even speak, and to have anyone who did not worship the image of the beast be put to death.

¹⁶It makes everyone—the small and great, the rich and poor, the free and slaves—to have a mark put on their right hands or on their foreheads, ¹⁷so that no one can buy or sell anything unless the person has the mark with the beast's name or the number of its name. ¹⁸This calls for wisdom. Let the one who understands calculate the number of the beast, for it is the number of a person. Its number is 666.

NOTES

13:11. *Then I saw another beast coming up from the earth.* This creature will be described as a lamb, but introducing it as a beast (*thērion*) suggests that it is dangerous, like the beast from the sea (NOTE on 13:1). The way John sees each beast "coming up" suggests power to dominate, just as the beasts symbolize empires that come from sea and land in Dan 7:3 and 7:17. John's readers would have correlated the beast from the sea with the Roman emperors (COMMENT on Rev 13:1–10) and the beast from the land with those who promoted the imperial cult. Interpreters differ over more precise identification of the group. A number of proposals have been made; the first offers a starting point for the approach developed in the COMMENT:

1. Aristocratic supporters of the imperial cult. Many of the imperial cult's supporters came from the social elite. They funded the erection of temples and statues, and some held imperial priesthoods. Many were members of urban councils and worked in civic administration (Friesen, "Beast," 52–59). The inscriptions that accompany their actions on behalf of the cult express gratitude for the benefits of imperial rule. In Asia Minor, "political, religious, and economic activities were so intertwined that a Christian who refused to honor the emperor in a religious way would have been limited in economic and political options" (Yarbro Collins, "'What,'" 82; cf. Friesen, "Beast," 62; Murphy).

2. Provincial council, or *koinon*, of Asia. This group had oversight of the three provincial temples in Asia: one dedicated to Augustus and Roma at Pergamum; another to Tiberius, Livia, and the Senate at Smyrna; and another to the Flavians—Vespasian, Titus, Domitian, and perhaps Domitia—at Ephesus. The council appointed provincial high priests and priestesses and oversaw sacrifices and festivals (Beale; Blount; Bovon, "Possession," 137). One problem with this proposal is that the council dealt with only the provincial temples and priesthoods, whereas many imperial cults operated at the municipal level. Another problem is that the council did not play a significant role in commerce, which is a prominent factor in Rev 13:16–18.

3. Imperial priesthood. This proposal is more focused than the previous one, since it points specifically to those who held priestly office in the imperial cult, whereas the provincial council included some who did not hold this office. At the same time, this proposal is not limited to those who were involved at the provincial level. Men and women also held local imperial priesthoods (Aune; Price, *Rituals*, 197–98). The most significant problem with this approach is that it is too narrow, as people could participate in the imperial cult in various ways without holding priestly office (Friesen, "Beast," 60).

4. Christians who accommodate pagan practice. The land beast is a false prophet (16:13; 19:20; 20:10). Within the Christian community there was a false prophet nicknamed Jezebel, who taught that it was acceptable to eat what had been sacrificed to Greco-Roman deities, presumably including offerings to the emperor (2:20). Just as the land beast masquerades as a lamb, Jezebel purports to follow Jesus the Lamb, yet both deceive people into false worship (Duff, *Who*, 113–25; cf. Beale; Wall). It seems likely that Revelation sees a connection between Jezebel and the false prophecy associated with the second beast. Yet the way the beast from the land encourages the world to make a statue for the ruler makes it unlikely that the figure represents a segment of the Christian community.

5. General support for Greco-Roman religion, including the imperial cult. Revelation is critical of all forms of idolatry (9:20; 21:8; 22:15). Since the imperial cult was linked to the worship of traditional deities, the author treats it all as false worship. Warnings

against idolatry can be addressed to people inside the church, like those who follow the teachings of Balaam and Jezebel (2:14, 20), as well as to society as a whole (Boring; Reddish; Roloff; Smalley; L. Thompson, *Book*, 164). This approach avoids reducing Revelation to a simple code in which each image has a single, well-defined meaning. The problem is that it generalizes too quickly. Revelation's parody of false worship focuses on patterns associated with the imperial cult.

It had two horns like a lamb, but it was speaking like a dragon. Since the lamb has two horns, some interpreters suggest that it is an aggressive ram (Dan 8:3; Aune). Yet this understanding is unlikely given Revelation's use of the term "lamb" (*arnion*) in connection with vulnerability and sacrifice (NOTE on Rev 5:6). A Passover lamb could be pictured with two horns (*t. Pesaḥ* 6:7). The creature's deceptively mild appearance is belied by its speech, which is like that of a dangerous dragon. The contrast between appearance and reality is like that in the saying, "Beware of false prophets, who come to you in sheep's clothing but inwardly are ravenous wolves" (Matt 7:15). Here the land beast speaks for the dragon by promoting idolatry (Rev 13:14).

13:12. *It exercises all the authority of the first beast in its presence.* The beast from the land plays an administrative role on behalf of the ruling power. In John's social world local officials did not formally derive their authority from Rome, but they worked under Roman auspices. The symbols of this implied relationship were part of urban life. At Ephesus, a municipal temple to Augustus was apparently located in the city's administrative center (Scherrer, "City," 4–6). At Miletus, an imperial altar stood in the courtyard of the building where the city council met (Friesen, *Imperial*, 71). Revelation assumes that the authority of the beast—the ruling power—takes tangible form in the political and administrative structures of the cities where the readers live.

It also makes the earth and all who live in it worship the first beast. The land beast will "make" people worship the ruler through deception and coercion (13:13–17). This visionary portrayal opposes the way the ruler cult was promoted at the provincial and municipal levels. Those who promoted the cult used various means of generating support.

First, people of influence initiated the building of imperial temples, altars, and statues. In 29 BCE provincial representatives asked Augustus for permission to build a temple to him, and permission was granted. Their efforts resulted in building the first provincial temple at Pergamum (Dio Cassius, *Rom. Hist.* 51.20.6–9). Later, the province asked permission to build a temple to Tiberius in order to show gratitude for court decisions that went in Asia's favor. In 26 CE representatives of eleven cities went to Rome to compete for the privilege of building the temple, and Smyrna eventually won (Tacitus, *Ann.* 4.55–56). To host such a temple was a matter of civic pride. The provincial temple at Ephesus, which was dedicated to the Flavian emperors about 89–90 CE, was also supported by leading citizens (Friesen, "Beast," 54–55; Herz, "Kaiserkult").

Wealthy patrons in other cities promoted the provincial temples. When the temple at Ephesus was dedicated, they sent dedications in order to show their cities' support (Friesen, *Twice*, 29–49). They also constructed municipal temples in their own cities. According to one first-century inscription, a benefactor "dedicated to the sons of Augustus a sanctuary and temple from his own money in the most prominent part of the square, on which his name also was inscribed, wanting to show his gratitude and piety to the whole [imperial] house. . . . He also founded at the harbor of the market a temple to Augustus god Caesar, so that no notable place should lack his goodwill and piety to the god [Augustus]" (IG 12 Supp. 124.16–23; Price, *Rituals*, 3). Altars and statues to the deified emperors were set up in forum areas, theaters, and public buildings and in the sanctuaries of a city's traditional deities (Tacitus, *Ann.* 4.2).

Second, imperial festivals were held at the provincial and local levels. These were popular events that cultivated public support for the cult. Processions from one part of a city to another were part of many religious celebrations, including those honoring the emperor. Participants might escort the animals that were garlanded for sacrifice and carry images of the emperor. Sacrifices were accompanied by prayers, banquets, and distributions of food, which reached a broad section of the populace. Athletic competitions were also held in connection with cult festivals. The provincial games, or *Sebasta Romaia*, lasted for several days and drew a wide range of participants (Price, *Rituals*, 3, 101–14). In the late first century CE, Ephesus held Olympic games honoring Domitian (Friesen, *Imperial*, 52; Krinzinger, "Spectacula").

The emperor also could be included in the worship of traditional Greco-Roman deities. At Ephesus, one group of worshipers made prayers and sacrifices to the emperors along with Demeter (Harland, *Associations*, 116–19). At Pergamum, an imperial festival was centered in the sanctuary of Asclepius (Friesen, *Imperial*, 74), and a group called the dancing cowherds had a dining hall with altars to Dionysus and Augustus (Figure 13; Radt, *Pergamon*, 196–99). Thyatira called itself the city of Augustus although its traditional patron was Apollo Tyrimnos (I.Thyat 960). At Philadelphia, games were held in honor of the local goddess Anaitis and the emperor (I.Phil 1480).

Third, the cult provided opportunities for social recognition. The men and women who served in the provincial cults typically came from the upper levels of society. To obtain such a position was an honor. The local cults provided opportunities for others to serve in the priesthoods. Groups of hymn singers from various cities traveled to the imperial temple at Pergamum to celebrate Augustus's birthday and other occasions. People gained social recognition by participating in this wider social network (Friesen, *Imperial*, 104–21).

whose mortal wound was healed. Revelation identifies the ruler cult especially with Nero, who had purportedly died a violent death but was rumored to be alive (NOTE on 13:3). This comment is part of the writer's parody of the imperial cult, since the cities of Asia had not established a cult honoring Nero. A temple to Nero might have been planned or begun at Ephesus in the 60s of the first century. Coins dating from 65/66 CE show Nero on one side and a temple—perhaps different from the Artemis temple—on the other and bear the title "temple warden" (*neokoros*). But as far as is known, no temple to Nero was actually built in Ephesus (Burrell, *Neokoroi*, 62–63). When the provincial temple was completed ca. 89/90, it honored the Flavian emperors—Domitian and his family. The temple at Aphrodisias included reliefs of Nero alongside those of other emperors. One shows him being crowned by his mother Agrippina, and another pictures his victory over Armenia (see Figure 34), but Nero is not given special prominence (Friesen, *Imperial*, 91, 148–49). Revelation centers the ruler cult on Nero because the author believes that Nero's brutality discloses the true character of imperial rule as a whole.

13:13. *It does great signs.* Jewish and early Christian sources ascribe miraculous signs to Moses (Exod 4:8–9; Deut 34:11), the apostles (Acts 2:43; 4:16), Paul (2 Cor 12:12), and Philip (Acts 8:6). Elijah (1 Kgs 17:8–24) and Elisha (2 Kgs 4:1–5:14) also worked miracles. Many assumed that working miracles showed that a person had legitimate authority from God (Mark 8:11; John 2:18; 1 Cor 1:22). By performing signs the beast from the land gives the impression that it possesses genuine prophetic authority and that the beast from the sea, whom it serves, is truly a godlike being.

In Greco-Roman contexts, wonders were used to legitimate a ruler's authority. A palm tree that miraculously sprang up at a temple portended the triumph of Julius Caesar (Caesar, *Bell. civ.* 3.105.6), and a statue that moved anticipated Vespasian's rise to become emperor (Tacitus, *Hist.* 1.86; Suetonius, *Vesp.* 5.7). It was said that Vespasian himself worked healing miracles, which heightened his prestige by showing that the gods favored him (Tacitus, *Hist.* 4.81.1–3; Suetonius, *Vesp.* 7.2; Bowersock, "Mechanics," 294–302).

so that it even makes fire come down from heaven to earth in the presence of the people. The ability to call down fire from heaven designated a person as a servant of God. This power was ascribed to Elijah (1 Kgs 18:24, 37–38; 2 Kgs 1:10, 12), David, Solomon, and Abraham (1 Chr 21:26; 2 Chr 7:1; *T. Ab.* 10:11; cf. Luke 9:54). The beast from the land mimics this sign to promote the worship of a false god. The heavenly fire also fits the author's parody of imperial claims. In the Greco-Roman world, the usual source of fire from heaven was Jupiter, or Zeus, who was pictured with a thunderbolt. An Asian inscription tells of fire flashing forth from a temple and people crying out in terror at what they took to be a manifestation of the god (Bowersock, "Mechanics," 295–96). In imperial ideology, Jupiter was often identified as the source of imperial authority (NOTE on Rev 13:2). The vision of the beast from the land plays on this theme by having a false prophet call forth a fiery bolt from heaven to give the appearance of heavenly approval for the deified ruler.

13:14. *It deceives those who live on the earth by the signs that it was allowed to do in the presence of the beast.* False prophets used miracles to lure people into false worship: "If a prophet or a dreamer of dreams arises among you and gives you a sign or a wonder, and the sign or wonder that he tells you comes to pass, and if he says, 'Let us go after other gods,' which you have not known, 'and let us serve them,' you shall not listen to the words of that prophet or dreamer of dreams. For the Lord your God is testing you, to know whether you love the Lord your God with all your heart and with all your soul" (Deut 13:1–3). This description informed the expectation that false prophets would arise at the end of the age to deceive people with miracles (Mark 13:22 par.). According to 2 Thess 2:9–10, the great opponent of Christ would be the man of lawlessness, the agent of Satan, "who uses all power, signs, lying wonders, and every kind of wicked deception." Some thought miracles would be performed by Beliar, who would come as a Nero-like ruler (*Sib. Or.* 2:167; 3:63–74; *Mart. Asc. Isa.* 4:1–14; cf. Peerbolte, *Antecedents*, 339–43). Revelation calls the miracle-working beast from the land a false prophet, placing it within this tradition of the eschatological deceiver (Rev 16:14; 19:20).

It told those who live on earth to make an image for the beast. The image (*eikōn*) is a statue of the seven-headed monster (13:15). Stories were told of Nebuchadnezzar (Dan 3:1) and Beliar setting up images for people to worship (*Mart. Asc. Isa.* 4:11) and of Caligula ordering his legate to place an imperial statue in the Jerusalem temple (Josephus, *Ant.* 18.261). In John's vision, however, the image is not set up by the ruler, but by the people, a practice that would have been familiar to early readers.

Influential citizens and benefactors established provincial and municipal temples to the emperor (NOTE on Rev 13:12), in which statues of the emperor were prominently displayed. Some depicted him in military garb, such as the image of Titus at Ephesus (Figure 8), Augustus at Pergamum (Figure 12), and probably Domitian at Laodicea (Figure 16). The statue of Tiberius at Smyrna apparently showed him in priestly garb (Figure 9). Some statues depicted emperors in the manner of Olympian gods (Price, *Rituals*, 181–86). A large cult statue, like the one at Ephesus, could be twenty-five feet tall; smaller images and paintings of the emperor were carried in processions (Price, *Rituals*, 189).

Imperial images were usually set up by individuals and groups from various cities rather than by Roman officials. One first-century inscription tells of imperial images being put on public display, with "the city providing . . . the statues" (*Rom. Civ.* 2:521). Some statues were intended for worship, while others were honorific images. Many were put up by associations such as the youth of the city or the worshipers of Dionysus; others were erected by private citizens (Price, *Rituals*, 174). By putting up imperial statues, individuals and associations fostered goodwill with the ruling power and asserted their place in civic life (Price, *Rituals*, 170–206; Friesen, *Imperial*, 23–131; Harland, *Associations*, 115–60).

which had been wounded by the sword and yet came to life again. See the NOTES on 13:3 and 13:12.

13:15. *It was allowed to give breath to the image of the beast, so that the image of the beast would even speak.* Jewish and Christian tradition insisted that statues were inanimate objects, in contrast to the living God (Isa 44:9–20; Wis 15:15–17; 1 Thess 1:9). There are several ways in which readers might have been expected to interpret a talking statue; the first is most likely:

1. Sorcery. Giving statues breath and the power of speech was identified with sorcery and here depicts the promoter of the ruler cult as a practitioner of the art. The assumption is that readers would condemn the practice (Rev 9:20; 18:23; 21:8; 22:15). Both ancient and modern interpreters have noted the similarities to sorcery (Irenaeus, *Haer.* 5.28.2; Victorinus; Andreas; Brighton; Charles; Bovon, "Possession"; Duff, *Who*, 116; Rodney L. Thomas, *Magical*, 68–81).
2. Hoax. The story of Bel and the dragon told of a statue that seemed to consume food but in reality was a hollow shell that priests entered by a secret passage so they could eat the food (Bel 1–26). In the second century CE a religious huckster and false prophet named Alexander created an oracular shrine at Abonoteichus on the southern shore of the Black Sea. For it he fashioned an image of a snakelike deity with an artificial head and hinged jaws that could be moved by cords. A small tube was inserted into the back of the head so that someone behind the scenes could talk through the tube and create the illusion that the idol was speaking (Lucian, *Alex.* 26; cf. Beale; Blount; Harrington; Reddish). Nevertheless, it is unlikely that John depicts a hoax since the land beast seems actually to animate the statue. Some interpreters have suggested that personnel at the imperial temples devised ways to simulate fire from heaven or to make the emperor's statue talk (S. Scherrer, "Signs"; Schüssler Fiorenza 85–86), but there is no evidence for imperial statues giving oracles (Aune 2:764; Friesen, "Myth," 310; Harland, *Associations*, 257).
3. Spontaneous animation. Many Greek and Roman writers agreed that statues were lifeless, even though they used them in worship (Plato, *Leg.* 11.931A; cf. Dio

Chrysostom, *Disc.* 12.59–61, 78). But popular piety assumed that statues could spontaneously sweat, move, or speak in order to communicate the will of the gods (Cicero, *Div.* 1.43.98; Plutarch, *Ant.* 60; Plutarch, *Cor.* 37.3–38.2; Lucian, *Philops.* 33; Lucian, *Syr. d.* 10). In Revelation, however, the statue does not speak spontaneously but is animated by the beast from the land.

and to have anyone who did not worship the image of the beast be put to death. The beast's action is like that ascribed to Nebuchadnezzar, who commanded people to worship the image he had set up or be killed in a fiery furnace, but the heroes refused to capitulate (Dan 3:4–6). A similar response of resistance is what the author of Revelation desires from the readers (Rev 13:10). Readers may have discerned analogies to Roman imperial practice. In the early second century CE, Pliny the Roman governor used a statue when trying to determine whether people were Christians:

> I considered that I should dismiss any who denied that they were or ever had been Christians when they repeated after me a formula of invocation to the gods and had made offerings of wine and incense to your [the emperor's] statue (which I had ordered to be brought into court for this purpose along with the images of the gods), and furthermore had reviled the name of Christ: none of which things, I understand, any genuine Christian can be induced to do. Others . . . did reverence to your statue and the images of the gods in the same way as the others, and reviled the name of Christ. (Pliny the Younger, *Ep.* 10.96.5–6)

Those who persisted in claiming to be Christians were executed. The emperor Trajan approved of Pliny's method but insisted that Christians were not to be hunted down (Pliny the Younger, *Ep.* 10.97.2). Stories of later Christian martyrs also emphasized refusals to worship imperial statues (*Mart. Apollonius* 7; *Mart. Pion.* 5; *Mart. Dasius* 7). What is striking is that it was typically the Roman governor rather than city officials who condemned Christians in this way, whereas it was the local leadership that most vigorously promoted imperial temples and statues. Revelation blends the traits of the Roman official with those of the local aristocracy to create a composite picture of authority.

13:16. *It makes everyone—the small and great, the rich and poor, the free and slaves.* The Romans broadly distinguished between an upper and a lower class, and within each group there were various strata. Upper-class status often included birth into a noble family and inherited wealth. Others, who acquired wealth, could advance their social status. Members of this class tended to be educated and cultured and likely held administrative positions. The lower classes included freeborn people of more modest means, freed slaves, and finally, slaves. Among the free population, status varied according to family background, occupation, citizenship, and wealth (MacMullen, *Roman*, 88–120; Harland, *Associations*, 27). Revelation envisions a situation in which no one is exempt from the beast's influence.

to have a mark put on their right hands or on their foreheads. In the visionary world, the mark of the beast is the opposite of the seal of God and the Lamb (7:3; 14:1). It does not have a direct connection with any one practice in the readers' social worlds. Rather, the imagery creates a web of associations:

1. Belonging. In the visionary world a seal on the forehead of the redeemed indicates that they belong to God (7:3; 14:1). Conversely, the mark on the forehead or right hand of others shows that they belong to the beast (13:16; 14:9; 20:4). The right hand is probably included because the mark is required for buying and selling, which involve the hands. Other sources say that the righteous had a sign of salvation on their foreheads and that the wicked had a sign of destruction (Ezek 9:4; *Pss. Sol.* 15:6–9; *Apoc. El.* 1:9). Unbelievers bear the stamp of this world, while believers bear the stamp of God (Ign. *Magn.* 5:2).

2. Commercial participation. Revelation contrasts those who have been purchased by the Lamb (5:9; 14:3–4) with those who belong to the beast and can purchase freely in the marketplace (13:16). In the readers' social worlds, the terms "mark" (*charagma*) and "image" (*eikōn*) were used for impressions on coins, which often bore the Roman ruler's portrait, name, and titles (Plutarch, *Mor.* 211B; 984F). Using such coinage would have been one way of handling the mark of the beast (Caird; Yarbro Collins, *Crisis*, 126–27; Kraybill, *Imperial*, 138–39). A mark with the emperor's name and date could also be stamped on official bills of sale and property agreements (Deissmann, *Bible*, 240–47). The mark in Revelation's visionary world cannot be reduced to a mark on a coin or document in the readers' social worlds, but such marks were among the reminders of the pervasiveness of the imperial commercial network.

3. Worship practices. On the one hand, the mark suggests that the beast mimics Jewish devotional practice. The faithful were to honor God's name (Exod 20:7) and to keep God's commandments before their eyes and upon their hand (13:9, 16; Deut 6:8; 11:18). Many Jews bound the text of God's command onto their foreheads and hands by leather bands known as phylacteries. Readers might have seen the land beast demanding a blasphemous counteraction, requiring that the sea beast's name be placed on the forehead and hand (Charles; Boxall; Lupieri). On the other hand, identifying marks were sometimes placed on devotees of a pagan god. In the third century BCE Jews in Alexandria had to have an ivy leaf, the sign of Dionysus, branded onto their bodies. Any who refused were executed (3 Macc 3:28–29). This practice was not widespread but is analogous to the way the mark of the beast binds people to false belief (Osborne; Reddish). See also the NOTE on the seal of God in Rev 7:3.

13:17. *so that no one can buy or sell anything unless the person has the mark with the beast's name or the number of its name.* The threat of exclusion from commercial life presses people in the vision to comply with the policies of the ruling power. The author is using parody rather than simply describing a known practice. There are several proposals regarding the basis of the parody. The first is most viable:

1. Pressures within trade associations. People often formed associations of those engaged in the same trade: textile and leather workers, dyers, potters, metalsmiths, fishers and fish sellers, bankers, merchants, slave traders, etc. (Harland, *Associations*, 39–40). Such associations sometimes dedicated monuments to emperors and officials in imperial administration, and their gatherings could include prayers or other religious rites. Linking the mark of the beast to commerce may point to the way Christians experienced pressure to publicly identify with the emperor if they participated in trade organizations (Aune, Giesen; Hemer, *Letters*, 126–27; Kraybill, *Imperial*, 135–41). Such situations inform the connection between worship and commerce.

The associations were voluntary and private social organizations that did not actually govern the public market or oversee the economic affairs of their members (A. Jones, *Roman*, 43). Moreover, buying and selling was not limited to the members of these groups. For example, traveling merchants sold goods at public fairs—and no one needed to belong to a guild in order to *purchase* goods in the market (Broughton, *Asia*, 868–81). The basis for what Revelation depicts probably has more to do with the more informal pressure that people might feel among associates who publicly identified with the imperial cult. The writer then expands this pressure into the specter of public acceptance of the cult becoming a requirement for business dealings of all sorts.

2. Using coins with the emperor's picture. Imperial coins regularly displayed the image of the current emperor. For Jews opposed to Roman rule, coins bearing the emperor's portrait could be considered a violation of the divine command not to make a graven image (Exod 20:4–6). The gospels say that when Jesus responded to question about taxes, he had his questioners produce a coin, which bore the emperor's portrait. The coin showed their connection to the imperial system (Mark 12:13–17 par.). Revelation envisions the beast's mark not only on the forehead, but on the right hand, perhaps because a person would hold a coin in the hand when making a sale (Caird; Murphy; Yarbro Collins, *Crisis*, 126–27; Kraybill, *Imperial*, 138–39; Taylor, "Monetary"). Although a reference to coinage is suggestive, it cannot be taken alone. In the vision of Babylon, the writer will issue a call for readers to disengage from all commercial practices deemed incompatible with the faith (COMMENT on Rev 18:4).

3. Organized action against Christians. Some interpreters have wondered whether Christians were subjected to a boycott. Analogies come from the third century, when people were required to obtain certificates showing that they made the sacrifices required by imperial authority (Ramsay, *Letters*, 105–11; cf. Beale; Keener). Others find no evidence of such formal mechanisms when Revelation was written—and some Christians were prosperous, therefore certainly not suffering from a boycott (3:17; Caird; Osborne).

13:18. *This calls for wisdom. Let the one who understands calculate the number of the beast.* This line is parallel to the exhortation at the end of the previous section. Where the author said, "Let the one with an ear hear," he assumed that the readers indeed had ears (13:9). Here, the idea is that at least some readers have the wisdom to calculate the number of the beast. To calculate (*psēphizein*) means adding up the numerical values of the letters of the beast's name, a practice known as *gematria*. Each letter in the Greek and Hebrew alphabets had a numerical value. The first nine letters stood for the numbers one through nine ($a = 1$, $b = 2$, etc.), the next nine letters for ten through ninety, and the remaining letters for multiples of one hundred. The Greek system included archaic letters, such as the digamma, or stigma (ς), for the number six. When one adds up the values of the letters of a word, the result is its calculation, or *psēphos* (*T. Sol.* 15:11). When different letter combinations yielded the same total, it was called an *equal calculation* (*isopsēphos*; *Greek Anth.* 11.334; IGR IV 743.7–8; Artemidorus, *Onirocritica* 4.24); when someone proposed a new way of making the calculation, it was a *new calculation* (*neopsēphon*; Suetonius, *Nero* 39). The use of various forms of the verb *psēphizein* for gematria make clear that it has that sense in Rev 13:18.

for it is the number of a person. Using gematria, "the number of a person" (*arithmos anthrōpou*) would be the numerical total of the letters in that person's name. Alternatively, some sources argue that *arithmos anthrōpou* should be translated as "man's number" (NIV), so the three sixes in the number of the beast signify humanity in general, since people were created on the sixth day (Gen 1:26–31). The beast may aspire to become a divine seven, but it remains a human six (Rowland; Smalley; Barr, *Tales*, 108). The expression has also been taken as a "human number" (RSV) as opposed to a mysterious angelic number (cf. Rev 21:17). What makes these interpretations unlikely is that words for "calculate" (*psēphizein*) were used for the adding up of the numerical values of letters in words (previous NOTE).

Its number is 666. On the history of interpretation, see §25E. This particular number functions in several ways. First, it represents a specific name. Readers have already learned that the beast is a blasphemous persecutor of the faithful, a tyrant who died yet was alive again. Later, the seven heads of the beast correspond to seven hills and kings, like those of Rome, and the beast burns the great city (17:9, 16). Given these traits, many sources conclude that the beast resembles Nero, who persecuted the church; who was said to have died, though some thought he was alive and would return; and who was implicated in the fire that destroyed much of Rome (NOTE on 13:3). A link to Nero is likely since other sources also consider Nero to be a beast and the embodiment of the devil (*Sib. Or.* 3:63; 5:343; 8:157; Philostratus, *Vit. Apoll.* 4.38; *Mart. Asc. Isa.* 4:1). If the Greek name Neron Caesar is written in Hebrew letters as נרון קסר/Nrwn Qsr, it equals 666 (*N* = 50, *r* = 200, *w* = 6, *n* = 50, *Q* = 100, *s* = 60, *r* = 200). The Latin form of the name Nero lacks the final *n*, which has a value of 50. When transliterated into Hebrew as קסר נרו/Nrw Qsr, the sum is 616, which is the number that appears as an alternative to 666 in some manuscripts (see below). Therefore, Nero's name works for both forms of the text.

Identifying the 666 with Nero by using the Hebrew alphabet has many proponents (e.g., Aune; Charles; Giesen; Keener; Müller; Roloff; Bauckham, *Climax*, 387–88), but others find it unpersuasive (Beale; Mounce; Thomas; Ulland, *Vision*, 299–314). One objection is that John wrote in Greek, telling his readers that the names Abaddon and Harmagedon come from Hebrew, which would be unnecessary if they knew that language (9:11; 16:16). Yet the reverse could also be true. Some of John's intended readers may have known Hebrew, which is why he notes Hebrew words. The practice of transliterating Latin names into Hebrew letters was probably known to at least some readers. A good example is a synagogue inscription from Sardis, a city where some readers lived. The text (mid-third to fourth centuries CE) transliterates what is probably the Latin name Severus into Hebrew letters (ביר[ס]ום/Sebîrûs; Cross, "Hebrew," 3–8). John could have transliterated Nero's name into Hebrew.

Another objection is that "Caesar" could be spelled קיסר/qysr (*y. Ber.* 9 [12d]; *b. Giṭ.* 56a), which has a value of 676. Nevertheless, the shorter form קסר/qsr is well-attested and is used to give the dates in documents. Some have noted a text from Murabbaʿat, which dates from the reign of Nero Caesar (נרון קסר/Nrwn Qsr; Mur XVIII, 1; DJD 2:101; Bauckham, *Climax*, 388). Now we can turn to more recent publications of papyri from Ketef Jericho. Among the commercial documents that use the short form קסר/qsr are a first-century CE Hebrew text, perhaps from the reign of Domitian (no. 9.11; DJD 38:68); an Aramaic text from the reign of Trajan in the early second century CE (no. 13.1; DJD 38:79); and perhaps an Aramaic bill of sale from the reign of Domitian (7 recto lower 1; DJD 38.57). The short form קסר/*qsr* is also used with a third-century CE date in the Dura-Europos synagogue (I.Syr 84A, 4). Moreover, ancient writers assumed that one could adjust spellings to attain a certain total when using gematria (Artemidorus, *Onirocritica* 1.11); therefore, John might have chosen a spelling that would yield 666.

Second, gematria could invite readers to connect names and traits. For example, someone noted that in Greek the name Nero (Nerōn) had the same numerical value as the words "he killed his own mother" (*idian mētera apekteine*). The equation underscored the opinion that being a matricide defined Nero's character (Suetonius, *Nero* 39). Making connections meant that one already knew the traits of a person and used numerical equivalence to emphasize them (Artemidorus, *Onirocritica* 4.24; Lucian, *Alex.* 11; *Greek Anth.* 11.334; *y. Ber.* 5a). Some have noted that if the Greek word for beast (*thērion*) is written in Hebrew letters as תריון/*trywn*, its value is 666 ($t = 400$, $r = 200$, $y = 10$, $w = 6$, $n = 50$). Revelation explains that this number corresponds to a man's name. Since the Hebrew forms of "beast" and "Nero Caesar" both equal 666, the calculation might point to the two being the same: the beast is a Nero-like figure. The genitive form of "beast" (*thēriou*) in Hebrew letters is תריו/*tryw*, which is 616, a number that fits the shorter form of Nero's name (Bauckham, *Climax*, 389; Klauck, "Do They," 693).

Third, a number can suggest certain characteristics that can be linked through gematria. For example, the letter rho (ρ) equals one hundred, which suggests symmetry, since it is ten squared, and in some contexts the letter was auspicious since the words *ep' agatha* (to the good) also had the value of one hundred in gematria. Yet context was crucial, since one hundred was also the total value of less positive words like "pasture" (*neme*), signifying shepherds, or "fetters" (*pedai*), for criminals (Artemidorus, *Onirocritica* 3.34). Similarly, the literary context is essential for the beast's number. The followers of the beast are marked with the number 666, and the followers of the Lamb number 144,000. These numbers are juxtaposed in Rev 13:18–14:1. The number 144,000 is twelve squared times a thousand, and it depicts the vast company of the redeemed (7:4–8, cf. 7:9). By way of contrast, the beast's number is based on twelve halved, which is six, and the sixes are multiplied by ten and a hundred, not by a thousand. The impression is that being marked with the beast's 666 is a debased alternative to belonging to the Lamb's 144,000 (cf. Bauckham, *Climax*, 398–99).

Other possibilities are less likely. Some interpreters assume that the number six is inherently imperfect (Beale; Beasley-Murray; Rowland; Smalley). Others point out that Jesus' name, when written in Greek (Iēsous), has a value of 888 ($I = 10$, $ē = 8$, $s = 200$, $o = 70$, $u = 400$, $s = 200$). This number goes beyond the perfect seven at every point (*Sib. Or.* 1:324–29). The same was true of a Hebrew name for God, which had three pairs of letters each adding up to eight (*OTP* 1:227). By comparison, some argue that the number of the beast repeatedly falls short of perfection. The problem is that ancient authors did not generally regard six as an imperfect number. For example, the beast in Revelation has a perfect seven heads, whereas the creatures around God's throne have only six wings (Yarbro Collins, *Cosmology*, 118). Finally, some note that 666 is the sum of all the numbers from one to thirty-six and that thirty-six is the sum of the numbers from one to eight. The eight is deemed significant because the beast of Rev 13 is identified with the eighth king in 17:11 (Bauckham, *Climax*, 390–97; Ulland, *Vision*,

309–14). However, this merely links the beast in Rev 13 with a king in Rev 17 without revealing anything more about it (Aune).

The number 666 is attested in many manuscripts ($\mathfrak{P}^{47}$ ℵ A P 046 051); in Irenaeus (*Haer.* 5.30.1); in Latin, Coptic, and Syriac versions; and in other texts (Hippolytus, *Antichr.* 48). The alternative reading 616 appears in some extant manuscripts ($\mathfrak{P}^{115}$ C), in others known to Irenaeus (*Haer.* 5.30.1), in Latin and Armenian versions, in Tyconius, and in some later writers (CCL 107:149–51). Some interpreters argue that 616 is the harder reading and yet could be authentic, since it is the numerical value of the Greek letters for Gaius Caesar (Gaios Kaisar: $G = 3$, $a = 1$, $i = 10$, $o = 70$, $s = 200$, $K = 20$, $a = 1$, $i = 10$, $s = 200$, $a = 1$, $r = 100$; Birdsall, "Irenaeus") or "Caesar god" (Kaisar Theos: $K = 20$, $a = 1$, $i = 10$, $s = 200$, $a = 1$, $r = 100$, $Th = 9$, $e = 5$, $o = 70$, $s = 200$; Deissmann, *Light*, 278 n. 3).

Most interpreters, however, conclude that 666 is original because of the breadth of its early attestation and the fact that a symmetrical number seems warranted by the context, since 666 is the counterpart to 144,000. In manuscripts in which the number was written in alphabetical signs, the variant could have arisen accidently by a change in the middle letter from xi to iota: χξϛ for 666 versus χιϛ for 616. Others suggest that the change to 616 was deliberate so that the number corresponded to familiar forms of a name like Nero Caesar (without the final *n*, which drops the total by fifty) in Hebrew letters (נרו קסר/Nrw Qsr) or Gaius Caesar in Greek letters (Aune; Metzger, *TCGNT*², 676; Michael, "666").

COMMENT

John's characterization of evil continues with the vision of the beast from the land, which is the third member of an alliance opposed to God and his people. On one side are God, who is earth's Creator (4:11; 10:6), and the Lamb, who was slain and yet lives (5:6). On the other side are Satan the dragon, who is one of earth's destroyers (11:18; 12:7–12), and the beast from the sea, which was slain and yet lives (13:1–3). Readers have also seen that the rightful claims of God and the Lamb are attested by the community of faith, which is portrayed as a pair of prophetic witnesses (11:3–13). By way of contrast, the dragon and beast from the sea have their own company of supporters, who are now represented by the beast that rises from the earth (13:11–12).

The portrait of the beast from the earth has multiple layers, which fuse biblical images with those from the Roman Empire. A similar layering technique is used in the visions of the two witnesses (11:3–13), the woman and the dragon (11:19–12:17), the beast from the sea (12:18–13:10), and Babylon the whore (17:1–18). At one level, Revelation draws on the traditional pairing of the sea monster Leviathan with the land monster Behemoth. Where the tyrannical beast rises from the sea, the beast that assists him now rises from the land (13:1, 11). At another level, the author invokes traditions about false prophets, who lead people astray with miraculous signs and wonders (13:13–14).

On Rev 13:11–18, see Duff, *Who*, 113–25; Esch-Wermeling, "Brückenschäge"; Friesen, "Beast"; Friesen, *Imperial*, 202–4; Friesen, "Myth"; Kraybill, *Imperial*, 135–39; Krinzinger, "Spectacula"; Marucci, "Gematrie"; Michael, "666" and "For It"; Oberweis, "Bedeutung"; Price, *Rituals*, 170–206; Siew, *War*, 175–81; Taylor, "Monetary"; Tóth, *Tier*, 44–196.

At still another level, the writer brings in allusions to the cult of the Roman emperors, which was popular in Asia Minor and involved making statues of the ruler to use in worship (13:14).

In later chapters John calls this beast the false prophet (*pseudoprophētēs*, 16:13; 19:20; 20:10). Like the dragon and the sea beast, it emits unclean spirits from its mouth in order to lure the kings of earth into battle on the great day of God (16:13). When the battle occurs, the fate of the false prophet and his allies discloses the symmetry of divine justice. The false prophet builds a career by deceiving people into deifying the ruler of the empire (13:12–15), yet in the end he and those he deceives meet the one who is "true," the rightful King of kings (19:11, 16). The false prophet may slay those who refuse to worship the sea beast and compel all people to receive the beast's mark (13:15–18), but eventually those who serve the beast as the false prophet demands are slain by the sword from Christ's mouth (19:20–21). The false prophet may call down fire from heaven to give the illusion of divine authority (13:13), but his pretensions are exposed when he is subjected to the wrath of heaven and brought to a fiery end (19:20).

The beast from the land is the opposite of the two witnesses depicted earlier (Resseguie 127–28). In terms of characterization it is a false prophet, since it promotes the worship of a false god (16:13; 19:20; 20:10), whereas the witnesses are true prophets, who attest the power of the true God (11:3, 6, 10). The land beast receives its authority from the beast (*exousia*; 13:12), but the witnesses receive their authority (*exousia*) from God (11:6). The land beast does impressive signs, such as calling down fire from heaven (13:13), whereas the witnesses have power to close the heavens and testify with fire from their mouths (11:5–6). The land beast expects all who live on earth to worship the sea beast, and it slays those who refuse (13:14–15); in contrast, the witnesses challenge all who live on earth with the claims of God and are slain by the beast as a result (11:7–10). The land beast has the appearance of a lamb (13: 11), but the witnesses die like Jesus the Lamb—and like Jesus, their hope is in God's power to bring resurrection (11:11–12).

Revelation's imagery makes polemical use of parody. Three factors are needed for parody to work (*NP* 10:546): First, the writer must deal with a text or topic whose main features are known to the readers. Second, the writer must alter and exaggerate certain features of the basic pattern. The genre includes "a mixture of the serious and the fantastic, the comic and the fabulous" (G. Carey, *Elusive*, 150–51). At the same time, the basic subject must still be recognizable. Third, the effect must be comic or satirical. Parody allows something that ordinarily seems impressive to be brought down to size so that it can be perceived as unworthy of respect.

The basis for the parody in 13:11–18 is a social pattern that was common in the cities of Asia, where the main supporters of the imperial cult were from the upper stratum of society. These men and women were wealthy, they often held positions in civic administration, and many served in the priesthoods of traditional deities and the imperial cult. Yet Revelation personifies this venerable group as a beast and uses satirical exaggeration to critique each aspect of their role. Politically, those who tout the benefits of imperial rule are pictured as tools of the state, who have authority to execute those who are noncompliant (13:12, 15). Religiously, these people not only dupe the populace into creating a statue of the ruler to worship, they even make the statue talk. Animating a statue seems to build them up by suggesting that they can invoke supernatural powers to back their claims about the ruler cult. Yet the comment actually undercuts their claims, for giving breath to a statue was a form of sorcery—something no respectable person would practice (13:14–15). Economically, these people do not merely oversee the local markets, as was the case in Asia Minor, but in the vision they control access by demanding that people show support for the ruling power by receiving the mark of the beast (13:16–18).

Parody is effective when, through the alterations and exaggerations, readers can see validity in the way it characterizes the basic subject. The writer describes a lamblike beast with a dragon's voice that slays those who resist the ruler cult, and yet readers know that they are not to look for a beast with that physical description. Rather, the parody discloses the destructive *character* of the forces at work in their world in a way that allows them to see analogies between the religious, social, and economic pressures portrayed in the vision and those in their own contexts.

The Beast from the Land and Idolatry (13:11–15)

John has seen one beast rise from the sea (13:1) and now tells of another coming up from the land (13:11). Basic to Revelation's worldview is that land and sea belong to the God who created them (4:11). In a rightly ordered universe, all creatures on earth and in the sea praise their Maker in concert with those around God's heavenly throne (4:6; 5:13). But the world is also the scene of conflict, for the destroyers of the earth (11:18) challenge the Creator (14:7). The principal destroyer is Satan, who was banished from heaven after the Messiah's exaltation. Wounded and angry, the devil comes to bring woe to earth and sea in the time that remains before his final demise (12:12).

Revelation assumes that the conflict between God and evil takes tangible political, religious, and economic forms. The empire claimed dominion over the world because Augustus and his successors brought peace and prosperity to sea and land (Horace, *Odes* 4.15; Plutarch, *Mor.* 824C; COMMENT on Rev 10:5–6). But in John's narrative, as Steven Friesen puts it, "the sea and land become sources of danger and oppression, not peace and plenty" ("Myth," 309). In the beast from the sea, evil is at work in an empire that dominates the world's peoples, deifies its own rulers, and persecutes the followers of Jesus (13:1–10). In the beast from the land, evil operates through those who promote the deification of the leaders of the state and who back these religious claims with their own political and economic influence (13:11–18).

The parody of the cult's supporters begins as John portrays them collectively as a figure like Behemoth, the beast from the land that was the counterpart to Leviathan, the monster in the sea. Behemoth was known for strength and power, its bones like bronze and limbs like iron; God alone could contend with it (Job 40:16, 18, 19). In the book of Job, Behemoth seems to lurk on land and in watery areas, but according to later tradition the monster lived on land (*1 En.* 60:7–8). Although God created both Behemoth and Leviathan, they personified chaotic forces, and God would destroy them at the end of the age, when they would become food for the righteous (*1 En.* 60:24; *4 Ezra* 6:49–52; *2 Bar.* 29:4). In Revelation's visionary world, the promoters of the ruler cult have power to execute the noncompliant, but by casting them in the role of Behemoth, the writer portends their own coming demise (19:20; Prigent; Roloff; Friesen, "Myth," 304–7).

John's Behemoth has two horns, "like a lamb" (Rev 13:11), making it seem remarkably unthreatening when compared with the ten-horned, seven-headed monster (13:2). What makes the beast from the land so dangerous, initially, is that it does not seem to pose a threat. It does not seem to be significantly different from Jesus the Lamb. The passage is provocative, pressing readers to ask whether they have too readily blurred the lines between the claims of the Lamb and those of the seemingly benign group that promotes the ruler cult. Recognizing that some readers find the situation to be ambiguous, John directs attention to what the beast says. Its speech is like that of a dragon, which shows that it is connected to Satan the dragon, and in verses to come the beast tells people to make an idol of the ruler (13:14). From John's perspective, that is demonic, not benign.

The land beast exercises all the authority of the first beast (13:12). Revelation portrays a chain of authority in which Satan the dragon gives authority (*exousia*) to the first beast (13:2, 4), and then that beast gives authority to its lamblike associate, which operates under the first beast's auspices, or "in its presence" (13:12). The leading figures in Asia Minor worked under imperial authority. Inscriptions show that many of the strongest supporters of imperial cults held important civic offices such as head of the council, financial officer of the council, secretary of the citizenry, city treasurer, and superintendent of public works (Friesen, "Beast," 55–57). By personifying the agents of the ruling power in lamblike guise, John agrees that they appear to be nonthreatening, but he will challenge this perception by disclosing how this agent of the beast *uses* its authority.

Whereas the beast from the sea exhibited blasphemous arrogance and dominated people of every tribe and nation (13:7), the beast from the land makes the earth worship the ruling power (13:12). It was characteristic of those who had local authority to call for displays of divine honor to be publicly given of the emperor (*Rom. Civ.* 2:521). The temples, festivals, and social networks that leading citizens created helped to generate popular support for the imperial cult (Note on 13:12).

Revelation's parody of the ruler cult intensifies as the land beast promotes the veneration of the beast "whose mortal wound was healed" (13:12), the monster who was "wounded by the sword and yet came to life again" (13:14). These traits identify the ruler cult with traditions about Nero, who had supposedly killed himself and yet was rumored to be alive (Note on 13:3). In the readers' social worlds, support for the imperial cult was widespread, but Nero had at most a minor role (Note on 13:12). The most prominent cult was that of Augustus, who was honored with the provincial temple at Pergamum, which was served by priests from various places, including Smyrna (I.Sard 8.90) and Thyatira (I.Thyat 1098; I.Sard 8.99). There was a local cult of Augustus in the administrative center at Ephesus and municipal cults in Thyatira, Sardis, Philadelphia, and many other cities (Notes on Rev 2:1, 18; 3:1, 7). Temples and divine honors were publicly given to Tiberius, Domitian, and the other Flavian emperors (Notes on 2:1, 8; 3:1, 14). Nero was not the focus of the imperial cult.

Making a Nero-like monster the center of the cult emphasizes that the practice of deifying leaders is not benign. The previous vision showed that in the legacy of Nero, the persecutor of the church, the empire shows its true face (Note on 13:3). For the writer of Revelation the heart of the cult cannot be construed as popular gratitude for imperial benefits; it is the deification of tyranny.

The beast from the land performs miraculous signs, creating the illusion that the worship it promotes is legitimate (13:13). Earlier, God's two witnesses had power to close up the heavens and to breathe fire as they prophesied (11:5). But the beast from the land calls down fire from heaven to show that it too is an agent of God. The scene is to some extent a parody of the story in which Elijah challenges the prophets of Baal to call down fire from heaven. Elijah said he would do the same and that the god who answered by fire was the true God (1 Kgs 18:20–40). In that story the false prophets failed to bring fire from heaven, but in Revelation the false prophet succeeds, giving the impression that the deified ruler he serves is truly divine. The action also fits Greco-Roman traditions. For example, it was said that as the future emperor Tiberius gained popular support for his leadership, a fire suddenly leapt up from an altar, purportedly showing divine approval for his aspirations to power (Dio Cassius, *Rom. Hist.* 54.9.6). Imperial ideology often made Zeus—the god of the lightning bolt—the source of imperial authority (NOTE on Rev 13:2). Imperial coins pictured Zeus holding a lightning bolt and scepter. To celebrate one of Domitian's military victories, coins were minted showing the emperor holding a lightning bolt (Fears, "Cult," 71, 79).

Yet signs can be performed by false prophets as well as by true ones (NOTE on Rev 13:14; cf. 16:13; 19:20; 20:10). The question is whether the miracle-worker turns people to God or leads them away from God—and the difference was not always clear. Readers at Ephesus tested those who claimed to be apostles and were not (2:2), but those at Pergamum and Thyatira seemed willing to accommodate practices associated with idolatry (2:14, 20). The messages to the churches explicitly warned against accommodating Greco-Roman religious practices, and later John denounced idolatry by linking it to demons, murder, sorcery, immorality, and theft (9:20–21). But in this vision he takes another approach, by portraying idolatry in a manner that presses readers to *see* its demonic character.

John has disparaged idols as lifeless objects that do not see or hear or walk (9:20). So it is initially surprising that the beast from the land defies John's critique by giving the statue breath (*pneuma*) and the ability to speak (13:15a). Since God gave breath (*pneuma*, 11:11) to the two witnesses who had been slain and gave mortals the power of speech (Exod 4:11), animating the statue might seem to display the height of divine power. The parody works by progressively elevating the beast through showing its impressive abilities and then toppling the beast from its lofty status by showing that these same abilities discredit it. Giving breath and speech to a statue was an act of sorcery. Ironically, the abilities that purport to demonstrate that this beast is an agent of the gods actually portray it as a sorcerer in the service of the devil.

Tales were told of magicians who could give breath to inanimate objects and make clay figurines and wooden objects move about like living beings (Ps.-Clement, *Recognitions* 3.47.2; Lucian, *Philops.* 14; 35; Apuleius, *Metam.* 2.1). Attempts to animate statues had a long tradition in Egypt. Practitioners used incantations and potions to infuse breath into the figurines, often in the hope of obtaining oracles from them, and this became popular in the Roman Empire during the first and second centuries CE. (PGM XII.30–34; Dodds, *Greeks*, 291–95). Readers would have understood that the beast does not work wonders by divine power but through the demonic power of magic (Bovon, "Possession," 138; Duff, *Who*, 116; Rodney L. Thomas, *Magical*, 68–81).

The beast that animates the statue can have those who refuse to worship it put to death, which inverts ordinary practice (Rev 13:15b). Actions identified with sorcery were considered to be socially deviant and dangerous, and laws were enacted against such practices. If found guilty, sorcerers could be put to death (Apuleius, *Metam.* 3.16; Apuleius, *Apol.* 47; *Rom. Civ.* 2:511, 536; MacMullen, *Enemies*, 121–27; Aune, *Apocalypticism*, 368–84). No legitimate sovereign would gain power by sorcery (Philostratus,

Vit. Apoll. 8.7.8). Yet in John's vision, the rules are turned upside down, for the demonic is now normative, not deviant. The sorcerer dominates society rather than lurking on its margins, and those who resist him are punished, not honored.

John's parody of support for the ruler cult goes beyond the conventional practices of his day. Sometimes, a person who was denounced to the authorities could be forced to make an offering before the statues of the emperors and traditional gods (NOTE on Rev 13:15), but this was not part of a systematic empirewide campaign to enforce imperial worship (Lampe and Luz, "Nachpaulinisches," 196–200; Hardy, *Christianity*, 166–67; S. Potter, *ABD* 5:231–35; P. Achtemeier, *1 Peter*, 34–36). Through his parody, John magnifies the instances when Jesus' followers faced death threats for refusing to venerate the gods of the empire. By magnifying the threat, he wants readers to see that this danger is not an aberration but an essential characteristic of a system in which imperial authority is made absolute (Harland, *Associations*, 256–59).

The Mark of the Beast and Commercial Pressure (13:16–18)

Revelation next says that the beast from the land puts a mark on people's foreheads or right hands (13:16). Such a mark places the recipients in the company of the sea beast, which has blasphemous names on its seven heads (13:1), and Babylon the whore, who displays her own name on her forehead (17:5). It also distinguishes them from the servants of God, who bear a seal on their foreheads (7:2–4). The mark contains the name, or number, of the satanic beast that was slain, just as the seal inscribes the faithful with the name of God and the Lamb who was slain (13:17; 14:1). Previous visions distinguished those who had the seal of God from those who lacked it (9:4), but now all people bear either the seal or the mark.

In the visionary world everyone belongs to God or God's adversary. The contrast was presumably not as clear in the readers' world, which is why the author presses the distinction as part of his call for perseverance and faithfulness to God, the Lamb, and the Christian community (13:10). Using the imagery of the mark and seal also blends elements from the commercial and religious spheres (NOTE on 13:16). The writer assumes that pressures from the marketplace will affect people's religious loyalties.

John pictures a situation in which those who receive the mark can buy and sell, while those who refuse it are excluded from the marketplace (13:17). The theme of commerce will be developed in the vision of Babylon, the city with traits of imperial Rome. John portrays the city as a whore with an insatiable desire for goods. Although the woman is repulsive, people are lured by her promises of wealth. They turn a blind eye to brutality and bloodshed in order to turn hefty profits (17:6; 18:3, 24). Babylon reduces everything to a commodity, with money to be made in gold, silver, ivory, grain, wine, and horses. Traders market slaves—literally "bodies"—and "the souls of human beings" (18:11–13). This city rides the beast that personifies imperial power. Yet Revelation warns that the destructive tendencies of the beast will be the undoing of its own empire. Those who use violence against the innocent become the victims of violence, and the whore with an insatiable appetite for material goods is consumed by her one-time allies (17:1–6, 16).

In the short term, receiving the mark seems to bring advantages. Those who publicly identify with the deified ruler escape the judgment of the ruling power and can take advantage of the commercial opportunities that the empire provides. But Revelation warns readers not to be fooled. Those who are marked as supporters of an oppressive regime do not escape judgment. Rather, they make themselves subject to God's judgment, which will bring loss rather than gain (14:9, 11; 16:2; 19:20; 20:4). This vision is paired with the one that follows, contrasting those who receive the beast's mark in order to buy (*agorazein*) and sell in the market with those who bear the seal of God because they have been bought (*agorazein*) by the Lamb's self-sacrifice (13:17; 14:3–4). The mark may give people a place in the economy of Babylon, but the seal provides access to New Jerusalem (14:1; 22:4).

John's visions do not offer a simple series of steps that readers can take in order to avoid entanglement in the beast's economy (Harland, *Associations*, 262). It is clear that the proper response to the vision is to resist receiving the beast's mark, but John does not spell out how that is to be done. The imagery has to do with resisting pressures to identify publicly with Roman authority in the realm of commerce, but the vision is evocative and cannot be reduced to a single practice, such as avoiding the use of imperial coinage (NOTES on 13:16–17). The vision presses for clarity about the readers' commitments, asking whether their identities are determined by the power to purchase goods in the market or by the power of the Lamb, whose blood has purchased them for God's kingdom (5:9). John observes that richness of faith can exist despite economic poverty (2:9) and that material prosperity can impoverish faith and community (3:17–18). Revelation expects that readers will have to work out the implications in the contexts in which they live.

John continues to challenge his readers by means of a riddle, inviting those who have a mind to calculate the number of the beast, which is 666 (13:18b). A riddle challenges people to see something the way the author sees it. The person who poses the riddle is initially in the position of having superior knowledge. Those who take up the challenge seek to demonstrate that they are equally knowledgeable by solving the riddle (*NP* 12:587). The subject matter needs to be familiar enough for the hearer or reader to have a chance of working out the solution, but the riddle maker poses the question in a manner that requires people to see the familiar in an unexpected way (Athenaeus, *Deipnosophistae* 10.448b–459b; *Greek Anth.* 14.1–64, 101–11). Riddles were used in Scripture (Judg 14:14), in Greek drama, and as games at Greek and Roman social gatherings (*NP* 12:590).

Implicit in every riddle is the query, "Do you see what I see?" As a means of persuasion, a riddle differs from a pronouncement that readers must either accept or dispute. Riddles pique curiosity, making readers want to know what the author sees. John says that those who have a mind (*nous*), or understanding, should be able to solve the riddle (Rev 13:18). On the one hand, he lays down a challenge that readers will want to accept, since they will want to show that they have understanding. On the other hand, John assumes that at least some of the readers will be able to guess the solution, just as they have the mind (*nous*) needed to connect the beast's seven heads with the hills and kings of Rome if given enough information (17:9).

The riddle uses gematria, the practice of adding up the numerical values of the letters in a word or name (*Greek Anth.* 14.20, 105). Gematria does not reveal new information but enables readers to make connections between things they already know. There are three steps in the process. First, readers must discern the traits of a person from the context. Second, they must think of a name of a person who might fit the traits. Third, they must see whether the name fits the number. Although some interpreters assume that

John used a numerical code to conceal his meaning from outsiders (Ford; Mounce), this is not the case. Revelation follows the practice of other ancient writers who provided enough information to help readers make the connections suggested by the gematria.

One example is found in an apocalyptic text that lists Roman rulers by noting well-known aspects of their reigns and the numerical values of their first initials. One has a first initial equivalent to the number ten (Greek *a*, for Augustus), and he hands power to another with an initial equivalent to three hundred (Greek *t*, for Tiberius), etc. (*Sib. Or.* 5:1–51). The satirist Lucian creates a parody of an oracle about a false prophet by giving numerical values of letters as clues to the false prophet's name (Lucian, *Alex.* 11). Another text says, "the son of the great God will come, incarnate, likened to mortal men on earth," with a name equaling 888. The author assumes that the clues will enable readers to recognize that the Greek letters in the name Jesus (*Iēsous*) add up to 888 (*Sib. Or.* 1:324–29). Another text tells of the "the one who is," a being with the earth under his feet and the stars around him, whose name equals 353. Even though the specific name is unclear, the context makes evident that it refers to God (*Sib. Or.* 1:137–46). By way of contrast, an inscription from Pompeii reads, "I love her whose number is 545" (Deissmann, *Light*, 277). Without knowing more of the context, readers will find it impossible to determine the woman's name. In Revelation, however, the context provides help.

Readers using gematria to solve John's riddle must first look at the portrait of the beast. They are to think of a beast that wears diadems and wields authority over the world, that speaks blasphemy and persecutes the faithful, that is said to have died and returned to life. In Rev 17:9–16 the beast is identified with seven hills and kings, and it burns the harlot city with fire. These literary cues prompt readers to think of Nero, who ruled the world from Rome, the city on seven hills. He persecuted the church, was implicated in a fire that destroyed much of the city, and was said to have died and yet to be alive (NOTE on 13:3). Readers must then look for a name whose letters add up to the correct total, and the name Nero Caesar does add up to 666 when written in Hebrew letters (NOTE on 13:18).

Those who succeed in doing the calculation join the community of those who have wisdom (13:18), which in this context means discerning the Nero-like qualities of the ruling power. By way of contrast, those who are unable to discover the solution fall into the category of those who lack wisdom—an unenviable position. The implication is that they must recognize that the writer knows more than they do, which adds rhetorical weight to the case he is building. From a literary perspective, the name and number inscribed on the beast's followers prepare for the contrast in the next verse, in which the followers of Jesus bear the name of the Lamb and his Father on their foreheads and their number is 144,000 (14:1).

29. Followers of the Lamb and the Beast (14:1–13)

14 [1]Then I looked, and there was the Lamb, standing on Mount Zion. With him were 144,000 who had his name and his Father's name written on their foreheads. [2]And I heard a sound from heaven that was like the sound of rushing water and like the sound of loud thunder. The sound I heard was like that of harpists playing their harps. ³They sang what seemed to be a new song in front of the throne and the four living creatures and the elders. And no one could understand the song except the 144,000, who had been purchased from the earth. ⁴They were not defiled with women. Now these who follow the Lamb wherever he goes are maidens. They were purchased from humankind as first fruit for God and the Lamb. ⁵In their mouth no lie was found; they are blameless.

⁶Then I saw another angel flying high overhead with eternal good news to proclaim to those who live on earth, and to every nation and tribe and language and people. ⁷He said in a loud voice, "Fear God and give him glory, for the hour of his judgment has come. Worship the one who made heaven and earth and the sea and springs of water." ⁸Another angel, a second one, followed and said, "Fallen, fallen is Babylon the great. She made all the nations drink the wine of her passionate immorality." ⁹Then another angel, a third one, followed them and said in a loud voice, "If any worship the beast and its image and receive a mark on their forehead or their hand, ¹⁰they will also drink of the wine of God's passionate anger, poured full strength into the cup of his wrath. They will suffer the pain of fire and sulfur before the holy angels and the Lamb. ¹¹The smoke of their painful suffering goes up forever and ever. There is no rest day or night for those who worship the beast and its image, or for the one who receives the mark with its name." ¹²This calls for the endurance of the saints, who keep the commandments of God and the faith of Jesus. ¹³And I heard a voice from heaven say, "Write: Blessed are the dead who die in the Lord from now on." "Yes," says the Spirit, "so they can rest from their labors, for their works follow them."

NOTES

14:1. *Then I looked, and there was the Lamb, standing on Mount Zion.* The fact that the Lamb is standing recalls that he was slain but has been restored to life (5:5–6). It is a militant posture: The dragon may stand on the seashore (12:18), but the Lamb stands on Zion.

With him were 144,000. The group can best be understood as the whole Christian community. Earlier, the 144,000 were said to come from the twelve tribes of Israel, yet they proved to be a countless multitude cleansed by the Lamb. The number indicates completeness (7:4, 9). Like all the redeemed, they have been purchased by Christ and bear God's name on their foreheads (5:9; 14:3–4; 22:4; Beale; Giesen; Prigent; Smalley). Alternatively, some interpreters limit the 144,000 to martyrs, arguing that following the Lamb implies violent death and that calling them "first fruit" (14:4) means they are only a part of the whole (Murphy; Yarbro Collins, *Crisis*, 127–28). This proposal is unlikely because following the Lamb means discipleship, and as first fruit they are distinguished from the rest of humankind, not from the rest of the church. Another proposal is that the 144,000 are those who survive until the end of the age since they bear the protective seal of God (Rev 7:3; Aune). This approach is unlikely, however, because the seal protects a person from divine wrath, not physical death.

who had his name and his Father's name written on their foreheads. The names show that the redeemed belong to God and the Lamb. The opposite is receiving the name of the beast, the agent of Satan (13:16–18). To be inscribed with the names of the Lamb and his Father is a sign of identity equivalent to the seal that was placed on the foreheads of the redeemed as a sign of protection and belonging (NOTE on 7:3).

In Revelation, John rarely refers to God as "Father," though other Christians did so. Here, God is the Father of Jesus (1:6; 3:5; 3:21; cf. Matt 11:27; Luke 2:26; John 5:17; 6:40). Revelation does not call God the Father of believers (Rom 1:7; 8:15; 1 Pet 1:17), although the idea is implied in calling the faithful God's children (Rev 21:7). The term "father" indicated respect. In Greco-Roman tradition, Zeus was regarded as the father of gods and humankind (Diodorus Siculus, *Libr.* 5.72.2; Dio Chrysostom, *Disc.* 53.12). Calling the emperors father (*patēr*) "gives them a certain authority over all" (Dio Cassius, *Rom. Hist.* 57.17.11; cf. Augustus, *Res* 35; Suetonius, *Aug.* 58.2). Emperors were "father of the country" (I.Eph 3801 II.8; I.Smyr 591.6; 731.3; 826.13; I.Thyat 1098.10). A contrast with imperial practice may be suggested by the way the redeemed bear the names of the Lamb and his Father on their foreheads (Rev 14:1), while others have the mark of the beast, which is the mark of the ruler, who in the Roman world was called father (13:16–18). For the author of Revelation, the legitimate authority and honor associated with the term "father" belongs to God, the Father of the Lamb.

14:2. *And I heard a sound from heaven that was like the sound of rushing water and like the sound of loud thunder.* Similar sounds introduced the opening vision of the exalted Jesus (1:15; cf. Ezek 1:24; 43:2), and thunder accompanied visions of God's throne and actions (Rev 4:5; 6:1; 8:5; 11:19). Here, as in 19:6, the imagery describes a multitude giving praise to God.

The sound I heard was like that of harpists playing their harps. The Greek harp, or kithara, had two vertical arms that were connected by a horizontal bar across the top and attached to a sound box at the bottom (Figures 22 and 23). It usually had seven strings, although some had as few as six or as many as nine or ten (Ps 33:2; *T. Job* 14:1; Plutarch, *Mor.* 238C; Pliny the Elder, *Nat.* 7.204). All the strings were the same length, but tuning pegs allowed musicians to adjust the tension of each string, varying the pitch. Musicians would cradle the kithara in their left arm and strum with their right hand, using a pick. Selected strings could be muted with the fingers of the left hand so only the desired notes would sound when strumming.

Singing to the accompaniment of a kithara was common, and the music could be either sad or joyful (Plutarch, *Mor.* 712F, 713D). In Revelation the mood is festive (cf. 1QHᵃ XIX, 22–23; 4Q511 10 8). The instrument was used for entertainment at banquets and contests (Philo, *Legat.* 12; I.Smyr 659.3, 24; Dio Chrysostom, *Disc.* 33.40). The Greeks and Romans used the kithara to accompany songs honoring their gods and heroes (Dio Chrysostom, *Disc.*, 2.28; Quintilian, *Inst.* 1.10.10; Lucian, *Salt.* 16). Kitharas also provided music in the Jerusalem temple (2 Chr 9:11; Ps 43:4), accompanying songs of praise and thanksgiving (Pss 92:3; 108:2; 147:7) and festive "new songs" (next NOTE).

By way of contrast, kitharas and other instruments were probably not used in first-century synagogues or Christian assemblies. Writers referred to the kithara as an illustration of articulate or inarticulate speech (1 Cor 14:7) or of harmony in the church (Ign. *Eph.* 4:1; Ign. *Phld.* 1:2), and later some explicitly said that Christians did not use instruments because of their connection to bawdy social life (Clement of Alexandria, *Paed.* 2.4.41; McKinnon, "Exclusion"; McKinnon, *Music*, 3–4, 32–35, 43). Revelation, however, transforms an image that had a place in the temple and in Greco-Roman practice into one that celebrates the work of God and the Lamb (Rev 5:8–9; 15:2–4).

14:3. *They sang what seemed to be a new song in front of the throne and the four living creatures and the elders.* The singers are probably the angels who accompanied the creatures and elders in 5:11–12 (Giesen) and not the 144,000 (Mounce; Pattemore, *People*, 184). New songs could praise God for his saving deeds and were often accompanied by stringed instruments (Pss 33:3; 40:3; 98:1, 5; 144:9; 149:1–3). The best manuscripts (A C) say that John heard "what seemed to be" (*hōs*) a new song, perhaps because the song is not exactly new; it was sung in Rev 5:9–10. On the elders and living creatures, see the NOTES on 4:4, 6.

And no one could understand the song except the 144,000, who had been purchased from the earth. The idea that only the redeemed could understand the song creates a suggestive contrast between the followers of the Lamb and the adherents of other traditions. The worshipers of Dionysus, Isis, and other deities had mysteries that were accessible only to initiates, who usually went through purification rites. They might say to outsiders, "I would tell you, if I were allowed to do so; you would learn about it, if you were allowed to do so" (Apuleius, *Metam.* 11.23.6; Klauck, *Religious*, 136–37). The imperial cult in Asia had its own mysteries, in which hymn singers played an important role (Friesen, *Imperial*, 113–16). In Revelation, those who are redeemed by the Lamb have the requisite purity and are privy to the meaning of the heavenly song (Brent, *Imperial*, 199).

Some translations take the Greek *mathein* to mean that no one was able to "learn" the song except the 144,000 (e.g., ESV, NET, NIV, NRSV). But the issue is not learning the words, but learning what the song means—that is, understanding it (cf. Matt 9:13). The new song speaks of being purchased by the Lamb, which the redeemed understand because they have received the benefits of Christ's death (NOTE on 5:9). To say they are purchased from (*apo*) the earth and humankind distinguishes those who believe from those who do not (14:3–4; cf. 5:9).

14:4. *They were not defiled with women.* Defilement (*molynein*) can occur through contact with something unclean or through sinful actions such as immorality, adultery, theft, idolatry, and murder (Isa 59:3; 65:4; cf. Rev 3:4). Defilement makes a person unfit to enter a holy place or the company of holy people. Nothing unclean is brought into New Jerusalem (21:27). Revelation does not assume that women are inherently unclean, since images of a woman giving birth and a woman at her wedding banquet are used in positive ways for the people of God, and New Jerusalem is pictured as a bride (Rev 12:1–6; 19:7; 21:2, 9–10). Rather, Revelation uses marital imagery in a positive way and links defilement to behaviors that violate the marriage relationship (cf. *Ep. Arist.* 152; *3 Bar.* 8:5). On one level the writer lists impurity along with sexual immorality (Rev 21:8, 27; 22:15). On another level he transfers connotations from illicit sexual relations to unfaithfulness toward God when using adultery, immorality, and prostitution metaphorically, as is the case with defilement here (2:14, 20–22; 17:4; 18:3; cf. Jer 3:1–10; Ezek 23:1–21; Hos 1–2).

Some interpreters assume that Rev 14:4 depicts those who have not defiled themselves with women as male virgins, since the term *parthenos*, or maiden, appears in the next line. With that assumption, there are several approaches to interpreting the imagery. First, some discern a military aspect in the image, since soldiers on duty were to abstain from sexual relations (Deut 23:9–10; 1 Sam 21:5). From this perspective the 144,000 are like troops in a holy war, and counting 12,000 from each of the twelve tribes is like taking a census of warriors (Rev 7:4–8; Num 1:2–3). The group gathers at Mount Zion, where Israel's king is to defeat his foes (Ps 2:6–9). There could also be a sacral dimension, since the redeemed are a priestly community, and defilement would prevent them from carrying out their priestly duties (Rev 5:10). Such purity was expected in the Dead Sea community, which saw itself as a priestly fellowship anticipating eschatological battle (1QM VII, 3–6; Bauckham, *Climax*, 230–32). Although this approach is suggestive, it should not be pressed, since military and priestly imagery is at best implicit in Rev 14:1–5, and purity regulations applied more broadly (Lev 15:18).

A second approach is that the 144,000 are contrasted with the angelic Watchers, who in primeval times defiled themselves with women and fell under divine judgment (Gen 6:2; *1 En.* 15:2–7; Olson, "Those"). But nothing in the context suggests that the faithful are being contrasted with heavenly beings. The threat of defilement from women comes most directly from the woman Jezebel and the "woman" Babylon, whose practices are compared to immorality and adultery (Rev 2:20–23; 17:1–6).

A third approach, which draws on gender and postcolonial studies, proposes that the imagery counters imperial ideals of masculinity. Depicting the faithful as those who have not defiled themselves with women is considered misogynistic, yet identifying them as virgins gives the males a feminine quality, since virginity was regularly ascribed to women, not men. The dominant Roman discourse emphasized that "real" men married, fathered children, and were the heads of their households; they were sexually dominant. Although Revelation is seen as androcentric, picturing Jesus' followers as male virgins fits the book's anti-imperialism by challenging models of masculinity associated with the empire (L. Huber, "Sexually"; Stenström, "Is Salvation"; Stenström, "Masculine"). A question affecting this approach is whether 14:4 concerns male virginity (next NOTE).

Now these who follow the Lamb wherever he goes are maidens. We begin a new sentence here since the verse repeats the word "these" (*houtoi*) three times, using three different images for the redeemed. The writer uses masculine imagery (14:4a), feminine imagery (14:4b), and harvest imagery (14:4c). Feminine imagery begins with the term *parthenoi*, which refers to maidens, or young women of marriageable age, commonly with the sense of physical virginity (Gen 24:16; Exod 22:16; *NewDocs* 4:224–25). The imagery anticipates the way the faithful will be depicted as the pure bride of the Lamb (Rev 19:7; 21:9). Although interpreters often assume that *parthenos* refers to male virgins, this is unlikely. The term is used for a male virgin in *Jos. As.* 4:7 and 8:1, but such usage is almost unprecedented. Even in the second century CE it was not clear that *parthenia* (virginity) could describe males; such usage became common only later (Achilles Tatius, *Leuc. Clit.* 5.20.5; BDAG 777 §b), which makes it unlikely here.

Confusion arises because many sources break Rev 14:4b in half. They take the first part, "for *parthenoi* are [they]," as an explanation of the previous comment about the redeemed not defiling themselves with women and assume that *parthenoi* must mean male virgins. The break leaves the rest of the sentence without a finite verb, requiring a paraphrase: "these [are] the ones who follow" (NAB) or "these follow" (NRSV). Grammatically, however, the words in 14:4b form a complete sentence: "these who follow" (*hoi akolouthountes*) is the subject, "are" (*eisin*) is the verb, and "maidens" (*parthenoi*) is the predicate. The initial *gar* (now) introduces the new feminine image in 14:4b and relates it to the theme of purity without suggesting that *parthenoi* (maidens) explains the masculine imagery that precedes it. This use of *gar* is common (BDAG 189 §2; cf. Rev 9:19; 16:14; 19:10; 21:25).

Maidens, or virgins, is a collective image for Zion and Israel, as well as for Christians who are pure in their devotion to Christ, just as young women are to be singularly committed to their betrothed (2 Kgs 19:21; Lam 2:13; Amos 5:2; 2 Cor 11:2). Since virginity was expected of young women approaching marriage, Revelation uses it as a metaphor for Christians who refrain from idolatry and other unfaithful practices, for they are well-suited to be the bride of the Lamb (Deut 22:13–21; Sir 7:24; Rev 19:7–8). Some interpreters think that John commends virginity as an ascetic ideal showing total commitment, since at least some in the Dead Sea community and the early church practiced celibacy (Matt 19:12; 1 Cor 7:8, 38; cf. Cyprian, FC 36:34–35; Methodius, ACW 27:47–48; Fulgentius, FC 95:316–17; Müller; Roloff; Yarbro Collins, *Crisis*, 129–31; *TLNT* 3:52). Most, however, take virginity as a metaphor for fidelity to God and Christ, since John uses antithetical terms such as immorality, adultery, and prostitution as metaphors for religious unfaithfulness (Caesarius, PL 35.2437).

Following the Lamb indicates discipleship, as in the gospels: "I will follow you wherever you go" (Matt 8:19 par.). The gospels sometimes link following to carrying the cross and the prospect of death (Matt 10:38 par.; Mark 8:34 par.; John 12:25–26; 1 Pet 2:21). Many interpreters think that in Revelation it points to martyrdom as true discipleship (Aune), though limiting the expression to martyrdom is not warranted.

They were purchased from humankind. The word "purchase" could connote redemption from bondage (NOTE on 5:9). Young women could be purchased out of slavery for marriage, and Jewish marriage contracts included assurances that the husband would redeem the woman if she was taken captive (Mur XX, 6; *m. Ket.* 4:8; Zimmermann, "Nuptial"). In Revelation, Jesus the Lamb plays the part of the faithful husband, who redeems the people who constitute his bride (Rev 5:9; 14:3–4).

as first fruit for God and the Lamb. In Jewish tradition the first fruits included grain, grapes, and other crops (Exod 34:22; Num 13:20), which were to be brought to the temple before the rest of the harvest took place (Lev 23:10–14; Deut 26:1–11). Cities in Asia and other places also offered first fruits to deities (I.Laod 4a.6; Pliny the Elder, *Nat.* 18.2.8) and occasionally used the term "first fruit" for people dedicated to the service of a god (Plutarch, *Mor.* 298F; 402A; Aune). Instead of *aparchē* (first fruit), a few manuscripts say that the redeemed are *ap' archēs* (from the beginning; 𝔓⁴⁷ ℵ), perhaps recalling that the redeemed are in the scroll of life from the foundation of the world (Rev 13:8).

14:5. *In their mouth no lie was found; they are blameless.* Lying is associated with uncleanness, immorality, false claims, and false prophecy (2:2; 3:9; 16:13; 21:8, 27; 22:15; Rom 1:25). Blasphemies come from the mouth of the beast (Rev 13:5), but there is no deception from the mouth of the redeemed (14:5; cf. Zeph 3:13). The word *amōmos* can mean being unblemished in a physical sense and blameless in a moral sense. Both aspects are at play here. The redeemed are without blame before God. Yet they are also called first fruit, and only first fruits without blemish were to be brought to the sanctuary (Lev 21:16–24; 22:21). Similarly, a bride was to be unblemished as she entered into marriage, which is fitting for those who are the bride of the Lamb (*m. Ket.* 7:7–8; Zimmermann, "Virginitäts-metapher," 50).

14:6. *Then I saw another angel flying high overhead with eternal good news to proclaim.* The angel is in mid-heaven, at the point where the sun is directly overhead (NOTE on Rev 8:13). Good news (*euangelizein/euangelion*) often meant that rebel forces or oppressive powers had been defeated in battle and that God and the rightful king prevailed (2 Sam 18:19, 31; Ps 68:11; Isa 40:9–10; 52:7; Nah 1:15). The good news of God's salvation was to be proclaimed from day to day, calling all nations to true worship (Ps 96:2; Bauckham, *Climax*, 286–89).

Good news was sometimes linked to imperial rule. Asia called the birth of the god Augustus good news because he brought peace to the world (*Rom. Civ.* 1:624). People at Sardis wore wreaths and made sacrifices at the good news that the emperor's son Gaius had come of age, and a benefactor at Laodicea provided feasts to celebrate such good news (I.Sard 8.14; I.Laod 82.12). Conversely, when imperial power became oppressive, the emperor's death or downfall was good news because it brought hope for liberation (Josephus, *Ant.* 18.228–29; Josephus, *J.W.* 4.656; Lucian, *Tyr.* 9). Similar dynamics appear in Christian passages that announce the good news of the coming of God's kingdom and his defeat of the powers of evil (Mark 1:14–15, 23–27). In Revelation the good news focuses on the establishment of God's reign and liberation from other powers that dominate the earth (Rev 11:15–18). The angel's good news is eternal because God's dominion is eternal, something that cannot be said of any earthly power, including Babylon or Rome, which was called the eternal city (Ovid, *Fast.* 3.72; *Sib. Or.* 3:46–56).

to those who live on earth, and to every nation and tribe and language and people. The Greek *epi* could mean that the angel proclaims a message "concerning" the judgment that will fall on the nations (Giesen), but it more probably is proclaimed "to" all people (cf. *epi* + accusative in Ezek 37:9 LXX; BDAG 402 §1). On nations, tribes, languages, and peoples, see the NOTE on Rev 5:9.

14:7. *He said in a loud voice, "Fear God and give him glory, for the hour of his judgment has come.* To fear God is to fear his judgment as well as to give him awe and reverence (Rev 11:18; 15:4; 19:5). God is glorified for his acts of creation, deliverance, and justice (4:11; 7:12; 15:4). Here, the angel announces the hour of judgment that will lead to the demise of Babylon (18:10; 19:2). The hour is akin to the Day of the Lord (NOTE on 6:17). The faithful hear the call to glorify God as an invitation to worship (Ps 22:23; Rev 4:11; 5:13; 7:12; 19:5), but the unfaithful hear it as a call to repentance, since God gives his glory to no one else. People are to turn and glorify him before judgment overtakes them (16:9; Josh 7:19; 1 Sam 6:5; Isa 24:15; 42:8–12; Jer 13:16).

"Worship the one who made heaven and earth and the sea and springs of water." Identifying God as the Creator accents his uniqueness and dominion over all other rulers (2 Kgs 19:15–19; Neh 9:6; Ps 146:3–6; Acts 4:24). If idolatry means worshiping created things rather than the God who made them (Wis 13:1–19; Rom 1:18–25; Acts 14:15), then the call to worship the Creator means turning from false belief to the God who is true. It was common to speak of Rome's rule over earth and sea (Philo, *Legat.* 8; NOTES

and COMMENT on Rev 10:6), but in Revelation it is God who exercises rightful rule over the creation, because he brought all things into being (4:11).

14:8. *Another angel, a second one, followed and said, "Fallen, fallen is Babylon the great.* This verse echoes Isa 21:9: "Fallen, fallen is Babylon, and all the images of her gods lie shattered on the ground" (cf. Jer 50:2; 51:8). Repeating a word like "fallen" underscores the tragedy of the great city's demise (Num 17:12). Using the past tense for a future occurrence in prophetic writings emphasized the certainty of a coming event (GHG §106n). This way of speaking made things vivid (Demetrius, *Eloc.* 214). Babylon could be called great because of its power and wealth (Dan 4:30; *Sib. Or. 4:93*), yet the city uses its power for tyranny, and its wealth stems from greed (Rev 18:10, 16, 19, 21). Some futuristic interpreters argue that Babylon literally refers to the city on the Euphrates River (9:14; 16:12), which will rise to world dominance at the end of the age (LaHaye; Thomas). Most, however, interpret the name symbolically, identifying Babylon with Rome, the city on seven hills (17:9; cf. Tertullian, *Marc.* 3.13; Tertullian, *Adv. Jud.* 9). On Babylon, see the NOTE on Rev 17:5.

"She made all the nations drink the wine of her passionate immorality." Here, *thymos* indicates "passionate immorality," whereas in 14:10 it means "passionate anger." The language recalls Jer 51:7: Babylon made "all the earth drunken; the nations drank of her wine, and so the nations went mad," yet suddenly, "Babylon has fallen." When applied to Rome, the language challenges the idea that Rome achieved dominion through virtue and good fortune (Plutarch, *Mor.* 317C). Its influence is depicted as debauchery.

14:9. *Then another angel, a third one, followed them and said in a loud voice, "If any worship the beast and its image.* See the NOTES and COMMENT on 13:4, 8, 14–15.

"and receive a mark on their forehead or their hand. See the NOTES on 13:16–18; cf. 16:2; 19:20; 20:4.

14:10. *"they will also drink of the wine of God's passionate anger, poured full strength into the cup of his wrath.* In 14:8 *thymos* was the "passionate immorality" of Babylon, but here it is the "passionate anger" of God. The Greek literally says that the wine is "mixed unmixed" in the cup of wrath (cf. *Pss. Sol.* 8:14). In Greek practice, one part wine was blended with one or two parts water in a mixing bowl before being poured into a cup; undiluted wine was full strength. Drinking to excess meant staggering and falling down, being out of one's mind and an object of contempt—all of which fit those brought low by divine judgment (Ps 75:8; Isa 51:17; Jer 51:7; Ezek 23:31–33). On divine wrath, see the NOTE on Rev 6:17.

"They will suffer the pain of fire and sulfur before the holy angels and the Lamb. A few Jewish and Christian martyrs were tormented with fire (2 Macc 7:5; Tacitus, *Ann.* 15.44; *Mart. Pol.* 11–15), but here the Lamb's opponents are subjected to fire. Fire and sulfur could be lethal (Rev 9:17–18) and are forms of punishment. God could use fire and sulfur against Sodom and Gomorrah (Gen 19:24), against the eschatological adversary named Gog (Ezek 38:22), and against Rome itself (*Sib. Or.* 3:54, 60). Instead of fiery rain, however, the imagery in Revelation points to the lake of fire and sulfur, where Satan, his allies, and the wicked will be thrown (Rev 19:20; 20:10; 21:8).

The idea that the wicked would be punished with fire was traditional. The gospels tell of the wicked being thrown into the furnace of fire (Matt 13:42, 50; 18:8–9; 25:41) and picture a rich man suffering the flames of Hades (Luke 16:23–26). Some interpreters ease the starkness of the scene by arguing that the torment of the unrepentant will end when the fire consumes them (Caird; cf. *1 En.* 48:9; *4 Ezra* 7:36–38, 61). Others insist that because repentance must always remain a possibility theologically, the torment cannot be endless (Smalley). The most direct reading of the text, however, is that it pictures torment without end (Beale; Osborne; Prigent).

14:11. *"The smoke of their painful suffering goes up forever and ever.* The smoke rising forever is like that from a city on which judgment has fallen (Isa 34:10; Rev 18:9, 18; 19:3). In Dan 3 people must worship the image that the king of Babylon has set up or be thrown into a furnace of fire. Here, the opposite occurs, for those who worship the image of the beast—a royal figure associated with Babylon—are thrown into the fire (deSilva, "Sociorhetorical," 85–87).

"There is no rest day or night for those who worship the beast and its image, or for the one who receives the mark with its name." The redeemed find rest after death (14:13), but the opponents of God find no rest (14:11; *1 En.* 63:6). God's servants give praise day and night, but his adversaries face torment day and night (Rev 4:8; 14:11). On worship of the beast, see the NOTES and COMMENT on 13:4, 8, 14–15. On the mark, see the NOTES on 13:16–18.

14:12. *This calls for the endurance of the saints, who keep the commandments of God and the faith of Jesus.* Endurance means steadfastness in the face of false teachings, physical threats, and other factors (1:9; 2:2; 3:10; 13:10). Here, it involves obedience to God's commandments, especially those that promote worship of God and guard against idolatry, blasphemy, sorcery, theft, murder, and other sins (2:14, 20; 9:20–21; 21:8). The text refers to keeping what is literally called "the faith of Jesus" (NOTE on 1:2). This can mean that people are holding on to the tradition received "from Jesus" (Beale), but it can also mean that they are to put their faith "in Jesus" and remain faithful "to Jesus." Such faith entails public witness to Jesus (2:13; 12:17).

14:13. *And I heard a voice from heaven say, "Write: Blessed are the dead.* There are seven beatitudes in Revelation (see Table 2). To be blessed (*makarios*) means well-being. On these expressions for well-being, see the INTRO IV.E.2.

"who die in the Lord from now on." The expression *ap' arti* means that the faithful who die "from now on" are blessed. At the same time, those who died previously are not excluded from blessing, since the martyrs in 6:9–11 are already at rest and have received white robes (Prigent). The assurance of blessing encourages those who face death for refusing to worship the beast (13:10). But it is not limited to those who die violently. Being blessed (*makarios*) is true of all the redeemed, who are promised life in the New Jerusalem (19:9; 22:7, 14; Giesen). An alternative is to read *ap' arti* as *aparti* (certainly) and to construe it as the beginning of a new sentence, so that it underscores the certainty of blessed rest (BDF §12.3; BDAG 97; Aune). This reading works well in manuscripts that lack the word "yes" ($\mathfrak{P}^{47}$ ℵ*), but it creates an awkward redundancy if one follows the best manuscripts (A C), which include "yes." The text would then read, "'Certainly, yes,' says the Spirit," which is unusually repetitive.

"Yes," says the Spirit, "so they can rest from their labors, for their works follow them." When someone was called blessed, it was common to give a reason for the blessing—for example, "Blessed are the poor in spirit, *for* theirs is the kingdom of heaven" (Matt 5:3): In Revelation the reason is provided by the Spirit, who emphasizes that the blessed dead will "rest from their labors, *for* their deeds follow them," which means that God favorably remembers what they have done. The Spirit responds to the unnamed voice with

"yes," which underscores the truth of what is said, much like "amen" (Rev 1:7; 22:20; Aune, *Prophecy*, 59–60, 283). The Spirit (singular) is God's agent of prophecy (2:7; 19:10; 22:17) and is different from the seven angelic spirits before the throne (1:4).

The prospect of rest after death was to some extent traditional. People could say that death brought relief from the struggles of this life and that burial meant being laid to rest (Josephus, *J. W.* 4.385; *Greek Anth.* 7.408). Some people assumed that death brought only rest (Seneca the Younger, *Marc.* 19.4–6; Lucretius, *De rer.* 3.915–30), but Revelation warns that dying does not guarantee rest, because God's opponents will face judgment (Rev 14:11). In some sources the restful state of the righteous after death was pictured as a kind of sleep (*L.A.B.* 3:10; 19:12; 28:10; 1 Thess 4:14), but the martyrs in Rev 6:9–11 are shown calling out to God. In some contexts rest is understood to be the final condition of the redeemed (Heb 4:10), but in Revelation the martyrs under the altar are told to rest for a little longer (Rev 6:11), which implies that rest continues until the resurrection, when the dead are brought to the fullness of life (Wright, *Resurrection*, 471).

COMMENT

Two visions now shape the readers' perspectives through the interplay of promise and warning. The first shows the promise of salvation on Mount Zion, known for God's presence and protection (Rev 14:1–5); the second warns of the fall of Babylon (14:6–11). The first centers on the Lamb and his followers, who bear his name and God's name on their foreheads; the second focuses on the beast and its followers, who worship its image and bear its name on their foreheads or hands. In one vision, those on Mount Zion are undefiled and chaste; in the other, those belonging to Babylon consume the wine of passionate immorality. The interplay between scenes of promise and warning culminates in the final exhortation to remain faithful, since God will not forget the saints, even in death (14:12–13).

As John narrates these visions, he discloses what belonging to the Lamb and belonging to the beast will mean for the future. He initially tells of music cascading down from heaven in a new song that the Lamb's followers can comprehend, and then he speaks of the smoke of torment rising up around the beast's worshipers forever. The beast may seem invincible (13:4), yet Revelation insists that it is not. Worshiping the beast may allow people to escape the judgment of the beast's agents for a time (13:15), but in the end it brings them under the judgment of God (14:9–11). Conversely, following the Lamb brings hardship and exclusion in the present time (13:8–10), yet the outcome is rest and a place among the blessed (14:12–13).

The themes of promise and warning anticipate scenes to come. The first vision refers to the followers of the Lamb as the "first fruit" of those who are redeemed from the earth (14:4), and this theme continues when harvest imagery is used for salvation later in the chapter (14:14–16). The second vision issues a warning to those who

On Rev 14:1–13, see Bauckham, *Climax*, 229–32; deSilva, "Sociorhetorical" and *Seeing*, 257–84; Hirschberg, *Das eschatologische*, 195–200; M. Hoffmann, *Destroyer*, 30–104; Olson, "Those"; Pattemore, *People*, 179–93; Rossing, *Choice*, 62–71; Siew, *War*, 189–98; Slater, *Christ*, 191–94; van Schaik, "Ἄλλος"; Zimmermann, "Virginitäts-metapher" and "Nuptial," 157–60.

drink the wine of Babylon's immorality (14:8), and again, this theme continues when God's opponents are trampled in the winepress of his wrath (14:18–20). The contrast between salvation on Mount Zion and the disaster falling on the allies of Babylon also foreshadows the conclusion of the Apocalypse, where Babylon meets a fiery demise (17:1–19:10) and New Jerusalem provides life and blessing from God and the Lamb (21:1–22:5).

The promises and warnings in this section presumably would have affected early readers of Revelation in different ways (deSilva, "Sociorhetorical"). For those confronted by pressure to compromise their loyalty to the Lamb, the visions offer encouragement to persevere, knowing that God will not abandon them. But for those who do not see making peace with the religious and commercial practices of the ruling power as a problem, the specter of judgment is a warning to change course. Rhetorically, the promise of salvation and the warning of judgment function differently but they serve the same end, which is that readers exhibit the faithful "endurance of the saints" (14:12).

The Lamb and the Redeemed on Mount Zion (14:1–5)

Visions of cosmic conflict have shown the seven-headed beast rising from the sea (13:1) and another beast, which looks like a lamb, rising from the land (13:11). But here, the true Lamb of God is on the high ground, Mount Zion, where the redeemed gather (14:1). The name Mount Zion recalls the hill on which Jerusalem was built. First, it has royal connotations, since it was David's capital and the place where the kings of Judah reigned (2 Sam 5:6–9; Ps 2:6). In Revelation, the name is suitable for the place where the Lamb stands, since he is the royal Lion of Judah, the messianic root of David, whose self-sacrifice establishes God's kingdom (Rev 5:5–10). Second, Mount Zion was the center of Israel's worship, since that was where the temple was located (Pss 9:11; 76:2; 132:13). Accordingly, John pictures songs of heavenly praise washing over Mount Zion, and he says that the redeemed are gathered in like first fruits being brought to the sanctuary (Rev 14:3–4). Third, Mount Zion was a source of divine help and a place of refuge, for there the Lord was to defeat his enemies and reign (Isa 4:2–6; 24:23; 31:4; Joel 2:32; Mic 4:7; 2 Bar. 40:1–3). Appropriately, John pictures the Lamb's followers finding a secure place there.

Many interpreters assume that John speaks of a heavenly Zion, since the Lamb stands there as he previously stood before God's heavenly throne (Rev 5:6–14; 7:9–17; cf. Heb 12:22–24; Gal 4:26; 2 Bar. 4:2–6; Giesen; Mounce; Slater, *Christ*, 191–94). Others think the Lamb is on earth, since music comes from heaven, which is above. They also assume that John follows Jewish sources in envisioning a messianic kingdom on earth, which will later be depicted as the thousand-year reign of the saints (Rev 20:4–6; *4 Ezra* 13:35; Aune; Murphy; Osborne; Thomas).

Literary cues, however, indicate that this vision of Zion anticipates New Jerusalem, not the millennial kingdom. The most significant cue is the nuptial theme that runs through the latter half of Revelation. In Rev 14:1–5, the sounds of rushing water, thunder, and song introduce a vision in which the redeemed are pictured as chaste maidens. The sense is that they are betrothed to the Lamb and follow him faithfully as they await their wedding day (COMMENT on 14:4). The sounds of rushing water, thunder, and heavenly worship are heard again when the wedding day of the Lamb has come and the bride has made herself ready (19:6–8). The motif culminates when the bride appears in splendor as the New Jerusalem (21:2, 9). The initial vision of Mount Zion and the maidens who follow the Lamb foreshadows the vision of New Jerusalem and the appearance of the Lamb's bride in glory (Zimmermann, "Nuptial"; Beasley-Murray; Boring).

Those accompanying the Lamb number 144,000 (14:1). This number is twelve times twelve thousand. It too anticipates life in New Jerusalem, the city that measures twelve thousand stadia on a side and whose walls are 144 cubits thick (21:16–17). Earlier, the number portrayed the followers of Jesus as heirs to the promises God made to Israel, since the 144,000 come from the twelve tribes. Yet this same group proved to be a countless multitude, redeemed by the Lamb from every tribe and nation (NOTES and COMMENT on 7:4; cf. §12A). Here again, 144,000 points to the vast company of those who belong to the Lamb and contrasts them with the followers of the beast, who are marked with 666, a number that seems diminished by comparison (13:18; 14:1).

The redeemed on Mount Zion bear the names of God and the Lamb on their foreheads, as they do in New Jerusalem (22:4). By way of contrast, those who belong to the beast receive his name or number on their foreheads or hands (13:16–18; 14:9, 11). The beast's mark identifies those who are willing to accept the claims of the ruling power in order to purchase (*agorazein*) goods without hindrance in the public market (13:17). By way of contrast, the redeemed bear the names of God and the Lamb on their foreheads as a sign that they have been purchased (*agorazein*) by the Lamb (14:3–4). Revelation recognizes that the desire of readers to participate in commercial life can make them affirm imperial claims in ways that the author thinks will violate their Christian commitments, especially in contexts in which maintaining their faith in a public way could entail personal sacrifice (NOTES and COMMENT on 13:16–17). So in addition to pointing to future blessings, the writer recalls the way the Lamb has already purchased the readers by his own sacrifice on their behalf. This would make it appropriate for them to respond by a willingness to experience sacrifice themselves.

John says that he heard sounds like rushing water, thunder, and harpists playing their harps (14:2). The context suggests worship (Pss 33:2; 43:4; 71:22; 150:3; 1 Macc 4:54). Literary cues link this vision to the previous one in which the heavenly beings around God's throne held harps as they sang a "new song" to the Lamb. Repeating the references to the harps and new song indicate that the scene in 14:1–5 should be understood in light of the earlier worship scene. There, the lyrics of the new song focused on the death of the Lamb, which redeems people of every nation:

> "You are worthy to receive the scroll and to open its seals,
> for you were slain and by your blood you purchased for God
> those of every tribe and language and people and nation,
> and you made them a kingdom and priests to our God
> and they will reign on earth." (5:9–10)

The literary connection helps readers discern why this new song can be understood only by the 144,000 (14:3b). The song gives glory to the slaughtered Lamb, and for those outside the Christian community, praising a crucified Messiah was incomprehensible.

Critics could charge that "this so-called Christ of yours was dishonorable and inglorious, so much that the last curse contained in the Law of God fell on him, for he was crucified" (Justin Martyr, *Dial.* 32.1; Hengel, *Crucifixion*, 1–10). The cross was "the tree of shame," not honor (Cicero, *Rab. Perd.* 4.13). To say that the victim of crucifixion was the agent of God's power was foolishness (1 Cor 1:18). Yet the new song identified the Lamb as the one who purchased (*agorazein*) people by his blood (Rev 5:9). Here, the 144,000 are said to have been purchased (*agorazein*) by the Lamb, which means they have received the benefits of his sacrifice (14:3). They understand the song's praise of the Lamb because they have been redeemed by him.

In the readers' world, harpists and singers praised various Greco-Roman deities, especially Apollo, who was often pictured holding a harp (Figure 23). At Ephesus singers devoted their music to the goddess Artemis (Diodorus Siculus, *Libr.* 2.47.2; cf. Dio Chrysostom *Disc.* 2.28; Quintilian, *Inst.* 1.10.10). At the imperial temple in Pergamum, choruses from cities throughout the province praised the god Augustus and his household (Friesen, *Imperial*, 104–13). Making God and the Lamb the focus of praise sets the followers of Jesus apart from others, but as the redeemed engage in such worship on earth, they join the song that the companies of heaven raise. The visions anticipate that the harps and songs that flourish in Babylon will come to an end (Rev 18:22), but those offered to God and the Lamb have abiding value. Therefore, this vision cycle ends by showing those who have conquered the beast standing by the sea of glass with harps in their hands (15:2). Their song of victory is like that of Moses at the sea, but it now centers on the triumph that comes through the Lamb and the hope that all nations will join in worshiping God (15:3–4).

John now describes the multitude in three ways. First, he uses masculine imagery to say that they are "not defiled with women" (14:4a). On a basic level this metaphor assumes that illicit sexual relations are defiling, making a person unfit to enter holy company. The language is then transferred to relationships with God. Previously, eating food offered to Greco-Roman deities was called immorality (*porneia*), yet some of John's early readers were being taught that it was acceptable to eat this food. Therefore, they are warned that such actions constitute religious adultery, since they violate their exclusive relationship to God (2:14, 20–22).

Revelation's use of sexual imagery culminates in the vision of Babylon the whore, the city that lures nations and kings into immorality (14:8; 17:1–6). Depictions of Babylon extend the metaphor of sexual infidelity to relationships marked by greed, violence against the saints, and godless arrogance (18:1–24). Although some interpreters equate Revelation's call for the faithful to remain pure with the need to avoid the Roman imperial cult (Giesen; Müller), the vision of the whore shows that the imagery is wider in scope. To say that the redeemed have not defiled themselves with women means that they resist the teachings of the woman Jezebel, who advocated an easy attitude toward Greco-Roman religious practices (2:20), and they reject the social and economic practices associated with Babylon the whore, the woman in scarlet (17:3).

Second, John shifts to feminine imagery for the redeemed, calling them maidens (*parthenoi*) who follow the Lamb (14:4b). Maidens are young women of marriageable age who have not had sexual relations. Portraying the redeemed as chaste *males* in 14:4a indicates that they resist the idolatry and sins associated with the whore, but depicting them as chaste *females* in 14:4b shows that they are prepared to be bride of the Lamb.

Their purity consists of righteous deeds (18:7–8; Zimmermann, "Nuptial"; Pattemore, *People*, 187). The shift from masculine to feminine imagery is as abrupt as saying that the redeemed number 144,000 and yet are numberless, or that they are pure because they wash in blood (7:4, 9, 14). When John says that the redeemed follow the Lamb wherever he goes, the language recalls how Israel was pictured as a bride, following God into the wilderness (14:4b; Jer 2:2; see below). Adding that the redeemed do not lie also fits this theme, since deception belongs to the allies of the beast but has no place in New Jerusalem the bride (Rev 13:14; 21:8, 27; 22:15). Finally, the redeemed are unblemished, or blameless, as befits a young woman anticipating her wedding day (14:5; *m. Ket.* 7:7–8).

The basis of the metaphor are the practices of betrothal that were common among Jews, Greeks, and Romans. At the time of betrothal, promises united the couple in an exclusive relationship that was tantamount to marriage. The couple would not actually live together until the wedding day, when the bride was taken to her bridegroom's home. Until that time, the young woman was expected to remain chaste (B. Cohen, *Jewish*, 279–347; Justinian, *Dig.* 23.1.1–18; Deut 22:23–24; Matt 1:18–25; *Jos. As.* 21:1). Faith binds people to Jesus the Lamb, much as a betrothed bride is bound to her bridegroom by solemn commitments. At the present time, believers do not live with the Lamb in the fullest sense but await the "wedding," when they will be raised to life in New Jerusalem. There, the Lamb and his bride will share the same dwelling (Rev 19:6–7; 21:2–3). During this period of betrothal, Jesus' followers are to remain chaste by refusing to yield to pressures that would violate their commitments to him (Zimmermann, "Nuptial," 157–60). In an ordinary sense, a major violation of betrothal was sexual infidelity. When transferred to discipleship, the notion of immorality (*porneia*) means that Jesus' followers are to resist false worship and the wrongful actions associated with it (2:14, 20; 14:8; 18:3).

Next, John moves from male and female imagery to that of the harvest, picturing the faithful as first fruit (Rev 14:4). The flow of thought follows the pattern set in Jer 2:2–3:

Jer 2:2–3	Rev 14:4
I remember . . . your love as a bride,	Now these are maidens
how you followed me in the wilderness	who follow the Lamb wherever he goes.
. . . Israel was holy to the Lord,	These were purchased from humankind
the first fruits of his harvest	as first fruit for God and the Lamb.

As in Jeremiah, Revelation's bridal imagery flows seamlessly into that of the harvest. Traditionally, the first fruits (*aparchē*) were the first ripe sheaves of grain or clusters of grapes, which were offered to God as a recognition of his claim upon the whole harvest (Exod 23:19). Although first fruit was sometimes a metaphor for a select few among the redeemed (Rom 16:5; 1 Cor 16:15), Revelation follows the pattern of Jer 2:3, in which the image includes the whole people of God. As first fruit was brought to the sanctuary (Deut 26:1–2), the redeemed are brought to the Lamb on Mount Zion (Rev 14:1). The 144,000 represent those who experience God's harvest of the earth as salvation and life.

Warnings Against Followers of the Beast (14:6–13)

The next vision has a more ominous tone as three angels appear in quick succession, bearing words of exhortation and warning. The first brings eternal good news (*euangelion*), a term suitable for the message of God's victory (14:6). Earlier, a mighty angel recalled how the prophets received good news (*euangelizein*) of God's reign. That message culminated in the announcement that the world had become the kingdom of the Lord and his anointed, which meant the destruction of the destroyers of the earth (Rev 10:7; 11:15–18; Isa 52:7). Now good news brought by the angel anticipates the fall of the despotic powers and points to God's rule over the nations, which is the climax of this series of visions (Rev 15:2–4).

The angel calls for the world to fear and glorify God. He addresses every nation, tribe, language, and people—the groups that have been lured into worshiping the beast (13:7; cf. 13:4, 16). Some interpreters argue that the angel signals that the time for repentance is past and that the nations now will be compelled to fear and glorify God as they fall under judgment (Beale; Giesen; Müller). Others, however, take the angel's message as a summons to repent. John recounted visions in which disasters fell on the ungodly only to have them refuse to repent so the movement toward judgment was interrupted (9:20–21; 10:1–11). Then, after witness was given and a lesser judgment fell, people came to fear and glorify God (11:13). The literary movement shows that repentance is God's desire (5:9; 15:3–4; Mounce; Osborne; Smalley; Bauckham, *Theology*, 98–104).

One reason people are to fear and glorify God is that the hour of judgment has come (14:7b). The plea for God to act justly was made by the martyrs, who demanded to know how long God would refrain from judgment, since delay meant that the faithful continued to suffer (6:10). Readers who identify with the victims will hear the announcement of judgment as good news because it means that the powers that slay the innocent and ruin the earth will be overthrown (18:20). But for those allied with the forces of injustice, the announcement of judgment is a threat, because God's action will bring an end to their dominion. Another reason to worship God is his power to create (14:7c). Beasts rise up from sea and land (13:1, 11), but Revelation repeatedly says that God made the sea and land (4:11; 10:5–6) and will not surrender his world to the forces that terrorize it (11:18; 14:7).

The second angel announces the fall of Babylon the great (14:8). Earlier, readers heard of "the great city" that encompassed the world's many peoples, tribes, languages, and nations. The city was identified with the sin of Sodom, the oppression of Egypt, and the hostility that led to Jesus' death in Jerusalem (11:8–10). Now the great city is called Babylon, the city that was once the center of an oppressive empire, and it has traits of Rome, the city on seven mountains or hills, which was the imperial power of John's own time (17:9; §35 COMMENT).

The charge is that Babylon the whore makes the nations drink the wine of her passionate immorality (14:8). The imagery evokes associations of a bawdy banquet where a prostitute makes clients drunk while luring them into sexual liaisons. The language is then applied to the way the nations of the world relate to the ruling power. On one level, the language challenges public rhetoric, which portrayed Rome as a fountainhead of virtue (Strabo, *Geographica* 6.4.2; Plutarch, *Mor.* 317c). Revelation charges that Rome was actually the source of immorality (*porneia*), its vices contaminating the empire (cf. *Sib. Or.* 5:386–96; Tacitus, *Ann.* 15.44; Lucian, *Nigr.* 16; Juvenal, *Satirae* 3; Rev 9:21; 21:9; 22:15). On another level, immorality connoted false worship. In Revelation's messages to the churches, John applied terms for sexual immorality to consuming what was offered to Greco-Roman deities (2:14, 20). Such food might be eaten at public festivals, at private meals in Greco-Roman temples, and at gatherings of associations where religious rites were observed (INTRO II.B.2). On yet another level, John uses the image of immorality for commercial networks, where relationships are based on an insatiable desire for luxury and a willingness to provide anything for a fee. He likens those seeking benefits from the empire to clients seeking pleasure from a prostitute (17:2; 18:3, 9), and he makes the mark of the beast a symbol for all who identify with the empire for economic advantage (13:17).

The third angel completes this sequence by disclosing the terrible consequences of worshiping the beast (14:9–10). The beast's devotees drink the wine of divine wrath and are eternally tormented with fire and sulfur in the presence of the angels and the Lamb. This gruesome scene is to some extent traditional (NOTE on 14:10), but one might ask whether it ascribes to God a brutality that might be better suited to the beast. In this regard, it is significant to remember that Revelation works with the idea of symmetry in judgment. The beast uses violence against the innocent, which is unjust, whereas God makes the perpetrators suffer the consequences of their own destructive tendencies.

Symmetry is evident in the metaphor of wine. Since Babylon the whore has made the nations drink the wine of her passionate immorality, she ultimately drinks the wine of God's passionate anger (14:8, 10). The "wine" of Babylon's passionate immorality is the seductive quality of conspicuous consumption and violence, which the nations imbibe (Rev 17:4–6). The vision of Babylon will show how those who use violence against others become the victims of violence, and how a society devoted to consumption is eventually consumed (NOTES and COMMENT on 17:16; 18:6). When these practices ruin those who do them, they function as the "wine" of divine wrath.

The symmetry continues in the image of fire. Earlier, the beast from the land, or false prophet, did signs in the presence of (*enōpion*) the beast and the public, calling fire from heaven to lure people into worshiping the beast, while slaying those who refused (13:12–16). Now, those who were lured to the beast by fire are engulfed by fire in the presence of (*enōpion*) the Lamb and the angels (14:10). Later, the beast uses fire to destroy Babylon (17:16), making the city's demise a fiery spectacle that others watch (18:9–10, 15, 17–18), as the smoke of the city's painful suffering (*basanismos*) goes up forever (18:10, 15; 19:3). Here, the allies of the beast, who brings fiery pain to others, are subjected to painful suffering (*basanismos*) in fire, as the angels and the Lamb look on (14:10–11). It seems incongruous that the Lamb, who endured suffering for the sake of others, now does nothing to alleviate suffering (5:9–10; 7:14–17). The underlying assumption is apparently that those who worship the beast effectively repudiate the Lamb, and their judgment is finally allowed to take its course. Since they have not wanted the redemption that the Lamb has offered, the Lamb allows their rejection to stand, and he does not interfere.

In contrast to this grim scene is the promise of rest for those who "die in the Lord," which offers encouragement. In an ordinary sense, labor (*kopos*) can refer to the efforts that people must make to earn a living (1 Thess 2:9; 2 Thess 3:8), but in Revelation it includes the labor involved in fostering faith and community in the face of opposition (Rev 2:2; cf. 1 Cor 15:58; 1 Thess 1:3). Since the term *kopos* can connote trouble (Job 5:6–7; Luke 11:7; 18:5), resting entails peace. The deeds (*erga*) mentioned here recall the works of love, faithfulness, and perseverance that the author commended in the messages to the assemblies (Rev 2:2, 19). In that context readers were warned that they were accountable for their deeds (2:23; 3:1, 15; 20:12), but the positive tone of this beatitude gives assurance that not even death will make God forget works of service (2:19; 3:8; cf. *4 Ezra* 8:33; *m. 'Abot* 6:9). It is challenging to follow (*akolouthein*) the Lamb (14:4), and yet the works of discipleship follow a person in blessing (14:13). The dead who have been allied with the beast have a future with no rest (*anapausis*, 14:11), while those who die in the Lord will be able to rest (*anapauesthai*, 14:13).

This interplay of warning and promise has an important rhetorical function. The specter of judgment in 14:9–11 functions as a warning, designed to move people to change course and avert judgment (cf. Philo, *Praem.* 163). Then the promise of rest in Rev 14:13 functions positively by encouraging hope for the blessings that come through the Lamb. The warning and promise function differently, but both are designed to foster "the endurance of the saints," which is the point of this section (14:12).

30. Harvest for Salvation and Reaping for Judgment (14:14–20)

14   ¹⁴Then I looked, and there was a white cloud. On the cloud was seated someone who looked like a human being. He had a gold laurel wreath on his head and a sharp sickle in his hand. ¹⁵Another angel came out of the temple, calling in a loud voice to the one seated on the cloud: "Use your sickle to reap the harvest, for the hour to harvest has come and the harvest of the earth is ready." ¹⁶So the one seated on the cloud swung his sickle over the earth, and the earth was harvested.

¹⁷Then another angel came out of the temple in heaven, and he also had a sharp sickle. ¹⁸Still another angel, who has power over fire, came out from the altar. He spoke with a loud voice to the one who had the sharp sickle and said, "Use your sharp sickle to cut the clusters of the vineyard of the earth, because its grapes are ripe." ¹⁹So the angel swung his sickle to the earth and cut the vineyard of the earth, and he put what he reaped into the great winepress of God's passionate anger. ²⁰Then the winepress was trampled outside the city, and the blood came out of the winepress as high as the horses' bridles for one thousand six hundred stadia.

NOTES

14:14. *Then I looked, and there was a white cloud.* Clouds indicate divine agency. They robe an angel (10:1), take witnesses to heaven (11:12), and bear Christ as a divine being (1:7). Clouds were a means of divine transport (Isa 19:1; Ps 104:3; Acts 1:9) and were connected to heavenly thrones (Ps 97:2; Sir 24:4; Virgil, *Aen.* 9.636–42). They could signal a theophany (Exod 16:10; Lev 16:2; Num 11:25; Mark 9:7 par.). The whiteness is heavenly, like the radiant hair of the exalted Christ, the garments of the faithful, and the throne of God (Rev 1:14; 3:5; 4:4; 19:11; 20:11).

On the cloud was seated someone who looked like a human being. The passage recalls Dan 7:13: "See, with the clouds of heaven there came one like a human being," or the Son of Man, who was given an everlasting kingdom so that all peoples should serve him. Revelation does not follow any known version of Dan 7:13 exactly. When saying that the figure is "like" a human being, the author uses *homoios* rather than *hōs* as in the Greek versions of Daniel, and he pictures the figure "sitting" rather than "coming." Earlier, John followed Dan 7:13 Theod. when he said that the figure would come "with the clouds" (NOTE on Rev 1:7), but here, he is closer to the LXX, for the figure appears "on" a cloud. Finally, John speaks of one cloud rather than many clouds (cf. Luke 21:27).

In many contexts the expression "Son of Man" (*huios anthrōpou*) simply meant "human being" (Ezek 2:1, 3, 6; Ps 144:3), and some sayings of Jesus use the expression to mean "I" (Matt 8:20). Someone who is "like a Son of Man" is "like a human being." Yet the figure comes on or with the clouds, which suggests that he is no ordinary person. Some propose that he is an angel, since angels could ride on clouds, wear wreathes, and participate in the eschatological harvest (*T. Ab.* 9:8; *Jos. As.* 14:8–9; Matt 13:39). The next verse refers to "another" angel, which could imply that the figure on the cloud is also an angel (Aune; Morris). Yet Revelation previously made clear that the exalted Christ is the one who comes with the clouds (Rev 1:7) and "looked like a human being" (1:13), making it likely that Christ is the figure in 14:14 (Carrell, *Jesus*, 175–95). Other Jewish and Christian writings use language from Dan 7:13 for a messianic figure (*1 En.* 46:1–3; 48:2; *4 Ezra* 13:3; Matt 26:64; Mark 14:62; Collins, *Daniel*, 306–7). On the final return of Christ, see the NOTE on Rev 22:7.

Daniel depicts the human one, or Son of Man, coming with the clouds to receive glory and an everlasting kingdom (Dan 7:13–14). Revelation elaborates by saying that he wears a gold wreath that signifies honor and he is seated in a manner suitable for a king. In some contexts the arrival of the Son of Man was envisioned as a time of redemption for the elect (Matt 24:30–31; Mark 13:26; 14:62; Luke 21:27; cf. *4 Ezra* 13:3, 12). This is probably the case in Rev 14:14–16, where the figure on the cloud harvests the earth, which may signify redemptive ingathering. Elsewhere, the Son of Man was pictured as a judge (*1 En.* 69:29; Matt 25:31) or the one who would defeat God's foes (*1 En.* 46:1–8; *4 Ezra* 13:1–11). Accordingly, some interpreters suggest that the figure in Rev 14:14 sits as judge (Yarbro Collins, *Cosmology*, 192; Huber, *Einer*, 230), perhaps alluding to Joel 3:12, where the Lord sits in judgment as the grain harvest and treading of grapes begins (Osborne). Although connotations of judgment are possible, the seated posture more probably connotes power to rule (Mark 14:62; Rev 4:2).

He had a gold laurel wreath on his head and a sharp sickle in his hand. A gold wreath (*stephanos*) signified victory in athletic contests and battle (NOTE on 2:10). The imagery was also used for dying faithfully, which is true of Christ, the slaughtered Lamb (5:5–6). Christ who conquered by faithful suffering appearing now on a white cloud with a gold wreath assures that the faithful who conquer in this way will receive the white robes and wreaths that have been promised to them (2:10; 3:11; 15:2).

Wreaths could also symbolize power to rule. Although it was customary for kings to wear a diadem rather than a wreath (NOTE on 12:3), the LXX and other Jewish texts used the term *stephanos* for the crowns worn by Israel's kings (2 Sam 12:30; Ps 21:3 [20:4 LXX]; Ezek 21:31; Josephus, *Ant.* 7.50), and Roman emperors were often pictured wearing wreaths (G. Stevenson, "Conceptual," 259–60). Here, Christ is the one like a human being, who was to exercise God-given dominion over the earth according to Dan 7:13–14 (Huber, *Einer*, 235). Later, Christ wears many diadems as he defeats the beast and dragon, which wear diadems of tyranny (12:3; 13:1; 19:12).

14:15. *Another angel came out of the temple, calling in a loud voice to the one seated on the cloud.* Some interpreters suggest that the ability to issue a command means that the angel is superior to the figure on the cloud (Aune; Morris), but this is unlikely. The angel comes from the temple, where God is present (7:15; 15:8), and he acts as a messenger by conveying God's command to the figure on the cloud (Giesen; Murphy).

"Use your sickle to reap the harvest. The language echoes Joel 3:13 (4:13 LXX): "Put in the sickle for the harvest is ripe." A sickle was a tool with a curved blade set into a handle. The term could be used for the tools used to harvest grain (Deut 23:25 LXX; Mark 4:29) and to cut grape vines (Isa 18:5; Columella, *Rust.* 4.25.1). A sickle is used for grain in Rev 14:15–16 and for grapes in 14:17–19. The sickle was often regarded as an instrument of peace rather than violence (Deut 16:9; Isa 2:4; Mic 4:3; 1 Sam 13:19–22), and the positive use seems dominant in Rev 14:15–16. This tool could also be used for cutting in the destructive sense. In the LXX of Zech 5:1–4, a flying sickle, rather than a flying scroll (MT), brings a curse on the land (cf. *Liv. Pro.* 3:5; Artemidorus, *Onirocritica* 2.24; *T. Ab.* 4:11; Aune). The threatening sense is prominent in Rev 14:17–19.

"for the hour to harvest has come and the harvest of the earth is ready." The grain is "ready," or literally "dry" enough, to be harvested. Some interpreters conclude that the angel has to tell Christ that the hour of harvest has come because the earthly Jesus said the timing of final events was known to God alone (Mark 13:32; Beale; Prigent; Smalley). This seems unlikely, however, since the exalted Christ of Revelation does not seem to be so limited in knowledge.

14:16. *So the one seated on the cloud swung his sickle over the earth, and the earth was harvested.* Harvesting can include both cutting and gathering up the grain (Ruth 2:3; Matt 13:30; 25:24; 2 Cor 9:6). Although harvesting could be an image for cutting down one's opponents in battle (Homer, *Il.* 11.67–71; Jer 9:22), the more positive sense of obtaining the crop seems dominant here (Sir 7:3; John 4:36–38; Gal 6:8).

14:17. *Then another angel came out of the temple in heaven, and he also had a sharp sickle.* Revelation envisions a temple in heaven, as do some Jewish and other early Christian writings (NOTE on 15:5). According to Israel's tradition, the earthly sanctuary was built following a heavenly plan (Exod 25:40), and some assumed that there was an actual sanctuary in heaven (Wis 9:8). The heavenly temple is where God is enthroned (Rev 7:15; G. Stevenson, *Power*, 284–301). Angels connected to the temple perform priestly duties by ministering at the altar and pouring out the contents of libation bowls (8:3–5; 15:5–8).

The counterpart to the heavenly temple is the community of faith on earth, which is pictured as a temple that is threatened by the nonbelieving world (COMMENT on 11:1–2). The temple theme shows God's solidarity with the earthly community in two ways: One is through visions in which the heavenly temple is opened and threatening portents are unleashed against the forces of evil (11:18–19; 15:5–8; 16:1, 17); the other is that the faithful are promised a place in God's temple, where they will be pillars and will serve him (3:12; 7:15). The temple theme culminates in the New Jerusalem, a city that has features of a sanctuary in which the faithful worship forever (22:5)—even though in that context the term "temple" is used for the presence of God and the Lamb rather than for the city itself (21:22).

14:18. *Still another angel, who has power over fire, came out from the altar.* Angels with power over fire and water (16:5) reflect Jewish traditions that linked angels to fire, wind, clouds, and thunder (*Jub.* 2:2; *1 En.* 60:11–21). The angel with authority over fire was sometimes said to judge or punish people (*L.A.B.* 38:3; *T. Ab.* 12:14; 13:11). Although earthly temples had two altars—one for incense and another for burnt offering—Revelation's heavenly temple has a single altar that combines both functions (NOTE on 6:9). It is possible that he comes out of the altar itself, since the martyrs were under the altar and voices come from the altar (6:9; 16:7). But since an angel is beside the altar in 8:5, it is more likely that readers are to picture him stepping out from behind the altar.

He spoke with a loud voice to the one who had the sharp sickle and said, "Use your sharp sickle to cut the clusters of the vineyard of the earth, because its grapes are ripe." The word *ampelos* commonly means grapevine, but it also can mean a vineyard (*Jos. As.* 25:2). Israel was called a vine (Jer 2:21) and a vineyard (Isa 5:1), but here the term is extended to the whole earth. Harvesting grapes involves cutting the clusters from the vine and gathering them. Here, the emphasis is on the cutting done with the sickle (Diodorus Siculus, *Libr.* 3.62.7), which connotes judgment (Isa 18:5; 24:13).

14:19. *So the angel swung his sickle to the earth and cut the vineyard of the earth, and he put what he reaped into the great winepress of God's passionate anger.* On the winepress, see the COMMENT. God's passionate anger was also mentioned in 14:10 and reminds readers of the "passionate immorality" (*thymos*) of Babylon from 14:8.

14:20. *Then the winepress was trampled outside the city.* The language echoes Joel 3:13: "Go in, tread, for the winepress is full. The vats overflow, for their wickedness is great." On one level the imagery draws on practices of winemaking, since workers in bare feet trampled grapes to squeeze out the juice (Judg 9:27). On another level the imagery connotes warfare, since a victorious army was said to trample its foes (Isa 25:10; Zech 10:5; Luke 21:24). Comparing military defeat to being trampled in a winepress was a way to speak of divine judgment (Lam 1:15). Dispensationalist interpreters take "the city" in a literal sense. They expect war at the end of the age to culminate in battle on the outskirts of Jerusalem (Joel 3:12–14; Zech 14:4; Thomas). But the city can better be understood as a metaphor for the believing community (cf. Rev 11:2), just as the vineyard is a metaphor for the earth and the sickle and winepress are metaphors for judgment.

and the blood came out of the winepress as high as the horses' bridles. A river or lake running with blood was a way to picture slaughter in war and divine judgment (Isa 34:3; Ezek 32:5–6; 2 Macc 12:16; *Sib. Or.* 5:372). The scale in John's vision is huge, with a torrent of blood perhaps five feet deep. It resembles traditional descriptions of an eschatological battle, when sinners will slay each other "until a stream shall flow with their blood" and a "horse shall walk through the blood of sinners up to his chest; and the chariot shall sink down up to its top" (*1 En.* 100:1–3; cf. *4 Ezra* 15:35–36). Telling of blood in battle rising as high as the horses' nostrils and flowing four miles into the sea emphasized the scale of the slaughter (*y. Taʿan.* 4:8; *Lam. Rab.* 2.2.4; Bauckham, *Climax*, 40–48). Revelation transforms this battle imagery by treating it as a comment on the vineyard imagery that preceded it. Just as the stream flowing from a winepress shows how much juice the grapes contained, the stream of blood shows how much violence the vineyard of earth contained. In this vision the earth's violence, or "blood," has reached a horrific level. The river reveals how much blood the earth contains, showing the need for God's judgment against it.

for one thousand six hundred stadia. A stade is a little more than six hundred feet, so the river of blood is flowing for about two hundred miles—much longer than in the sources noted above. The Greek number is sixteen hundred stadia, which equals four squared times ten squared and can be taken as a round figure, indicating completeness of judgment. Some interpreters argue for a more specific symbolism by noting that the earth has four corners (7:1) and that ten kings oppose God (16:14; 17:12), so squaring these numbers underscores the worldwide scope of judgment (Victorinus; Primasius; Bauckham, *Climax*, 47). Others take the number as forty squared, observing that forty was associated with punishment in the wilderness and the strokes of a lash (Num 14:33; Deut 25:3; Beasley-Murray). Literalistic interpreters argue that Palestine measures sixteen hundred stadia north to south and that at the battle of Harmagedon blood will flow from Megiddo in the north into the Jordan Valley (Osborne; Thomas). It is preferable, however, to assume that the imagery points to the immensity of judgment, not to geographical space.

The reading "one thousand six hundred" is well-attested (א^c A C 025 046). Some manuscripts refer to twelve hundred stadia (א*), perhaps because twelve connotes completeness. The reading 1,606 (*chiliōn hexakosiōn hex*) probably arose through an accidental repetition of the prefix *hex* (1876 2014). The variant of twenty-six hundred stadia (𝔓¹¹⁵) is probably an error (D. Parker, "New," 164).

COMMENT

This cycle of visions began when the heavenly temple was opened, signaling divine action against the destroyers of the earth (11:19), and it will culminate with the redeemed standing beside heaven's glassy sea (15:2–4). In between are scenes of conflict in which the dragon and beasts personify the political, religious, and economic forces that would pressure the followers of Jesus into compromising or abandoning their faith in order to obtain a more secure place in their social worlds (12:1–13:18). To give people incentive to remain faithful, the author offers an alternative perspective on the conflict through two pairs of visions. Each pair expands the horizon into the future so that readers can see that in the end the righteous will be delivered and the forces of evil destroyed.

The first set of visions contrasted the blessings promised to the followers of the Lamb, who are redeemed for God as "first fruit" (14:1–5), and the threats awaiting Babylon and the worshipers of the beast, who will drink the wine of divine wrath (14:6–11). The next pair of visions develops this imagery by picturing a grain harvest

On Rev 14:14–20, see Bauckham, *Climax*, 40–48; Carrell, *Jesus*, 175–95; M. Hoffmann, *Destroyer*, 30–104; K. Huber, *Einer*, 218–69, and "Ernte"; Slater, *Christ*, 153–60; G. Stevenson, "Conceptual"; van Schaik, "Ἄλλος"; Yarbro Collins, *Cosmology*, 189–95.

and the trampling of grapes from a vineyard. These harvest scenes are parallel to some extent: In each, a heavenly figure appears with a sickle, an angel comes out of the celestial temple and gives the command to reap, and the first figure reaps the earth. Yet in other respects the two scenes differ, leading to various interpretations, considered below. The approach taken here is that these scenes continue the alternation of promise and warning by using the image of the grain harvest for the ingathering of the faithful and the grape harvest for God's judgment against the wicked.

The agricultural imagery shapes the readers' perspectives on the world. Ordinarily, the times of growth and harvest moved in cyclical patterns. Grain fields that were green early in the season later became dry and golden, while the vineyards' small green grapes became large, deep red, and filled with juice. Workers reaped the harvest year after year, and commerce in grain and wine was part of the world's economic order (18:13). In John's vision, however, people do not tend the crops but *become* the crops; the present age no longer moves in cycles but is a single growing season with a final harvest; and the reaping of grain and treading of grapes no longer undergird the current world order but signify its end.

The vision is informed in part by Joel 3:13 (4:14 LXX), which speaks of a final battle in which the nations come to the valley of Jehoshaphat and God says,

> Put in the sickle for the harvest is ripe.
> Go in, tread, for the winepress is full.
> The vats overflow, for their wickedness is great.

It is not clear whether all of Joel's imagery originally came from the grape harvest (Wolff, *Joel*, 80–81) or whether it recalls both the grain and grape harvests (E. Achtemeier, *Book*, 333). But in either case the entire verse from Joel warns of divine action against the nations because of their wickedness. Joel pictures God sitting in judgment (3:12) as the multitudes assemble for battle (3:14). Revelation relates Joel's imagery to two distinct harvests—one of grain and the other of grapes—and seems to take the first as redemptive and the second as condemnatory. The writer also combines imagery from Joel with Dan 7:13, where the seated figure looks like a human being, or "Son of Man." Revelation assumes that this figure is Christ, who is to come on the clouds (Rev 1:7). By combining these texts, Revelation identifies the coming of Christ as the fulfillment of Dan 7:13 and the time of God's victory over of the nations.

The Harvest of the Faithful (14:14–16)

John sees a figure seated on a white cloud who is human in appearance, or literally "like a Son of Man" (14:14). Using this language from Dan 7:13 sets the figure apart from the many angels who appear in these scenes, enabling readers to identify him as the exalted Christ. John has already used language from Dan 7:13 to warn and encourage readers. Initially, he warned that the tribes of earth would grieve when Christ came with the clouds (Rev 1:7). Then readers were told that Christ, who was human in appearance, or "like a Son of Man," already walked among their congregations so that he could warn of judgment and offer hope (1:13; cf. 2:1–3:22). The vision of Christ on the cloud in 14:14 has the same potential to threaten and encourage.

The human one is seated on the cloud (4:14), much as God is seated on a throne (4:2; 5:1; 7:10; 19:4; 21:5). The posture suggests power to rule. Earlier, Christ was said to have taken his seat on God's throne because he conquered (3:21), and now he is enthroned on a white cloud with a gold wreath, which signifies conquest and victory (NOTE on 2:10). Revelation has said that Christ conquered by his sacrificial death, which frees people of every nation for life in God's kingdom (5:5–10). The problem is that Christ's reign continues to face opposition from hostile forces on earth, as the visions of the dragon and beasts make clear (12:1–13:18). Revelation assumes that opposition will continue until Christ's final coming, which is pictured here. At that time, Christ, who has already won victory through his death, will finally defeat the forces of evil so that God's kingdom will be unopposed (cf. 11:15–18).

An angel emerges from the temple to announce that the harvest of the earth is ready (14:15). The heavenly temple plays a dual role in Revelation. On the one hand, it is a source of hope for the faithful. There, God is worshiped as Creator of all things (4:11; cf. 10:6; 14:7), and the faithful are promised that they will join the heavenly company in God's temple (7:15). On the other hand, the temple is a source of threat for God's foes. As the Creator, God opposes the forces that now ruin the world he has made. Therefore, lightning and thunder have come from the temple as signs of God's judgment against the destroyers of the earth (11:18–19), and plagues will come from the temple in the next vision cycle (15:5–8).

The angel who comes out of the temple serves as God's messenger by directing the figure on the cloud to begin the grain harvest (14:15). The main interpretive question is whether the grain harvest should be understood positively or negatively. There are several options. First, some interpreters maintain that harvesting the wheat in 14:15, like cutting the grapes in 14:19–20, signifies divine judgment against the nations. They note that the angel says "the hour to harvest has come," perhaps recalling how a previous angel said "the hour of his judgment has come" (14:7) and readers were told of the fiery torment awaiting the followers of the beast. Earlier, Christ's coming on the clouds was said to bring grief for the tribes of earth (1:7). Moreover, his posture could mean that he sits in judgment, as God does in Joel 3:12. Since both the harvest and the winepress convey judgment against the wicked in Joel, one might assume that this is also true in Revelation. Other sources also use images of a grain harvest for God's condemnation of the wicked (Isa 17:5; Jer 51:33; Mic 4:12–13; Hos 6:11; Matt 3:12; Aune; Beale; Giesen; Müller; Hoffmann, *Destroyer*, 95–100; Yarbro Collins, *Cosmology*, 189–95).

Second, some interpreters argue that the grain harvest is a mixed judgment in which both the righteous and the wicked are gathered in, followed by the condemnation of the wicked in the winepress in the next scene. This approach recognizes that harvest imagery can connote *either* redemption or condemnation, as in Jesus' parable of the wheat and the weeds, which pictures a general ingathering of all people, after which the righteous enter God's kingdom and the wicked are subjected to punishment (Matt 13:24–30, 36–43; Oecumenius; Primasius; Mounce; Huber, *Einer*, 248–52; Huber, "Ernte").

Third, the grain harvest can be taken as a positive image for redemption and the grape harvest as a negative image of condemnation. There are compelling reasons for this approach. At the beginning of this chapter the redeemed were identified as "first fruit" (*aparchē*), which is a positive harvest image (Rev 14:4). Traditionally, the first fruit was set aside as an offering to God (Lev 2:12; 23:10; Deut 26:1–11), and Revelation used the image of first fruit when picturing the redeemed in the presence of the Lamb. This encouraging imagery continues as the figure on the cloud harvests the grain of earth. Harvesting could include both reaping and ingathering. By way of contrast, the negative imagery in previous scenes had to do with wine. The author showed the ungodly, who drank the wine of immoral passion, drinking the wine of God's anger, and this negative imagery will be developed in the vision of the winepress of God's wrath (Rev 14:10; 17–20).

Other reasons supporting this interpretation are that the vision in 14:14–16 concludes with the simple harvesting of grain, which was a positive image for bringing people into God's kingdom (Matt 9:37–38; Mark 4:29; Luke 10:2; John 4:35–38). By way of contrast, the vision of the vineyard ends with grapes being crushed in the winepress. When biblical texts refer to the harvest as judgment, they speak of grain being taken to the threshing floor and trampled underfoot, or being tossed into the air with a winnowing fork so that the chaff can be blown away by the wind or burned, and of separating the good seed from the weeds (Ps 1:4; Jer 51:33; Mic 4:12–13; Matt 3:12; 13:30; Luke 3:17; *4 Ezra* 4:28–32). None of this threatening imagery is developed in Rev 14:14–16, however, which suggests that the grain harvest is positive.

When all the factors are taken together, it seems best to interpret the grain harvest as an image for the ingathering of the faithful at the final coming of Christ (Bauckham, *Theology*, 94–98; cf. Blount; Boxall; Murphy; Osborne; Prigent; Resseguie; Smalley; Slater, *Christ*, 153–56). This approach recalls the early Christian expectation that Christ's return on the clouds would bring about the ingathering of the elect (Matt 24:30–31; Mark 13:26). The positive reading of the harvest imagery also fits the immediate literary context, in which those who have died in the Lord are called blessed (14:13), presumably because they have the hope of resurrection to life with Jesus the Lamb (14:1–5).

Reaping the Vineyard for Wrath (14:17–20)

The next scene begins when another angel comes out of the temple in heaven, holding a sickle as the figure on the cloud had done (14:17). Initially, it is unclear whether this angel brings salvation or judgment, but things take an ominous turn when a third angel comes out from the altar (14:18). Previously, the martyrs have called out from the altar, demanding to know how long God will delay in taking action against those who shed their blood (6:9–11). In the scenes that followed, cosmic disasters manifested divine wrath against the world, but the movement toward judgment was repeatedly interrupted in order that people could be sealed and redeemed (7:1–17) and that continued witness could be given to the unrepentant world (10:1–11:14; Bauckham, *Theology*, 84–88; Perry, *Rhetoric*, 209). But now the vision of the grape harvest shows that delay in judgment will not continue indefinitely. Action will be taken against the wicked, and when it does, the perpetrators of unjust violence will become the victims.

The vision depicts the earth as a vineyard full of ripe grapes (14:18). Grain is ready for harvest when it is dry (14:15), and grapes are ripe when filled with juice. The imagery is inspired in part by Joel 3:13, in which the grape harvest comes because human wickedness is so great. It is also analogous to Isa 5:7, in which Israel is the vineyard from which God "expected justice, but saw bloodshed." In Revelation the whole earth is pictured as a vineyard filled with blood, and at least some of this blood has come from the slaughter of the Lamb and the martyrs (Rev 5:9; 6:10; 7:14; 12:11). Subsequent visions repeat the message that earth has shed the blood of the prophets, saints, and witnesses to Jesus, as well as countless others (16:6; 17:6; 18:24; 19:2). Divine action needs to be taken against the earth because it is full of blood.

The grapes are thrown into the winepress of God's passionate anger and trampled (14:19). A winepress was a large flat basin that was either hewn out of rock or constructed by coating a stone-lined pit with plaster. Grapes were thrown into the basin, and workers trampled on them to squeeze out the juice. The liquid drained to the lowest side of the press and then was channeled into a second, lower basin where it could be collected. The imagery was a way of depicting the defeat of foes in battle, since the grapes were pulverized under the workers' feet (Joel 3:13; Isa 63:3).

John develops the wine imagery to show symmetry in God's judgment (Rev 14:19), following the pattern of previous scenes in which angels declared that Babylon made the nations drink the wine of her passionate immorality (14:8). That "wine" signified the intoxicating power of luxury, violence, and false worship (17:2; 18:3). The effect of wine becomes debilitating, and the same is true of avarice, brutality, and idolatry. When such practices become society's undoing, they function as the wine of divine wrath (14:10). In the vision of the grape harvest, a similar reversal takes place (14:19). Here, the vineyard that has become full of blood has its blood squeezed out in the winepress of wrath. Instead of drinking the wine, people become the wine. The perpetrators of violence ultimately fall victim to it themselves (14:19; cf. 18:6).

The wine is trampled outside the city (14:20). On one level the location continues the harvest imagery, since a winepress was typically located in a field outside of town (Matt 21:33). On a second level the imagery of the grape harvest shifts to that of battle, the idea being that blood shed "outside the city" means that those inside are spared divine judgment. In Revelation, the city (*polis*) is a metaphor for the community of faith (NOTE on Rev 11:2). The implication is that those who belong to the community, or city, are spared this final judgment. Previously, the Christian community, or city, was threatened, or trampled (*patein*), by the Gentiles (11:2); but now this situation is reversed as the ungodly themselves are trampled (*patein*) under divine wrath.

John does not indicate who does the trampling. It could be the angel who cut the grapes (Schüssler Fiorenza), or perhaps it is God, the divine warrior of Isa 63:3. In that passage God said, "I have trodden the winepress alone . . . I trod them in my anger and trampled them in my wrath" (Giesen; Osborne). More probably, however, Christ tramples the winepress. This vision foreshadows the battle in Rev 19:11–21, in which Christ returns to "trample the winepress of the wine of the passionate wrath of God the Almighty" (19:15; Bauckham, *Theology*, 97). The two scenes differ in some details: In 14:17–20 an angel reaps with a sickle and Christ tramples the winepress; while in 19:11–21 Christ is the only one said to act, and he uses the sword that comes from his mouth rather than a sickle. But through their use of the same winepress imagery for a battle connected to Christ's return, the two visions repeat the same basic message in different forms.

This scene, as in 19:11–21, envisions an end to the injustice that has plagued the world (cf. §39 COMMENT). The river of blood, which flows as high as a horse's bridle, shows the magnitude of the violence that has been done on earth (14:20). It reveals why divine justice cannot be delayed indefinitely. As Christ tramples the grapes, the amount of blood that is squeezed out shows how full of brutality the world has become. From this perspective the question is not, "Why is God's judgment so severe?" Rather, if one sees the earth as a vineyard already filled with blood, the question is like that of the martyrs: "Why has God not judged the wicked sooner?" (6:10).

31. All Nations Will Worship the Lord (15:1–4)

15 ¹Then I saw another great and awe-inspiring sign in heaven: seven angels with seven plagues, which are the last, for with them the anger of God is completed. ²Then I saw what appeared to be a sea of glass mixed with fire. Those who conquer the beast and its image and the number of its name were standing by the sea of glass, holding harps of God. ³They sing the song of Moses, the servant of God, that is, the song of the Lamb, saying,

> "Great and awe-inspiring are your works, Lord God Almighty.
> Just and true are your ways, King of the nations.
> ⁴Who will not fear you, Lord, and glorify your name,
> for you alone are holy.
> All nations will come and worship before you,
> for your acts of justice have been revealed."

NOTES

15:1. *Then I saw another great and awe-inspiring sign in heaven.* Heavenly signs like those of the woman and dragon disclose God's purposes (12:1, 3), whereas the signs performed by the beast's agents are deceptive (13:13–14; 16:14; 19:20).

seven angels with seven plagues, which are the last, for with them the anger of God is completed. This line introduces the series of visions that begins in 15:5, after a scene of heavenly praise. The pattern is like that in 8:2–6, where seven angels are given trumpets but use them only after a scene of heavenly prayer. The great and awesome plagues of Deut 28:59 and the sevenfold plagues of Lev 26:18, 21, 28 threaten disobedient Israel, but Revelation's final plagues press the beast's allies to repent.

15:2. *Then I saw what appeared to be a sea of glass mixed with fire.* God's crystal throne was pictured emitting fire and lightning, which mingled fire and water (*1 En.* 14:18–19; Dan 7:10; *2 En.* 29:1; Rev 4:5). Fire also suggests the trials that test faith (3:18; 1 Pet 4:12), and the conquerors here have passed through life's trials to the presence of God. Finally, fire can indicate judgment, much as hurling fire onto the earthly sea brings destruction and the beast's allies are subjected to fire (Rev 8:8–9; 14:10). The faithful stand beyond the fiery sea of judgment. Later, God's foes will be sent to the lake of fire, which is the final condemnation (19:20; 20:10).

Those who conquer the beast and its image and the number of its name. The Greek literally says they conquer "from" (*ek*) the beast. This could imply that they separate themselves from or are saved from the beast (BDF §212; MHT 3:260), though it may simply be a way of saying that they triumph over the beast (12:11). Related expressions occur in Greek and Latin (Pindar, *Isthm.* 6.60–61; Vellius Paterculus, *Rom. Hist.* 2.10.2; Aune).

were standing by the sea of glass, holding harps of God. Standing suggests triumph, like the redeemed who stand before God with palm branches signifying victory (7:9) or the Lamb who stands after being slaughtered and finally stands on Mount Zion (5:6; 14:1). Some translations picture the conquerors on the surface of the glassy sea (NAB; cf. 10:2), though they more likely sing beside the sea, as Israel did after the exodus (NIV, NRSV). The Israelites used tambourines (Exod 15:20), whereas here the redeemed use harps (NOTE on Rev 14:2). Calling them harps "of God" could mean they receive them "from God," as the angels receive trumpets from a heavenly source (8:2). The harps are also used "for God," that is, to praise him (cf. 1 Chr 16:42 LXX).

15:3. *And they sing the song of Moses, the servant of God.* Moses was often called God's servant (*doulos*; cf. 1 Kgs 8:56; Ps 105:26; *oiketēs*, Deut 34:5; *therapōn*, Josh 1:2; *pais*, Josh 1:7). Socially, servants were of low status (Rev 6:15), but to be God's servant was honorable. The title is used for John, the prophets, and all Christians (1:1; 2:20; 7:3; 10:7; NOTES on 1:1)

that is, the song of the Lamb, saying. Some interpreters suggest that the redeemed sing two different songs: the song of Moses from Exod 15, which is not quoted, *and* the song of the Lamb, which is quoted in Rev 15:3–4 (Thomas). Most, however, connect Moses and the Lamb to the one song that is quoted. The *kai* is explanatory ("indeed"), redefining the song of Moses as the one sung by those redeemed through the Lamb (Beale; Osborne).

"Great and awe-inspiring are your works, Lord God Almighty. "Great" and "awe-inspiring" traditionally described God and his acts of creation and deliverance (Jdt 16:13; Dan 9:4; Job 42:3 LXX; *Ep. Arist.* 155; Tob 12:22; Sir 43:29; Pss 111:2–4; 139:14). The expression Lord God Almighty reflects the Greek rendering of the Hebrew for Lord God of Hosts (NOTE on Rev 1:8). In the visions that are about to unfold, God's angels will perform great works of judgment against the beast and its allies (15:1).

"Just and true are your ways, King of the nations. Justice and truthfulness were virtues of a king in Israel's tradition (1 Kgs 3:28; 10:9; Ps 72:1; Prov 29:4) and the Greco-Roman world (Dio Chrysostom, *Disc.* 1.26; 2.54). When Augustus achieved supreme power and ended civil war, the Roman Senate and the people praised his justice, valor, clemency, and devotion (Augustus, *Res* 34; Aune). Although emperors did not officially call themselves kings, their conquests and dominion over the nations were celebrated in the imperial cult, and they were called kings by others. By way of contrast, those who have conquered the beast—with its traits of imperial Rome—use traditional biblical language to acclaim God's justice (Deut 32:4; Ps 145:17; Pr Azar 4) and call him King of the nations (Jer 10:7; cf. Pss 22:28; 47:8; 96:10). Elsewhere, Revelation calls Christ the King of kings (Rev 1:5; 5:9–10; 11:15; 17:14). Although many manuscripts read "King of the ages" ($\mathfrak{P}^{47}$ א^{*2} C; NIV), this is probably not original; it recalls a common title for God (Jer 10:10; Tob 13:7; *1 En.* 12:3; *Jos. As.* 16:16; 1 Tim 1:7). "King of the nations" (א^1 A 051) best fits the context (cf. Rev 15:4; *TCGNT*² 679–80; Aune; Smalley).

15:4. *"Who will not fear you, Lord, and glorify your name, for you alone are holy.* This rhetorical question assumes that all will fear and glorify God (Jer 10:6–7; cf. Exod 15:11; Pss 35:10; 89:8; Isa 40:25). Fear includes awe and reverence (Rev 11:13, 18). Glorifying God's name means ascribing honor to it, rather than blaspheming it, as the beast does (13:6). It was said that God "alone" is God, Lord, sovereign, king, just, almighty, and eternal (Ps 86:10; Isa 37:20; 1 Tim 6:15; 2 Macc 1:24–25). The term holy (*hosios*) was used for God (Deut 32:4; Ps 145:17; *Pss. Sol.* 10:5; Rev 16:5), but more often for devout people. Therefore, saying that God alone is holy means that he is singularly just and faithful. At Sardis and Philadelphia the god called Holy and Just (*Theos Hosios kai Dikaios*) was a Greco-Roman intermediary between the divine and human worlds (NOTES on Rev 3:1, 7; cf. S. Mitchell, *Anatolia*, 2:25–26; *NewDocs* 6:206–9). Revelation, however, ascribes these traits to God alone.

"All nations will come and worship before you. The translation begins a new sentence here in order to show the structure of the song (NAB, NIV, NRSV, REB). Although this is one of three successive lines that begin with the Greek *hoti* (for), it does not explain the previous line but restates the theme of worship that was introduced in 15:4a.

"for your acts of justice have been revealed." God's acts of justice, like the just ways mentioned in 15:3, include salvation for his people and the actions against the wicked that have preceded and will follow this section (16:5–7). The language may echo Ps 98:2, which tells of the acts that reveal God's justice in the sight of the nations (*Pss. Sol.* 2:10; Bauckham, *Climax*, 304).

COMMENT

The conquerors' song of praise beside the celestial sea in 15:2–4 brings the preceding series of visions to its climax. Conflict broke out when the dragon and beast persecuted the people of God in Rev 12–13, but the redeemed were encouraged by the sound of harps and a song coming down from heaven (14:1–5). Now, after warnings of judgment and the reaping of the earth, the faithful hold harps and sing of God's lordship, as at the end of other vision cycles (7:10–12; 11:15–18; 19:1–8). Before the final song in this vision cycle begins, however (15:2–4), the angels who will pour out bowls of plagues in the next vision series are introduced (15:1). The last vision in one series overlaps and interlocks with the first vision in the next series, showing that the two must be taken together. The singers may find that God's justice, truth, and holiness bring salvation, but they foreshadow the overthrow of the powers of injustice and deceit represented by the beast (Schüssler Fiorenza, *Book*, 172; Yarbro Collins, *Combat*, 47–49).

Conquerors Beside the Sea of Glass (15:1–2)

The redeemed stand by the sea of glass that stretches out before God's throne (4:6; 15:2a). The setting draws themes from the exodus to convey the meaning of salvation through the Lamb. Exodus themes appeared earlier, when a woman was threatened by a dragon and carried on an eagle's wings to the wilderness, much as Israel escaped from Pharaoh through the sea to the desert (12:1–6, 13–17). Now, after the horses of God's adversaries have been engulfed in a torrent of blood, the redeemed sing in triumph beside the crystal sea, much as Israel sang after Egypt's horses perished in the Red Sea (14:20; 15:2–4). The difference is that John's vision is cosmic in scale, for redemption no longer means crossing an earthly sea but crossing from earth to heaven; and deliverance is not

---

On Rev 15:1–4, see Bauckham, *Climax*, 296–307; Böttrich, "Das 'gläserne'"; deSilva, "Final," 225–28; Du Rand, "'Now'" and "Song"; Fenske, "Lied"; Jörns, *Das hymnische*, 126–32; Meynet, "Le cantique"; Moyise, "Singing."

simply an escape from death—since some conquerors do die (12:11)—but an overcoming of death through resurrection.

The faithful have conquered the beast by refusing to worship its image or receive its mark (15:2b). At the beginning of the book, promises were made to those who conquer, summoning readers to active engagement against the forces that threaten faith (2:7, 11, 17, 26; 3:5, 12, 21). At the end of the book, the conquerors have a place in the New Jerusalem (21:7). In between, however, Satan and his allies seek to dominate the world by deception and coercion (12:9; 13:14; 18:23), and the beast conquers the faithful by slaying them (11:7; 13:7). This creates a crisis of perception, since it would appear that the beast has triumphed and that resistance is futile. Yet the visions from heaven alter the readers' perspectives by showing that those who witness to God, even at the cost of their lives, are true conquerors. Capitulating to a lie is defeat, while refusing to do so is a victory, since it means that deception and coercion have not suppressed the truth. As the Lamb conquered by faithful suffering and was restored to life, those who attest to the truth of his victory have the promise of life in God's presence (5:5–6; 12:11; 15:2).

The conquerors include martyrs (Aune) and all the faithful (Beale; Giesen; Smalley). Revelation assumes that steadfast faith will accept martyrdom if it comes, but it does not expect all believers to be put to death (13:10; Bauckham, *Theology*, 88–94). In practical terms, the calls for readers to conquer meant engaging challenges ranging from overt hostility, to more subtle pressures to accommodate Greco-Roman worship, to the economic prosperity that produces complacency (Rev 2–3). Here, refusing to worship the beast's image means—at least in part—avoiding the imperial cult (Giesen; Roloff), whereas rejecting the mark is a broader summons to guard against commercial activities that lure people into identifying with the beast (NOTE on 13:17).

The Song of Moses and the Lamb (15:3–4)

The conquerors sing the song of Moses the servant of God, now called the song of the Lamb (15:3a). The contents echo a number of biblical passages in order to praise Israel's God. The title of the song recalls the song that God's "servant" Moses sang when the Egyptians were defeated by the sea during Israel's exodus from slavery (Exod 14:31; 15:1–18). This is fitting here since the singers celebrate victory over the tyrannical beast by heaven's glassy sea. The words of the song in Exod 15 differ from those in Revelation, but they share the themes of God's judgment on his enemies and deliverance of his people, his incomparable superiority, the nations fearing him, people coming to the place of worship, and his everlasting reign.

The general thematic connections are enriched by language from other biblical passages. The theme of God's incomparable holiness from Exod 15:11 creates a link with Jer 10:6–7, which declares that no one is like God and adds, "Who would not fear you, O King of the nations?" This in turn recalls Ps 86:8–10, which declares that God is incomparable because his works are great and awe-inspiring and that all nations will come and worship before him, for he alone is God. Finally, Ps 98:1–2 identifies God's triumph with the revelation of his justice. There are also allusions to a second song of Moses, which appears in Deut 32:1–43 and anticipates Israel's entry into the promised land, where the people will prove unfaithful and yet will be redeemed. Although some interpreters consider this a primary text for the song in Rev 15:3–4 (Fenske, "Lied"; cf. Beale), there are only a few connections. It is best to see the second song of Moses playing a supporting role by supplying references to God's name and greatness, and to his just and holy ways (Deut 32:3–4; Bauckham, *Climax*, 296–307; Meynet, "Le cantique"; Moyise, "Singing").

The lyrics of the song in Rev 15:3–4 do not reveal new information about God but celebrate the accomplishment of what readers would already have heard about God's justice, truth, and holiness. Some interpreters suggest that Revelation's song was already in use in churches known to John (Mounce; Smalley), but this is unlikely (INTRO IV.E.1). Yet some traditions understood that the song Moses sang at the sea anticipated that a new song of salvation would be sung in the future (*Mek.* "Shirata" 1.1–10, 73–86), and Revelation uses familiar motifs to create a song that has new elements. Recasting an older biblical song was not unique to Revelation. For example, Jewish writers created new lyrics for the songs ascribed to Deborah and Hannah (*L.A.B.* 32:1–18; 51:3–6). Revelation does something similar by reworking the song of victory at the sea.

John redefines the song of Moses by identifying it as "the song of the Lamb" (Rev 15:3a). He does not mention the Lamb in the song but defines it this way because God carries out his purposes through the Lamb. Earlier visions established a paradoxical pattern of fulfillment by announcing that the promise of the messianic Lion was fulfilled in the Lamb, who ransoms people from every nation to serve in God's kingdom (5:5–10). They also showed that the hope for the salvation of Israel's tribes would be realized in a multitude from every nation, who are redeemed by the blood of the Lamb (7:4–17). Now the conquerors sing to God as Israel, but instead of celebrating the destruction of their adversaries, as at the exodus, the singers tell of the nations being brought to worship the Lord (Bauckham, *Theology*, 101).

The song follows classic patterns of Hebrew poetry, which is appropriate since the redeemed acclaim the lordship of Israel's God (15:3b–4). The poetic structure also communicates the triumph of order over chaos, as the dissonant sounds of conflict in previous visions resolve into harmoniously structured praise. The song contains two pairs of strophes, each with two parts:

15:3	*15:4*
(a) Great and awe-inspiring are your works, Lord God Almighty.	Who will not fear, Lord, and glorify your name, for you alone are holy.
(b) Just and true are your ways, King of the nations.	All nations will come and worship before you, for your acts of justice have been revealed.

The strophes in 15:3 begin with praise and conclude with titles for God, while in 15:4 they call for worship and then explain the reason for it. The first two strophes feature pairs of adjectives, calling God's works "great and awe-inspiring" and "just and true" (15:3), while the next two center on verbs as people "fear" and "glorify" and then "come" and "worship" God (15:4). In Greek, the initial line of each strophe ends with the word *sou* (you/your), referring to God so that the singers repeatedly tell of *your* works, *your* ways, *your* name, and worship before *you*, evoking a sense of God's presence. The strophes move forward by acclaiming the greatness of God's actions in 15:3

and then pointing to the responses of reverence and worship in 15:4, yet they can also be read side by side, as shown above. The "a" lines make the greatness of God a counterpart to fear and glory, and the "b" lines center on God's justice and relationship to the nations.

The singers declare that God's works are great and awe-inspiring, and readers know that he creates, delivers, and rules the world (15:3; cf. 4:11; 7:10). Yet his claims clash with those of the beast, whose greatness leaves many in awe (13:3–4). The singers call God "Almighty," but the beast wields the power of Satan and seems to be invincible (13:2). Therefore, the next line of the song does not merely repeat but clarifies and intensifies the point, as is common in biblical poetry (Berlin, "Introduction," 304–5). God's ways are "just and true," which cannot be said of the beast, which works by coercion and deception; and God is King of the nations, despite the beast's purported authority over the nations (15:3; cf. 13:7). Identifying power with justice and truth recalls that the martyrs called the sovereign and true God to act with justice so that evil would not go unchecked (6:10). In visions to come, God's justice will mean pressing the violent to repent by giving them blood to drink and later turning evil against itself so that the beast destroys Babylon, its ally. Both actions are called just and true, and they show that God's justice is more than retribution (16:4–7; 17:16; 19:2); his goal is to rid the earth of the powers that would destroy it (11:18).

The conquerors ask, "Who will not fear, Lord, and glorify your name?" and then answer their own question by declaring, "All nations will come and worship before you" (15:4). Their words echo the most expansive hopes of the prophets, who spoke of all nations coming to worship the God of Israel (Isa 2:2–4; 66:23; Jer 16:19; Zech 8:22). Previously, God interrupted judgment so that his witnesses might work to bring many to fear and glorify him, which was his goal (Rev 11:13); and before stark visions of judgment, an angel called all nations to fear and glorify God, which is eternal good news (14:7). The problem is that others ask, "Who is like the beast?," which they think invincible, and during the plagues they curse God instead of glorifying him (13:4; 16:9, 11, 21). Therefore, God's victory means the defeat of the beast, Babylon, and their allies (19:17–21).

Since hope for the conversion of the nations stands in tension with warnings about God's judgment, some interpreters suggest that the nations do not so much worship as come into unwilling subjection to divine rule (Beale; Giesen; Müller; Roloff). Yet glorifying God is an act of worship, and the nations do bring glory to New Jerusalem, where they find healing at the tree of life (21:24–22:2). The tension between sweeping visions of judgments and unqualified visions of hope cannot be resolved in a simple logical fashion. Revelation places both types of visions before the readers in order to alienate them from the powers of destruction while drawing them to God, where life is found (Bauckham, *Theology*, 98–104; Boring 226–31; Smalley 388–89).

Fifth Cycle:
The Seven Bowls and
the Fall of Babylon (15:5–19:10)

32. General Comments on the Fifth Cycle

The fifth cycle of visions begins when seven angels appear to unleash the plagues that will bring the wrath of God to its culmination (Rev 15:1). The angels process from the heavenly temple with libation bowls, which they pour out on the earth, sea, rivers, and sky. The beast's kingdom is engulfed in darkness, and kings gather for battle at Harmagedon. Yet before the battle takes place, the final angel pours out his bowl, and the great city of Babylon is struck by an earthquake and hail (15:5–16:21). Readers have the impression that the end has come, yet even here, it has not. Having announced the devastation of Babylon, the author pauses in order to give readers a closer look at the city and the reasons for God's judgment against it (17:1–18).

Babylon is pictured as a grotesque whore who wears gold, jewels, and opulent purple and scarlet clothing. She rides the seven-headed beast, which is Satan's agent on earth. From her position of privilege, she corrupts the world's kings and peoples and is drunk with the blood of the saints. But a reversal occurs when the beast turns against the whore and destroys her so that the destructive forces that support Babylon the whore become her undoing (17:16). In scenes that follow, the angels declare that God's judgment has justly fallen on the city, while the kings, merchants, and seafarers who benefited from Babylon's commercial empire grieve its downfall (18:1–24). The cycle concludes with rejoicing in heaven over the demise of this tyrannical city and the news that the time has come to celebrate the marriage of the Lamb and his bride (19:1–10).

A. BABYLON THE WHORE IN THE HISTORY OF INTERPRETATION

Interpreters have long recognized that Revelation's Babylon has features of Rome and that the vision is a powerful critique of what the city represents. Yet differences emerged over what to make of the Roman elements, with some identifying the vision with future developments, others with the papacy, and still others with Rome as a general symbol of the sinful world. Hippolytus (d. 236) lived under imperial rule and considered Rome to be one of the many powers that would rise and fall before the six thousand years of history ended. He assumed, however, that Babylon was not the Rome of his own time but an evil kingdom that would arise in the future, nearer the time of the Antichrist (*Comm. Dan.* 4.22–24; *Antichr.* 36–42). A closer connection with imperial Rome was made by Victorinus (d. 304), who identified the heads of the beast that carried the whore with emperors from the first and second centuries and the whore's slaughtering of the saints with persecution under Decius. For him, the vision warned that the city would be destroyed in the future by a coalition of kings (*In Apoc.* 13.2; 14.2).

Many interpreters valued the stability brought by Roman rule and therefore generalized the significance of Babylon, taking the vision as a warning against sin. Tertullian (d. ca. 225) recognized that Babylon depicted imperial Rome, which would fall at the end of the age (*Adv. Jud.* 9; *Res.* 22), but like Cyprian, he construed the city's elegant clothes and jewels as a warning against the vice of ostentation (*Cor.* 13; *Cult. fem.* 2.12.2; Cyprian, *Hab. virg.* 12). Later, Tyconius (d. ca. 400) distinguished the city of the devil from the city of God—as Revelation contrasted Babylon and New Jerusalem. For him, the beast signified the devil's body on earth, and the whore symbolized all people who engage in sinful behavior (Babcock, *Tyconius*, 115–45; Weinrich, *Revelation*, 270). His approach was adopted by Augustine (d. 430), who regarded Babylon as the power of sin that is diffused throughout human society, and he was followed by most Latin interpreters (Primasius; Caesarius; Gregory the Great, *Moral.* 34.15 [26]; Bede; cf. INTRO I.A.3; O'Daly, *Augustine's*, 53–58).

In the east, Oecumenius (early sixth century) identified Babylon with Rome and argued that the heads of the beast that carries the city represented emperors from Nero in the first century to Diocletian in the fourth. He thought the Roman Empire was the context from which the Antichrist would arise in the last days (*In Apocalypsin* 9.8–19). Andreas (d. ca. 614) disagreed, insisting that Babylon corresponded to sinful people everywhere and that it also signified an oppressive empire that would appear at the end of the age (*In Apocalypsin* 18.53–54).

Antipapal interpretations of the Babylon vision emerged during the late Middle Ages when Rome was the center of ecclesiastical authority in the west. As calls for correction of abuses within the church were issued, some interpreters compared the depiction of the whore plying her trade to the church selling its benefices, and they took Babylon's corruption as a warning against unscrupulous prelates. The radical Franciscan Peter Olivi (d. 1298), who was adamant about the virtue of poverty, came close to identifying the wealthy institutional church with Babylon, and a similar connection was made by Dante (d. 1321) in his *Divine Comedy* (*Inferno* XIX.103–17; Burr, *Olivi's*, 47, 93–98).

More moderate views appeared in commentaries that construed Revelation as an outline of church history. Nicholas of Lyra (d. 1349) correlated chapters 1–16 with historical events from the first through the twelfth centuries but refused to speculate on how the vision of Babylon in chapters 17–18 might relate to more recent events or the papacy (INTRO I.B.4; Krey, "Many," 190). Martin Luther (d. 1456), however, reasserted the antipapal interpretation, and his German translation of the NT of 1522 included

Figure 31. The whore of Babylon wearing the papal tiara. Woodcut by Lucas Cranach, printed in Luther's German translation of the New Testament (September 1522).

illustrations of the whore wearing the papal tiara (Figure 31). Luther took the whore as a symbol of the papal empire from beginning to end (LuthW 35:408; 36:11).

The Reformed tradition also identified Babylon with the church under the papacy. In Britain, John Bale (d. 1563) identified the whore's jewelry and opulent clothing with Roman Catholic liturgical garb and the woman's deceptions with hypocrisy and false doctrine (*Image* 2.138–39). The Geneva Bible linked the whore's bloodthirsty tendencies to the violence that Catholics used against some of their critics. In North America, Jonathan Edwards (d. 1758) thought the periods of history outlined in the Apocalypse had progressed from the early apostolic church through the Reformation, which dealt a blow to the papal kingdom (Rev 16:10–11). He believed he was living at the time of the sixth bowl, when the diminishment of papal resources was symbolized by the drying up of the Euphrates (16:12–16). Edwards thought the collapse of papal Babylon, which was next in the sequence (16:17–18:24), might occur in the mid-nineteenth century, though complete victory would take longer (*Apocalyptic*, 13, 45, 381–427).

The radical reformer Thomas Müntzer (d. 1525) considered the whole social and religious hierarchy of the late medieval world to be the kingdom of the Antichrist. He saw Revelation's vision of the violent overthrow of Babylon as a summons for people to take up arms against the established order (INTRO I.C.3; Matheson, *Collected*, 157, 159, 193; McGinn, *Antichrist*, 214). In contrast, Pilgram Marpeck (d. 1556) thought the bloodthirsty whore depicted all who wrongly used violence to defend the gospel, including both Catholics and Lutherans (Klaassen, *Living*, 59). In response to the antipapal interpretations, some Roman Catholics argued that the vision of Babylon pertained to the future, when Rome had fallen away from the papacy, while others identified it with imperial Rome before the support and establishment of the church under Constantine and his successors (INTRO I.C.4).

Protestant groups that adopted a futuristic perspective broadened their use of the Babylon vision to critique both Catholics and other Protestants. After William Miller (d. 1849) predicted that Christ would return in 1843–44, opposition to his views intensified. One of his associates responded with a sermon on the line "Come out of her, my people" from Rev 18:4, urging the faithful to leave, or "come out of," the established churches, which had become Babylon, and to create a separate group of true believers, who expected the imminent return of Christ. This perspective continued among the Seventh-Day Adventists, who developed out of Miller's movement (Andrews, *Three*, chap. 3; cf. O'Leary, *Arguing*, 105–6).

Social reform movements in the nineteenth century focused more on the economic and political aspects of Revelation. Those advocating the abolition of slavery pointed out that the slave trade was characteristic of Babylon (Rev 18:13; Callahan, "Apocalypse," 60). William Lloyd Garrison (d. 1879) belonged to the Come-Outer movement, which was quite different from the followers of Miller noted above. Garrison and others used the admonition to "come out" of Babylon when urging people to separate themselves from institutions that tolerated slavery (Rev 18:4; 2 Cor 6:17). For Garrison, the United States itself was Babylon because its economy was based on human slavery and was doomed to the collapse portrayed in Rev 18 (Garrison, *From*, 492).

Dispensationalists distinguished an ecclesiastical Babylon, consisting of Catholics and some Protestants, from a political and commercial Babylon, which was the beast's empire (Scofield). In 1970 Hal Lindsey claimed that the whore's faithlessness characterized liberal Christian groups and warned that the World Council of Churches and ecumenical movements would create a global religious system that would support the Antichrist (*Late*, 122–34). As tensions between the United States and Iraq intensified in the late twentieth and early twenty-first centuries, some interpreters proposed that commercial Babylon would be rebuilt on the site of the ancient city in Iraq, where it would be tied to the oil industry (LaHaye 260–85).

Historical critics from the nineteenth century onward interpreted the vision of Babylon as a critique of imperial Rome. The significance for readers of later times was to be discerned by looking for analogies in their own contexts (INTRO I.D.3). More recent developments arising from literary and rhetorical studies, as well as the questions raised by feminist critiques of the passage, are discussed in §§35 and 36 COMMENTS.

B. LITERARY STRUCTURE

The Babylon vision plays a major role in the second half of Revelation. At the outset, the heavenly elders announce that the time has come "to destroy those who destroy the earth" (Rev 11:18). Then the author systematically introduces each of these destructive agents, including Satan the dragon (12:1–17); the seven-headed beast from the sea (13:1–10); the beast from the land, or false prophet (13:11–18; 16:13); and finally Babylon the whore (17:1–12). After this, the author traces the downfall of each figure in reverse order:

Satan is thrown from heaven to earth (12:1–17).
    Beast and false prophet conquer (13:1–18).
        Whore rides on the beast (17:1–12).
        Whore destroyed by the beast (17:13–18).
    Beast and false prophet are conquered (19:11–21).
Satan is thrown from earth into the abyss and lake of fire (20:1–3, 7–10).

The vision of the whore is a turning point, since she is the last to be introduced and the first to be overthrown. Structurally, this broad plot movement extends over several smaller vision cycles (11:19–15:4; 15:5–19:10; 19:11–22:5) and integrates each section into the story as a whole.

The seven bowl plagues and description of Babylon constitute the fifth major block of visions in Revelation. The previous cycle depicted conflict with the dragon and beasts, and it culminated in a song of victory beside heaven's glassy sea in 15:2–4. The new section starts with the appearance of seven angels and their movement out of the heavenly temple in 15:1 and 5–8. The conclusion of one block of visions overlaps with the opening scene of the next block. The same technique earlier connected the conclusion of the seal visions (8:1, 3–5) with the beginning of the trumpet series (8:2, 6; Schüssler Fiorenza, *Book*, 172–73; Yarbro Collins, *Combat*, 16–19; Yarbro Collins, *Crisis*, 112–15). By interlocking major sections, the author shows that they are to be taken together as parts of the same story of God's victory over evil. To emphasize the interconnection, the words that the saints use to celebrate God's justice in the climactic vision in 15:3–4 are echoed in 16:5–7 in the plague sequence. The repetition emphasizes that justice for the oppressed means judgment on those who oppress them.

The internal structure of this section modifies the pattern used for other plague sequences. The seal and trumpet visions group scenes into a pattern of 4 + 2 (interlude) + 1. Both series begin when four plagues occur in quick succession (6:1–8; 8:6–13). These are followed by two longer visions (6:9–17; 9:1–21) and an interlude, depicting the redemption and witness of the faithful (7:1–17; 10:1–11:14). Finally, there is a seventh vision of prayer or celebration in heaven (8:1; 11:15–18). The bowl visions expand the initial group to five plagues (16:1–11), which are followed by two longer plague visions (16:12–21) and the extended interlude on Babylon (17:1–18:24). As in the other sequences, a scene of heavenly celebration concludes the series (19:1–10). It is helpful to consider each section in turn.

The Plagues

The seven offering bowls are the third major series of plagues in Revelation (15:5–16:21) after the seven seals (4:1–8:5) and seven trumpets (8:6–11:18). The three plague sequences share some similar elements, such as the specter of war and the darkening of the sky, yet each also has unique features (see §18D; on the plagues and exodus traditions, see §18E). The plagues disclose different perspectives on divine justice. A key element is the way people respond to the plagues and how God then responds to their response. The first six seal visions elicit a question: "Who is able to stand?" (6:17). In response, the movement toward judgment is interrupted while readers are shown the answer: They see those redeemed by the Lamb standing in the presence of God (7:1–17), and the seventh seal brings prayerful silence (8:1). The first six trumpet plagues increase in intensity, but humanity refuses to repent (9:20–21), and judgment is again interrupted so the faithful can bear witness and others can learn to glorify God (10:1–11:14); then the seventh trumpet announces God's kingdom (11:15–18). The bowl plagues bring a still more hostile reaction, for people now curse God (16:9, 11, 21). When God's judgment falls on Babylon in 17:1–18:24, readers can see that the allies of destruction have persistently refused to change their ways, despite opportunities to do so. In this context God's justice means turning one destructive agent against another in order to overthrow these tyrannical powers and liberate those who have suffered under their dominion. The liberating aspect of divine justice is celebrated in 19:1–10.

The Interlude

The largest part of this section is the vision of Babylon (17:1–18:24), which is the counterpart to New Jerusalem (21:1–22:5). The contrast between these two cities is a major aspect of Revelation. The description of each city is introduced by one of the angels with the bowls of plagues, marking a clear literary contrast (17:1; 21:9). Babylon is portrayed as a whore, and New Jerusalem is a bride. Babylon is linked to brutality, materialism, and false worship, and New Jerusalem offers deliverance, blessing, and true worship. The whore intoxicates the nations with immorality, and the bride invites the nations to drink of the water that gives life. These contrasting images urge readers to resist the alluring and yet destructive practices associated with Babylon and to remain committed to the ways of the Lamb, which hold the promise of life in New Jerusalem (§35 COMMENT; Rossing, *Choice*, 161–64; Bauckham, *Theology*, 131–32; Deutsch, "Transformation," 123; Campbell, "Antithetical").

The Conclusion

The victory celebration in 19:1–10 is the climax of this block of visions, as in other cycles (8:1, 3–5; 11:15–18; 15:2–4). Because the visions of Babylon extend for two chapters, interpreters sometimes treat the bowls (15:1, 5–16:21) and Babylon (17:1–19:10) as separate sections (Bauckham, *Climax*, 22; cf. Blount; Giesen; Keener; Mounce; Murphy; Roloff), perhaps with the Babylon visions as an "appendix" to the bowls (Yarbro Collins, *Crisis*, 112). But given the pattern of including an interlude *within* a plague series (cf. 7:1–17; 10:1–11:14) and closing major sections with victory celebrations, it is best to include the Babylon visions within the section that begins with the warning of wrath in 15:1 and concludes with heavenly celebration in 19:1–10 (Schüssler Fiorenza, *Book*, 175; Boxall). Like other climactic scenes, this one looks back to the victory over Babylon that has just been won, while looking ahead to the wedding of the Lamb and the appearance of the bride in scenes to come (COMMENT on 19:1–10).

33. Five Bowls Poured on Earth and the Beast's Throne (15:5–16:11)

15   [5]Then, after these things, I looked and the temple—that is, the tent of witness in heaven—was opened. [6]And the seven angels, who have the seven plagues, came out of the temple. They were clothed in pure bright linen and were wearing gold sashes around their waists. [7]Then one of the four living creatures gave the seven angels seven gold offering bowls full of the anger of God, who lives forever. [8]The temple was filled with smoke from the glory and power of God, and no one could go into the temple until the seven plagues of the last angels were completed.

16   [1]Then I heard a loud voice from the temple say to the seven angels, "Go and pour out the seven offering bowls of the anger of God on the earth." [2]So the first angel went and poured out his offering bowl on the earth, and a nasty and terrible sore appeared on the people who had the mark of the beast and worshiped its image. [3]The second angel poured out his offering bowl on the sea, and it turned into blood, like the blood of a dead person, so that every living thing in the sea died. [4]The third angel poured out his offering bowl on the rivers and the springs of water, and they turned into blood. [5]Then I heard the angel of the waters say,

"You are just, O Holy One, who is and who was,
because you have given these judgments.
[6]Because they poured out the blood of saints and prophets,
you have given them blood to drink. They deserve it!"

[7]And I heard the altar say,

"Yes, Lord God Almighty, your judgments are true and just."

⁸The fourth angel poured out his offering bowl on the sun, and it was allowed to burn people with fire. ⁹The people were burned by intense heat, so that they cursed the name of God, who has power over these plagues. But they did not repent and give him glory. ¹⁰The fifth angel poured out his offering bowl on the throne of the beast, and darkness covered its kingdom. People bit their tongues because of their pain, ¹¹and they cursed the God of heaven because of their pains and their sores; but they did not repent of their works.

NOTES

15:5. *Then, after these things, I looked and the temple—that is, the tent of witness in heaven—was opened.* The writer of Revelation uses the term "temple" (*naos*) for the heavenly sanctuary as a whole (14:15, 17; 15:6, 8; 16:1, 17). He also calls the heavenly sanctuary "the tent of witness," identifying it with the tent sanctuary known from Israel's tradition. The usual Hebrew expression was "tent of meeting" (*'ōhel mô'ēd*), though it was also called the "tent of witness" (*'ōhel hā'ēduth*; Num 17:7 [17:22 MT]), since it housed the ark with the tablets of the law that bore witness to Israel's covenant with God (Exod 30:26, 36). In the LXX, both Hebrew expressions were rendered "tent of witness" (*skēnē tou martyriou*). Moses was said to have received the pattern for the tent while on Mount Sinai (Exod 25:9). According to tradition, he saw an actual heavenly sanctuary, like the one depicted here in Revelation (Wis 9:8; Heb 8:1–6; *2 Bar.* 4:5).

The tent of Moses' time (Exod 25:40) and the Jerusalem temple were said to be modeled after a heavenly pattern (1 Chr 28:19). According to 1 Kgs 8:4, the tabernacle was brought to the temple at the time that the temple was dedicated, helping identify the two earthly sanctuaries. Here, "tent" and "temple" are used for the one *heavenly* sanctuary. Similarly, the term "dwelling" (Hebrew, *mishkān*) could be used for an earthly tent and temple (Exod 26:1; Ps 132:7; 4Q504 1–2 IV, 2–3), as well as for God's heavenly chambers (4Q405 20 II, 21–22 7, 8). The earthly tent was a place where God revealed his glory and issued judgments against his opponents, and the same is true of the celestial tent (Exod 40:34; Num 14:10–12; Rev 15:8).

Jewish tradition sometimes referred to heaven as God's tent (Job 36:29) and temple (Pss 18:6; 29:9). Some writers also pictured a sacred structure within heaven—an outer "house" made of hailstones, whose walls were like stone slabs, and an inner "house" made of fire, where God's throne was located (*1 En.* 14:10–20; Nickelsburg, *1 Enoch*, 259–61). The *Songs of the Sabbath Sacrifice* from Qumran picture a more elaborate seven-part heavenly sanctuary, where angelic worship took place (Newsom, *Songs*, 39–58). Some of the DSS envision the worshiping community itself as a kind of temple, where the faithful shared in the worship offered in the heavenly temple through their prayers to God (Maier, *EDSS* 2:923–24; Davidson, *Angels*, 237–39). Other Jewish texts refer to angelic ministry in heaven without describing the structure of its sanctuary (*T. Levi* 3:4–6; 18:6) or tell of a temple that was created at the dawn of time and is now preserved in paradise (*2 Bar.* 4:1–7).

The writer of Hebrews pictures heaven as the holy of holies, where Christ is seated at God's right hand (Heb 8:1–6), while the forecourt of the tabernacle with its altar, table, and lampstand corresponds to earth and the present age (9:1–10:18). In Revelation the heavenly sanctuary is a single entity, rather than a structure with two parts. It is where God is enthroned (Rev 7:15), and it houses the incense altar and ark of the covenant (6:9; 8:3; 11:19).

In Revelation the earthly counterpart to the heavenly temple is the worshiping community, depicted as a temple under siege (11:1–2). The heavenly temple theme shows God's solidarity with the earthly community in two ways. First, the heavenly temple is the place from which plagues are unleashed against the forces of evil (11:18–19; 15:5–16:21). Second, the faithful are promised a place in God's temple, where they will be pillars and will serve him (3:12; 7:15). In the end, New Jerusalem has features of a sanctuary, though its only "temple" is the presence of God and the Lamb (21:22).

15:6. *And the seven angels, who have the seven plagues, came out of the temple.* Previously, angels emerging from the temple signaled the ingathering of the faithful and the judgment of the ungodly (14:15, 17), but now the angels bring only judgment (NOTE on 15:1). Some interpreters liken them to the six angelic figures—including one dressed in linen and girded—who mete out judgment on those who lack the mark of God in Ezek 9 (Stuckenbruck, *Angel*, 226–28; Giesen). Later, the plague angels interpret visions of Babylon and Jerusalem (Rev 17:1, 7, 15; 19:9; 21:9).

They were clothed in pure bright linen and were wearing gold sashes around their waists. John uses an unusual term, *linon*, for a linen garment (Aeschylus, *Suppl.* 120; P.Oxy. 1281.6), which some copyists apparently altered to the more typical *linoun* ($\mathfrak{P}^{47}$ [א]), as in the linen workers of Thyatira (*linourgoi*, I.Thyat 933.15). Other manuscripts say the angels were clothed with stone (*lithon*; A C), which patristic interpreters thought meant being clothed with Christ, the cornerstone (Gal 3:27; 1 Pet 2:4–8; Oecumenius; Andreas; Bede). Some argue that "stone" is the best reading, since one can wear precious stones (Ezek 28:13; Exod 28:15–21), and yet the idea is odd enough that copyists might have changed it to "linen" (Beale). It is more likely, however, that the unusual word for "linen" is original and that "stone" is a copyist's error (*TCGNT*[2] 680; Aune; Smalley). Elsewhere, the word for fine linen is *byssinos* (Rev 18:12, 16; 19:8, 14).

15:7. *Then one of the four living creatures gave the seven angels seven gold offering bowls full of the anger of God.* Offering bowls (*phialē*) were used in Jewish and Greco-Roman religious rites (see Figure 23; NOTE on 5:8). They were wide and shallow and were sometimes made of gold (1 Chr 28:17; Josephus, *Ant.* 3.150; Pindar, *Pyth.* 4.193). Such bowls could hold incense (Rev 5:8), flour mixed with oil (Num 7:13), or wine (Zech 9:15; Varro, *Ling. lat.* 5.122). The bowl visions extend the wine motif of the previous chapter, in which Babylon the whore made the world drunk on the wine of her immorality until God gave her the wine of wrath and the ungodly were trampled in the winepress (Rev 14:8, 10, 19–20).

who lives forever. God lives forever, in contrast to lifeless idols, and he is capable of fearful judgment (4:9; 9:20; 1 Thess 1:9; Heb 10:31). The beast's followers worship a statue that is magically animated, not the living god (Rev 13:15; 16:2).

15:8. *The temple was filled with smoke from the glory and power of God.* God's glory can overwhelm people; therefore, Israel's high priest shielded himself with a cloud of incense as he came into God's sanctuary (Lev 16:13). Here, however, smoke is generated by God's own glory, as at Sinai and in his heavenly throne room (Exod 19:18; Ps 18:6–8; Isa 6:4). It signals divine wrath (Deut 29:20). Where the smoke from incense permitted access to God, the smoke of glory now precludes access. Earlier, the smoke of incense went up as prayer (Rev 8:4), but here, the smoke comes from the God whose anger will afflict his adversaries.

and no one could go into the temple until the seven plagues of the last angels were completed. When Israel's tabernacle and first temple were dedicated, a cloud of glory filled them so the priests could not minister there (Exod 40:34–35; 1 Kgs 8:10–11; 2 Chr 5:13–14; 7:1–2). Here, God's glory is manifested in smoke. Some interpreters propose that no one could enter because the time for prayer (Lupieri) and intercession (Caird; Mounce; Reddish) had passed or because God's presence for the moment was one of wrathful judgment (Roloff). Nevertheless, preventing the angels from entering the temple for a time does not preclude the possibility of people on earth repenting in the face of the plagues they pour out (Smalley).

16:1. *Then I heard a loud voice from the temple say to the seven angels.* The unidentified voice presumably belongs to God (cf. Rev 16:17). In John's cultural context a voice from an earthly sanctuary might announce divine wrath, call for amending relationships with heaven, and warn of imminent catastrophe (Cicero, *Div.* 1.45.101; Ovid, *Metam.* 15.793; Statius, *Theb.* 7.407; Josephus, *J.W.* 6.299–300; Tacitus, *Hist.* 5.13.1). Here, the voice comes from the heavenly temple, where God calls for justice against his enemies (Ps 11:4–7; Isa 66:6).

"Go and pour out the seven offering bowls of the anger of God on the earth." Divine judgment meant that God would "pour out" wrath on his opponents (Ps 69:24; Jer 7:20; 10:25; Ezek 7:8; Zeph 3:8), and here the angels "pour out" bowls of anger on those who have "poured out" the blood of the saints (Rev 16:2, 6). Divine anger shows outrage at the presence of evil (Boring).

16:2. *So the first angel went and poured out his offering bowl on the earth.* In Israel priests poured out offering bowls within the sanctuary at the base of the altar (Exod 29:12; Lev 4:18, 25). In John's vision the angels move away from the sanctuary and pour the offering bowls onto the earth. Their movements invert Greco-Roman ritual (see COMMENT).

and a nasty and terrible sore appeared. Sores are boils, ulcers, or abscesses that erupt on the skin, fester, and ooze fluids. Painful and irritating, they are linked to uncleanness and fever (Job 2:7; 2 Kgs 20:1–7; Luke 16:21; Thucydides, *Pelop.* 2.49; Plutarch, *Mor.* 281C). God warned that painful sores would afflict the disobedient in Israel (Deut 28:27, 35). Here, they afflict those who bear the mark of the beast rather than the seal of the Lamb, much as a plague of sores before the exodus afflicted the Egyptians but not Israel (Exod 9:8–12; Rev 9:4). In John's cultural context, outbreaks of illness and skin disease were signs of divine wrath that made people seek out the divine will (Livy, *Rom. Hist.* 3.6–7; 4.30.8–9; 5.13.4–5), but in this vision cycle people remain opposed to God (Rev 16:9, 11).

on the people who had the mark of the beast and who worshiped its image. The beast's mark consists of its name and number (NOTES on 13:16–18). It identifies those who belong to the beast, in contrast to those who have been sealed with the name of God and the Lamb (NOTE on 7:3; cf. 14:1). Worshiping the beast means participating in the ruler cult, which in Revelation is a form of evil (13:4, 11–15). The mark, which exempted people from suffering under the authority of the beast, now becomes a sore, which afflicts people under the judgment of God.

16:3. *The second angel poured out his offering bowl on the sea.* Pouring offering bowls into the sea parodies Greco-Roman rites. Before embarking on a ship, someone might pour wine from a gold offering bowl into the sea, asking for the goodwill of Zeus, the help of wind and waves, and favorable weather (Pindar, *Pyth.* 4.193–200; Thucydides, *Pelop.* 6.32.1; Burkert, *Greek*, 71). Here, however, the bowl's contents come *from* God rather than being offered *to* the gods. They disturb the sea rather than quieting it, and they bring death rather than life.

and it turned into blood, like the blood of a dead person, so that every living thing in the sea died. Before the exodus, the Nile River turned to blood and its fish died, as they do here (Exod 7:20–21). John, however, focuses on the sea. The image of the sea turning to blood was a harbinger of bloodshed through civil war (Lucan, *Pharsalia* 1.547–48; Tacitus, *Ann.* 14.32). In Revelation these plagues lead to the conflicts that overthrow Babylon and the beast (Rev 17:1, 16; 19:11–21). The blood is compared to what one would find in a dead body, evoking images of blood that is congealed, thick, and cold (Galen, *Acut.* 15.782; Galen, *Progn.* 155; 177; Thompson). Just as diseased blood spreads contagion, blood like that of a corpse now spreads death (Artemidorus, *Onirocritica* 1.33). The text literally says that every living *psychē*, or soul, in the sea died. This does not refer to human beings (Beale) but to the deaths of creatures "in the sea" (cf. Rev 8:9).

16:4. *The third angel poured out his offering bowl on the rivers and the springs of water, and they turned into blood.* Moses turned the water of the Nile and other rivers in Egypt into blood (Exod 7:14–19; Pss 78:44; 105:29). In the Greco-Roman context a river or spring turning to blood was a sign of divine wrath and impending disaster (Cicero, *Div.* 1.43.98; Livy, *Rom. Hist.* 22.1.10). In response, people were to discern what offense had occurred and make amends with the deity (Julius Obsequens, *Prod.* 25). The beast's followers recognize that the bowl plagues convey God's wrath, but they refuse to repent (Rev 16:11).

16:5. *Then I heard the angel of the waters say.* Like the angel with power over fire in 14:18, this line reflects Jewish traditions that linked angels to elements such as fire, wind, clouds, and thunder (*Jub.* 2:2; *1 En.* 60:11–21; 61:10; 66:2; cf. 1QHᵃ IX, 8–13; 4Q287 2 4). The angel of the waters is different from the one pouring wrath into the waters.

"You are just, O Holy One, who is and who was, because you have given these judgments. On God's justice and holiness, see the NOTES on Rev 15:3–4. The repetition of these qualities emphasizes the fact that God's judgment is not arbitrary but is given to those who deserve it (Neh 9:33; Dan 9:14; *L.A.E.* 27:5; *T. Job* 43:13). God is traditionally known as the one who "is" (cf. Exod 3:14), but Revelation expands this to include all of time, so that God is "the one who is and was and is to come" (NOTE on Rev 1:4; cf. 4:8). Here and in 11:17 the reference to God's future coming is omitted, perhaps because in these visions God has come in judgment. The reason God has given "these judgments" will be explained in 16:6, where bloodshed is mentioned (Osborne).

God's justice has seemed slow in coming, because no action has been taken against those responsible for the martyrs' deaths (Rev 6:9–11). Therefore, the bowl visions emphasize the fact that God will deal justly against the wicked in the end. His justice is eschatological. Because the bowl plagues bring judgment on those who oppress the faithful, some interpreters call the angel's words of praise a judgment doxology (Betz,

"On") or a vindication formula, since they show that God is in the right (Staples, "Rev"; Yarbro Collins, "History"). Yet divine justice can be celebrated in various literary forms, and its character can best be seen in the context of the book (Aune; Jörns, *Das hymnische*, 132–35).

16:6. *"Because they poured out the blood of saints and prophets.* Pouring out blood is an idiom for murder (Gen 9:6; *Sib. Or.* 3:311–12). In this context the slain prophets are probably Christians who bear prophetic witness (Rev 11:10; 18:20; 22:6; Giesen; Mounce), and their violent deaths place them alongside the persecuted prophets of ancient Israel (1 Kgs 19:10; Neh 9:26; *Jub.* 1:12; Matt 23:31, 37 par.; 1 Thess 2:15).

"you have given them blood to drink. Giving bloodied water to those who have shed blood shows symmetry in judgment: "one is punished by the very things by which one sins" (Wis 11:16; cf. 2 Macc 5:10; 13:8; *T. Gad* 5:10; *L.A.B.* 43:5; 44:10; *m. Soṭah* 1:7–9; *t. Soṭah* 3–4; Winston, *Wisdom*, 232–33). In Israel's tradition it was a violation of God's law to consume blood (Lev 17:10–11; *1 En.* 7:5; 98:11). It was said that no one "who eats blood or sheds the blood of a person will remain upon the earth" but will go to the place of judgment (*Jub.* 7:29; cf. 21:18–20). Here, those who commit lawlessness by shedding blood now have their fill of lawlessness by drinking blood. Yet the symmetry does not mean exact retribution, since those who have shed blood do not have their own blood shed in this plague. There is restraint in the justice of God.

"They deserve it." The literal translation is "they are worthy." Previously, the godly were worthy of blessing (Rev 3:4), and God and the Lamb were worthy of praise for their acts of creation and redemption (4:11; 5:9). Here, the opposite is the case: The violent are worthy of divine judgment.

16:7. *And I heard the altar say, "Yes, Lord God Almighty, your judgments are true and just."* The voice does not come from the altar itself (Rowland) or from an angel (Osborne). Rather, John uses metonymy, calling something by the name of something in close relation to it (Lausberg, *Handbook* §565). The voice of the altar is probably the voice of the martyrs who are under the altar (6:9–11), just as a voice from the throne is the voice of someone on or near the throne (16:17; 19:5). The martyrs demanded that God bring judgment against those who shed their blood, and the altar has been linked to judgment against the wicked (6:9–10; 8:3–5; 9:13; 14:18). The response "Yes" (1:7; 14:13; 22:20), like "Amen," affirms that God is now seeing that justice is accomplished, showing that his ways are true and just, as in 15:3 and 19:2.

16:8. *The fourth angel poured out his offering bowl on the sun, and it was allowed to burn people with fire.* Fire from heaven would have been linked to divine wrath in a Greco-Roman context. Whether people were scorched by lightning or saw a ball of fire appear in the heavens, they would know that an offense had been committed against a god and that steps were needed to rectify the relationship (Julius Obsequens, *Prod.* 3; 52; 54). Similarly, if burning heat disrupted an ordinarily temperate climate, one might think that divine wrath was being carried out (Lucan, *Pharsalia* 1.646–47). But people refuse to repent in the face of divine judgment (Rev 16:9). By way of contrast, the faithful are given the promise of life with God, where they will not be struck by the sun or burning heat (7:16; cf. Ps 121:6; Isa 4:6; 49:10).

16:9. *The people were burned by intense heat, so that they cursed the name of God, who has power over these plagues. But they did not repent and give him glory.* Repentance means turning away from sin and false worship and turning toward God to glorify him, which is God's intent (Rev 11:13; 14:7), but these plagues again have the opposite effect (cf. 9:20–21; 16:11; cf. *T. Job* 16:7). Since the traditional penalty for blasphemy was death, it is significant that those who curse God are not killed at this point (Lev 24:16; Job 2:9). There is restraint in divine justice.

16:10. *The fifth angel poured out his offering bowl on the throne of the beast.* This passage uses metonymy (Lausberg, *Handbook* §565), where the word "throne" signifies the beast's power to rule. The presence of Satan's throne at Pergamum was revealed through the death of Antipas (Rev 2:13). Similarly, the throne of the beast refers to the power the beast exercises on Satan's behalf (13:2; Boxall). John's readers would have seen the beast's throne in Roman imperial authority (Blount; Giesen), but the imagery remains evocative and can be broader than that (Murphy; Roloff).

and darkness covered its kingdom. The beast's kingdom was created by its exercise of satanic authority over people of every tribe and nation (13:2, 7). Immersing it in darkness conveys divine wrath (cf. Lam 3:1–2). A plague of darkness fell on the Egyptians before the exodus (Exod 10:21–29). Darkness confined people and limited their movement, bringing terror and despair (Wis 17:1–18:4; Ps 107:10; John 9:4; 11:10). It was associated with the Day of the Lord, when God would defeat his adversaries (Ezek 32:7–9; Joel 2:10; Amos 5:18; 8:9; Zeph 1:15), especially at the end of the age (Note on Rev 6:12; Mark 13:34; *Sib. Or.* 5:349). In Greco-Roman sources the unusual onset of darkness, commonly by an eclipse of the sun or moon, was a sign of divine wrath, warning people of disaster and calling for reconciliation with the gods (Note on Rev 8:12). This is also true in Revelation, though the plague comes from the God of Israel.

People bit their tongues because of their pain. Pain or anguish involves both physical and emotional distress, and it arises from the cumulative experience of darkness and the sores, blood, and heat. Biting the tongue heightens the pain brought about by the plagues. It is analogous to those who gnash their teeth upon feeling the pain of divine judgment (Matt 8:12; 22:13; 25:30).

16:11. *and they cursed the God of heaven because of their pains and their sores; but they did not repent of their works.* Sores brought throbbing, agitated pain (Plutarch, *Mor.* 164F). Here, it afflicts those subject to the judgment of God. By way of contrast, the redeemed have the hope of life in New Jerusalem where there will be no more pain and anguish (Rev 21:4). The pain calls for repentance from certain "works," which in this context include worship of the beast. Referring to "works" in the plural suggests that worship of the beast is connected to other wrongful actions listed in Revelation, such as idolatry, murder, sorcery, fornication, theft, faithlessness, and deception (9:20–21; 21:8; 22:15). Some interpreters argue that the plagues primarily punish the wicked and manifest God's sovereignty by hardening their hearts, much as God hardened Pharaoh's heart before the exodus (Beale). The analogy, however, is more complex, since Pharaoh could both repent and harden his own heart (Exod 8:8, 15; 9:27, 34). A similar dynamic appears in Revelation: Plagues make many people refuse to repent (Rev 9:20–21), but an angel interrupts the movement toward judgment to allow the faithful to bear witness (10:1–11:12), and then many do come to glorify God (11:13). The beast's allies do not repent, but Revelation does not preclude repentance as a possibility (Blount; Harrington; Smalley).

COMMENT

The new cycle of visions continues the cosmic struggle between the Creator and the destroyers of the earth (11:18). Thus far, Satan the dragon has sought dominion over the world, using a beast from the sea and another from the land to extend his authority (13:1–4, 11–12). They work in league with Babylon the whore, whose empire encompasses land and sea (14:8; 17:1–6, 15). Yet the Apocalypse has identified God the Creator as the world's rightful Lord, and his angels now show his power over each sector of creation by pouring their offering bowls on earth and sea, as well as on rivers, springs, and the sun. Their actions encircle the beast's kingdom with a ring of threats, exposing the weakness of its power and the fallacy of taking part in the ruler cult, which treats the beast as sovereign (Blount). Sores afflict the beast's followers, and waves of the sea churn with blood; its allies are given blood to drink, and they suffer fiery heat. Only then does a plague plunge the beast's kingdom into darkness. Yet in the face of God's action, the allies of evil refuse to repent, setting the stage for more plagues to come (16:9, 11).

Structurally, the previous vision cycle concluded with a celebration of victory beside heaven's crystal sea (15:2–4). Yet before the song of triumph was sung, the new cycle of visions was introduced, as John saw seven angels with seven plagues; those seven angels now set about pouring out their plagues on earth (15:1, 5–8). The last scene of the previous cycle and the first scene of the new cycle overlap and interlock, so the themes of victory and judgment go together. The adjoining scenes contrast the triumphant outcome of faithfulness to God with the judgment on earth's destroyers. In one scene the worshipers of God stand victoriously beside the heavenly sea, and in the next sequence the followers of the beast are awash in a sea of blood. The conquerors celebrate God's kingship over the nations, but the plagues engulf the beast's kingdom in darkness. As a result, the faithful praise the name of God, while the followers of the beast curse it. The redeemed sing of God's justice, truth, and holiness because for them these things mean liberation, yet when the words of their song are echoed during the plague sequence, it is clear that justice for the oppressed means judgment on the oppressor (15:3–4; 16:5–7).

Thematically, the question of justice is integral to all three plague sequences. Each angel in this section has an offering bowl (*phialē*), an object first used to offer up the prayers of the saints in the heavenly throne room (5:8). Among the prayers were the martyrs' pleas for justice (6:9–11). Next, the prayers rise again at the heavenly altar (*thysiastērion*) and lead to the trumpet plagues that bring fire onto the earth without moving humanity to repent (8:3–5). Now the theme of the offering bowl returns, as judgments strike the earth, and a voice from the altar where the martyrs cried out now affirms that God has acted justly against those who shed the blood of the faithful.

The symmetrical arrangement of the first five bowl plagues highlights the theme of justice. This section is framed by references to the sores that afflict the worshipers of the beast (16:2, 11). In the middle, at the third bowl vision, divine justice itself is said to be symmetrical. There, an angel declares that those who have shed the blood of the saints and prophets are given blood to drink (16:5–7). The symmetrical form of this section

---

On Rev 15:5–16:11, see de Villiers, "Septet"; Jörns, *Das hymnische*, 132–39; Gallus, "Exodus"; Staples, "Rev"; Yarbro Collins, "History."

fits the symmetry of its view of justice. In the previous vision cycle God's truth and justice were part of the song that was sung by those who had conquered the beast. In their song, God's justice was a positive reason for the nations to worship him (15:2–4). Here, the theme takes a negative turn, as those who perpetrate injustice come under the justice of God (16:5–7).

The bowls repeat aspects of the seal and trumpet visions by revealing divine wrath and warning of the need for repentance, even as they advance the conflict. The bowl plagues now affect the whole world, rather than only a third of it as under the trumpets. The plagues do not take the lives of God's opponents, who remain alive and presumably could still choose to repent, though repentance does not occur. As the scale of the plagues intensifies, so does the intensity of opposition to God. After six seal plagues the world cried out in fear, "Who is able to stand?" (6:17), and after six trumpet plagues the response worsened into a hardened refusal to repent (9:20–21). Now, another step is taken, for people not only refuse to repent, but actively curse God (*blasphēmein*, 16:9, 11, 21). Since the scale of the plagues is cosmic and the response is adamant opposition, this pattern can go no further. With the bowls, "the anger of God is completed" (15:1). Yet readers will find that God's wrath has not yet run its course (Aune). His anger will continue as long as any of earth's destroyers remain active and will cease only after the agents of evil have been trampled in the winepress of his wrath (19:15; Smalley).

Seven Angels from the Heavenly Temple (15:5–8)

Opening the heavenly sanctuary initiates a new series of actions, as in previous cycles (4:1; 8:3–5; 11:19). By starting each vision cycle in the sanctuary, John identifies God as the ultimate source of the action. In the Greco-Roman context, the door of an earthly sanctuary being opened by an unseen power could portend either divine favor (Cicero, *Div.* 1.34.74; Virgil, *Aen.* 3.90–96) or defeat and misfortune (Dio Cassius, *Rom. Hist.* 64.8.1–2; Josephus, *J.W.* 6.293–96; Tacitus, *Hist.* 5.13). The same is true of the heavenly temple. Opening its door is encouraging for those whom God will redeem but ominous for the agents of evil, who will be defeated.

John refers to the celestial sanctuary as "the tent of witness," a name for Israel's sanctuary in the wilderness (NOTE on 15:5). Moses received the pattern for the tent on Mount Sinai, and some sources understood the pattern to be an actual heavenly tent, which was the model for the earthly sanctuary (Exod 25:9; Heb 8:1–5; Wis 9:8). According to the Pentateuch, the tent had an inner chamber that housed the ark of the covenant; a forecourt with a lamp, table, and incense altar; and an outer courtyard with a wash basin and an altar for burnt offering (Exod 25–30). John gives glimpses of God's throne, an altar, and the ark but does not indicate whether the heavenly sanctuary had other furnishings or even more than one chamber (Rev 4:2; 6:9; 8:3; 11:19; 16:17).

Calling the heavenly temple the tent of witness recalls the story of the exodus. The God who brought his people through the sea and sent plagues on those who oppressed them now brings the faithful to heaven's crystal sea, while sending plagues against those who afflict them (15:2–4; 16:1–21). There is a suggestive literary contrast: Readers were told that in his heavenly temple, God would spread his tent over the redeemed, sheltering them from thirst and heat (7:15); but in this plague sequence, the allies of the beast that blasphemes God's tent (13:6) receive blood to drink and suffer under burning heat (16:4–9).

When the heavenly sanctuary opens, seven angels emerge, robed in white linen like the priests (Lev 6:10; 16:4; 1QM VII, 10) and angels (Ezek 9:2–3; Dan 12:6; *Apoc. Zeph.* 6:12), who sometimes were pictured conducting priestly duties in heaven (4Q400 1 3; *T. Levi* 3:5). Gold sashes were worn by angels and the exalted Christ (Dan 10:5; Rev 1:13). The clothing has an aura of holiness. In the visionary world white robes are worn by servants of God, and bright linen adorns the companions of the returning Christ and those performing the righteous deeds (3:4–5; 6:11; 7:13–14; 19:8, 14).

In the cultural contexts of the readers, linen garments were also worn by devotees of Isis and other deities (*Rom. Civ.* 2:188; Plutarch, *Mor.* 352C). Furthermore, processions, such as that performed by the angels coming out of the temple, were a feature of religious life in the cities where John's readers lived. Participants dressed in white might carry offering bowls, baskets, jars, and other objects as they passed through crowds of onlookers to a sanctuary, where sacred action would take place (Apuleius, *Metam.* 11.10; G. Stevenson, *Power*, 297; Burkert, *Greek*, 99–101). The white-robed angels in John's vision do stage a procession, but they reverse the action. They carry bowls of wrath rather than symbols of bounty, and they move away from the sanctuary toward the world where God's adversaries seek dominion.

The angelic procession is met by one of the four living creatures who attend God's throne (Rev 15:7). With faces like a lion, ox, eagle, and human being, they are heavenly representatives of the created order who have called all things to praise God (4:6–8). In a former vision, the four creatures held gold offering bowls full of incense, which bore the prayers of the saints before the Lamb (5:8). Now, a living creature again holds gold offering bowls, but instead of bearing prayers before the Lamb, the bowls bear the wrath that will be poured out on the earth. It is peculiar to have a representative of creation give the angels bowls of wrath to strike the earth, yet the presence of this creature suggests that the goal of divine action is not the destruction of the earth, but the defeat of those who ruin it (11:18).

When the angels receive the bowls, the temple is filled with smoke from the glory of God (15:8). Similar manifestations occurred when God appeared at Mount Sinai (Exod 19:18), when Moses dedicated the tent sanctuary in the wilderness (Exod 40:34–38), when Solomon dedicated the temple (1 Kgs 8:10–11), and when Isaiah was called to prophesy (Isa 6:3–4). Such a display inspires awe and fear. By casting up an impenetrable veil of smoke, God ensures that the angels who are to pour out the plagues upon the earth will not be able to turn back until their task is completed. The smoke of incense that bore prayers for justice before God now becomes the smoke of judgment that comes from God (Rev 8:4; 15:8). The outcome will be smoke rising from a devastated Babylon, which was filled with the blood of the saints (18:9, 18; 19:3).

The Bowl Plagues Begin (16:1–11)

A voice from the temple commands the seven angels to "pour out" the bowls of wrath on the earth (16:1). The command shows the character of God's judgment, since his wrath falls on those who have "poured out" the blood of the saints (16:6). The vision inverts religious customs from John's world; that is, those who have typically poured out libations to the gods of the empire now have God's anger poured out on them.

Greco-Roman worshipers poured wine from a cup or offering bowl onto the earth as prayers for safety and success were offered to Zeus and other gods (Homer, *Il.* 9.162–81; 24.281–98; see Figure 23). Those departing on ships poured wine from an offering bowl into the sea and offered prayers (Pindar, *Pyth.* 4.193–200). In John's vision, the angels pour their offering bowls on earth and sea, but instead of prayers for blessing rising to heaven, the bowls bring divine anger from heaven. According to Greek custom, an offering of wine could be poured out at fellowship meals to signal peace and concord (Homer, *Od.* 3.41–42; Aristophanes, *Pax* 431–38; Burkert, *Greek*, 70–73). But John's vision reverses this as the libations poured from the bowls unleash hostilities against the adversaries of God.

The first five plagues take place in quick succession and are often compared to those that preceded Israel's exodus from Egypt (e.g., Gallus, "Exodus"; Beale; Blount; Boxall; Resseguie; see §18E). The context suggests this connection by mentioning the redeemed singing the song of Moses beside the sea, as Israel did after the exodus, and telling of angelic priests coming from the heavenly tent, the model for the sanctuary Israel used in the wilderness (Rev 15:1–8). The plagues include sores, water turning into blood, darkness, frogs, and hail, all of which have counterparts in the exodus story. Just as the plagues of Moses' time afflicted the Egyptians but not the Israelites, so those in Rev 16 strike the worshipers of the beast. As ten plagues once culminated in the overthrow of Pharaoh's army, the seven final plagues in Revelation lead to the downfall of the beast's kingdom.

Yet the plagues in Rev 16 also differ from those in Egypt at many points: Exodus tells of rivers turning to blood but says nothing about the sea or fiery heat. The main aspects of the last two bowl visions are warfare and earthquake, which are not part of the exodus plagues. To some extent, Rev 16 reshapes the tradition, as the bowls affect earth, water, fire, and air—the four elements that were understood to make up the world (Yarbro Collins, *Cosmology*, 107). The differences between Revelation's plagues and those of the exodus could reflect traditions that warned of various plagues striking the disobedient sevenfold (Lev 26:18, 21, 28; Campbell, "Findings"; Prigent) or traditions that anticipated plagues of fire, pestilence, earthquake, hail, and violence occurring at the end of the age (*Apoc. Ab.* 29:15–30:8; 1QM XI, 7–12; Beale; Smalley).

Significantly, the plague visions convey divine wrath using forms that would have been broadly familiar to John's readers. Outbreaks of infection and skin diseases, waves of blood in the sea, streams and springs flowing with blood, fire from heaven, darkness, earthquakes, and hail were widely thought to be signs of heavenly anger. Many of these signs portended destruction, especially through the kind of warfare depicted in the sixth bowl plague and the fall of Babylon and the beast (Rev 16:12–16; 17:16; 19:11–21). In Roman tradition, such signs called people to amend their relationships with the gods and warned that further disasters would occur if people persisted opposing divine will (Aune 2:416–19). The difference is that the plagues in Revelation signal a need to amend the world's relationship with the God of Israel, not the gods of the empire.

The first angel pours a bowl of wrath on the earth (16:2), which begins a series of plagues in which divine judgment fits the human offense (cf. Wis 11:16; 2 Macc 5:10; 13:8; *T. Gad* 5:10; *L.A.B.* 43:5; 44:10). The contents of the bowl affect those who bear the mark of the beast (Rev 13:16–18), in contrast to those sealed with the name of God and the Lamb (7:3; 14:1). People who received the mark and worshiped the beast expected to escape affliction by the beast's allies, but that mark is now matched by "a nasty and terrible sore," which afflicts people under the judgment of God. Yet there is divine restraint. Those who received the beast's mark seemed to escape the threat of death under the beast, while those who refused the mark were to be killed (13:15). God's plague is not a simple reversal of this practice. Painful though it is, the sore that God inflicts on the followers of the beast is less severe than the death that the beast inflicts upon the followers of the Lamb.

The second angel pours a bowl into the sea, and the waters turn into blood "like the blood of a dead person," and every living thing in the sea perishes (16:3). This goes beyond an earlier plague, when one-third of the sea was affected (8:9). John has depicted the beast rising from the sea to entwine people in a political and economic alliance that spans the seas (13:1). The seaborne commerce of the empire will be vividly presented in a vision in which the merchants who serve the beast transport their goods on the water (18:17–19). On a primary level, the vision of water turning into blood reveals that the beast may use the sea, but God created it, and the sea responds to his will. On a secondary level, the vision anticipates an indictment that falls on Babylon for the bloodshed it used to create its empire of the seas (18:24).

Theologically, this vision seems to create an internal contradiction: God is the Creator of the sea, and the creatures of the sea praise their Maker (5:13; 14:7); but the sea's creatures now perish in the plague of blood brought by God, which seems unjust (cf. 8:9). Nowhere does Revelation resolve this issue. Instead, the book focuses on a different incongruity: God is just and yet continues allowing the unjust to survive. This means that the plague is not yet full punishment. Rather, the vision of the sea turning to blood serves as a warning of a greater judgment to come. Those who have shed the blood of the saints find waves of blood washing up on their shores (6:10; 16:3). The beast left the corpses of the witnesses in the street, and the sea itself assumes the quality of a corpse (11:8–9; 16:3). The vision shows that God has spared the perpetrators of injustice not because he is indifferent, but because he has granted them time to repent—a point that will soon be made explicit (16:9, 11).

The third angel pours a bowl of wrath into the rivers and springs of water, which become as bloody as the sea (16:4). This again goes beyond the earlier trumpet plague, in which only a third of the rivers and springs were made bitter (8:11). It also creates a literary contrast, for God's opponents drink from springs and rivers of blood while the redeemed drink from the spring or river of life (7:17; 21:6). It seems incongruous that the rivers and springs that God created (14:7) now turn to blood. Yet the point is that the creation joins with the Creator in the service of divine justice. As in the exodus tradition, which informs this section, God enlists creation against Israel's foes so that "the elements of the universe—earth, fire, air, and water—carried out the assault" (Philo, *Mos.* 1.96; cf. Wis 5:20; 16:17, 24; 19:6; Josephus, *Ant.* 2.292).

The angel with authority over the water emphasizes the goal of justice by saying, "You are just, O Holy One, who is and who was, / because you have given these judgments" (Rev 16:5). This introduces a hymnic passage that is carefully structured in an A-B-B-A pattern. Its symmetry is an element of order in the middle of the chaos of the plagues. The first two lines declare God's justice and holiness and then give the reason: God has given these judgments (16:5). The reason for questioning God's justice has been his delay in dealing with those who kill the faithful (6:9–11). By not taking action, God has allowed oppression to continue. His justice is manifested when evil is overcome. The angel's words echo 15:3–4, in which the faithful sang of God's justice, inviting all nations to worship him. God's judgments are not against the created order but against the powers that have invaded it. God's justice threatens those allied with evil, yet it also provides incentive for all nations to worship him.

The next two lines include similar elements, but in reverse order: "Because they poured out the blood of the saints and prophets, / you have given them blood to drink. They deserve it!" (16:6). The angel begins with the explanation: Those who are judged have shed the blood of the saints and prophets. The declaration of justice follows: They deserve being given blood to drink. Previous visions showed the beast slaughtering the prophets and persecuting the saints (11:7; 13:6). The theme continues as Babylon the whore sits astride the beast, drunk with the blood of the saints and prophets (17:6; 18:24). Given the thirst for blood that the beast's allies have shown, God's judgment takes the form of giving them bloodied streams from which to drink.

The martyrs previously cried out from the altar, asking how long God would delay in seeing that justice was done (6:9–11), and here their voice speaks again from the altar, affirming that God has acted justly (16:7). Initially, this seems to follow the principle of retribution. There is poetic justice in people who have shed streams of blood being made to drink from blood-filled streams. Yet this is not punishment commensurate with the crime. The principle was that people were to be punished "life for life" (Exod 21:23; cf. Gen 9:6; Isa 49:26). Therefore, one might expect the wicked to be slain as they slew the saints, yet the perpetrators of injustice are not killed but are given blood to drink. There is restraint in the justice of God. The plague allows them to live, so that even here repentance remains a possibility.

The fourth angel pours a bowl onto the sun so that God's adversaries suffer fierce heat (Rev 16:8). Here, Revelation departs from previous patterns in which the sun became dark (6:13; 8:12), for the sun's heat is now intensified. The fire both afflicts the wicked and serves as a warning of their final defeat. God's judgment takes place when evil turns against evil and the beast destroys its own ally, Babylon, with fire (17:16; cf. 18:9, 18). Later, fire from heaven destroys Satan's armies (20:9), and the agents of evil are sent to the lake of fire (14:10; 19:20; 20:10–15). The fiery bowl plague allows the world to taste judgment without experiencing it fully.

In the Greco-Roman context, an intense experience of fiery heat could be taken as a sign of divine wrath, which called people to make amends with the gods (NOTE on 16:8). Here, however, people refuse to repent, as was the case before (9:20–21). More-over, they now take the additional step of blaspheming, or cursing, the name of God (16:9). Previously, the beast blasphemed, or cursed, God (13:6), and here his followers do the same, taking on the character of the sinister figure they serve (Caird).

The fifth angel pours a bowl of wrath on the throne of the beast with the result that the beast's kingdom is engulfed in darkness (16:10). The angels have encircled the beast's kingdom with a ring of threats against earth, sea, rivers, springs, and the sun, and now an angel strikes the center. The beast received its throne from Satan (13:2), and as Satan operates by deception and violence, these traits are also evident in the beast's manner of ruling (12:9, 17; 13:1–18). Its kingdom—displayed in the vision of Babylon—exists where people are brought under its rule by the lure of economic gain or threats of vio-lence (17:1–6; 18:1–24). The opposite of the beast's throne is God's throne, which is the center of a rightly ordered creation; and the opposite of the beast's kingdom is God's kingdom, which exists where the Lamb's self-sacrifice redeems people (4:1–11; 5:9–10; 11:15). God's angel does not destroy the beast's kingdom but immerses it in darkness, showing that superior power belongs to God. The plague shows that God can confine the beast as in the darkness of a prison, limiting its movements. The blackness foreshadows the beast's coming defeat (Ps 107:10–11; Isa 47:5; *Pss. Sol.* 15:10).

The bowl visions reveal the wrath of God and the obstinacy of God's opponents (Rev 16:11; Schüssler Fiorenza). Earlier visions made clear that God wants all nations to fear and glorify him (11:13; 14:7), and the plague sequences were interrupted so that people could be sealed for God and witness could be given (7:1–4; 10:4, 11; 11:1–13). Here again, the allies of the beast refuse to repent. By this point, it is clear that they have not simply been coerced into worshiping the beast in order to avoid affliction (cf. 13:16–17), because here they suffer affliction. They reveal their true loyalties by blaspheming God as the beast did (13:5–6; Bauckham, *Climax*, 31, 308).

34. Bowls Six and Seven: Harmagedon and Earthquake (16:12–21)

16 ¹²Then the sixth angel poured his offering bowl on the great river Euphrates, and its water was dried up, so that the way was made ready for the kings from the east. ¹³And I saw three unclean spirits, like frogs, come from the mouth of the dragon, the mouth of the beast, and the mouth of the false prophet. ¹⁴Now these are demonic spirits that do signs. They go out to the kings of the whole world, in order to gather them for the battle on the great day of God the Almighty. ¹⁵(See, I am coming like a thief! Blessed is the one who stays awake and clothed, so that he does not go around naked and exposed to shame.) ¹⁶And they gathered them at the place that is called in Hebrew, Harmagedon.

¹⁷Then the seventh angel poured his offering bowl into the air, and there was a loud voice from the temple, from the throne, saying, "It is done!" ¹⁸There were flashes of lightning and rumblings and peals of thunder, and a great earthquake occurred, the like of which has not occurred since there have been people on the earth, so great was the earthquake. ¹⁹The great city split into three parts, and the cities of the nations fell. Babylon the great was remembered before God, so that he gave her the wine-cup of his angry wrath. ²⁰Every island fled and the mountains disappeared. ²¹Huge hailstones weighing about a hundred pounds came down from heaven on the people, so that people cursed God for the plague of hail, because the plague was so terrible.

NOTES

16:12. *Then the sixth angel poured his offering bowl on the great river Euphrates.* Offering bowls were ordinarily poured out by those giving prayers to God, but here they bring

God's wrath onto earth (NOTES on 15:7; 16:2). The Euphrates, or "great river," was the idealized boundary of the promised land (Gen 15:18; Deut 1:7; Josh 1:4). The Assyrians and Babylonians who invaded Israel and Judah came from the Euphrates region (2 Kgs 23:29; 24:7). The city of Babylon was located beside the river, and Babylonian forces won victories there (Jer 46:2, 6, 10). After the exile, Jewish communities continued to exist along the Euphrates (*m. Ta'an.* 1:3), although the region beyond it was known for its foreign peoples (1QM II, 11). In the first century CE the Euphrates marked the eastern border of the Roman Empire, beyond which lived the Parthians (Strabo, *Geographica* 16.1.28).

and its water was dried up. Readers would discern God's action in this scene. The drying up of the river recalls how God parted the waters of the Red Sea to allow Moses and Israel to cross (Exod 14:21) and stopped the flow of the Jordan River so that Joshua (Josh 3:14–17), Elijah, and Elisha (2 Kgs 2:8, 14) could cross on dry ground. Later tradition ascribed a similar experience to Ezekiel (*Liv. Pro.* 3:8). When Caesar dried up a river by blocking its flow so that he could capture a city, people thought the action occurred by divine power (Caesar, *Bell. gall.* 8.40–43). In Revelation, the action shows creation responding to the will of its Creator.

so that the way was made ready for the kings from the east. Readers would have envisioned these kings coming from Parthia, which was east of the Euphrates and outside the Roman Empire. Some interpreters assume that this vision—together with that of the horseman in 6:1–2 and the cavalry at the Euphrates in 9:14—plays on persistent Roman fears of a Parthian invasion (Caird; Harrington; Reddish). Nevertheless, this fear may be overstated. The Romans were the ones who invaded Parthia, only to be repulsed in 53 and 36 BCE (Plutarch, *Crass.* 24.5–25.5; Plutarch, *Ant.* 34.3–5). At that time some Romans thought further attempts should be made to conquer Parthia (Virgil, *Aen.* 7.606; Horace, *Carm.* 1.12.53), but Augustus negotiated peace (Augustus, *Res* 29; Vellius Paterculus, *Rom. Hist.* 2.101). During the reign of Gaius Caligula, a Parthian king came peacefully across the Euphrates to show his friendship by paying homage to the Roman standards and the statues of the Caesars (Suetonius, *Gaius* 14.2–3). In Nero's time Rome and Parthia had disputes over borders but reached a settlement, and Nero gained favor with the Parthians by making their king's brother the ruler of Armenia (Tacitus, *Ann.* 15.1–19; Dio Cassius, *Rom. Hist.* 62.22.1–4; 63.5.2). The Parthians offered to assist Vespasian during the Roman civil war, then congratulated him for his victory in Judea and even asked the Romans for military assistance—though their request was refused (Tacitus, *Hist.* 4.51; Josephus, *J. W.* 7.105–6; Suetonius, *Dom.* 2.2; Aune 2:891–94). In the mid- to late first century CE there was little apparent danger of a Parthian invasion.

Revelation's vision of an invasion from the east probably draws on traditions about Nero and not on general uneasiness about the Parthians. Nero apparently committed suicide in 68 CE, but some people thought he remained alive. One form of the story tells of a Nero-like figure deceiving people, persecuting the faithful, and being worshiped by all. This story contributes to Revelation's portrayal of the beast (NOTE on 13:3). A second form of the tradition says that Nero fled to the Parthians but would one day return, crossing "the Euphrates with many myriads" to seize control of the empire through destructive war (*Sib. Or.* 4.119–24, 138–39; 5:361–65). This version seems to inform Revelation's portrayal of the Nero-like beast destroying Babylon/Rome

(Rev 17:16; Müller; Bauckham, *Climax*, 407–52). Some interpreters downplay the connection with the Nero legend because Revelation mentions only a group of eastern kings and not a Nero-like commander (Giesen; Smalley). But later kings do ally themselves with the Nero-like beast and burn the city set on seven hills, which fits the Nero tradition (Rev 17:9–18).

16:13. *And I saw three unclean spirits, like frogs.* Unclean spirits worked by demonic power (16:14; cf. Mark 7:25–26; Luke 4:33). Revelation compares the spirits to frogs, which could be associated with the underworld (Juvenal, *Satirae* 2.150). Ordinary plagues of frogs were repugnant (Exod 8:1–7; Pliny the Elder, *Nat.* 8.104; Aelian, *Nat. an.* 17.41), yet Revelation inverts this perception by showing people being enticed by the froglike spirits. Some interpreters assume that frogs signify impurity, but according to rabbinic tradition, frogs do not convey uncleanness (*m. Toh.* 5:1, 4). Rather, ancient writers compared empty speech and flattery to the meaningless croaking of frogs (Philo, *Somn.* 2.259; Dio Chrysostom, *Or.* 8.36; 66.22). In dreams, frogs signified cheats and beggars (Artemidorus, *Onirocritica* 2.15). Revelation's frog imagery points to the deceptive and hollow quality of what the agents of evil say.

come from the mouth of the dragon, the mouth of the beast, and the mouth of the false prophet. The dragon is an image for Satan (Rev 12:3). The beast from the sea or the abyss exercises Satan's authority in the political and military sphere by dominating the earth and persecuting the followers of Jesus. The traits of the beast mirror those of Roman emperors (13:1–10; cf. 11:7). The false prophet is the beast from the land, who deceived and coerced people into worshiping the ruler. The image parodied the practices of the urban elites who supported the Roman imperial cult (13:11–18).

This is the first time that "false prophet" (*pseudoprophētēs*) has been used for the third member of these three evil agents. In Israel's history prophets were deemed false if they said something would happen and it did not (Deut 18:22; Ezek 13:9–10). A false prophet lured people into false worship (Deut 13:1–5; 18:20; Matt 7:15; Luke 6:26; Acts 13:6; 2 Pet 2:1). At Thyatira, the prophetess Jezebel was considered false because her teachings promoted idolatry (Rev 2:20). By way of contrast, true prophets like those in 11:3–12 call people to worship the true God. True prophecy meant bearing witness to Jesus (19:10).

Revelation's portrayal of these three evil figures has similarities to traditions in other Jewish and Christian writings. First, a common expectation is that the activity of evil will intensify at the end of the age, and some sources give Satan, or Belial, a prominent role in the conflict. The Qumran *War Scroll* envisions Belial, the angel of darkness, enlisting allies for a final assault (1QM I, 5–12). Some sources expect Belial (CD VIII, 2; *Sib. Or.* 2:167; 3:63) or the deceiver (*Did.* 16:4) to come in an especially powerful way, but they also anticipate that he will be defeated (1QM XIV, 8–10; 1QS IV, 18–23; *T. Jud.* 25:3; *T. Levi* 18:12; *T. Dan* 5:10–11).

Second, Daniel pictures a tyrant arising at the end of the age to defy God and persecute the faithful (Dan 7:23–25). Other texts expect the tyrant to spread wickedness and oppress the righteous (*T. Mos.* 8:1–4; *2 Bar.* 36:7–11; *Barn.* 4:1–5). This figure was called the man of lawlessness and the agent of Satan (2 Thess 2:3–9). Like Revelation, some picture the tyrant as a Nero-like figure who will be the embodiment of Belial himself (*Sib. Or.* 3:63; *Mart. Asc. Isa.* 4:1–4).

Third, some scenarios include false prophets. The most common pattern is that multiple false prophets arise at the end of the age to deceive the elect (Matt 24:11; Mark 13:22). In 1 John the false prophets promote the work of the Antichrist in a world controlled by the evil one (1 John 4:1; 5:19). A common feature of that tradition is that the false prophets will perform miracles in order to impress people and lead them into false belief and practice (Matt 24:24; Mark 13:22). Some texts focus on one particular eschatological figure who deceives people through signs (2 Thess 2:9–10; *Did.* 16:4; *Mart. Asc. Isa.* 4:10–11; Peerbolte, *Antecedents*, 211, 342). Revelation combines all three traditions in a distinctive synthesis.

16:14. *Now these are demonic spirits that do signs.* Signs are miraculous deeds that purport to demonstrate divine power. They may be performed by true (Deut 34:11) or false (13:1–5) prophets; therefore, the signs do not guarantee authenticity (Matt 24:24 par.; 2 Thess 2:10). One could ascribe miracles to Satan (Mark 3:22) as well as to the action of God. In Revelation the signs are ascribed to demonic spirits and are presumably carried out through human agents.

They go out to the kings of the whole world, in order to gather them for the battle on the great day of God the Almighty. The kings of the whole world are a larger group than the kings of the east mentioned earlier (Rev 16:12). Their coming recalls the prophetic visions of a great battle, when many nations fight against God and his people before suffering a final defeat (Ezek 38:1–6; Zech 14:2; Joel 3:1–17; *4 Ezra* 13:33–34; 1QM XV, 1; XVI, 1). Although some manuscripts omit the definite article before "battle" ($\mathfrak{P}^{47}$ A 051), the evidence supports it, and it fits a context that recalls the well-known tradition of a specific battle with the nations at the end of the age (§39 COMMENT). It was said that a deceptive spirit from God once lured the idolatrous King Ahab into a battle where he was defeated (1 Kgs 22:19–23). Here, deceptive spirits also lure kings into war, but they come from the agents of evil, not from God. On "Almighty," see the NOTE on 1:8.

16:15. *See, I am coming like a thief!* The speaker is Jesus, and the image of the thief stresses the suddenness of his coming. The metaphor was used in sayings of Jesus and by early Christian writers (NOTE on 3:3; Bauckham, *Climax*, 104–9). Because the saying disrupts the flow of the vision, some interpreters regard it as an insertion from 3:3 (Aune). Most, however, take it as an integral part of the text. It is similar to the asides in 13:9–10 and 14:12–13, which call for faithfulness.

Blessed is the one who stays awake and clothed. This is the third of seven pronouncements of blessing, or beatitudes, in Revelation (Table 2; 1:3; 14:13; 16:15; 19:9; 20:6; 22:7, 14). To be blessed (*makarios*) is to receive favor from God (see INTRO IV.E.2). Rhetorically, a pronouncement of blessing encourages those who are faithful to continue their present course, yet it implicitly calls those who are lax to repent in order that they might receive God's favor. Some interpreters relate the metaphor to the idea that believers are "clothed" with Christ at baptism (Gal 3:27), suggesting that Revelation urges readers to hold on to baptismal grace (Tyconius; Brighton; Giesen), but the metaphor is broader and relates to faithfulness generally. For early Christians, vigilance meant believing that Christ is not dead but alive and that he will return. They are to express this conviction through living lives that are consistent with his message (Mark 13:34–37 par.; 1 Thess 5:6–8; *Did.* 16:1–2; NOTE on Rev 3:2).

so that he does not go around naked and exposed to shame. The passage pictures those who are not vigilant being caught unclothed, as an intruder might come upon a person who had undressed for sleep. Nudity was honorable for Greek athletes and statues of gods and heroes, but in most cases being seen unclothed was considered disgraceful (Gen 9:20–25; *Jub.* 3:30; 4Q166 II, 12–13). The LXX sometimes translated the Hebrew term for nakedness as "shame" (e.g., Isa 20:4; Ezek 16:36, 38). In a physical sense, seeing nakedness, or shame, sometimes meant seeing the genitals (Isa 47:3; Hos 2:10), but here it is a metaphor for those who are lax in faith (Rev 3:17). The context does not suggest that readers are to picture people being forcibly stripped, as Babylon will be stripped in defeat (17:16; cf. Isa 20:4; Ezek 16:37) or as temple guards were stripped as punishment for sleeping on duty (*m. Midd.* 1:2; Mounce). Rather, those who are spiritually complacent put themselves in danger of disgrace, like someone who is undressed and unduly relaxed. The warning draws on the sense that people feel disgrace when they do not measure up in the eyes of those whose opinions they value (Aristotle, *Rhet.* 2.6.23–27). Here, people are warned of the shame that the faithless will feel in the presence of Christ. The prospect of being shamed is designed to make people show greater zeal (Rev 3:18–19).

16:16. *And they gathered them in the place that is called in Hebrew, Harmagedon.* Harmagedon—or its more popular form Armageddon—is spelled in various ways in Greek manuscripts (*TCGNT*² 681). The name probably combines the Hebrew word *har*, meaning hill or mountain, with the name Megiddo, a city in northern Israel, although other derivations have been proposed and will be noted below (J. Paulien, *ABD* 1:394–95; Day, "Origin"). Some manuscripts shorten the name to Mageddon, showing that some copyists understood it to be Megiddo (1611 2053 2062).

Megiddo was located on the Jezreel plain at a strategic point on the route linking Egypt with Syria, and many battles were fought there. For readers of Revelation, the connotations of the name would have come from the Scriptures. Deborah's forces prevailed over Sisera and the Canaanites near Megiddo (Judg 5:19). The city was fortified by Solomon (1 Kgs 9:15), and King Ahaziah and King Josiah were killed nearby (2 Kgs 9:27; 23:29; 2 Chr 35:22). Megiddo is also pictured as a place of grief in Zech 12:11, a passage that describes God's final victory over the nations.

Revelation says the name Harmagedon is drawn from Hebrew. This comment suggests a special connection with Zech 12:11, which is the only place in the MT that Megiddo is spelled with a final *n* as Megiddon. Although extant manuscripts of the Greek OT sometimes include a final *n* in other passages (e.g., Magedōn in Josh 12:21 and 2 Chr 35:22; Mageddōn in 2 Kgs 9:27), the Hebrew form most closely resembling Revelation's usage is in Zech 12:11. The affinity with Zechariah shows that the name of Megiddo anticipates God's final victory over hostile nations.

It is odd to identify Megiddo as a hill or mountain (Hebrew, *har*) because the city was located on a large mound in a broad plain. The OT refers to the waters (Judg 5:19) and the plain or valley (2 Chr 35:22; Zech 12:11) of Megiddo but does not use the name for a mountain. Revelation evidently combines two texts: the name Megiddo from the battle vision in Zech 12, and the mountains from related battle scenes in Ezekiel (Ezek 38:8–21; 39:2, 4, 17). Mountain imagery being drawn from Ezekiel is likely because John later describes the carnage of this battle by using language from Ezek 39:17–20 (Rev 19:17–20). The name of the battle site, like the visions themselves, fuses elements from multiple biblical passages (Day, "Origin"; Beale; Boxall; Osborne).

One alternative proposal links Megiddo to Mount Carmel, which was nearby, since that was where Elijah defeated the prophets of Baal (Lohmeyer; Shea, "Location"). If John knew enough Palestinian geography to make this connection, however, he could not have expected his readers to do so. Another possibility is that the prefix *har-* comes from the Greek inferential particle *ara*, which in its enclitic form is *ar-*, so that the line reads that they gathered "in the place called in Hebrew, therefore, Megiddo" (Callahan, "Language," 482). Still another proposal is that the prefix *har-* derives from the Hebrew word *'ir*, meaning "city" of Megiddo. But this prefix most naturally means mountain, as in Hargarzim (Mount Gerizim) (Eusebius, *Praep. ev.* 9.17.5).

Interpreters who do not link Harmagedon to Megiddo usually try to discern a symbolic meaning by exploring possible meanings of the underlying Hebrew words. Precedent is found in Rev 9:11, in which the author plays on the Hebrew name Abaddon, which means destruction. When trying to determine the meaning of Harmagedon, one possibility is to follow the LXX of Zech 12:11, in which the word Megiddo is translated "cut down," from the Hebrew root *gdd*, "to cut," so that the name Harmagedon could anticipate God's opponents being cut down in battle (Oecumenius; Andreas; LaRondelle, "Biblical"; LaRondelle, "Etymology"; Jauhiainen, "OT"). Another proposal is to construe Har-magedon as *har-mo'ēd*, or "mountain of assembly." This approach suggests that the Hebrew letter *'ayin* (*yʿ*) is equivalent to the Greek gamma (*γ/g*; cf. the Hebrew name 'Amorah as the Greek Gomorra, Gen 19:24). This derivation could emphasize that Harmagedon is where kings assemble for battle (Rev 16:14), or it could allude to Isa 14:12–15, in which the king of Babylon is portrayed in mythological terms as one who attempts to put himself in the place of God on the mountain of assembly, only to be defeated (Boring; Roloff). Other interpreters identify the mountain of assembly with Jerusalem, where Israel assembled for worship and eschatological battles are to occur (Joel 2:30–3:3, 16–17; Zech 14:1–4; Loasby, "'Har-Magedon'").

A very different proposal is that John transcribed Hebrew words in reverse order. If Harmagedon is read backwards, it yields the place names Nod, where Cain was sent because of his sin (Gen 4:16), and Gomorrah, a city known for wickedness (19:24; Oberweis, "Erwägungen"; Giesen). This idea seems unlikely because John gives signals when special interpretation is expected (Rev 13:18; 17:9), and he does not do so here. Given the complexity of this name, some interpreters question whether readers would have found the name meaningful at all (Barr, *Tales*, 116), but the arguments for constructing the name as "mountain of Megiddo" seem plausible (Beale; Müller; Fekkes, *Isaiah*, 202–4).

16:17. *Then the seventh angel poured his offering bowl into the air, and there was a loud voice from the temple, from the throne.* The air is the region between earth and heaven. It is not so much the realm of demonic beings (Eph 2:2) as it is part of God's creation, like the sea, rivers, and heavenly bodies mentioned earlier (Rev 16:3, 4, 8). The voice from the throne belongs to God (19:5; 21:3), who sometimes calls for judgment from his temple (Isa 66:6).

saying, "It is done!" Completion is indicated by the Greek word *gegonen* in the third person singular: "It is done"; yet the completion of these plagues does not mean that God's purposes have been fully realized. The end comes only in the new creation, where Revelation uses the plural *gegonan* to announce that "all is done," because God makes all things new (Rev 21:6). Interpreters sometimes link God's statement "it is done" to Jesus saying "it is finished" on the cross (John 19:30; Beale; Osborne; Smalley), but there is little to suggest such a connection.

16:18. *There were flashes of lightning and rumblings and peals of thunder, and a great earthquake occurred.* These phenomena signal God's coming in power, as at Sinai (Exod 19:16–18; *4 Ezra* 3:18; *L.A.B.* 11:4–5). In the OT the earth shakes when God confronts his enemies (Judg 5:4–5; Mic 1:4; Nah 1:5), rules the nations (Ps 99:1), and judges the wicked (Isa 13:13; Jer 51:29). In later Jewish tradition the plague of hail on Egypt was accompanied by an earthquake, as it is here (Artapanus in Eusebius, *Praep. ev.* 9.27.33). In the Greco-Roman world, earthquakes were considered signs of divine wrath and portents of disaster, especially war (Cicero, *Div.* 1.18.35; 1.43.97; Pliny the Elder, *Nat.* 2.86.200; Ovid, *Metam.* 15.798). This fits the context in Revelation in which God's adversaries gather for a disastrous war (Rev 16:12–16; 19:11–21).

Jewish visionary texts anticipate that a great earthquake will accompany God's final defeat of his adversaries and the establishment of his kingdom (Ezek 38:20; *1 En.* 1:3–9; *T. Mos.* 10:4; *2 Bar.* 32:1). In some apocalyptic passages earthquakes are signs preceding the end of the age (Mark 13:8 par.; *2 Bar.* 27:7; 70:8; *4 Ezra* 9:3; *Apoc. Ab.* 30:6, 8), but in others an earthquake is part of God's judgment against the world, as it is in Rev 16 (cf. *Sib. Or.* 3:675–93; Bauckham, *Climax*, 199–209). According to Heb 12:27 the shaking of the universe will remove what is transient, but in Revelation the shaking is designed to overthrow a force that is hostile to God.

the like of which has not occurred since there have been people on the earth, so great was the earthquake. In the OT, afflictions of unparalleled severity include the plague of hail on Egypt (Exod 9:18, 24; cf. Joel 2:2; Jer 30:7), but Revelation's earthquake is more like the unprecedented disasters that apocalyptic texts envision at the close of the age (Dan 12:1; 1QM I, 12; *T. Mos.* 8:1; Mark 13:19 par.). The earthquake in Rev 16 is greater than those of previous visions (Rev 6:12; 8:5; 11:13, 19). During such an occurrence there was "a great bellowing roar," the "whole earth was upheaved, and buildings leaped into the air" so that "the crash of grinding and breaking timbers" was "most frightful" (Dio Cassius, *Rom. Hist.* 68.24.3–4).

Major earthquakes struck Asia at least six times between 27 BCE and 60 CE, damaging nearly all of the cities addressed by Revelation (J. Murray, "Urban," 145). Cities relied on imperial help after earthquakes, and the emperors who provided it were acclaimed as benefactors. Cities like Sardis and Philadelphia were especially grateful for assistance from Rome (NOTES on Rev 3:1, 7). In Rev 16, however, the earthquake destroys the great city itself, signaling God's judgment on Babylon/Rome (Murray, "Urban," 150–61). The ruling power will not play the role of benefactor, but victim.

16:19. *The great city split into three parts.* There are several approaches to interpreting "the great city" here. A combination of the second and third positions is most plausible; see the COMMENT:

1. Jerusalem. Some interpreters argue that in 11:8 the great city was where Jesus was crucified, and they assume that in 16:19 the great city must be different from Babylon, which is mentioned in the next line. This approach fits the prophetic idea that Jerusalem will be shaken in the end times (Zech 14:4; Oecumenius; Andreas; Ford; Lupieri; Thomas; Jauhiainen, *Use*, 119–21; Ruiz, *Ezekiel*, 265–69).

2. Babylon. Others assume that the great city of Rev 16:19a is Babylon, which is mentioned in 16:19b. This seems plausible, as such an interpretation also fits the wider context, which focuses on the destruction of Babylon (17:18; 18:10–21). From this perspective, the collapse of Babylon fulfills Israel's prophetic writings (Isa 13:19; Jer 50:14–15; 51:25–27) and apocalyptic tradition (*Sib. Or.* 5.438; Aune; Mounce; Prigent; Osborne).

3. The ungodly world as a whole. The "great city" is the whole world, just as Babylon is a realm that goes beyond any one city (Beale; Smalley).

and the cities of the nations fell. The prophetic oracles against the nations picture their rulers and cities being brought down. In addition to Babylon, cities like Damascus and Tyre, along with the towns of Moab, Philistia, Egypt, and other nations, were warned of their coming demise (Isa 13–23; Jer 46–51; Ezek 25–32). Apocalyptic texts included oracles against Babylon and other nations (*Sib. Or.* 3:350–488; 5:111–227, 286–446). Some warned that judgment would come upon the cities of Asia, which would fall through earthquakes and other disasters. Cities like Sardis, Laodicea, Ephesus, and Smyrna were among those doomed to fall (5:289–307). Revelation's vision signals the fulfillment of a longstanding tradition of God's judgment against the cities and nations that perpetrate idolatry and injustice.

Babylon the great was remembered before God, so that he gave her the wine-cup of his angry wrath. On Babylon, see the NOTE on Rev 17:5. People often prayed that God would not ignore injustice but remember it and bring it to an end (Ps 137:7; Neh 13:29). The martyrs asked that God would see that justice prevailed, and God now remembers the injustice and their prayers and takes action against Babylon, the perpetrator (Rev 18:5; cf. Hos 7:2; 8:13; 9:9; Jer 14:10). On the cup of divine wrath, see the NOTE on Rev 14:10.

16:20. *Every island fled and the mountains disappeared.* Previously, the islands and mountains were moved by an earthquake, but here they flee and disappear, a harbinger of an even greater judgment that will occur when earth and heaven flee before God (6:14; 20:11; Beale). Some islands were remote, so God making them flee points to his power over lands everywhere (Sir 47:16). Islands were associated with Gentile nations (Ps 72:10; 1 Macc 11:38). It was said that the Lord would judge their gods and make all the "islands of the nations" bow to him (Zeph 2:11; cf. *Sib. Or.* 5:121). Mountains connote strength and stability (Ps 125:1), and God making them vanish shows his greater power. Bringing down mountains can be a sign of deliverance, since it creates a level way for God's people (Isa 40:4; *Pss. Sol.* 11:4), but here it signals God coming to conquer his adversaries (Ps 97:5), especially at the end of the age (Ezek 38:20; *1 En.* 1:6; *Sib. Or.* 3:680; *T. Mos.* 10:4).

16:21. *Huge hailstones weighing about a hundred pounds came down from heaven on the people.* The hail is reminiscent of the plague before the exodus (Exod 9:24; see §18E), and it was sometimes included among the plagues expected at the end of the age (*Apoc. Ab.* 30:6). Hail was considered a form of divine punishment (Isa 30:30; Cicero, *Nat. d.* 2.5.14). In Rev 11:19 hail was a portent of the divine action that was about to begin, but here and in 8:7 it is part of a plague itself (*Sib. Or.* 3:692). Hailstones weighing one pound are extraordinary (Diodorus Siculus, *Libr.* 19.45.2), but these are one hundred times larger.

so that people cursed God for the plague of hail, because the plague was so terrible. The people's response goes beyond a refusal to repent of sin (9:20–21). Here, it includes blasphemy (*blasphēmein*), which in this context means that they cursed God (16:9, 11).

COMMENT

A voice from the heavenly temple (*naos*) has commissioned seven angels to pour out bowls of divine wrath. With each bowl, plagues have struck the sea, rivers, and sun, as well as the followers and kingdom of the beast (15:5–16:11). Now the angels pour out the remaining bowls, bringing the plagues to their conclusion. At the sixth bowl, the agents of evil send out demonic spirits to lure earth's kings to Harmagedon, anticipating the battle on the great day of God (16:12–16). Then at the seventh bowl, an earthquake strikes the great city of Babylon and huge hailstones fall on the earth (16:13–21). Readers have been warned that God will make Babylon drink the wine of his wrath (14:8), and when the city splits into three parts, it would seem that God's will has been accomplished. Therefore, the visions come full circle when a voice from the temple (*naos*) speaks again declaring, "It is done!" (16:17).

The first five bowl plagues have been described in quick succession, like the first four plagues in the seal and trumpet series (6:1–8; 8:6–13). Now the sixth and seventh bowl visions are narrated at greater length, like the fifth and sixth seal and trumpet visions (6:9–17; 9:1–21). The effect is to stretch out the action and to build intensity as the section approaches its culmination. Previously, the author placed an interlude *before* the seventh vision in the cycle, heightening the sense of delay in the coming of judgment (7:1–17; 10:1–11:14). In those series, the seventh vision was the climax, featuring prayer and celebration in heaven (8:1; 11:15–18). The bowl visions alter the pattern by placing the interlude concerning Babylon *after* the seventh plague (17:1–18:24), so the final scene of heavenly celebration is not numbered (19:1–10).

Altering the placement of the interlude affects the way each plague sequence functions in the book. In the seal and trumpet series, divine judgment seemed to unfold in an inexorable way until the interludes interrupted the progression before the end arrived, showing that God's final judgment was delayed so that people could be redeemed (7:1–17) and prophetic witness could be given to the world (10:1–11:14). The bowl plagues, however, show that God's justice will not delay forever. In this sequence all seven judgments are carried out without a pause against the unrepentant perpetrators of injustice. Accordingly, the interlude does not interrupt the movement toward justice; rather, it discloses more fully the reasons that God must finally free the world from the powers that oppress it.

The Sixth Bowl and Harmagedon (16:12–16)

The sixth angel pours out his offering bowl, prompting readers to expect a plague like those that have struck the beast and its allies in previous verses (16:12). Yet what occurs

On Rev 16:12–21, see Bauckham, *Climax*, 92–117, 199–209; Campbell, "Findings"; Day, "Origin"; Jauhiainen, "OT"; LaRondelle, "Etymology" and "Biblical"; Loasby, "Har-Magedon"; Murray, "Urban"; Oberweis, "Erwägungen"; Ruiz, *Ezekiel*, 258–91; Shea, "Location"; Steinmann, "Tripartite."

is that the Euphrates River dries up, which is a variation on the familiar theme of God's care for his people. The Red Sea parted so that Israel could cross on dry ground while Pharaoh's army was destroyed (Exod 14:21). The Jordan River dried up so that Joshua and Israel could conquer the promised land (Josh 3:17) and Elijah and Elisha could carry out their prophetic work (2 Kgs 2:8, 14). It was said that God would one day part the Euphrates to make a highway from Assyria to the promised land so that Israel's exiles could return (Isa 11:15–16; Zech 10:10–11; *4 Ezra* 13:43–47). What is surprising is that the Euphrates does not dry up to make a way for Israel but to allow kings from the east to invade.

The meaning of this invasion is disputed. One approach is to assume that the kings are coming to overthrow Babylon, the ruling power. If this is so, then these kings from the east must be different from the kings of the whole earth, who are mentioned later and are said to oppose God (Rev 16:14; Mounce; Roloff). From a literary perspective, it would make sense for the eastern kings to threaten Babylon, since the other plagues afflict the beast, Babylon, and their allies (16:2, 6, 10, 19). Moreover, the forces unleashed at the Euphrates in a previous vision attacked the ungodly (9:13–21), and the same might be true here. Cyrus, the Persian king from the east, once diverted the Euphrates so that his army could cross and conquer Babylon, and the eastern kings in John's vision might do the same (Herodotus, *Historiae* 1.190–91; Beale). Prophetic texts said that the nations would assemble against Babylon and that God would dry up its waters (Isa 13:4; Jer 50:38; 51:27–28). Revelation might envision something similar (Reddish; Jauhiainen, *Use*, 115).

From this perspective, the invasion of the eastern kings foreshadows the destruction of Babylon in Rev 17–18. It is also analogous to the Nero legends, which inform Revelation's portrayal of the beast and its allies. In previous chapters Revelation said that the beast had died and come to life. This recalls what was said about Nero, who had reportedly died and yet was said to be alive and hiding among the Parthians beyond the Euphrates, which was the eastern boundary of Rome's empire (NOTES on 13:3 and 16:12). Some people expected Nero to return, crossing the Euphrates with myriads of troops to wage destructive war and reclaim the throne of Rome (*Sib. Or.* 4.119–24, 138–39; 5:361–65). In light of this tradition, John's vision of the kings crossing the Euphrates suggests that they fit the pattern of Nero by coming to destroy Babylon/Rome, which is what the kings allied with the beast do in Rev 17:12–18 (Morris; Schüssler Fiorenza; Bauckham, *Climax*, 438–39).

An alternative is to see the kings coming to attack God and his people. This reading assumes that the eastern kings in 16:12 are allied with the kings of the whole world, who are God's adversaries in 16:14. All the kings cross the Euphrates to assemble at Harmagedon, preparing for the battle that results in their defeat in 19:11–21. As opponents of God and his people, the eastern kings are like the rulers of Assyria and Babylonia, who conquered Israel and Judah. Their coming fulfills the prophetic expectation that many nations will fight against Israel and Jerusalem in the end times (Ezek 38–39; Joel 3; Zech 12; 14; Brighton; Osborne; Thomas). In *1 En.* 56:5–8 angels stir up the Parthians and Medes in the east so that their armies come against Jerusalem, but the invading powers meet resistance, turn against each other, and bring about their own defeat.

The most viable approach is to combine the two lines of interpretation. On the main level of the vision the kings are opponents of God and his people. The angel dries up the Euphrates so the kings of the east can cross and join the kings in hostile action against God. Initially, it seems that allowing the kings to advance will give an advantage to God's enemies, but this actually serves God's purposes, since the kings gather to meet their final defeat by Christ in the battle in Rev 19:11–21. On a secondary level, however, Revelation does picture some of the kings turning against Babylon. They join the Nero-like beast that sets the city on fire (17:12–17). In different ways the overthrow of Babylon by its allies and the defeat of God's adversaries by Christ contribute to God's victory (Murphy).

Thus far, God's angels have carried out the plagues, but God's adversaries now take action by emitting unclean spirits from their mouths (16:13). Just as God sends seven spirits into the world in order to survey what is happening (5:6), Satan and his allies send out unclean spirits to bring people under the sway of evil. Those who belong to God are made clean by the blood of the Lamb (7:14; 22:14), but these spirits are unclean and bring people into the camp of the beast and Babylon, which defiles the world with idolatry, violence, and greed (17:4). The spirits are like frogs, which some interpreters compare to the plague of frogs that afflicted Egypt before the exodus (Exod 8:1–6; see §18E). Unlike the plague in Egypt, however, these froglike spirits come from Satan and his allies rather than from God. Their action might be more like that of Pharaoh's magicians, who called forth frogs in order to *mimic* God's power (8:7; Tyconius).

The imagery suggests that what the evil alliance says is as meaningless as the croaking of frogs (Lucian, *Merc. cond.* 28.4). The conflict between God and evil is a struggle between truth and falsehood. The dragon threatened the woman who represented God's people by pouring forth a destructive river from its mouth (Rev 12:15). The beast issued blasphemies from its mouth (13:5–6), and the words of the false prophet drew people into idolatry (13:11–18). Now the unclean spirits from the mouths of the dragon, beast, and false prophet lure kings into an alliance against God. By way of contrast, fire comes from the mouths of true prophets (11:5), and a sword comes from Christ's mouth (1:16; 19:15, 21). These images point to the superior power of the truth they bring.

The spirits do miraculous signs in order to gather the kings of the earth for battle (16:14). Signs purport to show divine authorization for the message of the miracle-worker. The beast from the land, or false prophet, called down fire from heaven and animated a statue in order to lure people into worshiping the beast. Such miracles had the quality of sorcery, which showed the false prophet's alliance with evil (NOTES and COMMENT on 13:13–14). Now the circle broadens as other agents perform deceptive wonders. People need discernment to tell which signs reveal the will of God. The traditional criterion is whether a sign draws people to God or sets them against God (Deut 13:1–3). When the demonic spirits use signs to lure the kings into battle, they promote rebellion against God and Christ, the true ruler of earth's kings (Rev 1:5; 17:14; 19:16). The kings may find a surrogate form of power in Babylon (17:2; 18:3), but God is Almighty (16:7, 14), which means the outcome of the battle is not in doubt. The battle will occur on "the great day of God" (16:14), recalling the expression "Day of the Lord," which sometimes refers to a future conflict when God will defeat those who oppose him (Isa 13:6, 9; Jer 46:10; Ezek 30:3; Zeph 1:14). Here, it portends defeat for God's enemies.

Against this backdrop of deception, Christ calls readers to be vigilant: "See, I am coming like a thief!" (Rev 16:15). The way these words intrude into the vision is as sudden and unexpected as Christ's coming will be. They warn that people must constantly be ready to avoid being caught unawares. The saying also startles readers by comparing Christ to a thief, an image with negative connotations (Matt 6:19; John 10:1). The readers are like vulnerable homeowners, who might suffer an unwanted intruder (Luke 12:39–40). The point is that no one knows when Christ will come, but the negative image also presses readers to ask why Christ presents himself as a thief instead of as a guest politely knocking at the door as in Rev 3:20 (Jack, *Texts*, 199). Previously, Christ was compared to a thief in order to startle self-satisfied Christians at Sardis and rob them of their complacency (3:3). Extending the saying to all readers is designed to have a similar effect (Resseguie 188).

This verse defines vigilance as remaining clothed or, literally, keeping one's garments (16:15). The point is like that of the parable about servants waiting for their master to return. They are to keep their garments wrapped around their waists so that they are ready for action (Luke 12:35–38), unlike those who become drowsy and undress for bed (Song 5:3; Neh 4:23; Bauckham, *Climax*, 105). The imagery is evocative and suggests multiple dimensions of meaning. On one level people keep their garments by believing and living the Christian faith (3:3). On another level white clothing connotes honor and everlasting life, so keeping one's garment also means holding on to the promise of salvation (3:5; 6:11; 7:9).

Finally, Christ warns that people will not want to go about naked so that others see their shame (16:15). The idea is that those roused from sleep will be indecently clad. Readers at Laodicea are said to be naked because of their complacency (3:17), and the implication is that to be found faithless in the presence of Christ would be as disgraceful as being seen unclothed in public; therefore, readers are to repent (3:18–19; Beale; Smalley). Rhetorically, the threat of shame was emotionally powerful (INTRO V.A.2). It would make readers distance themselves from what the nakedness represented. Like other asides in Revelation, the warning is intended to move readers to greater endurance and faithfulness (13:9–10; 14:12–13).

The theme of conflict resumes as hostile forces gather at a place called Harmagedon (16:16). John says that the name is a Hebrew term, and it seems to be based on the Hebrew word *har*, or mountain, along with the name Megiddo, a place in northern Israel. The author regularly uses biblical names because of their symbolic value. For example, he gives the names Balaam and Jezebel to his opponents in order to identify them with false teachers known from Scripture (2:14, 20). Later, the Hebrew name Abaddon discloses that the angel from the underworld has the character of "destruction" (9:11). The author calls the place that Jesus was crucified Sodom and Egypt to associate it with sin and oppression (11:8). Finally, he uses the name Babylon (14:8; 16:19) for a world power that includes Rome, the city set on seven hills (17:9). Given John's regular use of biblical names in a symbolic sense, the name Harmagedon is best taken symbolically as well.

The word "Harmagedon" is related to the place name Megiddo, which appears in Zechariah's account of God's final victory over the nations. The author paraphrases a portion of Zech 12 in the first chapter, warning that the tribes will grieve when they look on the one whom they have pierced (Zech 12:10, 12; Rev 1:7). The next verse of Zechariah speaks of mourning "as great as the mourning of Hadad-rimmon in the plain of Megiddo" (Zech 12:11). Revelation draws on this verse when using a form of "Megiddo" for the defeat of God's adversaries. It is not clear how the author of

Revelation understood the obscure reference to Hadad-rimmon in Zech 12:11a. The LXX took it to be a pomegranate orchard; the Targum construes it as the name of the Aramean who killed King Ahab (cf. 1 Kgs 15:18; 22:34; *b. Meg.* 3a; *b. Mo'ed Qaṭ.* 28b); and others consider it the name of a place or a pagan deity (Meyers and Meyers, *Zechariah*, 343). What is clear is that Megiddo sets the tone for grieving on the Day of the Lord. The prefix *har-*, which means mountain, recalls that in similar visions God is shown defeating his enemies on the mountains of Israel (Ezek 38:8–21; 39:2, 4, 17; NOTE on Rev 16:16).

The value of the name Harmagedon is that it portends defeat for those opposing God. Primary connotations come from the connection between Megiddo and grief in Zech 12:11, since the nations that gather at Harmagedon will come to grief when Christ defeats them in Rev 19:11–21. Secondary associations come from other battle stories. In Judg 5:19 Megiddo is associated with Deborah's victory over Israel's foes. God sent rain from heaven so that the Canaanite chariots bogged down in the mud and their army was defeated. Later, King Ahaziah, one of the allies of the idolatrous house of Ahab and Jezebel, met his death at Megiddo (2 Kgs 9:27). And King Josiah of Judah was killed near Megiddo because he refused to obey the word of the Lord (2 Chr 35:22). Taken together, these associations suggest that the name Harmagedon foreshadows the coming destruction of those who refuse to heed God.

The Seventh Bowl Shakes the World (16:17–21)

Hostile forces gather, but before a battle takes place, the seventh angel pours an offering bowl into the air (Rev 16:17). Along with the earth, water, and fire that were affected by the previous plagues, air is one of the four elements of the universe. By pouring bowls on each element, the angels show God's power over the whole created order (Yarbro Collins, *Cosmology*, 107). The goal is not the destruction of the earth, but the overthrowing of those who would ruin it (11:18). A voice comes from the throne of God, which is the center of true power, as opposed to the throne of the beast (16:10). God's voice from the celestial temple initially told angels to pour out their bowls, and now God speaks again, saying, "It is done!," indicating that the plagues have reached their culmination (16:1, 17). Yet God's wrath does not end here; it continues until evil has been completely overthrown (19:15). Only when the forces that threaten life are gone and all things are made new in the New Jerusalem will God say with absolute finality, "All is done!" (21:6). Creation rather than destruction is the goal.

Creation fights on the side of the Creator as God hems in his foes with lightning and thunder above and tremors on the earth below (16:18). Some earthquakes simply warn that God's wrath will come in the scenes that follow (8:5; 11:19). Others actually bring God's wrath upon the world. At the sixth seal an earthquake moved mountains and islands, terrifying people into asking who can stand (6:12–17). Before the seventh trumpet, an earthquake destroyed a tenth of a city, killing seven thousand and moving the rest to fear and glorify God (11:13). The final earthquake is more severe. Mountains and islands not only move, but disappear, and destruction is not limited to a tenth of a city but affects the "great city" and the cities of the nations (16:18).

The "great city" is a comprehensive image for the world in opposition to God (16:19a). In the vision of the beast and two witnesses, the great city encompassed the peoples of the world, combining traits of Babylon, Rome, Jerusalem, Sodom, and Egypt

(NOTE on 11:8). Later, the great city is identified with Babylon, which dominates the whole world and has characteristics of many cities, including Rome, Tyre, and Nineveh. The earthquake splits the city into three parts, so that it no longer has the aura of invincibility. Also affected are the nations that follow the beast and Babylon (13:7; 14:8). The collapse of their cities shows their vulnerability, and readers find that the only city that cannot be shaken is the New Jerusalem (3:12; 21:2). Hope for the nations lies in God's city, not their own (21:24).

God gives Babylon the wine cup of his wrath (16:19b). Babylon made all nations drink the wine of its immoral passion, which is the intoxicating power of idolatry, opulence, and violence (14:8). Babylon personifies the powers that have shed the blood of the prophets, saints, and witnesses to Jesus (17:6; 18:24). The martyrs have asked how long God will let injustice continue, and bowls filled with prayers have risen before his throne (5:8; 6:9–11; 8:3–4). Here, the contents of a bowl bring a response from God, who remembers the unjust acts that have been committed (18:5). There is symmetry in God's judgment, for he gives the wine of passionate wrath to the city that made others drunk with the wine of its passionate immorality (14:8, 10; 16:4). The symmetry is completed in the next chapter, where God directs evil to become evil's undoing so that Babylon is destroyed by its own allies (17:16).

The disappearance of islands and mountains, together with the great plague of hail, shows God working with the creation against his adversaries (16:20–21; cf. Wis 5:20–22). God used hail as a weapon in previous battles, and in some scenarios it was expected to fall on his foes in the future (Josh 10:11; Ezek 38:22; *Sib. Or.* 3:692). The one-hundred-pound hailstones in this plague are the size of stones hurled from a catapult (Josephus, *J.W.* 5.270). Hailstorms manifest God's power (Pss 78:47; 105:32) and carry out his vengeance (Wis 16:16; Sir 39:29), so one might understand the hail to be God's way of punishing the ungodly. Yet rather than describing the magnitude of the damage to crops, homes, or livestock (Exod 9:25) or telling of the number of people killed, the passage focuses on how people respond.

People curse God for the third time in this chapter (Rev 16:9, 11, 21). Some interpreters take this to mean that God has now ruled out opportunities for repentance, allowing his wrath to take its course (Beale). Nevertheless, the proper response to hail is that the ungodly should repent. During the unprecedented plague of hail before the exodus, Pharaoh confessed that he had sinned (Exod 9:22–35; Andreas), and other hailstorms were designed to make Israel turn to God (Hag 2:17). Similarly, the proper response to earthquakes has been to ask, "Who is able to stand?" (Rev 6:17) and to fear and glorify God (11:13). If people in this vision refuse to repent, it is not because God has prevented it but because they are firmly allied with God's opponents (Smalley). The same was true throughout 16:1–11. The severity of the plague makes clear that they have not simply been coerced into worshiping the beast in order to avoid affliction (13:16–17), because here they suffer affliction, yet refuse to honor God. They reveal their true loyalties by blaspheming God, as the beast did (13:5–6).

35. Interlude: Babylon the Whore (17:1–18)

17 ¹Then one of the seven angels who had the seven offering bowls came and said to me, "Come, I will show you the judgment on the great whore who is

seated on many waters. ²The kings of the earth have committed immorality with her, and those who dwell on the earth have become drunk from the wine of her immorality." ³Then he brought me in the Spirit to a desert. There I saw a woman seated on a scarlet beast that was full of blasphemous names. It had seven heads and ten horns. ⁴The woman was clothed in purple and scarlet and glittered with gold and jewels and pearls. In her hand she held a golden cup full of vile things and the impurities of her immorality. ⁵On her forehead was written a name, a mystery: "Babylon the great, the mother of whores and of the vile things of earth." ⁶I saw that the woman was drunk on the blood of the saints and the blood of the witnesses to Jesus. And I was completely amazed when I saw her.

⁷Then the angel said to me, "Why are you amazed? I will tell you the mystery of the woman and the beast that carries her, the one with seven heads and ten horns. ⁸The beast that you saw was and is not, and is about to come up from the abyss and go to destruction. Those who dwell on the earth, whose names have not been written in the scroll of life from the time the earth was made, will be amazed when they see the beast, because it was and is not and is to come. ⁹This calls for an understanding mind. The seven heads are seven mountains on which the woman is seated. They are also seven kings. ¹⁰Five have fallen, one is, and the other has not yet come. When he comes he must remain for only a little while. ¹¹As for the beast that was and is not, it is an eighth that belongs to the seven, and it is going to destruction. ¹²The ten horns that you saw are ten kings, who have not yet received royal power, but they will receive authority as kings for an hour, along with the beast. ¹³The kings are of one mind, and they give their power and authority to the beast. ¹⁴They will make war on the Lamb, but the Lamb will conquer them, for he is Lord of lords and King of kings, and those with him are called and chosen and faithful."

¹⁵Then he said to me, "The waters that you saw, where the whore is seated, are peoples and multitudes and nations and languages. ¹⁶As for the ten horns that you saw, they and the beast will hate the whore and will make her desolate and naked. They will eat her flesh and burn her up with fire. ¹⁷For God put into their hearts to do what is on his mind. That is why they will be of one mind and give their royal power to the beast, until the words of God have been completed. ¹⁸And the woman that you saw is the great city that has royal power over the kings of the earth."

NOTES

17:1. *Then one of the seven angels who had the seven offering bowls came and said to me.* The seven angels came from the heavenly temple and poured bowls of wrath on the earth in Rev 15–16. Noting that one of them now continues the revelation means that the vision of Babylon's fall is an extension of the bowl judgments. One of these angels will also show John the vision of New Jerusalem in 21:9, thereby establishing a contrast between Babylon the whore and Jerusalem the bride.

"Come, I will show you the judgment on the great whore. The term *pornē* can be used in a general way for a promiscuous woman or more specifically for a prostitute who provides sexual favors for money. The difference was not always clear since a woman might first receive gifts from her lovers and later expect payment for services (Seneca the Younger, *Ben.* 6.32.1).

Socially, not all prostitutes were alike. The most elite was the courtesan, or companion (*hetaira*) of a nobleman. She advanced her fortunes by sexually attracting men of wealth, and in return she often received jewelry and luxurious clothing. Wealth and social connections allowed her to engage in a sumptuous lifestyle (Petronius, *Satyricon* 126). Below the courtesans were the women and girls in ordinary brothels. Many of these were foreigners, captives, abandoned children, and girls from destitute families. Most turned to prostitution because they had no other means of support (Lucian, *Dial. meretr.* 6.1–2). Brothel owners provided food and clothing, but they were usually abusive, and conditions in brothels were foul. The trade went on "in dirty booths which are flaunted before the eyes in every part of the city, at the doors of the houses of magistrates and in the market-places, near government buildings and temples" (Dio Chrysostom, *Or.* 7.133–34; cf. Plautus, *Pseud.* 181; Horace, *Sat.* 1.2.31; Juvenal, *Satirae* 6.120–22). Taverns and inns sometimes had rooms called *cellae meretriciae* set aside for commercial sex. Some prostitutes worked alone and others with a pimp, finding clients along streets and roadways and using abandoned tombs for liaisons (Martial, *Epigrams* 1.34; Athenaeus, *Deipnosophistae* 570d). At the bottom of the scale were the slaves purchased by brothel owners or forced into prostitution by their masters. During the Roman period a large proportion of prostitutes seem to have been slaves (Demosthenes, *Orations* 59.18–19; Justinian, *Dig.* 37.14.7; Seneca the Elder, *Controversiae* 1.2; W. A. Krenkel, *CAM* 2:1291–97; Glancy and Moore, "How," 555–60).

The woman in John's vision has traits of both high-class and low-class prostitution. Her elegant clothing, gold, and jewels are appropriate for a courtesan; her clients include kings, and she rules like a queen (Rev 17:2; 18:7). Yet the woman is called a whore (*pornē*) rather than a courtesan (*hetaira*), and her drunken behavior is better suited to a street-side tavern than a nobleman's banquet room. A courtesan might be kept by one aristocrat for his pleasure, but the woman in Rev 17 serves a multitude of clients, like a low-class prostitute. Despite her conspicuous wealth, Revelation calls her a degraded "whore" (Glancy and Moore, "How," 560–62).

Revelation uses the image of prostitution to indict the city that rules the world. Feminine images for cities or nations were common (L. Huber, *Like*, 91–95). Biblically, Jerusalem (Isa 1:21) and the people of Israel (Jer 3:6–10; Ezek 16:15–22; 23:1–49; Hos 4:12–13; 5:3) were called prostitutes because their worship of various deities was considered religious promiscuity. It violated the covenant relationship with God, which was comparable to a marriage (Hos 2:5; Jer 2:20; 3:1–14; Ezek 16:36). In Revelation, however, the whore is linked to Babylon rather than Jerusalem, and she resembles Nineveh and Tyre, which were called prostitutes because of their political and commercial networks (Isa 23:16–17; Nah 3:4). All of these connotations are also combined with traits of Rome, the city that exerted political and economic dominion over the world in the first century CE.

Additional associations come from the use of feminine images to personify vice. It was common to picture vice as a seductive woman in garish attire and virtue as a woman in modest clothing. The standard legend told of Herakles meeting these two figures and rightly rejecting the seductive woman, which made him a good moral example (Xenophon, *Mem.* 2.1.21–22; Philostratus, *Vit. soph.* 482–84; Maximus of Tyre, *Orations* 14.1). Similarly, tyranny was depicted as a woman wearing purple and scarlet to cloak her oppressive practices. People were warned not to be fooled by appearances (Philostratus, *Vit. Apoll.* 6.10.5; Philo, *Sacr.* 21; Silius Italicus, *Punica* 15.25; Dio Chrysostom, *Or.* 1.81; Rossing, *Choice*, 78). Jewish sources personified wisdom as a virtuous woman (Prov 9:1–5; cf. 4Q185) and warned against the prostitute who draws one into vice (Prov 7:10–18; 4Q185; Philo, *Sacr.* 20–26). The contrast was a vivid way to shape values in antiquity (Rossing, *Choice*, 17–59; Yarbro Collins, "Portraits," 287–95).

"who is seated on many waters. An ordinary prostitute might sit in public places looking for clients (Rev 17:1b; Gen 38:14; Martial, *Epigrams* 6.66), but the great whore sits on or beside many waters. In one sense the preposition *epi* might mean that she sits "beside" the water, as Babylon was situated beside the Euphrates River and its network of canals. Judean exiles sat beside Babylon's waters and wept (Ps 137:1; Jer 51:13; Herodotus, *Historiae* 1.178, 185; Strabo, *Geographica* 16.1.9). Similarly, the city of Tyre sat beside the sea and had a trading empire that was likened to a network of prostitution (Isa 23:17; Ezek 27:3). Finally, ancient art pictured the goddess of Rome sitting beside the Tiber River (see the COMMENT) with an empire encompassing the Mediterranean Sea. In another sense, however, the *epi* means that she sits "on" many waters, since the waters symbolize the peoples over whom she rules (Rev 17:15). It is an image of dominion.

17:2. *"The kings of the earth have committed immorality with her.* Prostitution was legal in the Roman world, and some people thought it acceptable for men to use prostitutes as a sexual outlet (Horace, *Sat.* 1.2.31–32). Others thought it shameful for men—including kings—to do so, which is the sense in Revelation (Dio Chrysostom, *Or.* 7.133–34; Athenaeus, *Deipnosophistae* 569a; *Sib. Or.* 5:392; *Tg.* Jer 51:7). For a king to take up with a harlot queen showed that he was ruled by passion rather than discretion, which was considered degrading (Duff, *Who*, 110). The prophets used prostitution as a metaphor for political and economic alliances between kingdoms (Isa 23:17; Nah 3:4) and considered the worship of many gods to be promiscuous (2 Kgs 9:22; Hos 1:2; Mic 1:7). Here, the metaphor critiques rulers who entwined themselves socially and economically with Rome and adopted practices like the imperial cult. Revelation considers their behavior as degrading as that of the "lecherous and dissolute" men who sought to gratify their desires with a whore (Dio Chrysostom, *Or.* 7.134).

"and those who dwell on the earth have become drunk from the wine of her immorality." Drunkenness was disparaged since it could lead to a loss of judgment and indecent behavior (Gen 9:21; Prov 23:31–35; Jer 48:26; Eph 5:18). Here, the imagery points to the familiar scene of a prostitute making her clients drunk in order to lure them into illicit sexual relationships (Ezek 23:40–42; *T. Jud.* 13:5–6; Lucian, *Dial. meretr.* 6.2; Alciphron, *Ep. Court.* 13.11, 16, 18). It was said that the "spirit of immorality has wine for its servant" (*T. Jud.* 14:2; cf. *T. Reu.* 3:13–14).

As a metaphor, the language of drinking points to the way the world finds the opulence of the ruling power intoxicating, becoming numb to the violence and false worship that go along with it. The language echoes Jer 51:7, which says that Babylon made the earth drunk with her wine, which was taken to mean that those who imbibed of her sin became weak, confused, and liable for punishment (*Tg.* Jer 51:7). Earlier, Babylon was said to have made the peoples of the world drunk with the wine of her immoral passion, and this in turn becomes the wine of God's wrath, which brings the downfall of the city (Rev 14:8). There is symmetry in divine judgment, as Babylon's ruinous tendencies lead to its own ruin (18:6).

17:3. *Then he brought me in the Spirit to a desert.* "In the Spirit" means that John travels spiritually in a trance rather than physically (Aune) and that this journey takes place through the Spirit of God (Ezek 3:12; 8:3; Smalley). The Spirit enables John to see the visions of the exalted Christ, God's throne room, Babylon, and New Jerusalem (Rev 1:10; 4:2; 17:3; 21:10). Here, John is taken to a desert, which some interpreters consider to be a place of revelation (Giesen; Müller). It is more likely, however, that the city itself is in the desert and the setting foreshadows its fate, which will be desolation. Isaiah said that Babylon made the world a desert by conquest (Isa 14:17), and the OT oracle "fallen, fallen is Babylon" was issued from the desert (Isa 21:1–10; cf. 13:19–22; 14:22–23; Jer 50:12; Rev 18:2–3; Prigent). By the first century CE the actual city of Babylon was largely depopulated: "The great city has become a great desert" (Strabo, *Geographica* 16.1.5; cf. Pliny the Elder, *Nat.* 6.122). What John sees is a personification of Rome, rather than the actual Babylon. Nevertheless, the city in Revelation appears in a desert (*erēmos*) and finally becomes a desert (*erēmoun*) through destruction by its allies (Rev 17:16; 18:17, 19; Rossing, *Choice*, 71; Prigent; Roloff).

There I saw a woman seated on a scarlet beast that was full of blasphemous names. It had seven heads and ten horns. The woman sits on both the waters that represent the peoples over whom she rules (17:1, 15) and the beast that symbolizes the demonic power that undergirds her rule (17:3). The scarlet color of the woman's mount is like that of Satan, the red seven-headed dragon (12:3). The scarlet color also shows the deep affinity between the beast and the whore, who wears the red clothing that displays her wealth and mirrors her penchant for bloodshed (17:6; 18:24) and sin (Isa 1:18). Previously, the beast's heads had blasphemous names (Rev 13:1), but here, the beast is "full" of them. The blasphemous names recall the practice of calling emperors "god" (I.Smyr 591.4; I.Laod 15.1), "son of god" (I.Eph 252–53; I.Thyat 902–3), "lord and god" (Suetonius, *Dom.* 13.2), "master" (Philo, *Flacc.* 23), and "savior" (*Rom. Civ.* 1:624)—titles used for God and Christ in Revelation (NOTES on Rev 2:18; 4:11; 6:10; 7:10). For the writer, deifying the ruler is a form of opposing God.

17:4. *The woman was clothed in purple and scarlet and glittered with gold and jewels and pearls.* Descriptions of prostitutes often stress their lewdness (Athenaeus, *Deipnosophistae* 569b; Juvenal, *Satirae* 6.122), but John focuses on her opulence. Her gaudy clothing and jewelry come from illicit liaisons with clients and is worn to attract new lovers (Lucian, *Pisc.* 12; *T. Jud.* 13.4–5; Plautus, *Pseud.* 181). Purple, worn by nobles and the wealthy, indicated power and high status. It also cloaked statues of deities (Dan 5:7; 1 Macc 8:14; 11:57–58; Luke 16:19; John 19:2; Ep Jer 1:11; Plutarch, *Mor.* 646B; Lucian, *Nigr.* 15). Because it signified high status, many people spent large sums to purchase purple clothing. A freedman might imitate a senator by lounging about in purple clothes, while provincials fantasized about striking it rich and buying purple cloaks (Martial, *Epigrams* 2.29; Juvenal, *Satirae* 7.134–35; Lucian, *Nav.* 22). Scarlet signifies wealth, and scarlet cloth was a luxury item in Babylon's empire (Rev 18:12, 16;

2 Sam 1:24; Prov 31:21; Epictetus, *Diatribai* 3.22.10). An immoral woman wearing purple and scarlet in public emphasized her shamelessness (Jer 4:30; Martial, *Epigrams* 2.39; Lucian, *Dial. meretr.* 6.2). Yet even low-class prostitutes were sometimes given jewels and elegant clothing to wear in order to attract customers (Plautus, *Epid.* 191–92; Xenophon of Ephesus, *Ephesian Tale* 5.7; Glancy and Moore, "Who," 560–61).

In her hand she held a golden cup full of vile things and the impurities of her immorality. The language recalls Jer 51:7, in which Babylon is compared to a gold cup in the Lord's hand. Like the Targum of this passage, Revelation associates the cup with Babylon's sin (Aune). When used of food, "vile things" (*bdelygma*) are something so loathsome that no one should consume them (Lev 5:2; 11:13). Here, the vile things parallel "the impurities of her immorality." Both are metaphors. One traditional sense is that idolatry is vile (Deut 7:25; 29:16; 1 Kgs 11:5). Another sense is that vile things include immoral behavior, such as earning money by prostitution (Deut 23:18). Revelation combines "vile things" and "immorality" to mean idolatry (cf. Rev 2:14, 20; cf. Jer 13:27). The author also associates vile things with violence. The whore is drunk with the blood of the saints, and her cup is filled with vile things (Rev 17:4, 6). Shedding innocent blood and consuming blood of any sort were considered abhorrent in Israel's tradition (Lev 17:10–11; *1 En.* 7:5; 98:11; *Jub.* 7:29). Depicting the violence of the whore as a form of consuming blood fits the pattern of what is vile.

17:5. *On her forehead was written a name, a mystery.* Some prostitutes wore a band or garland around their foreheads, so having "the forehead of a prostitute" meant being brazenly immoral (Herodotus, *Historiae* 1.199; Jer 3:3; Court, *Myth*, 141). Some people have thought that prostitutes put their names on bands across their foreheads (*in fronte*, Seneca the Elder, *Controversiae* 1.2.7), although it is more probable that their names were displayed on signs outside their chambers (Juvenal, *Satirae* 6.122–23). Prostitutes used assumed names to suggest their characters: for example, Stratola (campaigner), Aristocleia (thoroughbred), and Lycisca (little wolf) (see Demosthenes, *Orations* 59.19.7; Plautus, *Pseud.* 179–80; Juvenal, *Satirae* 6.123). John's whore assumes the name of Babylon, which fits her oppressive character.

The name on Babylon's forehead identifies her as the mother of whores and the vile things of earth. This longer inscription is analogous to the way charges against a slave were tattooed on the slave's forehead as a degrading punishment. Slaves were not routinely marked, but one who ran away or committed some other offense could be punished by having the transgression tattooed on the forehead (Petronius, *Satyricon* 103.1–5; 105.11; Plautus, *Aul.* 325–26; Valerius Maximus, *Facta* 6.8.7). Even though the whore in Revelation is a queen (Rev 18:7), the inscription on her forehead announces her transgression to the world. It likens her to those who were considered the dregs of society: the tattooed slaves (C. Jones, "Stigma," 151).

The word "mystery" prefaces the inscription on the woman's forehead (NAB, NRSV) but is not part of the inscription itself (KJV, NIV). Some interpreters suggest that the woman has a secret name, much as the name of Rome's patron deity was kept secret so that it could not be used in spells (Pliny the Elder, *Nat.* 28.4.18; Plutarch, *Mor.* 278f; Aune). Nevertheless, this is unlikely. The woman's name is stated; the mystery concerns the meaning of the name, much as the mystery of the seven lampstands is that they signify churches (Rev 1:20). In contrast to the woman, who bears the inscription "mother of whores," Christ is inscribed with the name "King of kings and Lord of lords" on his robe and thigh (19:12, 16; Murphy).

Babylon the great. Babylon was the capital of an empire in the seventh and sixth centuries BCE, and it was called great because of its military power and splendor (Dan 4:30). By the late first century CE the term "great" was also used for Rome, the greatest city of the era and the center of an empire (Seneca the Younger, *Helv.* 6.3). Jewish authors saw analogies between the way Babylon destroyed the first temple in 587 BCE and Rome destroyed the second temple in 70 CE. The parallel suggested that Rome was a kind of Babylon (*Sib. Or.* 5:143, 159; *4 Ezra* 3:1–2, 29–31; 16:1; *2 Bar.* 10:2; 11:1; 67:7). The description of the besieged temple in Rev 11:1–2 is sometimes thought to reflect Rome's siege of Jerusalem, but this connection is not made explicit in the visions of Babylon in Rev 17–18.

For Christians the major similarity between the two cities was that Babylon was a world power in OT times as Rome was in their own time. The author of 1 Peter evidently writes from Rome but sends greetings from "Babylon" to Christians in Asia Minor, who are called "exiles" (1 Pet 1:1; 5:13). The sense is that Christians live in various places under Rome as Jewish exiles did under Babylon (P. Achtemeier, *1 Peter*, 354). Neither 1 Peter nor Revelation uses Babylon as a code name to conceal the author's meaning from the Romans. Revelation's critique of the city on seven hills (Rev 17:9) is clear enough for a Roman official to understand, and ancient Christian writers identified Revelation's Babylon with Rome (Tertullian, *Marc.* 3.13; Victorinus; Oecumenius; Primasius)

Some interpreters disagree, identifying Babylon with Jerusalem, the city pictured as a prostitute in the OT. They equate Babylon with the "great city" where Jesus was crucified (Rev 11:8) and note that Babylon persecutes Christians as Jerusalem persecuted Israel's prophets and the disciples of Jesus (Matt 23:29–39; Acts 8:1; 12:1–2). Picturing the whore riding the beast is said to show Jewish collaboration with Rome or perhaps with the Herodians. Just as the city rules over many peoples, Jerusalem oversaw the Jewish diaspora, and the whore's downfall resembles that of Jerusalem in Ezek 23:25–26 (Ford 283–93; Beagley, "*Sitz,*" 102–8; Barker, *Revelation*, 279–301; van de Water, "Reconsidering"; Lupieri). Few find this alternative convincing, however. The fact that the woman is located on seven hills, where she oversees a seaborne commercial empire and rules many nations, fits Rome much better (Biguzzi, "Is").

the mother of whores and of the vile things of earth. Some people called Rome the mother of all cities (Dionysius Periegetes, *Descriptio Periegesis* 356) and Italy the mother of all countries, uniting people everywhere in godly harmony (Pliny the Elder, *Nat.* 3.39). In Revelation, however, Babylon/Rome is the mother of all things ungodly, just as fornication is the mother of wicked deeds (*T. Sim.* 5:13; cf. Tob 4:13). The Greek word *pornōn* is in the genitive case and could be based on the masculine *pornos*, meaning that Babylon is the mother of male fornicators. But it is more probably based on the feminine *pornē*, identifying Babylon as the mother of female prostitutes (BDAG, 854–55). Vile things indicate false worship, as in Rev 17:4.

17:6. *I saw that the woman was drunk on the blood of the saints and the blood of the witnesses to Jesus.* Blood could be compared to red wine, and drinking blood could connote slaughter (Jer 46:10; Isa 34:5). Warriors, battlefields, and creatures feasting on the slain were said to be drunk with blood (Zech 9:15; Jdt 6:4; Ezek 39:18–19). The emperor Tiberius was said to have drunk blood as greedily as wine, since he was responsible for many deaths (Suetonius, *Tib.* 59.1). The imagery is especially repugnant from a Jewish perspective, which considers it unlawful to consume blood (Lev 17:10–11; *1 En.* 7:5; 98:11). Consuming any blood makes one liable to God's judgment (*Jub.* 7:29), so using the image as a metaphor for murder heightens the sense that the whore's actions must bring condemnation. The victims are the saints and witnesses to Jesus, two names for members of the Christian community. Christian blood was shed in Rome during the persecution under Nero (Tacitus, *Ann.* 15.44). Some interpreters see the whore's action as a travesty of partaking in Christ's blood during Holy Communion (Duff, *Who*, 102–5; King, "Travesty"), though it is not clear that sacramental imagery is involved here.

And I was completely amazed when I saw her. Being amazed (*thaumazein*) could mean being as perplexed and disturbed as Daniel was at his vision of four beasts and as Ezra was at a vision of an eagle with multiple heads (Dan 7:15; *4 Ezra* 12:3; Smalley). Some interpreters also liken this amazement to a person being baffled at seeing an unusual work of art (Lucian, *Herc.* 4; Callistratus, *Imagines* 6; Aune 2:927). Yet John's reaction is ambiguous. His amazement could mean that he is impressed by the whore, since the same word (*thaumazein*) is used for those who are impressed by the beast (Rev 13:3; 17:8). The way the angel corrects John's misguided astonishment implicitly corrects readers who are mistakenly impressed with the ways of Babylon/Rome (Giesen; Harrington; Murphy).

17:7. *Then the angel said to me, "Why are you amazed?* Jewish writings sometimes include an angelic guide who explains what a prophet or seer experiences in a vision. Earlier in Revelation the role of interpreter was played by a heavenly elder (Rev 5:5; 7:13–14), but here the role is played by an angel, which was more common (Ezek 40:3–4; Zech 1:7–6:15; Dan 7:16; 8:15; *1 En.* 21:5; 22:3; *2 Bar.* 55:3; *4 Ezra* 4:1; 5:31–32; 12:10).

"I will tell you the mystery of the woman and the beast that carries her, the one with seven heads and ten horns. A "mystery" has a hidden meaning, like that of the stars and lampstands (1:20), the whore's name (17:5), or a dream (Dan 2:30, 47). Some interpreters compare the manner of disclosure in this vision to a pattern in ancient literature, in which a writer gives a description (*ekphrasis*) of a work of art, then notes that an onlooker is baffled by it, and finally has a bystander explain its meaning. In Cebes's *Tabula*, for example, an old man explains a complex painting in which a woman with a cup signifies deception, a blind woman is Fortune, and courtesans symbolize vices (cf. Achilles Tatius, *Leuc. Clit.* 5.3–5; Aune 3:923–27; Rossing, *Choice*, 77). John's portrayal of the whore makes her as motionless as a painting, yet the text deals with a vision rather than a public work of art. More importantly, the angel relates the details to the powers that rule this age, as in apocalyptic texts like Dan 7 and *4 Ezra* 12, rather than giving instruction in practical morality, as in Cebes's *Tabula* (cf. Prigent; Smalley).

17:8. *"The beast that you saw was and is not, and is about to come up from the abyss and go to destruction.* The beast is the negative counterpart to the God who is and was and is to come (Rev 1:4, 8; 4:8). The language recalls a funereal epigram: "I was not, I came into being, I will not be anymore. That's no concern to me. That's life." Or "I was not, I am not, I do not care" (Klauck, *Religious*, 80). Echoing the funereal formula fits the career of a beast that brings death to others and then goes to destruction itself. According to 13:3, the beast is slain and returns to life, whereas in 17:8 it "was and is not, and is about to come up from the abyss." Both passages draw on legends concerning Nero that claimed he was not dead but alive and would return to assert power over Rome. The idea that the imperial beast was not dead but alive shapes the Nero tradition as a contrast to Jesus' death and resurrection (NOTES and COMMENT on 13:3). The warning that the beast would come up from the abyss in the future makes its future coming the counterpart to Christ coming again on the clouds of heaven (1:7; cf. Bauckham, *Climax*, 437–41; Beale). The beast's destruction will take place in the lake of fire (19:20).

"*Those who dwell on earth, whose names have not been written in the scroll of life from the time the earth was made.* On the scroll of life, see the NOTE on 13:8.

"*will be amazed when they see the beast, because it was and is not and is to come.* The people's amazement means being impressed by the beast, and their perspective will lead them to worship both the beast and Satan, the power behind the throne (cf. 13:3–4).

17:9. "*This calls for an understanding mind.* Revelation assumes that God is the source of wisdom (5:12; 7:12; Dan 2:20–23; Murphy) and here gives readers the clues they need to discern the significance of the beast. Although some interpreters suggest that the passage utilizes gematria, as the beast's number did (Rev 13:18; J. Schmidt, "Νοῦς"), this approach is unlikely. That passage asked readers to "calculate" the number of the beast, using the word *psēphizein*, which was typical of gematria. Nothing like that is suggested here.

"*The seven heads are seven mountains on which the woman is seated.* The most plausible reading is that this passage identifies the beast with Rome, the city set on seven hills. References to Rome's seven hills were widely known: "High on the hills, the seven, the city which rules the world" (Propertius, *Elegies* 3.111.57). With good leaders, "Rome shall even more proudly touch the heavens with its seven hills" (Statius, *Silv.* 4.1.6). The Greek word *horos* could indicate either a hill or a mountain, and it was used for the hills of Rome (Strabo, *Geographica* 5.3.7; Dionysius of Halicarnassus, *Ant. rom.* 2.50.1; cf. Varro, *Ling. lat.* 5.41; Pliny the Elder, *Nat.* 3.66; Virgil, *Aen.* 6.783; Ovid, *Trist.* 3.7.51–52; Martial, *Epigrams* 4.64.11–12; Juvenal, *Satirae* 9.130).

The seven heads are both mountains and kings. Such dual imagery fits Revelation: The seven spirits are pictured as torches before God's throne and as the eyes of the Lamb (Rev 4:5; 5:6). The dual imagery of mountains and kings underscores the beast embodying the power of both the city of Rome and its emperors. Other connotations fit this critique of imperial rule. Greco-Roman writers personified tyranny as a woman sitting on a mountain, much as the tyrannical whore sits on the seven mountains (Dio Chrysostom, *Or.* 1.78–84). Jewish writers pictured God's throne amid seven mountains, yet the arrogant whore sits on seven mountains as if attempting to take God's place (*1 En.* 18:6–8; 24:1–25:3; Thompson).

The main alternative interpretation is that the mountains in Rev 17:9b signify seven successive kingdoms (Ps 68:15–16; Jer 51:25) and that these kingdoms are represented by the kings in Rev 17:9c (cf. Dan 7:17, 23). From this perspective, the heads of the beast point to broad periods of time rather than specifically to the Roman Empire (Andreas; Beale). By following this approach, futuristic interpreters maintain that the beast signifies a series of kingdoms that will culminate at the end of the age (Seiss;

Walvoord; Thomas). This approach is improbable because Rome was so widely known as the city on seven hills.

"*They are also seven kings.* Identifying the beast's heads as kings is fitting, since the word "head" could signify the power to rule. Other writers depicted emperors or kings as the four heads of a monstrous leopard, the three heads of an eagle or other creature, and the head of an asp (Dan 7:6; 11:2; *4 Ezra* 12:22–26; Philostratus, *Vit. Apoll.* 5.13.1–2; CDᵃ VIII, 11). In John's vision the number seven is a given, since that is the number of heads on the beast. The imagery connects the beast with kingship. It does not invite speculation about which seven kings might be included in the group.

Identifying the seven heads with seven kings summarizes imperial rule. Roman historians referred to their own early history as a time spanning the reigns of seven kings (*Rom. Civ.* 1:59–61; Appian, *Bell. civ.* pref. 14). Historically, there were probably more kings during this early period, but the number was adjusted to the canonical seven, which became the accepted summary of kings in Rome's early history (Aune 3:948). By analogy, Revelation uses "seven" for the number of kings that will bring the story of Babylon/Rome to an end. Although emperors in the first century CE did not officially use the term "king," others called them kings (Josephus, *J. W.* 4.596; 1 Tim 2:2; 1 Pet 2:13). Interpreters have proposed many ways to connect the seven kings with specific emperors, but none of these proposals is convincing (Intro II.C.1–2).

17:10. "*Five have fallen, one is, and the other has not yet come. When he comes he must remain for a only little while.* The word "fallen" indicates that five kings died violently, just as Babylon's fall entails destruction (14:8; 18:2; 2 Sam 1:25). Many Roman emperors suffered violent deaths: Julius Caesar, Caligula, Galba, and Domitian were stabbed; Claudius was poisoned; Nero and Otho committed suicide; and Vitellius was beaten to death (Aune). The falling of rulers fits the general pattern of violent death, but since more than five perished this way, the passage does not allow readers to identify the kings with five specific emperors.

The sixth king is in power at the time of John's vision. Many interpreters have tried to determine who this king might be without reaching a satisfactory solution (Table 1 and Intro II.C.1–2). A seventh ruler is yet to come and will remain for a short time. Although several emperors reigned briefly in 69 CE, it is unlikely that the vision alludes to any of them. Brief reigns are a feature of the end of the age in apocalyptic writings (*4 Ezra* 12:30; *T. Mos.* 6:7). The author does not expect readers to identify the kings with known figures. The vagueness is comparable to *4 Ezra* 11–12, in which the Roman Empire is symbolized by an eagle with twelve wings, three heads, and eight smaller wings. It is clear that three wings and heads symbolize Julius Caesar, Augustus, and Tiberius, but the identities of the other wings are not apparent. Detailed connections are not expected (Friesen, *Imperial*, 141).

17:11. "*As for the beast that was and is not, it is an eighth that belongs to the seven, and it is going to destruction.* The imagery draws on legends concerning Nero, who "was" in power in the past, "was not" in power when Revelation was written, but was rumored to be returning in the future to bring destruction (Note on 13:3). Some interpreters argue that Domitian is the eighth king, a revivified Nero (Giesen). Various writers associated Domitian with Nero (Juvenal, *Satirae* 4.37–38; Marital, *Epigrams* 11.33; Pliny the Younger, *Pan.* 53). If John wrote during Domitian's reign, then he used the literary device of placing himself at an earlier point in time, during the reign of the sixth king

(Klauck, "Do," 687). It is more plausible, however, that John wrote during the reign of the sixth king and thought the seventh and eighth kings were still to come.

17:12. *"The ten horns that you saw are ten kings, who have not yet received royal power*. Like the dragon (Rev 12:3) and the fourth beast in Daniel (Dan 7:7–8, 20, 24), John sees a monster with ten horns (cf. Rev 13:1). Horns connote strength and power to save or destroy and could signify kingship (Ps 22:21; Luke 1:69). In Daniel the ten horns signify successive kings, but in Revelation the kings act as a coalition. Some interpreters identify them with the kings of the whole earth who ally themselves with the beast (Rev 16:14; 19:19; Beale; Prigent). But this is unlikely since a group of ten is more limited than all of earth's kings. Others identify them with the kings from the east who come to destroy Babylon/Rome (16:12). This interpretation is possible, since the imagery of the beast and the kings recalls expectations of Nero and his Parthian allies coming to seize Rome (Bauckham, *Climax*, 438).

"but they will receive authority as kings for an hour, along with the beast. Common political practices inform the imagery. Emperors granted royal authority to allies who reigned over certain regions while remaining subject to Rome (Augustus, *Res* 33; Suetonius, *Aug*. 48; Tacitus, *Agr*. 14.1). Examples of such kings include Herod the Great in Judea and Herod Agrippa in southern Syria (Luke 1:5; Josephus, *J.W.* 1.282–85; Acts 25:13). When a Parthian leader offered allegiance to Nero, the emperor responded, "I now declare you King of Armenia," for "I have power to take away kingdoms and to bestow them" (Dio Cassius, *Rom. Hist.* 62.5.3). Ordinarily, vassal kings received authority from Rome, but using the passive voice in Revelation suggests that these kings ultimately receive authority from God, as did the four horsemen (Rev 6:1–8; Beale; Osborne). They will carry out God's will by defeating the whore (17:16).

17:13. *"The kings are of one mind, and they give their power and authority to the beast*. Having "one mind" is a common political expression for citizens who agree on a common course of action. Such agreement enabled groups to prevail in war, as is the case here (Isocrates, *Or.* 4.138). Such harmony existing within a city or state or between nations (Dionysius of Halicarnassus, *Ant. rom.* 6.77.1) was considered a gift of the gods. In John's vision the kings exhibit a unity that is given by God and allows them to defeat the harlot city, their erstwhile ally (van Unnik, "MIA").

17:14. *"They will make war on the Lamb, but the Lamb will conquer them*. The ten kings differ from the kings of the whole earth in their hatred for the whore, but they are like the other kings in their opposition to the Lamb. This passage anticipates the battle of Rev 19:11–21 in which Christ defeats the beast and its allies by the sword that signifies his word.

"for he is Lord of lords and King of kings. See the NOTE on 19:16.

"and those with him are called and chosen and faithful." Christians are "called" to faith (Rom 1:6; 1 Cor 1:24) and "chosen" because God has a claim on them (1 Pet 2:9). Their response is to be "faithful," as were Christ and Antipas, who remained true to God at the cost of their lives (Rev 1:5; 2:10, 13). Those accompanying Christ may be the same as the 144,000 who follow the Lamb wherever he goes, although that group represented all the redeemed (14:1–5; cf. 7:3, 9; Prigent; Smalley).

Some interpreters argue that the Lamb's followers carry out divine retribution, like the warriors in the Qumran *War Scroll* and other texts (*1 En*. 90:19; 91:12; 95:3; 96:1; 98:12; *Apoc. Ab*. 29:19). They contrast this with a holy war in which the victory is won by God or his angels, as at the exodus (Exod 14:13–14; Isa 37:33–36; 1 En. 56:1–8; Aune; Osborne). This approach is not persuasive, however. In Revelation, Christ is the one who defeats the beast and its allies (Rev 17:14). At the battle in 19:11–21 Christ is accompanied by a group, but the weapon that brings victory is the sword of Christ's word. Christ's companions are not passive, since witness and suffering are forms of action (12:11; Bauckham, *Climax*, 234). But here, the victory is Christ's.

17:15. *Then he said to me, "The waters that you saw, where the whore is seated, are peoples and multitudes and nations and languages.* On the waters of Babylon, Rome, and other cities, see the NOTE on 17:1. Surging water was an image for invading peoples (Ps 144:7; Isa 8:6–7; 17:12–14; Jer 47:2), but here the waters are the peoples under Babylon's control.

17:16. *"As for the ten horns that you saw, they and the beast will hate the whore and will make her desolate and naked.* The ten kings who hate the whore are different from the kings who consort with her and grieve her downfall (18:3, 9–10). Conquering armies made cities desolate (*erēmoun*) by destroying and pillaging. This is a reminder that the whore personifies a city, since the term "desolate" was not used for attacks against women (Rossing, *Choice*, 87–92). Being stripped, however, fits both a woman and a city. Just as a woman might be stripped of her clothing by her captors, a city would be stripped of resources by its conquerors. The imagery was used for Jerusalem (Isa 3:17; Jer 13:26–27; Ezek 16:37–38; 23:10; 26–29; Hos 2:5, 12), but here it is more like the plundering of Nineveh (Nah 3:5) and Babylon (Isa 47:3). The scene creates a striking reversal of imperial art that depicts Roman emperors overpowering foreign nations pictured as partially unclothed women (see Figures 33 and 34). Here, the victim of imperial action is the beast's own city (Friesen, *Imperial*, 177).

"They will eat her flesh and burn her up with fire. On one level the language draws on punishments given to individual women. Queen Jezebel was accused of whoredom, or promoting unfaithfulness to the God of Israel. She fell from a window, and dogs ate her flesh (2 Kgs 9:30–37). As a metaphor, having one's flesh consumed indicates that others take over one's means of making a living (Ps 27:2; Mic 3:3). When extended to a fallen city, it indicates that all the city's resources are seized by the attackers. On a second level being physically burned was a punishment for prostitution and immoral behavior (Lev 20:14; 21:9), and the harlot is a city who is burned by her conquerors (Ezek 16:41; 23:25). Note that Revelation does not offer a consistent description of the fall of Babylon. It is variously said to fall through an earthquake (Rev 16:19), to be defeated by its allies (17:16), and to be devastated by plagues, pestilence, famine, and fire (18:8–9). Revelation uses multiple images to show the severity of God's judgment.

17:17. *"For God put into their hearts to do what is on his mind. That is why they will be of one mind.* Putting something into the heart is an idiom for providing divine direction (Exod 35:34; Neh 2:12). God's will is carried out by bringing destructive tendencies full circle so that evil destroys itself. Being of one mind indicates political concord, which here leads to destruction (NOTE on Rev 17:13).

"and give their royal power to the beast, until the words of God have been completed. Giving their royal power to the beast means that the kings recognize his sovereignty over them, and the result will be destruction. By way of contrast, the heavenly elders cast their laurel wreaths before God's throne, acknowledging his reign, and the outcome is joy (4:10). The completion of "the words of God" means that Babylon's fall fulfills the

words of the prophets (cf. 10:7). This passage recalls how Israel's prophets and earlier parts of Revelation prophetically announced the fall of Babylon (14:8; Isa 13–14; 21; 47; Jer 50–51).

17:18. *"And the woman that you saw is the great city that has royal power over the kings of the earth."* Babylon is "the great city," as was Rome, which was known as the greatest of cities (Horace, *Carm.* 4.3.13; Aelius Aristides, *Or.* 26.3, 9) and the master of the world (Virgil, *Aen.* 1.282; 7.603; Ovid, *Fast.* 5.93; *NW* 2.2:1605–13).

COMMENT

Babylon the great has played a cryptic role in Revelation up to this point. Previously, an angel declared that Babylon had fallen for making the nations drink of its passionate immorality, but no elaboration was given (Rev 14:8). Later, the outpouring of seven bowls of wrath culminated in an earthquake so violent that "the great city" was split into three parts and God gave Babylon the wine cup of his wrath (16:18–19). The vision cycle will conclude when the hosts of heaven sound "hallelujah" for God's judgment against the city (19:1–10). Yet before this victory celebration occurs, John gives an expanded description of Babylon and its demise (17:1–18:24).

God's judgment on Babylon is introduced by one of the angels who poured out the bowls in the previous chapter (17:1). The visions elaborate the seventh bowl plague by giving readers a clearer sense of the city's character and the reasons for God's action against it, but these scenes also include new elements. Nothing more is said about the earthquake that shattered the city at the seventh bowl plague. Instead, the city is now destroyed by its own allies, represented by the beast and a group of kings. Readers are shown *that* the city's reign of injustice must come to an end, but the different *ways* in which this devastation occurs indicate that the visions do not outline specific events that will bring it about.

The Babylon visions are an interlude that occurs after the seventh bowl plague (16:17–21) and before the final vision of celebration (19:1–10). The author varies the pattern established by the seal and trumpet visions, which included an interlude after the sixth plague vision and before the seventh vision of worship in heaven (7:1–17; 10:1–11:14). The two previous interludes provided responses to the question of the martyrs, who had asked how long God would wait before taking just action against those who had shed their blood (6:10). The interludes revealed that God extended the delay *before* carrying out final justice so that people could be sealed and redeemed (7:1–17) and witness could be given to an impenitent world (10:1–11:14). Now the Babylon visions

---

On Rev 17:1–18, see Beauvery, "L'Apocalypse"; Bergmeier, "Erzhure"; Biguzzi, "Is"; Campbell, "Antithetical"; Court, *Myth*, 122–53; de Villiers, "Composition" and "Rome"; Duff, *Who*, 83–112, Dyer, "Identity"; Friesen, *Imperial*, 136–41; Frilingos, *Spectacles*, 58–60, 103–7; Glancy and Moore, "How"; Humphrey, "Tale"; Keller, "Eyeing"; Kim, "Uncovering"; King, "Travesty"; Klauck, "Do"; Neufeld, "Sumptuous"; Pippin, "Eros"; Räpple, *Metaphor*; Rossing, *Choice*; Royalty, *Streets*, 187–94; Ruiz, *Ezekiel*, 292–378; Sals, *Biographie*, 49–144; J. Schmidt, "Νοῦς"; Slater, "King"; Streete, *Strange*, 150–58; van Unnik, "MIA"; Wengst, "Babylon"; Yarbro Collins, *Combat*, 170–90 and "Portraits."

show that the time of waiting *will end* with God acting justly against the perpetrators of injustice (17:1–18:24). The festive scenes that follow will celebrate this triumph of justice (19:1–10).

Babylon's fall marks a turning point in the story of evil's rise and fall, which spans the last half of Revelation. After Satan was expelled from heaven (12:7–12), he conjured up a seven-headed beast from the sea that blasphemed God and dominated the world (13:1–10). This monstrous tyrant was joined by the beast from the land, or false prophet, who deceived and coerced people into worshiping his master (13:11–18). John expands the picture by depicting Babylon the whore riding the seven-headed beast and reveling in brutality and greed (17:1–6). After successively portraying these agents of oppression, John traces their demise in reverse order, as the whore is destroyed by the beast (17:16), the beast and its associate are defeated by Christ (19:20), and Satan is finally imprisoned and thrown into the lake of fire (20:1–10):

Satan is thrown from heaven to earth (12:1–17).
    Beast and false prophet conquer (13:1–18).
        Whore rides on the beast (17:1–12).
        Whore destroyed by the beast (17:13–18).
    Beast and false prophet are conquered (19:11–21).
Satan is thrown from earth into the abyss and lake of fire (20:1–3, 7–10).

Babylon's demise also warns readers about the self-destructive power of evil, since the great city is destroyed by its own allies. In God's design, evil becomes evil's own undoing.

John shapes his readers' identities and commitments through contrasting feminine images. The positive images portray the people of God, and the negative images depict those opposed to God. Previously, the people of God were represented by a woman who was clothed with the sun and had a wreath of stars around her head. Her radiance suggests God-given glory (12:1). In contrast, the whore's sumptuous clothes and jewels are more garish than glorious, since they stem from illicit relationships. Her glittery appearance speaks of self-aggrandizement (17:4). Where the first woman is the mother of the Messiah and the faithful, the whore is the mother of whores and vile things (12:5, 17; 17:5).

What complicates this simple contrast is that even though the woman representing believers is pictured in a positive way, her experience is negative: She is persecuted by Satan the dragon and must find refuge in the desert and rely on nourishment from God. The prospect of such difficulties would make a reader wonder whether there is any reason to remain faithful (12:3–4, 13). The alternative, however, is to identify with the whore, who sits confidently astride the scarlet beast that is Satan's ally and who appears in the desert nourishing herself on the blood of the saints (17:3, 6). What encourages readers to remain faithful in the face of these two alternatives is the end of the stories: The woman personifying believers is divinely protected from the dragon in the desert, while the whore is destroyed by the seven-headed beast, which turns her into a desert (12:14–16; 17:16; Duff, *Who*, 85–87; Humphrey, *Ladies*, 107). The implication is that readers are best served by enduring opposition now in the hope of vindication in the end.

Visions of Babylon the whore and Jerusalem the bride continue this contrasting pattern. Each city is introduced by one of the angels with the bowls of plagues, making a clear literary connection (17:1; 21:9). The name Babylon connotes tyranny, materialism, and false worship, while the name Jerusalem connotes deliverance, blessing, and true worship. The whore debases relationships by turning them into commercial transactions, while the bride exemplifies honorable relationships. Babylon wears gold and pearls to attract clients for illicit liaisons, while Jerusalem is adorned with gold and pearls like a bride awaiting her groom (17:4; 21:2). The whore's way is defiling, while nothing is impure in Jerusalem the bride (17:4; 21:27). Kings revel in dishonorable relations with Babylon but are called to bring their glory to New Jerusalem (17:2; 21:24). The name on Babylon's forehead identifies her as the mother of whores and the vile things of earth, while the names on Jerusalem's gates and foundations are those of chosen tribes and faithful apostles (17:5; 21:12–14). The whore is drunk with blood and intoxicates the nations with immorality, while the bride invites the nations to drink of the water that gives life (17:2; 22:1–5; Rossing, *Choice*, 161–64; Bauckham, *Theology*, 131–32; Deutsch, "Transformation," 123; Campbell, "Antithetical").

Babylon personifies the arrogance, materialism, violence, and false belief that are at work in the readers' world. The contrasting vision of New Jerusalem discloses a God-centered harmony that is beyond the present world and will be realized in the new creation (21:1–2). Readers must live with the tension. They live in this age with an identity defined by the age to come. They cannot hope to create the New Jerusalem—that will be God's doing—and yet they are warned not to adopt the ways of Babylon. The writer does not respond to the tension by offering simple directives for readers to follow. Instead, his text engages the readers by pressing for clarity about their basic commitments. As he does this, he also challenges the readers to work out the implications by resisting practices incongruent with their faith in the contexts where they live (Harland, *Associations*, 262; Friesen, *Imperial*, 209).

The history of interpretation includes influential—and often problematic—ways of relating John's vision of the whore to the realm of time and space (see §32A). The approach taken here understands that in a primary sense Revelation's earliest readers would have identified Babylon with Rome, whose empire was supported by the imperial power that John depicts as a beast (17:4, 6, 9, 18; 18:11–20). Affirming a primary connection with Rome is important, since John understands that evil takes tangible forms. His vision is not about the timeless quality of evil but summons readers to resist the ruinous yet seductive forces of imperial society (Schüssler Fiorenza 119–31).

At the same time, the vision depicts forces that extend beyond Rome. The description of the whore combines prophetic critiques of a number of cities with elements from the imperial context in which John wrote, creating a multifaceted image. The woman is called Babylon, and her location beside many waters and her idolatry, brutality, and way of intoxicating the nations recall what the prophets said about Babylon (Jer 51:7, 13; Rev 17:1–5). She also resembles Nineveh, the capital of the Assyrian Empire. Cruel toward those it conquered, Nineveh was also a "prostitute, gracefully alluring, mistress of sorcery, who enslaves nations through her debaucheries" (Nah 3:4; Rev 17:1–2; 18:23). The great city in Revelation is also like Tyre, a city by the sea, whose vast commercial network enabled it to prostitute itself with the nations of the world (Isa 23:16–17; Rev 17:2).

The whore is Rome, yet more than Rome. The pattern is like that in earlier chapters of Revelation, in which the richly layered visions of witnesses and the great city (11:1–13), the woman and the dragon (12:1–17), and the beast from the sea (13:1–10) combined elements from multiple times and places into a single story. The traits of the whore are drawn from cities that existed long before Rome became a world power, and the fall of the whore does not bring an end to evil, since the beast continues to rage until the return of Christ, and Satan remains active even longer. The vision speaks to the imperial context in which Revelation was composed, with images that go beyond that context, depicting the powers at work in the world in ways that have subsequently engaged readers (Bauckham, *Theology*, 154–55; Friesen, *Imperial*, 177; Giesen 386–87).

Structurally, the passage is framed by references to the whore or woman seated on many waters (17:1, 18). The vision itself has two main sections. First, one of the bowl angels shows John a whore, who rides on the seven-headed beast, and John describes in detail what he sees (17:1–6). Second, the same angel gives John clues to the identity of the beast and whore (17:7–18). The explanation moves in two steps, each introduced by a comment about what the angel "said" or "says." The angel begins with the identity of the beast (17:7–14) and later comments on the gruesome fate of the whore (17:15–18). We consider each part in turn.

Description of the Whore and Beast (17:1–6)

An angel says, "Come, I will show you the judgment on the great whore who is seated on many waters" (17:1). These words introduce a feminine figure who personifies a ruling power. The imagery fits biblical portrayals of both Babylon, with its networks of rivers and canals, and Tyre, with its empire of the seas (NOTE on 17:1). It also fits first-century Rome, whose empire dominated the waters of "the Nile, who conceals the sources of his stream, and the Danube," as well as "the fiercely flowing Tigris" and "the monster-teeming Ocean that roars at the distant Britons" (Horace, *Carm.* 14.44–48). The angel warns that "judgment" will fall on the whore (Rev 17:16). For her trading partners, her demise will evoke an outpouring of grief (18:9–20), but for those oppressed by her reign, it elicits celebration (19:1–8).

Not all of John's readers would have shared his sharply critical stance toward the ruling power (L. Thompson, *Book*, 132). Those at Smyrna may have been threatened with imprisonment and death under the Roman authorities (2:9–10), and Roman officials were probably involved in the death of Antipas at Pergamum (2:13), but such violence does not seem to have been widespread. Other readers prospered under the Roman-era economic and political climate (3:17) and advocated a relaxed attitude concerning what had been sacrificed to Greco-Roman deities (2:14, 20). They would not have depicted Roman authority as John did.

John's critical view also differs from that of Paul, who insisted that government was established by God and was to be respected because it restrained wrongdoing (Rom 13:1–7; Dunn, *Romans*, 2:757–74). Early Christians did not pray to the emperor but offered prayers on his behalf and honored his authority (1 Tim 2:1–2; 1 Pet 2:13–17; P. Achtemeier, *1 Peter*, 179–82; J. H. Elliott, *1 Peter*, 484–502). Many Christians wanted to be seen as good, law-abiding members of Roman society, and they rejected the idea that their beliefs were a threat to imperial authority (Acts 16:21, 37; 17:7; 18:12–17; 19:35–41; 25:11; *1 Clem.* 60:4–61:2; Wengst, *Pax*, 89–118; cf. Gradl, "Kaisertum"). Since

John was conveying an anti-Roman message that not all of his readers shared, he had to alter the way they saw Roman authority.

John uses satire to shape the perspectives of his readers. Using stock features of a subject, a satirist exaggerates certain traits so that readers can still see the resemblance, but the subject now seems outlandish. If people can be startled into seeing as ridiculous what appears impressive or desirable, they will be more ready to resist it. Satirical elements appear in biblical texts that lampoon people who piously fashion an idol from half a piece of wood while cooking a meal over the other half (Isa 44:9–20) and critique the self-absorbed attitudes of a figure like Jonah (Marcus, *From*; Jemielity, *Satire*; Weisman, *Political*). Satire was a popular Roman genre (Quintilian, *Inst.* 10.1.93–94), and Roman writers such as Petronius, Persius, and Juvenal used it to mock the pretensions of the upper classes and those who tried to imitate them. Early Christians used satire in order to expose the foibles of Jesus' adversaries (C. R. Koester, "Comedy," 132–38). John used satire in his portrayal of the two beasts in Rev 13 and does so again in the picture of the harlot city.

The basis for John's satire is Rome's presentation of itself as a strong and virtuous ruling power. For example, a coin minted in Asia in 71 CE depicts Roma—the goddess who personified Roman power for the Greek world—as a noblewoman draped in battle dress, reclining on the seven hills of Rome. Her foot stretches out to the Tiber River in front of her, and her left hand rests on a short sword. Her appearance is one of strength and sobriety (Figure 32). Although readers may not have been familiar with the coin itself (Beale; Smalley), the imagery reflects a type that was well-known (H. Cohen, *Description*, 1:398; Aune 2:920–22; Beauvery, "L'Apocalypse"; Bergmeier, "Erzhure," plate 1; J. Schmidt, "Νοῦς"; Yarbro Collins, "Portraits," 294; cf. Court, *Myth*, 148–53).

John caricatures these Roman symbols in order to break the spell with which the great city bewitches the nations. Instead of a noblewoman, John pictures a debauched whore. Where one might expect an honorable exemplar of virtue, the harlot appears in a drunken stupor. Instead of sitting at ease on the seven hills, she clings to the back of an outrageous seven-headed beast. Her hand no longer holds a sword but raises a golden cup that one would expect to be filled with the finest wine, yet it contains vile sewage. The pretentious lady becomes a contemptible buffoon. This figure, who was revered in temples in the cities of Asia, is pictured as the "mother of whores and of the vile things of earth" (Rev 17:5).

Figure 32. Roman coin showing Roma seated on seven hills (71 CE). From Henry Cohen, *Description historique des monnaies frappées sous L'Empire Romain*, 398 no. 404.

The way John satirizes Rome might also play on images used in other religious traditions of the empire. Cybele the mother goddess was sometimes shown riding a leopard or lion, but here the great mother becomes the great whore, and her noble mount turns into a hideous monster (Godwin, *Mystery*, 114; Bovon, *New*, 142; Giesen; Müller; Schüssler Fiorenza). Dionysos could be pictured riding a tiger while clutching his flask of wine (Guzzo and d'Ambrosio, *Pompeii*, 30); the whore who rides the beast also grasps a wine cup and drinks with abandon—from a blend of bloodshed and idolatrous practice. The proper response is revulsion.

The city is labeled a "whore," which was degrading in both Jewish and Greco-Roman traditions. Marriage was esteemed, and prostitutes, who had liaisons with many clients, were viewed with contempt. They were considered brazen and shameless (Ezek 16:30; Terence, *Andria* 69–70, 797–980; Plautus, *Asin.* 504–44) and were said to be driven by lust. Instead of expressing virtue, they were considered slaves of uncontrolled desire (Juvenal, *Satirae* 6.125–32; Ezek 16:28; 23:5). Lacking all standards of decency, they provided services that were crude and impure (Johnson and Ryan, *Sexuality*, 93–94). John's vision develops these conventional elements into a critique of the ruling power's arrogance and insatiable desire.

The kings of the earth are said to have immoral sexual relations with the whore (Rev 17:2a). This point satirizes the political relationships that local rulers establish with the world's dominant power. The Romans found it advantageous to allow kings to govern some areas within its empire and along its borders. In public discourse such a king was called an "ally and friend" (*socius et amicus*) of Rome, emphasizing that the arrangement was based on mutual respect and abiding loyalty (Braund, *Rome*, 5–7, 23, 181–87). John's metaphor challenges this label by depicting political figures who seek to gratify their own desires by paying for the favors of the whore. This image critiques the way that kings and others in authority enhanced their own positions with Roman support, while allowing the Romans to drain the resources of their realms, supplying the empire's desire for gold, silver, slaves, and other trade goods (Notes on 18:11–13; cf. Isa 23:17).

The image of prostitution also serves Revelation's purposes because it reflects the practice of debasing sexual relationships into commercial transactions. Sexual intimacy was supposed to happen in the marriage relationship, and prostitution degraded it into something offered on a fee-for-service basis (Dio Chrysostom, *Or.* 7.133–34). At the street level, the degradation was clear; at the brothel the "women stand naked . . . Look at everything . . . The door is open. One obol [a small coin] . . . There is no coyness, no idle talk . . . Do whatever you wish. You come out. Tell her to go to hell. She is a stranger to you" (Athenaeus, *Deipnosophistae* 569e–f; Glancy and Moore, "How," 554). Revelation transfers this system of use and abuse to relationships with Rome. From the writer's perspective the façade of intimacy with the ruling power masks an underlying reality, which is that people traffic with Rome for pleasure and profit—nothing more.

Revelation also relates the notion of immorality (*porneia*) to Greco-Roman religious practices, such as eating what was offered to idols (Rev 2:14, 20). Since the kings of the earth (17:2) were Gentiles, they would have worshiped various deities regardless of their relationship to Rome. Therefore, their immoral liaisons *with the whore* point to what was uniquely part of a relationship with Rome: the imperial cult. Local authorities paid for the privilege of building temples to the emperor and goddess Roma; they bore the costs of imperial festivals and provided funds for singers to sound the emperor's praises (Price, *Rituals*, 78–100). From the perspective of Revelation, they are like clients paying to debase themselves with a harlot.

The inhabitants of the earth are said to be drunk with the wine of the whore's immorality (17:2b; cf. 14:8). The writer evokes images of a bawdy banquet in which a prostitute plies clients with wine while luring them into sexual liaisons. Metaphorically, this imagery challenges the public portrayal of Rome as the fountainhead of a virtuous society (Strabo, *Geographica* 6.4.2; Plutarch, *Mor.* 317c). John's imagery counters with a critique that resembles some of the common criticisms of Rome's decadence and obsession with luxury—vices that were contaminating the empire (*Sib. Or.* 5:386–96; Tacitus, *Ann.* 15.44; Lucian, *Nigr.* 16; Juvenal, *Satirae* 3). One might think the power symbolized by the sleazy woman would be repugnant, but John's vision pictures the populace overlooking this negative side of things because they find her boundless supply of luxuries intoxicating (Rev 18:11–13).

Drinking from the harlot's cup also has religious connotations: It means imbibing the vileness of false worship (17:4). The imperial cult had provincial temples at Ephesus, Smyrna, and Pergamum, along with the municipal cults in the other cities where John's readers lived (Notes on 2:1, 8, 12, 18; 3:1, 7, 14; cf. Friesen, *Imperial*, 205). From John's perspective, deifying the ruling power is an affront to God, yet people seem as oblivious to the problem as those deep in their cups. The problem was not that the ruler cult was an imposition—just the opposite. Deification of the emperors was widely accepted by the people. Since the whore is drunk with the blood of the saints (17:6), those who consort with her must also find violence intoxicating—they either find it exhilarating or are numb to it.

A scarlet beast with seven heads and ten horns carries the woman, representing the political power that undergirds her dominion (17:3). Readers have become acquainted with the beast from previous visions. Satan was pictured as a red dragon with seven heads that conjured up the beast in its own image (12:1–17). Rising from the sea, this seven-headed beast dominates the world (13:1–10). The beast was slain and yet living, making it the demonic counterpart to the slain and living Lamb (5:5–10). Where the Lamb is the agent of God, the beast is the agent of Satan. Where the Lamb redeems people of every tribe and nation, the beast oppresses them. Where the Lamb conquers by self-sacrifice, the beast conquers by sacrificing the faithful.

The beast has some traits that fit the imperial system as a whole. The earlier description of the beast combined elements from the four empires of Dan 7 with the military might, blasphemous claims, and persecution of the church that John associated with Rome (Rev 13:1–10). Here, the beast encompasses a series of rulers linked to Rome's seven hills, and the monster is full of blasphemous names, like those used for the deified emperors (17:3, 9). The beast also has traits of a specific emperor, namely, Nero. In the earlier vision, the beast was like Nero in that it persecuted the church and was said to have died and yet was alive (Note on 13:3). Here again, the beast is like Nero, who is no longer ruling and yet is expected to return (17:11). The sense is that in Nero, readers can see the empire's true face.

On the whore's forehead is inscribed a name, "Babylon the great" (17:5). The word "great" connotes power and wealth (Dan 4:30; *Sib. Or.* 4:93), and in Israel's tradition the name Babylon (Hebrew, Babel) exemplifies human arrogance, since there, people tried to build a tower to heaven (Gen 11:1–9; *Sib. Or.* 3:104). Zechariah saw a woman who personified wickedness being taken to the region of Babylon (Zech 5:5–11). The city was considered a predator, swallowing nations and gnawing their bones (Jer 50:7; 51:34). Opulent and haughty, Babylon lorded over many kingdoms, ruling with anger and violence (Isa 13:19; 14:4–6; 47:5; Jer 50:29). After burning the Jerusalem temple, the Babylonians exiled the people (Ps 137:1). With boundless hubris, Babylon was charged with trying to take the place of God (Isa 14:13–14; 47:10; Sals, *Biographie*). The name remained a potent symbol for an oppressive ruling power.

Babylon is the mother of whores and the vile things of earth (Rev 17:5). In ordinary practice an older prostitute trained younger girls to become prostitutes so they could work in her brothel. Outfitting the girls with the necessary clothing and makeup, the woman would instruct them in ways of providing pleasure to customers. If she purchased slaves in order to prostitute them, she might call them her own daughters so that customers would think the girls were freeborn and pay higher prices for their services (Demosthenes, *Orations* 59.19; Plutarch, *Per.* 24.5; Athenaeus, *Deipnosophistae* 568a). As a metaphor, the language points to how the ruling power draws others into following its ways. On one level the whore's vile things are idolatrous practices and her children are those who engage in false worship, as do the children of Jezebel (Rev 2:22–23; cf. Hos 2:2–5). More broadly, her vile practices are violent oppression of the faithful (Rev 17:6).

The whore is said to be drunk, which draws on common associations, since prostitutes were known for their love of wine and were depicted as drunkards (Plautus, *Pseud.* 181–82; Athenaeus, *Deipnosophistae* 570b; Alciphron, *Ep. Court.* 13.11, 16, 18; *T. Jud.* 13:5–6). Her cup is made of gold, as is fitting for the consort of kings, but instead of consuming fine wine, as one might expect (Martial, *Epigrams* 10.49), her cup is full of sewage. This scathing parody of elegance is revolting and designed to startle readers into recognizing the character of the ruling power. The expression "vile things" (*bdelygma*) points to false religious practices (Jer 13:27; 44:22; Ezek 5:9; 11:18). The imagery turns the idea that illicit sexual relations are defiling into a metaphor for the false worship and self-serving commercial practices of the empire (Rev 17:2; cf. 2:14, 20–22).

Then John adds that the woman drinks the blood of the saints and witnesses to Jesus (17:6). The portrayal of the bloodthirsty whore raises questions about the way the depiction of violence in the vision relates to the social world of the readers. By the time Revelation was written, some outbursts of violence against Christians had occurred, the most notorious of which happened in Rome during the reign of Nero (Tacitus, *Ann.* 15.44). Yet there had been no wholesale persecution of Christians in Asia Minor and Revelation's messages to the churches mention the death only of Antipas (Rev 2:13). Some interpreters assume that John predicts the onset of a persecution that will exceed those previously known (Mounce; Thomas). But it is more likely that he focuses on the present context of the readers. He magnifies the threat of imperial violence against Christians in order to disclose the *character* of the empire. The vision does not indicate how much violence it would take to fill Babylon's cup. Instead, it magnifies the phenomenon of violence against the followers of Jesus so readers come to see that in such actions the ruling power reveals its true nature (Giesen).

The Significance of the Whore and Beast (17:7–18)

John is amazed at the whore, prompting his angelic guide to give him—and his readers—an interpretation (17:7). This is not the first time a heavenly being has assisted John. When he was distraught that no one was worthy to open God's scroll, an elder directed attention to the Lion who conquered as a Lamb (5:4–6); and when John proved unable to identify the countless white-robed host, an elder explained that they were the redeemed (7:13–14). Here, an angel comments on the "mystery" of the woman and the beast, providing clues to their identities.

The beast "was and is not, and is about to come up from the abyss and go to destruction" (17:8). This description makes the beast the negative counterpart to God, "who is and who was and who is to come" (1:4). God's continuous existence in the present, past, and future shows that he is truly divine and worthy of worship (4:8; Neyrey, "'Without'"), whereas a beast that vacillates between presence and absence is no authentic deity. God is enthroned in heaven above, but the beast ascends from the abyss below. The beast once rose from the watery depths of the sea (13:1), but here and elsewhere it ascends from the smoky underworld, where the destroyer reigns and Satan will be incarcerated (9:2, 11; 11:7; 20:3). God the Creator brings all things into being (4:10–11), but the beast is an agent of destruction that ruins the earth and slaughters the faithful (11:7, 18). The Creator's purposes lead to a new creation (21:1), but the beast's actions result in its own demise. There is symmetry in divine judgment, for the beast that brings destruction finally suffers destruction itself (17:8; 19:20). The beast is also the negative counterpart to Christ the Lamb. God is "to come" (1:4; 4:8), and he does so through the coming of Christ for salvation and judgment (1:7; 22:7, 12, 20), but the beast's coming connotes oppression (Bauckham, *Climax*, 435).

Inhabitants of the earth are favorably impressed by the beast for at least two reasons (17:8b). One is that they are awed by the beast that "was and is not and is about to come," thinking that its ability to return makes it invincible and worthy of their loyalty. Invincibility was part of imperial ideology (NOTES on 13:3–4). The other reason is that their names have not been written in the scroll of life, which identifies those who have the hope of resurrection to life in the New Jerusalem. Since people are placed in the scroll from the time the world was made, their inclusion is an act of divine grace (NOTE on 13:8). Some interpreters infer that the opposite is also true, namely, that those who worship the beast have been divinely excluded from the scroll of life since the dawn of time (Beale). Yet Revelation does not have a notion of salvation in which God has eternally predestined many inhabitants of earth for condemnation. The book calls people everywhere to worship God (14:6–7), which presupposes that repentance is possible for them. There are also scenes in which the Lamb is said to redeem countless multitudes from every tribe (5:9–10; 7:9–14) and New Jerusalem stands open to receive nations and kings, who have shown hostility to God throughout Revelation (NOTES and COMMENT on 21:24–26). Hope for the healing of the nations continues into New Jerusalem (22:2). In Revelation the warnings of judgment work with the visions of hope in order to call people away from the ways of Babylon and toward true worship of God, which is the goal (11:13; 14:6–7; Giesen; Murphy; Smalley; Bauckham, *Climax*, 309–18; Boring 226–31).

What is said about the beast requires an understanding mind (*nous*, 17:9a). Something similar was said about using one's mind to calculate the beast's number (13:18). Since wisdom was highly valued in antiquity, the writer can expect that his readers will want to exhibit it. He helps them by disclosing the significance of the beast's heads, yet readers must put the clues together. This approach helps move readers to the author's point of view. Before readers can either accept or reject his message, they need to try to make sense of the clues—and to do so requires seeing the world as the author does.

First, readers learn that the seven heads of the beast represent seven mountains or hills (17:9b). Since Rome was commonly known as the city on seven hills, this detail allows readers to understand that the whore personifies Rome, even though the city is not named. The seven hills were a familiar element in Rome's presentation of itself, appearing in literature and pictures (Figure 32). Rome gazed "about her from her seven hills upon the whole world . . . the place of empire and the gods" (Ovid, *Trist.* 1.5.69–70). Since antiquity, this link to Rome has been widely recognized (Tertullian, *Adv. Jud.* 9; Victorinus; Oecumenius). Such a transparent allusion to Rome means that John does not use imagery to conceal his message but to reveal the opulence, arrogance, violence, and idolatry of the world's ruling power.

Next, readers learn that the seven heads also signify seven kings (Rev 17:9c). The angel gives two interpretations of the same "head" image. In a geographical sense the bejeweled city sits atop its mountains, but in a political sense it rests on its rulers. This aspect parodies the rhetoric in which Rome—with its ornate public buildings, many temples, and prosperous commercial networks—was situated on the largess of its emperors (Augustus, *Res* 19–21; Suetonius, *Aug.* 28.3; Strabo, *Geographica* 5.3.8). Just as portraying the city as a whore shows that its glamour is more garish than alluring, picturing the rulers who support her as the heads of a beast shows that her position rests on brutality, not benevolence.

Of the seven kings, five have fallen, one is reigning, and another is yet to come (Rev 17:10). These details have generated considerable speculation about which emperors John might have in mind (Table 1 and INTRO II.C.1–2). One approach traces a series of five emperors and identifies the reign of the sixth as the time that Revelation was written. But it is unclear where the sequence would begin. For example, counting could begin with Julius Caesar or Augustus, who mark the onset of the imperial era. Alternatively, the visions show the beast appearing after the Messiah's exaltation to heaven (12:5; 13:1), so the series could begin with Gaius Caligula, the first emperor after Christ, or perhaps with Nero, the great persecutor. Another problem is whether the list is to include all the emperors before John's time or only selected figures. Some interpreters count only the emperors who ruled for a significant length of time, others consider only deified emperors, and still others focus on emperors who died violently.

A second approach is to calculate the date of Revelation in order to identify the reigning emperor and then to count backwards to the five who have fallen. Given the uncertainties about Revelation's date, interpreters often must adjust the counting to make the sequence fit a particular theory about the date. We do well to recognize that the imagery was not designed to be used in this way, since readers would have known the identity of the reigning emperor and would not have needed to determine it. Moreover, it is not clear that identifying the five fallen kings has any bearing on the meaning of the vision as a whole. Their identities are inconsequential.

The most plausible interpretation is that seven is a round number representing the beast's power as a whole. Elsewhere in Revelation, the number seven shows completeness. The opening messages address seven churches, even though a different number could have been chosen since there were other churches in the region. Then plagues occur in cycles of seven visions, each cycle encompassing a full round of judgments. Similarly, the beast's seven heads signify the totality of its reign (Aune; Boring; Mounce; Murphy; Reddish). The point of identifying the current emperor as the sixth out of seven is to place readers near the end of the beast's dominion and yet warn that they are not really at the end, for another king must reign "for a little while" (*holigon*)—an indefinite period that makes calculation impossible (Bauckham, *Climax*, 406). "A little while," or a short time (*holigon*), is how long Satan rages on earth after his expulsion from heaven, and in the visionary world this period encompasses everything from Jesus' death and exaltation until his parousia (12:12). If "a little while" in the visionary world can include that much time, readers have no reason to think they can calculate the nearness of the end.

Repeating that the beast "was and is not" creates tensions in the interpretation (17:11). On the one hand this comment does not mean that the beast has no existence at all for John's readers. The monster's seven heads are the mountains on which the whore sits, and if the mountains exist, then the beast exists (17:9). Moreover, the seven heads are kings, one of whom reigns at the time John writes (17:10). Since one of the beast's heads is in power, the beast itself is a present reality (Giesen). On the other hand, the beast is especially identified with one of its heads, a figure who has ruled in the past, is not in power at the time of writing, and is to return in the future.

The imagery recalls stories about Nero, who had reigned before Revelation was composed and was likened to a tyrannical beast. Implicated in the fire that destroyed much of Rome, he unleashed a violent persecution against Christians, making Rome drunk with the blood of the saints (13:7; 17:6; Tacitus, *Ann.* 15.44). Although Nero's reign seemed to have ended when he killed himself, rumors persisted that he was alive and hiding among the Parthians. Some said he would come back, crossing the Euphrates with his allies to seize control of Rome (NOTE on 13:3). Traits of Nero appeared in the description of the beast in Rev 13, and here the beast returns to burn the imperial city (17:16). John does not expect Nero himself to return but weaves reminiscences of Nero into the portrayal of the beast to show that in Nero one can see the true nature of the empire (Aune; Bauckham, *Climax*, 384–452; Klauck, "Do").

The imagery places readers between the first and second comings of the beast (17:11). This idea fits the context in which John writes, since his readers are not facing widespread imperial persecution. Despite some local conflicts (2:9; 3:9), many seem prosperous and ready to accommodate the prevailing order (3:15–17). The vision of the beast warns them not to be deceived. The tyranny that has reared its head in the past might not be widely visible at present, but it is not gone; the beast's character has not changed (Boring; Murphy). John's vision warns against accommodation. Whenever the beast reappears, its end is to be destroyed—and that fate also threatens those who follow it.

The plot intensifies as the angel discloses that the beast's ten horns represent ten more kings (17:12). Revelation sometimes refers broadly to the "kings of the earth," who patronize the whore and join forces with the beast against God and the Lamb (16:14;

17:2, 18; 18:3), but the ten kings are a special group of the beast's allies. They may be the same as the kings from the east in 16:12 and are like the kings of the earth in their opposition to God and the Lamb (17:14). The difference is that the ten kings hate the whore and destroy her, while other kings grieve at her downfall (17:16; 18:9). The ten kings do not have royal power at the time Revelation is written but receive authority for an hour along with the returning beast. In Revelation's visionary world an hour is the length of time it takes to destroy Babylon, so reigning for an hour allows the ten kings to accomplish this grim task (18:10, 17, 19).

Relating Revelation's visionary world to the readers' world is complex. Futuristic interpreters assume that the vision predicts political developments at the end of the age, and some identify the kings with modern political entities (Lindsey, *Late*, 94; LaHaye and Jenkins, *Are*, 169). But this approach would have meant little to Revelation's first readers, and it involves selective literalism. For example, "ten" is taken as the exact number of kings, but the hour for which they rule is considered a general expression for "a short time"; the ten are said to be literal rulers, but the seven mountains and kings are symbols of kingdoms that span millennia. By way of contrast, historical interpreters usually correlate the images with political practices during John's time, when the Romans appointed vassal kings to govern parts of the empire. Since the beast has traits of Nero, the ten kings may be pictured as leaders accompanying Nero across the Euphrates to attack Rome. This is a much more helpful approach, but it too must work within limits. John says that the ten kings have not yet received royal power, which means that not even first-century readers could identify them with known political figures.

An alternative approach is to reframe the question. The issue is not whether readers can identify the kings, but whether they identify *with* them. The purpose of the vision is to shape the readers' commitments by contrasting the destructive consequences of allegiance to the beast with the life-giving outcome of allegiance to the Lamb. In an eerie spectacle of political concord, the kings put dissension aside and agree to give their might to the beast that embodies the ruinous force of Satan. Political unity was ordinarily lauded as a means of banishing the strife that destroys a city from within while providing strength against enemies from without (NOTE on 17:13). But in this case unity leads to the destruction of the city and the kings themselves. The issue, as John sees it, concerns who is served by such unity: the beast or the Lamb. Like the ten kings, those addressed by Revelation share a kingdom, but theirs is created by the redemptive work of Christ (1:5–6). Therefore, they are to emulate the heavenly elders, who step down from their thrones to cast their wreaths before God, declaring that those worthy of might are the God who creates and the Lamb who redeems (4:11; 5:12).

Two battles are depicted in the scenes that follow. The first foreshadows the end of the story, when kings battle the Lamb and are conquered by him (17:14). Preparations were made in 16:12–16, when the dragon, beast, and false prophet gathered kings for battle against God. The battle itself does not take place until 19:11–21, when Christ returns to defeat the beast and the allied kings with the sword from his mouth. The hostile kings are imposing, but the Lamb is the King of kings; he has a superior sovereignty. The Lamb has already conquered through his death, redeeming people for life in God's kingdom (1:5–6; 5:5–10). The problem is that those who belong to the

Lamb continue to be threatened by powers opposed to God, and as long as the threat is real, the Lamb's work is not done (13:7–10). Final victory will be won when the Lamb removes the threat by utterly defeating the agents of evil and death through his word (19:11–21; 1 Cor 15:24–26).

The angel introduces the second battle—the one that occurs at this point in the narrative—by revealing that the waters on which the whore sits represent peoples, multitudes, nations, and language groups (Rev 17:15). This imagery reflects the scope of Rome's empire, which encompassed peoples from the Atlantic coast to the Danube, Nile, and Tigris rivers farther east (Horace, *Carm.* 14.44–48). Its vast web of trade spanned the seas (Rev 18:11–20). Images in the imperial temple at Aphrodisias in Asia show Rome triumphing over nations ranging from the Egyptians, Arabs, and Judeans in the east to the Callaeci of western Spain (R. Smith, "Imperial," 96). The angel's comment also reflects the phenomenon of empire more broadly, since Babylon and other empires similarly wielded authority over many peoples, nations, and language groups (Dan 3:4; 5:19; 6:25; Jdt 3:8). The crux of the conflict is that the whore and beast wield authority over many nations, which in turn oppose the faithful (Rev 11:9 13:7); yet Christ redeems people of every tribe and nation, and it is God's desire that all these groups worship the Creator (5:9; 7:9; 14:6).

The vision climaxes when the beast and its ten horns vent their hatred for the whore by destroying her (17:16). Evil becomes evil's own undoing as those who dominate and ruin the earth end up ruining their own allies (11:18). The seven-headed dragon once chased the woman personifying God's people into the desert (12:1–6), but the seven-headed beast now turns the woman representing the ruling city into a desert. The whore wore purple, scarlet, gold, and jewels to display the wealth she received from clients and to lure others into her web, but these are stripped away in disgrace. The violent city that consumed the blood of the saints and witnesses to Jesus (17:6) now has her flesh consumed by the beast and its allies—a gruesome image for the sack of a city. In the end the city is burned, setting the stage for scenes of grief by her allies (18:9–10, 17–18). It can seem absurd for the beast that embodies imperial power to devastate the whore who personifies the imperial city. Yet the beast has traits of Nero, giving the spectacle a sordid realism. Nero may have ruled Rome, but he was also implicated in the fire that destroyed it (Tacitus, *Ann.* 15.38). In an ironic twist, destruction by fire means just that for the whore; it is "Nero all over again" (Boring 164).

Interpreters have often commented on the disturbing quality of Babylon's demise. A particular issue is the way the author uses feminine stereotypes to show God's action taking the form of violence against women (Pippin, "Eros"; Keller, "Eyeing"; Kim, "Uncovering"; Streete, *Strange*, 150–58). Some point out that the vision is not about women; rather, it uses feminine imagery when calling for resistance to Roman imperialism (Schüssler Fiorenza 12–15; Rossing, *Choice*, 87–90). Others respond that the use of such images does have a negative effect on the way readers perceive gender roles (Frilingos, *Spectacles*, 103–7; Glancy and Moore, "How," 568).

An important dimension of the question is how this imagery fits Revelation's understanding of justice. The writer works with a sense of symmetry, in which the perpetrators of violence become the victims of their own practices. Roman iconography celebrated the conquests of other nations that created the empire in which John's readers

Figure 33. Claudius subjugating Britain. Relief from the imperial temple at Aphrodisias (first century CE). New York University Excavations at Aphrodisias.

lived. For example, in a relief from the imperial temple at Aphrodisias, the emperor Claudius conquers a woman who personifies Britain (Figure 33). In another, Nero stands triumphant over a woman representing Armenia (Figure 34). In these sculptures, the women who symbolize nations are partially stripped and physically subjugated.

In John's vision, the pattern is reversed. The female figure is no longer one of the other nations but is Rome itself. The personified city is stripped and devastated by the same kind of violence that her rulers previously used against others. The brutality that created the empire now becomes the empire's undoing. The vision does not celebrate violence; rather, it warns that the city that thrives on the violence its rulers use against others will finally fall victim to these same destructive practices.

Divine justice is also reflected in the irony that the kings who have come together in one mind (*gnōmē*) in order to give power to the beast are actually carrying out the purpose, or mind (*gnōmē*), of God (17:17). In a remarkable move, God enables a group of opponents to put aside their differences and to agree on a common leader, achieving the unity that was considered a gift from heaven (Dio Chrysostom, *Or.* 39.8). Such concord allows the beast and its allies to devastate the great city, fulfilling the words of God that were spoken earlier: "Fallen, fallen is Babylon the great" (Rev 14:8). This message, voiced by the prophets (Isa 21:9; cf. Isa 13–14; 21; 47; Jer 50–51), will be repeated at the beginning of the next chapter (Rev 18:2). For John, connecting the actions to the words previously spoken shows the integrity of God. What God has spoken, he will do.

A haunting comment concludes the vision: "The woman that you saw is the great city that has royal power over the kings of the earth" (17:18). These words underscore the contrast between the ruling power's present grandeur and its sordid downfall. The vision would strike readers in the seven churches in various ways. For those threatened because of their beliefs, as at Smyrna, the passage offers encouragement to persevere, since God's purposes will prevail (2:9–10). For those at Pergamum and Thyatira, who adopt an easy attitude toward the immorality, or *porneia*, of idolatry, the fall of the whore, or *pornē*, warns that accommodation means having relationships that are debased and set people against God (2:14, 20). For readers exhibiting a complacency born of prosperity, as at Laodicea, the way the gaudy whore is stripped of her purple garments and gold baubles warns that material wealth is no ultimate source of security. The reward of the faithful is the refined gold and white garments that Christ provides (3:17–18). Rhetorically, John's goal is to give readers incentive to resist the beguiling social and economic forces represented by the whore.

Figure 34. Nero subjugating Armenia. Relief from the imperial temple at Aphrodisias (first century CE). New York University Excavations at Aphrodisias.

36. Interlude Continued: Fallen Is Babylon (18:1–24)

18 [1]After these things I saw another angel coming down from heaven with great authority, and the earth was filled with light from his glory. [2]He called out with a loud voice, saying, "Fallen, fallen is Babylon the great! It has become a home for demons and a lair for every unclean spirit, and a lair for every unclean bird, and a lair for every unclean and disgusting beast. [3]For all the nations have fallen because of the wine of her passionate immorality, and the kings of the earth committed immorality with her, and the merchants of the earth became rich from the power of her loose and extravagant ways."

[4]Then I heard another voice from heaven say, "Come out of her, my people, so that you do not take part in her sins and do not receive any of her plagues, [5]for her sins have stretched up to heaven, and God remembered her acts of injustice. [6]Give her what she herself has given to others. Give her back twice as much for what she has done. In the cup that she mixed, mix her twice as much. [7]To the extent that she glorified herself and indulged her loose and extravagant ways, give her pain and grief. For in her heart she says, 'I sit as a queen! I am not a widow. I will never see grief.' [8]This is why her plagues will come in just one day: deadly disease and grief and hunger. She will be consumed by fire, for the Lord God who judges her is powerful.

[9]"The kings of the earth who committed immorality and shared her loose and extravagant ways will weep and mourn over her when they see the smoke of her burning. [10]They will stand a long way off because they are afraid of the pain she suffers, and they will say, 'Oh no! Babylon, you great city, you powerful city, for in just one hour your judgment came.'

[11]"The merchants of the earth will weep and mourn over her, for no one buys their cargo anymore—[12]cargo of gold and silver and jewels and pearls, and fine linen and purple and silk and scarlet, and all the articles of citrus wood and all kinds of articles of ivory and all kinds of articles of fine wood and bronze and iron and marble, [13]and cinnamon and amomum and incense and fragrant ointment and frankincense, and wine and oil and fine flour and wheat, and cattle and sheep and horses and carriages, and slaves and souls of human beings—[14]'The ripe fruit your soul craved has gone from you. All your glitter and glamour are lost to you, never ever to be found again.' [15]The merchants who sold these things, who got so rich by her, will stand a long way off because they fear the pain she suffers. They will weep and mourn, [16]and say, 'Oh, no! The great city that wore fine linen and purple and scarlet, who glittered with gold and jewels and pearls—[17]in just one hour such great wealth was laid waste.'

"Every sea captain and every seafarer and the sailors and all who make their living on the sea stood a long way off. [18]They cried out as they saw the smoke from her burning and said, 'Who was like the great city?' ¹⁹They threw dust on their heads and were crying out, weeping and mourning, and they said 'Oh no! The great city, where all who have ships at sea became so rich by her wealth, for in just one hour she was laid waste.' ²⁰Rejoice over her, O heaven, and saints and apostles and prophets, because God has judged her as she judged you."

²¹Then a powerful angel picked up a stone that was like a large millstone and threw it into the sea. He said, "With such violent force will Babylon the great city be thrown down, and it will not be found anymore. ²²The sound of harpists and musicians and pipers and trumpeters will not be heard in you anymore. No craftsman of any kind will be found in you anymore. The sound of the hand mill will not be heard in you anymore. ²³The light of a lamp will not shine in you anymore. The sound of a bridegroom and a bride will not be heard in you anymore, because your merchants were the aristocrats of the earth, and all the nations were deceived by your sorcery. ²⁴In her was found the blood of the prophets and the saints and all who have been slain on the earth."

NOTES

18:1. *After these things I saw another angel coming down from heaven with great authority, and the earth was filled with light from his glory.* One of the seven angels who poured out plagues in 15:1–16:21 showed John the whore in 17:1, but now "another" angel speaks. He is not necessarily part of that group. He reflects divine glory (cf. 10:1–2; Exod 34:29; Matt 17:2–3). Some interpreters suggest that the angel is Christ (Primasius; Beale), but the term "angel" refers to a being other than Christ (Rev 22:8–9).

18:2. *He called out with a loud voice, saying, "Fallen, fallen is Babylon the great!"* The words recall those of Isaiah, who said, "Fallen, fallen is Babylon; and all the images of her gods lie shattered on the ground" (Isa 21:9; cf. 13:1–14:23; Jer 50:1–51:64; Rev 14:8). What was said earlier through the prophets is now being accomplished. In the OT Babylon was called great because of its power to rule the world (Dan 4:30). In Revelation the portrait of "Babylon" includes traits of imperial Rome, which in the first century was considered the greatest city on earth in size, military strength, and economic power (Seneca the Younger, *Helv.* 6.3). Yet this vision shows that even the most powerful city is doomed to fall. Some interpreters suggest that Babylon represents Jerusalem, but this is implausible (NOTE on Rev 17:5).

"It has become a home for demons and a lair for every unclean spirit, and a lair for every unclean bird. The language recalls prophetic announcements of the ruin of Babylon: "wild animals will lie down there, and its houses will be full of howling creatures; there ostriches will live, and there goat-demons will dance. Hyenas will cry in its towers, and jackals in the pleasant palaces" (Isa 13:21–22; cf. Jer 50:39; 51:37). Similar things were said about Edom (Isa 34:11–15), Jerusalem (Jer 9:10–11), and Nineveh (Zeph 2:13–14), so the judgment is typical of what happens to a faithless city. Babylon's broken walls create a home and a lair (*phylakē*) for despicable beings. Although the term *phylakē* could refer to a prison, here it is simply an enclosed space. Demons and unclean spirits were

said to inhabit desolate places, including devastated cities (Bar 4:35). Birds living in the ruined cities include ostriches, ravens, and owls; other unclean birds included eagles, vultures, buzzards, and hawks (Deut 14:12–18). Such birds feast on carrion following the defeat of Babylon's ally the beast (Rev 19:17–18).

"and a lair for every unclean and disgusting beast. Jackals, hyenas, and hedgehogs lived in ruined cities (Isa 13:21–22; 34:11; Jer 50:39; 51:37; 4Q179 1 I, 9). Some manuscripts omit this passage and relate "disgusting" to the birds in the previous line (א C 051). Others mention beasts but omit the spirits (1611) or the birds (A), and some include all of them (2329). A few interpreters omit the beasts, preferring the shorter reading (Aune; Osborne). It is best, however, to include all these creatures since the words "lair for every unclean" are repeated three times, followed by the mention of a spirit, bird, or beast. Given the repetition and the fact that different things are missing in different manuscripts, it seems probable that copyists accidentally skipped some items (*TCGNT*², 682–83; Schmid, *Studien*, 2:143–46).

18:3. *"For all the nations have fallen because of the wine of her passionate immorality.* This line echoes Jer 51:7: Babylon made "all the earth drunken; the nations drank of her wine, and so the nations went mad," yet suddenly, "Babylon has fallen." Babylon's passionate immorality is a metaphor for the debased pursuit of luxury, false worship, and brutality (Rev 17:2). Similar critiques appear elsewhere: "they have defiled themselves in the paths of licentiousness, and with wicked wealth . . . and debauchery and bragged about wealth and gain," taking the wine that is wickedness (CDª VIII, 5–11). In Revelation the nations are called to worship God (Rev 14:6), but here they are dominated by the beast and Babylon and come under divine judgment (13:7; 14:8; 17:15; 18:23). Yet God and Christ are the rightful rulers of the nations (15:3; 19:15), and Revelation extends hope that the nations will turn to God and live (15:4; 21:24; 22:2). The vision of New Jerusalem calls the nations away from the path of destruction into a different future.

There is broad manuscript support for reading "have fallen" from some form of *piptein* (*peptōka[si]n*, א A C 1006* 1611; *pepōtken*, 1854). Most modern editions, however, read "have drunk" from a form of *pinein* (*pepōka[si]n*, 1006ᶜ 2329; *pepōken*, P 051). Although less well-attested, this reading is said to make better sense, with the alternative "have fallen" said to have arisen through an error of the eye or ear, perhaps because of Babylon's having "fallen" in 18:2 (*TCGNT*², 683). Nevertheless, "have fallen" is a better attested and more difficult reading, yet one that is plausible, since those who drink to excess stagger and fall (Isa 24:20; Jer 25:27). Alternative readings could have arisen as errors of the eye or ear, or as attempts to ease a difficult reading. The variant "made to drink" from *potizein* is weakly attested and harmonizes Rev 18:3 with 14:8 (2042, NRSVᶠⁿ; Mounce). Reading "have fallen" continues a progression: The nations drink Babylon's wine (14:8), become intoxicated (17:2), and fall (18:3; Aune; Osborne).

"and the kings of the earth committed immorality with her. In Revelation the kings of the earth are hostile to God but favorable toward Babylon and lament its downfall (16:14; 17:2, 18; 18:9). The ten kings who hate and destroy Babylon are a smaller group (17:12, 16). Committing immorality with Babylon involves debased political relationships, self-serving commercial ties, and religious relationships that include the imperial cult (NOTE on 17:2).

"and the merchants of the earth became rich. Merchants travel in order to make a profit by buying goods and then selling them elsewhere. Much of their trade in the vision has to do with luxury items such as gold, silver, gems, and pearls, as well as trafficking in slaves (18:11–17a; 1 Macc 3:41). In Ezek 27:9–25, Tyre is the merchant city that entwines the world in its web of trade. In antiquity, merchants were emblematic of those driven by the desire for wealth. Some were thought dishonest. They "sail around looking for a depressed market; they mingle with agents and retailers; they buy and sell, submitting their own persons to unholy rates of interest, and striving after their capital." But if they fail to make a profit, "they climb into their lifeboats, wreck the ships, and pleading 'divine intervention' they personally deprive others of their lives" (Philostratus, *Vit. Apoll.* 4.32). It was said that greed sent people on commercial journeys to barter and make wealth dishonestly (Persius, *Satirae* 5.132–39; cf. Sir 26:29; 37:11).

"from the power of her loose and extravagant ways." The words "loose and extravagant ways" translate the rare Greek words *strēnos* (18:3) and *strēnian* (18:7, 9). Although these words can be translated as "luxury," the sense is more sharply negative. The meaning corresponds to "passionate immorality" (Rev 18:3, 9) and indicates sexual promiscuity (*T. Benj.* 9:1), eating and drinking to excess (Athenaeus, *Deipnosophistae* 3.127d), arrogance (2 Kgs 19:28), running wild (P.Oxy. 2783.24), and not working (P.Meyer 20.23). This type of behavior is linked to the merchants' wealth, thereby casting their commercial ventures in a negative light.

18:4. *Then I heard another voice from heaven say.* Since the voice refers to "my people," the speaker could be God; but the voice refers to God in the third person in 18:5, so it could be that Christ, an angel, or another member of the heavenly court now speaks. In any case, the voice expresses God's perspective (cf. 10:4).

"Come out of her, my people, so that you do not take part in her sins and do not receive any of her plagues. The language recalls prophetic exhortations to leave Babylon because of the city's sins: "Come out of her, my people! Save your lives, each of you, from the fierce anger of the Lord!" (Jer 51:45); "Flee from the midst of Babylon, save your lives, each of you! Do not perish because of her guilt, for this is the time of the Lord's vengeance; he is repaying her what is due" (Jer 51:6; cf. 50:8). Similarly, "Depart, depart, go out from there! Touch no unclean thing; go out from the midst of it, purify yourselves" (Isa 52:11). The city's sins involve idolatry, blasphemous arrogance, and violence. The plagues that fall on the city include deadly disease, famine, and fire (Rev 18:8).

18:5. *"for her sins have stretched up to heaven.* The city piles one sin upon another until the heap is as high as the skies (Jer 51:9; Ezra 9:6; Homer, *Od.* 15.329). The language shows the height of arrogance. By extending its transgressions to the gates of heaven, the city creates its own tower of Babel and shows contempt for the reign of God (Rev 18:7; Gen 11:4; Isa 14:13–14; Ezek 31:3, 10). Sins that reach heaven prompt God to act (Rev 18:5b; Jonah 1:2; *4 Ezra* 11:43). Just as the saints' prayers for help rise like incense before God (Rev 8:3–4), so do Babylon's sins. Each calls for a response from God. The language is hyperbolic—like that of the Hebrew prophets who inspired it (Heschel, *Prophets*, 1:3–26). Many readers would not have thought that the problem was so severe. Rhetorically, hyperbole is effective when readers are moved for a moment by its poetic exaggeration so that they see the character of something in bold terms (Lausberg, *Handbook* §909).

"and God remembered her acts of injustice. When God remembers his people, he acts on their behalf (1 Sam 1:19; Ps 25:6), but when he remembers injustice, he acts in judgment (Ps 109:14; Jer 14:10).

18:6. *"Give her what she herself has given to others.* The command "give her" (*apodote*) is in the second-person plural, and it is not clear who is to take action against Babylon. The plurals in Rev 18:6–7 could simply be indefinite, calling for judgment without specifying who should carry it out (Ruiz, *Ezekiel,* 403). Some interpreters think the plurals address punishing angels, like those in Rev 16 (Smalley), or the ten kings, who destroy Babylon (17:16; Roloff; Thomas), and some include God among those called into action (Beale). Yet it is not clear that the text has such specificity. A few argue that the plurals summon Christians to take vengeance on their enemies. They note that in 18:4 God's people are urged to leave Babylon, and since there is no explicit change in subject, they infer that God's people are called to avenge themselves in 18:6. This interpretation resembles Jewish texts in which the righteous slay the wicked (1QM I, 1; *1 En.* 90:19; 91:12; 95:3; 96:1; 98:12; *Apoc. Ab.* 29:19; Aune; S. M. Elliott, "Who"). However, this approach does not fit Revelation, in which agents of evil destroy each other (Rev 17:16) or are destroyed by Christ (17:14; 19:11–21). If the plurals address readers, they summon them to a prophetic vocation. They make God's opponents drink the cup of wrath, not by physically slaying them, but by pronouncing divine judgment (Jer 25:15–17; Rossing, *Choice,* 124).

"Give her back twice as much for what she has done. In the cup that she mixed, mix her twice as much. The previous directive says that punishment is to be equal to the offense: Since Babylon dealt violently with the faithful, she suffers the same kind of violence herself (Rev 19:2; Jer 50:15, 29; Ps 137:8). Here, the sense is intensified to double repayment (cf. Isa 40:2; Jer 16:18). Some interpreters suggest that the passage means that the wrongdoer is to be repaid an equivalent, or "duplicate," amount (Beale; Smalley; Thomas) or be punished in two ways—by both torment and grief or by suffering in both body and soul (cf. Baltzer, *Deutero-Isaiah,* 53; Holladay, *Jeremiah,* 479). Yet the context in Revelation is poetic denunciation and not a statement of strict legal practice, so the imagery should not be pressed. The author returns to punishments that are equal to the offense in the next verse.

18:7. *"To the extent that she glorified herself and indulged her loose and extravagant ways, give her pain and grief.* Glory is rightly given to God in worship (Rev 1:6; 4:9; 14:7; 15:4), but the whore has glorified herself, which is hubris (16:9). Those who have this attitude will be brought low (Prov 29:23; Dan 5:20; Luke 14:11). Babylon's self-glorification is expressed in her pursuit of luxury, idolatry, and shedding the blood of the saints (Rev 17:4–6). If Babylon's self-glorification and luxurious life have brought grief to others, she receives the same measure of pain and grief. Pain involves both physical and emotional agony (9:5; 14:10–11), as is evident by the smoke of torment that goes up from the city (18:10, 15). Grief is felt as a result of loss (18:8).

"For in her heart she says, 'I sit as a queen! I am not a widow. I will never see grief.' The words recall Isaiah's warning to Babylon: "Now therefore hear this, you lover of pleasures, who sit securely, who say in your heart, 'I am and there is no one besides me; I shall not sit as a widow or know the loss of children'" (Isa 47:8). The arrogant city will suffer what it thinks it cannot suffer (47:9; cf. 14:13–14). Similar soliloquies are ascribed to other cities that contribute to Revelation's depiction of the harlot city. God said to

Tyre, "Your heart is proud and you have said, 'I am a god; I sit in the seat of gods, in the heart of the seas'" (Ezek 28:2). Nineveh was "the exultant city that lived secure and said to itself, 'I am, and there is no one else'" (Zeph 2:15). And Rome was called queen and mistress of the world, thinking that she ruled an empire without end (Julius Frontinus, *De aquis* 2.88.1. Virgil, *Aen.* 1.279; Aune). When personified as a woman, Rome said, "I am alone, and no one will ravage me" (*Sib. Or.* 5.173).

Similar soliloquies occur in other sources, showing that the hubris motif would have been widely understood by Revelation's readers (Jer 5:12; Ovid, *Metam.* 6.170–202). Luxury and wealth foster arrogance, which leads to a downfall (*Sib. Or.* 2:133–34; Isa 14:15; Jer 5:14–17; Ezek 28:6–10). The device of imputing speech was used earlier to critique the Laodiceans, who said, "I am rich and have become wealthy and do not need anything," only to be warned of their need to repent (Rev 3:17). John's use of this literary form emphasizes the fact that the arrogant complacency he attributes to Babylon was also an issue for the Christians at Laodicea (M. Mathews, "Function").

18:8. *"This is why her plagues will come in just one day: deadly disease and grief and hunger. She will be consumed by fire, for the Lord God who judges her is powerful.* Destruction that comes in just one day (18:8) or hour (18:10, 17, 19) is swift and sudden (Isa 47:9). The plagues listed here fit a fallen city, since deadly disease and famine accompany a siege, people mourn those who die in battle, and defeated cities were sometimes burned by their captors (Lam 1:11; Zech 9:4; 2 Kgs 25:9). The language is analogous to that in Jer 50:34 (27:34 LXX), which says of the oppressed people of Israel that "their Redeemer is mighty [*ischyros*]; the Lord of hosts is his name," and he will bring trouble for "the inhabitants of Babylon."

18:9. *"The kings of the earth who committed immorality and shared her loose and extravagant ways will weep and mourn over her when they see the smoke of her burning.* In the first century the Romans allowed leaders governing regions in cooperation with the empire to call themselves kings (Rev 17:2; NOTE on 1:5). In Revelation kings represent the ruling class generally (6:15; Bauckham, *Climax*, 372). The kings commit immorality with Babylon as kingdoms consorted with Tyre the prostitute (Isa 23:17). As a metaphor, such immorality with Babylon connotes debased political relationships, self-serving commercial ties, and religious relationships that include the imperial cult (Ezek 27:33; cf. the NOTE on Rev 17:2). On "loose and extravagant ways," see the NOTE on 18:3. In Ezekiel's depiction of the fall of Tyre, kings are afraid (Ezek 26:15–17; 27:35). Babylon's allies would also bewail the city's downfall (Jer 51:8). On Babylon being burned, see the NOTE on Rev 17:16. The rising smoke is a visible sign of judgment (14:11; Isa 34:9–10).

18:10. *"They will stand a long way off because they are afraid of the pain she suffers, and they will say, 'Oh no! Babylon, you great city, you powerful city, for in just one hour your judgment came.'* The reactions of passersby show the effect of the devastation, as in the OT, in which they shake their heads in horror (Jer 18:16; 50:13; Ezek 5:14–15). Their standing "a long way off" shows their fear of suffering the same fate. Earlier, *ouai* announced that "woe" was coming on the ungodly (Rev 8:13; 12:12). Here, it expresses grief ("oh no!") at what has occurred (1 Kgs 13:30). The coming of judgment in just one hour fits the one-hour reign of the ten kings who destroy the city (Rev 17:12). It also connotes quick and unexpected destruction (Livy, *Rom. Hist.* 1.29.6). Although Babylon is called great and "powerful" (Rev 16:19; 17:18), this claim is now shown to be false since the city has fallen under the judgment of God, who is "powerful" (18:8).

18:11. *"The merchants of the earth will weep and mourn over her.* Ezekiel calls Tyre—a city that resembles Revelation's Babylon—"the merchant of the peoples on many coastlands" (Ezek 27:3). Tyre's vast trade network extended from Tarshish in southern Spain in the west to Greece, Asia Minor, Mesopotamia, and Arabia farther east (27:12–25). When Tyre's empire is destroyed, the merchants hiss in horror (27:36). Merchants of the Roman empire frequented ports throughout the Mediterranean, ventured south along the African coast to what today is Tanzania, and sailed eastward to the Arabian peninsula and India, which provided access to goods from China (Casson, *Periplus*). Merchants traveled the earth to bring goods to Rome: "Here is brought from every land and sea all the crops of the seasons and the produce of each land, river, lake, as well as the arts of the Greeks and barbarians, so that if someone should wish to view these things, he must either see them by traveling over the whole world or be in this city." At Rome it was possible "to see so many cargoes from India and even from Arabia Felix, if you wish, that one imagines that for the future the trees are left bare for the people there and that they must come here and beg for their own produce" (Aelius Aristides, *Or.* 26.11–12).

"for no one buys their cargo anymore. Merchants made a profit by buying merchandise at one place and selling it at another. To transport goods, they often leased space in ships (Rev 18:17). Their ventures required the support of investors, who expected a share of the profits (Casson, *Periplus*, 11–47). Maximizing profits was best done by trading in goods that could be resold at a high value, such as those listed in 18:12–13, which are mainly luxury items. Pliny the Elder identified the twenty-seven most costly items in the Roman world (*Nat.* 37.204), and eighteen of these are included as merchandise in Rev 18.

Fifteen of the twenty-nine products linked to Tyre in Ezek 27:12–24 are listed in Revelation. Revelation omits items such as tin, lead, mules, honey, goats, and carpets, which appear in Ezekiel, but adds pearls, silk, citrus wood, marble, and carriages, which were fashionable in the Roman world (Seneca the Younger, *Herc. Ot.* 659–69; Martial, *Epigrams* 9.59; Dio Chrysostom, *Or.* 3.93; 13.34). Some interpreters argue that Revelation summarizes what Ezekiel says about trade with Tyre without regard to the Roman imperial context (Prigent; Provan, "Foul"). It seems clear, however, that the goods listed blend items from the OT with those from John's context, just as the portrayal of the whore fuses traits of OT cities with those of imperial Rome (Bauckham, *Climax*, 338–83; Siitonen, "Merchants"; Aune).

18:12. *"cargo of gold and silver.* Gold and silver were valuable trade goods in the OT period (Ezek 27:12, 16). Gold was imported to Rome in large quantities, especially from Spain, where the mines were owned by the state. Gold epitomized ostentation, and critics charged that Roman conquests were driven by a desire for gold and that social status and personal happiness had come to be measured in gold (Pliny the Elder, *Nat.* 33.57, 152; Strabo, *Geographica* 3.2.10; Petronius, *Satyricon* 119; Lucian, *Nigr.* 15; 23). Silver, imported from Spain and other places, was used for jewelry, statues, mirrors, and lavish bathtubs. It adorned carriages, banquet couches, and women's bedsteads. Rich Romans ate from silver dishes, and some displayed wealth by purchasing silver dishes weighing a hundred pounds or more (Pliny the Elder, *Nat.* 33.95–96). Both gold and silver were used for statues of gods (NOTE on Rev 9:20).

.nd jewels and pearls. Jewels such as rubies, carnelian, chrysolite, moonstone, *.l,* onyx, jasper, sapphire, turquoise, and emerald were part of Tyre's trade empire (Ezek 27:16, 22; 28:13). Later, the Romans imported many of these items from India and others from Africa, Asia Minor, and elsewhere (Casson, *Periplus,* 42; Pliny the Elder, *Nat.* 37.79). Pearls are not mentioned in the OT but were highly valued during Roman times. The best came from India, though some were from the Red Sea and Persian Gulf (Pliny the Elder, *Nat.* 9.106; Athenaeus, *Deipnosophistae* 3.93).

"and fine linen and purple. These items connoted wealth and were part of the OT trade network (Ezek 16:13; 27:7, 16; Prov 31:21–22). Wealthier Romans wore fine linen. The best was imported from Egypt, Spain, and Asia Minor, and it was mentioned with purple and silk (Luke 16:19; Plutarch, *Mor.* 396B). Purple dye was expensive and made from shellfish; some purple dye was imported from Africa and Greece, but the most coveted came from Tyre. The dye's exorbitant price made purple a symbol of status and affluence (Pliny the Elder, *Nat.* 9.127–41). Some Asian cities produced and marketed linen and purple cloth (Acts 16:14; TAM 933; Magie, *Roman,* 1:48).

"and silk and scarlet. Silk, which originated in China, is not mentioned in the OT. It was sometimes brought to the Roman Empire overland by caravans or more often by ships coming from northwest India. Wealthy women wore silk. Some people thought it unseemly for men to wear it, but emperors and other men did so nonetheless (Dio Cassius, *Rom. Hist.* 57.15.1; 59.17.3; Pliny the Elder, *Nat.* 21.8; Plutarch, *Mor.* 145E; Josephus, *J.W.* 7.126). Scarlet dye came from insects in Galatia, North Africa, and elsewhere. It was less costly than purple and was used in luxury clothing (Pliny the Elder, *Nat.* 9.141; 22.3).

"and all the articles of citrus wood and all kinds of articles of ivory. Citrus wood came from North Africa, primarily Morocco, and was prized for its color and grain patterns, which were compared to markings on a peacock, leopard, or tiger. The wood is not mentioned in the OT, but citrus tables were the height of fashion among Romans, who spent enormous sums on them (Pliny the Elder, *Nat.* 13.91–102; Martial, *Epigrams* 10.98; 14.18; Petronius, *Satyricon* 119). Ivory was a sign of wealth and was a luxury trade item in the OT (Ezek 27:15; 1 Kgs 10:18; 22:39). High demand for ivory in Roman times reduced elephant populations in northern Africa and increased ivory importation from India (Pliny the Elder, *Nat.* 8.7; 12.5; Casson, *Periplus,* 42).

"and all kinds of articles of fine wood and bronze. Types of woods in Tyre's commercial network included local varieties such as fir, cedar, oak, and pine or boxwood, as well as African ebony (Ezek 27:5. 15). For Romans, the finer woods were maple and boxwood from Italy and Greece, cedar and cypress from Asia Minor, terebinth from Greece, and citrus from Morocco. Artisans used these woods to make expensive furnishings, boxes, doors, and other items, some inlaid with ivory. Though less common, ebony brought a high price (Pliny the Elder, *Nat.* 16.66, 70; Virgil, *Aen.* 10.136; Persius, *Satirae* 5.132–39; Meiggs, *Trees,* 279–99). Bronze was widely used in OT times and was traded at Tyre and other places (Ezek 27:13). For Romans, the most famous was Corinthian bronze, which was very expensive. With hues ranging from white to gold to reddish brown, it was said to be a blend of copper, gold, and silver. Wealthy collectors coveted figurines made from this bronze, which were status symbols (Murphy-O'Connor, "Corinthian").

"and iron and marble. Iron was a item in Tyre's trade network (Ezek 27:12, 19). The Romans obtained it from Spain and the alpine regions. When used for plows, agricultural tools, implements for quarrying and building, statues, and goblets it served peaceful purposes. On the military market, however, iron was turned into the swords and weapons that made "wars and slaughter and brigandage" more lethal; it was the metal "most hostile to mortality" (Pliny the Elder, *Nat.* 34.138–41; Diodorus Siculus, *Libr.* 5.13.1–2). Marble is not mentioned in the OT, but in Roman times it was in high demand for public and private use. Both the white and colored types were desirable. Ships were designed to transport heavy marble slabs and entire stone columns from Greece, Africa, Egypt, and parts of Asia Minor (Strabo, *Geographica* 12.8.14; Pliny the Elder, *Nat.* 36.1–8, 48–51; Seneca the Younger, *Ep.* 115.8; *NP* 8:281–92).

18:13. *"and cinnamon and amomum.* Cinnamon—like cassia wood, which came from the same plant—was traded for its aromatic properties (Exod 30:23–24; Ezek 27:19). It was grown in southern China and Southeast Asia, but the Romans thought it came from Arabia, northeast Africa, or India, since Roman merchants purchased it from Arabian and Indian traders. Alternatively, "cinnamon" may refer to a different spice, grown in Africa (Casson, *Periplus*, 122–24; Young, *Rome's*, 20). Romans used cinnamon in perfume, medicine, and incense and as a flavoring in wine (Pliny the Elder, *Nat.* 12.85–98; 13.15, 18; 14.107–8). Amomum, which is not mentioned in the OT, was an expensive aromatic substance from India; it was purchased at markets in Armenia, Media, Pontus, and other regions. The plant's pepperlike seeds were used in medicines and perfumes (Seneca the Younger, *Thy.* 948; Pliny the Elder, *Nat.* 12.48–49; 13.16; 26.34). Both cinnamon and amomum were lavishly used at Roman funerals (Persius, *Satirae* 3.104; 6.35).

"and incense and fragrant ointment and frankincense. Fragrant ointment (*myron*) was blended from substances like cinnamon, amomum, and myrrh (*smyrna*). Myrrh was a resin drawn from trees in southern Arabia and Somalia and imported for use in perfumes, medicines, and incense (Exod 30:23; Ezek 27:17 LXX; Pliny the Elder, *Nat.* 12.66–71). Inscriptions from Rome describe the wealthy reclining on fine couches and wearing perfume and sumptuous clothing: "wash, anoint yourselves with perfume, live in comfort and enjoy yourself, spend what you can—for whom are you keeping it?" (Connolly, *NewDocs* 4:130–31). Incense was made from cinnamon, myrrh, and frankincense—another resin imported from southern Arabia and Somalia (Exod 30:34; Josephus, *J. W.* 6.390). Romans burned incense to honor the gods and used large quantities at funerals (Pliny the Elder, *Nat.* 12.51–65, 83).

"and wine and oil. People of every social class consumed these items, which were trade goods in the OT (Ezek 27:17–18). Later, Roman markets included wines made in Italy as well as those from Spain, Sicily, Greece, and Asia (Horace, *Sat.* 2.8.15–17; Petronius, *Satyricon* 76; Juvenal, *Satirae* 14.270–71). Olive oil was produced throughout the empire and used for food, medicine, lighting, perfume, and rubbing on the body. Certain regions were known for fine wines and oils, which were traded as luxury items. Lesser quality wines and oils were used locally, but the merchants who imported them favored the better grades, which could be sold at higher prices (Strabo, *Geographica* 3.2.6; Pliny the Elder, *Nat.* 15.1–8, 18–19; *OCD* 1065).

"and fine flour and wheat. Grain was a staple that figured in OT trade (Ezek 27:17). Fine flour, used by the wealthy (Ezek 16:13), was white and finely ground, in contrast

to the darker and coarser types used in lower quality breads. In Roman times the best flour was made from Italian and North African wheat (Pliny the Elder, *Nat.* 18.82, 89, 102; Martial, *Epigrams* 13.10). Rome's population was probably between eight hundred thousand and one million people, creating an enormous market for grain. Fleets of cargo ships transported wheat from Egypt, North Africa, and other provinces (Lucian, *Nav.* 1–9; Acts 27:6). Emperors oversaw supplies of grain, but those procuring and shipping it were private contractors, who received inducements to transport grain to the city year-round and to make sure that the needs of the capital were met before those of other cities (Kraybill, *Imperial*, 107, 118).

"*and cattle and sheep*. Cattle were valued for their work, as well as for their milk and meat. Trained to pull plows and carts, they were widely used for working on farms and transporting goods. Many of the cattle in Italy were raised locally or shipped in from Sicily. Established landowners purchased cattle from different regions, each breed with distinctive traits. They enhanced their breeding stock with animals from Gaul, Asia, and especially Epirus in Greece (Columella, *Rust.* 6.1.1–2; Varro, *Rust.* 2.5.10; Strabo, *Geographica* 6.2.7). Sheep were traded with Tyre and were also part of the Roman economy (Ezek 27:14, 21). They were valued for wool, which was a staple in the textile industry, as well as for meat. Italian flocks included sheep of various types, and owners developed their breeding stock with imported animals from Gaul and Miletus in Asia. Some people paid high prices for Spanish breeding rams (Columella, *Rust.* 7.2.3–4; Pliny the Elder, *Nat.* 3.2.6; Strabo, *Geographica* 3.2.6).

"*and horses and carriages*. Horses symbolized wealth, power, and prestige and were valuable in international trade in the OT (Ezek 27:14; 1 Kgs 10:23–29; Isa 2:7; Esth 6:8). The Roman military used horses to pull chariots. In triumphal processions the horses displayed the strength of the victors (*NP* 6:506–10). Chariot racing was one of the most popular forms of entertainment, with competitors driving teams of two or four horses. Horses for chariot races were very expensive and were imported from North Africa, Spain, Sicily, Cappadocia, and Greece. The wealthy used horses and carriages for local transportation and travel to their country estates. The Greek term for a carriage, *rede*, corresponds to a Latin word for a four-wheeled vehicle. Since the wealthy on occasion could travel with a large entourage of friends and servants, they sometimes needed many carriages for a single trip (Horace, *Ep.* 1.15.10–13; Martial, *Epigrams* 3.47.5; 10.13.1; Suetonius, *Nero* 30.3). Wealthy women used two-wheeled carriages that were brightly decorated and draped with silk (Plutarch, *Mor.* 284A; Propertius, *Elegies* 4.8.15–22; Ovid, *Am.* 2.16.49–50). Carriages adorned with silver sold for exorbitant prices (Pliny the Elder, *Nat.* 33.140; Martial, *Epigrams* 3.62).

"*and slaves and souls of human beings*. Some of the people sold in slave markets were born as slaves; others were war captives (2 Macc 8:11; Dio Chrysostom, *Or.* 15.25). After Roman military victories, such as the suppression of the Jewish revolt in 70 CE, thousands of prisoners were sold (Josephus, *J. W.* 6.418–20; Philostratus, *Vit. Apoll.* 8.37). Others on the slave market were children who had been abandoned or abducted (Pliny the Younger, *Ep.* 10.66; Harris, "Towards"; Harrill, "Vice," 102–3). Although Revelation sometimes uses the term *douloi* for ordinary slaves (Rev 6:15; 13:16; 19:18) and for those who are slaves or servants of God (NOTE on 1:1), here the writer uses a different term: *sōmata*, or "bodies" (MM 621). A slave trader (see Figure 35) was a "merchant of bodies" (*sōmatemporos*). They traveled by land and sea looking for "bodies" to buy so they could resell them at a profit in slave markets (*Vita Aesopi* 20; *Periplus Maris Erythraei* 8, 36).

When taken alone, the use of the term "bodies" could be regarded as a conventional term for slaves, but in this context it underscores the demeaning quality of the slave trade, which debased people into "bodies" to be used by their owners (Bradley, *Slavery*, 52–54; Glancy, *Slavery*, 9–38). Potential buyers could strip a slave, as they might take the blanket off a horse, so that they could inspect the slave's body for defects (Seneca the Younger, *Ep.* 80.9). Slave traders used cosmetics to enhance the appearance and the sexual appeal of a slave's body (Pliny the Elder, *Nat.* 21.170; 24.35; 32.135). In the market, slaves had to jump and dance to demonstrate agility or inhale fumes to show they were not ill (Propertius, *Elegies* 4.5.51–21; Apuleius, *Apol.* 45).

Revelation counters this demeaning way of looking at slaves by adding that the merchants were selling not only "bodies," but "the souls of human beings" (*psychai anthrōpōn*). This expression is based on a Hebrew idiom that refers to people, including those sold as slaves (Ezek 27:13). Revelation uses it to emphasize that those trafficking in bodies are actually selling human lives. The slaves have souls (*psychai*), as do the persecuted believers mentioned elsewhere (Rev 6:9; 12:11; 20:4). In the immediate context, John also uses *psychē* for Babylon in order to create a contrast: Babylon's "soul" longs for expensive merchandise, while the "souls" of others are being sold to the city as commodities (18:13–14). Those who forget that the bodies and souls of slaves are made of the same substance as their masters become tyrants (Juvenal, *Satirae* 14.15–17).

Rome was the largest market for slaves in the first century CE. The trade was centered in the forum, where newly imported slaves stood with their feet whitened with chalk, surrounded by the din of auctioneers (Seneca the Younger, *Const.* 13.4; Pliny the Elder, *Nat.* 35.199–201; Juvenal, *Satirae* 1.111). Many slaves came from Asia Minor and the eastern Roman Empire (Harris, "Towards," 126–28; Bradley, *Slavery*, 31–56). Revelation's readers lived in regional centers of the slave trade, where Roman businesspeople were involved in human trafficking. Ephesus was a major center in the slave trade, with Latin inscriptions from dealers honoring their Roman patrons (I.Eph 646.6; 3025; *Vita Aesopi* 20; Varro, *Ling. lat.* 8.21). At Thyatira an inscription honors a slave trader for his civic service and his support for festivals honoring the emperor (I.Thyat 932). The slave dealers at Sardis had close ties to Roman businesspeople and honored a priest in the imperial cult (Herrmann, "Neues," 177; C. R. Koester, "Roman," 178–85). The way Revelation identifies the slave trade with Babylon/Rome indicts a practice that had a significant place in the cities where the readers lived.

18:14. *'The ripe fruit your soul craved has gone from you. All your glitter and glamour are lost to you, never ever to be found again.'* The city is now addressed in the second person. Some interpreters find this change from third to second person awkward and wonder whether the verse is out of place (Aune; Roloff). It can best be taken as giving voice to the lament of the merchants, which was introduced in Rev 18:11 and then interrupted by the long list of merchandise. The merchants speak directly to the city as the kings did in 18:10 (Osborne; Smalley). The word for fruit, *opōra*, connotes produce that has become ripe and sweet in the late summer. The translation "glitter and glamour" forms an alliterative pair, reflecting the Greek *lipara* and *lampra* (REB). They are bright and costly things, like the jewels and colorful clothing of the whore (18:16; Jas 2:2). The transient splendor of Babylon contrasts with the abiding radiance of New Jerusalem and its inhabitants (Rev 19:8; 22:1).

18:15. *"The merchants who sold these things, who got so rich by her, will stand a long way off because they fear the pain she suffers. They will weep and mourn.* See the NOTE on merchants in 18:3.

18:16. *"and say, 'Oh no! The great city that wore fine linen and purple and scarlet; who glittered with gold and jewels and pearls.* The city is personified as a woman who is adorned with the most expensive trade goods sold by the merchants (18:12). Her attire indicates wealth, yet since the woman is a prostitute, her opulent dress communicates shamelessness (17:4). Babylon the whore and New Jerusalem the bride both are adorned with gold, gems, and pearls and wear fine linen. The difference concerns the character of the city and the source of its brilliance, whether gained from debased relationships, as in Babylon, or from God, as in New Jerusalem.

18:17. *"in just one hour such great wealth was laid waste.* On one hour, see the NOTE on 18:10. Desolation comes from the burning of the city in 17:16.

"Every sea captain and every seafarer and the sailors and all who make their living on the sea stood a long way off. This list includes the occupations needed for seaborne commerce, as the listing of mariners, pilots, caulkers, rowers, traders, and fighters does in Ezek 27:25–32. A sea captain managed the ship; he might own the vessel or pilot one owned by someone else (Lucian, *Nav.* 7; 9; Plutarch, *Mor.* 807b). Sailors were the ordinary members of the crew. Those who trade or literally "work" on the sea could include all the occupations mentioned here, as well as fishermen (Alciphron, *Ep. Court.* 1.4.1–2). The context, however, emphasizes seaborne commerce (Demosthenes, *Orations* 33.4; Philostratus, *Vit. Apoll.* 4.32.3; Manganaro, "Le iscrizioni," 305).

A seafarer is literally one "who sails to a place" (*ho epi topon pleōn*). This unusual expression is well-attested in manuscripts of Revelation (A C 1006 1611 [א 046 0229 2329]) but has generated variants such as sailing "in ships" (051), "on the open sea" (2073), "on the river" (2053 2062), and "all the company in ships" (1 296 2049; KJV). Sailing to a place seems to mean sailing to a port (Acts 27:2; *Periplus Maris Erythraei* 6.1; 7.9; 8.6). The expression could refer to anyone traveling along the coasts (Aune), though this context implies travel to ports for commercial purposes (Giesen).

18:18. *"They cried out as they saw the smoke from her burning and said, 'Who was like the great city?'* To ask "Who was like" assumes that the object of admiration is incomparably great. The righteous often ask, "O Lord, who is like you?" to emphasize God's singular greatness (Ps 35:10; cf. 13:5; Isa 46:5), and the worshipers of the beast say, "Who is like the beast" in order to emphasize the greatness of God's adversary (Rev 13:4). Here, the mariners' question indicates that the city once appeared to be supremely grand but is no longer. Their words resemble those of the seafarers, who grieved the devastation of Tyre's commercial empire, saying, "Who was like Tyre, the one destroyed in the midst of the sea?" (Ezek 27:32).

18:19. *"They threw dust on their heads and were crying out, weeping and mourning.* Throwing dust on one's head was a gesture of grief (Josh 7:6; Job 2:12; Lam 2:12; Ovid, *Metam.* 8.526–32). The seafarers lamenting Tyre also do this, sitting in sackcloth and ashes (Ezek 27:30–31).

"and they said, 'Oh no! The great city, where all who have the ships at sea became so rich by her wealth. In the OT grieving seafarers recall the wealth involved in trade with

Tyre (Ezek 27:33). Later, it was said of Rome: "So many merchant ships arrive here, conveying every kind of goods from every people every hour and every day" that "the city is like a factory common to the whole earth"; the "arrivals and departures of the ships never stop" (Aelius Aristides, *Or.* 26.11, 13). Those engaging in seaborne commerce risked huge losses due to shipwrecks, but they hoped for large profits. Satirists pictured seafarers embarking with hopes of making millions and purchasing their own estates and said hyperbolically that there were more profit seekers at sea than there were men on shore (Juvenal, *Satirae* 14.274–83; Persius, *Satirae* 5.132–44). Investors were also among those who had ships at sea and who sought wealth through trade.

"'for in just one hour she was laid waste.' Sudden destruction in an hour is a recurring theme in Revelation (18:10, 17). Desolation is depicted as burning (18:9, 18) and becoming a wasteland (18:2). The whore was seen *in* a desolate place, and now she *becomes* one (17:3; cf. 4Q179 1 I, 12).

18:20. *"Rejoice over her, O heaven, and saints and apostles and prophets.* Many interpreters include this call to rejoice with the laments of the mariners that precede it (ESV, NAB, NIV, NRSV); others take it as the introduction to the angelic speech that follows (Beale; Rowland). However, it can best be understood as a final comment by the unnamed voice that narrates 18:4–20 (Yarbro Collins, "Revelation 18," 193). The words echo Jer 51:48: "Then the heavens and the earth, and all that is in them, shall shout for joy over Babylon, for the destroyers shall come against them" (cf. Isa 44:23; 49:13; Deut 32:43 LXX). Earlier in Revelation, heaven rejoiced when Satan was expelled from there, but earth experienced woe because Satan raged about the world (Rev 12:11). Now, heaven rejoices because the earth is rid of one destructive force, and in visions to come it will be delivered from the beast, false prophet, and Satan himself (19:20; 20:1–3, 10).

Saints are all members of the Christian community. Apostles are a more limited group, perhaps the twelve as in Rev 21:14 (Giesen) or perhaps a larger group that would include those called apostles in later times (2:2; Prigent). The prophets who are mentioned alongside the apostles are probably Christian prophets (11:18; 22:9) who worked in continuity with those of ancient Israel. Some interpreters think that these three groups represent the Christian community on earth, which can now rejoice with the heavens since the tyrannical city has fallen (Roloff). Others think they are in heaven, since the twelve apostles had presumably died, and the saints and prophets are said to have been slaughtered, like the martyrs under the heavenly altar (18:24; cf. 6:9–11; Giesen). In the next vision, rejoicing over Babylon's fall occurs in heaven (19:1–10), but the exhortation to rejoice is broad enough to include the earthly community.

"because God has judged her as she judged you." The Greek is awkward: "God judged your judgment from her" (*ekrinen ho theos to krima hymōn ex autēs*). It could mean that God has pronounced judgment against Babylon on behalf of the faithful (ESV, NRSV). The context, however, stresses that Babylon is to receive back what she gave to others (18:6). Having condemned the faithful, Babylon suffers condemnation from God (Aune; Osborne; Smalley).

18:21. *Then a powerful angel picked up a stone that was like a great millstone and threw it into the sea.* Two large millstones were used in mills powered by donkeys. The lower one was a stationary cone, and the upper one was hollowed out to fit over the cone. A donkey was tied to a wooden pole attached to the upper stone. As the animal walked in a circle around the mill, the upper stone rotated. Grain was poured through a hole in the upper stone and was ground as it passed between the stones (*NP* 8:909–15). Ordinary millstones were about thirty inches in diameter and very heavy (cf. Matt 18:6; Mark 9:42). The vision recalls the end of Jeremiah's oracle against Babylon, in which the prophet's messenger was to tie the scroll onto a stone and throw it into the Euphrates, saying, "Thus shall Babylon sink, to rise no more, because of the disasters that I am bringing on her" (Jer 51:63–64). Similarly, the stones and timber of Tyre—a city like the great city of Revelation—were to be cast into the sea (Ezek 26:12). Like Tyre, the great city in Revelation is never to be found again (26:21; Ruiz, *Ezekiel*, 469–70).

He said, "With such violent force will Babylon the great city be thrown down, and it will not be found anymore. Throwing down the stone anticipates the city being thrown down. Although Babylon has been destroyed by fire by this point in the book, the image of throwing down the stone is a reminder that in the readers' world the ruling power symbolized by Babylon remains, and its destruction is yet to come.

18:22. *"The sound of harpists and musicians and pipers and trumpeters will not be heard in you anymore.* The harp, or kithara, was held in one arm and strummed with a pick. Harps often accompanied singers. They were played to honor God or the gods (Ps 150:3; Dio Chrysostom, *Or.* 2:28) as well as for entertainment at contests and banquets (NOTE on Rev 14:2). The word "musicians" here is a general term. Lively music had a place at banquets, but not at funerals (Sir 22:6; 32:5–6; 49:1). Pipers played wind instruments with single or double reeds that were set in tubes with finger holes. Pipes were often played in pairs, one fingered by each hand. Sometimes used at funerals (Matt 9:23), pipes were also played for religious rites, especially in the cult of Dionysus, and at dramas, choral performances, weddings, and banquets (Plutarch, *Mor.* 643b; 1095ef). Trumpeters in the military gave signals to the troops (NOTE on Rev 8:2), but here they are entertainers who perform at theaters and banquets (Juvenal, *Satirae* 3.34; 10.214; Petronius, *Satyricon* 78). Although some musicians made a good income, they were considered lower class and morally dubious (Juvenal, *Satirae* 2.118; 6.76–77; Martial, *Epigrams* 5.56.8–9). The silencing of musicians recalls God's judgment against Tyre (Ezek 26:13) and to some extent against Babylon (see the NOTE below on the use of Jer 25:10).

"No craftsman of any kind will be found in you anymore. In the ancient world craftsmen included metalworkers, potters, weavers, dyers, tanners, woodworkers, sculptors, stonemasons, glassmakers, and those who made perfumes, bricks, and tents (Broughton, *Asia*, 817–39).

"The sound of a hand mill will not be heard in you anymore. Hand mills in the first century CE consisted of two stones. The lower stone was convex and the upper one was hollowed out to fit over it. By grasping a wooden handle attached to the upper stone, a person could rotate it, grinding the grain between the stones. Smaller than the large mill mentioned above (18:21), a hand mill was about twelve to eighteen inches in diameter (*NP* 8:911–13). It was an essential item in every household (Deut 24:6). Grinding flour was a regular chore for women or slaves (Exod 11:5; Matt 24:41; Juvenal, *Satirae* 8.67). The hand mill stopping signifies the end of daily life.

The language in this line and the next recalls Jeremiah's warning about the way Babylon would inflict divine judgment on Jerusalem: "I will banish from them the sound of gladness, the voice of the bridegroom and the voice of the bride, the sound of the millstones and the light of the lamp" (Jer 25:10 MT). Yet Jeremiah went on to say that God would punish Babylon by repaying its people according to what they had done (25:1–14). Revelation follows this line of thought by picturing a reversal. Where Jeremiah said that Babylon once silenced the sound of the millstone, the groom, and the bride, Revelation expects Babylon/Rome eventually to suffer these same things. There is symmetry in judgment.

18:23. *"The light of a lamp will not shine in you anymore.* Lamps were shallow covered dishes containing oil, and in the first century they had a spout in which a wick was placed. The most common were made of clay. Lamplight was a typical sign of life in a home, so extinguishing it was a metaphor for destruction (Job 18:6; 21:17). On the use of Jer 25:10, see the NOTE above.

"The sound of a bridegroom and bride will not be heard in you anymore. Wedding customs varied, but the bride and groom typically dressed in their finest, and a banquet was hosted for guests at the bride's home. The bride was escorted to the groom's home with a torchlight parade, and those accompanying the wedding party shouted and sang (2 Sam 17:3; Matt 9:15; 25:10; *CAM* 3:1349–50; NOTES and COMMENT on Rev 19:7–9). The cessation of the sound of the bridegroom and bride points to desolation (Jer 7:34; 16:9; Bar 2:23). Death would turn the wedding into mourning and its music into a funeral dirge (1 Macc 9:39–41). The prophets warned that Babylon would devastate Jerusalem and neighboring lands, taking away the light of lamps and the sounds of weddings (Jer 25:10). Here, the judgment is reversed, as Babylon suffers this fate. Prophetic promises concerning the joy of the wedding, with its connotations of redemption, will be fulfilled in the New Jerusalem (Isa 61:10; 62:4–5; Jer 33:11; Rev 21:2). On the use of Jer 25:10, see the NOTE above.

"because your merchants were the aristocrats of the earth. This language was formerly used for biblical Tyre, the city that provides the model for commercial Babylon in Revelation. Tyre was "the bestower of crowns, whose merchants were princes, whose traders were the honored of the earth" (Isa 23:8). In Revelation, the great city also has traits of Rome, and Roman businesspeople had prominent associations in the Asian cities where John's readers lived (Harland, *Associations*, 33–34, 285 n. 5).

Picturing merchants as the earth's aristocrats reverses ordinary perceptions, since merchants were considered dishonest and vulgar, worthy of being ranked with tax collectors and usurers. Those trading on a large scale were sometimes respected, but they were to retire to their country estates as soon as they accumulated wealth (Cicero, *Off.* 1.150–51). Satirists lampooned freed slaves and members of the lower classes who acquired wealth by merchandising and then put on the airs of aristocracy, as if wealth alone gave them status (Juvenal, *Satirae* 1.101–12). A freedman who made enormous sums by trading and then tried to play the part of the gentleman while retaining the boorish qualities of his origins was worthy of ridicule, not respect (Petronius, *Satyricon* 29–85; Royalty, *Streets*, 102–11). For satirists, such elevation of coarse merchants to the status of nobility was a matter of bad taste and impropriety; for John it signified a morally corrupt society driven by the profit motive.

"and all the nations of the earth were deceived by your sorcery. Sorcery in a literal sense usually involved the blending of potions from herbs, roots, and parts of animals. Often, the mixture was used with incantations that directed supernatural powers to do what the speaker desired (NOTE on 9:20). Although sorcery was known throughout

the ancient world, it was widely condemned. Theologically, sorcery was linked to demonic power (Irenaeus, *Haer.* 5.28.2) and was the opposite of the true worship of God (2 Chr 33:6; Philostratus, *Vit. Apoll.* 7.19; 8.8). Revelation links sorcery to deception and idolatry (Rev 2:20; 12:9; 13:14; 19:20; 20:3, 8, 10). The writer draws on the word's negative connotations to condemn Rome's ability to bring people under its influence. The language recalls how the prophets said that Babylon would be destroyed "in spite of your many sorceries and the great power of your enchantments" (Isa 47:9, 12). Nineveh was a prostitute who used sorcery and was threatened with destruction (Nah 3:4). Some texts also said that Rome craved sorcery (*Sib. Or.* 5.165). Sorcery is a suitable way to characterize Babylon, the city trafficking in evil and idolatry, whereas sorcery has no place in its counterpart, the New Jerusalem (Rev 9:21; 21:8; 22:15).

18:24. *"In her was found the blood of the prophets and the saints and all who have been slain on the earth."* The prophets are probably Christian prophets, as in 18:20, just as the saints are those in the Christian community. Revelation mentions the death of Antipas (2:13) and pictures other martyrs under the heavenly altar (6:9–11). The whore was drunk with the blood of the saints and witnesses to Jesus (16:6; 17:6). Some interpretations limit the passage to the deaths of Christians (Prigent), but the scope expands to include all who have been slain on the earth. The hyperbole recalls Jer 51:49, in which it was said, "Babylon must fall for the slain of Israel, as the slain of all the earth have fallen because of Babylon." Similar brutality could be ascribed to Rome, whose military conquests were sometimes denounced as butchery (Tacitus, *Agr.* 30.5). The pattern comes full circle as Babylon/Rome, which shed the blood of others, now meets its own demise (*Sib. Or.* 3:310–13; Philostratus, *Vit. Apoll.* 5.26.2).

COMMENT

Babylon the great was personified as a whore in the previous chapter. The traits were taken from prophetic indictments of Babylon, Nineveh, and Tyre, together with aspects of imperial Rome. That vision culminated in the city's fiery destruction, and the present chapter now explores the reasons for its demise. Aspects of the city that were noted before are considered more fully here. Despite the whore's disreputable profession, arrogance was suggested by her dominion over the kings of earth and by her shameless ostentation (17:1, 4, 18; 18:7). Obsession with luxury was shown by her gold, jewels, and expensive clothing (17:4; 18:12–17). False worship was evident in the religious connotations of Babylon's immorality, abomination, and impurity and by her reliance on the blasphemous claims of the beast (17:3–5; 18:3). Brutality was shown by her slaughter of the saints and witnesses to Jesus (17:6; 18:24). All these themes are now developed in scenes of judgment and lamentation (Yarbro Collins, *Crisis*, 123).

On Rev 18:1–24, see Bauckham, *Climax*, 338–83; Callahan, "Apocalypse"; Duff, *Who*, 61–70; Fekkes, *Isaiah*, 210–23; Friesen, *Imperial*, 204–9; Hylen, "Power"; Kraybill, *Imperial*; O'Donovan, "Political"; Perry, "Critiquing"; Räpple, *Metaphor*, 145–62; Rossing, *Choice*, 99–133; Royalty, *Streets*, 194–210; Ruiz, *Ezekiel*, 379–481; Shea, "Chiasm"; Siitonen, "Merchants"; Strand, "Some" and "Two"; R. Thomas, *Magical*, 32–37; Whitaker, "Falling"; Yarbro Collins, *Crisis*, 116–21; "Persecution"; and "Revelation 18."

The chapter has three main sections (Yarbro Collins, "Revelation 18," 198–99; Royalty, *Streets*, 197). The first (18:1–3) and third (18:21–24) are similar in form and content. In each, an angel announces the devastation of Babylon (18:1–2, 21–23a) and then gives several reasons for the city's fall (18:3, 23b–24). The charges that the city seduced kings and nations (17:2; 18:3; cf. 17:2) and shed innocent blood (18:24; cf. 17:6) are repeated from the previous vision. A new element is the prominence of merchants, who amass wealth and power in connection with Babylon (18:3, 23).

Rev 18:1–3	*Rev 18:21–24*
Announcement of the city's fall	Announcement of the city's fall
Nations drank her wine	Merchants became aristocrats
Kings committed immorality	Nations were deceived
Merchants have grown rich	Prophets, saints, and others were slain

Rev 18:4–20
Babylon will drink a double cup of wrath
Kings who committed immorality grieve
Merchants who grew rich grieve
Seafarers grieve as saints and prophets rejoice

The central section consists of the words of an unnamed heavenly voice (18:4–20). The voice sometimes condemns Babylon outright and sometimes mimics the city and those who mourn her destruction. Themes that appear in the introduction and conclusion of the chapter are developed in this middle part. The accusation that Babylon made the nations drunk becomes a warning that she will drink a double cup of wrath (18:4–8). The charge that kings reveled in immorality with the city is taken up as the heavenly voice imitates the kings who weep over the city's destruction (18:9–10). The charge that the merchants became rich through liaisons with the city is developed when the voice lists the vast supply of goods that were sold to the city and then expresses the grief of the merchants (18:11–17a) and seafarers (18:17b–19), who have lost their opportunity to make hefty profits. Having mimicked the grief of those who benefited from liaisons with Babylon, the voice concludes with its own perspective, which is to call for celebration on the part of those who have suffered under Babylon's rule, for her tyranny has ended (18:20).

Announcements of judgment and expressions of grief are the dominant literary forms in Rev 18, and all show that the city deserves to be condemned. On the surface the words "fallen, fallen" and a description of a dislocating scene seem to express sorrow for someone who has suffered calamity (2 Sam 1:17–27). In Jewish and Greco-Roman tradition, similar laments were made for devastated cities. When spoken for a city that one loves, the lament invites the hearer to share the grief (Lam 1; Aelius Aristides, *Or.* 18); but when spoken about an arrogant city or nation, such laments are ironic and warn that the powerful will receive their due. Words that seem to say "how sad" instead show that someone deserves to be brought down (Isa 14:4–23; Amos 5:1–3; Yarbro Collins, "Revelation 18"; Aune 3:975–79; Rossing, *Choice*, 102–18).

The chapter heightens the sense of loss by listing things pertaining to the city, one after another. There are lists of the despicable beings that inhabit the city (18:2), the judgments that have fallen on it (18:6–8), the luxury goods that no longer have buyers (18:12–13), and the signs of life that are no longer seen (18:22–23). As listeners hear the lists, they sense the magnitude of the coming disaster (Demetrius, *Eloc.* 63; Quintilian, *Inst.* 9.3.50). References to smoke rising and destruction striking in a single hour are made repeatedly, warning about the danger of associating with Babylon. The vision features not one but three groups of mourners, each looking at the city from a distance, visibly grieving, and saying "Oh no!" at the fall of the great city (Rev 18:9–10, 15–17a, 17b–19). To make clear that readers are not to sympathize with them, the voice explains that they are distraught because they have lost opportunities for immorality and profitmaking—losses that readers would presumably not find lamentable.

Revelation's portrayal of God's judgment on the great city is a sharp indictment of the imperial society in which the readers lived. As already noted, not all of John's readers would have shared his critical stance toward Rome (§35 COMMENT). Christians at Smyrna may have been impoverished and vulnerable (2:9–10), but those at Laodicea prospered in the Roman economy and seemed quite content with the current order of things (3:17). Therefore, the author tries to shape their perspectives so that they might see how Rome used the benefits of trade to make people accept a social and religious system that was at odds with the reign of God and the Lamb. In chapter 13 he showed how the beast from the land, which represented the urban elites, used economic pressure to promote the ruler cult, which deified a violent and tyrannical form of human authority. Then in chapter 17 he portrayed Babylon/Rome as a whore in order to indict a society driven by the desire for pleasure and profit in which people found brutality and bloodshed intoxicating. When the beast turns against the whore and devours her, the author shows how the destructive tendencies within a society become that society's undoing, thereby carrying out the judgment of God (17:16).

Chapter 18 continues disclosing the reasons for God's judgment on Babylon/Rome through criticisms that were made even by those outside the Christian community (Royalty, *Streets*, 208–9). Some Greek and Roman writers decried Rome's insatiable desire for luxury goods, as well as the conspicuous consumption of the upper classes and those who imitated them. The obsession with owning expensive items was considered decadent and the product of greed (Sallust, *Bell. cat.* 5.8; Seneca the Younger, *Ep.* 90.36; Petronius, *Satyricon* 119). Under Roman dominion human relationships were said to be debased and measured in money rather than character—"we become alternately merchants and merchandise; and we ask, not what a thing truly is, but what it costs"—and the result was a loss of integrity—"Call me a scoundrel, only call me rich!" (Seneca the Younger, *Ep.* 115.10, 14). Roman satirists ridiculed the insincerity and depravity that the pursuit of luxury created at Rome (Juvenal, *Satirae* 6.292–300), while philosophical writers urged people to pursue justice, temperance, honor, and friendship rather than wealth (Dio Chrysostom, *Or.* 3.93; 13.34). Still others idealized the austerity of previous generations as they lamented the loss of virtue in first-century Roman society (Pliny the Elder, *Nat.* 33.153).

Some of the Greek and Roman writers based their criticisms of imperial society on the common understanding of virtue (Perry, "Critiquing"), but Revelation invokes the judgment of God. The writer weaves together prophetic oracles against Babylon's arrogance, violence, and idolatry (Jer 50–51; Isa 13; 21; 47) with those condemning Tyre's commercial empire (Ezek 26–28). Rhetorically, the stream of allusions to the prophets has a cumulative effect. John envisions society as a city that has the traits of Babylon and

Tyre and therefore stands under prophetic judgment. For readers familiar with the OT, the use of biblical language heightens the sense that the righteous purposes of God will be carried out against the perpetrators of injustice (Bauckham, *Climax*, 345).

Theologically, the fall of Babylon/Rome is part of the victory of the Creator over the destroyers of the earth, which is the main theme in the second half of Revelation. In order to free the world from the ruinous forces that now try to dominate it, the Creator must "destroy those who destroy the earth" (Rev 11:18). The author has shown that in a rightly ordered universe all the creatures of earth and sea praise the Creator (4:11; 5:11–13). In contrast, Babylon has a voracious appetite, and its power is shown by the way it devours all that earth and sea can produce (18:11–17). The kingdom of the Creator is built through the Lamb, whose blood purchases and frees people (1:5–6; 5:9–10). In contrast, the kingdom of Babylon is built by corrupting the nations (18:3), shedding the blood of the innocent (18:24), and debasing people into commodities that can be bought and sold for profit (18:13).

Babylon's influence on the earth is destructive, and its future is that it will be destroyed. But God is the Creator, whose purposes culminate in new creation and New Jerusalem. Revelation contrasts Babylon with New Jerusalem to show the difference between two patterns of belief and practice, and what each means for the future. Babylon is a whore, a city where relationships are degraded into matters of pleasure and profit (18:3); but New Jerusalem is a bride, a city where relationships center on fidelity between God and his people (21:2, 9–10; §35 COMMENT). The kings and nations of the world are corrupted by Babylon and suffer loss when the city is ruined (18:9–10); yet the vision of New Jerusalem extends the prospect of a different future, for it shows kings and nations bringing their glory into God's city and finding healing there (21:24). Rhetorically, the scenes of Babylon's demise call readers to disengage from patterns of life that are ultimately destructive, whereas the vision of New Jerusalem calls them into the ways of God and the Lamb, where the future holds the promise of life (Rossing, *Choice*, 161–64; Bauckham, *Theology*, 131–32; Deutsch, "Transformation," 123; Campbell, "Antithetical").

An Angel Announces Babylon's Fall (18:1–3)

An angel declares, "Fallen, fallen is Babylon the great" (18:2). The city's fall was announced in 14:8, before it happened, showing the certainty of its occurrence. Here, the same words, which recall those of Israel's prophets (Isa 21:9; 13:1–14:23; Jer 50:1–51:64), are repeated after the vision of the city's demise. The repetition emphasizes that God will fulfill what has been spoken. The city's eerie desolation is partly a reversal of its former grandeur. It once attracted the most prestigious people on earth (Rev 17:2; 18:3), but now its smoldering ruins are suitable only for the demons and foul spirits that haunt its streets. Unclean birds and animals, such as vultures and hyenas, were supposed to live in deserted places outside a city's walls, but this city is now deserted, and the unclean creatures find a home within its walls. At the same time, the city's desolation is consistent with its character. The city, as a whore who rode a beast, is now the home of beasts, and the whore who drank impurity and abomination now is now filled with impure beings (17:3, 5). The city's allies once sent demonic spirits into the world to promote opposition to God (9:20; 16:14), and now God's judgment means that the demons live in the city itself.

Three reasons are given for Babylon's fall (18:3). First, the nations drank the wine of its passionate immorality. Just as a prostitute made clients drunk in order to involve them in sexual liaisons, the great city entwined the nations in its web of power through the intoxicating effect of commercial prosperity, which people accepted along with the empire's arrogance, idolatry, and violence (17:2). Second, the kings of the earth have committed immorality with Babylon. They established commercial ties with the great city in order to enhance their own positions, while engaging in false worship. Third, the merchants became rich by the city's loose and extravagant ways. The merchants were not included in Rev 17 but are given considerable attention in this chapter, where they appear alongside the shipmasters and sailors with whom they worked. Their role is to depict the great city as a society devoted to the pursuit of wealth and conspicuous consumption.

A Heavenly Voice Portrays the Mourners (18:4–20)

An unnamed heavenly voice speaks throughout 18:4–20, sometimes speaking directly from the heavenly perspective—which conveys the views of the author—and sometimes impersonating what Babylon and its allies would say. The voice speaks directly at the beginning and end of the passage, calling for the faithful to leave the city (18:4) and for the saints to rejoice at the city's demise (18:20). In between, the unnamed voice lets readers hear what is being said by Babylon and the kings, merchants, and seafarers who deal with her. Some readers find it confusing that this section seems to shift between mourning and celebrating the city's fall, but recognizing that the same heavenly voice speaks throughout this section allows readers to see its coherence. The voice urges readers to separate from the city and then shows why they should do so. The unnamed voice mimics the role of Babylon to show the height of the city's arrogance, which warrants judgment. Then it plays the roles of kings, merchants, and seafarers to show how even the city's allies will one day separate themselves from the city out of fear of sharing its punishment. Having seen that separation is inevitable, readers have incentive to separate themselves from the ways of Babylon now, rather than waiting and sharing the city's fate.

The voice begins with an exhortation: "Come out of her, my people, so that you do not take part in her sins and do not receive any of her plagues" (18:4). The voice uses the metaphor of fleeing from a doomed city in order to urge people to separate themselves from the patterns of life that Revelation ascribes to the dominant culture (cf. 2 Cor 6:17). The practical implications of the exhortation are not spelled out. The vision does not outline a social program for the churches of Asia to implement. Instead, its imagery is designed to challenge and shape the readers' basic commitments.

The vision warns that Babylon's brutality, arrogance, and obsession with luxury bring the city under divine judgment, and the readers must work out what it means to disengage from these practices in the contexts in which they live. Some interpreters propose that readers were being told to "come out" by avoiding participation in trade guilds and other commercial ventures linked to Rome. Since the meetings of these groups often involved expressions of loyalty to the emperor or the worship of Greco-Roman deities, withdrawing from such associations might have been one response to the exhortation (Yarbro Collins, "Persecution"; Kraybill, *Imperial*, 16, 100, 135–41; Bauckham, *Climax*, 376–77; Harland, *Associations*, 262). At the same time, the exhortation to withdraw from Babylon is evocative enough to fit multiple life situations—

which was also true of the warning about receiving the mark of the beast (NOTES and COMMENT on 13:16–18). The exhortation engages readers in a process of discernment in which they must continue to ask which commercial practices are incompatible with their commitments to God and the Lamb.

The heavenly voice says that Babylon's sins stretch up to heaven so that God now remembers her acts of injustice (*adikēmata*, 18:5). The indictment ties God's judgment against the city to the book's wider concern for justice (deSilva, *Seeing*, 72–75). The martyrs under the altar asked how long God would delay bringing justice (*ekdikein*) for the deaths of the faithful (6:10). Since God is just (*dikaios*, 15:3; 16:5, 7; 19:2), he cannot rightly ignore the suffering of the innocent. The theme continues here, where Babylon's acts of injustice include deceiving the nations, killing the faithful, and corrupting kings and nations (18:23–24). God allowing the perpetrators to continue unchecked would show moral indifference; therefore, Revelation will show God's justice unfolding in two ways. One is that justice means putting a stop to the destructive actions of the agents of evil, which begins with the fall of Babylon (17:16; 18:1–24) and will continue with the demise of the beast and false prophet (19:11–21) and then Satan himself (20:1–3, 7–10). The other dimension of justice will be the restoration of life for the faithful who have suffered, culminating in resurrection (20:4–6).

The voice says: "Give her what she herself has given to others. Give her back twice as much for what she has done. In the cup that she mixed, mix her twice as much" (18:6). Earlier, readers were warned that Babylon would drink the wine of God's wrath for making the nations drink the wine of the city's immorality (14:8–10). In ordinary usage wine has an initially pleasant intoxicating effect, but as more is consumed it becomes destructive to the drinker, who staggers, falls, and becomes an object of contempt. By analogy, Babylon's wine is the seductive quality of power, luxury, and violence, which the nations imbibe. When these forces lead to the destruction of those who consume them, they function as the wrath of God. The symmetry in judgment parodies the principle of generosity: If Babylon's insatiable desires ruin the world, let her have all the ruination she wants (19:2). If the whore has an insatiable thirst for violence, let her drink the cup of violence filled twice over (17:6).

Babylon the whore is judged because she glorified herself (18:7), whereas previous visions have insisted that true glory belongs to the God who created all things and to the Lamb who redeems people by his blood (4:11; 5:12–13; 7:12; 11:13; 14:7). The heavenly company has declared that God and the Lamb are worthy to rule (4:11; 5:13), but Babylon claims that she is sovereign, and her pride portends her fall (18:7). The city claims to be a queen, the most powerful of women, who could exert her influence in the social, political, and legal spheres and had access to wealth. She would be the last to go hungry. And Babylon contrasts itself with the widow, the most vulnerable of women. After experiencing grief at the loss of her husband, a widow had to depend on others for food, shelter, and protection from danger, and she often fell into poverty (Job 24:2–3; Ps 94:6; Isa 10:2; Mark 12:40). Because of its arrogance, Babylon will fall. Like other conquered cities, it will be comparable to a widow because of its losses (Isa 47:9; Lam 1:1; 4Q179 2 4–10; *Sib. Or.* 5:169).

In Rev 18:9 the first of three groups of mourners appear, each standing some distance away from the fallen city, watching the smoke curling up from its ruins. The heavenly voice continues to speak but now puts words in the mouths of the mourners, so readers can see how the loss of the city appears to Babylon's associates. Rhetorically, these scenes speak to those who are reluctant to "come out," or withdraw, from the empire's political and economic networks because of the loss it will entail (18:4). The portrayal of the grieving kings and merchants shows that loss will come and that placing one's trust in the seemingly invincible city is a tragic mistake.

The kings who grieve the downfall of Babylon the whore had reveled in immorality with her (18:9). The writer uses the language of sexual immorality in order to critique the way kings enhanced their own positions through ties with the empire. In ordinary practice kings were to show friendship and loyalty to the Roman emperors, but in Revelation this practice is pictured as the debased relationship of a client to a prostitute (NOTES and COMMENT on 17:2). Politically and economically, Revelation pictures kings consorting with the ruling power in order to satisfy their own desires. Committing immorality (*porneuein*) also has negative religious connotations in Revelation. When kings are faulted for their religious trafficking with the ruling power, the problem includes not only polytheism but the imperial cult, which Revelation identifies as the consummate form of idolatry (13:1–18).

The kings voice their grief by saying, "Oh no! Babylon, you great city, you powerful city, for in just one hour your judgment came," and yet they stand at a safe distance out of fear of having to suffer in the same way (18:10). The distancing shows that their primary concern is self-preservation. They debased themselves by consorting with the whore in order to obtain her benefits, but not out of any deeper bond. After Babylon's demise, the kings will distance themselves from the city, which raises the question: Why wait to separate from Babylon? (18:4). Refusing to separate now out of self-interest will only lead to loss and separation later, when the judgment of God comes.

The second group of mourners are the merchants, who traveled to buy goods in one market in order to sell them in another (18:11). Some merchants followed overland trade routes, but more traveled by sea since goods could be transported more cheaply in ships, allowing the merchants to make greater profits. Merchants were emblematic of people driven by the desire for wealth. Travel could be arduous, cargo could by lost through theft or storms at sea, and a shipwreck could take a merchant's life. Therefore, it was assumed that those who took such risks were driven by greed. A person ventured across the seas in order to "go back home from there with a tight-stuffed money bag" and "exult" in a "swollen purse" (Juvenal, *Satirae* 14.281–83; Persius, *Satirae* 5.132–39).

The goods handled by the merchants are listed in rapid succession, each connected with "and" (*kai*): gold *and* silver *and* jewels *and* pearls, etc. As readers hear of one thing after another—twenty-nine items in just two verses—they sense that the list could go on indefinitely (Demetrius, *Eloc.* 63; Quintilian, *Inst.* 9.3.50). Special attention is given to luxury items such as precious metals, gems, and expensive cloth. It was costly to transport goods, pay taxes, and reimburse investors, so traders favored commodities that had a high resale value in order to maximize profits. John underscores the sense of luxury by linking the merchants' wealth to the great city's "loose and extravagant ways" and its obsession with glamour, gold, jewels, and fine garments (Rev 18:3, 14–16).

The list of goods would have challenged John's readers in two ways. First, some people in the seven cities addressed by Revelation were *suppliers* of the textiles, wines, gems, marble, timber, horses, and slaves that fed the demand of the imperial markets (NOTES on 2:1, 8, 12, 18; 3:1, 7, 14). Readers with such commercial ties would find themselves standing with the merchants in this vision, bereft of their profits. Second, some people in the seven cities presumably aspired to be *consumers* of the luxury goods on the list. Rome may have set a standard for conspicuous consumption, but similar values were adopted by people in the provinces, who imagined buying gold, ivory, and carriages to display their affluence and win social recognition (Martial, *Epigrams* 9.59; Lucian, *Nav.* 22–23).

Gold was a sign of wealth and status. The wealthy wore gold rings and necklaces, had gold stitched into their garments, and wore shoes with gold buckles. People displayed the height of ostentation by setting lavish banquet tables with gold plates and cups and adorning their ceilings with gold. Traders imported gold statues of gods for the wealthy to dedicate at various temples (Seneca the Younger, *Ep.* 94.70; 115.9; Lucian, *Nigr.* 23; Philostratus, *Vit. Apoll.* 5.20). Silver tableware and serving dishes were also signs of status. The upper classes put silver on the basins in which they washed, the beds and couches on which they reclined, and the mirrors they used for grooming. They owned silver statues of the gods and trimmed their carriages in silver (Pliny the Elder, *Nat.* 33.128, 140–53). Jewels such as onyx, sapphire, jasper, beryl, and emerald were set into women's jewelry and men's rings; the finest goblets were encrusted with gems (Martial, *Epigrams* 5.11; 14.109; Juvenal, *Satirae* 5.37–45). Women also had pearls set in earrings, necklaces, bracelets, and anklets and had them sewn onto their clothing, slippers, and couches. By wearing pearls on gold chains, they could even sleep with these symbols of wealth (Pliny the Elder, *Nat.* 9.114–18; 33.40; 37.17).

Fine linen and purple were used for sumptuous garments (Luke 16:19). Among Romans, purple was traditionally worn by consuls, young men of noble families, senators, and people of rank. Because it was a status symbol, others spent large sums to purchase purple clothing. Satirists lampooned the newly rich with their purple cushions, the perfumed freedmen lounging about the theater in purple clothes and shoes like those of senators, the gentry who wore purple while living beyond their means, and the provincials fantasizing about striking it rich and buying purple cloaks (Martial, *Epigrams* 2.29; Juvenal, *Satirae* 7.134–35; Lucian, *Nav.* 22). Silk was used for elegant gowns, scented head wreaths, cushions on fine couches, and drapes on the carriages affluent women used. The height of extravagance was to have silk curtains protecting spectators from the sun at outdoor spectacles. Some called silk "a device of barbarian luxury" (Dio Cassius, *Rom. Hist.* 43.24.2; cf. Propertius, *Elegies* 4.8.15–22; Statius, *Silv.* 5.215). Scarlet clothing was another sign of affluence. A man from the lower classes might seek to impress people by swaggering about in a scarlet cloak while boasting about his purportedly noble ancestry and lucrative properties, and men plied young women with gifts of scarlet clothing in exchange for sexual favors (Martial, *Epigrams* 2.39; 4.28; 5.35; Petronius, *Satyricon* 28; 32).

Tables made of citrus wood were exorbitantly expensive, but fashionable Romans considered them essential. With an intricate grain, a lush color, and an ability to withstand wine spills, the wood was well-suited for tables used at banquets. The finest citrus tables cost hundreds of thousands of sesterces—as much as a large estate—but aspiring Roman men were obsessed with owning them (Pliny the Elder, *Nat.* 13.91–102; Dio Cassius, *Rom. Hist.* 61.10.3). Ivory was used for the legs of these stylish tables. It was also inlaid in ceilings and expensive furniture and was used for jewelry and carved boxes that held gold coins. Status-conscious people insisted that gaming pieces and knife handles be made of ivory. It was understood that ivory was meant for display (Juvenal, *Satirae* 11.126–34; Martial, *Epigrams* 14.5, 12, 14; Suetonius, *Nero* 31.2; Petronius, *Satyricon* 32; Lucian, *Nigr.* 23). Fine woods, like certain types of maple, were used for elegant tables. People aspiring to wealth dreamed of sleeping on beds made of imported cedar or terebinth. Furniture made from cheaper material was often covered with a veneer of fine wood to enhance its appearance (Horace, *Sat.* 2.8.10–11; Propertius, *Elegies* 3.7.49–50; Pliny the Elder, *Nat.* 16.231–32).

Bronze was used for items ranging from tools to statues of emperors and gods. Corinthian bronze was nearly as precious as gold. Artisans fashioned it into figurines, bowls, and dishes, which were status symbols for the upper classes. Collectors drove prices to such exorbitant levels that even the emperor complained. Wealthy Romans postured as connoisseurs of bronze, sniffing it in the market and claiming that it had a distinctive scent (Suetonius, *Tib.* 34.1; Pliny the Younger, *Ep.* 3.6; Pliny the Elder, *Nat.* 34.1, 6–8; Seneca the Younger, *Brev.* 12.2; Petronius, *Satyricon* 50).

Iron was important for Roman infrastructure. Iron tools were purchased in small quantities by farmers and artisans but in larger numbers by those who owned estates and mining operations. Iron bands were used in the monumental building projects sponsored by rich patrons, and large amounts of iron were used for the weapons carried by Roman legions (*NP* 6:941–43). Marble was a hallmark of affluence. It was said that Augustus found Rome in brick but left it in marble by constructing so many elegant temples and public buildings (Suetonius, *Aug.* 28.3). Marble was used for statues honoring the gods and notable people. Critics told of some people building marble mansions that were more splendid than temples and installing marble floors so they could have the thrill of walking on wealth (Pliny the Elder, *Nat.* 36.1–8, 48–51; Juvenal, *Satirae* 11.172; 14.86–95; Seneca the Younger, *Ep.* 16.8). Marble was often used as a façade, and this practice was said to be indicative of Roman life itself: stylish on the surface but crude underneath (Seneca the Younger, *Ep.* 115.9).

Cinnamon is the first of several imported spices listed in Revelation. It was blended in perfumes, burned as incense, and used as a flavoring in wine (Rev 18:13; Plutarch, *Mor.* 693C). Amomum was another imported spice used in perfume. People basking in luxury had their hair soaked with amomum (Martial, *Epigrams* 5.64.3). Fragrant ointments, often made from Arabian or African myrrh, were an essential part of the good life. People put fragrances on their bodies and in their bathtubs. Those at banquets put drops of perfume in their wine to enhance its aroma and flavor (Martial, *Epigrams* 14.110; Juvenal, *Satirae* 6.303). Critics considered perfume a wasteful luxury, since people wore it merely to call attention to themselves, and despite the high cost, the fragrances had no abiding value; they simply evaporated when used (Pliny the Elder, *Nat.* 13.20–23). Frankincense was regularly burned on altars to the gods in large civic sanctuaries and private homes, and it was used in large quantities at funerals. The wealthy were said to burn more incense to honor the dead than they did for any deity (Pliny the Elder, *Nat.* 12.83; Statius, *Silv.* 5.1.208–16).

All classes of Roman society consumed wine, making it a profitable commodity. Fashionable hosts, seeking to impress their guests, would offer them a selection of fine domestic and imported wines (Horace, *Sat.* 2.8.15–17). Everybody also used olive oil. The wealthy insisted on having the finest oil at their meals; others consumed the lower grades (Juvenal, *Satirae* 5.86–88). Fine flour was baked into the top-quality bread demanded by the upper classes, leaving coarser loaves to those of lesser standing (Juvenal, *Satirae* 5.67–75). Wheat merchants were part of an extensive network of trade in Rome. Private contractors shipped wheat from Egypt, North Africa, and other parts of the empire to Rome in order to meet the needs of the city's enormous population. Wheat was sold to individuals on the open market as well as to government officials, who doled out grain to city residents. To lessen the risk of public unrest due to food shortages, officials offered subsidies and other benefits to those bringing grain to the capital (Suetonius, *Claud.* 18–19; Lucian, *Nav.* 13).

Small farmers sold cattle and sheep locally, but Revelation includes these animals with the commodities handled by wealthy merchants. Established landowners built up their herds and flocks with breeds from various parts of the world. Patrons sponsoring civic events purchased cattle and sheep for public sacrifices—whereas those in the lower classes bought little meat (Juvenal, *Satirae* 12.11–13; Petronius, *Satyricon* 76; Rev 2:14, 20). Horses were essential for chariot racing, a favorite form of entertainment in Rome and throughout the empire. Large sums were spent to obtain horses with the speed and stamina needed to win. In the private sphere, the wealthy rode horses or had servants on imported horses accompany them as they rode in horse-drawn carriages. Satirists wrote of people fawning over the nobility in their carriages and of provincials dreaming of the status that horses and carriages would bring them (Pliny the Younger, *Ep.* 2.17; Horace, *Sat.* 1.6.107–9; Martial, *Epigrams* 10.13; 12.24; Lucian, *Nav.* 13; 22; Lucian, *Nigr.* 29; Juvenal, *Satirae* 4.1–7, 117–18; Suetonius, *Nero* 30.3).

Slaves are the last item Revelation mentions, bringing the list to its climax. People coveted the prestige that came from owning slaves. Many paid high prices for the premium slaves imported from Asia Minor, particularly from the regions of Phrygia and Cappadocia. Romans displayed high social status by being attended by slaves when entertaining guests or having slaves carry them in litters through the streets (Martial, *Epigrams* 3.62; 10.76; Juvenal, *Satirae* 11.146–47; Persius, *Satirae* 6.77; Harris, "Towards," 122–23). Provincials also regarded owning slaves a mark of success (Lucian, *Nav.* 22).

People may have coveted the status that came with *owning* slaves, but they regarded those who *traded* in slaves with contempt. John plays on the ancient ambivalence toward the slave trade by first mentioning that the merchants dealt in slaves, or literally "bodies," and then adding that they were selling "the souls of human beings" (Rev 18:13). By using two expressions rather than one, John emphasizes that selling slaves means trading in human lives. Slave traders were regarded as thieves and swindlers and were compared to pimps. Some of them abducted other people's slaves or kidnapped free people in order to sell them (Chariton, *Chaer.* 2.1.7–8; 1 Tim 1:10; Harrill, "Vice," 102–3). They catered to buyers with a sexual interest by using various techniques to enhance the attractiveness of the women and children they sold (Harrill, "Vice," 108–12). Since those who engaged in the slave trade were not respected, their principal motive was profit. To traffic in human lives was to "sell your soul for gain" (Persius, *Satirae* 6.75–78; cf. Seneca the Younger, *Ep.* 80.9; Seneca the Elder, *Controversiae* 1.2.9; Philostratus, *Vit. Apoll.* 4.22). Portraying Babylon/Rome as the center of the slave trade points to the seamy underside of its wealth.

The dynamics of slavery can be seen by comparing the imagery in Revelation to that of a slave trader's tombstone, which probably dates from the early first century CE (Figure 35). The man's name was Aulus Caprilius Timothy, and he called himself a slave

Figure 35. Slave trader's grave stele (early first century CE). Courtesy of Pierre Ducrey, *Le traitement des prisonniers de guerre dans la Grèce antique*, 2nd ed. (1968; Paris: De Boccard, 1999), pl. VIII.

trader, or "a merchant of bodies" (*sōmatemporos*). In the top panel the merchant reclines luxuriously on a couch at a funeral banquet. He holds a cup in one hand and faces a table with cakes and grapes. On the right is a horse and groom, which were symbols of status. The merchant's posture conveys a sense of ease, like Babylon in John's vision. The middle panel shows scenes of wine production and includes figures who carry baskets used for harvesting grapes and an amphora for wine. It was common for slave traders to bring jars of wine and other goods to the regions that supplied slaves. There, the wine would be exchanged for the slaves, who were taken to market for resale at a profit. The bottom panel depicts the slaves, who are being led away to market. Eight men are bound by their necks; behind them are two women and two children. The slave trader apparently walks in front (C. R. Koester, "Roman," 772–76).

The portrayal of Babylon in Revelation assumes that many people were attracted to a life of ease and prosperity, as shown in the top panel of the tombstone. The way the author challenges this perspective is comparable to directing attention downward through the festive scenes of winemaking to the unsavory picture of the slave trade at the bottom. The text—like the grave stele—shows that the luxury of the few (Rev 18:3) comes from the enslavement of the many (18:13). By analogy, readers are not to be beguiled by the empire's promises of wealth. Instead, they must ask who has paid the cost.

The merchants in John's vision tell the city: "The ripe fruit your soul craved has gone from you. All your glitter and glamour are lost to you, never ever to be found again" (18:14). The city is defined by its desires and ostentation. Grapes, apples, and pears were a regular part of banquets, served at the end of the meal. A wealthy host would serve choice fruits, their scent a feast in itself, leaving fruits past their prime to people of lesser standing (Juvenal, *Satirae* 5.150; Martial, *Epigrams* 10.94.6; Petronius, *Satyricon* 60). As a metaphor, ripe fruit stands for all the desirable things mentioned in previous verses. Repeating that the merchants grew rich by their relationship with the city, John shows that the city's materialistic obsessions are mirrored in the way her associates grieve (Rev 18:15–17a). Their words show that they think the prostitute's death is a pitiable waste. The whore's purple and scarlet gown, her gold, jewels, and pearls were so splendid that the merchants feel pained by such a loss of fine things.

The third group of mourners consists of those engaged in seaborne commerce (18:17b). Shipmasters piloted the vessels; sailors managed sails, rigging, and anchors; and traders leased space in the ships for exporting goods such as Italian wine and importing goods such as purple cloth, silver tableware, perfumes, and slaves (Casson, *Periplus*, 39–43; Juvenal, *Satirae* 12.29–51). Life aboard ship was cramped, and storms regularly ruined ships and took the lives of seafarers, yet people risked their lives and investments at sea in the pursuit of wealth (Petronius, *Satyricon* 76; Philostratus, *Vit. Apoll.* 4.32; Persius, *Satirae* 5.132–43; Propertius, *Elegies* 3.7). It was said that wherever the hope of gain calls, there the fleets gather, attracting those with the singular goal of profit (Juvenal, *Satirae* 14.265–83; Pliny the Elder, *Nat.* 2.118; Lucian, *Nav.* 13–15).

The seafarers lament, "Who was like the great city?" (Rev 18:18), echoing those who said, "Who is like the beast and who can make war against it?" (13:4). The object of admiration seemed to be incomparably great, but now the city's grandeur is gone, and in the next chapter the beast's appearance of incomparable strength will also be shown to be false. The profit motive emerges in the seafarers' lament: "Oh no! The great city, where all who have ships at sea became so rich by her wealth, for in just one hour she was laid waste" (18:19). Ordinarily, mariners and merchants grieved when storms sank their ships before they could bring their goods to market, thereby reducing them to poverty (Juvenal, *Satirae* 14.292–302). Here, however, the market itself—Babylon—is destroyed, taking with it their hopes of attaining fabulous riches. The end of the city means the loss of a lucrative business partner.

In 18:20 the heavenly voice, which has been speaking since 18:4, calls for rejoicing in heaven among three groups: the saints, apostles, and prophets. These groups are the counterpart to the three groups who mourn in 18:9–19. The celebration comes from the symmetry of divine judgment: The city that judged the faithful negatively finally receives a negative judgment from God. Revelation has repeatedly shown that God's justice cannot be equated with retribution. The movement toward a final judgment has been repeatedly interrupted so that repentance can occur (COMMENT on 19:2). Yet Revelation also gives assurance that justice will come. The perpetrators of violence are not allowed to continue indefinitely. Ending the destructive ways of the great city is one step in divine justice, and the other will be the gift of life that is given to the faithful through resurrection (11:18; 19:1–10).

An Angel Depicts Babylon's Fall (18:21–24)

The final section mirrors the opening of the vision, for an angel appears, announces the destruction of Babylon, and gives three reasons for the city's demise (cf. 18:3). Powerful angels have previously drawn attention to the sealed and open scrolls that revealed God's purposes (5:2; 10:1), and this third angel hurls a large millstone into the sea as a portent of Babylon's violent destruction (18:21). A large millstone was used to grind grain commercially rather than in the home, making it a suitable emblem for a city that consumed vast quantities of wheat (18:13). Ironically, the millstone sinks into the sea that had been integral to the city's wealth. The sea had once signified prosperity, since ships brought the world's goods across the sea to the city, whose empire dominated the waters (17:1; 18:17). But now the stone sinks into the sea as a symbol of the city's coming demise. Babylon will fall, but the God who created the sea will remain (10:6; 14:7).

The angel declares that the music of the harpists, pipers, and trumpeters will be silenced in the fallen city (18:22a). As before, many items are listed in quick succession, each linked with the word "and" (*kai*; cf. 18:12–13). This list conveys the magnitude of the devastation, since readers sense that the number of losses could be extended. Musicians playing harps and reed pipes regularly entertained at banquets. Harpists often sang as they played, and pipers accompanied the libations offered to the gods. At festivals, musicians played all night long, the music ranging from spirited songs to poignant laments, and contests among harpists and pipers were popular (Philo, *Legat.* 12; Plutarch, *Mor.* 712f–713c; Juvenal, *Satirae* 15.48–50; Lucian, *Ind.* 8–10; Dio Chrysostom, *Or.* 7.119). Trumpeters performed in city theaters and at banquets of wealthy patrons throughout the empire (Juvenal, *Satirae* 3.34; 6.249–50; 10.214; Petronius, *Satyricon* 53; 78), but now the trumpeters fall silent under judgment (Rev 8:2). Heavenly harpists have led songs of praise to God (5:8; 14:2), but those playing for the revelries in Babylon cease (18:22). Before, pipers brought levity, but now their silence means grief (Isa 5:12; 1 Macc 3:45). The absence of sound underscores the severity of the judgment (Isa 24:8–9; Ezek 26:13).

Artisans—the people who worked the materials the merchants brought to the city (18:12–13)—also vanish from the scene (Rev 18:22b). Goldsmiths and silversmiths produced tableware, jewelry, and statues dedicated to the gods and set gems and pearls in rings and necklaces. Weavers and dyers made cloth for garments, and carpenters fashioned furniture from fine woods. Artisans carved ivory into boxes and inlaid it on ceilings, and sculptors made statues of gods and notable figures out of bronze and marble. Blacksmiths made tools and weapons from iron, and perfumers turned resins into aromatic ointments. Leatherworkers, woolworkers, potters, and stonemasons all had a place in a great city. Such trades were practiced in the readers' cities (NOTES on 2:1, 8, 12, 18; 3:1, 7, 14). Their absence marks the end of the city's vitality. Grinding flour with a hand mill was an important part of daily life (18:22c; Deut 24:6). The chore was a regular one for women and slaves (Exod 11:5; Matt 24:41; Juvenal, *Satirae* 8.67). But now even the most essential daily work has ended.

Lamps were lit when the sun went down (Rev 18:23). In practical terms, lamps provided light for evening chores. Socially, they lighted up the space in which people ate and talked. During festivals, lamps were lit in the city streets and squares to allow nighttime celebration. The absence of lamplight marks the end of social life (18:23). Weddings were one of the most familiar forms of festivity in any city or village. The wedding banquet would be filled with the sounds of lively music, conversation, and dining; and shouts and singing would fill the streets as the bride was escorted to the groom's home (NOTES and COMMENT on 19:8–9). A city without these sounds is a place without joy.

The three reasons now given for the demise of the great city are variations on those noted at the beginning of the chapter (Rev 18:23b–24; cf. 18:3). First, its merchants are called the aristocrats of the earth. Aristocrats included the nobility, members of the royal court, and other highly respected people; in Revelation they are next to kings (6:15; cf. Prov 8:16; Sir 39:4; Dan 5:1; Mark 6:21). Aristocrats should exemplify the values of a society, but in Babylon that place of honor goes to merchants. John's vision plays on the common perception that merchants are driven by the desire for wealth. They purchase things only to sell them at a profit and are said to conceal the truth when marketing their wares to maximize their monetary advantage. Many readers would have agreed that portraying merchants as the aristocrats of a society was an indictment of that society (Royalty, *Streets*, 102–11).

Second, Babylon has deceived the nations with its sorcery (Rev 18:23c). This charge is similar to the accusation that the city made the nations drunk on the wine of immorality, since wine and sorcery alter people's perceptions (18:3). Sorcery was associated with the demonic realm, and its practitioners were seen as a threat to society. In both Jewish and Greco-Roman tradition, the practitioners of sorcery were to be condemned (Deut 18:10; Apuleius, *Metam.* 3.16; *Rom. Civ.* 2:511; MacMullen, *Enemies*, 121–27). Rather than opposing sorcery, however, the city that rules the world is said to practice it, luring people into illicit relationships through spells, as prostitutes were said to do (Lucian, *Dial. meretr.* 1; 4.4; *T. Reub.* 4:9). Earlier, the beast from the land played the role of sorcerer when promoting the worship of the beast from the sea (NOTES and COMMENT on Rev 13:11–15). Here, sorcery is a metaphor for the way the great city bewitches people into deifying the ruler making that wealth and ostentation the highest goods, and treating violence against the faithful as a matter of indifference (Rodney L. Thomas, *Magical*, 32–37).

Third, in the city was found the blood of prophets, saints, and all who have been slaughtered on earth (18:24). John has repeatedly listed what *will not* be found in the city anymore: luxuries, splendors, and artisans (18:14, 21, 22). When these are removed, what *is* found in the city is the blood of the Christian community and the peoples of the earth (Yarbro Collins, "Revelation 18," 199). Readers have been reminded about the deaths of Antipas and other Christian saints (2:13; 6:9; 12:11), but the judgment is extended to include "all" who have been slaughtered on earth. The comment is hyperbolic, as in the prophets, who charged that Babylon expanded its empire at a great cost of human life (Jer 51:49). Rome did the same as its armies overran neighboring peoples and purchased "peace stained with blood" (Tacitus, *Ann.* 1.10.4). Such images were part of the imperial cult (see Figures 29, 30, 33, 34).

Some readers may wonder whether Revelation opposes all that human culture has produced, since the author tells of the demise of political institutions, trade, and social life. Other NT writers are more positive about human government (Rom 13:1–7; 1 Pet 2:13–17), but John sees how the wealth of the few is paid for by the misery of the many, and how the security of some is obtained by the deaths of others. At the same time, John offers a contrasting picture of community life that is God-serving. The harpists fall silent in Babylon (Rev 18:22), but they continue to play for God and the Lamb (15:2). Bride and groom may not celebrate under God's judgment (18:23), but they will find reason to celebrate at the marriage supper of the Lamb (19:7, 9). Lamps are extinguished in Babylon, but in the New Jerusalem the presence of God serves as its abiding lamp (18:23; 21:23). Rhetorically, the negative images alienate readers from what Babylon represents, while the positive images call them to a different future.

37. Hallelujah! God Almighty Reigns (19:1–10)

19 ¹After these things I heard what sounded like a huge crowd in heaven, and they said,

"Hallelujah! Salvation and glory and power belong to our God,
²for his judgments are true and just,
for he judged the great whore, who ruined the earth with her immorality,
and he brought justice for the blood of his servants, which was shed by her own hand."

³Then they said a second time,

"Hallelujah! Smoke goes up from her forever and ever."

⁴And the twenty-four elders and the four living creatures fell down and worshiped God, who is seated on the throne, and they said,

"Amen. Hallelujah!"

⁵Then a voice came from the throne and said,

"Praise our God, all you his servants,
and you who fear him, both small and great."

⁶And I heard something that sounded like a huge crowd, that sounded like rushing water, that sounded like powerful thunder. They said,

"Hallelujah! For the Lord our God the Almighty reigns.
⁷Let us rejoice and celebrate and give him the glory,
for the wedding day of the Lamb has come
and his wife has made herself ready.
⁸She was given fine pure white linen to wear,
for the fine linen is the just deeds of the saints."

⁹Then he said to me, "Write this: Blessed are those who have been invited to the wedding banquet of the Lamb." He said to me, "These are the true words of God." ¹⁰Then I fell at his feet to worship him. But he said, "Do not do that! I am a fellow servant with you and your brethren who hold firmly to the witness of Jesus. Worship God! For the witness of Jesus is the Spirit of prophecy."

NOTES

19:1. *After these things I heard what sounded like a huge crowd in heaven.* In this context the heavenly company consists of the redeemed, including the "saints and apostles and prophets," who were called to rejoice in 18:20 (Giesen; Mounce; Smalley). They are compared to a "great crowd," recalling the "great crowd" from every nation who declare God's "salvation" (7:9–10; cf. 12:10) and those who conquered the beast and sang of God's justice and truth by heaven's crystal sea (15:3; 19:2). The vision could also suggest that the angelic hosts join the faithful in praising God and affirming his justice (5:11–13; 7:11–12; 16:5–6; Aune; Beale).

and they said, "Hallelujah. This is a transliteration of the Hebrew *hallĕlû-yāh*, which means "praise Yah(weh)." In Hebrew this expression is an imperative in the second person plural that summons a group to praise the Lord. When transliterated into Greek, it is not clear that the word itself calls for a group to give praise, but using the word in a setting of corporate worship suggests its significance. The analogous expression "praise our God" is used in 19:5. "Hallelujah" introduces many Hebrew psalms in the last third of the Psalter (e.g., Pss 106:1; 111:1; 150:1), and the LXX uses it to introduce still others (e.g., 119:1 [118:1]). It also concludes some psalms (e.g., 104:35; 106:48). Those who say "hallelujah" typically thank God for his faithfulness and saving actions on their behalf (e.g., Ps 105:1–2 [104:1–2 LXX]). Despite the prominence of "hallelujah" in the LXX version of the Psalter, the transliteration was used only occasionally in Greco-Jewish literature (*L.A.E.* 43:10; *Apoc. Sed.* 16:7; *Apoc. Mos.* 43:4) and Christian texts (*Gos. Bart.* 4.69–70; *Acts of Xanthippe* 19; *Apoc. Paul* 29–30).

"Salvation and glory and power belong to our God. Salvation comes from the removal of the threat Babylon posed, as it previously meant deliverance from earthly affliction (Rev 7:10, 14) and from Satan's accusations (12:10). Glory is the majesty that belongs to God (15:8; 21:23) and ascribing glory to God is an act of worship (4:9; 11:13; 14:7). God's "power" is shown in creating and delivering (4:11; 7:12), judging his foes (12:10; 14:7), and ruling the world he created (11:17).

19:2. *"for his judgments are true and just.* God's judgments are true to the commitments he has made, which include showing favor to his servants and destroying those who destroy the earth (11:18). Ending Babylon's reign is true to God's purposes, since a God who is just cannot allow evil to triumph (6:9–10; 15:3; 16:7; cf. Deut 32:4; Ps 145:17; Pr Azar 4).

"for he judged the great whore, who ruined the earth with her immorality. The language echoes prophetic warnings against Babylon for ruining the earth by military conquests (Jer 51:24–25 [28:24–25 LXX]). Revelation shifts the prophetic indictment to ruining the earth by immorality (*porneia*), which signifies the pursuit of luxury, false worship, and brutality. This imagery challenges Rome's public discourse, which claimed that its dominion was achieved through virtue and good fortune (Strabo, *Geographica* 6.4.2; Plutarch, *Mor.* 317C). From John's perspective, what Rome has done in corrupting others now leads to its own ruin (NOTES and COMMENT on Rev 14:8; 17:2; 18:3).

"and he brought justice for the blood of his servants, which was shed by her own hand." The Greek expression *ek cheiros autēs* can literally be translated that God brought justice for the blood of his servants "from her hand." There are two ways to construe this expression. The second is preferable:

1. The manner of divine judgment. Some interpreters take the Greek to mean that justice is now exacted "from the hand" of the whore. This approach emphasizes that God's judgment takes the form of retribution. The price for her misdeeds is exacted from her hand, so that she pays the price (cf. Gen 9:5; Deut 32:43; Ps 79:10). A common paraphrase is that God has avenged "on her" the blood of his servants (ESV, NAB, NIV, NRSV). The cry of the martyrs can be translated similarly, as a demand that God exact justice "from" (*ek*) those who dwell on earth, on account of the blood of the faithful that has been shed (Rev 6:11).
2. The reason for divine judgment. The whore is judged because of the blood that was shed "by her hand." This approach links "from her hand" to the shedding of blood that immediately precedes it. A similar expression occurs in 2 Kgs 9:7, where God declares that he will bring justice for the blood of the prophets and his servants, which was shed by the hand of Queen Jezebel (cf. Josephus, *Ant.* 9.108). The point is that God must take action against the whore because she was responsible for shedding blood (NET, NJB; Aune; Beale; Osborne; Smalley). Bloodshed was mentioned in 18:24, corruption was mentioned in 19:2b, and bloodshed is the reason again in 19:2c. The victory over Babylon is a response to the cry of the martyrs (NOTE on 6:10).

19:3. *Then they said a second time, "Hallelujah! Smoke goes up from her forever and ever."* Previously, the kings and shipmasters, who were allied with Babylon, grieved when they saw the smoke of her burning (18:9, 18). By way of contrast, the multitudes in heaven rejoice at seeing the smoke from Babylon's fiery downfall, since it marks the end of the city's tyranny. The image of smoke endlessly going up marks the finality of God's judgment (Isa 34:10; Rev 14:11).

19:4. *And the twenty-four elders and the four living creatures fell down and worshiped God, who is seated on the throne, and they said, "Amen. Hallelujah!"* On the elders and creatures, see the NOTES on 4:4 and 4:6. These figures regularly participate in the scenes of heavenly worship that conclude major cycles of visions (4:10; 5:8, 14; 7:11; 11:16; 19:4). "Amen" is a transliteration of a Hebrew word meaning "may it be so." It emphatically affirms what is said (1:6, 7; 22:20) and may conclude a statement of praise (5:14;

7:12; Rom 11:36; 16:27; Gal 1:5; Phil 4:20). It was combined with "hallelujah" or similar expressions (Ps 106:48; cf. 1 Chr 16:36) and was widely used in the early church (e.g., Rom 1:25; 1 Cor 14:16; Heb 13:21).

19:5. *Then a voice came from the throne.* The voice probably belongs to one of the elders or creatures beside God's throne, since they sometimes initiate praises (Rev 4:8–11). It is unlikely that this is God's voice, because the speaker refers to God in the third person in the next line. It is also unlikely that it is the voice of Christ, who shares the throne, since the voice calls for the worship of "our God." In Revelation Christ does not call others to give praise but receives praise from the heavenly host (5:6–14; 7:9). Even less likely is the possibility that the throne itself speaks (Philonenko, "Un voix"). This is a case of metonymy, in which John uses the word "throne" for someone who is on or by the throne (cf. Lausberg, *Handbook* §565). The point of the reference to the throne in Rev 19:5 is that the call to worship is divinely authorized. See also the metonymy in 16:7.

and said, "Praise our God, all you his servants, and you who fear him, both small and great." "Praise our God" has the same meaning as "hallelujah" in 19:6 (cf. Ps 150:1). The call for God's "servants" and "those who fear him" to give praise echoes Israel's worship tradition (Ps 135:1, 20). In Babylon, slaves were reduced to "bodies" that were bought and sold (Rev 18:13). By way of contrast, the slaves or servants of God are "purchased" by the blood of Christ and are given dignity and honor (Rev 5:9; 14:3; NOTE on 1:1). The categories "small and great" point to higher and lower social status (NOTE on 13:16).

19:6. *And I heard something that sounded like a huge crowd, that sounded like rushing water, that sounded like powerful thunder.* A great crowd in 19:1 included those in heaven, but now the group seems to include those on earth, since the call to praise in the previous verse included earthly worshipers. It is not unusual for worshipers to refer to themselves in the third person (e.g., Pss 28:8–9; 85:8–9). In Revelation, the crowd, the bride, and the wedding guests are all images for the people of God, including those in the earthly community of faith. The sounds of great waters and thunder are associated with the exalted Christ, God, and those allied with God (Rev 1:15; 4:5; 6:1; 14:2).

They said, "Hallelujah! For the Lord our God the Almighty reigns. Echoing the "hallelujah" now shows that the multitudes have responded to the call to give praise. The title "Lord God Almighty" is traditional (NOTE on 1:8). Here, the word "reigns" (*ebasileusen*) is in the aorist tense, which could mean that God "has begun to reign" (Aune; Beale). But as in psalms of praise, the aorist simply indicates the state of things: God reigns and his throne is everlasting (Ps 93:1–2 [92:1–2 LXX]; cf. 96:10 [95:10]; 97:1 [96:1]).

19:7. *"Let us rejoice and celebrate and give him the glory.* Rejoicing and celebrating were often paired (Matt 5:12; *T. Ab.* 11:7; *4 Bar.* 6:17; cf. Pss 97:1; 118:24; *1 En.* 104:13; Aune). But the language of Rev 19:7–8 is most like that of Isa 61:10: "I will *rejoice* greatly in the Lord; my soul shall *celebrate* in my God; for *he has clothed* me with the garments of salvation, he has covered me with the *robe of righteousness*, as a bridegroom decks himself with a garland, and as a *bride* adorns herself with her jewels" (Fekkes, *Isaiah*, 231–38).

"for the wedding day of the Lamb has come. This passage draws on several types of imagery:

1. Ordinary weddings. In common social practice, a bride and groom were initially bound together in a relationship of mutual commitment through the rite of be-

trothal. The man committed himself to be faithful to his wife and provide for her well-being; the woman also pledged her faithfulness. Her family usually arranged for the dowry. The wedding occurred some time later and included a banquet and a procession in which the bride was escorted to the groom's home, where the couple would live together (see COMMENT).

2. God as husband. A number of biblical writings picture God as a husband and Israel as his bride. These texts compared God's covenant relationship with Israel to a marriage: "I pledged myself to you and entered into a covenant with you," and "you became mine" as a bride (Ezek 16:8; cf. Jer 31:32; Isa 54:5; cf. 62:5). As a husband, God committed himself to love, care, and provide for his bride: "I will take you for my wife forever; I will take you for my wife in righteousness and in justice, in steadfast love and mercy. I will take you for my wife in faithfulness" (Hos 2:19–20). He provided "garments of salvation" for his bride to wear (Isa 61:10) and provided for her needs (Ezek 16:9–13). The wedding imagery also meant that God expected his people to be faithful to him, just as a bride was faithful to her husband (Jer 2:2; 3:20; L. Huber, *Like*, 103–12).

3. Messiah as bridegroom. Early Christians extended marital imagery from relationships with God to those involving Jesus. Some interpreters have explored possible precedents in Jewish sources (e.g., Zimmermann, "'Bräutigam'"), but Jewish sources from this period do not typically picture the Messiah as a bridegroom (J. Jeremias, *TDNT* 4:1101–3). The imagery does appear in multiple streams of Christian tradition, however. The parables of Jesus liken him to a bridegroom, in whose presence there is joy (Matt 19:15; Mark 2:19–20; Luke 5:34–35; *Gos. Thom.* 104). In the Johannine tradition, John the Baptist is pictured as the best man at a wedding where Jesus is the bridegroom, who draws people to himself as his bride (John 3:29). By providing wine at the wedding at Cana, Jesus implicitly claims the role of bridegroom (2:1–11). In the Pauline tradition, believers were compared to a young woman given to Christ as husband (2 Cor 11:2), and as the husband, Christ showed his devotion by giving himself completely for the church, his wife (Eph 5:28–32). The bridegroom image was common by the later first century (cf. *2 Clem.* 14:2).

4. Wedding as time of salvation. Some texts use banquet imagery for eschatological salvation and the arrival of God's kingdom (Isa 25:6; Matt 8:11–12; Luke 13:28–29; cf. Mark 14:25; Matt 26:29; Luke 22:18; *2 Bar.* 29:1–8). Banquet imagery was also used for resurrection, which brought deliverance from death and allowed people to wear white and celebrate with the Son of Man (*1 En.* 62:14–15). Although this eschatological banquet imagery was not specifically described as a wedding, the connection with joy and salvation meant that it could be linked to traditions like those in the prophets, who used nuptial imagery for deliverance from grief, oppression, and dishonor (Isa 61:10; 62:5; Roloff). Some Christian sources compare Christ to a bridegroom at his first coming (Mark 2:19–20), while others envision the wedding occurring with Christ's second coming and the resurrection (2 Cor 11:2; cf. 4:14). This sense of eschatological deliverance is developed in Revelation.

"and his wife has made herself ready." Most manuscripts refer to the "wife" (*gynē*) rather than the "bride" (*nymphē*) of the Lamb (א²). A young woman could be considered a wife after the betrothal, since that was the occasion when solemn promises were

made (*Jos. As.* 21:1). The word for a wife also means "woman," so the chaste wife, or woman, here is the opposite of Babylon, the debauched woman (Rev 17:3).

A woman might "make herself ready" for the wedding by anointing herself and putting on her dress and jewelry (Jer 2:32; *Jos. As.* 3:6–4:1; 18:6–7; *NP* 15:603; Safrai and Stern, *Jewish*, 2:758; L. Huber, *Like*, 131–32). When marital imagery was used for God's relationship to Israel, similar actions were mentioned (Ezek 16:8–13; Isa 49:18; 61:10). Revelation extends the idea of the bride's preparations from relationships with God to relationships with Jesus. In this context the emphasis is on the pure linen gown she will wear (Rev 19:8). Only later, in the vision of New Jerusalem, will more attention be given to the gold and jewels that are also part of her attire (21:2, 9–21).

19:8. *"She was given fine pure white linen to wear.* Pure white linen was suitable for the bride of God (Ezek 16:10; *Jos. As.* 3:6–4:1). It is closely related to the previously mentioned white robes, which signify purity, holiness, and honor (NOTE on 3:5). The imagery allows Revelation to bring together two fields of meaning: One is the process of purification that leads to wearing a white robe for worship in God's presence; the other is the purity appropriate for a bride at her wedding. Both the worship and the wedding scenes point to the hope of resurrection.

A white robe is an image for one's status before God. Readers are warned that sin makes their garments unclean, rendering them unfit for coming into God's presence (3:4). Therefore, they must wash their robes in the blood of the Lamb by receiving the benefits of Christ's death (7:14). Such cleansing provides access to New Jerusalem (22:14). The martyrs receive white robes as a promise of resurrection (6:11). Being clothed in splendor was a traditional way to refer to resurrection (*1 En.* 62:15–16; 1QS IV, 8; 2 Esd 2:39, 45; 1 Cor 15:53–54; 2 Cor 5:1–4; *Mart. Asc. Isa.* 4:16; 9:9, 17; Herm. *Sim.* 8.2.3).

"for the fine linen is the just deeds of the saints. In Rev 19:8 the way clothing is linked to just deeds has led to disputes about the connection between divine action and human action in the process of salvation. Two lines of thought have emerged. The first is most plausible:

1. The just deeds done by the believer constitute the garment. Most interpreters understand that the just deeds (*dikaiōmata*) are those of the bride, who is has "made herself ready" for the wedding (19:7). At *present*, Revelation assumes that the bridal garment is woven in the context of a relationship that Jesus the groom has already established with believers. It is related to images in which believers wash their robes in the blood of the Lamb (7:14; 22:14). Just deeds constitute the visible aspect of faith. In the *future*, the bridal gown is worn for resurrection, which is a gift of life that is given to believers by God. Revelation assumes that the deeds of faithful people follow them after death (14:13), the idea being that God remembers and values what they have done, allowing these deeds of justice to adorn them at the resurrection (Giesen; Mounce; Osborne; Reddish; Roloff; Smalley).

2. God's just deeds on behalf of the believer constitute the garment. The song in 15:4 celebrated God's deeds of justice (*dikaiōmata*). Since the wedding announcement says that the bride is literally "given" her white linen—presumably by God—some interpreters take the passage to mean that God performs just or saving actions on her behalf. Prophetic passages picture God as the one adorning his bride (Ezek 16:10;

Isa 61:10), and the same may be true here (Beale; Krodel; Morris). However, this view does not work well with the syntax or the wider thematic connections noted above.

19:9. *Then he said to me, "Write this: Blessed are those.* Where OT prophets were to "go and say" (Isa 6:9; Jer 2:2; Ezek 3:4), John is told to "write," so the prophetic word comes through his text (Aune, *Prophecy*, 275, 330–31). The message is that those who belong to God are blessed (*makarios*). This word for well-being occurs seven times in Revelation and anticipates the fullness of life that will come with the final defeat of evil and death (INTRO IV.E.2).

"who have been invited to the wedding banquet of the Lamb." Invitations to a marriage banquet could be given orally or in writing (Matt 22:1–10). For example, a written invitation could say, "Isidoros invites you to dine with him for the marriage of his daughter at the house of Titus the centurion" (P.Fay. 132), or "Thermouthis invites you to dine at the marriage of her daughter in her house tomorrow" (P.Oxy. 1579). In Revelation those invited to the Lamb's wedding banquet enjoy God's favor; they are "called" and "chosen" (Rev 17:14). The Lamb's wedding banquet is gracious, in contrast to the "banquet" on the battlefield in the next scene, where the allies of evil are defeated and are devoured by birds (Rev 19:17).

He said to me, "These are the true words of God." The angel emphasizes that the blessing promised to those invited to the Lamb's wedding banquet comes from God and is therefore reliable, or "true" (cf. 19:2; 21:5; 22:6). Some interpreters suggest that 19:9 underscores the truth of the whole book (22:6; Prigent), or at least its second half (Roloff). The focus here, however, concerns the validity of what God has just promised to the faithful through the angel.

19:10. *Then I fell at his feet to worship him. But he said, "Do not do that!* Ancient sources often mention someone involuntarily collapsing when encountering a heavenly figure, as John did before (1:17; cf. Tob 12:15–16; Matt 28:2–4; *T. Ab.* 9:1), or voluntarily prostrating themselves in worship, as John does here (*Jos. As.* 15:11). When such worship mistakenly occurs, the angel often tells the person not to worship him since he is not God (*Apoc. Zeph.* 6:11–15; *Mart. Asc. Isa.* 7:21; Bauckham, *Climax*, 120–32). Similarly, someone prostrating before another human being may be told not to do so, since the person being honored is not God (Acts 10:25–26; Aune). The angel's prohibition is *hora mē*, which is a short form of "see that you do not" (22:9; cf. *Did.* 6:1; Epictetus, *Diatribai* 2.9.3; Lucian, *Electr.* 6).

"I am a fellow servant with you and your brethren. In Revelation, God's servants (*douloi*) include John, the prophets, the martyrs, and all the members of the community of faith (Rev 1:1; 10:7; 19:2, 5). Here, the angel identifies himself as their "fellow servant" (*syndoulos*; cf. *Mart. Asc. Isa.* 8:5). This designation may seem peculiar, since angels serve as heavenly beings, whereas people are mortal and become God's servants by redemption (Rev 7:3; 19:20). Revelation includes both angels and people among God's servants, however, since both groups are instrumental in communicating the message of Jesus and both offer worship to God and the Lamb. In 22:9 the term "brethren" was used specifically for Christian prophets, but here it extends to all who hold firmly to testimony concerning Jesus.

"who hold firmly to the witness of Jesus. There are two main aspects of the witness of Jesus. First, the genitive "of Jesus" refers to the witness that comes *from* Jesus (Giesen;

Smalley; Hill, "Prophecy," 412; Bucur, "Hierarchy," 188). This witness from Jesus includes what he said and did in *the past* during his ministry on earth. Jesus was called "the faithful witness" because of what he said and the death that he died (Rev 1:5; 3:14). The witness from Jesus continues in *the present* through the messages given to John and other prophets. John received witness from Jesus through visions that he conveys through his writing (1:1–2). Therefore, to "hold firmly to the witness of Jesus" includes holding firmly to "the words of this book" (22:9).

Second, the witness "of Jesus" also suggests witness *concerning* Jesus, since he is the one through whom God works. To say that Jesus' witness to God is true means that Jesus himself is true (Aune). The same double sense appears in the expressions "word of God" and "commandments of God," where a word or commandment can both come from God and concern the worship that is given to God (1:9; 12:17; 20:4; Beale; Boring; Smalley; Slater, *Christ*, 89; Tonstad, *Saving*, 179–81).

"Worship God!" Worshiping God is contrasted with John's worship of the angel. Some interpreters have speculated that the worship of angels may have been a problem for John's readers (Harrington; Roloff), but this is unlikely since it was not mentioned in the messages to the churches in Rev 2–3 (Smalley). There is slight evidence that angel worship was a problem in early Christian Christianity (Col 2:18; Keener), but most of the warnings against worshiping angels are part of a literary motif that is designed to safeguard monotheism or the unique status of Christ. They do not critique actual cults of angels (Aune; Giesen; Prigent; Stuckenbruck, *Angel*, 101–3, 146–49).

"For the witness of Jesus is the Spirit of prophecy." On the "witness of Jesus," see the NOTE on 1:2. The expression "Spirit of prophecy" means that God's Spirit communicates the prophecy, since the Spirit brings the word of the exalted Jesus to the readers. Messages from the risen Jesus to the churches were conveyed through the Spirit (e.g., 2:1, 7, 8, 11; 22:16–17). The spiritual state in which John receives visions is said to be inspired by God's Spirit (1:10; 4:2; 17:3; 21:10), and these visions constitute the prophecy he receives from Jesus (1:2). Prophetic utterance was commonly ascribed to the Spirit (e.g., Num 11:25; Joel 2:28; Ezek 37:1, 4; Luke 1:67; 1 Thess 5:19–20; 1 Cor 12:1–3). Other sources also use the expressions "Spirit of prophecy" (*Tg. Onq.*; Gen 41:38; Num 11:25–26; *Tg.* Isa 61:1) or "prophetic Spirit" (Justin Martyr, *1 Apol.* 13.3; 31.1; Herm. *Man.* 11.9; Aune) for the Spirit of God that inspires prophecy.

COMMENT

The haunting specter of Babylon's demise in the previous chapter now gives way to songs of celebration. By juxtaposing scenes, John shows contrasting perspectives on the fall of the city. Three groups of mourners—kings, merchants, and seafarers—have been grieving the city's fiery destruction and the end of their profitable relationships with it. Each group lamented with repeated expressions of woe (*ouai*, Rev 18:10, 16, 19). Now

---

On Rev 19:1–10, see Boring, "Theology"; Bucur, "Hierarchy"; Fekkes, "His"; L. Huber, *Like*, 113–63; Jörns, *Das hymnische*, 144–60; G. W. H. Lampe, "Testimony"; MacLeod, "Heaven's"; McIlraith, "For"; Miller, "Nuptial"; Philonenko, "Une voix"; Roose, *"Zeugnis,"* 188–98; Rossing, *Choice*, 135–44; Ruiz, "Politics"; L. Thompson, *Book*, 53–73; M. Wilson, "Revelation 19.10"; Zimmermann, "'Bräutigam'" and "Nuptial."

the scene changes to show their counterparts, as three groups celebrate the end of the city's tyrannical reign. These groups include the heavenly multitude, the creatures and elders, and all God's servants. Each group rejoices by exclaiming "Hallelujah!" (19:1, 4, 6). In John's visionary world, Babylon's reign of deception has ended, and God's truth has prevailed (18:23; 19:2, 9). The city was responsible for the blood of the saints and prophets, but God has now brought justice for their blood (18:24; 19:2). In the devastated city no sound of musicians or artisans is heard, but from heaven praises ring out (18:22–23; 19:1, 6). Babylon has no place for a bridegroom and a bride, but the victory of God anticipates the wedding day of the Lamb and his bride (18:23; 19:7, 9).

The festive scene includes two main sections, incorporating praises and responses. In the first, there is celebration of God's rightful judgment against Babylon, which looks back to previous chapters. Given what has occurred, a great crowd in heaven gives a resounding "hallelujah," and their praise is echoed by the twenty-four elders and four living creatures, who fall down in worship (19:3–4). In the second section the worshipers look ahead to the wedding banquet that is to come, anticipating the vision of New Jerusalem as the bride in the final chapters of the book (21:2, 9–10). This wave of adulation begins when a voice from the throne calls all God's servants to praise, and a great crowd responds with "hallelujah" (19:5–8). An angel then pronounces a blessing on those invited to the wedding banquet.

At the end of the passage, John describes his own response in a surprising way. In contrast to the elders and creatures, who worshiped the God seated on the throne, John mistakenly venerates the angelic messenger. When he is told, "Worship God," this directive makes the focus of worship clear not only to John, but to his readers. These same elements occur in slightly different order at the end of the next vision cycle (22:6–9). Interpreters have proposed various ways to characterize the place of these scenes in the structure of the Apocalypse. The approach taken here is that they create a parallel pattern: The first occurrence marks the transition from the section on Babylon into the next series of visions, and the second occurrence marks the transition from the section on New Jerusalem into the epilogue.

The hymns in this section reflect the language and style of Hebrew poetry, which is fitting for a passage that celebrates the victory of Israel's God over his foes. The words "hallelujah" and "amen" are transliterations of Hebrew expressions, and themes of God's glory and justice often appear in the psalms (e.g., Pss 98:1; 106:1). The pattern of (1) issuing a call to praise God, (2) making a statement of praise, and (3) stating the reason for the praise is typical of Israel's worship (Westermann, *Psalms*, 47–52; Mc-Cann, *Theological*, 53–70). The initial call to praise was given in Rev 18:20, where a heavenly voice called worshipers to rejoice over Babylon's downfall. Now the remaining elements occur in the hymns in the first part of this passage (19:1–4; Murphy). In the second part, all three elements—call, praise, and reason—appear together in a well-developed sequence (19:5–8; Aune 3:1022). Initially, all God's servants are called to give praise, and they respond with "hallelujah." The reasons for praise are also given: They are to celebrate "for" God's judgments are true and just and "for" the wedding day of the Lamb has come (19:2, 6–7).

These hymns may reflect elements of Christian worship at the time Revelation was composed. It is unlikely that John wove existing hymns into his book, since themes like the defeat of the whore and wedding of the Lamb are so closely tied to the literary context; but using familiar forms would have enhanced the vision's ability to encourage readers to identify with the worshipers of God and to share the perspective of those who rejoice in this vision (INTRO IV.E.1).

Celebrating the Demise of the Whore (19:1–4)

A celestial voice issued a call to give praise for Babylon's fall in the previous vision: "Rejoice over her, O heaven, and saints and apostles and prophets, because God has judged her as she judged you" (18:20). The allies of Babylon might grieve the loss of the city's lively social and economic life, but for John this vibrant façade masked brutality, for the city shed the blood of many (18:24). In the new vision, John now hears the allies of heaven respond to the call to praise by celebrating the end of Babylon's tyranny: "Hallelujah! Salvation and glory and power belong to our God, for his judgments are true and just, for he judged the great whore, who ruined the earth with her immorality, and he brought justice for the blood of his servants, which was shed by her own hand" (19:1). The Apocalypse shows that the same event—the fall of Babylon—can be seen in two different ways: For those who profited under an unjust system, its collapse means loss, but for those who suffer under it, the end of the regime means salvation.

Praise begins with "Hallelujah!," a word that creates a refrain (19:1, 3, 4, 6). It is a transliteration of a Hebrew expression that is rooted in Israel's worship. The term comes from a subculture, not from the dominant culture, and here it celebrates the fall of Babylon the imperial city, whose traits include those of Rome. John assumes that some of his readers are inclined to minimize their distinctive faith commitments by eating what had been offered to Greco-Roman deities, yet this vision tacitly challenges such accommodation by praising God with language from Israel's tradition and affirming the sovereignty of the true God over all rivals to the throne (19:1; Ruiz, "Praise").

Several reasons for praising God are given (19:2). First, saying that "his judgments are true and just" characterizes God's actions broadly. The whore and the beast operate through deception rather than truth (13:14; 18:23). They adopt the tactics of Satan, the deceiver, who seeks the unjust condemnation of the faithful (12:9–10). Previous visions have warned that the faithful will face the power of untruth on earth and may come under the unjust judgment of the beast when they refuse to capitulate. Yet there are also promises that God will not abandon his people but give them a future beside heaven's crystal sea, where they will sing of his truth and justice (15:2–3). Now God's commitment to truth and justice is emphasized again, since these characterize the actions that bring "salvation" for his people (19:1–2).

Second, God has "judged the great whore, who destroyed the earth with her immorality" (19:2). The central conflict in Revelation is between the Creator and the destroyers of the earth (4:11; 10:6; 11:18), one of whom is the whore. When the heavenly company said that the time had come for God to destroy those who destroy the earth, they played on two senses of the verb *diaphtheirein*, which can mean both ruining something morally and destroying it so that it no longer exists (NOTE on 11:18). This vision repeats that Babylon the whore destroyed, or ruined (*phtheirein*), the earth, adding that the destruction occurred through her immorality (*porneia*). This is a term for sexual immorality that Revelation extends to include the pursuit of economic gain along with false worship and violence (17:2; 18:3). There is symmetry in divine justice (18:6; 19:2; cf. Wis 11:17; 2 Macc 5:10; 13:8; *T. Gad* 5:10; *L.A.B.* 43:5; 44:10; *m. Soṭah*

1:7–9; *t. Soṭah* 3–4). The city that ruins the world through its alliance with the beast is finally ruined when the beast turns against it (Rev 17:3, 16). The whore who lured earth's kings into immoral relationships is stripped bare by kings (17:2, 16). The society that was notorious for conspicuous consumption (18:11–17) is itself consumed (17:16). Evil becomes evil's own undoing.

Third, praise is given because God has "brought justice for the blood of his servants, which was shed by her hand" (19:2). The theme of justice was introduced when the martyrs under the heavenly altar asked how long God would refrain from bringing justice against those who had shed their blood (6:10). As long as God delays judgment, the innocent continue to suffer. The initial response to the martyrs was cryptic. They were given white robes as assurance of vindication and resurrection, but they were also told to rest until other witnesses had finished their work (6:11). The visions that followed showed that wrath alone would not make people repent, so the movement toward judgment was repeatedly interrupted in order that people might be sealed for God (7:1–17) and the Christian community might continue bearing witness (10:1–11:14). When the bowls of wrath turned rivers and springs into blood, the voices from the altar declared that it was just for God to give the perpetrators of injustice blood to drink (16:4–7). Yet even here the opponents of God remained alive. Only when repeated calls for repentance were rejected (16:9, 11) did God turn evil's destructive power against itself in order to deliver those who suffered under it (Bauckham, *Theology*, 80–88; Perry, *Rhetoric*, 102; Tavo, *Woman*, 174).

The heavenly voices declare that smoke goes up from the ruined Babylon "forever and ever" as a sign that its devastation is permanent (19:3). Readers again find that the specter of judgment can be interpreted in two different ways: The kings and merchants were grief-stricken when they saw the smoke of the city's burning because it signaled the end of profitable political and trade relationships (18:9, 18). In contrast, those who suffered under its rule can rejoice because the continual smoke means that there will be no resurgence of its tyranny (19:3). Rhetorically, these contrasts would affect John's readers in different ways. For those who currently suffer, like those at Smyrna (2:9–11), the assurance that God's justice will prevail offers encouragement to remain faithful in the face of threats. But for those who are wealthy, like those at Laodicea (3:16), these visions are a summons to move beyond complacency and to identify with the victims, so that when God's justice is done, they too will have reason to celebrate, like the twenty-four elders and the four living creatures, who add their "amen" to the swelling wave of sound (19:4).

Celebrating the Lamb and the Bride (19:5–10)

The waves of praise from the vast heavenly crowd have surged inward toward the center, to the throne of God, where the elders and creatures bow in worship. Now the direction is reversed, as the call to praise comes "from the throne" and moves outward to involve all of God's servants (19:5). The line separating the hosts in heaven from the faithful on earth fades in this call to worship, as does the boundary between the text and the readers. All are to worship God (L. Thompson, *Book*, 53–63).

The call to worship also cuts across the lines of social class, since it addresses "both small and great," those of low and high social status (19:5). John has included kings, nobles, and generals, the rich and the powerful among the great. Further down are people such as merchants, shipmasters, and sailors; and at the lowest end of the spectrum are the small, who are the poorest freedmen and slaves (NOTES on 6:15; 18:11, 17). The variety of social classes in the visions is helpful, since John's readers include those who are impoverished and (2:9; 3:8) and some who are wealthy (3:16). John assumes that the wealthy may be especially inclined to accommodate the ways of imperial power, yet he recognizes that belief and unbelief do not follow class lines. He warns that those from all social classes can fall under the influence of the beast (13:16; 19:18) and will face the judgment of God (6:15; 20:12). Yet he also understands that there is a place for people of every social class within the faith community (11:18; 19:5), just as there is one for people from every ethnic and language group (5:9; 7:9).

John compares what he hears to the sound of "a great crowd," "rushing water," and "powerful thunder" (19:6). In a previous vision such sound signified a new song that only the 144,000 who were with the Lamb could understand (14:1–5). Here, the chorus makes its message plain by saying, "Hallelujah! For the Lord our God the Almighty reigns" (19:6; Murphy). The theme of God's reign is a familiar part of Israel's worship, yet the *way* God reigns is a mystery (10:7), since powers hostile to God now work in the world, concealing his reign (13:1–4; 17:18). John's visions give readers a reason to reaffirm the traditional belief in the reign of God by disclosing the outcome of God's purposes—the defeat of evil and deliverance of the faithful—even if this does not seem evident at present.

The crowd continues the festive tone by declaring that "the wedding of the Lamb has come" (19:7). The wedding imagery evokes a wealth of positive associations that are the opposite of those suggested by the whore and her immorality (19:2). Ideally, marriage was to be a lifelong partnership based on mutual consent and affection (Ps.-Phoc. 195–97; Plutarch, *Mor.* 138C; 142D; 143A; 144D). In practice, marriages often fell short, but nuptial imagery conveyed values that were widely held. In John's social context, the ideals of marriage were often associated with the emperors and their wives. Augustus enshrined marital fidelity in law (Suetonius, *Aug.* 34). The imperial temple at Aphrodisias pictured the deified Claudius and his wife Agrippina clasping hands in a picture of marital harmony. The imperial temple at Laodicea was dedicated to both Domitian and his wife Domitia. Although their relationship was sometimes turbulent, the city's coins picture them looking at each other in an image of concord (Figure 16; Friesen, *Imperial*, 62, 178; L. Huber, *Like*, 119–20). Revelation's visions run counter to such official portraiture by depicting imperial power as a beast and its consort as a whore. Their relationship was not marked by fidelity but faithlessness, for the whore drew kings into immoral relations, and the beast turned against her and burned her with fire (Rev 17:2, 16).

The Lamb and his bride provide the positive contrast, depicting a relationship based on mutual fidelity (19:7). The bridegroom is called "the Lamb," who is a royal figure, the King of kings (17:14). Biblically, one could picture the groom at a royal wedding as a victorious figure on a horse, with a sword on his thigh and a commitment to truth and justice (Ps 45:1, 3, 4, 7). These images are used for Christ in the next scene (Rev 19:11–15; Zimmermann, "Nuptial," 163–65). Jesus the Lamb has conveyed love through redemptive suffering (1:5; 5:9; 7:14). This sacrifice has proved him worthy of royal power (5:12) and shows that he will be "faithful and true" to his people, who are identified as his bride (19:11).

The heavenly company declares that the wedding day of the Lamb "has come" (*ēlthen*, 19:7). In ordinary practice a wedding announcement was joyous news about the "the day long-awaited" (P.Oxy. 3313). But if readers assume that the wedding will occur immediately, the next scenes alter this expectation. Instead of coming directly to his marriage celebration, the Lamb is called away to battle. Babylon has fallen, but the beast and its allies remain a threat and must be defeated before the wedding can take place. It was understood that a man was not to marry just before going into war. According to Jewish tradition, a newly married man was not to set out with the army but was to remain home with his wife (Deut 24:5). In Roman practice, soldiers were not to marry until their military service was completed. For soldiers "to live with their wives in wedlock" was "considered incompatible with military discipline and with preparedness and readiness for war" (Herodian, *Historiae* 3.8.5; cf. *Rom. Civ.* 2:374, 479). From a literary perspective, the announcement of the wedding followed by a delay is a way of assuring readers that the end will indeed come, even though they have no way of knowing how long it will be before it does.

The Lamb's bride is called his wife (*gynē*) before the wedding (Rev 19:7), drawing on the practice of betrothal, which was common among Jews, Greeks, and Romans. This was a formal agreement that was tantamount to marriage. The promises could be made orally (Justinian, *Dig.* 23.1.7), though in the Greco-Roman period there were sometimes records of the dowry, the husband's pledge to provide for his wife, and commitments to fidelity (Philo, *Spec.* 3.72; Safrai and Stern, *Jewish*, 2:756). During the period of betrothal, the woman was expected to remain chaste (Deut 22:23–24; Matt 1:18–25; *Jos. As.* 21:1).

Revelation makes Christian discipleship analogous to betrothal. Faith binds people to Jesus the Lamb, much as a betrothed bride is bound to her husband by solemn commitments. John previously depicted the faithful as "maidens" (*parthenoi*), who remain chaste by refusing to yield to pressures that would violate their commitments (NOTE on Rev 14:4; Zimmermann, "Nuptial," 157–60). In an ordinary sense, a major violation of betrothal was sexual infidelity. When transferred to discipleship, this meant that Jesus' followers were to resist false worship and the wrongful actions associated with it, which the seer calls "immorality" (*porneia*; 2:14, 20; 14:8; 18:3). This imagery was not unique. Paul told the Corinthians, "I promised you in marriage to one husband, to present you as a chaste virgin to Christ," meaning that they were to remain committed until Christ's second coming (2 Cor 11:2). At the resurrection, they would be presented to him as at a wedding (cf. 4:14). Until then, they were to resist forms of teaching that would lead them to compromise their commitment to Jesus (11:2–4).

In preparation for the wedding (*gamos*), the "bride has made herself ready" (19:7). In common practice, the wedding was the time that the bride was taken to live with her husband in his home (19:7; Plutarch, *Mor.* 271E; Justinian, *Dig.* 23.2.5). The central event was not an exchange of vows, since the solemn commitments were made earlier at the betrothal. More attention was given to the wedding procession, when the bride was escorted to the groom's home (1 Macc 9:37–39; Catullus, *Poems* 61.31–32, 76–81; *NP* 15:605–11; *CAM* 2:895–96; 3:1349–50; Safrai and Stern, *Jewish*, 2:757–58). The analogy is that Jesus' followers are now committed to him like a betrothed bride, yet they do not live with him in the fullest sense. The "wedding" will occur with resurrection to life in New Jerusalem, where the Lamb and the bride will fully share the same dwelling (Rev 21:2–3).

Clothing was an important part of ordinary weddings, and the same is true for the bride of the Lamb (19:8). The clothing of a bride was to reflect modesty and chastity, while conveying beauty and elegance. Traditional attire included a wreath, veil, and often a long white tunic (L. Huber, *Like*, 130–33; *NP* 15:606, 609). To some extent, the Lamb's bride reflects traditional customs by wearing a robe made from fine linen. Her robe is pure (*katharos*), which suggests that she is undefiled by relationships that violated her commitment to the Lamb, and it is bright, suggesting beauty (*Jos. As.* 18:5). Elegance is shown by the fine linen fabric (Luke 16:19; Ezek 16:13; *Jos. As.* 3:6–4:1; Plutarch, *Mor.* 396B). For the whore, fine linen was simply one of the countless items purchased from her trade partners, and she wore it with the purple and scarlet she used to seduce her clients (Rev 18:12, 16). The bride, however, adorns herself "for her husband" (21:2).

The passage says that it was given, or allowed (*edothē*), that she wear pure bright fine linen (19:8). The passive voice leaves the source of her garment unstated. On the one hand, this might suggest that her linen robe is given to her by God, much as white robes were given to the martyrs earlier (6:11). Culturally, there is some evidence that a bride would be given a fine robe to wear by her parents (Pliny the Younger, *Ep.* 5.16.7). Biblically, God was pictured providing the garment of salvation and fine linen for his bride (Isa 61:10; Ezek 16:10). Theologically, this fits the idea that the purity and honor signified by the fine linen are gifts from God. On the other hand, the passive voice could suggest that she is allowed to wear fine linen, perhaps implying that she has woven the garment herself. Some brides did weave the gowns that they wore on their wedding day (L. Huber, *Like*, 129; Safrai and Stern, *Jewish*, 2:757). By analogy, this would fit a context in which the Lamb's bride is adorned with her own just deeds, which are mentioned in the next line.

The heavenly company explains that the fine linen the bride wears consists of "the just deeds of the saints" (19:8). To some extent, one can read this imagery in light of conventional values. A bride weaving the clothing she wore on her wedding day reflected industry, care for the family, and a faithful presence in the home (L. Huber, *Like*, 123–24). By way of analogy, the kinds of deeds that are fitting for a believer include love, faith, service, and perseverance (Rev 2:19; McIlraith, "For"). Yet Revelation's description of the bride does not focus on domesticity. Instead, John speaks about the bride doing deeds that are just (*dikaiōmata*, Rev 19:8). This moves beyond typical gender roles by making the bride's actions congruent with those of God, who is called just (*dikaios*), since his deeds of justice (*dikaiōmata*, 15:4) mean the defeat of evil. The whore's deeds of injustice (*adikēmata*, 18:5) included violence and greed, and the bride's deeds of justice are the opposite. In the Apocalypse, love, faith, and service have a militant quality, since they reflect allegiance to God and the Lamb and resistance to the ways of God's opponents.

The imagery shifts from the bride to the guests when an angel speaks of those who are "invited to the wedding banquet of the Lamb" (19:9). The people of God are both the bride and the guests in this passage. As elsewhere, the author uses two or more images for the same group in the same context (e.g., 7:4, 9; 14:4). In some contexts the banquet was hosted by the bride's family (P.Fay. 132; P.Oxy. 1579). Afterward, the guests would join the torchlight procession to the groom's house. There could also be meals at the groom's home in the days after the wedding (John 2:1–11; *CAM* 3:1338–39; *NP* 15:605, 611; Safrai and Stern, *Jewish*, 2:757–59). Invitations were sent to family and friends, who would join the festivities. People could attend the wedding banquet because they enjoyed the favor of the host. The analogy is that readers have been "invited" to the wedding banquet of the Lamb through the words of God (Rev 19:9), which are extended through those who hold firmly to the witness of Jesus (19:10).

To receive the invitation is to be "blessed" (*makarios*), which suggests another variation on common practice (19:9). At an ordinary wedding the guests would take part in the procession that led the bride to the groom's home. Along the way, people would shout blessings (*makarismoi*) to the couple, wishing them happiness, prosperity, and children (*OCD* 927). Here, however, the guests are called "blessed," since they are given the hope of life and well-being, which will culminate in life in New Jerusalem (22:14; (Intro IV.E.2).

The initial outburst of celebration in this section culminated with the elders and living creatures bowing before God's throne (19:4), but after a second round of praises John bows in mistaken worship of an angel, who must tell him to worship God instead (19:10). In this context John's action is so incongruous as to be humorous. Despite the swelling choruses of praise to God, John missed his cue. There were literary conventions in which people were so impressed by an angel that they mistakenly bowed in worship (Note on 19:10), but in this context the heavenly voices have made the focus of worship clear. Rhetorically, however, John's account of his mistake reinforces his credibility as a witness. By acknowledging where he was mistaken and corrected (cf. 17:6), he underscores that what he says is faithfully presented. Moreover, worship was an issue in the congregations Revelation addresses. John has penned sharp reproofs to those who are willing to eat what had been linked to the worship of Greco-Roman deities (2:14, 20). As John himself accepts correction about the focus of worship, readers should accept correction about the focus of worship in their contexts.

Revelation distinguishes God and the exalted Jesus, who can be worshiped, from angels and human beings, who cannot. John uses expressions like "Alpha and Omega" and "first and last" for God and the risen Christ (1:8, 17; 21:6; 22:13), and yet he retains a monotheistic perspective. There is only one throne, which God and Jesus share (3:21; 22:3). Jesus is not a second deity, who is worshiped alongside God. Rather, the worship of Jesus is included in the worship of the one God, since it is through Jesus that God's purposes are accomplished (5:13; 7:10; 22:3). By way of contrast, angels are grouped with human beings and are considered servants of God. Both groups are alike in that they give worship to God and the Lamb but do not receive it (5:11–12; 7:9–12; Bauckham, *Theology*, 54–65).

The angel's command to worship God is then linked to "the Spirit of prophecy" (19:10). This association reflects the essential connection between prophecy and worship that informs the book as a whole. Revelation was composed in a context in which the difference between true and false prophecy was disputed. The message to Thyatira, for example, challenges the legitimacy of Jezebel, who called herself a prophetess but taught that it was acceptable to eat what had been sacrificed to Greco-Roman deities (2:20). Later, John pictures a beastlike false prophet, who promotes the worship of the great beast from the sea, which was a form of the ruler cult (13:11–18; 16:13; 19:20).

The principal criterion for distinguishing true from false prophecy in Revelation is whether a prophet moves people to worship God or lures people away from God (INTRO III.A.1; §8 COMMENT; cf. Deut 13:1–11; Philo, *Spec. Laws* 1.315; Matt 24:11; 1 Cor 12:1–3; 1 John 4:1–3). The angel links the Spirit of prophecy to "the witness of Jesus," which encompasses the witness that comes from the earthly Jesus and is transmitted through the tradition of the early church, and the witness that comes from the exalted Jesus, which is conveyed through the Spirit to prophets like John and his associates (NOTE on 19:10). Accordingly, the community could test a prophet's message by asking whether a message that purportedly came from the risen Jesus was congruent with what had already been received from the earthly Jesus (cf. 1 Cor 12:1–3; 1 John 4:1–3). Since Jesus himself is "the faithful witness," whose death makes people into priests that serve his God (Rev 1:5–6), a prophet claiming to have received witness from the risen Jesus by means of the Spirit of prophecy should do the same, that is, the message should direct people to the worship of God.

Sixth Cycle:
From the Beast's Demise to
New Jerusalem (19:11–22:5)

---

38. General Comments on the Sixth Cycle

The sixth cycle of visions begins after the announcement that "the wedding day of the Lamb has come and his wife has made herself ready" (Rev 19:7). One might expect the celebration to begin, but in Revelation's visionary world the bride does not appear until a thousand years have passed. Instead, Christ—the groom at this wedding (19:7, 9)—comes on a white horse to defeat the agents of evil. The beast and false prophet are thrown into the lake of fire, and their allies are slain with the sword from Christ's mouth (19:11–21). Instead of the festive "wedding banquet of the Lamb" (19:9), readers find "the great banquet of God," in which the birds feast on corpses on the battlefield (19:17). The rout continues as Satan is bound with a chain and confined to the abyss for a thousand years, only to be released and hurled into the lake of fire (20:1–3, 7–10).

As the agents of evil are defeated, the faithful who suffered under their rule are vindicated. The martyrs, who represent the faithful, are resurrected to reign with Christ for a thousand years (20:4–6); then all the dead are raised for judgment (20:11–15), and a new heaven and earth appear (21:1–22:5). The bride of the Lamb descends in splendor (21:2). She is New Jerusalem, the counterpart to Babylon the whore. In this dazzling city Revelation's vision cycles come to their end, as an angelic guide leads John to the tree of life and the river of living water, which flows from the throne of God and the Lamb (22:1–5).

A. HISTORY OF INTERPRETATION

Revelation's depiction of the defeat of the beast, the binding of Satan, and the thousand-year reign of the saints is one of the most disputed sections of the book. Interpreters disagree over whether Revelation expects Jesus and his followers literally to reign on earth in the future or whether the millennial kingdom should be taken figuratively. Since Revelation is the only canonical book to mention such a thousand-year

741

period, debates are especially intense among those trying to fit the passage into a comprehensive system of eschatology. In many cases the notion of the millennial kingdom is broadened to include various hopes for a future golden age, even if these scenarios have little to do with Revelation.

Western Interpretation to 350: Future Age on Earth Versus Life in Heaven After Death

An early form of the idea that Christ would establish a thousand-year kingdom on earth in the future is linked to Papias of Hierapolis (d. ca. 130), who is said to have known Revelation (Andreas, *In Apocalypsin* pref.) and to have collected sayings attributed to Jesus and the disciples (Eusebius, *Hist. eccl.* 3.39.1, 12). Papias believed that after the resurrection of the dead, Christ would establish a kingdom in which every vine would have ten thousand branches and every branch ten thousand twigs; every cluster would have ten thousand grapes and each grape yield gallons of wine (quoted in Irenaeus, *Haer.* 5.33.3–4). Although this picture of lavish abundance does not derive from Rev 20:4–6 (cf. *2 Bar.* 29:5–7), it became a feature of certain forms of millennialism.

The Christian apologist Justin Martyr (d. ca. 165) mentioned the millennium when arguing that Christianity was the fulfillment of Jewish Scripture. He recognized that prophecies concerning the glorification of Jerusalem had not yet been realized (e.g., Ezek 40–48; Isa 54:11–12; 60:1–3, 11; Zech 14:7–8), but he argued that they would be fulfilled when Christ reigned with the saints for a thousand years. In a move that later interpreters would repeat, he identified Revelation's millennium as the time when people will "build houses and inhabit them" and "plant vineyards and eat their fruit" without fear. In that day the "wolf and the lamb shall feed together," and "the lion shall eat straw like the ox" (Isa 65:21, 25). Only then will the last judgment take place and the faithful enter into life everlasting (*Dial.* 80–81).

Irenaeus (d. ca. 200) incorporated this view of the millennium into a comprehensive view of history. Noting that God had created the world in six days and rested on the seventh (Gen 1:1–2:4), he reasoned that if each day of creation symbolized a thousand years (Ps 90:4; 2 Pet 3:8), then the created order would last for six thousand years and the millennial reign of the saints would be the final period of blessedness for the world (*Haer.* 5.28.3; cf. *Barn.* 15:1–5). Irenaeus expected the present age to culminate in the defeat of the Antichrist and in the bodily resurrection of the saints for life on earth (*Haer.* 4.20.11; 5.30.4). Belief in a bodily resurrection and an earthly millennium were important because they affirmed the goodness of creation and justice of God. Since God created the world to be good, it was right for him to restore it to perfection and abundance at the end of the age, as Papias had said. And since Christians lost their lives within the created order, it would be just for God to give them life again on earth before the last judgment (*Haer.* 5.32.1; 5.33.3; Daley, *Hope*, 28–32).

The futuristic perspective provoked opposition from the Roman presbyter named Gaius (early third century), who thought hope for an earthly millennium was essentially lust for pleasure (Intro I.A.1), but the view of Tertullian (d. ca. 225) concerning the millennium was more positive, like that of Irenaeus (*Fug.* 12; *Marc.* 3.25). Commodian (mid-third century) varied the pattern by assuming that the heavenly Jerusalem (Rev 21:2) would descend during the millennium rather than after it (*Instructiones* 1.41,

44). Lactantius (d. ca. 325) enriched the scenario by blending biblical texts with Greco-Roman oracles ascribed to Trismegistus, Hystapes, and the Sibyls to show that all these prophetic traditions pointed to the future in similar ways (*Inst.* 7.14–27; Daley, *Hope*, 66–68; Fàbrega, "Laktanz"; Dochhorn, "Laktanz").

The main alternative to the futuristic perspective was that "the first resurrection" in Rev 20:4–6 referred to the souls of the martyrs being raised to reign with Christ in heaven immediately after death. For Hippolytus (d. 236) and Cyprian (d. 258) the millennial kingdom signified the blessed state of the dead in heaven. Such prospects for an immediate postmortem reward gave people incentive to remain faithful in the face of persecution (Hill, *Regnum*, 160–69, 192–201).

The perspective of Victorinus (d. 304) was more futuristic. He thought the grape harvest in Rev 14:18–20 and the warrior trampling the winepress of wrath in 19:11–16 both pointed to the defeat of the Antichrist. By relating Revelation to prophetic visions about the subjugation of the nations (e.g., Isa 60:10; 61:5), he concluded that some of the defeated nations would serve the saints in the millennial kingdom. He assumed that the New Jerusalem of Rev 21:1–22:5 would descend during the millennium, rather than after it, and that vines would yield their bounty on the scale of "ten thousand"—recalling the ideas of Papias and Irenaeus (Victorinus, *In Apoc.* 14.3–21.6; Hill, *Regnum*, 35–39).

Eastern Interpretation to 350: Spiritual Perspectives

Clement of Alexandria (d. ca. 215) emphasized that spiritual training prepared souls for a place with God after death. He thought perfected souls would join the twenty-four heavenly elders in judging the world. When souls became angelic, they would be taught by true angels for a thousand years, perhaps construing the millennium as a period of postmortem heavenly instruction (*Ecl.* 57.4; Hill, *Regnum*, 174–75). Origen (d. 254) coupled spiritual interpretation with rejection of the idea of an earthly millennium where people would eat, drink, and enjoy marital relations, since desires for bodily pleasure were contrary to virtue. He urged people to eat and drink of divine wisdom instead. Revelation's vision of "the first resurrection" showed that those who remained true to their baptisms would enter heavenly blessedness when they died, and the gem-like appearance of New Jerusalem also signified spiritual transformation after death (*Princ.* 2.11.2–3; *Hom. Jer.* 2.3; Hill, *Regnum*, 176–89).

Methodius (d. ca. 311), agreed that the millennial hope did not involve physical pleasure, but he criticized Origin for not giving the human body a place in the process of salvation. People had incentive to strive for sexual purity now because in the future they would be raised bodily to be with Christ. In the present age the faithful are like the woman of Rev 12, who is threatened by the sins symbolized by the dragon; but those who purify themselves have the hope of resurrection to the millennium of rest and celebration, followed by transformation to incorruptible life (*Symp.* 8.5–13; 9.1, 5; Daley, *Hope*, 61–64). Sharper criticism of Origen's views came from the Egyptian bishop Nepos (mid-third century), who insisted that there would be a thousand-year kingdom on earth (Eusebius, *Hist. eccl.* 7.24.1). But Dionysius of Alexandria (d. 264) and other eastern writers countered that the millennium had to be understood spiritually (INTRO 1.A.2; Eusebius, *Hist. eccl.* 3.24.18–25.4; 3.39.13; 7.24.1; Epiphanius, *Pan.* 77.36.5–6).

From 350 to 700: The Millennium as the Present Age of the Church

Tyconius (d. ca. 400) marked a turning point in the debate when he identified the millennium with the current situation of the church. He noted that in Revelation the millennium began when Satan was bound (Rev 20:2) and that in the gospels Jesus bound Satan by performing exorcisms (Matt 12:29; Mark 3:27). By seeing these texts together, Tyconius argued that the thousand-year kingdom began with the ministry of Jesus. His interpretation made sense of the fact that even though Christianity had overcome opposition and spread throughout the Roman Empire, the church still struggled with sin and evil. For Tyconius such conflict was to be expected during the millennium, since Satan was only bound and would not be annihilated until the end of time. Until then, the righteous and the unrighteous would exist side by side (INTRO 1.A.3).

Augustine (d. 430) once accepted the traditional idea that history would last for six thousand years, with the millennium as the seventh period of rest for the world (*Civ.* 20.7), but he later agreed with Tyconius that the millennium was a present reality. People entered it through the "first resurrection" (Rev 20:4–6), which meant spiritually dying and rising in baptism (*Civ.* 20.6; cf. Rom 6:4). The second resurrection would be the bodily resurrection at the end of time (Rev 20:11–13; cf. John 5:28–29; 1 Cor 15:35–58). Satan was now confined to "the abyss" of human hearts, where wickedness would reside until God destroyed it. For Augustine, the millennium was not the idyllic period of rest at the end of history; true rest would come only when time ceased and people entered the Sabbath rest of eternity (*Civ.* 20.7; 22.30).

Jerome (d. 420) agreed that Revelation did not promise a millennial kingdom of physical pleasure and called such ideas a "fable" (*Comm. Dan.* 7:17). After revising Victorinus's commentary, he added a postscript arguing that the millennium symbolized a life of perfect obedience and chastity, which fit the growing interest in monasticism. The vision of New Jerusalem provided similar spiritual instruction. The city's precious stones were those people who withstood persecution, and its twelve gates of pearl signified the apostles' teaching (SC 423:127–29). In the city stands a single throne, showing the unity of the Trinity, and the river of life is the grace of the Spirit flowing through Scripture (FC 48:8–9). The ecclesiastical perspective of Tyconius and Augustine, along with the moral and spiritual emphasis in Jerome's edition of Victorinus, defined western perspectives on the millennium for centuries (Primasius; Caesarius; Bede; Beatus; cf. Matter, "Apocalypse," 41; Hasitschka, "Ankunft").

In the east, Oecumenius (early sixth century) proposed a Christological interpretation, identifying Rev 20:1–6 with the earthly ministry of Jesus. He assumed that with God, a thousand years could equal one day (Ps 90:4; 2 Pet 3:8) and that Christ's incarnation brought the "day" of salvation, symbolized by the thousand years. Christ bound the devil by his exorcisms, and the "first resurrection" occurred when the apostles rose spiritually by coming to faith. Oecumenius's most distinctive idea was that the millennium ended with Christ's ministry and the devil had already been released to threaten people until the end of the age (Rev 20:3, 7–10). More conventional was Andreas of Caesarea (d. ca. 614), who followed the tradition in thinking that the millennium extended from Christ's incarnation to his second coming and that people entered it by the spiritual death and resurrection that came through baptism.

Interpretation from 700 to 1500:
The Millennium as the Coming Phase of History

Early medieval interpreters accepted the tradition that the millennium was the present age of the church, but some also began envisioning a coming age of peace on earth. Bede (d. 735) noted this idea in his treatment of the seven seals. He thought the seals outlined periods of world history, culminating in the cosmic disasters of the sixth seal, which signified persecution by the Antichrist. Since the seventh seal ushered in a period of silence (8:1), he thought there would be a time of rest after the Antichrist and before the last judgment. For support he invoked Jerome, who thought Daniel envisioned a forty-five-day respite after the demise of the Antichrist (Bede, *In Apoc.* 8.1). Other Latin writers developed this idea, claiming that the peaceful period after the Antichrist would allow for the conversion of pagans (Honorius Augustodunensis, d. ca. 1156) and Jews (Otto of Freising, d. 1158) to Christianity and for the reform of the church itself (Gerhoh of Reichersberg, d. 1169; Lerner, "Medieval," 51–57).

Joachim of Fiore (d. 1202) went further by identifying the peaceful period after the Antichrist with the millennial vision of Rev 20:1–6. He divided history into the era of the Father, which was characterized by marriage, and that of the Son, which featured celibate clergy. Conflict with the Antichrist would soon bring the era of the Son to an end, but afterward, the era of the Spirit would fulfill the monastic ideal of contemplation. That coming era would be the reign of the saints pictured in 20:1–6. Joachim thought Revelation's reference to a thousand years symbolized completeness and that the new age would actually be quite short. When it was over, a second Antichrist would appear for the final persecution of the church before the last judgment (20:7–10; Lerner, "Millennialism," 346–48; McGinn, *Antichrist*, 140–41).

The idea that Rev 20 referred to a literal thousand-year period came through a revision of Augustine's belief that the millennium was the present situation of the church in its struggle with sin. The Franciscan Peter Olivi (d. 1298) proposed that the millennium began when Satan was bound by Constantine, whose conversion led to the Christianizing of the Roman Empire. A thousand years later, in the fourteenth century, the period would culminate in conflict with the Antichrist, which Olivi saw beginning in the Franciscans' struggle for church reform. When the new spiritual age arrived, it would last perhaps seven hundred years, allowing time for the world to be converted before the end (Burr, *Olivi's*, 167–72). John of Rupescissa (d. ca. 1366) decided that even more time was needed to bring in the glorious future and concluded that the coming spiritual age would last for the full thousand years of Rev 20:1–6 (Lerner, "Millennialism," 351–54).

A different form of millennialism appeared in the early fifteenth century among the Taborites, the radical followers of Jan Hus (d. 1415). Rather than looking for a spiritual millennium, the Taborites sought prosperity in a kingdom that would overturn the current social order and endure until the general resurrection of the dead. Some hoped it would last for a thousand years, during which there would be no private property, kings, or taxation. In such a kingdom all would have equal rights to fishponds, meadows, and forests, and goods would be so abundant that coins would not be necessary (Lerner, "Millennialism," 355–56; Potestà, "Radical," 126–30).

From 1500 to 2000: Present, Postmillennial, and Premillennial Views

Protestant reformers of the sixteenth century generally rejected belief in a future millennial kingdom. Martin Luther (d. 1546) followed Augustine in identifying the millennium as the present time of the church, but by taking the thousand years in a general sense, he could say that the period was reaching its end and that the Turkish armies threatening Europe at the time were Gog and Magog, whose defeat would lead to the last judgment (Rev 20:7–10; LuthW 35:408–9). Luther and his followers explicitly rejected the idea that the saints would inherit an earthly kingdom and annihilate the godless before the last judgment (Augsburg Confession of 1530, art. 17). Their opposition was directed in part against radicals like Thomas Müntzer (d. 1525), who advocated violent overthrow of the social order (INTRO I.C.3). Also in view were Anabaptists like Augustin Bader (d. 1530), whose ecstatic experiences convinced him that the present age would end on Easter of 1530. He thought that at that time the Turks would overrun Christendom for two and half years, but then the thousand-year reign of the saints would begin and government and taxation would be abolished. Because his views were considered dangerous, Bader was executed (Clasen, *Wiedertäufer*, 114–17).

John Calvin (d. 1564) rejected the idea of a future thousand-year kingdom (*Institutes* 3.25.5), as did Heinrich Bullinger (d. 1575) in chapter 11 of the Second Helvetic Confession of 1566 and Thomas Cranmer (d. 1556) in article 41 of the Forty-Two Articles of 1553 (Backus, *Reformation*, 108–11). Yet questions about the flow of history continued to generate interest in the millennium. John Bale (d. 1563) accepted the traditional idea that the thousand years began when Satan was bound at the time of Christ, but he gave it a Protestant spin by claiming that the period ended in the year 1000 when Satan was set loose during the papacy of Sylvester II, who was charged with sorcery. Bale thought he was living after the millennium, when Satan had been unleashed and worked through the papacy, which threatened the faithful before the last judgment. Thomas Brightman (d. 1607) thought Rev 20 actually mentioned two millennial periods. One was the thousand-year confinement of Satan (20:1–3), which began with Constantine and ended with Satan's release during the invasion of the Ottoman Turks around 1300. At that time the second millennium began, when many people were spiritually resurrected through the reform of the church and could serve as Christ's witnesses on earth (20:4–6). If Christians were now in that second millennial period, they had incentive to work for the visible renewal of the church on earth (Smolinski, "Apocalypticism," 38–39).

Other interpreters insisted that the millennium was still to come. Johann Heinrich Alsted (d. 1638) argued that it would begin with the "first resurrection" (20:4, 6), which would be a literal, physical resurrection in the future, rather than a type of spiritual renewal, as others assumed. Similarly, Joseph Mede (d. 1638) said that the world was still threatened by the Antichrist, who was to reign for 1,260 years (cf. 11:3; 12:6), beginning with the fall of Rome in the fifth century and continuing until 1716 or 1736. Then the saints would be raised bodily to reign in heaven, while the faithful who had not died would reign on earth (Smolinski, "Apocalypticism," 39–40).

By the eighteenth century, belief in a future millennial age was common in Britain and North America, and many thought it would come through progress in evangelism and social reform. Jonathan Edwards (d. 1758) considered Revelation to be a map of history, which showed how the beast—identified as the papacy—would gradually be overthrown by the spread of the gospel and God's outpouring of the Spirit. Through spiritual renewal, society would be transformed so that in the millennial age people everywhere would glorify God and love and peace would prevail (Stein, *Apocalyptic*, 17–21, 334–41; McDermott, *One*, 37–92). Edwards' student Samuel Hopkins (d. 1803) thought advances in technology, medicine, and communication were bringing humanity closer to a millennial quality of life (Smolinski, "Apocalypticism," 62).

In the nineteenth century this perspective was known as *postmillennialism*, which meant that Christ was expected to return for judgment *after* the millennial ideals had been realized. The vision of Christ coming on a white horse wielding a sword from his mouth was not taken to be his final coming but as a symbol for the evangelism that leads to the millennial age (Rev 19:11–21; Warfield, *Biblical*, 647). Alexander Campbell (d. 1866), the founder of the Disciples of Christ, established a journal called *The Millennial Harbinger* to promote the political and religious changes he felt were needed to bring in the millennial age. Charles Finney (d. 1875) tried to hasten the coming of the millennium through mass evangelism, the control of alcohol abuse, and the abolition of slavery. After the Civil War, however, those committed to social reform dropped the idea of bringing in the millennial age and worked with a more open-ended sense of the future (Moorhead, "Apocalypticism").

The main alternative to postmillennialism was to think that the millennium would arrive through sudden change. That view, known as *premillennialism*, expects conditions on earth to worsen until Christ returns *before* the millennial age to establish his kingdom on earth. William Miller (d. 1849) became disillusioned with the idea that the millennial age would come through the reform of social institutions and concluded that it would begin only with the sudden destruction of worldly kingdoms at Christ's return (INTRO I.D.2). Some of his followers formed the Seventh-Day Adventist Church, which taught that at the beginning of the millennium the faithful would be raised to reign with Christ in heaven, while Satan was bound in the abyss, which would be the earth, desolated by the battle of Armageddon. After the thousand years the wicked would be judged, and the faithful would descend from heaven with New Jerusalem. For Jehovah's Witnesses, which grew out of the nineteenth-century Adventist tradition, the millennium is to be a probationary period during which people have the opportunity to live godly lives before the last judgment. At that time, the 144,000 will rule with Christ in heaven while the great multitude lives on earth (Rev 7:4–9). The release of Satan in 20:7–10 will be the final test of character before the judgment (Penton, *Apocalypse*, 193–96).

The most influential premillennial approach was developed by John Nelson Darby (d. 1882) and others (INTRO I.D.2). In this schema the present age is to end with Armageddon, which is understood to be a literal battle. The armies of the Antichrist are to assemble in northern Israel (Rev 16:12–16; Joel 3:9–11), but they will be defeated in Transjordan (Isa 63:1–3) and the Valley of Jehoshaphat (Joel 3:12–13), and Christ will make a victory ascent up the Mount of Olives (Zech 14:3–5; cf. Rev 19:11–21; LaHaye and Ice, *Charting*, 63–64). At that point the millennial kingdom begins, when Satan is bound, Jews accept Christianity, and people live long and prosperous lives on earth (Boyer, *When*, 318–24).

Modern historical interpretation shifts the focus from the future to Revelation's ancient context. Interpreters note similarities between the binding of Satan and scenes in Jewish texts, commenting on the way Revelation adapts and transforms the motif (NOTE on 20:1). Many suggest that the millennial reign of the saints is the writer's attempt to reconcile two different eschatologies: One is the prophetic hope for a golden age and restoration of the Davidic monarchy (e.g., Isa 11:1–9; Amos 9:11–15; *Pss. Sol.* 17:21–32); the other is the apocalyptic expectation that history will end through God's intervention to defeat the forces of evil, transform the cosmos, and establish an eternal kingdom (Dan 7:23–27; 11:40–12:3; *T. Mos.* 10:1–10). The idea is that John accommodated both views by envisioning a temporary messianic kingdom before the last judgment, new creation, and eternal reign of God (Charles 2:142–43; Aune 3:1104–8; Müller 334–35; Reddish 384).

Precedents for the idea of a temporary messianic kingdom appear in several Jewish texts. The earliest is the *Apocalypse of Weeks* (*1 En.* 93:3–10; 91:11–17), which divides history into ten time periods, or weeks. In the eighth week the righteous execute justice on the wicked and the temple is rebuilt; in the ninth week righteousness extends to the whole world; and in the tenth week there is a final judgment and new creation. Although Revelation includes some of these elements, it is not clear that the eighth week in the *Apocalypse of Weeks* consists of a temporally limited kingdom, and at no point is a messiah mentioned. It is difficult to take this passage as precedent for a temporally defined messianic kingdom (Stephens, *Annihilation*, 213).

The Messiah does play a prominent role in *4 Ezra* 7:26–30, which says that at the end of the age the heavenly Jerusalem and a blessed land will be manifested. At that time the Messiah, who is God's Son, will be revealed, and those with him will rejoice for four hundred years. Then the Messiah and all other people will die, and the earth will return to its primeval silence for seven days until the dead are raised for judgment (cf. 11:46; 12:34; 13:48–49; Stone, *Fourth*, 204–6, 215–16).

Again, Revelation includes similar motifs but develops them differently. Nowhere does Revelation limit the Messiah's reign to a set number of years. The messianic kingdom was established through Jesus' death and resurrection (Rev 1:5; 12:5), and it continues through the defeat of the beast and the thousand years when Satan is bound (19:11–20:3). Christ's reign does not end when the thousand years are over, for he continues to reign with God forever in New Jerusalem (22:1–4). Moreover, those redeemed by the Messiah already constitute a kingdom, where they serve as priests of God (1:5–6; 5:9–10). Through resurrection from the dead, they share fully in Christ's reign and continue serving as priests during the thousand years (20:4–6). At that point they do not die, as the Messiah's companions do in *4 Ezra* 7:28–29; instead, they continue living and reigning in the new creation (Rev 22:5).

Finally, several scenes in *2 Baruch* envision a temporary messianic kingdom. In 29:3–30:1 the Messiah's coming inaugurates a time of phenomenal abundance, when every vine will have a thousand branches and every grape will produce gallons of wine. The monsters Leviathan and Behemoth will meet their ends, and people will feast on them, as well as on manna that descends from heaven. The period ends when the Messiah returns to glory and the dead are raised for judgment. From 39:7 to 40:1–3 the Messiah liberates the world by slaying the tyrant that oppresses it on Mount Zion and establishing a dominion that will endure until the world of corruption has ended. During the Messiah's reign, people will live at peace with one another and in harmony with the natural world (cf. Isa 11:6–9). There will be no pain during childbirth, and heavy labor will not be needed to produce food, for the earth will freely yield its bounty (*2 Bar.* 72:2–74:3).

The scenes of abundance and harmony in *2 Baruch* resemble the millennial views of Papias, Justin, and Irenaeus, yet they differ from Rev 20:4–6, which says only that the redeemed reign with Christ and serve as priests. Interpreters even debate whether the resurrected martyrs are in heaven or on earth, since the location is not stated (COMMENT on 20:6). *Second Baruch* assumes that the provisional messianic kingdom will fulfill prophetic texts about a time when people will not die prematurely, sorrow will be replaced by joy, and wild animals will live in peace under the guidance of a child (Isa 11:6–9; 51:11; 65:20–25; *2 Bar.* 73:1–6). Yet none of this is included in Revelation.

Comparing the thousand years in Rev 20:1–6 to the temporary messianic kingdoms in Jewish apocalyptic writings obscures the function of the vision in Revelation. From a literary perspective, the thousand-year period is only one phase in the book's stylized depiction of God's victory over evil, which shows how Satan is banished from heaven to earth (12:7–12), then from earth to the abyss (20:1–3), and finally to the lake of fire (20:7–10). The Messiah reigns throughout the process, from his birth and exaltation to God's throne (12:5), to his return as King of kings (19:16), and to his sharing of God's throne in New Jerusalem (22:1, 3). Those redeemed by the Messiah already constitute "a kingdom" (1:6; 5:9–10). They are raised to reign with Christ for a thousand years (20:4–6), and they continue sharing in the kingdom forever in the new creation (22:5).

Conclusion

Since the second century, Revelation's vision of the millennium has been linked to expectations for the transformation of the earth. What is striking is that almost none of the usual elements of this transformation appears in Rev 20:1–6. Nothing is said about the earth yielding superabundant harvests, animals peacefully coexisting with each other and human beings, increased longevity, or the restoration of Jerusalem (Hill, *Regnum*, 238; Stephens, *Annihilation*, 213). Many of the aspects of this lavish picture are taken from the Jewish prophets, and from antiquity to the present, many interpreters have assumed that the millennium will be the time when the prophetic texts will be fulfilled. So it is significant that Rev 20:1–6 makes almost no allusion to OT texts. Rather, the vision of the new creation, which paraphrases Isaiah, Ezekiel, and other texts, makes it clear that the new creation is where Revelation expects the prophetic hopes to be realized (NOTES on Rev 21:1–7). The millennium does not have this role in Revelation.

The millennium is connected to the theme of the justice of God (Bauckham, *Theology*, 106–8). The scenes in which Satan is bound and finally defeated assure readers that evil will not be permitted to continue forever. Since God is just, he will bring the activity of evil to an end for the sake of those who are now its victims. Since the devil threatened the followers of Jesus with imprisonment (Rev 13:10), the devil himself is subjected to imprisonment (20:1–3, 7–10). Moreover, true justice means acting for the well-being of those who have suffered. By raising the martyrs to life, the vision shows that death will be overcome through resurrection. Just as Jesus has already risen as the first among many to come (1:5), the martyrs represent the faithful who will be the first to rise at the close of the age as a step toward the final resurrection that will end the power of death (20:4–6, 14; 21:4).

B. LITERARY STRUCTURE

God's battle against Satan and his allies is a major theme in the second half of the book of Revelation. The direction is set by the words of the heavenly elders, who announce that the time has come to "destroy those who destroy the earth" (11:18). The chapters that follow successively introduce the destroyers, including Satan the dragon, the beast and false prophet, and Babylon the whore. Then the author traces their downfall in reverse order:

Satan is thrown from heaven to earth (12:1–17).
    Beast and false prophet conquer (13:1–18).
        Whore rides on the beast (17:1–12).
        Whore destroyed by the beast (17:13–18).
    Beast and false prophet are conquered (19:11–21).
Satan is thrown from earth into the abyss and lake of fire (20:1–3, 7–10).

The sixth vision cycle marks the final phase of the conflict. Babylon has now fallen, but the beast, false prophet, and Satan remain. These destroyers must be defeated for the life-giving purposes of the Creator and the Lamb to be fully realized in the new creation.

The other major theme is God's vindication of his people, which the heavenly elders also announced. They said that it was time for the dead to be judged and for God to reward his servants, including the prophets, the saints, and all who fear God's name (11:18). The sixth cycle brings their words to fulfillment, for the faithful are judged graciously and given a place in Christ's kingdom (20:4–6), then all the dead are judged at the final resurrection (20:11–15), and the redeemed are given a place in New Jerusalem, where they live in the radiant presence of God and the Lamb forever (22:1–5).

Structurally, the broad plotline extends over several smaller vision cycles and integrates each section into the story as a whole (11:19–15:4; 15:5–19:10; 19:11–22:5). Since a few cycles include seven numbered visions, some interpreters suggest that the final cycle is made up of seven unnumbered visions with an appendix describing New Jerusalem. In this scheme, the formula "and I saw" (*kai eidon*) introduces each of the seven visions (Farrer, *Rebirth*, 57; Yarbro Collins, *Crisis*, 112; Murphy xi–xii). However, this formula occurs eight times in the main body of the section (19:11, 17, 19; 20:1, 4, 11, 12; 21:1) and a ninth time in 21:22, where it does not introduce a new vision (Bauckham, *Climax*, 5–6). The interpretation given below does not assume that there are seven distinct visions in this final series.

The interpretation of the sixth vision cycle given below assumes that the text moves from conflict to victory, as earlier vision cycles have done. Some interpreters differ in their understanding, arguing that the battles in 19:11–21 and 20:7–10 offer two versions of the same scene (R. F. White, "Reexamining"; McKelvey, "Millennium"; Mathewson, "Re-examination"). They reason that recapitulation is part of the book's style, that both battles end up with the adversaries in the lake of fire, and that both include elements from the defeat of Gog in Ezek 38–39. This approach is unlikely because although Revelation repeats similar scenes in successive vision cycles (e.g., 14:18–20; 19:11–21), it does not do so *within* the same vision cycle. The action is stylized and moves progressively to the final defeat of evil. (On the use of Ezekiel in these scenes, see the COMMENT on 20:7–10.) Reading the section as a narrative sequence that moves from conflict to new creation does *not* mean that it should be taken as an outline of coming events. Revelation portrays God's final victory over evil without giving readers a way to translate it directly into the world of time and space.

The most important structural feature of the sixth cycle is that two plotlines crisscross. The downfall of the beast, false prophet, and Satan forms the first. With each step, these destructive agents are overcome and finally subjected to a common fate in the lake of fire (19:11–21; 20:1–3, 7–10). The writer underscores the continuity by weaving images from Ezekiel's vision of the defeat of Gog into two different scenes. The summoning of the birds to feast on the slain occurs early in the section (Ezek 39:17–20; Rev 19:17–18), and the fiery demise of Gog and other hostile nations occurs later (Ezek 38:1–23; Rev 20:7–9). Images from the same part of Ezekiel can be included at two different points because Revelation presents this as one extended battle.

The second plotline concerns God's vindication of his people. The interconnected scenes move from the resurrection of the martyrs, who represent the faithful (20:4–6), to the general resurrection (20:11–15), to the new creation (21:1–22:5). The writer again takes material that was traditionally part of one scene and distributes it over two scenes. Some sources said that at the end of the age there would be a resurrection of the righteous and the unrighteous—regularly listed in that order—followed by a judgment in which the faithful would be blessed and the wicked punished (Dan 12:2; *1 En.* 51:1–2; Acts 24:15; John 5:28–29; *4 Ezra* 7:32–44; cf. *2 Bar.* 30; 50–51). Accordingly, Revelation begins with the resurrection of the just in Rev 20:4–6 and then the resurrection and judgment of everyone else in 20:11–15. The extension of the resurrection theme through two scenes shows that they belong to one sustained plotline, which culminates with the redeemed in New Jerusalem (21:1–22:5).

Revelation portrays a conflict between God the Creator, whose purposes triumph in new creation (4:11; 21:1), and his opponents the destroyers, whose attempt to dominate the world brings about their own ruin (11:18; 19:20; 20:10). The scenes of resurrection show God's power to give life, as the faithful who have died are resurrected (20:4) and then Death, Hades, and the sea are forced to give up the rest of the dead (20:13). In the end, all agents of death are abolished, as Death and Hades are thrown into the lake of fire, and the sea ceases to exist so that the new creation is filled with life (20:14; 21:1, 4).

The conclusion to the book (22:6–21), which follows the vision of New Jerusalem, forms the counterpart to the introduction (1:1–8), creating a literary frame around the six vision cycles. Some interpreters propose that the conclusion starts later, at 22:10, because in 22:6–9 John again mistakenly tries to worship the revealing angel and is directed to worship God, paralleling the scene that concluded the Babylon visions (19:10; Aune; Giblin; Schüssler Fiorenza). It is true that transitional scenes in Revelation often interweave themes from adjacent sections (Bauckham, *Climax*, 5; Longenecker, "Linked"), but it is helpful to treat 22:6 as the beginning of the conclusion because this is where the writer introduces the themes that will be repeated throughout the final section. These include the announcement that Jesus is coming soon (22:7, 12, 20) and the insistence on keeping the prophecy in this book (22:7, 9, 10, 18, 19; cf. Giesen; Mounce; Prigent; Satake).

39. The Beast and False Prophet Are Conquered (19:11–21)

19 [11]Then I saw heaven opened, and there was a white horse. Its rider was called faithful and true, and he judges and makes war with justice. [12]His eyes were like a flame of fire, and on his head were many diadems. He has a name written on him that no one knows but he himself. [13]He wore a robe dyed with blood, and his name was called the Word of God. [14]The armies of heaven were following him on white horses, and they wore fine linen that was white and pure. [15]From his mouth comes a sharp sword that he will use to strike down the nations, and he is the one who will rule them with an iron rod. He is the one who will trample the winepress of the wine of the passionate wrath of God the Almighty. [16]He has a name written on his robe, on his thigh: King of kings and Lord of lords.

[17]Then I saw an angel standing in the sun, and he called out with a loud voice and said to all the birds flying high overhead, "Come and gather for the great banquet of God. [18]Come and eat the flesh of kings and the flesh of generals and the flesh of the powerful and the flesh of horses and their riders, the flesh of all, both free and slave, both small and great." [19]Then I saw that the beast and the kings of the earth and their armies had gathered to make war against the rider on the horse and his army. [20]But the beast was captured, along with the false prophet who had done signs in its presence, the signs by which he deceived those who received the mark of the beast and worshiped its image. The two of them were thrown alive into the lake of fire that burns with sulfur. [21]And the rest were killed by the sword that comes from the mouth of the rider on the horse; and all the birds ate their fill of their flesh.

NOTES

19:11. *Then I saw heaven opened.* Previously, an open door in heaven allowed John to enter God's throne hall (4:1), but here, a divine warrior comes out to battle God's foes (19:11). Visions of heaven opening often signal divine revelation (Ezek 1:1; Matt 3:16; Acts 10:11; *T. Abr.* 7:3; Herm. *Vis.* 1.1.4) or actions of God against his opponents (Rev 11:19; 15:5; Isa 64:1; 3 Macc 6:18–19). In Greco-Roman tradition the sound of armies in heaven was a sign of impending conflict on earth (Tacitus, *Hist.* 5.13; Josephus, *J. W.* 6.298–99; Ovid, *Metam.* 15.784). In Revelation the heavenly warrior not only portends the coming of conflict, but is the agent who overthrows the enemies of God (Berger, "Prodigien," 1450).

and there was a white horse. Its rider was called faithful and true. The returning Christ has been pictured on a white cloud (Rev 14:14), and here he arrives on a white horse. He is faithful and true (3:14), as is God (3 Macc 2:11; Rev 6:10; 15:3; 16:7; 19:2; cf. 21:5; 22:6). White is associated with God's throne (20:11), Christ's head and hair (1:14), and the robes of the saints, martyrs, and heavenly elders (3:4, 18; 4:4; 6:11). White can connote purity (19:14). Victorious military leaders sometimes had white horses (Herodotus, *Historiae* 7.40; 9.63; Dio Cassius, *Rom. Hist.* 43.14.3), as does Christ, who comes to win victory. Earlier, a rider on a white horse appeared when the first of the seven seals was opened (Rev 6:2), and some interpreters identify him as Christ. Most, however, do not make this connection since the rider at the first seal is parallel to the three riders that follow, and all of them symbolize forces that threaten society (Note on 6:2).

The word "called" (*kaloumenos*) is missing in some manuscripts (A 051); it appears before "faithful" in some (1611 1841), after "faithful" in others (ℵ), and after "true" in still others (2028). Some interpreters prefer to omit the word because it does not fit Revelation's style and may have been added, since "faithful and true" seem to be a title elsewhere (3:14; Aune; Smalley). Yet it is more likely that the word was accidentally omitted, especially if "called" came after "faithful" and before "and" (*kai*), which starts with the same Greek letters as *kaloumenos* (*TCGNT*² 685–86). There is no clear reason for the word to have been added.

and he judges and makes war with justice. John's vision recalls Isa 11:1–4, which describes the ideal king from David's line who will "judge the poor with righteousness," treat the vulnerable fairly, and slay the wicked with the breath of his lips (cf. Pss 9:8–12; 72:2–4). Revelation develops the imagery in 19:15–16, where the King of kings strikes down hostile nations with the sword from his mouth.

Isaiah's picture of the ideal king contributed to Jewish messianic expectations. In *Pss. Sol.* 17:26 and 29 the Davidic Messiah leads and judges with righteousness and uses his word and an iron rod to subdue ungodly nations (17:21–24; cf. 18:6–8). The Dead Sea pesher on Isa 11 pictures the Davidic king arising at the end of days and apparently taking part in the final battle against the nations, when he will defeat the wicked and rule over the nations and Magog (4Q161 8–10 III, 18–22; cf. 1Q28b V, 24–25; on Magog see the Note on Rev 20:8). In another text the messianic figure from Isa 11 slays an adversary of God during the eschatological war (4Q285 5 1–6; 11Q14 1 I, 7–13). The *War Scroll* mentions the messianic star of Jacob in its account of the final battle, suggesting that the Davidic Messiah will take part in defeating the nations (1QM XI, 6). Similar images are used in later apocalyptic writings (*4 Ezra* 12:32–33; 13:8–11, 37–38; cf. *2 Bar.* 40:1–2; 72:1–2; Collins, *Scepter*, 52–78).

The Pauline tradition includes a militant dimension in the expectation of Christ's return. Paul pictures the risen Christ seated at God's right hand, where he will reign until he has put all his enemies under his feet (1 Cor 15:25; cf. Ps 110:1). The end will come when Christ has defeated every ruler, authority, and power and when death is destroyed through the resurrection that will occur at Christ's final coming (1 Cor 15:24, 26). A more extensive picture appears in 2 Thess 1:7–2:12, which warns of an outbreak of rebellion against God in the future. At that time, the man of lawlessness, who is

Satan's agent, will take his seat in the temple and declare himself to be God. Recalling Isa 11, the passage says Christ will destroy this agent of evil with the breath of his mouth (2 Thess 2:8). Neither Pauline passage pictures Christ on a horse doing battle with a beast as Revelation does, but these texts share a conviction that Christ will return to judge and redeem individuals and to remove the powers that threaten human life and well-being (De Boer, *Defeat*, 134–36; Rowland 703–4).

Other NT references to the final coming of Christ expect him to bring salvation (1 Cor 1:7; 1 Thess 1:10; Heb 9:28; 1 John 3:2) and the resurrection of the dead (1 Thess 4:13–18; cf. John 14:2–3). Yet scenarios in the gospels lack the militant dimension found in the Pauline tradition and Revelation. The Synoptic Gospels warn that before Christ's return the nations will make war and the faithful will be persecuted (Mark 13:1–13; Matt 24:3–14; Luke 21:5–24). They promise that when the Son of Man comes on the clouds, he will gather the elect together (Mark 13:24–27; Matt 24:29–31; Luke 21:25–28). Some expect the wicked to be judged (Matt 24:50–51; 25:31–46) but do not picture Christ making war. Like the Synoptics, Revelation shares traditions about the Son of Man coming on the clouds (NOTES on Rev 1:7; 14:14) and arriving like a thief (NOTES on 3:3; 16:15). Although these traditions are not integrated in the battle scene in 19:11–21 (McKelvey, "Millennium"; R. A. Campbell, "Triumph"), they contribute to Revelation's expectation that Christ's return will bring both deliverance and judgment.

19:12. *His eyes were like a flame of fire.* Eyes emitting flames or rays indicated divine power (Apollodorus, *Library* 2.4.9; Suetonius, *Aug.* 79.2) or angelic status (Dan 10:6; *1 En.* 106:5–6). In Revelation, Christ's fiery eyes suggest spiritual power (Rev 1:14; 4:5; 5:6; cf. Dan 10:6) and the ability to search human hearts and minds (Rev 2:18, 23). Fire purifies (3:18) and destroys (8:5–7). The fiery-eyed warrior now comes to destroy the agents of evil.

and on his head were many diadems. A diadem was a band worn around the head to signify kingship (1 Macc 6:15; 13:32). Roman emperors generally refused to wear diadems in order to avoid the impression that they were instituting monarchy, preferring the wreath, which symbolized victory. But the Romans did confer diadems on vassal kings to confirm their rights to rule locally (Suetonius, *Jul.* 79.2; Suetonius, *Cal.* 22.1; Dionysius of Halicarnassus, *Ant. rom.* 3.61.3). Since a diadem was a cloth band and not a large jeweled crown, a ruler could wear more than one to show that he ruled a number of regions; for instance, two diadems showed dominion over Egypt and Asia (1 Macc 11:13; Josephus, *Ant.* 13.113). Parthian coins pictured their rulers wearing diadems, sometimes with multiple strands at the end. These coins often include the title "King of kings," which is also used for Jesus, the diademed rider in Rev 19:11–16 (Shore, *Parthian*, 141–42; D. A. Thomas, *Revelation*, 130–32). Kings who had tyrannical tendencies (Dio Chrysostom, *Disc.* 1.79) or rebelled against the ruling power might claim diadems for themselves (Josephus, *Ag. Ap.* 1.98–100), as the dragon and the beast do (Rev 12:3; 13:1). But Christ, whose royal authority is granted by God, is depicted as the legitimate ruler of earth's kings (1:5; 19:16).

He has a name written on him that no one knows but he himself. Some interpreters suggest that Christ's secret name is inscribed on the diadems (Beale; Smalley), but this is unlikely since the word for "diadems" is plural, and the Greek words for "he has" (*echōn*) and "name" (*onoma*) are singular. The name could be written on the head

(Blount), but it is probably inscribed on Christ's robe, as is clear in 19:16. Several inter-pretations of the name have been proposed. The first is most plausible:

1. The name inscribed on Jesus' robe: King of kings and Lord of lords. This interpreta-tion recognizes that John's vision moves from concealment to disclosure. Christ may have a "name written" that is known only to him (19:12), but he is free to reveal the name; and the text does so in 19:16 where the "name inscribed" is "King of kings and Lord of lords." This movement from secrecy to disclosure also occurs in 17:5, where the whore has a "name inscribed." Her name is "a mystery," but the writer reveals that the name is "Babylon the great." Elsewhere, a text says that God has "the secret name" and yet reveals that the name is Sabaoth, which is fitting for the God of gods (*Pr. Jac.* 15). Secrecy and disclosure occur in the same context (Aune).

2. A name that will remain unknown until the end of time. Knowing someone's name could imply having power over that person, and keeping a name hidden prevented it from being wrongfully used in an oath or invocation (Gen 32:29; Judg 13:17–18; *Jos. As.* 15:12; *1 En.* 69:14). In the Greco-Roman world people were said to know tra-ditional names for the gods but not the names the gods used for themselves, unless a deity revealed that name (Plato, *Crat.* 400de; Iamblichus, *De mysteriis* 7.4; Aune). Some interpreters see an analogy in Revelation, in which Christ hides his name to protect his power. Full disclosure of Christ's identity awaits the consummation of God's purposes at the end of the age (*Mart. Asc. Isa.* 8:7; 9:6; Kraft; Murphy; Os-borne; Thomas; cf. Origen, *Comm. Jo.* 2.60; Oecumenius; Primasius).

3. The divine name of God. The God of Israel was said to have "the great name which no one can know" (*4 Bar.* 6:13), even though the name was revealed in Scripture. According to Exod 6:3, the patriarchs knew God as El Shaddai but did not know the name Yahweh, which was revealed to Moses. In Jewish practice, the divine name was not to be spoken aloud (Josephus, *Ant.* 2.276). A reason to think that the rider's name is the traditional name for God is that Christ shares many traits with God: Both are "faithful and true," both judge and make war with justice, and as the Word of God, Christ carries out God's purposes (Rev 19:11, 13). Earlier, Revelation men-tioned Christ's "new name" in the same context as God's name (3:12). Therefore, some interpreters conclude that it is not the name itself that is hidden but the *sig-nificance* of the name and the way Christ will fulfill God's purposes (Beale; Prigent; Smalley). This and the previous interpretation are unlikely, however, because the name inscribed on Christ is disclosed in 19:16: "King of kings and Lord of lords."

19:13. *He wore a robe dyed with blood.* The word *baptein* means "dipped" and was used for dyed fabrics (Josephus, *J.W.* 4.563; Lucian, *Ver. hist.* 1.17). Christ's robe is dyed with blood rather than with ordinary pigment. Some manuscripts say the robe was "spattered" (*rantizein, rainein,* and these verbs compounded with *peri-*), but "dyed" is well-attested and sufficiently odd that copyists might have altered it (*TCGNT*[2] 686–87). Babylon the whore wears purple and scarlet garments to show the opulence of her reign (Rev 17:4; 18:16), but Christ is the King of kings whose royal robes are dyed with blood, recalling his self-sacrifice (BDAG 166). There are two principal in-terpretations concerning the source of the blood. The most probable is that this is Christ's own blood. Revelation says that Jesus' blood (*haima*) advances God's kingdom by delivering people from sin (1:5; 5:9). Jesus' blood makes the robes of the redeemed white (7:14), like the robes of those who follow him into battle. His blood also brings victory over evil (12:11), and here he defeats the satanic beast and false prophet. Since Christ appears in a bloodstained robe *before* the battle begins, the blood must be his own (Origen, *Comm. Jo.* 2.61; Oecumenius; Bede; Boring; Boxall; Giesen; Harrington; Lupieri; Vanni, *L'Apocalisse*, 323). It is unlikely that his robe is stained with the blood of the martyrs (Rev 6:10; 16:6; 17:6; 18:24; 19:2; Primasius; Caird) because Christ's blood makes the robes of others white, rather than their blood making his robe red (7:14).

A second interpretation is that it is the blood of Christ's enemies. Revelation's battle scene draws on Isa 63:1–3, in which God is portrayed as a warrior who has trampled the winepress of wrath so that his robes are red with the blood of his enemies. Since Jesus tramples the winepress in Rev 19:15, one might assume that his robe too is spattered with his adversaries' blood. Traditionally, such imagery was used for the Messiah. When paraphrasing Gen 49:11, which speaks of the lionlike ruler from Judah, the Targumim say: "How beautiful is the King Messiah, who is to arise from among those of the house of Judah. He girds his loins and goes forth to battle against those that hate him; and he kills kings with rulers, and makes the mountains red from the blood of their slain . . . His garments are rolled in blood; he is like a presser of grapes" (*Tg. Neof.* and *Frg. Tgs.* Gen 49:11). Revelation has already shown Christ trampling the winepress of God's wrath and making the blood of his foes flow in rivers (Rev 14:19–20). Here, he tramples the winepress again, and one might assume that his bloodstained robe anticipates the outcome of the battle (Aune; Blount; Mounce; Müller; Murphy; Osborne; Prigent; Roloff; Thomas; Decock, "Symbol," 175).

There are two problems with this approach. First is the sequence. The action in this scene moves progressively. Christ comes for battle in 19:11–16, and the action then occurs in 19:17–21. He has the sword in 19:15 and then uses it in 19:21. Birds are summoned to a banquet in 19:17–18, and then they eat when the battle is over in 19:21. Christ's robe has already been dyed in blood by 19:13, and he only now comes to trample the winepress of wrath. Therefore, the blood that has already been shed is best taken to be Christ's own. Second, Revelation transforms older images in light of Jesus' death and resurrection. In 5:5–6, John invoked the image of the lionlike ruler from Judah from Gen 49:11, but he did not follow the targumic interpretation quoted above. Instead, he showed that the promise of the conquering Lion was realized in the slain Lamb. The pattern in Rev 19:13 is similar. The vision of the divine warrior has similarities to Isa 63:1–3, but the imagery is recast so that Christ comes to the battle in robes stained with his own blood, since his sacrificial death has been his path to victory (Maier, *Apocalypse*, 189).

and his name was called the Word of God. Only here in Revelation does "word" (*logos*) function as a title for Christ. Since the term is also used for Christ in John 1:1 and 1:14 (cf. 1 John 1:1; Ign. *Magn.* 8:2; Heb 1:2), some interpreters assume that Revelation and the gospel were written by the same person (Origen, *Comm. Jo.* 2.42; Cyprian, *Test.* 2.3) or that Revelation reflects a later stage in the Johannine tradition (Taeger, *Johannesapokalypse*, 207–8). Yet a direct connection is unlikely (Schüssler Fiorenza, *Book*, 97–99). The gospel focuses on the preexistent Word, who created all things and became incarnate (John 1:1, 14), whereas Revelation envisions the Word coming at the end of the age to judge God's foes (Rev 19:13). Even though the gospel identifies Jesus as God's agent of judgment (John 5:22; 12:48), it does not use *logos* as a title in such contexts (Frey, "Erwägungen," 403–9). The gospel draws on traditions that personified God's creative Word, or wisdom (Sir 24:3; Wis 9:1–2, 9), whereas Revelation is closer to traditions that personified God's Word judging the Egyptians at the exodus: "your all-powerful word leaped from heaven, from the royal throne, into the midst of the land that was doomed, a stern warrior carrying the sharp sword of your authentic command, and stood and filled all things with death" (Wis 18:15–16). It is unlikely that there is a direct connection between Revelation's *logos* imagery and that of the Fourth Gospel (Intro II.D.1).

19:14. *The armies of heaven were following him on white horses, and they wore fine linen that was white and pure.* This heavenly army could consist of saints or angels. Some scenarios pictured both groups coming with Christ at the end of the age (*Mart. Asc. Isa.* 4:14–17), and there are reasons to do this (Aune; Beale; Mounce; Osborne; Smalley; Pattemore, *People*, 193):

1. Saints. The armies wear fine linen like the bride who represents the people of God (Rev 19:8). The martyrs (6:11) and other faithful Christians (3:5) wear white robes. Like the heavenly riders, the redeemed follow the Lamb wherever he goes (14:4). In a previous reference to the battle against the beast, Christ is accompanied by the faithful (17:14), and that is probably true here (Primasius; Apringius; Bede; Giesen; Murphy; Prigent; Thomas; McNicol, *Conversion*, 53).
2. Angels. Angels in bright linen brought plagues against the beast and his followers (Rev 15:6–16:21). In Jewish tradition, angelic hosts constituted an army (Josh 5:13–15). God was pictured coming with his holy ones, or angels (Deut 33:2), especially to battle his foes (Ps 68:17) and win victory at the end of the age (Zech 14:5; *1 En.* 1:9; Jude 14–15; *T. Levi* 3:3). In Christian tradition, Christ was expected to return with a multitude of angels (Matt 16:27; Mark 8:38; Luke 9:26), an event linked to his kingship, his acts of judgment (Matt 25:31; 2 Thess 1:6–8), and the ingathering of the faithful (Mark 13:26–27; Oecumenius; Roloff). Both saints and angels may be included in Rev 19:14.

19:15. *From his mouth comes a sharp sword that he will use to strike down the nations.* The sword from Christ's mouth is mentioned repeatedly in Revelation (1:16; 2:12, 16; 19:15, 21). Here, the language paraphrases Isa 11:4: "he shall strike the earth with the rod of his mouth, and with the breath of his lips he shall kill the wicked." Isaiah speaks of a ruler from David's line, whom later Jewish tradition identified as the Messiah, who would destroy the unlawful nations with the word of his mouth (*Pss. Sol.* 17:24, 35; 4Q161 8–10 III, 15–19; *1 En.* 62:2) and slay the wicked with his breath (1Q28b V, 24–25; *4 Ezra* 13:9–11, 37–38). Early Christians used similar imagery for the returning Christ (2 Thess 2:8). A distinctive element is that in Revelation a sword—rather than a rod or breath—comes from the Messiah's mouth (cf. 4Q161 8–10 III, 22). The image is reminiscent of Isa 49:2, in which God makes the mouth of his servant "like a sharp sword" (Fekkes, *Isaiah*, 119–22). See the Note on Rev 1:16.

and he is the one who will rule them with an iron rod. The imagery in the previous verse was inspired by Isa 11:4, which originally had the king striking the earth with the rod of his mouth, but Revelation changed it to the sword from Christ's mouth. Now the writer weaves in the image of the rod by recalling the iron rod of Ps 2:9 LXX. Elements from Isa 11:1–5 and Ps 2:9 were combined and interpreted messianically in

Jewish sources (*Pss. Sol.* 17:23–24, 35; 1Q28b V, 24–26), which suggests that Revelation draws on a tradition (NOTE on Rev 2:27).

The verb *poimainein* literally means "to shepherd." Ordinarily, a shepherd used a wooden rod to direct the flock with blows (Plato, *Crit.* 109b) and to fend off predators (1 Sam 17:34–36). An iron rod points to severe action (*Num. Rab.* 12:3). In a transferred sense, a ruler would shepherd people by governing and defending them. His rod symbolized authority (Ps 45:6–7; Mic 7:14). Coins minted at Rome and Ephesus in the late first century CE show Vespasian wearing the wreath of victory on one side and Domitian riding a horse and holding a rod or scepter in his left hand on the other side (Figure; RIC 2:85, 88, 89, 97). By way of contrast, Revelation portrays Christ as the rider with the rod. Christ's claim to authority is higher than that of his rivals, including those in the empire, and it is different in kind, for Christ is allied with God, the Creator, and he comes to rid the world of the destructive forces that now work within it.

He is the one who will trample the winepress of the wine of the passionate wrath of God the Almighty. The language recalls Isaiah, in which God comes in a bloodstained garment and says: "I have trodden the winepress alone, and from the peoples no one was with me; I trod them in my anger and trampled them in my wrath" (Isa 63:3; cf. 63:6). In Revelation, Christ is God's agent and does the trampling. In winemaking, workers in bare feet trampled grapes in a winepress to squeeze out the juice (Judg 9:27), while in warfare, a victorious army was said to trample its foes by defeating them on the battlefield (Isa 25:10; Zech 10:5; Luke 21:24). Comparing military action to trampling in a winepress depicted divine judgment: "Go in, trample, for the winepress is full. The vats overflow for their wickedness is great" (Joel 3:13; cf. Lam 1:15).

This part of Revelation's battle scene recalls an earlier vision in which the earth, described as a vineyard, was reaped and the harvest was trampled in the winepress of God's anger (Rev 14:17–20). The two scenes differ in detail: In 14:17–20 an angel reaps with a sickle, whereas in 19:11–21 Christ wages war with the sword from his mouth. But both scenes allude to a battle with horses (14:20; 19:18) in which Christ is the agent of judgment who tramples the winepress (14:20; 19:15). The two visions repeat the same message in different forms, pointing to Christ defeating the agents of injustice who have plagued the world (COMMENT on 14:17–20).

Figure 36. Roman coin showing Vespasian with a laurel wreath on one side and Domitian on horseback with a rod on the other (76 CE). Courtesy of the Classical Numismatic Group (cngcoins.com).

19:16. *He has a name written on his robe, on his thigh.* The Greek includes the conjunction *kai*, so the name could be written "on his robe *and* on his thigh" (ESV, NIV, NRSV). But *kai* probably introduces an appositive (BDAG 495 1c), so the name is written only once: on the robe, on the part that covers the thigh (Aune). The thigh is where the sword typically hung (Exod 32:27; Ps 45:3), suggesting that the name inscribed there has a militant aspect. There were analogies in ancient statuary: A figure's thigh might be inscribed with "To Zeus, king of the gods" (Pausanius, *Descr.* 5.27.12; cf. Cicero, *Verr.* 2.4.43 §93; *NW* 2:1635–36). In Revelation, the inscription on Christ's thigh asserts that supreme kingship belongs to him.

King of kings and Lord of lords. God was called King of kings (2 Macc 13:4; 3 Macc 5:35; Philo, *QG* 4.76) and Lord of lords (Deut 10:17; Ps 136:3), and both titles could be used together (*1 En.* 9:4; Dan 4:37 LXX). Similar expressions include "God of gods" and "Lord of kings" (Dan 11:36; *1 En.* 63:2, 4). Here and in Rev 17:14 Christ shares these titles of God. In the Greco-Roman world, Zeus was called the King of kings (Dio Chrysostom, *Disc.* 2.75), but Revelation reserves that title for Christ (cf. "the ruler of the kings of the earth" in Rev 1:5). John's use of the title may have a polemical quality since the title King of kings was used for the rulers of Babylon (Ezek 26:7; Dan 2:37), Persia (Ezra 7:12), and Parthia (Suetonius, *Cal.* 5; Dio Cassius, *Rom. Hist.* 37.6.1–3; 65.11.3). Yet here it is Christ who bears these titles as he fights against the beast allied with Babylon and wins the victory.

19:17. *Then I saw an angel standing in the sun.* Previously, angels stood at the four corners of the earth (Rev 7:1) and on sea and land (10:5) to make announcements. Here, an angel stands in the sun, which is another part of God's creation. The sun sent scorching heat on God's opponents (16:8). Now the angel stands in the sun to announce the defeat of the beast, much as a radiant angel announced Babylon's fall (18:1–2; Beale).

and he called out with a loud voice and said to all the birds flying high overhead, "Come and gather for the great banquet of God. The birds are in mid-heaven, or overhead, the place from which an eagle announced woe and an angel called the earth to worship God (Note on 8:13; 14:6). The language recalls Ezek 39:17: "Speak to the birds of every kind and to all the beasts of the field: Assemble and come, gather from all around to the sacrificial feast that I am preparing for you . . . and you shall eat flesh and drink blood." Like Ezekiel, Revelation summons the birds, but it omits Ezekiel's reference to beasts, perhaps to avoid confusion with the beast that Christ defeats. Revelation calls the meal a banquet (*deipnon*) rather than a sacrifice, as Ezekiel does, thereby making slaughter of the wicked on the battlefield the counterpart to the faithful sharing in the wedding banquet of the Lamb (Rev 19:9; Bøe, *Gog*, 278–83).

19:18. *"Come and eat the flesh of kings and the flesh of generals and the flesh of the powerful and the flesh of horses and their riders, the flesh of all, both free and slave, both small and great."* This language continues the paraphrase of Ezekiel, who said, "You shall eat the flesh of the mighty, and drink the blood of the princes of the earth," and be filled "with horses and charioteers, with warriors and all kinds of soldiers" (Ezek 39:18, 20). Revelation expands the list to include the whole society, both free and slave, as well as lower and higher social classes ("small and great"). These same groups were terrified by signs of divine wrath at the sixth seal (Notes on Rev 6:15). They asked, "Who can stand?" (6:17), and their question was followed by an interruption of judgment. But in the vision of the final battle, these groups ask no questions. They persist in their opposition to Christ and fall under his judgment.

Revelation uses a part of Ezek 39 here for the defeat of the beast and more of Ezek 38–39 for the final victory over Satan in Rev 20:7–10 (Bøe, *Gog*, 371–79). Although a thousand years separates the two battle scenes (20:1–6), the writer can use the same section of Ezekiel in both visions because both are part of the story of God's victory over evil. See the Notes and Comment on 20:7–10.

19:19. *Then I saw that the beast and the kings of the earth and their armies had gathered to make war against the rider on the horse and his army.* Revelation develops a traditional motif of the nations attacking Israel, only to suffer a decisive defeat. In Ps 2:1–11 the nations and kings conspire against the Lord and his anointed, but God's king subdues them with his rod of iron as Christ does in Rev 19:1–21 (cf. Acts 4:25–26). Prophetic texts envision the attack by the nations occurring in the future. According to Ezek 38–39, Gog from Magog will lead horsemen from many nations against Israel, only to be defeated—his troops becoming food for the birds and beasts. In Joel 3 the nations that attack Jerusalem are trampled like grapes in a winepress (cf. Rev 19:15), and in Zech 12–14 their defeat ushers in God's reign over the earth.

Apocalyptic texts expect the final assault by the nations to occur at the end of the present age. Some picture God's angels provoking the nations to make this attack, since it will lead to their defeat (*1 En.* 56:5–8). In the Dead Sea *War Scroll* the hostile nations are dominated by Belial, the angel of darkness (1QM I, 1–7; XV, 2). The nations oppose the sons of light, whose company receives help from the angels (XIII, 10; XVII, 6–7) and probably the Messiah (XI, 6–7). In *4 Ezra* 13:5–11 the coming of the Messiah seems to provoke the climactic attack of the nations, which are then destroyed by the Messiah's fiery breath (cf. *2 Bar.* 70:2–10; 72:1–6; *T. Jos.* 19:8). In still other scenarios the nations' attack stems from their own desire for dominion (*Sib. Or.* 3:657–68; Peerbolte, *Antecedents*, 250–55, 311–13, 329).

Revelation identified Satan, the beast, and the false prophet as the agents who gather the kings at Harmagedon in 16:14, and they mount the attack in 19:19. The vision combines the tradition about the final assault by the nations with expectations concerning the rise of an eschatological tyrant (see §25D). The result is that the agents of evil gather the nations in an effort that ultimately leads to their own demise.

19:20. *But the beast was captured.* The beast and false prophet are involuntarily apprehended. They do not surrender or sue for peace, as those who expect defeat might do (Tacitus, *Ann.* 12.18–19). The one doing the capturing is presumably Christ (Aune) and not the heavenly armies (Osborne), which play no active role. In ordinary warfare a defeated leader might be killed (Josh 10:28, 30, 37) or taken captive, perhaps to be displayed in a triumphal procession and then executed (Augustus, *Res* 4; Josephus, *J.W.* 7.153–54). A captive leader might be spared because of his status (1 Sam 15:8), noble character (Tacitus, *Ann.* 12.36–37), or usefulness in negotiation (1 Kgs 20:31–34; 1 Macc 8:7). But the beast and false prophet are relegated to the lake of fire and have no place in the kingdom of God.

along with the false prophet who had done signs in its presence, the signs by which he deceived those who received the mark of the beast and worshiped its image. The false prophet was earlier depicted as the beast from the land, which personified the supporters of the ruler cult. The signs the prophet performed included calling fire from heaven and animating a statue as a sorcerer might do (NOTES and COMMENT on 13:11–15). The mark of the beast signified identification with the ruling power and its deification of human authority (NOTES and COMMENT on 13:16–18).

The two of them were thrown alive into the lake of fire that burns with sulfur. Being taken alive to the underworld is horrific punishment. In Jewish sources such a fate was suitable for rebels, such as Korah and other wicked people (Num 16:33; Ps 55:15), and for sinners defeated in battle at the end of the age (*1 En.* 56:8). Greco-Roman sources consider being taken alive to the realm of the dead to be a grim fate (Euripides, *Tro.* 442; Ovid, *Metam.* 9.403–12; Ovid, *Ars* 3.9–16; *NW* 2:1637–38). The horror of this punishment was widely understood. Moreover, fire and sulfur are destructive (Rev 9:17–18). Jewish sources tell of fire and sulfur from heaven destroying Sodom and Gomorrah (Gen 19:24; Luke 17:29), the wicked (Ps 11:6), and Gog, the eschatological adversary (Ezek 38:22). Some writers pictured a place of punishment burning with fire and sulfur, as the lake of fire does here (Isa 30:33; 66:24; Rev 14:10; 4Q525 15 6).

Revelation has woven the traits of Leviathan into its image of the beast from the sea (COMMENT on Rev 13:1) and the traits of Behemoth into the description of the false prophet, or beast from the land (COMMENT on 13:11). Some writers expected the righteous to feast on these monsters at the end of the age (*1 En.* 60:7–8, 24; *2 Bar.* 29:4; *4 Ezra* 6:49–52). But in Revelation the opponents of God are burned rather than eaten. Their fiery end is like that of the fourth beast in Dan 7:11 (Lupieri). Ironically, Revelation's beast has personified the tyrannical power of the state, but in the end it is burned—a punishment the Romans used for enemies of the state (Justinian, *Dig.* 48.19.8.2)

The reference to a *lake* of fire is unusual. In Revelation the fiery lake is different from Hades, which is the place where the dead are kept until final resurrection (Rev 20:13). Other sources, however, refer to Hades (Luke 16:23–24) and Gehenna (Matt 5:22; 18:9) as the place of fiery torment to which sinners (Matt 13:42, 50; Mark 9:43, 47–48; *4 Ezra* 7:38) or the devil and his angels (Matt 25:41; cf. *Mart. Asc. Isa.* 4:14) will be sent. In Revelation, Death and Hades are thrown into the lake of fire along with Satan (Rev 20:10, 14). The lake also differs from the abyss, which in Revelation is the realm of demons (NOTE on 9:1). Other sources speak of rebellious angels being confined in a fiery abyss (*1 En.* 10:6, 13; 21:7–10), but in Revelation, Satan is released from the abyss and then hurled into the fiery lake (Rev 20:10). Greco-Roman sources told of a lake in the underworld and pictured rivers of fire there (Plato, *Phaed.* 113ab; Virgil, *Aen.* 6.550–51), but they did not refer specifically to a lake of fire. Revelation presents a distinctive fusion of the images of a lake and a place of burning (Bertrand, "L'Étang"; Aune). The place of punishment is the counterpart to heaven's fiery sea of crystal, where the redeemed gather in celebration (Rev 15:2).

19:21. *And the rest were killed by the sword that comes from the mouth of the rider on the horse.* In ordinary warfare complete victory might involve slaying all of one's foes (Polybius, *Histories* 3.116.10–11; Josephus, *J.W.* 7.214). The conquerors might also destroy buildings and fields to prevent their use by their opponents (Caesar, *Bell. gall.* 4.35) or to show religious devotion (Tacitus, *Ann.* 13.57). Israel sometimes slaughtered their opponents as they acquired territory (Num 21:35). Destruction of those who worshiped other gods was a sign of divine judgment against idolatry (Exod 22:20) and a means of preventing them from leading Israel into apostasy (Deut 20:17–18;

N. Lohfink, *TDOT* 5:180–99). Revelation follows Israel's tradition to the extent that the slaughter of the beast's forces is an act of divine judgment (Giblin). But the vision differs from the scenes of warfare noted above in that the battle is won solely by the Messiah without the aid of human armies (COMMENT below; cf. *4 Ezra* 13:1–13; *2 Bar.* 40:1–2; 72:1–6; *T. Mos.* 10:2, 10; Bauer, *Das tausendjährige*, 155–60). The only weapon used is the sword that comes from Christ's mouth. The battle is won by the word of truth (NOTE on Rev 19:15).

and all the birds ate their fill of their flesh. In a previous vision the adversaries of God's witnesses left the witnesses' corpses unburied as a show of contempt (11:9–10). Here, the situation is reversed as birds consume the unburied corpses of God's enemies (1 Kgs 14:11; 16:4; 21:24). Having one's body be food for birds was considered a horrific judgment (Deut 28:26; Jer 7:33; 16:4; 19:7; 34:20; *Sib. Or.* 3:644; Homer, *Il.* 13.831).

COMMENT

Victory over the beast and false prophet has been anticipated throughout the second half of Revelation. Heavenly voices declared that the time had come to destroy those who destroy the earth (Rev 11:18). Satan was cast down to earth, where he persecuted the saints (12:1–17). Satan's allies included the beast and false prophet, who exerted dominion over the nations (13:1–18), as well as the whore, who personified the city that ruled the world (17:1–15). The turning point came when the beast turned against the whore, destroying her with fire (17:16). Her downfall brought grief to her clients but joy to those who suffered under her tyranny (18:1–24), and heavenly voices announced that the time had come for the Lamb to claim his bride (19:7–9). Before the marriage festivities can begin, however, the Lamb must complete his military service by defeating the beast and false prophet (19:11–21). This will leave only Satan, whose final episodes are reported in the next chapter.

The description of the battle scene draws heavily on biblical imagery. The portrayal of the heavenly warrior is like that of the anointed king of Ps 2:1–11, who subdues hostile nations with an iron rod. He is also the ideal ruler, who brings justice and slays the wicked with the force of his mouth (Isa 11:1–5). His robe is stained red, like the robe of God the warrior, who tramples his foes as in a winepress (Isa 63:1–6; cf. Joel 3:11–13). Since Christ is the bridegroom (Rev 19:7–9), his portrait recalls a psalm celebrating the wedding of a victorious king: "Gird your sword on your thigh, O mighty one . . . In your majesty ride on victoriously for the cause of truth and to defend the right" (Ps 45:3–4; Farrer, *Rebirth*, 169–70; Mealy, *After*, 64–65; Aune 3:1046–47). His opponents include the kings and nations of earth, who were traditionally expected to attack Israel at the end of the age (NOTE on Rev 19:19). The battle is especially reminiscent of Ezek 39:17–20, in which birds are summoned to devour the corpses.

Some interpreters also suggest that the scene resembles a Roman triumphal procession (Aune 3:1050–52; R. A. Campbell, "Triumph"; D. A. Thomas, *Revelation*, 74–89;

On Rev 19:11–21, see Bauer, *Das tausendjährige*, 125–63; Bertrand, "L'Étang"; Bøe, *Gog*, 246–54, 276–300; Bredin, *Jesus*, 200–14; Herms, *Apocalypse*, 227–41; M. Hoffmann, *Destroyer*, 169–211; McKelvey, "Millennium"; McNicol, *Conversion*, 41–56; Mealy, *After*, 59–94; Moyise, "Does"; Vanni, *L'Apocalisse*, 318–28.

Blount). The victorious general would ride through the streets of Rome in a chariot drawn by four white horses, while senators and magistrates walked alongside. Some in attendance rode horses. The victor wore a purple robe and head wreath and held an ivory scepter. After Vespasian suppressed the Jewish revolt, his triumphal procession included displays of booty, such as gold head wreaths, along with moving stages that showed the enemy being slain, cities being devastated, and prisoners being taken. When the procession was over, one of the leading rebels was executed (Josephus, *J. W.* 7.123–57; cf. Versnel, *Triumphus*, 56–57, 95).

John's vision in Rev 19:11–21 is both similar to and different from a Roman triumph. Christ rides a horse rather than a chariot, and he comes to win a battle rather than simply to celebrate the completion of one. He wears diadems rather than a wreath, has a robe colored with blood rather than purple dye, and wields a rod of iron rather than of ivory. In the end, the beast and false prophet are taken captive but are not placed on parade; they go directly to the lake of fire. The similarities to a Roman triumph fit the pattern of symmetry in divine justice: The beast with Roman traits, who repeatedly celebrated victory over others (11:7; 13:7), is finally subjected to the victory of Christ. Yet the scene in Revelation is sufficiently different from a typical triumph to show that Christ is not simply replicating Roman patterns. His victory is of a different kind.

John follows a pattern of conflict in which victory is won by divine action without the assistance of human armies. The classic example was the exodus, when God destroyed the Egyptian forces at the sea while Israel looked on (Exod 14:13–14). Some prophetic (Isa 63:3) and apocalyptic (*T. Mos.* 10:7) texts also envision God defeating hostile nations in the future. There were several ways for God to achieve his victory; all are reflected in Revelation:

1. God could make the foes of Israel destroy each other. God had done this in the past (2 Chr 20:22–24), and some expected him to do so again at the end of the age (Ezek 38:21; *1 En.* 56:5–8). This type of victory occurs in Rev 17:16, where the beast turns against Babylon and burns the city.
2. God could send fiery swords, hail, and brimstone from heaven to destroy Israel's foes (*Sib. Or.* 3:663–97). Such plagues are used against Gog in Ezek 38:22. Heavenly fire brings victory in Rev 20:7–10.
3. God could use a special agent. In the past an angel mysteriously slaughtered the Assyrian army (2 Kgs 19:32–35; Isa 37:33–36), and some sources thought an angel would win victory in the future (*T. Mos.* 10:2). Others drew inspiration from Isaiah's description of the king who could destroy the wicked with his breath and expected the Messiah to triumph in this way at the final battle (Isa 11:1–5; *4 Ezra* 13:1–13; Notes on Rev 19:11 and 15). This option is reflected in Revelation, when Christ slays the beast's forces with the sword of his mouth (19:21).

Human agents do not play a military role in the battle against the beast in Rev 19:11–21 or against Satan in 20:1–3, 7–10. These visions differ from holy war in which people slay their enemies while attributing victory to God (Josh 6:2, 21; 8:1–2; Judg 4:15–16; 1 Sam 7:10–11) and from texts in which the righteous fight alongside angelic helpers (1QM I, 2; XV, 1 to XVI, 10; 1QH[a] XIV, 29–33). Instead, the faithful conquer (*nikan*) the beast in a penultimate way through faithful witness. They win victories when they refuse to capitulate to falsehood even at the cost of their lives, and the outcome of their resistance will be resurrection (Rev 2:7, 11, 17; 12:11; 15:2; Bauckham, *Climax*, 210–37). In the climactic battle the saints and angels may appear with Christ (NOTE on 19:14), but it is Christ who brings the threat posed by the beast to an end.

A perennial question concerns the relationship of the battle in the visionary world to the world in which the readers live. Older spiritual interpretations saw the battle as a spiritual conflict in every age, whereas futuristic interpreters often insist that Revelation predicts a gathering of armies in northern Israel (see §38A). John's language, however, makes a literal interpretation problematic. Spatial movements in the vision are not like those in the ordinary world. Earthly cavalry prepare to assault a warrior who comes from heaven (19:19), and the beast and false prophet are hurled from earth into the lake of fire (19:20). The action is described metaphorically, since Christ's sword comes from his mouth and his victory is pictured as trampling a winepress (19:15). More important, the beast and false prophet personify networks of political and social influence. Such forces were at work in the Roman imperial world, and yet the beast and false prophet exhibit traits that go beyond Roman practice (§§27–28 COMMENT). The battle vision does not allow readers to calculate *where* evil will be defeated; rather, it gives assurance of the fact *that* it will be defeated, giving the faithful encouragement to resist what the beast and false prophet represent.

The goal of the battle is not to destroy the earth but "to destroy those who destroy the earth" (11:18). Earth is God's creation (4:11; 10:6; 14:7), and the beast and false prophet ruin it through falsehood, oppression, and violence. For the sake of the earth and the faithful within it, God must end the reign of these destructive agents so that life can flourish (Rossing, "For," 173). The martyrs under the altar demanded to know how long God would refrain from taking action against those who shed the blood of the innocent (6:10). Delay seemed to allow the perpetrators of injustice to continue afflicting the faithful. Scenes that followed showed God postponing his final acts of judgment so that people could be sealed and witness could be given to the world (7:1–17; 10:1–11:13). Along the way, warning visions showed the ungodly being pressed to change their ways (9:20–21; 16:9, 11). The point is that if the delay does not bring repentance, then the perpetrators of injustice must finally be removed for the sake of those who suffer (Barr, "Doing"; Boring 112–19; Schüssler Fiorenza, *Book*, 46–48).

Christ the Warrior (19:11–16)

Heaven opens and a rider on a white horse appears (19:11). Although unnamed, his traits show that he is Christ (M. Hoffmann, *Destroyer*, 176–81). The first vision in Revelation centered on the exalted Christ, who had flaming eyes and a sword coming from his mouth (1:14, 16; 2:12, 18). In that vision Christ was already present with his followers, walking among the lampstands that represented the seven churches. He was called "faithful and true" (3:14), and he confronted members of the Christian community with words of reproof and warning (Schüssler Fiorenza 105). Now the one who is "faithful and true" appears again with eyes aflame and the sword from his mouth, not to judge his followers this time, but to judge the adversaries of God (19:11, 15).

Christ comes to bring justice into a war that has been raging throughout the second half of the book (19:11). The aggressor is Satan, pictured as a dragon wearing seven diadems in order to show his aspiration for dominion over the world (12:3). Satan tried to devour the Messiah at his birth, only to be foiled when Christ was taken to God's heavenly throne (12:4–6). Then war (*polemos*) broke out in heaven, and Satan was thrown down to earth, where he continued making war against God's people (12:7, 17). Satan was joined by the beast, which wore ten diadems and made war against the faithful (13:1, 7; cf. 11:7). Then Satan, the beast, and the false prophet gathered the kings of the earth at Harmagedon for a war against God (16:12–16). Since the agents of evil have unleashed a destructive war, God's justice will be accomplished through Christ, who wears "many diadems" as a sign of rightful power (19:12). He turns the tide of battle by destroying the forces that would destroy the earth (11:18).

Christ is inscribed with a name that only he knows (19:12). The servants of God (7:3; 14:1) and the allies of the beast have names on their foreheads (13:16–18), as does Babylon (17:5). But Christ's name is on the robe that covers his thigh (19:16). Although the name is secret, the text reveals that it is King of kings and Lord of lords (NOTES on 19:12, 16). The full significance of Christ's identity as King and Lord has been hidden, which is presumably why his opponents think they can defeat him in this battle (cf. 1 Cor 2:6–8). The implication is that not even Christ's followers know the full extent of his lordship until he discloses it.

A major dimension of Christ's identity is revealed by his robe, which has been dyed with his own blood (NOTE on Rev 19:13). The imagery recalls that Christ shed his blood out of love (1:5), to deliver people of every nation from sin (1:5–6; 5:5–10). Therefore, Christ's coming for battle does not signal a reversal in his character, as if the meek Lamb now becomes the vengeful warrior (Moyise, "Does," 813–14). Instead, this victory completes the conquest of sin and evil that began with Christ's witness and crucifixion (1:5; Boring; Giesen). In Revelation, Christ's death was an act of resistance, marking his refusal to abandon God's truth in order to capitulate to falsehood (Blount, *Can*, 47–50). The blood he shed for the sake of others enables them to serve in the kingdom of God (1:5–6; 5:9–10; 7:13–17). The problem is that those redeemed by the blood of the Lamb suffer on earth because of the forces of evil (6:9–10; 12:11; 17:6). Therefore, the love and justice of God converge by bringing an end to the political, social, and religious evils symbolized by the beast and false prophet.

Christ is called "the Word of God" (19:13), an expression previously used in a general way for God's revelation of his identity and purposes (1:2). The God of Revelation has a sovereign claim upon a world where other powers vie for the readers' loyalties. The faithful have received the spoken "word of God," which calls for their faithfulness and promises salvation (19:9), and they are to hold on to God's word in the face of conflict and death (1:9; 6:9; 20:4). The battle vision reverses this situation. Instead of the faithful suffering for the sake of God's word, the Word acts for the sake of the faithful by subduing the forces of evil.

The armies of heaven, wearing fine linen robes, accompany Christ on white horses (19:14). Their appearance contrasts with the demonic riders from the underworld, who wear breastplates radiating fire and sulfur and have hideous fire-breathing horses with lions' heads (9:17). They also differ from the cavalry in Rome's armies, who wore helmets and breastplates and carried pikes, shields, and quivers of darts (Josephus, *J. W.* 3.96). Their wearing linen rather than armor suggests that they have no reason to fear the beast; and they carry no weapons because the battle will be won by Christ (Rev 19:21). Their linen robes are like those of a bride on her wedding day (19:8). Such garments connote the purity that comes from the Lamb, who redeems people from sin by making their robes white by his blood (7:14). The redeemed live out their status by righteous actions, which constitute the bright pure garment that signifies the visible aspect of faithfulness (19:8; Miller, "Nuptial," 315–16). White robes indicate purity and honor and are suitable for worship (NOTE on 3:5). The heavenly hosts serve as witnesses to Christ's victory (Mealy, *After*, 78–80).

The portrayal of Christ uses several metaphors. First, his sword comes from his mouth (19:15). This detail fits the pattern of using images to depict the power of speech. On the side of evil, the dragon tried to destroy the woman who represents God's people by spewing water from his mouth (12:15). Later, the dragon and its allies emitted frog-like spirits from their mouths to gather kings for battle (16:13). Such images convey the destructive quality of falsehood. On the side of God, the witnesses subdue their opponents with fire from their mouths, an image for prophetic speech (NOTE on 11:5). Then Christ, who is God's Word (19:13), defeats the agents of evil with the word from his mouth, making it a victory of truth over deception.

Second, Christ will rule the nations with "a rod of iron" (19:15). This metaphor was used earlier when the child who would wield the iron rod escaped from the dragon to God's throne in heaven (12:5). The satanic dragon continued to threaten Christ's followers on earth (12:17), and it set the beast over the nations (13:7); but in the end the nations are brought under Christ's rule and the faithful will share in his reign, symbolized by the iron rod (2:26–28). Given the starkness of the rod imagery, it is surprising that the nations willingly bring their glory to the city where Christ reigns (21:24–26). That final vision calls the nations to a future in which Christ's iron rod will not need to be used.

Third, Christ tramples the winepress of divine wrath (19:15). Previously, Babylon the whore made the nations drunk with the "wine of her passionate immorality," which signified idolatry, opulence, and violence (14:8; 18:3). The imagery indicted Roman imperialism, which lured people with economic opportunity and impressed them with the empire's military strength, even as it deified human rulers. Such a society was capable of killing the faithful so that the whore was drunk on the blood of the saints (17:6). Making a play on the words wine (*oinos*) and passion (*thymos*), John points to the symmetry in divine judgment. The nations that drink the wine of the whore's passionate immorality are trampled in the winepress of the wine of God's passionate wrath. Instead of drinking the wine, they become the wine. Those who perpetrated the violence now suffer it themselves.

Christ is called King of kings and Lord of lords (19:16). These titles were ordinarily reserved for God but here are given to Christ, who acts on God's behalf. The writer recognizes that there is a place for human kingship but finds that kings are swayed by the forces of evil and use their authority for destructive ends (16:12, 14; 17:2, 12, 18; 18:3, 9). By way of contrast, Christ uses his royal authority to build God's kingdom by redeeming people (5:9–13). The battle vision warns that the kings who are allied with the destroyers of the earth will finally be defeated (11:18; 19:18, 19), while the vision of New Jerusalem extends the hope that earth's kings might finally receive life under the rule of the Creator and the Lamb (21:24).

Victory over the Beast and Its Allies (19:17–21)

An angel summons flocks of birds to "the great banquet [*deipnon*] of God" to eat the flesh of God's opponents, who are about to be slain on the battlefield (19:17). This grisly feast is the counterpart to the joyous wedding banquet (*deipnon*) of the Lamb (19:9). The juxtaposition uses contrasting pairs of visions to shape the readers' perspectives. Previous visions have shown that people bear either the seal of God or the mark of the beast (7:3; 13:16–14:1) and belong either to the whore or to the bride (17:1–2; 19:7–8; Bauckham, *Theology*, 131–32; Rossing, *Choice*, 161–65; Wengst, "Babylon"). The banquet motif points to the outcome of basic commitments. The faithful have a place at Christ's wedding banquet, whereas the beast's allies can anticipate becoming a meal for birds in the battlefield banquet of God (19:9, 17).

Revelation announces that those who fall in battle will include "all, both free and slave, both small and great" (19:18). Just as the Lamb's followers come from all strata of society (11:18; 19:5), so do the allies of the beast (13:16). In the imperial age, kings ruled vassal states allied with Rome, and here they join the beast. Generals (*chiliarchoi*) were leaders of a thousand men—or in Roman practice, commanders of six hundred—and the term was extended to various high-ranking personnel (I.Eph 3032.5; Mark 6:21; Acts 21:31). The powerful were known for courage in battle (Heb 11:34). Horses and riders supported the Roman infantry (Josephus, *J.W.* 3.96–97). Free men were recruited as soldiers (Pliny the Younger, *Ep.* 10.29–30; *Rom. Civ.* 2:449–50), and their personal slaves served in camp (Tacitus, *Hist.* 2.87; 4.23). Slaves were sometimes armed in last, desperate attempts to increase troop strength (Caesar, *Bell. civ.* 1.24, 75; Livy, *Rom. Hist.* 22.59.12). People from lower classes became foot soldiers, and those from higher classes served as officers (Watson, *Roman*, 37). In this battle, however, social status means nothing. Those opposed to God, whether king or slave, meet the same fate.

As the birds gather in anticipation of the carnage (Rev 19:17), the forces of the beast gather in order to provide it (19:19). Satan, the beast, and the false prophet deceived earth's kings into participating in this battle, where they meet the word of truth (16:13–14; 19:11, 13; Resseguie 114–15). The kings gathered at Harmagedon, a name portending their defeat (NOTE on 16:16). The beast and its allies have had opportunities to change course but have not done so (16:9, 11). The time has come to destroy the destroyers of the earth, fulfilling what the elders said earlier (11:18).

The beast and false prophet are captured at the beginning of the battle (19:20). Until now, many have asked, "Who is like the beast and who can make war against it?" (13:4). They have assumed the beast is invincible; but readers know this is not true, since the beast is the agent of the dragon, which was defeated in heaven (12:7–12). The battle fully shows the weakness of the beast, which is captured before the fight begins. Similarly, the false prophet called down fire from the sky, as if he could make heaven do his bidding (13:13–15). But here the powers of heaven make him do their bidding by taking him prisoner. Earlier, the false prophet brought about the deaths of those who did not worship the beast (13:15b), but now the situation is reversed. He brings about the deaths of those who *do* worship the beast—since those he deceived are slain (19:21). The beast and false prophet were once held in high honor, but now they are disgraced war captives (Livy, *Rom. Hist.* 22.59.1; Tacitus, *Hist.* 4.80). In ordinary war, some prisoners salvaged a bit of honor by fighting valiantly and capitulating only when all hope was gone (Livy, *Rom. Hist.* 22.59.2–8). But the agents of evil are captured at the outset and thus robbed of any vestige of respect.

The beast and false prophet are thrown into the lake of fire, which removes them from the world (19:20). Their fiery demise fits their characters. The beast destroyed the whore with fire so that the smoke of her burning "goes up from her forever" (17:16; 18:9, 18; 19:3). Now the beast that inflicted fire on others suffers it himself. The false prophet called down fire from heaven in order to beguile people into false worship (13:13), but now he is subjected to fire under heaven's judgment. Revelation shows that those who follow the Lamb may encounter resistance in the present, but they are promised life with God beside heaven's fiery sea of glass (14:4; 15:2). In contrast, those allied with the beast will follow it to the lake of fire, where it is joined by the devil, Death, and Hades (20:10, 14, 15; 21:8).

The rest of the beast's allies are slain by the sword from Christ's mouth (19:21). Rather than destroying the earth, the battle results in the destruction of earth's destroyers (11:18). The previous visions showed that these forces refused to repent (9:20–21; 16:9, 11). They carried out the designs of the beast, and since they would not change, they must be removed for the sake of those who suffered under their dominion. The allies of the beast once destroyed the whore by devouring her flesh (17:16); what they did to others is what they now receive: Birds devour their flesh (19:21; Bøe, *Gog*, 297).

Revelation's battle vision depicts the utter destruction of the kings of earth and their allies. Yet elsewhere, the kings and nations worship God and come to New Jerusalem, where the tree of life provides healing (Rev 15:2–4; 21:24; 22:2). Some interpreters try to turn the incongruity into a logical sequence by assuming that some of the ungodly must survive the battle in 19:17–21 so that Satan can deceive them after the millennial reign of the saints (Osborne 688). But the contrast between scenes of destruction and scenes of redemption can better be understood rhetorically. The judgment scenes warn people against continuing to follow the destructive ways of the beast, and the scenes of salvation call people to ally themselves with God and the Lamb. The goal is to secure the allegiance of the readers in John's present (Bauckham, *Theology*, 102–3; Boring 200).

40. Millennial Kingdom, Defeat of Satan, Last Judgment (20:1–15)

20 ¹Then I saw an angel coming down from heaven, holding in his hand the key to the abyss and a huge chain. ²And he seized the dragon, the ancient serpent, who is the devil and Satan, and bound him for a thousand years. ³He cast him into the abyss, then locked and sealed it over him, in order that he might not deceive the nations anymore until the thousand years were over. After this he must be released for a short time.

⁴Then I saw thrones, and people sat down on them, and judgment was given in their favor. And those I saw were the souls of those who had been beheaded because of the witness of Jesus and the word of God, who had not worshiped the beast or its image and had not received the mark on their fore-

heads or on their hands. They came to life and reigned with Christ for a thousand years. ⁵The rest of the dead did not come to life until the thousand years were over. This is the first resurrection. ⁶Blessed and holy are those who have a share in the first resurrection. Over these the second death has no power, but they will be priests of God and of Christ, and will reign with him for a thousand years.

⁷And when the thousand years are over, Satan will be released from his prison. ⁸He will go out to deceive the nations that are at the four corners of the earth, Gog and Magog, to assemble them for battle. Their number is like the sand of the sea. ⁹And they came up across the breadth of the earth and surrounded the camp of the saints, the beloved city; but fire came down from heaven and devoured them. ¹⁰And the devil who had deceived them was thrown into the lake of fire and sulfur, where the beast and the false prophet also were, and painful suffering will be inflicted on them day and night forever and ever.

¹¹Then I saw a great white throne and the one who is seated on it. Before his face the earth and heaven fled away, and no place was found for them. ¹²And I saw the dead, great and small, standing before the throne, and scrolls were opened. Another scroll was also opened, which is the scroll of life. And the dead were judged according to their works, by what was written in the scrolls. ¹³And the sea gave up the dead that were in it, and Death and Hades gave up the dead that were in them, and they were judged, each one of them, according to their works. ¹⁴Then Death and Hades were thrown into the lake of fire. This is the second death, the lake of fire. ¹⁵And if any were not found written in the scroll of life, they were thrown into the lake of fire.

NOTES

20:1. *Then I saw an angel coming down from heaven, holding in his hand the key to the abyss and a huge chain.* Several keys are mentioned in Revelation. An angel used a key to open the abyss, which is the realm of the demonic beings below the earth (9:1). At that point, the demonic beings came out, but here, an angel uses the key to lock Satan in. Elsewhere, Jesus has the key to Death and Hades, which is where the dead are kept until the final resurrection (NOTE on 1:18). That key shows that Christ has the power to confine or release people from death, just as he has the key of David, which opens the way to God's presence (3:7). Chains were used to bind war captives (2 Kgs 25:7; Jer 40:1; Josephus, *J. W.* 3.402; Tacitus, *Ann.* 12.36) and other prisoners. The larger the chain, the more severe the punishment (Justinian, *Dig.* 48.19.8.6). Apocalyptic tradition has supernatural figures being bound with chains as punishment for wrongdoing (*1 En.* 54:3–4; *2 Bar.* 56:13; *Sib. Or.* 2:289; Jude 6; 2 Pet 2:4), as happens to Satan here.

20:2. *And he seized the dragon, the ancient serpent, who is the devil and Satan, and bound him.* On terms for Satan, see the NOTES on Rev 12:9. Seizing and binding was used for criminals (Mark 6:17; cf. John 18:12). Binding (*dein*) was also a term for neutralizing a demon (Tob 8:3; Mark 3:27 par.) and Satan (*T. Levi* 18:12). Prisoners were chained for transport and often wore chains in prison—on one or both hands, one or both legs, and perhaps around the neck (Rapske, *Paul*, 206–9). Apocalyptic sources have people (Matt 22:13) and Satan (*1 En.* 10:4–6; cf. 18:14) bound hand and foot before being cast into the darkness. Here, Satan is bound while imprisoned in the abyss.

The motif of binding evil beings appears in various ancient sources. Some told of evil figures being bound in the distant past. One said that many demons were bound in Noah's time and that some remained active during the present age under Satan's authority (*Jub.* 10:11). Others said that when the heavenly watchers transgressed before Noah's time (Gen 6:1–4), they were bound (*Jub.* 5:6, 10; Jude 6; 2 Pet 2:4; *2 Bar.* 56:13), and God's angels cast them into darkness until the final judgment, when they were taken to a place of fiery torment (*1 En.* 10:4–5, 11–12; cf. 88:1–3). Revelation depicts an angel binding Satan and imprisoning him for later fiery punishment, but the action occurs at the end of the age rather than in primeval times.

Other texts envisioned the future, when God would gather the kings of earth and host of heaven like prisoners in a pit who would be punished later (Isa 24:21–22; cf. *1 En.* 53:3–5; 54:1–6). In Revelation's vision of the future the kings are not bound but are destroyed on the battlefield; Satan alone is bound (Rev 19:17–20:3). Isaiah spoke of a single mythic tyrant trying to exalt himself above God and yet being brought down to Sheol (Isa 14:12–15). But there, the tyrant's fall led to death rather than to temporary imprisonment, as is the case with Satan in Revelation (Nickelsburg, *1 Enoch*, 221, 225).

for a thousand years. This length of time encompasses both the binding of Satan (Rev 20:2) and the reign of the saints (20:4). As the period during which Satan is bound, the number is distinctive. Texts that told of the watchers being bound from primeval times until the final judgment defined the period as seventy generations (*1 En.* 10:12) or ten thousand years (18:16; 21:6). Those that told of the future said that the kings and heavenly host would be imprisoned for "many days" before being punished (Isa 24:22). Some envisioned souls being subjected to a kind of purgatory in the underworld for a thousand years (Plato, *Resp.* 10.615a, 621d; Virgil, *Aen.* 6.748; *NW* 2:1640–42), but Revelation focuses on Satan, not on the transmigration of souls (Oecumenius).

20:3. *He cast him into the abyss, then locked and sealed it over him.* The door to the abyss is shut, or locked (*klein*), presumably with the key (*kleis*) held by the angel (Rev 20:1). Sealing meant that wax or clay was placed along the edge of the door and stamped with a distinctive marking, like the impression produced by a signet ring (7:2). Sealing did not physically strengthen the closure but deterred unauthorized people from attempting to open the door unobserved, as a broken seal would show tampering (Dan 6:17; Bel 14; Matt 27:66). What is sealed can be opened only by God's authority. In Rev 20:7 the abyss is called Satan's prison.

in order that he might not deceive the nations anymore until the thousand years were over. In the ancient world, set prison terms were not given out as punishment (Justinian, *Dig.* 48.19.8.9). One purpose of prison was to hold people until a sentence could be imposed. This function fits the accounts of the evil watchers, who are imprisoned until the final judgment (NOTE on Rev 20:2), but in Revelation, Satan's imprisonment is followed by temporary release rather than immediate punishment. A second purpose of imprisonment was to prevent further wrongdoing and to make the offender submit to the authorities (Rapske, *Book*, 14–15). This fits Revelation's millennium, when Satan is incarcerated to prevent further acts of deception.

After this he must be released for a short time. Some texts tell of evil figures being bound until the end of the age (NOTE on 20:2), but Revelation is unique in envisioning the devil's temporary release before the end. Since the short time of Satan's banishment to earth was three and a half years (12:6, 12), some interpreters assumed that the short time of his release would also be three and a half years (Augustine, *Civ.* 20.8). Revelation, however, does not specify the time. To say that Satan must (*dei*) be released indicates that it is the will of God and will actually lead to Satan's defeat (cf. *dei* in Rev 1:1; 22:6). This idea is similar to Ezekiel's oracles concerning Gog, who devised battle plans against Israel (Ezek 38:11–12) only to find that God used Gog's own schemes to defeat him (Ezek 38:4, 17; 39:2; Bøe, *Gog*, 302).

20:4. *Then I saw thrones, and people sat down on them.* The identity of those sitting down must be inferred. A combination of the first two interpretations given below is most plausible, so that the martyrs represent all the faithful:

1. Resurrected martyrs. Revelation usually mentions a throne and then identifies who is sitting on it (Rev 4:2, 4; 14:14, 20; 20:11). Accordingly, those who take their seats in 20:4a are identified as those who have been beheaded for their witness in 20:4b. Earlier it was said that those who conquer would take their seats on Christ's throne, just as Christ took his seat on God's throne (3:21). Since the martyrs are exemplary conquerors (12:11), they seem to be the figures taking their seats on thrones (Aune; Mounce; Murphy; Yarbro Collins, *Crisis*, 128–29).

2. All the faithful. This vision centers on the martyrs but is not limited to them. The messages to the churches promised that all who conquer by remaining faithful will take their seats on thrones with Christ (3:21). Readers were told that all the redeemed are priests and members of God's kingdom, who will reign on earth (5:10), and this promise is reaffirmed here, where all who are resurrected are priests who reign with Christ (20:4, 6), just as all the redeemed will do in New Jerusalem (22:5). The gospels say that the disciples will sit on twelve thrones and judge the tribes of Israel (Matt 19:28; Luke 22:30), but Revelation extends this promise from the twelve to all the followers of Jesus (*Mart. Asc. Isa.* 9:17–18; Beale; Giesen; Prigent; Smalley).

3. Heavenly court. Some interpreters propose that the twenty-four elders sit on the thrones, as in previous visions (Rev 4:4; 11:16). The elders announced the coming defeat of evil, judgment of the dead, and rewarding of the saints (11:16–18), so it could be fitting for them to appear in the context where these things occur. The next line mentions judgment, and the elders could serve as the heavenly court, as in Dan 7:9 (Mealy, *After*, 103–10). This interpretation is unlikely, however, because John usually mentions a throne and then identifies the one seated there, but this vision does not refer to the elders or other heavenly beings. Moreover, John always pictures the elders *sitting* on thrones, using the present participle of *kathēnai* (4:4; 11:16); he never pictures them *taking their seats* (*kathizein*).

and judgment was given in their favor. The dative pronoun *autois* can be translated in two ways. The first is preferable:

1. Judgment was given *for* them, or "in their favor." The resurrected saints sit on thrones because God has judged them favorably. Condemned by the world, they

are vindicated by God. The martyrs asked for justice in 6:10, and God acted in their favor with his negative judgment against Babylon and the beast (18:8, 20; 19:2, 11). Now God's positive judgment is evident in the martyrs' resurrection to life in Christ's kingdom (20:4). This approach recalls Dan 7:22, in which at the end of the age "judgment was given for the holy ones of the Most High," and the time arrived for them to possess the kingdom. The faithful will not be subject to the second death (Rev 20:6) since they are already judged favorably by God (Beale; Giesen; Roloff; Smalley).

2. Authority to judge was given *to* them (ESV, NAB, NASB, NIV, NRSV). The idea here is that a heavenly court gives judgment along with God (Dan 7:9–10) in the same way an earthly court might give judgment along with a king (Ps 122:5). If those on the thrones are the *elders*, then they participate in God's favorable judgment of the martyrs; but if those on the thrones are the *martyrs or the redeemed*, then they receive authority to judge other people—a pattern reflected in other sources (1QpHab V, 4; Wis 3:7–8; Matt 19:28; Luke 22:30; 1 Cor 6:1–2; Aune; Harrington; Mounce; Murphy; Osborne). However, there is no suggestion that the saints judge anyone during the millennium or afterward. In Revelation judgment is consistently ascribed to God (Rev 14:7; 16:5, 7; 20:12–13) and Christ (19:11).

And those I saw were the souls of those who had been beheaded because of the witness of Jesus and the word of God. If the martyrs are on the thrones, then the initial *kai* (and) introduces a comment that clarifies their identity. It does not introduce a new group. The term *pelekizein* means being beheaded by an ax (Josephus, *Ant*. 20.117). Roman law provided for different forms of punishment, depending on the crime and the social status of the person convicted. Beheading was used for those of higher status (Justinian, *Dig*. 48.19.8.1–2; Eusebius, *Hist. eccl*. 5.1.47; Aune). Accounts of Christian martyrdoms say that Paul and others were beheaded (*Acts Paul* 11.3; Eusebius, *Hist. eccl*. 2.25.5; *Acts Scill*. 14, 17; *Mart. Potamiaena* 6; cf. Acts 12:2). The Romans used more brutal forms of execution for those of lower status. Some Christians were burned (*Mart. Pol*. 15:1), crucified (Tacitus, *Ann*. 15.44; Eusebius, *Hist. eccl*. 2.25.5; 3.1), and killed by wild animals (Ign. *Rom*. 4:1; Eusebius, *Hist. eccl*. 5.1.56). Earlier, John "saw under the altar the souls of those who had been slain [*esphagmenōn*] because of the word of God and the testimony that they had given" (Rev 6:9). The parallel shows that "beheaded" (*pepelekismenōn*) in 20:4 is a general term for all who have been "slain" for the faith. On witness to Jesus and the word of God, see the NOTE on 1:2.

who had not worshiped the beast or its image and had not received the mark on their foreheads or on their hands. The image of the beast is linked to the ruler cult (NOTE on 13:14). The beast's mark consists of the name, or number, of the beast, just as the seal of God seems to include the names of God and Jesus. The mark identifies those who belong to the beast and enables them to buy and sell. They are spared judgment by the beast but are subject to the judgment of God (NOTES on 13:16–18). The identity of those who refuse to worship the beast has been taken in two ways. In the COMMENT the two will be combined, with the martyrs treated as representatives of the whole community of faith:

1. A further description of the martyrs. Having mentioned those beheaded for their witness, John introduces a new clause with *kai hoitines* (and who). These words comment on what precedes them. The words are used this way in 1:7, where John

mentions "every eye" and then explains that this includes "those who pierced him." Although the pronoun *hoitines* is in the nominative case, it can modify what precedes it even if the antecedent is in a different case (Mussies, *Morphology*, 93). *Hoitines* also describes what precedes it when not prefaced by *kai* (e.g., 2:24; 17:12; see BDAG 729, 2b). Revelation speaks of all who refused to worship the beast being killed (13:15; Aune; Mounce; Murphy; Reddish). The imagery warns readers against seeking an escape route (Mealy, *After*, 110–15, 119).

2. A wider group of nonmartyred believers. This reading assumes that *kai* (and; also) and the shift to the nominative pronoun *hoitines* means that John is expanding the horizon beyond the martyrs. This interpretation fits the wider context, where those who refuse to accept the beast's mark are barred from commerce but are not necessarily killed (13:16–17). The promises of salvation are given to those who die in the Lord (14:13) and are not limited to those who die violently. What is said of those in the millennial kingdom is true of all the faithful: They share in Christ's reign and serve as priests (1:6; 5:10; 20:6), and they are blessed (1:3; 14:13; 16:15; 19:9; 22:7, 14). Therefore, all the faithful must be included (Beale; Giesen; Müller; Prigent; Smalley). The two approaches can be combined by treating the martyrs as emblematic of the whole church (Bauckham, *Theology*, 88–94, 107–8; Osborne).

They came to life. The aorist *ezēsan* is ingressive, "came to life." This word creates a contrast with the rest of the dead, who do not come to life until the thousand years are over (20:5). The aorist form is used for the resurrections of Jesus (2:8; Rom 14:9) and the beast (Rev 13:14). John saw the *psychai*, or souls, of the martyrs crying out under the altar (6:9), but such souls are not alive in the true sense until they are brought to life through resurrection (*1 En.* 103:4). Rather than speaking of souls becoming disembodied through death and reembodied through resurrection, the word "soul" is used for the whole person (Rev 18:13), who undergoes death (12:11) and is raised to endless life. One could speak of the death and resurrection of the *psychē* (John 10:11, 15, 17; 12:25) and of the body (2:19, 21; 1 Cor 15:35–49). The use of comparable expressions for the raising of Jesus and the souls of the martyrs (Rev 2:8; 20:5) fits the idea that resurrection involves the whole person (cf. the NOTE on 20:14).

and reigned with Christ. The saints reign (*basileuein*) with Christ (Rev 20:4), in contrast to the kings (*basileis*), who opposed Christ and suffered death (19:19). Some interpreters assume that reigning means that the saints exercise dominion over the nations during this period (Victorinus). Yet that is not stated. The idea is that they share in the blessings of Christ's rule (Giesen).

for a thousand years. The saints reign for a thousand years while Satan is bound (NOTE on 20:2), but their reign does not end at that point. They continue reigning in the New Jerusalem (22:5). Various reasons have been given for the thousand years; the first is most plausible:

1. One thousand is a round number that indicates completeness and, as ten cubed, symmetry. Elsewhere, Revelation uses multiples of 1,000 to suggest completeness. Those who belong to God and the Lamb include 12,000 from the twelve tribes, for a total of a 144,000 (7:3–8; 14:1, 3). The redeemed have a place in New Jerusalem, which is a cube measuring 12,000 stadia on each side (21:16). The shape conveys a sense of wholeness. When used for time, 1,000 years suggests vastness (Josephus,

Ant. 1.108; Dio Chrysostom, *Disc.* 17.20; Lucian, *Nav.* 44). Like the number 144,000, John does not use 1,000 because it comes from an established eschatological tradition; rather, the numbers create impressions through common associations (Yarbro Collins, *Cosmology*, 85; Smalley).

2. Jewish traditions. Some sources envisioned a righteous or messianic kingdom being established for a time at the end of this age. The *Apocalypse of Weeks* divided history into ten periods, or weeks, of unspecified length. The eighth period would bring the defeat of wickedness, and the ninth would see righteousness manifested everywhere, until the tenth period ushered in the last judgment and new heaven. Nothing is said about the Messiah's role in this scenario (*1 En.* 91:12–17). In *4 Ezra* 7:26–30 the present age ends with the coming of the Messiah and a kingdom that endures for four hundred years. Then the Messiah dies and the world returns to primeval silence before the resurrection and last judgment. In *2 Baruch* the Messiah defeats evil and ushers in phenomenal abundance and peace for an unspecified period before the resurrection (29:3–30:1; 40:1–4; 72:2–74:3).

Problems in taking these traditions as a basis for Rev 20:1–6 are discussed in §38A. Here, we simply note that they say nothing about a thousand years. Sayings ascribed to first- and second-century rabbis expect the days of the Messiah to last forty, sixty, seventy, four hundred, six hundred, one thousand, or two thousand years (*b. Sanh.* 99a; *Midr. Ps.* 90 §17; *Pesiq. Rab.* 1.7). The variety shows that expectations for a thousand years were not common. Some interpreters have attempted to trace this idea to a first-century rabbi such as Eliezer ben Hyrcanus (Str-B 3:826), but this approach is tenuous, since the written sources are late and it is not clear which views can be ascribed to him.

Elsewhere, *Jub.* 23:27 envisions a future in which people will live for a thousand years, though this is not the duration of a kingdom. More common is the observation that Gen 1:1–2:4 says that God created the world in seven days and Ps 90:4 says that for God a thousand years are like a day (cf. 2 Pet 3:8). If God created the world in six days and rested on the seventh, and if one day equals a thousand years, then one might conclude that the world will endure for six thousand years before the abiding seventh day of salvation (*Barn.* 15; *2 En.* 32:2–33:1). Accordingly, one might assume that the final period of this age should last a thousand years (Charles; Harrington; Kraft; Mounce; Müller; Murphy; Osborne; Prigent; Roloff). However, this view relies on a passage in *2 Enoch* that is quite late (Aune); and more importantly, outside of chapter 20, the writer of Revelation does not structure all of time in blocks of a thousand years, making it unlikely that he does so here.

3. Non-Jewish traditions. Zoroastrian tradition divided the final era of history into three periods of a thousand years. It also mentions the confinement and later release of a demon in connection with the final thousand-year period. If one posits Persian influence on Jewish apocalyptic thought, this idea could lie behind the idea of a millennial kingdom (Bousset; J. Sanders, "Whence"). But since there is no evidence of Zoroastrian periodization elsewhere in Revelation, it is unlikely that there is a connection here.

20:5. *The rest of the dead did not come to life until the thousand years were over.* The rest of the dead have been understood in two ways; the first is preferable:

1. The ungodly. If all the faithful are raised to share in the millennial kingdom, then "the rest" of the dead are the ungodly. After the beast's capture, the rest of his army perished, and they included people of every social class (Rev 19:21). They remain in Hades while the beast is in the abyss. According to this view, the resurrection depicted later in the chapter involves only the ungodly, who are raised to face final judgment (20:12–13; Giesen; Osborne).

2. The ungodly and the faithful who were not martyred. If only the martyrs are raised for the millennium, then all other people, both righteous and unrighteous, remain dead until the resurrection depicted later. This approach fits the idea that martyrs receive their favorable judgment from God in 20:4, whereas those who stand in the final judgment include both the wicked, who are condemned, and those inscribed in the scroll of life, who are redeemed (20:11–15; Smalley). What makes this second interpretation less likely is that the martyrs seem to represent all the faithful. Revelation does not clearly distinguish the faithful who die violently from those who die nonviolently. What is true for the martyrs is true for all the faithful.

This is the first resurrection. This expression has been construed in several ways. Each has precedents in the history of interpretation (see INTRO I.A). Here, the first is considered most viable:

1. Resurrection of the faithful to endless life. This approach takes the word "resurrection" as a collective term for raising a group of the dead to life at the end of the age, which was a common idea (Matt 22:31; Luke 14:14; Acts 23:6; 1 Cor 15:12; Heb 6:2). This perspective fits the present context, in which the righteous dead are brought to life as a group (Rev 20:4). Such an approach assumes continuity between Jesus' resurrection and the resurrection of the faithful. Just as Jesus died and came to life, never to die again (1:18; 2:8), the faithful who have died are restored to endless life that begins in the millennium (20:4) and continues in New Jerusalem (21:4; 22:4–5). Since Jesus' resurrection brought him to complete life, not merely to an intermediate state of existence, the same is true of the faithful. The righteous experience resurrection "first," before others do, and there is no suggestion that they undergo another type of resurrection when the rest are brought to life later (20:5, 12–13). There is no reference to a "second" resurrection since each person is raised only once. Rather, some are raised here, and others are raised on a second occasion, at the end of the millennial vision (Aune; Boring; Giesen; Lupieri; Mounce; Reddish).

2. Intermediate state between physical death and final resurrection. Some interpreters observe that in Revelation the first (*prōtos*) things belong to this age and pass away (21:1, 4). They propose that the first resurrection means entering an afterlife that continues throughout the present age but will be followed by a qualitatively different resurrection at the end of the age—one that leads to life in the new heaven and earth. Since those who die in the Lord and those who share in the first resurrection are blessed (14:13; 20:6), then death might be equated with the first resurrection. Revelation's visions of the martyrs under the altar and the saints before God's throne might depict the souls who have experienced a spiritual resurrection to a provisional afterlife (6:9–11; 7:9–17; 15:2–4) and await bodily resurrection at the last judgment (20:11–21:8; Beale; Smalley; Kline, "First"; James Hughes, "Revelation"; Giblin, "Millennium").

This approach is not persuasive. Although it is possible to use resurrection language for both present existence and final resurrection (John 5:24–29; 11:25–26; Rom 6:4–5), there is no suggestion of that here (Osborne). Revelation does not limit coming to life to a spiritual state, whether speaking of Jesus, the righteous, or "the rest" of humanity (Rev 2:8; 20:4, 5). The scenes in 7:9–17 and 15:2–4 are not of a provisional afterlife that the righteous enter upon death. They are glimpses of the new creation.

3. Earthly life beginning with baptism. The first resurrection can be understood as Christ's resurrection, which believers share through faith and baptism (Rom 6:4). Or one might think of it as a person first coming to true life through baptism (Augustine, *Civ.* 20.6; Caesarius) or faith (Oecumenius). From this perspective the millennium depicts the faithful throughout time sharing new life in Christ in anticipation of the final resurrection that accompanies the last judgment (Prigent; P. Hughes, "First"; Shepherd, "Resurrections"). A major problem with this approach is that the context is resurrection to life after bodily death (i.e., beheading in Rev 20:4). It cannot be equated with the newness of life that comes through baptism or faith.

20:6. *Blessed and holy are those who have a share in the first resurrection.* This is the fifth of seven statements of blessing (*makarios*), or beatitudes, in Revelation (see Table 2). It fits the life that comes through resurrection (INTRO IV.E.2). The word "holy" (*hagios*) describes God (4:8; 6:10) and Christ (3:7). The redeemed, who are set apart for service to God, are already holy (*hagioi*), and they face resistance from God's opponents (13:7, 10; 14:12). Nevertheless, being holy or set apart for God now has a future through the promise of resurrection. Those who have a share (*meros*) in the first resurrection will also share in the tree of life and New Jerusalem (22:19). The opposite is a share in the lake of fire (21:8).

Over these the second death has no power. See the NOTE on 20:14.

but they will be priests of God and of Christ, and will reign with him for a thousand years. The language recalls Exod 19:6, in which Israel is called "a kingdom of priests and a holy nation." It could also echo Isa 61:6: "you shall be called the priests of the Lord" and "ministers of the holy one." Earlier, the redeemed were called priests of God (Rev 1:6; 5:10), but here they also serve Christ. In those contexts they were said to constitute a kingdom, whereas here they share Christ's reign. See the NOTES on 1:6 and 5:10.

20:7. *And when the thousand years are over, Satan will be released from his prison.* This is the "short time" of Satan's release (20:3). Releasing a prisoner of war could display clemency on the part of the victor (Diodorus Siculus, *Libr.* 11.92.4; Tacitus, *Ann.* 14.12), and here it could reflect the clemency of God. The proper response was for a captive to show gratitude and obedience (Josephus, *Ant.* 10.40; Tacitus, *Ann.* 12.37), but Satan continues his rebellion and therefore must be halted permanently.

20:8. *He will go out to deceive the nations that are at the four corners of the earth.* The nations have been understood in several ways. The first is most plausible:

1. Ordinary nations. Revelation consistently refers to "nations" as groups of people. They can be redeemed by Christ (5:9; 7:9) or deceived (18:23; 20:3) and swayed by evil (13:7; 14:8; 18:3; Beale; Mounce; Smalley; Reddish). The passage draws on Ezekiel's vision of Gog, whose allies include various nations: Meshech and Tubal to the north of Israel, Persia to the east, Cush to the south, Put to the west, etc. (Ezek 38:2–6). Revelation universalizes this idea by saying that the nations come from "the four corners of the earth," emphasizing totality (*T. Ash.* 7:2), since enemy

nations come from every direction (*4 Ezra* 13:5; Bøe, *Gog*, 308–11). Yet they are ordinary nations.

2. Nations that survive the battle of Rev 19:11–21. The battle seems to destroy all of Christ's opponents (19:18, 21), but the vision also mentions Christ's rule over the nations (19:15), and other passages tell of the nations worshiping God after the defeat of the beast (15:2–4). Revelation could imply that those who did not join the beast's army would survive the battle of 19:11–21 even if they were not followers of Christ. Since these nations come from the four corners of the earth, they might have been distant from the conflict (Beasley-Murray; Osborne). What makes this approach implausible is that Revelation does not envision a neutral position in the battle (Mealy, *After*, 121–22).

3. Nations that were slain in the battle and resurrected immediately after the millennium. The martyrs are raised at the beginning of the millennium and "the rest" of the dead come to life afterward (20:5). John has pictured the ungodly remaining in Hades for the thousand years that Satan is confined to the abyss. One might argue that when Satan is released from the abyss, the allies of the beast who were slain in 19:17–21 are released from the realm of the dead so they can all take part in this final battle (Mealy, *After*, 120–42). The problem is that 20:11–15 describes the dead being raised for judgment rather than for battle. It is unlikely that both visions describe the same event.

4. Beings from the underworld. The four corners of the earth could be the entrances to the underworld (*1 En.* 18:14), where demons or spirits of the dead resided. This could fit Rev 7:1, where four angels hold back destructive winds at the four corners of the earth, and then demonic hordes (9:1–11) and the beast (11:7) "come up" from the abyss to threaten people—much as the nations "come up" for battle in 20:9. Ezekiel pictured nations hostile to God going down to the pit (Ezek 32:18–23). They include Meshech and Tubal, which are identified with Gog and Magog (32:26; 38:2). They could come out of the abyss for this final battle (Kraft; Krodel; Schüssler Fiorenza; Rissi, *Future*, 34–36). Problems with this view are that the nations are never identified in this way elsewhere in Revelation, and none of the traditions associated with Gog and Magog identify them as demonic spirits (Bøe, *Gog*, 315–18).

5. Those born during the millennial age who reject the gospel. Dispensationalist interpreters expect a future millennium to fulfill OT promises concerning fruitful life for people and their descendants. They assume that many people will be born during this period (Rev 20:4–6). The idea is that people will be given the opportunity to come to faith, and those who refuse will constitute the hostile nations at the end of the millennial age (20:7–10; LaHaye; Thomas). However, this view is based on texts such as Isa 65:17–25, which John connects with the New Jerusalem (Rev 21:1–22:5), not with the millennium. It also interprets the OT texts with a kind of literalism that does not fit Revelation's recasting of OT imagery.

Gog and Magog. Ezekiel tells of a battle in which a prince named Gog from the land of Magog will assault Israel in the end times (Ezek 38:2–3, 8). Revelation both appropriates and transforms the passage. One aspect of this transformation is that in Revelation Gog is no longer an individual prince and Magog is no longer a place; both are names for hostile nations. Precedent may have come from texts that name Magog as the ancestor of a people (Gen 10:2; 1 Chr 1:5; Josephus, *Ant.* 1.123), allowing Magog to be included among the nations (4Q161 8–10 III, 21). Some sources treated Gog and Magog as a pair of nations (*Sib. Or.* 3.319, 512; 4Q523 5; *3 Enoch* 45:5). The way Gog and Magog come to include all hostile nations is analogous to the way the one seven-headed beast in Revelation encompasses all the threatening empires pictured in Dan 7:1–8. Another aspect is that Revelation places Gog and Magog under the influence of Satan. There may have been precedent for this, since the Qumran *War Scroll* associates the nations assembled by Gog with the hordes of Belial (1QM XI, 8, 16).

Revelation also splits Ezekiel's vision of Gog and Magog into two parts. The first consists of the battle that takes place before the millennium, when the nations are defeated by the Messiah and devoured by birds (Rev 19:17–21). Ezekiel mentions the birds but not the Messiah's role in the battle (Ezek 39:17–20), although there were traditions in which the Messiah won the victory, as in Rev 19. The LXX of Num 24:7, which differs from the MT, says that a king will arise from Jacob to rule over Gog. The Isaiah pesher from Qumran goes further, with the Davidic Messiah defeating the nations and ruling over Magog (4Q161 8–10 III, 10–21). Similarly, the Targumim say, "At the very end of the days Gog and Magog ascend on Jerusalem and they fall at the hand of King Messiah" (*Frg. Tg.* and *Tg. Neof.* Num 11:26). In the second part Gog and Magog are destroyed by fire from heaven after the millennium (Rev 20:7–10). In this passage no specific role is ascribed to the Messiah. The fire from heaven implies that Gog and Magog are destroyed directly by God, as in Ezek 39:6 (cf. 1QM XI, 16–18). On this two-stage use of Ezekiel, see the COMMENT.

to assemble them for battle. Assembling troops was a common feature in descriptions of battles (Judg 6:33; 1 Sam 13:5; 1 Macc 3:59), including the assembling of Gog's army (Ezek 38:7, 13; 1QM XI, 16). Other texts envision Beliar (1QM I, 1–5; XVIII; *T. Dan* 5:10–11) or angels (*1 En.* 56:5–8) gathering forces for the eschatological conflict, as Satan does here. In Rev 16:13–14 demonic spirits sent by Satan, the beast, and the false prophet gather the nations for battle at Harmagedon. In the battle the armies are led by the beast and false prophet, who are captured (19:19–21). Therefore, in Revelation, Satan alone must gather the nations for their final battle.

Their number is like the sand of the sea. The sand is a common metaphor for large armies (Josh 11:4; Judg 7:12; 1 Sam 13:5). The irony is that although the armies in this vision are as numerous as the sand of the sea, their leader ends up in the lake of fire (Rev 20:10).

20:9. *And they came up across the breadth of the earth.* The phrase "come up" was used for armies going into battle (Judg 4:10; 1 Sam 7:7), including the forces of Gog (Ezek 38:11, 16). Coming "across the breadth of the earth" indicates the distance that the army needed to travel in order to attack (Hab 1:6 LXX). Since they come from the four corners of the earth, the scale is vast (Rev 20:8), and the land becomes their highway (*1 En.* 56:6).

and surrounded the camp of the saints. Armies surrounded an opposing force or a city in order to prevent people from fleeing or supplies from being brought in (2 Kgs 6:14–15; Jdt 7:20; Luke 21:20; Josephus, *J. W.* 3.148; 4.557). The move also facilitated an attack from all sides (1 Macc 13:42; 15:41; Arrian, *Anabasis* 5.23.3; 5.24.4; 6.6.8). The word *parembolē* was used for the Israelite camp in the wilderness, which was moved as they journeyed (Exod 17:1; 19:16; Num 4:5 LXX). Since God was present there, the camp was holy, and those within it had to be clean (Lev 14:8; Num 5:2–3; Deut 23:14).

The term was also used for military camps and armies (1 Macc 3:15). Ancient Israel was considered a fighting force (Deut 2:14; Josh 1:11), and the Qumran community called its members the "camps of the saints" who would take part in the final battle with evil (1QM III, 5). In Revelation the camp of the saints is the Christian community.

the beloved city. In this context the words "camp" and "city" are synonyms. In Jewish sources Jerusalem, or Zion, was the city God loved (Pss 78:68; 87:1–2; Sir 24:11), and it was sometimes identified as the camp of Israel (4Q394 3–7 II, 16–17; 8 IV, 10; cf. Heb 13:11–14). The most literal interpretations assume that the city is the earthly Jerusalem (Thomas), but it is better to take "the beloved city" as a metaphor for the Christian community. Previously, the community was pictured as "the holy city," threatened by an unbelieving world (Rev 11:2), and those who belong to the community are beloved by Christ (1:5; 3:19).

but fire came down from heaven and devoured them. Ezekiel said that God would judge Gog with pestilence, bloodshed, rain, hail, fire, and sulfur (Ezek 38:22), but fire is the principal agent of divine wrath (39:6; cf. 2 Kgs 1:10, 12; Luke 9:54). On the Day of the Lord it falls on the nations (Zeph 3:8; *Sib. Or.* 3:672–73). The simplest reading is that fire came "from heaven" (A 2053^{com}), but other sources add that it was "from God" (ℵ^2 P 051), which is a logical interpretation (cf. Gen 19:24; 1 Kgs 18:38). Earlier, birds devoured the allies of the beast (Rev 19:21), and now fire devours the allies of Satan.

20:10. *And the devil who had deceived them was thrown into the lake of fire and sulfur, where the beast and the false prophet also were.* The action is evidently performed by God, who has the devil thrown into the lake of fire. The theme of Beliar being devoured by fire appears in writings from Qumran (11Q13 III, 7) and *T. Jud.* 25:3. On the lake of fire, see the NOTE on Rev 19:20.

and painful suffering will be inflicted on them day and night forever and ever. Painful suffering is sometimes pictured as sharp physical pain (9:5) like the sensation of burning (14:10–11). The beast brought painful suffering to Babylon by burning the city, so that its smoke rose forever and ever (17:16; 18:9, 15; 19:3), and now the beast, false prophet, and Satan suffer similar torment in fire forever and ever.

20:11. *Then I saw a great white throne and the one who is seated on it.* The principal throne in Revelation belongs to God, the source of rightful power (4:2, 10; 5:1; 7:10). The throne is white, which can connote purity (19:14) and suggests glory (21:23). In Dan 7:9, God's throne is fiery and his clothing is white (cf. *1 En.* 14:18–21). Revelation seems to envision God (cf. Rom 14:10) rather than Christ sitting in judgment (Matt 25:31; 2 Cor 5:10). Since Christ shares God's throne (Rev 3:21; 12:5), some interpreters suggest that here he shares the role of judge (Beale; Osborne; Smalley), but Christ's role is implicit at best.

Before his face the earth and heaven fled away, and no place was found for them. On the day of wrath the mountains and islands move (6:14), and at the judgment on Babylon the islands flee and mountains disappear (16:20). What is "not found" (Rev 18:14, 21, 22) and has "no place" (cf. Dan 2:35) is gone (Giesen). Earlier, no place was found for Satan in heaven (Rev 12:8), but now no place is found for earth or heaven at all. This action prepares for the new heaven and earth (21:1).

20:12. *And I saw the dead, great and small, standing before the throne.* The great and small are people of various levels of society. Earlier, the redeemed stood before the throne in praise (7:9); here, humanity stands before the throne for judgment.

and scrolls were opened. These scrolls are the heavenly records of human deeds. Ordinary kingdoms kept records and could reward people for notable actions (Esth 6:1–3), and it was said that God also had record books. Recording people's deeds meant that people would be remembered and they would be held accountable for those deeds (Isa 65:6; Mal 3:16; *1 En.* 81:1–4; 89:61–72; 97:6; 104:7; *Mart. Asc. Isa.* 9:22; *m. 'Abot* 2:1). The corollary is that the scrolls also hold God to account, since the faithful are promised that God will remember their efforts (Rev 14:13).

John refers to multiple scrolls of deeds, perhaps because it was said that righteous deeds were recorded in one scroll and sins in another (*T. Ab.* 12:12; *Apoc. Zeph.* 7:1–11). Some texts pictured the names of the righteous being inscribed in one scroll and the names of sinners in another (*Jub.* 30:21–23). This is not the case in Revelation, in which the names of the redeemed are in the scroll of life, which is in a separate category. The scrolls were to be opened at the final judgment so that people could be rewarded or punished (Dan 7:10; *1 En.* 47:3; *4 Ezra* 6:20; *2 Bar.* 24:1; Baynes, *Heavenly*).

Another scroll was also opened, which is the scroll of life. The scroll of life is the list of people who receive the gift of life with God (Rev 3:5; 13:8; 17:8; 20:15; 21:27). Sometimes, references to "the scroll of the living" (Ps 69:28) and "the scroll" that God has written (Exod 32:32) identify people who are alive and assume that being blotted out of the book means dying. To be listed in the scroll of life indicates preservation (4Q504 1–2 VI, 14) and to be blotted out means death (4Q381 31 8). In Revelation and other sources, being recorded in the scroll entails a glorious future in God's city (Isa 4:3), deliverance from the abyss and Hades (*Apoc. Zeph.* 9:1–2) and resurrection to future life (Dan 12:1).

Some texts assume that people are placed in the scroll as a consequence of their righteousness (*Apoc. Zeph.* 3:6–9; *T. Jac.* 7:27; *Jub.* 30:21–22; Herm. *Sim.* 2.9; *Odes Sol.* 9:11–12). Others, however, thought of people being inscribed in God's scroll through divine election (1QM XII, 1–3) or grace, which gives them citizenship in heaven and everlasting life (*Jos. As.* 15:4; Luke 10:20; Phil 3:20–4:3). This idea is similar to Revelation, in which God inscribes people in the scroll from the foundation of the world (Rev 13:8; 17:8). At the last judgment people are accountable for their actions as inscribed in the scrolls of deeds, but they are saved by grace by having their names in the scroll of life. See the Notes on 3:5 and 13:8.

And the dead were judged according to their works, by what was written in the scrolls. Being judged according to one's deeds is an important theme (Jer 17:10; Ps 62:12). Although some texts spoke of being judged by Christ (Matt 16:27; 25:31–46; John 5:27–29; 2 Cor 5:10), Revelation and other texts assume that final judgment belongs to God (*Sib. Or.* 2:214–20; *4 Ezra* 7:33; 1 Pet 1:17). Paul speaks of people's work being tested and perhaps destroyed by fire on the Day of the Lord (1 Cor 3:13–15), but Revelation and other sources focus only on the outcome of judgment as blessing or punishment.

20:13. *And the sea gave up the dead that were in it, and Death and Hades gave up the dead that were in them.* John seems to picture those who have died on earth being kept in Hades, the realm under the earth, until the last judgment (*2 Bar.* 42:8; 50:2; cf. Isa 26:19; Dan 12:2). Those who died at sea are a separate category. It was said that "the souls of those who have met their end in the deep never go down to Hades, but wander in the same spot about the face of the waters" (Achilles Tatius, *Leuc. Clit.* 5.16.2; cf. Propertius, *Elegies* 3.7.25; *NW* 2:1644). Even these will be raised for judgment (*1 En.* 61:5; *Sib. Or.* 2:233).

and they were judged, each one of them, according to their works. See the NOTE on Rev 20:12.

20:14. *Then Death and Hades were thrown into the lake of fire.* This statement can best be taken to mean that the role of Death and Hades is ended. In the new creation death will be no more (21:4; cf. Isa 24:8). The thought is similar to 1 Cor 15:26, in which the end of the age brings the destruction of death (Giesen; Mounce; Osborne; Prigent; Smalley). Some interpreters argue that Death and Hades signify the wicked people who were kept by these powers, so throwing Death and Hades into the lake of fire means punishing the wicked (Aune; Beale; Mealy, *After*, 181). But this interpretation is unlikely because at this point the dead have been removed from Death and Hades (Rev 20:13). Instead, the vision depicts the end of Death and Hades themselves (*L.A.B.* 3:10). Similarly, the sea, which also gave up its dead, has no place in the new creation (Rev 20:13; 21:1). On the lake of fire, see the NOTE on 19:20.

This is the second death, the lake of fire. The second death is the punishment of the wicked after their resurrection at the end of the age (2:11; 20:6, 14; 21:8). Like Revelation, Jewish sources identify the second death with the fires of Gehenna (*Tg.* Isa 65:5–6; Beale). Where ordinary death deprives a person of life in this age, the second death deprives a person of life in the age to come (*Tg.* Jer 51:40, 57). It means pain, despair, and disgrace, in contrast to blessing and everlasting life (*Tg.* Isa 65:13–15; *Tg. Onq.* Deut 33:6). Jewish texts do not refer to ordinary death as a merely physical occurrence, as if only the body dies, or picture the second death as something that affects only the soul. They assume that each type of death affects the whole person. Jewish sources assume that even the body can be subject to the second death (*Tg.* Isa 65:6). This idea differs from Greco-Roman sources that equate types of death with aspects of a person's being. Plutarch says that an initial death separates the soul and mind from the body, and a second death separates the mind from the soul, making true blessedness possible (*Mor.* 942F). In Revelation and Jewish sources, however, ordinary death and the second death affect the whole person. Contrary to Plutarch, the second death never brings blessing.

20:15. *And if any were not found written in the scroll of life, they were thrown into the lake of fire.* The idea that those condemned by God will be sent to a place of fire appears in both Jewish tradition (Isa 66:24; *1 En.* 90:24–27; *4 Ezra* 7:36, 38; *2 Bar.* 44:15) and Christian tradition (Matt 5:22; 18:9; Mark 9:43; Luke 16:23–24). Although people are judged by their works (Rev 20:12–13), the scroll of life is the final basis for judgment.

COMMENT

Revelation 20 continues the epic drama of God's victory over evil. The vision cycle began as Christ came to judge and "make war with justice" (19:11), and the theme

---

On Rev 20:1–15, see Bauer, *Das tausendjährige*, 163–99; Bauckham, *Climax*, 56–70; Baynes, *Heavenly*; Bøe, *Gog*; R. A. Campbell, "Triumph"; de Villiers, "Prime"; Giblin, "Millennium"; Glasson, "Last"; Gourgues, "Thousand-Year"; James A. Hughes, "Revelation"; Kline, "First"; Mathewson, "Re-examination"; McKelvey, "Millennium"; Mealy, *After*, 95–142; Poythress, "Genre"; J. Sanders, "Whence"; Schüssler Fiorenza, *Priester*, 291–344; Shepherd, "Resurrections"; D. Smith, "Millennial"; Taeger, *Johannesapokalypse*, 163–71; Vivian, "Gog"; R. F. White, "Reexamining."

of divine justice now shapes John's portrayal of the battle's aftermath in two pairs of scenes. In scenes one and three, Satan becomes a war captive, chained in the abyss for a thousand years. When released, he renews his attack, is defeated, and is hurled into the lake of fire. Here, God's justice brings evil to an end (20:1–3, 7–10). In scenes two and four, people are given a fitting judgment by God. Those who suffered for their faith are judged favorably and raised to reign with Christ. Then the rest of the dead are brought before God's throne and judged according to what they have done (20:4–6, 11–15). The alternating scenes reflect larger plotlines that intersect in this chapter (§40 COMMENT).

Two complementary dimensions of justice inform this passage. One is the conviction that a just God will not allow evil to continue afflicting the vulnerable. Thus far, the agents of evil have persistently refused to halt their attempt to dominate the earth, and even after a thousand-year incarceration, Satan remains incorrigible. Since the perpetrators of evil have refused to change, justice requires that their activities be brought to an end for the sake of the world (20:1–3, 7–10). The other dimension is human accountability. Those who come under the sway of evil are not exempted from responsibility for their actions. God is not indifferent toward evildoing but will hold people accountable for what they do—though his justice is tempered with mercy. Similarly, he will not forget the faithful who suffer, but his justice will give them life in his kingdom (20:4–6, 11–15).

Debates over this chapter typically focus on relating the visionary world to the readers' world. Futuristic interpreters often argue for direct connections, anticipating that in the time to come the saints will reign on earth for a thousand years before the last judgment. Others maintain that the thousand years is an indefinite period that began when Satan was bound at Jesus' first coming and will continue until Christ's return. These and other views are summarized in §38A. The approach taken here is that John's readers would have seen themselves living in the time when Satan and the beast were at work, and not in the millennial age after the beast was defeated and Satan was bound. For them, the end of evil remained a future hope. But this approach also recognizes that the visionary world does not outline a chronological sequence of events that can be correlated directly with the readers' world.

In literary terms, the latter half of Revelation encompasses two principal time periods. One extends for the three and a half years that Satan is restricted to the earth, where he uses the beast, false prophet, and whore to make war against the saints (12:6, 17; 13:5–7). During this conflict Satan's agents exercise authority and subject the faithful to imprisonment and death by the sword (13:10). The other period lasts for a thousand years, and the situation is reversed. The devil, who had the faithful taken captive, is now chained in prison, and those who were beheaded for their faith are brought to life so they can reign (20:1–6).

Three and a Half Years	Thousand Years
Satan and his agents wield authority.	Faithful reign with Christ.
Faithful are imprisoned.	Satan is imprisoned.
Faithful are slain with the sword.	The beheaded are resurrected.

The vision of the thousand years enables readers to see how the evil perpetrated on the righteous eventually comes full circle. Just as the whore who brought others to grief eventually comes to grief (18:6–8) and the beast that burned the whore with fire is subjected to fire (17:16; 19:20), the devil who imprisoned the faithful is thrown into prison before receiving his final sentence (2:10; 13:10; 20:1–3, 10).

The two periods fit the pattern of presenting readers with contrasting pairs of visions (Friesen, *Imperial*, 159). Elsewhere, the beast is the opposite of the Lamb, and the whore is the opposite of the bride. Such images do not suggest that readers will actually *see* a debauched woman riding on a seven-headed monster; rather, they disclose the *character* of the destructive yet alluring forces in the readers' social worlds. The same is true of Revelation's use of time. The three and a half years that Satan imprisons and kills the saints is a short time in the visionary world, and it shows that the time in which evil can operate is limited. In contrast, the thousand-year period in which Satan is imprisoned and the saints live and reign is vast, and it leads to endless life in the new creation.

Yet it is clear that readers will not *see* time moving in this way. The three and a half years that Satan threatens the saints begins with the Messiah's birth and exaltation (12:5–6, 12–17) and continues until Christ's return (19:11–20:3). For readers in the late first century, the time between Christ's first and second comings had already become an indefinite period of more than three and a half years. The vision assures readers that evil will end without allowing them to calculate when this will occur in terms of ordinary chronology. Similarly, the vision of the thousand years during which Satan is bound and the saints reign encourages readers to trust in God's vindication, but it does not mean that this period can be equated with a timespan in the readers' world.

The Binding of Satan (20:1–3)

The final vision cycle began as heaven opened, the warrior Christ came to defeat his foes, and an angel summoned birds to the battlefield (19:11, 17). Now an angel comes down from heaven to continue the rout of evil (20:1). He holds in his hand the key to the abyss, where demonic forces dwell in smoky gloom. The abyss's inhabitants include grotesque locusts, a sinister angel called the destroyer, and the beast that arises to threaten the saints (9:2–11; 11:7; 17:8). Yet the key to the abyss belongs in heaven, whose agents limit what the powers of the abyss can do. Earlier, the key to the abyss was given to an angel, who opened the abyss and unleashed a demonic plague (9:1). But now an angel uses the key to lock the abyss once Satan has been imprisoned there. Theologically, evil's origin is never explained; its existence is presupposed. Revelation's question is how God will deal with it. The descent of the angel with the key and chain shows that the powers and realms of evil, whatever their origin, are ultimately under the rule of God.

The angel apprehends Satan the dragon, who instigated the great battle against Christ in the previous scene (20:2). Together with the beast and false prophet, Satan lured the kings of the earth to Harmagedon (16:13–16), but their armies were annihilated and the beast and false prophet were captured (19:17–21). This left only Satan, who is now taken into custody. Like the beast and false prophet, he remains unwavering in his opposition to God until he is captured—which will also be true after his release

(19:20; 20:7–8). Previously, the devil worked through the social and political forces represented by the beast and false prophet to create the illusion that evil was invincible (13:4), but this scene marks a reversal. Satan the dragon made war against the saints, and they faced the prospect of becoming war captives (12:17; 13:10), but here the dragon is taken captive (20:2). He wore diadems to display his royal honor (12:3), but now he is reduced to a disgraced prisoner of war (Livy, *Rom. Hist.* 22.59.1; Tacitus, *Hist.* 4.80). Revelation does not give Satan the prestige of operating on the same level with God. One of God's subordinates puts the devil in chains, which was degrading (2 Tim 1:16; Josephus, *J. W.* 4.628; Seneca the Elder, *Controversiae* 9.1.7; Justinian, *Dig.* 49.7.3).

The angel casts Satan into the abyss, which is locked and sealed, so that he cannot deceive the nations for a thousand years (20:3). This action continues the story of the progressive demise of evil. One form of Satan's activity has already been halted. He formerly denounced people before God's throne, which ended when the Messiah was exalted and Satan was expelled from heaven so that his influence was limited to the earth (12:7–12). A second form of Satan's activity has been to deceive people (12:9). He draws people into the belief that dominion belongs to earth's destroyers (11:18) rather than to the Creator and the Lamb (12:5; 15:3). When nations are deceived, they deify human authority (13:14) and follow the materialistic and violent course of Babylon/Rome (18:3, 23). Therefore, Satan's banishment from heaven is followed by incarceration in the abyss, which halts his activity for a thousand years. The scene might be compared to intensifying the treatment of an unrepentant malefactor. If banishment brings no change in behavior, then imprisonment is the next step (Seneca the Younger, *Ira* 1.16.2–3).

The vision of Satan's demise speaks to the situation of John's readers. In the messages to the churches, evil had multiple faces (de Villiers, "Prime"). First, the devil worked through those who denounced believers and threatened them with ten days in prison and death (2:9–10; 3:9), as well as in the execution of Antipas (2:13). In such a situation one response would be for Christians to abandon their beliefs in order to preserve their lives. However, Revelation reverses this picture by disclosing that Satan rages about the earth not because he is invincible, but because he has already been defeated in heaven (12:7–12); and finally he will be subjected to prison—not for ten days, but for a thousand years (2:10; 20:2–3). Second, Satan worked more subtly through teachings that encouraged the accommodation of polytheism, which weakened a commitment to the one God (2:20, 24). The vision in 20:1–3 affirms that God will prevail, giving Christians incentive to resist both the overt and more subtle pressures to relinquish their commitments.

This understanding differs from those interpreters who maintain that 20:1–3 pictures Satan's activity being restricted but not halted. Their argument is that Satan was bound during the ministry of Jesus (Mark 3:27; John 12:31; Col 2:15) and that the reign of the saints in Rev 20:4–6 spans the time between the first and second comings of Christ. Since evil continues throughout the time of the church's existence (2 Cor 4:4; 1 Tim 3:7; 2 Tim 2:26; 1 Pet 5:8), the binding of Satan is understood to merely limit rather than to stop the devil's activity. This approach makes it possible for one to fit Rev 20 into a comprehensive NT eschatology without a future millennial age (Augustine, *Civ.* 20.7; Primasius; Andreas; Beale; Prigent; Smalley).

However, this approach does not fit the literary movement of Revelation. John pictures the period between Christ's exaltation and return as the time of Satan's banishment from heaven to earth, where he deceives the nations and persecutes the saints (Rev 12:1–17). By way of contrast, in 20:1–3 Satan is confined in the abyss, which means that he cannot deceive the nations "anymore" (*eti*), just as defeat in heaven meant that he had no place there "any longer" (12:8) and Babylon's fall meant that life was not found there "anymore" (18:21–23). Satan does not deceive anyone during the millennium (20:4–6), but deception resumes afterward (20:7–8; Mounce; Osborne). If the vision of Satan persecuting the faithful in 12:1–17 shows the present character of earthly life, the vision of Satan's binding assures people that the present situation is not the final one. Evil will be defeated in ways that are not now evident (Boring; Giesen; Murphy).

The Reign of the Saints (20:4–6)

Divine justice has thus far taken the form of halting the activity of evil. Now its second form is the vindication of the righteous. The language of the passage is imprecise, but reasons for the interpretation developed here are given in the NOTES. John sees thrones, which connote royal authority, and he pictures those who were slain for their witness to Jesus taking their seats on the thrones (20:4). This scene recalls the vision of the martyrs under the altar, who demanded to know how long God would refrain from bringing justice for the shedding of their blood (6:9–10). The martyrs' question received a partial answer in the judgments that led to the fall of the whore, beast, false prophet, and Satan (18:8, 20; 19:2, 11). But for John true justice involves more than actions *against* the perpetrators of evil; it means acting *for* the well-being of those who have suffered. This positive act of justice occurs here as they receive favorable judgment from God.

The figures John sees had been beheaded (20:4), implying that they had been formally condemned by the ruling power. If their deaths came through negative judgment by God's opponents, their resurrection expresses the positive judgment of God. The reason given for the death sentence is their witness to the word of God, which centers on God's claim to dominion over the world he created, and their witness to Jesus, the slain and living Lamb. In the visionary world, those who bear witness find themselves at odds with the beast, which personifies the ruling power, and their resistance costs them their lives (cf. 13:1–10).

This depiction of the martyrs has affinities with the social worlds of John's readers, even as it goes beyond their experiences. The faithful are said to have been killed for refusing to worship the beast's image, which early readers would have connected to the imperial cult, which was popular in Asia Minor (20:4). They also refused to accept the beast's mark, which consisted of its name or number and signified the social and economic pressures that moved people to identify with the ruling power (20:4; NOTE and COMMENT on 13:16). Given the visions of the land beast coercing people into worshiping the ruling power (13:15) and of Babylon/Rome drunk with the blood of the saints (16:6; 17:6; 18:24), interpreters have sometimes assumed that Revelation's concern with the martyrs reflects a heightened threat of imperial persecution. But the evidence is that in the first century, persecution was locally instigated and sporadic; even under Domitian there is little to suggest intensified efforts to force people in Asia Minor to participate in the imperial cult (INTRO II.C.2; III.A.3; III.B.1). At the same time, violence occasionally occurred. Jesus and Antipas were slain (1:5; 2:13), believers in Smyrna were threatened (2:9–10), and Revelation may allude to the deaths of Christians in Rome under Nero (COMMENT on 13:7; 17:6).

John's focus on believers who suffer violent death takes the issue of violence beyond the readers' experiences in order to disclose the character of those experiences. His visions depict a fundamental clash between the claims of God and the claims of a society that deifies its rulers—the martyrs are emblematic of the church as a whole. Jesus conquered by suffering death faithfully (5:6), and his followers also conquer by remaining faithful to the point of death (12:11); but faithfulness, rather than a violent death, is the key point. John does not assume that every faithful Christian will be beheaded or killed violently (COMMENT on 13:10), but he does assume that faithfulness involves a willingness to accept martyrdom if necessary (Bauckham, *Theology*, 88–94, 107–8; Krodel; Osborne). Revelation envisions a future in which those suffered who because of the negative judgment of other people are vindicated by God. Just as Jesus the faithful witness was slain, "came to life" (*ezēsen*), and now lives forever (2:8; cf. 1:18), God brings other slain witnesses to life (*ezēsan*, 20:4). There is no suggestion that they die again when the thousand years are over; for them, life continues in New Jerusalem. The same is true for all the redeemed. John calls this "the first resurrection" (20:5). Here, resurrection (*anastasis*) is a collective term for bringing the redeemed as a group from death into life. In contrast, "the rest of the dead" do not come to life until the thousand years are over; they remain in Hades, the realm of the dead (NOTE on 1:18). The stages in Revelation's depiction of resurrection are to some extent distinctive, but they have affinities with the depiction in other sources. Some Jewish texts envisioned a resurrection at the end of the age (Dan 12:2; *4 Ezra* 7:26–32; *2 Bar.* 30:1–5), but early Christians believed that resurrection occurred in stages: Jesus had already been raised, and his resurrection would be followed by the resurrection of others in the future (1 Cor 6:14; 2 Cor 4:14). Paul traces a two-part sequence of resurrection: "Christ the first fruits, then at his coming those who belong to Christ" (1 Cor 15:23; cf. 1 Thess 4:13–18). For Paul, Jesus' resurrection occurs first and sets the pattern for others. Similarly, Revelation shares the idea that resurrection happens in stages, with Jesus being "the firstborn" of the many dead who will rise later (Rev 1:5).

Revelation is unusual in dividing the future resurrection into two phases, but even this element has affinities with two types of tradition. First is the idea that the righteous will rise while the ungodly remain in the realm of the dead. There is precedent for this idea in Isaiah, which says that the faithful who have suffered and died will rise and live (Isa 26:19), whereas there are also the dead who do not rise; remaining in death is their punishment (26:14). Other texts also say that the righteous—especially those who suffer—will be raised, whereas God will leave the wicked in the realm of the dead (2 Macc 7:14; cf. *Pss. Sol.* 3:11–12; *1 En.* 91:10; 92:3; Nickelsburg, *Resurrection*, 94–95). In these scenarios, resurrection is a blessing reserved for the faithful. This pattern is similar to the first resurrection in Rev 20:4–6.

Second, some texts anticipate a resurrection of both the righteous and the unrighteous—regularly listed in that order—followed by a judgment in which the faithful are blessed and the wicked are punished (Dan 12:2; *1 En.* 51:1–2; Acts 24:15; John 5:28–29; *4 Ezra* 7:32–44; cf. *2 Bar.* 30; 50–51). This pattern is more closely related to the final judgment scene in Rev 20:11–15, in which those who are raised are judged according to their works. Revelation is like these sources in picturing a resurrection of the just and the unjust, but it is distinctive in putting the resurrection of these groups in a sequence, with parts of the sequence separated by a thousand years (Aune; Lupieri; Müller).

Those who participate in the first resurrection are the "blessed and holy" who serve as priests (*hiereis*) of God and Christ (20:6). According to Revelation, people become priests through Christ's blood, which cleanses them from sin so they can come into the presence of God (1:6; 5:10; 7:14–15). Their priestly role involves directing worship toward the one true God in a context in which the focus of worship is disputed (Friesen, *Imperial*, 182). The principal alternative is the ruler cult (20:4), though Revelation's critique also extends to other polytheistic traditions (2:14, 20; 9:20). But in this vision there is a reversal. Those who were killed for refusing to worship the dragon and the beast are raised to continue serving as priests to God and Christ (13:4, 15; 20:4). Their priestly service does not end after a thousand years but continues in New Jerusalem, where God and the Lamb are the temple, or focus, for worship (21:22) and they worship in God's presence with God's name on their foreheads, as was customary for high priests (22:3–4; cf. the NOTES and COMMENT on 5:10).

The resurrected saints also reign (*basileusousin*) with Christ for a thousand years (20:6). Although some interpreters compare this vision to the interim messianic kingdom mentioned in Jewish texts (*4 Ezra* 7:28; *2 Bar.* 29:1–30:1; see §38A), Revelation's perspective is different. The writer does not equate the messianic kingdom with the thousand years mentioned in Rev 20:1–6. The Messiah's reign began with Jesus' resurrection and exaltation to God's throne (3:21; 12:5), so Christ is *already* the ruler of the kings of the earth (1:5; 17:14; 19:16). Through his death he redeems people who already constitute "a kingdom" where the reign of God and Christ is recognized (1:6; 5:10), even as agents of evil set up alternative centers of power (13:2, 4). The point of 20:4–6 is that just as Christ reigns in God's kingdom through his resurrection, the faithful will share more fully in Christ's reign through their own resurrections. Christ's reign does not end when the thousand years are over; he continues to share the throne of God (22:1, 3). Likewise, the saints' reign does not end after a thousand years; it extends into New Jerusalem, where they continue reigning forever (22:5).

John does not say whether the saints reign on earth or in heaven. On the one hand, he could be speaking of earth. In the previous scene an angel came down from heaven and confined Satan to the abyss, making the earth free of his influence (20:1–3), and in what follows, Satan gathers the nations from the four corners of the earth to attack the camp of the saints, which one might assume is also on earth (20:7–10). Earlier, the redeemed were said to be a kingdom and priests who would reign on earth (5:10). Since the same language is used for the millennium, one could infer that the earth is where the saints reign during the thousand years (20:6).

On the other hand, some interpreters argue that the vision focuses on heaven. The souls of the martyrs were previously under the heavenly altar (6:9), and there is no suggestion that their resurrections involve a descent to earth. The faithful were to sit down on Christ's throne as he sat down on God's throne (3:21), and the throne of God is in heaven, as are the thrones of the elders (4:2, 4; 11:16; cf. 7:9–17; 15:2). The binding of Satan in 20:1–3 seems to rid earth of evil for a thousand years, but it would not be unusual to shift from earth to heaven in 20:4–6, since such shifts occur elsewhere (e.g., 12:7–12, 13–17). Finally, since the nations of earth try to attack the saints in 20:7–10, their camp could be on earth, but the kings of earth tried to attack Christ, who appeared in heaven (19:11, 19), so Revelation could picture earthly nations attempting to attack heavenly saints (Giblin, "Millennium"; Gourgues, "Thousand-Year").

John's vagueness about the location needs to shape perspectives on this vision. Many interpreters have pictured the millennial kingdom as the place where biblical promises concerning peace and prosperity are realized and where the natural order is transformed into a paradise where the wolf and the lamb feed together and the lion eats straw like the ox (Isa 65:20–25; see §38A). But Rev 20:4–6 says nothing of this, reserving the transformation of the world for the new creation (Isa 65:17; Rev 21:1). John speaks of the saints' location in relational rather than in geographical terms. Each time readers might expect him to say the saints "reigned on earth," he says only that they "reigned with Christ" (20:4, 6). Witness to Christ may now be the cause of conflict and death, but the reign of Christ leads to the saints' resurrection. Having shown that this is the character of God's justice, John leaves other questions unanswered.

Victory over Satan and His Allies (20:7–10)

After a thousand years Satan is released, though the reason is not immediately apparent (20:7). Some interpreters suggest that tradition required that John include the conflict with Gog, which Ezek 38–39 pictures at the end of the age, before the vision of New Jerusalem in Ezek 40–48 (Boring; Kraft; Krodel). Yet this is unlikely because John already included part of Ezekiel's vision—the summoning of the birds—in Rev 19:17–21, making it unnecessary for him to deal with the prophecy again. An alternative is to ask the prior question: Why was Satan imprisoned at all rather than being sent directly to the lake of fire like the beast and false prophet (19:20)?

We have seen how the imprisonment showed the symmetry of divine justice, for the devil who took the faithful captive (2:10–11; 13:10) was himself taken captive. His release continues the process of revelation by demonstrating Satan's incorrigible character. Upon his release, Satan resumes his deception of the nations, showing that his is a case of unrelenting evil (20:8). Earlier, the devil battled Michael and his angels, but he was thrown down to earth and immediately began persecuting the people of God (12:13–17). He gathered kings for war (16:13–14), but after their defeat he was confined to the abyss (19:19–20:3). Even then, after his release, he continues summoning the nations for war (20:7–11). Since Satan does not change, God must finally bring his activity to an end.

Satan gathers nations from the four corners of the earth (20:8). Since the nations seemed to have been destroyed in the previous battle (19:17–21), interpreters have tried to explain where they come from at this point, but John does not clarify this issue (NOTE on 20:8). The same problem arises later, for the nations all seem to be destroyed in 20:9, yet there is still a place for them in New Jerusalem (21:24, 26; 22:2). Such non sequiturs in the visionary world make it difficult to translate these scenes into coherent sequences of events in the readers' world. What they do is to show that allegiance to God holds the promise of life, whereas deception by Satan brings the opposite (Bauckham, *Theology*, 102–3).

The nations are called Gog and Magog (20:8), names mentioned in Ezek 38–39. The prophet said that a prince named Gog from the land of Magog would attack those people living securely on the mountains of Israel, but God would destroy Gog's armies by fire, and the birds would feast on the slain. Revelation transforms this scenario. Gog is no longer an individual and Magog is not a place, but both represent the nations collectively (NOTE on Rev 20:8). They are also allies of Satan, who is not mentioned in Ezekiel, and they attack the Christian community.

What is peculiar is that Ezekiel's vision is linked to two scenarios in Revelation. One is the birds feasting on the slain (Ezek 39:17–20), which occurs in the battle *before* the millennium (Rev 19: 17–21). The other is Gog and Magog's attack and their destruction by fire (Ezek 38:1–16; 39:6), which are set *after* the millennium (Rev 20:7–10). Some interpreters maintain that Revelation depicts the same battle twice, since repetition is part of the book's style. Their proposal is that in the two battles that frame the millennium, readers see that Satan, the beast, and the false prophet gather the nations to fight, but the powers of heaven defeat their armies, and the agents of evil end up in the lake of fire (19:11–21; 20:7–10). So if John depicts the same battle twice, it would not be surprising that he uses the same oracles of Ezekiel twice (R. F. White, "Reexamining"; McKelvey, "Millennium"; Mathewson, "Re-examination").

A problem with this approach is the differences between the scenes. In the first battle, the beast and false prophet come against Christ, and Christ's sword wins the victory. In the second battle, Satan, Gog, and Magog come against the saints, and heavenly fire wins the victory; Christ plays no visible role. The first battle occurs after the whore's fiery demise and the second after a thousand years of peace. The first leads to Satan's temporary binding and the second to his final defeat (Bøe, *Gog*, 372). Elsewhere, Revelation repeats elements in different vision cycles (e.g., 14:18–20; 19:1–16) but does not do so within the same cycle.

An alternative is to note that the two battles are part of the same plotline, which concerns God's defeat of evil, even though the two scenes play distinctive literary roles. The plot moves forward as John traces the fall of the whore (17:1–18:24), the defeat of the beast and false prophet (19:11–21), and finally the binding and climactic victory over Satan (20:1–3, 7–10). Tracing a series of events in the visionary world does not mean that the scenes correspond to a series of distinct events in the readers' world. First, note the fluidity in Revelation's use of the OT. If the vision of Babylon in Rev 18 fused prophetic judgments against multiple cities into the vision of a single city's demise, Rev 19–20 does the opposite by translating Ezekiel's singular judgment against Gog into multiple battle scenes. Sometimes the sequence of visions in Revelation corresponds to those in Ezekiel, and sometimes it differs. John does not assume that there is a one-to-one correspondence between an OT prophecy and its fulfillment in an eschatological event (Bøe, *Gog*, 367, 378). Second, the adversaries in John's visionary world correspond in part to entities in the readers' world, yet they cannot simply be equated with them. The whore personified a city that was Rome and yet was larger than Rome, just as the beast personified Roman imperialism and yet was more than that (§§27 and 35 COMMENT; Friesen, *Imperial*, 177). Therefore, their defeat cannot be equated with the fall of one particular city or regime.

The battle unfolds as nations come up against the camp of the saints, which is a metaphor for the Christian community (20:9). The word "camp" (*parembolē*) suggests the prospect of movement, like the camp of Israel on its journey through the wilderness. The sense is that as long as evil is present, the Christian community has not fully "arrived" (Boring). It also suggests that the saints are a military force (NOTE on 20:9).

Previously, the Lamb conquered by suffering death (5:5–6), and those who followed him conquered Satan by witnessing to God and the Lamb (12:11; Bauckham, *Theology*, 76–80). In this final battle, the community continues to be the militant counterpart to the nations that have been deceived, but they play a defensive role. God wins the victory.

Another metaphor for the community is the beloved city (20:9). Initially, John pictured the faithful as the holy city being trampled by unbelieving nations (11:2). Later, he pictured a reversal at the return of Christ, when the agents of oppression were trampled outside the city (i.e., outside the community of faith; 14:20). Now the faithful are again called a city (*polis*), which distinguishes them from Satan's allies. Previous visions showed that the world is dominated by "the great city" (*polis*) of Babylon/Rome, which was doomed to fall (17:18; 18:10), yet Christians constituted the community, or city, where the reign of God and the Lamb was already acknowledged (11:2). At this point in the story, the saints in Revelation have been dwelling in safety for a thousand years, yet the battle vision shows that even here they have no security except in God (Caird). The worshiping community is the harbinger of the holy city, New Jerusalem, where God's reign will be fully and finally manifested (21:2).

Like the previous battle (19:11–21), this scene follows a pattern of conflict in which God's adversaries are defeated by divine action without the assistance of human armies (§39 COMMENT). Heavenly fire was one of the things God would use against Gog, according to Ezek 39:6, but in Revelation such fire also signals the reversal of evil's fortunes. The false prophet called down fire from heaven to deceive people into worshiping the beast—which was actually worshiping Satan (13:4, 13–14)—but now those who are deceived are destroyed by the fire sent by God.

Finally, Satan is thrown into the lake of fire where the beast and false prophet are (20:10; cf. 19:20). Revelation speaks of Satan being tormented there day and night forever (Mounce). The scene reflects the idea that punishment should be given in proportion to deeds (18:7). Accordingly, Satan the fiery red dragon, who tried to devour (*katesthiein*) the Messiah (12:3–4), sees his allies devoured by fire before he is also subjected to a fiery end (20:9–10). The devil once accused the faithful "day and night" (12:10), but now he is tormented "day and night." In Revelation, Satan's opposition to God is unending, and his fiery fate is likewise unending. The lake of fire removes the prospect of an exit for the agents of evil.

Resurrection and Last Judgment (20:11–15)

The previous battle scene depicted God's justice as victory over the forces of evil. Now the scene changes to a courtroom, and justice has to do with individual accountability (20:11). John sees a great white throne, which signifies God's authority to judge (6:16; 19:1–4) and to redeem (7:9–17). The satanic dragon challenged the Creator by establishing a rival throne for the beast (13:2; 16:10), and where Satan had his throne, the faithful were slain (2:13). Now Satan and the beast have been overcome, but God's throne remains, as it will in the New Jerusalem (21:3, 5; 22:1, 3). The sense of divine power is palpable. God created earth and heaven (10:6; 14:7), and these flee from God's presence (20:11). In a previous scene people wanted earth to shelter them from God's judgment (6:15–17), but in the end this is not possible.

The dead from all ranks of society stand before the throne (20:12). Death, Hades, and the sea give up all their dead, so that no one is exempted from judgment (20:13). Some of these are the unfaithful, who were not part of the first resurrection (20:5). Accordingly, one might assume that the faithful are not part of this judgment since they have already been raised and judged favorably by God (20:4; Giesen). Yet the context suggests that both the righteous and the unrighteous now stand before God. Note that both groups include people of higher and lower rank (11:18; 13:16; 19:5, 18). The works of those both inside (2:2, 5, 23; 3:1–2, 8, 15) and outside (9:20; 16:11) the Christian community are subject to divine scrutiny, and each receives a suitable reward (11:18; 22:12). Since the scroll of life is opened at the last judgment (20:12, 15), the redeemed whose names are in the scroll are presumably part of the scene, though they are not condemned (3:5; 13:8; 17:8).

Judgment is based on the scroll of life and the scrolls of deeds (20:12). Each has its own function. The scrolls of deeds recall a tradition in which good and bad actions were recorded in an appropriate ledger (NOTE on 20:12). The sense is that God's judgment is not arbitrary but is based on written evidence (Mounce; Smalley; cf. Dan 7:10; *1 En.* 47:3; *4 Ezra* 6:20; *2 Bar.* 24:1). This scene differs from court cases in the readers' social worlds, in which judges would make decisions only after hearing arguments by the prosecution and defense (*Rhetorica ad Herennium* 2.1–31; Quintilian, *Inst.* 3.9). Here, no arguments are presented. Satan formerly acted as the accuser (Rev 12:10–12), but he no longer has that role. The vision mentions only the judge, the people, and the record.

Judging the dead according to their works presupposes a standard of accountability (20:12). Revelation does not include a comprehensive list of righteous and unrighteous actions, but some things can be inferred: On the positive side is worship of the Creator and the Lamb (4:11; 5:11–14; 14:8). Christ showed love, so those who follow him are to do works of love (1:5; 2:4–5, 19). Since God (6:10; 15:3) and Christ (3:7, 14; 19:11) are true, God's people are to reject what is false (2:2). Since God (21:5; 22:6) and Christ (1:5; 3:14; 19:11) are faithful, people are also to show fidelity (2:19). On the negative side, the opposite of true worship is idolatry (2:14, 22; 9:20; 21:8; 22:15). As God is the Creator, his opponents are the destroyers (11:18). As God and Christ are true and faithful, their opponents exhibit falsehood and infidelity (9:21; 21:8, 27; 22:15). Christ provides cleansing (7:14), but those who embrace what is defiled reject what he offers (17:14; 21:8, 27).

The other factor in judgment is the scroll of life, a kind of citizenship roster containing the names of those who will have life in New Jerusalem (20:12; cf. Isa 4:3; Rev 21:27). Revelation says that people are written in the scroll of life from the foundation of the world (13:8; 17:8). The implication is that being named in the scroll is a gift of God rather than the result of one's good deeds. It is a form of grace, which should be encouraging to readers (NOTES on 3:5; 13:8). The problem is that Revelation says that those whose names are *not* in the scroll of life will be punished, which might suggest that some are predestined to condemnation (20:15).

Logically, one might argue that if God graciously inscribes people in the scroll from the foundation of the world, then he must also intentionally exclude people. But Revelation undercuts this logic in two ways. First, the scroll of life is linked to the Lamb

(13:8; 21:27), and the visions of those redeemed by the Lamb are expansive. Scenes of heavenly worship tell of the Lamb redeeming people from every tribe and nation, giving countless numbers a place before God's throne, where they drink from the water of life (5:9–10; 7:9–17). These elements characterize life in New Jerusalem (21:1–7; 22:1–5), where those written in the Lamb's scroll of life have their place (21:27). The expansiveness of the visions of salvation encourages hope. Second, Revelation has repeatedly interrupted the movement toward final judgment to make room for repentance (7:1–3; 10:1–11), showing that God's desire is for all people to turn from idolatry to true worship (9:20–10:11; 14:6–7; 15:3–4; 16:9, 11).

Revelation presents a tension: People are judged according to their works, yet they are saved by the favor connoted by the scroll of life (Boring; Harrington). Judgment is not a purely human affair in which those whose good deeds outnumber their evil deeds are saved and the rest are condemned. Neither does God simply choose to redeem some and condemn others. Logically, the tension is awkward, but rhetorically, it shapes the readers' perspectives in two ways: On the one hand, people are accountable for what they do, so they must not capitulate to evil but resist it. When they fail, the proper response is repentance (22:14). On the other hand, the forces of evil are so pervasive that resistance can seem futile, but the scroll of life gives assurance that salvation is ultimately God's doing. This gives people reason for hope and perseverance (13:8–10), knowing that the scope of redemption is wide (7:9–17).

The final judgment ends the work of Death and Hades (20:13). They are sometimes pictured as places that can be locked or opened with a key (1:18), and they are also depicted as sinister beings that hold people captive (6:8). Before the judgment, they "give up" their dead, which means they have no absolute right over people. They do God's bidding by relinquishing those they hold (*1 En.* 51:1; *L.A.B.* 3:10; 32:13; 33:3; *4 Ezra* 4:41–43; 7:32; *2 Bar.* 21:23; Bauckham, *Climax*, 56–70). Then God deals with them as he dealt with the beast, false prophet, and Satan—by throwing them into the lake of fire (Rev 20:14). The end of death is the counterpart to resurrection: As God brings the dead to life, he also terminates death's power to hold anyone captive. In the New Jerusalem, death has no place (21:4).

Judgment ends with the opponents of God in the lake of fire, which is also called "the second death" (20:14). Revelation refrains from using terms like physical death and spiritual death and assumes that both death and resurrection affect the whole person. Ordinary death affects both the righteous and the wicked, whereas the second death afflicts only those condemned by God. In Revelation those who belong to God and the Lamb may suffer and be condemned by their earthly opponents, but their future is endless life in the presence of God and the Lamb (22:3–5). Conversely, those allied with evil may now elude condemnation, but their future is the second death in the lake of fire, along with Satan, the beast, the false prophet, Death, and Hades (19:20; 20:10, 14–15). John's visions disclose the divergent outcomes of relationships with God and God's adversaries.

Some interpreters argue that Revelation depicts condemnation as annihilation rather than ongoing suffering (Boismard, "Le sort"; Harrington). For example, when Babylon fell, the smoke of her burning went "up from her forever and ever" (19:3; cf. 18:9–10), yet the context was one of utter destruction, for "it will not be found anymore" (18:21). Moreover, those in the lake of fire include the beast and false prophet, who are not individuals but personifications of social and political forces, along with Death and Hades. One can imagine a political system and death coming to an end, but it is hard to see how they could suffer torment. Most interpreters acknowledge that Revelation assumes some form of continued existence for God's opponents (Osborne; Reddish; Smalley), but these observations help to show that the judgment they receive cannot be understood in a simple physical sense.

The prospect of eternal punishment also seems incongruent with the mercy of God (Harrington). The issue is not limited to Revelation, since other NT passages picture the wicked being punished in a similar way (Matt 5:22; 18:9; Mark 9:43; Luke 16:23–24). Two things may be said about this paradox. First, some people in antiquity found it assuring to think that death simply meant the cessation of existence. If the future held no judgment, but only an end to existence, then there was nothing to fear (Lucretius, *De rer.* 3.861–69; Diogenes Laertius, *Lives* 9.124–25). A popular tomb inscription of the time read, "I did not exist, I do not exist, I do not care" (Klauck, *Religious*, 80). Revelation, however, does not include this option. Death is not an escape. Second, the specter of final judgment is designed to evoke the readers' repentance rather than resignation. Those who show unrelenting opposition to God are warned of the prospect of unrelenting judgment (21:8; 22:15), but the corollary is the promise that those who "wash their robes" have a place in God's New Jerusalem (22:14).

41. New Heaven and New Earth (21:1–8)

21 ¹Then I saw a new heaven and a new earth, for the first heaven and the first earth passed away, and the sea was no more. ²And I saw the holy city, New Jerusalem, coming down out of heaven from God, made ready as a bride beautifully dressed for her husband. ³And I heard a loud voice from the throne, saying, "See, here is the dwelling of God with humankind. He will dwell with them and they will be his peoples, and God himself will be with them as their God. ⁴He will wipe away every tear from their eyes, and death will be no more, neither mourning nor crying nor pain anymore, for the first things have passed away." ⁵Then the one seated on the throne said, "See, I am making all things new." He also said, "Write, because these words are trustworthy and true." ⁶Then he said to me, "All is done. I am the Alpha and the Omega, the beginning and the end. To the one who thirsts, I myself will give freely from the spring of the water of life. ⁷Those who conquer will inherit these things. I will be their God and they will be my sons and daughters. ⁸But for the cowardly and faithless and vile and murderers and immoral and sorcerers and idolaters and all the liars, their share will be in the lake that burns with fire and sulfur, which is the second death."

NOTES

21:1. *Then I saw a new heaven and a new earth.* This allusion to Isa 65:17a has some affinities with the MT, "For behold, I create new heavens and a new earth" (Fekkes,

Isaiah, 228) and some with the LXX, "For there will be the new heaven and the new earth" (Aune). The wording is probably the author's paraphrase. Also see Isa 66:22: "the new heavens and the new earth, which I will make." The word "new" (*kainos*) emphasizes the difference from what has gone before, as in "the new song" previously (Rev 5:9; 14:3). It can also encompass some continuity, like the same person being given a new name (2:17; 3:12). In the Hebrew text of Isa 65:17 the newness comes from God creating (*bār'a*). This could mean that the new heaven and earth will be as different from the old as the current heaven and earth are from the prior chaos (Gen 1:1). Alternatively, one might think of God's creative action transforming the existing world from sorrow into blessedness (Isa 41:19–20; 45:8; 65:18).

In Jewish writings, expectations for a new creation took a variety of forms: The earth would be purged of evil and continue, and heaven would pass away before a new heaven appeared (*1 En.* 91:14, 16); the earth would be transformed (*Jub.* 1:29; 4:26; *1 En.* 45:4–5); the world would cease and another earth and heaven would begin (*L.A.B.* 3:10; 32:17); or what was corruptible would disappear and all else would be renewed (*2 Bar.* 32:6; 44:9, 12; 57:2). Some were merely vague about the process (*1 En.* 72:1; 1 QS IV, 25; Stephens, *Annihilation*, 46–116).

Early Christian texts speak of a future renewal or rebirth (Matt 19:28), which could refer to the transformation of the existing world but could also point to a qualitatively new state after the end of this world (24:29, 35; D. Sim, "Meaning"). For Paul the new creation came into being through Christ's crucifixion, and others participate in it in the present when they die to sin and are brought into the life that comes through faith (2 Cor 5:17; Gal 6:15; Furnish, *II Corinthians*, 332–33; Martyn, *Galatians*, 572–74). Paul also anticipates that in the future the creation will be set free from its bondage to decay, so that it participates in the glorious transformation of those whom God raises from the dead (Rom 8:18–25). In Revelation, the new heaven and earth remain in the future. Given the range of meanings associated with notions of new creation, its character must be discerned from the context (see the COMMENT).

for the first heaven and the first earth passed away. This line echoes Isa 65:17b: "the first things shall not be remembered or come to mind" (cf. 43:18). In Isaiah, the word "first" (*prōtos*) is used for the former troubles that are no longer remembered (65:16), but Revelation uses "first" for the created heaven and earth, which no longer exist. Revelation, like some other apocalyptic writings, envisions heaven or earth passing away (*1 En.* 91:16; *2 Bar.* 44:9–12; *T. Job* 33:4) or ceasing (*L.A.B.* 3:10; *2 En.* 65:6), without specifying how this might occur. "Pass away" simply means that something ends (*apēlthan*, Rev 21:1; cf. 9:12; 11:14). Texts that told of the world's end were not anticreation; they typically understood God to be the Creator and did not expect matter to vanish into nothingness (Adams, *Stars*, 99).

There were various perspectives on the end of the world. First, some Jewish writings considered heaven and earth to be inherently transient, so they eventually would perish, wear out, or pass away like smoke (Ps 102:25–27; Isa 51:6). Later texts spoke of the world reaching the end of its lifespan (*4 Ezra* 5:50–55; 14:18; *2 Bar.* 85:10). In one scenario the Messiah and all people die natural deaths, and the world returns to primeval silence before the emergence of a new world. The cosmos is not annihilated but sleeps as the dead sleep before resurrection (*4 Ezra* 7:29–32). Second, some OT passages told of God's judgment against his adversaries resulting in the destruction of heaven and earth (Isa 13:9–13; 34:4; Jer 4:23–28; Joel 2:30–31; Nah 1:4–5; Zeph 1:2–3; Hag 2:21–22). Since these texts are poetic, warnings of cosmic catastrophe could be taken as metaphors for political upheaval (Wright, *New*, 333), but some seem to envision an actual collapse of the created order (e.g., Isa 24:19–20; Adams, *Stars*, 25–51). Later texts link God's judgment to the shaking of the earth at the end of the present age (*1 En.* 1:3–9; *T. Mos.* 10:4–6). Third, some Jewish writers told of God judging the earth by fire (Zeph 1:18; 3:8; Josephus, *Ant.* 1.70; *L.A.E.* 49:3). Others expected all things on earth (Ps.-Sophocles frg. 2 [*OTP* 2:826]) or even the earth itself (*Sib. Or.* 3:80–92) to be consumed by fire and then refashioned (*Sib. Or.* 4:171–83; van der Horst, "Elements").

Christian tradition includes sayings of Jesus that refer to the darkening of celestial bodies and shaking of heaven at the end of the age (Matt 24:29; Mark 13:24–25; Luke 21:25–26). When connected to Jesus' statement that "heaven and earth will pass away," the sense is that these heavenly signs signal the end of the cosmic order (Matt 5:18; 24:35; Mark 13:31; Luke 21:33; Adams, *Stars*, 133–81). Similarly, Heb 12:26–27 warns that God will shake both heaven and earth at the end of the age, doing away with what is transient, so that only what belongs to God's kingdom remains (cf. Heb 1:10–12; C. R. Koester, *Hebrews*, 103, 195–96, 542–53). Finally, 2 Pet 3:10–13 says that heaven will pass away and the elements will be dissolved with fire before the coming of the new heaven and earth. This idea is similar to the Stoic notion that the cosmos will be dissolved into fire and later remade (van der Horst, "Elements"). But where Stoics thought the world would repeatedly undergo conflagrations and that each new world would be identical to the old ones, 2 Peter envisions dissolution occurring only once before the appearance of a qualitatively new world (Adams, *Stars*, 127–28, 217).

Revelation refers to the final defeat and judgment of the wicked by fire (Rev 17:16; 19:20; 20:9–10, 14), but not to a final end of the world. At the sixth seal, Revelation includes traditional signs of cosmic collapse, as the heavenly bodies become dark and the earth is shaken (6:12–17), but instead of the end, the forces of destruction are halted so that people can be redeemed (7:1–3). The book focuses on the destruction of earth's destroyers (11:18), not on the destruction of the earth itself.

and the sea was no more. Sea, earth, and heaven are three principal parts of the created order (5:13; 10:6; 14:7). Some apocalyptic texts include the sea's disappearance among the tribulations at the end of the age (*T. Mos.* 10:6; *T. Levi* 4:1; *Sib. Or.* 5:447–48; Giesen; Mounce; Müller), but it is not a common theme. The first two of the following interpretations of Revelation's perspective are most viable:

1. Sign of the new order. The prior age was dominated by Babylon/Rome, the city seated on many waters (Rev 17:1), whereas New Jerusalem will have central place in the new creation, which lacks a sea (21:1–2). The absence of the sea underscores the difference between Babylon's brutal dominion, which relied on seaborne commerce (18:17, 19), and the new order in God's city. Just as Babylon fell and was not found anymore (*eti*), the sea it relied on for its economy does not exist anymore (*eti*, 18:21–23; 21:1; Andreas; Rossing, *Choice*, 144–47).
2. End of death. Death, Hades, and the sea all held people captive but have now had to give up their dead (Note on 20:13). The first two powers—Death and Hades— were thrown into the lake of fire (20:14). The process is completed when the third

power—the sea—is eliminated (21:1). Therefore, John uses parallel expressions to say that the sea was "no more" and death will be "no more" (*ouk eti*, 21:1, 4).

3. End of chaos and evil. Many texts assume that the sea uniquely symbolized threats to the created order (Gen 1:2). In the OT, God set limits for the sea (Jer 5:22) and he dried up its waters (Pss 18:15; 77:16; Jer 51:36; Nah 1:4; Hab 3:8; *1 En.* 101:7). Monsters in the sea had to be controlled and defeated (Job 7:12; 26:12; Pss 74:13–14; 89:9–10; Isa 27:1). In Revelation, Satan stands by the sea, the beast rises from it, and the whore is seated on it (12:18–13:1; 17:1; cf. Dan 7:2–3). From this perspective, the end of the sea marks the end of the evil it symbolizes (Aune; Mounce; Murphy; Prigent; Reddish; T. Schmidt, "And the Sea"). This approach is unlikely, however, because both sea and land are susceptible to evil in Revelation. Jewish tradition linked Leviathan with the sea and the monster Behemoth with the land (*1 En.* 60:7–8; *4 Ezra* 6:49–52; *2 Bar.* 29:4), and Revelation links one beast to the sea and another to the earth (Rev 13:1, 11). The writer assumes that the demonic abyss opens onto the earth (9:1–3) and that earth is filled with opponents of God (11:10; 13:14; 18:3). The sea is no more evil than the land.

4. New exodus imagery. God dried up the sea at Israel's exodus from Egypt (Exod 14:21–22; Ps 106:9). The exodus was a paradigm for God's future acts of deliverance, when sorrow and sighing would end (Isa 51:10–11; Zech 10:10–11), as they do in New Jerusalem (Rev 21:4). The book of Wisdom said that at the exodus "the whole creation in its nature was fashioned anew" (Wis 19:6), and here, overcoming the sea is part of the new creation (Mathewson, "New"; Beale; Ford). A problem with this approach is that when Revelation draws on exodus motifs, it makes the allusion clear (e.g., Rev 15:3; 16:1–21), which is not the case here.

5. Removal of a barrier. Revelation tells of a glassy sea before the throne of God (4:6). If the sea in 21:1 could be identified with the heavenly sea, then its absence would signal the removal of the barrier separating people from God (Mealy, *After*, 193–200). There is little to suggest, however, that 21:1 refers to the heavenly sea. Alternatively, one might consider the sea as a barrier between John on Patmos and his readers in Asia Minor (Boring). But this interpretation is unlikely because the sea also was a means of connecting people by ship (8:9; 18:17–19).

21:2. *And I saw the holy city, New Jerusalem, coming down out of heaven from God.* Calling Jerusalem the holy city was common, since the temple was there (Neh 11:1; Isa 48:2; 52:1; Tob 13:8; 1 Macc 2:7; Matt 27:53). In Revelation the city is holy even though it has no temple because God and the Lamb are there (Rev 21:22). Some texts expected Jerusalem to be called by a new name, such as My Delight Is in Her (Isa 62:2, 4; Beale). But it was rare to call the city itself "new" (*T. Dan* 5:12; NOTE on Rev 21:10). The context recalls how God promised that in creating a new heaven and earth he would also create Jerusalem rejoicing (Isa 65:17–19). John envisions the realization of this hope.

made ready as a bride beautifully dressed for her husband. This imagery recalls texts about God's redemption of Zion: "I will rejoice greatly in the Lord," for "he has clothed me with the garments of salvation . . . as a bride adorns herself with her jewels" (Isa 61:10; cf. 52:1). The people of the restored city will be like the ornaments a bride wears (Isa 49:18). Although Israel was sometimes pictured as a faithless bride (Jer 2:2, 20; Ezek

16:8–22), Revelation recalls OT promises of a redeemed Zion, a bride who would be a source of joy (Mathewson, *New*, 44–49). Jewish prayers asked that mourners would be consoled in the hope that God would "renew the works of the heavens and of the earth," that he would "console them in Jerusalem" and like a bridegroom "live with his bride forever," filling earth with his glory (4Q434a 1–3, 6–7; Weinfeld, "Grace"). Such hopes are fulfilled and surpassed in New Jerusalem, where heaven and earth are made new, mourning is banished, and the redeemed live forever as a bride with her husband. Traditionally, God was Zion's husband (Isa 54:5–6; 62:4–5; L. Huber, *Like*, 103–14), but Revelation identifies the city as the bride of Christ (Rev 19:7; 21:9). Jewish sources typically do not picture the Messiah as a bridegroom, but in early Christian circles faith in Jesus the bridegroom was likened to a marriage (Matt 25:1–13; Mark 2:20; John 3:29; 2 Cor 11:2; Eph 5:25–32).

21:3. *And I heard a loud voice from the throne, saying.* Unnamed voices come from the midst of the four living creatures (Rev 6:6), from heaven (10:4, 8; 11:12; 12:10; 14:2; 18:4), from the heavenly temple (16:1, 17), and from the throne (16:17; 19:5). They are often loud (11:12; 12:10; 16:1, 17) and come from groups (12:10; 14:2–3). This voice comes from the throne, but it probably does not belong to God since it refers to God in the third person. God speaks in the first person in 21:5a. Nevertheless, coming from the throne means that this voice has divine authority.

"See, here is the dwelling of God with humankind. The Greek word for dwelling is *skēnē*, which the LXX used for the tent (*'ōhel*, Exod 33:7–11), or tabernacle (*mishkan*, 25:9), where God dwelled with Israel in the wilderness and manifested his glory (40:34–38). Similar terms for "dwelling" were extended to the earthly temple (Pss 43:3; 84:1; 132:7; 4Q504 1–2 IV, 2), Jerusalem (Ps 46:4), and the heavenly sanctuary (NOTE on Rev 15:5). The related verb *skēnoun*, or "to dwell," is used in the next line of Rev 21:3, where it is linked to God's covenant. The text resembles Lev 26:11–12, in which God said, "I will make my dwelling among you" and "will be your God, and you shall be my people" (Rissi, *Future*, 57; Prigent).

An even stronger connection can be made with Ezek 37:27: "My dwelling shall be with them; and I will be their God, and they shall be my people." The promise in Ezekiel is followed by a description of a city with twelve gates, where God would dwell with Israel and reveal his glory (43:7, 9) as in Rev 21:9–22:5 (Mathewson, *New*, 51–52). One difference from Ezekiel is that Revelation's city has no temple, since God and the Lamb are its temple (Rev 21:22). Another is that in Revelation God's dwelling is among humankind, not just Israel. It was said that the OT tabernacle was formerly God's dwelling "among humankind" (Ps 78:60; van Ruiten, "Intertextual," 500–501), which is essentially "among Israel." Revelation expands this idea to humankind more broadly (see the COMMENT). Some interpreters propose that the Greek *skēnē* recalls the Hebrew *shekinah*, a rabbinic term for divine presence (Giesen; Mounce; Osborne), but this is unlikely since the term *shekinah* was not commonly used before the second century CE (C. R. Koester, *Dwelling*, 71–72, 124).

"He will dwell with them and they will be his peoples. The verb "to dwell" (*skēnoun*) repeats the idea of "dwelling" (*skēnē*) from the previous line. Previously, God (Rev 7:15) and the redeemed (12:12; 13:6) were said to dwell in heaven, but here God's dwelling comes down from heaven. The language recalls God's covenant with Israel: "I will be their God and they will be my people" (Jer 7:23; 30:22; 31:1, 33; 32:38; Ezek 11:20;

36:28; 37:23; Bar 2:35; 11Q19 LIX, 13). This formula also accompanied God's promise to dwell with Israel (Lev 26:11–12; Zech 8:3, 8; Exod 29:45; *Jub*. 1:17; 11Q19 XXIX, 7–8) and the Christian community (2 Cor 6:16). New Jerusalem is the fulfillment of this hope.

Some manuscripts read "people" in the Greek singular (*laos*; P 051 1006), and others, "peoples" (*laoi*; א A 046 2030 2050). "People" is the usual covenant formula (Lev 26:12; Jer 24:7; Ezek 37:23; Zech 2:11). If the singular is original, then the Greek plural for "peoples" could have arisen to make the word match the plural subject and verb (*autoi . . . esontai*). Many English translations use "people" (ESV, NAB, NAS, NIV, NJB), but it is more likely that "peoples" is the original and that the variant arose to make the word fit the traditional covenant formula (NRSV). Revelation can use the singular for God's people collectively (Rev 18:4), but they come from many peoples (5:9; 7:9); the context pictures the redemption of many nations (21:24, 26; 22:2; cf. Isa 25:6; 56:7; Ps 47:8). "Peoples" is synonymous with "humankind" in 21:3a (Bauckham, *Climax*, 310–13; Aune; Smalley; Mealy, *After*, 223; cf. McNicol, *Conversion*, 72–75). See the COMMENT.

"and God himself will be with them as their God. Some manuscripts include the final words "their God" (*autōn theos*; A 2030 2050 2053), sometimes reversing the sequence (051 1854). Other manuscripts omit the words (א 1778 2081). Since the words seem redundant, they were probably original and later deleted to simplify the style (Aune; Smalley). When God is "with" people, they are protected and thrive (Exod 3:12; Num 23:21; Deut 20:1; 31:6; Isa 8:10; 41:10; Jer 42:11).

21:4. *"He will wipe away every tear from their eyes, and death will be no more, neither mourning nor crying nor pain anymore.* Isaiah's vision of a new heaven and earth pointed to the end of untimely death (Isa 65:19–20), but in Revelation death is abolished altogether. This line recalls Isa 25:8: "He will swallow up death forever, and the Lord God will wipe away tears from all faces" (cf. Rev 7:17). Other passages say that when the redeemed come to Zion, "sorrow and sighing shall flee away" (Isa 35:10; 51:11), and in Jerusalem "no more shall the sound of weeping be heard" or "the cry of distress" (Isa 65:19; cf. Jer 31:16; *4 Ezra* 8:54; *T. Ab*. 20:14). Greek and Roman writers said that death was not to be feared because it ended suffering (Euripides, *Orest*. 1522; Lucretius, De *rer*. 3.905; Dio Chrysostom, *Disc*. 642; Plutarch, *Mor*. 611C), but Revelation considers death an adversary that must be defeated (cf. 1 Cor 15:26; *4 Ezra* 8:53; *2 Bar*. 21:23; *L.A.B*. 3:10; 33:3). Death can be faced because it ultimately will end with resurrection and new creation. Grief ends because evil ends (*T. Mos*. 10:1).

"for the first things have passed away." This line echoes Isa 65:16–17, in which the first, or former, troubles of exile are forgotten with the creation of the new heaven and earth (NOTE on Rev 21:1b). The language also resembles Isa 43:18–19a: "Do not remember the former things or consider the things of old. I am about to do a new thing." In this passage from Isaiah the "former things" are God's past deeds of salvation, which people are not to remember because God is going to do something even more remarkable. In Revelation the first or former things are death, mourning, crying, and pain, which belong to the past and are gone (Fekkes, *Isaiah*, 257). Isaiah's promise that God will do a new thing is reiterated in Rev 21:5. For Paul, the old has already passed away in Christ (2 Cor 5:17), though the defeat of death remains in the future (1 Cor 15:27); Revelation also emphasizes the future dimension.

21:5. Then the one seated on the throne said, "See, I am making all things new." When God says in Isa 43:19, "I am doing a new thing," the context is Israel's deliverance from Babylon in a new exodus, with God giving people water from rivers in the desert. Revelation expands this to making "all things" (*panta*) new. Deliverance from Babylon is complete (Rev 17–18) and God's people now come to New Jerusalem, where they drink the water of life (21:6; Mathewson, *New*, 60–64). The verb "to make" (*poiein*), which was used for God's creating (Rev 14:7) and redeeming in Christ (1:6; 3:12; 5:10; Osborne), is now used comprehensively for new creation.

He also said, "Write, because these words are trustworthy and true." OT prophets were told to "go and say" (Isa 6:9; Jer 2:2; Ezek 3:4), but John is told to write (Aune, *Prophecy*, 275, 330–31). In Isa 65:16, which is part of the background, God is called *'amēn*, which could be translated as "true" (LXX) or "faithful" (Aquila), words used here in Revelation (Beale). The trustworthy and true words John is given (Rev 19:9; 22:6) fit the character of the true God (6:10; 15:3) and Christ his faithful and true witness (3:14; 19:11).

21:6. Then he said to me, "All is done. The verb *gegonan* is perfect tense, third person plural, with the first aorist ending—*an* ($\aleph^1$ A; cf. Rom 16:7). The peculiar form probably led to the variant *gegona*, which is first person singular and agrees with *egō* (I; $\aleph^*$ 025 046 051). Manuscripts with this variant also omit the verb *eimi* (am; next NOTE) so that *gegona egō* becomes a form of "I am." Others adopt the usual third person plural ending—*asin* (1006; Oecumenius) (see Aune; Smalley; *TCGNT*[1], 767). The unusual form of the plural may be linked to "all things," which become new (Satake), though it also underscores the fulfillment of God's "words" (Osborne). At the first creation God spoke and things were done (*egeneto*, Gen 1:3, 6, 9, 11; John 1:3; U. Sim, *Das himmlische*, 80). In the new creation all is done (*gegonan*) when God makes all things new.

"I am the Alpha and the Omega, the beginning and the end. On alpha and omega, see the NOTE on Rev 1:8, where the expression is used for God, and the NOTE on 22:13, where it is said of Christ. God is called first and last in Isaiah, which contrasts him with rival claimants to the throne (Isa 41:4; 44:6; 48:12), and that same context says God declared things from "the beginning" (40:21; 41:26). Later Jewish texts refer to God as "the beginning and the end of all things" because he orders creation (Josephus, *Ant.* 8.280; Josephus, *Ag. Ap.* 2.190; Philo, *Plant.* 93; Aristobulus frg. 4 [*OTP* 2:841]). In Revelation God not only creates all things, but directs history toward the defeat of evil and the new creation. In antiquity it was said that Zeus "holds the beginning and the end and the middle of all things that exist" (Plato, *Leg.* 4.715e; cf. Ps.-Aristotle, *De Mundo* 7; Plutarch, *Mor.* 601B; Aune), but John limits that language to the God of Israel and his Messiah (Rev 21:6; 22:13). Some manuscripts omit the verb *eimi* (am), as in 22:13 ($\aleph$ 025 046 051), but others include it, as in 1:8 (A 1006 1841 2053). The full form "I am" (*egō eimi*) echoes the divine name and underscores God's singular position (Exod 3:14; Deut 32:39; Isa 45:18).

"To the one who thirsts, I myself will give freely from the spring of the water of life. Thirst was a metaphor for the need for God (Pss 42:2; 63:1). God was the source of life and could therefore be called the spring of life and living water (Ps 35:10; Jer 2:13; 17:13; 4Q504 1–2 V, 2). By extension, "spring of life" was used for the wisdom that enabled people to live as God intends (Prov 10:11; 13:14; 14:27; 16:22; Sir 21:13; *1 En.* 48:1; 49:1; 1QH[a] XVI, 7–8, 12–16).

In Revelation drinking the water of life means resurrection to endless life in God's presence. The language echoes Isa 55:1: "Ho, everyone who thirsts, come to the waters . . . Come, buy wine and milk without money and without price." Isaiah's context pictures deliverance as a new exodus and return to Zion, as Israel is given abundant water in the wilderness (Isa 41:17–18; 43:20; 44:3–4; 48:21; 49:10; Fekkes, *Isaiah*, 260–64). In Revelation, however, the water flows from New Jerusalem, where fullness of life is given (cf. Ezek 47:1–12; Zech 14:8; Joel 3:18; NOTES on Rev 22:1–2).

The expression "living water" was used for flowing water (Gen 26:19; Lev 14:6) and for water that gives life (Jer 2:13; *Barn.* 11:2), but Revelation uses the somewhat different expression "water of life." Living water is important in John's gospel (John 4:10, 14; 7:37–39), but a direct connection with Revelation is unlikely. In the gospel the water flows from Jesus and is identified with the Spirit, whereas in Revelation it flows from New Jerusalem. Similarities arise because the gospel, like Revelation, draws on biblical motifs (see INTRO II.D.1).

21:7. *"Those who conquer will inherit these things.* Conquering means persevering in faith (NOTE on 2:7). Inheritance means receiving a share (*meros*) of something good, rather than the share of punishment given to the wicked (NOTE on Rev 21:8). It could include a place in God's city of Jerusalem (*Pss. Sol.* 7:2; 9:1; 17:23). In the NT, inheritance is associated with eternal life (Mark 10:17; Luke 10:25), a share in God's kingdom (Matt 25:34; Gal 5:21), and salvation (Eph 1:14; Heb 1:14). In Rev 21:7 the inheritance of "these things" includes a share in the new creation, New Jerusalem, deathless life, relationship with God, and the water of life (21:1–6; Aune).

"I will be their God and they will be my sons and daughters. The traditional covenant formula was "I will be their God and they will be my people" (e.g., Jer 31:1, 33; Ezek 36:28), which was paraphrased earlier (NOTE on Rev 21:3). Here, the language is modified to reflect the practice of adoption, which uses the expression "he will be my son" (Kraeling, *Brooklyn*, no. 8.5, 8, 9; cf. Exod 2:10). In the OT, God promised an heir to David's throne and said, "I will be a father to him and he shall be a son to me" (2 Sam 7:14; 1 Chr 17:13; 22:10; 28:6). Accordingly, the kings of Israel could be considered adopted sons of God (Pss 2:7; 89:26–27). In Jewish tradition the promise of sonship from 2 Sam 7:14 was used primarily for the Messiah (4Q174 1–3 i 11), and Christians used it for Jesus as the Son of God (Heb 1:5). At the same time, the promise could be extended to Israel (*Jub.* 1:24; *T. Jud.* 24:3) and the Christian community (2 Cor 6:18), perhaps because father and child imagery was used for God's relationship to his people (Jer 31:9; Deut 14:1; Hos 1:10). Elsewhere in the NT, God is called the Father of believers (Matt 6:9; Luke 11:2; John 20:17; Rom 1:7; 1 Cor 1:3; 1 Pet 1:17), but Revelation reserves "Father" for God's relationship to Jesus (Rev 1:6; 2:28; 3:5, 21; 14:1).

21:8. *"But for the cowardly and faithless and vile.* This is one of three lists in Revelation of people doing wrongful actions (cf. 9:20–21; 22:15). The first three items appear only on this list. Being cowardly was shameful and corrupting (Sir 2:12; 4 Macc 6:20–21; Philo, *Virt.* 26; Epictetus, *Diatribai* 1.9.33), but it was not ordinarily judged as harshly as it is here. Exceptions were punishments for troops guilty of cowardice in battle (Polybius, *Histories* 6.38.1–3; Josephus, *J.W.* 5.482–83). By analogy, cowardice in Revelation means relinquishing one's faith in the battle against evil (*TLNT* 1:301). Faithlessness showed a lack of commitment (Wis 14:25; Philo, *Sacr.* 22; Philo, *Spec. Laws* 2.8; Epictetus, *Diatribai* 1.3.7). Here, it is the opposite of faith, which includes loyalty to God and Christ (Rev 2:10; 17:14). If Jesus (1:5; 3:14; 19:11) and Antipas (2:13) are faithful and resist evil, the faithless are the opposite (2 Cor 6:14–15; Tit 1:15; Luke 12:46). Faithfulness warrants inheritance (cf. P.Oxy. 494.9), but faithlessness does not. The vile are those who practice idolatry (Deut 7:25–26; 1 Kgs 21:26; Hos 9:10) and sexual immorality (Lev 18:26–30). In Revelation this is especially linked to the ways of the whore (NOTES on Rev 17:4–5).

"and murderers and immoral and sorcerers and idolaters and all the liars. All three vice lists in Revelation include murder, immorality, sorcery, and idolatry (cf. 9:20–21; 22:15). Murder was condemned and punished under both Jewish and Roman law (Exod 21:12–14; Justinian, *Dig.* 48.8.3.5). Immoral people were those who engaged in illicit sexual relations. In practice, some forms of immorality were tolerated though disparaged, whereas others, such as adultery, were punished (Josephus, *Ag. Ap.* 2.215; *Rom. Civ.* 1:603). In Rev 21:8 immorality may include both illicit sexual conduct and infidelity to God (Rev 17:2, 4; 18:3; 19:2).

Sorcerers manipulated supernatural powers through potions and incantations. This practice was considered deviant, dangerous, and liable to punishment (NOTE on Rev 9:20; Rodney Thomas, *Magical*, 22–44). Idolatry encompassed traditional Greco-Roman polytheism and the imperial cult. Polytheism was condemned in Judaism and early Christianity, which distinguished Jews and Christians from the wider Greco-Roman society (NOTES and COMMENT on 9:20; 13:4). Lying was a vice (Philo, *Sacr.* 22; Plutarch, *Mor.* 464B) that could range from the small untruths that were disparaged (Sir 7:13) to greater acts of deception such as making false statements under oath, which subjected a person to divine wrath (Zech 5:3–4; Pliny the Younger, *Pan.* 64.3). In Revelation, lying characterizes those who use deception to promote idolatry (Rev 16:13; 19:20).

"their share will be in the lake that burns with fire and sulfur, which is the second death." The word "share" (*meros*) could be used for inheritance (P.Oxy. 105.4, 6, 9, 11; Appian, *Bell. Civ.* 3.13.94; Luke 12:13; 15:12). It is the opposite of the inheritance given to the faithful (Rev 21:7). On the lake of fire, see the NOTE on 19:20. On the second death, see the NOTE on 20:15.

COMMENT

New creation brings the final vision cycle—and the entire book of Revelation—to its culmination. This section summarizes God's redemptive action in light of what has

---

On Rev 21:1–8, see Adams, *Stars*, 237–39; Deutsch, "Transformation"; Du Rand, "New"; Georgi, "Visionen"; Giesen, "Lasterkataloge"; Graz, "Das herabsteigende"; Gundry, "New"; Haacker, "Neuer"; Heide, "What"; Herms, *Apocalypse*, 190–94; Hirschberg, *Das eschatologische*, 203–44; Hock, "From"; L. Huber, *Like*, 163–76; Kitzberger, "Wasser"; P. Lee, *New*, 267–75; Mathewson, *New*, 28–94, and "New"; McNicol, *Conversion*, 71–75; Mealy, *After*, 190–235; C. Müller, "Gott"; Müller-Fieberg, "Literarische"; Oesch, "Intertextuelle"; Pattemore, *People*, 197–212; Pezzoli-Olgiati, *Täuschung*, 161–71; Roloff, "Neuschöpfung" and "Weltgericht"; Rossing, *Choice*, 144–53; Royalty, *Streets*, 214–25; T. Schmidt, "And the Sea"; U. Sim, *Das himmlische*, 66–91; Söllner, *Jerusalem*, 188–204; Stephens, *Annihilation*, 227–57; Tavo, *Woman*, 294–344; van Ruiten, "Intertextual"; Vanni, *L'Apocalisse*, 253–76; Vögtle, "Dann"; Zimmermann, "Nuptial," 169–74.

gone before and introduces themes developed in the next section: John now sees New Jerusalem descend, and later he gets a closer look at the city (21:2, 9–21); a heavenly voice announces God's presence with humankind, and later John beholds the city where God's servants see his face (21:3, 22–27; 22:3–5); and God promises the water of life to the thirsty, and later John sees the water of life flowing from the throne (21:6; 22:1–2).

The passage unfolds in three parts, each with its own voice. First, John tells of seeing the new heaven and earth appear and New Jerusalem descending (21:1–2). Second, an unnamed voice from the throne discloses the meaning of what John sees, identifying the city as God's dwelling place, where death and grief no longer exist (21:3–4). Third, God speaks, underscoring the newness and finality of what John sees and distinguishing the life promised to the faithful from the second death of the wicked (21:5–8). Some interpreters attempt to arrange the passage in a chiastic structure that begins and ends with newness (21:1a, 5a) and has pairs of statements about former things passing away (21:1b, 4c), sea and death no longer existing (21:1c, 4b), and the holy city descending as God's dwelling (21:2–4a; van Ruiten, "Intertextual," 475–76; Aune; Mathewson, *New*, 33). Nevertheless, this approach is unlikely because God's utterance in 21:5a introduces a new section with distinctive elements (Georgi, "Visionen," 358). Moreover, the theme of God and his people, or children, recurs in a way that does not fit the chiasm (21:3, 7).

Nearly every verse in this section recalls passages from the prophets, weaving older themes into a new vision of promise. The dominant passage is Isa 65:17–19, which speaks of the new heaven and earth; the end of the first, or former, things; and a Jerusalem in which people no longer weep. Other passages are brought into this basic framework. Jerusalem appears in splendor like a bride beautifully dressed for her husband, as in Isa 52:1 and 61:10. The announcement of God dwelling among humankind marks the fulfillment of texts such as Ezek 37:27 and Zech 2:10–11 and 8:8. Saying that God will wipe away every tear from people's eyes and that death will be no more evokes Isa 25:8. The announcement that God makes all things new recalls Isa 43:19, and other lines use prophetic language for God as the beginning and the end (44:6) and the source of the water of life (55:1). (Details are given in the Notes.) Theologically, this pervasive use of biblical language reaffirms the faithfulness of God, which is central to the passage (Rev 21:5). The sense is that what was promised through the prophets will be fulfilled.

New Heaven and Earth (21:1–2)

John says, "I saw a new heaven and a new earth," taking up one of the most expansive prophetic visions of God's future (21:1a; Isa 65:17). Like other apocalyptic writings, Revelation assumes that a future for human beings includes a future for the world (*1 En.* 91:16; *2 Bar.* 44:12; Note on Rev 21:1). Although some interpreters suggest that John has little interest in cosmology (Giesen; Müller; Satake), the creation and its future are integral to his message (Bauckham, *Theology*, 47–53; Schüssler Fiorenza 110; Rossing, "For"). Previous visions showed that God has a rightful claim over the world because he created it (4:11; 10:6; 14:6–7). Therefore, every creature in heaven, on earth, under the earth, and in the sea ascribes rightful power to God and the risen Christ, who is the ruler of creation (3:14; 5:13). The same will be true of the future: God will rightly be worshiped because the new heaven and earth come from his creative action.

In John's vision the first heaven and earth are gone (21:1b). The reason is shown by the repeated use of the words "first" (*prōtos*) and "passed away" (*apēlthan*) in 21:1 and 4: The first heaven and earth that passed away were inextricably linked to other first things that passed away, including death, mourning, crying, and pain. That world was defined by the clash between the reign of God and Christ and that of the destroyers of the earth (11:18; Schüssler Fiorenza 109). In the plague scenes, the earth, sea, and sky were enlisted in a battle that affected the whole created order.

Significantly, Revelation does not picture God destroying the first heaven and earth. Some early Christian writers expected the world to be annihilated by fire (2 Pet 3:10, 12; Justin Martyr, *1 Apol.* 20.1–4; 60.8–9; Justin Martyr, *2 Apol.* 2.2–3; Theophilus, *Autol.* 2.37–38; Minucius Felix, *Octavius* 11.1–3; Augustine, *Civ.* 20.16). Revelation, however, refers only to the demise of the wicked by fire, not to a fiery destruction of the cosmos (Rev 17:16; 19:20; 20:9–10, 14). Portents of judgment included heaven vanishing and mountains and islands being shaken (6:12–17), but destruction was halted and the created order remained (7:1–3). Later, islands fled and mountains disappeared at Babylon's fall (16:20), yet heaven and earth continued (19:11; 20:1, 7–9). Only when God appeared in judgment did earth and heaven flee (20:11). The world in which death was operative is gone (Stephens, *Annihilation*, 242–43).

Theologically, the new heaven and earth represent God's faithfulness to creation, not his abandonment of it. Interpreters often ask whether the new creation is a renewal of the first one (Harrington; Hirschberg, *Das eschatologische*, 212–16; P. Lee, *New*, 268) or a replacement of it (Roloff, "Weltgericht," 123–26; Roloff, "Neuschöpfung"; Vögtle, "Dann"; Giesen; Müller). But these categories are inadequate. On the one hand, there is a clear discontinuity between the first heaven and earth that pass away and the new heaven and earth that appear. The new is not a natural outgrowth of the old; it comes from God's new act of creation. On the other hand, there is also continuity, in that people who live in the present creation have a future in the new creation.

In Revelation, the redemption of the world is like that of human beings. The people who belong to the first heaven and earth are given life by the Creator; they cannot generate life on their own. Then after death they must be given life through resurrection. Such new life does not simply restore things to their previous condition; it is qualitatively different (NOTES and COMMENT on 20:4–6, 12–13). The same thing happens on the cosmic scale when the heaven and earth in which death operates pass away. Heaven and earth lack the capacity to become new; they must be "made new" by God (21:5). Through this new act of creation—analogous to resurrection—they are taken beyond the threat of destruction to participate in God's eternity (Bauckham, *Theology*, 49; Stephens, *Annihilation*, 256–57; Beale; Smalley).

Heaven and earth are made new, yet the sea is "no more" (21:1c). Interpreters often think that the sea symbolizes chaos. Yet Revelation assumes that both sea and land are God's creations and that both are threatened by evil (10:6; 14:7; 12:12). One beast rises from the sea and another from the land (13:1, 11), and the shaft of the demonic abyss opens onto the land rather than the sea (9:1–3). The sea is not a distinctive symbol for evil; rather, it is gone because it held the dead, who have now been raised, so the sea has lost that function. The sea had also been dominated by Babylon's oppressive empire (17:1–6), so the absence of the sea signals the onset of a new order (NOTE on 21:1).

John sees the city descending from heaven (21:2). On the one hand, the new city has the name and title of its predecessor: Jerusalem, the holy city (Neh 11:1; Isa 51:1). On the other hand, New Jerusalem does not refurbish the earthly city; it is of a different order. The foundations and walls of the former Jerusalem were built from the ground up (Neh 2:17; 6:15; Josephus, *J. W.* 5.142–55), but New Jerusalem comes from heaven down, its fantastic size and gemlike structures beyond anything human hands can make (NOTES and COMMENT on Rev 21:9–22:5). Some ancient sources imagined a heavenly Jerusalem that was the counterpart to the earthly city (NOTE on 21:10), and interpreters often assume that Revelation refers to the descent of this preexisting city (Giesen; Lupieri; Roloff). But calling Jerusalem new means that the city—like the new heaven and earth—comes from God's new creative action (Schüssler Fiorenza, *Priester*, 349–50; Söllner, *Jerusalem*, 192).

The city is "made ready as a bride beautifully dressed for her husband" (21:2c). The previous vision cycle concluded by announcing the wedding of the Lamb (19:7). There, the bride was the people of God, who were adorned with bright pure linen (19:8). Now, the bride is a city (21:19–21). The bejeweled appearance of New Jerusalem fits the dual role of city and bride. A bride wore gold and jewels on her wedding day (Ezek 16:10–13; *Jos. As.* 3:6–4:1; 18:5–6; *T. Jud.* 13:5; Pliny the Younger, *Ep.* 5.16.7), and in visions of the future, Jerusalem the city would be built with gems and gold (Isa 54:11–14; Tob 13:16–17). Therefore, the restoration of Zion could be compared to a bride being adorned with jewels (Isa 52:1; 61:10).

The city's descent is like the bride appearing on her wedding day. The marriage was announced in Rev 19:7–9, but only now does the bride come into view. In antiquity, the wedding was when the bride was taken to the groom's home (1 Macc 9:37; Matt 25:1–13; Safrai and Stern, *Jewish*, 758; Plutarch, *Mor.* 271D–E; Justinian, *Dig.* 23.2.5). Here, the imagery shifts: The bridal city *becomes* the home—the dwelling of God with humankind (Rev 21:3; L. Huber, *Like*, 128, 175). God can dwell with people because the relationship will be a covenant, like a marriage. An early form of the marriage covenant said, "She is my wife and I her husband from this day forever" (Kraeling, *Brooklyn*, nos. 2.3–4; 7:4; cf. Tob 7:12). One text says, "I have given you for a bride to Joseph today, and he himself will be your bridegroom forever and ever" (*Jos. As.* 19:5). Similarly, God's intention to take Israel as his wife culminates in his saying, "you are my people," and the people responding "you are my God" (Hos 2:23; cf. 2:16, 20; Mathewson, *New*, 55).

The bridal imagery of Rev 21:2 shapes the way readers are to see their present situations (Deutsch, "Transformation," 111–13). John has already depicted the faithful as maidens, betrothed to the Lamb (14:4). At the present time, he is not visibly with them, but through their faithfulness they are preparing the splendid gown they will wear on the wedding day (19:7–8). What calls them to remain faithful despite pressure to fall into faithlessness—called immorality, or *porneia*—is the promise of the day when they will live with the bridegroom forever (21:2–3). The alternative is to adopt the ways of the whore, who entices people into compromising their commitments for social and economic advantage (17:1–6; 18:9–19). Together, the repulsive portrayal of Babylon the whore and the appealing picture of Jerusalem the bride encourage readers to remain true to God and the Lamb, their betrothed, resisting social, economic, and religious pressures to do otherwise.

The Dwelling of God (21:3–4)

As the city descends, a voice proclaims: "Here is the dwelling of God with humankind. He will dwell with them and they will be his peoples, and God himself will be with them as their God" (21:3). Previous visions pictured God's dwelling (*skēnē*) as a tent or temple in heaven, drawing on the idea of a celestial counterpart to the earthly tent where God dwelled with Israel in the wilderness (NOTE on 15:5). The beast cursed God's dwelling (13:6), and angels processed from it to pour plagues on the beast and its allies (15:5–8), but the defeat of evil and onset of a new creation alters this situation. God's dwelling is no longer in heaven but descends from heaven, and it is no longer a source of judgment but manifests God's presence with humankind. This dwelling is an entire city with characteristics of a sanctuary. According to Ezek 37:27, God said, "My dwelling shall be with them; and I will be their God, and they shall be my people"; then the prophet describes a city with twelve gates and a temple where God's glory is present (Ezek 40:1–5; 43:1–5; 48:30–35). Revelation also identifies a twelve-gated city as God's dwelling, but it is a city that is a thousand times greater than the one in Ezekiel, one where the temple is not a building but is God himself and the Lamb (Rev 21:15–22).

The passage marks the consummation of God's covenant promise, "I will be their God and they will be my people" (Jer 30:22; 31:1; Ezek 37:23). The covenant was repeatedly broken by Israel's faithlessness, so prospects for its realization came from God's persistence (Jer 31:31–34; 32:33, 37–38; Ezek 36:25–28). Sin, judgment, and death constitute barriers between God and people, which must be overcome for God to dwell with them (Lev 26:11–12; Zech 8:3, 8; Exod 29:45). This process is complete in New Jerusalem, where God's dwelling (*skēnē*) is with people and he dwells (*skēnoun*) with them, bringing life and well-being. Earlier it was said that where God made his dwelling, no one would suffer hunger, thirst, or scorching heat—all of which diminish life—for grief would be taken away and the redeemed would drink from the water of life (Rev 7:15–17). Accordingly, in New Jerusalem death, grief, and thirst are gone; only life remains (21:3–6).

Traditionally, God promised to make his dwelling with Israel, but here he makes his dwelling with humankind (21:3a). The word "humankind" (*anthrōpoi*) has referred to unrepentant human beings (9:20), who opposed God (16:9, 21), allied themselves with the beast (16:2), and were subject to divine judgment (9:4–6, 10, 15, 18; 16:8). Yet here they are redeemed. Revelation also departs from the usual formulations by saying that the redeemed will be his "peoples" (*laoi*), rather than his "people" (*laos*, 18:4). Elsewhere, the word "people" is used alongside nations, tribes, language groups, and kings (5:9; 7:9; 10:11; 11:9; 13:7; 14:6; 17:15). "Peoples" in the Greek plural has not been used for the faithful but for the faithless inhabitants of the great world city where Christ was crucified (11:9), who live under the dominion of the whore (17:15). Yet here too it is used for the redeemed.

Some interpreters limit "humankind" and "peoples" to the faithful Christians who come *out of* every nation and conquer by remaining faithful (5:9–10; 21:7), since the faithless have all been condemned to the lake of fire (21:8; Giesen; Müller; Osborne; Herms, *Apocalypse*, 191–94; Mealy, *After*, 228). But others plausibly argue that the New Jerusalem vision extends the hope of redemption to all peoples, to humanity as a whole. The context draws from the most expansive visions in the OT: "I will come and dwell in your midst, says the Lord. Many nations shall join themselves to the Lord on that day, and shall be my people" (Zech 2:10–11; Hirschberg, *Das eschatologische*, 239–41); similarly, the defeat of death will be a blessing for all peoples (Isa 25:6; 56:7). This expansive scope fits a context in which the kings of the earth, who opposed God and were destroyed in battle (Rev 16:14; 17:2; 18:3, 9; 19:18–20), come into New Jerusalem (21:24), and where the nations, who were dominated by evil and destroyed by heavenly fire (13:7; 17:15; 18:3, 23; 20:8–9), find New Jerusalem to be a place of light and healing (21:24, 26; 22:2; Roloff; Bauckham, *Climax*, 311; Mathewson, *New*, 51–52). The main objection is that such an expansive reading of the text seems to undercut Revelation's warnings of judgment (21:8; 22:15).

The issue is how to read Revelation's language. If the vision is taken as a prediction that every human being will be saved in the end, then the warnings of judgment make little sense; conversely, if the visions of judgment are taken as predictions about the complete destruction of kings and nations (19:19–20; 20:7–9), then it is equally hard to explain where the nations and kings in New Jerusalem will come from (21:24, 26). The passage can better be read as an invitation, as a vision of the future to which God *calls* all human beings. Sweeping visions of judgment warn about the devastating consequences of the reign of the beast, and expansive visions of redemption promise a glorious future under the reign of God. Both futures remain open in Revelation; the question is whether people respond to the message with faith or rejection. The vision of redemption includes all humanity because this is the future to which all humanity is *called* (Bauckham, *Theology*, 103; Boring 226–31).

The final words of the unnamed voice give people incentive to persevere, trusting that God "will wipe away every tear from their eyes, and death will be no more, neither mourning nor crying nor pain anymore, for the first things have passed away" (21:4). The language speaks to readers in a world where no one is immune from suffering (C. Müller, "Gott"). Death is pictured as a grim rider, taking life through violence, famine, and disease (6:8; Vanni, *L'Apocalisse*, 263). The height of injustice is the fact that the faithful can be afflicted and killed by those under the sway of evil (2:9–10; 6:9; 13:7–10, 15; 17:6; 18:24). Yet according to Revelation, the readers will not avoid death by abandoning their commitments, because that would subject them to divine judgment (16:10–11). One could adopt the ways of Babylon, but evil will turn against itself when the beast destroys Babylon and brings mourning (*penthos/penthein*) to the city and its allies (18:7–8, 11, 15, 19). Therefore, readers are to look to the future, knowing that although the faithful may suffer death now, death will release them and be abolished (20:13–14).

All Things New (21:5–8)

Finally, God speaks in what is often considered the rhetorical climax of the book (21:5; Aune, *Apocalypticism*, 65; Georgi, "Visionen," 359; Hellholm, "Problem," 44). Although John understands his entire text to be a revelation from with God (1:1), God rarely speaks directly. It is often unclear whether a voice from the throne belongs to God or to another heavenly being (e.g., 16:17; 19:5). Nevertheless, God clearly spoke in the introduction, where he said, "I am the Alpha and the Omega" (1:8). Now he speaks again in similar words so that his speech frames the book.

God's announcement, "See, I am making all things new" (21:5), repeats the theme of a new heaven and earth. God speaks from the throne, where he formerly sat in judgment over the inhabitants of the former creation (20:11), but now he brings about a new creation by his word (Mathewson, *New*, 61). Previously, the hosts in heaven glorified God because he made "all things" (*panta*, 4:11), Here, God announces that he makes "all things new" (*kaina panta*, 21:5). Where Isa 43:19 (MT) declared that God was doing "a new thing," Revelation extends God's action to "all things"—the new heaven, the new earth, the New Jerusalem, and all they contain (Rev 21:1–2).

God's command to John is one word: "Write"; the terseness connotes authority (21:5; Demetrius, *Eloc.* 7). First, writing puts God's commitments in a form that is not to be altered—a point emphasized in 22:18–19. John began to write at Christ's command (1:11; 2:1, 8, 12, etc.), and unnamed voices told him to write of the blessings promised to the faithful (14:13; 19:9). God gives the final command to write, affirming that his words are trustworthy and true (21:5; cf. 19:9; 22:6). The reliability of the message fits God's character (6:10; 15:3). Second, writing allows the words of God and Christ to be communicated in various churches. John was told to "write and send" the message (1:3, 11), and his text is to remain open and accessible to all readers (22:10).

The single word *gegonan* (all is done, 21:6) signals the completion of God's purposes. The introduction to Revelation said that the book would disclose what must soon take place (*genesthai*, 1:1). The narrative progressed through scenes of cosmic conflict, until the final series of plagues occurred and a voice from the throne said, "It is done" (*gegonen*, 16:17). Yet at that point, the action continued with the demise of Babylon, the beast, and Satan. Only when all things have been made new does God say with finality, "All is done" (21:6). His purposes end not with judgment, but with the new creation.

God now declares, "I am the Alpha and the Omega, the beginning and the end" (21:6). Forms of the alpha and omega expression are used for God (1:8; 21:6) and Christ (1:17; 22:13) in the opening and concluding chapters of the book, creating a frame around the whole. Using the word "end" (*eschatos*) for God points to the internal movement of Revelation. G. B. Caird observed that the author takes readers through one series of visions after another, offering glimpses of triumph before quickly moving on: "If from time to time we have been puzzled because he has brought us to the end, which turned out after all to be less than final, we now see why. The end is not an event but a person" (266). The book reveals what "the end" is by revealing who God is. As Richard Bauckham writes: "God precedes all things, as their Creator, and he will bring all things to eschatological fulfillment. He is the origin and goal of all history. He has the first word, in creation, and the last word, in new creation" (*Theology*, 27). The flow of the visions discloses the character of God, who makes all things new (21:5).

Several images depict the redeemed. Initially, they are the thirsty who receive the water of life (21:6b). Metaphorically, thirst designates the need for life with God, who lives forever (4:9–10; 7:2; 10:6; 15:7). Such thirst is fully met when the barriers to life with God—sin, evil, and death—are overcome through resurrection to life in New Jerusalem. In the first creation God made springs of water (14:7), yet these became contaminated vehicles of judgment (8:10–11; 16:4–5). The spring of water in the new creation holds the promise of deathless life in true relationship with God. Some interpreters suggest that the water of life is a present reality that the faithful receive (22:17;

Giesen; Taeger, *Johannesapokalypse*, 35–43), but the verb "will give" in 21:6 points to the future and scenes of New Jerusalem (Satake; Mathewson, *New*, 84–85).

The imagery next shifts to conquering (*nikan*), a verb with military and athletic connotations (21:7; cf. the NOTE on 2:7). Some visions have shown the beast conquering by inflicting death on the faithful (11:7; 13:7), but others have shown a transformed sense of conquering, in which the Lamb conquers by enduring suffering and death (5:5–6). The deaths of the Lamb and those who follow him are victories in part because they show a militant refusal to capitulate to evil. In them, truth triumphs over falsehood (12:11; 15:2; Bauckham, *Theology*, 88–94; C. R. Koester, "Church," 274–76). Yet the final victory is that of life over death, which occurs through resurrection. The messages to the seven churches pointed to this victory with promises to those who conquer. They anticipate Revelation's final chapters, in which the risen conquerors eat from the tree of life (2:7; 22:2) and do not suffer the second death (2:11; 21:7–8). The promise of eating the hidden manna anticipates the final banquet in the new creation (2:17; 19:9; 21:2). The promise of the morning star, which signifies Christ, anticipates sharing his authority in deathless reign (2:28; 22:16). The promises of remaining in the scroll of life (3:6; 21:27), being inscribed with the names of New Jerusalem, God, and Christ (3:12; 21:2; 22:4) and having a place on the throne (3:21; 22:3–5) are fully realized through resurrection to life in God's city.

Next the imagery shifts to inheritance (21:7a). Ordinarily, inheritance began as a promise that a testator would give possessions to heirs in the future, after the testator's death. The testator's commitment to the heirs, who were usually family members, was shown by inscribing the promise in a will (P.Oxy. 490.7; 494.30). Specific items in an ordinary will could include a place for the heirs to live and provisions for their livelihoods (P.Oxy. 104.9–31; 105.5–10; 489.8–9; 493.2–3). Here, inheritance from God is not given after the testator's death but after his abolition of death; the heirs do not dwell in the home the deceased has vacated but in the city where the living God is present; and the sustenance they receive is the water of life (21:1–6). Access to Babylon came through commercial transactions and debased relationships with the whore (18:3, 11–13), but life in New Jerusalem comes honorably, as an inheritance given by God (Royalty, *Streets*, 223).

Inheritance is linked to adoption when God says to the heir, "I will be their God and they will be my sons and daughters" (21:7b). Previously, covenant language had marital overtones, and the redeemed were depicted through feminine imagery as a bride (21:2–3). Here, the covenant language echoes the practice of adoption, and the redeemed are identified through masculine imagery as sons. The word "daughters" is added to the translation because the promise extends to all God's people. In ordinary practice, a boy who was adopted as a son had the right to inherit his father's estate (P.Oxy. 1206.6–10; Cicero, *Dom.* 35; Cicero, *Fam.* 13.19; Gal 4:5–7). Those whom God adopts inherit a share in his city. The language has royal connotations since God said of the heir to David's throne, "I will be a father to him and he shall be a son to me" (2 Sam 7:14; NOTE on Rev 21:7). Jesus is the primary heir since he is God's Son in a singular sense (2:18), but the term "son" is now extended to the redeemed, who share in the reign of God and the Lamb (22:5). Some early Christians told of people being adopted as God's sons and daughters in the present, through the work of the Spirit and the evoking of faith (Rom 8:14–15; Gal 3:26; 4:5–6), but Revelation uses language of adoption and sonship for the new life that comes through resurrection from the dead (cf. Rom 8:23).

Ordinarily, the opposite of inheritance is disinheritance (P.Oxy. 2757 ii.8, 12; 2857.4, 9, 11; *Sel. Pap.* 85), yet here it is an inheritance, or "share," of punishment (Rev 21:8). The author lists eight types of people who come under judgment. Such lists illustrated things to be avoided (cf. 9:20–21; 22:15). Jewish writings also list wrongful behaviors (1QS III, 9–11; Wis 14:25–26; Philo, *Sacr.* 22; Philo, *Post.* 52; Philo, *Conf.* 117), as do early Christian writings (e.g., Mark 7:21–22 par.; Rom 1:29–31; 1 Cor 5:10–11; 6:9–10; Gal 5:19–21; Col 3:5; 1 Tim 1:9–10; 2 Tim 3:2–5; 1 Pet 4:3, 15; *Did.* 2:2–7; *Barn.* 20:1–2; Conzelmann, *1 Corinthians*, 100–1). Like the vice lists in popular philosophy, these reinforced basic principles for conduct (Berger, "Hellenistische," 188–92). In Revelation the list has been shaped to fit the context (Murphy; Osborne; Roloff; Smalley).

Rather than beginning with classic vices, John leads with cowardice and faithlessness, which were issues for Christians facing both overt and subtle pressures to compromise their commitments (Beale; Roloff). The last five items include four—murder, immorality, idolatry, and lying—that are prohibited in the Decalogue (Exod 20:4, 13, 14, 16; cf. Jer 7:9; Mark 10:19; Rom 13:9; Aune), and the final item—sorcery—is forbidden in Exod 22:18. This pattern fits Revelation's emphasis on keeping the commandments of God (Rev 12:17; 14:12). John's list also includes idolatry, a practice that was rejected by Jews and Christians but not by Greeks and Romans, whose religious traditions were polytheistic. Nevertheless, the central place given to the critique of idolatry in Revelation (2:14, 20; 9:20; 13:14–15; 14:9, 11; 15:2; 16:2; 19:20; 20:4; 22:15) shapes the way all other items on the list are understood (Prigent; Giesen, "Lasterkatalog," 218–24).

Contrasts made within Revelation show that behaviors on this list are understood as opposition to God. If the conquerors persevere in the face of evil (2:10 21:7), the *cowardly* are the opposite (21:8). They are like soldiers who abandon their positions and allow the forces of evil to have their way (Plutarch, *Mor.* 73F; 215F). Such cowardice was associated with people who crave luxuries, like those provided by the whore (Plutarch, *Mor.* 32F; Dio Chrysostom, *Disc.* 4.115). The *faithless* are the opposite of faithful witnesses, like Jesus (Rev 1:5; 3:14; 19:11) and Antipas (2:13). Since faithfulness means serving a faithful God in love (2:19; 21:5; 22:6) and resisting violent and deceptive powers (2:10; 13:10; 14:12), John assumes that the faithless support evil. The *vile* share the traits of Babylon the whore, whose vile practices included idolatry and violence against the saints (17:4–6). In contrast, the faithful are undefiled (3:4; 14:4). *Murderers* take another's life. The Lamb and his followers may suffer wrongful death (1:18; 5:6; 6:9), but their opponents perpetrate it (2:10, 13; 11:7; 13:7–10, 15; 17:6; 18:24). The *immoral* engage in illicit sexual relations, although the term also suggests religious infidelity (cf. 2:14, 20; 17:2, 4; 18:3; 19:2). The opposite is to live as chaste followers of the Lamb, who is the bridegroom for his people (14:4; 19:7–8).

Sorcerers illicitly manipulate supernatural forces (9:21; 22:15). The beast from the land performed sorcery by animating a statue of the great beast for people to worship (Note on 13:15), and Babylon's intoxicating wealth and brutality were a kind of sorcery that kept people under her dominion (18:23). True worship means honoring the God who created and justly rules the world (4:11; 14:7; 15:3–4). *Idolaters* practice the opposite, and Revelation insists that idolatry is demonic (9:20). The height of idolatry is deifying the ruling power and honoring it with a statue (13:11–15). Finally, God (6:10; 15:3) and Jesus (3:7, 14; 19:11) are true, whereas Satan (12:9; 20:8), the false prophet (13:14; 16:13; 19:20), and the whore (18:23) seek dominion through deception. The Lamb's followers adhere to the truth rather than a lie (14:5), but *liars* embrace falsehood against the purposes of God (2:2, 9, 20; 3:9; 22:15).

Revelation's list of wrongful actions has an important rhetorical function. The author warns that those who are committed to God in the present will experience conflict with evil, yet they are promised a future with God (21:7). He also warns that those who disassociate themselves from God in the present effectively align themselves with the agents of evil. The warning is that in the future the separation from God will be made permanent. The vision's rhetorical function is to shape the readers' responses in the present. The promises work positively to foster commitment in the confidence that God will prevail. The warnings work negatively by seeking to turn readers away from the forces that draw them away from God. Together, the promises and warnings serve the same end, which is to encourage readers to persevere (13:10; 14:12; Boring; Osborne; Smalley; Rossing, *Choice*, 156).

The warning in 21:8 is set within a broader pattern of judgment. Earlier, it was said that those not inscribed in the scroll of life will go to the lake of fire (20:15), whereas here, those who practice wrongdoing are sent there (21:8). Together, these and other passages create a tension in which people are accountable for what they do and yet are saved by the divine favor conveyed by the scroll of life (COMMENT on 20:11–15). According to Revelation, access to God's city is not reserved for those who have never sinned, but for those who are cleansed by the blood of Christ (7:14; 22:14; Boring; Smalley). The heavenly voice identifies sins in order to move readers to reject sins and to trust in the redemption that Christ provides, while remaining part of the community that conquers by resisting evil.

42. The New Jerusalem (21:9–22:5)

21 ⁹Then one of the seven angels who had the seven offering bowls full of the seven last plagues came and spoke with me. He said, "Come, I will show you the bride, the wife of the Lamb." ¹⁰And he transported me in the Spirit to a great high mountain, and he showed me the holy city, Jerusalem, coming down out of heaven from God. ¹¹It had the glory of God. Its radiance was like a jewel, like jasper that was clear as crystal. ¹²It had a great high wall with twelve gates. By the gates were twelve angels, and on the gates were written the names of the twelve tribes of the sons of Israel: ¹³on the east three gates and on the north three gates and on the south three gates and on the west three gates. ¹⁴The wall of the city has twelve foundations and on them are the twelve names of the twelve apostles of the Lamb.

¹⁵The one who spoke with me had a gold measuring rod with which to measure the city and its gates and its wall. ¹⁶Now the city is laid out as a square. Its length is the same as its width. He measured the city with the rod, twelve thousand stadia. The length and width and height are equal. ¹⁷He also measured

the thickness of its wall, 144 cubits as a person—or rather an angel—measures things. [18]The wall was built of jasper and the city was pure gold, like pure glass. [19]The foundations of the city wall are adorned with every kind of jewel. The first foundation is jasper, the second sapphire, the third chalcedony, the fourth emerald, [20]the fifth sardonyx, the sixth carnelian, the seventh chrysolite, the eighth beryl, the ninth topaz, the tenth chrysoprase, the eleventh jacinth, the twelfth amethyst. [21]And the twelve gates are twelve pearls, each one of the gates was of a single pearl. And the main street of the city is pure gold, as transparent as glass.

[22]Now I did not see a temple in the city, because its temple is the Lord God Almighty and the Lamb. [23]The city does not need the sun or the moon to shine on it, for the glory of God is its light and its lamp is the Lamb. [24]The nations will walk by its light, and the kings of the earth will bring their glory into it. [25]Its gates will never be shut by day, and there will be no night there. [26]They will bring the glory and the honor of the nations into it. [27]But nothing common will enter it, nor anyone who does what is vile and deceitful, but only those who are written in the Lamb's scroll of life.

22 [1]Then he showed me the river of the water of life, bright as crystal. It was flowing from the throne of God and the Lamb [2]through the middle of the city's main street. On each side of the river is the tree of life, which produces twelve crops of fruit, bearing its fruit each month, and the leaves of the tree are for the healing of the nations. [3]And there will be no curse anymore. The throne of God and the Lamb shall be in it, and his servants will worship him. [4]They will see his face, and his name will be on their foreheads. [5]Night will be no more. They will not need the light of a lamp or the light of the sun, for the Lord God will shine on them, and they will reign forever and ever.

NOTES

21:9. *Then one of the seven angels who had the seven offering bowls full of the seven last plagues came.* The seven angels who poured out offering bowls brought plagues of sores, rivers of blood, scorching heat, and darkness on the beast's allies and showed kings gathering for disastrous war (16:1–16). But here, one of those angels reveals the opposite: the city that offers healing, the river of life, the light of God's glory, and hope for kings and nations (21:23–22:5).

and spoke with me. He said, "Come, I will show you the bride, the wife of the Lamb." In Ezek 40:4 an angelic figure showed the prophet a vision of the temple and city. In similar texts a figure shows a seer visions of a new (2Q24 1 3; 4Q554 1 II, 15) or heavenly (*Apoc. Zeph.* 3:1; 5:1–4) Jerusalem. Revelation uses both the words "wife" (*gynē*, 19:7; 21:9; cf. *Jos. As.* 21:1) and "bride" (*nymphē*, Rev 21:2) for the Lamb's betrothed. The bridal imagery functions in several ways:

1. It completes the depiction of Jesus' followers, who at present are like betrothed maidens, devoted to the Lamb, whose deeds of righteousness adorn them like a bridal

gown (14:4; 19:7–8; Zimmermann, "Nuptial"). The descent of New Jerusalem is like the wedding, when the bride is taken to the bridegroom's home. The twist in John's vision is that the bride is not simply taken to her groom's dwelling—she is the dwelling, the city were God dwells with humankind (21:2–3).

2. The Lamb's wife (*gynē*) is New Jerusalem, which is the opposite of Babylon the whore, the woman (*gynē*) who rode the beast (17:3). On the contrast, see the COMMENT.

3. Less directly, New Jerusalem continues the story of the woman (*gynē*) who gave birth to the Messiah and was persecuted by Satan (12:1–6, 13–17). For the persecuted mother, God's action takes the form of preservation in the face of evil, but for the bride, the form is endless life in the presence of God. Together, the women in Rev 12 and 21 depict the present struggle and future glory, respectively, of God's people (Humphrey, *Ladies*, 103–18; Tavo, *Woman*, 338–41).

21:10. *And he transported me in the Spirit to a great high mountain.* The words "in the Spirit" indicate a spiritual state brought about by God's Spirit (NOTE on 1:10; cf. 4:2; 17:3). A mountain was the place where Moses saw the pattern of the tabernacle (Exod 24:15–25:10) and where later tradition said that Zephaniah saw the heavenly city (*Apoc. Zeph.* 3:1–3; 5:1–6). Closest to Revelation is Ezekiel being taken to a mountain where he saw a glorified Jerusalem that was located on a mountain (Ezek 40:2). Some think Revelation's New Jerusalem is also on a mountain, fulfilling the promise that Zion would be the highest of mountains, where God would reign and the nations would worship (Ps 48:1–3; Isa 2:2; 24:23; Joel 3:17; Mic 4:1–2; Zech 14:1–11; *1 En.* 25:3; *Jub.* 4:26; Caesarius; Bede; Bauckham, *Theology*, 132–33; Mathewson, *New*, 99). Such connections are not entirely clear in the text, however.

and he showed me the holy city, Jerusalem, coming down out of heaven. Revelation's vision of New Jerusalem draws on prophetic images of the city's glorification. Some prophets anticipated a refurbishing of the earthly city (Jer 30:18–22; 31:38–40). Others depicted an earthly city whose splendor exceeded that of ordinary cities. In Isaiah the glorified Jerusalem belongs to the new heaven and earth (Isa 65:17–19). The city is adorned with jewels (54:11–12), its beauty like that of a bride (61:10). It is like Eden (51:3), radiant with God's glory (60:1–2). God's people gather there, and the nations come to its light, for its gates will always be open (51:11; 60:3–5; 60:11). Ezekiel tells of a square city, with twelve gates for the twelve tribes (Ezek 48:30–35). In it is a temple where God's glory is manifest (43:1–5). A river flows from the temple, and trees bear fruit each month, their leaves bringing healing (47:1, 12). Zechariah says that God will be a wall of fire around the city and will manifest his glory there (Zech 2:5). The redeemed gather in it, the nations come to it, and its temple is pure (8:3, 20–23; 14:16, 21). Living water flows from the city in endless day (14:7–8). Revelation includes all of these elements, except the temple, so New Jerusalem fulfills promises made in the prophets (P. Lee, *New*, 6–52).

Other Jewish writings develop these motifs. Some pictured the earthly city robed in eternal glory (Bar 5:1–9; cf. *Pss. Sol.* 11:1–9; Sir 36:19). Tobit pictures Jerusalem built with jewels and gold, where God's people gather and the nations come to its light (Tob 13:9, 11, 16). Yet unlike Revelation, Tobit envisions an earthly city with a temple (14:5–7). In the Dead Sea text known as the *Description of New Jerusalem*, an angel shows the author a city twenty by fourteen miles in size. Its walls are built of gold and jewels (4Q554 2 II, 13–15) and its twelve gates are named for the sons of Israel (4Q554 1 I, 13–II, 10). Its streets are laid out in a grid and paved with white stones (5Q15 1 I, 6–7). It may have a spring (4Q554 4 1–2). But in contrast to Revelation, this city has a temple with gold walls (11Q18 10 I, 2). It is not clear whether the city plays a role in Israel's future battle against the nations (4Q554 2 II, 14–22; García Martínez, *Qumran*, 201) or comes from Israel's triumph over them (DiTommaso, *Dead*, 173–75). A different development of biblical motifs appears in the *Temple Scroll*, in which the ideal sanctuary of the present age—rather than the city—has twelve gates named for the sons of Israel (11Q19 XXXIX, 12–13; cf. 4Q365a 2 II, 1–4; García Martínez, "Temple"). One of the *Sibylline Oracles*, written after the destruction of the temple in 70 CE, envisions the city being built on a huge scale, its walls extending to the coast. It will be more brilliant than the sun, with a temple and tower that touch the clouds, though in contrast to the city in Revelation, it remains an earthly city (*Sib. Or.* 5:249–55, 420–27; P. Lee, *New*, 197–205).

Some writers tell of a Jerusalem that already exists in heaven and will be revealed at the end of the age. In *1 En.* 24–26 the tree of life is linked to a primordial Jerusalem, which anticipates the future paradisiacal Jerusalem where the redeemed will live (cf. *Jub.* 4:26; *T. Dan* 5:12). Later, the earthly Jerusalem is shown being removed and replaced by a new city (*1 En.* 90:28–29). Some texts assume that the new city comes from heaven, though this is not clear (Nickelsburg, *1 Enoch*, 312–18, 404–5). Jewish apocalypses written after the fall of Jerusalem in 70 CE say that God created the true Jerusalem and paradise at the dawn of time, and when the earthly city falls, the heavenly one is preserved by God (*2 Bar.* 4:1–7; *4 Bar.* 5:35). In these sources the present existence of a heavenly Jerusalem gives hope for the city's future restoration (*2 Bar.* 6:9; 32:4; *4 Ezra* 8:52; 13:36). In *4 Ezra* the city is personified as a woman (*4 Ezra* 10:27–28, 44–45, 53–54), like the imagery in Revelation (Rev 21:2, 10). But in *4 Ezra* 7:26 the city is revealed before the resurrection and last judgment rather than after it, as in Revelation. More importantly, Revelation does not envision the restoration of Jerusalem but centers on a city of another order in the new creation (Hirschberg, *Das eschatologische*, 224–29; Söllner, *Jerusalem*, 262–96).

Among Christians, Paul symbolically equates the earthly Jerusalem of the present age with Jewish law and connects the heavenly Jerusalem to the promise of deliverance in Christ. For him, those who believe the promise belong to the heavenly city (Gal 4:26; Phil 3:20). Hebrews calls the heavenly Jerusalem the city that is to come, which will remain after the created order is shaken at the end of the age. The faithful enter the city through resurrection, which is also true in Revelation (Heb 11:10, 16; 12:22–24; C. R. Koester, *Hebrews*, 486, 544–53). Interpreters often assume that Revelation pictures a Jerusalem that now exists in heaven coming down to earth in the new age (Giesen; Lupieri; Roloff). But Revelation is distinctive. None of the other Jewish or Christian sources clearly depicts a heavenly city descending to earth as Revelation does (DiTommaso, *Dead*, 123–49). Moreover, Revelation called Jerusalem "new" (Rev 21:2), emphasizing that the city—like the new heaven and earth—comes from God's new creative action (Schüssler Fiorenza, *Priester*, 349–50).

In Revelation the future Jerusalem both resembles and differs from its earthly predecessor. In terms of worship, Jerusalem was where the temple was built (1 Kgs 8:27–30; Ezra 5:2; 6:14–15). The New Jerusalem is the consummate place of worship, yet it has no temple edifice, for God and the Lamb are its temple (Rev 21:22; 22:3). In terms of governance, Jerusalem was where kings ruled over Israel (2 Sam 5:5–9; 1 Kgs 11:42). In New Jerusalem the throne of God and the Lamb is central, and all the redeemed share in their reign (Rev 22:3–5).

from God. Ancient cities honored the memory of their founders with coins and monuments: for example, Romulus and Remus at Rome (Livy, *Rom. Hist.* 1.6.4), an Athenian king's son at Ephesus (Strabo, *Geographica* 14.1.3), an Amazon at Smyrna (Strabo, *Geographica* 12.3.21), a Hellenistic king at Philadelphia (W. Gasque, *ABD* 5:304–5). God is the founder of New Jerusalem and is therefore worthy of the highest honor from its citizens (cf. Heb 11:10).

21:11. *It had the glory of God. Its radiance was like a jewel, like jasper that was clear as crystal.* The eschatological Jerusalem and its temple were pictured as the place of God's glory, and Revelation fulfills this hope (Ezek 43:1–5; Zech 2:5; Isa 60:1–3; cf. Bar 5:1–2; *Pss. Sol.* 17:31). The word *phōstēr* usually refers to a light-giving body. Therefore, some interpreters think that the *phōstēr* is Christ himself, since he is the city's lamp and morning star (Rev 21:23; 22:16; Oecumenius; Primasius; Andreas; Vanni, "La dimension"). But more probable is that the city's *phōstēr* is the "radiance" of its own foundations, walls, and streets.

21:12. *It had a great high wall.* City walls were monumental structures that conveyed a sense of grandeur (Strabo, *Geographica* 16.1.5; Aelius Aristides, *Orations* 25.7; Owens, *City*, 75, 87–88, 121). For earthly Jerusalem to lack walls was a disgrace and to have fine walls showed honor (Neh 2:17; 6:15–16; 1 Macc 4:60; Isa 26:1; Josephus, *J.W.* 5.142–48). Ephesus, Smyrna, Pergamum, and Laodicea had walls dating to pre-Roman times (Strabo, *Geographica* 14.1.4, 21). Rome's walls were considered sacred and inviolable (Plutarch, *Mor.* 271A). New Jerusalem's massive walls reflect the incomparable majesty of God. Its qualities of jasper and crystal are like those of the divine presence John described earlier (Rev 4:3, 6). Traditionally, a wall provided protection (Josephus, *J.W.* 2.218; Caesar, *Bell. civ.* 2.2), but when New Jerusalem descends, all of God's opponents have been defeated, and the gates are always open.

with twelve gates. New Jerusalem's twelve gates do not correspond to those of the historical Jerusalem but to the city envisioned by Ezekiel (Ezek 48:30–34; cf. 4Q365a 2 II, 1–4; 4Q554 1 I, 13 to II, 10; 11Q19 XXXIX, 12–13). Like walls, gates could be monumental. Ephesus had the Magnesia, Koressos, and harbor gates around its perimeter (I.Eph 27.424–25) and another gate by the agora (see Figure 3; NOTE on Rev 21:13). Pergamum had an imposing main gate (Radt, *Pergamon*, 80–83), and Laodicea had several gates, including a new one dedicated to Domitian (I.Laod 24). John depicts gates in New Jerusalem that are beyond anything given by an earthly benefactor.

By the gates were twelve angels. The primary role of the angels is to signal the presence of God (Satake). Some interpreters think they also prevent evildoers from entering (Rev 21:27), as gatekeepers did in the earthly Jerusalem and its temple (1 Chr 23:5; 26:1–9; Neh 3:29) and as Isa 62:6 says, "Upon your walls, O Jerusalem, I have posted sentinels." The LXX identified the sentinels as guards, and later tradition construed them as angels, like those said to control the heavenly gates (*Exod. Rab.* 18:5; *Mart. Asc. Isa.* 10:27). Just as cherubim once barred the way to the tree of life in Eden, one might imagine them guarding the tree in New Jerusalem (Gen 3:24; Rev 22:2; Aune; Rowland; Smalley; Fekkes, *Isaiah*, 264–65; Mathewson, *New*, 103–4). Nevertheless, the idea that the angels guard the gates is unlikely, since the city descends after the devil and the wicked have been banished and evil no longer threatens. Moreover, the city's gates remain open for the nations (Rev 21:25).

and on the gates were written the names of the twelve tribes of the sons of Israel. Historically, Jerusalem's gates were named for tribes like Ephraim (Neh 8:16) and Benjamin (Jer 37:13), as well as other things, such as the Corner Gate (2 Kgs 14:13), Valley Gate (2 Chr 26:9), Dung Gate (Neh 2:13), and Sheep Gate (Neh 3:1; John 5:2). The city envisioned by Ezekiel had gates named for all twelve tribes (Ezek 48:30–35). Later depictions of a restored Jerusalem or temple also name gates for the twelve tribes in varying sequences (4Q365a 2 II, 1–4; 4Q554 1 I, 13 to II, 10; 11Q19 XXXIX, 12–13; XL, 11 to XLI, 11; Peuch, "Names"). Revelation includes a distinctive list of tribal names in 7:4–8, but not here.

21:13. *on the east three gates and on the north three gates and on the south three gates and on the west three gates.* Three city gates face each of the four principal directions, as in Ezek 48:30–34, though the sequence of directions in Revelation follows Ezek 42:15–20, which deals with the temple. Here, as elsewhere, Revelation uses temple patterns for the city (Mathewson, *New*, 101–2). Some interpreters suggest that the directions have cosmological significance, since heaven was said to have twelve gates for the winds (*1 En.* 34–36) and the zodiac had twelve parts (Müller). More plausible is that the directions show that New Jerusalem is perfectly oriented without conveying special cosmological meaning.

21:14. *The wall of the city has twelve foundations and on them are the twelve names of the twelve apostles of the Lamb.* Foundations of an ordinary city wall were laid on bedrock. The lower courses were below ground level, but the upper courses were often visible (Vitruvius, *Arch.* 1.5.1, 7; Luke 6:48). In Revelation the city descends from heaven, so its entire foundation is visible. John seems to picture twelve large foundation stones. Metaphorically, those who established or led a community were its "foundations." At Qumran this term was used for the twelve men on the community council (1QS VIII, 1–6; XI, 8), who were also identified as the gemlike foundation stones of New Jerusalem (4Q154 1 I, 1–2). Early Christians considered Christ (1 Cor 3:11) and the apostles and prophets to be their foundations (Eph 2:20), and Revelation follows tradition by placing the apostles' names on the foundation stones of New Jerusalem.

21:15. *The one who spoke with me had a gold measuring rod to measure the city and its gates and its wall.* In Ezekiel the angelic figure uses a rod, or literally a reed, that was six long cubits in size (Ezek 40:3) and in the DSS one that is seven cubits (4Q554 1 III, 18–19; 5Q15 1 I, 2–4). Both of these are a little over ten feet in length. In Roman times, measuring reeds ranged from seven and a half to nine and a half feet (Heron, *Geometria* 4.11; 21.13). In Revelation, however, the reed is angelic in size (Rev 21:17). Previously, John was given a rod to measure the temple and city that symbolized God's people. In that context measuring signified preservation (11:1–2). Here, the measuring reveals the perfection of the city.

21:16. *Now the city is laid out as a square. Its length is the same as its width.* "Four-sided" (*tetragōnos*) suggests completeness or perfection (Plato, *Prot.* 344a; Aristotle, *Rhet.* 3.11.2). Some ancient cities and sacred areas had this form (Strabo, *Geographica* 12.4.7; I.Smyr 753.31). Ezekiel envisioned a square city (Ezek 48:16) and holy of holies in the temple (41:4). Babylon was square (Herodotus, *Historiae* 1.178), and Rome once had quadrilateral form (Dionysius of Halicarnassus, *Ant. rom* 2.65.3; Plutarch, *Rom.* 9.4). The square shape was used for Roman military camps and some provincial cities (Josephus, *J. W.* 3.77; Owens, *City*, 110, 127, 135). Nineveh was rectangular (Diodorus Siculus, *Libr.* 2.3.2). New Jerusalem gives the ideal form cosmic dimensions (Kraybill, *Imperial*, 211–13; U. Sim, *Das himmlische*, 103).

He measured the city with the rod, twelve thousand stadia. A stade (*stadios*) was the length of a stadium, about 600 feet, so 12,000 stadia is about 1,500 miles. Some Jewish texts pictured an idealized Jerusalem as a rectangle measuring 14 by 20 miles (4Q554 1 I–II; García Martínez, *Qumran*, 186), or as a city extending to Joppa, 35 miles away (*Sib. Or.* 5:252), or to Damascus, 140 miles away (*Cant. Rab.* 7.5.3). In the second century CE it was said that Rome's walls figuratively enclosed the world, from Britain to Mesopotamia (Aelius Aristides, *Orations* 26.82), and a third-century CE Jewish source pictured Rome as a square measuring 9,000 stadia on each side, which is three-fourths the size of New Jerusalem (*b. Meg.* 6b; Aune). It is not clear that readers would have known such claims concerning Rome, but New Jerusalem's huge size gives it a grandeur that surpasses that of earthly cities.

Revelation uses the number twelve for God's people, including the tribes and apostles (Rev 21:12, 14). The number 12,000 was used for those sealed out of the twelve tribes of Israel (7:4–8). Using this number for the dimensions of New Jerusalem is appropriate, since the city signifies the future blessedness of those who have been sealed (Giesen; Bauckham, *Climax*, 399).

The length and width and height are equal. The city wall is 12,000 stadia, or 1,500 miles, high. In comparison, the wall of first-century Jerusalem was said to be 20 cubits high (30 feet; Josephus, *J. W.* 5.155). Some writers told of city walls ranging from 70 cubits high (105 feet; Jdt 1:2) to 200 royal cubits high (340 feet; Herodotus, *Historiae* 1.178). In the DSS New Jerusalem's wall is 49 cubits high (73.5 feet; 4Q554 2 II, 14). The closest analogy to the extraordinary height in Revelation is a vision of Jerusalem with a tower reaching the clouds (*Sib. Or.* 5:424–25).

The distinctive aspect of New Jerusalem is that it is a cube, whose height equals its length and width. The shape makes the city comparable to the holy of holies in Israel's sanctuaries, which were cubic: 10 cubits per side in the tabernacle (15 feet; Exod 26:15–16; Josephus, *Ant.* 3.115, 122) and 20 cubits in Solomon's temple (30 feet; 1 Kgs 6:20; cf. Ezek 41:4). Like the holy of holies, the walls of New Jerusalem are covered with gold (1 Kgs 6:20; Rev 21:18). Where God's glory once filled the holy of holies, it now fills New Jerusalem (Exod 40:34; 1 Kgs 8:11; Rev 21:23–24). The massive size of the cubic city exhibits holiness on a cosmic scale.

21:17. *He also measured the thickness of its wall, 144 cubits.* After measuring the city's length, width, and height, the angel measures the wall's thickness (Aune; Osborne; Satake), which is why the unit changes from a stade (600 feet) to a cubit (1.5 feet). The action is like that in Ezekiel, in which the angelic figure measures both the thickness and length or height of walls (Ezek 40:5; 41:5, 9, 12; cf. 4Q554 2 II, 13–14). Thickness was noted in descriptions of the walls of Jerusalem (Josephus, *J. W.* 5.154), Babylon (Herodotus, *Historiae* 1.178; Strabo, *Geographica* 16.1.5), and other cities (Jdt 1:2; Vitruvius, *Arch.* 1.5.3). Although some interpreters think that here the angel measures the wall's height (Beale; Giesen; Harrington), it is unlikely that the seer would say that the city's height equaled its width (12,000 stadia) and then add that its "great high wall"

(Rev 21:12) was only 144 cubits tall. A textual variant could suggest that the angel measures the city' "edge" (Hernández, "Scribal"), though the thickness of the wall seems to be the point.

as a person—or rather an angel—measures things. A standard cubit was the distance from the elbow to the tip of the middle finger. According to the measure of a person (Deut 3:11), this would be about 18 inches. The figure in Ezek 40:5 uses a longer cubit, about 20.4 inches in length. Some interpreters take John to mean that the angel was using the ordinary human measurement, which would mean that the wall was 144 cubits, or 216 feet, thick—remarkably thin for a wall 1,500 miles long (NIV, NRSV; Mounce; Osborne). Most acknowledge that the 144 cubits is symbolic and need not be architecturally plausible (Giesen; Roloff). Yet it seems likely that John gives cohesion to his symbolism by explaining that what he first identified as human measurement was actually angelic measurement—the expression "which is" (*ho estin*) signals a transferred meaning (cf. Rev 4:5; 5:6, 8). Since an angel can stand on both land and sea (10:1–2), the 144 angelic cubits would be incomparably larger than ordinary human measure and therefore appropriate for the size of New Jerusalem's wall (Caird).

21:18. *The wall was built of jasper and the city was pure gold, like pure glass.* The rare word *endōmēsis* was used in inscriptions that publicized how a sanctuary or other structure was built (I.Smyr 753.30; I.Did 112.20; I.Strat 112.4; I.Trall 147a.9). John uses it for the material in the wall of New Jerusalem. The main text behind Rev 21:18–21 is Isa 54:11–12, a poem about God's intention to restore Zion as a city set with jewels. Another text pictured God himself as a wall of fire around the city (Zech 2:1–5). In Revelation the wall is made of jasper, a stone with God's own radiance (Rev 4:3). Jasper was a green-, blue-, purple-, or rose-colored gem (Pliny the Elder, *Nat.* 37.115–18). The city is also made of gold, which fulfills hopes found in some texts about New Jerusalem (Tob 13:16; cf. 4Q5542 II, 15; 11Q18 10 I, 1).

21:19. *The foundations of the city walls are adorned with every kind of jewel.* In the Roman world benefactors built temples, towers, and other structures "from the foundations" and "adorned" them (I.Eph 429.2; 438.8; TAM 2/408.10–11). But adorning foundations with gems was extraordinary. Precious stones and metals were normally reserved for the upper structure (1 Chr 29:2; Josephus, *J.W.* 5.201–13, 222). In New Jerusalem the foundations themselves are gems, giving grandeur of another order. Such foundations would be laid by God (Isa 54:11; *4 Ezra* 10:27; Heb 11:10).

21:19b–20. Having said that gems adorn New Jerusalem's foundations, John now says that each foundation stone *is* a huge gem. The main background for this vision is from Isa 54:11: "I am about to set your stones in antimony [LXX carbuncle, ruby], and lay your foundations with sapphires." The stones listed have affinities with two OT texts. First, the high priest's breastplate had twelve stones set in gold and arranged in four rows, each stone representing one of the twelve tribes (Exod 28:17–20; 39:10–13). Second, the King of Tyre is said to have been in Eden, adorned with jewels set in gold (Ezek 28:13). The MT of Ezekiel then lists nine of the stones that also appear on the high priest's breastplate, though in a different order. The LXX expands Ezekiel's list to twelve and includes the same gems as in Exodus. Nevertheless, the stones in the LXX do not always match those in the MT, and the sequence differs. Comparing lists of stones (Table 6) is difficult because it is not clear how some Hebrew and Greek terms should be understood (Söllner, *Jerusalem*, 216–24). The last several stones listed in Table 6 do

Table 6. The Stones in New Jerusalem's Foundations

Rev 21:19–20, New Jerusalem	Exod 28:17 (MT), High priest/tribes	Ezek 28:13 (MT), Eden	Exod/Ezek (LXX)
Jasper	Jasper	Jasper	Jasper
Sapphire	Sapphire	Sapphire	Sapphire
Emerald	Emerald	Emerald	Emerald
Carnelian	Carnelian	Carnelian	Carnelian
Beryl	Beryl?	Beryl?	Beryl
Topaz	Topaz	Topaz	Topaz
Amethyst	Amethyst	—	Amethyst
Jacinth	Jacinth?	—	Ligurion?
Chrysolite	Moonstone?	Moonstone?	Chrysolite
Chalcedony	Agate?	—	Agate
Sardonyx	Onyx	Onyx	Onyx
Chrysoprase	Turquoise?	Turquoise?	Carbuncle

Note: Items are arranged by type rather than sequence.

not seem to have counterparts in the MT or LXX lists. The lists in other Jewish sources show a similar variety. It seems likely that John freely adapted the OT lists.

The primary function of the list of gems comes from its cumulative effect: Naming gem after gem conveys the city's overwhelming majesty. The list also magnifies the hope for Jerusalem's glorification. Some texts said the city would one day be built with jewels, mentioning just a few types of gems (Isa 54:11–12; Tob 13:16), but Revelation's list is longer, suggesting that God would both fulfill and surpass expectations for the future. Other interpretive dimensions emerge when the gems are related to key themes in the literary context:

1. Bridal imagery. An elegant bride would wear jewels on her wedding day (Ezek 16:10–13; *Jos. As.* 3:6–4:1; 18:5–7; *T. Jud.* 13:5; Pliny the Younger, *Ep.* 5.16.7). New Jerusalem is the bride of the Lamb, and she is adorned for her life with the Lamb (Rev 21:2, 9).

2. Priestly imagery. In New Jerusalem all of God's people are priests and have his name inscribed on their foreheads, as the high priest did on his turban (1:6; 5:10; 20:6; 22:4; cf. Exod 28:38). The entire city bears the names of the tribes and is filled with God's presence. Therefore, it is appropriate that the city itself have twelve gems, since Israel's high priest wore a breastplate with twelve gems, which represented the twelve tribes, when he came into God's presence in the sanctuary (Exod 28:17–21).

3. Creation imagery. The twelve stones associated with Eden fit a context that locates the tree and river of life in New Jerusalem. The imagery of creation is transformed to fit God's new creation, which is the context for the city. There was some overlapping of priestly and paradisiacal traditions, since the high priest's breastplate was said to include stones from Havilah, a place associated with Eden, and the stones were to shine with glory at the end of the age (*L.A.B.* 26:12–13; *2 Bar.* 6:7–9).

Some interpreters link the stones to the twelve parts of the zodiac (Malina; Müller; cf. Philo, *Mos.* 2.133; Josephus, *Ant.* 3.186), but the context does not develop this connection (Bergmeier, "Jerusalem," 104–6; Reader, "Twelve," 451–54).

The first foundation is jasper, the second sapphire, the third chalcedony, the fourth emerald.

Jasper referred to precious stones in various colors ranging from green to blue, purple, and rose (Pliny the Elder, *Nat.* 37.115–18). In Revelation this stone characterizes God (Rev 4:3) and the city wall (21:11, 18; Isa 54:12 LXX). Sapphires were described as blue and heavenly, with gold specks that made them glitter (Pliny the Elder, *Nat.* 37.119–20; Philostratus, *Vit. Apoll.* 1.25.3). They were associated with God's presence (Exod 24:10; Ezek 1:26; 10:1) and with glorified Jerusalem's foundations and gates (Isa 54:11 LXX; Tob 13:17; 2Q24 3 2). Chalcedony may have been a stone that was cloudy with a whitish or grayish hue (Pliny the Elder, *Nat.* 37.116). The gem called a *smaragdos* had an intense green color, so it could be called an emerald (Pliny the Elder, *Nat.* 37.62–75). It was to be part of glorified Jerusalem's gates (Tob 13:17).

21:20. *the fifth sardonyx, the sixth carnelian, the seventh chrysolite, the eighth beryl, the ninth topaz, the tenth chrysoprase, the eleventh jacinth, the twelfth amethyst.* Sardonyx had tan and white layers, which were suitable for cameos (Juvenal, *Satirae* 6.380; Pliny the Elder, *Nat.* 37.86–89). Carnelian was known for its red color, which made it suitable for God's presence (Pliny the Elder, *Nat.* 37.105–6; Rev 4:3). Chrysolite was golden like the sun (Pliny the Elder, *Nat.* 37.126; Diodorus Siculus, *Libr.* 2.52.3). Beryl, with its rich green hue, was similar to an emerald (Pliny the Elder, *Nat.* 37.76; Juvenal, *Satirae* 5.38). Topaz was a "pleasing transparent stone, similar to glass," which sparkled with a golden luster (Diodorus Siculus, *Libr.* 3.39.5; Strabo, *Geographica* 16.4.6). Chrysoprase was golden with a greenish hue (Pliny the Elder, *Nat.* 37.77, 113). Jacinth was blue or perhaps rose-colored (Achilles Tatius, *Leuc. Clit.* 2.11.3). Amethyst was deep red or purple (Pliny the Elder, *Nat.* 37.80, 121).

21:21. *And the twelve gates are twelve pearls, each one of the gates was of a single pearl.* Ordinary pearls were rather small, which made them suitable for rings, earrings, and ornaments on clothing (Pliny the Elder, *Nat.* 9.114, 116; 1 Tim 2:9). Yet pearls were said to be worth as much or more than gold (Athenaeus, *Deipnosophistae* 3.93b; Arrian, *Indica* 8.13). People paid exorbitant prices for them (Suetonius, *Jul.* 50.2; Matt 13:45–46; Pliny the Elder, *Nat.* 9.106; 37.204). Pearls the size of gates would be inconceivably large and costly (cf. *1 En.* 18:7).

Jan Fekkes (*Isaiah*, 241–44) suggests that Revelation's imagery here stems from Isa 54:12, which said that Jerusalem's gates would be "stones of *'eqdah*." Some ancient interpreters related this rare word to the Hebrew root *qdh*, which means "kindle" and thus something sparkling. Accordingly, translators pictured the gates as crystal (LXX), carbuncles (*Tg.* Isa 54:12), or sapphires and emeralds (Tob 13:16). Alternatively, the root *qdh* in Aramaic means to "bore," or hollow out, so other translators of Isa 54:12 pictured stones that were bored or carved (Aquila; Symmachus; Vulgate). Since holes were bored into the pearls used in jewelry, John may have pictured the gates of pearl this way. A similar interpretation appears in rabbinic texts (*Midr. Ps.* 87:2; *b. B. Bat.* 75a; *b. Sanh.* 100a).

And the main street of the city is pure gold, as transparent as glass. Streets in ancient cities typically were not paved, and as such, they were liable to be dusty and muddy.

Paving a street was costly, but it made movement easier and contributed to a city's pride (Strabo, *Geographica* 14.1.37; Owens, *City*, 157). At Ephesus the main street was paved in honor of Artemis and the emperor Domitian (see Figure 6; I.Eph 3008; cf. I.Smyr 826). In New Jerusalem the paving is a gift from God (Tob 13:16). Like the gold flooring in the holy of holies, it fits the place of God's presence (1 Kgs 6:30). In Revelation's visionary world, God's witnesses were slain in "the main street [*plateia*] of the great city," which represents humanity alienated from God (Rev 11:8). But the street of New Jerusalem holds the promise of life. There are several ways to picture the street:

1. The city's main street. This is the most plausible interpretation. Cities like Ephesus and Pergamum had one central street connecting different parts of the city (I.Eph 3071.22; Radt, *Pergamon*, 83; Owens, *City*, 80, 87; cf. Josephus, *J.W.* 1.425). When the Romans aided Sardis in rebuilding after the earthquake of 17 CE, the city constructed a new colonnaded main street. In Smyrna the main street was called the Golden Way (Aelius Aristides, *Orations* 17.10; 18.6). A central thoroughfare was typical of ancient cities, and in some a second major street ran perpendicular to it (Strabo, *Geographica* 17.1.8, 10; Diodorus Siculus, *Libr.* 17.52.3). Given the symmetry of New Jerusalem, John seems to picture one golden street extending from the central gate on one side of the city to the central gate on the opposite side (Osborne; Smalley).

2. The city's open square. In the OT the square was inside the city gate (Gen 19:2; Judg 19:15; 2 Sam 21:12; 2 Chr 32:6), and in Greco-Roman cities the agora, or forum, was in the heart of the city (Aune). Accordingly, one might envision a wide golden street extending across New Jerusalem and opening out into a golden plaza in the city center (U. Sim, *Das himmlische*, 39–40, 115–16; cf. *Apoc. Zeph.* 5:3).

3. A collective term for all the city's streets (Beale; Harrington). This approach, although it is the least plausible, fits Tob 13:16, which expected Jerusalem's "streets" to be paved with ruby and stones of Ophir (cf. the white paving stones in 4Q554 1 II, 16–23; 5Q15 1 I, 6). But Rev 21:21 envisions one golden avenue.

21:22. *Now I did not see a temple in the city.* Jewish texts regularly expected a new or glorified Jerusalem to have a temple (Ezek 40–48; Zech 14:16–21; Tob 14:5; *1 En.* 91:13; *2 Bar.* 32:4; 11Q18 10 I, 2; *Sib. Or.* 5:422), even in the new creation (*Jub.* 1:17, 28). Therefore, some interpreters wonder whether Revelation reflects the kind of anti-temple viewpoints that appear in other sources (Aune 3:1166–67, 1188–91; Rowland 725–29).

The Dead Sea community thought the Jerusalem temple had been corrupted by its priesthood (1QpHab XII, 8–9) and understood their own community to perform priestly functions (1QS VIII, 4–10; IX, 3–6). They also thought of a heavenly sanctuary where worship took place (4Q400–405), yet they hoped for the earthly temple's restoration (11Q19 XXIX, 8–10) and expected New Jerusalem to have a temple (2Q24 4 3; 11Q18 19 1–2; 20 2; García Martínez, *Qumran*, 199–200; Maier, *EDSS* 2:923–24). According to the gospels, Jesus criticized practices that turned the temple into a house of trade or den of robbers rather than a house of prayer (Matt 21:13; Mark 11:17; Luke 19:46; John 2:16), and he spoke of its destruction (Mark 13:2 par.). Yet he also taught in the temple and apparently spoke of its rebuilding, though not as an ordinary structure (next NOTE).

Other sources assumed that God was transcendent and did not dwell in temples made with human hands. Yet those who accepted this principle typically thought it acceptable to build earthly temples, whether the authors were Jewish (1 Kgs 8:27–30; Bar 1:8; 3:24; Philo, *Cher.* 99–100; Josephus, *J. W.* 5.458–59) or Greek (Plutarch, *Mor.* 477C; 1034B). Some early Christians, however, argued that even the Jerusalem temple violated the principal of not making houses for God (Acts 7:47–50; cf. 17:24; *Barn.* 16:1–2).

Like the DSS, Revelation speaks of a heavenly "temple" (Rev 11:19; 15:5–8) and considers the community of faith to be God's earthly temple (11:1–2), but unlike the DSS, Revelation does not suggest that the historical Jerusalem temple was defiled by wrong practice. Early Christian writers could use temple imagery for the Christian community (1 Cor 3:16–17; 2 Cor 6:16; Eph 2:21; 1 Pet 2:5) while affirming that the historical temple was legitimate (1 Cor 9:13). Revelation's perspective is not primarily anti-temple; rather, its positive references to the heavenly and earthly temples suggest that John considered the concept of a temple to be valid, so that it could be used for God and the Lamb (next NOTE; G. Stevenson, *Power*, 268–69; Söllner, *Jerusalem*, 224–38).

because its temple is the Lord God Almighty and the Lamb. Revelation is unusual in calling God himself a "temple." The imagery occurs only rarely (Isa 8:14; *Barn.* 16:1). The crucified and risen Christ is identified as the temple in John 2:19–21. In that context the implication was that Jesus functioned as the temple because in him atonement was made and the divine presence was revealed (C. R. Koester, *Symbolism*, 86–89). But in the Fourth Gospel, Christ is the temple or focus of worship for the Christian community in the present, while Revelation calls God and Christ the temple of New Jerusalem in the future. The texts develop the motif in different ways. (On Revelation and John's gospel, see INTRO II.D.1).

The way John's gospel identifies the crucified and risen Jesus with the temple is based on a saying of Jesus that concerns the destruction and rebuilding of the temple. A similar temple saying is mentioned in the Synoptic Gospels, but since it is ascribed to false witnesses, it is not clear whether the gospel writers thought it to be genuine (Matt 26:61; Mark 14:48). If they did, they may have understood the temple that Jesus would raise up to be the Christian community, rather than the risen Christ himself (Juel, *Messiah*, 205–9; 1 Cor 3:16–17; 2 Cor 6:16; Eph 2:21; 1 Pet 2:5; cf. the believer as temple in 1 Cor 6:19; *Barn.* 16:7–10).

21:23. *The city does not need the sun or the moon to shine on it, for the glory of God is its light and its lamp is the Lamb.* The language recalls Isa 60:19: "The sun shall no longer be your light by day, nor for brightness shall the moon give light to you by night; but the Lord will be your everlasting light, and your God will be your glory" (cf. Isa 60:1–2, 20; 24:23; Ps 104:2). The parallel reference to God's glory and the Lord's light in Isa 60:19 becomes a dual reference to the glory of God and the lamp of the Lamb (who is "Lord," Rev 19:16; Fekkes, *Isaiah*, 266–68). Identifying Christ as the lamp may recall Ps 132:17, in which God prepares a lamp for his anointed one. Light was a messianic image (11Q5 XXVII, 2; *1 En.* 48:4; Luke 2:32; John 8:12). Just as Israel's sanctuaries were illumined by lamps (Exod 25:37; 2 Chr 13:11; Josephus, *J. W.* 5.216–17), here the light shines throughout the city. In scenes of judgment the sun brought scorching heat against the beast's allies (Rev 16:8), but now the sun is gone, which signals blessing (7:16). The light of sun and moon was dimmed in judgment (6:12; 8:12; 9:2; cf. *4 Ezra* 7:38–44), but here their light gives way to the greater glory of God. The fall of Babylon meant that no lamp shone there (Rev 18:23), but New Jerusalem is perpetually lit by the lamp of the Lamb.

21:24. *The nations will walk by its light, and the kings of the earth will bring their glory into it.* It was said of Zion, "Nations shall come to your light, and kings to the brightness of your dawn," and "the wealth of the nations shall come to you" (Isa 60:3, 5; cf. 60:11; Mathewson, *New*, 165–75; Aune). The hope is that the nations will come to learn God's ways (Isa 2:2–4; Mic 4:1–4; Jer 3:17; Pss 22:27–28; 86:9; 138:4). This includes true worship, which the prophets depicted as the nations keeping the feast of Booths (Zech 14:16–19), serving as priests and Levites (Isa 66:18–21), and offering gifts to God (Zeph 3:9–10; Tob 13:11; *1 En.* 10:21–22; *Pss. Sol.* 17:31; *Sib. Or.* 3:772–73). This hope for the nations differs from Jewish sources that expected the nations to be annihilated at the end of the age (*4 Ezra* 12:33; 13:37–38; 1QM XV, 2; XVIII, 12) or to be defeated and to bring tribute to Jerusalem as subject peoples (Isa 60:10–14; 61:5–6; Zech 14:14; *Pss. Sol.* 17:30–31; 1QM XII, 13–14).

21:25. *Its gates will never be shut by day, and there will be no night there.* The language recalls Isa 60:11: "Your gates shall always be open; day and night they shall not be shut, so that nations shall bring you their wealth, with their kings led in procession." The sense, however, has shifted so that the kings are not subjects on display but are worshipers of God (previous NOTE). Moreover, in Isaiah the gates stand open day and night, but in Revelation the night is gone. This recalls Zech 14:7, which tells of the time when it "shall be continuous day . . . not day and not night, for at evening time there shall be light."

21:26. *They will bring the glory and the honor of the nations into it.* This line continues the echo of Isa 60:11, though the sense has changed. In Isaiah the nations and kings are subservient to Israel (cf. Isa 49:23; 1QM XII, 13–15), but in Revelation the nations willingly honor God. Some interpreters think bringing glory means bringing wealth or treasure (NAB, NJB), but Revelation typically pairs giving "glory" and "honor" when referring to worship (Rev 4:9, 11; 5:12–13; 7:12), which is the case here.

21:27. *But nothing common will enter it, nor anyone who does what is vile and deceitful.* This line recalls Isa 52:1, in which Jerusalem is "the holy city," since "the uncircumcised and the unclean shall enter you no more" (cf. 35:8). The original promise was that Jerusalem would never again be defiled by foreign invaders. Revelation underscores the absolute purity of the city and shows that the kings and nations who enter are no longer unclean. What is unclean, or "common" (*koinos*), is the opposite of what is holy.

Traditional sources of defilement included unclean animals, diseased people, and corpses (Lev 11:5, 28, 40; 13:1–8, 34; Num 19:11–13; Acts 10:14), as well as sexual misconduct, homicide, idolatry, and sin generally (Lev 18:20, 23–30; Num 35:33–34; Josh 22:17; Isa 1:16; 6:5–7). Here it is linked to what is vile and deceitful (NOTES on Rev 21:8). Traditionally, the strictest purity standards governed admission to the temple, and foreigners and unclean people were to be barred from the future sanctuary (Ezek 44:6–9; cf. 4Q174 I, 1–4). Certain unclean things were also excluded from the city itself (Josephus, *Ant.* 12.145–46), and visions of a restored or eschatological Jerusalem speak of holiness extending to the entire city (Zech 14:19–20; *Pss. Sol.* 17:30; 11Q19 XLVII, 3–5). In Revelation, this hope is realized in New Jerusalem.

but only those who are written in the Lamb's scroll of life. The scroll of life was like a register of citizens of New Jerusalem (Isa 4:3; Phil 3:20; 4:3; NOTE on Rev 13:8). Ordinary cities kept registers in order to identify those who had the benefits of citizenship, including Roman citizenship (*politographein*; I.Eph 8.40; IG 853.15; Sherwin-White, *Roman*, 314–16; J. Winter, *Life*, 52–55). People could be removed from the register for serious crime (Dio Chrysostom, *Disc.* 31.84; *NP* 3:370; 4:259), and the practices mentioned in Rev 21:27a are deemed incompatible with registration in the scroll of life (U. Sim, *Das himmlische*, 124–25).

22:1–2a. *Then he showed me the river of the water of life, bright as crystal.* The prophets envisioned a stream flowing from glorified Jerusalem (Isa 33:20–21; Ezek 47:1; Zech 13:1; 14:8; Joel 3:18; cf. *1 En.* 53:6–7; 4Q554 4 1–2). On one level the water brings life by quenching human thirst for God (NOTE on Rev 21:6); on another level the water suggests cleansing from sin (Zech 13:1; cf. Joel 3:18 with Num 25:1–2). Cleansing fits Revelation's subtheme of the purity of New Jerusalem (Rev 21:27). Some interpreters have linked the water to baptism (Primasius; Caesarius), but this connection is not evident in the context.

It was flowing from the throne of God and the Lamb through the middle of the city's main street. Some sources end the sentence after "Lamb" and think the tree of life is "in the middle of the street," just as it once stood "in the middle of the garden" in Gen 2:9 (NA[27], NJB). But it is best to put the period after "street," since Revelation regularly begins sentences with *kai* (and) and only rarely with prepositions (e.g., Rev 4:1; 7:15; 9:18; 22:15; Aune). Thus the river flows "in" or "through" the middle of the street (ESV, NAB, NIV, NRSV). Rome, Ephesus, Smyrna, and other cities had rivers beside them, but a river *in* the street was ordinarily undesirable. For example, the "river" in the elegant main street of one city was an open drain created by rainwater and sewage. Such a "river" in the street endangered the city's health and beauty (Pliny the Younger, *Ep.* 10.98–99; cf. Strabo, *Geographica* 14.1.37). In New Jerusalem the river in the street is pure and gives life. It is a sign of blessing (Artemidorus, *Onirocritica* 2.27).

22:2b. *On each side of the river is the tree of life.* Ezekiel used the singular "tree" in a collective sense for the many trees that grew on both sides of the river (Ezek 47:7, 12), while the creation story spoke of one tree of life in Eden (Gen 2:9–10; 3:22). Some interpreters think that Revelation uses "tree" in Ezekiel's collective sense, so that Eden's one tree of life becomes a forest of trees along each side of the river in New Jerusalem (Andreas; Aune; Beale; Müller; Osborne; Roloff; Smalley). Others think Revelation transforms Ezekiel's many trees into a single tree of life as in Genesis (Murphy; Prigent; Satake). This understanding is likely, given the paradisiacal imagery in the context. Just as the river flows from beneath the throne of God and the Lamb, it flows under the tree of life, whose roots extend to both banks.

In Jewish tradition the tree of life was a metaphor for wisdom (Prov 3:18; cf. 1QH[a] XVI, 5–6) and those bearing wisdom's fruits (Prov 11:30; 13:12; 15:4; *Pss. Sol.* 14:3). In *Tg. Neof.* Gen 3:24 the law is a tree of life, and observing its precepts leads to sharing the tree of life in the world to come. Christians identified Jesus as the tree of life since he embodied wisdom (Oecumenius; cf. Hippolytus, *Fr. Prov.* 17.2; Apringius; Bede) and called the cross "the tree" (Gal 3:13; Acts 5:30) that gave life to others (Caesarius; Hemer, *Letters*, 42–44; Boxall; Lupieri; Thompson). In Revelation, Jesus promises access to the tree but is not himself the tree (Rev 2:7).

which produces twelve crops of fruit, bearing its fruit each month. Where Ezek 47:12 spoke of many trees bearing fruit each month, Revelation says that the one tree bears twelve fruits. This could mean twelve different kinds of fruit (Victorinus; Aune), but the next clause explains that twelve fruits mean a harvest of fruit in each of the twelve months (Andreas; Satake).

and the leaves of the tree are for the healing of the nations. Formerly, the beast awed people by appearing to undergo a healing from a mortal wound (Rev 13:3, 12), and the beast deceived and oppressed the nations. Those who came under its influence received sores and agony (16:2, 10–11). In New Jerusalem healing is considered genuine, offering fullness of life in relationship with God. Ordinary leaves were used for healing sores, wounds, eye and stomach problems, and other ailments. They were eaten or ground up and mixed with wine and then drunk or made into salves (Pliny the Elder, *Nat.* 21.78, 127, 150, 158, 163; 22.37, 49, 50, 59; 23.3, 4). In New Jerusalem the leaves bring healing or wholeness in relationship to God.

22:3. *And there will be no curse anymore.* If the word *katathema* refers to that which is accursed (ESV, NAB, NRSV), it emphasizes that nothing abominable is in the city (21:27). But it probably refers to the curse itself, which is taken away (I.Kourion 131.15; NIV, NJB). First, it refers to the curse imposed by God, after human beings sinned by eating from the tree of the knowledge of good and evil. That curse included laboring for food and pain in childbearing. As a result, people were banished from the garden and separated from the tree of life that would grant immortality (Gen 3:17–24). In New Jerusalem the curse is removed because sin is gone and people now come to the tree of life (Rev 22:2; Giesen; Prigent; Smalley). Second, the language echoes Zech 14:11, which promises that Jerusalem will not fall under the curse of war (MT, *ḥērem*; LXX, *anathēma*) but will be secure (Aune; Mathewson, *New*, 201–3). In New Jerusalem God's battle with evil has ended. Babylon, the beast, and Satan have been vanquished (Rev 17:16; 19:20; 20:10), and the nations that come to Jerusalem do so as worshipers, not as foes. The curse of war is gone.

The throne of God and the Lamb shall be in it, and his servants will worship him. Revelation often uses the word *proskyneuein* for worship (e.g., 4:10; 5:14; 7:11), but here the verb is *latreuein*, which was used for all who serve God in fear, love, obedience, and prayer (Deut 10:12–13; Josh 24:24; Luke 1:74–75; 2:37; Rom 1:9–10; 2 Tim 1:3). The term was used for priestly service (Heb 8:5; 9:9; Rev 7:15), and it fits the priestly character of the redeemed in Rev 22:3–4. On "servant," see the NOTE on 1:1.

22:4. *They will see his face.* To see God's face meant unmediated communion with him. One barrier to this was the difference between divine majesty and human limitation. God's radiant majesty made it impossible for humans to see him and remain alive (Exod 33:20–23; Ovid, *Metam.* 3.287–309; cf. Xenophon, *Mem.* 4.3.13–14; *Sib. Or.* 3:17; 1 Tim 6:16). A second barrier was sin. Those who transgressed in Eden wanted to hide from God's face (Gen 3:8; cf. Isa 6:5), and sinners who come before God's face encounter judgment (Rev 6:16). Some sources told of people who were able to see God (Gen 32:31; Exod 24:11; 33:11; Num 12:8; Judg 13:22; *Mart. Asc. Isa.* 3:9), but the dominant idea was that truly seeing God's face was impossible (John 1:18; 1 John 4:12; Ps.-Orpheus 22–24 [*OTP* 2:800–801]; Aune). People might desire to "see God's face," in the sense of receiving favor from him (Job 33:26; Pss 17:15; 24:6), but unmediated communion with God is an eschatological hope (Matt 5:8; Heb 12:14; 1 Cor 13:12; 1 John 3:2; *4 Ezra* 7:98). Only in New Jerusalem is it fully realized.

and his name will be on their foreheads. Just as God has written the names of those entering New Jerusalem in his scroll (Rev 13:8; 17:8; 21:27), so has he written his own name on them. Just as the names of the tribes and apostles are engraved on the city (21:12, 14), so God's name is put on its inhabitants. Here, "name" is singular, though elsewhere it includes the names of God and the Lamb (14:1). An angel put a seal with the name on the foreheads of the redeemed to show that they belonged to God (7:3). In contrast, the beast's heads bore blasphemous names (13:1), the whore had "Babylon" on her brow (17:3, 5), and the beast's followers bore his name or number on their foreheads (13:17). Those who bore God's name were protected from divine wrath but not from earthly suffering, since the beast's allies persecuted them. Yet bearing the name was assurance that they would be protected through suffering and brought to life in God's presence (NOTE on 7:3).

22:5. *Night will be no more. They will not need the light of a lamp or the light of the sun, for the Lord God will shine on them.* This line recalls Isa 60:19: "The sun shall no more be your light by day, nor for brightness shall the moon give you light by night; but the Lord will be your everlasting light, and your God will be your glory" (cf. Rev 21:23). Night belongs to the old order, not the new (Zech 14:7; Rev 21:25). The darkening of heavenly bodies signaled divine judgment and the presence of evil (6:12; 8:12; 9:2; 16:10), but both have now passed. Night is no more, just as the threats posed by the sea, death, pain, grief, and the curse are no more (21:1, 4; 22:3). For God to shine on people connotes blessing and favor (Num 6:25; Pss 4:6; 31:16; 80:3; 89:15; 4Q542 1 I, 1–2).

and they will reign forever and ever. The language resembles Dan 7:18: "the holy ones of the Most High shall receive the kingdom and possess the kingdom forever." Since Dan 7:27 adds that "all dominions shall serve and obey them," some interpreters assume that Revelation envisions a similar form of dominion (Beale; Thomas). This understanding is unlikely, however, since here and in Rev 20:4–6 reigning means sharing the fullness of Christ's rule. Revelation does not say that others are *being* ruled (Giesen; Müller; on ruling the nations with an iron rod, see the NOTES and COMMENT on 2:26–27). Some suggest that the reign of the saints in New Jerusalem fulfills the Hellenistic ideal of shared city governance (Georgi, "Visionen," 372; U. Sim, *Das himmlische*, 139). There is at most a limited connection, however, since the vision distinguishes God and the Lamb from the rest of the populace. Others reign with them, but no one takes their place. Others give worship, but only God and the Lamb receive it (22:3).

COMMENT

The appearance of a new heaven and earth, and New Jerusalem descending from God, brought the final vision cycle to a climax (21:1–8). The themes introduced there are

On Rev 21:9–22:5, see Bachmann, "Ausmessung"; Bergmeier, "Jerusalem"; Böcher, "Zur Bedeutung"; Boneva, "La spatialisation"; Fuller Dow, *Images*, 180–221; Fekkes, *Isaiah*, 238–78; Frenschkowski, "Utopia"; Georgi, "Visionen"; Gundry, "New"; Hirschberg, *Das eschatologische*, 244–90; Hock, "From"; L. Huber, *Like*; Jart, "Precious"; Kitzberger, "Wasser"; P. Lee, *New*, 275–300; Maier, *Apocalypse*, 192–97; Mathewson, *New*, 95–215; C. Müller, "Gott"; Oesch, "Intertextuelle"; Pattemore, *People*, 197–212; Pezzoli-Oligiati, *Täuschung*, 161–86; Rapp, "Das herabsteigende"; Räpple, *Metaphor*, Reader, "Twelve"; Rossing, *Choice*, 151–61 and "River"; Royalty, *Streets*, 214–39; Schille, "Apokalyptiker"; U. Sim, *Das himmlische*; Söllner, *Jerusalem*, 204–61; Tavo, *Woman*, 295–344; Vanni, "La dimension"; F. Winter, "Aspekte."

now developed: the city, the bride, God's presence with many peoples, no uncleanness, and the water of life. The previous passage was dominated by sound, as voices from the throne declared the end of death and grief and announced God's presence among humankind. Now there is a visually rich depiction of New Jerusalem in four phases. First, John is shown the city from a distance, so that he can see its glory, walls, and gates (21:9–14). Second, the angel measures the city, revealing its perfect dimensions, the jewels on its foundations, its gates of pearl, and golden street (21:15–21). Third, attention shifts to those who have a place in the city, including God and the Lamb, who give it light, and the nations and kings, who bring their glory into it (21:22–27). Finally, John looks to the center of the city, where the water of life flows from the throne of God and the Lamb, the tree of life bears fruit, and the redeemed see the face of God (22:1–5).

Cities have been a major motif in Revelation. The opening chapters addressed readers in seven cities of Asia Minor. The messages identified issues readers faced in their contexts, from persecution to accommodation and complacency due to wealth. Readers were called to renewed commitment to God in the cities where they lived (1:9–3:22). The middle of the book reveals that local issues are part of a larger struggle between God and evil in "the great city," which is called Babylon and has features of imperial Rome. Violence, false worship, and the pursuit of wealth characterize that city, which ultimately will fall (11:8; 17:1–18:24). The end of the book turns to New Jerusalem, the city of God and the Lamb. John envisions a city that belongs to the future, yet he encourages readers to exhibit trust and perseverance in the present, since he takes readers beyond the limitations of cities in this world to see how God's purposes are realized in life, truth, and glory (21:9–22:5).

Rhetorically, the New Jerusalem vision is an encomium praising the city. When speakers in antiquity gave such encomia, they not only described the features of a city, but commended the values reflected in it. While telling of streets, gates, temples, and the people who lived there, they emphasized beauty, concord, piety, and honor (Aelius Aristides, *Orations* 17; 26; Balch, "Two"; Royalty, *Streets*, 217). Revelation's description of New Jerusalem draws on the biblical prophets, while including Greco-Roman themes. The city's symmetry is perfect and its walls majestic; its streets and gates are elegant and its inhabitants worship continually. To some extent New Jerusalem is an ideal city on a cosmic scale (Georgi, "Visionen"; U. Sim, *Das himmlische*, 137–40; Kraybill, *Imperial*, 211–14; F. Winter, "Aspekte"; cf. Gilchrest, *Revelation*, 12–82).

Yet the central question concerns the city's power structure. For ancient theorists, the city was a divinely ordained form of political life, a monarch expressing Zeus's governance of the people (Aristotle, *Pol.* 1253a; 1278b; 1284b). For Stoics, structuring life around urban ideals fit the divine ordering of the cosmos, and Plutarch observed that Alexander the Great gave such ideas political form as "he conquered through force of arms" and "brought together into one body all people everywhere" (*Mor.* 329C). Later, the conquests of Augustus and his successors made Rome the hub of a world empire, whose dominion was said to have arisen through divine providence (*Rom. Civ.* 1:624, 627; Maier, *Apocalypse*, 193–94).

Physical aspects of cities in the empire reflected the Roman power structure. The Romans and their allies built new cities and refurbished old ones. Augustus could boast that he found Rome made of brick and left it in marble to show "the majesty of the empire" (Suetonius, *Aug.* 28.3). He built new temples, porticoes, a basilica, and a theater;

he added to the forum and finished the house for the Senate (Augustus, *Res* 19–21). In Asia Minor, a monumental gate at Ephesus was dedicated to Augustus and his family; and a new paved street, colonnade, and part of the theater were inscribed to Domitian and Artemis (see Figures 3, 4, 5, 6; I.Eph 2034; 3005; 3008; 3092). The massive new stadium at Laodicea was dedicated to Titus and its gate to Domitian and Zeus (I.Laod 15; 24). The temples erected for the imperial cult were civic landmarks (Owens, *City*, 74–93, 121–63; U. Sim, *Das himmlische*, 32–41).

The New Jerusalem vision reflects a different power structure. Its defining element is the presence of God and the Lamb, and the features of the city reflect the character of their rule (Rev 21:22–23; 22:1, 2, 5). God's fundamental identity is the Creator, who is worthy of power because he brought all things into being (4:11). As the Creator, God rid the earth of its destroyers, and his work culminated in new creation (11:18; 21:1). The radiant structures of his city encircle the Creator's throne, which pours forth water to show the life that comes from his reign; and the city's gates and street lead to the tree of life, where people receive food and healing (22:1–2).

The slain and living Lamb shares God's throne (22:1, 3). The Lamb brings people of every nation into God's kingdom through his death (5:9–10; 7:9–14). His actions differ from those of the beast, which exercises imperial power through violent conquest (11:7; 13:7). The Lamb conquers through the sacrifice that gives life to others (5:5–6; 12:11). Those who belong to New Jerusalem are the Lamb's bride, married to his redemptive suffering. The city's foundations are the apostles who follow the path of the Lamb, and the nations are illumined by his light (21:9, 14, 23; Maier, *Apocalypse*, 196; Kraybill, *Apocalypse*, 177–78).

John's description of this city is cosmic; the city's size and majesty are overwhelming. The vision does not allow God's kingdom to be equated with any earthly city. Revelation resists the idea that any form of social and political organization can claim to be the final one. New Jerusalem critiques the power structures of this world from a perspective that is not captive to this world. The vision calls for renewed trust in God in the present by showing that God's purposes extend far beyond the present, culminating in a future for the world that can be glimpsed through faith but never controlled.

Description of the City (21:9–14)

One of the angels who brought the seven last plagues invites John to look closely at the city. Previously, one of the angels said, "Come, I will show you the judgment on the great whore" (17:1), and now one says, "Come, I will show you the bride, the wife of the Lamb" (21:9). There is a clear literary connection between the scenes. The whore is Babylon, personifying a society driven by desires for pleasure and profit. She wears the gold, jewels, and pearls that come from her illicit trade (17:4). The world signified by Babylon operates by violence and deception. It beguiles people with promises of wealth, while making them worship rulers who slaughter the innocent (17:1–6; 18:23–24). Kings and nations may revel in the prosperity Babylon brings, but the arrangement is morally degrading and makes them numb to injustice (17:2; 18:3, 9, 23).

In contrast, New Jerusalem is the bride, personifying the community that follows the Lamb. She is adorned with gold, jewels, and pearls, as is fitting for a bride (21:2, 18–21). The bride is characterized by fidelity to the Lamb, and her garments are acts of justice (14:4; 19:7–8). She has nothing to do with impurity and deception (21:27).

Kings and nations share the splendor of the bridal city by walking in light, not by the relentless pursuit of wealth. They give glory to the Creator and the Lamb, which is honorable, rather than debasing themselves through false worship (21:24–26; Bauckham, *Theology*, 131–32; Deutsch, "Transformation," 123; Wengst, "Babylon").

The portrayals of Babylon and Jerusalem are designed to shape the commitments of the readers. The vision of Babylon challenges those who find imperial society alluring by showing that its violence and obsession with wealth are repulsive. Readers are called to disengage from what the city represents, since the society that destroys others will finally suffer destruction itself (17:16; 18:4). The vision of New Jerusalem gives readers positive incentive to remain faithful to God and the Lamb, since the future holds the promise of life in God's city. Babylon holds no future for a bride and groom (18:23), but in New Jerusalem the redeemed will share in the wedding banquet of the Lamb (19:7, 9). Demons dwell in Babylon (18:2), but New Jerusalem will be the dwelling of God (21:3). Readers now live in the world dominated by Babylon, but they are to live as citizens of New Jerusalem, letting the traits of that city shape their lives in the present in the confidence that the future belongs to God (Schüssler Fiorenza, *Book*, 187–92; Rossing, *Choice*, 155–65).

The angelic tour of the city recalls prophetic texts concerning Jerusalem's glorification. Ezekiel provides the template for Revelation's final chapters. John has already included battle scenes with birds feasting on carrion and Gog and Magog being defeated (Ezek 38–39; Rev 19:17–21; 20:7–10) and has announced resurrection and God's dwelling among people (Ezek 37:11–14, 27; Rev 20:2–6, 11; 21:3). The New Jerusalem vision now adds an angel with a measuring rod, a city with twelve gates named for the tribes, the presence of God's glory, and the river and fruit-bearing trees (Ezek 40–48; Rev 21:9–22:5; cf. Sänger, ed., *Ezechielbuch*). Into this framework the writer weaves elements from other prophetic texts, including the gemlike appearance of the city, its continual light, flowing water, and the nations coming to worship (Isa 54:11–12; 60:1–3, 11; Zech 14:7–8, 16). Theologically, the use of prophetic imagery reaffirms the integrity of the God who reigns there. The sense is that God will be true to what was spoken through the prophets.

New Jerusalem comes down from heaven. Unlike other writers, John does not anticipate the glorification of the earthly city (NOTE on Rev 21:10). Revelation was written after the Roman destruction of Jerusalem in 70 CE, but it gives little if any attention to that event. The vision of the holy city under siege uses biblical imagery to symbolize the Christian community being threatened by the unbelieving world, but it does not deal with the fate of the actual city (11:1–2). The depiction of Rome as Babylon makes no mention of the loss of the temple (17:1–18:24). The transcendent quality of the city John envisions means that no earthly city, not even Jerusalem, can claim to be the focus of God's kingdom. God's reign is of another order (Giesen; Smalley; Roloff, "Neuschöpfung," 131; Hirschberg, *Das eschatologische*, 216, 243).

There is some debate about what New Jerusalem signifies. Some interpreters treat the city primarily as a place (Royalty, *Streets*, 215–18, 239), but others see it personifying the future of God's people (Gundry, "New") or reflecting God's own presence (Rapp, "Das herabsteigende"). It is best to take all three dimensions into account (Aune; Osborne; Bauckham, *Theology*, 132–43; Pattemore, *People*, 199–201; Söllner, *Jerusalem*, 256–59; Zimmermann, "Nuptial," 174). As a place, the city shares God's own glory

(21:11). Its radiance resembles jasper, like God on his throne (4:3). The New Jerusalem vision does not equate hope with the prospect of going to a different place. Entering the city means coming into the presence of God (21:3, 23; 22:4–5).

The city also personifies the future glory of God's people. The bridal imagery is relational. Using it for the city shows that those now wedded to the Lamb through faith will have a future with him through resurrection. The list of gems adorning the city suggests the elegant attire a bride would wear when taken to the groom's home, anticipating the glory that the redeemed will share in endless life with God and the Lamb. (21:2, 19–21). The expression "holy city" was used symbolically for the worshiping community, which was besieged by the unbelieving world and yet protected by God (11:1–2). Calling New Jerusalem the holy city gives assurance that the community that now worships in a conflicted situation will have a future in which worship takes place freely in God's presence (21:10; 22:3–4).

The character of God's people is suggested by the city's gates and foundations, which are named for the tribes of Israel and the apostles of the Lamb (21:12–14). Inscribing names on public structures mirrors Greco-Roman practice. Such inscriptions shaped a city's identity and reflected its power structures. As Augustus refurbished Rome, he stipulated that the names of his sons were to be inscribed on the basilica and the name of his son-in-law on the theater (Augustus, *Res* 20–21). In Asia Minor, the inscription over the gate by the agora at Ephesus (4–2 BCE) read, "To the Emperor Caesar Augustus, son of the deified, high priest, consul twelve times, tribune twenty times," and it named members of the imperial family and the benefactors who erected the gate (I.Eph 3006). The gate built at Laodicea in 84–85 CE was inscribed, "To Zeus most great, the savior, and to emperor Domitian Caesar Augustus Germanicus, high priest most great, exercising the authority of tribune for the fourth time, consul for the twelfth time, father of the fatherland" (I.Laod 24). Such inscriptions identify the city with the gods, rulers, and patrons of the empire.

New Jerusalem's inscriptions tell a different story. Its public structures name the leading figures in the history of the community to which John's readers belong. Including the apostles along with the tribes does not mean that John envisions the creation of a "new" Israel (Beale; Giesen; Prigent, Satake; Smalley). Both the tribes and the apostles belong to one and the same people of God (Osborne; Friesen, *Imperial*, 183; P. Lee, *New*, 280). The pattern was introduced earlier, when John heard that those protected by God included twelve thousand from each of the twelve tribes, recalling God's promise to preserve his people. But what John saw was a countless multitude from every nation. The idea was that God's promise to preserve Israel was fulfilled in saving people from many nations through the blood of the Lamb (7:4–14). Belonging to God's city means sharing in the redemption that extends from ancient Israel to the Christian community. The inscriptions on the gates and foundations reflect that story and identity (Gilchrest, *Revelation*, 83–275).

The City's Size and Gems (21:15–21)

The angel measures New Jerusalem to show its impeccable design. In the Greco-Roman world the ideal city was a square. Walls were built around the perimeter and a broad avenue stretched from the main gate on one side to the main gate on the opposite side, creating a central axis. An agora, or forum, was built along the main street in the heart of the city. Other streets might be arranged in a grid pattern, with gates added as needed (Owens, *City*, 80, 91, 150). To some extent, New Jerusalem's perfect symmetry, impressive walls and gates, and elegant avenue fit the established patterns (21:15–21).

Yet John describes a city so enormous that it beggars the imagination. Ezekiel envisioned the glorified Jerusalem as a square that measured 1.5 miles on each side (Ezek 48:30–35), but John pictures a city a thousand times larger, measuring 1,500 miles on each side. Then he transforms the square into a cube, with its height matching its length and width. This compounds the sense of symmetry and perfection, yet it requires that readers imagine a city towering 1,500 miles above its foundations, which is almost inconceivable (Rev 21:16). John uses human categories like cubits but makes clear that the scale is angelic (21:17), placing the realization of God's designs beyond the limits of this world.

John magnifies the sense of splendor by telling of a city made of gold with walls of jasper and foundations made of gems (21:18–20). Ordinary pearls were small enough to wear on necklaces, but those in New Jerusalem are so huge that each pearl forms a gate through which kings and nations can pass. The main street is not merely paved—rare enough in antiquity—but covered with gold (21:21). The details were inspired by Isa 54:11–12 and other texts that envisioned a glorified Jerusalem being constructed of gems and gold (Notes on Rev 21:18–21). Using biblical language for the city reflects the character of its God. Theologically, the idea is that God will not only be true to the promises he made through the prophets but will realize them in an almost unimaginable way.

New Jerusalem has a fantastic quality that bears some resemblance to Lucian's depiction of the Isle of the Blessed, where heroes were said to go when they died (*Ver. hist.* 11–13). The similarities were striking enough that an ancient Christian scholiast wondered whether Lucian had drawn from Revelation (Maier, *Apocalypse*, 193; Frenschkowski, "Utopia"):

> The city itself is all of gold and the wall around it of emerald. It has seven gates, all of single planks of cinnamon. The foundations of the city and the ground within its walls are of ivory. There are temples of all the gods, built of beryl, and in them great monolithic altars of amethyst, on which they make their great burnt offerings. Around the city runs a river of the finest myrrh, a hundred royal cubits wide and five deep, so that one can swim in it comfortably. For baths they have large houses of glass, warmed by burning cinnamon; instead of water there is hot dew in the tubs. . . . Nobody grows old . . . it is always spring there. . . . The grapevines yield twelve vintages a year, bearing every month.

What is striking about the passage is not simply what Lucian says, but why he says it. Lucian is challenging the classic beliefs about a blessed afterlife by satirizing them. He calls his satire *A True History*, but through whimsical exaggeration he makes clear that everything he is saying is untrue. Venerable beliefs about a city near the Elysian Fields become laughable when Lucian depicts a place that is not merely pleasant, but absurd in its luxury, allowing people to swim in perfume and bathe in hot dew. The literary context adds fanciful details such as a sea of milk, people with feet made of cork, and trees producing loaves of baked bread.

Revelation's New Jerusalem vision also challenges conventional beliefs, but in a different way. John pushes human imagination to its limits in order to show that God's city cannot be identified with any earthly city. No form of political organization can claim to be the final one. Rome was called "the eternal city" (Ovid, *Fast.* 3.72), its empire established by the providence of the gods and its imposing buildings showing "the majesty of the empire" (Vitruvius, *Arch.* 1.pref.2). But visions of Babylon's demise and New Jerusalem's cosmic splendor show that God's designs are of another order. The vastness of the description undercuts human pretensions by showing that no city can ever be equated with the kingdom of God on earth

Life Within the City (21:22–27)

John says, "I did not see a temple in the city," a comment that sets New Jerusalem apart from Greco-Roman cities, in which temples were a regular feature of civic life (Rev 21:22a). The temple to Artemis at Ephesus was a major landmark and center for pilgrimage. Smyrna had a temple to the mother goddess and Pergamum a temple to Athena, and all three cities had provincial temples to the emperors and smaller sanctuaries for other deities. Cities throughout Asia Minor had multiple temples (NOTES on 2:1, 7, 12, 18; 3:1, 7, 14). In Rome, Augustus built thirteen new temples, including those to Apollo, Jupiter, Minerva, Mars, and the deified Julius; and he refurbished eighty-two more (Augustus, *Res* 19–21). Plutarch could state categorically that a "city without holy places," no traveler "will ever see" (Plutarch, *Mor.* 1125E). John would agree, since the city he reveals is of another sort.

What makes John's comment about "no temple" especially surprising is that the temple was the central feature of the historical Jerusalem, and John's description of New Jerusalem draws heavily from Ezekiel's vision of the glorified city, which emphasizes the temple's importance (Ezek 40–48). Jewish tradition concerning the future Jerusalem regularly assumed there would be a temple there (NOTE on Rev 21:22). John transforms the tradition, in part, by giving the entire city the traits of a sanctuary. Where Ezekiel described the dimensions of the future temple's walls and foundations, Revelation deals with those of the city. Where Ezekiel envisioned a river flowing from a temple filled with God's glory, Revelation says the entire city is illumined by God's glory and the river flows from God's throne. Revelation's New Jerusalem has the cubic shape and golden surface of the holy of holies, and in it the redeemed worship God with his name on their foreheads, like high priests (Rev 21:16; 22:4; Vogelgesang, "Interpretation," 76–78; Mathewson, *New*, 112–13).

But the main point of transformation is that the only "temple" in New Jerusalem is the presence of God and the Lamb (21:22). Ordinary temples mediated access to God. In Israel, the temple included several courts and chambers, and access was limited. Moving from one court to the next required progressively higher levels of holiness, so the inner chamber was accessible only to the high priest and only once during the year (Lev 16:2). Greek and Roman temples often had sacred precincts. Some temples were closed; others restricted access to priests or other groups, and some were more open. Yet temples were places set apart for the gods (G. Stevenson, *Power*, 42–54). New Jerusalem has no temple because no structure mediates the presence of God and the Lamb. The barriers of sin and evil have been removed. All worshipers in the city can see God's face

(Rev 22:4). God and the Lamb are the city's temple because their presence is accessible to all (G. Stevenson, *Power*, 268–69).

Up to this point, the temple theme in Revelation involved the contrast between a heavenly and an earthly temple. The heavenly temple was where God's throne was located, and it was the place from which action was taken against the forces of evil. In the heavenly temple the pleas from the faithful rose up and divine wrath was summoned down on an unjust world, where the allies of the beast coerced and deceived people into false worship (6:9; 8:3–5; 11:19; 14:15, 18; 15:5–8; 16:1, 7, 17). The counterpart to the celestial sanctuary was the community of faith on earth. The community is where the redeemed served as priests and worshiped God as the hosts do in heaven, despite threats from the unbelieving world (1:5; 5:10; 11:1–2).

Given the conflict, those being socially marginalized were called pillars in God's temple and were promised a place in New Jerusalem (3:12). John also envisioned Jesus' followers coming through earthly suffering to deathless life in God's temple (7:14–15). In New Jerusalem these promises are both kept and transformed, so life in the temple proves to be life in the presence of God and the Lamb, who are the temple (21:22).

The horizon expands when John says that the city is illumined by the glory of God and the Lamb; the nations walk in its light, and the kings of earth bring their glory into it (21:23–24). The scene raises again the question of the city's power structure. Roman writers could call Rome the "light of the whole world and the citadel of all nations" (Cicero, *Cat.* 4.11) and celebrated the way nations were brought to Rome through conquest. Virgil pictured Augustus, seated at the threshold of "shining Apollo" in Rome, as conquered peoples and their gifts were paraded before him (*Aen.* 8.714–28). An inscription from Asia Minor praised Caligula as "the new Sun God" and said that the empire's vassal kings would "join in giving illumination by their own rays, so that the majesty of his immortality should be more venerable" (*Rom. Civ.* 2:31).

The New Jerusalem vision focuses on the redemption of kings and nations rather than their subjugation. The language is biblical, recalling prophetic texts about nations and kings being drawn to the light of God's glory in Zion (Isa 60:3; cf. Mic 4:1–4; Jer 3:17; Pss 22:27–28; 86:9; 138:4; Tob 13:11; *Pss. Sol.* 17:31). Not only Israel but the nations have the possibility of walking in the light of the Lord (Isa 2:2–5). Earlier in Revelation the heavenly chorus called God the "King of the nations" and said, "All nations will come and worship before you" because God's acts of justice are revealed (Rev 15:3–4). Where Ezekiel envisioned the trees of New Jerusalem providing leaves for healing, John adds that the healing is for the *nations*; the goal is their redemption (Rev 22:2; Bauckham, *Climax*, 314–15; Kraybill, *Apocalypse*, 177–78)

The vision calls the nations to a future different from the one in previous visions. John has seen nations allied with the destroyers of the earth, including Satan, the beast, and Babylon, (11:18; 13:7; 14:8; 18:3, 23; 20:3). The nations rejoiced at the slaughter of God's witnesses (11:9) and trampled the holy city in a display of contempt (11:2). When they made a final assault against God's city, they were destroyed by heavenly fire (20:8–9). Yet New Jerusalem offers the prospect of a different future, in which the nations no longer trample God's city but walk in its light. Walking in light meant doing what is true, just, and in harmony with God's will (Prov 4:18; 8:20; Rom 13:13; Eph 5:8; 1 John 1:7). The image of light connoted life and well-being, which is what the nations receive in God's city (Pss 56:13; 97:11; Bar 5:9).

Similarly, the kings of the earth have been seduced by Babylon (Rev 17:2, 18; 18:3, 9–10) and swayed by Satan, so they make war against the Lamb and are destroyed by the sword from his mouth (16:14; 19:19–21). But again, New Jerusalem extends the prospect of a different future in which kings bring their glory into God's city. Some texts suggest that the kings do so as subjects bringing tribute (Isa 60:5–7, 11; Hag 2:6–9; 4Q504 1–2 IV, 1–13; 1QM XII, 14–15; cf. Fekkes, *Isaiah*, 270). But in Revelation "giving glory" is an act of worship, which honors the Creator and the Lamb (Rev 4:9, 11; 5:12, 13; 7:12; 11:13; 14:7; 19:1, 7; Bauckham, *Climax*, 312–16; Mathewson, *New*, 164–75; Osborne).

Some interpreters maintain that the hostile kings and nations of previous chapters have now been annihilated, so those in New Jerusalem must be a different group. They equate "the nations" with the believers who came out of many nations into the Christian community (5:9–10; 7:9) and call them "kings of the earth," since believers reign in New Jerusalem. They point out that Revelation cannot envision the salvation of all kings and nations, since that would make the earlier scenes of judgment irrelevant (Beale; Giesen; Lupieri; Müller; cf. Osborne; Herms, *Apocalypse*, 197–256).

The approach taken here is that Revelation provides two contrasting visions of the future. The scenes of judgment, in which nations and kings are destroyed, warn of the devastating consequences of allegiance to evil. Those who ally themselves with the destroyers of the earth ultimately suffer destruction themselves. In contrast, the scenes of salvation, in which nations and kings come to New Jerusalem, promise life in God and the Lamb. Both futures remain open; the question is how the world will respond. The New Jerusalem vision is not a simple statement that all will be saved. Rather, the scene holds out the prospect of what life with God can mean for kings and nations, because it is the future to which all are *called* (14:6–7; Sweet; Bauckham, *Theology*, 103; Boring 226–31; Mathewson, *New*, 174–75).

Similar dynamics pertain to the warning that nothing unclean can be brought into the city (21:27a). The visions have linked uncleanness, abomination, and falsehood (16:13; 17:4–5; 18:2) to the activity of Satan, the beast, the false prophet, and Babylon (12:9; 13:5–6, 14; 14:5; 22:15). Since all these agents of evil have been overthrown, there seems to be no point in including the warning in the New Jerusalem vision. But the passage addresses the readers, who live before the end, when the forces of evil are active. It warns that those who adopt the ways of evil defile themselves, making themselves unfit to enter God's presence. Persisting in that course of action threatens to make the situation permanent, excluding them from God's city (Harrington; Müller; Sweet; Mathewson, *New*, 181–82).

The warning is coupled with the promise that there is a place in the city for those in the Lamb's scroll of life (21:27). People are written in the scroll from the foundation of the world, which makes it an act of divine favor (NOTE on 13:8; cf. 17:8). At the last judgment, people are held accountable for what they do, yet access to God's city ultimately comes from inclusion in the scroll, which is an act of grace (20:12–15; §40 COMMENT). The point of the scroll is not to narrow the prospect of salvation. Revelation links the scroll to the Lamb, who redeems a countless multitude from every nation (5:9–10; 7:9–14). Where the preceding warning about impurity was designed to move people to resist sin and evil in the present, the promise of life through the scroll of the Lamb fosters hope for the future.

The Throne of God and the Lamb (22:1–5)

The throne of God and the Lamb has a central place in New Jerusalem, and creation imagery manifests the character of their reign (22:1). In Revelation's initial throne room scene, God was surrounded by four beings with faces of a lion, ox, eagle, and human being. As representatives of the created order they praised God for creation (4:6–11), until every living thing of earth, sea, sky, and under the earth praised God and the Lamb together (5:13; 10:6). Now in the final throne room scene, God and the Lamb rule as one. Together, God's acts of creation and justice (10:6; 15:3) and the Lamb's redemption through love and self-sacrifice (1:5–6; 5:9–14; 7:14) overcome evil and death and culminate in giving life.

Revelation does not envision a simple return to a primeval paradise, but pictures a river and fruit-bearing tree in the heart of a city. In Genesis, the first city was built outside the garden of Eden, not within it (Gen 4:17), but other texts anticipated that glorified Jerusalem would be like Eden (Isa 51:3). Jewish tradition added that God preserved paradise and true Jerusalem for the redeemed at the end of the age (*2 Bar.* 4:1–7; *Jub.* 4:26; *T. Dan* 5:12). Revelation's vision of New Jerusalem points to the realization of such hopes, while depicting the created world and the urban world as a harmonious whole.

The river of life, which flows from the throne, is a vivid way to show that the reign of God and the Lamb is a source of life for others (Rev 22:1). The water imagery also fits urban motifs, because an effective ruler would ensure that water was brought into a city. Rome relied on a network of aqueducts, and the water showed the beneficence of the emperor (Frontinus, *Aqueducts* 1.4, 11, 88, 89). In Asia Minor, Hellenistic kings built an extensive network of aqueducts at Pergamum, and the other cities addressed by Revelation also had aqueducts (see Figure 11; Notes on Rev 2:8, 12, 18; 3:1, 7, 14). Augustus provided two aqueducts at Ephesus, while a wealthy patron added a third, dedicating it to Augustus, Tiberius, and Artemis (see Figure 4; Note on 2:1).

Revelation reverses the pattern: Water is not brought in from outside but flows from the heart of the city, as envisioned by the prophets. Where prophetic texts had a river flowing from the temple, Revelation has it flow from the throne, because God and the Lamb have become the temple (Ezek 47:1–12; Zech 13:1; 14:8; Joel 3:18). Such a river is a sign of God's presence and blessing (Ps 46:4). As "the water of life," the river gives life. Theologically, people receive it when the barriers to life with God—sin, evil, and death—are overcome. At present, readers may be cleansed from sin by the Lamb (1:5; 7:14), and they share in the Lamb's victory over evil by remaining faithful (12:11). But fullness of life comes when sin and evil no longer threaten and death is fully overcome through resurrection (20:14; 21:4). Since life in that sense belongs to the new creation, New Jerusalem is where the water of life is found.

The tree of life grows over the river, its roots extending to both banks (22:2). The imagery is suggestive since in the Greco-Roman world sacred trees grew above springs, and some of the springs were said to have healing properties (Pausanias, *Descr.* 4.34.4; 8.19.2; 8.23.4; Frontinus, *Aqueducts* 1.4). Sacred trees appear in traditions linked to cities like Ephesus (Hemer, *Letters*, 41–47) and Smyrna (Pausanias, *Descr.* 7.5.2), as well as other places (Pausanias, *Descr.* 1.30.2; 2.31.8; Pliny the Elder, *Nat.* 12.3). They were popularly linked to Zeus, Athena, and other deities (Pausanias, *Descr.* 8.23.5; Nilsson, *Geschichte*, 1:209–12).

The New Jerusalem vision poses a counterclaim, since its tree of life is connected to God, the Lamb, and the biblical tradition of Eden. God created the tree of life at the dawn of time and placed it in a garden with the tree of knowledge. The first human beings were not to eat from the tree of knowledge, and when they did so, they were banished from the garden so they would not eat from the tree of life and live forever (Gen 2:9, 17; 3:1–24). Later tradition emphasized the tree's beauty and exquisitely sweet fragrance, its leaves that never withered, and its lovely fruit. At present, no one has the right to touch it, but at the consummation of the age, its fruit will be given to the chosen (1 En. 24:4–25:6; cf. Apoc. Mos. 28:4; 4 Ezra 8:52; T. Levi 18:11; Tg. Neof. Gen 3:24).

Revelation depicts the realization of such hopes by combining Eden's tree of life with the many trees Ezekiel associated with the glorified Jerusalem (Ezek 47:12). The tree is a continual source of food, for it bears a crop each month, and those who hunger now will not hunger in God's city (7:16). The trees in Ezekiel had "leaves for healing" (Ezek 47:12; cf. 4 Ezra 7:123), but John expands this to include healing for "the nations," as noted above (Rev 22:2). Just as all people have been barred from the tree of life because of sin, Revelation extends the hope of salvation to all nations through the reign of God and the Lamb. The text calls them to turn to the source of life (cf. 14:6–7).

The fullness of God's reign means that the curse will be "no more" (ouk estai eti, 22:3). According to Genesis, people first incurred God's curse in Eden, when they disobeyed God and hid from his face. Because of sin, they bore the curse of hard labor for food, along with pain and separation from the tree of life, so they were subject to death (Gen 3:8–24). In New Jerusalem, sin has been overcome, so the curse can be removed. Heavy labor has ended, and the tree of life bears fruit continually (Rev 22:2). Like the curse, pain, grief, and death are no more, and people can look into the face of God (21:4; 22:3, 5).

The vision would have been broadly appealing in the imperial world, where utopian scenes included fresh flowing water and trees yielding fruit continually (Hesiod, Opera et dies 161–73). Virgil used such imagery to celebrate the reign of Augustus, picturing the new imperial age as the time when every land would produce all kinds of fruit without cultivation. Flowers and spices would spring up everywhere, and there would be such abundance that merchants would no longer need to transport goods across the sea (Ecl. 4.18–39). From the perspective of Revelation, however, the empire is the opposite of the ideal. Babylon is the imperial city that drains the world of its produce, merchants continually transporting goods by ship to meet the city's voracious appetite (Rev 18:11–14). Relentless consumption makes Babylon the antithesis of New Jerusalem, where the reign of God and the Lamb is manifested in what is produced and given (Georgi, "Visionen," 369–70; Bauckham, Theology, 135; Maier, Apocalypse, 195; Rossing, "River"; U. Sim, Das himmlische, 126).

In the city, God and the Lamb rule as one and are worshiped as one (22:3). Revelation's perspective is monotheistic and highly critical of worship given to anyone other than God, including angels (19:10; 22:8–9). For the writer, Jesus is not a second deity alongside God but the one through whom God acts to accomplish his purposes. The coming of God occurs in the coming of Jesus (1:4, 7, 8; 22:12), and salvation from God is enacted through the Lamb, so worshipers honor both together (7:10). The lordship of God is exercised in the lordship of Jesus (1:8; 19:16), so there is only one throne, not two (7:17; 22:1). Where John mentions the reign of God and Christ together, he uses a singular verb (11:15) or singular pronoun. Worship is given to "him," not "them" (22:3). The worship of Jesus is understood to be within the monotheistic worship of God (Giesen; Smalley; Bauckham, *Theology*, 60–65).

The worshipers see God's face and bear his name on their foreheads (22:4). Earlier, Christ promised to write the name of God, New Jerusalem, and his own name on the faithful, and the New Jerusalem vision shows that the outcome of Jesus' action is life in God's presence (3:12). Bearing the name also fits the priestly calling of the redeemed. The people of Israel constituted God's "priestly kingdom" (Exod 19:6), though access to the inner court of the sanctuary was limited to Israel's high priest, who wore God's name on the turban over his forehead (Exod 28:38; Josephus, *Ant.* 3.178; Josephus, *J. W.* 5.235–36; Philo, *Spec. Laws* 1.72). Revelation extends the role of "kingdom and priests" to those of every nation, who are redeemed by the Lamb (Rev 1:6; 5:10; cf. Isa 61:6; 66:21). In New Jerusalem the role of high priest is also extended to all the redeemed, who bear God's name on their foreheads, serve in God's presence, and see God's face—which not even the high priest had been allowed to do (Schüssler Fiorenza, *Priester*, 385–89; Mathewson, *New*, 212–14).

Priestly service was an important source of identity in the Roman world. Inscriptions from Asia Minor recognize the leading men and women who served in the priesthoods of Artemis, Athena, Zeus, and other deities and in the cults of the emperors. The role often included underwriting the costs of festivals, but it brought status and public honor (NOTES on Rev 2:1, 7, 12, 18; 3:1, 7, 14). When viewed from a common social perspective, Jesus' followers had no priesthood. Yet Revelation gives the whole community a priestly role that involves offering prayer and praise to God in contexts of competing claims concerning worship. Their honor comes not from the public, but from God and culminates in service in New Jerusalem (20:6; 22:3–4).

The redeemed also reign forever in God's unending light (22:5). At present, the faithful constitute "a kingdom" (1:6; 5:10), because they recognize that legitimate power belongs to the Creator and the Lamb (4:11; 5:12–13; 7:12). Revelation depicts the current context as one of conflict, in which other forces vie for dominion, but expects God and the Lamb to exercise their royal power by defeating earth's destroyers and bringing in the kingdom (11:15, 18; 12:10; 19:6). A decisive step is taken when the faithful are resurrected to reign with Christ during the thousand years when Satan is bound (20:4–6) and their reign continues in New Jerusalem, where death itself is gone (22:5). The redeemed have no independent dominion. They reign by sharing fully in the life brought about through the reign of God and the Lamb.

43. Conclusion to the Book (22:6–21)

22   ⁶Then he said to me, "These words are trustworthy and true. The Lord, the God of the spirits of the prophets, sent his angel to show his servants what things must soon take place.

⁷"See, I am coming soon!

"Blessed is the one who keeps the words of the prophecy in this scroll."

⁸I, John, am the one who heard and saw these things. And when I heard and saw them, I fell down to worship at the feet of the angel who showed them to me. ⁹But he said to me, "Do not do that! I am a fellow servant with you and your brothers the prophets, and with those who keep the words of this scroll. Worship God!"

¹⁰Then he said to me, "Do not seal up the words of the prophecy contained in this scroll, because the time is near. ¹¹Let the unjust still do injustice and the filthy still be filthy. Let the just still do what is just and the holy still be holy.

¹²"See, I am coming soon, and my reward is with me to repay each according to his work.

¹³"I am the Alpha and the Omega, the first and the last, the beginning and the end.

¹⁴"Blessed are those who wash their robes so that they may have the right to the tree of life and may enter the city by the gates. ¹⁵Outside are the dogs and the sorcerers and the immoral and the murderers and the idolaters and everyone who loves and practices deception.

¹⁶"I, Jesus, sent my angel to bear witness to all of you about these things for the assemblies. I am the root and descendant of David, the bright morning star."

¹⁷The Spirit and the bride say, "Come."
Let the one who hears say, "Come."
And let the one who is thirsty come.
Let the one who wishes receive the water of life as a gift.

¹⁸"I myself bear witness to everyone who hears the words of the prophecy in this scroll: If anyone adds to them, God will add to that person the plagues that are written in this scroll, ¹⁹and if anyone takes away from the words of this scroll of prophecy, God will take away that person's share in the tree of life and the holy city, which are written in this scroll." ²⁰The one who bears witness to these things says, "Yes, I am coming soon."

Amen. Come Lord Jesus!
²¹The grace of the Lord Jesus be with all.

NOTES

22:6 *Then he said to me, "These words are trustworthy and true.* The speaker is probably the angel who showed John the city (21:9, 15; 22:1; Mounce; Osborne; Prigent), though some interpreters propose that the speaker is Christ (Charles; Schüssler Fiorenza) or the angel who revealed the whole book to John (1:1; Aune; Satake; Smalley). But since the text does not signal a change and refers to the "sent" angel in the third person (22:6c), readers are presumably to continue picturing the angel from 21:9–22:5. The language is similar to Dan 2:45, which said of things to come, "the dream is true and its interpretation is trustworthy" (Beale).

"and the Lord, the God of the spirits of the prophets. The spirit of a prophet is the faculty within a person that allows one to prophesy. The prophet's spirit is understood to be the vehicle for God's Spirit, which inspires prophecy (Joel 2:28; Luke 1:67; Acts 11:27–28). The God of the spirits has authority over the spirits of the prophets and all people (Num 16:22; 27:16; *Jub.* 10:3; Heb 12:9; *1 Clem.* 64:1), as well as over spiritual beings (2 Macc 2:34; *1 En.* 37:2; 39:12; cf. 1QH XVIII, 8; Knibb, *Ethiopic,* 190–91). Therefore, the prophets are accountable to God. Some interpreters assume that in this context the prophets include all Christians, since the two witnesses in Rev 11:3 portray the prophetic vocation of the whole Christian community (Smalley). But here John focuses on those were specifically designated prophets in the early church (Rev 22:9; Aune; Giesen).

sent his angel to show his servants. In this passage God sends the angel, whereas in 22:16 Jesus does. The pattern recalls 1:1, in which the revelation came from God to Jesus to the angel to John. It fits the broad literary structure, with God giving a scroll to Christ, who opens it, and an angel giving the scroll to John (5:1, 8; 10:2, 9; Mazzaferri, *Genre,* 265–79; Bauckham, *Climax,* 243–57). The visions do not consistently focus on a single revealing angel but include other angels who disclose things (e.g., 17:1; 21:9; Carrell, *Jesus,* 119–27). The servants include all of John's Christian readers (NOTES on 1:1).

what things must soon take place. The language resembles Dan 2:28–29, which said that God "made known . . . what must happen in the last days" (cf. 2:45). Both passages emphasize the necessity (*dei*) of what must happen and have an eschatological perspective (cf. Mark 13:7), but Revelation adds "soon," since the message pertains to the readers and is not reserved for distant generations, as in Daniel (NOTE on Rev 1:1). The word *dei* (must) indicates that God's purposes will be carried out, but it does not signify a rigid determinism (COMMENT on 1:1).

22:7. *"See, I am coming soon!* This saying occurs repeatedly in Revelation (2:16; 3:11; 22:7, 12, 20), along with other references to Christ's coming (1:7; 2:5; 3:3; 16:15). The promise of Christ's coming was integral to early Christian tradition. Its principal aspects include the ingathering and rewarding of the righteous (14:14–17; 22:12) and judgment on God's adversaries (19:11–21). The Pauline writings say that when Christ comes at the end of the age, the ingathering will mean resurrection of the dead and transformation of those still living (1 Thess 4:14–17; 2 Thess 2:1; 1 Cor 15:23; Phil 3:20–21; Col 3:3–4). They expect Christ to give people what they deserve (1 Cor 4:4–5) and to defeat God's opponents, including death (1 Thess 1:10; 2 Thess 1:7–10; 2:8; 1 Cor 15:24). Therefore, Christians are to pray for Christ to come (1 Cor 16:22; Dunn, *Theology,* 294–315). The Synoptic Gospels identify Jesus as the Son of Man who will come on the clouds (cf. Dan 7:13) to gather in the elect (Matt 24:29–31; 26:64; Mark 13:24–27; 14:62; Luke 21:25–28; Acts 1:11) and to judge individuals and nations (Matt 16:27; 25:31–32). John's gospel expects Jesus to come and gather believers into his Father's house (John 14:1–3). Later tradition anticipates the transformation of the faithful at Christ's coming (1 John 2:28–3:2).

How soon Jesus would come is unclear in early Christian texts. Some suggest he would come within a generation (Matt 24:34; Mark 13:30), while others say that God alone knows the time (Matt 24:36; Mark 13:32; Acts 1:7). The proper response to his delay is to remain watchful (Matt 24:46; 25:1–13, 19; Mark 13:34–37; Luke 12:35–46; 21:34–36). John's gospel corrects the mistaken impression that the beloved disciple would live until Christ's coming (John 21:22–23) and affirms that Christ already comes to make his home among the faithful. His presence is revealed by the Spirit (14:23, 26; C. R. Koester, *Word*, 149–51, 182–86). Paul writes as if Jesus will come in his own lifetime (1 Thess 4:17), but other texts leave the timing open (1 Tim 6:14–15; 2 Tim 4:8; Tit 2:13). Some writers speak of Jesus' coming as imminent (Jas 5:7–9; Heb 9:28; 10:37), while 2 Peter responds to the delay by saying that with God, one day is like a thousand years, and that the added time allows for repentance (2 Pet 3:8–9; Rowland, *NIDB* 4:384–85; Adams, "'Coming'").

Some interpreters propose that for Revelation "soon" actually means that Christ will come "suddenly," whenever that might be, or that John's visions have taken him to the end of the age and from that perspective Christ's final coming appears to be "soon" (Beale; Osborne). Others say that John was simply mistaken regarding the timing (Boring 73). Some focus on the way Christ's future coming becomes a present reality in worship (Giesen). Others distinguish the eternal realm of God from the temporal realm of human life, proposing that from the divine perspective, Christ's coming is always imminent because his reign presses in on each generation (Smalley). On imminence and delay in Revelation, see the COMMENT.

"Blessed is the one. This is the sixth of seven statements about the "blessed" (*makarios*; 1:3; 14:13; 16:15; 19:9; 20:6; 22:14; INTRO IV.E.2, Table 2).

"who keeps the words of the prophecy in this scroll." As prophecy, Revelation includes things pertaining to the future, but it does not equate prophecy with prediction. The criterion for true prophecy is whether the message fosters obedience to God or promotes false worship and unethical conduct (cf. Deut 13:1–3; Matt 7:15–20; 1 John 4:1–3; 1 Cor 12:1–3; *Did.* 11–12; cf. Aune, *Prophecy*, 217–29). Therefore, to keep the prophecy is to heed its call for fidelity to God, Christ, and the Christian community (Rev 1:3; 2:26; 3:3, 8, 10; 12:17; 14:12; 22:9).

22:8. *I, John, am the one who heard and saw these things.* The use of the first person and the name "John" distinguish the writer's words from those of Jesus in 22:7. On John's identity, see INTRO II.A. On one level, this statement fits traditions about prophets seeing and hearing God's word (Jer 23:18). Before issuing an oracle about the star from Jacob (cf. Rev 22:16), Balaam gave his name and spoke of hearing God's words and seeing a vision (Num 24:15–17). Later, this pattern was used for Enoch and others (*1 En.* 1:2; Nickelsburg, *1 Enoch*, 138; *4 Ezra* 3:1; *2 Bar.* 13:1; *3 Bar.* 4:1; *Apoc. Zeph*^A 7 [*OTP* 1:508]). At the conclusion of Daniel, the seer says, "I Daniel," when recounting what he saw (Dan 12:5). Throughout Revelation, John refers to what he saw (e.g., Rev 1:12; 7:9; 13:1; 19:11; 21:1) and heard (e.g., 1:10; 6:1; 12:10; 19:1; 21:3). On a second level, official documents often concluded with a person making a statement in the first person and stating his name (P.Ryl. 172.27–28; P.Fay. 93.19–20; P.Lond. 332.27). A statement by a witness, concerning what had been seen and heard could conclude this way (*Sel. Pap.* 254). The language underscores the solemn truth of John's words (cf. Jesus in Rev 22:16, 18).

And when I heard and saw them, I fell down to worship at the feet of the angel who showed them to me. John was once overcome by the majesty of Jesus and fell at his feet but was told not to fear (1:17; cf. Tob 12:15–16; Matt 28:2–4; *T. Abr.* 9:1). When he falls down in worship before an angel, however, he is corrected (cf. *Jos. As.* 15:11). It seems unlikely that John mistook the angel for Christ (Beale), but the different scenes do distinguish Christ, who can be worshiped, from angels, who cannot (Stuckenbruck, *Angel*, 245–73). Since a nearly identical encounter with an angel occurs in Rev 19:10 and 22:8–9, some interpreters consider the repetition to be a result of editing (Aune; Charles). Yet the repetition does two things. First, the use of the same scene to conclude the descriptions of Babylon and New Jerusalem indicates that those two visions show contrasting sides of the same question, which is the worship of God. Second, it reaffirms John's connection to the readers. Like them, he is capable of misconstruing the focus of worship. Since he accepts repeated correction, the implication is that readers should do the same.

22:9. *But he said to me, "Do not do that! I am a fellow servant with you and your brothers the prophets, and with those who keep the words of this scroll.* The prohibition *hora mē* is a short form of "see that you do not" (*Did.* 6:1; Epictetus, *Diatribai* 2.9.3; Lucian, *Electr.* 6). Since the word "brother" can include all Christians (Rev 1:9; 19:10; cf. 6:11; 12:10), some interpreters think the prophets are identical to all who keep the words of the scroll (Beale; cf. Andreas; Primasius). But the passage distinguishes a group of prophets from the larger group of believers (Aune; Osborne). On circles of Christian prophets, see INTRO III.A.1.

"Worship God!" This scene reinforces the proper focus for worship without suggesting that veneration of angels was a major problem for the readers (NOTE on 19:10).

22:10. *Then he said to me, "Do not seal up the words of the prophecy contained in this scroll, for the time is near.* The speaker is presumably the angel (Aune; Mounce), not Christ (Giesen). This command differs from Daniel, in which the seer was told to seal up his text until the end of time (Dan 8:26; 12:4, 9). The *Testament of Moses* said that a revelation to Moses was to be preserved in a jar until the future day of recompense (1:17–18), and Enoch was said to have written for later generations, though the mode of preserving the text is not mentioned (*1 En.* 1:2). A variation is that Ezra was to make some texts public and to circulate other revelations among a select group (*4 Ezra* 14:6, 45–46). The pattern of delayed disclosure is used in pseudonymous writings ascribed to figures such as Daniel, Enoch, Moses, and Ezra, who lived centuries before the texts were written. These texts were said to have been sealed up or secretly preserved in order to account for the fact that they were not previously known (Collins, *Daniel*, 341–42). Revelation, however, is explicitly addressed to the writer's contemporaries. Some interpreters suggest that John thought the age was about to end, so there would be no future generations (Blount; Müller; Schüssler Fiorenza, *Book*, 49), but Revelation's approach to time is more fluid (see the COMMENT). John's book is immediately relevant because it depicts a conflict with hostile forces that is already under way.

22:11. *"Let the unjust still do injustice and the filthy still be filthy. Let the just still do what is just and the holy still be holy.* The language recalls Dan 12:10: "Many shall be purified, cleansed, and refined, but the wicked shall continue to act wickedly." A difference is that Daniel speaks descriptively of some being purified and others continuing in wickedness, whereas Revelation uses imperatives. The imperative functions rhetorically to indicate the possible responses to the message, as in Ezek 3:27: "Let those who will hear, hear; and let those who refuse to hear, refuse." Some interpreters propose that the command to continue in injustice shows that the end is so close that repentance is no longer possible (Mounce; Prigent; Roloff). Others relate such commands to divine sovereignty: God has determined who belongs to the Lamb and to the beast, and each group will inevitably respond to his word with acceptance or rejection (Beale; cf. Osborne). These approaches miss the rhetorical function of the verse, which is to startle readers into changing their behavior (Blount; Giesen; Müller). The goal is to move the "filthy" to "wash their robes" (Rev 22:11, 14).

The verb "to be filthy" in a few manuscripts is *rypanthētō*, from *rypainein* (א 1854; NA[27]), but in most it is *rypareuthētō*, from *rypareuein* (046 1006 1841 2329), which is found only here in Greek literature. As the best-attested and yet most difficult reading, it is probably original. John evidently coined this verb as a derivative of the previous noun *ryparos* (Aune). Coining a word in this way was a familiar practice (Demetrius, *Eloc.* 96–98; Lausberg, *Handbook* §§547–51). It enables John to create a sequence in which each noun in Rev 22:11 is followed by a corresponding verbal expression.

22:12. *"See, I am coming soon, and my reward is with me to repay each according to his work.* On Jesus' coming, see the NOTES and COMMENT on 22:7. Reward (*misthos*) can refer to something positive (1 Cor 3:8) or negative (2 Macc 8:33). The language recalls Isa 40:10: "See, the Lord God comes with might . . . his reward is with him, and his recompense before him." The LXX translates a similar saying in Isa 62:11 to read "the savior" comes with reward, which could invite messianic interpretation of the theme (Fekkes, *Isaiah*, 276–78). Yet most sources understood that it was God who would repay people according to their deeds (Pss 28:4; 62:12; Prov 24:12; Jer 17:10; *Pss. Sol.* 2:16, 34; 17:8; Rom 2:6; 2 Tim 4:14; cf. *1 Clem.* 34:3; *4 Ezra* 7:35). Revelation modifies the tradition by ascribing God's actions to Christ, a pattern that anticipates a similar shift in the next verse (cf. Matt 16:27; John 5:25–29).

22:13. *"I am the Alpha and the Omega, the first and the last, the beginning and the end.* On "Alpha and Omega," see the NOTE on Rev 1:8. On the "first and last," see the NOTE on 1:17 (cf. 2:8). On "beginning and end," see the NOTE on 21:6. Revelation ascribes to Christ a role at the beginning and end of all things. Other NT writers gave Christ a role in creation, often by identifying him as the embodiment of God's word or wisdom (1 Cor 8:6; Col 1:15–17; Heb 1:2; John 1:1–4; Brown, *Gospel*, 1:521–24; Lincoln, *Colossians*, 597–98; C. R. Koester, *Hebrews*, 186–88). God created by his word (Gen 1:3; Ps 33:6), and Revelation calls Christ God's word (*logos*, Rev 19:13), which could include a creative role, though this association is not developed in the book. God's wisdom was also said to have been present in the beginning (LXX *archē*), participating in creation (Prov 8:22–31; cf. Wis 9:9; Sir 24:3). Using similar language, Revelation calls Christ "the *archē* of God's creation," which could suggest he is creation's beginning or origin, though it more probably means he is its ruler (Rev 3:14). The extent to which Revelation develops a word or wisdom Christology is unclear (Dunn, *Christology*, 247). Identifying both God and Jesus as the end assumes that God exercises his eschatological role as redeemer, judge, and ruler through Christ (Col 1:16; Heb 1:2; cf. John 5:21–29; 17:1–5, 24).

22:14. *"Blessed are those who wash their robes.* Since no change is indicated, the speaker is probably Christ (Giesen), rather than John (Smalley) or the angel (Vanni, "Liturgical"). This is the last of the seven references to the "blessed" (*makarios*; 1:3; 14:13; 16:15; 19:9; 20:6; 22:7; INTRO IV.E.2, Table 2). The unclean were not to come into contact with other people or to appear in God's presence (NOTE on 21:27). Since uncleanness could be physical, purification involved washing one's clothes and body (Lev 11:25; 13:6; 14:8; Num 31:24; 4Q274 1 I, 3; 4Q512 10–11 6; 11Q19 XLIX, 17–20; L, 8, 13; LI, 4–5). When the uncleanness arose from sin, washing garments was to be accompanied by repentance and a change in one's manner of life (Num 8:21). Such washing was done before meeting God at Mount Sinai (Exod 19:10–14) and entering the sanctuary (Num 8:7, 15; 11Q19 XLV, 7–10). Here, washing is a metaphor for the removal of sin that occurs through repentance and faith in the redemptive action of Christ (Rev 7:14). Although some interpreters suggest that baptismal washing is involved (Prigent), it is not the focus. The verb "wash" is in the active voice and present tense, indicating ongoing repentance and faith rather than the singular washing of baptism, which was done to a person by someone else (Aune; Giesen).

The reading "wash their robes" is well attested (א A 1006 1841 2050 2053), and a similar expression is used in Rev 7:14. The alternative reading is "those who do the commandments" (046; KJV; Goranson, "Text"). Revelation used a similar expression earlier—though it said "keeping" (*tērein*) rather than "doing" (*poiein*) the commandments (12:17; 14:12)—but this variant in 22:14 has weak support. Since *poiountes tas entolas* is similar to *plynontes tas stolas*, the variant could have arisen through an error of the eye or ear.

"so that they may have the right to the tree of life. Eating from the tree of life means everlasting life in God's presence (NOTE on 22:2). It was said of the tree: "no flesh has the right to touch it until the great judgment" when its fruit will be given to the chosen (*1 En.* 25:4–5). According to *Tg. Neof.* Gen 3:22–24, those who observe God's commandments will eat from the tree of life. By way of comparison, Revelation understands that the redeemed will obey the commandments (Rev 12:17; 14:12) but assumes that access to the tree comes from the cleansing provided by Christ (7:14). The expression *exousian epi* can mean having "authority over" something. This can be threatening (6:8; 13:7; 16:9), but here, authority over the tree of life means authority to eat from it and live (Osborne).

"and may enter the city by the gates. Those with a place in a redeemed Jerusalem were told, "Go through, go through the gates" (Isa 62:10; Beale). To the righteous it was said, "Open the gates, so that the righteous nation that keeps faith may enter in" (Isa 26:2). Similar language was used for entering the sanctuary (Ps 118:19–20), and in Revelation the righteous enter New Jerusalem, the place of worship (Rev 22:3, 11). Some sources expected the redeemer to open the gates of paradise so that the redeemed could enter and eat from the tree of life (*T. Levi* 18:10, 14). In Revelation Christ does this through his self-sacrifice (Rev 7:14; 22:14).

22:15. *"Outside are the dogs and the sorcerers and the immoral and the murderers and the idolaters and everyone who loves and practices deception.* For most behaviors listed here, see the NOTES on 21:8 (cf. 9:20–21; 21:27). New to this list are dogs. In Jewish texts dogs ate what was unclean (Exod 22:15; Ps.-Phoc. 185). Calling someone a dog showed contempt (1 Sam 17:43; 2 Kgs 8:13; Homer, *Il.* 11.360; Homer, *Od.* 17.248). In a specific sense, Deut 23:18 refers to male prostitutes as dogs, which could mean that Revelation uses the term for the sexually immoral (Aune; Ford). But it was also used for fools (Prov 26:11), greedy rulers (Isa 56:10), Gentiles (Mark 7:27), those contemptuous of the gospel (Matt 7:6), false teachers (Phil 3:2), unbelievers (*Did.* 9:5), and heretics

(2 Pet 2:21–22; Ign. *Eph.* 7:1). In Revelation the dogs may be the unclean, cowards, or abominable (cf. Rev 21:8, 27). Some ancient writers wanted dogs excluded from the holy city (4Q394 8 IV, 8–9; Philonenko, "'Dehors'"). Some Greco-Roman groups kept dogs out of sanctuaries (Plutarch, *Mor.* 290B–C), but others admitted them (Strelan, "Outside"). In Revelation, the dogs are the unrepentant, who are excluded because sin has no place in God's city.

22:16. *"I, Jesus, sent my angel to bear witness.* Both the angel and Jesus bear witness (22:16, 18, 20). Official documents, such as the wills that governed inheritance, often concluded with the names of witnesses, who identified themselves by saying "I am" (*eimi*) and stating their ages and distinguishing physical marks (P.Oxy. 105.14–20; 491.18–25; 492.18–24). As the key witness, Jesus now gives his name before addressing a possible loss of inheritance (Rev 22:18–19). His distinguishing features are messianic titles (22:16b), introduced with the expression *egō eimi*, which has divine overtones (1:8, 17).

"to all of you about these things for the assemblies. The "you" (*hymin*) is plural, and the identity of the intended recipients is disputed. The first interpretation is most plausible:

1. A group of prophets within the Christian community. The plural in 22:9 probably recalls the group of prophets who were mentioned in 22:6. Since John belongs to the circle of prophets (22:9), they serve as his emissaries. They deliver his message *epi*—"for" or "to"—the churches (Aune, *Apocalypticism*, 250–60; Biguzzi, "Chaos"; Schüssler Fiorenza, *Book*, 146; Müller; Osborne).
2. "You" as synonymous with "the churches." The plural could mean that the message is simply addressed to all of John's readers (Sweet). Grammatically, however, this view is improbable since it would mean the churches are given a message for the churches (Aune). Some interpreters suggest that *epi* means "concerning" the churches (cf. 10:11; Yarbro Collins, *Crisis*, 39; Prigent; Satake). This usage is unusual, however. Others note that some manuscripts read *en* (A 1006 1841 2329), so that the angel addresses "you" who are "in" the churches (Beale). Deleting the preposition altogether gives the same effect (Andreas). Yet *epi* has good attestation (‭א‬ 051 2030 2050 241) and is the most difficult reading, so it is probably original.
3. The angels of the seven churches (Smalley). In the early chapters a message was addressed to the angel of each church (1:20; 2:1, 8, 12, etc.). Here this is unlikely, however, since the focus is on Jesus sending his angel (singular). On the mediating angel, see the Note on 1:1.

"I am the root and descendant of David, the bright morning star." The root of David is a messianic title that recalls Isa 11:1, 10 (Note on Rev 5:5). The descendent (*genos*) of David is a related title (Ign. *Eph.* 20:2; Ign. *Trall.* 9:1; Ign. *Smyr.* 1:1), echoing the promise that David's offspring would establish God's kingdom (2 Sam 7:12; 4Q174 1 I, 10; John 7:42; Rom 1:3). The morning star recalls the oracle of Balaam, who said that a star would rise from Jacob to rule the nations (Num 24:17). Jewish sources took the star to be a messianic figure (*T. Levi* 18:3; *T. Jud.* 24:1; 4Q175 12). In CD VII, 18–20, the star is the interpreter of the law and his scepter is a royal figure, but in 1QM XI, 6, the star defeats Israel's foes (Collins, *Scepter*, 61–80). Here Revelation follows the messianic interpretation by identifying Jesus as the star. By way of contrast, a comet, or "star," was

said to have appeared after Julius Caesar's death, signifying his deification. The star was pictured on imperial coins, and the symbol was bequeathed to Augustus and Tiberius, who shared imperial rule (Horace, *Odes* 1.12.47; Valerius Maximus, *Mem.* 1.pref; cf. the morning star in Statius, *Silvae* 4.1.1–4; Whitaker, "Falling"). In Revelation Christ is the legitimate ruler, who grants his followers a share in his reign, signified by the star.

22:17. *The Spirit and the bride say, "Come."* Some interpreters identify the Spirit and bride with the voice of the Christian community in which the Spirit is now at work. It is preferable, however, to take the Spirit and bride as voices from the visionary world, which readers overhear in John's narration. "Come" (*erchou*) is in the second person singular. Some interpreters see this as an invitation to come to Christ in faith. Their approach is to understand all three occurrence of "come" here as addressing the world, calling for repentance and faith (Beale; Blount; Mounce; Osborne). Most, however, read "come" as a response to Jesus, who has repeatedly announced his coming (22:7, 12). The prayer "come" is a response to his word, as is clearly the case in 22:20 (Aune; Boxall; Giesen; Reddish; Roloff; Smalley).

Let the one who hears say, "Come." Texts were read aloud in groups (1 Thess 5:27; Col 4:16) and by individuals in private (Acts 8:30; Pliny the Younger, *Ep.* 3.5.10–12). Revelation was to be read in the assembly but here uses the singular to call each person to respond (Rev 1:3; cf. 2:7, 11, etc.; 22:18).

And let the one who is thirsty come. Let the one who wishes receive the water of life as a gift. The language recalls Isa 55:1, in which God says, "Ho, everyone who thirsts, come to the waters" and buy "without price" (Fekkes, *Isaiah*, 260–64). In Revelation thirst signifies a need for God, and the water of life is obtained through resurrection to life in New Jerusalem (NOTE on Rev 21:6).

22:18. *"I myself bear witness to everyone who hears the words of the prophecy in this scroll.* Some interpreters suggest that John now speaks (Prigent; Roloff; Smalley), but since Jesus is the speaker in 22:16 and the witness in 22:20, he probably speaks here (Blount; Giesen; Osborne). Sayings have been verified by oath (10:5–7) and by stating that "these words are trustworthy and true" (19:9; 21:5; 22:6). Now Jesus himself bears "witness," as one would do in an official document. In the legal sphere, a person's share in inheritance was dealt with by a will (P.Oxy. 105.4, 6, 9, 11). The will would conclude with people stating their names and "I bear witness" (*martyrō*, P.Oxy. 105.13, 14; cf. 489.24, 26; 490.15, 16). This language also appears in solemn agreements (P.Oxy. 3483.11, 12). Since Revelation speaks of retaining or losing a share in God's city (Rev 22:19), it is fitting that Jesus has stated his name (22:16) and now attests the contents.

"If anyone adds to them, God will add to that person the plagues that are written in this scroll. The usual Greek form of the word pair "add/take away" was *prosthenai/aphelein* (Deut 4:2 LXX; 1 Macc 8:30; Philo, *Mos.* 2.34; Josephus, *Ag. Ap.* 1.42). For the word "add," however, Revelation uses *epitheinai*, which was also used for inflicting blows, or plagues (Acts 10:30; 16:23). There are two main approaches to interpretation:

1. Warning not to falsify the scroll's message by one's teaching or manner of life. Exhortations not to add or take away from God's word usually focused on the need for complete obedience and avoiding false teaching (Prov 30:6; 11Q19 LIV, 6–7; *Barn.* 19:11; Eusebius, *Hist. eccl.* 5.16.3). The language recalls Deuteronomy: "You must neither add anything to what I command you nor take away anything from it," and "You must diligently observe everything that I command you; do not add

to it or take anything from it" (Deut 4:2; 12:32). These passages do not address only copyists, who transcribe the text, but call Israel to be obedient. Those passages make adding or taking away equivalent to disobedience, especially through idolatry and false prophecy. Revelation combines these texts with another that warns idolaters, "All the curses written in this book will descend on them," for they will suffer calamity "in accordance with all the curses of the covenant written in this book of the law" (Deut 29:20–21). In a context in which John's opponents accommodate idolatry (Rev 2:2, 14, 20), this passage warns against deviating from Revelation's call for teaching and a manner of life that are faithful to God (Beale; Prigent; Smalley; R. Thomas, "Spiritual," 208; Tilly, "Textsicherung," 232–47). An analogy is Paul's curse on those who alter the gospel through their preaching (Gal 1:6–9).

2. Warning against tampering with the written text. Because texts could be altered as they circulated (Dio Chrysostom, *Disc.* 42.4), a writer might say, "I ask those who read my books not to add or remove anything from the present contents" (Artemidorus, *Onirocritica* 2.70). Revelation goes further, invoking a conditional curse on those who alter the text. The first part states that if a certain action is performed, the punishment in the second part will be implemented by divine action (cf. Deut 28:15–19; CIG 2664.5–6). To preserve the integrity of the LXX translation of Jewish law, "they commanded that a curse should be laid, as was their custom, on anyone who should alter the version by any change to any part of the written text, or any deletion either" (*Ep. Arist.* 311; the accounts in Philo, *Mos.* 2.34, and Josephus, *Ant.* 12.109, lack the curse). Sacred writings were to be preserved without alteration (Josephus, *Ag. Ap.* 1.42; *1 En.* 104:10–13; Nickelsburg, *1 Enoch*, 533–34). Accordingly, Rev 22:18–19 can be read as a warning against altering John's text (Irenaeus, *Haer.* 5.30.1; Aune; Hiecke and Nicklas, "*Worte*," 72–82; Reddish; Royalty, "Don't"). In the COMMENT the call for faithful obedience is primary and the implications for preserving the text are secondary.

22:19. *"and if anyone takes away from the words of this scroll of prophecy, God will take away that person's share in the tree of life and in the holy city, which are written in this scroll."* In Deut 4:1–2 those who faithfully adhere to God's word can enter the promised land; in Rev 22 they can enter New Jerusalem. The word "share" (*meros*) indicates inheritance (NOTE on Rev 21:8). The insistence on not adding or taking away anything has been called a canonization formula, which makes a text function as normative Scripture. Some think John is appealing to the idea of canonization to establish the authority of his own text (Bousset; Royalty, "Don't"). Nevertheless, the word pair "add/take away" was widely used in contexts that did not pertain to the canonical status of a text. The word pair affirmed accuracy in reporting (Josephus, *Ant.* 1.17; Josephus, *J.W.* 1.26; Chariton, *Chaer.* 3.1.5–6). A warning against adding or taking away was designed to safeguard the integrity of a message (van Unnik, "De la règle"; Aune).

22:20. *The one who bears witness to these things says, "Yes, I am coming soon."* On witness, see the NOTE on 22:16. On Jesus' coming, see the NOTE and COMMENT on 22:7.

Amen. Come Lord Jesus! This saying was used in early Christian worship. The Aramaic form is *maranatha*, which can be interpreted either as a prayer, *marana tha* ("Our Lord, come"), or as a confession, *maran atha* ("Our Lord comes" or "has come"). The Greek form in Revelation is a prayer that is used after the conditional curse that warns against altering the message. Paul used the Aramaic form in a similar way after a conditional curse that warns those who have no love for the Lord (1 Cor 16:22–23). An analogous pattern appears in the *Didache*, which refers to the Eucharist: "If anyone is holy, let him come; if anyone is not, let him repent. Maranatha! Amen" (*Did.* 10:6).

Some interpreters argue that Revelation, 1 Corinthians, and the *Didache* all reflect eucharistic practice, which would mean that the invitation for the thirsty to come in Rev 22:17 would be an invitation to the meal, and the prayer for Jesus' coming would focus on his presence within the worshiping community (Blount; Giesen; Harrington; Roloff; Smalley). A eucharistic setting is clear in the *Didache*. In 1 Corinthians some think Paul reflects a eucharistic connection, since the meal anticipates Christ's future coming (1 Cor 11:25; K. G. Kuhn, *TDNT* 4:466–72; Schrage, *Der erste*, 4:472–73), but others think the ending of 1 Corinthians simply presses for clarity of commitment in view of Christ's future coming (Eriksson, *Traditions*, 114–19; Thistleton, *First*, 1348–52). The absence of clear allusions to the Lord's Supper in Revelation makes a eucharistic setting unlikely here, and the invitation to come and drink refers to the water of New Jerusalem, not the Eucharist (Rev 22:1; Satake; Müller; Osborne).

22:21. *The grace of the Lord Jesus be with all.* Revelation's closing resembles those of Pauline letters:

The grace of the Lord Jesus	be with you	1 Cor 16:23
The grace of our Lord Jesus	be with you	Rom 16:20
The grace of our Lord Jesus Christ	be with you	1 Thess 5:28
The grace of the Lord Jesus Christ . . .	be with you all	2 Cor 13:13
The grace of our Lord Jesus Christ	be with you all	2 Thess 3:18
The grace of the Lord Jesus Christ	be with your spirit	Phil 4:23; Phlm 25
The grace of our Lord Jesus Christ	be with your spirit	Gal 6:18

Later forms read "Grace be with you" (Col 4:18; 1 Tim 6:21; cf. 2 Tim 4:22) or "with you all" (Tit 3:15) or "with all who love our Lord Jesus Christ" (Eph 6:24). Variations appear in other texts (Heb 13:25; *1 Clem.* 65:2; *Barn.* 21:9), but not in 1 and 2 Peter, the Johannine Epistles, or Jude. The letters of Ignatius and Polycarp conclude with forms of "be strong" (*errōsthe*). Revelation follows the Pauline pattern. The writer assumes that Jesus is Lord (Rev 17:14; 19:16) but uses the expression "Lord Jesus" only here and in the responsive "Come, Lord Jesus" of the previous verse. The author may be using an expression that circulated among the Pauline churches.

Manuscript evidence varies at several points. First, some add "Christ" (046 051 94 1006 1854) or read "our Lord Jesus Christ" (205 254 2067); but the shorter reading "Lord Jesus" is well attested (א A 1611 2053 2062), and the longer versions echo the conclusions of many of the Pauline letters noted above. Second, some ask that grace be with "all" (A; ESV, NAB), while others specify "all of you" (296; KJV) or "all of us" (2050), and still others read "the saints" (א; cf. NIV), "your saints" (2329), "all the saints" (051; NRSV), or "all his saints" (2030). The two shortest and best attested readings are "all" and "the saints." The others seem to be expansions, some reflecting Pauline patterns. Of the shorter readings, some interpreters argue that "the saints" is original since it is not used in Pauline conclusions but is used for Christians in Revelation (Rev 5:8; 8:3–4; 11:18, etc.). They also assume that John would limit grace to believers and not extend it to all (Aune). Yet better manuscript evidence supports "all" (A), which also differs from

Paul, who regularly includes "you." Since the variants show a tendency toward greater specificity among the recipients, it seems likely that the simple "all" is the original reading that was later changed (*TCGNT*[2], 690–91; Beale; Osborne; Smalley). Third, a final amen is included in some manuscripts (א 046 051), but not others (A 1006 1841). If the word were original, it is unlikely to have been omitted; therefore, it seems to be a scribal addition.

COMMENT

The description of New Jerusalem brought readers into the future, to the water and tree of life, where God's servants worship and reign in everlasting light (Rev 22:1–5). An exchange between John and an angel forms a literary bridge between the majesty of the city and the book's concluding admonitions (22:6–9). The entire conclusion also makes a transition from the visionary world to the readers' world (22:6–21). Its principal function is to shape the way readers receive the text. Repeated references to "this scroll" (22:7, 9, 10, 18, 19) enjoin readers to see John's work as a whole, as a message from God and the risen Jesus to the Christian community (22:6, 16).

The conclusion of Revelation (22:6–21) is the counterpart to its introduction (1:1–8). Readers were initially told that the message of the book came from God and Jesus through an angel to John, to show God's servants what must soon take place; and at the end this pattern is repeated (1:1; 22:6, 16). Both the introduction and conclusion say that this book is a prophecy (1:3; 22:7, 10, 18, 19), that those who keep it are blessed (1:3; 22:7), and that the time is near (1:3; 22:10). God and Christ are called the Alpha and Omega (1:8; 22:13), and Christ is said to be coming (1:7; 22:7, 12, 20). John speaks in his own name, attesting what he heard and saw (1:1–2, 4; 22:8). The readers are identified as those in the churches (1:4; 22:16), and responses include "yes" and "amen" (1:7; 22:20). The fact that the book is framed in this way means that its final form is designed to be read as a whole (Mounce; Roloff; Sänger, "Amen," 81–85).

Epistolary features enhance the framing effect. The salutation "grace to you" is matched by an epistolary conclusion, "The grace of the Lord Jesus be with all" (1:4; 22:21). Revelation lacks the personal greetings that conclude many Greco-Roman and Pauline letters, but other epistolary features are present in a modified way:

1 Cor 16:21–23	Rev 22:16–21
I, Paul write this greeting	I, Jesus . . . bear witness
Let anyone be accursed who has no love for the Lord	If anyone adds . . . God will add the plagues . . .
Our Lord, come!	Come, Lord Jesus!
The grace of the Lord Jesus be with you.	The grace of the Lord Jesus be with all.

On Rev 22:6–21, see Biguzzi, "Chaos"; Boring, "Voice"; Goranson, "Text"; Hartman, "Form"; Hiecke and Nicklas, "*Worte*"; Kowalski, "Prophetie"; Longenecker, "Linked"; Philonenko, "Dehors"; Royalty, "Don't"; Sänger, "Amen"; Strelan, "Outside"; Robert Thomas, "Spiritual"; Tilly, "Textsicherung"; Vanni, "Liturgical"; Whitaker, "Falling."

Like Paul's use of his own name, the first person "I, Jesus" is a verbal signature that identifies him as the authority behind the message (Weima, *Neglected*, 207). Where one might expect exhortations, Paul pronounces a conditional curse (*anathēma*) on anyone who effectively denies the gospel message—that is, who has no love for the Lord—and couples this with a prayer that the Lord will come (*maranatha*; 1 Cor 16:22; Eriksson, *Traditions*, 294–95). Similarly, Revelation places a conditional curse on anyone who falsifies the prophetic message and follows it with the prayer that the Lord might come. Revelation's concluding greeting of grace from the Lord Jesus follows those of Pauline letters (NOTE on Rev 22:21).

Interpreters sometimes suggest that Revelation and 1 Corinthians conclude in similar ways because both were to be read during corporate worship. In some gatherings, speakers brought prophetic words from God, while others uttered prayers or added "Amen" (1 Cor 11:4–5; 14:15–16, 29–32). A similar interplay of voices is evident in Rev 22:6–21. As Revelation was read aloud (1:3), listeners would have heard John's narration of his visionary experience along with words from the exalted Christ given prophetically in the first person: "I am coming soon" (22:7, 12). The Spirit and bride say "Come," and there are direct invitations for listeners to respond, so that all might say, "Amen. Come, Lord Jesus" (22:17, 20). Revelation not only directs people to "worship God," but includes responsive forms that invite readers into such worship (22:9; Vanni; "Liturgical"). Some interpreters relate Revelation's conclusion to a eucharistic setting (Giesen; Harrington; Prigent; Roloff; Karrer, *Johannesoffenbarung*, 252), but the absence of clear references to the Eucharist in Revelation makes this unlikely. The interplay between prayer, prophetic word, and response seems to mirror the broader worship life within John's churches (Müller 282; Biguzzi, "Chaos," 207–8; Kowalski, "Prophetie"; Thompson, *Book*, 54–56; on hymns, see the INTRO IV.E.1).

Revelation is designed to shape the commitments of those who hear it, and its conclusion has the features of persuasive speech. There is no reason to think that John was rhetorically trained, but speakers in antiquity often reiterated main themes in their conclusions (*Rhetorica ad Herennium* 2.30.47; Quintilian, *Inst.* 6.1.1; Lausberg, *Handbook* §§431–42). The same was true of letters, whose conclusions could function rhetorically (Eriksson, *Traditions*, 280–84; Rossing, *Choice*, 159–61). Revelation has sharply contrasted the destructive consequences of following the beast with the blessings given to followers of the Lamb. In the conclusion these antitheses are repeated in succinct form, so that listeners will consider what it means to keep or lose a share in New Jerusalem (Rev 22:11, 14–15, 18–19). Stylistically, contrasts are made by juxtaposing word pairs like unrighteous and righteous, filthy and holy, and coining a new word to fit the parallel structure (NOTE on 22:11). Through paronomasia, the author plays on different meanings of "add" and "take way" to show the correlation between action and result (22:18–19; Aune; on paronomasia, see INTRO V.B.3).

On the emotional level, the conclusion elicits fear and hope—which play a role in persuasion (Aristotle, *Rhet.* 2.5.1–22; deSilva, *Seeing*, 182–85). The repeated references to Christ's imminent coming generate a sense of expectancy that can take two forms: For the ungodly it will mean judgment and exclusion from God's city, but for the faithful it will mean salvation. The grim portrayal of the ungodly is designed to repel listeners, while the invitation to come to the water of life generates a desire to be included among the faithful (22:17; Cicero, *Inv.* 1.52.98). For John's persecuted readers, the warnings and promises are a call to remain faithful in the face of opposition (Rev 2:8–11; 3:7–13). For other readers, who are complacent and accommodate polytheistic practices, they are a call to repent and "wash their robes" (22:14). In both cases, however, the desired outcome is the same: perseverance in faith.

Acceptance of the message assumes that the audience has confidence in the speaker (Aristotle, *Rhet.* 1.2.4). Aspects of the conclusion emphasize John's credibility, but throughout the passage John becomes less visible as Christ emerges as the primary speaker. Christ's voice breaks in using the first person, "I am coming soon" (22:7, 12). At points it is not clear whether a statement is made by an angel or Jesus (22:10–11, 14–15), Jesus or John (22:18–19), but in the end, Jesus' voice is clearly heard (22:20). Although some interpreters take this ambiguity as a sign of disorderly composition (Charles; Ford; Kraft), it reflects an underlying unity. The assumption is that the book's message originates with God and the exalted Jesus, who send it to the readers through the angel and John. John acts independently when he mistakenly worships the angel (22:8–9), but where the speaker's identity is left unclear, readers are to hear Christ addressing them *through* the angel and John (Mounce; Roloff; Boring, "Voice"). The language recalls divine speech from Deuteronomy, Isaiah, Daniel, and other biblical passages, enhancing the sense that readers encounter a divine word in John's text (see the NOTES).

Some interpreters divide the passage into five or more parts (Aune; Beale; Osborne), but a simpler proposal is to read it in three sections (cf. Biguzzi, "Chaos"). First is the interchange between John and the angel (22:6–9). Here, God is the originator of the message and the focus of worship. The angel and readers are God's servants, and all are called to "keep" the message of the prophetic book. Christ speaks briefly in the middle of the opening section, announcing his coming. Second is a section on the just and the unjust, those who are promised a place in God's city and those who are warned of exclusion (22:10–15). Again, Christ announces his coming in the middle of the section but now continues speaking until the end. Third, the passage returns to the theme of the prophetic book (22:16–20). This section is framed by statements that identify Jesus as the book's authenticating witness. As before, another voice sounds in the middle—but instead of Christ announcing his coming, the Spirit and bride say "come" and invite hearers to do the same. The epistolary greeting concludes the section.

Keeping the Prophecy of This Book (22:6–9)

As the vision of New Jerusalem fades, the angelic guide calls the words John has received "trustworthy and true," repeating a scene played out earlier (22:6a; cf. 19:9–10). The language tacitly emphasizes how the message is to be received. Previously, angels told of the reliability of specific sayings, and this emphasis now extends to the whole book (19:9; 21:5). The integrity of the message comes from the character of God and Christ, who are trustworthy and true (3:14; 6:10; 15:3; 19:11). Then God is called "the God of the spirits of the prophets" (22:6b). In one sense this means that the message comes from the God who inspires prophets. This includes John, who writes the message, along with the other prophets who will deliver his text to the readers (22:9, 16). The prophets are to be heard as God's emissaries. In another sense the spirits within the prophets are accountable to God, and the prophets are not to alter the message (22:18–19). Accountability to God is important in a social context in which some, who call themselves apostles and prophets, advocate views that are at odds with John's message (2:2, 14, 20; Biguzzi, "Chaos").

John has been shown "what things must soon take place," creating a sense that God is about to act (22:6c). At the same time, the internal dynamics of the book caution against trying to determine what "soon" means chronologically. The angel speaks in the plural about "what things" must take place, which include more than Christ's final coming. By using this expression in both the introduction and the conclusion (1:1; 22:6), the author shows that the things to take place "soon" encompass all the visions in the book. These begin with messages to the seven churches and culminate in the new heaven and earth. If the book anticipates what must soon take place (*genesthai*, 1:1), the horizon extends to the point where God can say "all is done" (*gegonan*, 21:6) in the new creation—which occurs after visions of the saints reigning for a thousand years.

What takes place in the visionary world does not translate into a clear sequence of events in the readers' world. The seal visions depict threats of conquest, violence, hardship, and death that are difficult to locate at one moment in time, and when the great day of wrath seems to arrive, the progression is interrupted by scenes of redemption (6:17; 7:1–17). The trumpet visions show plagues falling on the earth, but their function is to disclose the ineffectiveness of wrath in bringing repentance (9:20–21). They do not lay out an inexorable series of events, since the sequence is again interrupted and John is told to prophesy again *in between* the sixth and seventh trumpets (10:1–11). By that point two woes have occurred, and a third is coming "soon" (9:12; 11:14). The third woe is equivalent to the seventh trumpet, which follows immediately, yet the seventh trumpet vision extends the story by announcing God's kingdom and summarizing the entire second half of the book. Readers are hard-pressed to determine what "soon" means.

That pattern persists in the second half of Revelation, where visionary time has no straightforward connection to ordinary time. The visions portray the Christian community's conflict with evil, which lasts for three and a half years (12:6; 13:5), yet it begins when Christ is exalted to heaven and Satan is thrown down to earth (12:5, 7–9), and it ends when Christ returns and Satan is bound (19:11–20:3). The time the devil rages is "short" in the visionary world, but it encompasses the entire span between Christ's first and final comings (12:12). For John's earliest readers, the time since Christ's first coming had already lasted for one or two generations—much more than three and a half years. Revelation may disclose "what things must soon take place," but the imagery, interrupted sequences, and symbolic use of time mean that readers cannot translate the visions into a straightforward series of events in their own world (Maier, *Apocalypse*, 123–59; Bauckham, *Theology*, 157–59).

The question of time continues when Jesus interjects, "See, I am coming soon" (22:7a). The saying is repeated twice more, heightening the sense of anticipation (22:12, 20). Hope for the coming of Jesus took various forms (Note on 22:7). In Revelation it has several dimensions. First, the Jesus who died and rose years before the book was written is understood to be already present. The inaugural vision shows that Christ is now among the seven churches, walking in their midst (1:12–20). Second, the Christ who is already present may "come" for judgment in contingent and local ways. Readers are warned that "if" they do not repent, Christ will come to them in judgment (2:5, 16; 3:3). Such judgment could mean losing status as a congregation (2:5) or facing Christ's judgment—the sword from his mouth (2:16). But if repentance does occur, the implication is that Christ will not come in this way. Third, Christ is expected to come to bring the final defeat of evil and redemption of his people. Instead of a local or contingent coming, every eye will see him (1:7). He will gather the redeemed from the earth and bring a definitive end to the beast and false prophet, who sought dominion over the world (14:14–17; 19:11–21).

Some interpreters identify Christ's words "I am coming soon" in 22:7, 12, and 20 (cf. 2:25; 3:11) with his final coming (Aune; Blount; Murphy; Osborne), others with his local comings (Giesen), and still others think both may be included (Beale; Boxall). From a literary perspective, it is significant that Revelation uses nearly identical language for both the local and final comings of Christ, so they are not sharply distinguished. Whether dealing with local idolatry at Pergamum or the idolatrous beast and false prophet that oppress the world, Christ comes to make war with the sword of his mouth (2:16; 19:15). Whether speaking of the complacent at Sardis or a battle with the hostile kings of earth, Christ says he is coming like a thief (3:3; 16:15). In both his local and final comings Christ gives people what their "works" deserve (2:5; 3:2–3; 22:12). To be clear, Revelation does not reduce Christ's coming to a present spiritual encounter with individuals. The book does envision a final defeat of evil for the world as a whole (Blount). Yet Revelation also assumes that Christ is already present and uses language that blurs the lines between his local and final comings. The result is that the word "soon" calls readers to persevere in hope, even as differences between visionary time and ordinary time caution them to resist calculating what "soon" means in chronological terms (cf. Frey, "Was erwartet").

Christ says, "Blessed is the one who keeps the words of the prophecy in this scroll" (22:7b). This recalls the introduction, where John's text was called prophecy (1:3; cf. 22:10, 18, 19). In Revelation prophecy is a special form of communication from God to a human recipient. The prophetic message includes calls for repentance and warnings of judgment (2:5, 16; 3:3; 14:7), exhortations to be faithful and promises of blessing (2:10; 3:11; 7:14; 13:10; 14:12–13). In Revelation, the criterion for true prophecy is not simple prediction. False prophets are not denounced for making incorrect predictions but for promoting false worship (2:20; 13:11–18; 16:13–14; 19:20), whereas true prophets are like the witnesses clothed in sackcloth, who summon people to repentance (11:3, 10). True prophecy directs people to God and Jesus (19:10). This is why people are to respond to John's prophecy by "keeping" it—by resisting sin, obeying God's commandments, holding firmly to the message of Jesus, and living in a manner consistent with it (2:26; 3:3, 8; 12:17; 14:12). "Keeping" the words means worshiping God, washing one's robe through repentance, and rejecting forms of behavior that are inconsistent with the faith (22:8, 14–15).

John attests to his experience using his own name (22:8a; cf. 1:1, 4, 9), not the name of a figure from the past, as other apocalyptic writers did (Dan 12:5; *1 En.* 1:2; 93:2; *4 Ezra* 3:1; see the INTRO I.A and IV.A.1). Since John was apparently known among his readers, their reception of the message would depend in part on whether they trusted him (Aristotle, *Rhet.* 1.2.4; deSilva, *Seeing*, 127–28). He shapes their perception by indicating that he is not the book's author but like his readers is one who "hears" the message (Rev 22:8a, 18a). Then, for the second time, he recounts his own mistaken response to what he saw and heard. He fell down to worship the angel and was told not to do so (19:10; 22:8b–9). This reinforces John's credibility. By acknowledging where he was mistaken, he underscores that what he says is faithfully presented (Quintilian, *Inst.* 4.1.8–10). Moreover, by accepting correction a second time, John gives readers incentive to do the same, by receiving correction through his text.

The angel identifies himself as God's servant (*doulos*, 22:9), a term also used for prophets, martyrs, and all believers (1:1; 10:7; 19:2, 5). Although angels are heavenly beings and people are mortal, they are alike in that both receive messages from God and offer worship to God (5:11–12; 7:11). Mistakenly worshiping angels was probably not an issue for John's readers (NOTES on 19:10), but the line between true and false worship and idolatry was not always clear, as is evident from disputes over food offered to idols (2:14, 20). Therefore, the book contrasts the worshipers of the dragon and beast, who belong to Babylon (13:4; 14:9; 16:2; 17:2), with the worshipers of God and the Lamb, who have a place in New Jerusalem (7:9–15; 15:2–4; 22:3). The visions of Babylon's fall and New Jerusalem's descent are followed by nearly identical scenes in which an angel tells John, "Worship God" (19:9–10; 22:6–9). Babylon's fall may warn of God's judgment against evil while New Jerusalem promises redemption, but the implications of both visions are the same. Readers are to worship the God who is the source of both judgment and hope (Bauckham, *Climax*, 133–35; Stuckenbruck, *Angel*, 253–55; Smalley).

The Just and the Unjust (22:10–15)

John is told, "Do not seal up the words of the prophecy contained in this scroll, because the time is near" (22:10). This point distinguishes Revelation from apocalyptic writings that were said to have been kept secret until the end times (NOTE on 22:10). From its inception, Revelation was designed to be an open book that addressed issues facing its earliest readers, and modern historical interpretation takes that setting into account when exploring the significance of the text. The command not to seal it up also fits Revelation's literary structure (Mazzaferri, *Genre*, 265–79; Bauckham, *Climax*, 243–57). Initially, God gave a scroll to the Lamb, who broke its seals (5:1–7; 6:1–17; 8:1). An angel gave the unsealed scroll to John, who was told to eat it and prophesy (10:1–11). When he did so, his words depicted the faithful bearing witness in the face of opposition (11:1–13), and that theme was developed in the second half of the book (see §23 COMMENT). The message that has been unsealed is not to be resealed, since the call to bear witness speaks to the immediate context of the readers.

The scroll is left open because "the time is near," which raises the question, "Time for what?" One might assume that *the end* of time is near, the time (*kairos*) to judge the dead, reward the saints, and destroy the destroyers of the earth (11:18). Or one might assume that the time of Christ's coming is near (22:7, 12, 20). But as considered above, Revelation plays on multiple senses of what Christ's presence and coming entail. The Messiah's exaltation to God's throne and Satan's expulsion from heaven mean that divine action against the destroyers of the earth is already under way, but how long it will last remains unclear.

Instead, readers are shown that it is time for Jesus' followers to bear prophetic witness. The announcements of God's imminent action assure them that a just God will put things right, while visions that delay the end create opportunity for witness to be given, in order that people might repent. At points, Revelation gives the impression that time is moving in a relentless path toward judgment, as plague after plague is revealed. But the writer interrupts the progression before the final scene, in order to show people being sealed for God and bearing witness to the world (7:1–17; 10:1–11:14). The goal is that through the community's witness, in the time before the end, the world might be called to the Creator and the Lamb. John's scroll is to remain unsealed because it is a word of witness that is relevant for the time that is at hand (1:2; 22:16, 20; Bauckham, *Theology*, 157–59).

The exhortations that follow distinguish two groups—the just and unjust—whose current situation is the focus of this section (22:11):

Let the unjust still do injustice
and the filthy still be filthy.
Let the just still do what is just
and the holy still be holy.

Lines one and three contrast the unjust (*adikōn*) with the just (*dikaios*), and lines two and four contrast the filthy with the holy. The portrayal of the beast and whore show how unrighteousness or injustice (*adikēma*, 18:5) is related to idolatry, deception, brutality, and materialism (13:1–18; 17:1–6; 18:3). Such behaviors (cf. 22:15) show a person's allegiance to evil. Conversely, God and Christ are committed to what is right and just (15:3–4; 19:11), so they oppose evil and deliver those who have suffered (6:10; 16:5, 7; 19:2). Those who do what is right follow the ways of God and Christ (19:8). Similarly, filth is the defilement that comes from sin (Zech 3:3; Ign. *Eph.* 16:2). It is related to idolatry, violence, and other sins that link a person to the whore and exclude one from God's presence (Rev 17:4–6; 21:8, 27). The holy are committed to a God who is holy (4:8; 6:10); they reject the sins that defile (3:4; 14:4) and have a place in God's New Jerusalem (21:2).

The exhortations to do what is just and to remain holy are direct appeals for faithfulness, while the exhortations to persevere in injustice and filth are *ironic*, designed to provoke a change in one's pattern of life. Other examples of ironic exhortation are the summons to come to the sanctuary at Bethel and transgress (Amos 4:4–5) or to fill up the measure of evil (Matt 23:32; cf. Jer 7:21; Herm. *Vis.* 2.3.4). An ironic exhortation says, "Go ahead, follow the path of evil—you will see where it leads." To make the point clear, readers are told about the judgment awaiting the impenitent (Rev 22:14–15). Rhetorically, the direct and the ironic exhortations function differently—the first reinforces current faithfulness, while the second presses for repentance—but they serve the same end, which is a renewed commitment to God (Blount; Giesen; Müller; Reddish; Smalley).

At this point Christ again interjects, "I am coming soon," adding that his reward is with him (22:12b; cf. 22:7). Reward is linked to the question of divine justice (11:18). It is understood that people embark on a path of discipleship through Christ's self-sacrifice, which redeems them for God's kingdom (1:5; 5:9–10; 14:3–4). But following Christ is costly to some believers, who lose social status and even their lives (2:9–10; 3:8; 6:9–11; 13:15; 17:6; 18:24; 20:4). It would be unjust for Christ to abandon them while allowing the ungodly to have their way. So the redeemed are called to be true to Christ in the face of evil, confident that he will be true to them, bringing them to life in his kingdom. At the same time, those perpetrating injustice will not be allowed to continue indefinitely. The destroyers of the earth will eventually suffer destruction themselves (11:18; 17:16; 19:20–21).

Repayment according to a person's works is part of Revelation's complex understanding of judgment (22:12c). Readers were told that Christ knows their works, which may express either faithfulness to Christ and love for his people (2:2, 19; 3:8) or a lack of commitment (3:1–2, 15) and persistence in sin (2:6, 22; cf. 9:20). Later visions show the symmetry in judgment. Those whose works exhibit faithfulness may suffer, but they will not be abandoned, for God will not forget what they have done (14:13). Conversely, the demise of the whore shows that those who are destructive receive what they meted out to others (18:6). The assumption is that those who do the kinds of works listed in 22:15 show that they reject God and will have no place in God's city. People are judged for what they do, but the pattern makes room for repentance (22:14). They are ultimately saved by being inscribed in the scroll of life through divine grace (20:12; §40 Comment).

In this passage Christ's role is fused with that of God. The high Christology is expressed in calling Christ the Alpha and Omega (22:13). Forms of this expression frame the book:

God: I am the Alpha and Omega (1:8)
Christ: I am the first and the last (1:17)
God: I am the Alpha and the Omega,
            the beginning and the end (21:6)
Christ: I am the Alpha and Omega, the first and the last,
            the beginning the end (22:13)

When used for God, these expressions identify him as the one who precedes all things as their Creator and the one who brings all things to their fulfillment. When used of Christ, they have the same meaning. As God is the beginning of all things, his role as Creator has been explicit (4:11; 10:6; 14:7); Christ's role in creation is implicit. Calling Christ the *archē* of creation identifies him as its ruler (3:14). The Lamb's scroll of life is linked to the world's foundation (13:8). Revelation also calls Christ the Word (*logos*) of God, a term other sources use for God's creative power (John 1:1–4; Heb 1:2), though this connection is not developed in Revelation. Identifying both God and Christ as the end of all things is much clearer. Revelation calls God the one who is to come (Rev 1:4, 8; 4:8) and the judge of human deeds (20:11–15), and it also refers to Christ this way (22:12). God's coming as redeemer, judge, and ruler occurs through Christ's coming (Sänger, "Amen").

Revelation uses language for Christ that was typically reserved for God alone: "I am the first and I am the last; besides me there is no god" (Isa 44:6). Revelation extends this language to Jesus, while retaining a monotheistic perspective. Christ is not worshiped as a second deity alongside God but within the worship of the one true God. All creation gives glory to God and the Lamb (Rev 5:13), and the redeemed ascribe salvation to them (7:10). Yet there is only one throne for God and the Lamb, and in New Jerusalem the redeemed do not worship "them" but worship "him," taking God and the Lamb as a single focus (22:3; Bauckham, *Theology*, 54–65).

The last of seven references to the "blessed" speaks to the current situation of the readers as it promises future well-being (22:14). Washing one's robes is an image for repentance. Some people at Sardis were said to have soiled their clothing through unfaithfulness to Christ (3:4). Babylon's uncleanness came from false worship, violence, and materialism (17:4). Such sins defile people and exclude them from God's city (21:27; 22:15). Yet access to God's city is not limited to those who have never sinned. Rather, it is given to those who are cleansed by turning from sin and claiming the benefits of Christ's death—that is, those who wash their robes in the blood of the Lamb (7:14).

Entering the city means having access to the tree of life (22:14). According to Genesis, people were barred from the tree because of sin, so all were subject to death (Gen 3:22, 29). But when sin is overcome, death is as well, so it has no place in New Jerusalem (Rev 21:4). People enter God's city through resurrection to endless life, signified by the tree (22:2). Where people were told to "come out" of Babylon by disengaging from that city's destructive ways of life (18:4), they are called to "enter" New Jerusalem by its gates, which continually stand open on all sides of the city (21:13, 21; Rossing, *Choice*, 59, 154). The gates are named for the tribes of Israel, and those who enter have a rightful place among God's people (21:12).

A list of those excluded from God's city shows the future of the unrepentant (22:15). Like the items on previous lists, these behaviors express a fundamental opposition to God (9:20–21; 21:8, 27). Sorcery is linked to the false prophet and Babylon (13:15; 18:23). Immorality connotes illicit sexual relations and the infidelity to God personified by the whore (17:2, 4; 18:3; 19:2). Where God and Christ give life (1:18; 2:7, 10; 4:9–10; 10:6; 21:6), a murderer takes it away (2:10, 13; 11:7; 13:7–10, 15; 17:6; 18:24). If true worship is given to the God who creates and the Lamb who redeems, idolatry is the false worship given to those who destroy the earth (11:18; 13:4, 11–15). Where God and the Lamb work through truth, Satan (12:9; 20:8), the false prophet (13:14; 16:13; 19:20), and the whore (18:23) seek dominion through deception (NOTE on 21:8). The function of the list in 22:15 is to press the unclean to repent and "wash their robes" (22:14). When read descriptively, as a picture of the ungodly lingering outside the city gate in the new creation, the verse is incongruous (Barr, *Tales*, 147). But just as the promise of blessing in 22:14 is designed to draw people to hope in God, the warning in 22:15 is designed to move them from sin to repentance.

Testimony of Jesus and Final Greeting (22:16–21)

The one who has repeatedly announced his coming (22:7, 12–13) finally identifies himself: "I, Jesus" (22:16). Jesus spoke in the first person in the opening chapters (1:17–18; 2:2, 9, 13, etc.) and now concludes by stating his name. The force of the name can be seen by comparison with other texts. First, Revelation and Daniel are apocalypses in which the seer states his name in the conclusion (Dan 12:5; Rev 22:8). Revelation, however, goes further by having *Jesus* state his name, making him the authority behind the visions (22:16). Second, Revelation has features of a letter (INTRO IV.A.3). The Pauline letters were usually dictated to a scribe (Rom 16:22) and sometimes included Paul's name and final comments in his own hand (1 Cor 16:21–24; Col 4:18; 2 Thess 3:17; Phlm 17; cf. Gal 6:11). By way of analogy, Revelation concludes with Jesus' verbal signature. Third, like the name of a witness at the end of an official document, Jesus' name attests to the truth of what is said (NOTES on 22:16, 18).

Rhetorically, stating one's name brings the force of the speaker's character to bear on what is said. For example, Paul invokes his personal credibility when declaring, "I, Paul, am telling you," adding "I testify" (Gal 5:2–3; cf. 1 Cor 10:1; Eph 3:1; Col 1:23; 4:18; 1 Thess 2:18). Listeners are to pay attention because of *what* is being said and *who* is saying it (Aristotle, *Rhet.* 1.2.3–4). Therefore, Jesus' credentials are summed up in messianic titles. The "root and descendant of David" recalls Isa 11:1, 10 and has identified Jesus as the only one worthy to reveal the contents of God's scroll (NOTE on Rev 5:5). As the royal Messiah, Jesus builds the kingdom (5:10; 11:15), defeats evil (Isa 11:4; Rev 19:15), and shares the throne of God (22:3).

As the "bright morning star," Jesus is the ruler who arises from Judah according to Num 24:17 (NOTE on Rev 22:16). The morning star was of singular brilliance (Sir 50:6) and it signaled a new day (*Jos. As.* 14:1; 2 Pet 1:19; Martial, *Epigrams* 8.21). Readers have now seen the splendor of his reign culminating in the eternal day of New Jerusalem, which is illumined by his light (Rev 21:23). The one in whom biblical promises are fulfilled now attests the validity of John's text. The titles are introduced with "I am" (*egō eimi*), which recalls the divine name. The expression has been used where God speaks (1:8; cf. 21:6) and where Christ shares the characteristics of God, such as being first and last and the one who searches minds and hearts (1:17; 2:23). Divine overtones are fitting here, since Jesus shares God's identity as Alpha and Omega (22:13), and like God he sends the angel with Revelation's message (22:6, 16). There is divine authorization for the book.

John's message was sent to readers through emissaries. In antiquity it was common for letters to be carried by business travelers, but others could be commissioned for the task (Rom 16:1–2; 2 Cor 7:6–8; Phil 2:25, 29; Col 4:7–8, 16; Phlm 17–19; M. Mitchell, "New"; Klauck, *Ancient*, 65). Revelatory texts could also be sent this way. In a vision Hermas was told to "write two little books and send one to Clement and one to Grapte. Clement shall then send it to the cities abroad . . . in this city you shall read it yourself with the elders who are in charge of the church" (Herm. *Vis.* 2.4.3). John apparently sent his message through emissaries that belonged to his prophetic circle (NOTE on Rev 22:16; Aune, *Apocalypticism*, 250–60).

Previously, Jesus interrupted John's narration to announce his coming (22:7, 12), but here the pattern is reversed as John interrupts by having the Spirit and bride ask Jesus to come (22:17). In the visionary world the Spirit sometimes works in silence, enabling John to see things (1:10; 4:2; 17:3; 21:10), and it conveys the words of the risen Christ (2:1, 7, 8, 11, etc.). On occasion the Spirit speaks in its own voice, responding to what another heavenly voice has said (14:13). This occurs here, as the Spirit responds to the risen Christ. Although some interpreters identify the Spirit's voice with that of the church, which is moved by the Spirit (Harrington; Prigent), or with the voice of John and other prophets (Beale; Bauckham, *Theology*, 118; Giesen; Roloff; Smalley), this is unlikely. John is narrating what he heard in the visionary world, so that through his words the readers hear the Spirit's words (Aune).

The Spirit is joined by the bride, who personifies the future people of God. Some interpreters identify the bride with the Christian community of the present, whose hearers are to say "come" (Giesen; Roloff). But this is unlikely. The bride is the city that descends in the new creation (21:2, 9), the city that epitomizes the hope of salvation (22:14, 18, 19). The voice of the bride comes from the future into the present, awakening the desire to meet the bridegroom at his coming (Bauckham, *Climax*, 167–68; Rossing, *Choice*, 161; Blount; Osborne).

John now shifts from narration to exhortation: "Let the one who hears say, 'Come'" (22:17b). Words that come from the visionary world are designed to evoke a response in the ordinary world. Each listener is called to become a speaker by joining those who ask Jesus to "come." This one-word petition affirms the message of the book and aligns the listener with those who anticipate Jesus' coming as salvation. These worshipers discern the character of God's reign and await the accomplishment of his designs. The outward movement from heavenly to earthly worship (22:17ab) is analogous to earlier scenes in which the acclamation that began around the throne of God and the Lamb was taken up by successive waves of worshipers until all creation joined in (5:8–14).

John's voice becomes indistinguishable from that of Jesus when all who thirst are invited to receive the water of life (22:17cd; cf. 21:6). In the first of these parallel lines, thirst (*dipsōn*) shows a *need* for God, who is the source of life (cf. Pss 42:2; 63:1). The barriers to fullness of life with God include sin, evil, and death. The second line recognizes that this need can lead to the *desire* (*thelōn*) for the life that God and Christ give (cf. Rev 7:17; 21:6). Some interpreters maintain that the invitation to "come" means that readers receive the water of life in the present (Giesen; Taeger, *Johannesapokalypse*, 49). This perspective fits the Fourth Gospel, in which living water is an image for the Spirit (John 4:10, 14; 7:37–39) and eternal life begins in the present (5:24), but Revelation locates the water of life in New Jerusalem (Rev 22:1). For the thirsty, the water of life is a promise of a future in which the barriers of sin, evil, and death are overcome through resurrection to life in God's city (Satake; Müller; Bauckham, *Climax*, 168).

The exalted Jesus now warns against altering the message in the book. By saying "I myself bear witness," he brings his own credibility to bear on the message (22:18). John's earliest readers held Christ in highest esteem. He is the faithful witness (1:5; 3:14), whose own death testified to the truth of God's reign in the face of opposition. A two-part warning follows (22:18–19). Concerning the words of prophecy in this book:

> If anyone adds to them
> > God will add to that person the plagues that are written in this scroll,
> and if anyone takes away from the words of this scroll of prophecy,
> > God will take away that person's share in the tree of life and the holy city,
> > which are written in this scroll.

The plague visions threatened the unrepentant with suffering and death through demonic powers (e.g., 9:4–6, 18, 20) and God's prophets and angels (11:6; 15:1–16:21). The plagues on Babylon included death, grief, famine, and fiery destruction (18:4, 8). Conversely, the vision of New Jerusalem has promised deathless life in God's city (22:1–5). The warning continues the symmetrical pattern of judgment. If the words are trustworthy and true (22:6), then alteration is an act of deception, which is contrary to the ways of God. To falsify the message allies a person with those who oppose God and who are therefore excluded from God's city (22:15; cf. 2:20; 12:9; 13:14; 18:23; 19:20; 20:8).

On a primary level this passage warns against falsifying the message of Revelation through one's teaching and manner of life. The literary context does not focus on those who might alter the text while copying it but addresses each person who "hears" the words in the Christian assembly (22:17b, 18a; cf. 2:7, 11, 17, etc.). Hearers have already been told to "keep" what is written in the book and that they are blessed through faithfulness to God and Christ (1:3; 22:7, 9). Since "keeping" means obeying the message, then "adding and taking away" are the opposite and connote disobedience. The language used here recalls passages from Deuteronomy in which the principal issue was complete obedience to God and a rejection of idolatry and false prophecy (NOTE on 22:18; Beale; Prigent; Smalley; Robert Thomas, "Spiritual," 208; Tilly, "Textsicherung," 244–47).

On a secondary level the passage cautions against tampering with the text itself. The book of Revelation was to circulate among the seven churches noted in 1:11, and it eventually found a wider audience. Ancient writers were concerned about careless copying. Referring to his own writing, Irenaeus said, "I adjure you, who shall copy this book, by our Lord Jesus Christ, by his glorious advent when he comes to judge the living and the dead, that you compare what you transcribe and correct it with this copy" (Eusebius, *Hist. eccl.* 3.20.3). Revelation, however, is concerned with those who might alter the message *willfully*, not simply through careless copying. Revelation was composed in a context of conflicting prophetic teachings (Rev 2:20). Even those within John's communities may have assumed that prophetic messages were to be evaluated and, if necessary, modified by others (1 Cor 14:29–30; Aune, *Prophecy*, 217–29). Accordingly, tampering with the written text would be a form of disobedience, though alteration could also include verbally misrepresenting the message in one's teaching (Aune; Biguzzi, "Chaos," 205).

Jesus concludes his witness by saying for the third time, "I am coming soon" (Rev 22:20a; cf. 22:7, 12), which invites the response: "Amen. Come, Lord Jesus!" (22:20b). The petition encompasses several dimensions of meaning. First, it is addressed directly to Christ, which presupposes that Christ is already present among the readers. They can speak to him because he now walks among them (1:12–20; 2:1). Second, the petition has an eschatological aspect, asking Christ to come in a final way to defeat evil and bring the redeemed deathless life (22:12–14; Aune; Satake). Third, the petition is flexible enough to include "comings" that are less than final. Christ spoke of coming to specific congregations for provisional disciplinary action (2:5, 16; 3:3). By extension, Christ could "come" in gracious ways that are less than ultimate. The Aramaic petition for Christ's coming was used this way in some eucharistic services (*Did.* 10:6; Blount; Giesen). To say "come, Lord Jesus" addresses the Christ who is present with language that is eschatological but open to other meanings (Beale; Smalley).

The final verse is an epistolary conclusion: "The grace of the Lord Jesus be with all" (22:21). It differs from Greco-Roman letters, which typically concluded "be strong" (*errōso, errōsthe*) or "fare well" (*eutychei*). Sometimes wishes for the recipient's good health were added (J. White, *Light*, 194–202). Revelation closely follows conventions of Pauline letter closings (NOTE on 22:21). First, the basic term is *charis*, or grace, which in Revelation appears only in the epistolary introduction and conclusion (1:4; 22:21). The term frames the text and invites readers to see both the encouraging and confrontational visions as expressions of grace. Second, the grace has Jesus as its source. Some

Christian letters left the source of grace unspecified (Col 4:18; 1 Tim 6:21; Tit 3:15; Heb 13:25), but Revelation does not. Third, John extends the final greeting to "all." A more common expression in Pauline and Greco-Roman letters was "all of you" (Weima, *Neglected*, 28–34), but the sense is the same. Although the words to the churches in Rev 2–3 include sharp reproofs, the book's message is given that they might be blessed (Rev 1:3), so it is fitting for a final word of grace to be extended to all the readers addressed by the book.

Index of Modern Authors

Baird, William, 83, 160
Balch, David L., 88, 102, 160, 192, 528, 554, 556, 826
Ball, David Mark, 161, 220
Balsdon, J. P. V. D., 161, 242
Baltzer, Klaus, 161, 700
Bandstra, Andrew J., 161, 217, 220, 381, 382, 389
Bandy, Alan S., 123, 161
Barclay, John M. G., 92, 161, 275, 329
Barker, Margaret, 161, 675
Barnes, Robin, 53, 161
Barnett, Paul, 161, 559
Barr, David L., 65, 70, 115, 121, 156, 161, 169, 172, 176, 179, 195, 221, 224, 225, 246, 253, 278, 291, 382, 385, 387, 388, 505, 524, 570, 597, 661, 764, 855
Barth, Markus, 161, 335
Bauckham, Richard, 52, 65, 70, 85, 101, 105, 107, 112, 113, 118, 161, 216, 218, 219, 223, 226, 227, 228, 229, 230, 243, 249, 251, 252, 254, 265, 271, 298, 313, 326, 328, 331, 336, 340, 349, 369, 384, 386, 387, 392, 400, 402, 404, 405, 409, 412, 413, 418, 419, 420, 421, 423, 426, 427, 430, 431, 442, 443, 447, 452, 472, 474, 476, 478, 480, 482, 485, 486, 487, 488, 489, 494, 497, 500, 502, 504, 505, 507, 508, 510, 511, 512, 516, 519, 525, 526, 537, 549, 550, 552, 554, 562, 565, 570, 571, 574, 576, 579, 588, 597, 598, 610, 612, 615, 620, 626, 629, 630, 633, 634, 635, 636, 643, 656, 658, 659, 662, 664, 665, 667, 677, 679, 680, 683, 684, 689, 691, 701, 702, 711, 714, 715, 731, 735, 739, 749, 750, 752, 764, 767, 768, 773, 781, 786, 788, 790, 792, 798, 802, 803, 806, 807, 808, 812, 816, 828, 832, 833, 835, 836, 838, 850, 852, 853, 854, 856, 857
Bauer, Thomas Johann, 162, 762, 781
Baynes, Leslie, 162, 316, 477, 487, 576, 780, 781
Beagley, Alan James, 162, 278, 327, 485, 504, 675
Beale, Gregory K., 123, 140, 156, 162, 212, 216, 217, 218, 219, 227, 228, 229, 244, 245, 255, 270, 277, 287, 288, 289, 290, 301, 309, 312, 313, 320, 325, 326, 327, 331, 332, 333, 336, 337, 340, 356, 360, 361, 365, 374, 377, 381, 383, 389, 390, 394, 396, 398, 409, 411, 414, 415, 416, 417, 418, 421, 427, 430, 431, 434, 435, 444, 446, 448, 452, 456, 458, 466, 467, 468, 476, 477, 480, 482, 483, 486, 490, 494, 497, 504, 505, 508, 513, 516, 519, 524, 529, 542, 544, 546, 547, 552, 553, 566, 567, 571, 576, 589, 593, 596, 597, 598, 607, 614, 620, 624, 628, 632, 634, 636, 645, 647, 649, 653, 661, 662, 663, 665, 667, 669, 677, 679, 685, 689, 697, 700, 708, 726, 727, 728, 731, 732, 754, 755, 757, 759, 771, 772, 773, 775, 776, 779, 781, 784, 796, 799, 803, 809, 816, 820, 823, 825, 829, 833, 838, 839, 840, 841, 842, 843, 844, 845, 847, 849, 851, 856, 858
Bean, George Ewart, 162, 334
Beard, Mary, 162, 369, 390, 452, 511, 582, 585
Beasley-Murray, George, 67, 156, 162, 175, 184, 196, 551, 598, 617, 626, 777
Beauvery, Robert, 162, 681, 685
Becker, Jürgen, 162, 184, 387
Beckwith, Ibson T., 70, 76, 157, 219, 377, 528
Beirich, Gregory S., 162, 355
Bell, Albert A., 72, 73, 162
Benko, Stephen, 162, 528, 554
Berger, Klaus, 162, 264, 402, 440, 451, 452, 453, 503, 504, 505, 753, 809
Berger, Paul R., 163, 342
Bergmeier, Roland, 163, 216, 374, 529, 681, 685, 819, 825
Berlin, Adele, 163, 636
Bertrand, Daniel A., 163, 761, 762
Betz, Hans Dieter, xxiii, 163, 262, 290, 470, 647
Biguzzi, Giancarlo, 163, 229, 249, 266, 356, 404, 405, 493, 574, 576, 675, 681, 843, 847, 848, 849, 850, 858
Birdsall, J. N., 163, 599
Black, Matthew, 163, 216, 401, 484, 497, 505, 548
Blanke, Helmut, 161, 335
Bleek, Friedrich, 61, 164, 439, 538

Blount, Brian K., 87, 157, 164, 213, 216, 227, 269, 271, 287, 288, 312, 313, 314, 341, 356, 384, 386, 401, 409, 418, 427, 428, 431, 434, 446, 449, 461, 477, 480, 497, 508, 519, 589, 593, 629, 643, 649, 650, 653, 755, 756, 763, 765, 840, 841, 844, 846, 851, 853, 857, 858

Böcher, Otto, 164, 173, 174, 178, 196, 201, 440, 825

Bøe, Sverre, 164, 461, 759, 760, 762, 768, 771, 777, 781, 789

Boesak, Allan Aubrey, 64, 164

Boismard, Marie Emile, 164, 792

Boneva, Krassimira, 164, 825

Borgen, Peter, 164, 275, 278, 281, 327, 329, 330

Borger, Rykle, 164, 287

Boring, M. Eugene, 90, 91, 108, 109, 111, 132, 157, 164, 211, 214, 219, 220, 221, 222, 224, 225, 228, 229, 236, 250, 252, 299, 390, 394, 395, 413, 425, 435, 438, 444, 446, 452, 458, 476, 478, 480, 488, 492, 493, 498, 553, 555, 559, 570, 587, 590, 617, 636, 646, 661, 689, 691, 693, 732, 756, 764, 765, 768, 775, 785, 788, 789, 792, 796, 806, 810, 833, 839, 847, 849

Bosworth, A. B., 164, 395

Böttrich, Christfried, 164, 363, 366, 633

Bousset, Wilhelm, 62, 67, 68, 157, 164, 301, 353, 400, 427, 441, 477, 499, 504, 528, 538, 556, 774, 845

Bovon, François, 164, 249, 250, 589, 593, 603, 686

Bowersock, G. W., 164, 592

Boxall, Ian, 157, 195, 246, 262, 265, 268, 292, 300, 340, 341, 356, 357, 369, 372, 384, 394, 398, 399, 410, 413, 434, 435, 437, 449, 476, 480, 484, 486, 488, 497, 507, 514, 515, 543, 595, 629, 643, 649, 653, 661, 756, 823, 844, 851

Boyer, Paul S., 61, 164, 438, 538, 539, 747

Bradley, Keith R., 165, 706

Branick, Vincent, 88, 165

Braund, David C., 165, 686

Bredin, Mark R. J., 165, 276, 278, 280, 762

Brent, Allen, 165, 535, 609

Briggs, Robert A., 165, 326, 327, 332, 398, 541

Brighton, Louis A., 80, 157, 593, 659, 665

Brooke, George J., 165, 366

Broughton, T. R. S., 93, 165, 256, 272, 284, 295, 338, 339, 448, 596, 709

Brown, Raymond E., xv, xxiii, 67, 81, 83, 165, 533, 543, 841

Bruce, F. F., 165, 265

Brunt, John C., 100, 165

Brütsch, Charles, 157, 369

Buchinger, Harald, 44, 165

Bucur, Bogdan G., 165, 216, 220, 265, 732

Burr, David, 46, 47, 166, 537, 638, 745

Burrell, Barbara, 166, 259, 284, 311, 591

Busch, Peter, 166, 528, 529, 542, 547, 550, 554, 556, 558

Buttrey, Theodore V., 166, 378

Büyükkolanci, Mustafa, 198, 337, 342

Byron, John, 166, 212

Cadbury, Henry Joel, 100, 166

Cadoux, Cecil John, 166, 272, 273, 278, 339

Caird, G. B., v, 74, 157, 306, 309, 320, 324, 336, 355, 400, 409, 413, 414, 415, 427, 441, 447, 449, 452, 456, 459, 474, 476, 478, 480, 483, 485, 497, 500, 504, 516, 519, 546, 550, 559, 569, 595, 596, 614, 646, 655, 657, 756, 790, 807, 817

Callahan, Allen D., 140, 141, 166, 640, 661, 711

Camille, Michael, 166, 467

Campbell, Gordon, 166, 643, 653, 664, 681, 683, 714

Campbell, R. Alastair, 166, 361, 362, 754, 762, 781

Carey, Greg, 136, 166, 220, 223, 299, 303, 478, 487, 493, 508, 576, 578, 600

Carrell, Peter R., 166, 223, 248, 249, 253, 476, 487, 623, 626, 838

Casson, Lionel, 166, 449, 702, 703, 704, 722

Charles, J. Daryl, 166, 382

Charles, R. H., 62, 67, 76, 81, 85, 115, 123, 140, 152, 219, 242, 255, 263, 264, 274, 290, 295, 301, 324, 325, 353, 357, 362, 365, 376, 380, 382, 393, 395, 396, 398,

Charles, R. H. (*continued*)
  400, 405, 414, 418, 431, 441, 449, 457,
  458, 461, 466, 471, 477, 481, 482, 484,
  485, 497, 500, 504, 505, 507, 515, 528,
  547, 548, 578, 593, 595, 597, 748, 774,
  837, 840, 849
Charlesworth, James H., xxiii, 167, 514
Christe, Yves, 167, 351
Clasen, Klaus-Peter, 167, 746
Cohen, Boaz, 167, 619
Cohen, Henry, 167, 685
Collins, John J., xv, 64, 69, 104, 105, 107,
  167, 205, 218, 297, 302, 487, 530, 548,
  572, 580, 623, 753, 840, 843
Constantinou, Eugenia Scarvelis, 40, 154,
  167
Conzelmann, Hans, 167, 809
Cook, John Granger, 77, 167
Corsten, Thomas, xl, 167, 337, 342
Court, John M., 75, 78, 157, 167, 233, 313,
  357, 397, 446, 543, 674, 681, 685
Coutsoumpos, Panayotis, 167, 291
Cross, Frank Moore, 167, 597
Cuss, Dominique, 167, 576

Daley, Brian E., 37, 38, 167, 742, 743
Dalrymple, Rob, 167, 423, 487
Daniel, E. Randolph, 45, 167, 232
Danker, Frederick W., xix, 168, 278
Davidson, Maxwell J., 168, 644
Davies, W. D., 163, 168, 324
Davis, R. Dean, 168, 366, 373, 382
Day, John, 168, 660, 661, 664
De Boer, Martinus C., 168, 754
Decock, Paul B., 168, 756
Deissmann, Adolf, 143, 168, 220, 243, 277,
  400, 595, 599, 606
Denis, Albert-Marie, 168, 210
Deppermann, Klaus, 54, 55, 168
deSilva, David A., 96, 103, 132, 135, 136,
  137, 168, 220, 221, 222, 223, 229, 251,
  252, 266, 268, 269, 270, 303, 316, 347,
  348, 492, 507, 558, 576, 579, 585, 614,
  615, 616, 633, 716, 848, 851
Deutsch, Celia, 168, 643, 683, 714, 801,
  804, 828
Dieterich, Albrecht, 62, 168
DiTommaso, Lorenzo, 168, 813

Dochhorn, Jan, 168, 534, 535, 548, 549,
  554, 567, 743
Dodds, E. R., 169, 603
Doglio, Claudio, 169, 219
Doniger, Wendy, 169, 528, 559
Doyle, Thomas, 198, 423
Dräger, Michael, 169, 310, 335
Draper, J. A., 169, 423, 427, 428
Drury, John, 56, 169
Du Rand, Jan A., 169, 633, 801
Ducrey, Pierre, 169, 721
Duff, Paul B., 91, 96, 169, 274, 278, 298,
  303, 306, 589, 593, 599, 603, 672, 676,
  681, 682, 711
Dulk, Mattijs den, 169, 303
Dunbabin, Katherine M. D., 169, 299, 344
Dunn, James D. G., 170, 274, 298, 578,
  684, 838, 841
Düsterdieck, Friedrich, 157, 353, 538
Dyer, Charles H., 170, 681

Ebner, Martin, 159, 170, 171, 177, 183, 574
Ebrard, Johannes Heinrich August, 157
Ego, Beate, 170, 364, 366
Ehrman, Bart D., 145, 188
Elliott, Edward B., 157
Elliott, J. K., 145, 170
Elliott, John H., 75, 88, 170, 328, 578, 684
Elliott, Susan M., 170, 700
Emmerson, Richard K., 166, 167, 170, 171,
  181, 185, 187, 539
Engen, John H. van, 43, 170
Enroth, Anne Marit, 170, 238, 264
Eriksson, Anders, 170, 846, 848
Esch-Wermeling, Elisabeth, 159, 170, 177,
  183, 574, 599
Ewald, Heinrich, 157, 439

Fàbrega, Vallentin, 170, 743
Farrer, Austin, 170, 524, 750, 762
Fears, J. Rufus, 94, 170, 581, 603
Fee, Gordon, 157, 170, 288
Fekkes, Jan, III, 123, 170, 290, 324, 325,
  326, 368, 402, 404, 423, 430, 546, 661,
  711, 728, 732, 757, 793, 798, 800, 814,
  819, 821, 825, 833, 841, 844
Fenske, Wolfgang, 171, 633, 634
Feuillet, André, 171, 485, 546

Firth, Katharine R., 171, 537
Fitzmyer, Joseph A., 171, 474, 486
Flanigan, C. Clifford, 44, 171
Flint, Peter, 172, 202
Fontenrose, Joseph, 171, 545
Ford, J. Massyngberde, 157, 222, 233, 242, 243, 287, 313, 337, 387, 459, 461, 485, 500, 513, 528, 606, 662, 675, 796, 842, 849
Fox, Kenneth A., 171, 263
Frankfurter, David, 171, 275, 278
Fredriksen, Paula, 37, 171
Frenschkowski, Marco, 171, 441, 505, 825, 830
Frey, Jörg, 67, 81, 83, 139, 163, 169, 170, 171, 173, 176, 180, 181, 183, 191, 200, 201, 205, 757, 851
Friedrich, Nestor Paulo, 171, 303, 306
Friesen, Steven J., 63, 64, 73, 76, 77, 79, 94, 99, 120, 128, 129, 172, 217, 228, 233, 242, 244, 251, 259, 260, 265, 273, 278, 281, 284, 286, 287, 291, 303, 322, 327, 330, 334, 335, 361, 366, 367, 368, 388, 390, 391, 465, 469, 480, 481, 490, 515, 518, 528, 553, 558, 559, 570, 574, 576, 578, 579, 580, 581, 583, 585, 586, 587, 589, 590, 591, 593, 599, 601, 602, 609, 618, 678, 680, 681, 683, 684, 687, 711, 736, 783, 787, 789, 829
Frilingos, Christopher A., 172, 387, 681, 693
Frye, Northrop, 172, 412
Fuller Dow, Lois K., 172, 825
Furnish, Victor Paul, 172, 794

Gallus, Laslo, 172, 650, 653
García Martínez, Florentino, 172, 813, 816, 820
Garnsey, Peter, 172, 408
Garrison, William Lloyd, 172, 640
Gaston, Lloyd, 172, 264
Genovese, Eugene D., 59, 172
Georgi, Dieter, 172, 801, 802, 806, 825, 826, 835
Geyser, Albert S., 172, 202, 423
Giblin, Charles Homer, 157, 173, 223, 366, 484, 486, 498, 500, 504, 505, 512, 751, 762, 775, 781, 788

Gieschen, Charles A., 173, 245, 249, 253, 476, 487
Giesen, Heinz, 74, 76, 112, 131, 157, 173, 213, 216, 219, 227, 229, 239, 242, 243, 244, 246, 248, 269, 270, 274, 281, 287, 289, 290, 293, 301, 313, 318, 324, 325, 327, 331, 332, 336, 337, 340, 341, 361, 362, 373, 377, 389, 394, 397, 400, 405, 409, 415, 416, 421, 425, 430, 431, 432, 434, 435, 438, 441, 446, 450, 452, 456, 457, 458, 459, 460, 461, 466, 467, 470, 475, 477, 479, 481, 482, 483, 484, 485, 486, 490, 497, 498, 499, 504, 505, 507, 508, 513, 515, 516, 519, 524, 541, 542, 547, 550, 551, 563, 567, 570, 571, 575, 585, 587, 595, 597, 607, 609, 612, 614, 616, 618, 620, 624, 628, 630, 634, 636, 643, 645, 648, 649, 658, 659, 661, 673, 676, 678, 684, 686, 688, 689, 691, 707, 708, 726, 730, 731, 732, 752, 756, 757, 765, 771, 772, 773, 775, 779, 781, 785, 791, 795, 797, 801, 802, 803, 804, 805, 808, 809, 813, 816, 817, 824, 825, 828, 829, 833, 836, 838, 839, 840, 841, 842, 844, 846, 848, 851, 853, 856, 857, 858
Gilchrest, Eric J., 173, 826, 829
Glad, Clarence E., 173, 348
Glancy, Jennifer A., 173, 671, 674, 681, 686, 693, 706
Glasson, Thomas Francis, 173, 781
Godwin, Joscelyn, 173, 528, 529, 686
Gollinger, Hildegard, 173, 524, 529, 543, 547, 554
Goodenough, Erwin R., 173, 433
Goranson, Stephen, 173, 842, 847
Gordley, Matthew E., 130, 173
Gordon, Robert P., 173, 460, 462
Gourgues, Michel, 173, 781, 788
Gradl, Hans-Georg, 111, 173, 578, 684
Grant, Frederick C., 174, 529
Grappe, Christian, 174, 193, 404, 423
Graz, Ursula Rapp, 174, 801
Green, E. M. B., 195, 233, 337, 342
Grelot, Pierre, 174, 543
Gummerlock, Francis X., 174, 354
Gundry, Robert H., 174, 197, 326, 476, 801, 825, 828
Gunkel, Hermann, 62, 174, 528

Lambrecht, Jan, 175, 184, 196, 206, 274, 278, 356, 357, 404, 433, 434, 524, 576
Lampe, G. W. H., 184, 732
Lampe, Peter, 184, 276, 604
LaRondelle, Hans K., 184, 661, 664
Lausberg, Heinrich, 135, 142, 143, 184, 246, 298, 328, 338, 366, 374, 381, 412, 420, 472, 509, 561, 648, 649, 699, 728, 841, 848
Laws, Sophie, 184, 382, 387
Lazenby, J. F., 198, 249
Le Frois, Bernard J., 184, 543
Lee, Dal, 116, 184
Lee, Pilchan, 184, 801, 803, 812, 813, 825, 829
Lefebvre, Philippe, 184, 423
Leipoldt, Johannes, 50, 185
Lembke, Markus, 149, 185
Lenski, Richard Charles Henry, 158, 251
Lerner, Robert E., 43, 46, 185, 537, 745
Levine, Amy-Jill, 64, 185
Levine, Lee I., 185, 290, 320
Lewis, Suzanne, 44, 185
Lieu, Judith, 185, 275
Lincoln, Andrew T., 185, 841
Lindsey, Hal, 61, 185, 539, 641, 692
Loasby, Roland E., 185, 661, 664
Lohmeyer, Ernst, 158, 661
Lohse, Eduard, 185, 275, 278, 281, 329, 330
Lona, Horacio E., 77, 185
Longenecker, Bruce W., 185, 752, 847
Lücke, Friedrich, 61, 185
Lülsdorff, Raimund, 185, 249
Lumsden, Douglas W., 185, 353
Lupieri, Edmundo F., 158, 248, 275, 290, 327, 329, 394, 401, 448, 465, 480, 500, 595, 646, 662, 675, 756, 761, 775, 787, 804, 813, 823, 833
Luz, Ulrich, 184, 276, 604

Maas, Martha, 186, 378
MacLeod, David J., 186, 382, 732
MacMullen, Ramsay, 128, 186, 470, 594, 603, 724
Magie, David, 186, 286, 321, 338, 448, 703
Maier, Harry O., 116, 186, 223, 387, 413, 421, 487, 504, 559, 563, 644, 756, 820, 825, 826, 827, 830, 835, 850

Maitland, Samuel R., 186, 439
Malay, Hasan, xxiv, 186, 214, 265, 295, 296, 310
Malherbe, Abraham J., 186, 234, 261, 402, 533
Malina, Bruce J., 97, 158, 222, 246, 353, 361, 387, 459, 542, 819
Mamiani, Maurizio, 53, 186
Manganaro, Giacomo, xl, 186, 240, 242, 249, 707
Marcus, David, 186, 578, 685
Marshall, John W., 186, 276, 278, 487, 500
Martin, Dale B., 186, 212
Martyn, J. Louis, 187, 794
Marucci, C., 186, 599
Mason, Hugh J., 187, 336
Mason, Steve, 187, 275, 329
Matheson, Peter, 155, 187, 640
Mathews, Mark D., 187, 342, 346, 701
Mathews, Susan F., 187, 402, 404
Mathewson, David, 123, 187, 227, 377, 382, 751, 781, 789, 796, 797, 799, 801, 802, 804, 806, 807, 808, 812, 814, 815, 822, 824, 825, 831, 833, 836
Matter, Ann E., 40, 42, 187, 354, 744
Mattingly, Harold, xxiv, 187
Mayo, Philip L., 187, 275, 278, 327, 328
Mazzaferri, Frederick David, 91, 105, 187, 223, 384, 405, 476, 483, 487, 488, 493, 838, 852
McCann, J. Clinton, Jr., 187
McDermott, Gerald R., 187, 747
McDonald, Lee Martin, 35, 187
McDonald, Patricia M., 187, 382, 388
McDonough, Sean M., 187, 215, 220, 226, 366, 370
McGinn, Bernard, 35, 37, 42, 43, 45, 46, 47, 48, 161, 166, 167, 170, 171, 181, 185, 187, 188, 193, 195, 197, 438, 439, 526, 536, 537, 538, 539, 573, 640, 745
McIlraith, Donal A., 188, 732, 738
McKelvey, R. J., 188, 751, 754, 762, 781, 789
McKinnon, James, 188, 609
McNicol, Allan J., 188, 757, 762, 798, 801
Mealy, J. Webb, 188, 762, 766, 771, 773, 777, 781, 796, 798, 801, 805

Meeks, Wayne A., 102, 188
Meer, Frederick van der, 188, 440
Meiggs, Russell, 188, 448, 703
Menken, Maarten J. J., 188, 218, 220
Merkt, Andreas, 165, 167, 169, 175, 178, 191, 194, 195, 202, 203
Metzger, Bruce M., xxv, 35, 38, 40, 50, 51, 145, 188, 599
Meyers, Carol L., 188, 498, 668
Meyers, Eric M., 188, 498, 668
Meynet, Roland, 189, 633, 635
Michael, Michael George, 189, 599
Michaels, J. Ramsey, 158, 394
Mildenberg, Leo, 189, 378, 541
Millar, Fergus, 189, 365, 371, 391
Miller, Kevin E., 189, 732, 766
Minear, Paul S., 189, 485, 500, 505, 506, 553
Minnis, Alastair J., 43, 189
Mitchell, Margaret M., 189, 225, 856
Mitchell, Stephen, 189, 214, 296, 322, 334, 335, 633
Mommsen, Theodor, 189, 286
Moore, Stephen D., 173, 671, 674, 681, 686, 693
Moorhead, James H., 63, 189, 747
Morris, Leon, 66, 158, 480, 578, 623, 624, 665, 731
Morton, Russell, 129, 189, 382, 383, 423
Mottahedeh, Patricia Erhart, 189, 378, 541
Mounce, Robert H., 66, 74, 76, 96, 158, 248, 249, 270, 280, 290, 295, 301, 324, 325, 326, 330, 331, 337, 340, 356, 366, 373, 387, 394, 398, 400, 418, 421, 425, 427, 430, 431, 434, 435, 444, 446, 450, 458, 459, 461, 466, 467, 475, 476, 477, 478, 481, 482, 483, 484, 485, 490, 497, 500, 504, 505, 507, 516, 519, 524, 528, 542, 551, 569, 586, 597, 606, 609, 616, 620, 628, 635, 643, 646, 648, 660, 663, 665, 688, 691, 698, 726, 730, 752, 756, 757, 771, 772, 773, 774, 775, 776, 781, 785, 790, 791, 795, 796, 797, 817, 837, 840, 841, 844, 847, 849
Moyise, Steve, 65, 123, 182, 188, 189, 195, 229, 307, 382, 387, 413, 633, 635, 762, 765

Müller, Christoph G., 190, 801, 806, 825
Müller, Ulrich B., 75, 107, 109, 112, 158, 225, 234, 244, 248, 287, 331, 340, 365, 377, 431, 434, 570, 597, 611, 618, 620, 628, 636, 658, 661, 673, 686, 748, 756, 773, 774, 787, 795, 802, 803, 805, 815, 819, 823, 825, 833, 840, 841, 843, 846, 848, 853, 857
Müller-Fieberg, Rita, 190, 801
Munck, Johannes, 190, 440
Murphy, Frederick J., 75, 89, 112, 115, 131, 158, 212, 216, 221, 222, 225, 235, 244, 246, 250, 252, 263, 265, 269, 273, 275, 286, 289, 290, 293, 295, 301, 314, 316, 318, 319, 324, 328, 329, 330, 336, 337, 356, 360, 361, 382, 384, 394, 395, 398, 400, 413, 415, 418, 421, 428, 431, 432, 435, 438, 444, 446, 450, 456, 458, 466, 467, 477, 484, 485, 494, 497, 498, 504, 505, 507, 514, 515, 524, 528, 547, 558, 567, 570, 589, 596, 607, 616, 624, 629, 643, 649, 666, 675, 676, 677, 689, 691, 733, 736, 750, 755, 756, 757, 771, 772, 773, 774, 785, 796, 809, 823, 851
Murphy-O'Connor, Jerome, 190, 703
Murray, James S., 190, 662, 664
Murray, Michele, 190, 275, 278, 327
Mussies, G., 83, 190, 287, 364, 467, 773
Musurillo, Herbert, 190, 242, 287, 368

Nanz, Christian, 190, 551
Neufeld, Dietmar, 190, 274, 312, 681
Newsom, Carol A., 190, 644
Neyrey, Jerome H., 97, 186, 190, 215, 328, 689
Nickelsburg, George W. E., 69, 190, 377, 457, 516, 644, 770, 786, 813, 839, 845
Nicklas, Tobias, 33, 66, 146, 165, 167, 169, 175, 177, 178, 182, 191, 194, 195, 202, 203, 845, 847
Nielsen, Harald, 191, 348
Nielsen, Kirsten, 191, 423
Nielsen, Kjeld, 191, 433
Nikolakopoulos, Konstantin, 40, 191
Nilsson, Martin P., 191, 834
North, John, 162, 369, 390, 452, 511, 582, 585
Nutton, Vivian, 191, 339, 348

Index of Subjects

beast from the land, 588–604. *See also* false prophet, the great

beast from the sea: activity of, 499; description of, 569–74, 577, 676–77, 681, 687. *See also* Antichrist; 666

beatitudes, 130–32

Beatus, 44, 353, 744

Bede, 41, 353

Behemoth, 532, 580, 599–601, 748, 761, 796

Belial, 461, 513, 530–32, 549–50, 557, 658, 760, 778

Berengaudus, 41, 44

book of life. *See* scroll of life

bowl plagues: and the exodus tradition, 445–47, 666; and other plague cycles, 443–45

bridal imagery, 610–11, 618–19, 710, 728–30, 736–39, 796, 804, 811–12, 818, 844, 856–57

Brightman, Thomas, 232, 437, 746

Brorson, Hans Adolf, 50

Bullinger, Heinrich, 51–52, 746

Calvin, John: on Antichrist, 537; on millennium, 746; on Revelation, 51

canonical status of Revelation, 35, 38, 48–50

character of author of Revelation, 136–37, 223

character portrayal in Revelation, 116–19

Chimera, 467, 473

church historical approach to Revelation, 46–48, 232, 354, 438–40, 526, 536, 638, 645. *See also* Joachim of Fiore; Lyra, Nicholas of

city: the beloved, 779, 790, 796; the great, 119, 266, 486, 500, 506, 509, 662–63, 668–69, 675, 790; the holy, 75, 438, 486, 495–96, 572, 804, 812

Clement of Alexandria, 33–34, 66–67, 74, 100, 149, 243, 743

conquering: as faithfulness, 265, 270–71, 376, 388–89, 552, 631–36; 800; Roman, 406, 583–84, 587, 694

creation: in apocalyptic texts, 105, 513; new, 120–22, 125, 271, 282, 430–31, 793–810, 818, 823; in relation to God

and Christ, 116–17, 119, 133, 220, 230, 242, 367–71, 390–92, 479, 490, 554, 660, 669, 764; suffering of, 450, 453, 650, 652, 654

creatures, the four living: in the history of interpretation, 351–53; significance of, 364, 369

crown. *See* wreath imagery

Cyprian: on Antichrist, 535; on Babylon, 638; on martyrs' prayer, 353; on millennium, 743, on Revelation, 32, 231

Daniel: and apocalyptic genre, 104; as model for visions in Revelation, 249, 253, 362, 367–68, 383, 389, 479, 486–95, 498, 531, 533, 548, 563, 572–73, 577, 580, 582, 839–40, 855; on Son of Man, 218, 623; Theodotian's text of, 218, 245

Darby, John Nelson, 60, 747. *See also* dispensationalist interpretation of Revelation

date of Revelation, 71–79

Dead Sea Scrolls: on apocalyptic material, 64; on Belial, 461, 472, 532, 549; on biblical interpretation, 481; on celibacy, 611; on eschatological battle, 426, 432, 658, 679–80, 753, 760, 778–79, 813; on Greek biblical text, 124, 220; on heavenly scenes, 360, 365, 644; on Michael, 548; on Nero's name in Hebrew, 597–98; on New Jerusalem, 812–13, 816, 820; on Psalm 2, 302; on temple, 821; on woman giving birth, 529–30

death, second, 278, 282, 781, 792, 801

denunciation of Jesus' followers to authorities, 274–75, 279–80, 292

destroyers of the earth, 516–17

determinism, 222, 472

devil. *See* Satan

Dionysius of Alexandria, 34, 68, 80, 139

dispensationalist interpretation of Revelation, 60–61, 232–33, 255, 325–26, 351, 355, 421, 437–39, 527, 543, 540, 551, 563, 625, 640–41, 777

Dolcino, Fra, 232

Domitian: and Asia Minor, 77–78, 256–58, 272–73, 295, 322, 327, 334, 814, 820, 827, 829; and banishment of John, 243; coins of, 253, 260, 265, 323, 335, 581,

603, 736, 758; and date of Revelation, 65, 71, 74–78, 94, 678; and imperial cult, 64, 259–60, 265, 296, 298, 322, 335, 349, 365–66, 581, 583, 589, 591, 593, 602; and Judaism, 77, 280; and Nero, 540, 559, 571; as persecutor, 76–77, 578; practices of, 361, 386, 502

dragon, 544–46, 558

Edwards, Jonathan, 53, 640, 747
Eichhorn, Gottfried, 61
elders, the twenty-four, 360–63, 368–69, 519–20
emotional effect of Revelation, 134–36
Ephesus: description of, 256; social, economic, and religious life in, 256–61, 266–67
Erasmus, Desiderius: on authorship and canonical status of Revelation, 48, 67; on Greek text of Revelation, 145
ethnic background of readers, 87–88
Euphrates, 395, 406, 466, 471–72, 571, 656–57, 665, 691–92
exodus imagery, 126, 377, 437, 445–46, 448–53, 458, 463, 468, 542, 554, 557–58, 565–67, 632–35, 642, 646–54, 663, 666, 669, 763, 796
Eyck, Jan van, 44

false prophet, the great, 118, 499, 517, 521–22, 530, 588–93, 599–600, 658, 666, 760–69, 855. *See also* beast from the land; prophets
forty-two months, visionary significance of, 120–21, 438, 486–87, 495, 562, 572, 585
Francis of Assisi, 45–46, 355, 537
Franciscans, Spiritual, 46, 355, 537. *See also* Olivi, Peter John
Frederick II, 46, 536–39

Gaius, the Roman elder, 31–32, 67
Garrison, William Lloyd, 640
gematria, 597–99, 605–6
Geneva Bible, 52, 354, 438, 440, 640
genre of Revelation, 104–12
Gerardo of Borgo San Donnino, 45, 438
Glossa ordinaria, 43

God: as creator, 367, 479, 490; portrayal of, 116–17, 367–71. *See also* Alpha and Omega; creation; justice, symmetry in
Gog and Magog, 776–78, 788–89
Grotius, Hugo, 53

Hades, 247–48, 254, 397–98, 408, 792–93
Handel, George Frideric, 58
Harmagedon, 660–61, 667–68, 767–68
Hebrew: biblical text, 123–24, 336; in gematria, 540, 596–99; John's knowledge of, 69, 140, 546, 548, 660–61, 667, 726; poetic forms, 635, 733–34
Hippolytus: on Antichrist, 535; on Babylon, 638; on Revelation, 32
Hoffmann, Melchior, 54–55, 355, 440, 537
house churches, 88
Howe, Julia Ward, 58
Hugh of St. Cher, 43
Hus, Jan, 47, 54, 355, 440, 745
Hut, Hans, on Revelation, 54
hymns based on Revelation, 50, 58–59
hymns within Revelation, 127–30, 518, 733–34

Immaculate Conception, 56, 527, 543
immorality, literal and metaphorical, 138, 262–63, 288–89, 293, 306, 469–70, 613, 618–21, 671–75, 686–87, 701, 717, 727, 734, 737, 804, 809, 842, 855
imperial cult: in Asia Minor, 93–95, 574, 578–84, 589–91; at Ephesus, 259; and heavenly throne vision, 370–71, 385, 392; at Laodicea, 334; on Patmos, 242; at Pergamum; 284–85; at Philadelphia, 322; at Sardis, 311; at Smyrna, 273; at Thyatira, 296
inheritance, 217, 301, 383, 800–801, 808–9, 844–45
interludes within Revelation, 113, 141, 356–57, 405, 424, 442–43, 487–91, 505, 642, 664, 681
Irenaeus: on Antichrist, 534–35; on author, 66, 80, 243; on date, 74, 77; on millennium, 742; on Revelation, 30–31, 353, 355, 437–38; on text, 144
Isis, 215, 220, 256, 259, 284, 528–29, 544–45, 556–57, 609

256, 258, 299, 273, 284, 366, 694; legend of surviving death, 126, 570–71, 581, 602, 657; the number 666 and, 597–99; persecution of Christians, 570, 586, 602

New Jerusalem, description of, 810–36

Newton, Isaac, 52–53

Nicolai, Philipp, 50

Nicolaitans, 88–89, 262–64

Nicolas de Gorran, 43

144,000: in the history of interpretation, 355–56; significance of, 417, 424–27, 607–8, 617

Oecumenius: on Antichrist, 536; on Babylon, 638; on millennium, 744, 776; on Revelation, 39; on text of Revelation, 144, 149–50

Old Testament: Hebrew or Greek versions informing Revelation, 123–24; types of usage in Revelation, 123–25

Olivi, Peter John, 46, 638

Origen: on Antichrist, 536; on millennium, 743; on Revelation, 33–34

Papias, 34, 742

Pareus, David, 61

parody, 116, 138, 263, 288, 300, 412–13, 520, 566, 578–80, 590–92, 595, 600–606, 685, 688, 713, 830

parousia, 838–39. *See also* Jesus

Parthians, 126, 394–95, 406–7, 471–72, 657, 665, 691

Patmos: description of, 239–40; social, economic, and religious life on, 240–42, 251

Pauline tradition: in Revelation, 83–84

peace, Roman, 395–96, 407

Pergamum: description of, 282–84; social, economic, and religious life in, 284–86

persecution, 96–98, 276–82

Peter Lombard, 43

Peter of Tarentaise, 232

Philadelphia: description of, 312–22; social, economic, and religious life in, 322–23, 327–28

Philips, Dirk, 55

plagues: comparison of cycles in Revelation, 443–45; exodus and Greco-Roman traditions, 445–54, 474

Pliny the Younger, on trials of Christians, 96–99, 276, 280, 292, 594

plot of Revelation, 121–22

preterist interpretation of Revelation, 57

priests: as description of early Christians, 228, 389–90; Greco-Roman, 240–42, 259, 272–73, 296, 311, 322, 334; in New Jerusalem, 836

Primasius: on Babylon, 638, 695; on millennium, 714, 784; on Revelation, 40–41

prophecy: as literary genre, 107–9, 221, 224, 229; spirit of, 732, 739–40

prophets: Christian, 90–91, 214, 224, 299, 507–8; false, 91, 214, 224, 262, 305–6, 501, 532–34, 592–93, 600–603, 658–59, 666, 739–40, 851; Greco-Roman, 214, 298; Jewish, 213–14, 299, 305–6, 481

Purim, 502

Python, 528, 545, 547, 555–56

Qumran. *See* Dead Sea Scrolls

Quodvultdeus, 38, 527

Radical and Anabaptist interpretations of Revelation, 53–55. *See also* Müntzer, Thomas

Reformed interpretation of Revelation, 50–53, 351, 537, 640

relegation of John to an island, 242–43

resurrection: the first, 775–76, 785–88; final, 779–80, 790

rhetorical aspects of Revelation, 110, 132–44, 222–23, 227, 268–69, 281, 298, 305, 318, 328, 337–38, 356, 374, 381, 405, 412, 420, 424, 430, 472, 509, 521, 558, 561, 578, 606, 616, 622, 659, 695, 699, 713, 717, 735, 739, 768, 792, 806, 810, 826, 840–41, 848, 853, 856

Ribera, Francisco, 56–57

Richard of St. Victor, 43

riddle, 605–6

Roman Catholic interpretation of Revelation, 55–58, 537–39, 640

Rome: early Christian attitudes toward, 684–85; on seven hills, 677, 690

Rupert of Detutz, 43

666: in the history of interpretation, 538–40; significance of, 596–99

sacrificial meat as issue for Christians, 99–101, 293

Sardis: description of, 309–10; social, economic, and religious life in, 310–12

Satan: binding of, 769–70, 783–85; expulsion from heaven, 549–51, 554–55, 563–65; final defeat of, 776–79, 788–90

Satan's throne, 286–87

satire. *See* parody

Saturnalia, 502, 510

Scofield, Cyrus, 60. *See also* dispensationalist interpretation of Revelation

scroll of God: as sealed, 374, 383–84; as open, 476–77, 482, 488–94

scroll of life, 314–15, 319–20, 574–75, 587, 689, 791–92, 810, 822–23, 833

seal of God, 415–17, 425–26, 825

seals, seven: in the history of interpretation, 353–55; and literary structure, 356–57, 405–6; and other plague cycles, 443–45; and Synoptic apocalypse, 357–58

seven churches. *See* assemblies addressed by Revelation; messages to the seven assemblies

Simmons, Menno, 54

slave or servant as designation for Christians, 211–12

slave trade, 705–6, 720–22

Smyrna: description of, 271–72; social, economic, and religious life in, 272–74; 278–79, 316

Son of God, 297–98, 304

Son of Man, 245, 252–53, 623, 627–28

sorcery, 87, 92, 469–70, 474, 593, 601, 603–4, 710–11, 724, 801, 809–10, 855

source criticism of Revelation, 62, 69–71, 440–41

spatial and temporal settings in Revelation, 119–21

Spirit: and Christ, 108–9, 237–38, 251–52; inspiration through, 224–25, 243, 251–52, 264–65, 270, 732

spirits: of prophets, 838, 849; the seven, 216

spiritual: interpretation of Revelation, 30–45, 48–49, 53–55, 353, 355, 537,

743–47, 764; nature of John's experience, 251–52

stars, seven, 248–49, 253

structure, literary, of Revelation, 112–15, 234–38, 356–57, 442–43, 524–25, 641–43, 750–52

styles of writing in Revelation, 139–41

synagogue of Satan, 276, 280–81, 330

Synoptic traditions, 84–85, 357–58

Taborites, 745

temple imagery, 332, 438–39, 484–86, 494–96, 628, 644–45, 664, 820–21, 831–32

temples, Greco-Roman, 94, 100, 256, 259–60, 265, 272–73, 284–85, 310–11, 322, 327, 334–35, 339, 406, 409, 541, 572, 574, 585–86, 590–94, 602, 693, 736, 831

temporal perspective of Revelation, 222–23

Tertullian: on Babylon, 638; on Revelation, 32

text of Revelation, 144–50

three and a half years, as biblical formula, 562–63, 572–73

Thyatira: description of, 295; social, economic, and religious life in, 295–97, 303

title of Revelation, 209–10

tree of life, 265–66, 823–24, 834–35, 842, 855

Trent, Council of, 55–56

tribulation. *See* affliction, the great

Trinitarian interpretation of Revelation, 36, 38–39

trumpet plagues: and the exodus tradition, 445–47; in the history of interpretation, 437–38; and other plague cycles, 443–45

Tyconius: on Antichrist, 535–36; on Babylon, 638; on Revelation, 36–37

Typhon, 528, 545, 556–57, 561, 569

Ubertino of Casale, 46, 355, 537

underworld, 120, 247–48

unity of Revelation, 69–71

Victorinus: on Babylon, 638; on Revelation, 33

wealth, as issue for Christians, 101–3, 274, 338, 344–46, 673, 698–99, 701–10, 717–25, 828. *See also* Franciscans, Spiritual; Olivi, Peter John

wedding. *See* bridal imagery

Wesley, Charles, 58

white robe, 314, 318–19, 347, 371, 400, 428, 730–31

whore: in ancient world, 671–72, 674, 686–87, 688; demise of, 734–35. *See also* Babylon

witness, concept of, 212–13, 732

witnesses, the two, 439–40, 496–98, 505–12

woman clothed with the sun: in the history of interpretation, 525–27; in mythic sources, 528–30; significance of, 542–44, 560–63

word pictures, 138–39

wreath imagery, 277–78, 365

Wyclif, John, 47, 354, 537

Zion, 616–17

Zwingli, Ulrich, 50–51